Europe on a Shoestring

Scandinavia
p131

Russia &
the Baltic Coast
p773

Great Britain &
Ireland
p49

Germany,
Austria &
Benelux
p201

Central &
Eastern Europe
p671

France &
Switzerland
p307

Balkans
p583

Spain &
Portugal
p377

Italy, Greece & Turkey
p471

Mark Bak hmond,
Andrea Schulte-Peevers, Andy Symington, Nicola Williams

PLAN YOUR TRIP

KOPRIVSHTITSA,
BULGARIA P748

ON THE ROAD

PARIS, FRANCE P310

WARSAW, POLAND P691

Contents

CAUSEWAY COAST,
NORTHERN IRELAND P126

ON THE ROAD

**LAKE DISTRICT,
GREAT BRITAIN P81**

**SAN SEBASTIÁN,
SPAIN P392**

**COPENHAGEN,
DENMARK P134**

Contents

SURVIVAL GUIDE

SPECIAL FEATURES

Welcome to Europe

Whatever your budget (or lack of), it is impossible to tour Europe and not be awestruck by its immense beauty, epic history, cultural diversity and uncanny knack for throwing up the unexpected.

Urban Adventure

Some of Europe's headline locations can suck up your cash like a herd of thirsty elephants. But for every London or Paris there's a more affordable Lviv or Porto. Scattered among the 40 countries covered in this guide, ranging from Iceland to Turkey, there are hundreds of fascinating cities, towns and villages to discover. Take a taxi tour of the mural art of Belfast, ride the ferry across the Bosphorus in İstanbul, enjoy an ice cream on Venice's Piazza San Marco – many of Europe's most memorable experiences needn't break the bank, and a surprising amount can be done for free. Be flexible and you'll soon find your funds stretching further than you ever imagined.

Glorious Scenery

Europe's lovely landscapes are the gift that keeps on giving. Stride across English meadows or the sand dunes of the Baltic states. Sail down Norwegian fjords or Germany's Rhine. Climb, ski or just marvel at the Swiss and French Alps. Relax on Croatian beaches or Greek islands. Explore the honeycombed hills of Cappadocia or cycle past Dutch tulip fields in full bloom. Picture-postcard views are around every corner, whichever route you take.

Cultural Giant

With thousands of years of civilisation under its belt, Europe's cultural diversity is its trump card. Religions, philosophies and artistic movements that changed the world developed in Athens, Rome, Moscow, Leipzig, Vienna – the list is endless. Europe has 450-odd Unesco World Heritage sites – the most of any continent – with just over 50 in Italy alone! Be it climbing up Skellig Michael off Ireland's west coast, soaking up the architectural majesty of Granada's Alhambra, or witnessing whirling dervishes in action, Europe's range of cultural attractions is gargantuan and unsurpassed.

Party House

Europe has some of the best nightlife in the world. Globally famous DJs keep the party going in London, Berlin and Paris, all of which also offer top-class entertainment, especially theatre and live music. Other key locations for high-energy nightlife include Moscow, Belgrade, Budapest and Madrid, while those hankering for something cosier can add Dublin's pubs or Vienna's cafes to their itinerary. Continue to party on the continent's streets at a multiplicity of festivals and celebrations, from city parades attended by hundreds of thousands to intimate concerts in an ancient amphitheatre.

Why I Love Europe

By Brendan Sainsbury, Writer

Like many young travellers, I began my life on the road in the late 1980s with a £140 Inter-rail ticket. Not having travelled outside Britain as a child, I'll never forget the excitement of arriving at Paris' Gare du Nord after dark to explore the 'City of Light'. Since then I've travelled around Europe multiple times, returning regularly to my favourite places (Andalucía, the Loire, the Dolomites, London and the English Lake District) and revelling in the diversity, intensity and complexity of this multilayered continent that I'll need at least 10 lifetimes to explore properly.

For more about our writers, see p896

Above: Preikestolen (Pulpit Rock; p175), Norway

Europe

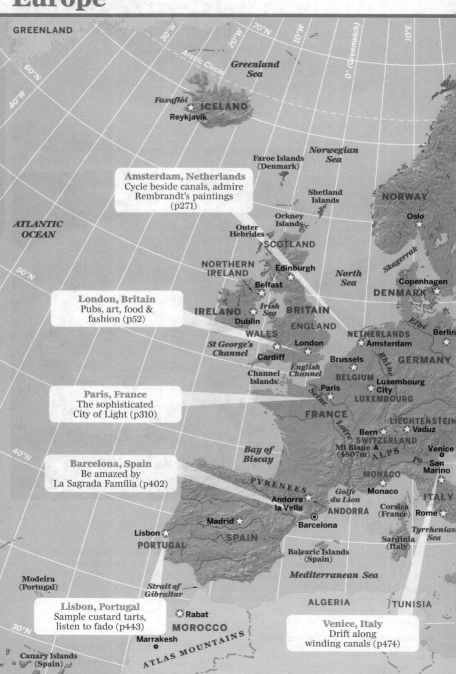

GREENLAND

Greenland Sea

Faxaflói ⭐ ICELAND
Reykjavík

Norwegian Sea

Faroe Islands
(Denmark)

Amsterdam, Netherlands
Cycle beside canals, admire
Rembrandt's paintings
(p271)

Shetland
Islands

NORWAY

Oslo ⭐

ATLANTIC OCEAN

Orkney
Islands

Outer
Hebrides

SCOTLAND

Skagerrak

Copenhagen ⭐

*North
Sea*

DENMARK

NORTHERN
IRELAND

Edinburgh ⭐

Belfast ⭐

London, Britain
Pubs, art, food &
fashion (p52)

IRELAND ⭐

*Irish
Sea*

BRITAIN

Elbe

Berlin ⭐

Dublin

ENGLAND

NETHERLANDS
⭐ Amsterdam

GERMANY

WALES

St George's
Channel

Cardiff ⭐

London ⭐

Rhine

Brussels
⭐

BELGIUM

Luxembourg
City ⭐

Channel
Islands

*English
Channel*

Paris, France
The sophisticated
City of Light (p310)

Paris ⭐

LUXEMBOURG

Seine

FRANCE

LIECHTENSTEIN

Bern ⭐

⭐ Vaduz

SWITZERLAND

Mt Blanc ▲
(4807m)

ALPS

Venice
○

*Bay of
Biscay*

Loire

Po

San
Marino

Barcelona, Spain
Be amazed by
La Sagrada Família (p402)

PYRENEES

MONACO

Monaco ⭐

ITALY

Andorra
la Vella ⭐

*Golfe
du Lion*

ANDORRA

Corsica
(France)

Rome ⭐

Madrid ⭐

Barcelona ◉

Lisbon ⭐

SPAIN

PORTUGAL

Sardinia
(Italy)

*Tyrrhenian
Sea*

Balearic Islands
(Spain)

Mediterranean Sea

Modeira
(Portugal)

*Strait of
Gibraltar*

Lisbon, Portugal
Sample custard tarts,
listen to fado (p443)

⭐ Rabat

MOROCCO

ALGERIA

TUNISIA

Venice, Italy
Drift along
winding canals (p474)

Marrakesh
○

Canary Islands
(Spain)

ATLAS MOUNTAINS

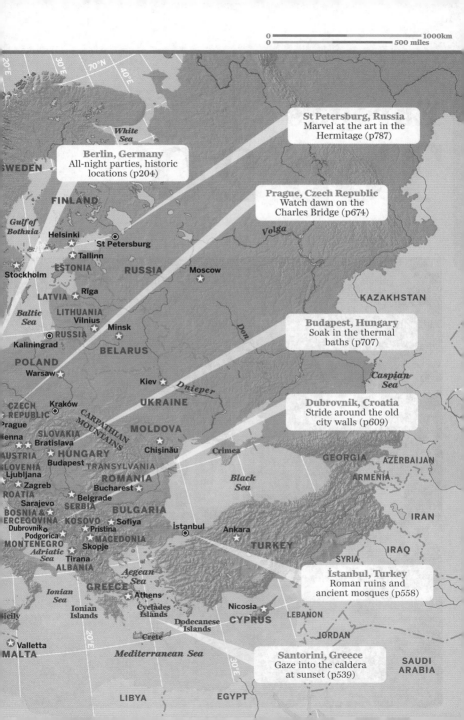

St Petersburg, Russia
Marvel at the art in the
Hermitage (p787)

Berlin, Germany
All-night parties, historic
locations (p204)

Prague, Czech Republic
Watch dawn on the
Charles Bridge (p674)

Budapest, Hungary
Soak in the thermal
baths (p707)

Dubrovnik, Croatia
Stride around the old
city walls (p609)

İstanbul, Turkey
Roman ruins and
ancient mosques (p558)

Santorini, Greece
Gaze into the caldera
at sunset (p539)

0   1000km
0   500 miles

SWEDEN

*White
Sea*

FINLAND

*Gulf of
Bothnia*

Helsinki
St Petersburg
Tallinn
ESTONIA

Volga

Stockholm

RUSSIA

Moscow

LATVIA
Rīga

KAZAKHSTAN

*Baltic
Sea*

LITHUANIA
Vilnius
Minsk

RUSSIA
Kaliningrad

BELARUS

POLAND
Warsaw

Kiev
Dnieper

*Caspian
Sea*

UKRAINE

CZECH
REPUBLIC
Prague
Kraków

CARPATHIAN
MOUNTAINS

MOLDOVA

Don

Vienna
SLOVAKIA
Bratislava
HUNGARY
AUSTRIA
SLOVENIA
Ljubljana
Budapest
Chişinău
Crimea

*Black
Sea*

GEORGIA
AZERBAIJAN

TRANSYLVANIA

Zagreb
CROATIA
Sarajevo
BOSNIA &
HERCEGOVINA
Dubrovnik
Podgorica
MONTENEGRO

ROMANIA
Bucharest

ARMENIA

Belgrade
SERBIA
KOSOVO
Pristina
MACEDONIA
Skopje

BULGARIA
Sofiya

İstanbul
Ankara

IRAN

TURKEY

SYRIA
IRAQ

*Adriatic
Sea*
Tirana
ALBANIA

*Aegean
Sea*

GREECE
Athens

Nicosia
CYPRUS
LEBANON

*Ionian
Sea*

Ionian
Islands

Cyclades
Islands

JORDAN

Sicily

Valletta
MALTA

Dodecanese
Islands
Crete

Mediterranean Sea

SAUDI
ARABIA

LIBYA
EGYPT

Europe's
Top 20

London Nightlife

1 Can you hear that, music lovers? That's London (p52) calling – from the numerous theatres, concert halls, nightclubs, pubs and even tube stations, where on any given night hundreds, if not thousands, of performers are taking to the stage. Search for your own iconic London experience, whether it's the Proms at the Royal Albert Hall, an East End singalong around a clunky pub piano, a theatre performance in the West End, a superstar DJ set at Fabric or a floppy-fringed guitar band at a Hoxton boozer.

Lost in Venice

2 There's something magical about Venice (p474) on a sunny winter's day. With far fewer tourists around and the light sharp and clear, it's the perfect time to lap up the city's unique and magical atmosphere. Ditch your map and wander the shadowy backlines of Dorsoduro while imagining secret assignations and whispered conspiracies at every turn. Then visit two of Venice's top galleries, the Gallerie dell'Accademia and the Peggy Guggenheim Collection, which houses works by many of the giants of 20th-century art.

OLI SCARFF / STAFF / GETTY IMAGES ©

STEVANZZ / GETTY IMAGES ©

Scaling Paris' Eiffel Tower

3 Initially designed as a temporary exhibit for the 1889 Exposition Universelle (World Fair), the elegant, webbed-metal art-nouveau design of Paris' Eiffel Tower (p310) has become the defining fixture of the French capital's skyline. Its 1st floor incorporates two glitzy glass pavilions housing interactive history exhibits; outside them, peer d-o-w-n through glass flooring to the ground below. Visit at dusk for the best day and night views of the glittering City of Light, and toast making it to the top at the sparkling Champagne Bar.

Ancient Rome

4 Rome's famous seven hills (actually, there are nine) offer some superb vantage points. A favourite is the Palatino (p500), a gorgeous green expanse of evocative ruins, towering umbrella pines and unforgettable views over the Roman Forum. This is where it all began, where Romulus supposedly founded the city and where the ancient Roman emperors lived in unimaginable luxury. Nowadays, it's a truly haunting spot; as you walk the gravel paths you can almost sense the ghosts in the air. Right: Palatino (Palatine Hill; p500)

Remembering the Berlin Wall

5 Even after nearly three decades, it's hard to comprehend how the Berlin Wall (p208) separated the city for 28 years. The best way to examine its role and ramifications is to make your way – on foot or by bike – along the Berlin Wall Trail. Passing the Brandenburg Gate and analysing graffiti at the East Side Gallery, the world's largest open-air mural collection, the path brings it all into context. It's heartbreaking and hopeful and sombre, but integral to understanding Germany's capital today.

Left: East Side Gallery artwork, *My God, Help Me to Survive This Deadly Love* (1990; Dmitry Vrubel)

©CHANTAL/GETTY IMAGES

Santorini

6 On first view, startling Santorini (p539) grabs your attention and doesn't let it go. The submerged caldera, surrounded by lava-layered cliffs topped by villages that look like a sprinkling of icing sugar, is one of nature's great wonders, best experienced by a walk along the clifftops from the main town of Fira to the northern village of Oia. The precariousness and impermanence of the place is breathtaking. Recover from your efforts with Santorini's ice-cold Yellow Donkey beer in Oia as you wait for its famed picture-perfect sunset.

Prague

7 Prague's big attractions – Prague Castle (p674) and Old Town Square – are highlights of the Czech capital, but for a more insightful look at life after the Velvet Revolution, head to local neighbourhoods around the centre. Working-class Žižkov and energetic Smíchov are crammed with pubs, while elegant, tree-lined Vinohrady features a diverse menu of cosmopolitan restaurants. Prague showcases many forms of art, including both iconic works from the last century and more recent, equally challenging pieces.

Imperial Vienna

8 Imagine what you could do with unlimited riches and Austria's top architects at your hands for 640 years: you have the Vienna (p283) of the Habsburgs. The graceful Hofburg whisks you back to the age of empires as you marvel at the treasury's imperial crowns, the equine ballet of the Spanische Hofreitschule (Spanish Riding School) and Empress Elisabeth's chandelier-lit apartments. The palace is rivalled in grandeur only by Schloss Schönbrunn and also the baroque Schloss Belvedere, both set in exquisite landscaped gardens.
Above: Schloss Belvedere (p289)

Amsterdam by Boat

9 To say Amsterdammers love the water is an understatement. Sure, the city (p271) made its first fortune in maritime trade, but that's ancient history. You can stroll next to the canals and check out some of the thousands of houseboats. Or, better still, go for a ride. From boat level you'll see a whole new set of architectural details, such as the ornamentation bedecking the bridges. And when you pass the canalside cafe terraces, you can just look up and wave. Top: *Bridge of the Rainbow,* by Gilbert Moity, Amsterdam Light Festival

Budapest

10 Straddling both sides of the Danube River, with the Buda Hills to the west and the Great Plain to the east, Budapest (p707) is perhaps the most beautiful city in Eastern Europe. Parks brim with attractions, the architecture is second to none and museums are filled with treasures. And with pleasure boats sailing up the Danube Bend, Turkish-era thermal baths belching steam and a nightlife throbbing till dawn most nights, it's easy to see why the Hungarian capital is one of the continent's most delightful cities to visit. Bottom: Gellért Baths (p711)

Quirky Barcelona

11 One of Spain's top sights, La Sagrada Família (p403), modernist brainchild of Antoni Gaudí, remains a work in progress more than 90 years after its architect's death. Inspired by nature and barely restrained by a Gothic style, Barcelona's quirky temple soars skyward with an almost playful majesty. The improbable angles and departures from architectural convention will have you shaking your head in disbelief, but the detail of the decorative flourishes on the Passion and Nativity facades are worth studying for hours.

Below: Interior of La Sagrada Família

İstanbul

12 Straddling Europe and Asia, and serving stints as the capital of the Byzantine and Ottoman Empires, İstanbul (p558) is one of the world's great cities. Marvel at the historical highlights in Sultanahmet – the Aya Sofya, Blue Mosque, Topkapı Palace and Grand Bazaar. Then take time to experience the vibrant contemporary life of this huge metropolis. Cross the Galata Bridge, passing ferries and fish-kebab stands, to Beyoğlu, where the nightlife thrives from chic rooftop bars to rowdy taverns.

Bottom: Grand Bazaar (p560)

Lisbon

13 With its labyrinthine alleyways, hidden courtyards and curving, shadow-filled lanes, the Alfama is a magical place to lose all sense of direction and delve into the soul of the Portuguese capital (p443). On the journey, you'll pass bread-box-sized grocers, brilliantly tiled buildings and cosy taverns filled with easygoing chatter, with the aroma of chargrilled sardines and the mournful rhythms of fado drifting in the breeze. Then you round a bend and catch sight of steeply pitched rooftops leading down to the glittering river, the Tejo.

St Petersburg

14 Marvelling at how many masterpieces there are in the Hermitage; window-shopping and people-watching along Nevsky Prospekt; gliding down canals past the grand facades of palaces and golden-domed churches; enjoying a ballet at the beautiful Mariinsky Theatre; having a banquet fit for a tsar then dancing till dawn at a dive bar in a crumbling ruin – Russia's imperial capital (p787) is a visual stunner and hedonist's delight, best visited at the height of summer, when the White Nights see the city party around the clock.

Top Right: Church of the Saviour on the Spilled Blood (p787)

Tallinn

15 The Estonian capital (p800) is rightly famous for its two-tiered chocolate-box Old Town with landscapes of intertwining alleys, picturesque courtyards and red-rooftop views from medieval turrets. But be sure to step outside the Old Town walls and experience Tallinn's other treasures: no visit is complete without sampling its stylish restaurants plating up fashionable New Nordic cuisine, its buzzing, Scandinavian-influenced design community, its ever-growing number of museums – such as Kumu, the city's award-winning modern-art repository – or its progressive contemporary architecture.

Dubrovnik

16 Get up close and personal with the city by walking Dubrovnik's spectacular city walls (p609), as history is unfurled from the battlements. No visit is complete without a leisurely walk along these ramparts, the finest in the world and Dubrovnik's main claim to fame. Built between the 13th and 16th centuries, they are still remarkably intact today, and the vistas over the terracotta rooftops and the Adriatic Sea are sublime, especially at dusk when the sundown makes the hues dramatic and the panoramas unforgettable.

Athens

17 Magnificent ruins of its ancient civilisation are scattered across the mainland and islands of Greece, but it's in its capital Athens (p527) that the greatest and most iconic of those monuments still stands. High on a rocky outcrop overlooking the city, the Acropolis epitomises the glory of ancient Greece with its graceful Parthenon. Other impressive ruins littering this resilient, vibrant city include the mammoth Temple of Olympian Zeus and two agoras (marketplaces – one Greek, one Roman) mingling with first-rate museums. Top right: Temple of Olympian Zeus (p531)

The Matterhorn

18 It graces Toblerone packages and evokes stereotypical *Heidi* scenes, but nothing prepares you for the allure of the Matterhorn (p366). As soon as you arrive at the timber-chalet-filled village of Zermatt, this mighty mountain looms above you, mesmerising you with its chiselled, majestic peak. Gaze at it from a tranquil sidewalk cafe, hike in its shadow along the tangle of alpine paths above town with cowbells clinking in the distance or pause to admire its sheer size from a ski slope.

Bay of Kotor

19 There's a sense of secrecy and mystery to the Bay of Kotor (p630). Grey mountain walls rise steeply from steely blue waters, getting higher and higher as you progress through their folds to the hidden reaches of the inner bay. Here, ancient stone settlements hug the shoreline, with Kotor's medieval alleyways concealed in its innermost reaches behind hefty stone walls. Talk about drama! But you wouldn't expect anything else of the Balkans, where life is exuberantly Mediterranean and lived full of passion on these ancient streets.

Transylvania

20 The Romanian region (p729) that so ghoulishly inspired Irish writer Bram Stoker to create his *Dracula* has some seriously spooky castles. Monumental Bran Castle, south of Braşov, is suitably vampiric. The castle is nestled high amid the Carpathians, a relatively underexplored mountain range that's ideal for all manner of outdoor activity, including hiking, trekking, mountain biking and skiing.
Bottom: Bran Castle (p734)

Need to Know

For more information, see Survival Guide (p847)

Currency
Euro (€), Pound (£), Swiss franc (Sfr), Rouble (R)

Languages
English, French, German, Italian, Spanish, Russian, Hungarian, Greek, Turkish

Visas
EU citizens don't need visas to visit other EU countries. Australians, Canadians, New Zealanders and Americans don't need visas for visits of less than 90 days.

Money
ATMs are common; credit and debit cards are widely accepted.

Mobile Phones
Europe uses the GSM 900 network. Coming from outside Europe, buy a prepaid local SIM.

Time
Britain, Ireland and Portugal (GMT); Central Europe (GMT plus one hour); Greece, Turkey and Eastern Europe (GMT plus two hours); Russia (GMT plus three hours)

When to Go

- desert, dry climate
- warm to hot summers, mild winters
- warm to hot summers, cold winters
- mild summers, cold winters
- cold climate

Sweden
GO May-Sep

Russia
GO May-Sep & Dec-Jan

Britain
GO Apr-Oct

Germany
GO May-Sep

Czech Republic
GO Apr-Oct

France
GO Apr-Jun & Sep-Oct

Italy
GO Apr-Jun & Sep-Oct

High Season
(Jun–Aug)

➡ Everybody comes to Europe and all of Europe hits the road.

➡ Hotel prices and temperatures are at their highest.

➡ Expect all the major attractions to be nightmarishly busy.

Shoulder
(Apr–May & Sep–Oct)

➡ Crowds and prices drop, except in Italy, where it's still busy.

➡ Temperatures are comfortable but it can be hot in southern Europe.

➡ Overall these are the best months to travel in Europe.

Low Season
(Nov–Mar)

➡ Outside ski resorts, hotels drop their prices or close down.

➡ The weather can be cold and days short, especially in northern Europe.

➡ Some places, such as resort towns, are like ghost towns.

Useful Websites

Lonely Planet (www.lonely planet.com/europe) Destination information, hotel bookings, traveller forum and more.

The Man in Seat Sixty-One (www.seat61.com) Encyclopaedic site dedicated to train travel, plus plenty of other tips.

Hidden Europe (www.hidden europe.co.uk) Fascinating magazine and online dispatches from all the continent's corners.

Discover Europe (www.visit europe.com) Information about travel in 33 member countries.

Spotted by Locals (www.spottedbylocals.com) Insider tips for cities across Europe.

Nomadic Matt (www.nomadic-matt.com) Backpacking and budget-travel tips and tricks for the savvy Europe-bound.

Opening Hours

In most of Europe businesses are open 9am to 6pm Monday to Friday, and 9am to 1pm or 5pm on Saturday. In smaller towns there may be a one- to two-hour closure for lunch. Some shops close on Sunday.

Businesses also close on national holidays and local feast days. Banks have the shortest opening times, often closing between 3pm and 5pm and occasionally even shutting for lunch.

Restaurants typically open from noon until midnight and bars open around 6pm or 7pm. Museums usually close on Monday or (less commonly) on Tuesday.

Emergency Number

The phone number ☏112 can be dialled free for emergencies in all EU states. See individual countries for country-specific emergency numbers.

Daily Costs

Budget:
Less than €60

➡ Dorm beds: €10–20

➡ Admission to museums: €5–15

➡ Pizza or pasta: €8–12

Midrange:
€60–200

➡ Double room in a small hotel: €50–100

➡ Short taxi trip: €10–20

➡ Meals in good restaurants: around €20 per person

Top end:
More than €200

➡ Stay at iconic hotels: from €150

➡ Car hire: from around €30 per day

➡ Theatre tickets: €15–150

Arriving in Europe

Schiphol Airport, Amsterdam (p277) Trains to the centre (20 minutes).

Heathrow Airport, London (p66) Trains (15 minutes) and tube (one hour) to the centre.

Aéroport de Charles de Gaulle, Paris (p327) Many buses (one hour) and trains (30 minutes) to the centre.

Frankfurt Airport, Frankfurt (p237) Trains (15 minutes) to the centre.

Leonardo da Vinci Airport, Rome (p514) Buses (one hour) and trains (30 minutes) to the centre.

Barajas Airport, Madrid (p390) Buses (40 minutes) and metro (15 minutes) to the centre.

Exchange Rates

Australia (A$1)	€0.69	£0.58
Canada (C$1)	€0.70	£0.60
Japan (¥100)	€0.81	£0.69
NZ (NZ$1)	€0.66	£0.56
US (US$1)	€0.96	£0.81

For current exchange rates, see www.xe.com.

Euro Reading List

➡ *A Time of Gifts* (1977), *Between the Woods and the Water* (1986) and *The Broken Road: From the Iron Gates to Mount Athos* (2013) Patrick Leigh Fermor's classic trilogy about walking, aged 18, from Hoek van Holland to İstanbul in 1934.

➡ *Neither Here nor There: Travels in Europe* (1992; Bill Bryson) Twenty years after his 1970s European tour Bryson retraces his steps with humour and acute observation.

➡ *Nul points* (2007) European travels inspired by the continent's greatest song contest, by the British writer and humorist, Tim Moore.

➡ *Rite of Passage: Tales of Backpacking 'round Europe* (2003; Edited by Lisa Johnson) Young travellers conquer Europe for the first time.

➡ *Once Upon a Time in the West Country* (2016) and *One Hit Wonderland* (2003) Two of five comic travelogues by Tony Hawks, the ultimate insatiably curious traveller who once played the Moldovans at tennis and traipsed around Ireland with a fridge.

For much more on **getting around**, see p859

PLAN YOUR TRIP NEED TO KNOW

First-Time Europe

For more information, see Survival Guide (p847)

Checklist

➡ Make sure your passport is valid for six months past arrival.

➡ Check if you require visas.

➡ Check the airline baggage restrictions.

➡ Inform your debit-/credit-card company you're heading away.

➡ Arrange for appropriate travel insurance.

➡ Check if you need an International Driving Permit to rent a car.

➡ Check the validity of your mobile phone in Europe.

What to Pack

Flip-flops (thongs) for overnight trains, hostel bathrooms and the beach.

Hiking boots for Europe's walks.

Ear plugs – especially helpful in hostels.

Antimosquito plugs – useful in summer, particularly in the Baltic and Scandinavia.

European plug adapters.

Unlocked mobile phone for use with a local SIM card.

Top Tips for Your Trip

➡ Trains have long been one of the most efficient and fun ways of getting around Europe – and most countries have a good rail network.

➡ Check online for availability of advance reservations for particularly popular sights.

➡ Europe is biking heaven – rent wheels in Amsterdam, Copenhagen or to get around the French countryside.

➡ This is your ultimate opportunity to use a foreign language. Learn 20 basic phrases in three different European tongues.

➡ Get off the beaten track. Dodge the crowds in the Scottish Highlands, rural Poland or the plains of central Spain.

What to Wear

Cities Smart-casual is the way to go, particularly if dining out or attending the theatre. A light sweater or waterproof jacket is useful in spring and autumn.

Countryside Casual is fine and the further south you go in Europe, the more relaxed fashion becomes. Bring sturdy shoes.

Beach resorts Bikini tops and bare male chests are fine on the sand but cover up in beach restaurants and on the street.

Sleeping

For major cities and resorts, book a night or two in advance. Elsewhere you can usually just turn up and find a room.

Hostels There's no shortage of these across Europe, including more contemporary 'poshtels' and 'flashpacker' hostels with design-chic private rooms and stylish four-bed 'dorms'.

B&Bs and homestays Great for character-filled accommodation and connecting with locals.

Camping Cheap, but campsites are seldom dead-central.

Safe Travel

With terrorist attacks on the rise it's easy to become a little paranoid about how safe travel across Europe currently is. To ease your mind, consider the following points:

➡ Statistically you are many times more likely to be killed in a car crash or by gun crime than you are of becoming a victim of terrorism in Europe.

➡ Register with your own country before you travel so that you can be more easily found or contacted in an emergency (see http://dfat.gov.au/travel in Australia and https://step.state.gov in the USA).

➡ Stay in touch with friends and family back home so they always know where you are.

For more information, see p853.

Money

➡ ATMs are common and the easiest way to get cash. But always have a back-up option should you lose your card or encounter a technical glitch.

➡ Much of Western Europe generally uses a chip-and-pin system for added security – you'll need a four-digit PIN to use your card.

➡ To ensure your plastic works wherever you go, tell banks and credit-card providers your travel dates and the countries you plan to visit.

Tipping

Tipping isn't such a big deal in Europe as it is, say, in North America. If you tip, 5% to 10% will usually suffice.

Montmartre, Paris (p310)

Etiquette

Kissing A handshake is fine with strangers but across Continental Europe cheek-skimming kisses – at least two, but up to four – are the way to greet friends.

Language Europe has dozens of languages and it would be impossible to learn them all. But learning a few simple phrases and useful words in the language of each country you plan to visit will go a long way.

Religion At churches, mosques or other religious buildings be respectful and dress modestly: take off your hat and cover shoulders, torsos and thighs.

Eating

➡ Most hostels have kitchens and you learn a lot about a country by shopping in the supermarkets and corner shops.

➡ Search out weekly morning markets – there's no finer opportunity for mingling with locals. Take your own recyclable shopping bag or basket.

➡ While it might be tempting to favour restaurants with a menu in English, the very best (and best-loved by locals) rarely offer a translation.

➡ Avoid 'tourist menus' but do look out for places that offer a bargain set lunch – this can be a great way of sampling food at fancy restaurants usually beyond your budget.

➡ For popular places, reserve anything from a day to a month in advance.

©ANSHARPHOTO/SHUTTERSTOCK

If You Like...

Castles & Palaces

Versailles, France The vast formal palace against which all others are measured includes the Hall of Mirrors and sumptuous gardens. (p328)

Scloss Neuschwanstein, Germany In the heart of the Bavarian Alps, this is everybody's (including Disney's) castle fantasy. (p227)

State Hermitage Museum, Russia Now housed in the Winter Palace, a golden-green baroque building St Petersburg is unmatched for tsarist splendour. (p787)

Bran Castle, Romania Better known as Dracula's Castle, this Transylvanian beauty is straight out of a horror movie. (p734)

Alhambra, Spain This Islamic palace in Granada is a World Heritage–listed wonder. (p432)

Windsor Castle, Britain The world's largest and oldest continuously occupied fortress is one of the British monarch's principal residences. (p68)

Topkapı Palace, Turkey Tour the opulent pavilions and Treasury of the former court of the Ottoman empire in İstanbul. (p560)

Loire Valley, France More seriously turreted, chateaux dripping in gold leaf than anywhere else in Europe. Chambord is the Renaissance heavyweight. (p337)

Beaches & Islands

Santorini, Greece The name Santorini conjures up images of perfect golden beaches and the reality will not disappoint. (p539)

Albanian Riviera, Albania The stuff of legend among backpackers, this region offers swarming hotspots and sublime underdeveloped coastline. (p644)

Menorca, Spain Beaches so beautiful you think they might be dreams are tucked away in little coves in the prettiest of the Balearic Islands. (p418)

Black Sea Coast, Bulgaria Bulgaria guards the best beaches on the Black Sea, especially if you avoid the big resorts and head to Sozopol. (p754)

Hvar Island, Croatia Famed for its verdancy and lilac fields, this luxurious and sunny island is the jumping-off point for the wooded Pakleni Islands. (p608)

Isle of Skye, Scotland A 50-mile-long smorgasbord of velvet moors, jagged mountains, sparkling lochs and towering sea cliffs. (p95)

Sensational Scenery

The Alps, Switzerland There's no competition for the most stunning landscape in Europe – beautiful Switzerland. (p365)

Fjords, Norway Like steep gashes cutting into a precipitous coastline, Norway's fjords are simply unmissable. (p175)

West Coast of Ireland Wind-whipped headlands, hidden bays and mossy green clifftops battle against the wild Atlantic. (p117)

High Tatras, Slovakia Pristine snowfields, mountain lakes, thundering waterfalls, undulating pine forests and shimmering alpine meadows. (p690)

Vatnajökull National Park, Iceland Skaftafell is the jewel in the crown of this collection of peaks and glaciers. (p194)

Nightlife

Berlin, Germany There's nothing quite like arriving at superclub Berghain to dance from sunrise to sundown. (p217)

London, Britain A multifarious scene from a quiet session at the local pub to a full-blown night on the tiles of East London. (p52)

Moscow, Russia Once famed for its strict door policies, Moscow has spawned a slew of new, democratically run bars and clubs. (p776)

Madrid, Spain Has more bars per capita than anywhere else on earth and no one goes to bed here before killing the night. (p380)

Reykjavík, Iceland Join in the *djammið*, a raucous weekend pub crawl around the Icelandic capital's vibrant cafe-bar scene. (p190)

Belgrade, Serbia The Serbian capital is one of the liveliest places to party the night away, especially in its summer *splavovi* (floating clubs) on the Danube. (p658)

Fantastic Food & Drink

Copenhagen, Denmark Yes, Denmark's capital is the place to sample Europe's most sought-after menus and cool New Nordic cuisine. (p134)

San Sebastián, Spain The Basque powerhouse hosts an impressive array of Michelin-starred restaurants. (p392)

Lyon, France Forget Paris, the gastronomic capital of La Belle France is undoubtedly Lyon, a city that will have gourmands swooning. (p341)

İstanbul, Turkey Grilled meats, kebaps and a marvellous array of meze (small dishes) can be sampled in this paradise for food lovers. (p558)

Champagne, France Guided tours at prestigious Champagne houses end with tastings bien sûr. In Reims and Épernay, there are plenty more places to drink France's famous bubbles. (p339)

Adreneline Rush

Jungfraujoch, Switzerland Make the once-in-a-lifetime trip up to Europe's highest train station at 3454m. Be rewarded with staggering, million-dollar views of the Alps and Europe's mightiest peaks. (p369)

Top: Versailles (p328), France

Bottom: High Tatras (p690), Slovakia

Norrland, Sweden Explore the icy wastelands of northern Sweden in the most thrilling way possible: by snowmobile or dog sled. (p155)

Mostar, Bosnia and Hercegovina Screw up your courage and learn from professional divers how to safely jump off Stari Most. (p622)

Bovec and Bled, Slovenia The capital of active sports in Eastern Europe is Slovenia, with everything from canyoning to hydrospeeding. (p592)

Pont du Gard, France Skip, dance and prance across the top tier of the world's finest Roman aqueduct. Paddle beneath it in a canoe and cliff jump with locals into the river below. (p349)

Tarifa, Spain The wind is always blowing big-time here, considered by many to be the best spot on the Med for windsurfing and kitesurfing. (p438)

Art Collections

Musée du Louvre, France It's not just Paris' museum, it's the world's; treasures collected from Europe and all over the planet in exhaustive quantity. (p314)

Florence, Italy From the Duomo, to the Uffizi, to the Ponte Vecchio – the entire Renaissance in one city. (p487)

Hermitage, Russia Housed in the Winter Palace, the hermitage is one of the world's greatest art collections, stuffed full of treasures from Egyptian mummies to Picasso. (p787)

Van Gogh Museum, Netherlands Despite his troubled life and struggles with madness, Van Gogh's superb creations are gloriously easy to enjoy in Amsterdam. (p271)

Madrid, Spain With the Prado, Thyssen and Reina Sofía within a single golden mile of art, Madrid is a premier destinations for art lovers. (p380)

Bilbao, Spain For fans of modern art, there is no more iconic one-stop shop than the shimmering Museo Guggenheim. (p394)

Music

Berlin, Germany Everything from the world's most acclaimed techno venue to the Berlin Philharmonic can be seen in Germany's music-obsessed capital. (p211)

Irish music, Ireland The Irish love their music and it takes little to get them singing; the west coast hums with music pubs, especially in Galway. (p119)

Fado, Portugal Portuguese love the melancholic and nostalgic songs of fado; hear it in Lisbon's Alfama district. (p451)

Trubači, Serbia While this wild brass music is celebrated en masse at Guča each August, ragtag *trubači* bands wander the streets of many Serbian towns year-round. (p658)

Seville, Spain Few musical forms capture the spirit of a nation quite like passionate flamenco, and Seville is its cradle. (p425)

Cafes & Bars

Vienna's coffee houses, Austria Unchanged in decades and heavy with the air of refinement; pause for a cup served just so. (p291)

Irish pubs, Ireland Come and join the warm and gregarious crowds of locals in any pub in Ireland for a true cultural experience. (p106)

Paris' cafe society, France What's more clichéd: the practised curtness of the Parisian waiter or the studied boredom of the customer? (p310)

Amsterdam's tiny havens, Netherlands The Dutch call them 'brown cafes' for the former tobacco stains on the walls, but they're still cosy, warm and invariably friendly. (p276)

Bourse cafes, Belgium Many of Brussels' most iconic cafes are within stumbling distance of the city's Bourse and are great places to sample Belgian beer. (p256)

Reykjavík, Iceland The weekend pub crawl *djammið* in Iceland's party-fun capital is a local institution and rite of passage for any new arrival. (p190)

Historical Sites

Stonehenge, Britain The UK's most iconic – and mysterious – archaeological site, dating back some 5000 years. (p68)

Pompeii, Italy Wander the streets and alleys of this great ancient city, buried by a volcanic eruption. (p512)

Athens, Greece Ancient wonders include the Acropolis, Ancient Agora, Temple of Olympian Zeus and more. (p527)

Moscow's Kremlin, Russia The seat of power to medieval tsars and modern tyrants alike, Moscow's vast Kremlin offers incredible history lessons. (p776)

Dachau, Germany The first Nazi concentration camp is a harrowing introduction to WWII's horrors. (p222)

Carnac, France Predating Stonehenge by around 100 years, Carnac in windswept Brittany safeguards the world's greatest concentration of megalithic sites. (p335)

Month by Month

January

It's cold but most towns are relatively tourist-free and hotel prices are rock bottom. Head to Eastern Europe's ski slopes for wallet-friendly prices, with Bosnia and Bulgaria your best bets.

✹ Orthodox Christmas, Eastern Europe

Christmas is celebrated in different ways in Eastern Europe: many countries celebrate on Christmas Eve (24 December), with an evening meal and midnight Mass. In Russia, Ukraine, Belarus, Moldova, Serbia, Montenegro and Macedonia, Christmas falls in January, as per the Julian calendar.

✹ Kiruna Snöfestivalen, Sweden

In the last weekend of January this Lapland snow festival (www.snofestival en.com), based around a snow-sculpting competition, draws artists from all over Europe. There's also a husky-dog competition and a handicrafts fair.

February

Carnival in all its manic glory sweeps the Catholic regions. Cold temperatures are forgotten amid masquerades, street festivals and general bacchanalia. Expect to be kissed by a stranger.

✹ Carnaval, Netherlands

Pre-Lent is celebrated with greater vigour in Maastricht than anywhere else in northern Europe. While the rest of the Netherlands hopes the canals will freeze for ice skating, this Dutch corner cuts loose with a celebration that would have done its former Roman residents proud.

✹ Carnevale, Italy

In the period before Ash Wednesday, Venice goes mad for masks (www.venice-carnival-italy.com). Costume balls, many with traditions centuries old, enliven the social calendar in this storied old city. Even those without a coveted invite are swept up in the pageantry.

✹ Carnivals, Croatia

For colourful costumes and nonstop revelry head to Rijeka, where Carnival is the pinnacle of the year's calendar (www.rijecki-karneval.hr). Zadar and Samobor host Carnival celebrations too, with street dancing, concerts and masked balls.

✹ Fasching, Germany

Germany doesn't leave the pre-Lent season solely to its neighbours. Karneval is celebrated with abandon in the traditional Catholic regions including Bavaria, along the Rhine and particularly vibrantly in Cologne (www.koelner karneval.de).

March

Spring arrives in southern Europe. Further north the rest of the continent continues to freeze, though days are often bright.

✯✯ St Patrick's Day, Ireland

Parades and celebrations are held on 17 March in Irish towns big and small to honour the beloved patron saint of Ireland. While elsewhere the day is a commercialised romp of green beer, in his home country it's time for a parade and celebrations with friends and family.

☆ Budapest Spring Festival, Hungary

This two-week festival in March/April is one of Europe's top classical-music events (www.springfestival. hu). Concerts are held in a number of beautiful venues, including stunning churches, the opera house and the national theatre.

April

Spring arrives with a burst of colour, from the glorious bulb fields of Holland to the blooming orchards of Spain. On the most southern beaches it's time to shake the sand out of the umbrellas.

✯✯ Semana Santa, Spain

There are parades of penitents and holy icons in Spain, notably in Seville, during Easter week (www.semana-santa.org). Thousands of members of religious brotherhoods parade in traditional garb before thousands of spectators. Look for the pointed *capirotes* (hoods).

✯✯ Settimana Santa, Italy

Italy celebrates Holy Week with processions and passion plays. 'v Holy Thursday Rome is thronged with the faithful and even nonbelievers are swept up in the emotion and piety of hundreds of thousands thronging the Vatican and St Peter's Basilica.

✯✯ Orthodox Easter, Greece

The most important festival in the Greek Orthodox calendar has an emphasis on the Resurrection, so it's a celebratory event. The most significant part is midnight on Easter Saturday, when candles are lit and fireworks and a procession hit the streets.

✯✯ Feria de Abril, Spain

Hoods off! A weeklong party in Seville in late April counterbalances the religious peak of Easter (http://feriadesevilla.anda-lunet.com). The beautiful old squares of this gorgeous city come alive during the long, warm nights for which the nation is known.

✯✯ Koninginnedag, Netherlands

The nationwide celebration of Queen's Day on 27 April is especially fervent in Amsterdam, awash with orange costumes and fake Afros, beer, dope, leather boys, temporary roller coasters, clogs and general craziness.

May

May is usually sunny and warm and full of things to do – an excellent time to visit Europe. It's not too hot or too crowded, though you can still expect the big destinations to feel busy.

✯✯ Queima das Fitas, Portugal

Coimbra's annual highlight is this boozy week of fado music and revelry that begins on the first Thursday in May (www. queimadasfitascoimbra. pt), when students come out to celebrate the end of the academic year.

🍺 Beer Festival, Czech Republic

An event dear to many travellers' hearts, this Prague beer festival (www. ceskypivnifestival.cz) offers lots of food, music and – most importantly – around 70 beers from around the country from mid- to late May.

☆ Brussels Jazz Marathon, Belgium

Around-the-clock jazz performances hit the city of Brussels during the second-last weekend in May (www.facebook.com/ brusselsjazzmarathon). The saxophone is the instrument of choice for this international-flavoured city's most joyous celebration.

June

The huge summer travel season hasn't started yet, but the sun has broken through the clouds and the weather is generally gorgeous across the continent.

🎭 Festa de São João, Portugal

Elaborate processions, live music on Porto's plazas and merrymaking all across Portugal's second city. Squeaky plastic hammers (for sale everywhere) come out for the unusual custom of whacking one another. Everyone is fair game – expect no mercy.

🎭 White Nights, Russia

By mid-June the Baltic sun just sinks behind the horizon at night, leaving the sky a grey-white colour and encouraging locals to forget routines and party hard. The best place to join the fun is St Petersburg, where balls, classical-music concerts and other summer events keep spirits high.

☆ Hellenic Festival, Greece

The ancient theatre at Epidavros and the Odeon of Herodes Atticus are the headline venues of Athens' annual cultural shindig (www.greekfestival.gr). The festival, which runs from mid-June to August, features music, dance, theatre and much more.

☆ Glastonbury Festival, Britain

Glastonbury's youthful summer vibe peaks for this long weekend of music, theatre and New Age shenanigans (www.glastonburyfestivals.co.uk). It's one of England's favourite outdoor events and more than 100,000 turn up to writhe around in the grassy fields (or deep mud) at Pilton's (Worthy) Farm. Every six years the festival indulges in a fallow year for its pastures to rejuvenate – meaning no fest in 2018 (but back with a vengeance in 2019).

☆ Roskilde Festival, Denmark

Northern Europe's largest music festival (www.roskilde-festival.dk) rocks Roskilde each summer. It takes place in late June but advance ticket sales are on offer in December and the festival usually sells out.

July

One of the busiest months for travel across the continent – with outdoor cafes, beer gardens and beach clubs all hopping with activity. Expect beautiful – even steamy – weather anywhere you travel.

🎭 Il Palio, Italy

Siena's great annual event is the Palio (2 July and 16 August; www.thepalio.com), a pageant culminating in a bareback horse race round Il Campo. The city is divided into 17 *contrade* (districts), of which 10 compete for the *palio* (silk banner), with emotions exploding.

🎭 Running of the Bulls, Spain

Fiesta de San Fermín (Sanfermines) is the weeklong, nonstop Pamplona festival (www.bullrunpamplona.com) with the daily *encierro* (running of the bulls) as its centrepiece. Anything can happen, but it rarely ends well for the bull. The anti-bullfighting event, the Running of the Nudes (www.runningofthenudes.com), takes place two days earlier.

☆ Festival d'Avignon, France

Rouse your inner thespian with Avignon's performing-arts festival in the south of France. Street acts in its fringe fest are as inspired as those on official stages.

☆ EXIT, Serbia

Eastern Europe's most talked-about music festival (www.exitfest.org) takes place within the walls of the Petrovaradin Citadel in Serbia's second city, Novi Sad. Book early as it attracts music lovers from all over the continent with big international acts headlining.

☆ Gentse Feesten, Belgium

Ghent is transformed into a 10-day party of music and theatre (www.gentsefeesten.be), a highlight of which is a vast techno celebration called 10 Days Off.

🎭 Medieval Festival of the Arts, Romania

The beautiful Romanian city of Sighişoara hosts open-air concerts, parades and ceremonies, all glorifying medieval Transylvania and taking the town back to its fascinating 12th-century origins.

☆ Bažant Pohoda, Slovakia

Slovakia's largest music festival (www.pohodafestival.sk) represents all genres of music from folk and rock to orchestral over eight different stages. It's firmly established as one of Europe's biggest and best summer music festivals.

☆ Ultra Europe, Croatia

Held over three days in Split's Poljud Stadium, this electronic music fest (www.ultraeurope.com) includes a huge beach party.

☆ Paléo Festival Nyon, Switzerland

More than 250 shows and concerts are staged for this premier music festival (http://yeah.paleo.ch) held above the town of Nyon.

August

Everybody's going someplace as half of Europe shuts down to enjoy the traditional month of holiday with the other half. If it's near the beach, from Germany's Baltic to Spain's Balearics, it's mobbed and the temperatures are hot, hot, hot!

☆ Amsterdam Gay Pride, Netherlands

Held at the beginning of August, this is one of Europe's best GLBT events (www.amsterdamgaypride.nl). It's more about freedom and diversity than protest.

☆ Salzburg Festival, Austria

Austria's most renowned classical-music festival (www.salzburgfestival.at) attracts international stars from late July to the end of August. That urbane person sitting by you having a glass of wine who looks like a famous cellist, probably is.

☆ Zürich Street Parade, Switzerland

Zürich lets its hair down with an enormous techno parade (www.streetparade.com). All thoughts of numbered accounts are forgotten as bankers, and everybody else in this otherwise staid burg, party to orgasmic, deep-base thump, thump, thump.

☆ Notting Hill Carnival, Britain

This is Europe's largest – and London's most vibrant – outdoor carnival (www.thelondonnottinghillcarnival.com), where London's Caribbean community shows the city how to party. Food, frolic and fun are just a part of this vast multicultural two-day celebration.

☆ Edinburgh International Festival, Britain

Three weeks of innovative drama, comedy, dance, music and more (www.eif.co.uk). Two weeks overlap with the celebrated Fringe Festival (www.edfringe.com), which draws acts from around the globe. Expect cutting-edge productions that often defy description.

☆ Guča Trumpet Festival, Serbia

Guča's Dragačevo Trumpet Assembly (www.guca.rs) is one of the most exciting and bizarre events in all of Eastern Europe. Hundreds of thousands of revellers descend on the small Serbian town to damage their eardrums, livers and sanity in four cacophonous days of celebration.

September

It's cooling off in every sense, from the northern countries to the romance started on a dance floor in Ibiza. Maybe the best time to visit: the weather's still good and the crowds have thinned.

☆ Oktoberfest, Germany

Despite its name, Germany's legendary beer-swilling party (www.oktoberfest.de) starts mid-September in Munich and finishes a week into October. Millions descend for litres of beer and carousing that has no equal. If you didn't plan ahead, you'll have to sleep in Austria.

☆ Festes de la Mercè, Spain

Barcelona knows how to party until dawn and it outdoes itself for the Festes de la Mercè (around 24 September). The city's biggest celebration has four days of concerts, dancing, *castellers* (human-castle builders), fireworks and *correfocs* – a parade of fireworks-spitting dragons and devils.

October

Another good month to visit – almost everything is still open, while prices and visitor numbers are way down. Weather can be unpredictable, though, and even cold in northern Europe.

☆ Belfast International Arts Festival, Northern Ireland

After 50 years of being hosted at Queen's University, this huge arts festival (www.belfastinternational-artsfestival.com) reinvented itself in 2015 and is now held at a wider cache of Belfast venues. The city sheds its gritty legacy and celebrates the intellectual and the creative without excessive hype.

🍷 Wine Festival, Moldova

Wine-enriched folkloric performances in Moldova draw oenophiles and anyone wanting to profit from the 10-day visa-free regime Moldova introduces during the festival.

November

Autumn leaves have fallen and snow is about to across much of Europe. Even the temperate zones around the Mediterranean Sea can receive chilly, rainy and blustery weather. Most seasonal attractions have closed for the year.

🎆 Guy Fawkes Night, Britain

Bonfires and fireworks erupt across Britain on 5 November, recalling the foiling of a plot to blow up the Houses of Parliament in the 1600s. Try to seek out a viewpoint on higher ground in London to see glowing explosions erupt everywhere across the city.

☆ Iceland Airwaves, Iceland

Roll on up to Reykjavík for Iceland Airwaves (www.icelandairwaves.is), a great music festival featuring both Icelandic and international acts.

December

Despite freezing temperatures this is a magical time to visit Europe, with Christmas decorations brightening the dark streets. Prices remain surprisingly low provided you avoid Christmas and New Year's Eve.

🎆 Natale, Italy

Italian churches set up an intricate crib or a *presepe* (nativity scene) in the lead-up to Christmas. Some are quite famous, and many date back hundreds of years and are venerated for their spiritual ties.

🛍 Christmas Markets

In December, Christmas markets (www.christmas-markets.com) are held across Europe, with particularly good ones in Germany, Austria, Slovakia and Czech Republic. The most famous are in Nuremberg and Vienna. Slovak Christmas markets are regarded as some of Europe's best and a great opportunity to taste *medovina* (mead) and *lokše* (potato pancakes).

Plan Your Trip
Itineraries

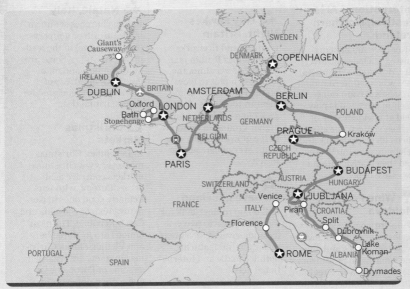

8 WEEKS **First-Time Europe**

This combo of major league countries and left-field destinations provides an irresistible mix of world-famous sights and unforgettable experiences for the first-time European traveller.

Ease into the first two weeks with Ireland and Great Britain. The atmosphere of a **Dublin** bar provides the perfect introduction, followed by a few days exploring the city's museums and literary haunts. It costs nothing to walk across the Unesco-listed **Giant's Causeway** in Northern Ireland, which leaves more money to enjoy your next stop: **London**. The city is pricey, but affordable if you focus on its free museums and parks. Travel west to marvel at **Stonehenge** and wander the historic streets of **Oxford** and **Bath**.

Return to London to board the Eurostar or a low-cost airline flight (often cheaper) for the next couple of weeks to hop around some of the continent's iconic northern metropolises. In **Paris** you will be dazzled by the Louvre, Eiffel Tower and Versailles. Check out more classic art, plus *those* cafes, in enchanting **Amsterdam**. Get a taste of Scandinavia in **Copenhagen**, the

Piran (p595), Slovenia

coolest kid of the Nordic bloc. And unleash your inner party animal in **Berlin**, where you can also see the remains of the wall.

Go through the former Iron Curtain to the gorgeous old Polish royal capital of **Kraków**, miraculously spared destruction in WWII. If you thought that was stunning wait till you see the architectural glories of **Prague**. Continue to **Budapest** to freshen up in thermal baths and enjoy cafes and bars, followed by a visit to Slovenia's eco-friendly capital **Ljubljana**.

The Venetian-style seaside resort of **Piran** is a good starting point for a jour-ney down the scenic Dalmatian Coast via **Split** and **Dubrovnik**, both with ancient ruins to explore. End up off the beaten track in Albania, where you can sail on a ferry across beguiling **Lake Koman** and relax at a beachside campsite in **Dry-mades** on the Albanian Riviera.

Cruise across the Adriatic on one of the ferry services to Italy, where your final week's pit stops include hauntingly beauti-ful **Venice**, the exquisite Renaissance time capsule of **Florence**, and **Rome**.

East to West

This trans-European journey kicks off in the east, a dynamic part of Europe where it's still possible to encounter under-the-radar experiences. Then enjoy a more leisurely pace of life along the balmy Mediterranean coast as you continue west towards the resorts of Spain and Portugal.

Begin in Russia's capital **Moscow**, where the imposing Kremlin and adjacent Red Square are guaranteed to strike you with awe. Take an overnight train to **St Petersburg**, home to the magnificent art collection of the Hermitage and gorgeously restored imperial palaces. Another overnight train will whisk you to Latvia's lovely art-nouveau captial **Rīga**, where you can get a taste of the Baltic. If the weather's fine consider a day trip to the chic beach resort of **Jūrmala**.

Poland's capital **Warsaw** is a vibrant city that's survived all that history could throw at it. Continue into Ukraine and spend a few days in Unesco World Heritage–listed **Lviv**, which oozes Central European charm. Move on to **Transylvania** and sharpen your fangs at 'Dracula's' castle in **Bran**. Romania's dynamic capital **Bucharest** is next, with its good museums, parks and trendy cafes.

Sofia, Bulgaria's relaxed capital, is another recommended pitstop en-route to the beautiful, chaotic **İstanbul**: when you've had your fill of sightseeing you can relax in a hamam (Turkish steam bath).

Explore the ancient world with the Acropolis in **Athens**, then island-hop to volcanic **Santorini**. Pick up the pace by flying to Spain where the genius of Gaudí, cultural riches and glorious food beckon in supercool **Barcelona**. Zip north to Basque seaside resort **San Sebastián**, with its delicious food scene, and to the Museo Guggenheim in happening **Bilbao**. End in energetic **Madrid**, home to some of Europe's finest galleries and bars.

Head south to see the beautiful Moorish architecture of the Alhambra in **Granada** and the stunning Mezquita of **Córdoba**. Cross to Portugal where the fascinating capital **Lisbon** offers a lamplit old quarter and superb *pastéis de nata* (custard tarts) in the waterside Belém district.

Top: Mezquita (Mosque; p429), Córdoba, Spain
Bottom: Blackheads House (p817), Rīga, Latvia

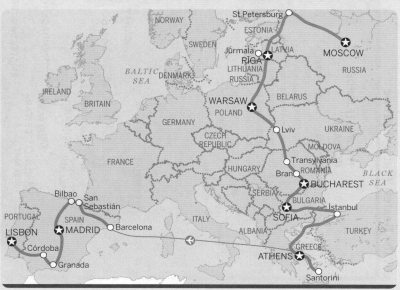

Off the Beaten Track – Europe

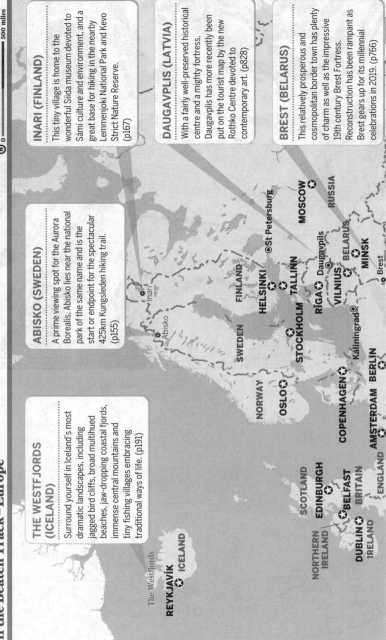

INARI (FINLAND)

This tiny village is home to the wonderful Siida museum devoted to Sámi culture and environment, and a great base for hiking in the nearby Lemmenjoki National Park and Kevo Strict Nature Reserve. (p167)

DAUGAVPILS (LATVIA)

With a fairly well-preserved historical centre and a mighty fortress, Daugavpils has more recently been put on the tourist map by the new Rothko Centre devoted to contemporary art. (p828)

BREST (BELARUS)

This relatively prosperous and cosmopolitan border town has plenty of charm as well as the impressive 19th century Brest Fortress. Reconstruction has been rampant as Brest gears up for its millennial celebrations in 2019. (p766)

ABISKO (SWEDEN)

A prime viewing spot for the Aurora Borealis, Abisko lies near the national park of the same name and is the start or endpoint for the spectacular 425km Kungsleden hiking trail. (p155)

THE WESTFJORDS (ICELAND)

Surround yourself in Iceland's most dramatic landscapes, including jagged bird cliffs, broad multihued beaches, jaw-dropping coastal fjords, immense central mountains and tiny fishing villages embracing traditional ways of life. (p191)

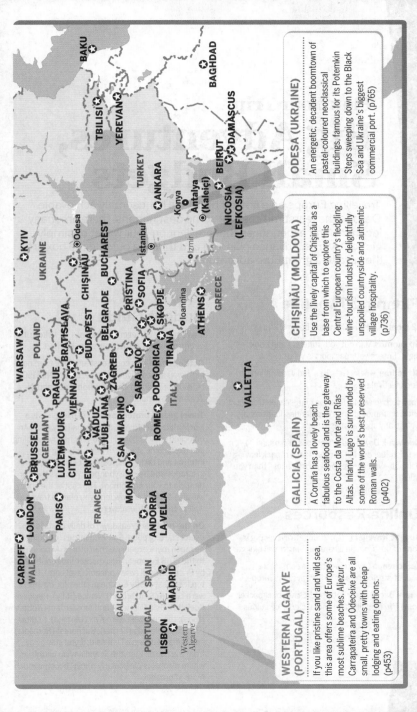

WESTERN ALGARVE (PORTUGAL)

If you like pristine sand and wild sea, this area offers some of Europe's most sublime beaches. Aljezur, Carrapateira and Odeceixe are all small, pretty towns with cheap lodging and eating options.
(p453)

GALICIA (SPAIN)

A Coruña has a lovely beach, fabulous seafood and is the gateway to the Costa da Morte and Rías Altas. Inland, Lugo is surrounded by some of the world's best preserved Roman walls.
(p402)

CHIŞINĂU (MOLDOVA)

Use the lively capital of Chişinău as a base from which to explore this Central European country's fledgling wine-tourism industry, delightfully unspoiled countryside and authentic village hospitality.
(p736)

ODESA (UKRAINE)

An energetic, decadent boomtown of pastel-coloured neoclassical buildings, famous for its Potemkin Steps sweeping down to the Black Sea and Ukraine's biggest commercial port. (p765)

Plan Your Trip

Big Adventures, Small Budgets

Travelling Europe on a limited budget is handsomely achievable. Despite the fearsome costs of some destinations, there are many locations and experiences that are light on your wallet or simply gloriously free. Advance planning and thinking outside the box are the keys to a great Euro adventure.

Planning Timeline

12 months before Calculate budget. Start saving.

Six months Map out your itinerary and book flight. Ensure your passport is valid.

Six to four weeks Get visas and vaccinations. Book festival tickets.

Four to two weeks Reserve high-season transport and accommodation in popular destinations, as well as any specialist activities.

One week Download travel apps and music playlist. Test out full backpack and repack leaving half out – you can get by with much less than you think.

Online Resources

Budget Traveller (http://budgettraveller.org) Tons of tips from an award-winning travel blogger.

Eurocheapo (www.eurocheapo.com) More budget-stretching advice on travelling Europe.

Savvy Backpacker (http://thesavvybackpacker.com) Trip planning and useful city price guides.

Budget Guide

2 are many different elements to take into account when planning your budget.

Getting there This could cost anything from nothing, if you already live in Europe, to, say, NZ$1500 (€960) for a return air ticket from Auckland, New Zealand, to London.

Travel gear & protection A good backpack is a worthwhile investment, plus a small day pack. An unlocked smart phone is also very handy, enabling you to combine staying in touch, surfing the internet and taking photos. Don't skimp on travel insurance and be sure your policy covers theft or damage to your equipment. The cost of the policy will also depend on how long you plan to travel, as well as the countries covered.

On the road Our breakdown of daily costs is a useful starting point. Some countries are going to be much more expensive than others. According to the 2018 European Backpacker Index published by Price of Travel (www.priceoftravel.com), the top five most costly European cities for travellers were Zürich (Switzerland), Venice (Italy), Reykjavik (Iceland), Oslo (Norway) and Amsterdam (Netherlands); the cheapest were Kyiv (Ukraine), Kraków (Poland), Belgrade (Serbia), Bucharest (Romania) and Sofia (Bulgaria). That said, if you stay away from the booze, then the Scandinavian countries, where alcohol is particularly pricey, become much more affordable.

Time of year Avoid high season (June to August, and over Christmas and New Year, and winter school holidays in ski resort areas) and you will find prices are lower, particularly for accommodation and transport. Even for busy times, booking transport well in advance or using some kind of travel pass can cut your costs considerably.

All this said, you could assume a rock-bottom budget of €60/40/35 a day for an expensive/midrange/cheap country. This would entail a pretty spartan standard of accommodation and eating with little more than the occasional beer. Add at least €30 more to each of these daily amounts to account for more comfort and fun during your travels.

Accommodation

Hostels and camping are among the cheapest forms of accommodation. Also consider sites that link travellers with thousands of global residents who'll let you occupy their couch, spare room or even their garden in your own tent – and sometimes show you around town – for free.

Couchsurfing (www.couchsurfing.com)

Camp in My Garden (http://campinmygarden.com)

Global Freeloaders (www.globalfreeloaders.com)

Hospitality Club (www.hospitalityclub.org)

5W (www.womenwelcomewomen.org.uk)

Stay 4 Free (www.stay4free.com)

Check the rules of each organisation. And always let friends and family know where you're staying.

Swopping homes (see www.homeexchange.com), house-sitting (using sites such as www.housecarers.com or www.mindmyhouse.com) and pet-sitting (www.trustedhousesitters.com) are other cheap ways of staying in another place without forking out a cent.

Discount Cards

Camping Cards

The Camping Card International (CCI; www.campingcardinternational.com) is an ID that can be used instead of a passport when checking into a camping ground. Many camping grounds offer a small discount if you sign in with one and it includes third-party insurance.

Transport Passes

If you plan to visit more than a few countries, or one or two countries in-depth, you might save money with a rail pass.

European citizens and residents qualify for a one-month InterRail pass (www.interrail.eu). There are special rates if you're under 26 years old. Children under 12 are free.

Non-European citizens can apply for a Eurail pass (www.eurail.com) valid in 28 countries for up to three months.

Student Cards

The International Student Identity Card (www.isic.org), available for students, teachers and under-26s, offers thousands of worldwide discounts on transport, museum entry, youth hostels and even some restaurants. Apply for the cards online or via issuing offices, which include STA Travel (www.statravel.com).

For under-26s, there's also the European Youth Card (www.euro26.org). Many countries have raised the age limit for this card to under 30.

City & Museum Passes

Enquire at tourist offices about passes that provide free and/or discounted entry to many key local attractions, experiences and services. Many museums offer cheaper combo tickets covering two or three museums in town. These can work out to be good value, but do your sums before you buy.

Best Budget Experiences

The following are our picks for the best locations, sights and experiences across Europe for budget travellers:

Great Britain & Ireland

Great Britain Entry to London's amazing selection of museums and galleries usually costs nothing, and it's free entry to Glasgow and Edinburgh's premier cultural storehouses, too. The inspiring landscapes of the Lake District or along Hadrian's Wall can be appreciated gratis.

Ireland Dublin's Trinity College and the National Gallery are a couple of the city's free attractions. In Northern Ireland, Derry's city walls and the People's Gallery Murals are both no-charge highlights.

Scandinavia

Denmark Copenhagen's National Museum and National Gallery are both free. So is a wander in the intriguing alternative 'republic' of Christiania or a peek at the *Little Mermaid*. Plus, free walking tours can show you around town.

Sweden Some major state-run museums in Stockholm, such as the excellent Historiska Museet, are free. Sign up online for a free walking tour of the city (http://freetourstockholm. com). Test your parkour skills for free using the purpose-built obstacle course in city park Nydalsparken.

DAILY COSTS

COUNTRY	BUDGET (€)	MIDRANGE (€)	TOP END (€)
Albania	<50	50-120	>120
Austria	<100	100-200	>200
Belgium	<100	100-200	>200
Bosnia & Hercegovina	<60	60-130	>130
Britain	<80	80-160	>160
Bulgaria	<50	50-120	>120
Croatia	<60	60-130	>130
Czech Republic	<80	80-200	>200
Denmark	<120	120-220	>220
Estonia	<60	60-120	>120
Finland	<120	120-250	>250
France	<110	110-220	>220
Germany	<100	100-200	>200
Greece	<60	60-120	>120
Hungary	<60	60-130	>130
Ireland	<60	60-120	>120
Italy	<100	100-250	>250
Kosovo	<60	60-130	>130
Latvia	<60	60-120	>120
Lithuania	<60	60-120	>120
Luxembourg	<100	100-200	>200
Macedonia	<60	60-120	>120
The Netherlands	<100	100-200	>200
Norway	<140	140-220	>220
Poland	<50	50-90	>90
Portugal	<60	60-130	>130
Romania	<50	50-120	>120
Russia	<20	20-50	>50
Serbia	<60	60-130	>130
Slovakia	<50	50-120	>120
Slovenia	<50	50-100	>100
Spain	<80	80-180	>180
Sweden	<110	110-220	>220
Switzerland	<180	180-270	>270
Turkey	<50	50-100	>100
Ukraine	<20	20-50	>50

Finland It's a cheap ferry ride from Helsinki to the fortress islands of Suomenlinna, with a fascinating view of the harbour on the way. Once there, you can wander the fortifications to your heart's content.

Norway Not known as a budget destination, but Oslo's iconic opera house is free to wander around, while Bergen's classic Bryggen district is the city's major highlight.

Iceland Grab a bike from Reykjavík and head out to explore the Golden Circle attractions, none of which charge admission. Many more of Iceland's natural wonders are free to visit.

Germany, Austria & Benelux

Germany A trio of iconic Berlin attractions are free: the Brandenburg Gate is a symbol of the city; the nearby Reichstag offers marvellous city views from its roof terrace and glass dome; and the al fresco Berlin Wall Memorial is essential viewing. In Hamburg, see the harbour for a pittance by jumping on one of the regular ferry services.

Austria There is no cheaper thrill in Austria than a hair-raising motor along the 36 hairpins of Grossglockner Road, with staggering views of snow-capped mountain peaks and plunging waterfalls guaranteed. Rub shoulders with 28 dwarfs, scale a staircase encrusted with angels and relive scenes from *The Sound of Music* – all for free at Salzburg's Schloss Mirabell.

Belgium Brussels' magnificent Grand Place is one of the world's most unforgettable city squares. Nearby, the cheeky Manneken Pis statue, a tiny statue of a boy urinating, is a major drawcard. Or track down Tin Tin, Lucky Luke and other comic-strip heroes emblazoned on building facades all over the capital.

Luxembourg City It's not a cheap town, but it's a beautiful one; wandering its ramparts is its most spectacular attraction. Plus, for just €2, you can head out to explore anywhere in this small country by train or bus.

The Netherlands It costs nothing to spend a glorious afternoon in Amsterdam's Vondelpark, a slice of idyllic Dutch life on a sunny day.

France & Switzerland

France It doesn't cost a cent to scamper up, cartwheel across or simply laze on the golden sands and gorge on extraordinary sea views of Dune du Pilat, Europe's largest sand dune. In Paris catch a free fashion show in the city's flagship department store Galeries Lafayette, track down

stunning street art and whittle away a Sunday at the world's largest flea market, Marché aux Puces de St-Ouen.

Switzerland Let your hair down and boogie with the best of them at Europe's largest street party, aka Zürich's wild and wacky, larger-than-life Street Parade in August. Urban swimming is wildly popular in Bern, Basel and Zürich. Then of course, there's Europe's biggest plain waterfall, the thunderous Rheinfall – free, totally free.

Spain & Portugal

Spain Madrid's art-rammed Museo del Prado is free in the late afternoon. The nearby Reina Sofía and Museo Thyssen-Bornemisza are also free at certain times. Santiago de Compostela, one of Europe's most memorable cathedrals, is free to enter, as is Barcelona's Mercat de la Boqueria covered market.

Portugal Accommodation in Portugal offers the best value in Western Europe, and eating out certainly doesn't break the budget either. The extraordinary cathedral in Braga doesn't charge admission.

Italy, Greece & Turkey

Italy The Vatican museums, including the Sistine Chapel, are free on the last Sunday of the month, while blockbuster Roman sights like the Pantheon and Trevi Fountain are always free. Explore the Cinque Terre, an endless network of seaside hiking trails linking five beautiful medieval villages teetering perilously on cliff edges.

Greece The Meteora monasteries, perched atop towering rock pinnacles, make for an otherworldly setting. See the world from the viewpoint of 11th-century hermit monks. With world-famous climbing, once-secret hiking trails, stunning chapels and truly dramatic views, you'll understand why they stayed so long.

Turkey Is there a more Turkish experience than visiting a grand, historic hamam? Head to İstanbul for a cultural soak.

Balkans

Albania For just a handful of lekë, ride the ferry down enormous Lake Koman on a three-hour voyage through a chain of spectacular mountain gorges, stopping off at various tiny hamlets on the way. Some travellers enjoy the scenery so much they do the journey in both directions in one day; others continue to the Accursed Mountains for more stunning scenery.

FESTIVALS & ACTIVITIES

Fancy going to Glastonbury, one of Europe's top festivals? Know that in 2017 a ticket cost £238 plus £5 booking fee, and that dedicated festival fans were already registering for the 2019 fest in late 2017. Attendance at Europe's biggest musical parties doesn't come cheap, but there are scores of smaller, less costly festivals that you could check out, particularly over the summer. See Must Love Festivals (http://mustlovefestivals.com) for ideas.

Likewise if you have particular activities in mind – say, a cooking course, yoga or skiing – look into where you might get the best value. A cooking course in İstanbul is likely to be far cheaper than one in Paris. Head to Eastern Europe's ski slopes for wallet-friendly prices, with Bosnia and Bulgaria your best bets.

Kosovo The Pristina Bear Sanctuary, a superb NGO-run project in the countryside around the Kosovan capital can be visited for free (though donations are accepted), and the journey here is part of the fun. The resident bears have all been rescued from restaurants where they were once kept as caged 'mascots', and it's wonderful to see them finally enjoying good living conditions.

Slovenia Lake Bled is lovely to behold from almost any vantage point and makes a stunning backdrop for the 6km walk along the perimeter. It doesn't cost a penny and is beautiful any time of year.

Central & Eastern Europe

Belarus The centre of Minsk is surprisingly attractive: a uniform conurbation that features colourful 1950s architectural flourishes that are far grander than you might expect from Soviet-era style.

Czech Republic Kutná Hora's Sedlec Ossuary (aka the 'Bone Church') is at the top of every backpacker's must-do list. It's cheap to enter and relatively easy to get to from Prague by bus or train.

Georgia The best way to experience Georgia on a budget is simply to stroll through old Tbilisi, with its winding lanes, balconied houses, leafy squares and handsome churches.

Hungary No trip to Budapest is complete without a dip in the pool and hot tub, and the Széchenyi Baths are the most popular and accessible.

Moldova Try to make it over to the country's separatist, Russian-speaking region of Transdniestr. It's a time-warp kind of place, where the Soviet Union reigns supreme and busts of Lenin line the main boulevards.

Poland It's free to enter the grounds of the Auschwitz-Birkenau Memorial & Museum to bear witness to one of history's greatest crimes: the murder of more than a million Jews and many others by Nazi German occupiers in WWII.

Romania Bucharest's enormous Palace of Parliament is the world's second-largest administrative building and a testament to the egos of dictators. Students pay half price for the guided tour.

Slovakia The High Tatras feature true Alpine peaks, arising seemingly in the middle of nowhere. There are miles of excellent hiking trails, and entry to the mountains is free.

Ukraine Lviv's Ploshcha Rynok, the city's amazing market square, lies at the heart of the Unesco-protected heritage zone. It's free to enjoy.

Russia & the Baltic Coast

Russia Moscow's Red Square, Lenin's Tomb and Gorky Park are among its not-to-be-missed free attractions. Time your visit to St Petersburg's magnificent Hermitage Museum for the first Thursday of the month, when it's free entry to all.

Baltic States There's no charge for enjoying the beaches at Pärnu in Estonia, Jūrmala in Latvia and the golden sand dunes of the Curonian Spit National Park in Lithuania.

Plan Your Trip
Getting Around Europe

For many, trains or buses will be the preferred mode of Euro transport. Flights are useful for covering distances quickly and are affordable if booked in advance. If time isn't an issue, then cycling can get you from one end of the continent to the other, and keep you fit.

Air

In the face of ever-increasing competition from low-cost airlines, many national carriers have dropped their prices and regularly offer special deals. Some, such as British Airways, have even adopted the low-cost model of online booking, where the customer can opt to buy a one-way flight, or piece together their own return journey from two one-way legs. For a comprehensive overview of which low-cost carriers fly to or from different European cities, check out the excellent www.fly cheapo.com.

Air Passes

Depending on which airline you fly into Europe, you may be able to purchase one of the following air passes. Check the details carefully and compare prices with budget airlines, taking into account taxes and any luggage surcharges.

Visit Europe Pass (www.oneworld.com/flights/single-continent-fares/visit-europe)

Europe Airpass (http://www.staralliance.com/en/airpass-details)

SkyTeam (www.skyteam.com)

Transport Options

Train Europe's train network is fast and efficient but rarely a bargain, unless you book well in advance or use a rail pass wisely.

Bus Usually taken for short trips in more remote areas, though long-distance intercity buses can be cheap.

Car You can hire a car or drive your own through Europe. Roads are excellent but petrol is expensive. Alternatively, hook up with other drivers keen to car share.

Ferry Boats connect Britain and Ireland with mainland Europe; Scandinavia to the Baltic countries and Germany; and Italy to the Balkans and Greece.

Air Speed things up by flying from one end of the continent to the other.

Bicycle Slow things down on a two-wheeler; a great way to get around just about anywhere.

Charter Flights

Charter flights are organised by tour operators for travellers who have purchased a holiday package that includes transport and accommodation. Depending on when you fly it can be a very good deal. Certain charter airlines such as Condor (www.condor.com) also sell flights directly, without the accommodation packages.

Train

Comfortable, frequent and reliable, trains are *the* way to get around Europe.

➡ Many state railways have interactive websites publishing their timetables and fares, including Germany (www.bahn.de) and Switzerland (www.sbb.ch), which both have pages in English. Eurail (www.eurail.com) links to 28 European train companies.

➡ The very comprehensive Man in Seat 61 (www.seat61.com) is a gem, while the US-based Budget Europe Travel Service (www.budgeteuropetravel.com) can also help with tips.

➡ European trains sometimes split en route to service two destinations, so even if you're on the right train, make sure you're also in the correct carriage.

➡ A train journey to almost every station in Europe can be booked via the French railways

website Oui SNCF (www.oui.sncf), which also sells InterRail and other passes.

International Rail Passes

If you're covering lots of ground, a rail pass (which usually needs to be purchased in your home country) is the way to go. For more information on specific passes, see International Rail Passes (p863) in the Transport chapter.

➡ You can buy online from sites such as www.raileurope.com, www.railpass.com and www.interrail.eu. If you're already in Europe arrange for the pass to be sent to parents or friends, then forwarded on.

➡ Compare prices of point-to-point ticket charges and rail passes before purchasing to make absolutely sure you'll break even.

➡ Shop around as prices do vary between outlets. When weighing up options, look into cheap deals that include advance-purchase reductions, one-off promotions or special circular-route tickets.

➡ Pass-holders must always carry their passport with them for identification purposes. The railways' policy is that passes cannot be replaced or refunded if lost or stolen.

National Rail Passes

National rail operators might also offer their own passes, or at least a discount card, offering substantial reductions on tickets purchased (eg the Bahn Card in Germany or the Half-Fare Card in Switzerland).

Check your options at individual train-operator sites via http://uk.voyages-sncf.com/en. Such discount cards are usually only good value it if you're staying in the country a while and doing a lot of travelling.

Bus

If you really want to make your budget go further then buses are always going to be a cheaper (but slower) form of transport around Europe.

There are a huge number of bus companies on the market offering cheap tickets. Search for the most competitive fare and convenient route with ComparaBUS (www.comparabus.com).

SLEEPING IN AIRPORTS

Sometimes the cheapest flights are for very early morning departures or late arrivals after public transport has stopped for the night. In such cases, it may be worth checking out whether it's possible to snooze at the airport – it's cheaper than paying for a hotel room for what would probably only be a short night anyway.

Start your research with the entertaining Guide to Sleeping in Airports (www.sleepinginairports.net): in Europe, airports in Munich, Helsinki, Tallinn and Zürich make it into the world's top 10 airports to sleep in. Among the worst for kipping the night: London's Luton, Santorini, Pisa and Paris' Aéroport de Beauvais.

FlixBus (www.flixbus.com) has its own app, free wi-fi and plug sockets on board its buses and, at the last count, linked 1400 destinations in 26 countries.

Megabus (http://uk.megabus.com) offers discount bus tickets throughout the UK and to cities in Belgium, France, Germany, Italy, the Netherlands, Ireland and Spain.

Bus Passes

Eurolines (www.eurolines.com) Europe's biggest organisation of international buses, comprised of various national companies, operates under the name Eurolines. The Eurolines Pass (www.eurolines-pass.eu) allows you to visit a choice of 50 cities across Europe over 15/30 days. In high season (mid-June to mid-September) the pass costs €270/350 for those aged under 26, or €320/425 for those 26 and over. It's cheaper in other periods.

Busabout (www.busabout.com) Offers a 'hop-on, hop-off' service around Europe, stopping at major cities. Buses are often oversubscribed, so book each sector to avoid being stranded. It departs every two days from May to the end of October.

Car

While driving a car (p860) will give you the greatest flexibility in the places you can see across Europe, it will also be the most expensive way to travel unless you happen to be travelling in a group that can share the cost.

If that's not the case then hitching (p862) is another option – it's never entirely safe, though, and we cannot recommend it.

Car Sharing

A variation on hitching is car sharing, whereby you hook up with other drivers heading to the same place as you with empty seats in their car. You only pay a small contribution to the driver's costs, making it a cheap way to get around. Lifts are arranged and paid for in advance online using a car-pooling service such as Bla Bla Car (www.blablacar.com), Drive2Day (www.drive2day.de) or Europe Carpooling (http://www.europe-carpooling.com).

When searching for a ride, Bla Bla Car has a 'ladies only' filter allowing women to only accept lifts with other female drivers and passengers.

Another increasingly popular means of getting from A to B is renting a car from a local through a car-pooling service such as Drivy (www.drivy.co.uk), which connects ride-seekers with car owners in the UK, France, Spain, Germany, Austria and Belgium.

Student noticeboards in colleges are often another good car-pooling source.

Bicycle

Much of Europe is ideally suited to cycling. Popular cycling areas include the whole of the Netherlands, the Belgian Ardennes, the west of Ireland, the upper reaches of the Danube in southern Germany and anywhere in northern Switzerland, Denmark or the south of France. Exploring the small villages of Turkey and Eastern Europe also provides up-close access to remote areas.

A primary consideration on a cycling trip is to travel light, but you should take a few tools and spare parts, including a puncture-repair kit and an extra inner tube. Panniers are essential to balance your possessions on either side of the bike frame. Wearing a helmet is not compulsory in most countries, but is certainly sensible.

Seasoned cyclists can average 80km a day, but it depends on what you're carrying and your level of fitness.

Cyclists' Touring Club (CTC; www.ctc.org.uk) The national cycling association of the UK runs organised trips to Continental Europe.

European Cyclists' Federation (www.ecf.com) Has details of 'EuroVelo', the European cycle network of 12 pan-European cycle routes, plus tips for other tours.

Holland Cycling Routes (www.hollandcycling-routes.com) The complete lowdown on peddling around the Netherlands.

France Vélo Tourisme (https://en.francevelotourisme.com) Loads of information on exploring France by bicycle.

SwitzerlandMobility (www.veloland.ch/en/cycling-in-switzerland.html) Details of Swiss national routes and more.

Regions at a Glance

Europe is like an old-fashioned sweet shop – too many tempting options! To stop your head from spinning we've divided this guide's On the Road chapters into clusters of neighbouring countries that share not only borders but often overlapping histories and cultures. Rather than spreading your travels thinly across broad swathes of Europe, consider the benefits of concentrating on a smaller region. The key elements of each region are spelled out so you'll know where to go if you're looking for beaches and nightlife rather than history and culture.

Great Britain & Ireland

History
Landscape
Nightlife

The Romans came 2000 years ago and so should you. Capitals London and Dublin simply rock but also make time to see some of the region's other highlights, from the Scottish Highlands to Ireland's pubs.

p49

Scandinavia

Cities
Forests
Outdoor Adventures

Design-savvy cities that know how to party and pristine swathes of nature perfect for outdoor pursuits and Zen moments are among the prime draws of this region that includes Denmark, Finland, Iceland, Norway and Sweden.

p131

Germany, Austria & Benelux

Landscapes
Cities
Drinking

Edgy architecture, art and culture are enlivened by beer halls and convivial cafes in this region. History is writ large across a region that includes incredible castles and WWII memorials.

p201

France & Switzerland

Food & Drink
Art
Mountains

Gastronomic delights, classic works of art and awe-inspiring landscapes are the major highlights on this twinset of nations spanning the Alps and stretching from the English Channel to the shores of the Med.

p307

Spain & Portugal

Beaches
Scenery
Food & Drink

When much of the rest of Europe is shivering you can be sure of some sunshine on the Iberian Peninsula. And even if the weather isn't playing ball, there are plenty of cultural attractions including amazing museums and fabulously tasty food.

p377

Italy, Greece & Turkey

History
Beaches
Food & Drink

Crucibles of the ancient world, the attractions of this Mediterranean trio encompass ruins, beaches and budget-friendly gastronomic goodies. The southeastern Med's warmth is also reflected in the friendliness of the locals.

p471

Balkans

Beaches
Festivals
Scenery

Travel here may not be as smooth as other parts of Europe, but that means it's still possible to discover some off-the-radar treasures, such as Albania's amazing beaches. There are also ancient towns, cool cities and fantastic festivals.

p583

Central & Eastern Europe

Food & Drink
Scenery
Outdoor Adventures

The combination of mountain rusticity with old-world style captivates here. Come for half-timbered villages and graffiti-decorated Renaissance squares as well as alpine activities, outdoor cafes and beer halls.

p671

Russia & the Baltic Coast

Architecture
History
Scenery

Moscow and St Petersburg are full of architectural and artistic must-sees, but it's not all about Russia. It's easy to travel between the Baltic States, each with their very own distinct cultures and bewitching scenery.

p773

On the
Road

Great Britain & Ireland

Best Traditional Pubs

➡ Lamb & Flag (p63)

➡ Bear Inn (p74)

➡ Café Royal Circle Bar (p89)

➡ Horse Shoe (p93)

➡ John Mulligan's (p106)

Best Places to Stay

➡ Clink78 (p62)

➡ Safehouse (p83)

➡ Isaacs Hostel (p103)

➡ Vagabonds (p123)

Why Go?

Great Britain, which includes England, Wales and Scotland, can be traversed from tip to toe in around half a day. However, you could spend a lifetime exploring this historic and beautiful island – from ancient Stonehenge and the great medieval cathedrals of Westminster, Canterbury and York to the colleges of Oxford and Cambridge Universities and the castles and magnificent scenery of Wales and Scotland.

West across the Irish Sea, lies Ireland, made up of the Republic and the British province of Northern Ireland. Postcard-perfect Ireland isn't a fantasy. You'll find it along the peninsulas of the southwest, in the brooding loneliness of Connemara and the dramatic wildness of the Causeway Coast. Although a very modern country, timeless traditions endure. Linger in the yard of a thatched-cottage pub on a warm evening and you'll experience a country that has changed little in generations.

Fast Facts

Capitals London (England), Cardiff (Wales), Edinburgh (Scotland), Belfast (Northern Ireland), Dublin (Republic of Ireland)

Currency Pound (£; Great Britain and Northern Ireland); euro (€; Republic of Ireland)

Emergency ☑999 (Great Britain and Northern Ireland); ☑999 or ☑112 (Republic of Ireland)

Languages English, Scottish Gaelic, Welsh (Great Britain); English, Irish (Ireland)

Mobile Phones Most foreign phones work in Great Britain and Ireland (beware roaming charges); local SIMs and basic handsets available

Visas Not required for most EU citizens and citizens of Australia, New Zealand, USA and Canada

Great Britain & Ireland Highlights

1 London

Experiencing the many delights of one of the world's greatest capital cities. (p52)

2 Oxford

Getting lost among the dreaming spires of this ancient university town. (p72)

3 Bath

Visiting Roman baths and admiring grand Georgian architecture. (p69)

4 Snowdonia National Park

Climbing or riding the train up the 1085m mountain. (p83)

5 Manchester

Diving into the northern powerhouse's wealth of cultural institutions and cracking nightlife scene. (p80)

Shetland Islands

Lerwick

NORTH SEA

Orkney Islands

Stromness   Kirkwall
South Ronaldsay

Thurso   Wick
Helmsdale

Fraserburgh

Ullapool

Elgin   Aberdeen
Moray
Firth   Nairn   Stonehaven

Cairngorms
National Park   Montrose

Inverness   Kingussie   SCOTLAND

Loch
Ness

Kyle of
Lochalsh

Lewis
Stornoway

The
Minch

Tarbert   Harris

Uig

Dunvegan   7
Isle of
Skye

Fort
Augustus

Ben Nevis
(1344m)   Perth   Dundee
St Andrews

Fort William

Glencoe   Stirling

Kinlochleven

Loch Lomond
& Trossachs
National Park   Loch
Lomond

Dumbarton   Glasgow   Hamilton
Mallaig

Mull   Oban   Lanark

Iona   Tarbert   Kilmarnock
Brodick

Arran   Ayr

Jura

Islay   Mull of
Kintyre

Campbeltown

North Uist

Lochmaddy

South Uist

Lochboisdale

Barra

Sea
of the
Hebrides

St Kilda

ATLANTIC
OCEAN

Berwick-upon-Tweed

Edinburgh   6

Peebles   Kelso

Melrose

Jedburgh   Northumberland
National Park

Lanark

Dumfries   Galloway
Forest Park

Coleraine

Derry/Londonderry

Buncrana

200 km

100 miles

N

6 Edinburgh
Striding along the Royal Mile up to Edinburgh Castle. (p84)

7 Isle of Skye
Being wowed by the magnificent scenery of the Scottish highlands and islands. (p95)

8 Belfast
Taking a black taxi tour of West Belfast's murals and paying a visit to Titanic Belfast. (p120)

9 Galway
Experiencing the *craic* of Ireland's liveliest city in music-filled pubs. (p117)

10 Dublin
Meandering through museums, pubs and literary haunts. (p99)

ENGLAND

London

POP 8.65 MILLION

Everyone comes to London with preconceptions. Whatever yours are, prepare to have them exploded by this endlessly intriguing city. Its streets are steeped in fascinating history, magnificent art, imposing architecture and popular culture. When you add a bottomless reserve of cool to this mix, it's hard not to conclude that London is one of the world's great cities, if not the greatest.

It's certainly not a cheap city, but with some careful planning and a bit of common sense, you can find excellent bargains and freebies among the popular attractions. And many of London's best assets – its wonderful parks, bridges, squares and boulevards, not to mention many of its landmark museums – come completely free.

◉ Sights

◉ Westminster & St James's

★ **Westminster Abbey**   CHURCH
(Map p62; ☑ 020-7222 5152; www.westminster-abbey.org; 20 Dean's Yard, SW1; adult/child £22/9, cloister & gardens free; ⏰ 9.30am-3.30pm Mon, Tue, Thu & Fri, to 6pm Wed, to 1.30pm Sat; ⊜ Westminster) A splendid mixture of architectural styles, Westminster Abbey is considered

---

DON'T MISS

CHANGING OF THE GUARD

A London 'must see', this is when the Old Guard (Foot Guards of the Household Regiment) comes off duty to be replaced by the New Guard on the forecourt of **Buckingham Palace**. Lasting around 45 minutes, the ceremony usually takes place daily at 11am in June and July and on Sunday, Monday, Wednesday and Friday, weather permitting, during the rest of the year, but be sure to check the website before setting out. Alternatively, catch the changing of the mounted guard at **Horse Guards Parade** (Map p62; http://changing-guard. com/queens-life-guard.html; Horse Guards Parade, off Whitehall, SW1; ⏰ 11am Mon-Sat, 10am Sun; ⊜ Westminster, Charing Cross, Embankment).

---

the finest example of Early English Gothic (1190–1300). It's not merely a beautiful place of worship – the Abbey also serves up the country's history cold on slabs of stone. For centuries, the country's greatest have been interred here, including 17 monarchs from Henry III (died 1272) to George II (1760). Never a cathedral (the seat of a bishop), Westminster Abbey is what is called a 'royal peculiar', administered by the Crown.

★ **Houses of Parliament**   HISTORIC BUILDING
(Palace of Westminster; Map p62; www.parliament. uk; Parliament Sq, SW1; ⊜ Westminster) **FREE** A visit here is a journey to the heart of UK democracy. Officially called the Palace of Westminster, the Houses of Parliament's oldest part is 11th-century **Westminster Hall**, one of only a few sections that survived a catastrophic fire in 1834. Its roof, added between 1394 and 1401, is the earliest known example of a hammerbeam roof. The rest is mostly a neo-Gothic confection built by Charles Barry and Augustus Pugin for 20 years from 1840. The palace's most famous feature is its clock tower, officially the Elizabeth Tower but better known as **Big Ben** (Map p62; ⊜ Westminster).

★ **Tate Britain**   GALLERY
(☑ 020-7887 8888; www.tate.org.uk/visit/tate-britain; Millbank, SW1; ⏰ 10am-6pm, to 9.30pm on selected Fri; ⊜ Pimlico) **FREE** The older and more venerable of the two Tate siblings celebrates British works from 1500 to the present, including those of Blake, Hogarth, Gainsborough, Hepworth, Whistler, Constable and Turner, as well as vibrant modern and contemporary pieces from Lucian Freud, Francis Bacon and Henry Moore. Join a free 45-minute **thematic tour** (⏰ 11am, noon, 2pm & 3pm daily) and 15-minute **Art in Focus** (⏰ 1.15pm Tue, Thu & Sat) talks.

★ **Buckingham Palace**   PALACE
(Map p62; ☑ 0303 123 7300; www.royalcollection. org.uk/visit/the-state-rooms-buckingham-palace; Buckingham Palace Rd, SW1; adult/child/under 5yr £24/13.50/free; ⏰ 9.30am-7pm (to 6pm Sep) Jul-Sep only; ⊜ Green Park, St James's Park) Built in 1703 for the Duke of Buckingham, Buckingham Palace replaced St James's Palace as the monarch's official London residence in 1837. Queen Elizabeth II divides her time between here, Windsor Castle and, in summer, Balmoral castle in Scotland. If she's in residence, the square yellow, red and blue Royal Standard is flown; if not, it's the Union Flag. Some 19

LONDON PARKS

London's central parks (find details of them all at www.royalparks.org.uk) are among its prime assets and they're all free to explore.

Start with **Hyde Park** (Map p64; www.royalparks.org.uk/parks/hyde-park; ⊙5am-midnight; ◉Marble Arch, Hyde Park Corner, Queensway). At 145 hectares, this is central London's largest open space with an astonishing variety of landscapes and trees. The Serpentine lake separates it from **Kensington Gardens** (Map p64; ✆0300 061 2000; www.royalparks.org.uk/parks/kensington-gardens; ⊙6am-dusk; ◉Queensway, Lancaster Gate), where you'll find the **Serpentine Galleries** (Map p64; ✆020-7402 6075; www.serpentinegalleries.org ⊙10am-6pm Tue-Sun; ◉Lancaster Gate, Knightsbridge) FREE showing great contemporary art for free.

Across Hyde Park Corner is the aptly named **Green Park** (Map p62; www.royalparks.org.uk/parks/green-park; ⊙5am-midnight; ◉Green Park), followed by lovely **St James Park** south of the Mall. Should you hunger for more greenery, head north to the elaborate and formal **Regent's Park** (www.royalparks.org.uk; ⊙5am-dusk; ◉Regent's Park, Baker St).

lavishly furnished **State Rooms** are open to visitors when Her Royal Highness (HRH) takes her holidays from late July to September.

⊙ West End

★ British Museum   MUSEUM
(Map p66; ✆020-7323 8299; www.britishmuseum.org; Great Russell St & Montague Pl, WC1; ⊙10am-5.30pm Sat-Thu, to 8.30pm Fri; ◉Russell Sq, Tottenham Court Rd) FREE The country's largest museum and one of the oldest and finest in the world, this famous museum boasts vast Egyptian, Etruscan, Greek, Roman, European and Middle Eastern galleries, among others. It is frequently London's most-visited attraction, drawing 6.5 million visitors annually.

Don't miss the **Rosetta Stone**, the key to deciphering Egyptian hieroglyphics, discovered in 1799; the controversial **Parthenon Sculptures**, taken from the Parthenon in Athens by Lord Elgin (then the British ambassador to the Ottoman Empire); and the large collection of **Egyptian mummies**.

★ National Gallery   GALLERY
(Map p62; ✆020-7747 2885; www.nationalgallery.org.uk; Trafalgar Sq, WC2; ⊙10am-6pm Sat-Thu, to 9pm Fri; ◉Charing Cross) FREE With some 2300 European masterpieces on display, this is one of the world's great art collections, with seminal works from every important period in the history of art – from the mid-13th to the early 20th century, including masterpieces by Leonardo da Vinci, Michelangelo, Titian, Van Gogh and Renoir.

Many visitors flock to the East Wing (1700–1900), where works by 18th-century British artists such as Gainsborough, Constable and Turner, and seminal Impressionist and post-Impressionist masterpieces by Van Gogh, Renoir and Monet await.

★ Trafalgar Square   SQUARE
(Map p62; ◉Charing Cross) Trafalgar Square is the true centre of London, where rallies and marches take place, tens of thousands of revellers usher in the New Year and locals congregate for anything from communal open-air cinema and Christmas celebrations to political protests. It is dominated by the 52m-high **Nelson's Column** and ringed by many splendid buildings, including the National Gallery (p53) and the church of **St Martin-in-the-Fields** (Map p62; ✆020-7766 1100; www.stmartin-in-the-fields.org; Trafalgar Sq, WC2; ⊙8.30am-1pm & 2-6pm Mon, Tue, Thu & Fri, 8.30am-1pm & 2-5pm Wed, 9.30am-6pm Sat, 3.30-5pm Sun; ◉Charing Cross).

National Portrait Gallery   GALLERY
(Map p62; ✆020-7321 0055; www.npg.org.uk; St Martin's Pl, WC2; ⊙10am-6pm Sat-Wed, to 9pm Thu & Fri; ◉Charing Cross, Leicester Sq) FREE What makes the National Portrait Gallery so compelling is its familiarity; in many cases, you'll have heard of the subject (royals, scientists, politicians, celebrities) or the artist (Andy Warhol, Annie Leibovitz, Lucian Freud) but not necessarily recognise the face. Highlights include the famous 'Chandos portrait' of William Shakespeare, the first artwork the gallery acquired (in 1856) and believed to be the only likeness made during the playwright's lifetime, and a touching sketch of novelist Jane Austen by her sister.

GREAT BRITAIN AT A GLANCE

Don't Miss

London's museums Institutions bright and beautiful, great and small, wise and wonderful – London's got them all. The range is vast, from the major British Museum to the specialist Sir John Soane's Museum. You could spend weeks exploring them without even scratching the surface. And most are free!

Edinburgh A city of many moods that's famous for its festivals and especially lively in the summer. Edinburgh is also worth visiting out of season for sights such as the castle silhouetted against a blue spring sky with a yellow haze of daffodils misting the slopes below the esplanade.

Bath Thanks to its natural hot springs, the Romans built a health resort here. The waters were rediscovered in the 18th century, and Bath became the place to see and be seen by British high society. The stunning Georgian architecture of grand townhouses and sweeping crescents (not to mention Roman remains, a beautiful cathedral and a cutting-edge 21st-century spa) means Bath demands your undivided attention.

Isle of Skye Of all Scotland's many islands, Skye is one of the most famous and best loved by visitors, thanks to a mix of history, accessibility (the ferry from the mainland has been replaced by a bridge) and sheer beauty. With jagged mountains, velvet moors and towering sea cliffs, Skye's scenery never fails to impress.

Stonehenge Mysterious and compelling, Stonehenge is Britain's most iconic ancient site. People have been drawn to this myth-laden ring of bluestones for the last 5000 years, and we still don't know quite why it was built.

Itineraries

One Week

This circular whistle-stop tour ticks off Britain's greatest hits in an action-packed fortnight. Start with a full day in Britain's greatest city, **London**, simply walking the streets to admire the world-famous sights: Buckingham Palace, Tower Bridge, Trafalgar Sq and more. Then head southwest to **Salisbury**, across to the iconic menhirs of Stonehenge, then onwards to the beautiful historic city of **Bath**. Continue to **Cardiff**, the Welsh capital. Retrace your path slightly across the classic English countryside to reach the renowned university city of **Oxford**. Not far away from Oxford is **Stratford-upon-Avon**, for everything Shakespeare.

Two Weeks

Head north at the start of week two, spending a night in **Manchester**, where you can enjoy this industrial city's rich heritage and hedonistic nightlife. Continue north to Scotland's capital, **Edinburgh**, for another great castle, before recrossing the border to **York** for its glorious cathedral and historic city walls. Keep going south to reach **Cambridge**, another landmark university city. Then enjoy the last few days back in **London**, immersed in galleries, museums, luxury shops, street markets, West End shows, East End cafes – or whatever takes your fancy.

Essential Food & Drink

Bacon sandwich The breakfast of champions. Debate rages over the choice of sauce – red (tomato ketchup) or brown (spicy pickled fruit sauce).

Beans on toast A comforting childhood classic of tinned baked beans poured over buttered toast, served in many cafes as a breakfast or lunch dish.

Fish and chips The nation's favourite takeaway meal, served in hundreds of chip shops all over the country.

Scotch egg This masterpiece of culinary engineering consists of a hardboiled egg wrapped in sausage meat, coated in breadcrumbs and deep-fried.

Getting Around

Transport in Britain can be expensive compared with Continental Europe; bus and rail services are sparse in the more remote parts of the country. For timetables, check out www.traveline.info. Tourist offices can provide maps and information.

Bus Cheaper and slower than trains, but useful in more remote regions that aren't serviced by rail.

Car Useful for travelling at your own pace, or for visiting regions with minimal public transport. Cars can be hired in every town or city.

Train Relatively expensive, with extensive coverage and frequent departures throughout most of the country.

When to Go

London

°C/°F **Temp**

Rainfall Inches/mm

J F M A M J J A S O N D

Jun–Aug Weather at its best. Accommodation rates peak – especially for August school holidays.

Mar–May, Sep & Oct Crowds reduce. Prices drop. Weather is often good.

Nov–Feb Wet and cold. Snow falls in mountain areas, especially up north. Some places shut for winter.

Arriving in Great Britain

Heathrow Airport (London) Trains, London Underground (tube) and buses to central London run from just after 5am to before midnight (night buses run later); fares are from £5.70 to £21.50. Taxis to central London from Heathrow cost from £45 to £85 (more at peak hours).

Edinburgh Airport Frequent trams (£5.50) and buses (£4.50) head to Edinburgh city centre. Night buses run every 30 minutes from 12.30am to 4am (£4). Taxis cost £18 to £28; it's about 20 to 30 minutes to the city centre.

Best in Print

Notes from a Small Island (Bill Bryson; 1995) An American's fond and astute take on Britain.

Raw Spirit (Iain Banks; 2003) An enjoyable jaunt around Scotland in search of the perfect whisky.

Slow Coast Home (Josie Drew; 2003) The chatty tale of a 5000-mile cycle tour through England and Wales

Resources

BBC (www.bbc.co.uk)

Visit Britain (www.visit britain.com)

Traveline (www.traveline.info)

Set Your Budget

Dorm beds: £15–30

Cheap cafe/pub meal: £7–11

Long-distance coach: £15–40 (200 miles)

Central London

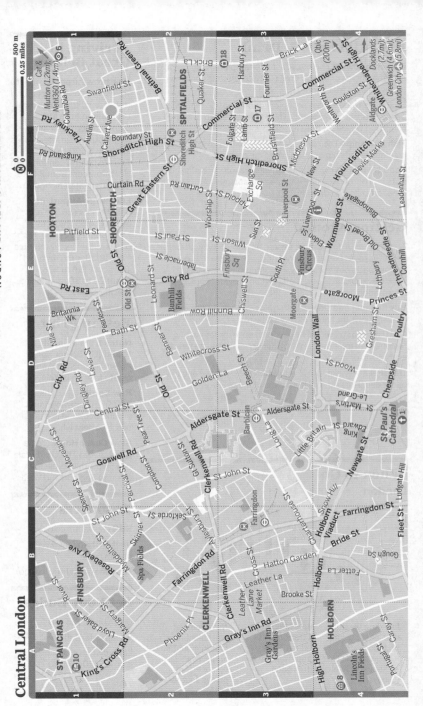

0 — 500 m
0 — 0.25 miles

G
F
E
D
C
B
A

Cat &
Mutton (1.2km);
Neti360 (1.4km) ⑥

Kingsland Rd
Hackney Rd
Columbia Rd
Austin St
Swanfield St
Calvert Ave
Boundary St
Bethnal Green Rd

SPITALFIELDS
Brick La
⑱
Quaker St
Hanbury St
Fournier St
Brick La

Commercial St
⑰
Folgate St
Lamb St
Brushfield St

Qbic
(200m)

Commercial St
Wentworth St
Goulston St
Whitechapel High St
Aldgate
Docklands
Greenwich (4.6mi);
London City (5.8mi)

Shoreditch
High St
Shoreditch High St
Middlesex St
Houndsditch
Bevis Marks

HOXTON
Pitfield St
OLD ST
SHOREDITCH
Curtain Rd
Great Eastern St
Curtain Rd
Worship St
Appold St
Exchange
Sq
New St
Bishopsgate
Leadenhall St

East Rd
Old St ⑪
Leonard St
City Rd
St Paul St
Tabernacle St
Wilson St
Finsbury
Sq
Liverpool St
Eldon St
Wormwood St
Old Broad St
Threadneedle St
Cornhill

Britannia
Wk
Nile St
Peerless St
Bath St
Banner St
Bunhill
Fields
Bunhill Row
Chiswell St
South Pl
Finsbury
Circus
Moorgate
Moorgate
London Wall
Gresham St
Princes St
Lothbury
Poultry

City Rd
Lever St
Dingley Rd
OLD ST
Whitecross St
Beech St
London St
Wood St
St Martin's
Le-Grand
Cheapside

Central St
Moreland St
Pear Tree St
Golden La
Barbican
Aldersgate St
Little Britain
King
Edward St
St Paul's
Cathedral ①

Goswell Rd
Gt Sutton St
Compton St
Clerkenwell Rd
Aldersgate St
Long La
Newgate St
Ludgate Hill

Spencer St
St John St
Percival St
St John St
Sekforde St
Farringdon
⑭
Snow Hill
Holborn
Viaduct
Farringdon St
Fleet St

FINSBURY
Rosebery Ave
Myddelton St
Skinner St
Aylesbury St
Spa Fields
Farringdon Rd
CLERKENWELL
Clerkenwell Rd
Leather
Lane
Leather La
Hatton Garden
Holborn
Bride St
Fetter La
Gough Sq

River St
Lloyd Baker St
Margery St
Phoenix Pl
Clerkenwell Rd
Leather
Lane
Market
Brooke St
Holborn
High Holborn
HOLBORN

ST PANCRAS
King's Cross Rd ⑩
Gray's Inn Rd
Gray's
Inn
Gardens
Lincoln's
Inn Fields
⑧
Portugal St
Carey St

57

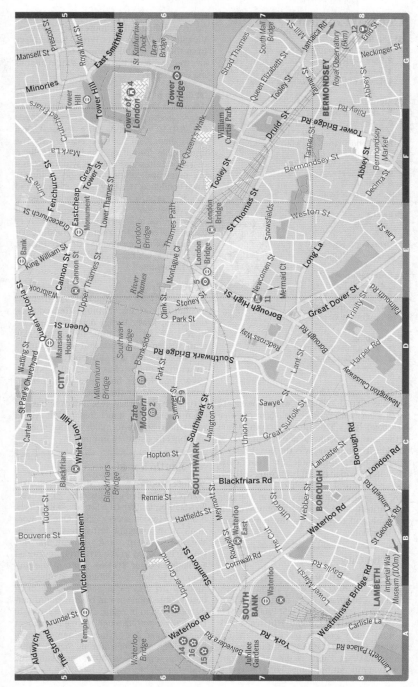

Central London

Sir John Soane's Museum MUSEUM
(Map p56; ☎ 020-7405 2107; www.soane.org; 12 Lincoln's Inn Fields, WC2; ⊙ 10am-5pm Wed-Sun; ⊕ Holborn) FREE This little museum is one of the most atmospheric and fascinating in London. The building was the beautiful, bewitching home of architect Sir John Soane (1753–1837), which he left brimming with his vast architectural and archaeological collection, as well as intriguing personal effects and curiosities. The museum represents his exquisite and eccentric tastes, persuasions and proclivities.

⊙ The City

★ St Paul's Cathedral CATHEDRAL
(Map p56; ☎ 020-7246 8357; www.stpauls.co.uk; St Paul's Churchyard, EC4; adult/child £18/8; ⊙ 8.30am-4.30pm Mon-Sat; ⊕ St Paul's) Towering over diminutive Ludgate Hill in a superb position that's been a place of Christian worship for over 1400 years (and pagan before that), St Paul's is one of London's most magnificent buildings. For Londoners, the vast dome is a symbol of resilience and pride, standing tall for more than 300 years. Viewing Sir Christopher Wren's masterpiece from the inside and climbing to the top for sweeping views of the capital is an exhilarating experience.

★ Tower of London CASTLE
(Map p56; ☎ 0844 482 7777; www.hrp.org.uk/tower-of-london; Petty Wales, EC3; adult/child £24.80/11.50, audio guide £4/3; ⊙ 9am-4.30pm Tue-Sat, from 10am Sun-Mon; ⊕ Tower Hill) The unmissable Tower of London (actually a castle of 22 towers) offers a window into a gruesome and compelling history. A former royal residence, treasury, mint, armoury and zoo, it's perhaps now most remembered as the prison where a king, three queens and many nobles met their deaths. Come here to see the colourful **Yeoman Warders** (or Beefeaters), the spectacular **Crown Jewels**, the soothsaying ravens and armour fit for a *very* large king.

★ Tower Bridge BRIDGE
(Map p56; ⊕ Tower Hill) One of London's most recognisable sights, familiar from dozens of movies, Tower Bridge doesn't disappoint in real life. Its neo-Gothic towers and sky-blue suspension struts add extraordinary elegance to what is a supremely functional structure. London was a thriving port in 1894 when it was built as a much-needed crossing point in the east, equipped with a then-revolutionary steam-driven bascule (counter-balance) mechanism that could raise the roadway to make way for oncoming ships in just three minutes.

⊙ South Bank

★ Tate Modern GALLERY
(Map p56; www.tate.org.uk; Bankside, SE1; ⊙ 10am-6pm Sun-Thu, to 10pm Fri & Sat; ⦿; ⊕ Blackfriars, Southwark, London Bridge) FREE One of London's most amazing attractions, this outstanding modern- and contemporary-art gallery is housed in the creatively revamped **Bankside Power Station** south of the Millennium Bridge. A spellbinding synthesis of modern art and capacious industrial brick design, Tate Modern has been extraordinarily successful in bringing challenging work to the masses, both through its free permanent collection and fee-paying big-name temporary exhibitions. The stunning Switch House extension opened in 2016, increasing the available exhibition space by 60%.

Shakespeare's Globe HISTORIC BUILDING
(Map p56; ☑ 020-7902 1500; www.shakespeares-globe.com; 21 New Globe Walk, SE1; adult/child £17/10; ⊘ 9.30am-5pm; 🚻; ⊖ Blackfriars, London Bridge) Unlike other venues for Shakespearean plays, the new Globe was designed to resemble the original as closely as possible, which means having the arena open to the fickle London skies, leaving the 700 'groundlings' (standing spectators) to weather London's spectacular downpours. Visits to the Globe include tours of the theatre (half-hourly) as well as access to the exhibition space, which has fascinating exhibits on Shakespeare and theatre in the 17th century.

👁 Kensington & Hyde Park

★ **Victoria & Albert Museum** MUSEUM
(V&A; Map p64; ☑ 020-7942 2000; www.vam.ac.uk; Cromwell Rd, SW7; ⊘ 10am-5.45pm Sat-Thu, to 10pm Fri; ⊖ South Kensington) FREE The Museum of Manufactures, as the V&A was known when it opened in 1852, was part of Prince Albert's legacy to the nation in the aftermath of the successful Great Exhibition of 1851. It houses the world's largest collection of decorative arts, from Asian ceramics to Middle Eastern rugs, as well as Chinese paintings, Western furniture, fashion from all ages and modern-day domestic appliances. The (ticketed) temporary exhibitions are another highlight, covering anything from David Bowie retrospectives to designer Alexander McQueen, special materials and trends.

★ **Natural History Museum** MUSEUM
(Map p64; www.nhm.ac.uk; Cromwell Rd, SW7; ⊘ 10am-5.50pm; ⊖ South Kensington) FREE This colossal and magnificent-looking building is infused with the irrepressible Victorian spirit of collecting, cataloguing and interpreting the natural world. The **Dinosaurs Gallery** (Blue Zone) is a must for children, who gawp at the animatronic T-Rex, fossils and excellent displays. Adults for their part will love the intriguing Treasures exhibition in the **Cadogan Gallery** (Green Zone), which houses a host of unrelated objects each telling its own unique story, from a chunk of moon rock to a dodo skeleton.

Science Museum MUSEUM
(Map p64; ☑ 020-7942 4000; www.sciencemuseum.org.uk; Exhibition Rd, SW7; ⊘ 10am-6pm; ⊖ South Kensington) FREE With seven floors of interactive and educational exhibits, this scientifically spellbinding museum will mesmerise adults and children alike, covering everything from early technology to space travel. A perennial favourite is **Exploring Space**, a gallery featuring genuine rockets and satellites and a full-size replica of the 'Eagle', the lander that took Neil Armstrong and Buzz Aldrin to the moon in 1969. The **Making the Modern World Gallery** next door is a visual feast of locomotives, planes, cars and other revolutionary inventions.

GREAT BRITAIN & IRELAND LONDON

> **DON'T MISS**
>
> ## LONDON MARKETS
>
> Visitors are rightly drawn to London's famed markets. A treasure trove of small designers, unique jewellery pieces, original framed photographs and posters, colourful vintage pieces and bric-a-brac, they are the antidote to impersonal, carbon-copy shopping centres.
>
> Among the most popular are **Camden Market** (www.camdenmarket.com; Camden High St, NW1; ⊘ 10am-6pm; ⊖ Camden Town, Chalk Farm), **Old Spitalfields Market** (Map p56; www.oldspitalfieldsmarket.com; Commercial St, E1; ⊘ 10am-5pm Mon-Fri & Sun, 10am-6pm Sat; ⊖ Liverpool St), **Portobello Road Market** (www.portobellomarket.org; Portobello Rd, W10; ⊘ 8am-6.30pm Mon-Wed, Fri & Sat, to 1pm Thu; ⊖ Notting Hill Gate, Ladbroke Grove) and **Borough Market** (Map p56; www.boroughmarket.org; 8 Southwark St, SE1; ⊘ 10am-5pm Wed & Thu, 10am-6pm Fri, 8am-5pm Sat; ⊖ London Bridge). There are dozens of others, such as Brick Lane's excellent **Sunday UpMarket** (Map p56; www.sundayupmarket.co.uk; Old Truman Brewery, 91 Brick Lane, E1; ⊘ 11am-6pm Sat, 10am-5pm Sun; 🚇 Shoreditch High St) and **Columbia Road Flower Market** (Map p56; www.columbiaroad.info; Columbia Rd, E2; ⊘ 8am-3pm Sun; ⊖ Hoxton), which only pop up on the weekend. Camden and Old Spitalfields are both mainly covered, but even the outdoor markets are busy, rain or shine.

The River Thames

A FLOATING TOUR

London's history has always been determined by the Thames. The city was founded as a Roman port nearly 2000 years ago and over the centuries since then many of the capital's landmarks have lined the river's banks. A boat trip is a great way to experience the attractions.

There are piers dotted along both banks at regular intervals where you can hop on and hop off the regular services to visit places of interest. The best place to board is Westminster Pier, from where boats head downstream, taking you from the City of Westminster, the seat of government, to the original City of London, now the financial district and dominated by a growing band of skyscrapers. Across the river, the once shabby and neglected South Bank now bristles with as many top attractions as its northern counterpart, including the slender Shard.

In our illustration we've concentrated on the top highlights you'll enjoy from a waterborne

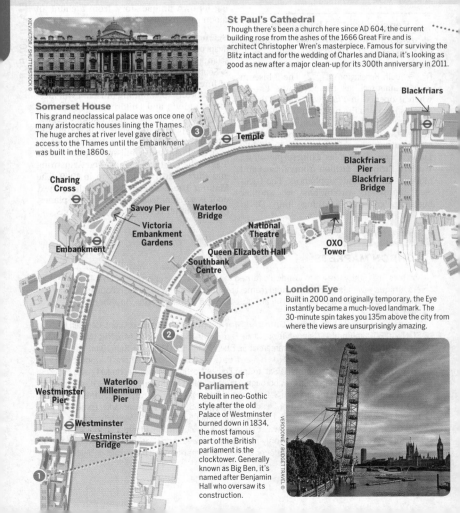

St Paul's Cathedral
Though there's been a church here since AD 604, the current building rose from the ashes of the 1666 Great Fire and is architect Christopher Wren's masterpiece. Famous for surviving the Blitz intact and for the wedding of Charles and Diana, it's looking as good as new after a major clean-up for its 300th anniversary in 2011.

KIEV.VICTORY / SHUTTERSTOCK ©

Somerset House
This grand neoclassical palace was once one of many aristocratic houses lining the Thames. The huge arches at river level gave direct access to the Thames until the Embankment was built in the 1860s.

Blackfriars

Temple

Blackfriars Pier
Blackfriars Bridge

Charing Cross

Savoy Pier

Waterloo Bridge

Victoria Embankment Gardens

Embankment

National Theatre

OXO Tower

Queen Elizabeth Hall
Southbank Centre

London Eye
Built in 2000 and originally temporary, the Eye instantly became a much-loved landmark. The 30-minute spin takes you 135m above the city from where the views are unsurprisingly amazing.

Westminster Pier

Waterloo Millennium Pier

Houses of Parliament
Rebuilt in neo-Gothic style after the old Palace of Westminster burned down in 1834, the most famous part of the British parliament is the clocktower. Generally known as Big Ben, it's named after Benjamin Hall who oversaw its construction.

Westminster
Westminster Bridge

VERDOONE / BUDGET TRAVEL ©

vessel. These are, from west to east, the **❶ Houses of Parliament**, the **❷ London Eye**, **❸ Somerset House**, **❹ St Paul's Cathedral**, the **❺ Tate Modern**, **❻ Shakespeare's Globe**, the **❼ Tower of London** and **❽ Tower Bridge**.

In addition to covering this central section of the Thames, boats can also be taken upstream as far as Kew Gardens and Hampton Court Palace, and downstream as far as Greenwich and the Thames Barrier.

BOAT HOPPING

Thames Clippers hop-on/hop-off services are aimed at commuters but are equally useful for visitors, operating every 15 minutes on a loop from piers at Westminster, Embankment, Waterloo, Blackfriars, Bankside, London Bridge and the Tower. Oyster cardholders get a discount off the boat ticket price.

30 St Mary Axe (Gherkin)

Tower of London
It's not the tallest building in London anymore, but with the Crown Jewels and execution site, the 900-year-old Tower still overshadows the city's other attractions. From the river you can clearly see Traitors' Gate through which enemies of the crown entered the prison.

Cannon St

Leadenhall Building (Cheese Grater)

Millennium Bridge

Monument

Southwark Bridge

20 Fenchurch St (Walkie Talkie)

Bankside Pier

London Bridge

Southwark Cathedral

London Bridge Pier

HMS Belfast

Tower Pier

London Bridge

Shard

City Hall

Tate Modern
Directly across the river from St Paul's, this museum of modern art is the world's most visited. Built as a power station in the late 1940s, its industrial architecture is as popular as its artworks, while a splendid new extension was completed in 2016.

Shakespeare's Globe
The reconstructed Globe stands on the river a few hundred metres from where the original stood (and burnt down in 1613 during a performance). The life's work of American actor Sam Wanamaker, the theatre runs a hugely popular season from April to October each year.

Tower Bridge
It might look as old as its namesake neighbour but one of the world's most iconic bridges was only completed in 1894. Not to be confused with London Bridge upstream, this one's famous raising bascules allowed tall ships to dock at the old wharves to the west and are still lifted up to 1000 times a year.

West End & Westminster

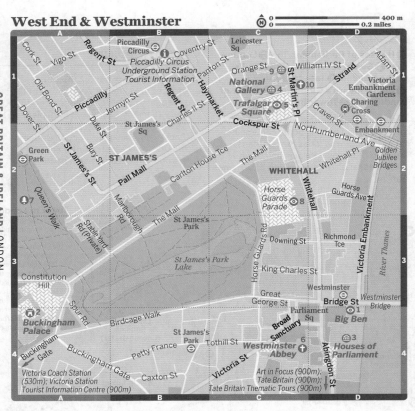

West End & Westminster

◎ Top Sights
1 Big Ben	D4
2 Buckingham Palace	A4
3 Houses of Parliament	D4
4 National Gallery	C1
5 Trafalgar Square	C1
6 Westminster Abbey	C4

◎ Sights
7 Green Park	A2
8 Horse Guards Parade	C2
9 National Portrait Gallery	C1
10 St Martin-in-the-Fields	C1

🛏 Sleeping

During university holidays (generally mid-March to late April, late June to September, and mid-December to mid-January), student dorms and halls of residence are open to paying visitors. Agencies include **LSE Vacations** (☎020-7955 7676; www.lsevacations.co.uk; s/tw/tr incl breakfast from £45/65/90; 🛜), whose eight halls include **Bankside House** (Map p56; ☎020-7955 7676; 24 Sumner St, SE1; s/tw/tr/q incl breakfast from £68/89/119/133; 🛜; ⊖Southwark) and **High Holborn Residence** (Map p66; ☎020-7107 5737; 178 High Holborn, WC1; s/d from £36/45; 🛜; ⊖Holborn).

★**Clink78**   HOSTEL €
(Map p56; ☎020-7183 9400; www.clinkhostels.com/london/clink78; 78 King's Cross Rd, WC1; dm/r incl breakfast from £16/65; @🛜; ⊖King's Cross St Pancras) This fantastic 630-bed hostel is housed in a 19th-century magistrates' courthouse where Charles Dickens once worked as a scribe and members of the Clash stood trial in 1978. It features pod beds (including overhead storage space) in four- to 16-bed dormitories. There's a top kitchen with a huge dining area and a busy bar – Clash – in the basement.

St Christopher's Village   HOSTEL €

(Map p56; ☑ 020-7939 9710; www.st-christophers.
co.uk; 163 Borough High St, SE1; dm/r incl breakfast
from £11.40/50; 🛜; ⊖ London Bridge) This 230-
bed party-zone hostel has new bathrooms,
fresh paint, pod beds with privacy curtains,
reading lights, power sockets (British and
European) and USB ports, and refurbished
common areas. Its two bars, Belushi's and
Dugout, are perennially popular. Dorms
have four to 33 beds (following the introduction of triple bunks); breakfast and linen are
included.

Qbic   DESIGN HOTEL €

(☑ 020-3021 3300; www.qbichotels.com; 42 Ad-
ler St, E1; r from £54; ✳🛜; ⊖ Aldgate East) 🖉
There's a modern feel to this snappy hotel,
with white tiling, neon signs, and vibrant
art and textiles. Rooms are sound-insulated,
mattresses excellent and rain showers powerful. Prices vary widely depending on when
you book, and the cheapest are windowless.

✕ Eating

Eating in London can be pricey. If your
budget is limited, check out some home-
grown chains such as Pret a Manger (www.
pret.co.uk), Real Greek (www.therealgreek.
com), Tas (www.tasrestaurants.co.uk) and
Wagamama (www.wagamama.com). They're
all good value and made even cheaper by
regular voucher offers: check out www.
vouchercodes.co.uk and www.myvoucher
codes.co.uk.

★ Padella   ITALIAN €

(Map p56; www.padella.co; 6 Southwark St, SE1;
dishes £4-11.50; ⊗ noon-3.45pm & 5-10pm Mon-
Sat, noon-3.45pm & 5-9pm Sun; 🖉; ⊖ London
Bridge) Yet another fantastic addition to the
foodie enclave of Borough Market (p59),
Padella is a small, energetic bistro specialising in handmade pasta dishes, inspired by
the owners' extensive culinary adventures in
Italy. The portions are small, which means
that, joy of joys, you can (and should!) have
more than one dish. Outstanding.

Talli Joe   INDIAN €

(Map p66; ☑ 020-7836 5400; www.tallijoe.com;
152-156 Shaftesbury Ave, WC2; dishes £4-11.50;
⊗ noon-10.30pm Mon-Sat, to 4pm Sun; ⊖ Leicester
Sq, Tottenham Court Rd) Talli Joe is a colourful
and very new breed of Indian restaurants
serving 'half plates' (meaning share portions). The menu has been composed by the

legendary Joe, who has travelled the length
and breadth of India for regional dishes. So
expect the unexpected: from Keralan fish
curry and Bohri chicken from Gujarat to a
Kolkatta street snack of five-spiced potatoes.

Mildreds   VEGETARIAN €

(☑ 020-7484 1634; www.mildreds.co.uk; 45 Lex-
ington St, W1; mains £7-12; ⊗ noon-11pm Mon-Sat;
🛜🖉; ⊖ Oxford Circus, Piccadilly Circus) Central
London's most inventive vegetarian restaurant, Mildreds is crammed at lunchtime so
don't be shy about sharing a table in the
sky-lit dining room. Expect the likes of Sri
Lankan sweet-potato and cashew-nut curry,
ricotta and truffle tortellini, Middle Eastern
mezze, wonderfully exotic (and filling) salads and delicious stir-fries. There are also
vegan and gluten-free options.

🍺 Drinking & Nightlife

For up-to-the-minute listings see *Time Out*
or the *Evening Standard*.

★ Lamb & Flag   PUB

(Map p66; ☑ 020-7497 9504; www.lambandflag-
coventgarden.co.uk; 33 Rose St, WC2; ⊗ 11am-11pm
Mon-Sat, noon-10.30pm Sun; ⊖ Covent Garden)
Everybody's favourite pub in central London, pint-sized Lamb & Flag is full of charm
and history, and is on the site of a pub that
dates from at least 1772. Rain or shine, you'll
have to elbow your way to the bar through
the merry crowd drinking outside. Inside
are brass fittings and creaky wooden floors.

Cat & Mutton   PUB

(☑ 020-7249 6555; www.catandmutton.com;
76 Broadway Market, E8; ⊗ noon-11pm Mon, to
midnight Tue-Thu, to 1am Fri, 10am-1am Sat, noon-
11.30pm Sun; ⊖ London Fields) At this fabulous
Georgian pub, Hackney hipsters sup pints
under the watchful eyes of hunting trophies,
black-and-white photos of old-time box-
ers and a large portrait of Karl Marx. If it's
crammed downstairs, as it often is, head up
the spiral staircase to the comfy couches. DJs
spin funk, disco and soul on the weekends.

Netil360   ROOFTOP BAR

(www.netil360.com; 1 Westgate St, E8; ⊗ noon-
8.30pm Wed & Sun, to 10.30pm Thu-Sat Apr-Nov;
🛜; ⊖ London Fields) Perched atop Netil
House, this uber-hip rooftop cafe-bar offers
incredible views over London, with brass telescopes enabling you to get better acquaint-
ed with workers in the Gherkin. In between
drinks you can knock out a game of croquet

Hyde Park

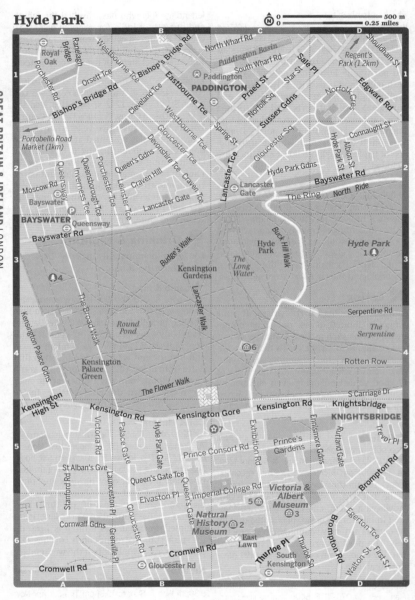

on the AstroTurf, or perhaps book a hot tub for you and your mates to stew in.

Brew By Numbers   MICROBREWERY
(Map p56; www.brewbynumbers.com; 79 Enid St, SE1; ⊙6-10pm Fri, 11am-8pm Sat; ⊜Bermondsey)

This microbrewery's raison d'être is experimentation. Everything from its 'scientific' branding (the numbers refer to the type of beer – porter, pale ale etc – and recipe) to its enthusiasm for exploring new beer styles and refashioning old ones (*saison* for instance, an

Hyde Park

old Belgian beer drunk by farm workers) is about broadening the definition of beer.

☆ Entertainment

Some of the world's best theatre can be seen in London. Enquire at each theatre's box office about cut-price standby tickets or limited late releases for otherwise sold-out shows. Student standby tickets are sometimes available one hour or so before performances start. On the day of performance, you can buy discounted tickets, sometimes up to 50% off, for West End productions from **Tkts Leicester Square** (www.tkts.co.uk/leicester-square; The Lodge, Leicester Sq, WC2; ⊙ 10am-7pm Mon-Sat, 11am-4.30pm Sun; ⊖ Leicester Sq).

★ **National Theatre**   THEATRE
(Royal National Theatre; Map p56; ☑ 020-7452 3000; www.nationaltheatre.org.uk; South Bank, SE1; ⊖ Waterloo) England's flagship theatre showcases a mix of classic and contemporary plays performed by excellent casts in three theatres (Olivier, Lyttelton and Dorfman). Artistic director Rufus Norris, who started in April 2015, made headlines in 2016 for announcing plans to stage a Brexit-based drama.

Travelex tickets, costing just £15 and which you can book in advance, are available for certain performances; same-day tickets, which you must buy in person at the box office, cost £15 to £18; Friday Rush tickets cost £20, and are released online every Friday at 1pm for performances the following week. Under-18s pay half price.

Southbank Centre   CONCERT VENUE
(Map p56; ☑ 0844 875 0073; www.southbank-centre.co.uk; Belvedere Rd, SE1; ⊖ Waterloo) The Southbank Centre comprises several venues – **Royal Festival Hall** (Map p56; ☑ 020-7960 4200), **Queen Elizabeth Hall** (QEH; Map p56)

and Purcell Room – hosting a wide range of performing arts. As well as regular programming, it organises fantastic festivals, including London Wonderground (circus and cabaret), Udderbelly (a festival of comedy in all its guises) and Meltdown (a music event curated by the best and most eclectic names in music).

Royal Opera House   OPERA
(Map p66; ☑ 020-7304 4000; www.roh.org.uk; Bow St, WC2; tickets £4-270; ⊖ Covent Garden) Classic opera in London has a fantastic setting on Covent Garden Piazza and coming here for a night is a sumptuous – if pricey – affair. Although the program has been fluffed up by modern influences, the main attractions are still the opera and classical ballet – all are wonderful productions and feature world-class performers.

Midweek matinees are usually cheaper than evening performances, and restricted-view seats cost as little as £4. Discounted tickets for each day of the week (two per customer available to the first 49 people in the queue) priced from £4 to £68 go on sale on Friday at 1pm; students must apply for special standby tickets (£10) by email. Half-price standby tickets four hours before the performance are very occasionally available. Free lunchtime recitals are held on Mondays, when possible, in the Crush Room or Paul Hamlyn Hall, depending on the program, though ongoing building works have recently seen the venue moved to the nearby Swiss Church London at 79 Endell St.

★ **Royal Albert Hall**   CONCERT VENUE
(Map p64; ☑ 0845 401 5034; www.royalalberthall.com; Kensington Gore, SW7; ⊖ South Kensington) This splendid Victorian concert hall hosts classical music, rock and other performances, but is famously the venue for the BBC-sponsored Proms. Booking is possible, but from mid-July to mid-September Proms punters queue for £5 standing (or 'promenading') tickets that go on sale one hour before curtain-up. Otherwise the box office and prepaid-ticket collection counter are through door 12 (south side of the hall).

ⓘ Information

Visit London (www.visitlondon.com) can fill you in on everything from attractions and events to tours and accommodation. Kiosks are dotted about the city and can also provide maps and brochures; some branches are able to book theatre tickets.

Bloomsbury

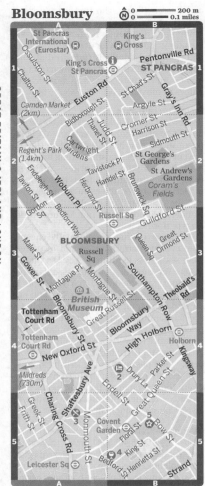

Heathrow Airport (Terminal 1, 2 & 3 Underground station concourse; ⏰7.30am-8.30pm)

King's Cross St Pancras Station (Map p66; Western Ticket Hall, Euston Rd N1; ⏰8am-6pm)

Liverpool St Station (Map p56; ⏰8am-6pm)

Piccadilly Circus Underground Station (Map p62; ⏰9am-4pm)

Victoria Station (⏰8am-6pm; 🚇Victoria)

ⓘ Getting There & Away

BUS

Long-distance buses (called 'coaches' in Britain) terminate at **Victoria Coach Station** (164 Buckingham Palace Rd, SW1; 🚇Victoria).

TRAIN

Most of London's main-line rail terminals are linked by the Circle line on the tube.

Euston Manchester, Liverpool, Glasgow

King's Cross Cambridge, York, Edinburgh

Liverpool Street Stansted Airport (Express), Cambridge

London Bridge Gatwick Airport

Paddington Heathrow Airport (Express), Oxford, Bath, Cardiff

St Pancras Gatwick and Luton Airports, Canterbury, Paris Eurostar

Victoria Gatwick Airport (Express)

Waterloo Salisbury

ⓘ Getting Around

TO/FROM THE AIRPORTS

Heathrow Airport Trains, the tube and buses to London run from just after 5am to before midnight (night buses run later and 24-hour tube runs Friday and Saturday) and cost £5.70 to £21.50; taxi £46 to £87. From 2018 express trains run along the Elizabeth Line (Crossrail).

Gatwick Airport Trains to London run from 4.30am to 1.35am and cost £10 to £20; hourly buses to London run 24/7, and cost from £5; taxi is about £100.

London City Airport DLR trains to central London run from 5.30am to 12.30am Monday to Saturday, and 7am to 11.15pm Sunday, and cost from £2.80; taxi is around £30.

Luton Airport Trains to London run from 7am to 10pm and cost from £14; buses running 24/7 to London cost £10; taxi will cost about £110.

Stansted Airport Trains to London run from 5.30am to 1.30am and cost £23.40; 24/7 buses run to London and cost from £12; a taxi will cost from £130.

BICYCLE

Cycling is generally a good way to get around the city, although traffic can be intimidating for less confident cyclists. The city has tried hard to im-

Bloomsbury

prove the cycling infrastructure, however, opening new 'cycle superhighways' for commuters and launching **Santander Cycles** (☑ 0343 222 6666; www.tfl.gov.uk/modes/cycling/santander-cycles), which is particularly useful for visitors. **Transport for London** (www.tfl.gov.uk) publishes 14 free maps of London's cycle routes. You can order them online or by ringing 0843 222 1234.

PUBLIC TRANSPORT
Boat

Thames Clippers (www.thamesclippers.com; all zones adult/child £9.90/4.95) run regular services between Embankment, Waterloo (London Eye), Blackfriars, Bankside (Shakespeare's Globe), London Bridge, Tower Bridge, Canary Wharf, Greenwich, North Greenwich and Woolwich piers, from 6.55am to around midnight (from 9.29am weekends). Its River Roamer tickets (adult/child £18.50/9.25) give freedom to hop on and hop off boats on most routes all day.

Bus

London's red double-decker buses afford great views of the city, but be aware that the going can be slow, thanks to traffic jams and dozens of commuters getting on and off at every stop. Bus services normally operate from 5am to 11.30pm.

Underground, DLR & Overground

The London Underground ('the tube'; 11 colour-coded lines) is part of an integrated-transport system that also includes the **Docklands Light Railway** (DLR; www.tfl.gov.uk/dlr), a driverless overhead train operating in the eastern part of the city, and Overground network (mostly outside of Zone 1 and sometimes underground).

The first trains operate from around 5.30am Monday to Saturday and 6.45am Sunday. The last trains leave around 12.30am Monday to Saturday and 11.30pm Sunday.

Additionally, the Victoria and Jubilee lines, plus most of the Piccadilly, Central and Northern lines, run all night on Friday and Saturday to get revellers home (on what is called the 'Night Tube'), with trains every 10 minutes or so. Fares are off-peak.

Tickets & Passes

➡ The cheapest and most convenient way to pay for public transport is to buy an Oyster Card, a smart card on which you can store credit. The card works on the entire transport network and can be purchased from all tube and train stations and some shops.

➡ Oyster Cards will know whether to charge you per journey, for a return or for a day Travelcard.

➡ You need to pay a £5 deposit per Oyster Card, which you will get back when you return the card, along with any remaining credit.

➡ If you're staying for more than just a few days, consider getting a weekly or monthly pass (which can be loaded on to the Oyster Card).

WORTH A TRIP

CANTERBURY

Canterbury tops the charts for English cathedral cities. Many consider the World Heritage–listed **cathedral** (www.canterbury-cathedral.org; adult/child/concession £12.50/8.50/10.50, tours £5/4, audio guide £4/3; ⊙ 9am-5.30pm Mon-Sat, 12.30-2.30pm Sun) to be one of Europe's finest, and the town's narrow medieval alleyways, riverside gardens and ancient city walls are a joy to explore. Staff at the **tourist office** (☑ 01227-862162; www.canterbury.co.uk; 18 High St; ⊙ 9am-6pm Mon-Wed & Fri, to 8pm Thu, to 5pm Sat, 10am-5pm Sun; 🖥) located in the Beaney House of Art & Knowledge, can help book accommodation, excursions and theatre tickets. The city's **bus station** (St George's Lane) is just within the city walls. There are two train stations: Canterbury East for London Victoria (from £11.30, two hours), and Canterbury West for London's Charing Cross and St Pancras stations (from £13.60, one hour).

➡ Paper tickets are still available but are more expensive than Oyster Card fares.

➡ Contactless cards can be used instead of Oyster Cards (they benefit from the same 'smart-fare' system); just check for international fees with your card issuer.

TAXI

Black cabs are available for hire when the yellow sign above the windscreen is lit; just stick your arm out to signal one. Fares are metered, with the flagfall charge of £2.60 (covering the first 248m during a weekday), rising by increments of 20p for each subsequent 124m.

Minicabs, which are licensed, are cheaper (usually) competitors of black cabs. Unlike black cabs, minicabs cannot legally be hailed on the street; they must be hired by phone or directly from one of the minicab offices (every high street has at least one and most clubs work with a minicab firm to send revellers home safely).

Windsor & Eton
POP 31,225

Dominated by the massive bulk of Windsor Castle, these twin towns have a rather surreal atmosphere, with the morning pomp and ceremony of the changing of the guards in Windsor, and the sight of schoolboys dressed in formal tailcoats wandering the streets of tiny Eton, home to Eton College, the largest and most famous public (meaning private and fee-paying) school in England.

◉ Sights

★ Windsor Castle   CASTLE
(☑ 03031-237304; www.royalcollection.org.uk; Castle Hill; adult/child £21.20/12.30; ⊙ 9.30am-5.15pm Mar-Oct, 9.45am-4.15pm Nov-Feb; last admission 1hr 15min before closing; all or part of castle subject to occasional closures; ♿; ☐ 702 from London Victoria, ☒ London Waterloo to Windsor & Eton Riverside, ☒ London Paddington to Windsor & Eton Central via Slough) The world's largest and oldest continuously occupied fortress, Windsor Castle is a majestic vision of battlements and towers. It's used for state occasions and is one of the Queen's principal residences; if she's at home, the Royal Standard flies from the Round Tower. Join a free guided tour (every half-hour) of the wards or take a handheld multimedia tour of the lavish **State Apartments** and beautiful chapels. Some sections may be off-limits if in use. Book tickets online to avoid queues.

★ Windsor Great Park   PARK
(☑ 01753-860222; www.windsorgreatpark.co.uk; Windsor; ⊙ dawn-dusk) **FREE** Stretching from Windsor Castle almost all the way southwest to Ascot, Windsor Great Park covers just under 8 sq miles and features a lake, walking tracks, a bridleway, gardens and a deer park with 500 free-roaming red deer. Its popular **Long Walk** is a 2.7-mile jaunt south from King George IV Gate, south of the castle, to the 1831 Copper Horse statue of George III on Snow Hill, the park's highest point. From Windsor, public access is via Park St.

ℹ Information

Tourist Office (☑ 01753-743900; www.windsor.gov.uk; Old Booking Hall, Windsor Royal Shopping Arcade, Thames St; ⊙ 10am-5pm Apr-Sep, to 4pm Oct-Mar) Pick up a heritage walk map (£2.20).

ℹ Getting There & Away

Reading Buses (www.reading-buses.co.uk) coaches head to/from London Victoria (from £6, two hours).

Trains from Windsor & Eton Riverside (Dachet Rd) go directly to London Waterloo (£10.50, 55 minutes). Trains from Windsor & Eton Central (Thames St), changing at Slough for London Paddington (£10.50, 26 to 40 minutes), are quicker.

Salisbury & Stonehenge
POP 40,300

Centred on a majestic cathedral that's topped by the tallest spire in England, Salisbury makes an appealing Wiltshire base. It's been an important provincial city for more than a thousand years, and its streets form an architectural timeline ranging from medieval walls and half-timbered Tudor townhouses to Georgian mansions and Victorian villas. Salisbury is also the access point for tours to nearby Stonehenge, Britain's most iconic archaeological site.

◉ Sights

★ Stonehenge   ARCHAEOLOGICAL SITE
(EH; ☑ 0370 333 1181; www.english-heritage.org.uk; near Amesbury; adult/child same-day tickets £19.50/11.70, advance booking £17.50/10.50; ⊙ 9am-8pm Jun-Aug, 9.30am-7pm Apr, May & Sep, 9.30am-5pm Oct-Mar; ℗) An ultramodern makeover at ancient Stonehenge has brought an impressive visitor centre and the closure of an intrusive road (now restored to grassland). The result is a far stronger sense of historical context, with dignity and mystery returned to an archaeological gem.

A pathway frames the ring of massive stones. Although you can't walk in the circle, unless on a recommended **Stone Circle Access Visit** (☑ 0370 333 0605; adult/child £38.50/23.10), you can get close-up views. Admission is through timed tickets – secure a place well in advance.

★ Salisbury Cathedral   CATHEDRAL
(☑ 01722-555120; www.salisburycathedral.org.uk; The Close; requested donation adult/child £7.50/3; ⊙ 9am-5pm Mon-Sat, noon-4pm Sun) England is endowed with countless stunning churches, but few can hold a candle to the grandeur and sheer spectacle of 13th-century Salisbury Cathedral. This early English Gothic-style structure has an elaborate exterior decorated with pointed arches and flying buttresses, and a sombre, austere interior designed to keep its congregation suitably pious. Its statuary and tombs are outstanding; don't miss the daily tower tours and the cathedral's original, 13th-century copy of the **Magna Carta** (⊙ 9.30am-5pm Mon-Sat, noon-4pm Sun Apr-Oct, 9.30am-4.30pm Mon-Sat, noon-3.45pm Sun Nov-Mar).

★ Salisbury Museum   MUSEUM
(☑ 01722-332151; www.salisburymuseum.org.uk; 65 The Close; adult/child £8/4; ⊙ 10am-5pm Mon-Sat

GLASTONBURY

To many people, Glastonbury is synonymous with the **Glastonbury Festival of Contemporary Performing Arts** (www.glastonburyfestivals.co.uk; tickets from £238; ⊙ Jun or Jul), a frequently mud-soaked extravaganza of music, theatre, dance, cabaret, carnival and spirituality that's been held on and off on farmland in Pilton, just outside Glastonbury, for the last 40-plus years (bar the occasional off year to let the farm recover).

Outside of the festival, the area is still worth visiting for the scattered ruins of **Glastonbury Abbey** (☑ 01458-832267; www.glastonburyabbey.com; Magdalene St; adult/child £7.50/4.50; ⊙ 9am-8pm Jun-Aug, to 6pm Mar-May, Sep & Oct, to 4pm Nov-Feb) and **Glastonbury Tor** (NT; ☑ 01278-751874; www.nationaltrust.org.uk; ⊙ 24hr) FREE, a grassy hump about a mile from town, topped by the ruins of St Michael's Church. According to local legend, the tor is said to be the mythical Isle of Avalon, King Arthur's last resting place. It's also allegedly one of the world's great spiritual nodes, marking the meeting point of many mystical lines of power known as ley lines.

Bus 37/375/376 runs to Wells (£3.50, 15 minutes, several times an hour), which has a train station.

year-round, plus noon-5pm Sun Jun-Sep) The hugely important archaeological finds here include the Stonehenge Archer, the bones of a man found in the ditch surrounding the stone circle – one of the arrows found alongside probably killed him. With gold coins dating from 100 BC and a Bronze Age gold necklace, it's a powerful introduction to Wiltshire's prehistory.

ⓘ Information

Tourist Office (☑ 01722-342860; www.visitsalisbury.co.uk; Fish Row; ⊙ 9am-5pm Mon-Fri, 10am-4pm Sat, 10am-2pm Sun; 🛜)

ⓘ Getting There & Away

Direct National Express bus services include Bath (£11.20, one hour and 25 minutes, one daily) and London (£8.10, three hours, three daily) via Heathrow.

The **Stonehenge Tour** (☑ 01202-338420; www.thestonehengetour.info; adult/child/family £30/20/90) leaves Salisbury's railway station half-hourly from June to August, and hourly between September and May.

Half-hourly train connections include Bath (£5, one hour) and London Waterloo (£9.10, 1½ hours).

Bath

POP 88,900

Britain is littered with beautiful cities, but precious few compare to Bath. Home to some of the nation's grandest Georgian architecture – not to mention one of the world's best-preserved Roman bathhouses – this slinky, sophisticated, snooty city, found-ed on top of natural hot springs, has been a tourist draw for nigh on 2000 years.

Bath's heyday really began during the 18th century, when local entrepreneur Ralph Allen and his team of father-and-son architects, John Wood the Elder and Younger, turned this sleepy backwater into the toast of Georgian society, and constructed fabulous landmarks such as the Circus and Royal Crescent.

◉ Sights

⭐**Roman Baths**   HISTORIC BUILDING
(☑ 01225-477785; www.romanbaths.co.uk; Abbey Churchyard; adult/child/family £17.50/10.25/48; ⊙ 9.30am-5pm Nov-Feb, 9am-5pm Mar–mid-Jun, Sep & Oct, 9am-9pm mid-Jun–Aug) In typically ostentatious style, the Romans construct-ed a complex of bathhouses above Bath's three natural hot springs, which emerge at a steady 46°C (115°F). Situated alongside a temple dedicated to the healing goddess Sulis-Minerva, the baths now form one of the best-preserved ancient Roman spas in the world, and are encircled by 18th- and 19th-century buildings. Bath's premier at-traction can get very busy. To dodge the worst of the crowds, avoid weekends, and July and August.

⭐**Royal Crescent**   ARCHITECTURE
Bath is famous for its glorious Georgian ar-chitecture, and it doesn't get any grander than this semicircular terrace of majestic townhouses overlooking the green sweep of Royal Victoria Park. Designed by John Wood the Younger (1728–82) and built

Bath

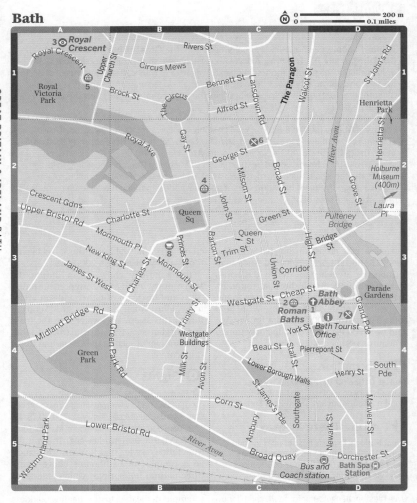

between 1767 and 1775, the houses appear perfectly symmetrical from the outside, but the owners were allowed to tweak the interiors, so no two houses are quite the same. **No 1 Royal Crescent** (☎01225-428126; www.no1royalcrescent.org.uk; 1 Royal Cres; adult/child/family £10.30/5.10/25.40; ☺10am-5pm) offers you an intriguing insight into life inside.

★ **Bath Abbey** CHURCH
(☎01225-422462; www.bathabbey.org; Abbey Churchyard; suggested donation adult/child £4/2; ☺9.30am-5.30pm Mon, 9am-5.30pm Tue-Fri, to 6pm Sat, 1-2.30pm & 4.30-6pm Sun)

Looming above the city centre, Bath's huge abbey church was built between 1499 and 1616, making it the last great medieval church raised in England. Its most striking feature is the west facade, where angels climb up and down stone ladders, commemorating a dream of the founder, Bishop Oliver King.

Tower tours (☎01225-422462; adult/child £8/4; ☺10am-5pm Apr-Aug, 10am-4pm Sep & Oct, 11am-4pm Nov-Mar, hourly Mon-Fri, every half hour Sat) leave on the hour from Monday to Friday, and every half-hour on Saturdays.

Bath

Jane Austen Centre   MUSEUM
(☑ 01225-443000; www.janeausten.co.uk; 40 Gay St; adult/child £12/6.20; ⊙ 9.45am-5.30pm Apr-Oct, 10am-4pm Sun-Fri, 9.45am-5.30pm Sat Nov-Mar) Bath is known to many as a location in Jane Austen's novels, including *Persuasion* and *Northanger Abbey*. Although Austen lived in Bath for only five years, from 1801 to 1806, she remained a regular visitor and a keen student of the city's social scene. Here, guides in Regency costumes regale you with Austen-esque tales as you tour memorabilia relating to the writer's life in Bath.

Holburne Museum   GALLERY
(☑ 01225-388569; www.holburne.org; Great Pulteney St; ⊙ 10am-5pm Mon-Sat, 11am-5pm Sun) **FREE** Sir William Holburne, the 18th-century aristocrat and art fanatic, amassed a huge collection, which now forms the core of the Holburne Museum, in a lavish mansion at the end of Great Pulteney St. The museum houses a roll call of works by artists including Turner, Stubbs, Hoare and Gainsborough, as well as 18th-century majolica pottery and porcelain.

🛏 Sleeping & Eating

Bath YHA   HOSTEL €
(☑ 0345 371 9303; www.yha.org.uk; Bathwick Hill; dm £23, d/q from £49/69; ⊙ check in 3-11pm; P @ 🏠) Split across an Italianate mansion and a modern annex, this impressive hostel is a steep climb (or a short hop on bus U1 or U18) from the city. The listed building means the rooms are huge, and some have

period features such as cornicing and bay windows.

Adventure   CAFE, BAR €
(☑ 01225-462038; www.adventurecafebar.co.uk; 5 Princes Bldgs, George St; mains £5-10; ⊙ 8am-3am Mon-Fri, from 9am Sat & Sun; 🏠🗷) This cafe-bar offers something to everyone at most times of the day: morning cappuccino, lunchtime ciabatta and late-night beer and cocktails. There's great outdoor seating at the back.

🍷 Drinking

Café Retro   CAFE €
(☑ 01225-339347; www.caferetro.co.uk; 18 York St; mains £5-10; ⊙ 9am-5pm; 🏠) A poke in the eye for the corporate coffee chains. The paint job's scruffy, the crockery's ancient and none of the furniture matches, but that's all part of the charm: this is a cafe from the old school, and there are few places better for burgers, butties or cake. Takeaways (in biodegradable containers) are available from Retro-to-Go next door.

★ Colonna & Smalls   CAFE
(☑ 07766 808 067; www.colonnaandsmalls.co.uk; 6 Chapel Row; ⊙ 8am-5.30pm Mon-Fri, from 8.30am Sat, 10am-4pm Sun; 🏠) If you're keen on caffeinated beans, this is a cafe not to miss. A mission to explore coffee ensures that there are three guest espresso varieties and smiley staff happy to share their expertise. They'll even tell you that black filter coffee – yes, filter coffee – is actually the best way to judge high-grade beans.

ⓘ Information

Bath Tourist Office (☑ 01225-614420; www.visitbath.co.uk; 2 Terrace Walk; ⊙ 9.30am-5.30pm Mon-Sat, 10am-4pm Sun, closed Sun Nov-Jan) Calls to the tourist office are charged at the premium rate of 50p per minute.

ⓘ Getting There & Away

Bath's **bus and coach station** (Dorchester St) is near the train station. National Express coaches run direct to London (£1, 3½ hours, four daily) and London Heathrow (£1, two hours, twice daily).

Bath Spa station is at the south end of Manvers St. Direct services include Cardiff Central (£10, one hour, hourly), London Paddington (£8, 1½ hours, half-hourly) and Salisbury (£5, one hour, hourly).

Oxford

POP 159,994

One of the world's most famous university cities, Oxford is a beautiful, privileged place. It is steeped in history and studded with august buildings, yet maintains the feel of a young city, thanks to its large student population. It's a wonderful place to ramble: the oldest colleges date back 750 years, and little has changed inside the hallowed walls since then (with the notable exception of female admissions, which only began in 1878).

⊙ Sights

★ **Bodleian Library**   LIBRARY

(☑ 01865-287400; www.bodleian.ox.ac.uk/bodley; Catte St; Divinity School £1, or £3.50 with audio tour; guided tours £6-14; ⊙9am-5pm Mon-Sat, 11am-5pm Sun) Oxford's Bodleian Library is one of the oldest public libraries in the world and quite possibly the most impressive one you'll ever see. Visitors are welcome to wander around the central quad and the foyer exhibition space. For £1 you can visit the **Divinity School**, but the rest of the complex is only accessible on guided tours. Check timings online or at the information desk. Advance tickets are available for extended tours only; others must be purchased on the day.

★ **Christ Church**   COLLEGE

(☑ 01865-276492; www.chch.ox.ac.uk; St Aldate's; adult/child £10/9 Jul & Aug, £8/7 Sep-Jun; ⊙10am-5pm Mon-Sat, 2-5pm Sun; last admission 4.15pm)

DON'T MISS

PUNTING IN OXFORD

A quintessential Oxford experience, punting is all about sitting back and quaffing Pimms (the typical English summer drink) as you watch the city's glorious architecture float by. Which, of course, requires someone else to do the hard work – punting is far more difficult than it appears. If you decide to go it alone, a deposit for the punt is usually charged. Most punts hold five people including the punter. The most central location to hire a punt is **Magdalen Bridge Boathouse** (☑ 01865-202643; www.oxfordpunting.co.uk; High St; chauffeured 4-person punts per 30min £32, punt rental per hr £22; ⊙9.30am-dusk Feb-Nov).

The largest of all of Oxford's colleges, with 650 students, and the one with the grandest quad, Christ Church is also most popular with visitors. Its magnificent buildings, illustrious history and latter-day fame as a location for the *Harry Potter* films bring tourists in droves. The college was founded in 1524 by Cardinal Thomas Wolsey, who suppressed the 9th-century monastery existing on the site to acquire the funds for his lavish building project.

★ **Ashmolean Museum**   MUSEUM

(☑ 01865-278000; www.ashmolean.org; Beaumont St; ⊙10am-5pm Tue-Sun, 10am-8pm last Fri of month) **FREE** Britain's oldest public museum, second in repute only to London's British Museum, was established in 1683 when Elias Ashmole presented Oxford University with a collection of curiosities amassed by the well-travelled John Tradescant, gardener to Charles I. Today the museum's four floors feature interactive displays, a giant atrium, glass walls with views into galleries on different levels and a beautifully sited rooftop restaurant. Collections span the world in bright, spacious galleries in one of Britain's best examples of neoclassical architecture.

★ **Pitt Rivers Museum**   MUSEUM

(☑ 01865-270927; www.prm.ox.ac.uk; South Parks Rd; ⊙noon-4.30pm Mon, 10am-4.30pm Tue-Sun; ⊛) **FREE** Hidden away through a door at the back of the **Oxford University Museum of Natural History** (☑ 01865-272950; www.oum. ox.ac.uk; Parks Rd; ⊙10am-5pm; ⊛) **FREE**, this wonderfully creepy anthropological museum houses a treasure trove of half a million objects from around the world – more than enough to satisfy any armchair adventurer. One of the reasons it's so brilliant is the fact there are no computers, interactive displays or shiny modern gimmicks. Dim lighting lends an air of mystery to the glass cases stuffed with prized booty of Victorian explorers.

Magdalen College   COLLEGE

(☑ 01865-276000; www.magd.ox.ac.uk; High St; adult/child £6/5; ⊙10am-7pm late Jun-late Sep; 1pm-dusk or 6pm, whichever's earlier, late Sep-late Jun) Set amid 40 hectares of private lawns, woodlands, river walks and deer park, Magdalen (*mawd*-lin), founded in 1458, is one of the wealthiest and most beautiful of Oxford's colleges. It has a reputation as an artistic college. Some of its notable students

Oxford

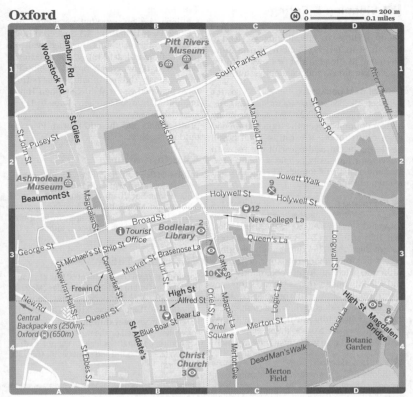

have included writers Julian Barnes, Alan Hollinghurst, CS Lewis, John Betjeman, Seamus Heaney and Oscar Wilde, not to mention Edward VIII, TE Lawrence 'of Arabia', Dudley Moore and Cardinal Thomas Wolsey.

Radcliffe Camera   LIBRARY
(📞 01865-287400; www.bodleian.ox.ac.uk; Radcliffe Sq; tours £14; ⊘ Only accessible on Bodleian tours, Wed 9.15am, Sat 9.15am, Sun 11.15am & 1.15pm) The sandy-gold Radcliffe Camera is the quintessential Oxford landmark and undoubtedly one of the city's most photographed buildings. This beautiful, light-filled circular, columned library and reading room that focuses on the humanities was built between 1737 and 1749 in grand Palladian style, and has Britain's third-largest dome. The only way to see the interior is to join an extended 1½-hour tour (£14) of the Bodleian Library.

Oxford

◉ Top Sights

◉ Sights

⊕ Activities, Courses & Tours

⊗ Eating

◉ Drinking & Nightlife

🛏 Sleeping & Eating

When it comes to eating out, Oxford offers plenty of choice to suit all budgets. Head to Walton St in Jericho, Banbury Rd in Summertown, St Clement's St or Cowley Rd for a good selection of independent restaurants.

Central Backpackers HOSTEL €
(☏ 01865-242288; www.centralbackpackers.co.uk; 13 Park End St; dm £22-28; 🛜) A welcoming budget option between the train station and town centre, above a bar, this small hostel has basic, bright and cheerful dorms, with lockers, for four to 12 people, a rooftop terrace and a small TV lounge. There's a six-bed women-only dorm.

★ Edamamé JAPANESE €
(☏ 01865-246916; www.edamame.co.uk; 15 Holywell St; mains £7-10.50; ⊙ 11.30am-2.30pm Wed, 11.30am-2.30pm & 5-8.30pm Thu-Sat, noon-3.30pm Sun; 🖉) The queue out the door speaks volumes about this tiny, deliciously authentic place. All light wood, dainty trays and friendly bustle, this is Oxford's top spot for gracefully simple, flavour-packed Japanese cuisine. Dishes include fragrant chicken miso ramen, tofu stir-fry and, on Thursday nights, sushi. No bookings; arrive early and be prepared to wait. Cash only at lunch.

★ Vaults & Garden CAFE €
(☏ 01865-279112; www.thevaultsandgarden.com; University Church of St Mary the Virgin, Radcliffe Sq; mains £7-10.50; ⊙ 9am-6pm; 🛜🖉) 🍃 Hidden in the vaulted 14th-century Old Congregation House of the University Church, this buzzy local favourite serves a wholesome seasonal selection of soups, salads, pastas, curries, sandwiches and cakes, including vegetarian and gluten-free options. It's one of Oxford's most beautiful lunch venues, with additional tables in a pretty garden overlooking Radcliffe Sq. Arrive early to grab a seat.

🍷 Drinking & Nightlife

Bear Inn PUB
(☏ 01865-728164; www.bearoxford.co.uk; 6 Alfred St; ⊙ 11am-11pm Mon-Thu, 11am-midnight Fri & Sat, 11.30am-10.30pm Sun) Arguably Oxford's oldest pub (there's been a pub on this site since 1242), the atmospherically creaky Bear requires all but the most vertically challenged to duck their heads when passing through doorways. A curious tie collection covers the walls and ceilings, and there are usually a couple of worthy guest ales and artisanal beers.

Turf Tavern PUB
(☏ 01865-243235; www.turftavern-oxford.co.uk; 4-5 Bath Pl; ⊙ 11am-11pm; 🛜) Squeezed down a narrow alleyway, this tiny medieval pub (dating from at least 1381) is one of Oxford's best loved. It's where US president Bill Clinton famously 'did not inhale'; other patrons have included Oscar Wilde, Stephen Hawking and Margaret Thatcher. Home to 11 real ales, it's always crammed with students, professionals and the odd tourist. Plenty of outdoor seating.

ℹ Information

Tourist Office (☏ 01865-686430; www.experienceoxfordshire.org; 15-16 Broad St; ⊙ 9am-5.30pm Mon-Sat, 10am-4pm Sun Jul & Aug; 9.30am-5pm Mon-Sat, 10am-4pm Sep-Jun) Covers the whole of Oxfordshire; stocks printed Oxford walking guides and books official walking tours.

ℹ Getting There & Away

Services to/from Oxford's central **bus station** (Gloucester Green) include Cambridge (Megabus/X5, £8.70/13.50, 3¾ hours) and London Victoria (X90/Oxford Tube, £10/15, 1¾ hours).

Oxford's main **train station** (Botley Rd) is conveniently placed on the western side of the city centre. Destinations include London Paddington (£5, 1¼ hours) and Manchester (£31.30, 2¾ hours).

Stratford-upon-Avon

POP 27,455

The author of some of the most quoted lines ever written in the English language, William Shakespeare was born in Stratford in 1564 and died here in 1616. Experiences linked to his life in this unmistakably Tudor town range from the touristy (medieval re-creations and Bard-themed tearooms) to the humbling (Shakespeare's modest grave in Holy Trinity Church) and the sublime (taking in a play by the world-famous Royal Shakespeare Company).

⊙ Sights & Activities

★ Shakespeare's Birthplace HISTORIC BUILDING
(☏ 01789-204016; www.shakespeare.org.uk; Henley St; adult/child £17.50/11.50; ⊙ 9am-5pm Apr-Aug, 9am-4.30pm Sep & Oct, 10am-3.30pm Nov-Mar) Start your Shakespeare quest at the house where the world's most popular playwright supposedly spent his childhood days. In fact,

the jury is still out on whether this really was Shakespeare's birthplace, but devotees of the Bard have been dropping in since at least the 19th century, leaving their signatures scratched on to the windows. Set behind a modern facade, the house has restored Tudor rooms, live presentations from famous Shakespearean characters, and an engaging exhibition on Stratford's favourite son.

★ **Shakespeare's New Place**   HISTORIC SITE
(✆ 01789-338536; www.shakespeare.org.uk; cnr Chapel St & Chapel Lane; adult/child £12.50/8; ⏰ 10am-5pm Apr-Aug, to 4.30pm Sep & Oct, to 3.30pm Nov-Feb) When Shakespeare retired, he swapped the bright lights of London for a comfortable townhouse at New Place, where he died of unknown causes in April 1616. The house was demolished in 1759, but an attractive Elizabethan knot garden occupies part of the grounds. A major restoration project has uncovered Shakespeare's kitchen and incorporated new exhibits in a reimagining of the house as it would have been. You can also explore the adjacent **Nash's House**, where Shakespeare's granddaughter Elizabeth lived.

Anne Hathaway's Cottage   HISTORIC BUILDING
(✆ 01789-338532; www.shakespeare.org.uk; Cottage Lane, Shottery; adult/child £12.50/8; ⏰ 9am-5pm Apr-Aug, 9am-4.30pm Sep & Oct, 10am-3.30pm Nov-Mar) Before tying the knot with Shakespeare, Anne Hathaway lived in Shottery, 1 mile west of the centre of Stratford, in this delightful thatched farmhouse. As well as period furniture, it has gorgeous gardens and an orchard and arboretum, with examples of all the trees mentioned in Shakespeare's plays. A footpath (no bikes allowed) leads to Shottery from Evesham Pl. The **City Sightseeing** (✆ 01789-299123; www.city-sightseeing.com; adult/child 24hr £16.82/8.41, 48hr £25.52/13; ⏰ 9.30am-5pm Apr-Sep, to 4pm Oct-Mar) bus stops here.

🛏 Sleeping & Eating

Stratford-upon-Avon YHA   HOSTEL €
(✆ 0345 371 9661; www.yha.org.uk; Wellesbourne Rd, Alveston; dm/d/glamping from £13/58/49; P ☎) Set in a large 200-year-old mansion 1.5 miles east of the town centre, this superior hostel attracts travellers of all ages. Of its 32 rooms and dorms, 16 are en suite, as are four-person camping pods with kitchenettes. There's a canteen, bar and kitchen. Buses X15, X18 and 18A run here from Bridge St. Wi-fi is available in common areas.

Fourteas   CAFE €
(✆ 01789-293908; http://thefourteas.co.uk; 24 Sheep St; dishes £4.60-7.55, afternoon tea with/without Prosecco £20/15; ⏰ 9.30am-5pm Mon-Sat, 11am-4.30pm Sun) Breaking with Stratford's Shakespearean theme, this tearoom takes the 1940s as its inspiration with beautiful old teapots, framed posters and staff in period costume. As well as premium loose-leaf teas and homemade cakes, there are hearty breakfasts, delicious sandwiches (fresh poached salmon, brie and grape), a hot dish of the day and indulgent afternoon teas (gluten-free options available).

☆ Entertainment

★ **Royal Shakespeare Company**   THEATRE
(RSC; ✆ box office 01789-403493; www.rsc.org.uk; Waterside; tours adult £7-9, child £4.50-5, tower adult/child £2.50/1.25; ⏰ tour times vary, tower 10am-5pm Sun-Fri, 10am-12.15 & 2-5pm Sat mid-Mar–mid-Oct, 10am-4.30pm Sun-Fri, 10am-12.15pm Sat mid-Oct–mid-Mar) Stratford has two grand stages run by the world-renowned Royal Shakespeare Company – the Royal Shakespeare Theatre and the **Swan Theatre** (✆ 01789-403493; www.rsc.org.uk; Waterside) on Waterside – as well as the smaller **Other Place** (✆ box office 01789-403493; www.rsc.org.uk; 22 Southern Lane). The theatres have witnessed performances by such legends as Lawrence Olivier, Richard Burton, Judi Dench, Helen Mirren, Ian McKellan and Patrick Stewart. Various one-hour **guided tours** take you behind the scenes.

Zipping up the lift of the Royal Shakespeare Theatre's tower rewards with panoramic views over the town and River Avon. Spectacular views also unfold from its 3rd-floor Rooftop Restaurant, which opens to a terrace.

Contact the RSC for performance times, and book well ahead. There are often special deals for under-25-year-olds, students and seniors, and a few tickets are held back for sale on the day of the performance, but get snapped up fast.

🛈 Information

Tourist Office (✆ 01789-264293; www.shakespeares-england.co.uk; Bridge Foot; ⏰ 9am-5.30pm Mon-Sat, 10am-4pm Sun) Just west of Clopton Bridge.

🛈 Getting There & Away

National Express coaches and other bus companies run from Stratford's Riverside bus station (behind the Stratford Leisure Centre on Bridge-way). Services include London Victoria (£7.70, three hours, three daily) and Oxford (£10.10, 70 minutes, daily).

By train from London Marylebone station you'll need to change at Dorridge (£6.50. two hours).

Cambridge

POP 123,900

Abounding with exquisite architecture, exuding history and tradition and renowned for its quirky rituals, Cambridge is a university town extraordinaire. The tightly packed core of ancient colleges, the picturesque riverside 'Backs' (college gardens) and the leafy green meadows surrounding the city give it a more tranquil appeal than its historic rival Oxford.

👁 Sights

Cambridge University comprises 31 colleges, though not all are open to the public. Opening hours are only a rough guide, so contact the colleges or the tourist office for more information.

★ **King's College Chapel** CHURCH
(✆01223-331212; www.kings.cam.ac.uk; King's Pde; adult/child £9/£6; ⊙9.30am-3.15pm Mon-Sat, 1.15-2.30pm Sun term time, 9.30am-4.30pm daily university holidays) In a city crammed with showstopping buildings, this is a scene-stealer. Grandiose 16th-century King's

---

PUNTING ON THE CAMBRIDGE BACKS

Behind the Cambridge colleges' grandiose facades and stately courts, a series of gardens and parks lines up beside the river. Collectively known as the Backs, the tranquil green spaces and shimmering waters offer unparalleled views of the colleges and are often the most enduring image of Cambridge for visitors.

Gliding a self-propelled punt along the Backs is a blissful experience – once you've got the hang of it. You can always opt for a relaxing chauffeured punt, which costs around £20 to £28 per hour; 45-minute chauffeured trips of the Backs cost about £15 to £19 per person. One-way trips to Grantchester (1½ hours) start at around £18 per person.

College Chapel is one of England's most extraordinary examples of Gothic architecture. Its inspirational, intricate 80m-long fan-vaulted ceiling is the world's largest and soars upwards before exploding into a series of stone fireworks. This hugely atmospheric space is a fitting stage for the chapel's world-famous choir; hear it sing during the free and magnificent **evensong** during term time (5.30pm Monday to Saturday, 10.30am and 3.30pm Sunday).

★ **Trinity College** COLLEGE
(✆01223-338400; www.trin.cam.ac.uk; Trinity St; adult/child £3/1; ⊙10am-4.30pm Jul-Oct, to 3.30pm Nov-Jun) The largest of Cambridge's colleges, Trinity offers an extraordinary Tudor gateway, an air of supreme elegance and a sweeping Great Court – the largest of its kind in the world. It also boasts the renowned and suitably musty **Wren Library** (✆01223-338400; Trinity St; ⊙noon-2pm Mon-Fri year-round, plus 10.30am-12.30pm Sat term time) **FREE**, containing 55,000 books dated before 1820 and more than 2500 manuscripts. Works include those by Shakespeare, St Jerome, Newton and Swift – and AA Milne's original *Winnie the Pooh;* both Milne and his son, Christopher Robin, were graduates.

★ **Fitzwilliam Museum** MUSEUM
(www.fitzmuseum.cam.ac.uk; Trumpington St; by donation; ⊙10am-5pm Tue-Sat, noon-5pm Sun) **FREE** Fondly dubbed 'the Fitz' by locals, this colossal neoclassical pile was one of the first public art museums in Britain, built to house the fabulous treasures that the seventh Viscount Fitzwilliam bequeathed to his old university. Expect Roman and Egyptian grave goods, artworks by many of the great masters and some quirkier collections: banknotes, literary autographs, watches and armour.

🛏 Sleeping & Eating

Cambridge YHA HOSTEL €
(✆0345-371 9728; www.yha.org.uk; 97 Tenison Rd; dm £25, d £60; @🤝) A smart, friendly, recently renovated, deservedly popular hostel with compact dorms and good facilities. Handily, it's near the railway station.

★ **Urban Shed** SANDWICHES €
(✆01223-324888; www.theurbanshed.com; 62 King St; sandwiches from £5; ⊙8.30am-5pm Mon-Fri, 9am-5.30pm Sat, 10am-5pm Sun; 🐾) Somewhere between a retro goods shop and a sandwich bar, unorthodox Urban Shed has

a personal service ethos so strong that regular customers have a locker for their own mug. Decor teams old aeroplane seats with cable-drum tables, their own-blend coffee is mellow and the sandwiches range is superb.

Fitzbillies CAFE €
(☑ 01223-352500; www.fitzbillies.com; 52 Trumpington St; mains £9-12; ⊙ 8am-6pm Mon-Fri, from 9am Sat, from 9.30am Sun) Cambridge's oldest bakery has a soft, doughy place in the hearts of generations of students, thanks to its ultrasticky Chelsea buns and other sweet treats. Pick up a bagful to take away or munch in comfort in the quaint cafe.

ℹ️ Information

Tourist Office (☑ 01223-791500; www.visitcambridge.org; The Guildhall, Peas Hill; ⊙ 9.30am-5pm Mon-Sat Nov-Mar, plus 11am-3pm Sun Apr-Oct)

ℹ️ Getting There & Away

Buses leave from Parkside. Destinations include Gatwick (from £15, 3¾ hours, 12 daily), Heathrow (from £12, 2¾ hours, hourly), Oxford (Megabus/X5, £8.70/13.50, 3¾ hours) and Stansted (from £6, 45 minutes, 10 daily).

The train station is 1.5 miles southeast of the centre. Destinations include London King's Cross (£24, one hour, two to four per hour) and Stansted (£10.40, 30 minutes, hourly).

York

POP 198,000

Nowhere in northern England says 'medieval' quite like York, a city of extraordinary cultural and historical wealth that has lost little of its pre-industrial lustre. A magnificent circuit of 13th-century walls encloses

ℹ️ YORK PASS

Using a **York Pass** (www.yorkpass.com) can save you money. It covers access to more than 30 pay-to-visit sights in and around York, including York Minster, Jorvik and Castle Howard. You can buy it at York tourist office or online.

a spider's web of narrow streets with the awe-inspiring York Minster at its heart.

◉ Sights

★**York Minster** CATHEDRAL
(☑ 01904-557200; www.yorkminster.org; Deangate; adult/child £10/free, incl tower £15/5; ⊙ 9am-6pm Mon-Sat, 12.30-6pm Sun, last admission 4.30pm Mon-Sat, 3pm Sun) The remarkable York Minster is the largest medieval cathedral in all of northern Europe, and one of the world's most beautiful Gothic buildings. Seat of the archbishop of York, primate of England, it is second in importance only to Canterbury, seat of the primate of *all* England – the separate titles were created to settle a debate over the true centre of the English church. If this is the only cathedral you visit in England, you'll still walk away satisfied.

★**National Railway Museum** MUSEUM
(www.nrm.org.uk; Leeman Rd; ⊙ 10am-6pm Apr-Oct, to 5pm Nov-Mar; 🅿️ 🚼) **FREE** While many railway museums are the sole preserve of lone men in anoraks comparing dog-eared notebooks and getting high on the smell of machine oil, coal smoke and nostalgia, this place is different. York's National Railway Museum – the biggest in the world, with more than 100 locomotives – is so well presented and crammed with fascinating stuff

YORK'S CITY WALLS

If the weather's good, don't miss the chance to walk York's City Walls (www.yorkwalls.org.uk), which follow the line of the original Roman walls and give a whole new perspective on the city. Allow 1½ to two hours for the full circuit of 4.5 miles or, if you're pushed for time, the short stretch from Bootham Bar to Monk Bar is worth doing for the views of the minster.

Start and finish in the Museum Gardens or at **Bootham Bar** (on the site of a Roman gate), where a multimedia exhibit provides some historical context, and travel clockwise. Highlights include **Monk Bar**, which is the best-preserved medieval gate and still has a working portcullis, and **Walmgate Bar**, England's only city gate with an intact barbican.

York

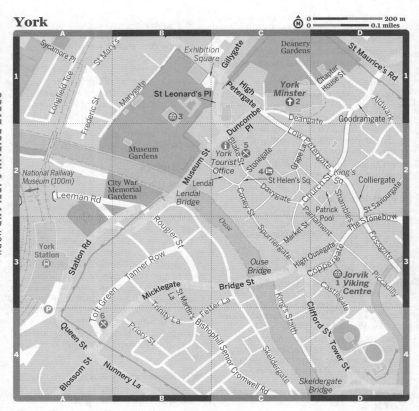

York

◎ Top Sights
1 Jorvik Viking Centre	D3
2 York Minster	C1

◎ Sights
3 Yorkshire Museum	B1

🛏 Sleeping
4 Fort	C2

✕ Eating
5 Mannion's	C2
6 Your Bike Shed	A4

that it's interesting even to folk whose eyes don't mist over at the thought of a 4-6-2 A1 Pacific class thundering into a tunnel.

★ Jorvik Viking Centre
MUSEUM

(☑ ticket reservations 01904-615505; www.jorvik-viking-centre.co.uk; Coppergate; adult/child £11/8; ◎10am-5pm Apr-Oct, to 4pm Nov-Mar) Interactive multimedia exhibits aimed at bringing history to life often achieve exactly the opposite, but the much-hyped Jorvik manages to pull it off with aplomb. Thoroughly restored and reimagined following flood damage in 2015, it's a smells-and-all reconstruction of the Viking settlement unearthed here during excavations in the late 1970s, experienced via a 'time-car' monorail that transports you through 9th-century Jorvik (the Viking name for York). You can reduce time waiting in the queue by booking your tickets online.

Yorkshire Museum
MUSEUM

(www.yorkshiremuseum.org.uk; Museum St; adult/child £7.50/free; ◎10am-5pm) Most of York's Roman archaeology is hidden beneath the medieval city, so the superb displays in the Yorkshire Museum are invaluable if you want to get an idea of what Eboracum was like. There are maps and models of Roman

York, funerary monuments, mosaic floors and wall paintings, and a 4th-century bust of Emperor Constantine. Kids will enjoy the dinosaur exhibit, centred on giant ichthyosaur fossils from Yorkshire's Jurassic coast.

Sleeping & Eating

★ Fort
HOSTEL €

(☑ 01904-620222; www.thefortyork.co.uk; 1 Little Stonegate; dm/d from £22/85; 🖥) This boutique hostel showcases the work of young British designers, creating affordable accommodation with a dash of character and flair. There are six- and eight-bed dorms, along with six doubles, but don't expect a peaceful retreat – the central location is in the middle of York's nightlife, and there's a lively club downstairs (earplugs are provided!).

York YHA
HOSTEL €

(☑ 01629-592 700; www.yha.org.uk; 42 Water End, Clifton; dm/tw from £15/39; P🖥) Originally the Rowntree (Quaker confectioners) mansion, this handsome Victorian house makes a spacious and child-friendly youth hostel, with most of its rooms four-bed dorms. It's often busy, so book early. It's about a mile northwest of the city centre; there's a riverside footpath from Lendal Bridge (poorly lit, so avoid after dark). Alternatively, take bus 2 from the train station or Museum St.

★ Mannion & Co
CAFE, BISTRO €

(☑ 01904-631030; www.mannionandco.co.uk; 1 Blake St; mains £7-12; ⊙ 9am-5pm Mon-Sat, 10am-4.30pm Sun) Expect to queue for a table at this busy bistro (no reservations), with its maze of rustic, wood-panelled rooms and

selection of daily specials. Regulars on the menu include eggs Benedict for breakfast, a chunky Yorkshire rarebit made with home-baked bread, and lunch platters of cheese and charcuterie from the attached deli. Oh, and pavlova for pudding.

Your Bike Shed
CAFE €

(☑ 01904-633777; www.yourbikeshed.co.uk; 148-150 Micklegate; mains £4-7; ⊙ 9am-5pm Mon-Sat, to 4pm Sun; 🖥) Reinvigorated by the 2014 Tour de France (which began in Yorkshire) and the annual Tour de Yorkshire (from 2015), York's cycling scene has latched onto this cool cafe and bike workshop. Fitted out with recycled furniture and classic bikes, it serves reviving portions of halloumi burger, pie and peas, and carrot cake to hungry cyclists, washed down with excellent coffee.

ℹ Information

York Tourist Office (☑ 01904-550099; www.visityork.org; 1 Museum St; ⊙ 9am-5pm Mon-Sat, 10am-4pm Sun) Visitor and transport info for all of Yorkshire, plus accommodation bookings, ticket sales and internet access.

ℹ Getting There & Away

For bus timetables, call **Traveline Yorkshire** (☑ 0871 200 2233; www.yorkshiretravel.net) or check the computerised 24-hour information points at the train station and Rougier St. All local and regional buses stop on Rougier St, about 200m northeast of the train station. Connections include London (from £14, 5½ hours, daily).

From this major railway hub there are direct connections to Edinburgh (£17/10, 2½ hours, hourly), London King's Cross (£22, two hours, hourly) and Manchester (£8.90, 1½ hours, every 15 minutes).

WORTH A TRIP

CASTLE HOWARD

Stately homes may be two-a-penny in England, but you'll have to try pretty damn hard to find one as breathtakingly stately as **Castle Howard** (☑ 01653-648 333; www.castle-howard.co.uk; adult/child house & grounds £18.95/9.95, grounds only £11.95/7.95; ⊙ house 10am-4pm, grounds 10am-5pm, last admission 4pm; P). A work of theatrical grandeur and audacity set in the rolling Howardian Hills, 15 miles northeast of York, this is one of the world's most beautiful buildings, instantly recognisable from its starring role in both the TV series and film of *Brideshead Revisited*, based on Evelyn Waugh's 1945 novel of nostalgia for the English aristocracy.

There are several organised tours from York; check with the tourist office for up-to-date schedules. Stephenson's of Easingwold (www.stephensonsofeasingwold.co.uk) bus 181 links York with Castle Howard (£10 return, 40 minutes, four times daily Monday to Saturday year-round, three on Sunday May to September).

Manchester

POP 527,240

The uncrowned capital of the north is well deserving of the title. It has a rich history and culture, easily explored in its myriad museums and galleries. You can also dine, drink and dance yourself into happy oblivion in the swirl of hedonism that is one of Manchester's most cherished characteristics.

⊙ Sights

★ Museum of Science & Industry   MUSEUM

(MOSI; ☑0161-832 2244; www.msimanchester.org. uk; Liverpool Rd; suggested donation £3, special exhibits £6-8; ◎10am-5pm; ☒1 or 3, ☒Deansgate-Castlefield) FREE Manchester's rich industrial legacy is explored in this excellent museum set within the enormous grounds of the old Liverpool St Station, the oldest rail terminus in the world. The large collection of steam engines, locomotives and original factory machinery tells the story of the city from the sewers up, while a host of new technology looks to the future. Take Metrolink to Deansgate-Castlefield or Metroshuttles 1 or 3.

★ People's History Museum   MUSEUM

(☑0161-838 9190; www.phm.org.uk; Left Bank, Bridge St; ◎10am-5pm) FREE The story of Britain's 200-year march to democracy is told in all its pain and pathos at this superb museum, housed in a refurbished Edwardian pumping station. You clock in on the 1st floor (literally: punch your card in an old mill clock, which managers would infamously fiddle with so as to make employees work longer) and plunge into the heart of Britain's struggle for basic democratic rights, labour reform and fair pay.

★ Manchester Art Gallery   GALLERY

(☑0161-235 8888; www.manchesterartgallery.org; Mosley St; ◎10am-5pm Fri-Wed, to 9pm Thu; ☒St Peter's Square) FREE A superb collection of British art and a hefty number of European masters are on display at the city's top gallery. The older wing has an impressive selection of 18th- and 19th-century paintings, as well as the country's best assemblage of Pre-Raphaelite art. There's also a permanent collection of pre-17th-century art, with works predominantly from the Dutch and early Renaissance masters. The gallery runs a free, hour-long highlights tour from 2pm to 3pm Thursday to Sunday.

Whitworth Art Gallery   GALLERY

(☑0161-275 7450; www.whitworth.manchester. ac.uk; University of Manchester, Oxford Rd; ◎10am-5pm Fri-Wed, to 9pm Thu; ☒15, 41, 42, 43, 140, 143 or 147 from Piccadilly Gardens) FREE Manchester's second most important art gallery has a wonderful collection of British watercolours. It also houses the best selection of historic textiles outside London, and has galleries devoted to the work of artists from Dürer and Rembrandt to Lucian Freud and David Hockney. To reach here catch bus 15, 41, 42, 43, 140, 143 or 147 from Piccadilly Gardens.

John Rylands Library   LIBRARY

(☑0161-306 0555; www.library.manchester.ac.uk/ rylands; 150 Deansgate; ◎10am-5pm Tue-Sat, noon-5pm Mon & Sun; ☒all city centre) FREE Less a library and more a cathedral to books, Basil Champneys' stunning building is a breathtaking example of Victorian Gothic, particularly the Reading Room, complete with high-vaulted ceilings and stained-glass windows. The collection of early printed books and rare manuscripts is equally impressive, and includes a Gutenberg Bible, the earliest extant New Testament text and the country's second-largest assembly of works by Britain's first printer, William Caxton. There's a free 30-minute tour at 3pm Wednesdays and Fridays.

⫚ Sleeping & Eating

Manchester's choice of restaurants is second only to London. Spinningfields, just off Deansgate, has some of the most interesting spots in the centre, while the Northern Quarter is great for offbeat cafes and organic eats.

★ Manchester YHA   HOSTEL €

(☑0345-371 9647; www.yha.org.uk; Potato Wharf; dm/d from £15/65; ℗ @ ☎; ☒Deansgate-Castlefield) This purpose-built canalside hostel in the Castlefield area is one of the best in the country. It's a top-class option with four- and six-bed dorms, all with bathrooms, as well as three doubles and a host of good facilities. Potato Wharf is just left off Liverpool Rd.

♟ Drinking & Nightlife

★ Port Street Beer House   CRAFT BEER

(www.portstreetbeerhouse.co.uk; 39-41 Port St; ◎noon-midnight Sun-Fri, to 1am Sat; ☒Piccadilly Gardens) Fans of real ale love this Northern Quarter boozer with its seven hand pulls, 18 draught lines and more than 100 beers from around the world, including gluten-free ales and some heavy hitters: Brewdog's Tactical

Nuclear Penguin is a 32% stout, but at £45 a bottle you won't need more than one. It hosts regular tastings and tap takeovers.

North Tea Power CAFE
(☑ 0161-833 3073; www.northteapower.co.uk; 36 Tib St; ☉ 8am-7pm Mon-Fri, from 9am Sat, 10am-6pm Sun; ☎) The name may say tea, but the interior of this cafe screams coffee shop. North Tea Power is one of Manchester's early adopters on the artisanal coffee scene, with the requisite communal tables, industrial pillars and Macbook-wielding tribe. As well as flat whites, aeropress and pour-overs, the menu features a load of loose-leaf teas, cakes and all-day breakfast options.

☆ Entertainment

★ **HOME** ARTS CENTRE
(☑ 0161-200 1500; www.homemcr.org; 2 Tony Wilson Pl, First St; tickets £5-20; ☉ box office noon-8pm, bar 10am-11pm Mon-Thu, to midnight Fri-Sat, 11am-10.30pm Sun; ☐ all city centre) One of Britain's best new arts centres, Home has two theatre spaces that host provocative new works in a variety of contexts, from proscenium sets to promenade pieces. The five cinema screens show the latest indie releases as well as classics. There's also a ground-floor bar and a cafe on the 1st floor.

ⓘ Information

Tourist Office (www.visitmanchester.com; 1 Piccadilly Gardens; ☉ 9.30am-5pm Mon-Sat, 10.30am-4.30pm Sun; ☐ Piccadilly Gardens) This is a self-service tourist office, with brochures and interactive maps to help guide visitors.

ⓘ Getting There & Around

The excellent public transport system can be used with a variety of Day Saver tickets. For enquiries about local transport, including night buses, contact **Travelshop** (☑ 0161-244 1000; www.tfgm.com; 1 Piccadilly Gardens; ☉ 7am-6pm Mon-Sat, 10am-6pm Sun).

Manchester Airport (☑ 0808-169 7030; www.manchesterairport.co.uk) is 12 miles south of the city. Frequent trains connect with Manchester Piccadilly Station (£5, 20 minutes) while buses (£4.10, 30 minutes) go to Manchester Coach Station (p81). A taxi takes 25 to 40 minutes, and costs £20 to £30.

National Express (www.nationalexpress.com) serves most major cities almost hourly from the **Coach Station** (Chorlton St). Destinations include London (£5, five hours, hourly).

Manchester Piccadilly is the main station for most train services across Britain. Destinations include London Euston (£23, two hours, hourly).

Lake District National Park

The Lake District (or Lakeland, as it's often known round these parts) is by far and away the UK's most popular national park. Every year, some 15 million people pitch up to explore the region's fells and countryside, and it's not hard to see why. Ever since the Romantic poets arrived in the 19th century, its postcard panorama of craggy hilltops, mountain tarns and glittering lakes has been stirring the imaginations of visitors.

◉ Sights

Stretching for 10.5 miles between Ambleside and Newby Bridge, **Windermere** isn't just the queen of Lake District lakes – it's also the largest body of water anywhere in England, closer in stature to a Scottish loch. It's been a centre for tourism since the first trains chugged into town in 1847, and it's still one of the national park's busiest spots.

Grasmere is a gorgeous little Lakeland village, all the more famous because of its links with Britain's leading Romantic poet, William Wordsworth. Literary pilgrims will want to see **Dove Cottage** (☑ 015394-35544; www.wordsworth.org.uk; adult/child £8.95/free; ☉ 9.30am-5.30pm Mar-Oct, 10am-4.30pm Nov, Dec & Feb), his former home.

The main town of the north Lakes, **Keswick** sits beside lovely Derwent Water, a

---

WORTH A TRIP

HADRIAN'S WALL

Named in honour of the emperor who ordered it built, Hadrian's Wall was one of Rome's greatest engineering projects, a spectacular 73-mile testament to ambition and the practical Roman mind. It was constructed between AD 122 and 128 to separate Romans and Scottish Picts.

A variety of buses along the route of the wall are covered by the **Hadrian's Wall Rover Ticket** available from bus drivers and tourist offices, where you can also get timetables. The railway line between Newcastle and Carlisle (Tyne Valley Line; £15.90, 1½ hours, hourly) has stations at Corbridge, Hexham, Haydon Bridge, Bardon Mill, Haltwhistle and Brampton. Not all services stop at all stations.

silvery curve studded by wooded islands and criss-crossed by puttering cruise boats, operated by the **Keswick Launch** (☑ 017687-72263; www.keswick-launch.co.uk; round-the-lake pass adult/child/family £10.75/5.65/25.50).

🛌 Sleeping

There are more than 20 YHA hostels, many of which can be linked by foot if you wish to hike. In addition to the four excellent campsites run by the National Trust (near Ambleside, Great Langdale, Wasdale and Coniston), there are more great places to sleep under the stars.

★ Ambleside YHA   HOSTEL €

(☑ 0345 371 9620; www.yha.org.uk/hostel/ambleside; Lake Rd; dm £18-32; P 🛜) One of the YHA's flagship Lake District hostels, this huge lakeside house is a fave for activity holidays (everything from kayaking to ghyll scrambling). Great facilities (kitchen, bike rental, boat jetty and bar) mean it's heavily subscribed, so book well ahead. Families can book out dorms as private rooms. The hostel is halfway between Ambleside and Windermere on Lake Rd (the A591).

ℹ️ Information

The national park's main visitor centre is at **Brockhole** (☑ 015394-46601; www.brockhole. co.uk; ⊙ 10am-5pm), just outside Windermere, and there are tourist offices in **Windermere** (☑ 015394-46499; www.windermereinfo. co.uk; Victoria St, Windermere Town; ⊙ 8.30am-5.30pm), **Bowness** (☑ 0845 901 0845; bownesstic@lake-district.gov.uk; Glebe Rd, Bowness-on-Windermere; ⊙ 9.30am-5.30pm), **Ambleside** (☑ 015394-32582; tic@thehubof ambleside.com; Central Bldgs, Market Cross; ⊙ 9am-5pm), **Keswick** (☑ 017687-72645; www. keswick.org; Moot Hall, Market Pl; ⊙ 9.30am-4.30pm; 🛜), **Coniston** (☑ 015394-41533; www. conistontic.org; Ruskin Ave; ⊙ 9.30am-4.30pm Mon-Sat, 10am-2pm Sun) and **Carlisle** (☑ 01228-598596; www.discovercarlisle.co.uk; Greenmarket; ⊙ 9.30am-5pm Mon-Sat, 10.30am-4pm Sun).

All have information on local sights, activities, accommodation and public transport and can help with accommodation bookings.

ℹ️ Getting There & Away

To get to the Lake District via the main West Coast train line, you need to change at Oxenholme for Kendal and Windermere.

National Express coaches run direct from London Victoria and Glasgow to Windermere and Kendal.

WALES

Cardiff

POP 346,000

Welsh capital since only 1955, Cardiff has embraced the role with vigour, emerging in the new millennium as one of Britain's leading urban centres. Caught between an ancient fort and an ultramodern waterfront, compact Cardiff seems to have surprised even itself with how interesting it has become.

👁 Sights

★ Cardiff Castle   CASTLE

(☑ 029-2087 8100; www.cardiffcastle.com; Castle St; adult/child £12.50/9, incl guided tour £15.75/11; ⊙ 9am-6pm Mar-Oct, to 5pm Nov-Feb) There's a medieval keep at its heart, but it's the later additions to Cardiff Castle that really capture the imagination. During the Victorian era, extravagant mock-Gothic features were grafted onto this relic, including a clock tower and a lavish banqueting hall. Some but not all of this flamboyant fantasy world can be accessed with a regular castle entry; the rest can be visited as part of a guided tour.

★ National Museum Cardiff   MUSEUM

(☑ 0300 111 2333; www.museumwales.ac.uk; Gorsedd Gardens Rd; ⊙ 10am-5pm Tue-Sun) FREE Devoted mainly to natural history and art, this grand neoclassical building is the centrepiece of the seven institutions dotted around the country that together form the Welsh National Museum. It's one of Britain's best museums; you'll need at least three hours to do it justice, but it could easily consume the best part of a rainy day.

★ Wales Millennium Centre   ARTS CENTRE

(☑ 029-2063 6464; www.wmc.org.uk; Bute Pl, Cardiff Bay; ⊙ 9am-7pm) The centrepiece and symbol of Cardiff Bay's regeneration is the superb Wales Millennium Centre, an architectural masterpiece of stacked Welsh slate in shades of purple, green and grey topped with an overarching bronzed steel shell. Designed by Welsh architect Jonathan Adams, it opened in 2004 as Wales' premier arts complex, housing major cultural organisations such as the Welsh National Opera, National Dance Company, BBC National Orchestra of Wales, Literature Wales, HiJinx Theatre and Tŷ Cerdd (Music Centre Wales).

CONWY

A visit to Britain's most complete walled town should be high on the itinerary for anyone with even a mild crush on things historic. The World Heritage–listed **castle** (Cadw; 01492-592358; www.cadw.wales.gov.uk; Castle Sq; adult/child £8.95/5.80; 9.30am-5pm Mar-Jun, Sep & Oct, to 6pm Jul & Aug, 10am-4pm Mon-Sat, from 11am Sun Nov-Feb; P) dominates the town, as it has done ever since Edward I first planted it here in the late 13th century.

For a small town, Conwy really packs in the historical interest. All within a short stroll of each other, Conwy's three key properties – **Plas Mawr** (Cadw; www.cadw.wales.gov.uk; High St; adult/child £6.50/4.20; 9.30am-5pm Easter-Sep, to 4pm Oct), **Aberconwy House** (NT; www.nationaltrust.org.uk; Castle St; adult/child £4.60/2.30; 10am-5pm late Feb-Oct) and **Royal Cambrian Academy** (01492-593413; www.rcaconwy.org; Crown Lane; 11am-5pm Tue-Sat) FREE – encapsulate the town's rich heritage and its continuing role in the Welsh art scene. Conwy's train station is just inside the town walls, on Rosemary Lane. Most buses stop by the train station.

🛏 Sleeping & Eating

★ Safehouse
HOSTEL €

(029-2037 2833; www.safehousehostel.com; 3 Westgate St; dm/d without bathroom from £14/39;) There aren't too many hostels with a grand Victorian sitting room to rival Safehouse's. Built in 1889, this lovely red-brick office building has been thoughtfully converted into a boutique hostel with private rooms and four- to 12-bed dorms. Each bunk bed has its own built-in locker and electrical socket. It's on a busy road, so earplugs are a sensible precaution.

Coffee Barker
CAFE €

(Castle Arcade; mains £5.50-8.50; 8.30am-5.30pm Mon-Sat, 11am-4.30pm Sun;) This vast cafe and gelateria sits at the entrance to one of Cardiff's Victorian arcades. It's best known for its coffees, indulgent stacks of pancakes and thick milkshakes served in glass milk bottles. Despite its size, soft chairs and quirky decor give it a cosy vibe. It's almost always busy so expect to queue before slumping into the sofas.

🍷 Drinking & Nightlife

Gwdihŵ
BAR

(029-2039 7933; www.gwdihw.co.uk; 6 Guildford Cres; 3pm-midnight Mon-Wed, noon-2am Thu-Sat, 4pm-midnight Sun) The last word in Cardiff hipsterdom, this cute little bar has an eclectic line-up of entertainment (comedy, DJs and lots of live music, including micro festivals that spill over into the car park), but it's a completely charming place to stop for a drink at any time. If you're wondering about the name, it's the Welsh take on an owl's call.

ℹ Information

Tourist Office (029-2087 3573; www.visitcardiff.com; Wales Millennium Centre, Bute Pl, Cardiff Bay; 10am-6pm Mon-Sat, to 4pm Sun) Information, advice and souvenirs.

ℹ Getting There & Away

AIR

Cardiff Airport (01446-711111; www.cardiff-airport.com) is 12 miles southwest of the city. Buses connect either directly with Central bus station or Rhoose Cardiff Airport train station.

BUS

Cardiff's Central bus station is due to reopen near the train station in a revitalised Central Square in 2018. See www.traveline.cymru for details.

National Express (www.nationalexpress.com) coaches depart from **Cardiff Coach Station** (Sophia Gardens), with destinations including London (from £5, 3½ hours, four daily). Megabus (£4.30) also connects Cardiff with London.

TRAIN

Direct services from Cardiff Central station include London Paddington (£12, two hours, hourly), Bath (£10, one hour, hourly) and Manchester (£23.50, three hours, hourly).

Snowdonia National Park

Snowdonia National Park (Parc Cenedlaethol Eryri; www.eryri-npa.gov.uk) was founded in 1951, making it Wales' first national park. Around 350,000 people travel to the national park to climb, walk or take the train to the summit of Mt Snowdon (1085m), Wales' highest mountain.

On a clear day the views from the mountain stretch to Ireland and the Isle of Man. Even on a gloomy day you could find yourself above the clouds. At the top is the striking **Hafod Eryri** (⊙ 10am-20min before last train departure; 🛜) visitor centre. Clad in granite and curved to blend into the mountain, it's a wonderful building, housing a cafe, toilets and ambient interpretative elements built into the structure itself.

Six paths of varying length and difficulty lead to the summit, all taking around six hours return, or you can cheat and catch the **Snowdon Mountain Railway** (☏ 01286-870223; www.snowdonrailway.co.uk; Llanberis; adult/child return diesel £29/20, steam £37/27; ⊙ 9am-5pm mid-Mar–Oct), opened in 1896 and still the UK's only public rack-and-pinion railway. However you get to the summit, take warm, waterproof clothing, wear sturdy footwear and check the weather forecast before setting out.

🛏 Sleeping

YHA Snowdon Pen-y-Pass   HOSTEL €
(☏ 08453-719534; www.yha.org.uk; A4086; dm/tw £24/59) This superbly situated hostel has three of Snowdon's trails literally on its doorstep. Comprehensively refurbished in 2014, it has a new kitchen, Mallory's Cafe/Bar (named for a past patron who perished on Everest) and some of the best rooms of any of the park's YHAs (half of which are en suite). It's 5.5 miles up the A4086 from Llanberis.

YHA Snowdon Bryn Gwynant   HOSTEL €
(☏ 08453-719108; www.yha.org.uk; Nantgwynant; dm/tw £20/60; ⊙ Mar-Oct; 🅿 🛜) Bryn Gwynant has the most impressive building and the most idyllic setting of all Snowdonia National Park's youth hostels, occupying a slate Victorian mansion overlooking Lake Gwynant to Snowdon. It's located 4 miles east of Beddgelert, near the start of the Watkin Path.

❶ Getting There & Away

Stops on the three major rail routes into or around the park – the Cambrian, North Wales Coast and Conwy Valley Lines – include Betws-y-Coed, Porthmadog, Barmouth, Caernarfon, Machynlleth, Llandudno and Conwy. There's also the seasonal Ffestiniog and Welsh Railways.

Bus services are more extensive, reaching towns not on the rail network. There's also the Snowdon Sherpa, five bus lines linking trailheads and principal towns in the Snowdon area. It's £1.50 per ride, or £5 for a day pass.

SCOTLAND

Edinburgh

POP 498,810

Edinburgh is a city that begs to be explored. Its Old Town is filled with quirky, come-hither nooks that tempt you to walk just a little bit further. And every corner turned reveals sudden views and unexpected vistas – green sunlit hills, a glimpse of rust-red crags, a blue flash of distant sea.

But there's more to Edinburgh than sightseeing. This is a city of pub crawls and impromptu music sessions, mad-for-it clubbing and all-night parties, overindulgence and wandering home through cobbled streets at dawn. All these superlatives come together at festival time in August, when it seems as if half the world descends on Edinburgh for one enormous party. If you can possibly manage it, join them.

◉ Sights

Edinburgh's main attractions are concentrated in the city centre – on and around the Old Town's Royal Mile between the castle and Holyrood, and in the New Town. A major exception is the **Royal Yacht Britannia** (www.royalyachtbritannia.co.uk; Ocean Terminal; adult/child incl audio guide £16/8.50; ⊙ 9.30am-6pm Apr-Sep, to 5.30pm Oct, 10am-5pm Nov-Mar, last entry 1½hr before closing; 🅿; 🚍 11, 22, 34, 36, 200, 300), which is in the redeveloped docklands district of Leith, two miles northeast of the centre.

★ Edinburgh Castle   CASTLE
(☏ 0131-225 9846; www.edinburghcastle.gov.uk; Castle Esplanade; adult/child £18.50/11.50, audioguide £3.50/£1.50; ⊙ 9.30am-6pm Apr-Sep, to 5pm Oct-Mar, last entry 1hr before closing; 🚍 23, 27, 41, 42, 67) Edinburgh Castle has played a pivotal role in Scottish history, both as a royal residence – King Malcolm Canmore (r 1058–93) and Queen Margaret first made their home here in the 11th century – and as a military stronghold. The castle last saw military action in 1745; from then until the 1920s it served as the British army's main base in Scotland. Today it is one of Scotland's most atmospheric and popular tourist attractions.

★ Real Mary King's Close   HISTORIC BUILDING
(☏ 0131-225 0672; www.realmarykingsclose.com; 2 Warriston's Close, High St; adult/child £15.50/9.50;

⊙10am-9pm Apr-Oct, 9am-5.30pm Mon-Thu, 9.30am-9pm Fri & Sat, to 6.30pm Sun Nov, 10am-5pm Sun-Thu, to 9pm Fri & Sat Dec-Mar; ⊟23, 27, 41, 42) Edinburgh's 18th-century City Chambers were built over the sealed-off remains of Mary King's Close, and the lower levels of this medieval Old Town alley have survived almost unchanged amid the foundations for 250 years. Now open to the public, this spooky, subterranean labyrinth gives a fascinating insight into the everyday life of 17th-century Edinburgh. Costumed characters lead tours through a 16th-century townhouse and the plague-stricken home of a 17th-century gravedigger. Advance booking recommended.

National Museum of Scotland
MUSEUM

(☑0300-123 6789; www.nms.ac.uk/national-museum-of-scotland; Chambers St; fee for special exhibitions varies; ⊙10am-5pm; ⚕; ⊟45, 300) FREE Broad, elegant Chambers St is dominated by the long facade of the National Museum of Scotland. Its extensive collections are spread between two buildings, one modern, one Victorian – the golden stone and striking modern architecture of the new building, opened in 1998, is one of the city's most distinctive landmarks. The five floors of the museum trace the history of Scotland from its geological beginnings to the 1990s, with many imaginative and stimulating exhibits. Audio guides are available in several languages.

Scottish Parliament Building
NOTABLE BUILDING

(☑0131-348 5200; www.parliament.scot; Horse Wynd; ⊙9am-6.30pm Tue-Thu, 10am-5pm Mon, Fri & Sat in session, 10am-5pm Tue-Thu in recess; ⚕; ⊟6, 300) FREE The Scottish parliament building, on the site of a former brewery, was officially opened by the Queen in October 2004. Designed by Catalan architect Enric Miralles (1955–2000), the ground plan of the parliament complex is said to represent a 'flower of democracy rooted in Scottish soil' (best seen looking down from Salisbury Crags). Free, one-hour guided tours (advance booking recommended) include a visit to the Debating Chamber, a committee room, the Garden Lobby and a Member of the Scottish Parliament's (MSP) office.

Arthur's Seat
VIEWPOINT

(Holyrood Park; ⊟6, 300) The rocky peak of Arthur's Seat (251m), carved by ice sheets from the deeply eroded stump of a long-extinct volcano, is a distinctive feature of Edinburgh's skyline. The view from the summit is well worth the walk, extending from the Forth Bridges in the west to the distant conical hill of North Berwick Law in the east, with the Ochil Hills and the Highlands on the northwestern horizon. You can hike from Holyrood to the summit in around 45 minutes.

🛏 Sleeping

Safestay Edinburgh
HOSTEL €€

(☑0131-524 1989; www.safestay.com; 50 Blackfriars St; dm £34-40, tw £139; @ 🛜; ⊟300) A big, modern hostel, with a convivial cafe where you can buy breakfast, and mod cons such as keycard access and charging stations for mobile phones, MP3 players and laptops. Lockers in every room, a huge bar and a central location just off the Royal Mile make this a favourite among the young, party-mad crowd – don't expect a quiet night!

Budget Backpackers
HOSTEL €

(☑0131-226 6351; www.budgetbackpackers.com; 9 Cowgate; dm £17-24, tw £68; @ 🛜; ⊟2) This fun spot piles on the extras, with bike storage, pool tables, laundry and a colourful chill-out lounge. You'll pay a little more for four-bunk dorms, but larger dorms are great value. The only downside is that prices increase at weekends, but otherwise it's a brilliant spot to doss.

🍴 Eating

★ Mums
CAFE €

(☑0131-260 9806; www.monstermashcafe.co.uk; 4a Forrest Rd; mains £9-12; ⊙9am-10pm Mon-Sat, 10am-10pm Sun; 🛜⚕; ⊟2, 23, 27, 41, 42, 300) 🍴 This nostalgia-fuelled cafe serves up

---

FESTIVAL CITY

Edinburgh hosts an amazing number of festivals throughout the year, notably the **Edinburgh International Festival** (☑0131-473 2000; www.eif.co.uk; ⊙Aug), the **Edinburgh Festival Fringe** (☑0131-226 0026; www.edfringe.com; ⊙Aug) and the **Military Tattoo** (☑0131-225 1188; www.edintattoo.co.uk; ⊙Aug), all in August. **Hogmanay**, Scotland's New Year's celebrations, is also a peak party time.

Royal Mile

A GRAND DAY OUT

Planning your own procession along the Royal Mile involves some tough decisions – it would be impossible to see everything in a single day, so it's wise to decide in advance what you don't want to miss and shape your visit around that. Remember to leave time for lunch, for exploring some of the Mile's countless side alleys and, during festival time, for enjoying the street theatre that is bound to be happening in High St.

The most pleasant way to reach the Castle Esplanade at the start of the Royal Mile is to hike up the zigzag path from the footbridge behind the Ross Bandstand in Princes Street Gardens (in springtime you'll be knee-deep in daffodils). Starting at **① Edinburgh Castle** means that the rest of your walk is downhill. For a superb view up and down the length of the Mile, climb the **② Camera Obscura's Outlook Tower** before visiting **③ Gladstone's Land** and **④ St Giles Cathedral**.

CLAUDIO DIVIZIA / SHUTTERSTOCK ©

ROYAL VISITS TO THE ROYAL MILE

1561: Mary, Queen of Scots arrives from France and holds an audience with John Knox.
1745: Bonnie Prince Charlie fails to capture Edinburgh Castle, and instead sets up court in Holyroodhouse.
2004: Queen Elizabeth II officially opens the Scottish Parliament building.

Edinburgh Castle
If you're pushed for time, visit the Great Hall, the Honours of Scotland and the Prisons of War exhibit. Head for the Half Moon Battery for a photo looking down the length of the Royal Mile.

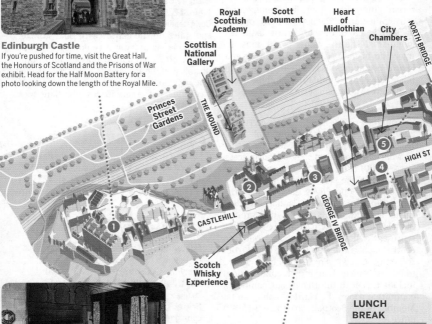

DE AGOSTINI / W. BUSS / GETTY IMAGES ©

Gladstone's Land
The 1st floor houses a faithful recreation of how a wealthy Edinburgh merchant lived in the 17th century. Check out the beautiful Painted Bedchamber, with its ornately decorated walls and wooden ceilings.

LUNCH BREAK

Burger and a beer at **Holyrood 9A**; steak and chips at **Maxie's Bistro**; slap-up seafood at **Ondine**.

If history's your thing, you'll want to add **⑤ Real Mary King's Close**, **⑥ John Knox House** and the **⑦ Museum of Edinburgh** to your must-see list.

At the foot of the mile, choose between modern and ancient seats of power – the **⑧ Scottish Parliament** or the **⑨ Palace of Holyroodhouse**. Round off the day with an evening ascent of Arthur's Seat or, slightly less strenuously, Calton Hill. Both make great sunset viewpoints.

TAKING YOUR TIME

Minimum time needed for each attraction:
Edinburgh Castle two hours
Gladstone's Land 45 minutes
St Giles Cathedral 30 minutes
Real Mary King's Close one hour (tour)
Scottish Parliament one hour (tour)
Palace of Holyroodhouse one hour

Real Mary King's Close
The guided tour is heavy on ghost stories, but a highlight is standing in an original 17th-century room with tufts of horsehair poking from the crumbling plaster, and breathing in the ancient scent of stone, dust and history.

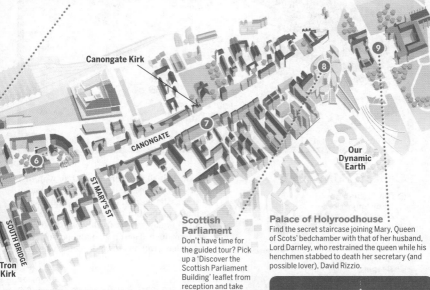

Canongate Kirk

CANONGATE

Our Dynamic Earth

ST MARY'S ST

SOUTH BRIDGE

Tron Kirk

Scottish Parliament
Don't have time for the guided tour? Pick up a 'Discover the Scottish Parliament Building' leaflet from reception and take a self-guided tour of the exterior, then hike up to Salisbury Crags for a great view of the complex.

Palace of Holyroodhouse
Find the secret staircase joining Mary, Queen of Scots' bedchamber with that of her husband, Lord Darnley, who restrained the queen while his henchmen stabbed to death her secretary (and possible lover), David Rizzio.

St Giles Cathedral
Look out for the Burne-Jones stained-glass window (1873) at the west end, showing the crossing of the River Jordan, and the bronze memorial to Robert Louis Stevenson in the Moray Aisle.

PHOTOGROFF30/ SHUTTERSTOCK ©

HEARTLAND ARTS / SHUTTERSTOCK ©

DAVID IONUT/ SHUTTERSTOCK ©

Central Edinburgh

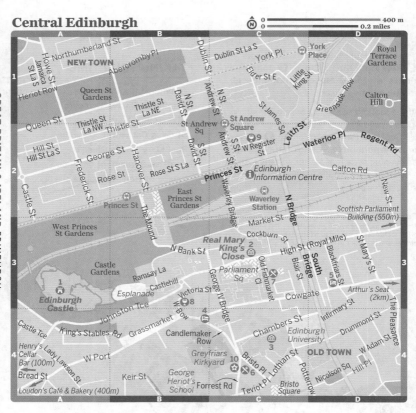

N 0 ——— 400 m
0 ——— 0.2 miles

Central Edinburgh

classic British comfort food that wouldn't look out of place on a 1950s menu – bacon and eggs, bangers and mash, shepherd's pie, fish and chips. But there's a twist – the food is all top-quality nosh freshly prepared from local produce. There's also a good selection of bottled craft beers and Scottish-brewed cider.

Wings FAST FOOD €
(☑ 0131-629 1234; www.wingsedinburgh.com; 5/7 Old Fishmarket Close; per portion £3.50; ⊙ 4-11pm Mon, noon-11pm Tue-Sun; ☐ 23, 27, 41, 42) Eateries don't come much simpler. Order some bowls of barbecued chicken wings (six wings per portion) with the sauce of your choice (a couple of dozen to choose from, whether soused in tequila and lime juice or slathered with hot chilli) and a drink. If you're still hungry, order more. Genius. Great sci-fi/comic-book decor too.

★ **Loudon's Café & Bakery** CAFE €€
(www.loudons.co.uk; 94b Fountainbridge; mains £8-13; ⏲ 7.30am-5pm Mon-Fri, 8am-5pm Sat & Sun; 🌐 ♿ 👶; 🚌 1, 34, 300) A cafe that bakes its own organic bread and cakes on the premises, ethically sourced coffee, daily and weekend newspapers scattered about, even some outdoor tables – what's not to like? All-day brunch (8am to 3pm) served at weekends includes eggs Benedict, warm spiced quinoa with dried fruit, and specials such as blueberry pancakes with fruit salad.

🍷 **Drinking & Nightlife**

Café Royal Circle Bar PUB
(📞 0131-556 1884; www.caferoyaledinburgh.co.uk; 17 West Register St; ⏲ 11am-11pm Mon-Wed, to midnight Thu, to 1am Fri & Sat, to 10pm Sun; 🌐; 🚌 Princes St) Perhaps *the* classic Edinburgh pub, the Café Royal's main claims to fame are its magnificent oval bar and its Doulton tile portraits of famous Victorian inventors. Sit at the bar or claim one of the cosy leather booths beneath the stained-glass windows, and choose from the seven real ales on tap.

★ **Bow Bar** PUB
(www.thebowbar.co.uk; 80 West Bow; ⏲ noon-midnight Mon-Sat, to 11.30pm Sun; 🚌 2, 23, 27, 41, 42) One of the city's best traditional-style pubs (it's not as old as it looks), serving a range of excellent real ales, Scottish craft gins and a vast selection of malt whiskies, the Bow Bar often has standing-room only on Friday and Saturday evenings.

☆ **Entertainment**

The comprehensive source for what's-on info is *The List* (www.list.co.uk).

★ **Sandy Bell's** TRADITIONAL MUSIC
(www.sandybellsedinburgh.co.uk; 25 Forrest Rd; ⏲ noon-1am Mon-Sat, 12.30pm-midnight Sun; 🚌 2, 23, 27, 41, 42, 45) This unassuming pub is a stalwart of the traditional music scene (the founder's wife sang with the Corries). There's music almost every evening at 9pm, and from 3pm Saturday and Sunday, plus lots of impromptu sessions.

Henry's Cellar Bar LIVE MUSIC
(📞 0131-629 2992; www.facebook.com/Henryscellarbar; 16 Morrison St; admission free-£10; ⏲ 9pm-3am Sun & Tue-Thu, 8pm-3am Mon, 7pm-3am Fri & Sat; 🚌 all Lothian Rd buses) One of Edinburgh's most eclectic live-music venues, Henry's has something going on most nights of the week, from rock and indie to 'Balkan-inspired folk' and from funk and hip-hop to hardcore, staging both local bands and acts from around the world.

ℹ️ **Information**

Edinburgh Tourist Office (Edinburgh iCentre; 📞 0131-473 3868; www.visitscotland.com/info/services/edinburgh-icentre-p234441; Waverley Mall, 3 Princes St; ⏲ 9am-7pm Mon-Sat, 10am-7pm Sun Jul & Aug, to 6pm Jun, to 5pm Sep-May; 🌐; 🚌 St Andrew Sq) Includes an accommodation booking service, currency exchange, gift and bookshop, internet access and counters selling tickets for Edinburgh city tours and Scottish Citylink bus services.

ℹ️ **Getting There & Around**

AIR

Edinburgh Airport (EDI; 📞 0844 448 8833; www.edinburghairport.com), 8 miles west of the city, has numerous flights to other parts of Scotland and the UK, Ireland and mainland Europe. There's a **VisitScotland Information Centre** (📞 0131-473 3690; www.visitscotland.com; East Terminal, Edinburgh Airport; ⏲ 7.30am-7.30pm Mon-Fri, to 7pm Sat & Sun) in the airport's terminal extension.

Edinburgh Trams (www.edinburghtrams.com) run from the airport to the city centre (one way/return £5.50/8.50, 33 minutes, every six to eight minutes from 6am to midnight).

BUS

Scottish Citylink (📞 0871 266 3333; www.citylink.co.uk) buses connect Edinburgh with all of Scotland's cities and major towns, including Glasgow (£7.90, 1¼ hours, every 15 minutes) and Inverness (£19.40, 3½ to 4½ hours, hourly). **National Express** (📞 0871 781 8181; www.nationalexpress.com) runs a direct coach service from London (£27, 9½ hours, daily). Also check with **Megabus** (📞 0141-352 4444; www.megabus.com) for cheap intercity bus fares (from as little as £5) from Edinburgh to London, Glasgow and Inverness.

TRAIN

Edinburgh's main terminus is Waverley train station. Trains arriving from, and departing for, the west also stop at Haymarket station, which is more convenient for the West End.

ScotRail (📞 0344 811 0141; www.scotrail.co.uk) runs a regular shuttle service between Edinburgh and Glasgow (£12.90, one hour, every 15 minutes), and frequent daily services to all Scottish cities, including Inverness (from £16.80, 3½ hours, seven daily). There are also regular trains to London King's Cross (£32.50, 4½ hours, hourly) via York (£17/10, 2½ hours, hourly).

Glasgow

POP 596,500

Disarmingly blending sophistication and earthiness, Scotland's biggest city has evolved over the last couple of decades to become one of Britain's most intriguing metropolises.

At first glance, the soberly handsome Victorian buildings, legacies of wealth generated from manufacturing and trade, suggest a staid sort of place. Very wrong. They are packed with stylish bars, top-notch restaurants, hedonistic clubs and one of Britain's best live-music scenes. The place's sheer vitality is gloriously infectious: the combination of edgy urbanity and the residents' legendary friendliness is captivating.

◉ Sights

Glasgow's main square, situated in the city centre is the grand **George Square**, which was built in the Victorian era to show off the city's wealth, and dignified by statues of notable Scots, including Robert Burns, James Watt, John Moore and Sir Walter Scott.

Glasgow

Mackintosh House 4
Hillhead St
Gibson St
Great Western Rd
Maryhill Rd
WEST END
University Ave
Kelvin Way
River Kelvin
Eldon St
W Princes St
Rupert St
W Princes St
St Georges Cross
New City Rd
Bunhouse Rd
Argyle St
3 Kelvingrove Art Gallery & Museum
Park Circus
Park Quad
Woodlands Rd
8
Park Tce
Woodlands Tce
Lynedoch St
St Georges Rd
Junction 17
Buccleuch St
Garnet St
Kelvingrove Park
Gray St
Sauchiehall St
Royal Tce
Woodside Tce
Woodside Pl
9
Sauchiehall St
Berkeley St
Eldersie St
North St
Sauchiehall St
Charing Cross
India St
Newton St
Elmbank St
Holland St
Kelvinhaugh St
Argyle St
St Vincent Cres
St Vincent St
Clydeside Expressway
Minerva St
Finnieston St
Argyle St
Bothwell St
Pitt St
Riverside Museum (700m); Tall Ship (750m)
Millennium Bridge (Pedestrian Only)
Anderston
Stobcross St
Elliot St
Lancefield St
Hydepark St
Cheapside St
Warroch St
Washington St
Bell's Bridge
Lancefield Quay
Anderston Quay
Govan Rd
River Clyde
Kingston Bridge
Springfield Quay
Paisley Rd
House for an Art Lover (2.8km)
Morrison St

★ **Kelvingrove Art Gallery
& Museum** GALLERY, MUSEUM
(☎ 0141-276 9599; www.glasgowmuseums.com;
Argyle St; ☺ 10am-5pm Mon-Thu & Sat, from 11am
Fri & Sun) FREE A magnificent stone building,
this grand Victorian cathedral of culture is a
fascinating and unusual museum, with a bewildering variety of exhibits. You'll find fine
art alongside stuffed animals, and Microne-
sian shark-tooth swords alongside a Spitfire
plane, but it's not mix 'n' match: rooms are
carefully and thoughtfully themed, and the
collection is a manageable size. It has an excellent room of Scottish art, a room of fine
French Impressionist works, and quality Renaissance paintings from Italy and Flanders.

★ **Riverside Museum** MUSEUM
(☎ 0141-287 2720; www.glasgowmuseums.com;
100 Pointhouse Pl; ☺ 10am-5pm Mon-Thu & Sat,
from 11am Fri & Sun; ♿) FREE This visually impressive modern museum at Glasgow Harbour owes its striking curved forms to late
British-Iraqi architect Zaha Hadid. A transport museum forms the main part of the collection, featuring a fascinating series of cars
made in Scotland, plus assorted railway lo-
cos, trams, bikes (including the world's first
pedal-powered bicycle from 1847) and model

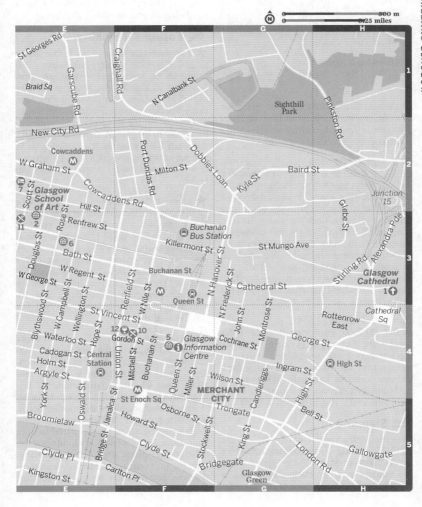

Glasgow

Clyde-built ships. An atmospheric recreation of a Glasgow shopping street from the early 20th century puts the vintage vehicles into a social context. There's also a cafe.

★ **Glasgow Cathedral** CATHEDRAL
(HES; ☑ 0141-552 6891; www.historicenvironment. scot; Cathedral Sq; ⊙ 9.30am-5.30pm Mon-Sat, 1-5pm Sun Apr-Sep, 10am-4pm Mon-Sat, from 1pm Sun Oct-Mar) Glasgow Cathedral has a rare timelessness. The dark, imposing interior conjures up medieval might and can send a shiver down the spine. It's a shining example of Gothic architecture, and unlike nearly all of Scotland's cathedrals, survived the turmoil of the Reformation mobs almost intact. Most of the current building dates from the 15th century.

Burrell Collection GALLERY
(☑ 0141-287 2550; www.glasgowlife.org.uk; Pollok Country Park; ⊙ closed) FREE One of Glasgow's top attractions, this outstanding museum 3 miles out of town houses everything from Chinese porcelain and medieval furniture to paintings by Cézanne. It's closed for refurbishment, and is due to reopen in 2020.

🛏 Sleeping

Glasgow Metro Youth Hostel HOSTEL €
(☑ 0141-354 0109; www.hostellingscotland.org. uk; 89 Buccleuch St; s £32-45; ⊙ late Jun-Aug; 🛜) Student accommodation belonging to the nearby Glasgow School of Art provides the venue for this summer hostel. All rooms are comfortable singles, many with en suite, there are kitchen facilities and it's a very good deal for solo travellers or groups. It's slightly cheaper midweek.

Glasgow SYHA HOSTEL €
(☑ 0141-332 3004; www.hostellingscotland.org.uk; 8 Park Tce; dm/s/tw £29/52/69; @🛜) Perched on a hill overlooking Kelvingrove Park in a charming townhouse, this place is one of Scotland's best official hostels. Dorms are mostly four to six beds with padlock lockers, and all have their own en suite. The common rooms are spacious, plush and good for lounging about. There's no curfew, it has a good kitchen, and meals are available.

🍴 Eating & Drinking

★ **Saramago Café Bar** CAFE, VEGAN €
(☑ 0141-352 4920; www.cca-glasgow.com; 350 Sauchiehall St; mains £8-12; ⊙ food noon-10pm Sun-Wed, to 11.30pm Thu-Sat; 🛜🍴) In the airy atrium of the Centre for Contemporary Arts, this place does a great line in eclectic vegan fusion food, with a range of top flavour combinations from around the globe. The upstairs bar has a great deck on steep Scott St and packs out inside with a friendly hipstery crowd enjoying the DJ sets and quality tap beers.

★ **Riverhill Coffee Bar** CAFE €
(☑ 0141-204 4762; www.riverhillcafe.com; 24 Gordon St; rolls £4-5; ⊙ 7am-5pm Mon-Fri, from 8am Sat, from 10am Sun; 🛜) ✎ Chain cafes plaster Glasgow's centre, so it's a joy to come across this tiny place, which offers great coffee and hot chocolate as well as delicious filled rolls and tempting pastries. Ingredients are sustainably sourced and seriously tasty. It's extremely friendly; you'd come every day if you lived nearby.

★ **Ox & Finch** FUSION €€
(☑ 0141-339 8627; www.oxandfinch.com; 920 Sauchiehall St; small plates £4-10; ⊙ noon-10pm; 🛜🍴) This fashionable place could almost sum up the thriving modern Glasgow eating scene, with a faux-pub name, sleek but comfortable contemporary decor, tapas-sized dishes and an open kitchen. Grab a cosy booth and be prepared to have your taste buds wowed with innovative, delicious creations designed for sharing, drawing on French and Mediterranean influences but focusing on quality Scottish produce.

Horse Shoe   PUB

(☎ 0141-248 6368; www.thehorseshoebarglasgow.
co.uk; 17 Drury St; ⊙ 10am-midnight Sun-Fri, from
9am Sat) This legendary city pub and popular
meeting place dates from the late 19th century and is largely unchanged. It's a picturesque spot, with the longest continuous bar
in the UK, but its main attraction is what's
served over it – real ale and good cheer. Upstairs in the lounge is some of the best-value
pub food (three-course lunch £4.50) in town.

ℹ Information

Glasgow Tourist Office (www.visitscotland.
com; 158 Buchanan St; ⊙ 9am-5pm Mon-Sat,
10am-4pm Sun Nov-Apr, 9am-6pm Mon-Sat,
10am-4pm Sun May, Jun, Sep & Oct, 9am-7pm
Mon-Sat, 10am-5pm Sun Jul & Aug; ☎) In
the Gallery of Modern Art (GoMA; ☎ 0141-287
3050; www.glasgowmuseums.com; Royal Exchange Sq; ⊙ 10am-5pm Mon-Wed & Sat, until
8pm Thu, 11am-5pm Fri & Sun).

ℹ Getting There & Around

AIR

Glasgow International Airport (GLA; ☎ 0344
481 5555; www.glasgowairport.com; ☎) Ten
miles west of the city. Handles international
and domestic flights.

Glasgow Prestwick Airport (PIK; ☎ 0871 223
0700; www.glasgowprestwick.com) Thirty
miles southwest of Glasgow. Used by Ryanair
and some other budget airlines, with connections mostly to southern Europe.

There are buses every 10 or 15 minutes from
Glasgow International Airport to Buchanan bus

station (p93) via Central and Queen Street train
stations (single/return £7/9.50, 25 minutes).
This is a 24-hour service. You can include a day
ticket on the bus network for £9 total.

There are also buses from Buchanan bus station direct to/from Edinburgh Airport (£11.40,
one hour, half-hourly).

BUS

All long-distance buses arrive at and depart
from **Buchanan bus station** (☎ 0141-333 3708;
www.spt.co.uk; Killermont St; ☎).

Megabus (☎ 0141-352 4444; www.megabus.
com) is your first port of call if you're looking
for the cheapest fare on many major bus
routes, including to Edinburgh and London. National Express (p89) also runs daily to several
English cities.

Scottish Citylink (☎ 0871 266 3333; www.
citylink.co.uk) has buses to Edinburgh (£7.90,
1¼ hours, every 15 minutes) and to most major
towns in Scotland.

TRAIN

As a general rule, Glasgow Central station
serves southern Scotland, England and Wales,
and Queen Street station serves the north and
east. Buses run between the two stations every
10 minutes. There are direct trains to London's
Euston station; they're much quicker (advance
purchase single £62, full fare off-peak/peak
£134/183, 4½ hours, more than hourly) and
more comfortable than the bus.

ScotRail (p89) destinations include Edinburgh
(£12.90, one hour, every 15 minutes) and Inverness (£11.80, 3½ to four hours, six daily, four on
Sunday).

DON'T MISS

THE GENIUS OF CHARLES RENNIE MACKINTOSH

Charles Rennie Mackintosh (1868–1928) is to Glasgow what Gaudí is to Barcelona. A
designer, architect and master of the art-nouveau style, his quirky, linear and geometric
designs are seen all over Glasgow. Many of his buildings are open to the public and the
one not to miss is his masterpiece, the **Glasgow School of Art** (☎ 0141-353 4526; www.
gsa.ac.uk; 167 Renfrew St; tours adult/child £7/3.50, from Jun 2019 £14/7; ⊙ 10am-4.30pm,
from Jun 2019 9am-5.30pm), restored and reopened in 2018 after it was damaged in fire in
2014.

If you're a fan, the Mackintosh Trail ticket (£10), available at the tourist office or any
Mackintosh building, gives you a day's free admission to his creations, plus unlimited bus
and subway travel. Highlights include the following:

Willow Tearooms (www.mackintoshatthewillow.com; 217 Sauchiehall St)

Mackintosh House (☎ 0141-330 4221; www.hunterian.gla.ac.uk; 82 Hillhead St; adult/child
£6/3; ⊙ 10am-5pm Tue-Sat, 11am-4pm Sun)

House for an Art Lover (☎ 0141-353 4770; www.houseforanartlover.co.uk; Bellahouston
Park, Dumbreck Rd; adult/child £6/4.50; ⊙ check online, roughly 10am-4pm Mon-Fri, to noon
Sat, to 2pm Sun)

Inverness & Loch Ness

POP 61,235

Inverness has a great location astride the River Ness at the northern end of the Great Glen. In summer it overflows with visitors intent on monster hunting at nearby Loch Ness, but it's worth a visit in its own right for a stroll along the picturesque River Ness, a cruise on Loch Ness and a meal in one of the city's excellent restaurants.

◉ Sights

Loch Ness Centre & Exhibition MUSEUM
(☑ 01456-450573; www.lochness.com; adult/child £7.95/4.95; ☉ 9.30am-6pm Jul & Aug, to 5pm Easter-Jun, Sep & Oct, 10am-4pm Nov-Easter; Ⓟ 🖮) This Nessie-themed attraction adopts a scientific approach that allows you to weigh the evidence for yourself. Exhibits include the original equipment – sonar survey vessels, miniature submarines, cameras and sediment coring tools – used in various monster hunts, as well as original photographs and film footage of sightings. You'll find out about hoaxes and optical illusions, as well as learning a lot about the ecology of Loch Ness – is there enough food in the loch to support even one 'monster', let alone a breeding population?

WORTH A TRIP

LOCH LOMOND

The 'bonnie banks' and 'bonnie braes' of Loch Lomond have long been Glasgow's rural retreat. The main tourist focus is on the loch's western shore, along the A82. The eastern shore, followed by the West Highland Way long-distance footpath, is quieter. The region's importance was recognised when it became the heart of **Loch Lomond & the Trossachs National Park** (www.lochlomond-trossachs.org) – Scotland's first national park, created in 2002.

The main centre for Loch Lomond boat trips is Balloch, where **Sweeney's Cruises** (☑ 01389-752376; www.sweeneyscruiseco.com; Balloch Rd) offers a range of outings, including a one-hour cruise to Inchmurrin and back (adult/child £10.20/7, five times daily April to October, twice daily November to March). Balloch is connected to Glasgow by bus (£5, 1½ hours, at least two per hour) or train (£5.60, 45 minutes, every 30 minutes).

Urquhart Castle CASTLE
(HES; ☑ 01456-450551; adult/child £9/5.40; ☉ 9.30am-8pm Jul-Aug, to 6pm Apr, May & Sep, to 5pm Oct, to 4.30pm Nov-Mar; Ⓟ) Commanding a superb location 1.5 miles east of Drumnadrochit, with outstanding views (on a clear day), Urquhart Castle is a popular Nessie-hunting hotspot. A huge visitor centre (most of which is beneath ground level) includes a video theatre (with a dramatic 'reveal' of the castle at the end of the film) and displays of medieval items discovered in the castle. The site includes a gift shop and a restaurant, and is often very crowded in summer.

🛏 Sleeping & Eating

Bazpackers Backpackers Hotel HOSTEL €
(☑ 01463-717663; www.bazpackershostel.co.uk; 4 Culduthel Rd; dm/d £18/60; @ 🛜) 🍃 This may be Inverness' smallest hostel (34 beds), but it's hugely popular. It's a friendly, quiet place – the main building has a convivial lounge centred on a wood-burning stove, and a small garden and great views (some rooms are in a separate building with no garden). The dorms and kitchen can be a bit cramped, but the showers are great.

Velocity Cafe CAFE €
(☑ 01463-419956; www.velocitylove.co.uk; 1 Crown Ave; mains £4-7; ☉ 8am-5pm Mon-Wed & Fri, to 9pm Thu, 9am-5pm Sat, 10am-5pm Sun; 🛜 🖉 🖮) 🍃 This cyclists' cafe serves soups, sandwiches and salads prepared with organic, locally sourced produce, as well as yummy cakes and coffee. There's also a workshop where you can repair your bike or book a session with a mechanic.

ⓘ Information

Inverness Tourist Office (☑ 01463-252401; www.visithighlands.com; 36 High St; ☉ 9am-5pm Mon & Wed-Sat, from 10am Tue, 10am-3pm Sun, longer hours Mar-Oct; 🛜) Bureau de change and accommodation booking service; also sells tickets for tours and cruises.

ⓘ Getting There & Around

AIR

Inverness Airport (INV; ☑ 01667-464000; www.invernessairport.co.uk) is at Dalcross, 10 miles east of the city, off the A96 towards Aberdeen. There are scheduled flights to Amsterdam, London, Manchester, Dublin, Orkney, Shetland and the Outer Hebrides, as well as other places in the UK.

OTHER BRITISH HIGHLIGHTS

Cornwall The southwestern tip of Britain is ringed with rugged granite sea cliffs, sparkling bays, picturesque fishing villages and white sandy beaches.

Liverpool The city's waterfront is a World Heritage Site crammed with top museums including the International Slavery Museum and the Beatles Story.

Pembrokeshire Wales' western extremity is famous for its beaches and coastal walks, as well as being home to one of Britain's finest Norman castles.

Glen Coe Scotland's most famous glen combines those two essential qualities of Highlands landscape: dramatic scenery and deep history.

Climbing Ben Nevis Join the 100,000 people who reach the 1344m peak, the highest point in the British Isles.

BUS

Services depart from Inverness bus station (Margaret St) and include Edinburgh (£30, 3½ to 4½ hours, hourly) and Glasgow (£30, 3½ to 4½ hours, hourly). For London (£18.40, 13 hours, daily) you'll usually need to change at Glasgow.

If you book far enough in advance, Megabus offers fares from as little as £1 for services to Glasgow and Edinburgh, and £10 to London.

Buses from Inverness to Fort William run along the shores of Loch Ness (six to eight daily, five on Sunday); those headed for Skye turn off at Invermoriston. There are bus stops at Drumnadrochit (£3.20, 30 minutes) and Urquhart Castle car park (£3.50, 35 minutes).

TRAIN

There are services to Edinburgh (£16.80, 3½ hours, seven daily), Glasgow (£11.80, 3½ to four hours, six daily, four on Sunday) and London (£46, eight to nine hours, one daily direct; others require a change at Edinburgh).

Isle of Skye

POP 10,000

The second-largest of Scotland's islands is a 50-mile-long patchwork of velvet moors, jagged mountains, sparkling lochs and towering sea cliffs. Skye takes its name from the old Norse *sky-a,* meaning 'cloud island', a Viking reference to the often mist-enshrouded **Cuillin Hills**, Britain's most spectacular mountain range. The stunning scenery is the main attraction, including the cliffs and pinnacles of the **Old Man of Storr, Kilt Rock** and the **Quiraing**, but there are plenty of cosy pubs to retire to when the rain clouds close in. There are also dozens of art galleries and craft studios (ask at Portree tourist office for the free *Gallery & Studio Trails* booklet).

The tourist hordes tend to stick to Portree, Dunvegan and Trotternish – it's almost always possible to find peace and quiet in the island's further-flung corners. Come prepared for changeable weather: when it's fine it's very fine indeed, but all too often it isn't.

⊙ Sights & Activities

Skye offers some of the finest – and in places, the roughest and most difficult – walking in Scotland. The Cuillin Hills is a playground for rock climbers, and the two-day traverse of the Cuillin Ridge is the finest mountaineering expedition in the British Isles. The sheltered coves and sea lochs around Skye's coast also provide water lovers with magnificent sea-kayaking opportunities.

Dunvegan Castle   CASTLE
(⍲ 01470-521206; www.dunvegancastle.com; adult/child £14/9; ⊘ 10am-5.30pm Easter–mid-Oct; Ⓟ)
Skye's most famous historic building, and one of its most popular tourist attractions, Dunvegan Castle is the seat of the chief of Clan MacLeod. In addition to the usual castle stuff – swords, silver and family portraits – there are some interesting artefacts, including the Fairy Flag, a diaphanous silk banner that dates from some time between the 4th and 7th centuries, and Bonnie Prince Charlie's waistcoat and a lock of his hair, donated by Flora MacDonald's granddaughter.

Aros Centre   CULTURAL CENTRE
(⍲ 01478-613750; www.aros.co.uk; Viewfield Rd; exhibition £5; ⊘ 9am-5pm; Ⓟ🅗) FREE On the southern edge of Portree, the Aros Centre is a combined visitor centre, book and gift shop, restaurant, theatre and cinema. The new St Kilda Exhibition details the history and culture of these remote rocky outcrops,

and Xbox technology allows you to take a virtual tour of the islands.

🛏 Sleeping & Eating

Portree Youth Hostel   HOSTEL €

(SYHA; ☑ 01478-612231; www.syha.org.uk; Bayfield Rd; dm/tw £26/78; [P] 🛜) This brand new SYHA hostel (formerly Bayfield Backpackers) has been completely renovated and offers brightly decorated dorms and private rooms, a lounge with views over the bay, and outdoor seating areas, with an ideal location in the town centre just 100m from the bus stop.

Café Arriba   CAFE €

(☑ 01478-611830; www.cafearriba.co.uk; Quay Brae; mains £6-12; ☉ 7am-6pm May-Sep, 8am-5pm Tue-Sat Oct-Apr; ☑) 🖉 Arriba is a funky little cafe, brightly decked out in primary colours and offering delicious flatbread melts (bacon, leek and cheese is a favourite), as well as the best choice of vegetarian grub on the island, ranging from a veggie breakfast fry-up to falafel wraps with hummus and chilli sauce. Also serves excellent coffee.

ⓘ Getting There & Away

BOAT

Despite the bridge, there are still a couple of ferry links between Skye and the mainland. Ferries also operate from Uig on Skye to the Outer Hebrides.

The **CalMac** (☑ 0800 066 5000; www.calmac. co.uk) ferry between Mallaig and Armadale (30 minutes, eight daily Monday to Saturday, five to seven on Sunday) is very popular on weekends and in July and August. Book ahead if you're travelling by car.

Skye Ferry (☑ 07881 634726; www.skyeferry. co.uk; car with up to 4 passengers £15; ☉ Easter-mid-Oct) runs a tiny vessel (six cars only) on the short Kylerhea to Glenelg crossing (five minutes, every 20 minutes). The ferry operates from 10am to 6pm daily (till 7pm June to August).

BUS

Scottish Citylink run buses from Glasgow to Portree (£43.30, seven hours, three daily), and Uig (£43.30, 7½ hours, two daily) via Crianlarich, Fort William and Kyle of Lochalsh. There is also an Inverness to Portree service (£26.40, 3¼ hours, four daily).

ⓘ Getting Around

Getting around the island by public transport can be a pain, especially if you want to explore away from the main Kyleakin–Portree–Uig road. Here, as in much of the Highlands, there are fewer buses on Saturday and only a handful of Sunday services.

Stagecoach (www.stagecoachbus.com) operates the main bus routes on the island, linking all the main villages and towns. Its Skye Dayrider/Megarider ticket gives unlimited bus travel for one day/seven days for £8.50/32. For timetable info, call **Traveline** (☑ 0871 200 22 33; www.travelinescotland.com).

Great Britain Survival Guide

ⓘ Directory A–Z

ACCOMMODATION

Accommodation can be difficult to find during holidays (especially around Easter and New Year) and major events (such as the Edinburgh Festival). In summer, popular spots (York, Canterbury, Bath etc) get very crowded, so booking ahead is essential. Local tourist offices often provide an accommodation booking service for a small fee.

Hostels The two main types are those run by the Youth Hostels Association (www.yha.org. uk) and Scottish Youth Hostels Association (www.syha.org.uk); and independent hostels, most of which are listed in the Independent Hostels Guide (https://independenthostels. co.uk). The simplest hostels cost between £13 and £17 per person per night. Larger hostels with more facilities are £18 to £30. London's YHA hostels cost from £32.

B&Bs Bed and breakfast (B&B) is a great British institution. At smaller places it's pretty much a room in somebody's house; larger places may be called a 'guesthouse' (halfway between a B&B and a full hotel). Prices start from around £30 per person for a simple bedroom and shared bathroom; for around £35 to £45 per person you get a private bathroom – either down the hall or an en suite.

Camping Campsites range from farmers' fields with a tap and basic toilet, costing from £5 per person per night, to smarter affairs with hot showers and many other facilities, charging up to £15. You usually need all your own equipment.

LGBT TRAVELLERS

Resources include the following:

Diva (www.divamag.co.uk)

Gay Times (www.gaytimes.co.uk)

Switchboard LGBT+ Helpline (www.switchboard.lgbt; 0300 330 0630)

INTERNET RESOURCES

Visit Britain (www.visitbritain.com) Comprehensive national tourism website.

OPENING HOURS

Banks 9.30am to 4pm or 5pm Monday to Friday; main branches 9.30am to 1pm Saturday

Post offices 9am to 5pm (5.30pm or 6pm in cities) Monday to Friday, 9am to 12.30pm Saturday (main branches to 5pm)

Pubs 11am to 11pm Sunday to Thursday, 11am to midnight or 1am Friday and Saturday

Restaurants lunch noon to 3pm, dinner 6pm to 10pm; hours vary widely

PUBLIC HOLIDAYS

In many areas of Britain, bank holidays are just for the banks – many businesses and visitor attractions stay open.

New Year's Day 1 January

Easter March/April (Good Friday to Easter Monday inclusive)

May Day First Monday in May

Spring Bank Holiday Last Monday in May

Summer Bank Holiday Last Monday in August

Christmas Day 25 December

Boxing Day 26 December

TELEPHONE

The UK uses the GSM 900/1800 network, which covers the rest of Europe, Australia and New Zealand, but isn't compatible with the North American GSM 1900. Most modern mobiles can function on both networks – but check before you leave home just in case.

Area codes in the UK do not have a standard format or length. In our reviews, area codes and phone numbers have been listed together, separated by a hyphen.

Other codes include ☑ 0500 or ☑ 0800 for free calls, ☑ 0845 for local rates, ☑ 087 for national rates and ☑ 089 or ☑ 09 for premium rates.

Mobile phones start with ☑ 07 and calling them is more expensive than calling a landline.

Dial ☑ 100 for an operator and ☑ 155 for an international operator as well as reverse-charge (collect) calls.

To call outside the UK, dial ☑ 00, then the country code, the area code (you usually drop the initial zero) and the number.

ⓘ Getting There & Away

AIR

London is served by five airports; Heathrow (www. heathrow.com) and Gatwick (www.gatwickairport. com) are the busiest. Regional airports include Cardiff (p83), Manchester (p81), Edinburgh (p89) and Glasgow (p93).

LAND
Bus

The international network Eurolines (www. eurolines.com) connects a huge number of

European destinations via the Channel Tunnel or ferry crossings. Services to and from Britain are operated by National Express (www.nationalexpress.com).

Train

The quickest way to Europe from Britain is via the Channel Tunnel. High-speed Eurostar (www. eurostar.com) passenger services shuttle at least 10 times daily between London and Paris (2½ hours) or Brussels (two hours) via the Channel Tunnel. The normal one-way fare between London and Paris/Brussels costs around £145; advance booking and off-peak travel gets cheaper fares as low as £29 one way.

Vehicles use the Eurotunnel (www.eurotunnel.com) at Folkestone in England or Calais in France. The trains run four times an hour from 6am to 10pm, then hourly. The journey takes 35 minutes. The one-way cost for a car and passengers is between £75 and £100 depending on time of day; promotional fares often bring it down to £59 or less.

Travelling between Ireland and Britain, the main train–ferry–train route is Dublin to London, via Dun Laoghaire and Holyhead. Ferries also run between Rosslare and Fishguard or Pembroke (Wales), with train connections on either side.

SEA

Ferries sail from southern England to French ports in a couple of hours; other routes connect eastern England to the Netherlands, Germany and northern Spain, and Ireland from southwest Scotland and Wales.

The main ferry routes between Britain and mainland Europe include Dover to Calais or Boulogne (France), Harwich to Hook of Holland (Netherlands), Hull to Zeebrugge (Belgium) or Rotterdam (Netherlands), and Portsmouth to Santander or Bilbao (Spain). Routes to and from Ireland include Holyhead to Dun Laoghaire. Competition from the Eurotunnel and budget airlines means ferry operators discount heavily at certain times of year. The short cross-channel routes such as Dover to Calais or Boulogne can be as low as £20 for a car plus up to five passengers, although around £50 is more likely.

If you're a foot passenger, or cycling, crossings can start from as little as £10 each way. Broker sites covering all routes and options include www.aferry.co.uk and www.directferries.co.uk.

❶ Getting Around

For travellers on a budget, public transport is the best way to go. Cheapest but slowest are long-distance buses (called coaches in Britain). Trains are faster but much more expensive.

AIR

Britain's domestic air companies include British Airways (www.britishairways.com), Loganair (www.loganair.co.uk), EasyJet (www.easyjet.com) and Ryanair (www.ryanair.com). On most shorter routes (eg London to Newcastle, or Manchester to Bristol), it's often faster to take the train once airport downtime is factored in.

BUS

Long-distance buses nearly always offer the cheapest way to get around. Many towns have separate stations for local buses and intercity coaches; make sure you're in the right one.

National Express (www.nationalexpress.com) is England's main coach operator. North of the border, Scottish Citylink (www.citylink.co.uk) is the leading coach company. Tickets are cheaper if you book in advance and travel at quieter times. As a rough guide, a 200-mile trip (eg London to York) will cost around £15 to £30 if booked a few days in advance.

Also offering cheap fares (from £1) is Megabus (www.megabus.com), which serves about 30 destinations around Britain.

Fares listed are for the cheapest advance purchase ticket.

Bus Passes

National Express offers discount passes to full-time students and under-26s, called Young Persons Coachcards. They cost £10 and give 30% off standard adult fares. Also available are coachcards for people over 60, families and travellers with a disability.

For touring the country, National Express offers Brit Xplorer passes, allowing unlimited travel for seven/14/28 days (£79/139/219).

CAR & MOTORCYCLE

Car rental is expensive in Britain; you'll pay from around £130 per week for the smallest model and around £190 per week for a medium-sized car (including insurance and unlimited mileage). All the major players including Avis, Enterprise, Hertz and Budget operate here.

Using a rental-broker site such as Kayak (www.kayak.com) can help find bargains. It's illegal to drive a car or motorbike in Britain without (at least) third-party insurance. This is included with all rental cars.

TRAIN

About 20 different companies operate train services in Britain, while Network Rail operates tracks and stations. For some passengers this system can be confusing at first, but information and ticket-buying services are mostly centralised. If you have to change trains, or use two or more train operators, you still buy one ticket – valid for the whole journey. The main railcards and passes are also accepted by all train operators.

Centralised ticketing service cover all train services in a single site, and make a small booking fee on top of every ticket price. The main players include National Rail Enquiries (www.nationalrail.co.uk), QJump (www.qjump.co.uk), Rail Easy (www.raileasy.co.uk) and Train Line (www.thetrainline.com).

Classes, Costs & Reservations

Rail travel has 1st and standard classes. Travelling 1st class costs around 50% more than standard. At weekends some train operators offer 'upgrades' to 1st class for an extra £5 to £25 on top of your standard class fare, payable on the spot.

The earlier you book, the cheaper it gets. You can also save if you travel 'off-peak' (ie days and times that aren't busy). If you buy online, you can have the ticket posted (UK addresses only), or collect it from station machines on the day of travel.

There are three main fare types:

Anytime Buy anytime, travel anytime – usually the most expensive option.

Off-peak Buy anytime, travel off-peak (what is off-peak depends on the journey).

Advance Buy in advance, travel only on specific trains (usually the cheapest option).

Fares listed are for the cheapest advance purchase ticket.

Train Passes

If you're staying in Britain for a while, railcards (www.railcard.co.uk) are available:

16–25 Railcard For those aged 16 to 25, or a full-time UK student.

Senior Railcard For anyone over 60.

Family & Friends Railcard Covers up to four adults and four children travelling together. Railcards cost £30 (valid for one year, available from major stations or online) and get 33% discount on most train fares, except those already heavily discounted. With the Family card, adults get 33% and children get 60% discounts, so the fee is easily repaid in a couple of journeys.

Various local train passes are also available covering specific areas and lines – ask at a local train station to get an idea of what's available.

National Passes

For country-wide travel, BritRail (www.britrail.net) passes are available for visitors from overseas. They must be bought in your country of origin (not in Britain) from a specialist travel agency. Available in seven different versions (including England only; Scotland only; all Britain; and UK and Ireland) for periods from four to 30 days.

IRELAND

Dublin

POP 1,345,402

Sultry rather than sexy, Dublin exudes personality as only those who've managed to turn careworn into carefree can. The halcyon days of the Celtic Tiger (the Irish economic boom of the late 1990s), when cash cascaded like a free-flowing waterfall, have long since disappeared, and the city has once again been forced to grind out a living. But Dubliners still know how to enjoy life. They do so through their music, art and literature – things that Dubs often take for granted but, once reminded, generate immense pride.

There are world-class museums, superb restaurants and the best range of entertainment available anywhere in Ireland – and that's not including the pub, the ubiquitous centre of the city's social life and an absolute must for any visitor. And should you wish to get away from it all, the city has a handful of seaside towns at its edges that make for wonderful day trips.

⦿ Sights

Dublin's finest Georgian architecture, including its famed doorways, is found around **St Stephen's Green** (⊘dawn-dusk; 🚇all city centre, 🚇St Stephen's Green) and **Merrion Square** (⊘dawn-dusk; 🚇all city centre) just south of Trinity College; both are prime picnic spots when the sun shines.

O'Connell St, Dublin's grandest avenue, is dominated by the needle-like **Spire** (O'Connell St; 🚇all city centre, 🚇Abbey). It rises more than 120m from the spot once occupied by a statue of Admiral Nelson, which was blown up by the Irish Republican Army (IRA) in 1966. Nearby is the 1815 **General Post Office** (📞01-705 7000; www.anpost.ie; Lower O'Connell St; ⊘8am-8pm Mon-Sat; 🚇all city centre, 🚇Abbey), an important landmark of the 1916 Easter Rising, when the Irish Volunteers used it as a base for attacks against the British army.

ⓘ DISCOUNT CARDS

Dublin Pass (adult/child one day €52/31, three day €83/52) Saving heavy-duty sightseers a packet this pass provides free entry to over 25 attractions (including the Guinness Storehouse), discounts at 20 others and guaranteed fast-track entry to some of the busiest sights. To avail of the free Aircoach transfer to and from the airport, order the card online so you have it when you land. Otherwise, it's available from any Discover Ireland Dublin Tourism Centre.

Heritage Card (adult/child and student €40/10) This card entitles you to free access to all sights in and around Dublin managed by the Office of Public Works (OPW). You can buy it at OPW sites or Dublin Tourism offices.

⭐ **Trinity College** HISTORIC BUILDING
(📞01-896 1000; www.tcd.ie; College Green; ⊘8am-10pm; 🚇all city centre) **FREE** Ireland's most prestigious university is a bucolic retreat in the heart of the city. Just ambling about its cobbled squares it's easy to imagine it in those far-off days when all good gentlemen (for they were only men) came equipped with a passion for philosophy and a love of empire. The student body is a lot more diverse these days, even if the look remains the same. See also p94.

⭐ **Old Library & Book of Kells** LIBRARY
(www.tcd.ie; Library Sq; adult/student/family €11/9.50/22, fast-track €14/12/28; ⊘8.30am-5pm Mon-Sat, 9.30am-5pm Sun May-Sep, 9.30am-5pm Mon-Sat, noon-4.30pm Sun Oct-Apr; 🚇all city centre) Trinity's greatest treasures are found within the Old Library, built by Thomas Burgh between 1712 and 1732. The star of the show is the **Book of Kells**, a breathtaking illuminated manuscript of the four Gospels of the New Testament, created around AD 800 by monks on the Scottish island of Iona, but more stunning still is the 65m **Long Room**, the library's main chamber, which houses around 200,000 of the library's oldest volumes.

⭐ **Guinness Storehouse** BREWERY, MUSEUM
(www.guinness-storehouse.com; St James's Gate, South Market St; adult/child from €17.50/16, Connoisseur Experience €55; ⊘9.30am-7pm Sep-Jun,

IRELAND AT A GLANCE

Don't Miss

Dublin Ireland's capital and largest city has enough distractions to keep visitors engaged for at least a few days. From world-class museums and entertainment to superb dining and top-grade hotels, Dublin has all the baubles of a major international metropolis, plus friendly locals and Guinness.

Galway city One word to describe Galway city? Craic! Ireland's liveliest city literally hums through the night at music-filled pubs where you can hear three old guys playing spoons and fiddles or a hot, young band. Join the locals as they bounce from place to place, never knowing what fun lies ahead but certain of the possibility.

Rock of Cashel Soaring up from the green Tipperary pastures, this ancient fortress takes your breath away at first sight. The seat of kings and churchmen who ruled over the region for more than a thousand years, its impervious walls guard an awesome enclosure with a complete round tower, a 13th-century Gothic cathedral and the most magnificent 12th-century Romanesque chapel in Ireland.

Causeway Coast Spot *Game of Thrones* filming locations as you follow the rugged coastline for 16.5 spectacular kilometres, passing Ballintoy Harbour and the geological wonder of the Giant's Causeway's outsized basalt columns, as well as cliffs and islands, sandy beaches and ruined castles.

Titanic Belfast The construction of the world's most famous ocean liner is celebrated in high-tech, multimedia glory at this wonderful museum. Explore virtually every detail of the *Titanic*'s construction and place yourself in the middle of the industrial bustle that was Belfast's ship-yards at the turn of the 20th century.

Itineraries

One Week

This round-the-island tour conveniently takes in a big chunk of Ireland's major scenic and heritage highlights. Start in cosmopolitan **Dublin**, including visits to Trinity College and the Book of Kells as well as a sample of Guinness in its home town. Cross the border into Northern Ireland and head to **Belfast**. Go northwest along the Antrim coast to the spectacular **Giant's Causeway**; along the way, *Game of Thrones* fans can check out Ballintoy Harbour, which stood in for the Iron Islands' Lordsport Harbour in the TV series. Continue around the coastline and head south via **Connemara National Park**, one of Ireland's scenic highlights.

Two Weeks

Devote at least a day to **Galway city** exploring its colourful streets and wonderful pubs. Spend another day exploring the world-famous Ring of Kerry, ending in **Killarney National Park**, right on the edge of Killarney itself. Visit Ireland's second city, **Cork**. Go north through medieval **Kilkenny**, which is also a centre for arts and crafts and home to many good places to eat, drink and shop. Head back to Dublin for a final day of sightseeing.

Essential Food & Drink

Potatoes The mashed potato dishes colcannon and champ (with cabbage and spring onion, respectively) are two of the tastiest recipes in the country.

Soda bread Made with bicarbonate of soda and buttermilk, this is a superbly tasty bread, and is often on the breakfast menus at B&Bs.

Stout While Guinness has become synonymous with stout the world over, few outside Ireland realise that there are two other major producers competing for the favour of the Irish drinker: Murphy's and Beamish & Crawford, both based in Cork city.

Whiskey At last count, there were almost 100 different types of Irish whiskey, brewed by only three distilleries – Jameson's, Bushmills and Cooley's.

Getting Around

Transport in Ireland is efficient and reasonably priced to and from major urban centres; smaller towns and villages along those routes are well served. Service to destinations not on major routes is less frequent and often impractical.

Bicycle Dublin operates a bike-share scheme with over 100 stations spread throughout the city.

Bus An extensive network of public and private buses make them the most cost-effective way to get around; there's service to and from most inhabited areas.

Car The most convenient way to explore Ireland's every nook and cranny. Cars can be hired in every major town and city; drive on the left.

Train A limited (and expensive) network links Dublin to all major urban centres, including Belfast in Northern Ireland.

When to Go

Dublin

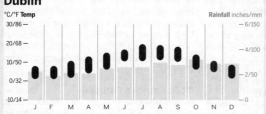

°C/°F **Temp**   **Rainfall** inches/mm

Jun–mid-Sep Weather at its best. Accommodation rates at their highest (especially in August).

Mar–May & mid-Sep–Oct Weather often good: sun and rain in May; 'Indian summers' and often warm in September.

Nov–Feb Cold and wet weather throughout the country; fog can reduce visibility.

Arriving in Ireland

Dublin Airport Private coaches run every 10 to 15 minutes to the city centre (€7). Taxis take 30 to 45 minutes and cost €20 to €25.

Dun Laoghaire Ferry Port Public bus takes around 45 minutes to the centre of Dublin; DART (suburban rail) takes about 25 minutes. Both cost €3.25.

Belfast International Airport Airport Express 300 bus runs hourly from Belfast International Airport (one way/return £7.50/10.50, 30 to 55 minutes). A taxi costs around £30.

Top Phrases

Hello. *Dia dhuit.*

Goodbye. *Slán.*

Excuse me. *Gabh mo leithscéal.*

Sorry. *Tá brón orm.*

You're welcome. *Tá fáilte romhat.*

Resources

Failte Ireland (www.discover ireland.ie) Official tourist board website – practical info and a huge accommodation database.

Northern Ireland Tourist Board (www.nitb.com) Official tourist site.

Set Your Budget

➡ Dorm bed: Ireland €12–20, Northern Ireland £18–25

➡ Cheap meal in cafe or pub: Ireland €8–15, Northern Ireland £7–11

➡ Intercity bus travel (200km trip) €12–25.

9am to 8pm Jul & Aug; 🚌 13, 21A, 40, 51B, 78, 78A, 123 from Fleet St, 🚊 James's) The most popular visit in town is this multimedia homage to Guinness in a converted grain storehouse that is part of the 26-hectare brewery. Across its seven floors you'll discover everything about Guinness before getting to taste it in the top-floor **Gravity Bar**, with its panoramic views. The floor directly below has a very good restaurant. Pre-booking your tickets online will save you time and money.

★ Chester Beatty Library MUSEUM

(📞 01-407 0750; www.cbl.ie; Dublin Castle; ⏰ 10am-5pm Mon-Fri, 11am-5pm Sat, 1-5pm Sun year-round, closed Mon Nov-Feb, free tours 1pm Wed, 2pm Sat & 3pm Sun; 🚌 all city centre) FREE This world-famous library, in the grounds of **Dublin Castle** (📞 01-677 7129; www.dublincastle.ie; Dame St; guided tours adult/child €10/4, self-guided tours €7/3; ⏰ 9.45am-5.45pm, last admission 5.15pm), houses the collection of mining engineer Sir Alfred Chester Beatty (1875–1968), bequeathed to the Irish state on his death. Spread over two floors, the breathtaking collection includes more than 20,000 manuscripts, rare books, miniature paintings, clay tablets, costumes and other objects of artistic, historical and aesthetic importance.

Little Museum of Dublin MUSEUM

(📞 01-661 1000; www.littlemuseum.ie; 15 St Stephen's Green N; adult/student €10/8; ⏰ 9.30am-5pm, to 8pm Thu; 🚌 all city centre, 🚊 St Stephen's Green) This award-winning museum tells the story of Dublin over the last century via memorabilia, photographs and artefacts donated by the general public. The impressive collection, spread over the rooms of a handsome Georgian house, includes a lectern used by JFK on his 1963 visit to Ireland and an original copy of the fateful letter given to the Irish envoys to the treaty negotiations of 1921, whose contradictory instructions were at the heart of the split that resulted in the Civil War.

★ National Gallery MUSEUM

(www.nationalgallery.ie; W Merrion Sq; ⏰ 9.15am-5.30pm Mon-Wed, Fri & Sat, to 8.30pm Thu, 11am-5.30pm Sun; 🚌 4, 7, 8, 46A from city centre) FREE A magnificent Caravaggio and a breathtaking collection of works by Jack B Yeats – William Butler's younger brother – are the main reasons to visit the National Gallery, but not the only ones. Its excellent collection is strong in Irish art, and there are also high-quality collections of every major European school of painting.

National Museum of Ireland – Archaeology MUSEUM

(www.museum.ie; Kildare St; ⏰ 10am-5pm Tue-Sat, 2-5pm Sun; 🚌 all city centre) FREE Ireland's most important cultural institution was established in 1877 as the primary repository of the nation's archaeological treasures. These include the most famous of Ireland's crafted artefacts, the **Ardagh Chalice** and the **Tara Brooch**, dating from the 12th and 8th centuries respectively. They are part of the Treasury, itself part of Europe's finest collection of Bronze and Iron Age gold artefacts, and the most complete assemblage of medieval Celtic metalwork in the world.

Dublin City Gallery – the Hugh Lane GALLERY

(📞 01-222 5550; www.hughlane.ie; 22 N Parnell Sq; ⏰ 9.45am-6pm Tue-Thu, to 5pm Fri, 10am-5pm Sat, 11am-5pm Sun; 🚌 7, 11, 13, 16, 38, 40, 46A, 123 from city centre) FREE Whatever reputation Dublin has as a repository of world-class art has a lot to do with the simply stunning collection at this exquisite gallery, housed in the equally impressive Charlemont House, designed by William Chambers in 1763. Within its walls you'll find the best of contemporary Irish art, a handful of Impressionist classics and Francis Bacon's relocated studio.

★ National Museum of Ireland – Decorative Arts & History MUSEUM

(www.museum.ie; Benburb St; ⏰ 10am-5pm Tue-Sat, 2-5pm Sun; 🚌 25, 66, 67, 90 from city centre, 🚊 Museum) FREE Once the world's largest military barracks, this splendid early neoclassical grey-stone building on the Liffey's northern banks was completed in 1704 according to the design of Thomas Burgh (he of Trinity College's Old Library). It is now home to the Decorative Arts & History collection of the National Museum of Ireland, with a range of superb permanent exhibits ranging from a history of the Easter Rising to the work of iconic Irish designer Eileen Gray (1878–1976).

★ St Patrick's Cathedral CATHEDRAL

(www.stpatrickscathedral.ie; St Patrick's Close; adult/child €6.50/free; ⏰ 9.30am-5pm Mon-Fri, 9am-6pm Sat, 9-10.30am & 12.30-2.30pm Sun; 🚌 50, 50A, 56A from Aston Quay, 54, 54A from Burgh Quay) Ireland's largest church is St Patrick's Cathedral, built between 1191 and 1270 on the site of an earlier church that had stood here since the 5th century. It was here that St Patrick himself reputedly baptised the local Celtic chieftains, making this bit of ground some fairly sacred turf: the well in question is in the adjacent **St Patrick's Park**, which was once a slum but is now a lovely spot to sit and take a load off.

★ **Kilmainham Gaol**   MUSEUM
(☎ 01-453 2037; www.kilmainhamgaolmuseum. ie; Inchicore Rd; adult/child €8/4; ⏰ 9am-6.45pm Jun-Sept, 9.30am-5.30pm rest of year; ☐ 69, 79 from Aston Quay, 13, 40 from O'Connell St) If you have *any* desire to understand Irish history – especially the juicy bits about resistance to British rule – then a visit to this former prison is an absolute must. This threatening grey building, built in 1796, played a role in virtually every act of Ireland's painful path to independence, and even today, despite closing in 1924, it still has the power to chill. Book online as far in advance as possible to get your preferred time.

☞ Tours

★ **Historical Walking Tour**   WALKING
(☎ 01-878 0227; www.historicaltours.ie; Trinity College Gate; adult/student/child €12/10/free; ⏰ 11am & 3pm May-Sep, 11am Apr & Oct, 11am Fri-Sun Nov-Mar; ☐ all city centre) Trinity College history graduates lead this 'seminar on the street' that explores the Potato Famine, Easter Rising, Civil War and Partition. Sights include Trinity, City Hall, Dublin Castle and Four Courts. In summer, themed tours on architecture, women in Irish history and the birth of the Irish state are also held. Tours depart from the College Green entrance.

Trinity College Walking Tour   WALKING
(Authenticity Tours; www.tcd.ie/visitors/tours; Trinity College; tours €6, incl Book of Kells €14; ⏰ 10.15am-3.40pm Mon-Sat, to 3.15pm Sun May-Sep, fewer midweek tours Oct & Feb-Apr; ☐ all city centre, ☐ College Green) A great way to see Trinity's grounds is on student-led walking tours, which depart from the College Green entrance every 20 to 40 minutes.

🛏 Sleeping

★ **Isaacs Hostel**   HOSTEL €
(☎ 01-855 6215; www.isaacs.ie; 2-5 Frenchman's Lane; dm/tw from €16/70; @ 🛜; ☐ all city centre, ☐ Connolly) The northside's best hostel – hell, for atmosphere alone it's the best in town – is in a 200-year-old wine vault just around the corner from the main bus station. With summer barbecues, live music in the lounge, internet access, colourful dorms and even a sauna, this terrific place generates consistently good reviews from backpackers and other travellers.

★ **Generator Hostel**   HOSTEL €
(☎ 01-901 0222; www.generatorhostels.com; Smithfield Sq; dm/tw from €16/70; @ 🛜; ☐ Smithfield) This European chain brings its own brand of funky, fun design to Dublin's hostel scene, with bright colours, comfortable dorms (including women-only) and a lively social scene. It even has a screening room for movies. Good location right on Smithfield Sq, next to the **Old Jameson Distillery** (www.jamesonwhiskey.com; Bow St; adult/student/child €18/15/9, masterclasses €55; ⏰ 10am-5pm Mon-Sat, 10.30am-5pm Sun; ☐ 25, 66, 67, 90 from city centre, ☐ Smithfield).

Jacob's Inn   HOSTEL €
(☎ 01-855 5660; www.jacobsinn.com; 21-28 Talbot Pl; dm/d from €11/70; 🛜; ☐ all city centre, ☐ Connolly) Sister hostel to Isaacs around the corner, this clean and modern hostel offers spacious accommodation with private

---

CAMPUS ACCOMMODATION

Trinity College (☎ 01-896 1177; www.tcd.ie/summeraccommodation; Accommodations Office, Trinity College; s/d from €79/129; ⏰ May–mid-Sep; P @ 🛜; ☐ all cross-city) The closest thing to living like a student at this stunningly beautiful university is crashing in their rooms when they're on summer holidays. Rooms and two-bed apartments in the newer block have their own bathrooms; those in the older blocks share facilities, though there are private sinks. Breakfast is included.

Dublin City University (DCU; ☎ 01-700 5736; www.summeraccommodation.dcu.ie; Larkfield Apartments, Campus Residences, Dublin City University; s/d from €80/120; ⏰ mid-Jun–mid-Sep; ☐ 11, 11A, 11B, 13, 13A, 19, 19A from city centre) This accommodation is proof that students slum it in relative luxury. The modern rooms have plenty of amenities at hand, including a kitchen, common room and fully equipped health centre. The Glasnevin campus is only 15 minutes by bus or car from the city centre.

Dublin

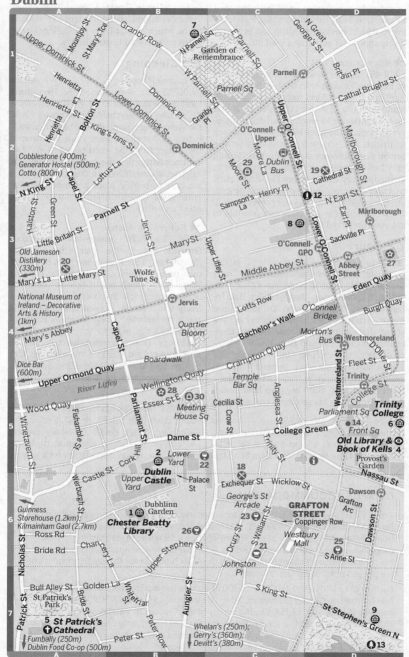

A **B** **C** **D**

Upper Dominick St
Mountjoy St
St Mary's Tce
Granby Row
N Parnell Sq
E Parnell Sq
N Great George's St

7
Garden of
Remembrance
Parnell Sq
W Parnell Sq
Parnell
Brita'in Pl
Cathal Brugha St

Henrietta St
Dominick Pl
Granby Pl
Lower Dominick St

Henrietta La
Henrietta St
Bolton St
King's Inns St
O'Connell-
Upper
Moore La
Moore St
Upper O'Connell St
Marlborough St

Cobblestone (400m);
Generator Hostel (500m);
Cotto (800m)
Capel St
Dominick
29
Dublin
Bus
19
Cathedral St

N King St
Parnell St
Jervis St
Sampson's
La
Henry Pl
12
N Earl St
Earl Pl
Marlborough

Harbour St
Green St
Little Britain St
Mary St
Upper Liffey St
8
O'Connell-
GPO
Lower O'Connell St
Sackville Pl

Old Jameson
Distillery
(330m)
20
Little Mary St
Middle Abbey St
Abbey
Street
27

Mary's La
Wolfe
Tone Sq
Jervis
Lotts Row
Eden Quay

National Museum of
Ireland – Decorative
Arts & History
(1km)
Mary's Abbey
Capel St
Quartier
Bloom
Bachelor's Walk
O'Connell
Bridge
Burgh Quay
Westmoreland

Dice Bar
(600m)
Upper Ormond Quay
Boardwalk
River Liffey
Crampton Quay
Morton's
Bus
Fleet St
D'Olier St
Westmoreland St
Trinity

Wood Quay
Parliament St
Wellington Quay
Essex St E
28
30
Temple
Bar Sq
Cecilia St
Anglesea St
Temple Bar Sq
College St
Trinity
College

Winetavern St
Fishamble St
Meeting
House Sq
Crow St
Trinity St
College Green
14
Parliament Sq
Front Sq
6
Old Library & ⊙
Book of Kells **4**

Dame St
2
Lower
Yard
22
Provost's
Garden

Nicholas St
Castle St
Cork
Hill
Upper
Yard
Dublin
Castle
Palace
St
18
Exchequer St
George's St
Arcade
Wicklow St
Nassau St
Dawson

Werburgh St
Ross Rd
Dubhlinn
Garden
1
Chester Beatty
Library
26
23
GRAFTON
STREET
Coppinger Row
Westbury
Mall
Grafton
Arc
Dawson St
25
S Anne St

Guinness
Storehouse (1.2km);
Kilmainham Gaol (2.7km)
Bride Rd
Chancery La
Upper Stephen St
S William St
21
Johnston
Pl
S King St

Bull Alley St
Golden La
Whitefriar St
Peter Row
Aungier St

Patrick St
St Patrick's
Park
5 St Patrick's
⊙ Cathedral
Peter St
Whelan's (250m);
Gerry's (360m);
Devitt's (380m)
St Stephen's Green N
9
13

Fumbally (250m);
Dublin Food Co-op (500m)

A **B** **C** **D**

bathrooms and outstanding facilities, including some wheelchair-accessible rooms, a bureau de change, bike storage and a self-catering kitchen.

✕ Eating

★ **Fumbally** CAFE €
(☏ 01-529 8732; www.thefumbally.ie; Fumbally Lane; mains €5-9.50; ☺ 8am-5pm Tue-Fri, 10am-5pm Sat, plus 7-9.30pm Wed; ☐ 49, 54A from city centre) A bright, airy warehouse cafe that serves

SELF-CATERING

If you're looking to self-cater, there are some excellent options, especially south of the river, including **Fallon & Byrne** (www.fallonandbyrne.com; Exchequer St; mains €5-10; ⊘ 8am-9pm Mon-Fri, 9am-9pm Sat, 11am-7pm Sun; ⊒ all city centre), the **Dublin Food Co-op** (www.dublin-food.coop; 12 Newmarket; ⊘ 10am-7pm Wed & Fri, to 8pm Thu, 9.30am-5pm Sat, 11am-5pm Sun; ⊒ 49, 54A, 77X from city centre) in Newmarket and the **Temple Bar Food Market** (www.facebook.com/TempleBarFoodMarket; Meeting House Sq; ⊘ 10am-5pm Sat; ⊒ all city centre) – not to mention a fine selection of cheesemongers and bakeries. North of the river, the traditional **Moore Street Market** (Moore St; ⊘ 8am-4pm Mon-Sat; ⊒ all city centre) is the city's most famous, where the colour of the produce is matched by the language of the spruikers.

healthy breakfasts, salads and sandwiches – while the occasional guitarist strums away in the corner. Its Wednesday dinner (mains €16) is an organic, locally sourced exploration of the cuisines of the world that includes a single dish (and its vegetarian variant) served in a communal dining experience; advance bookings suggested.

★**M&L** CHINESE €
(☎ 01-874 8038; www.mlchineserestaurant.com; 13/14 Cathedral St; mains €9-13; ⊘ 11.30am-10pm Mon-Sat, noon-10pm Sun; ⊒ all city centre) Beyond the plain frontage and the cheap-looking decor is Dublin's best Chinese restaurant... by some distance. It's usually full of Chinese customers, who come for the authentic Szechuan-style cuisine – spicier than Cantonese and with none of the concessions usually made to Western palates (no prawn crackers or curry chips).

Gerry's CAFE €
(6 Montague St; Irish fry-up €6.50; ⊘ 8am-2pm Mon-Fri, to 2.30pm Sat; ⊒ 14, 15, 65, 83) A no-nonsense, old-school 'caff' (the British Isles' equivalent of the greasy spoon) is rarer than hen's teeth in the city centre these days, which makes Gerry's something of a treasure. You won't find a more authentic spot to enjoy a traditional Irish fry-up. If you want healthy, it always does porridge, but what's the point?

★**Oxmantown** CAFE €
(www.oxmantown.com; 16 Mary's Abbey, City Markets; sandwiches €5.50; ⊘ 7.30am-4pm Mon-Fri; ⊒ Four Courts, Jervis) Delicious breakfasts and excellent sandwiches make this cafe one of the standout places for daytime eating on the north side of the Liffey. Locally baked bread, coffee supplied by Cloud Picker (Dublin's only microroastery) and meats sourced from Irish farms are the ingredients, but it's the way it's all put together that makes it so worthwhile.

Cotto MEDITERRANEAN €
(www.cotto.ie; 46 Manor St; mains €11-15; ⊘ 6-10pm Wed-Sun, 11am-3.30pm Sat & Sun; ⊒ 25, 25A, 66, 67 from city centre) Some of the very best pizzas in town are beautifully prepared in this lovely spot, which is run by the same folks behind Oxmantown. Ingredients are local, but the end result is straight out of *la cucina Italiana*. Weekend brunches are a nice mix of Irish (sausage rolls, black pudding sandwiches) and Mediterranean (eggs shakshuka with grilled flatbreads and labneh).

🍷 Drinking & Nightlife

The plethora of pubs in Temple Bar is a favourite place to start. We urge you to explore further afield: the pubs around Grafton St are a great mix of old-style pubs and stylish modern spots. Camden St, southwest of St Stephen's Green, is very popular, as is Dawson St and Merrion Row – the latter has a couple of long-established favourites.

North of the Liffey has a selection of fine old pubs and genuine locals (read: visitors will be given the once-over), but there are a handful of popular bars, including the long-running gay bar **George** (www.thegeorge.ie; 89 S Great George's St; weekends after 10pm €5-10, other times free; ⊘ 2pm-2.30am Mon-Fri, 12.30pm-2.30am Sat, 12.30pm-1.30am Sun; ⊒ all city centre).

★**Toner's** PUB
(☎ 01-676 3090; www.tonerspub.ie; 139 Lower Baggot St; ⊘ 10.30am-11.30pm Mon-Thu, to 12.30am Fri & Sat, 11.30am-11pm Sun; ⊒ 7, 46 from city centre) Toner's, with its stone floors and antique snugs, has changed little over the years and is the closest thing you'll get to a country pub in the heart of the city. Next door, Toner's Yard is a comfortable outside space. The shelves and drawers are reminders that it once doubled as a grocery shop.

★**John Mulligan's** PUB
(www.mulligans.ie; 8 Poolbeg St; ⊘ 10.30am-11.30pm Mon-Thu, to 12.30am Fri & Sat, noon-11pm

Sun; 🖥 all city centre) This brilliant old boozer is a cultural institution, established in 1782 and in this location since 1854. A drink (or more) here is like attending liquid services at a most sacred, secular shrine. John F Kennedy paid his respects in 1945, when he joined the cast of regulars that seems barely to have changed since.

★ Grogan's Castle Lounge   PUB
(www.groganspub.ie; 15 S William St; ⊙10.30am-11.30pm Mon-Thu, to 12.30am Fri & Sat, 12.30-11pm Sun; 🖥 all city centre) This place, known simply as Grogan's (after the original owner), is a city-centre institution. It has long been a favourite haunt of Dublin's writers and painters, as well as others from the alternative bohemian set, who enjoy a fine Guinness while they wait for that inevitable moment when they're discovered.

★ Kehoe's   PUB
(9 S Anne St; ⊙10.30am-11.30pm Mon-Thu, to 12.30am Fri & Sat, noon-11pm Sun; 🖥 all city centre) This classic bar is the very exemplar of a traditional Dublin pub. The beautiful Victorian bar, wonderful snug and side room have been popular with Dubliners and visitors for generations, so much so that the publican's living quarters upstairs have since been converted into an extension – simply by taking out the furniture and adding a bar.

★ Long Hall   PUB
(51 S Great George's St; ⊙10.30am-11.30pm Mon-Thu, to 12.30am Fri & Sat, noon-11pm Sun; 🖥 all city centre) A Victorian classic that is one of the city's most beautiful and best-loved pubs. Check out the ornate carvings in the woodwork behind the bar and the elegant chandeliers. The bartenders are experts at their craft, an increasingly rare attribute in Dublin these days.

★ Cobblestone   PUB
(www.cobblestonepub.ie; N King St; ⊙4.30-11.30pm Mon-Thu, to 12.30am Fri & Sat, 1.30-11.30pm Sun; 🖥 Smithfield) It advertises itself as a 'drinking pub with a music problem', which is an apt description for this Smithfield stalwart – although the traditional music sessions that run throughout the week can hardly be described as problematic. Wednesday's Balaclava session (from 7.30pm) is for any musician who is learning an instrument, with musician Síomha Mulligan on hand to teach.

Clement & Pekoe   CAFE
(www.clementandpekoe.com; 50 S William St; ⊙8am-7pm Mon-Fri, 10am-6pm Sat, noon-6pm Sun; 🖥 all city centre) Our favourite cafe in town is this contemporary version of an Edwardian tearoom. Walnut floors, art-deco chandeliers and wall-to-wall displays of handsome tea jars are the perfect setting in which to enjoy the huge range of loose-leaf teas and carefully made coffees, along with a selection of cakes.

☆ Entertainment

For events, reviews and club listings, pick up a copy of the fortnightly music review *Hot Press* (www.hotpress.com), or go online to read Totally Dublin (www.totallydublin.ie). Friday's *Irish Times* (www.irishtimes.com) has a pullout section called 'The Ticket' that has reviews and listings of all things arty.

★ Devitt's   LIVE MUSIC
(📞01-475 3414; www.devittspub.ie; 78 Lower Camden St; ⊙from 9pm Thu-Sat; 🚌14, 15, 65, 83) Devitt's – aka the Cusack Stand – is one of the favourite places for the city's talented musicians to display their wares, with sessions as good as any you'll hear in the city centre. Highly recommended.

Whelan's   LIVE MUSIC
(📞01-478 0766; www.whelanslive.com; 25 Wexford St; 🚌16, 122 from city centre) Perhaps the city's most beloved live-music venue is this mid-size room attached to a traditional bar. This is the singer-songwriter's spiritual home: when they're done pouring out the contents of their hearts on stage, you can find them filling up in the bar along with their fans.

Workman's Club   LIVE MUSIC
(📞01-670 6692; www.theworkmansclub.com; 10 Wellington Quay; free-€20; ⊙5pm-3am; 🖥 all city centre) A 300-capacity venue and bar in the former working-men's club of Dublin. The emphasis is on keeping away from the mainstream, which means everything from singer-songwriters to electronic cabaret. When the live music at the Workman's Club (Twitter: @WorkmansClubs) is over, DJs take to the stage, playing rockabilly, hip-hop, indie, house and more.

Abbey Theatre   THEATRE
(📞01-878 7222; www.abbeytheatre.ie; Lower Abbey St; 🖥 all city centre, 🚆 Abbey) Ireland's national theatre was founded by WB Yeats in 1904 and was a central player in the development of a consciously native cultural identity. In

2017 it appointed Neil Murray and Graham McLaren of the National Theatre of Scotland as its new directors, and they have promised an exciting new program that will fuse traditional and contemporary fare.

Bord Gáis Energy Theatre THEATRE
(☑01-677 7999; www.grandcanaltheatre.ie; Grand Canal Sq; ☒Grand Canal Dock) Forget the uninviting sponsored name: Daniel Libeskind's masterful design is a three-tiered, 2100-capacity auditorium where you're as likely to be entertained by the Bolshoi Ballet or a touring state opera as you are to see *Disney on Ice* or Barbra Streisand. It's a magnificent venue – designed for classical, paid for by the classics.

❶ Information

A handful of official-looking tourism offices on Grafton and O'Connell Sts are actually privately run enterprises where members pay to be included.

Dublin Visitor Centre (www.visitdublin. com; 25 Suffolk St; �l9am-5.30pm Mon-Sat, 10.30am-3pm Sun; ☐all city centre) General visitor information on Dublin and Ireland, as well as an accommodation and booking service.

---

❶ LEAP CARD & FARE SAVER PASSES

Leap Card (www.leapcard.ie) A plastic smart card available in most newsagents. Once you register it online, you can top it up with whatever amount you need. When you board a bus, Luas or suburban train, just swipe your card and the fare – usually 20% less than a cash fare – is automatically deducted.

Freedom of the City (adult/child €33/16) Three-day unlimited travel on all bus services, including Airlink and Dublin Bus Hop-On, Hop-Off tours as well as entry to the Little Museum of Dublin and a Pat Liddy walking tour.

Luas Flexi Ticket (one/seven/30 days €7/26/100) Unlimited travel on all Luas services.

Rambler Pass (five/30 days €31.50/157.50) Valid for unlimited travel on all Dublin Bus and Airlink services, except Nitelink.

Visitor Leap Card (one/three/seven days €10/19.50/40) Unlimited travel on bus, Luas and DART, including Airlink, Nitelink and Xpresso bus.

---

❶ Getting There & Away

AIR

Located 13km north of the city centre, **Dublin Airport** (☑01-814 1111; www.dublinairport.com) has two terminals: most international flights (including most US flights) use Terminal 2; Ryanair and select others use Terminal 1. Both terminals have the usual selection of pubs, restaurants, shops, ATMs and car-hire desks.

There is no train service from the airport to the city centre. Buses cost around €7 one way and take around 45 minutes; taxis cost around €25, taking about 25 minutes.

BOAT

Dublin Port Terminal (☑01-855 2222; Alexandra Rd; ☐53 from Talbot St) is 3km northeast of the city centre. Operators include the following:

Irish Ferries (☑0818 300 400; www.irishferries.com; Ferryport, Terminal Rd South) Holyhead in Wales; €200 return, three hours.

P&O Irish Sea (☑01-407 3434; www.poferries. com; Terminal 3) Liverpool; €180 return, 8½ hours or four hours on fast boat.

An express bus transfer to and from Dublin Port is operated by **Morton's** (www.mortonscoaches.ie; adult/child €3/1.50; �l7.15am, 1.30pm & 7pm). Otherwise, regular bus 53 serves the port from Talbot St. Inbound ferries are met by timed bus services that serve the city centre.

BUS

The main bus terminal **Busáras** (☑01-836 6111; www.buseireann.ie; Store St; ☒Connolly) is just north of the river behind Custom House.

It's possible to combine bus and ferry tickets from major UK centres to Dublin on the bus network. The journey between London and Dublin takes about 12 hours and costs from €29 return (€41 for a single!). For details, contact **Eurolines** (☑0870 514 3219; www.eurolines.com).

From here, **Bus Eireann** (☑1850 836 6111; www.buseireann.ie) buses serve the whole national network, including buses to towns and cities in Northern Ireland.

TRAIN

Dublin has two main train stations:

Heuston Station (☑01-836 5421; ☒Heuston) On the western side of town near the Liffey, for services to Cork, Galway, Killarney, Limerick and most other points south and west.

Connolly Station (☑01-836 3333; ☒Connolly, ☒Connolly Station) North of the Liffey, behind the Custom House, with services to Belfast.

Connolly Station is a stop on the DART line into town; the Luas Red Line serves both Connolly and Heuston stations.

❶ Getting Around

BICYCLE

One of the most popular ways to get around the city is with the blue bikes of Dublinbikes (www. dublinbikes.ie), a public bicycle-rental scheme with more than 100 stations spread across the city centre. Purchase a €10 smart card (and pay a credit-card deposit of €150) or a three-day card online or at any station before 'freeing' a bike for use, which is then free of charge for the first 30 minutes and €0.50 for each half-hour thereafter.

BUS

The **Dublin Bus Office** (☑ 01-873 4222; www. dublinbus.ie; 59 Upper O'Connell St; ⊗ 8.30am-5.30pm Tue-Fri, to 2pm Sat, 9am-5.30pm Mon; ▣ all city centre) has free single-route timetables for all its services. Buses run from around 6am (some start at 5.30am) to about 11.30pm.

Local buses cost from €2 to €3.30 for a single journey. You must pay the exact fare when boarding; drivers don't give change.

TRAIN

The **Dublin Area Rapid Transport** (DART; ☑ 01-836 6222; www.irishrail.ie) provides quick train access to the coast as far north as Howth (about 30 minutes) and as far south as Greystones in County Wicklow. Pearse Station is convenient for central Dublin south of the Liffey, and Connolly Station for north of the Liffey. There are services every 10 to 20 minutes, sometimes more frequently, from around 6.30am to midnight Monday to Saturday. Services are less frequent on Sunday. A one-way DART ticket from Dublin to Dun Laoghaire or Howth costs €3.25.

TRAM

The Luas (www.luas.ie) light-rail system has two lines: the green line (running every five to 15 minutes) connects St Stephen's Green with Sandyford in south Dublin via Ranelagh and Dundrum; the red line (every 20 minutes) runs from the Point Village to Tallaght via the north quays and Heuston Station.

There are ticket machines at every stop or you can use a tap-on, tap-off Leap Card, which is available from most newsagents. A typical short-hop fare (around four stops) is €2.30.

From 2018, a new cross-city line will connect the green and red lines with a route from St Stephen's Green through Dawson St and around Trinity College and over the river.

TAXI

All taxi fares begin with a flagfall of €3.60 (€4 from 10pm to 8am), followed by €1.10 per kilometre thereafter (€1.40 from 10pm to 8am).

Taxis can be hailed on the street. Numerous taxi companies, such as **National Radio Cabs** (☑ 01-677 2222; www.nrc.ie), dispatch taxis by radio. You can also try MyTaxi (www.mytaxi. com), a taxi app.

The Southeast

Kilkenny

POP 26,512

Kilkenny is the Ireland of many visitors' imaginations. Built from dark-grey limestone flecked with fossil seashells, Kilkenny (from the Gaelic 'Cill Chainnigh', meaning the Church of St Canice) is also known as 'the marble city'. Its picturesque 'Medieval Mile' of narrow lanes and historic buildings strung between castle and cathedral along the bank of the River Nore is one of the southeast's biggest tourist draws. It's worth braving the crowds to soak up the atmosphere of one of Ireland's creative crucibles – Kilkenny is a centre for arts and crafts, and home to a host of fine restaurants, cafes, pubs and shops.

⊙ Sights

★ **Kilkenny Castle**　　　CASTLE
(☑ 056-770 4100; www.kilkennycastle.ie; The Parade; adult/child €8/4; ⊗ 9.30am-5.30pm Apr-Sep, to 5pm Mar, to 4.30pm Oct-Feb) Rising above the River Nore, Kilkenny Castle is one of Ireland's most visited heritage sites. Stronghold of the powerful Butler family, it has a history dating back to the 12th century, though much of its present look dates from Victorian times.

During the winter months (November to January) visits are by 40-minute guided tours only, which shift to self-guided tours from February to October. Highlights include the Long Gallery with its painted roof and carved marble fireplace. There's an excellent tearoom in the former castle kitchens, all white marble and gleaming copper.

★ **St Canice's Cathedral**　　　CATHEDRAL
(☑ 056-776 4971; www.stcanicescathedral.ie; St Canice's Pl; cathedral/ round tower/ combined €4/3/6; ⊗ 9am-6pm Mon-Sat, 1-6pm Sun Jun-Aug, shorter hours Sep-May) Ireland's second-largest medieval cathedral (after St Patrick's in Dublin) has a long and fascinating history. The first monastery was built here in the 6th century by St Canice, Kilkenny's patron saint. The present structure dates from the 13th to 16th centuries, with extensive 19th-century reconstruction, its interior housing ancient grave slabs and

Kilkenny

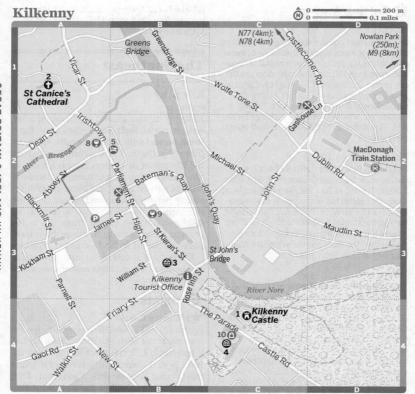

Kilkenny

the tombs of Kilkenny Castle's Butler dynasty. Outside stands a 30m-high round tower, one of only two in Ireland that you can climb.

Medieval Mile Museum　　　MUSEUM
(☎ 056-781 7022; www.medievalmilemuseum.ie; 2 St Mary's Lane; adult/child €7/3; ⊙10am-6pm Apr-Oct, 11am-4.30pm Nov-Mar) Dating from the early 13th century, St Mary's Church has been converted into a fascinating modern museum that charts the history of Kilkenny in medieval times. Highlights include the Rothe Chapel, lined with ornate 16th- and 17th-century tombs carved from local limestone, remnants of the 17th-century timber roof above the crossing, and a selection of 13th- and 14th-century grave slabs. A huge interactive map of Kilkenny allows you to explore maps and documents relating to the medieval city.

National Craft Gallery
GALLERY

(🖉 056-779 6147; www.nationalcraftgallery.ie; Castle Yard; ⊙10am-5.30pm Tue-Sun; 🖼) FREE Contemporary Irish crafts are showcased at these imaginative galleries, set in former stables across the road from Kilkenny Castle, next to the shops of the **Kilkenny Design Centre** (🖉 056-772 2118; www.kilkennydesign. com; Castle Yard; ⊙10am-7pm). Ceramics dominate, but exhibits often feature furniture, jewellery and weaving from the members of the Crafts Council of Ireland. Family days are held the third Saturday of every month, with a tour of the gallery and free hands-on workshops for children. For additional workshops and events, check the website.

🛏 Sleeping & Eating

Kilkenny Tourist Hostel
HOSTEL €

(🖉 056-776 3541; www.kilkennyhostel.ie; 35 Parliament St; dm/tw from €17/42; @🖻) Inside an ivy-covered 1770s Georgian townhouse, this fairly standard, 60-bed IHH hostel has a sitting room warmed by an open fireplace, and a timber- and leadlight-panelled dining room adjoining the self-catering kitchen. Excellent location, but a place for relaxing rather than partying.

Mocha's Vintage Tearooms
CAFE €

(www.facebook.com/thevintagetearoomsby-mocha; 4 The Arches, Gashouse Lane; mains €7-14; ⊙8.30am-5.30pm Mon-Sat) A cute retro tearoom with picture-cluttered walls and rose-patterned china. As well as tea and cakes, there's a breakfast menu (until 11.30am) with a choice of bagels or a full Irish fry-up, and hot lunch specials including fish and chips.

★Foodworks
BISTRO, CAFE €€

(🖉 056-777 7696; www.foodworks.ie; 7 Parliament St; lunch mains €14, 3-course dinner €30; ⊙noon-4.30pm Sun-Wed, noon-9.30pm Thu-Sat; 🖻🖼) 🌱 The owners of this cool and casual bistro keep their own pigs and grow their own salad leaves, so it would be churlish not to try their pork belly stuffed with black pudding, or confit pig's trotter – and you'll be glad you did. Delicious food, excellent coffee and friendly service make this a justifiably popular venue; it's best to book a table.

🍷 Drinking & Nightlife

★Kyteler's Inn
PUB

(🖉 056-772 1064; www.kytelersinn.com; 27 St Kieran's St; ⊙11am-midnight Sun-Thu, to 2am Fri & Sat) Dame Alice Kyteler's old house was built back in 1224 and has seen its share of history: she was charged with witchcraft in 1323. Today the rambling bar includes the original building, complete with vaulted ceiling and arches. There is a beer garden, a courtyard and a large upstairs room for the live bands (nightly March to October), ranging from trad to blues.

John Cleere's
PUB

(🖉 056-776 2573; www.cleeres.com; 22 Parliament St; ⊙11.30am-11.30pm Mon-Thu, to 12.30am Fri & Sat, 1-11pm Sun) One of Kilkenny's finest venues for live music, theatre and comedy, this long bar has blues, jazz and rock, as well as trad music sessions on Monday and Wednesday. Food is served throughout the day, including soup, sandwiches, pizza and Irish stew.

ℹ Information

Kilkenny Tourist Office (🖉 056-775 1500; www.visitkilkenny.ie; Rose Inn St; ⊙9am-6pm Mon-Sat, 10.30am-4pm Sun) Stocks guides and walking maps. Located in Shee Alms House, dating from 1582 and built in local stone by benefactor Sir Richard Shee to help the poor.

ℹ Getting There & Away

Bus Éireann (p108) and DublinCoach (http://www.dublincoach.ie/) services stop at the train station and on Ormonde Rd (nearer the town centre); JJ Kavanagh (www.jjkavanagh. ie) buses to Dublin airport stop on Ormonde Rd only. Services include Cork (€15, 2½ hours, every two hours), Dublin (€14.50, 2¼ hours, two daily) and Dublin airport (€20, two to three hours, seven daily).

MacDonagh train station (Dublin Rd) is a 10-minute walk northeast of the town centre. Services include Dublin Heuston (€25.85, 1½ hours, six daily).

The Southwest

Cork

POP 208,669

Ireland's second city is first in every important respect – at least according to the locals, who cheerfully refer to it as the 'real capital of Ireland'. It's a liberal, youthful and cosmopolitan place that was badly hit by economic recession but is now busily reinventing itself with spruced-up streets, revitalised stretches of waterfront, and – seemingly – an artisanal coffee bar on every corner. There's a bit of a hipster scene, but the best of the city is still happily traditional – snug pubs with

Cork

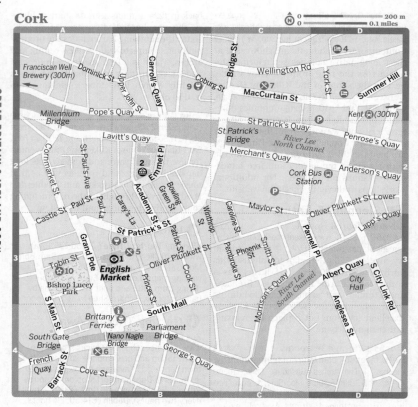

Cork

live-music sessions, restaurants dishing up top-quality local produce, and a genuinely proud welcome from the locals.

◉ Sights

The best sight in Cork is the city itself – soak it up as you wander the streets. A new conference and events centre, complete with 6000-seat concert venue, tourist centre, restaurants, shops, galleries and apartments, is scheduled to open in 2019 as the focus of the new **Brewery Quarter** (the former Beamish & Crawford brewery site, fronted by the landmark mock-Tudor 'counting house'), a block west of the English Market.

Shandon, perched on a hillside overlooking the city centre to the north, is a great spot for the views alone, but you'll also find galleries, antique shops and cafes along its old lanes and squares. Those tiny old row houses, where generations of workers raised huge families in very basic conditions, are now sought-after urban pieds-à-terre. Pick up a copy of the *Cork Walks – Shandon* leaflet from the tourist office (p114) for a self-guided tour of the district.

★ English Market
MARKET

(www.englishmarket.ie; main entrance Princes St; ⊙8am-6pm Mon-Sat) It could just as easily be called the Victorian Market for its ornate vaulted ceilings and columns, but the English Market is a true gem, no matter what you name it. Scores of vendors set up colourful and photogenic displays of the region's very best local produce, including meat, fish, fruit, cheeses and takeaway food. On a sunny day, take your lunch to nearby **Bishop Lucey Park**, a popular alfresco eating spot.

★ Cork City Gaol
MUSEUM

(✆021-430 5022; www.corkcitygaol.com; Convent Ave; adult/child €8/5; ⊙9.30am-5pm Apr-Sep, 10am-4pm Oct-Mar) This imposing former prison is well worth a visit, if only to get a sense of how awful life was for prisoners a century ago. An audio tour (€2 extra) guides you around the restored cells, which feature models of suffering prisoners and sadistic-looking guards. Take a bus to UCC – from there walk north along Mardyke Walk, cross the river and follow the signs uphill (10 minutes).

Crawford Art Gallery
GALLERY

(✆021-480 5042; www.crawfordartgallery.ie; Emmet Pl; ⊙10am-5pm Mon-Sat, 11am-4pm Sun, to 8pm Thu) FREE Cork's public gallery houses a small but excellent permanent collection covering the 17th century through to the modern day. Highlights include works by Sir John Lavery, Jack B Yeats and Nathaniel Hone, and a room devoted to Irish women artists from 1886 to 1978 – don't miss the pieces by Mainie Jellet and Evie Hone.

🛏 Sleeping

Sheila's Hostel
HOSTEL €

(✆021-450 5562; www.sheilashostel.ie; 4 Belgrave Pl, off Wellington Rd; dm/tw from €16/50; @🖜) Sheila's heaves with young travellers, and it's no wonder given its excellent central location. Facilities include a sauna, lockers, laundry service, a movie room and a barbecue. Cheaper twin rooms share bathrooms. Breakfast is €3 extra.

Brú Bar & Hostel
HOSTEL €

(✆021-455 9667; www.bruhostel.com; 57 MacCurtain St; dm/tw incl breakfast from €17/50; @🖜) This buzzing hostel has its own internet cafe, with free access for guests, and a fantastic bar, popular with backpackers and locals alike. The dorms (each with a bathroom) have four to six beds and are both clean and stylish – ask for one on the upper floors to avoid bar noise. Breakfast is included.

🍴 Eating

★ Farmgate Cafe
CAFE, BISTRO €

(✆021-427 8134; www.farmgate.ie; Princes St, English Market; mains €8-14; ⊙8.30am-5pm Mon-Sat) 🍃 An unmissable experience at the heart of the English Market, the Farmgate is perched on a balcony overlooking the food stalls below, the source of all that fresh local produce on your plate – everything from crab and oysters to the lamb in your Irish stew. Go up the stairs and turn left for table service, or right for counter service.

Quay Co-op
VEGETARIAN €

(✆021-431 7026; www.quaycoop.com; 24 Sullivan's Quay; mains €7-11; ⊙11am-9pm Mon-Sat, noon-9pm Sun; 🖉🖬) 🍃 Flying the flag for alternative Cork, this cafeteria offers a range of self-service vegetarian dishes, all organic, including big breakfasts and rib-sticking soups and casseroles. It also caters for gluten-, dairy- and wheat-free needs, and is amazingly child-friendly.

WORTH A TRIP

ROCK OF CASHEL

The iconic and much-photographed **Rock of Cashel** (www.heritageireland. ie; adult/child €8/4; ⊙9am-7pm early Jun–mid-Sep, to 5.30pm mid-Mar–early Jun & mid-Sep–mid-Oct, to 4.30pm mid-Oct–mid-Mar) is one of Ireland's true highlights. The 'rock' is a fortified hill, the defences of which shelter a clutch of historical, religious monuments. The site has been a defensive one since the 4th century and its compelling features include the towering 13th-century Gothic cathedral, a 15th-century four-storey castle, an 11th-century round tower and a 12th-century Romanesque chapel.

The rock is a five-minute stroll along Bishop's Walk from appealing market town **Cashel**. There are eight buses daily between Cashel and Cork (€16, 1¾ hours) via Cahir (€6, 20 minutes, six daily). The bus stop for Cork is outside the Bake House on Main St. The Dublin stop (€16, 2½ hours, six daily) is opposite.

Tara's Team Room
TEAHOUSE €

(☑ 021-455 3742; www.facebook.com/tarastearoom; 45 McCurtain St; ☺ 9am-6pm Mon-Sat, 10am-5pm Sun) You'll search a long time to find a cuter cafe in Ireland than this place. The vintage decor manages to be kitsch yet charming and food is served on china plates. Good for a meal or just a fresh cake and tea (made with leaves of course). Service is prompt and smiling. Mains are priced €8 to €12.

🍷 Drinking & Nightlife

★ Sin É
PUB

(☑ 021-450 2266; www.facebook.com/sinecork; 8 Coburg St; ☺ 12.30-11.30pm Mon-Thu, to 12.30am Fri & Sat, to 11pm Sun) You could easily spend an entire day at this place, which is everything a craic-filled pub should be – long on atmosphere and short on pretension (Sin É means 'that's it!'). There's music every night from 6.30pm May to September, and regular sessions Tuesday, Friday and Sunday the rest of the year, much of them traditional but with the odd surprise.

★ Franciscan Well Brewery
PUB

(☑ 021-439 3434; www.franciscanwellbrewery.com; 14 North Mall; ☺ 1-11.30pm Mon-Thu, to 12.30am Fri & Sat, to 11pm Sun; 🛜) The copper vats gleaming behind the bar give the game away: the Franciscan Well brews its own beer. The best place to enjoy it is in the enormous beer garden at the back. The pub holds regular beer festivals together with other small independent Irish breweries.

★ Mutton Lane Inn
PUB

(☑ 021-427 3471; www.facebook.com/mutton.lane; Mutton Lane; ☺ 10.30am-11.30pm Mon-Thu, to 12.30am Fri & Sat, 2-11pm Sun) Tucked down the tiniest of alleys off St Patrick's St, this inviting pub, lit by candles and fairy lights, is one of Cork's most intimate drinking holes. It's minuscule, so try to get in early to bag the snug, or perch on the beer kegs outside.

☆ Entertainment

Cork's cultural life is generally of a high calibre. To see what's happening grab *WhazOn?* (www.whazon.com), a free monthly leaflet available from the tourist office, news agencies, shops, hostels and B&Bs.

★ Triskel Arts Centre
ARTS CENTRE

(☑ 021-472 2022; www.triskelart.com; Tobin St; tickets €6-10; ☺ box office 10am-5pm Mon-Sat; 🛜)

A fantastic cultural centre housed partly in a renovated church building – expect a varied program of live music, installation art, photography and theatre at this intimate venue. There's also a cinema (from 6.30pm) and a great cafe.

ℹ️ Information

Cork City Tourist Office (☑ 021-425 5100; www.discoverireland.ie/corkcity; Grand Pde; ☺ 9am-5pm Mon-Sat year-round, plus 10am-5pm Sun Jul & Aug) Souvenir shop and information desk. Sells Ordnance Survey maps.

ℹ️ Getting There & Around

AIR

Cork Airport (☑ 021-431 3131; www.corkairport.com) is 8km south of the city. **Bus Éireann** (☑ 021-455 7178; www.buseireann.ie) service 226A shuttles between the train station, bus station and Cork Airport every half-hour between 6am and 10pm (€5.60, 30 minutes). A taxi to/from town costs €22 to €26.

BOAT

Brittany Ferries (☑ 021-427 7801; www.brittanyferries.ie; 42 Grand Pde) sails to Roscoff (France) weekly from the end of March to October. The crossing takes 14 hours; fares vary widely. The ferry terminal is at Ringaskiddy, 15 minutes by car southeast of the city centre along the N28. Taxis cost €30 to €38. Bus Éireann runs a service from Cork (South Mall) to link up with departures (€8, 40 minutes); confirm times on its website.

BUS

Bus Éireann (p114) operates from the **bus station** (cnr Merchant's Quay & Parnell Pl), while **Aircoach** (☑ 01-844 7118; www.aircoach.ie) and **Citylink** (☑ 091-564 164; www.citylink.ie; 🛜) services depart from St Patrick's Quay, across the river. **GoBus** (☑ 091-564 600; www.gobus.ie; 🛜) uses a stop around the corner on Parnell Pl. Services include Dublin (from €14, three hours, six to nine services daily), Kilkenny (€22, three hours, twice daily) and Kilarney (€28, two hours, hourly).

TRAIN

Kent Train Station (☑ 021-450 6766) is north of the River Lee on Lower Glanmire Rd, a 10- to 15-minute walk from the city centre. Bus 205 runs into the city centre (€2, five minutes, every 15 minutes). Services include Dublin (€66, 2¼ hours, eight daily), Galway (€63, four to six hours, seven daily, two or three changes) and Killarney (€28, 1½ to two hours, nine daily).

Killarney

POP 14,504

In the tourism game for more than 250 years, Killarney is a well-oiled machine set in the midst of sublime scenery spanning lakes, waterfalls and woodland spreading beneath a skyline of 1000m-plus peaks. Competition keeps standards high and visitors on all budgets can expect to find good restaurants, great pubs and comfortable accommodation.

◉ Sights & Activities

The town itself can easily be explored on foot in an hour or two. However, Killarney's biggest attraction, in every sense, is the nearby Killarney National Park. Killarney's tourist office (p116) stocks walking guides and maps. **Killarney Guided Walks** (📞087 639 4362; www.killarneyguidedwalks.com; adult/child €9/5) leads guided explorations.

The 214km **Kerry Way** (www.kerryway.com), the Republic's longest way-marked footpath, starts and ends in Killarney. It takes around 10 days to complete the whole route; if you have less time it's worth hiking the first three days as far as Glenbeigh, from where a bus or a lift could return you to Killarney.

★**Killarney National Park**   PARK
(www.killarneynationalpark.ie) **FREE** Enclosed within Killarney's 10,236-hectare (25,280-acre) national park are beautiful Lough Leane (the Lower Lake or 'Lake of Learning'), Muckross Lake and the Upper Lake, as well as the Mangerton, Torc, Shehy and Purple Mountains. Areas of oak and yew woodland stretch for miles. This is wonderful walking and biking country.

Gap of Dunloe   NATURAL FEATURE
The Gap of Dunloe is a scenic valley squeezed between Purple Mountain and Carrauntoohil (at 1040m, Ireland's highest peak). In summer it is a tourist bottleneck crammed with coaches depositing crowds of day trippers for one-hour pony-and-trap rides through the pass. Rather than joining the hordes, think about hiring a bike and cycling the route.

🛏 Sleeping & Eating

★**Fleming's White Bridge**
Caravan & Camping Park   CAMPGROUND €
(📞064-663 1590; http://killarneycamping.com; White Bridge, Ballycasheen Rd; sites per vehicle plus 2 adults €26, hiker €10; ⊙mid-Mar–Oct; 📶)
A lovely, sheltered, family-run campsite 2.5km southeast of the town centre off the N22, Fleming's has a games room, bike hire, campers' kitchen, laundry and free trout fishing on the river that runs alongside. Your man Hillary at reception can arrange bus, bike and boat tours.

Súgán Hostel   HOSTEL €
(📞087 718 8237; www.suganhostelkillarney.com; Lewis Rd; dm/tw from €15/40; 📶) Behind its publike front, 250-year-old Súgán is an amiably eccentric hostel with an open fire in the cosy common room and low, crazy-cornered ceilings and hardwood floors. Check in at the adjacent Lord of the Rings–themed bar, a handy spot for a pint of Guinness once you're settled in.

Khao   ASIAN €
(📞064-667 1040; 66 High St; mains €11-12; ⊙noon-10.30pm; 🍴) Fiery spices waft from this cosy spot, which sizzles up authentic stir-fries and wok-fried noodles along with rich curries, rice dishes and noodle soups. All of its produce is organic, and vegetarian choices abound. The two-course lunch menu, served between noon and 5pm, is a fantastic deal. Takeaway is available.

Lir Café   CAFE €
(📞064-663 3859; www.lircafe.com; Kenmare Pl; dishes €3-7; ⊙8am-9pm; 📶) Contemporary Lir Café brews some of Killarney's best coffee. Food is limited to toasties, cakes, biscuits and the real treat, handmade chocolates, including Bailey's truffles.

🍷 Drinking & Nightlife

★**O'Connor's**   PUB
(http://oconnorstraditionalpub.com; 7 High St; ⊙10.30am-11pm Mon-Thu, to 12.30am Fri & Sat, 12.30-11pm Sun) Live music plays every night at this tiny traditional pub with leaded-glass doors, which is one of Killarney's most popular haunts. In warmer weather, the crowds spill out onto the adjacent lane.

★**Celtic Whiskey Bar**
& Larder   BAR
(📞064-663 5700; www.celticwhiskeybar.com; 93 New St; ⊙10.30am-11.30pm Mon-Thu, to 12.30am Fri & Sat, to 11pm Sun) Of the thousand-plus whiskeys stocked at this stunning contemporary bar, over 500 are Irish, including 1945 Willie Napier from County Offaly and 12-year-old Writers' Tears from County Carlow. One-hour courses (from €15) include

Killarney

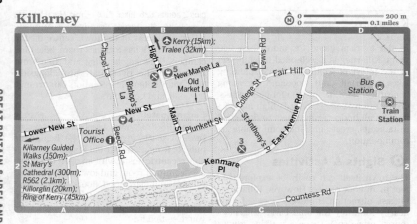

Killarney

🛏 Sleeping
1 Súgán Hostel C1

🍽 Eating
2 Khao B1
3 Lir Café C2

🍸 Drinking & Nightlife
4 Celtic Whiskey Bar & Larder B2
5 O'Connor's B1

the introductory Distiller's Apprentice and a blend-your-own Blender's Challenge. A dozen Irish craft beers are on tap; sensational food (mains €10.50 to €24.50) is served until 10pm.

ℹ Information

Tourist Office (☎ 064-663 1633; http://killarney.ie; Beech Rd; ⏰ 9am-5pm Mon-Sat; 📶) Killarney's tourist office can handle most queries and is especially good with transport intricacies.

ℹ Getting There & Around

AIR
Kerry Airport (KIR; ☎ 066-976 4644; http://kerryairport.ie) is at Farranfore, 17km north of Killarney on the N22. There are daily flights to Dublin and London's Luton and Stansted airports.

Bus Éireann (www.buseireann.ie) has hourly services between Killarney and Kerry Airport (€5.60, 20 minutes). A taxi to Killarney costs about €20.

BICYCLE
Bicycles are ideal for exploring the scattered sights of the Killarney region, many of which are accessible only by bike or on foot.

Many of Killarney's hostels and hotels offer bike rental. Alternatively, try **O'Sullivan's Bike Hire** (☎ 064-663 1282; www.osullivanscycles. com; Beech Rd; per day/week €15/80).

BUS
Bus Éireann operates from the **bus station** (Park Rd). For Dublin you need to change at Cork (€25, two hours, hourly) – the train is much faster.

TRAIN
From Killarney's **train station** (Fair Hill), just east of the centre, there are one or two direct services per day to Cork (€10, 1½ hours) and Dublin (€21, 3¼ hours); otherwise you'll have to change at Mallow.

Ring of Kerry

The Ring of Kerry is the longest and the most diverse of Ireland's big circle drives, combining jaw-dropping coastal scenery with emerald pastures and villages.

The 179km circuit usually begins in Killarney and winds past pristine beaches, the island-dotted Atlantic, medieval ruins, mountains and loughs (lakes). The coastline is at its most rugged between Waterville and Caherdaniel in the southwest of the peninsula. It can get crowded in summer, but even then, the remote Skellig Ring can be uncrowded and serene – and starkly beautiful.

The Ring of Kerry can easily be done as a day trip, but if you want to stretch it out, places to stay are scattered along the route.

Killorglin and Kenmare have the best dining options, with some excellent restaurants; elsewhere, basic (sometimes very basic) pub fare is the norm.

❶ Getting There & Around

Bus Éireann (p108) runs a once-daily Ring of Kerry bus service (No 280) from late June to late August. Buses leave Killarney at 11.30am, arriving back at Killarney (€23.50) at 4.45pm. En route, stops include Killorglin (€8, 30 minutes), Cahersiveen (€17.50, 1½ hours), Waterville (€20, 1¾ hours) and Caherdaniel (€21.80, 2¼ hours).

Travel agencies and hostels in Killarney offer daily coach tours of the Ring for about €25, year-round, lasting from 10.30am to 5pm.

The West Coast

Galway

POP 79,934

Designated the European Capital of Culture for 2020, arty, bohemian Galway (Gaillimh) is one of Ireland's most engaging cities. Brightly painted pubs heave with live music, while restaurants and cafes offer front-row seats for observing buskers and street theatre. Remnants of the medieval town walls lie between shops selling handcrafted Claddagh rings, books and musical instruments; bridges arch over the salmon-stuffed River Corrib; and a long promenade leads to the seaside suburb of Salthill, on Galway Bay, the source of the area's famous oysters.

◎ Sights

★ Galway City Museum   MUSEUM

(www.galwaycitymuseum.ie; Spanish Parade House, Merchant's Rd; ☺10am-5pm Tue-Sat year-round, noon-5pm Sun Easter-Sep) **FREE** Exhibits at this modern museum covering the city's history from 1800 to 1950 include an iconic Galway hooker fishing boat, a collection of *currachs* (boats made of a framework of laths covered with tarred canvas), and sections covering Galway and the Great War, and the city's cinematic connections.

★ Spanish Arch   HISTORIC SITE

The Spanish Arch is thought to be an extension of Galway's medieval city walls, designed to protect ships moored at the nearby quay while they unloaded goods from Spain, although it was partially destroyed by the tsunami that followed the 1755 Lisbon earthquake. Today it reverberates with buskers and drummers, and the lawns and riverside form a gathering place for locals and visitors on sunny days, as kayakers negotiate the tidal rapids of the River Corrib.

Lynch's Castle   HISTORIC BUILDING

(Shop St; ☺10am-4pm Mon-Wed & Fri, 10am-5pm Thu) **FREE** Now an AIB Bank, this excellent example of a town castle was built around the 15th century (the exact date is unknown), though much of what you see today dates from around 1600. The facade's stonework includes ghoulish gargoyles and the coats of arms of Henry VII, the Lynches (the most powerful of the 14 ruling Galway tribes) and the Fitzgeralds of Kildare. On the ground floor, interpretive panels cover

---

OFF THE BEATEN TRACK

SKELLIG MICHAEL

The jagged, 217m-high rock of **Skellig Michael** (www.heritageireland.ie; ☺May–Sep) **FREE** is the larger of the two Skellig Islands and a Unesco World Heritage site. If it looks familiar that's because the island is a location in recent Star Wars movies. Early Christian monks survived at this forbidding site from the 6th until the 12th or 13th century. The 12km crossing can be rough but is well worth making. There are no toilets or shelter, so bring something to eat and drink, and wear stout shoes and weatherproof clothing.

Trips usually run from May until September, depending on weather (there are no sailings on two days out of seven, on average). You can depart from Portmagee, Ballinskelligs or Caherdaniel. There is a limit on the number of daily visitors, with boats licensed to carry no more than 12 passengers each, so book ahead; the cost is around €75 per person. Check to make sure operators have a current licence; the OPW (Office of Public Works; www.opw.ie) can provide advice.

Boats leave in the morning and return at 3pm, and give you around two hours on the rock, which is the bare minimum to visit the monastery, look at the birds and have a picnic.

GREAT BRITAIN & IRELAND GALWAY

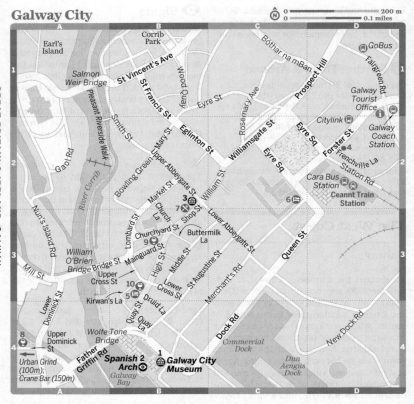

Galway City

its history and architecture; the magnificent fireplace is a highlight.

🛏 Sleeping

★ Kinlay House
HOSTEL €

(☎ 091-565 244; www.kinlaygalway.ie; Merchant's Rd, Eyre Sq; dm/d €25/70; @ 🛜) Easygoing staff and a brilliant location right by Eyre Sq make this large, brightly lit hostel a winner. Freshly renovated in 2017, superb amenities include a self-catering kitchen and a cosy TV lounge with a pool table. The four- to eight-bed dorms and private rooms come with electric sockets and USB points; dorms have curtains screening each bunk.

Barnacles
HOSTEL €

(☎ 091-568 644; www.barnacles.ie; 10 Quay St; dm/d from €15/60; 🛜) Housed in a medieval building with a modern extension, this well-run hostel has clean rooms named after the city's 14 tribes and an epicentral location surrounded by pubs. There's a spacious self-catering kitchen and cosy common room with a big gas fireplace and games consoles. Breakfast includes scones and soda bread. From June to August there's a minimum two-night stay.

✖ Eating & Drinking

Most pubs in Galway have live music at least a couple of nights a week, whether in an informal trad session or a headline act. **Róisín Dubh** (www.roisindubh.net; 9 Upper Dominick St; ⊙5pm-2am Sun-Thu, to 2.30am Fri & Sat) is the best place for bands; **Tig Cóilí** (www.tigcoiligalway.com; Mainguard St; ⊙10.30am-11.30pm Mon-Thu, 10.30am-12.30am Fri & Sat, 12.30pm-11pm Sun) excels at trad sessions.

Urban Grind   CAFE €
(www.urbangrind.ie; 8 West William St; dishes €3.50-8.50; ⊙8am-6pm Mon-Wed, 8am-11pm Thu & Fri, 9am-11pm Sat Jun–mid-Sep, 8am-6pm Mon-Fri, 9am-6pm Sat mid-Sep–May) Creative hub Urban Grind whips up fantastic breakfasts (cinnamon porridge; organic ciabatta with grilled chorizo and poached egg) and lunches (black and white bean tortilla with avocado and lime mayo; glazed beef brisket with horseradish relish), and brews some of Galway's best coffees and loose-leaf teas. Craft beers and boutique wines are served until late Thursday to Saturday in summer.

McCambridge's   CAFE, DELI €
(www.mccambridges.com; 38/39 Shop St; dishes €5-14; ⊙cafe 8.30am-5.30pm Mon-Wed, 8.30am-9pm Thu-Sat, 9.30am-6pm Sun, deli 8am-7pm Mon-Wed, 8am-9pm Thu-Sat, 9.30am-6pm Sun) Superb prepared salads are among the perfect picnic ingredients at this gourmet food emporium. All high ceilings, blond wood and busy staff, the upstairs cafe is lovely with a changing menu of modern Irish fare such as Galway Hooker beef stew, and over 100 craft beers from Ireland's west. Brunch is served until 4.30pm on Sunday.

★ Crane Bar   PUB
(www.thecranebar.com; 2 Sea Rd; ⊙10.30am-11.30pm Mon-Fri, 10.30am-12.30am Sat, 12.30pm-11pm Sun) West of the Corrib, this atmospheric, always crammed two-storey pub is the best spot in Galway to catch an informal *céilidh* (traditional music and dancing session). Music on both levels starts at 9.30pm.

★ Tigh Neachtain   PUB
(www.tighneachtain.com; 17 Upper Cross St; ⊙11.30am-midnight Mon-Thu, 11.30am-1am Fri, 10.30am-1am Sat, 12.30-11.30pm Sun) Painted a bright cornflower blue, this 19th-century corner pub – known simply as Neáchtain's (*nock*-tans) or Naughtons – has a wraparound terrace for watching Galway's passing parade, and a timber-lined interior with a roaring open fire, snugs and atmosphere to spare. Along with perfectly pulled pints of Guinness and 130-plus whiskeys, it has its own range of beers brewed by Galway Hooker.

❶ Information

Galway Tourist Office (☑091-537 700; www.discoverireland.ie; Forster St; ⊙9am-5pm Mon-Sat) Galway's large, efficient tourist office can help arrange tours and has reams of information on the city and region.

❶ Getting There & Around

BICYCLE
Galway's bike-share scheme (www.bikeshare.ie/galway.html) has 16 stations around town. For visitors, €3 (with €150 deposit) gets you a three-day pass. The first 30 minutes of each hire is free; up to two hours is €1.50.

BUS
Bus Éireann (www.buseireann.ie) operates daily services to all major cities in the Republic and the North from **Cara Bus Station** (☑091-562

WORTH A TRIP

CLIFFS OF MOHER

Star of a million tourist brochures, the Cliffs of Moher in County Clare are one of the most popular sights in Ireland. But like many an ageing star, you have to look beyond the famous facade to appreciate its inherent attributes. In summer the site is overrun with day trippers, but there are good rewards if you're willing to walk along the cliff tops for 10 minutes to escape the crowds.

The landscaped **Cliffs of Moher Visitor Centre** (☑065-708 6141; www.cliffsofmoher.ie; adult/child incl parking €6/free, O'Brien's Tower €2/1; ⊙9am-9pm Jul & Aug, 9am-7.30pm Mon-Fri, to 8pm Sat & Sun Jun & Sep, shorter hours rest of year) has exhibitions about the cliffs and their natural history. A number of bus tours leave Galway every morning for here, including **Lally Tours** (☑091-562 905; http://lallytours.com; tours adult/child from €25/15).

000; Station Rd), near the train station. Services include Dublin (€15.70, 3¾ hours, hourly) and Dublin Airport (€15.50, four hours, hourly). **Citylink** (www.citylink.ie; ticket office 17 Forster St; ⊙office 9am-6pm; 🛜) services depart from **Galway Coach Station** (New Coach Station; Fairgreen Rd). Destinations include Cork (€22, three hours, five daily), Dublin (€15, 2½ hours, hourly) and Dublin Airport (€21, 2½ hours, hourly). Also from Galway Coach Station, **GoBus** (www.gobus.ie; Galway Coach Station; 🛜) has frequent services to and from Dublin (3½ hours) and Dublin Airport (three hours). Fares start at €18.

TRAIN

From the train station, just off Eyre Sq, Irish Rail (www.irishrail.ie) runs up to 10 direct trains daily to/from Dublin's Heuston Station (from €18, 2¼ hours).

Connemara

With its shimmering black lakes, pale mountains, lonely valleys and more than the occasional rainbow, Connemara in the northwestern corner of County Galway is one of Ireland's most gorgeous corners. It's prime hill-walking country with plenty of wild terrain, none more so than the Twelve Bens, a ridge of rugged mountains that form part of **Connemara National Park** (www.connemaranationalpark.ie; off N59; ⊙24hr) FREE.

Connemara's 'capital', **Clifden** (An Clochán), is an appealing Victorian-era country town with an oval of streets offering evocative strolls. The **Sky Road** is a spectacular 15km cycling and driving route looping out to the township of Kingston and back to Clifden, taking in some rugged, stunningly beautiful coastal scenery en route. Set out clockwise from the southern side for the best views, which peak at sunset.

🛏 Sleeping & Eating

Clifden Bay Hostel   HOSTEL €
(🗭087 776 9345; http://clifdenbayhostel; 1 Market St; dm €17-23; ⊙reception 9am-5pm) Right in the centre of town, this cheery hostel is set in a cream-coloured house framed by big picture windows, with sunlit rooms and 34 beds. The adjoining bar has wi-fi and live music until late most nights.

Connemara Hamper   DELI €
(www.connemarahamper.com; Market St; dishes €3-8.50; ⊙9.30am-6pm Mon-Sat year-round, noon-6pm Sun Jul & Aug) Irish farmhouse cheeses, Connemara smoked salmon, pâtés, dips, jams, chutneys, savoury ready-to-eat dishes such as chicken-and-leek pies and sweet treats including cakes and biscuits from this terrific deli make ideal picnic ingredients, along with all-natural wines.

ℹ Information

Tourist Office (www.discoverireland.ie; Galway Rd/N59; ⊙9.30am-6pm Easter–mid-Oct) Helpful staff at Clifden's seasonal tourist office can suggest activities including walking routes.

ℹ Getting There & Away

Bus Éireann (www.buseireann.ie) and Citylink (www.citylink.ie) have several services daily to and from Galway. Fares start at €15.50 and the trip takes 90 minutes (two hours on the Bus Éireann service, which goes via Roundstone).

Northern Ireland

POP 1.85 MILLION

An exploding food scene, hip cities and the stunning Causeway Coast: there's plenty to pull visitors to the North. When you cross from the Republic into Northern Ireland you'll notice a couple of changes: the road signs are in miles and the prices are in pounds sterling – you're in the UK. At the time of research, there was no border checkpoint and not even a sign to mark the crossing point.

Brexit may change all that. Negotiations with the EU are unlikely to be finalised any time soon, but border towns are bracing themselves for the possible return of a 'hard border' with passport and custom controls. It's a bitter pill to swallow for a province that voted to remain in the EU. The issue brings renewed uncertainty, but nobody wants to see a return to the violence of the Troubles that ended with the Good Friday Agreement two decades ago. An atmosphere of determined optimism remains.

Belfast

POP 333,000

Belfast is in many ways a brand-new city. Once shunned by travellers unnerved by tales of the Troubles and sectarian violence, in recent years it has pulled off a remarkable transformation from bombs-and-bullets pariah to a hip-hotels-and-hedonism party town.

The old shipyards on the Lagan continue to give way to the luxury apartments of the Titanic Quarter, whose centrepiece – the stunning, star-shaped edifice housing the Titanic Belfast centre, covering the ill-fated liner's construction here – has become the city's number-one tourist draw; it was even named the world's leading tourist attraction at the 2016 World Travel Awards.

New venues keep popping up – already this decade historic Crumlin Road Gaol and SS *Nomadic* opened to the public. They all add to a list of attractions that includes beautifully restored Victorian architecture, a glittering waterfront lined with modern art, a fantastic and fast-expanding foodie scene and music-filled pubs.

◉ Sights

★ Titanic Belfast
MUSEUM
(www.titanicbelfast.com; Queen's Rd; adult/child £18/8; ⊙9am-7pm Jun-Aug, to 6pm Apr, May & Sep, 10am-5pm Oct-Mar; ⌂Abercorn Basin) The head of the slipway where the *Titanic* was built is now occupied by the gleaming, angular edifice of Titanic Belfast, an unmissable multimedia extravaganza that charts the history of Belfast and the creation of the world's most famous ocean liner. Cleverly designed exhibits enlivened by historical images, animated projections and soundtracks chart Belfast's rise to turn-of-the-20th-century industrial superpower, followed by a high-tech ride through a noisy, smells-and-all recreation of the city's shipyards. Tickets also include entry to the **SS Nomadic** (www.nomadicbelfast.com; Hamilton Dock, Queen's Rd; adult/child £7/5; ⊙9am-7pm Jun-Aug, to 6pm Apr, May & Sep, 10am-5pm Oct-Mar). Built in Belfast in 1911, this little steamship is the last remaining vessel of the White Star Line. It once ferried 1st- and 2nd-class passengers between Cherbourg Harbour and the ocean liners that were too big to dock at the French port.

★ Ulster Museum
MUSEUM
(www.nmni.com; Botanic Gardens; ⊙10am-5pm Tue-Sun; ♿; ⌂Botanic) FREE You could spend hours browsing this state-of-the-art museum, but if you're pressed for time don't miss the **Armada Room**, with artefacts retrieved from the 1588 wreck of the Spanish galleon *Girona;* the **Egyptian Room**, with Takabuti, a 2500-year-old Egyptian mummy unwrapped in Belfast in 1835; and the **Early Peoples Gallery**, with the bronze Bann Disc, a superb example of Celtic design from the Iron Age.

★ Ulster Folk Museum
MUSEUM
(http://nmni.com/uftm; Cultra; folk museum adult/child £9/5.50, transport & folk museum £11/6; ⊙10am-5pm Tue-Sun Mar-Sep, 10am-4pm Tue-Fri, 11am-4pm Sat & Sun Oct-Feb; ♿; ⌂Cultra) Farmhouses, forges, churches, mills and a complete village have been reconstructed at this excellent museum, with human and animal extras combining to give a powerful impression of Irish life over the past few hundred years. From industrial times, there are redbrick terraces from 19th-century Belfast and Dromore. Another highlight is the **Picture House**, a silent cinema that was housed in a County Down hayloft from 1909 to 1931. There's even a corner shop dating from 1889 selling sweets from glass jars.

★ Crown Liquor Saloon
HISTORIC BUILDING
(www.nationaltrust.org.uk/the-crown-bar; 46 Great Victoria St; ⊙11.30am-11pm Mon-Sat, 12.30-10pm Sun; ⌂Europa Bus Centre) FREE There are not many historical monuments that you can enjoy while savouring a pint of beer, but the National Trust's Crown Liquor Saloon is one of them. Belfast's most famous bar was refurbished by Patrick Flanagan in the late 19th century and displays Victorian decorative flamboyance at its best (he was looking to pull in a posh clientele from the train station and Grand Opera House opposite). Despite being a tourist attraction, the bar fills up with locals come 6pm.

★ Cave Hill Country Park
PARK
(www.belfastcity.gov.uk; Antrim Rd; ⊙7.30am-dusk; ⌂1A to 1G) FREE The view from the summit of Cave Hill (368m) takes in the whole sprawl of the city, the docks, Belfast Lough and the Mourne Mountains – on a clear day you can see Scotland. Cave Hill Country Park spreads across the hill's eastern slopes, with several waymarked walks and an **adventure playground** (☎028-9077 6925;

ⓘ BELFAST VISITOR PASS

The **Belfast Visitor Pass** (per one/two/three days £6.50/11/14.50) allows unlimited travel on bus and train services in Belfast and around, and discounts on admission to Titanic Belfast and other attractions. You can buy it online at www.translink.co.uk and at airports, main train and bus stations, the Metro kiosk on Donegall Sq and the Visit Belfast Welcome Centre.

Belfast

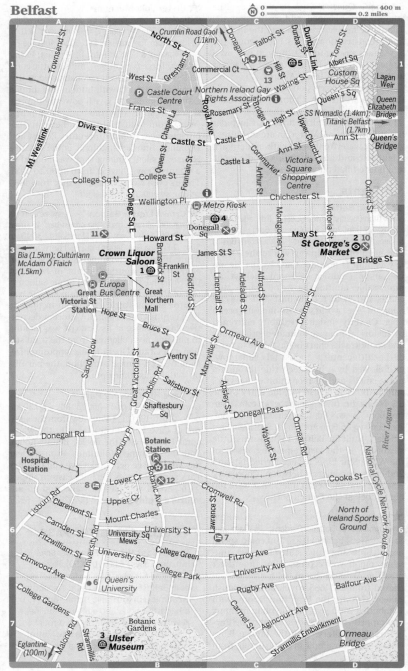

Belfast

◎ Top Sights
1 Crown Liquor Saloon B3
2 St George's Market D3
3 Ulster Museum A7

◎ Sights
4 City Hall C3
5 Oh Yeah Music Centre C1

⊕ Activities, Courses & Tours
6 Belfast Bike Tours A7

🛏 Sleeping
7 Global Village Backpackers C6
8 Vagabonds A6

✗ Eating
9 Bobbin Coffee Shop C3
10 George's of the Market D3
11 John Long's A3
12 Maggie May's B5

🍷 Drinking & Nightlife
13 Duke of York C1
14 Filthy Quarter B4
15 John Hewitt C1

✪ Entertainment
16 Belfast Empire B5

child 3-14yr £2.50; ⊙ 10am-8pm Jul & Aug, shorter hours Apr-Jun & Sep, Sat & Sun only Oct-Mar; ➡ 1A to 1G).

★ **St George's Market**   MARKET
(www.belfastcity.gov.uk; cnr Oxford & May Sts; ⊙ 6am-3pm Fri, 9am-3pm Sat, 10am-4pm Sun; ➡ Belfast Central) Ireland's oldest continually operating market was built in 1896. This Victorian beauty hosts a Friday **variety market** (flowers, produce, meat, fish, homewares and second-hand goods), a Saturday **food and craft market** (food stalls to look out for include Suki Tea, Ann's Pantry bakers and Hillstown Farm) and a **Sunday market** (food, local arts and crafts and live music). **George's of the Market** (✆ 028-9024 0014; http://georgesbelfast.com; Oxford St; brunch £3.50-8, express lunch £7, dinner £12.50-25; ⊙ 10am-2.30pm Tue, 10am-2.30pm & 5-9.30pm Wed-Sat, 10am-4pm Sun; ➡ Belfast Central) ➴ overlooks the action.

★ **Crumlin Road Gaol**   HISTORIC BUILDING
(✆ 028-9074 1500; www.crumlinroadgaol.com; 53-55 Crumlin Rd; tour adult/child £9/6.50; ⊙ 10am-5.30pm, last tour 4.30pm; ➡ Agnes St) Guided tours of Belfast's notorious Crumlin Road Gaol take you from the tunnel beneath Crumlin Rd, built in 1850 to convey prisoners from the courthouse across the street (and allegedly the origin of the judge's phrase 'take him down'), through the echoing halls and cramped cells of C-Wing, to the truly chilling execution chamber. Advance tour bookings are recommended. The jail's pedestrian entrance is on Crumlin Rd; the car-park entrance is reached via Cliftonpark Ave to the north.

☞ Tours

Black taxi tours of West Belfast's murals are offered by a large number of taxi companies and local cabbies. These can vary in quality and content, but in general they're an intimate and entertaining way to see the sights. Drivers will pick you up from anywhere in the city centre.

Several companies also offer day-long bus tours around filming locations used for *Game of Thrones* – visit https://discovernorthernireland.com/explore/game-of-thrones-guided-tours.

🛏 Sleeping

★ **Vagabonds**   HOSTEL €
(✆ 028-9023 3017; www.vagabondsbelfast.com; 9 University Rd; dm £15-17, d & tw £50; @ 🛜; ➡ Shaftesbury Sq) Comfy bunks, lockable luggage baskets, private shower cubicles, a beer garden, a pool table and a relaxed atmosphere are what you get at one of Belfast's best hostels, run by a couple of experienced travellers. It's conveniently located close to both Queen's and the city centre.

Global Village Backpackers   HOSTEL €
(✆ 028-9031 3533; http://globalvillagebelfast.com; 87 University St; dm £14.50-16.50, d £44; @ 🛜; ➡ Botanic Ave) In a 19th-century brick terrace house close to Queen's University, Global Village combines period fireplaces and stained-glass windows with bright wall murals and wall-mounted guitars. There's a sociable kitchen and dining area, a beer garden and a barbecue.

✗ Eating

Maggie May's   CAFE €
(✆ 028-9032 2662; www.maggiemaysbelfastcafe.co.uk; 50 Botanic Ave; mains £4.50-7.50; ⊙ 8am-11pm Mon-Sat, 9am-11pm Sun; ✔ ➴; ➡ Botanic) This is a classic little cafe with cosy wooden booths, murals of old Belfast and a host of hungover students wolfing down huge

Ulster fry-ups. The all-day breakfast menu includes French toast and pancake stacks, while lunch can be soup and a sandwich or a burger.

John Long's   FISH & CHIPS €

(☏ 028-9032 1848; www.johnlongs.com; 39 Athol St; fish & chips £4.50-7; ⏱ 11.45am-6.30pm Mon-Fri, to 6pm Sat; 🚇 Europa Bus Centre) A wonderfully down-to-earth Belfast institution, this 1914-opened chippie is hidden in an inconspicuous red-brick building adjoining a car park, and is covered in mesh grills (a legacy of having its windows blown out when the nearby Europa Hotel was bombed). Inside, it fries up classic cod and chips in beef dripping, served at 1970s Formica booths. Cash only.

Bobbin Coffee Shop   CAFE €

(www.loafcatering.com; Donegall Sq S; mains £3.50-7.50; ⏱ 9am-5pm Mon-Wed & Fri, to 7.30pm Thu, 10am-5pm Sat & Sun; 🚼; 🚇 Donegall Sq) The elegant cafe inside Belfast's City Hall (www.belfastcity.gov.uk; Donegall Sq; ⏱ guided tours 11am, 2pm & 3pm Mon-Fri, noon, 2pm & 3pm Sat & Sun Oct-May, plus 10am & 4pm Mon-Fri, 4pm Sat & Sun Jun-Sep; 🚇 Donegall Sq) FREE is run by the social enterprise and catering company Loaf, which provides training and work experience for people with learning disabilities and autism. The wholesome, fresh-baked goods and meals include sausage rolls with home-made relish, Irish stew, sandwiches and toasties.

Bia   CAFE €

(☏ 028-9096 4184; www.culturlann.ie; 216 Falls Rd; mains £8-22; ⏱ 9am-6pm Mon-Thu, to 9pm Fri & Sat, 10am-4pm Sun; 🚼🚼; 🚇 Broadway) Inside the Irish-language and arts centre Cultúrlann McAdam Ó Fiaich (www.culturlann.ie; ⏱ 9am-5.30pm Mon-Fri, 9.30am-5pm Sat, 1-4pm Sun) FREE, Bia (meaning 'food') serves home-cooked stews, soups, roasts, steaks, burgers and lighter bites such as cakes, scones and pastries.

🍷 Drinking & Nightlife

★ Duke of York   PUB

(☏ 028-9024 1062; www.dukeofyorkbelfast.com; 11 Commercial Ct; ⏱ 11.30am-midnight Mon, to 1am Tue-Sat, 1-9pm Sun; 🚇 Queen's Sq) In a cobbled alleyway off buzzing Hill St, the snug, traditional Duke feels like a living museum. There's regular live music; local band Snow Patrol played some of their earliest gigs here. Outside on Commercial Ct, a canopy of umbrellas leads to an outdoor area covered

with murals depicting Belfast life; it takes on a street-party atmosphere in warm weather.

★ John Hewitt   PUB

(www.thejohnhewitt.com; 51 Donegall St; ⏱ 11.30am-1am Mon-Fri, noon-1am Sat, 7pm-1am Sun; 🚇 Queen's Sq) Named for the Belfast poet and socialist, the John Hewitt is one of those treasured bars that has no TV or gaming machines, just the murmur of conversation. It's a good place to try Jawbox gin, made by the bar's owner Gerry White, and craft beers from Lisburn's Hilden brewery (☏ 028-9266 0800; www.hildenbrewery.com; Hilden House, Grand St; tour £10; ⏱ tours by reservation noon Wed-Fri). There are regular sessions of folk, jazz and bluegrass from 9pm.

Eglantine   PUB

(www.eglantinebar.com; 32 Malone Rd; ⏱ 11.30am-midnight Sun-Tue, to 1am Wed-Sat; 📶; 🚇 Eglantine Ave) The 'Eg' is a local institution, and widely reckoned to be the best of Belfast's many student pubs. It serves good beer and decent food, and hosts numerous events: Monday is quiz night and Tuesday is open-mic night; other nights see DJs spin and bands perform. Bonus: *Pac-Man* machine.

★ Filthy Quarter   BAR

(www.thefilthyquarter.com; 45 Dublin Rd; ⏱ 1pm-1am Mon-Sat, to midnight Sun; 🚇 Dublin Rd) Four individually and collectively fabulous bars make up the Filthy Quarter: retro-trad-style, bric-a-brac-filled Filthy McNastys, hosting local musicians from 10pm nightly; the fairy-lit Secret Garden, a two-storey beer garden with watering cans for drinks coolers; Gypsy Lounge (Tuesday, Thursday, Friday, Saturday and Sunday nights), with a gypsy caravan DJ booth; and a chandelier- and candelabra-adorned cocktail bar, Filthy Chic.

☆ Entertainment

A good place to get the low-down on live music and club nights is the Oh Yeah Music Centre (www.ohyeahbelfast.com; 15-21 Gordon St; ⏱ museum 11am-3pm Mon-Fri, noon-5pm Sat; 🚇 Queen's Sq) FREE.

Other resources include the Visit Belfast Welcome Centre, Big List (www.thebiglist.co.uk) and Culture Northern Ireland (www.culturenorthernireland.org).

★ Belfast Empire   LIVE MUSIC

(www.thebelfastempire.com; 42 Botanic Ave; entry live bands £3-22.50; ⏱ 11.30am-1am Mon-Sat,

12.30pm-midnight Sun; Botanic) A converted late-Victorian church (reputed to be haunted) with three floors of entertainment, the Empire is a legendary live-music venue. Look out for stand-up comedy and quiz nights too.

ⓘ Information

Visit Belfast Welcome Centre (028-9024 6609; http://visit-belfast.com; 9 Donegall Sq N; ⊙9am-7pm Mon-Sat, 11am-4pm Sun Jun-Sep, 9am-5.30pm Mon-Sat, 11am-4pm Sun Oct-May; ; Donegall Sq) Provides stacks of information about the whole of Northern Ireland and books accommodation. Services include left luggage (not overnight), currency exchange and free wi-fi. There's also a gift shop selling local crafts and souvenirs.

ⓘ Getting There & Away

Contact **Translink** (028-9066 6630; www.translink.co.uk; Europa Bus Centre) for timetable and fares information for buses and trains.

AIR

Belfast International Airport (Aldergrove; 028-9448 4848; www.belfastairport.com; Airport Rd) is 30km northwest of the city; **George Best Belfast City Airport** (BHD; 028-9093 9093; www.belfastcityairport.com; Airport Rd) is 6km northeast of the city centre.

BOAT

Apart from services with **Stena Line** (08447 707070; www.stenaline.co.uk; Victorial Terminal, 4 West Bank Rd; trips from £79; 96) and **Steam Packet Company** (08722 992 992; www.steam-packet.com; Albert Quay; return fares from £87), car ferries to and from Scotland and England dock at Larne, 37km north of Belfast. Trains to the terminal at Larne Harbour depart from Great Victoria St station.

BUS

There is an **information point** (Great Victoria St, Great Northern Mall; ⊙8am-6pm Mon-Fri, 8.30am-5pm Sat) at Belfast's **Europa Bus Centre** (028-9066 6630; www.translink.co.uk; ⊙5am-11pm Mon-Fri, 5.45am-11pm Sat, to 10.15pm Sun), where you can pick up regional bus timetables. Contact **Translink** for timetable and fares information.

National Express (0871 781 8181; www.nationalexpress.com) runs a daily coach service between Belfast and London via the Cairnryan ferry, Dumfries, Manchester and Birmingham. **Scottish Citylink** (0871 266 3333; www.citylink.co.uk) operates three buses a day from Glasgow to Belfast, via the Cairnryan ferry.

TRAIN

Belfast has two main train stations: **Great Victoria St** (Great Victoria St, Great Northern Mall) and **Belfast Central** (East Bridge St). If you arrive by train at Central Station, your rail ticket entitles you to a free bus ride into the city centre. A local train also connects with Great Victoria St.

Destinations offered by **Northern Ireland Railways** (NIR; 028-9066 6630; www.translink.co.uk/Services/NI-Railways) include Dublin (£30, 2¼ hours, eight daily Monday to Saturday, five Sunday).

ⓘ Getting Around

TO/FROM THE AIRPORT

Belfast International Airport Airport Express 300 bus runs to the Europa Bus Centre (one way/return £7.50/10.50, 30 to 55 minutes). The first bus from Belfast/the airport is at 4.20am/4.55am, then buses run at least once an hour until 11.30pm (from Belfast) and 12.15am (from the airport). A taxi costs about £30.

George Best Belfast City Airport Airport Express 600 bus runs to the Europa Bus Centre (one way/return £2.50/3.80, 15 minutes) every 20 minutes between 6am and 9.30pm Monday to Saturday, and every 40 minutes on Sunday. A return ticket is valid for one month. A taxi fare to the city centre is about £10.

BICYCLE

Belfast Bikes (034-3357 1551; www.belfastbikes.co.uk; registration per 3 days £5, bikes per 30min/1hr/2hr/3hr free/£0.50/1.50/2.50; ⊙24hr) Belfast's bike-share scheme provides bikes at 40 docking stations throughout the city. Register online or via the app. If the bike is lost, stolen or damaged, your credit card will be charged £120.

Belfast Bike Tours (07812 114235; www.belfastbiketours.com; £15; ⊙10.30am & 2pm Mon, Wed, Fri & Sat Apr-Aug, Sat only Sep-Mar; Queen's University) Guided tours; also rents out bikes.

BUS

Metro (028-9066 6630; www.translink.co.uk) operates Belfast's bus network. Most city services depart from various stops on and around Donegall Sq, at City Hall and along Queen St. You can pick up a free bus map (and buy tickets) from the **Metro kiosk** (Donegall Sq; ⊙8am-5.30pm Mon-Fri) at the northwest corner of the square.

Buy your ticket from the driver (change given); fares within the city zone are £2. You can also buy Metro dayLink Cards (£3.50) from the Metro kiosk, the **Visit Belfast Welcome Centre** or the **Europa Bus Centre**, giving you unlimited bus travel within the City Zone all day Monday to Saturday.

If you plan on using city buses a lot, it's worth buying a Metro Smartlink Travel Card (available from the same places). The card costs an initial fee of £1, plus £10.50 per 10 journeys – you can get it topped up as you want. When you board the bus, you simply place the card on top of the ticket machine and it automatically issues a ticket.

The Causeway Coast

Ireland isn't short of scenic coastlines, but the Causeway Coast between Portstewart and Ballycastle – climaxing in the spectacular rock formations of the Giant's Causeway – and the Antrim Coast between Ballycastle and Belfast are as magnificent as they come.

◉ Sights

★ **Giant's Causeway**   LANDMARK
(www.nationaltrust.org.uk; ⊙ dawn-dusk) FREE
This spectacular rock formation – Northern Ireland's only Unesco World Heritage site – is one of Ireland's most impressive and atmospheric landscape features, a vast expanse of regular, closely packed, hexagonal stone columns looking for all the world like the handiwork of giants. The phenomenon is explained in the **Giant's Causeway Visitor Experience** (☑ 028-2073 1855; 60 Causeway Rd; adult/child £10.50/5.25; ⊙ 9am-7pm Jul & Aug, to 6pm Mar-Jun, Sep & Oct, to 5pm Nov-Feb) ✎, housed in a new, ecofriendly building half-hidden in a hillside above the sea. Visiting the Giant's Causeway itself is free of charge, but you pay to use the car park on a combined ticket with the visitor centre; parking-only tickets aren't available. The Visitor Experience admission fee is reduced by £1.50 if you arrive by bus, by bike or on foot.

From the centre it's an easy 10- to 15-minute walk downhill to the Causeway itself, but a more interesting approach is to follow the clifftop path, then descend the Shepherd's Steps. For the less mobile, a minibus shuttles from the visitor centre to the Causeway (£2 return).

🛏 Sleeping

There are several hostels along the coast, including the excellent **Sheep Island View Hostel** (☑ 028-2076 9391; www.sheepislandview. com; 42A Main St; dm/s/tw £18/25/45; P @ 🕏), **Ballycastle Backpackers** (☑ 028-2076 3612; www.ballycastlebackpackers.net; 4 North St; dm/tw from £17.50/35, cottages £80; P @ 🕏) and **Bushmills Hostel** (☑ 028-2073 1222; www.

hini.org.uk; 49 Main St; dm £16-20, tr £53; ⊙ closed 11.30am-2.30pm Jul & Aug, 11.30am-5pm Mar-Jun, Sep & Oct; @ 🕏).

ℹ Getting There & Away

As well as the seasonal bus services **Antrim Coaster** (Bus 252; ☑ 028-9066 6630; www.translink.co.uk; Bus Rambler unlimited day travel adult/child £9/4.50; ⊙ Easter, May bank-holiday weekends, Jul & Aug; 🕏) and **Causeway Rambler** (Bus 402; ☑ 028-9066 6630; www.translink.co.uk; Bus Rambler unlimited day travel adult/child £9/4.50; ⊙ Easter-Sep), and the **Giant's Causeway & Bushmills Railway** (☑ 028-2073 2844; infogcbr@btconnect.com; return adult/child £5/3), bus 172 from Ballycastle (£4.40, 30 minutes, eight daily Monday to Friday, three Saturday and Sunday) to Coleraine (£4.40, 25 minutes) and Bushmills (£2, five minutes) stops here year-round. From Coleraine, trains run to Belfast or Derry.

Derry/Londonderry

POP 107,900

Northern Ireland's second-largest city continues to flourish as an artistic and cultural hub. Derry's city centre was given a striking makeover for its year as the UK City of Culture 2013, with the new Peace Bridge, Ebrington Sq, and the redevelopment of the waterfront and Guildhall area making the most of the city's splendid riverside setting.

There's lots of history to absorb here, from the Siege of Derry to the Battle of the Bogside and Bloody Sunday – a stroll around the 17th-century city walls that encircle the city is a must, as is a tour of the Bogside murals – along with taking in the burgeoning live-music scene in the city's lively pubs.

◉ Sights

★ **Derry's City Walls**   WALLS
(⊙ dawn-dusk) FREE The best way to get a feel for Derry's layout and history is to walk the 1.5km circumference of the city's walls. Completed in 1619, Derry's city walls are 8m high and 9m thick, and are the only city walls in Ireland to survive almost intact. The four original gates (Shipquay, Ferryquay, Bishop's and Butcher's) were rebuilt in the 18th and 19th centuries, when three new gates (New, Magazine and Castle) were added.

★ **Guildhall**   NOTABLE BUILDING
(☑ 028-7137 6510; www.derrystrabane.com/Guildhall; Guildhall St; ⊙ 10am-5.30pm) FREE
Standing just outside the city walls, the neo-Gothic Guildhall was originally built in

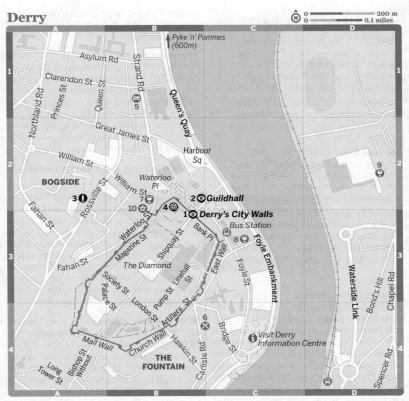

Derry

1890, then rebuilt after a fire in 1908. Its fine stained-glass windows were presented by the London livery companies, and its clock tower was modelled on London's Big Ben. Inside, there's a historical exhibition on the Plantation of Ulster, and a tourist information point.

Tower Museum MUSEUM
(www.derrystrabane.com/towermuseum; Union Hall Pl; adult/child £4/2; ⊙10am-5.30pm, last entry 4pm) Head straight to the 5th floor of this award-winning museum inside a replica 16th-century tower house for a view from the top. Then work your way down through the excellent **Armada Shipwreck** exhibition, and the **Story of Derry**, where well-thought-out exhibits and audiovisuals lead you through the city's history, from the founding of the monastery of St Colmcille (Columba) in the 6th century to the Battle of the Bogside in the late 1960s. Allow at least two hours.

OTHER IRISH HIGHLIGHTS

Dingle (65km west of Killarney) The charms of this special spot have long drawn runaways from across the world, making this port town a surprisingly cosmopolitan and creative place.

Glendalough (50km south of Dublin) Nestled between two lakes, this lovely spot is one of Ireland's most significant monastic sites.

Kinsale (28km south of Cork) This picturesque yachting harbour has been labelled the gourmet capital of Ireland; it certainly contains more than its fair share of international-standard restaurants.

Slieve League (120km southwest of Derry/Londonderry) Spend a day walking along the top of these awe-inspiring cliffs via the slightly terrifying One Man's Path to Malinbeg, near Glencolumbcille.

People's Gallery Murals PUBLIC ART
(Rossville St) The 12 murals that decorate the gable ends of houses along Rossville St, near Free Derry Corner, are popularly referred to as the People's Gallery. They are the work of 'the Bogside Artists' (Kevin Hasson, Tom Kelly, and Will Kelly, who passed away in 2017). The three men lived through the worst of the Troubles in Bogside. The murals can be clearly seen from the northern part of the City Walls.

🛏 Sleeping & Eating

Hostel Connect HOSTEL €
(☎ 028-7137 2101; http://hostelconnect.co.uk; 51 Strand Rd; dm £15-18, d £44-48; @ 🖭) This bright, centrally located hostel offers small but neat doubles and twins as well as six-, nine- and 15-bed dorms with wooden bunks. There's a big living room and a kitchen for preparing meals, and a breakfast of bagels, fruit and toast is included. All rooms share bathrooms.

★ Pyke 'n' Pommes STREET FOOD €
(www.pykenpommes.ie; behind Foyle Marina, off Baronet St; mains £4-16; ☺ noon-5pm Fri & Sat, to 4pm Sun-Thu; 🖉 🖭) 🍴 Derry's single-best eatery is this quayside shipping container. Chef Kevin Pyke's delectable, mostly organic burgers span his signature Notorious PIG (pulled pork, crispy slaw, beetroot and crème fraîche) and Veganderry (chickpeas, lemon and coriander) to his Legenderry

Burger (Wagyu beef, pickled onions and honey-mustard mayo). His Pykeos fish tacos are another hit.

Primrose Cafe CAFE €
(www.facebook.com/primrosederry; 15 Carlisle Rd; dishes £3.50-7; ☺ 8am-5pm Mon-Sat, 10am-5pm Sun; 🖭) The Primrose prospers by sticking to the classics and doing them really well: scones, cookies, cheesecake, gateau and meringue pie, all baked fresh daily, plus brunch items like waffles, Greencastle smoked kipper and avocado French toast.

🍷 Drinking & Entertainment

★ Peadar O'Donnell's PUB
(www.peadars.com; 59-63 Waterloo St; ☺ 11.30am-1.30am Mon-Sat, 12.30pm-12.30am Sun) Done up as a typical Irish pub/grocery (with shelves of household items, shopkeeper's scales on the counter and a museum's-worth of old bric-a-brac), Peadar's has rowdy traditional-music sessions every night and often on weekend afternoons as well. Its adjacent **Gweedore Bar** hosts live rock bands every night, and a Saturday-night disco upstairs.

★ Walled City Brewery MICROBREWERY
(☎ 028-7134 3336; www.walledcitybrewery.com; 70 Ebrington Sq; ☺ 5-11pm Tue-Thu, 2.30-11.30pm Fri & Sat, 2-10pm Sun) Housed in the former army barracks on Ebrington Sq, Walled City Brewery is an exciting new craft brewery and restaurant run by master brewer and Derry local James Huey. As well as having 10 craft beers on tap, Walled City serves top-notch grub, such as house-smoked beer-braised pulled pork (mains £14 to £24).

Sandino's Cafe-Bar BAR
(http://sandinoscafebar.com; 1 Water St; ☺ 11.30am-1am Mon-Sat, noon-midnight Sun) From the posters of Che and the Free Palestine flag to the fairtrade coffee and gluten-free beer, this relaxed cafe-bar exudes a liberal, left-wing vibe. DJs spin from Thursday to Saturday in Club Havana; there's regular live music too.

ℹ Information

Visit Derry Information Centre (☎ 028-7126 7284; www.visitderry.com; 44 Foyle St; ☺ 9am-5.30pm Mon-Fri, 10am-5pm Sat & Sun; 🖭) A large tourist information centre with helpful staff and stacks of brochures for attractions in Derry and beyond. Also sells books and maps and can book accommodation. **Claudy Cycles** (☎ 028-7133 8128; www.claudycycles.com;

Visit Derry Information Centre; bike hire per half-/full day £8/12) can be rented here.

ℹ Getting There & Around

City of Derry Airport (☑ 028-7181 0784; www.cityofderryairport.com; Airport Rd, Eglinton) is about 13km east of Derry along the A2 towards Limavady. There are direct flights to London Stansted (daily), Liverpool (twice weekly) and Glasgow International (four days a week), plus summer routes to Spain.

The **bus station** (☑ 028-7126 2261; Foyle St) is just northeast of the walled city. Services include Belfast Europa Bus Centre (£12, 1¾ hours, half-hourly Monday to Friday, hourly Saturday and Sunday) and Galway (£16.50, 5½ hours, five daily).

Derry's train station is on the eastern side of the River Foyle; a free Rail Link bus connects it with the bus station. Services include Belfast (£12, 2½ hours, nine daily Monday to Saturday, six on Sunday).

Ireland Survival Guide

ℹ Directory A–Z

ACCOMMODATION

Hostels in Ireland can be booked solid in summer. An Óige (https://anoige.ie) and Hostelling International Northern Ireland (HINI; www.hini.org.uk) are branches of Hostelling International (HI); An Óige has 25 hostels in the Republic, while HINI has five in the North. Other hostel associations include Independent Holiday Hostels of Ireland (http://hostels-ireland.com) and the Independent Hostel of Ireland (www.independenthostelsireland.com).

From June to September a dorm bed at most hostels costs €12 to €25 (£10 to £18). Many hostels now have family and double rooms.

Typical B&Bs cost around €40 to €60 (£35 to £50) per person a night (sharing a double room), though more luxurious B&Bs can cost upwards of €70 (£60) per person. Most B&Bs are small, so in summer they quickly fill up.

Commercial campgrounds typically charge €15 and €25 (£12 to £20) for a tent or campervan and two people. Unless otherwise indicated, prices quoted for 'campsites' are for a tent, car and two people.

INTERNET RESOURCES

Entertainment Ireland (http://entertainment.ie) Countrywide entertainment listings.

Failte Ireland (www.discoverireland.ie) Official tourism site.

Tourism Northern Ireland (https://www.tourismni.com) Official tourism site.

LGBT TRAVELLERS

Resources include the following:

Cara-Friend (www.cara-friend.org.uk/projects/glyni) Voluntary LGBT counselling, information, health and social-space organisation.

Gaire (www.gaire.com) Message board and info for a host of gay-related issues.

National Lesbian & Gay Federation (NLGF; ☑ 01-671 9076; http://nxf.ie) Publishes the monthly *Gay Community News* (https://gcn.ie).

Northern Ireland Gay Rights Association (☑ 0771-957 6524; www.nigra.co.uk; Belfast LGBT Centre, 23-31 Waring St)

Outhouse (☑ 01-873 4932; www.outhouse.ie; 105 Capel St; ☐ all city centre) Top gay, lesbian and bisexual resource centre in Dublin.

OPENING HOURS

Hours in both the Republic and Northern Ireland are roughly the same.

Banks 10am to 4pm Monday to Friday (to 5pm Thursday)

Pubs 10.30am to 11.30pm Monday to Thursday, 10.30am to 12.30am Friday and Saturday, noon to 11pm Sunday (30 minutes 'drinking up' time allowed); closed Christmas Day and Good Friday

Restaurants Noon to 10.30pm; many close one day of the week

Shops 9.30am to 6pm Monday to Saturday (to 8pm Thursday in cities), noon to 6pm Sunday

PUBLIC HOLIDAYS

The following are public holidays in both the Republic and Northern Ireland:

New Year's Day 1 January

St Patrick's Day 17 March

Easter (Good Friday to Easter Monday inclusive) March/April

May Holiday 1st Monday in May

Christmas Day 25 December

St Stephen's Day (Boxing Day) 26 December

ℹ SLEEPING PRICE RANGES

Sleeping prices are listed at high-season rates (low-season rates can be 15% to 20% less), based on two people sharing a double, and include a private bathroom unless otherwise stated.

Republic of Ireland

€ less than €80

€€ €80–180

Northern Ireland

£ less than £50

££ £50–120

ⓘ EATING PRICE RANGES

Eating price indicators are used to indicate the cost of a main course at dinner:

Republic of Ireland

€ less than €12

€€ €12–25

Northern Ireland

£ less than £12

££ £12–20

St Patrick's Day and St Stephen's Day holidays are taken on the following Monday when they fall on a weekend. In the Republic, nearly everywhere closes on Good Friday even though it isn't an official public holiday. In the North, most shops open on Good Friday, but close the following Tuesday.

TELEPHONE

Area codes in the Republic have three digits except for Dublin, which has a two-digit code (01). Always use the area code if calling from a mobile phone, but you don't need it if calling from a fixed-line number within the area code.

In Northern Ireland, the area code for all fixed-line numbers is 028, but you only need to use it if calling from a mobile phone or from outside Northern Ireland. To call Northern Ireland from the Republic, use 048 instead of 028, without the international dialling code.

ⓘ Getting There & Away

AIR

Ireland's main airports:

Cork Airport (p114) Airlines servicing the airport include Aer Lingus and Ryanair.

Dublin Airport (p108) Ireland's major international gateway airport, with direct flights from the UK, Europe, North America and the Middle East.

Shannon Airport (SNN; ☑ 061-712 000; www.shannonairport.ie; ☎) In County Clare; has a few direct flights from the UK, Europe and North America.

Northern Ireland's airports:

Belfast International Airport (p125) Has direct flights from the UK, Europe and North America.

SEA

Competition from budget airlines has forced ferry operators to discount heavily and offer flexible fares.

A useful website is www.aferry.co.uk, which covers all sea-ferry routes and operators to Ireland. Main operators include the following:

Brittany Ferries (www.brittanyferries.com) Cork to Roscoff; April to October.

Irish Ferries (www.irishferries.com) Dublin to Holyhead ferries (up to four per day year-round); and France to Rosslare (three times per week).

P&O Ferries (www.poferries.com) Daily sailings year-round from Dublin to Liverpool, and Larne to Cairnryan. Larne to Troon runs March to October only.

Stena Line (www.stenaline.com) Daily sailings from Holyhead to Dublin Port, from Belfast to Liverpool and Cairnryan, and from Rosslare to Fishguard.

ⓘ Getting Around

BICYCLE

Ireland is a great cycling destination. However, dodgy weather, many very narrow roads and some very fast drivers are major concerns. A good tip for cyclists in the west is that the prevailing winds make it easier to cycle from south to north.

Buses will carry bikes, but only if there's room. For trains, bear in mind:

➡ Intercity trains charge up to €10 per bike.

➡ Book in advance (www.irishrail.ie), as there's only room for two bikes per service.

BUS

Bus Éireann (p108) The Republic's main line.

Translink (☑ 028-9066 6630; www.translink.co.uk) Northern Ireland's main bus service; includes Ulsterbus and Goldline.

CAR & MOTORCYCLE

Advance rates start at around €20 per day for a small car (unlimited mileage). Shop around and use price comparison sites as well as company sites (which often have deals not available on booking sites).

Other tips:

➡ Most cars are manual; automatic cars are available, but they're much more expensive to hire.

➡ If you're travelling the Republic into Northern Ireland, it's important to be sure that your insurance covers journeys to the North.

➡ The majority of hire companies won't rent you a car if you're under 23 and haven't had a valid driving licence for at least a year.

TRAIN

Irish Rail (Iarnród Éireann; ☑ 1850 366 222; www.irishrail.ie) Operates trains in the Republic.

Translink NI Railways (☑ 028-9066 6630; www.translink.co.uk) Operates trains in Northern Ireland.

Scandinavia

Best Places to Sleep

➡ Icehotel (p156)

➡ Generator Hostel (p135)

➡ Vandrarhem af Chapman & Skeppsholmen (p147)

➡ Pensjonat Jarlen (p180)

Best Places to Eat

➡ Høst (p141)

➡ Lysverket (p178)

➡ Slippurinn (p192)

➡ Kuu (p162)

Why Go?

Effortlessly chic cities and remote forests; rocking festivals and the majestic aurora borealis; endless day and perpetual night: Scandinavia's menu is anything but bland.

Stolid Nordic stereotypes dissolve in the region's vibrant capitals. Crest-of-the-wave design can be seen across them all, backed up by outstanding modern architecture, excellent museums, acclaimed restaurants and a sizzling nightlife.

The great outdoors is rarely greater than in Europe's big north. Epic expanses of wilderness and intoxicatingly pure air mean that engaging with nature is an utter pleasure. It's rare to find such inspiring landscapes that are so easily accessible.

Despite the scary subzero winter temperatures, there's still a wealth of things to do: skiing, sledding behind huskies or reindeer, taking snowmobile safaris, spending romantic nights in snow hotels, visiting Santa Claus and gazing at the soul-piercing northern lights.

Explosive summer's long days are filled with festivals, beer terraces and wonderful boating, hiking and cycling.

Fast Facts

Capitals Copenhagen (Denmark), Stockholm (Sweden), Helsinki (Finland), Oslo (Norway), Reykjavík (Iceland)

Emergency ☑112

Currency krone (Dkr, Denmark), krona (Skr, Sweden), euro (€, Finland), krone (Nkr, Norway), króna (Ikr, Iceland)

Languages Danish, Swedish, Finnish, Norwegian, Icelandic, Sámi languages

Time Zone Central European (Denmark, Sweden, Norway; UTC/GMT plus one hour), Eastern European (Finland; UTC/GMT plus two hours), Western European (Iceland; UTC/GMT)

Country Codes ☑45 (Denmark), ☑46 (Sweden), ☑358 (Finland), ☑47 (Norway), ☑354 (Iceland)

Population 5.7 million (Denmark), 9.9 million (Sweden), 5.5 million (Finland), 5.2 million (Norway), 334,300 (Iceland)

Scandinavia Highlights

1 Copenhagen
Shopping and noshing in Scandinavia's capital of cool. (p134)

2 Stockholm
Touring urban waterways, exploring t museums and wandering the Old Town. (p146)

3 Helsinki
Immersing yourself in Helsinki for the latest in Finnish design and nightlife. (p158)

4 Rovaniemi
Crossing the Arctic Circle, visiting the Arktikum museum, and Santa in Lapland. (p167)

5 Kiruna Hiking reindeer-filled landscapes, exploring Sámi culture and sleeping in the Icehotel. (p156)

6 Lofoten Heading for the Arctic Ocean and arguably Europe's most beautiful archipelago. (p181)

7 Hurtigruten
Journeying Norway's coast on the Hurtigruten ferry. (p181)

8 Fjordland
Exploring the southwestern fjords from Bergen. (p175)

9 Vatnajökull National Park
Discovering Skaftafell glacier and the icebergs at Jökulsárlón. (p194)

10 Reykjavík
Partying till dawn on the weekend pub crawl *djammið* in Iceland's lively capital, then hitting excellent museums, shops and cafes. (p184)

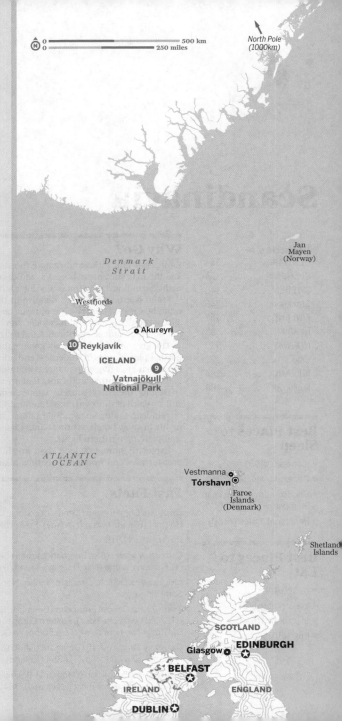

DENMARK

Copenhagen

POP 1.7 MILLION

Copenhagen is the coolest kid on the Nordic block. Edgier than Stockholm and worldlier than Oslo, the Danish capital gives Scandinavia the X-factor. While this 850-year-old harbour town has managed to retain much of its historic good looks – think copper spires and cobbled squares – the focus here is on the innovative and cutting edge. Denmark's over-achieving capital is home to a thriving design scene, its streets awash with effortlessly hip shops, cafes and bars, world-class museums and art collections, intelligent new architecture, and a galaxy of Michelin-starred restaurants.

◉ Sights

★**Tivoli Gardens**   AMUSEMENT PARK
(☑ 33 15 10 01; www.tivoligardens.com; Vesterbrogade 3; adult/child 3-7yr 120/50kr, Fri after 7pm 175/100kr; ◷ 11am-11pm Sun-Thu, to midnight Fri & Sat early Apr-late Sep, reduced hours rest of year; ⊞; ☐ 2A, 5C, 9A, 12, 14, 26, 250S, ⑤ København H) Dating from 1843, tasteful Tivoli wins fans with its dreamy whirl of amusement rides, twinkling pavilions, carnival games and open-air stage shows. Visitors can ride the renovated, century-old **roller coaster**, enjoy the famous Saturday evening **fireworks display** or just soak up the story-book atmosphere. A good tip is to go on Friday during summer when the open-air Plænen stage hosts free rock concerts by Danish bands (and the occasional international superstar) from 10pm – go early if it's a big-name act.

Indeed, Tivoli is at its most romantic after dusk, when the fairy lights are switched on, cultural activities unfold and the clock tower of the neighbouring Rådhus soars in the moonlight like the set of a classic Disney film.

ⓘ COPENHAGEN CARD

Copenhagen Card (www.copenhagencard.com; adult/child 10-15yr 24hr 389/199kr, 48hr 549/279kr, 72hr 659/329kr, 120hr 889/449kr) Discount tourist card offering admission to 79 museums and attractions, as well as free public transport. Each adult card includes up to two children aged under 10.

★**Nationalmuseet**   MUSEUM
(National Museum; ☑ 33 13 44 11; www.en.natmus.dk; Ny Vestergade 10; adult/child 85kr/free; ◷ 10am-5pm Tue-Sun; ⊞; ☐ 1A, 2A, 9A, 14, 26, 37, ⑤ København H) For a crash course in Danish history and culture, spend an afternoon at Denmark's National Museum. It has first claim on virtually every antiquity uncovered on Danish soil, including Stone Age tools, Viking weaponry, rune stones and medieval jewellery. Among the many highlights is a finely crafted 3500-year-old Sun Chariot, as well as bronze *lurs* (horns), some of which date back 3000 years and are still capable of blowing a tune.

Nyhavn   CANAL
(Nyhavn; ☐ 1A, 26, 66, 350S, Ⓜ Kongens Nytorv) There are few nicer places to be on a sunny day than sitting at an outdoor table at a cafe on the quayside of the Nyhavn canal. The canal was built to connect Kongens Nytorv to the harbour and was long a haunt for sailors and writers, including Hans Christian Andersen. He wrote *The Tinderbox, Little Claus and Big Claus* and *The Princess and the Pea* while living at No 20, and also spent time living at Nos 18 and 67.

★**Designmuseum Danmark**   MUSEUM
(www.designmuseum.dk; Bredgade 68; adult/child 100kr/free; ◷ 11am-5pm Tue & Thu-Sun, to 9pm Wed; ☐ 1A, Ⓜ Kongens Nytorv) The 18th-century Frederiks Hospital is now the outstanding Denmark Design Museum. A must for fans of the applied arts and industrial design, its fairly extensive collection includes Danish textiles and fashion, as well as the iconic design pieces of modern innovators like Kaare Klint, Poul Henningsen and Arne Jacobsen.

Christiania   AREA
(www.christiania.org; Prinsessegade; ☐ 9A, Ⓜ Christianshavn) Escape the capitalist crunch and head to Freetown Christiania, a hash-scented commune straddling the eastern side of Christianshavn. Since its establishment by squatters in 1971, the area has drawn nonconformists from across the globe, attracted by the concept of collective business, workshops and communal living. Explore beyond the settlement's infamous 'Pusher St' – lined with shady hash and marijuana dealers who do not appreciate photographs – and you'll stumble upon a semi-bucolic wonderland of whimsical DIY homes, cosy garden plots, eateries, beer gardens and music venues.

WORTH A TRIP

A MODERN ART DRAWCARD: LOUISIANA

The extraordinary Louisiana (www.louisiana.dk; Gammel Strandvej 13, Humlebæk; adult/student/child 125/110kr/free; ⊘11am-10pm Tue-Fri, to 6pm Sat & Sun) museum of modern and contemporary art should be high on your 'to do' list even if you're not normally a gallery-goer. Along with its ever-changing, cutting-edge exhibitions, much of the thrill here is the glorious presentation. A maze-like web of halls and glass corridors weaves through rolling gardens in which magnificent trees, lawns, a lake and a beach view set off monumental abstract sculptures (Henry Moore, Jean Arp, Max Ernst, Barbara Hepworth etc), making them feel like discovered totems.

Louisiana is in the pretty coastal town of Humlebæk, 30km north of Copenhagen. From Humlebæk train station, the museum is a 1.5km signposted walk northeast. Trains to Humlebæk run at least twice hourly from Copenhagen (92kr, 35 minutes) but if you're day-tripping, the 24-hour Copenhagen ticket (adult/child 130/65kr) is much better value.

Statens Museum for Kunst
MUSEUM

(☑33 74 84 94; www.smk.dk; Sølvgade 48-50; adult/child 110kr/free; ⊘11am-5pm Tue & Thu-Sun, to 8pm Wed; ☐6A, 26, 42, 184, 185) FREE Denmark's National Gallery straddles two contrasting, interconnected buildings: a late-19th-century 'palazzo' and a sharply minimalist extension. The museum houses medieval and Renaissance works and impressive collections of Dutch and Flemish artists, including Rubens, Breughel and Rembrandt. It claims the world's finest collection of 19th-century Danish 'Golden Age' artists, among them Eckersberg and Hammershøi, foreign greats like Matisse and Picasso, and modern Danish heavyweights including Per Kirkeby.

★Rosenborg Slot
CASTLE

(☑33 15 32 86; www.kongernessamling.dk/en/rosenborg; Øster Voldgade 4A; adult/child 110kr/free, incl Amalienborg Slot 145kr/free; ⊘9am-5pm mid-Jun–mid-Sep, reduced hours rest of year; ☐6A, 42, 184, 185, 350S, Ⓜ Nørreport, Ⓢ Nørreport) A 'once upon a time' combo of turrets, gables and moat, the early-17th-century Rosenborg Slot was built in Dutch Renaissance style between 1606 and 1633 by King Christian IV to serve as his summer home. Today the castle's 24 upper rooms are chronologically arranged, housing the furnishings and portraits of each monarch from Christian IV to Frederik VII. The pièce de résistance is the basement Treasury, home to the dazzling crown jewels, among them Christian IV's glorious crown and Christian III's jewel-studded sword.

Little Mermaid
MONUMENT

(Den Lille Havfrue; Langelinie, Østerport; ☐1A, ◐ Nordre Toldbod) New York has its Lady Liberty and Sydney its (Danish-designed) Opera House. When the world thinks of Copenhagen, the chances are they're thinking of the *Little Mermaid*. Love her or loathe her (watch Copenhageners cringe at the very mention of her), this small, underwhelming statue is arguably the most photographed sight in the country, as well as the cause of countless 'Is that it?' shrugs from tourists who have trudged the kilometre or so along an often windswept harbourfront to see her.

☞ Tours

Canal Tours Copenhagen
BOATING

(☑32 96 30 00; www.stromma.dk; Nyhavn; adult/child 80/40kr; ⊘9.30am-9pm late Jun–mid-Aug, reduced hours rest of year; ☒; ☐1A, 26, 66, 350S, Ⓜ Kongens Nytorv) Canal Tours Copenhagen runs one-hour cruises of the city's canals and harbour, taking in numerous major sights, including Christiansborg Slot, Christianshavn, the Royal Library, Opera House, Amalienborg Palace and the *Little Mermaid*. Embark at Nyhavn or Ved Stranden. Boats depart up to six times per hour from late June to late August, with reduced frequency the rest of the year.

⨳ Sleeping

★Generator Hostel
HOSTEL €

(☑78 77 54 00; www.generatorhostel.com; Adelgade 5-7; dm/d from 130/595kr; @ 🛜; ☐350S, 1A, 26, Ⓜ Kongens Nytorv) A solid choice for 'cheap chic', upbeat, design-literate Generator sits on the edge of the city's medieval core. It's kitted out with designer furniture, slick communal areas (including a bar and outdoor terrace) and friendly, young staff. While the rooms can be a little small, all are bright and modern, with bathrooms in private rooms and dorms.

DENMARK AT A GLANCE

Don't Miss

Copenhagen Denmark's high-achieving capital is home to a thriving design scene, a futuristic metro system, and clean, green developments. Its streets are awash with effortlessly hip shops, cafes and bars; world-class museums and art collections; brave new architecture; and no fewer than 15 Michelin-starred restaurants.

Skagen Skagen is an enchanting place, both bracing and beautiful. It lies at Denmark's northern tip and acts as a magnet for much of the population each summer, when the town is full to capacity yet still manages to charm. In the late 19th century, artists flocked here, infatuated with the radiant light's impact on the rugged landscape.

Viking history The Vikings were not just plunderers but also successful traders, extraordinary mariners and insatiable explorers. Getting a feel for the Viking era is easy, whether visiting the ship-burial ground of Ladby, the Viking forts of Zealand, the longship workshops at Roskilde or the many museums that seek to recreate the era with live re-enactments.

Lego in Billund A long way from the capital, unassuming Billund is the home town of the Lego Company and unofficial HQ for happy wholesome families. Here, the Legoland theme park and the inspired new Lego House (designed to resemble gigantic Lego bricks) are geared to celebrate the 'toy of the century' in detail-rich ways that will delight your child, and your inner child.

Cycling Is Denmark the world's best nation for cycling? Probably, thanks to its extensive national network of cycle routes, terrain that is either flat or merely undulating, and a culture committed to two-wheeled transport.

Itineraries

One Week

To cover the classic sites, start in **Copenhagen** and soak up the riches (cultural, culinary, retail) of the capital. From there, it's a short hop west to investigate Denmark's royal and Viking heritage at **Roskilde**. Then grab a hefty dose of childhood nostalgia, investigating Lego-themed treats in **Billund**.

Two Weeks

Follow the one week itinerary but add in a visit to Hamlet's castle in **Helsingør** and hop north to luminous **Skagen** for art, beaches and fresh seafood. Finally, stop by cosmopolitan **Aarhus**, the country's second city.

Essential Food & Drink

New Nordic flavours Sample Nordic produce cooked with groundbreaking creativity.

Smørrebrød Rye or white bread topped with anything from beef tartare to egg and prawns, the open sandwich is Denmark's most famous culinary export.

Sild Smoked, cured, pickled or fried, herring is a local staple.

Kanelsnegle A calorific delight, the 'cinnamon snail' is a sweet, buttery pastry, sometimes laced with chocolate.

Koldskål A cold, sweet buttermilk soup eaten in summer, made with vanilla and traditionally served with crunchy biscuits such as *kammerjunkere*.

Beer Carlsberg may dominate, but Denmark's expanding craft brewers include Mikkeller, Amager Bryghus and Bryghuset Møn.

Getting Around

Transport in Denmark is reasonably priced, quick and efficient. Plan your journey on www.rejseplanen.dk.

Train Reasonably priced, with extensive coverage of the country and frequent departures.

Car Denmark is perfect for touring by car; they can be hired in larger towns. Drive on the right.

Bike Extensive bike paths link towns throughout the country. Bikes can be hired in every town.

Bus All large cities and towns have a local and regional bus system. Long-distance buses run a distant second to trains (but are cheaper).

Ferries Boats link virtually all of Denmark's populated islands.

When to Go
Copenhagen

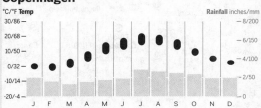

Mid-Jun–mid-Aug Long daylight hours, with many concerts and festivals. Busy campgrounds, beaches and sights.	**May–mid-Jun & mid-Aug–Sep** A good time to travel, with generally mild weather and lighter crowds.	**Oct–Apr** Cool and wet with short daylight hours, but *hygge* (cosiness) is in full swing.

Arriving in Denmark

Copenhagen International Airport Denmark's main airport. Trains leave every 10 minutes (36kr, 12 minutes), connecting the airport to Copenhagen Central Station (København Hovedbanegården). By taxi it's a 20-minute journey between the airport and city centre; cost is 250kr to 300kr. Metro line M2 runs 24 hours from the airport (station: Lufthavnen) to many neighbourhoods (eg Christianhavn, Kongens Nytorv, Nørreport, Frederiksberg), but doesn't run through Copenhagen Central Station.

Top Phrases

Hello. Goddag.

Goodbye. Farvel.

Please. Vær så venlig.

Thank you. Tak.

Excuse me. Undskyld mig.

Resources

Visit Denmark (www.visitdenmark.com) Info ranges from the practical to the inspirational.

Rejseplanen (www.rejseplanen.dk) Journey planner.

Denmark.dk (www.denmark.dk) Hugely informative on diverse subjects.

Set Your Budget

➡ Dorm bed: 150–300kr

➡ Double room in budget hotel: 500–700kr

➡ Cheap meal: under 125kr

➡ 24-hour City Pass for Copenhagen transport: 80kr

Central Copenhagen (København)

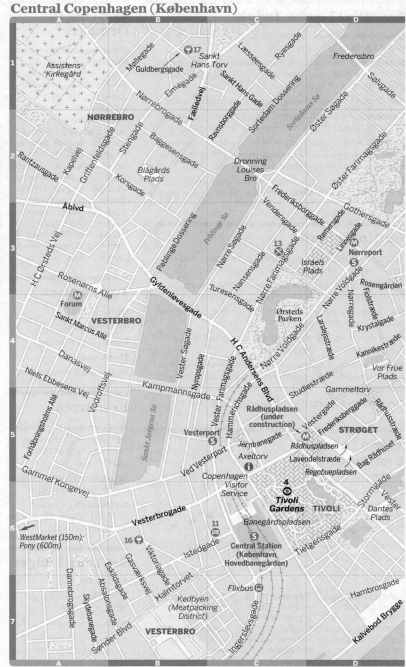

Assistens Kirkegård

Møllegade

17 Sankt Hans Torv

Guldbergsgade

Læssøesgade

Ryesgade

Fredensbro

Elmegade

Sankt Hans Gade

Sølvgade

Nørrebrogade

Fælledvej

Ramsborggade

Sortedam Dossering

Sortedams Sø

Øster Søgade

NØRREBRO

Stengade

Baggesensgade

Dronning Louises Bro

Øster Farimagsgade

Rantzausgade

Kapelvej

Griffenfeldsgade

Blågårds Plads

Korsgade

Frederiksborggade

Rømersgade

Gothersgade

Åblvd

Peblinge Dossering

Peblinge Sø

Nørre Søgade

Vendersgade

Linnésgade

Nørreport

H C Ørsteds Vej

Rosenørns Allé

Forum

Gyldenløvesgade

Nansensgade

Nørre Farimagsgade

13

Israels Plads

Rosengården

Fiolstræde

Nørregade

Nørre Voldgade

VESTERBRO

Sankt Marcus Allé

Turesensgade

Ørsteds Parken

Krystalgade

Danasvej

Vester Søgade

Nyropsgade

H C Andersens Blvd

Nørre Voldgade

Larslejsstræde

Kannikestræde

Niels Ebbesens Vej

Vodroffsvej

Kampmannsgade

Vester Farimagsgade

Hammerichsgade

Studiestræde

Vor Frue Plads

Gammeltorv

Fornåbningsholms Allé

Sankt Jørgens Sø

Vesterport

Rådhuspladsen (under construction)

Vestergade

Frederiksberggade

Rådhusstræde

STRØGET

Jernbanegade

Rådhuspladsen

Bag Rådhuset

Gammel Kongevej

Ved Vesterport

Axeltorv

Lavendelstræde

Regnbuepladsen

Stormgade

Copenhagen Visitor Service

4

Tivoli Gardens

TIVOLI

Vester

Dantes Plads

Vesterbrogade

11

Banegårdspladsen

Tietgensgade

WestMarket (150m); Pony (600m)

16

Istedgade

Central Station (København Hovedbanegården)

Hambrosgade

Viktoriagade

Eskildsgade

Gasværksvej

Halmtorvet

Flixbus

Ingerslevsgade

Kalvebod Brygge

Dannebrogsgade

Skydebanegade

Absalonsgade

Sønder Blvd

Kødbyen (Meatpacking District)

VESTERBRO

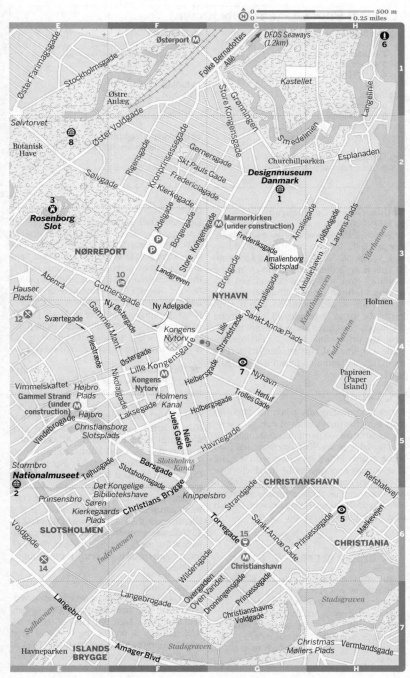

Central Copenhagen (København)

⊚ Top Sights
1 Designmuseum Danmark	G2
2 Nationalmuseet	E5
3 Rosenborg Slot	E3
4 Tivoli Gardens	C6

⊚ Sights
5 Christiania	H6
6 Little Mermaid	H1
7 Nyhavn	G4
8 Statens Museum for Kunst	E2

⊕ Activities, Courses & Tours
9 Canal Tours Copenhagen	F4

⊜ Sleeping
10 Generator Hostel	F3
11 Urban House Copenhagen by MEININGER	C6

⊗ Eating
12 DØP	E4
13 Høst	C3
14 Lillian's Smørrebrød	E6

⊖ Drinking & Nightlife
15 Christianshavns Bådudlejning og Café	G6
16 Mikkeller Bar	B6
17 Rust	B1

★ **Urban House Copenhagen by MEININGER** HOSTEL, HOTEL €

(☏89 88 32 69; www.urbanhouse.me; Colbjørnsensgade 5-11, Vesterbro; dm/d from 140/530kr; @ 🛜; 🚊2A, 5C, 9A, 10, 14, 250S, Ⓢ København H) This huge hostel spans a trio of historic buildings close to Central Station and Vesterbro's on-trend venues. Slumber options range from single rooms to dorms with bunks for up to 12 people; all have private bathrooms. Bed linen and towels are included in the price, while in-house facilities include a communal kitchen, laundry, games room, small cinema and even a tattoo parlour!

✗ Eating

Beneath Copenhagen's galaxy of Michelin stars is a growing number of hot spots serving innovative contemporary Danish fare at affordable prices. The international food scene is also lifting its game, with a spate of new places serving authentic dishes like pho, ramen and tacos made using top-notch produce. Keeping them company are veritable city institutions serving classic Danish fare, including smørrebrød.

> ### ⓘ CHEAP SLEEPS
>
> Budget accommodation has received a boost in recent years with hip, low-frill chains WakeUp Copenhagen (www.wakeupcopenhagen.com) and Generator Hostel (https://generatorhostels.com). Reserve rooms in advance, especially during the busy summer season.

DØP HOT DOGS €

(☏30 20 40 25; www.døp.dk; Købmagergade 50; hot dogs from 35kr; ⊙11am-6.30pm Mon-Sat; 🚊14, Ⓜ Nørrebro, Ⓢ Nørrebro) 🍴 Danes love a good *pølse* (sausage), and hot-dog vans are ubiquitous across Copenhagen. DØP is the best, with a van right beside Rundetårn (Round Tower). Everything here is organic, from the meat and vegetables to the toppings. Options range from a classic Danish roasted hot dog with mustard, ketchup, remoulade, pickles and onions both fresh and fried, to a new-school vegan tofu version.

★ **WestMarket** MARKET €

(☏70 50 00 05; www.westmarket.dk; Vesterbrogade 97, Vesterbro; meals from 50kr; ⊙bakeries & coffee shops 8am-7pm, food stalls 10am-10pm; 🛜♿; 🚊6A) From dodgy shopping arcade to cool street-food hub, WestMarket peddles grub from all corners of the globe: from ramen, bao and lobster rolls to risotto, bubbling pizza and tapas. For a Scandi experience, hit **Kød & Bajer** (☏30 54 60 88; www.koedogbajer.dk; Vesterbrogade 97, Stall C12; ⊙11am-9pm) for harder-to-find Nordic craft beers and snacks like dried moose, bear and elk sausages, then settle down at **Gros** (☏60 45 11 02; www.groshverdagskost.dk; Vesterbrogade 97, Stall C6; meals 98kr; ⊙11am-9pm; 🛜🖉) 🍴 for a modern take on retro Danish dining classics.

Lillian's Smørrebrød DANISH €

(☏33 14 20 66; http://lillians-smorrebrod.dk; Vester Voldgade 108; smørrebrød from 17kr; ⊙6am-2pm Mon-Fri; 🚊1A, 2A, 9A) Tiny 1970s throwback Lillian's is one of the best and least costly smørrebrød places in town. Decked out in white deli-style tiles, with kitsch artwork and just a handful of tables, its generous, open-faced sandwiches are classic: think marinated herring, chicken salad and roast beef with remoulade. However, while the coffee here is also a bargain, you'll get a much better cup elsewhere.

Pony
NEW NORDIC €€

(☑33 22 10 00; www.ponykbh.dk; Vesterbrogade 135, Vesterbro; 2-/3-/4-course menu 325/425/485kr; ☉5.30-10pm Tue-Sun; ☐6A) This is the cheaper bistro spin-off of Copenhagen's Michelin-starred Kadeau. While the New Nordic grub here is simpler, it's no less nuanced and seasonal; think cured brill with gooseberries and dried brill roe, or roasted wolf fish with summer cabbage, black cabbage, nasturtiums and crispy grains. The on-point wines are organic and from smaller producers, and the vibe intimate and convivial.

Drinking & Nightlife

Copenhagen is packed with a diverse range of drinking options – slinky cocktail hideouts, rowdy and nicotine-stained *bodegas* (pubs), and everything in between.

★ Mikkeller Bar
BAR

(☑33 31 04 15; http://mikkeller.dk; Viktoriagade 8B-C, Vesterbro; ☉1pm-1am Sun-Wed, to 2am Thu & Fri, noon-2am Sat; ☎; ☐6A, 9A, 10, 14, 26, ⑤København H) Low-slung lights, green floors and 20 brews on tap: cool, cult-status Mikkeller flies the flag for craft beer, its rotating cast of suds including Mikkeller's own acclaimed creations and guest drops from microbreweries from around the globe. Expect anything from tequila-barrel-aged stouts to yuzu-infused fruit beers. The bottled offerings are equally inspired, with cheese and snacks to soak up the foamy goodness.

Christianshavns Bådudlejning og Café
BAR

(☑32 96 53 53; www.baadudlejningen.dk; Overgaden Neden Vandet 29; ☉9am-midnight Jun-Aug, reduced hours rest of year; ☎; ☐2A, 9A, 37, 350S, Ⓜ Christianshavn) Right on Christianshavn's main canal, this festive, wood-decked cafe-bar is a wonderful spot for drinks by the water. It's a cosy, affable hang-out, with jovial crowds and strung lights. There's grub for the peckish and gas heaters and tarpaulins to ward off any northern chill. The cafe plans to resume its rental of little rowboats in 2018.

SPLURGE

The phenomenal popularity of **Høst** (☑89 93 84 09; http://hostvakst.dk; Nørre Farimagsgade 41; 3-/5-course menu 350/450kr; ☉5.30pm-midnight, last order 9.30pm; ☐37, Ⓜ Nørreport, ⑤Nørreport) is easy to understand: award-winning interiors and New Nordic food that's equally fabulous and filling. The set menu is superb, with three smaller 'surprise dishes' thrown in and evocative creations like baked flounder with roasted chicken skin, shrimp, peas and an apple-vinegar fish stock, or a joyful rose-hip sorbet paired with Danish strawberries, a green strawberry puree, meringue and herbs.

Rust
CLUB

(☑35 24 52 00; www.rust.dk; Guldbergsgade 8, Nørrebro; ☉hours vary, club usually 8.30pm-5am Fri & Sat; ☎; ☐3A, 5C, 350S) A smashing, multilevel place attracting one of the largest, coolest, most relaxed crowds in Copenhagen. Live acts focus on alternative or upcoming indie rock, hip-hop or electronica. At 11pm, the venue transforms into a club, with local and international DJs pumping out anything from classic hip-hop to electro, house and more.

ℹ Information

Copenhagen Visitors Centre (☑70 22 24 42; www.visitcopenhagen.com; Vesterbrogade 4A, Vesterbro; ☉9am-8pm Mon-Fri, to 6pm Sat & Sun Jul & Aug, reduced hours rest of year; ☎; ☐2A, 6A, 5C, 12, 14, 26, 66, 250S, ⑤København H) Copenhagen's excellent and informative information centre has a cafe and lounge with free wi-fi; it also sells the Copenhagen Card (p134).

ℹ Getting There & Away

➜ Copenhagen's user-friendly **international airport** (☑32 31 32 31; www.cph.dk; Lufthavnsboulevarden, Kastrup; Ⓜ Lufthavnen, ⑤København Lufthavn) is Scandinavia's busiest hub, with direct flights to cities in Europe, North America and Asia.

➜ **DFDS Seaways** (☑33 42 30 00; www.dfdsseaways.com; Dampfærgevej 30; ⑤Nordhavn) runs one daily service to/from Oslo (one-way from 675kr, 17¼ hours), which leaves from Søndre Frihavn, just north of Kastellet.

SCANDINAVIA HELSINGØR

LEGOLAND

The attractions of the 'company town' of Billund (built around a little Danish product you might know: Lego) are so geared to families you might feel a little, well, underdressed if you visit without your own set of excited offspring. But don't let that stop you from embracing your inner child and allocating the wondrous **Legoland** and awesome new **Lego House** some generous time in your itinerary.

Legoland (☑ 75 33 13 33; www.legoland.dk; Nordmarksvej; adult/child 379/359kr; ⊗ 10am-8pm or 9pm Jul–mid-Aug, shorter hours Apr-Jun & mid-Aug–early Nov, closed early Nov-Mar; P ♿) Mind-blowing Lego models, fun rides and the happy-family magic associated with great theme parks have transformed Legoland into Denmark's most visited tourist attraction outside of Copenhagen. It's a great day outing (you'll need a day to do it justice) and it sits smack-bang in the middle of Jutland, 1km north of Billund.

The heart of Legoland is **Miniland** – 20 million plastic Lego blocks snapped together to create miniature cities and replicate global icons (and re-create scenes from *Star Wars* movies).

Lego House (☑ 82 82 04 00; www.legohouse.com; Ole Kirks Plads 1; Experience Zones ticket 199kr; ⊗ 9.30am-8.30pm most days) Opened in 2017 in the heart of Billund, Lego House is a hands-on 'experience centre' with a thoroughly brilliant design that resembles a stack of 21 gigantic Lego bricks. It is marketed as the 'Home of the Brick' and incorporates top-quality museum displays of the company's history, plus exhibition areas and rooftop terraces. The ground level (home to eateries and a Lego shop) has free public access; access to the Experience Zones requires a prebooked ticket (with allocated entry time).

➜ **Eurolines** (www.flixbus.com; Ⓢ København H) operates buses to several European cities. The ticket office is behind Central Station.

➜ All long-distance trains arrive at and depart from Københavns Hovedbanegård (Central Station). Destinations include Hamburg (from 627kr, 4½ hours, several daily), Odense (308kr, 1¼ to two hours, at least twice hourly) and Aarhus (418kr, 2¾ to 3½ hours, one to three hourly).

❶ Getting Around

➜ Copenhagen has an extensive public transit system consisting of a metro, rail, bus and ferry network. All tickets (billets) are valid for the whole network. Click onto the very handy www.rejseplanen.dk for routes and schedules.

➜ The cheapest ticket, (24/12kr per adult/child aged 12 to 15 years) covers two zones, offers unlimited transfers and is valid for one hour. Children under 12 travel free if accompanied by an adult.

➜ If you plan on exploring sights outside the city, you're better off buying a 24-hour ticket (all zones 130/65kr per adult/child) or a seven-day FlexCard (all zones 675kr).

➜ Alternatively, you can purchase a Rejsekort (www.rejsekort.dk), a touch-on, touch-off smart card valid for all zones and all public transport across Denmark.

➜ Copenhagen vies with Amsterdam as the world's most bike-friendly city. Most streets have cycle lanes and there's a high-tech city-bike scheme.

Helsingør

POP 46,830

The main sight at the busy port town of Helsingør (Elsinore) is imposing Kronborg Slot, a brute of a castle that dominates the narrowest point of the Øresund.

◎ Sights

★**Kronborg Slot**   CASTLE
(www.kronborg.dk; Kronborgvej; interior adult/student 140/130kr; ⊗ 10am-5.30pm Jun-Sep, 11am-4pm Apr & May, 11am-4pm Tue-Sun Oct-Mar) Best known as the Elsinore Castle of Shakespeare's *Hamlet,* this Unesco World Heritage site is a vast Renaissance masterpiece topped by baroque green-copper spires. It's ringed by moats, fortifications and powerful Vaubanesque star bastions that you can discover without a ticket. But it's well worth the entry fee to explore the inner palace's rooms, tapestries, ceiling paintings and viewpoints and, best of all, to delve into the spooky maze of casemates – subterranean dungeon passages barely lit by flickering paraffin lamps.

★**M/S Museet for Søfart**   MUSEUM
(Maritime Museum of Denmark; www.mfs.dk; Ny Kronborgvej 1; adult/child 110kr/free; ⊗ 10am-6pm Jul & Aug, 11am-5pm Sep, closed Mon rest of year)

Ingeniously built into a dry dock beside Kronborg Slot, this subterranean museum merits a visit as much for its design as for its informative multimedia galleries. These explore Denmark's maritime history and culture in dynamic, contemporary ways. Alongside nautical instruments, sea charts and wartime objects, exhibitions explore themes including the representation of sailors in popular culture, trade and exploitation in Denmark's overseas colonies, and the globe-crossing journeys of modern shipping containers.

✖️ Eating

Rådmand Davids Hus   DANISH €
(☑ 49 26 10 43; Strandgade 70; dishes 48-108kr; ☺ 10am-5pm Mon-Sat; 🛜) What better place to gobble down Danish classics than a snug, lopsided 1694 house, complete with cobbled courtyard? Refuel with honest, solid staples or special 'shopping lunches', typically a generous plate of salad, salmon pâté and slices of pork, cheese and homemade rye bread. Leave room for the Grand Marnier pancakes.

ℹ️ Getting There & Away

Trains to Copenhagen (108kr, 45 minutes) run about three times hourly from early morning to around midnight.

Scandlines car ferries (☑ 33 15 15 15; www. scandlines.dk; adult/child 40/28kr, car with up to 9 passengers single/day return 380/390kr; ☺ 24hr) take 20 minutes to sail to/from Helsingborg in Sweden.

Roskilde

POP 50,390

Most foreigners who have heard of Roskilde know it either as the home of one of Europe's best music festivals or the site of several remarkable Viking ship finds, housed in an excellent, purpose-built museum. To the Danes, however, it is a city of great royal and religious significance, and was capital city long before Copenhagen.

👁️ Sights

★ Roskilde Domkirke   CATHEDRAL
(www.roskildedomkirke.dk; Domkirkestræde 10; adult/pensioner/child 60/40kr/free; ☺ 10am-6pm Mon-Sat, 1-6pm Sun Apr-Sep, to 4pm Oct-Mar) The crème de la crème of Danish cathedrals, this twin-spired giant was started by Bishop Absalon in 1170, but has been rebuilt and tweaked so many times that it's now a superb showcase of 850 years' worth of Danish architecture. As the royal mausoleum, it contains the crypts of 37 Danish kings and queens and is now a Unesco World Heritage site. The entry fee includes a comprehensive, full-colour 48-page guidebook.

★ Viking Ship Museum   MUSEUM
(Vikingskibsmuseet; ☑ 46 30 02 00; www.viking eskibsmuseet.dk; Vindeboder 12; adult/child May–mid-Oct 130kr/free, mid-Oct–Apr 85kr/free; ☺ 10am-5pm late Jun–mid-Aug, to 4pm rest of year, boat trips daily mid-May–Sep; 🅿️ 🚻) Five original Viking ships, discovered at the bottom of Roskilde Fjord, are displayed in the main hall of this must-see museum. A short walk away, the same ticket gives access to the workshops of **Museumsø** (incl in Viking Ship Museum ticket adult/child May–mid-Oct 130kr/free, mid-Oct–Apr 85kr/free; ☺ 10am-5pm late Jun–mid-Aug, to 4pm mid-Aug–late Jun), where archaeological and reconstruction work takes place, and **Nordic longboats** (per person 100kr; ☺ May-Sep) depart. There are free 45-minute guided tours in English at noon and 3pm daily from late June to the end of August and at noon on weekends from May to late June and in September.

★ Ragnarock   MUSEUM
(www.museumragnarock.dk; Rabalderstræde 16; adult/child 90kr/free; ☺ 10am-5pm Tue & Fri-Sun, to 10pm Wed & Thu; 🅿️; 🚌 202A) Within a startling architectural statement of a building, this spirit-lifting, highly interactive museum delivers a multisensory, experiential and often humorous journey through the evolution of rock music and youth culture from the 1950s to the present. Walls of headphones let you listen to music time capsules, and spin-to-hear turntables explain about gramophones. Play with interactive musical lights, learn why toilets were integral to Danish music production and practise various dance steps on the hot-spot stage beside the 'world's biggest mirror ball'.

🎉 Festivals & Events

Roskilde Festival   MUSIC
(www.roskilde-festival.dk; Darupvej; tickets from 1995kr; ☺ early Jul) Denmark's answer to Glastonbury, Roskilde Festival is northern Europe's largest music festival, a week-long summer binge of bands and booze.

ℹ Getting There & Away

Trains run frequently between Copenhagen and Roskilde (84kr, 25 minutes). Holders of the Copenhagen Card get free train travel to Roskilde.

Aarhus

POP 269,000

Aarhus (*oar*-hus), Denmark's second-largest city, is busy staking a claim for visitor attention, and building a reputation as an emerging European destination for savvy city-breakers, festival-goers, art and food fans, and those looking beyond the capital-city conga. It's a great place to explore – compact, photogenic and friendly.

⊙ Sights

★ARoS Aarhus Kunstmuseum   MUSEUM

(☑87 30 66 00; www.aros.dk; Aros Allé 2; adult/child 130kr/free; ☺10am-5pm Tue & Thu-Sun, to 10pm Wed; ♿) Inside the cubist, red-brick walls of Aarhus' showpiece art museum are nine floors of sweeping curves, soaring spaces and white walls showcasing a wonderful selection of Golden Age works, Danish modernism and an abundance of arresting and vivid contemporary art. The museum's cherry-on-top is the spectacular Your Rainbow Panorama, a 360-degree rooftop walkway offering views of the city through its glass panes in all shades of the rainbow.

★Den Gamle By   MUSEUM

(The Old Town; ☑86 12 31 88; www.dengamleby. dk; Viborgvej 2; adult/child 135kr/free; ☺10am-5pm, hours vary by season; ♿) The Danes' seemingly limitless enthusiasm for dressing up and re-creating history reaches its zenith at Den Gamle By. It's an engaging, picturesque open-air museum of 75 half-timbered houses brought here from all corners of Denmark and reconstructed as a provincial market town from the era of Hans Christian Andersen. Recreated neighbourhoods from 1927 and 1974 are the newest additions.

🛏 Sleeping & Eating

City Sleep-In   HOSTEL €

(☑86 19 20 55; www.citysleep-in.dk; Havnegade 20; dm 190kr, d without/with bathroom 460/520kr; @ 🛜) This central hostel used to house seamen and is a real one-off with its rambling layout of sitting rooms, terraces, rooms and dorms. There is a large communal kitchen and a bar-cafe with regular live music. Colourful murals cover the walls and the furnishings are an eclectic and comfortable mishmash of styles and eras.

★Aarhus Street Food   FOOD HALL €

(www.aarhusstreetfood.com; Ny Banegårdsgade 46; mains 50-150kr; ☺11.30am-9pm Sun-Thu, to 10pm Fri & Sat; 🛜🍴) 🌿 A former garage at the back of the **bus station** (Rutebilstation; Fredensgade 45) now houses a buzzing street-food venue serving everything from pizza slices to bumper burgers, by way of Thai curries and Vietnamese *bánh mì*. The place has fast become one of *the* places to meet, greet and graze in town – on-site bars stay open until midnight Friday and Saturday.

🍷 Drinking & Entertainment

Aarhus is the nation's music capital, with no shortage of quality music gigs in venues from dignified concert halls to beer-fuelled boltholes. For the low-down click onto www. visitaarhus.com or www.aoa.dk.

★Strandbaren   BAR

(www.facebook.com/strandbarenaarhus; Pier 4, Havnebassin 7; ☺May-Sep) Plonk shipping containers and sand on a harbourfront spot and voila: beach bar. This chilled hang-out at **Aarhus Ø** offers food, drink, flirting and weather-dependent activities and events. Check hours and location on the Facebook page (harbour redevelopment may require an annual location change; opening hours are 'when the sun is shining'). Bus 33 comes here, but cycling is best.

ℹ Information

VisitAarhus (☑87 31 50 10; www.visitaarhus. com; Hack Kampmanns Plads 2; ☺10am-4pm Mon-Sat, 11am-2pm Sun) Has an info desk inside Dokk1 (☑89 40 92 00; www.dokk1.dk; Hack Kampmanns Plads 2; ☺8am-10pm Mon-Fri, 10am-4pm Sat & Sun; ♿).

ℹ Getting There & Away

Trains to Copenhagen (one way 388kr, three to 3½ hours), via Odense (244kr, 1½ hours), leave Aarhus roughly half-hourly.

Abildskou (☑32 72 93 86; www.abildskou. dk) bus 888 runs up to 10 times daily between Aarhus and Copenhagen (149kr to 249kr, 3½ to 4½ hours), stopping at the capital's train station, bus station or airport.

Skagen

POP 8200

The town of Skagen (pronounced 'skain') is a busy working harbour and Denmark's northernmost settlement, just a couple of kilometres from the dramatic sandy spit beloved of artists, where the country finally peters out at Grenen, a slender point of wave-washed sand where seals bask and seagulls soar.

Sights

★ **Gammel Skagen**   VILLAGE, BEACH

There's a touch of Cape Cod in refined Gammel Skagen ('Old Skagen', also known as Højen), renowned for its gorgeous sunsets, upmarket hotels and well-heeled summer residents.

It was a fishing hamlet before sandstorms ravaged this windswept area and forced many of its inhabitants to move to Skagen on the more protected east coast. It's a pleasant bike ride 4km west of Skagen: head towards Frederikshavn and turn right at Højensvej, which takes you to the waterfront.

★ **Grenen**   BEACH

Appropriately enough for such a neat and ordered country, Denmark doesn't end untidily at its most northerly point, but on a neat finger of sand just a few metres wide. You can actually paddle at its tip, where the waters of the Kattegat (an arm of the Baltic Sea) and Skagerrak (part of the North Sea) clash, and you can put one foot in each sea – but not too far. Bathing here is forbidden because of the ferocious tidal currents.

Sleeping & Eating

Danhostel Skagen   HOSTEL €

(☑98 44 22 00; www.danhostelskagen.dk; Rolighedsvej 2; dm/s/d 180/525/625kr; ☺Mar-Nov; 🅿🛜) Always a hive of activity, this hostel is modern, functional and spick-and-span. It's decent value, particularly for families or groups. Low-season prices drop sharply. It's 1km towards Frederikshavn from the Skagen train station (if you're coming by train, get off at Frederikshavnsvej). Breakfast/linen costs 60/60kr.

Skagen Fiskerestaurant   SEAFOOD €€

(☑98 44 35 44; www.skagenfiskerestaurant.dk; Fiskehuskajen 13; mains 120-299kr; ☺11am-10pm Apr-Oct, shorter hours rest of year) This dockside place has a winning sales pitch: fresh, casual cafe fare at lunch and dinner (*fiskefrikadeller*, creamy fish soup, fish and chips), an in-demand outdoor terrace and summertime live music. It's rustic and fun – you know a place doesn't take itself too seriously when the floor is covered in sand.

❶ Getting There & Away

Trains run hourly to Frederikshavn (60kr, 35 minutes), where you can change for destinations further south.

The summertime bus 99 connects Skagen with other northern towns and attractions.

Denmark Survival Guide

❶ Directory A–Z

ACCOMMODATION

➡ Campgrounds, hostels and B&B accommodation generally offer an excellent standard of accommodation and are good ways to secure comfort on a budget.

➡ During July and August it's advisable to book ahead.

LGBT TRAVELLERS

➡ Given Denmark's high degree of tolerance for alternative lifestyles of all sorts, it's hardly surprising that Denmark is a popular destination for gay and lesbian travellers.

➡ Copenhagen in particular has an active, open gay community with a healthy number of venues, but you'll find gay and lesbian venues in other cities as well (as well as mainstream venues that are welcoming to all).

➡ A useful website for travellers with visitor information and listings is www.rainbowbusinessdenmark.dk. Also see www.oaonline.dk.

➡ The main gay and lesbian festival of the year is Copenhagen Pride (www.copenhagenpride.dk), a week-long queer fest that takes place in August.

MONEY

➡ One krone is divided into 100 øre. There are 50 øre, 1kr, 2kr, 5kr, 10kr and 20kr coins. Notes come in denominations of 50, 100, 200, 500 and 1000 kroner.

> **❶ PRICE RANGES**
>
> The following price ranges refer to a double room in high season.
>
> € less than 700kr
>
> €€ 700–1500kr
>
> €€€ more than 1500kr

ℹ JUTLAND FERRY PORTS

Ferries to Sweden, Norway and Iceland run from two ports at the top tip of Jutland: Frederikshavn (Stena Line to Gothenburg and Oslo) and Hirtshals (Color Line & Fjord Line to Bergen, Kristiansand, Stavanger, Langesund and Larvik (Norway), Smyril Line to Seyðisfjörður (Iceland) via Tórshavn (Faroe Islands). See www.directferries.com for all routes.

Trains run from Copenhagen via Odense, Aarhus and Aalborg to Frederikshavn; change at Hjørring for Hirtshals.

➜ ATMs are widely available. Credit cards are accepted in most hotels, restaurants and shops.

➜ Hotel and restaurant bills and taxi fares include service charges in the quoted prices. Further tipping is unnecessary, although rounding up the bill is not uncommon when service has been especially good.

OPENING HOURS

Banks 10am to 4pm Monday to Friday

Bars 4pm to midnight, to 2am or later Friday and Saturday

Cafes 8am to 5pm or midnight

Restaurants noon to 10pm

Shops 10am to 6pm Monday to Friday, to 4pm Saturday and some Sundays

Supermarkets 8am to 9pm

TELEPHONE

➜ All telephone numbers in Denmark have eight digits; there are no area codes.

➜ Country code: ☏ 45.

➜ International access code: ☏ 00.

➜ Local SIM cards with data packages are easily available and cheap.

ℹ Getting There & Around

For getting around in Denmark, the essential website is www.rejseplanen.dk. Download the app for easy mobile access.

AIR

The majority of overseas flights into Denmark land at **Copenhagen International Airport** (p141) in Kastrup, about 9km southeast of central Copenhagen.

BUS

Copenhagen is well connected to the rest of Europe by daily (or near daily) buses. Eurolines operates most international routes.

Within the country, all large cities and towns have a local and regional bus system. Long-distance buses run a distant second to trains.

BOAT

➜ Ferry connections are possible between Denmark and Norway, Sweden, Germany, Poland (via Sweden), Iceland and the Faroe Islands. Check www.directferries.com for details.

➜ Boats link virtually all of Denmark's populated islands.

TRAIN

➜ Denmark has a very reliable train system with reasonable fares and frequent services. **Danske Statsbaner** (☏ 70 13 14 15; www.dsb.dk) runs virtually all train services in Denmark.

➜ There are regular international links from Copenhagen to Sweden (via the bridge) and Germany (via ferry).

SWEDEN

Stockholm

☏ 08 / POP 932,000

Beautiful capital cities are no rarity in Europe, but Stockholm is near the top of the list for sheer loveliness. Its 14 islands rise starkly out of the surrounding ice-blue water, each boasting saffron-and-cinnamon buildings that stand honeyed in sunlight and frostily elegant in cold weather. The city's charms are irresistible. From its movie-set Old Town (Gamla Stan) to its ever-modern fashion sense and impeccable taste in food and design, the city acts like an immersion school in aesthetics.

◉ Sights

Stockholm is strewn across 14 islands connected by more than 50 bridges. Gamla Stan, the old town, is Stockholm's historic and geographic heart.

★ **Kungliga Slottet** PALACE
(Royal Palace; ☏ 08-402 61 30; www.theroyalpalace.se; Slottsbacken; adult/child 160/80kr, combo ticket incl Riddarholmen adult/child 180/90kr; ◉ 9am-5pm daily Jul & Aug, 10am-5pm daily May-Jun & Sep, 10am-4pm Tue-Sun Oct-Apr; 🚌 43, 46, 55, 59 Slottsbacken, 🚇 Gamla Stan) Kungliga Slottet was built on the ruins of Tre Kronor castle, which burned down in 1697. The north wing survived and was incorporated into the new building. Designed by court

architect Nicodemus Tessin the Younger, it took 57 years to complete. Highlights include the decadent Karl XI Gallery, inspired by Versailles' Hall of Mirrors, and Queen Kristina's silver throne in the Hall of State.

Nobelmuseet
MUSEUM
(☑08-54 43 18 00; http://nobelcenter.se; Stortorget; adult/child 120kr/free; ☺9am-8pm Tue-Sun Jun-Aug, shorter hours rest of year; ☒53, ☒Gamla Stan) Nobelmuseet presents the history of the Nobel Prizes and their recipients, with a focus on the intellectual and cultural aspects of invention. It's a slick space with fascinating displays, including short films on the theme of creativity, interviews with laureates like Ernest Hemingway and Martin Luther King, and cafe chairs signed by the visiting prize recipients (flip them over to see!).

★Stadshuset
NOTABLE BUILDING
(City Hall; www.stockholm.se/stadshuset; Hantverkargatan 1; adult/child 100/50kr, tower 50kr/free; ☺9am-3.30pm, admission by tour only; ☒3, 62 Stadshuset, ☒Rådhuset) The mighty Stadshuset dominates Stockholm's architecture. Topping off its square tower is a golden spire and the symbol of Swedish power: the three royal crowns. Entry is by guided tour only; tours in English take place every 30 minutes from 9am until 3.30pm in summer, and less frequently the rest of the year. The tower is open for visits every 40 minutes from 9.15am to 4pm or 5pm from May to September; it offers stellar views and a great thigh workout.

★Vasamuseet
MUSEUM
(www.vasamuseet.se; Galärvarvsvägen 14; adult/child 130kr/free; ☺8.30am-6pm Jun-Aug, 10am-5pm Thur-Tue, to 8pm Wed Sep-May; ℗; ☒44, ☒Djurgårdsfärjan, ☒7) A good-humoured glorification of some dodgy calculations, Vasamuseet is the custom-built home of the massive warship Vasa; 69m long and 48.8m tall, it was the pride of the Swedish crown when it set off on its maiden voyage on 10 August 1628. Within minutes, the top-heavy vessel tipped and sank to the bottom of Saltsjön, along with many of the people on board.

★Skansen
MUSEUM
(www.skansen.se; Djurgårdsvägen; adult/child 180/60kr; ☺10am-6pm, extended hours in summer; ℗; ☒69, ☒Djurgårdsfärjan, ☒7) The world's first open-air museum, Skansen was founded in 1891 by Artur Hazelius to provide an insight into how Swedes once lived. You could easily spend a day here and not see it all. Around 150 traditional houses and other exhibits dot the hilltop – it's meant to be 'Sweden in miniature', complete with villages, nature, commerce and industry. Note that prices and opening hours and days vary seasonally; check the website before you go.

ABBA: The Museum
MUSEUM
(☑08-12 13 28 60; www.abbathemuseum.com; Djurgårdsvägen 68; adult/child 250/95kr; ☺9am-7pm Mon-Fri Jun-Aug, shorter hours rest of year; ☒67, ☒Djurgårdsfärjan, Emelie, ☒7) A sensory-overload experience that might appeal only to devoted ABBA fans, this long-awaited and wildly hyped cathedral to the demigods of Swedish pop is almost aggressively entertaining. It's packed to the gills with memorabilia and interactivity – every square inch has something new to look at, be it a glittering guitar, a vintage photo of Benny, Björn, Frida or Agnetha, a classic music video, an outlandish costume or a tour van from the band members' early days.

🏃 Activities

Strömma Kanalbolaget
BOATING
(☑08-12 00 40 00; www.stromma.se; Svensksundsvägen 17; 200-400kr) This ubiquitous company offers tours large and small, from a 50-minute 'royal canal tour' around Djurgården (200kr) to a 50-minute ABBA tour, which visits places where ABBA: The Movie was shot and drops you off at the ABBA museum (p147) (315kr). There are also hop-on, hop-off tours by bus (from 300kr), boat (180kr) or both (400kr).

🛏 Sleeping

★City Backpackers
HOSTEL €
(☑08-20 69 20; www.citybackpackers.org; Upplandsgatan 2a; dm 300-360kr, s/d/tr from 550/690/920kr, breakfast 65kr; ☺@☎; ☒T-Centralen) The closest hostel to Centralstationen has clean rooms, friendly staff, free bike hire and excellent facilities, including sauna, laundry and kitchen (with a free stash of pasta). En suite private rooms are also available. Bonus for female guests: there are four- and eight-bed female-only dorms if you prefer, and you can borrow a hairdryer from reception.

★Vandrarhem af Chapman & Skeppsholmen
HOSTEL €€
(☑08-463 22 66; www.stfchapman.com; Flaggmansvägen 8; dm/s/d from 325/595/940kr;

SWEDEN AT A GLANCE

Don't Miss

Stockholm The nation's capital calls itself 'beauty on water', and it certainly doesn't disappoint in the looks department. Stockholm's many glittering waterways reflect slanted northern light onto spice-hued buildings, and the crooked cobblestone streets of Gamla Stan are magical to wander.

Winter sports Winter sports in Lapland are a major draw. To go cross-country skiing, just grab a pair of skis and step outside; for downhill sports, be it alpine, heli-skiing or snowboarding, Åre is your best bet. And those are far from your only options.

Göteborg The humble sibling to Stockholm's confident polish, Göteborg is a city of slick museums, raw industrial landscapes, pleasant parks, can-do designers and cutting-edge food.

Hiking Sweden has some absolutely gorgeous hiking trails, most of which are well maintained and supplied with conveniently located mountain huts along the way. The season is relatively short, but it's worth a bit of extra planning to get out into the wilderness: its natural landscape is one of Sweden's best assets.

Medieval Visby It's hard to overstate the beauty of the Hanseatic port town of Visby, itself the justification for making the ferry trip to Gotland. Inside its thick medieval walls are twisting cobblestone streets, fairy-tale cottages draped in flowers and gorgeous ruins atop hills with stunning Baltic views.

Itineraries

One Week

Spend a few days exploring the sights in and around stylish capital **Stockholm**. Then, make your way west toward **Göteborg**, Sweden's so-called second city, a worthy destination in its own right. Then join in the feasting, archery and medieval fun in the historic town of **Visby**.

Two Weeks

Spend your second week heading north, to enjoy the terrace bars and cafes of **Östersund**, a Unesco-designated 'city of gastronomy'. Continue to **Kiruna**, outpost of the north, to explore some of the world's last truly wild landscapes. Start with a hike in the accessible but vast and untamed **Abisko National Park**, a short train ride from Kiruna. From Kiruna, zip over to **Jukkasjärvi** for a look at the famed Icehotel and a chance to visit a Sami reindeer camp.

Essential Food & Drink

Swedish cuisine, once viewed as meatballs, herring and little else, has had the New Nordic makeover and showcases local produce, blending traditional techniques and contemporary experimentation.

Swedish menu essentials:

Coffee To fit in, eight or nine (OK, four) cups a day is about right; luckily, the country's cafes are a delight.

Reindeer & game Expect to see reindeer and other delicious game on the menu, especially up north in Sami cooking.

Alcohol Beer is everywhere, and improving; but try a shot of *brännvin* (aquavit) with your pickled herring, too.

Fish Salmon and cod are ubiquitous and delicious, and herring smoked, cured, pickled or fried is fundamental. Tasty lake fish include Arctic char and pike-perch.

Getting Around

Transport in Sweden is reliable and easy to navigate. Roads are generally in good repair, and buses and trains are comfortable, with plenty of services on board and in stations. There's a good trip planner at https://reseplanerare.resrobot.se.

Car Expensive but great if you want to explore smaller roads and remote places; especially ideal for camping and outdoor activities.

Bus More thorough coverage than the train network, and often equally quick and cheap (if not more so).

Train Affordable and extensive; speed depends on whether the route is local, regional or express.

When to Go

Stockholm

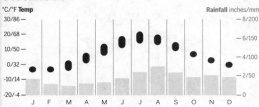

| | Mid-Jun–Aug | Sep–Oct | Nov–May |

Mid-Jun–Aug Season starts at midsummer with warm weather. Most sights and accommodation will be open.

Sep–Oct Weather is still good; many tourist spots are closed, but you'll have the rest all to yourself.

Nov–May Best season for winter-sports adventures, the northern lights and holiday markets.

Arriving in Sweden

Stockholm Arlanda Airport The Arlanda Express train runs from the airport to Stockholm central station (adult/child one way 280/150kr, 20 minutes, every 10 to 15 minutes). Airport buses (Flygbussarna) also run to the city centre (adult/child one way 99/89kr, 45 minutes, every 10 minutes).

Gothenburg Landvetter Airport Flygbussarna buses run from the airport to the city centre (adult/child one way 95/79kr, 30 minutes, every 15 minutes).

Top Phrases

Hello. Hej.

Goodbye. Hej då.

Please/Thank you. Tack.

Excuse me. Ursäkta mig.

Yes/No. Ja/Nej.

Resources

Visit Sweden (www.visitsweden.com) Official tourism website.

Swedish Institute (www.si.se/English) Scholarly info on Swedish culture.

The Local (www.thelocal.se) News from Sweden in English.

Set Your Budget

➡ Dorm bed or campsite: 250–450kr

➡ Fast-food meal (kebab, quiche, sandwich): 65–85kr

➡ 24-hour bus and metro ticket: 120kr

Stockholm

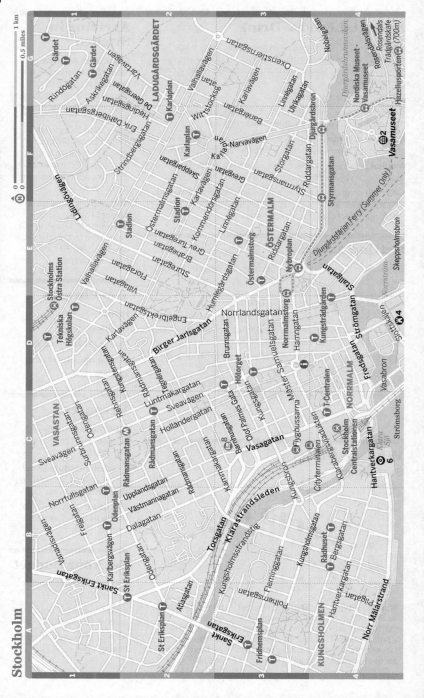

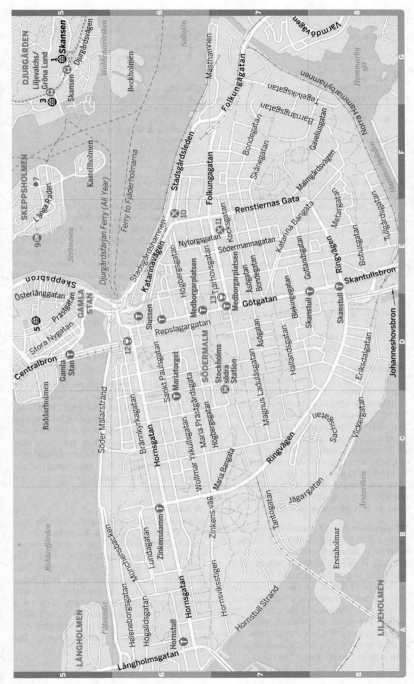

Stockholm

⊖@ॿ; 📵65 Skeppsholmen) The *af Chapman* is a storied vessel that has done plenty of travelling of its own. It's anchored in a superb location, swaying gently off Skeppsholmen. Bunks are in dorms below deck. Apart from showers and toilets, all facilities are on dry land in the Skeppsholmen hostel, including a good kitchen, a laid-back common room and a TV lounge.

✕ Eating

Stockholm is a city of foodies. Its epicurean highlights don't come cheap, but you can find great value in the abundant cafes, coffee shops and vegetarian buffets.

★ Rosendals Trädgårdskafe   CAFE €€
(📞08-54 58 12 70; www.rosendalstradgard.se; Rosendalsterrassen 12; mains 99-145kr; ⊕11am-5pm Mon-Fri, to 6pm Sat & Sun May-Sep, closed Mon Feb-Apr & Oct-Dec; 🅿🍴; 📵44, 69, 76 Djurgårdsbron, 🛳7) 🍴 Set among the greenhouses of a pretty botanical garden, Rosendals is an idyllic spot for heavenly pastries and coffee or a meal and a glass of organic wine. Lunch includes a brief menu of soups, sandwiches (such as ground-lamb burger with chanterelles) and gorgeous salads. Much of the produce is biodynamic and grown on-site.

★ Hermans Trädgårdscafé   VEGETARIAN €€
(📞08-643 94 80; www.hermans.se; Fjällgatan 23B; buffet 195kr, desserts from 35kr; ⊕11am-9pm; 🍴; 📵2, 3, 53, 71, 76 Tjärhovsplan, 🚇Slussen) 🍴 This justifiably popular vegetarian buffet is one of the nicest places to dine in Stockholm, with a glassed-in porch and outdoor seating on a terrace overlooking the city's glittering skyline. Fill up on inventive, flavourful veggie and vegan creations served from a cosy, vaulted room – you might need to muscle your way in, but it's worth the effort.

Meatballs for the People   SWEDISH €€
(📞08-466 60 99; www.meatballs.se; Nytorgsgatan 30, Södermalm; mains 179-195kr; ⊕11am-10pm Mon-Thu, to midnight Fri & Sat, limited hours Jul & Aug; 🍴; 🚇Medborgarplatsen) The name says it all. This restaurant serves serious meatballs, including moose, deer, wild boar and lamb, served with creamed potatoes and pickled vegetables, and best washed down with a pint of Sleepy Bulldog craft beer. It's a novel twist on a traditional Swedish dining experience, accentuated by the rustic decor and delightful waiting staff.

🍷 Drinking & Entertainment

★ Akkurat   BAR
(📞08-644 00 15; www.akkurat.se; Hornsgatan 18; ⊕3pm-midnight Mon, to 1am Tue-Sat, 6pm-1am Sun; 🚇Slussen) Valhalla for beer fiends, Akkurat boasts a huge selection of Belgian ales as well as a good range of Swedish-made microbrews and hard ciders. It's one of only two places in Sweden to be recognised by a Cask Marque for its real ale. Extras include a vast wall of whisky and live music several nights a week.

★ Kvarnen   BAR
(📞08-643 03 80; www.kvarnen.com; Tjärhovsgatan 4; ⊕11am-1am Mon & Tue, to 3am Wed-Fri, noon-3am Sat, noon-1am Sun; 🚇Medborgarplatsen) An old-school Hammarby football fan hang-out, Kvarnen is one of the best bars in Söder. The gorgeous beer hall dates from 1907 and seeps tradition; if you're not the clubbing type, get here early for a nice pint and a meal (mains from 210kr). As the night progresses, the nightclub vibe takes over. Queues are fairly constant but justifiable.

ℹ️ Information

Stockholm Visitor Center (📞 08-50 82 85 08; www.visitstockholm.com; Kulturhuset, Sergels Torg 3; ⏱9am-7pm Mon-Fri, 9am-4pm Sat, 10am-4pm Sun May–mid-Sep, shorter hours rest of year; 📶; 🚇T-Centralen) The main visitors centre occupies a space inside Kulturhuset on Sergels Torg.

ℹ️ Getting There & Away

➡ Stockholm's and Sweden's main airport, **Arlanda** (ARN; 📞10-109 10 00; www.swedavia. se/arlanda), is 45km north of the city centre.

➡ Stockholm is connected by ferry to Turku and Helsinki in Finland via the Åland archipelago, and also to Tallinn (Estonia), Riga (Latvia) and St Petersburg (Russia).

➡ Most long-distance buses arrive at and depart from **Cityterminalen** (www.cityterminalen.com; ⏱7am-6pm), which is connected to Centralstationen.

➡ Stockholm is the hub for national and international train services run by **Sveriges Järnväg** (SJ; 📞0771-75 75 75; www.sj.se).

ℹ️ Getting Around

➡ The **Arlanda Express** (www.arlandaexpress. com; Centralstationen; one-way adult/child 280/150kr, 2 adults one-way in summer 350kr) airport train service from Centralstationen takes 20 minutes to reach Arlanda.

➡ A cheaper option is the **Flygbuss** (www.flygbussarna.se; Cityterminalen) service between Stockholm Arlanda and Cityterminalen. Buses (119kr, 50 minutes, every 10 or 15 minutes) leave from stop 11 in Terminal 5. Tickets are cheapest online.

➡ **Storstockholms Lokaltrafik** (SL; 📞08-600 10 00; www.sl.se; Centralstationen; ⏱SL Center Sergels Torg 7am-6.30pm Mon-Fri, 10am-5pm Sat & Sun, inside Centralstationen 6.30am-11.45pm Mon-Sat, from 7am Sun) runs all *tunnelbana* (metro) trains, local trains and buses within Stockholm county. Refillable SL travel cards (20kr) can be loaded with single-trip or unlimited-travel credit.

Uppsala

📞 018 / POP 214,559

Drenched in history but never stifled by the past, Uppsala has the party vibe of a university town to balance out its large number of important buildings and general atmosphere of weighty cultural significance. It's a terrific combination, and one that makes the town both fun and functional, not to mention very rewarding for the interested traveller.

⊙ Sights

★**Domkyrka**   CHURCH (Cathedral; 📞018-430 35 00; www.uppsaladomkyrka.se; Domkyrkoplan; ⏱8am-6pm, tours in English 11am & 2pm Mon-Sat, 4pm Sun Jul & Aug) FREE The Gothic Domkyrka dominates the city and is Scandinavia's largest church, with towers soaring an inspiring 119m. The interior is imposing, with the French Gothic ambulatory flanked by small chapels. Tombs here include those of St Erik, Gustav Vasa and the scientist Carl von Linné. Regular tours in English are conducted in July and August and at other times by appointment.

★**Gamla Uppsala**   ARCHAEOLOGICAL SITE (www.arkeologigamlauppsala.se; ⏱24hr; 🅿; 🚌2) FREE One of Sweden's largest and most important burial sites, Gamla Uppsala (4km north of Uppsala) contains 300 mounds from the 6th to 12th centuries. The earliest are also the three most impressive. Legend has it they contain the pre-Viking kings Aun, Egil and Adils, who appear in *Beowulf* and Icelandic historian Snorre Sturlason's *Ynglingsaga*. More recent evidence suggests the occupant of Östhögen (East Mound) was a woman, probably a female regent in her 20s or 30s.

ℹ️ Information

Destination Uppsala Tourist Centre (📞018-727 48 00; www.destinationuppsala.se; Kungsgatan 59; ⏱10am-6pm Mon-Fri, to 3pm Sat, plus 11am-3pm Sun Jul & Aug) Located directly in front of the train station, the tourist office has helpful advice, maps and brochures about the whole county.

ℹ️ Getting There & Away

Upplands Lokaltrafik (📞0771-14 14 14; www. ul.se) bus 801 shuttles between Uppsala and Arlanda Airport (91kr, 40 minutes).

SJ Rail (Statens Järnvägar; 📞0771-75 75 75; www.sj.se/en) operates regular services to/from Stockholm (from 105kr, 40 minutes).

Göteborg

📞 031 / POP 580,000

Though often caught in Stockholm's shadow, gregarious, chilled-out Göteborg (*yur-te-borry*, Gothenburg in English) actually has greater appeal for many visitors (and resident Swedes) than the fast-paced capital. Some of the country's finest talent hails from the streets of this cosmopolitan port, including music icons José González and Soundtrack of Our Lives. Neoclassical architecture lines its tram-rattled streets, grit-hip cafes hum with bonhomie, and there's always some cutting-edge art and architecture to grab your attention.

◉ Sights

The Haga district is Göteborg's oldest suburb, dating back to 1648. A hard-core hippie hang-out in the 1960s and '70s, its cobbled streets and vintage buildings are now a gentrified blend of cafes, op shops and boutiques.

★ Konstmuseum   GALLERY
(www.konstmuseum.goteborg.se; Götaplatsen; adult/child 40kr/free; ⏲11am-6pm Tue & Thu, to 8pm Wed, to 5pm Fri-Sun; ♿; ☐4 Berzeliigatan) Home to Gothenburg's premier art collection, Konstmuseet displays works by the French Impressionists, Rubens, Van Gogh, Rembrandt and Picasso; Scandinavian masters such as Bruno Liljefors, Edvard Munch, Anders Zorn and Carl Larsson have pride of place in the **Fürstenburg Galleries**.

Other highlights include a superb sculpture hall, the **Hasselblad Center** with its annual *New Nordic Photography* exhibition, and temporary displays of next-gen Nordic art.

★ Universeum   MUSEUM
(www.universeum.se; Södra Vägen 50; adult/child 250/195kr; ⏲10am-6pm, to 8pm Jul & Aug; P♿; ☐2 Korsvägen) In what is arguably the best museum for kids in Sweden, you find yourself in the midst of a humid rainforest, complete with trickling water, tropical birds and butterflies flitting through the greenery and tiny marmosets. On a level above, roaring dinosaurs maul each other, while next door, denizens of the deep float through the shark tunnel and venomous beauties lie coiled in the serpent tanks. In the 'technology inspired by nature' section, stick your children to the Velcro wall.

⌂ Sleeping

★ STF Göteborg City   HOSTEL €€
(☎031-756 98 00; www.svenskaturistforeningen. se; Drottninggatan 63-65; hostel r from 995kr, hotel s/d from 1400/1500kr, breakfast 85kr; @☎; ☐1 Brunnsparken) This large super-central hostel is all industrial chic in the cafe/dining area

and lounge; and plush comfort on each of its individually themed floors. All rooms are private, with en suite bathroom, luxe carpeting and comfortable bed-bunks, and – rarity of rarities! – your bed linen and towels are provided for you.

✗ Eating & Drinking

Kungsportsavenyn brims with beer-downing tourists, but there are still some savvier options. The Linné district is home to several friendly student hang-outs serving extremely cheap beer.

Saluhall Briggen   MARKET €
(www.saluhallbriggen.se; Nordhemsgatan 28; ⏲9am-6pm Mon-Fri, to 3pm Sat; ☐1 Prinsgatan) This covered market will have you drooling over its bounty of fresh bread, cheeses, quiches, seafood and ethnic treats. It's particularly handy for the hostel district.

Ölhallen 7:an   BEER HALL
(Kungstorget 7; ⏲11am-midnight Sun-Tue, to 1am Wed-Sat; ☐3, 4, 5, 7, 10 Kungsportsplatsen) This well-worn Swedish beer hall – the last remaining from its era – hasn't changed much in over 100 years. It attracts an interesting mix of bikers and regular folk with its homey atmosphere and friendly service. The illustrations lining the walls are Liss Sidén's portraits of regulars in the old days.

❶ Information

Tourist Office (☎031-368 42 00; www.goteborg.com; Kungsportsplatsen 2; ⏲9.30am-8pm late Jun–mid-Aug, shorter hours rest of year) Central and busy; has a good selection of free brochures and maps.

❶ Getting There & Away

➧ Stena Line runs ferries to Kiel in Germany (foot passenger one-way/return from 500kr) and Fredrikshavn in Denmark (foot-passenger one-way from 200kr).

➧ Bus services include Copenhagen (from 239kr, 4¾ hours, four daily), Malmö (from 119kr, 3½ to four hours, seven to nine daily), Oslo (from 229kr, 3½ hours, five to 10 daily) and Stockholm (from 159kr, 6½ to seven hours, four to five daily).

➧ Trains run to Copenhagen (472kr, 3¾ hours, hourly), Malmö (195kr, 2½ to 3¼ hours, hourly), Oslo (305kr, four hours, three daily) and Stockholm (430kr, three to five hours, one to two an hour).

Gotland

☑ 0498

Gorgeous Gotland, an island adrift in the Baltic, has much to brag about: a Unesco-lauded medieval capital, truffle-sprinkled woods, dining hot spots, talented artisans and more hours of sunshine than anywhere else in Sweden. It's also one of the country's richest historical regions, with around 100 medieval churches and countless prehistoric sites.

ⓘ Getting There & Away

Year-round car ferries between Gotland and both Nynäshamn (just south of Stockholm) and Oskarshamn (between Stockholm and Malmö) are operated by **Destination Gotland** (☑ 0771-22 33 00; www.destinationgotland.se; Korsgatan 2, Visby).

Visby

The Unesco-listed medieval port town of Visby alone warrants a trip to Gotland. Within its sturdy city walls await twisting cobbled streets, fairy-tale wooden cottages, evocative church ruins and steep hills with impromptu Baltic views. The wining and dining options are similarly superb. It gets very busy in summer.

◉ Sights

★**Gotlands Museum**   MUSEUM
(☑ 0498-29 27 00; www.gotlandsmuseum.se; Strandgatan 14; incl Konstmuseet adult/child 120kr/ free; ☺ 11am-4pm Tue-Sun; 🖭) Gotlands Museum is one of the mightiest regional museums in Sweden. While highlights include amazing 8th-century, pre-Viking picture stones, human skeletons from chambered tombs and medieval wooden sculptures, the star turn is the legendary Spillings treasure horde. At 70kg it's the world's largest booty of preserved silver treasure.

★**Visby Sankta Maria Domkyrka**   CATHEDRAL
(Visby Saint Maria Cathedral; www.visbydf.se; Norra Kyrkogatan 2; ☺ 9am-9pm Jul & Aug, to 5pm rest of year) Visby's church ruins contrast with the stoic and utterly awe-inspiring Sankta Maria *kyrka*. Built in the late 12th and early 13th centuries and heavily touched up over the years, its whimsical towers are topped by baroque cupolas. Soak up the beautiful stained-glass windows, carved floor slabs and ornate carved reredos. The cathedral is used for intimate music concerts in summer. The best place to view the cathedral is from behind – climb all those stairs up the hillside for astounding views.

ⓘ Information

Gotlands Turistbyrå (☑ 0498-20 17 00; www. gotland.info; Donners Plats 1; ☺ 8am-7pm daily summer, 9am-5pm Mon-Fri & 10am-4pm Sat rest of year) The tourist office is conveniently located at Donners Plats and can help with accommodation and advise on what is going on during your stay. It also organises free tours during the summer months.

Around Gotland

Renting a bicycle and following the well-marked Gotlandsleden cycle path is one of the best ways to spend time on Gotland. It loops all around the island, sometimes joining the roadways but more often winding through quiet fields and forests. You can hire cycles at several locations in Visby.

Norrland

Norrland, the northern half of Sweden, is a paradise for nature lovers who enjoy hiking, skiing and other outdoor activities; in winter in particular, the landscape is transformed by snowmobiles, dog sleds and the eerie aurora borealis. The far north is home to the Sámi people and their reindeer.

Östersund

☑ 063 / POP 49,806

This pleasant town by Storsjön lake, in the chilly waters of which is said to lurk Sweden's answer to the Loch Ness monster, is an

---

OFF THE BEATEN TRACK

ABISKO

A stunning hiking destination and one of the best spots in Sweden for viewing the aurora borealis. Abisko lies near the national park of the same name and is the start- or end-point for the 425km Kungsleden hiking trail. The hostel, trailhead and national park are at Abisko Turiststation, 4km west of the principal village. Abisko is easily reached from Kiruna or Narvik, Norway, by bus or train.

excellent activity base and gateway town for further explorations of Norrland.

◎ Sights & Activities

Östersund is a major winter sports centre. You can also ask at the tourist office about monster-spotting lake cruises in summer.

★ Jamtli   MUSEUM

(www.jamtli.com; Museiplan; adult/child 70kr/free, late June–late Aug free; ⊙11am-5pm daily late Jun-late Aug, Tue-Sun rest of year; P ⚑) Jamtli, 1km north of the centre, consists of two parts: the open-air museum, comprising painstakingly reconstructed wooden buildings, complete with enthusiastic guides wearing 19th-century period costume; and the indoor museum, home to the **Överhogdal Tapestries**, the oldest of their kind in Europe – Christian Viking relics from AD 1100 that feature animals, people, ships and dwellings. Another fascinating display is devoted to Storsjöodjuret (the lake monster), including taped interviews with those who claim they have seen it, monster-catching gear and a pickled monster embryo.

🛏 Sleeping & Eating

STF Ledkrysset Hostel   HOSTEL €

(☑063-10 33 10; http://ostersundledkrysset.se; Biblioteksgatan 25; dm/s/d 180/350/520kr; 🛜) This well-run, central hostel is in a converted old fire station and is your best shoestring bet.

ⓘ Getting There & Away

SJ departures include two trains daily to Stockholm (701kr, five hours) via Uppsala. There are onward connections to Trondheim, Norway. Bus and summer train options head further north.

Kiruna

☑0980 / POP 22,900

Scarred by mine works, Kiruna may not be the most aesthetically appealing city, but its proximity to great stretches of hikeable wilderness, the iconic Icehotel and the proliferation of winter activities make it an excellent base.

Due to danger of collapse from mining, plans are a foot to move the entire city a couple of miles northwest within the space of 20 years; the town centre move is already under way.

👉 Tours

Active Lapland   SNOW SPORTS

(☑076-104 55 08; www.activelapland.com; Solbacksvägen 22; tours from 1250kr) This experienced operator offers 2½-hour dog-sled rides (1250kr), rides under the northern lights (highly recommended), and airport pick-ups by dog sleigh (5400kr). They'll even let you drive your own dog sled (3200kr).

🛏 Sleeping & Eating

★ SPiS Hotel & Hostel   HOSTEL €

(☑0980-170 00; www.spiskiruna.se; Bergmästaregatan 7; dm/d from 305/535kr, hotel s/d 995/1195kr; P 🛜) This catch-all hotel-and-hostel combo features modern hotel rooms and cosy dorms in central Kiruna. There's a deli, bakery and top-quality restaurant as part of the complex, plus a handy communal guest kitchen and an even handier supermarket just a few minutes' stroll away. Look for the orange building.

ⓘ Information

Tourist Office (☑0980-188 80; www.kiruna lapland.se; Lars Janssonsgatan 17; ⊙8.30am-

---

DON'T MISS

ICEHOTEL

The winter wonderland that is the **Icehotel** (☑0980-668 00; www.icehotel.com; Marknadsvägen 63; s/d/ste from 2400/3300/5400kr, cabins from 2000kr; ⊙Dec-Apr; P 🛜) in Jukkasjärvi, 18km east of Kiruna, is an international phenomenon. The enormous hotel building is constructed using 30,000 tonnes of snow and 4000 tonnes of ice, with international artists and designers coming to contribute innovative ice sculptures every year. In the ice rooms, the beds are made of compacted snow and covered with reindeer skins and serious sleeping bags, guaranteed to keep you warm despite the -5°C temperature inside the rooms. Come morning, guests are revived with a hot drink and a sauna. The attached Ice Church is popular for weddings, while the ice bar and restaurants provide refreshment. Nonguests can visit the Icehotel in winter and take part in a range of activities and guided tours. Summer activities include ice-sculpting and a look at next season's building blocks in a chilled warehouse.

6pm Mon-Fri, to 4pm Sat & Sun) Located inside the Folkets Hus visitor centre, the tourist office offers internet access and can book various tours. Also has an excellent model of how Kiruna will look after the 'move'.

❶ Getting There & Away

➡ Kiruna Airport, 7km east of the town, has flights with SAS and Norwegian to Stockholm.

➡ There's a daily bus to Narvik (Norway; 320kr, 2¾ hours) via Abisko. Other departures include Jukkasjärvi (48kr, 30 minutes, two to six daily).

➡ There is a daily overnight train to Stockholm (from 696kr, 17½ hours). Other destinations include Narvik (Norway; 227kr, 3½ to 3¾ hours) via Abisko (199kr, 1½ to two hours).

Sweden Survival Guide

❶ Directory A–Z

ACCOMMODATION

Sweden has hundreds of hostels (vandrarhem), usually with excellent facilities. There's a scarcity of dormitories; hostels are more likely to have singles and doubles. They keep very short reception opening times, so prebook by telephone. Before leaving, you must clean up after yourself; cleaning materials are provided.

DISCOUNT CARDS

Göteborg, Malmö, Stockholm and Uppsala have tourist cards that get you into their major attractions and offer parking, travel on public transport and discounts at participating hotels, restaurants and shops.

LGBT TRAVELLERS

Sweden is a famously liberal country that has been a leader in establishing LGBT rights.

A good source of local information is the free monthly magazine QX. You can pick it up at many clubs, shops and restaurants in Stockholm, Göteborg and Malmö.

MONEY

➡ Sweden uses the krona (plural kronor) as currency. One krona is divided into 100 öre.

➡ Credit and debit cards are extremely widely used, even for small purchases, and a few stores and museums are even cash-free.

➡ Tipping isn't expected, except at dinner (when around 10% for good service is customary).

OPENING HOURS

Banks 9.30am to 3pm Monday to Friday; some city branches 9am to 5pm or 6pm.

Bars & pubs 11am or noon to 1am or 2am.

❶ PRICE RANGES

The following room prices are for a double room in the summer season (mid-June through August); standard weekday prices during the rest of the year might be twice as high. Breakfast is normally included in hotel room prices, but usually costs extra in hostels.

€ less than 800kr

€€ 800–1600kr

€€€ more than 1600kr

Restaurants 11am to 2pm and 5pm to 10pm; often closed on Sunday and/or Monday.

Shops 9am to 6pm Monday to Friday, 9am to 1pm Saturday.

Supermarkets 8am or 9am to 7pm or 10pm.

Systembolaget (alcohol shop) 10am to 6pm Monday to Friday, 10am to 2pm (often until 5pm) Saturday, sometimes with extended hours on Thursday and Friday evenings.

Tourist offices Usually open daily Midsummer to mid-August, Monday to Friday only the rest of the year.

TELEPHONE

➡ Country code: 46. International access code: 📞 00.

➡ Local SIM cards are readily available; data packages are relatively cheap.

❶ Getting There & Around

AIR

Stockholm Arlanda (p153) links Sweden with major European and North American cities. **Göteborg Landvetter** (www.swedavia.se/landvetter; 🚌 Flygbuss) is Sweden's second-biggest international airport. **Stockholm Skavsta** (Nyköping Airport (NYO); 📞 0155-28 04 00; www.skavsta.se/en; General Schybergs Plan 22, Nyköping; 🚌 Flygbussarna) is located 100km south of Stockholm, near Nyköping, and is mainly used by Ryanair flights. **Sturup Airport** (📞 010-109 45 00; www.swedavia.com/malmo; Malmö-Sturup) in Malmö serves the south of the country and is also a major international hub.

BUS

Eurolines connect Sweden's major cities with many other European destinations. Swebus Express runs to Copenhagen. There are many cross-border buses to Norway.

Swebus Express (📞 0771-21 82 18; www.swebus.se) has the largest network of express buses, but they only serve the southern half of the country. **Svenska Buss** (☑ 0771-67 67 67; www.svenskabuss.se) and **Nettbuss** (☑ 0771-15 15 15; www.nettbuss.se) also connect many southern towns and cities with Stockholm; prices are often slightly cheaper than Swebus Express prices, but services are less frequent.

In the north, bus connections with Stockholm are provided by several smaller bus operators. There are also services into Finland and Norway.

FERRY

Sweden has numerous international ferry connections to Denmark, Norway, Finland, Germany, Poland, Estonia and Latvia. Check www.directferries.com for all routes.

TRAIN

Sweden is linked by rail to Denmark and the rest of Europe via the Öresund bridge. Trains shuttle between Copenhagen and Malmö, where you can change to Swedish services. There are some through trains to Stockholm and Göteborg. There are regular train services between Sweden and Norway.

Sweden has an extensive and reliable railway network, and trains are almost always faster than buses.

Inlandsbanan (☑ 0771-53 53 53; www.inlandsbanan.se; Storsjöstråkket 19, Östersund) One of the great rail journeys in Scandinavia is this slow and scenic 1300km route from Kristinehamn to Gällivare.

Sveriges Järnväg (SJ; ☑ 0771-75 75 99; www.sj.se) National network covering most main lines, especially in the southern part of the country.

Tågkompaniet (☑ 0771-44 41 11; www.tagkompaniet.se) Operates excellent overnight trains

---

SAUNAS

For centuries the sauna has been a place to bathe, meditate, warm up and even give birth, and most Finns still use it at least once a week. Bathing is done in the nude (public saunas are nearly always sex-segregated) and Finns are quite strict about its nonsexual – even sacred – nature. Shower first. Once inside (with a temperature of 80°C to 100°C; 176°F to 212°F), water is thrown onto the stove using a *kauhu* (ladle), producing *löyly* (steam). A *vihta* (whisk of birch twigs and leaves) is sometimes used to lightly strike the skin, improving circulation. Cool off with a cold shower or preferably by jumping into a lake. Repeat. The sauna beer afterwards is also traditional.

---

from Göteborg and Stockholm north to Kiruna and Narvik.

FINLAND

Helsinki

☑ 09 / POP 629,512

It's fitting that harbourside Helsinki, capital of a country with such watery geography, melds so graciously into the Baltic. Half the city seems liquid, and the complex, undulating coastlines include any number of bays, inlets and islands. The design scene here is legendary, whether you're browsing showroom brands or taking the backstreet hipster trail. The city's gourmet side is also flourishing, with new places that offer locally sourced tasting menus popping up at dizzying speed.

⊙ Sights & Activities

★**Ateneum**   GALLERY
(www.ateneum.fi; Kaivokatu 2; adult/child €15/free; ⊙10am-6pm Tue & Fri, to 8pm Wed & Thu, to 5pm Sat & Sun) Occupying a palatial 1887 neo-Rennaissance building, Finland's premier art gallery offers a crash course in the nation's art. It houses Finnish paintings and sculptures from the 'golden age' of the late 19th century through to the 1950s, including works by Albert Edelfelt, Hugo Simberg, Helene Schjerfbeck, the von Wright brothers and Pekka Halonen. Pride of place goes to the prolific Akseli Gallen-Kallela's triptych from the Finnish national epic, the *Kalevala*, depicting Väinämöinen's pursuit of the maiden Aino.

★**Kiasma**   GALLERY
(www.kiasma.fi; Mannerheiminaukio 2; adult/child €14/free, 1st Sun of month free; ⊙10am-5pm Tue & Sun, to 8.30pm Wed-Fri, to 6pm Sat) Now one in a series of elegant contemporary buildings in this part of town, curvaceous and quirky metallic Kiasma, designed by Steven Holl and finished in 1998, is a symbol of the city's modernisation. It exhibits an eclectic collection of Finnish and international contemporary art, including digital art, and has excellent facilities for kids. Its outstanding success is that it's been embraced by the people of Helsinki, with a theatre and a hugely popular glass-sided cafe and terrace.

★ **Design Museum**   MUSEUM
(www.designmuseum.fi; Korkeavuorenkatu 23;
adult/child €12/free; ☺11am-6pm Jun-Aug, 11am-
8pm Tue, to 6pm Wed-Sun Sep-May) An unmissable stop for Finnish design aficionados,
Helsinki's Design Museum has a permanent
collection that looks at the roots of Finnish
design in the nation's traditions and nature.
Changing exhibitions focus on contemporary design – everything from clothing to
household furniture. From June to August,
30-minute tours in English take place at
2pm on Saturday and are included in admission. Combination tickets with the nearby
Museum of Finnish Architecture (Arkkite-
htuurimuseo; ☑045-7731-0474; www.mfa.fi; Kasar-
mikatu 24; adult/child €10/free, combination ticket
with Design Museum €15/free; ☺11am-6pm Tue &
Thu-Sun, to 8pm Wed) are a great-value way to
see the two museums.

★ **Suomenlinna**   FORTRESS
(Sveaborg; www.suomenlinna.fi) Suomenlinna,
the 'fortress of Finland', straddles a cluster
of car-free islands connected by bridges.
The Unesco World Heritage site was originally built by the Swedes as Sveaborg in the
mid-18th century. Several museums, former
bunkers and fortress walls, as well as Finland's only remaining WWII submarine, are
fascinating to explore; its **tourist office**
(☑029-533-8420; ☺10am-6pm May-Sep, to 4pm
Oct-Apr) has info. Cafes and picnic spots are
plentiful.

Ferries (www.hsl.fi; one-way/return
€3.20/5, 15 minutes, four hourly, fewer in
winter) depart from the passenger quay at
Helsinki's kauppatori.

★ **Kotiharjun Sauna**   SAUNA
(www.kotiharjunsauna.fi; Harjutorinkatu 1; adult/
child €13/7; ☺2-9.30pm Tue-Sun) Helsinki's
only original traditional public wood-fired
sauna dates back to 1928. It's a classic experience, where you can also get a scrub down
and massage (from €30). There are separate
saunas for men and women; bring your own
towel or rent one (€3). It's a 150m stroll
southwest of the Sörnäinen metro station.

★ **Allas Sea Pool**   SWIMMING
(www.allasseapool.fi; Katajanokanlaituri 2; day
ticket adult/child €12/6, towel rental €5; ☺6.15am-
11pm Mon-Fri, 8am-11pm Sat & Sun) Constructed
from Finnish fir, this 2016-built swimming
complex sits right on the harbour against a
spectacular city backdrop. It incorporates a
bracing Baltic seawater pool, two freshwater

> **DON'T MISS**
>
> ## DESIGN SHOPPING
>
> Helsinki is a design epicentre, from
> fashion to the latest furniture and
> homewares. Central but touristy Espla-
> nadi has the chic boutiques of Finnish
> classics. The most intriguing area to
> browse is nearby Punavuori, with a great
> retro-hipster vibe and numerous bou-
> tiques, studios and galleries to explore.
> A couple of hundred of these are part
> of **Design District Helsinki**, whose
> invaluable map you can find at the tour-
> ist office.

pools (one for adults, one for kids; both heated to 27°C; 80.6°F) and three saunas (male,
female and mixed). Regular events include
DJs or full-moon all-night nude swimming.
Its restaurant serves Nordic cuisine.

🛏 Sleeping

Hostel Diana Park   HOSTEL €
(☑09-642-169; www.dianapark.fi; Uudenmaanka-
tu 9; dm/s/d from €32/62/75; 🛜) More like a
guesthouse, Helsinki's most characterful
and laid-back hostel occupies the 3rd (top)
floor of a walk-up building in a lively street
of bars and restaurants. Its 50 beds are
spread across 15 rooms; all share bathrooms
but have in-room sinks. Private rooms offer
more peace and there's a great lounge for socialising. Breakfast costs €7.

Hostel Domus Academica   HOSTEL €
(☑09-1311-4334; www.hostelacademica.fi; Hieta-
niemenkatu 14; dm/s/d/tr from €31/58/85/109;
☺Jun-Aug; 🅿@🛜♨) Finnish students live
well, so take advantage of this summer residence: a clean, busy, environmentally sound
spot with a pool and sauna. Its 326 modern en-suite rooms come with kitchenettes
(crockery is in the common room) and Finnish textiles. Dorms sleep up to three. Breakfast costs €8.50. HI discount. Rates include
a morning sauna.

🍴 Eating

Good budget options are in short supply: cafes offer lunch choices and there are plenty
of self-catering opportunities.

★ **Vanha Kauppahalli**   MARKET €
(www.vanhakauppahalli.fi; Eteläranta 1; ☺8am-6pm
Mon-Sat, plus 10am-5pm Sun Jun-Aug; 🖋) 🌶

FINLAND AT A GLANCE

Don't Miss

Design shopping in Helsinki Functional, elegant, outrageous or wacky: the choice is yours. The capital's decidedly nonmainstream chic is best explored by browsing the vast variety of design shops that spatter its centre.

National park hiking The country's wonderful forests provide excellent hiking opportunities – highlights include Lapland's protected areas and the hilly Karhunkierros trail near Kuusamo.

Summer cottages The symbol of the Finnish summer is a cosy cottage perched on a blue lake, with a little rowboat, a fishing pier and perhaps its own swimming beach. The simplest rustic cabins have outside loos and water drawn from a well, while the most modern designer bungalows have every creature comfort.

Sámi culture Finland's indigenous northerners have used technology to ease the arduous side of reindeer herding while maintaining an intimate knowledge of Lapland's natural world. Their capital, Inari, and the nearby Lemmenjoki National Park are the best places to begin to learn about Sámi culture and traditions.

Lakeland Finland's beautiful eastern Lakeland seems to have more water than land, so it'd be a crime not to get out on it. You can take three days to paddle the family-friendly Oravareitti (Squirrel Route), or head out into Kolovesi and Linnansaari national parks to meet freshwater seals.

Itineraries

One Week

Kick off in capital **Helsinki**, prowling the buzzing Design District and unwinding in excellent restaurants and bars. Hit Suomenlinna or an island restaurant to get a feel for the archipelago, and day trip to historic **Porvoo's** enchanting wooden buildings.

Grab the train to gorgeous **Savonlinna**, where the stunning castle hosts an opera festival.

Two Weeks

Head to harbour city **Turku**, then up north to the capital of Lapland, **Rovaniemi**, a great base for outdoor activities. Push on further north to **Inari** to explore national parks and Sámi culture.

Essential Food & Drink

Coffee Finland's staple, best accompanied with a *pulla* (cardamom-flavoured pastry).

Offbeat meats Unusual meats appear on menus: reindeer is a staple up north; elk and bear are available during autumn's hunting season.

Fresh food The kauppahalli (market hall) offers a stunning array of produce. In summer, stalls at the kauppatori (market square) sell delicious fresh vegetables and fruit.

Alcoholic drinks Beer is a staple, and microbreweries are on the increase. Finns also love dissolving things in vodka – try a shot of *salmiakkikossu* (salty-liquorice flavoured) or *fisu* (Fisherman's Friend–flavoured).

Fish Salmon is ubiquitous, and lake fish include Arctic char, lavaret, pike-perch and scrumptious fried *muikku* (vendace).

Getting Around

A useful combined journey planner for Finland's public-transport network is online at www.journey.fi.

Bus Around the same price as trains, but slower. They cover the whole country and rarely need booking.

Car Hire widely available; week or weekend deals booked in advance are much better than sky-high day rates. Automatic transmission is rare; book well in advance and expect a hefty premium. Drive on the right.

Air Generally expensive, but you can get some good deals on Lapland routes.

Train Generally modern and comfortable, with good coverage. Book busy routes in advance.

When to Go

Helsinki

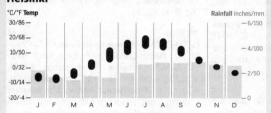

Jul Peak season, with numerous festivals across the country, though Helsinki is quiet.

Jun & Aug Fewer insects up north; quieter than July and most attractions are open.

Sep–May Short, cool days. Aurora-spotting chances are highest in October, November and March.

Arriving in Finland

Helsinki-Vantaa Airport

Trains on the airport rail link (€5, 30 minutes, 5.05am to 12.05am) serve the city. Local buses (24 hours) and faster Finnair buses (5am to 1.10am) run into the city (30 to 50 minutes). Taxis cost €45 to €50 to the city centre (30 minutes). Cheaper shared airport taxis cost from €29.50 per person.

Top Phrases

Hello. Moi.

Goodbye. Näkemiin.

Thank you. Kiitos.

Excuse me. Anteeksi.

Yes. Kyllä/Joo.

No. Ei.

Resources

Metsähallitus (www.nationalparks.fi) Excellent resource, with detailed information on Finland's national parks and protected areas.

Finnish Tourist Board (www.visitfinland.com) Comprehensive official site.

This is Finland (https://finland.fi) Maintained by the Ministry of Foreign Affairs; informative and entertaining.

Set Your Budget

➡ Dorm bed: €25–35

➡ Bike hire per day: €10–20

➡ Lunch buffet: €8–14

➡ Two-hour bus/train to next town: €8–30

Helsinki

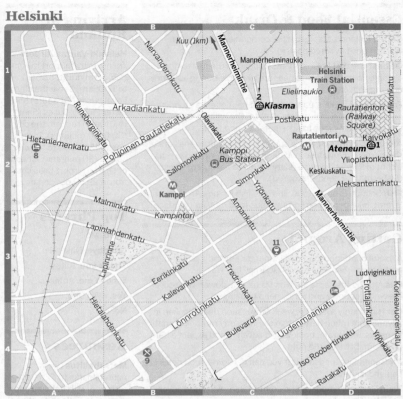

Alongside the harbour, this is Helsinki's iconic market hall. Built in 1888 it's still a traditional Finnish market, with wooden stalls selling local flavours such as liquorice, Finnish cheeses, smoked salmon and herring, berries, forest mushrooms and herbs. Its centrepiece is its superb cafe, **Story** (www.restaurantstory.fi; snacks €3.20-10, mains €12.80-17; ☺ kitchen 8am-3pm Mon-Fri, to 5pm Sat, bar to 6pm Mon-Sat; 🖉) 🍴. Look out too for soups from Soppakeittiö.

Soppakeittiö SOUP €
(www.sopakeittio.fi; Vanha Kauppahalli; soups €9-10; ☺ 11am-5pm Mon-Sat; 🖉) A great place to warm the cockles in winter, this soup stall inside the Vanha Kauppahalli (p159) is renowned for its bouillabaisse, which is almost always on the menu. Other options might include cauliflower and goat's cheese, smoked reindeer or potato and parsnip. There are also branches at the **Hietalahden**

Kauppahalli (www.hietalahdenkauppahalli.fi; Lönnrotinkatu 34; ☺ 8am-6pm Mon-Thu, to 10pm Fri & Sat; 🖉) 🍴 in Kamppi, and **Hakaniemen Kauppahalli** (www.hakaniemenkauppahalli.fi; Hämeentie 1; ☺ 8am-6pm Mon-Fri, to 4pm Sat; 🖉) 🍴 in Kallio.

⭐**Kuu** FINNISH €€
(🕿 09-2709-0973; www.ravintolakuu.fi; Töölönkatu 27; mains €19-30, 2-/3-course lunch menus €24/28, 4-course dinner menus €47-51; ☺ 11.30am-midnight Mon-Fri, 2pm-midnight Sat, 4-11pm Sun) Traditional Finnish fare is given a sharp, contemporary twist at Kuu, which creates dishes from local ingredients such as smoked reindeer heart with pickled forest mushrooms, poached pike-perch with Lappish fingerling potatoes, and liquorice ice cream with cloudberry soup. Wines aren't cheap, but there are some interesting choices. Its casual bistro sibling, KuuKuu, is located 800m south.

Helsinki

⊙ 9am-6pm Mon-Sat, to 4pm Sun mid-May–mid-Sep, 9am-6pm Mon-Fri, 10am-4pm Sat & Sun mid-Sep–mid-May) Busy multilingual office with reams of information on the city. Also has an office at the airport (www.visithelsinki.fi; Terminal 2, Helsinki-Vantaa Airport; ⊙10am-8pm May-Sep, 10am-6pm Mon-Sat, noon-6pm Sun Oct-Apr).

🍷 Drinking & Entertainment

Finns don't mind a drink and Helsinki has some of Scandinavia's most diverse nightlife. Some bars and club nights have a minimum age of 20 or older, so check event details on websites before you arrive.

Bar Loose   BAR, CLUB
(www.barloose.com; Annankatu 21; ⊙8pm-4am Wed-Sat, 11pm-4am Sun; 🛜) The scarlet interior seems too stylish for a rock bar, but that's what Bar Loose is, with portraits of guitar heroes lining one wall and an eclectic crowd upstairs. Downstairs is a club area, with live music more nights than not and DJs spinning everything from metal to mod/retro classics. Drinks are decently priced.

ℹ Information

Helsinki City Tourist Office (☎ 09-3101-3300; www.visithelsinki.fi; Pohjoisesplanadi 19;

ℹ Getting There & Away

➜ **Helsinki-Vantaa airport** (www.helsinki-vantaa.fi), Finland's main air terminus, is served from many European and intercontinental cities. It's 19km north of Helsinki.

➜ International ferries travel to Stockholm, Tallinn, St Petersburg and German destinations.

THE CALL OF KALLIO

For Helsinki's cheapest beer (around €3 to €4 a pint), hit working-class Kallio (near Sörnäinen metro station), north of the city centre. Here, there's a string of dive bars along Helsinginkatu, but on this street as well as on the parallel Vaasankatu and crossing Fleminginkatu you'll find several more characterful bohemian places: go for a wander and you'll soon find a venue you like.

WORTH A TRIP

PORVOO

Finland's second-oldest town is an ever-popular day trip or weekender from Helsinki. Porvoo (Swedish: Borgå) officially became a town in 1380, but even before that it was an important trading post. The town's fabulous historic centre includes the famous brick-red former warehouses along the river that once stored goods bound for destinations across Europe. During the day, Old Town craft shops are bustling with visitors, but staying on a weeknight will mean you could have the place more or less to yourself. The old painted buildings are spectacular in the setting sun.

Bus services depart for Porvoo from Helsinki's Kamppi bus station about every 30 minutes (€9 to €15, one hour).

There is also regular fast-boat service to Tallinn.

➡ **Kamppi bus station** (www.matkahuolto. fi; Salomonkatu) has departures to all Finland centres. **OnniBus** (www.onnibus.com; Kamppi bus station, Salomonkatu) runs budget routes to several Finnish cities.

➡ Helsinki's **train station** (Rautatieasema; www.vr.fi; Kaivokatu 1) has a central location, linked to the metro (Rautatientori stop) and a short walk from Kamppi bus station. There are train services all over Finland and also to Russia.

❶ Getting Around

➡ Trains run from the airport to central Helsinki every 10 minutes (€5, 30 minutes). Bus services also run between the airport and the train station.

➡ With a flat inner city and well-marked cycling paths, Helsinki is ideal for cycling. Get hold of a copy of the Helsinki cycling map at the tourist office.

➡ The city's public-transport system HSL operates buses, metro and local trains, trams and a ferry to Suomenlinna. A one-hour flat-fare ticket for any HSL transport costs €3.20 when purchased on board or €2.90 when purchased in advance. You can buy rechargeable cards and multiday tickets at the tourist office, R-kioski shops and elsewhere.

Turku

📋 02 / POP 187,600

The historic castle and cathedral point to the city's rich cultural history when it was capital, and contemporary Turku is a hotbed of experimental art and vibrant festivals, thanks in part to its spirited population from its university (the country's second largest), who make Turku's nightlife young and fun. As the first city many visitors encounter arriving by ferry from Sweden and Åland, it's a splendid introduction to the Finnish mainland.

◉ Sights

★ Turun Linna   CASTLE

(Turku Castle; 📞 02-262-0300; www.turku.fi/turunlinna; Linnankatu 80; adult/child €10/5; ⊙ 10am-6pm daily Jun-Aug, Tue-Sun Sep-May) Founded in 1280 at the mouth of the Aurajoki, mammoth Turku Castle is easily Finland's largest fortress. Highlights include two dungeons and sumptuous banqueting halls, as well as a fascinating historical museum of medieval Turku in the castle's Old Bailey. Models depict the castle's growth from a simple island fortress to a Renaissance palace. Guided tours in English run four to six times daily from June to August.

★ Aboa Vetus & Ars Nova   MUSEUM, GALLERY

(www.aboavetusarsnova.fi; Itäinen Rantakatu 4-6; adult/child €10/5.50; ⊙ 11am-7pm) Art and archaeology unite here under one roof. Aboa Vetus (Old Turku) draws you underground to Turku's medieval streets, showcasing some of the 37,000 artefacts unearthed from the site (digs still continue). Back in the present, Ars Nova has contemporary art exhibitions upstairs. English-language tours lasting 45 minutes (included in admission) take place daily from 11.30am in July and August.

★ Turun Tuomiokirkko   CATHEDRAL

(Turku Cathedral; 📞 040-341-7100; www.turunseurakunnat.fi; Tuomiokirkonkatu 1; cathedral free, museum adult/child €2/1; ⊙ cathedral & museum 9am-6pm) The 'mother church' of Finland's Lutheran faith, Turku Cathedral towers over the town. Consecrated in 1300, the colossal brick Gothic building was rebuilt many times over the centuries after damaging fires, but it still looks majestic and historic. Upstairs, a small museum traces the stages of the cathedral's construction, and contains medieval sculptures and religious paraphernalia. Free summer organ concerts (www.turkuorgan.fi) take place at 8pm Tuesday. English-language

Turku

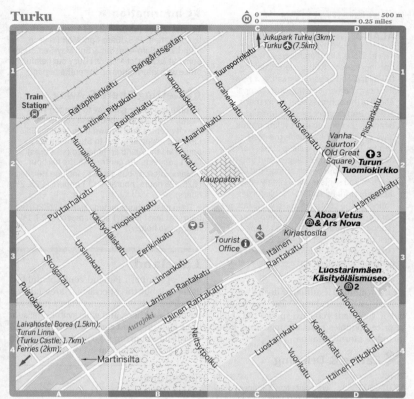

services are held at 4pm every Sunday except the last of the month year-round.

⭐**Luostarinmäen
Käsityöläismuseo** MUSEUM
(Luostarinmäki Handicrafts Museum; ☎02-262-0350; www.turku.fi/handicraftsmuseum; Vartio-vuorenkatu 2; adult/child €6/4; ⏰10am-6pm daily Jun-Aug, Tue-Sun May & Sep, 10am-4pm Tue-Sun late Nov–early Jan) When the savage Great Fire of 1827 swept through Turku, the lower-class quarter Luostarinmäki escaped the flames. Set along tiny lanes and around grassy yards, the 19th-century wooden workshops and houses now form the out-door handicrafts museum, a national treas-ure since 1940. All the buildings are in their original locations, including the workshops of 30 artisans (among them a silversmith, a watchmaker, a baker, a potter, a shoemaker, a printer and a cigar shop), where artisans in period costume ply their trades.

Turku

🛏 Sleeping

Laivahostel Borea HOSTEL €
(☎040-843-6611; www.msborea.fi; Linnankatu 72; dm/s/tw/d/tr/q from €30/51/82/92/112/135; 🅿🛜) Built in Sweden in 1960, the enormous passenger ship SS *Bore* is docked outside the Forum Marinum museum, just 500m north-east of the ferry terminal. It now contains an

OFF THE BEATEN TRACK

ÅLAND

The glorious Åland archipelago is a geopolitical anomaly: the islands belong to Finland and speak Swedish, but have their own parliament, flag and stamps. Åland is the sunniest spot in northern Europe and its sweeping white-sand beaches and flat, scenic cycling routes have great appeal. Outside the lively capital, Mariehamn, a sleepy haze hangs over the islands' tiny villages, and finding your own remote beach among the 6500 skerries and islets is surprisingly easy. A lattice of bridges and free cable ferries connects the central islands, while larger car ferries run to the archipelago's outer reaches. Several ferries head to Åland, including those that connect Turku and Helsinki with Stockholm. Bikes are the best way to explore and are easily rented.

award-winning HI-affiliated hostel with 120 vintage en-suite cabins. Most are squishy, but if you want room to spread out, higher-priced doubles have a lounge area. Rates include a morning sauna.

✕ Eating & Drinking

Tintå BISTRO €€
(☑02-230-7023; www.tinta.fi; Läntinen Rantakatu 9; mains lunch €7.50-14.50, dinner €17-32, pizza €13-16; ⊙11am-midnight Mon-Thu, to 2am Fri, noon-2am Sat, to 10pm Sun) With a cosy exposed-brick interior, this riverside wine bar is also a great bet for weekday lunches, gourmet pizzas and classy mains (such as raspberry and rhubarb salmon or Moroccan-style lamb skewers). Grab a glass of wine and a seat on the summer terrace, and watch the world go by.

**Panimoravintola
Koulu** MICROBREWERY
(School Brewery-Restaurant; www.panimoravintolakoulu.fi; Eerikinkatu 18; ⊙11am-2am) In a former school, complete with maps on the wall, a menu scrawled on a blackboard and a playground-turned-summer beer garden, this fantastic brewpub only serves what it brews – around five lager-style beers that change with the seasons, and a couple of interesting ciders flavoured with tart cranberries and blackcurrants. The exception is the whisky collection, with 75 or so to sample.

ℹ Information

Tourist Office (☑02-262-7444; www.visitturku.fi; Aurakatu 4; ⊙8.30am-6pm Mon-Fri year-round, plus 9am-4pm Sat & Sun May-Sep, 10am-3pm Sat & Sun Oct-Mar; 🛜) Busy but helpful office with information on the entire region.

ℹ Getting There & Away

➜ Turku is a major gateway to Sweden via Åland. The harbour, about 3km southwest of the city centre, has its own train station. Silja Line and Viking Line sail to Stockholm (11 hours) via the Åland archipelago (six hours). Bus 1 connects the centre with the harbour.

➜ Major intercity bus services include Helsinki (€25, 2½ hours, hourly) and Tampere (€25, 2½ hours).

➜ Train destinations include Helsinki (€20, two hours, at least hourly) and Tampere (€23, 1¾ hours, two hourly).

Lakeland

Most of southern Finland could be dubbed 'lakeland', but this spectacular area takes it to extremes. It often seems there's more water than land here, and what water it is: sublime, sparkling and clean, reflecting sky and forests like a mirror. It's a land that leaves an indelible impression on every visitor.

Savonlinna

📋 015 / POP 34,905

One of Finland's prettiest towns, Savonlinna shimmers on a sunny day as the water ripples around its centre. Set on islands between Haapavesi and Pihlajavesi lakes, it's a classic Lakeland settlement with a major attraction: perched on a rocky islet is one of Europe's most visually dramatic castles, Olavinlinna. The castle hosts July's world-famous opera festival in a great setting.

◉ Sights & Activities

From June to August, Savonlinna passenger harbour is buzzing with dozens of daily scenic cruises.

★**Olavinlinna** CASTLE
(St Olaf's Castle; ☑029-533-6941; www.kansallismuseo.fi; adult/child €9/4.50; ⊙11am-5.15pm Jun–mid-Aug, 10am-3.15pm mid-Aug–mid-Dec & Feb-May) Built directly on rock in the middle of the lake (now accessed via bridges), this heavily restored 15th-century fortification was constructed as a military base on the Swedes' restless eastern border. The

currents in the surrounding water ensure that it remains unfrozen in winter, which prevented enemy attacks over ice. To visit the castle's upper levels, including the towers and chapel, you must join an hour-long guided tour. Guides bring the castle to life with vivid accounts of its history.

★☆ Festivals & Events

Savonlinna Opera Festival MUSIC
(Savonlinnan Oopperajuhlat; ☑ 015-476-750; www.operafestival.fi; Olavinkatu 27; ☺ early Jul-early Aug) This internationally renowned event is Finland's most famous festival, with an enviably dramatic setting: the covered courtyard of Olavinlinna Castle.

🛏 Sleeping & Eating

The lakeside **kauppatori** is the place for casual snacking. A traditional *lörtsy* (turnover) comes savoury with meat (*lihalörtsy*) or sweet.

Kesähotelli Vuorilinna HOSTEL €
(☑ 015-73950; www.spahotelcasino.fi; Kylpylaitoksentie; s €55-119, d €65-149; ☺ Jun-Aug; 🅿🐾) Spread over four buildings used by students during term time, this 220-room hostel is operated by Savonlinna's Spa Hotel Casino. Located on lovely Vääräsaari, it is accessed via footbridge from the city centre. Cheaper rooms share a bathroom and kitchen (no utensils). The lack of wi-fi is disappointing, but free use of the spa facilities at the next-door hotel compensates.

ℹ Information

Visit Savonlinna (http://visitsavonlinna. fi; Riihisaari; ☺ 10am-5pm Tue-Sun Sep-Apr, 9am-5pm Mon-Fri & 10am-5pm Sat & Sun May, 10am-5pm daily Jun-Aug) Maps and brochures are available in the Riihisaari (Lake Saimaa Nature & Culture Centre; ☑ 044-417-4466; www.savonlinna.fi/museo; adult/child €7/3, incl Olavinlinna €10/4.50; ☺ 10am-5pm Tue-Sun Sep-Apr, 9am-5pm Mon-Fri & 10am-5pm Sat & Sun May, 10am-5pm daily Jun-Aug).

ℹ Getting There & Away

➜ There are several express buses a day from Helsinki (€30, five to 5½ hours).

➜ Trains from Helsinki (€48, 4¼ hours) and Joensuu (€25, 2¼ hours) both require a change in Parikkala.

➜ In summer, boats connect Savonlinna with other Lakeland towns.

Lapland

Extending hundreds of kilometres above the Arctic Circle, Lapland is Finland's true wilderness and casts a powerful spell. The midnight sun, the Sámi peoples, the aurora borealis (Northern Lights) and the wandering reindeer are all components of Lapland's magic, as is good old ho-ho-ho himself, who 'officially' resides up here.

Rovaniemi

☑ 016 / POP 62,231
A tourism boom town, the 'official' terrestrial residence of Santa Claus is the capital of Finnish Lapland and a more-or-less obligatory northern stop. Its wonderful Arktikum museum is the perfect introduction to the mysteries of these latitudes, and Rovaniemi is a good place from which to organise activities. It's also Lapland's transport hub.

⊙ Sights & Activities

Rovaniemi is great for winter (snowmobiling, skiing and husky-sledding) and summer activities, offering frequent departures with multilingual guides.

★ **Arktikum** MUSEUM
(www.arktikum.fi; Pohjoisranta 4; adult/child €12/5; ☺ 9am-6pm Jun-Aug, 10am-6pm Tue-Sun mid-Jan–May & Sep-Nov, 10am-6pm Dec–mid-Jan) With its beautifully designed glass tunnel stretching out to the Ounasjoki, this is one of Finland's finest museums. One half deals

SCANDINAVIA LAPLAND

OFF THE BEATEN TRACK

INARI

The tiny village of Inari (Sámi: Anár) is Finland's most significant Sámi centre and it boasts the wonderful **Siida** (www. siida.fi; Inarintie 46; adult/child €10/5; ☺ 9am-7pm Jun-Aug, to 6pm Sep, 10am-5pm Wed-Mon Oct-May) museum, the place to begin to learn something of their culture and environment. Inari is also a great base for locations such as Lemmenjoki National Park and the Kevo Strict Nature Reserve – primo hiking spots. The village sits on Lapland's largest lake, Inarijärvi; a couple of campsites provide budget cabin accommodation. Two daily buses hit Inari from Rovaniemi (€60.10, five hours) and continue to Norway.

with Lapland, with information on Sámi culture and the history of Rovaniemi; the other offers a wide-ranging display on the Arctic, with superb static and interactive displays focusing on flora and fauna, as well as on the peoples of Arctic Europe, Asia and North America. Downstairs an audiovisual – basically a pretty slide show – plays on a constant loop.

Lapland Safaris OUTDOORS
(☑016-331-1200; www.laplandsafaris.com; Koskikatu 1; ⏱4hr/overnight snowmobile tours €99/680) Lapland Safaris is the largest and best-established of Rovaniemi's tour operators, with an impressive variety of options. Snowmobiling is big in winter; in summer there are hiking trips (six hours; from €99) and fishing excursions (three hours; from €89).

🛏 Sleeping

Guesthouse Borealis GUESTHOUSE €
(☑044-313-1771; www.guesthouseborealis.com; Asemieskatu 1; s/d/tr/apt from €58/68/99/175; Ⓟ🛜) Friendly owners and proximity to trains make this family-run spot a winner. Rooms are simple, bright and clean, and guests can use a kitchen. Breakfast, served in an airy dining room, features Finnish porridge. The two apartments each have their own entrance and full kitchen; one has a private balcony and private sauna.

OFF THE BEATEN TRACK

HIKING IN LAPLAND

Northern Finland's great swaths of protected forests and fells make it one of Europe's prime hiking destinations. Head to the Karhunkierros near Kuusamo for a striking terrain of hills and sharp ravines, which are never prettier than in autumn. The **Urho Kekkonen National Park** in Lapland is one of Europe's great wildernesses; the spectacular gorge of the **Kevo Strict Nature Reserve** and the fell scenery of **Pallas-Yllästunturi National Park** are other great northern options. A network of camping huts makes itinerary planning easy and are good spots to meet Finns. The key resource for walking is the excellent national parks website www.outdoors.fi.

🍴 Eating & Drinking

Cafe & Bar 21 CAFE €
(www.cafebar21.fi; Rovakatu 21; dishes €10-14; ⏱11am-8.30pm Mon & Tue, to 9.30pm Wed & Thu, to 11pm Fri, noon-11pm Sat, noon-8.30pm Sun; 🛜) A reindeer-pelt collage on the grey-concrete wall is the only concession to place at this artfully modern designer cafe-bar. Black-and-white decor makes it a stylish haunt for salads, superb soups, tapas and its house-speciality waffles (both savoury and sweet), along with creative cocktails. The bar stays open late.

Kauppayhtiö BAR
(www.kauppayhtio.fi; Valtakatu 24; ⏱11am-9pm Tue-Thu & Sun, to 3.30am Fri, 1pm-3.30am Sat; 🛜) Almost everything at this oddball gasoline-themed bar-cafe is for sale, including colourful plastic tables and chairs, and retro and vintage toys, as well as new streetwear and Nordic clothing at the attached boutique. DJs play most evenings and there are often bands at weekends – when it's rocking, crowds spill onto the pavement terrace. Its burgers are renowned. Bonus: pinball machines.

ℹ Information

Tourist Office (☑016-346-270; www.visitrovaniemi.fi; Maakuntakatu 29; ⏱9am-5pm Mon-Fri mid-Aug–mid-Jun, plus 10am-3pm Sat mid-Jun–mid-Aug; 🛜) On the square in the middle of town.

ℹ Getting There & Away

➡ Rovaniemi's airport is a major winter destination for charter flights. Finnair and Norwegian fly daily from Helsinki.

➡ Night buses serve Helsinki (€83.90, 12¾ hours, up to four daily). Daily connections serve just about everywhere else in Lapland. Some buses head on north into Norway.

➡ One direct train per day runs from Rovaniemi to Helsinki (€80, eight hours), with two more services requiring a change in Oulu (€14, 2¼ hours).

Finland Survival Guide

ℹ Directory A–Z

ACCOMMODATION

➡ Many accommodation choices open only in summer, usually campsites or converted student residences.

➡ Almost all campgrounds have cabins or cottages for rent, which are usually excellent value: from €40 for a basic double cabin.

DON'T MISS

VISITING SANTA

The southernmost line at which the sun does not set on at least one day a year, the Arctic Circle (Napapiiri in Finnish) crosses the Sodankylä road 8km north of Rovaniemi. Surrounding the marker is **Santa Claus Village** (www.santaclausvillage. info; Tarvantie 2, Napapiiri; ⊗ 9am-6pm Jun-Aug, 10am-5pm mid-Jan–May, Sep & Nov, 9am-7pm Dec–mid-Jan) FREE, a touristy complex of shops, winter activities and cottage accommodation. Santa Claus Post Office (www.santaclaus.posti.fi) here receives over half a million letters yearly from children (and adults) all over the world. But the top attraction for most is, of course, Santa himself, who sees visitors year-round in a rather impressive grotto (www.santaclauslive.com), where a huge clock mechanism (it slows the earth's rotation so that Santa can visit the whole world's children on Christmas night) eerily surrounds those queuing for an audience. The portly saint is quite a linguist, and an old hand at chatting with kids and adults alike. A private chat (around two minutes) is absolutely free, but you can't photograph the moment, and official photos of your visit start at an outrageous €25. Bus 8 heads here from Rovaniemi train station (€3.90, 25 minutes, up to three hourly 6.30am to 6.30pm) passing through the centre of town.

DISCOUNT CARDS

Finland's three main cities offer visitors a discount card that gives free public transport, admission to sights, and discounts on activities and restaurants. They can be worthwhile if you are planning a sightseeing-heavy itinerary.

LGBT TRAVELLERS

Finland's cities are open, tolerant places and Helsinki, though no Copenhagen nor Stockholm, has a small but welcoming gay scene.

MONEY

➡ Finland uses the euro (€). The one- and two-cent coins used in other eurozone nations are not accepted in Finland.

➡ Credit cards are widely accepted and Finns are dedicated users of the plastic even to buy a beer or cup of coffee.

➡ Service is considered to be included in bills, so there's no need to tip at all unless you want to reward exceptional service. Door staff in bars and restaurants expect a cloakroom tip if there's no mandatory coat charge.

OPENING HOURS

Many attractions in Finland, particularly outdoor ones, only open for a short summer season.

Alko (state alcohol shop) 9am to 8pm Monday to Friday, to 6pm Saturday

Banks 9am to 4.15pm Monday to Friday

Businesses & shops 9am to 6pm Monday to Friday, to 3pm Saturday

Nightclubs 10pm to 4am Wednesday to Saturday

Pubs 11am to 1am (often later on Friday and Saturday)

Restaurants 11am to 10pm, lunch 11am to 3pm. Last orders generally an hour before closing.

TELEPHONE

➡ Country code: ☎ 358. International access code: ☎ 00.

➡ Local SIM cards with data packages are easily available and cheap.

Getting There & Away

Finland is easily accessed from Europe and beyond. There are direct flights from numerous destinations, while Baltic ferries are another good option.

AIR

Finland is easily reached by air, with direct flights to **Helsinki airport** (p163) from many European, American and Asian destinations.

BOAT

➡ The daily Stockholm–Helsinki and Stockholm–Turku ferries are popular ways to get here. There are several other Sweden–Finland services.

➡ Helsinki is linked to nearby Tallinn, Estonia, by very regular ferries and fast ferries.

PRICE RANGES

The following price ranges refer to a double room in high season.

€ less than €70

€€ €70–160

€€€ more than €160

→ Other ferries connect Finland with Russia and Germany. See www.directferries.com for all routes.

BUS

There are bus connections with Russia and, in the far north, with Norway and Sweden.

TRAIN

Finland's only international trains are to/from Moscow and St Petersburg in Russia. There is no train between Finland and Sweden, but train passes give significant discounts on ferry and bus connections.

🛈 Getting Around

→ A useful combined journey planner for Finland's public transport network is online at www.journey.fi.

→ There are competitive fares on domestic flights from Helsinki to Rovaniemi in Lapland that can compare to the train price.

→ Bus is the main form of long-distance transport, with a far more comprehensive network

than the train. Ticketing is handled by Matkahuolto (www.matkahuolto.fi), the excellent website of which has all timetables.

→ State-owned Valtion Rautatiet runs Finnish trains: a fast, efficient service, with prices roughly equivalent to buses on the same route. Discounted advance fares are available online.

NORWAY

Oslo

POP 666,759

Oslo is home to world-class museums and galleries to rival anywhere else on the European art trail and is fringed with forests, hills and lakes. Add to this mix a thriving cafe and bar culture and top-notch restaurants and the result is a thoroughly intoxicating place in which to forget about the fjords for a while.

Oslo

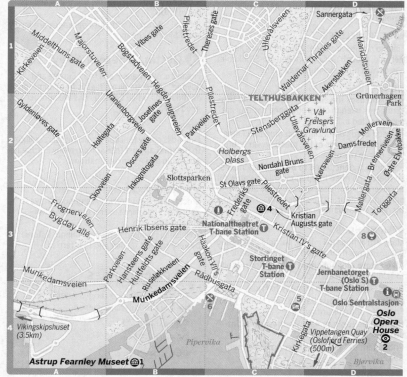

Sights

Astrup Fearnley Museet — GALLERY

(Astrup Fearnley Museum; ☏ 22 93 60 60; www.
afmuseet.no; Strandpromenaden 2; adult/child
120kr/free; ⊙ noon-5pm Tue, Wed & Fri, to 7pm Thu,
11am-5pm Sat & Sun; ⛴ Aker brygge) Designed
by Renzo Piano, this private contemporary
art museum is housed in a wonderful building of silvered wood, with a sail-like glass
roof that feels both maritime and at one
with the Oslofjord landscape. While the
museum's original collecting brief was con-
ceptual American work from the '80s (with
artists of the ilk of Jeff Koons, Tom Sachs,
Cindy Sherman and Richard Prince well
represented), it has in recent times broad-
ened beyond that, with, for example, a room
dedicated to Sigmar Polke and Anselm
Kiefer.

Vikingskipshuset — MUSEUM

(Viking Ship Museum; ☏ 22 13 52 80; www.khm.
uio.no; Huk Aveny 35; adult/child 80kr/free;

⊙ 9am-6pm May-Sep, 10am-4pm Oct-Apr; ⛴ 91)
Around 1100 years ago, Vikings dragged
up two longships from the shoreline and
used them as the centrepiece for grand ceremonial burials, most likely for important
chieftains or nobles. Along with the ships,
they buried many items for the afterlife:
food, drink, jewellery, furniture, carriages, weapons, and even a few dogs and
servants for companionship. Discovered
in Oslofjord in the late 19th century, the
ships are beautifully restored and offer an
evocative, emotive insight into the world of
the Vikings.

Nasjonalgalleriet — GALLERY

(National Gallery; ☏ 21 98 20 00; www.nasjonal-
museet.no; Universitetsgata 13; adult/child 100kr/
free, Thu free; ⊙ 10am-6pm Tue, Wed & Fri, to 7pm
Thu, 11am-5pm Sat & Sun; ⛴ Tullinløkka) Norway's national gallery houses the nation's
largest collection of traditional and modern art, and many of Edvard Munch's best-
known creations are on permanent display
here, including his most renowned work,
The Scream. There's also an impressive collection of European art, with works by Gauguin, Claudel, Picasso and El Greco, plus
Manet, Degas, Renoir, Matisse, Cézanne
and Monet. Nineteenth-century Norwegian
artists have a strong showing here too, including key figures such as JC Dahl and
Christian Krohg.

Oslo Opera House — ARCHITECTURE

(Den Norske Opera & Ballett; ☏ 21 42 21 21; www.
operaen.no; Kirsten Flagstads plass 1; foyer free;
⊙ foyer 10am-9pm Mon-Fri, 11am-9pm Sat, noon-
9pm Sun; Ⓣ Sentralstasjonen) The centrepiece

SCANDINAVIA OSLO

NORWAY AT A GLANCE

Don't Miss

Geirangerfjorden The 20km chug along Geirangerfjord, a Unesco World Heritage site, must rank as the world's loveliest ferry journey. Long-abandoned farmsteads still cling to the fjord's near-sheer cliffs, while ice-cold cascades tumble, twist and gush down to emerald-green waters.

Bergen Set amid a picturesque and very Norwegian coastal landscape of fjords and mountains, Bergen is one of Europe's most beautiful cities. A celebrated history of seafaring trade has bequeathed to the city the stunning (and Unesco World Heritage–listed) waterfront district of Bryggen, an archaic tangle of wooden buildings.

Oslo Norway's capital is already bursting at the seams with top-notch museums, art galleries and a glacier-white opera house that could make even Sydney jealous, but in the past couple of years it has achieved a striking rebirth of its waterfront district complete with daring architecture, a grade-A modern-art gallery, new restaurants and even a beach.

Tromsø A cool 400km north of the Arctic Circle, is northern Norway's most significant city with, among other superlatives, the world's northernmost cathedral, brewery and botanical garden. Its busy clubs and pubs – more per capita than in any other Norwegian town – owe much to the university and its students.

Lofoten Islands Few visitors forget their first sighting of the Lofoten Islands. The jagged ramparts of this astonishing island chain rise abruptly from the sea in summer greens and yellows or the stark blue and white of winter, their razor-sharp peaks stabbing at a clear, cobalt sky or shrouded mysteriously in swirling mists.

Itineraries

One Week

After a couple of days exploring the fine galleries and museums of **Oslo**, take the scenic Oslo–Bergen railway, one of the most spectacular rail journeys on earth. From Oslo, the line climbs gently through forests, plateaus and ski centres to the beautifully desolate **Hardangervidda Plateau**, home to Norway's largest herd of wild reindeer and numerous hiking trails. At Myrdal, take the Flåmsbana railway down to **Flåm**, from where fjord cruises head up the incomparable Nærøyfjord. Trains then carry you on to **Bergen**, arguably Norway's prettiest city.

Two Weeks

Head north; linger in **Trondheim** for a couple of days then head to the standout **Lofoten Islands**. **Tromsø** is a university town par excellence. Its Polar Museum captures the spirit of Arctic exploration, its Arctic Cathedral wonderfully evokes the landscapes of the north, while the surrounding peaks host a wealth of summer and winter activities.

Essential Food & Drink

Reindeer Roast reindeer *(reinsdyrstek)* is something every non-vegetarian visitor to Norway should try at least once: best eaten rare to medium-rare.

Elk Known elsewhere in the world as moose, elk *(elg)* comes in a variety of forms, including as a steak or burger.

Salmon One Norwegian contribution to international cuisine that you shouldn't miss is salmon.

Meatballs Traditional Norwegian meatballs served with mushy peas, mashed potatoes and wild-berry jam is a local, home-cooked favourite.

Coffee If Norway has a national drink, it's coffee. Most Norwegians drink it black and strong.

Getting Around

Air SAS and Norwegian have extensive domestic networks. Widerøe services small towns.

Boat Ferries, many of which take cars, connect offshore islands to the mainland, while the Hurtigruten sails from Bergen to Kirkenes and back every day of the year.

Bus Services along major routes are fast and efficient. Services to smaller towns can be infrequent, sometimes with no services at all on weekends.

Car Roads are in good condition, but travel times can be slow thanks to winding roads, heavy summer traffic with few overtaking lanes, and ferries.

Train Trains reach as far north as Bodø, with an additional branch line connecting Narvik with Sweden further north. Book in advance for considerably cheaper minipris tickets.

When to Go

Oslo

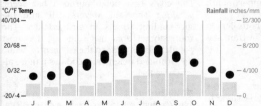

Mid-Jun–mid-Aug Accommodation and transport often booked out. Accommodation prices mostly at their lowest.

May–mid-Jun & mid-Aug–Sep A good time to travel, with generally mild, clear weather and fewer crowds.

Oct–Apr Short, cold days and many attractions closed. Northern lights and other wintry activities available.

Arriving in Norway

Gardermoen International Airport (Oslo) Trains connect the airport to the city centre (19 to 26 minutes, 90kr) up to six times hourly from around 4am to midnight. Buses (adult/child 160/80kr) take 40 minutes. Taxis cost 750kr to 1150kr (30 minutes to one hour).

Flesland Airport (Bergen) Airport bus connects the airport with downtown (adult one way/return 90/160kr, 45 minutes) up to four times hourly from 3.50am to just after midnight.

Top Phrases

Hello. God dag.

Goodbye. Ha det.

Please. Vær så snill.

Thank you. Takk.

Excuse me. Unnskyld.

Resources

Visit Norway (www.visit-norway.com) Norwegian Tourist Board site ranging from practical to inspirational. Check out its excellent apps.

Fjord Norway (www.fjord-norway.com) Focused on Norway's star attractions.

Set Your Budget

➡ Dorm bed: from €35

➡ Hut or cabin: from €55

➡ Double in B&B or guesthouse: up to €80

➡ Supermarket picnic fare and cheaper lunch specials: up to €14

of the city's rapidly developing waterfront is the magnificent Opera House, considered one of the most iconic modern buildings of Scandinavia. Designed by Oslo-based architectural firm Snøhetta and costing around €500 million to build, the Opera House opened in 2008, and resembles a glacier floating in the waters of the Oslofjord. Its design is a thoughtful meditation on the notion of monumentality, the dignity of cultural production, Norway's unique place in the world and the conversation between public life and personal experience.

Munchmuseet   GALLERY
(Munch Museum; ☑ 23 49 35 00; www.munchmuseet.no; Tøyengata 53; adult/child 100kr/free; ⊙ 10am-4pm, to 5pm mid-Jun–late Sep; ⊤ Tøyen) A monographic museum dedicated to Norway's greatest artist Edvard Munch (1863–1944), and housing the largest collection of his work in the world: 28,000 items including 1100 paintings and 4500 watercolours, many of which were gifted to the city by Munch himself (although his best-known pieces, including *The Scream,* are held in the Nasjonalgalleriet).

To get here, take a bus or the T-bane to Tøyen, followed by a 300m signposted walk.

☞ Tours

Norway in a Nutshell   TOURS
(Fjord Tours; ☑ 81 56 82 22; www.norwaynutshell.com) For maximum sights in minimal time. From Oslo, the typical route includes a train across Hardangervidda to Myrdal, a descent along the dramatic Flåmbanen, a cruise along Nærøyfjorden to Gudvangen, a bus to Voss, a connecting train to Bergen for a short visit, then an overnight return rail trip to Oslo (including a sleeper compartment); the return tour costs 2790kr.

You can also do one-way tours to Bergen (1890kr). Book at tourist offices or train stations.

🛏 Sleeping

Oslo Vandrerhjem Haraldsheim   HOSTEL €
(☑ 22 22 29 65; www.haraldsheim.no; Haraldsheimveien 4; incl breakfast with/without bathroom dm 350/290kr, d 660/560kr; @ 📶; 🚊 Sinsenkrysset) A pleasant, if hard-to-find, hostel 4km from the city centre. It has 24-hour reception and 268 beds in clean four-bed dorms or private rooms (some of the ones in the new building have balconies). There are kitchen and laundry facilities. Linen costs 50kr. Take tram

12, 15 or 17, or bus 31 or 32 to Sinsenkrysset, then walk five minutes uphill.

★ Saga Poshtel Oslo   HOSTEL €€
(☑ 23 10 08 00; www.sagahoteloslocentral.no; Kongens gate 7; dm/d 520/1100kr; 📶; 🚊 Øvre Slottsgate) A crossover hostel-hotel (posh-tel, if you didn't already get it), smartly designed and very central, with a big social lounge with decent wi-fi. Rooms are basic but spotless; there are lots of doubles, plus four- and six-bunk-bed dorms, all with en suites.

🍴 Eating

★ Syverkiosken   HOT DOGS €
(☑ 967 08 699; Maridalsveien 45; hot dogs from 20kr; ⊙ 9am-11.30pm Mon-Fri, from 11am Sat & Sun; 🚊 34) It might look like a hipster replica, but this hole-in-the-wall *pølser* (hot dogs) place is absolutely authentic and one of the last of its kind in Oslo. Dogs can be had in a potato bread wrap in lieu of the usual roll, or with both, and there's a large range of old-school accompaniments beyond sauce and mustard.

Pipervika   SEAFOOD €€
(www.pipervika.no; Rådhusbrygge 4; mains 175-250kr, shrimp per kg 130kr; ⊙ 7am-11pm; 🚊 Aker brygge) If the weather is nice, nothing beats a shrimp lunch, with fresh shrimp on a baguette with mayonnaise and a spritz of lemon eaten dockside. The revamped fisherman's co-op still does takeaway peel-and-eat shrimp by the kilo, but you can now also relax with a sushi plate, oysters or a full seafood menu including fish burger on brioche or killer fish and chips.

🍷 Drinking & Entertainment

The city's best neighbourhood bar scene is along Thorvald Meyers gate and the surrounding streets in Grünerløkka. The Youngstorget area has some of the most popular places close to the city centre, while the Grønland neighbourhood has a more alternative feel.

★ Kulturhuset   BAR, PUB
(http://kulturhusetioslo.no; Youngs gate 6; ⊙ 8am-3.30am Mon-Fri, from 11am Sat & Sun; 🚊 Brugata) The Norwegian notion of culture being an interactive, collective enterprise combines here with their exceptional ability to have a good time. The city's 'culture house' moved into this beautiful, rambling old four-storey building in 2017, but it feels as if it's been part of the Oslo fabric for years.

ℹ Information

Oslo Visitor Centre (☑ 81 53 05 55; www.
visitoslo.com; Jernbanetorget 1; ⊙ 9am-6pm;
⬚ Sentralstasjon) Right beside the main train
station. Sells transport tickets as well as the
useful Oslo Pass; publishes free guides to the
city.

ℹ Getting There & Away

➡ **Oslo Gardermoen International Airport**
(https://avinor.no/flyplass/oslo), located
50km north of town, is the city's principal
airport. Some airlines also operate 'Oslo' services to/from Torp, some 123km southwest of
Oslo, and Rygge, around 60km southeast of
the centre.

➡ Ferries run daily to Copenhagen and Fredrikshavn in Denmark, and to Kiel in Germany in
summer.

➡ All trains arrive and depart from Oslo S in
the city centre. Long-distance buses arrive
and depart from the adjacent Galleri Oslo Bus
Terminal.

ℹ Getting Around

➡ All public transport is covered off by the
Ruter (https://ruter.no/en/) ticketing system. Oslo offers an efficient public-transport
system with an extensive network of buses,
trams, underground trains (T-bane) and
ferries.

➡ Gardermoen airport is linked to the centre by
bus and train.

The Western Fjords

This spectacular region has truly indescrib-
able scenery. Lysefjord, Hardangerfjord,
Sognefjord and Geirangerfjord are all variants on the same theme: steep crystalline
rock walls dropping with sublime force
straight into the sea, often decorated with
waterfalls, and small farms harmoniously
blending into the natural landscape. Bergen and Stavanger are engaging, lively cities that have attractive historic quarters.

Stavanger

POP 123,369

Said by some to be the largest wooden city
in Europe, Stavanger's old quarter climbs
up the slopes around a pretty harbour. Stavanger is also one of Norway's liveliest urban centres and an excellent base to explore
stunning Lysefjord.

◉ Sights

★ **Gamle Stavanger**   AREA
Gamle (Old) Stavanger, above the western
shore of the harbour, is a delight. The Old
Town's cobblestone walkways pass between
rows of late-18th-century whitewashed
wooden houses, all immaculately kept and
adorned with cheerful, well-tended flow-
erboxes. It well rewards an hour or two of
ambling.

Stavanger Domkirke   CHURCH
(Håkon VIIs gate; 30kr; ⊙ 9am-6pm Jul & Aug, 9am-
4pm May-Jun & Sep, shorter hours rest of year) This
beautiful church is an impressive but understated medieval stone cathedral dating from
approximately 1125; it was extensively renovated following a fire in 1272 and contains
traces of Gothic, baroque, Romanesque
and Anglo-Norman influences. Despite restoration in the 1860s and in 1940, and the
stripping of some features during the Reformation, the cathedral is, by some accounts,
Norway's oldest medieval cathedral still in
its original form.

🛏 Sleeping

★ **Thompsons B&B**   B&B €
(☑ 51 52 13 29; www.thompsons-bed-and-break-
fast.com; Muségata 79; s/d with shared bathroom
400/500kr; 🅿) You won't find a bigger bargain in Stavanger than this homey B&B.

DON'T MISS

LYSEFJORD

All along the 42km-long Lysefjord, the
granite glows with an ethereal, ambient
light, even on dull days. This is many
visitors' favourite fjord, and there's no
doubt that it has a captivating beauty.
Boat trips run from Stavanger along the
fjord, but the area's most popular outing
is the hike (think two hours) to the top of
incredible **Preikestolen** (Pulpit Rock),
25km east of Stavanger. You can inch
up to the edge of its flat top and peer
604m straight down a sheer cliff into
the blue water for some intense vertigo.
Boat-bus-hike combinations run here
from Stavanger May to mid-September;
book tickets from **Norled** (www.norled.
no; Lysefjord cruise adult/child/family
450/280/1100kr, Preikestolen boat-and-
bus-ticket 320kr), the tourist office or
Fiskespiren Quay.

Housed in a 1910 villa in a peaceful residential area, this four-bed B&B has a home-away-from-home vibe engendered by the warm and welcoming owner, Sissel Thompson. Rooms are cosy and comfortable, and the traditional Norwegian breakfast, taken around the downstairs dining table, is generous.

✗ Eating & Drinking

★ **Renaa Xpress Sølvberget**   NORWEGIAN €€
(Stavanger Kulturhus; ☑ 51 55 11 11; www.restaurantrenaa.no; Sølvberggata 2; panini 89-98kr, salads 170kr, pizzas 180-199kr; ⊙ 10am-10pm Mon-Thu, to midnight Fri & Sat, noon-10pm Sun) One of three Renaa restaurants in Stavanger, this upmarket cafe pretty much corners the lunchtime market. Go for the daily soup deal, tuck into a huge salad, enjoy a panino topped with *Parmaskinke* (Parma ham) or *røkelaks* (smoked salmon), or order a wood-fired, wild-yeasted pizza (available from 3pm). Needless to say, the cake, pastries and coffee are delicious, too.

★ **Bøker & Børst**   BAR
(☑ 51 86 04 76; www.bokerogborst.webs.com; Øvre Holmegate 32; ⊙ 10am-2am) With all the decorative chic of a well-worn living room – complete with book-lined shelves, retro floor-lamps and old wallpaper – this lovely coffee bar is a fine spot to while away a few hours. There are plenty of beers on tap, plus

---

ℹ FJORD TOURS FROM BERGEN

There are dozens of tours of the fjords from Bergen; the **tourist office** (p178) has a full list and you can buy tickets there or purchase them online. Most offer discounts if you have a **Bergen Card** (www.visitbergen.com/bergencard; adult/child 24hr pass 240/90kr, 48hr 310/1120kr, 72hr 380/150kr). For a good overview, pick up the *Round Trips – Fjord Tours & Excursions* brochure from the tourist office, which includes tours offered by a range of private companies.

Fjord Tours (☑ 81 56 82 22; www.fjordtours.com) and **Rodne Fjord Cruises** (☑ 55 25 90 00; www.rodne.no; Torget; adult/child/family 550/350/1250kr; ⊙ 10am & 2.30pm daily Mar-Oct, 10am Wed-Fri, noon Sat & Sun Nov-Feb) are the key operators.

---

pub-type snacks and pastries, and a covered courtyard at the back.

ℹ Information

Stavanger Turistforening DNT (☑ 51 84 02 00; www.stf.no; off Muségata; ⊙ 10am-4pm Mon, Wed, Fri & Sat, 10am-6pm Tue & Thu) Information on hiking and mountain huts.

Tourist Office (☑ 51 85 92 00; www.regionstavanger.com; Strandkaien 61; ⊙ 9am-8pm Jun-Aug, 9am-4pm Mon-Fri, 9am-2pm Sat Sep-May) Local information and advice on Lysefjord and Preikestolen.

ℹ Getting There & Away

➜ Bus destinations include Bergen (475kr, 5½ hours, hourly) and Oslo (742-811kr, 9½ hours, three daily) via Kristiansand.

➜ Trains run to Oslo (997kr, eight hours, up to five daily) via Kristiansand.

➜ Fjord Line ferries run daily to Hirtshals in Denmark (10½ hours).

Bergen

POP 278,121
Surrounded by seven hills and fjords, Bergen is a charming city. With the World Heritage–listed Bryggen and buzzing Vågen harbour as its centrepiece, Bergen climbs the hillsides with timber-clad houses, while cable cars offer stunning views from above.

◉ Sights

★ **Bryggen**   HISTORIC SITE
FREE Bergen's oldest quarter runs along the eastern shore of Vågen Harbour (*bryggen* translates as 'wharf') in long, parallel and often leaning rows of gabled buildings. Each has stacked-stone or wooden foundations and reconstructed rough-plank construction. It's enchanting, no doubt about it, but can be exhausting if you hit a cruise-ship and bus-tour crush.

★ **KODE**   GALLERY
(☑ 53 00 97 04; www.kodebergen.no; Rasmus Meyers allé; adult/child 100kr/free, includes all 4 museums, valid 2 days)) A catch-all umbrella for Bergen's art museums, KODE showcases one of the largest art-and-design collections in Scandinavia. Each of the four buildings has its own focus: **KODE 1** (Nordahl Bruns gate 9; ⊙ 11am-5pm) houses a national silver collection and the renowned Singer art collection; **KODE 2** (Rasmus Meyers allé 3) is for contemporary exhibitions; **KODE 3** (Rasmus Meyers allé 7; ⊙ 10am-6pm) majors in Edvard

Bergen

Munch; and **KODE 4** (Rasmus Meyers allé 9; ⊘11am-5pm; ⊛) focuses on modern art.

🛏 Sleeping & Eating

Bergen Vandrerhjem YMCA HOSTEL €
(⌕55 60 60 55; www.bergenhostel.no; Nedre Korskirkealmenning 4; dm/s/d 215/600/850kr) This wallet-friendly hostel has a lot in its favour: the dorms are great value, the decor inside is sparklingly clean, the kitchen is well equipped and there's a cracking harbour-view roof terrace. Even better – all rooms have en suite and minifridge. The downsides: the location can be noisy, and rates are hiked in summer.

Citybox HOSTEL, HOTEL €
(⌕55 31 25 00; www.citybox.no; Nygårdsgaten 31; s from 799kr, d 899-999kr, f 1545kr; ⊛) Norway's first hostel-hotel minichain began in Bergen, and it's still doing brisk business – especially since a 2017 extension that added a whole new wing. It's a long way from budget-digs territory – this is more like a smart hotel, with clean white walls, soft beds and fluffy duvets. The decor is simple, but it's a real bargain for Bergen.

★ Torget Fish Market SEAFOOD €
(Torget; lunches 99-169kr; ⊘7am-7pm Jun-Aug, 7am-4pm Mon-Sat Sep-May) For most of its history, Bergen has survived on the fruits of the sea, so there's no better place for lunch than

SPLURGE

If you're going to blow the budget on one meal in Norway, make it at **Lysverket** (☑ 55 60 31 00; www.lysverket. no; KODE 4, Rasmus Meyers allé 9; lunch mains 165-195kr, lunch sharing menu with/without dessert 295/395kr, 4-/7-course menu 745/995kr; ☺ 11am-1am Tue-Sat). Chef Christopher Haatuft is pioneering his own brand of Nordic cuisine, which he dubs 'neo-fjordic' – in other words, combining modern techniques with the best fjord-sourced produce. His food is highly seasonal, incredibly creative and full of surprising textures, combinations and flavours. Savour every mouthful.

the town's lively fish market, where you'll find everything from salmon to calamari, fish and chips, prawn baguettes and seafood salads. If you can afford it, the sides of smoked salmon are some of the best in Norway.

Pingvinen NORWEGIAN €€
(☑ 55 60 46 46; www.pingvinen.no; Vaskerelven 14; daily specials 119kr, mains 159-269kr; ☺ noon-3am) Devoted to Norwegian home cooking, Pingvinen is the old favourite of *everyone* in Bergen. They come for meals their mothers and grandparents used to cook, and the menu always features at least one of the following: fish-cake sandwiches, reindeer, fish pie, salmon, lamb shank and *raspeballer* (sometimes called *komle*) – west-coast potato dumplings. Note that whale is served here.

☆ Entertainment

Garage LIVE MUSIC
(☑ 55 32 19 80; www.garage.no; Christies gate 14; ☺ 3pm-3am Mon-Sat, 5pm-3am Sun) Garage has taken on an almost mythical quality for music lovers across Norway. They do have the odd jazz and acoustic act, but this is a rock-and-metal venue at heart, with well-known Norwegian and international acts drawn to the cavernous basement. Stop by for their Sunday jam sessions in summer.

❶ Information

Bergen Tourist Information Centre (☑ 55 55 20 00; www.visitbergen.com; Strandkaien 3; ☺ 8.30am-10pm Jun-Aug, 9am-8pm May & Sep, 9am-4pm Mon-Sat Oct-Apr) You can't miss Bergen's tourist office – it's in a hulking

great edifice on the waterfront. The staff are superb, helping organise fjord tours, public transport, hiking routes and who knows what else. They publish the free *Bergen Guide*, and sell admission, excursion and public-transport tickets. It gets very, very busy: arrive early or be prepared to queue.

❶ Getting There & Away

➡ There are ferry services to Hirtshals in Denmark. This is also the southernmost point of the **Hurtigruten coastal ferry** (p181) that runs right up to the Norwegian Arctic.

➡ Bus destinations include Oslo (498kr to 577kr, 10 hours, four daily) and Stavanger (475kr, 5½ hours, six daily).

➡ The spectacular train journey between Bergen and Oslo (349kr to 905kr, 6½ to eight hours, five daily) runs through the heart of Norway. Early bookings can secure you some great discounts.

Sognefjorden

Sognefjorden, the country's longest (204km) and deepest (1308m) fjord, cuts a deep slash across the map of western Norway. In places, sheer walls rise more than 1000m above the water.

FLÅM
POP 450

At the head of Aurlandsfjorden, Flåm sits in a truly spectacular setting beside Sognefjord. The main attraction here is the stunning mountain railway that creeps up into the surrounding peaks and offers truly eye-popping panoramas. Unfortunately it's far from a well-kept secret, and on the busiest summer days the tiny village can find itself swamped by several thousand visitors.

🏃 Activities

★ Flåmsbana Railway RAIL
(www.visitflam.com/en/flamsbana; adult/child one way 360/180kr, return 480/240kr) This 20km-long engineering wonder hauls itself up 864m of altitude gain through 20 tunnels. At a gradient of 1:18, it's the world's steepest railway that runs without cable or rack wheels. It takes a full 45 minutes to climb to Myrdal on the bleak, treeless Hardangervidda plateau, past thundering waterfalls (there's a photo stop at awesome Kjosfossen). The railway runs year-round, with up to 10 departures daily in summer, dropping to four in winter.

🛏 Sleeping

★Flåm Camping & Hostel
HOSTEL, CAMPGROUND €

(📞940 32 681; www.flaam-camping.no; Nedre Brekkevegen 12; 1-/2-person tent 120/205kr, dm/s/tw/q 335/550/920/1315kr, with shared bathroom 260/450/720/995kr; ⊗Mar-Nov; 🅿🛜) Everyone's favourite when looking for a budget place in Flåm, this conveniently positioned hostel and campground has accommodation options to suit all wallets: bunk-bed dorms, singles, twins, triples and quads, in simple lodge buildings with pine walls and colourful fabrics. There's also tonnes of green grassy space for caravans and campers and it's just a short walk to the marina.

🍷 Drinking & Nightlife

Ægir Bryggeri
BREWERY

(📞57 63 20 50; www.flamsbrygga.no/aegir-bryggeripub; Flåmsbrygga; ⊗noon-10pm May-mid-Sep, 6-10pm mid-Sep-Apr) Looking for all the world like a stave church, Ægir Brewery, all appealing woodwork and flagstones, offers six different kinds of draught beer, all brewed on the spot. It also does a tasty creative take on Norwegian comfort food as well as burgers and pizzas (160kr to 210kr).

ℹ Getting There & Away

➡ Flåm is the only Sognefjorden village with a rail link, via the magnificent Flåmsbana railway. There are train connections to Oslo and Bergen at Myrdal.

➡ Buses run to Bergen (285kr to 350kr, three hours), among other local destinations.

Geirangerfjorden

Scattered cliffside farms, most long abandoned, still cling to the towering, near-sheer walls of twisting, 20km-long emerald-green Geirangerfjord, a Unesco World Heritage site. Geiranger village has a fabulous location at the head of the fjord, but gets overrun by visitors and cruise ships. The one-hour scenic ferry trip along the fjord between Geiranger and Hellesylt is as much mini-cruise as means of transport – take it even if you've no particular reason to get to the other end.

👁 Sights & Activities

Flydalsjuvet
VIEWPOINT

Somewhere you've seen that classic photo, beloved of brochures, of the overhanging rock Flydalsjuvet, usually with a figure gazing down at a cruise ship in Geirangerfjord. The car park, signposted Flydalsjuvet, about 5km uphill from Geiranger on the Stryn road, offers a great view of the fjord and the green river valley, but doesn't provide the postcard view down to the last detail.

For that, you'll have to drop about 150m down the hill, then descend a slippery and rather indistinct track to the edge. Your intrepid photo subject will have to scramble down gingerly and with the utmost care to the overhang about 50m further along. If it's a selfie, we advise care when walking backwards.

👉 Tours

★Geiranger Fjordservice
BOATING

(📞70 26 30 07; www.geirangerfjord.no; Homlong; 1½hr tours adult/child 250/135kr) This long-running company runs sightseeing boat trips up and down the fjord from Geiranger. The standard 1½-hour trip runs up to five times daily in midsummer, just once daily in April and October, and not at all from November to March.

From mid-June to August, it also operates a smaller, 15-seater RIB boat (adult/child 695/395kr) and runs kayaking tours (525/469kr), all from its base at Homlong, 2km from Geiranger.

🛏 Sleeping

Geirangerfjorden Feriesenter
CAMPGROUND €

(📞951 07 527; www.geirangerfjorden.net; Grande; lakefront campsite for car, tent & 2 adults 255kr, cabin from 990kr; ⊗late Apr-mid-Sep; 🅿🛜) A more

DON'T MISS

SOGNEFJORDEN BY BOAT

It may get overrun in summer, but the classic **boat trip** (www.thefjords.no; one way/return 400/870kr) heads up Nærøyfjord to Gudvangen (five daily), with a connecting bus to Voss for trains to Bergen or Oslo. The **tourist office** (📞57 63 33 13; www.visitflam.com; Stasjonsvegen; ⊗8.30am-8pm Jun-Aug, to 4pm May & Sep) sells tickets.

From May to September, **Norled** (📞51 86 87 00; www.norled.no; Kong Christian Frederiks plass 3) runs a direct ferry to Bergen (adult/child 825/415kr, 5½ hours). There are good discounts if you buy in advance online.

HARDANGERFJORD

Running from the Atlantic to the steep wall of central Norway's Hardangervidda Plateau, Hardangerfjord is classic Norwegian fjord country. There are many beautiful corners, although our picks would take in **Eidfjord**, **Ulvik** and **Utne**, while **Folgefonna National Park** offers glacier walks and top-level hiking. You can easily explore Hardangerfjord from Bergen; www.hardangerfjord.com is a good resource.

tranquil option than camping in town is to head along the northern shore to this lovely spot, with spacious pitches, well-maintained facilities and particularly pretty, well-decorated cabins. If you don't mind not being beside the water, you can save 300kr.

❶ Getting There & Away

➡ From mid-June to mid-August, sightseeing buses make the spectacular run from Geiranger to Åndalsnes (adult/child 478/239kr, three hours, twice daily), known as the 'Golden Route'.

➡ The car ferry between Geiranger and Hellysylt is a stunner. There are four to eight sailings a day between May and early October (adult/child one way 260/130kr, return 360/180kr, 1½ hours).

➡ From mid-April to mid-October, the Hurtigruten coastal ferry makes a detour from Ålesund (departs 9.30am) to Geiranger (departs 1.30pm) on its northbound run.

Northern Norway

With vibrant cities and some wondrous natural terrain, you'll be mighty pleased with yourself for undertaking an exploration of this huge territory that spans the Arctic Circle.

Trondheim

POP 190,464

Trondheim, Norway's original capital, is nowadays the country's third-largest city after Oslo and Bergen. With wide streets and a partly pedestrianised heart, it's a simply lovely city with a long history. Fuelled by a large student population, it buzzes with life, has some good cafes and restaurants, and is rich in museums.

◉ Sights

★ **Nidaros Domkirke** CATHEDRAL

(☑73 89 08 00; www.nidarosdomen.no; Kongsgårdsgata; adult/child/family 90/40/220kr, tower 40kr, with Archbishop's Palace & crown jewels 180/90/440kr; ⊙9am-6pm Mon-Fri, to 2pm Sat, to 5pm Sun mid-Jun–mid-Aug, shorter hours rest of year) Nidaros Cathedral is Scandinavia's largest medieval building, and the northernmost Gothic structure in Europe. Outside, the ornately embellished, altar-like west wall has top-to-bottom statues of biblical characters and Norwegian bishops and kings, sculpted in the early 20th century. Several are copies of medieval originals, nowadays housed in the adjacent museum. Note the glowing, vibrant colours of the modern stained-glass in the rose window at the west end, a striking contrast to the interior gloom.

★ **Archbishop's Palace** MUSEUM, HISTORIC BUILDING

(Kongsgårdsgata; adult/child/family 90/40/220kr, crown jewels 90/40/220kr, with cathedral & crown jewels 180/80/440kr; ⊙10am-5pm Mon-Fri, 10am-3pm Sat, noon-4pm Sun mid-Jun–mid-Aug, shorter hours rest of year) The 12th-century archbishop's residence (Erkebispegården), commissioned around 1160 and Scandinavia's oldest secular building, is beside the cathedral. In its west wing, you'll find Norway's **crown jewels** and its **museum**. After visiting the statues, gargoyles and carvings from the cathedral, drop to the lower level with a selection of the myriad artefacts revealed during the museum's late-1990s construction.

★ **Rockheim** MUSEUM

(www.rockheim.no; Brattørkaia 14; adult/concession/child 130/100/free; ⊙11am-6pm Tue-Sun) This terrific museum is devoted to pop and rock music, mainly Norwegian, from the 1950s until yesterday. It's a dockside temple to R&B, where a huge projecting roof featuring Norwegian record covers extends above an equally vast converted warehouse. Within, there's plenty of action and interaction (mix your own hip-hop tape, for example). Home of Rock is on the quayside, very near Pirbadet and the fast-ferry landing stage.

🛏 Sleeping

★ **Pensjonat Jarlen** GUESTHOUSE €

(☑73 51 32 18; www.jarlen.no; Kongens gate 40; s/d/tr 540/690/960kr, cat or dog 100kr; ☏) Price, convenience and value for money are a winning combination here. After a 2010 overhaul, the rooms at this central spot have a contemporary look and are outstanding, although some bathrooms could do with a spruce-up. Some rooms have polished floor-boards, others carpet, and most have a hot plate and fridge thrown in.

Eating & Drinking

Ravnkloa Fish Market
SEAFOOD €

(☑73 52 55 21; www.ravnkloa.no; Munkegata; snacks from 50kr, mains 140-215kr; ☺10am-5pm Mon-Fri, to 4pm Sat) Everything looks good at this fish market that doubles as a cafe with quayside tables out the front. The fish cakes are fabulous and it also does shrimp sandwiches, mussels and a fine fish soup. In addition to seafood, it sells an impressive range of cheeses and other gourmet goods.

Antikvariatet
CAFE, BAR

(☑942 20 557; Nedre Bakklandet 4; drinks from 79kr; ☺2pm-1.30am Tue-Fri, noon-1.30am Sat & Sun) Now this is our kind of place – craft beers on tap, shelves lined with books, views over the water and regular live gigs. Unsurprisingly it's popular with students and trendy types, and it's in a delightful location among the wooden houses of the Bakklandet. You'll have to be lucky to snaffle a balcony table.

Information

Tourist Office (☑73 80 76 60; www.visittrond-heim.no; 1st fl, Nordre gate 11; ☺9am-6pm mid-Jun–mid-Aug, to 6pm Mon-Sat rest of year) In the heart of the city, with stacks of information and an accommodation booking service.

Getting There & Away

➡ The bus and train stations are adjoining.
➡ Bus services include Bergen (808kr, 14 hours, one overnight).
➡ There are two to four trains daily to/from Oslo (937kr, 6½ hours). Two head north to Bodø (1088kr, 9¾ hours).

Lofoten

You'll never forget your first approach to the Lofoten Islands by ferry. The islands spread their tall, craggy physique against the sky like some spiky sea dragon and you wonder how humans eked out a living in such inhospitable surroundings.The four main islands are all linked by bridges or tunnels, with buses running the entire length of the Lofoten road (E10) from Fiskebøl in the north to Å at road's end in the southwest.

Sights & Activities

Lofoten's principal settlement, Svolvær, makes a pretty spot from which to base your explorations, with steep mountains rising sharply in the background and a busy harbour. The still-active fishing village of Henningsvær, perched at the end of a thin promontory, is the lightest, brightest and trendiest village in the archipelago, while Å is a very special place at what feels like the end of the world on the western tip of Lofoten. Its shoreline is lined with red-painted fisherfolk's shanties on stilts over the water.

Svolværgeita
HIKING, CLIMBING

You'll see it on postcards all over Lofoten – some daring soul leaping between two fingers of rock high above Svolvær. To hike up to a point just behind the two pinnacles (355m), walk northeast along the E10 towards Narvik, past the marina, then turn left on Nyveien and right on Blatind veg. The steep climb begins just behind the children's playground.

The climb takes around half an hour, or an hour if you continue up to the summit of Floya. To actually climb Svolværgeita and take the leap, you'll need to go with a climbing guide – ask the tourist office for recommendations or try **Northern Alpine Guides** (☑942 49 110; www.alpineguides.no; Kalleveien 21).

Sleeping

Å-Hamna Rorbuer & Vandrerhjem
HOSTEL €

(☑76 09 12 11; www.lofotenferie.com; dm 280kr, 2-4 bed cabins 1200-1700kr, 6-bed cabin 2150kr) Most of the *rorbuer* (fisher's huts) in Å have

---

WORTH A TRIP

THE HURTIGRUTEN

Norway's legendary **Hurtigruten** (☑81 00 30 30; www.hurtigruten.com) coastal ferry has been a lifeline linking coastal towns and villages and is now one of the most popular ways to explore Norway. A Hurtigruten ferry heads north from Bergen nightly, pulling into 35 ports on its six-day journey to Kirkenes, where it then turns around and heads back south. The return journey takes 11 days and covers a distance of 5200km. In agreeable weather (by no means guaranteed) the fjord and mountain scenery along the way is nothing short of spectacular.

Lofoten

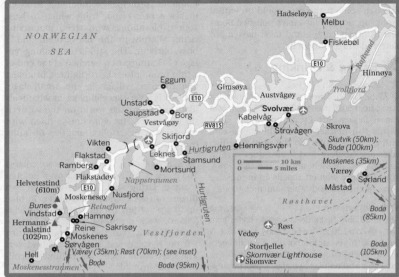

been turned into holiday cabins, offering the chance for an atmospheric night's sleep. Wood-clad inside and out, the cabins are simple but cosy, and some are furnished with antiques and fishing ephemera.

❶ Getting There & Around

➡ From the south, the easiest way for non-drivers to reach Lofoten is the foot-passenger-only express boat between Bodø and Svolvær (476kr, three to 3½ hours).

➡ Getting around is easy. Buses run the entire E10 from the Fiskebøl–Melbu ferry in the north to Å at road's end in the southwest. Tourist offices sell an excellent Lofoten cycling guide (259kr).

Tromsø

POP 72,681

Simply put, Tromsø parties. By far the largest town in far-northern Norway and the administrative centre of Troms county, it's lively with an animated street scene, a respected university, the hallowed Mack Brewery, and more pubs per capita than any other Norwegian town. Its corona of snow-topped peaks provides arresting scenery, excellent summer hiking and great winter skiing and dog-sledding.

❂ Sights & Activities

Winter activities include chasing the northern lights, cross-country skiing, reindeer- and dog-sledding, snowshoe safaris, ice fishing and snowmobiling. In summer try hiking, fishing, glacier trekking and sea kayaking. The tourist office can book things for you.

★ **Arctic Cathedral** CHURCH
(Ishavskatedralen; ☑ 476 80 668; Hans Nilsens veg 41; adult/child 50kr/free, organ recitals 70-170kr; ⊙9am-7pm Mon-Sat, 1-7pm Sun Jun–mid-Aug, 3-6pm mid-Aug–mid-May, from 2pm Feb) The 11 triangles of the Arctic Cathedral (1965), aka Tromsdalen Church, suggest glacial crevasses and auroral curtains. The glowing stained-glass window that occupies the east end depicts Christ descending to earth. The west end is filled by a futuristic organ and icicle-like lamps of Czech crystal. Unfortunately, its position beside one of Tromsø's main thoroughfares somewhat spoils the serenity outside. It's on the southern side of the Bruvegen bridge, about 1km from town. Take bus 20 or 24.

★ **Polaria** MUSEUM, AQUARIUM
(☑ 77 75 01 11; www.polaria.no; Hjalmar Johansens gate 12; adult/child 130/65kr; ⊙10am-7pm mid-May–Aug, 10am-5pm Sep–mid-May) This Arctic-

themed attraction provides a multimedia introduction to northern Norway and Svalbard. Kick things off by watching the two films *In the Land of the Northern Lights* and *Spitsbergen – Arctic Wilderness,* then follow the Arctic walkway past exhibits on shrinking sea ice, the aurora borealis, aquariums of cold-water fish and – the big draw – some yapping, playful bearded seals (feeding time is at 12.30pm year-round, plus 3pm in summer or 3.30pm in winter).

🛏 Sleeping

Smart Hotel Tromsø   HOTEL €
(☑415 36 500; www.smarthotel.no/en/tromso; Vestregata 12; d from 695kr; 🛜) The northernmost outpost of this budget mini-chain offers some of the best rates in town, and it's a fine base – as long as you don't mind the boxy rooms, basic facilities and institutional decor (battleship-grey is the colour of choice, combined with graffiti-style slogans like 'You Are Smart'). It's deservedly popular, so book ahead. The buffet breakfast costs 110kr.

🍴 Eating & Drinking

★**Risø**   CAFE €
(☑416 64 516; www.risoe-mk.no; Strandgata 32; mains 95-179kr; ⊙7.30am-5pm Mon-Fri, 9am-5pm Sat) You'll find this popular coffee and lunch bar packed throughout most of the day: young trendies come in for their hand-brewed Chemex coffee, while local workers pop in for the daily specials, open-faced sandwiches and delicious cakes. It's small, and the tables are packed in tight, so you might have to queue.

Ølhallen Pub   PUB
(☑77 62 45 80; www.olhallen.no; Storgata 4; ⊙10am-7.30pm Mon-Wed, 10am-12.30am Thu-Sat) Reputedly the oldest pub in town, and once the hang-out for salty fishermen and Arctic sailors, this is now the brewpub for the excellent **Mack Brewery** (Mack Ølbryggeri; www.mack.no; Storgata 5). There are 67 ales to try, including eight on tap – so it might take you a while (and a few livers) to work your way through them all.

ℹ Information

Tourist Office (☑77 61 00 00; www.visittromso.no; Kirkegata 2; ⊙9am-5pm Mon-Fri, 10am-5pm Sat & Sun Jan-Mar & mid-May–Aug, shorter hours rest of year; 🛜) Tromsø's busy, efficient tourist office is in a detached building

beside the harbour, and provides booking services and local info. Wi-fi is free.

ℹ Getting There & Away

➡ SAS and Norwegian have direct flights to many Scandinavian cities.

➡ There are up to three daily express buses to/from Narvik (280kr, 4¼ hours) and one to/from Alta (620kr, 6½ hours), where you can pick up a bus for Honningsvåg, and from there, on to Nordkapp, Europe's northernmost mainland point.

Norway Survival Guide

ℹ Directory A–Z

ACCOMMODATION
Staying within a tight budget is difficult in Norway, and you'll either need to stay at campground (in a tent or a simple cabin), hostels or guesthouses; within the budget category, it's rare that you'll have a private bathroom.

LGBT TRAVELLERS
Norwegians are generally tolerant of gay culture, though attitudes aren't quite as liberal as Denmark or Sweden. Oslo has the liveliest gay scene.

MONEY
➡ Credit and debit cards are widely used, even for small transactions.

➡ One Norwegian krone (Nkr1) equals 100 øre.

➡ Service charges and tips are included in restaurant bills and taxi fares; tipping on a North American scale is not expected. It is, however, customary to round up the bill.

THE AURORA

The aurora borealis (northern lights), an utterly haunting and exhilarating sight, is often visible to observers above the Arctic Circle. It's particularly striking during the dark winter; in summer the sun more or less renders it invisible.

To see the lights, you want a dark, clear night with high auroral activity. October, November and March are often optimal for this. Then it's a question of waiting patiently outside, preferably between the hours of 9pm and 2am, and seeing if things kick off. The Aurora Forecast app helps you predict auroral activity on the hoof.

ⓘ PRICE RANGES

The following price ranges relate to a double room with private bathroom in high season and, unless stated otherwise, include breakfast:

€ less than 750kr

€€ 750–1400kr

€€€ more than 1400kr

OPENING HOURS

These standard opening hours are for high season (mid-June to mid-August) and tend to decrease outside that time.

Banks 8.15am to 3pm Monday to Wednesday and Friday, to 5pm Thursday

Central Post Offices 8am to 8pm Monday to Friday, 9am to 6pm Saturday; otherwise 9am to 5pm Monday to Friday, 10am to 2pm Saturday

Restaurants noon to 3pm and 6pm to 11pm; some don't close between lunch and dinner

Shops 10am to 5pm Monday to Wednesday and Friday, to 7pm Thursday, to 2pm Saturday

Supermarkets 9am to 9pm Monday to Friday, to 6pm Saturday

TELEPHONE

➡ All telephone numbers in Norway have eight digits; there are no separate area codes.

➡ Country code: ☑ 47

➡ International access code: ☑ 00

➡ Local SIM cards with data packages are easily available and cheap.

ⓘ Getting There & Around

AIR

➡ Norway is well linked to other European countries by air. Norwegian (www.norwegian.com) is Europe's best budget airline, with a wide network. The country's principal airport is **Oslo Gardermoen** (p175).

➡ Due to the time and distances involved in overland travel within Norway, even budget travellers may want to consider a segment or two by air. The major Norwegian domestic routes are quite competitively priced.

BOAT

International ferry connections are possible between Norway and Denmark, Germany and Sweden. Check www.directferries.com for all routes.

A great way to explore the coast is the **Hurtigruten coastal ferry** (p181).

BUS

Swebus Express (☑ 0200 218 218; www.swebusexpress.se) has the cheapest buses between Oslo and Swedish cities. **Eurolines** (www.eurolines.com) also has many international routes. In the north, cross-border buses link Norway with Russia and Finland.

Within Norway, there's an excellent network of long-distance buses. **Nor-Way Bussekspress** (www.nor-way.no) operates the largest network. **Lavprisekspressen** (www.lavprisekspressen.no) operates the cheapest services if you get the right moment online. **Nettbuss** (www.nettbuss.no) also has a large network.

TRAIN

➡ Norway is connected to Sweden by train at several points. There are regular connections to Oslo from Stockholm and Göteborg. Rail services between Sweden and Norway are operated by **Norwegian State Railways** (Norges Statsbaner, NSB; ☑ press 9 for English 81 50 08 88; www.nsb.no) or **Swedish Railways** (p158).

➡ Within Norway, Norwegian State Railways runs an excellent though limited system of lines connecting Oslo with Stavanger, Bergen, Trondheim and other southern cities. Rail lines reach as far north as Bodø (you can also reach Narvik by rail from Sweden); further north you're limited to buses and ferries.

ICELAND

Reykjavík

POP

The world's most northerly capital combines colourful buildings, wild nightlife and a capricious soul to brilliant effect. You'll find Viking history, captivating museums, cool music, and offbeat cafes and bars. And it's a superb base for touring Iceland's natural wonders. Reykjavík's heart lies between Tjörnin (the Pond) and the harbour, and along Laugavegur, with nearly everything for visitors within walking distance.

◉ Sights

★ **Reykjavík Art Museum – Hafnarhús**   GALLERY

(☑ 411 6400; www.artmuseum.is; Tryggvagata 17; adult/child kr1600/free; ⊙ 10am-5pm Fri-Wed, to 10pm Thu) Reykjavík Art Museum's Hafnarhús is a marvellously restored warehouse converted into a soaring steel-and-concrete exhibition space. Though the well-curated exhibitions of cutting-edge contemporary Icelandic art change frequently (think installations, videos, paintings and sculpture), you can always count on the comic-book-style paintings of Erró (Guðmundur Guðmundsson), a political artist who has donated several thousand works to the museum. The cafe, run by Frú Lauga (☎534 7165; www.frulauga.is; Laugalækur 6; ⊘11am-6pm Mon-Fri, to 4pm Sat; ☒) ☞ farmers market, has great harbour views.

★ **National Museum**   MUSEUM
(Þjóðminjasafn Íslands; ☎530 2200; www.nationalmuseum.is; Suðurgata 41; adult/child kr2000/free; ⊘10am-5pm May–mid-Sep, closed Mon mid-Sep–Apr; ☐1, 3, 6, 12, 14) This superb museum displays artefacts from settlement to the modern age. Exhibits give an excellent overview of Iceland's history and culture, and the free smartphone audio guide adds loads of detail. The strongest section describes the Settlement Era – including the rule of the chieftans and the introduction of Christianity – and features swords, drinking horns, silver hoards and a powerful **bronze figure of Thor**. The priceless 13th-century **Valþjófsstaðir church door** is carved with the story of a knight, his faithful lion and a passel of dragons.

Settlement Exhibition   MUSEUM
(Landnámssýningin; ☎411 6370; www.reykjavikmuseum.is; Aðalstræti 16; adult/child kr1600/free; ⊘9am-6pm) This fascinating archaeological ruin/museum is based around a 10th-century **Viking longhouse** unearthed here from 2001 to 2002, and other settlement-era finds from central Reykjavík. It imaginatively combines technological wizardry and archaeology to give a glimpse into early Icelandic life. Don't miss the fragment of **boundary wall** at the back of the museum that is older still (and the oldest human-made structure in Reykjavík). Among the captivating high-tech displays, a wraparound panorama shows how things would have looked at the time of the longhouse.

★ **Hallgrímskirkja**   CHURCH
(☎510 1000; www.hallgrimskirkja.is; Skólavörðustígur; tower adult/child kr900/100; ⊘9am-9pm Jun-Sep, to 5pm Oct-May) Reykjavík's immense white-concrete church (1945–86), star of a thousand postcards, dominates the skyline and is visible from up to 20km away. Get an unmissable view of the city by taking an elevator trip up the

74.5m-high **tower**. In contrast to the high drama outside, the Lutheran church's interior is quite plain. The most eye-catching feature is the vast 5275-pipe **organ** installed in 1992. The church's size and radical design caused controversy, and its architect, Guðjón Samúelsson (1887–1950), never saw its completion.

★ **Icelandic Phallological Museum**   MUSEUM
(Hið Íslenzka Reðasafn; ☎561 6663; www.phallus.is; Laugavegur 116; adult/child kr1500/free; ⊘10am-6pm) Oh, the jokes are endless here, but although this unique museum houses a huge collection of penises, it's actually very well done. From pickled pickles to petrified wood, there are 286 different members on display, representing all Icelandic mammals and beyond. Featured items include contributions from sperm whales and a polar bear, minuscule mouse bits, silver castings of each member of the Icelandic handball team and a single human sample – from deceased mountaineer Páll Arason.

✵ Festivals & Events

★ **Iceland Airwaves**   MUSIC
(www.icelandairwaves.is; ⊘Nov) You'd be forgiven for thinking Iceland is just one giant music-producing machine. Since the first edition of Iceland Airwaves was held in 1999, this fab festival has become one of the world's premier annual showcases for new music (Icelandic and otherwise).

☞ Tours

Reykjavík is the hub for tours to amazing landscapes and activities around Iceland.

Reykjavík Excursions   BUS
(Kynnisferðir; ☎580 5400; www.re.is; BSÍ Bus Terminal, Vatnsmýrarvegur 10) The largest and most popular bus-tour operator (with large groups) has an enormous booklet full of summer and winter programs (tours from kr9000 to kr47,900). Extras include horse riding, snowmobiling and themed tours tying in with festivals. Also offers 'Iceland on Your Own' bus tickets and passports for transport, and operates the Flybus to the Keflavík International Airport.

Elding Adventures at Sea   WILDLIFE
(☎519 5000; www.whalewatching.is; Ægisgarður 5; adult/child kr11,000/5500; ⊘harbour kiosk 8am-9pm; ☐14) ☞ The city's most established and ecofriendly outfit, with an included

ICELAND AT A GLANCE

Don't Miss

Reykjavík Petite Reykjavík boasts all the treats you'd expect of a European capital – such as excellent museums and great shopping – and the city's ratio of coffee houses to citizens is nothing short of staggering. These crank up the intensity after hours, when tea is swapped for tipples and the dance moves are broken out.

Vatnajökull National Park Europe's largest national park covers nearly 14% of Iceland and safeguards mighty Vatnajökull, the largest ice cap outside the poles (it's three times the size of Luxembourg). Scores of outlet glaciers flow down from its frosty bulk, while underneath it are active volcanoes and mountain peaks.

Vestmannaeyjar An offshore archipelago of craggy peaks, Vestmannaeyjar is a mere 30-minute ferry ride from the mainland, but feels miles and miles away in sentiment. A boat tour of the scattered islets unveils squawking seabirds, towering cliffs and postcard-worthy vistas of lonely hunting cabins perched atop rocky outcrops.

Jökulsárlón A ghostly procession of luminous-blue icebergs drifts serenely through a 25-sq-km lagoon before floating out to sea. This surreal scene (handily, right next to the Ring Road) is a natural film set.

Getting into hot water Iceland's unofficial pastime is splashing around in its surplus of geothermal water. You'll find 'hot-pots' everywhere from downtown Reykjavík to the isolated peninsular tips of the Westfjords. Not only are they incredibly relaxing but they're the perfect antidote to a hangover and a great way to meet the locals (this is their social hub; the equivalent of the local pub or town square).

Itineraries

One Week

Start in **Reykjavík**, enjoying the city's museums, cafes and bars while getting acclimatised. Then complete the day-long **Golden Circle** with stops at glittering **Gullfoss**, surging **Geysir**, and historic **Þingvellir National Park**, where you'll witness the tearing apart of the continental plates.

Two Weeks

With two weeks you can circumnavigate the island on the famous Ring Road, which loops you near the most popular sights.

Glide through **Akureyri**, Iceland's unofficial northern capital and head to the geological treasure chest of the **Mývatn** region next.

Heading on to the southeast, jump on a snowmobile to discover the vast ice cap at **Vatnajökull**. Don't miss the glacial lagoon at **Jökulsárlón**. You can warm up your hiking legs in **Skaftafell**. Then tackle the awesome trek from **Skógar** to **Þórsmörk**, a verdant interior valley.

Essential Food & Drink

The incredible local fish and lamb should be high on your hit-list. You may be considering the 'novelty value' of sampling the likes of whale, puffin and even *hákarl* (fermented Greenland shark), but please do consider your actions.

Skyr Rich and creamy yoghurt-like staple, sometimes sweetened with sugar and berries.

Hangikjöt Literally 'hung meat', usually smoked lamb, served in thin slices (it's traditionally a Christmas dish).

Harðfiskur Brittle pieces of wind-dried haddock ('fish jerky'?), usually eaten with butter.

Pýlsur Icelandic hot dogs, made with a combination of lamb, beef and pork.

Liquorice Salt liquorice and chocolate-covered varieties fill the supermarket sweets aisles.

Getting Around

Car The most common way for visitors to get around. Vehicles can be expensive to rent but provide great freedom. A 2WD vehicle will get you almost everywhere in summer. Driving into the highlands and on F roads requires 4WDs.

Bus A decent bus network operates from around mid-May to mid-September, shuttling you between major destinations and into the highlands. Outside these months, services are less frequent (and even nonexistent). Find an invaluable online map at www.publictransport.is.

Air If you're short on time, domestic flights can help you get around efficiently.

When to Go

Reykjavík

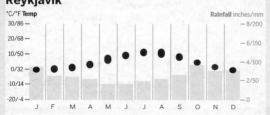

Jun–Aug Visitors descend en masse, especially to Reykjavík and the south. Prices peak; prebookings are essential.

May & Sep Optimal visiting conditions if you prefer smaller crowds and lower prices over cloudless days.

Oct–Apr Brief spurts of daylight; long nights with possible northern lights viewings.

Arriving in Iceland

Keflavík International Airport Iceland's primary international airport, 48km west of Reykjavík. Flybus, Airport Express and Airport Direct have buses connecting the airport with Reykjavík. Strætó (www.bus.is) bus 55 connects the BSÍ bus terminal and the airport (kr1680, nine daily Monday to Friday in summer). Airport Express also goes to Borgarnes and Akureyri in summer. Taxis available to Reykjavík but are not heavily utilised because of the high cost (about kr15,000), and the ease of bus connections.

Top Phrases

Hello. Halló.

Goodbye. Bless.

Yes/No. Já/Nei.

Thank you. Takk.

Excuse me. Fyrirgefðu.

Resources

Visit Iceland (www.visiticeland.com) Iceland's official tourism portal.

Safe Travel (www.safetravel.is) Stay safe while travelling.

Reykjavík Grapevine (www.grapevine.is) Great English-language newspaper and website.

Set Your Budget

➡ Camping: kr1200–1800

➡ Dorm bed: kr4500–7000

➡ Hostel breakfast: kr1800–2000

➡ Grill-bar grub or soup lunch: kr1500–2200

Central Reykjavík

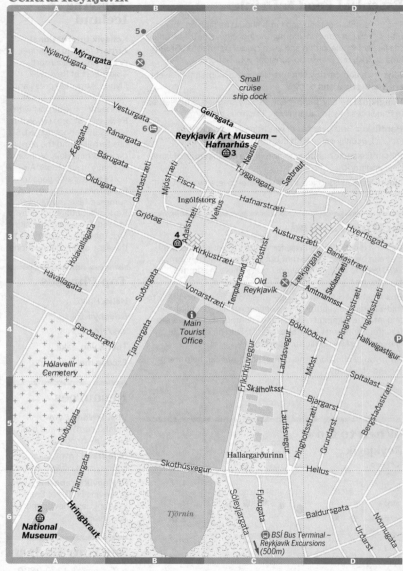

whale exhibition and refreshments sold on board. Elding also offers angling (adult/child kr14,200/7100) and puffin-watching (adult/child from kr6500/3250) trips and combo tours, and runs the ferry to Viðey. Offers pick-up.

🛏 Sleeping

★ Reykjavík Downtown Hostel

HOSTEL €

(☎ 553 8120; www.hostel.is; Vesturgata 17; 4-/10-bed dm kr10,100/7400, d with/without bathroom kr28,000/24,500; @ 🖥) Squeaky clean and

Central Reykjavík

KEX Hostel　　　　　　　　　　　　HOSTEL €

(☑ 561 6060; www.kexhostel.is; Skúlagata 28; dm 4-/16-bed kr7900/4900, d with/without bathroom kr39,700/25,500; @ ☎) An unofficial head-quarters of backpackerdom and popular local gathering place, KEX is a mega-hostel with heaps of style (think retro vaudeville meets rodeo) and sociability. Overall it's not as prim as the other hostels – and bath-rooms are shared by many – but KEX is a favourite for its lively restaurant-bar with water views and interior courtyard.

✖ Eating

★ Sægreifinn　　　　　　　　　　SEAFOOD €

(Seabaron; ☑ 553 1500; www.saegreifinn.is; Geirs-gata 8; mains kr1350-1900; ⏰ 11.30am-11pm mid-May–Aug, to 10pm Sep–mid-May) Sidle into this green harbourside shack for the most fa-mous lobster soup (kr1400) in the capital, or choose from a fridge full of fresh fish skewers to be grilled on the spot. Though the origi-nal sea baron sold the restaurant some years ago, the place retains a cosy, laid-back feel.

★ Gló　　　　　　　　　ORGANIC, VEGETARIAN €

(☑ 553 1111; www.glo.is; Laugavegur 20b; mains kr1400-2000; ⏰ 11am-9pm Mon-Fri, 11.30am-9pm Sat & Sun; ☎ ☑) Join the cool cats in this airy upstairs restaurant serving fresh, large daily specials loaded with Asian-influenced herbs and spices. Though not exclusively vegetarian, it's a wonderland of raw and organic foods, with a broad bar of

well run, this effortlessly charming hos-tel gets such good reviews that it regularly lures large groups and the nonbackpacker set. Enjoy friendly service, a guest kitchen and excellent rooms. Discount kr700 for HI members.

SCANDINAVIA REYKJAVIK

THE BLUE LAGOON

In a magnificent black-lava field, the milky teal **Blue Lagoon** (Bláa Lónið; ☑ 420 8800; www.bluelagoon.com; adult/child from kr6990/free; ⊘ 7am-midnight Jul–mid-Aug, to 11pm mid-May–Jun, 8am-10pm Jan–mid-May & mid-Aug–Sep, to 9pm Oct-Dec) is fed water from the futuristic Svartsengi geothermal plant; with its silver towers, roiling clouds of steam, and people daubed in white silica mud, it's an other-worldly place. Those who say it's too commercial and too crowded aren't wrong, but you'll be missing something special if you don't go. Pre-booking is essential.

The superheated water (70% sea water and 30% fresh water, at a perfect 38°C; 100.4°F) is rich in blue-green algae, mineral salts and fine silica mud, which condition and exfoliate the skin – it sounds like advertising speak, but you really do come out as soft as a baby's bum. The water is hottest near the vents where it emerges, and the surface is several degrees warmer than the bottom.

The lagoon has been developed for visitors, with an enormous, modern complex of changing rooms, plus a spa, a hotel, restaurants, a rooftop viewpoint and a gift shop, and is landscaped with hot-pots, steam rooms, a sauna, a bar and a piping-hot waterfall that delivers a powerful hydraulic massage – like being pummelled by a troll.

Towel or bathing-suit hire is 700kr. The complex is just off the road between Keflavík and Grindavík. Bus services run year-round, as do tours (which sometimes offer better deals than a bus ticket plus lagoon admission).

elaborate salads, from root veggies to Greek, to choose from. It also has branches in **Laugardalur** (☑ 553 1111; Engjateigur 19; mains kr1250-2000; ⊘ 11am-9pm Mon-Fri; 🕸🎋) 🍴 and **Kópavogur** (Hæðasmári 6; mains kr1300-2300; ⊘ 11am-9pm Mon-Fri, 11.30am-9pm Sat & Sun; 🕸🎋) 🍴.

★**Messinn**   SEAFOOD €€
(☑ 546 0095; www.messinn.com; Lækjargata 6b; lunch mains kr1850-2100, dinner mains kr2700-4100; ⊘ 11.30am-3pm & 5-10pm; 🕸) Make a beeline to Messinn for the best seafood that Reykjavík has to offer. The speciality here is the amazing pan-fry dishes: your pick of fish is served up in a sizzling cast-iron skillet, accompanied by buttery potatoes and salad. The mood is upbeat and comfortable, and the staff are friendly.

🍷 Drinking & Nightlife

Reykjavík is renowned for its weekend *djammið,* when folks buy booze from Vín-búðin (state alcohol shop), have a pre-party at home, then hit the town at midnight. Many of the cafes around town morph into bars at night. Minimum drinking age is 20.

★**Kaffibarinn**   BAR
(☑ 551 1588; www.kaffibarinn.is; Bergstaðastræti 1; ⊘ 3pm-1am Sun-Thu, to 4.30am Fri & Sat; 🕸) This old house with the London Underground symbol over the door contains one of Reykjavík's coolest bars; it even had a starring role in the cult movie *101 Reykjavík* (2000). At weekends you'll feel like you need either a famous face or a battering ram to get in. At other times it's a place for artistic types to chill with their Macs.

★**Kaffi Vínyl**   CAFE
(☑ 537 1332; www.facebook.com/vinilrvk; Hverfis-gata 76; ⊘ 8am-11pm; 🕸) This light shining in the Reykjavík coffee, restaurant and music scene is popular for its chilled vibe, music and delicious vegan and vegetarian food.

ⓘ Information

Main Tourist Office (Upplýsingamiðstöð Ferðamanna; ☑ 411 6040; www.visitreykjavik. is; Ráðhús City Hall, Tjarnargata 11; ⊘ 8am-8pm) Friendly staff and mountains of free brochures, plus maps, Reykjavík City Card and Strætó city bus tickets. Books accommodation, tours and activities.

ⓘ Getting There & Around

➜ International flights operate through **Keflavík International Airport** (KEF; ☑ 425 6000; www. kefairport.is), 48km west of Reykjavík.

➜ Flybus, Airport Express and Airport Direct have buses connecting the airport with Reykjavík. Strætó (www.bus.is) bus 55 connects the BSÍ bus terminal and the airport (kr1680, nine daily Monday to Friday in summer).

➜ Strætó operates regular, easy buses around Reykjavík and its suburbs; it also operates long distance buses.

The Golden Circle

The Golden Circle takes in three popular attractions all within 100km of the capital: Þingvellir, Geysir and Gullfoss. It is a tourist circuit loved (and marketed) by thousands. The Golden Circle offers the opportunity to see a meeting point of the continental plates and site of the ancient Icelandic parliament (Þingvellir), a spouting hot spring (Geysir) and a roaring waterfall (Gullfoss), all in one doable-in-a-day loop. Visiting under your own steam – by bike or hire car – allows you to visit at off-hours and explore exciting attractions further afield. Almost every tour company in the Reykjavík area offers a Golden Circle excursion (from bus to bike to super-Jeep), often combinable with other sights as well.

◉ Sights

★ **Þingvellir National Park**   NATIONAL PARK
(www.thingvellir.is) Þingvellir National Park, 40km northeast of central Reykjavík, is Iceland's most important historical site. The Vikings established the world's first democratic parliament, the **Alþingi** (pronounced *ál-thingk-ee*, also called Alþing), here in AD 930. The meetings were conducted outdoors, and as with many saga sites, there are only the stone foundations of ancient encampments. The site has a superb natural setting, in an immense, fissured rift valley, caused by the meeting of the North American and Eurasian tectonic plates, with rivers and waterfalls.

★ **Geysir**   GEYSER
FREE One of Iceland's most famous tourist attractions, Geysir (gay-zeer; literally 'gusher') is the original hot-water spout after which all other geysers are named. Earthquakes can stimulate activity, though eruptions are rare. Luckily for visitors, the very reliable geyser, Strokkur, sits alongside. You rarely have to wait more than five to 10 minutes for the hot spring to shoot an impressive 15m to 30m plume.

★ **Gullfoss**   WATERFALL
(Golden Falls; www.gullfoss.is) **FREE** Iceland's most famous waterfall, Gullfoss is a spectacular double cascade dropping a dramatic 32m. As it descends, it kicks up magnificent walls of spray before thundering down a rocky ravine. On sunny days the mist creates shimmering rainbows, while in winter the falls glitter with ice. Although it's a popular sight, the remote location still makes you feel the ineffable forces of nature that have worked this landscape for millennia.

Above the falls there's a small tourist information centre, shop and cafe.

The South

As you work your way eastwards from Reykjavík, Rte 1 (the Ring Road) emerges into austere volcanic foothills punctuated by surreal steam vents, around Hveragerði, then swoops through a flat, wide coastal plain, full of verdant horse farms and greenhouses, before the landscape suddenly begins to grow wonderfully jagged, after Hella and Hvolsvöllur. Mountains thrust upward on the inland side, some of them volcanoes wreathed by mist (eg Eyjafjallajökull, site of the 2010 eruption), and the first of the awesome glaciers appears, while enormous rivers like the Þjórsá cut their way to the black-sand beaches rimming the Atlantic.

Throughout, roads pierce deep inland to realms of lush waterfall-doused valleys and awe-inspiring volcanoes. Public transport (and traffic) is solid along the Ring Road, which is studded with interesting settlements.

SCANDINAVIA THE GOLDEN CIRCLE

OFF THE BEATEN TRACK

THE WESTFJORDS

The Westfjords is where Iceland's dramatic landscapes come to a riveting climax and where mass tourism disappears – only about 14% of Iceland's visitors ever see the region. Jagged bird cliffs and broad, multihued dream beaches flank the south. Rutted dirt roads snake north along jaw-dropping coastal fjords and over immense central mountains, revealing tiny fishing villages embracing traditional ways of life. In the far north, the **Hornstrandir** hiking reserve crowns the quiet region. **Ísafjörður** is the major bus hub in the Westfjords and accessible from Reykjavík. West Travel (www.westfjordsadventure.is) runs limited bus services in the region. Local ferries also zip around the area.

Vestmannaeyjar

Jagged and black, the Vestmannaeyjar (sometimes called the Westman Islands) form 15 eye-catching silhouettes off the southern shore. The islands were formed by submarine volcanoes around 11,000 years ago, except for Surtsey, the archipelago's newest addition, which rose from the waves in 1963. Surtsey was made a Unesco World Heritage site in 2008, but its unique status means that it is not possible to land there except for scientific study.

Heimaey is the only inhabited island. Its little town and sheltered harbour lie between dramatic *klettur* (escarpments) and two ominous volcanoes – blood-red Eldfell and conical Helgafell. These days Heimaey is famous for its puffins (around 10 million birds come here to breed); Þjóðhátíð, Iceland's biggest outdoor festival; and its new volcano museum.

◉ Sights

★ **Eldheimar**   MUSEUM
(Pompeii of the North; ☑ 488 2700; www.eldheimar.is; Gerðisbraut 10; adult/child kr2300/1200; ⊙ 11am-6pm daily May-Sep, 1-5pm Wed-Sun Oct-Apr) More than 400 buildings lie buried under lava from the 1973 eruption, and on the edge of the flow 'Pompeii of the North' is a new museum revolving around one house excavated from 50m of pumice, along what was formerly Suðurvegur. The modern volcanic-stone building allows a glimpse into the home with its crumbling walls and intact but toppled knick-knacks, and is filled with multimedia exhibits on the eruption and its aftermath, from compelling footage and eyewitness accounts to the home-owners' story.

★ **Eldfell**   VOLCANO
The 221m-high volcanic cone Eldfell appeared from nowhere in the early hours of 23 January 1973. Once the fireworks finished, heat from the volcano provided Heimaey with geothermal energy from 1976 to 1985. Today the ground is still hot enough in places to bake bread or char wood. Eldfell is an easy climb from town, up the collapsed northern wall of the crater; stick to the path, as the islanders are trying to save their latest volcano from erosion.

★ **Eldfellshraun**   NATURAL FEATURE
Known as Eldfellshraun, the new land created by the 1973 lava flow is now criss-crossed with a maze of other-worldly hiking tracks that run down to the fort at Skansinn and the area where the lava meets the town's houses, and all around the bulge of the raw, red eastern coast. Here you'll find small black-stone beaches, the Gaujulundur lava garden and a lighthouse.

★☆ Festivals & Events

★ **Þjóðhátíð**   MUSIC
(National Festival Þjóðhátíð Vestmannaeyjar; www.dalurinn.is; kr23,900; ⊙ Jul or Aug) Three-day Þjóðhátíð is the country's biggest outdoor festival. Held at Herjólfsdalur festival ground over the last weekend in July or the first weekend in August, it involves music, dancing, fireworks, a big bonfire, gallons of alcohol and, as the night progresses, lots of drunken sex (it's something of a teen rite of passage), with upwards of 17,000 people attending.

⊨ Sleeping & Eating

Aska Hostel   HOSTEL €
(☑ 662 7266; www.askahostel.is; Bárustigur 11; dm/d/q without bathroom kr5400/12,900/27,100; ⊛) This cheery yellow historic building is home to a good hostel in the village centre with bright, modern rooms and welcoming staff.

★ **Slippurinn**   ICELANDIC €€
(☑ 481 1515; www.slippurinn.com; Strandvegur 76; lunch kr2200-3000, dinner mains kr3490-6990, set menu kr7990-11,990; ⊙ noon-2.30pm & 5-10pm early May–mid-Sep; ⊛) Lively Slippurinn fills the upper storey of a beautifully remodelled old machine workshop that once serviced the ships in the harbour and now has great views to it. The food is delicious Icelandic with a level of creativity that sets it above most restaurants in the country. Ingredients are exquisite and combinations of fish, local produce and locally sourced meats divine.

ⓘ Getting There & Away

Eimskip's ferry **Herjólfur** (☑ 481 2800; www.eimskip.is; per adult/child/bicycle/car kr1410/760/760/2220) sails from Landeyjahöfn (about 12km off the Ring Road between Hvolsvöllur and Skógar) to Heimaey year-round. The journey takes about 30 minutes. Passengers should book ahead in high season.

Getting to or from Landeyjahöfn, **Strætó** (p200) bus 52 runs from Reykjavík (4200kr, 2¼ hours, three daily in summer).

Skógar

Skógar nestles under the Eyjafjallajökull ice cap just off the Ring Road. This little tourist settlement is the start (or occasionally end) of the fantastic 23km day hike over the Fimmvörðuháls Pass to Þórsmörk, and is one of the busiest activities centres in the southwest. At its western edge, you'll see the dizzyingly high waterfall, Skógafoss, and on the eastern side you'll find a fantastic folk museum.

⊙ Sights

★**Skógar Folk Museum**   MUSEUM
(Skógasafn; ☑ 487 8845; www.skogasafn.is; adult/child kr2000/free; ⊙ 9am-6pm Jun-Aug, 10am-5pm Sep-May) The highlight of little Skógar is the wonderful Skógar Folk Museum, which covers all aspects of Icelandic life. The vast collection was put together by Þórður Tómasson over roughly 75 years – he retired as the museum's curator at the age of 92. There are also restored buildings – a church, a turf-roofed farmhouse, cowsheds – and a huge, modern building that houses an interesting transport and communication museum, a basic cafe and a shop.

★**Sólheimajökull**   GLACIER
One of the easiest glacial tongues to reach is Sólheimajökull. This icy outlet glacier unfurls from the main Mýrdalsjökull ice cap and is a favourite spot for glacial walks and ice climbing. Rte 221 leads 4.2km off the Ring Road to a small car park and the **Arcanum Glacier Café** (Café Solheimajökull; ☑ 547 1500; www.arcanum.is; snacks kr750-1375; ⊙ 9.30am-5pm May-Sep, reduced hours Oct-Apr; ☎), from where you can walk the 800m to the ice along a wide track edging the glacial lagoon. Don't attempt to climb onto the glacier unguided.

★**Skógafoss**   WATERFALL
This 62m-high waterfall topples over a rocky cliff at the western edge of Skógar in dramatic style. Climb the steep staircase alongside for giddy views, or walk to the foot of the falls, shrouded in sheets of mist and rainbows. Legend has it that a settler named Þrasi hid a chest of gold behind Skógafoss...

🛌 Sleeping

Skógar HI Hostel   HOSTEL €
(☑ 487 8780; www.hostel.is; dm/d kr4750/12,900; ☎) A solid link in the HI chain, this spot is located a stone's throw from Skógafoss in an old school with utilitarian rooms. There's a guest kitchen and a laundry.

❶ Getting There & Away

Strætó bus 51 runs here from Reykjavík twice daily (5040kr, 2½ hours). Sterna and Reykjavík Excursions services also pass through in summer.

Landmannalaugar & Þórsmörk

Two of the most renowned inland spots of southern Iceland are Landmannalaugar, where vibrantly coloured rhyolite peaks meet bubbling hot springs, and Þórsmörk, a gorgeous, forested valley tucked away from the brutal northern elements under a series of ice caps. They are linked by the rightly famous 55km Laugavegurinn hike,

---

DON'T MISS

JÖKULSÁRLÓN

A host of spectacular, luminous-blue icebergs drift through Jökulsárlón glacier lagoon, right beside the Ring Road between Höfn and Skaftafell. It's worth spending a couple of hours here, admiring the wondrous ice sculptures (some of them striped with ash layers from volcanic eruptions), scouting for seals or taking a boat trip.

The icebergs calve from Breiðamerkurjökull, an offshoot of Vatnajökull, crashing down into the water and drifting towards the Atlantic Ocean. They can spend up to five years floating in the 25-sq-km-plus, 260m-deep lagoon, melting, refreezing and occasionally toppling over with a mighty splash, startling the birds. They then move on via Jökulsá, Iceland's shortest river, out to sea.

Although it looks as though it's been here since the last ice age, the lagoon is only about 80 years old. Until the mid-1930s Breiðamerkurjökull reached the Ring Road; it's now retreating rapidly (up to a staggering 500m per year), and the lagoon is consequently growing.

Iceland's most popular trek (for more information, check Ferðafélag Íslands' website: www.fi.is). Since these areas lie inland on roads impassable by standard vehicles, most visitors access them on tours or amphibious buses from the southern Ring Road. Þórsmörk, one of Iceland's most popular hiking destinations, can be done as a day trip from Reykjavík.

Skaftafell & Vatnajökull National Park (Jökulsárgljúfur)

Skaftafell, the jewel in the crown of Vatnajökull National Park (Jökulsárgljúfur), encompasses a breathtaking collection of peaks and glaciers. It's the country's favourite wilderness: hundreds of thousands come yearly to marvel at thundering waterfalls, twisted birch woods, the tangled web of rivers threading across the sandar (sand deltas) and brilliant blue-white Vatnajökull with its myriad ice tongues.

Icelandic Mountain Guides (IMG; ✆ Reykjavík 587 9999, Skaftafell 894 2959; www.mountainguides.is; ⊙ 8.30am-6pm May-Sep, reduced hours Oct-Apr) and **Glacier Guides** (✆ 562 7000; www.glacierguides.is; ⊙ 8.30am-6pm Apr-Oct, reduced hours Nov-Mar) lead glacier walks and adventure tours.

The **visitor centre** (✆ 470 8300; www.vjp. is; ⊙ 8am-9pm Jun-Aug, 9am-7pm May & Sep, 9am-6pm Oct & Nov, 9am-5pm Dec-Apr; 🛜) has a **campground** (sites per adult/teen/child kr1700/800/free; ⊙ May-Sep; 🛜) and summertime cafe. Various buses and transports travelling between Reykjavík and Höfn stop here.

The North

Iceland's mammoth and magnificent north is a wonderland of moon-like lava fields, belching mudpots, epic waterfalls, snow-capped peaks and whale-filled bays. The region's top sights are variations on one theme: a grumbling, volcanically active earth.

Akureyri

POP 18,200

Little Akureyri, with its surprising moments of big-city living, is the best base in the north. From here you can explore by car or bus, and tour the region's highlights.

Skaftafell National Park

↪ Tours

★ **Saga Travel** ADVENTURE TOUR
(✆ 558 8888; www.sagatravel.is; Kaupvangsstræti 4; ⊙ booking office 7.30am-5pm Jun-Aug, reduced hours rest of year) Saga offers a rich and diverse year-round program of excursions and activities throughout the north. It includes obvious destinations such as Mývatn, Húsavík (for whale watching) and Askja in the highlands, but also offers innovative tours along themes such as food or art and design. Check out Saga's full program online, or drop by its central booking office.

Jökulsárgljúfur

ℹ Information

Tourist Office (✉ 450 1050; www.visitakureyri. is; Hof, Strandgata 12; ⏱ 8am-6.30pm mid-Jun–mid-Sep, shorter hours rest of year; ☎) This friendly, efficient office is inside Hof (✉ 450 1000; www.mak.is). There are loads of brochures, maps, internet access and a great design shop. Knowledgable staff can advise on tours and transport. There's a complex array of opening hours outside of summer; the office generally closes at 4pm in winter, and 5pm in spring and autumn.

ℹ Getting There & Away

Akureyri's **bus station** (Hafnarstræti 82) is the hub for bus travel in the north provided by SBA-Norðurleið and Sterna; Strætó operates from a stop in front of Hof. (Note: there is talk of building a central bus terminal that will serve all operators, so it pays to double-check departure points.) If you need to return to Reykjavík, consider taking an all-terrain bus route through the interior highlands, rather than along Rte 1. Buses run to Mývatn, Egilsstaðir, Húsavik, Reykjavík and other destinations.

Mývatn Region

Undisputed gem of the northeast, Mývatn (*mee*-vaht) lake and the surrounding area are starkly beautiful, an otherworldly landscape of spluttering mudpots, weird lava formations, steaming fumaroles and volcanic craters.

Reykjahlíð, at the northern end of the lake, is more an assortment of accommodation than a true town, but it makes the best base.

◉ Sights

The sights along Mývatn's eastern lakeshore, close to Reykjahlíð, can be linked together on an enjoyable half-day hike. Steaming vents and craters await at Krafla, an active volcanic region 7km north of the Ring Road.

🛌 Sleeping

Akureyri Backpackers   HOSTEL €
(✉ 571 9050; www.akureyribackpackers.com; Hafnarstræti 98; dm kr4900-5800, d without bathroom kr20,300; ☎) Supremely placed in the town's heart, this backpackers has a chilled travellers' vibe and includes a tour-booking service and a popular bar. Rooms spread over three floors: four- to eight-bed dorms, plus private rooms with made-up beds are on the top floor. Minor gripe: there are toilets and sinks on all levels but showers are in the basement, as is the free sauna.

★ **Dimmuborgir**   NATURAL FEATURE
The giant jagged lava field at Dimmuborgir (literally 'Dark Castles') is one of the most fascinating flows in the country. A series of nontaxing, colour-coded walking trails runs through the easily anthropomorphised landscape. The most popular path is the easy Church Circle (2.3km). Ask at the **cafe** (✉ 464 1144; www.kaffiborgir.is; mains kr1950-3950; ⏱ 10am-9pm Jun-Aug, reduced hours Sep-May, closed mid-Dec–Feb) here about free guided ranger walks in summer.

1. Reykjavík, Iceland
The unmistakable Hallgrímskirkja (p185) dominates the city's skyline.

2. Lofoten, Norway
Astoundingly beautiful views over a village in the Lofoten Islands (p181).

3. Lapland, Sweden
The aurora borealis (northern lights; p183) dances across Scandinavian skies on clear nights.

4. Stockholm, Sweden
Kungliga Slottet (Royal Palace; p146) houses an ornate chapel.

★ Hverfjall
NATURAL FEATURE

Dominating the lava fields on the eastern edge of Mývatn is the classic tephra ring Hverfjall (also called Hverfell). This near-symmetrical crater appeared 2700 years ago in a cataclysmic eruption. Rising 452m from the ground and stretching 1040m across, it is a massive and awe-inspiring landmark in Mývatn.

★ Leirhnjúkur
NATURAL FEATURE

Krafla's most impressive, and potentially most dangerous, attraction is the Leirhnjúkur crater and its solfataras, which originally appeared in 1727, starting out as a lava fountain and spouting molten material for two years before subsiding.

In 1975, the Krafla Fires began with a small lava eruption by Leirhnjúkur, and after nine years of on-and-off action Leirhnjúkur became the ominous-looking, sulphur-encrusted mudhole that tourists love today. The earth's crust here is extremely thin and in places the ground is ferociously hot.

🛏 Sleeping

Hlíð
CAMPGROUND, GUESTHOUSE €

(☑464 4103; www.myvatnaccommodation.is; Hraunbrún; sites per person kr1600, dm kr5000, d incl breakfast kr25,000, cottage kr36,500; @🛜) Sprawling, well-run Hlíð is 300m uphill from the **church** and offers a full spectrum: camping, sleeping-bag dorms and rooms with kitchen access, no-frills huts, self-contained cottages sleeping six, and en suite guesthouse rooms. There's also a laundry, playground and bike hire.

ⓘ ARRIVING AT SEYÐISFJÖRÐUR

The Norröna ferry from Denmark arrives at Seyðisfjörður in the east. It's a good introduction to the country: made up of multicoloured wooden houses and surrounded by snowcapped mountains and cascading waterfalls, it's picturesque and the most historically and architecturally interesting town in east Iceland.

There's tourist information in the ferry terminal. From here, **FAS** (☑472 1515, 893 2669) runs a bus service to Egilsstaðir (1050kr, around 45 minutes) to coincide with the ferry arrival and departure.

ⓘ Getting There & Away

All buses pick up/drop off passengers at the information centre in Reykjahlíð. Tourist bus services run to Akureyri, Reykjavík, Egilsstaðir and more.

Húsavík

POP 2240

Húsavík, Iceland's whale-watching capital, has become a firm favourite on travellers' itineraries – and with its colourful houses, unique museums and stunning snowcapped peaks across the bay, it's easily the northeast's prettiest fishing town.

⊙ Sights

★ Húsavík Whale Museum
MUSEUM

(Hvalasafnið; ☑414 2800; www.whalemuseum.is; Hafnarstétt; adult/child kr1900/500; ⊙8.30am-6.30pm daily May-Sep, 10am-4pm Mon-Fri Oct-Apr) This excellent museum provides all you ever need to know about the impressive creatures that visit Skjálfandi bay. Housed in an old harbourside slaughterhouse, the museum interprets the ecology and habits of whales, conservation and the history of whaling in Iceland through beautifully curated displays, including several huge skeletons soaring high above (they're real!).

☞ Tours

North Sailing
WILDLIFE

(☑464 7272; www.northsailing.is; Garðarsbraut; 3hr tours adult/child kr10,500/4500) The original whale-watching operator, with a fleet of lovingly restored traditional boats. Its four-hour 'Whales, Puffins & Sails' tour (adult/child kr14,000/5600) is on board an old schooner; when conditions are right, sails are hoisted and engines cut. Some four-hour tours are on the schedule as a carbon-neutral option; the ship is run on renewable energy instead of fossil fuel.

Gentle Giants
WILDLIFE

(☑464 1500; www.gentlegiants.is; Garðarsbraut; 3hr tours adult/child kr10,300/4200) Gentle Giants has a flotilla of old fishing vessels for its standard three-hour tours, plus a fleet of high-speed rigid inflatable boats (RIBs) offering a way to cover more ground in the bay (RIB tours from kr19,000). It also runs special trips ashore on Flatey (Flat Island) for birdwatching, and fast (and pricey) RIB day trips to Grímsey.

🛏 Sleeping & Eating

Húsavík Hostel HOSTEL **€**
(📞858 5848; www.husavikhostel.com; Vallholtsve-
gur 9; dm/d without bathroom kr6500/15,840; 📶)
This is the only in-town budget option, and
its 21 beds are popular. There are bunk-filled
dorm rooms and a couple of private rooms
(which include linen), plus kitchen, but no
real lounge space. Management is friendly
and offers good local information.

★ Naustið SEAFOOD **€€**
(📞464 1520; www.facebook.com/naustid; Ás-
garðsvegur 1; mains kr2000-4900; ⏱noon-10pm)
In a new location away from the harbour,
buttercup-yellow Naustið wins praise for its
super-fresh fish and a simple concept that's
well executed: skewers of fish and vegetables, grilled to order. There's also fish soup
(natch), fish tacos and langoustine, plus
home-baked rhubarb cake for dessert.

ℹ Information

Tourist Information Centre (📞464 6165;
www.visithusavik.is; Hafnarstétt; ⏱8.30am-
6.30pm daily May-Sep, 10am-4pm Mon-Fri Oct-
Apr) In the lobby of the **Whale Museum** (p198),
with plentiful maps and brochures.

ℹ Getting There & Away

SBA-Norðurleið (📞550 0700; www.sba.
is) services (departing from in front of Gamli
Baukar restaurant, on the waterfront) include
bus 641a to Akureyri (3700kr, 1½ hours, one
daily mid-June to August) and bus 650a to
Mývatn (3500kr, 55 minutes, one daily mid-
June to August).

Strætó (📞540 2700; www.straeto.is) services
(departing from N1 service station) include bus
79 to Akureyri (2520kr, 1¼ hours, three daily).

Iceland Survival Guide

ℹ Directory A–Z

ACCOMMODATION

For visits between May and September travellers
should book accommodation well in advance
(no need to prebook campsites). All hostels and
some guesthouses and hotels offer cheaper
rates if guests use their own sleeping bags.
Generally, accommodation prices are very high
compared to mainland European lodging.

Iceland has 35 well-maintained hostels administered by Hostelling International Iceland (www.
hostel.is). In Reykjavík and Akureyri, there are
also independent backpacker hostels. Bookings

---

are recommended at all of them, especially from
June to August.

LGBT TRAVELLERS

Icelanders have a very open, accepting attitude
towards homosexuality, though the gay scene is
quite low-key, even in Reykjavík.

MONEY

➜ The Icelandic unit of currency is the króna
(plural krónur), written as kr here, and often
written elsewhere as Ikr or ISK.

➜ Coins come in denominations of 1kr, 5kr,
10kr, 50kr and 100kr.

➜ Notes come in denominations of 500kr,
1000kr, 2000kr, 5000kr and 10,000kr.

➜ Credit cards reign supreme, even in the most
rural reaches of the country (PIN required for
purchases). ATMs are available in all towns.

➜ As service and VAT are always included in
prices, tipping isn't required in Iceland.

OPENING HOURS

Banks 9am to 4pm Monday to Friday

Cafe-bars 10am to 1am Sunday to Thursday,
10am to between 3am and 6am Friday and
Saturday

Cafes 10am to 6pm

Post offices 9am to 4pm or 4.30pm Monday to
Friday (to 6pm in larger towns)

Restaurants 11.30am to 2.30pm and 6pm to
9pm or 10pm

Shops 10am to 6pm Monday to Friday, 10am to
4pm Saturday; some Sunday opening in Reykjavík malls and major shopping strips

Supermarkets 9am to 8pm (later in Reykjavík)

Vínbúðin (government-run alcohol stores)
Variable; many outside Reykjavík only open for
a couple of hours per day

TELEPHONE

➜ All telephone numbers in Iceland have seven
digits; there are no area codes.

➜ Country code: 📞354

➜ International access code: 📞00

➜ Local SIM cards with data packages are easily
available and cheap.

ℹ Getting There & Away

AIR

A growing number of airlines (including budget carriers) fly to Reykjavík's **Keflavík International Airport** (p190) from destinations in Europe and North America. Some airlines have services only from June to August.

FERRY

Smyril Line (www.smyrilline.com) operates a pricey but well-patronised weekly car ferry, the *Norröna*, from Hirsthals (Denmark) through Tórshavn (Faroe Islands) to Seyðisfjörður in east Iceland from late March until October. Limited winter passage is possible (departures are weather-dependent) – see the website. Fares vary widely.

ℹ Getting Around

A decent bus network operates from around mid-May to mid-September, shuttling you between major destinations and into the highlands. Outside these months, services are less frequent (even nonexistent). Find an invaluable online map at www.publictransport.is.

Many bus services can be used as day tours (the bus spends a few hours at the final destination and stops at points of interest en route). Main bus companies include the following:

Reykjavík Excursions (☑ 580 5400; www.re.is)

SBA-Norðurleið (☑ 550 0700; www.sba.is)

Sterna (☑ 551 1166; www.icelandbybus.is)

Strætó (☑ 540 2700; www.bus.is)

Germany, Austria & Benelux

Best Castles & Palaces

➡ Schloss Neuschwanstein (p227)

➡ Amsterdam Royal Palace (p273)

➡ Château de Bouillon (p266)

➡ Château de Vianden (p268)

Best Iconic Sights

➡ Munich Hofbräuhaus (p226)

➡ Keukenhof Gardens (p277)

➡ Manneken Pis (p250)

➡ In Flanders Fields (p265)

Why Go?

Tradition and modernity combine to dazzling effect in this sizeable chunk of old Europe that will likely soar beyond your expectations. Berlin, Munich, Amsterdam, Brussels, Salzburg and Vienna are all high on the list of must-see places. But bountiful riches await as much in these hopping metropolises as in storybook villages, lyrical valleys, undulating mountain roads and vine-draped river banks.

Castles and chocolate, tulips and cuckoo-clocks, Alps and canals: all the icons are here to be discovered along with the region's noble cathedrals, grand palaces, art galleries full of Old Masters, and charismatic traditional cafes, beer halls and pubs.

But these countries aren't like staid museums. From the devastation of wars came opportunities for regrowth and innovation. Cities like Leipzig, Düsseldorf, Rotterdam and Antwerp are hotbeds of modern architecture, edgy cultural happenings and contemporary zeitgeist – real drivers of the exciting 21st-century scene in central Europe.

Fast Facts

Capitals Berlin (Germany), Amsterdam (Netherlands), Brussels (Belgium), Luxembourg (Luxembourg), Vienna (Austria)

Emergency ☎112

Currency Euro (€)

Languages German, Dutch, French, Letzeburgesch

Country codes ☎49 (Germany), ☎31 (Netherlands), ☎32 (Belgium), ☎352 (Luxembourg), ☎43 (Austria)

Population 81.1 million (Germany), 16.9 million (Netherlands), 11.2 million (Belgium), 553,000 (Luxembourg), 8.7 million (Austria)

Time zone Central European (UTC/GMT plus one hour)

Germany, Benelux & Austria Highlights

1 Berlin Preparing for total immersion in a cultural and party scene in Europe's capital of alternative cred. (p204)

2 Munich Jumping on board for beer fests, BMWs, Alpine excursions and more in Bavaria's stylish metropolis. (p222)

3 The Romantic Rhine Snapping a postcard-perfect village along this beautiful stretch of river. (p250)

4 Brussels Imbibing the atmosphere and your fill of lambic beers in Belgium's stylish capital. (p252)

5 Bruges Appreciating the beautiful canal scenes of this heart-winning Flanders town. (p262)

6 Delft Taking in the townscapes of Vermeer's work and the blue-and-white ceramics of this pretty Dutch town. (p277)

7 Amsterdam Rejoicing in your urbanity in this fun and handsome icon of cool. (p271)

8 Salzburg Acquainting yourself with Mozart in this city of *Sound of Music* fame. (p296)

9 Vienna Roaming Habsburg palaces between coffee stops in Austria's magnificent capital. (p283)

GERMANY

Berlin

030 / POP 3.61 MILLION

Berlin is a bon vivant, passionately feasting on the smorgasbord of life and never taking things – or itself – too seriously. Its unique blend of glamour and grit is bound to mesmerise anyone keen to connect with its vibrant culture, superb museums, fabulous food, intense nightlife and tangible history. When it comes to creativity, the sky's the limit in Berlin, Europe's newest start-up capital. In the last 20 years, the city has become a giant lab of cultural experimentation thanks to an abundance of space, cheap rent and a free-wheeling spirit that nurtures and encourages new ideas. All this trendiness is a triumph for a city that staged a revolution, was headquartered by Nazis, then bombed to bits, divided in two and finally reunited – and that was just in the 20th century! Must-sees and aimless explorations – Berlin delivers it all in one exciting and memorable package.

◉ Sights

Key sights such as the Reichstag, Brandenburger Tor and Museumsinsel cluster in the walkable historic city centre – **Mitte** – which

---

ⓘ SIGHTSEEING ON THE CHEAP

Bus 100 & bus 200 Get a crash course in 'Berlinology' by hopping on bus 100 or 200 at Zoologischer Garten or Alexanderplatz and letting major landmarks whoosh by for the price of a standard bus ticket. Bus 100 goes via the Reichstag and Tiergarten; 200 via Potsdamer Platz.

Museumspass Berlin (www.visitberlin.de/en/museum-pass-berlin; adult/reduced from €29/14.50) Buys admission to the permanent exhibits of about 30 museums for three consecutive days, including big draws like the Pergamonmuseum.

Tip-based city tours Several companies offer city walking tours in English. Try Alternative Berlin Tours (http://alternativeberlin.com) or New Berlin Tours (http://www.neweuropetours.eu).

---

also cradles the mazelike hipster quarter around Hackescher Markt.

★ Reichstag
HISTORIC BUILDING

(Map p210; www.bundestag.de; Platz der Republik 1, Visitors' Service, Scheidemannstrasse; ⊙ lift 8am-midnight, last entry 9.45pm, Visitors' Service 9am-3pm Mon, to 4pm Tue-Thu, to 1.30pm Fri; 🚌 100, Ⓢ Brandenburger Tor, Hauptbahnhof, Ⓤ Brandenburger Tor, Bundestag) **FREE** It's been burned, bombed, rebuilt, buttressed by the Wall, wrapped in fabric and finally turned into the modern home of the German parliament by Norman Foster: the 1894 Reichstag is indeed one of Berlin's most iconic buildings. Its most distinctive feature, the glittering glass dome, is serviced by a lift and affords fabulous 360-degree city views. For guaranteed access, make free reservations online; otherwise try scoring tickets at the **Reichstag Service Centre** (www.bundestag.de; Scheidemannstrasse; ⊙ 8am-8pm Apr-Oct, to 6pm Nov-Mar; 🚌 100, Ⓢ Brandenburger Tor, Ⓤ Brandenburger Tor) for the same or next day. Bring ID.

★ Brandenburger Tor
LANDMARK

(Brandenburger Gate; Map p210; Pariser Platz; Ⓢ Brandenburger Tor, Ⓤ Brandenburger Tor) A symbol of division during the Cold War, the landmark Brandenburg Gate now epitomises German reunification. Carl Gotthard Langhans found inspiration in Athens' Acropolis for the elegant triumphal arch, completed in 1791 as the royal city gate. It stands sentinel over Pariser Platz, a harmoniously proportioned square once again framed by banks, a hotel and the US, British and French embassies, just as it was during its 19th-century heyday.

★ Holocaust Memorial
MEMORIAL

(Memorial to the Murdered Jews of Europe; Map p210; ☎ 030-2639 4336; www.stiftung-denkmal.de; Cora-Berliner-Strasse 1; audioguide €3; ⊙ field 24hr, information centre 10am-8pm Tue-Sun Apr-Sep, to 7pm Oct-Mar, last entry 45min before closing; Ⓢ Brandenburger Tor, Ⓤ Brandenburger Tor) **FREE** Inaugurated in 2005, this football-field-sized memorial by American architect Peter Eisenman consists of 2711 sarcophagi-like concrete columns rising in sombre silence from undulating ground. You're free to access this maze at any point and make your individual journey through it. For context visit the subterranean **Ort der Information** (Information Centre; Map p210; ☎ 030-7407 2929; www.holocaust-mahnmal.de;

Berlin

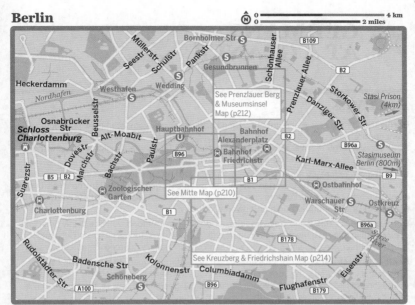

Cora-Berliner-Strasse 1; audioguide €3; ⊙ 10am-8pm Tue-Sun Apr-Sep, to 7pm Oct-Mar, last admission 45min before closing; ⒮ Brandenburger Tor, ⓤ Brandenburger Tor) **FREE** whose exhibits will leave no one untouched. Audioguides and audio translations of exhibit panels are available.

Pergamonmuseum MUSEUM
(Map p212; ☏ 030-266 424 242; www.smb.museum; Bodestrasse 1-3; adult/concession €18/9; ⊙ 10am-6pm Fri-Wed, to 8pm Thu; 🚌 100, 200, TXL, ⒮ Hackescher Markt, Friedrichstrasse) Opening a fascinating window on to the ancient world, this palatial three-wing complex unites a rich feast of classical sculpture and monumental architecture from Greece, Rome, Babylon and the Middle East, including the radiant-blue Ishtar Gate from Babylon, the Roman Market Gate of Miletus and the Caliph's Palace of Mshatta. Renovations put the namesake Pergamon Altar off limits until 2019. Budget at least two hours for this amazing place and be sure to pick up the free and excellent audioguide.

Neues Museum MUSEUM
(New Museum; Map p212; ☏ 030-266 424 242; www.smb.museum; Bodestrasse 1-3; adult/concession €12/6; ⊙ 10am-6pm Fri-Wed, to 8pm Thu; 🚌 100, 200, TXL, ⒮ Hackescher Markt)

David Chipperfield's reconstruction of the bombed-out Neues Museum is now the residence of Queen Nefertiti, the showstopper of the Egyptian Museum, which also features mummies, sculptures and sarcophagi. Pride of place at the Museum of Pre- and Early History (in the same building) goes to Trojan antiquities, a Neanderthal skull and the 3000-year-old 'Berliner Goldhut', a golden conical hat. Skip the queue by buying your timed ticket online. Entry must be made during the designated 30-minute time slot.

LOCAL KNOWLEDGE

HITLER'S BUNKER

Berlin was burning and Soviet tanks advancing relentlessly when Adolf Hitler put a bullet into his brain on 30 April 1945 in the labyrinthine *Führerbunker*. Today a parking lot covers the **site** (Map p210; cnr In den Ministergärten & Gertrud-Kolmar-Strasse; ⊙ 24hr; ⒮ Brandenburger Tor, ⓤ Brandenburger Tor), revealing its dark history only via an information panel with a diagram of the vast bunker network, construction data and the site's post-WWII history.

GERMANY AT A GLANCE

Don't Miss

Berlin The city's glamour and grit are bound to mesmerise anyone keen on exploring its vibrant culture, edgy architecture, fabulous food, intense parties and palpable history. Nearly three decades after the Wall's collapse, the German capital is increasingly grown up without relinquishing its indie spirit and penchant for creative improvisation.

Munich If you're looking for Alpine clichés, Munich will hand them to you in one chic and compact package. But the Bavarian capital also has plenty of unexpected trump cards under its often bright-blue skies. Folklore and age-old traditions exist side by side here with sleek BMWs, designer boutiques and high-powered industry.

German food & drink If you crave traditional German comfort food, you'll certainly find plenty of places to indulge in a meat-potato-cabbage diet. These days, though, 'typical' German fare is lighter, healthier, creative and prepared with seasonal and locally sourced ingredients.

Schloss Neuschwanstein Commissioned by Bavaria's most celebrated (and loopiest) 19th-century monarch, King Ludwig II, Schloss Neuschwanstein rises from the mysterious Alpine forests like a bedtime-storybook illustration. All turrets and towers, the sugary folly is said to have inspired Sleeping Beauty's Castle at Disneyland.

Romantic Rhine As the mighty Rhine flows from Mainz to Koblenz, the landscape's unique face-off between rock and water creates a magical mix of the wild (churning whirlpools, dramatic cliffs), the agricultural (near-vertical vineyards), the medieval (hilltop castles, half-timbered hamlets), the legendary (Loreley) and the modern (in the 19th-century sense: barges, ferries, passenger steamers and trains).

Itineraries

One Week

Bookended by two of Germany's most fun cities, this road trip is a fine introduction for first-timers to the top of the pops of German culture, character, architecture and landscapes. Kick off in **Berlin** to sample its top-notch museums, old and bold architecture and nice-to-naughty nightlife. Next head to show-stopping **Dresden**, sitting proud and pretty in its baroque splendour on the Elbe River. Push south to **Nuremberg**, with its evocative walled medieval centre, and on to **Munich** to wrap up a day of palace- and museum-hopping with an evening in a beer garden.

Two Weeks

Get up early to beat the crowds swarming 'Mad' King Ludwig II's Schloss Neuschwanstein in **Füssen**. In the afternoon, point the compass north for the **Romantic Road**, possibly overnighting in Dinkelsbühl or Rothenburg ob der Tauber. Next, cut west to historic **Heidelberg**, with its romantically ruined fortress, then north to the **Romantic Rhine**. Take the slow boat up the river past fairy-tale villages, vineyards and hilltop castles before winding up in cosmopolitan **Cologne** for church-hopping, great art and rustic beer halls.

Essential Food & Drink

Bread Tasty and textured, often mixing wheat and rye flour, and available in 300 varieties, German bread is a world-beater.

Sausage There are more than 1500 sausage types, all commonly served with bread and a sweet (*süss*) or spicy (*scharf*) mustard (*Senf*). The most popular variety is the Bratwurst.

Schwarzwälder Kirschtorte (Black Forest gateau) A multilayered chocolate sponge, cream and kirsch confection, topped with morello cherries and chocolate shavings.

Beer Few things are as deeply ingrained in the German psyche as the love of beer. The 'secret' of the country's golden nectar dates back to the 1516 Reinheitsgebot (purity law) passed in Bavaria, demanding breweries use just four ingredients – malt, yeast, hops and water.

Getting Around

Germans are whizzes at moving people around, and the public transport network is one of the best in Europe. The best ways of getting around the country are by car and by train.

Train Extensive network of long-distance and regional trains with frequent departures; fairly expensive but numerous deals available.

Car Useful for travelling at your own pace or for visiting regions with no or minimal public transport. Cars can be hired in every town and city. Drive on the right.

Bus Cheaper and slower than trains and with a growing long-haul network. Regional bus services fill the gaps in areas not served by rail.

Air Only useful for longer distances, eg Hamburg to Munich or Berlin to Munich.

When to Go

Berlin

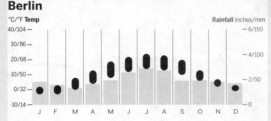

Jul & Aug Busy roads and long lines at key sights; festivals celebrate everything from music to wine and sailing to samba.

Apr–Jun & Sep–Oct Smaller crowds and lower prices; sunny, temperate weather.

Nov–Mar Shorter hours at key sights; December Christmas markets; ski resorts busiest in January and February.

Arriving in Germany

Frankfurt Airport S-Bahn train lines S8 and S9 link the airport with the city centre in 15 minutes several times hourly for €4.55. Taxis make the trip in 20 to 30 minutes and average €30.

Munich Airport The S1 and S8 trains link the airport with the city centre in 40 minutes (€10.80). The Lufthansa Airport Bus (€10.50) departs every 20 minutes and takes about the same time as the train. A taxi costs about €60.

Top Phrases

Hello. Guten Tag.

Goodbye. Auf Wiedersehen.

Yes/No. Ja/Nein.

Please. Bitte.

Thank you. Danke.

Resources

German National Tourist Office (www.germany.travel)

Deutsche Welle (www.dw.com)

Facts About Germany (www.tatsachen-ueber-deutschland.de/en)

Deutschland Online (www.magazine-deutschland.de)

Online German course (www.deutsch-lernen.com)

Set Your Budget

➡ Hostel, camping or private room: €15–30

➡ Sausage snack: €2

➡ Public transport day pass: €5–7

The Berlin Wall

The construction of the Berlin Wall was a unique event in human history, not only for physically bisecting a city but by becoming a dividing line between competing ideologies and political systems. It's this global impact and universal legacy that continue to fascinate people more than a quarter century after its triumphant tear-down. Fortunately, plenty of original Wall segments and other vestiges remain, along with museums and memorials, to help fathom the realities and challenges of daily life in Berlin during the Cold War.

Our illustration points out the top highlights you can visit to learn about different aspects of these often tense decades. The best place to start is the ❶ **Gedenkstätte Berliner Mauer**, for an excellent introduction to what the inner-city border really looked liked and what it meant to live in its shadow. Reflect upon what you've learned while relaxing along the former death strip, now the ❷ **Mauerpark**, before heading to the emotionally charged exhibit at the ❸ **Tränenpalast**, an actual border-crossing pavilion. Relive the euphoria of the

Brandenburg Tor
People around the world cheered as East and West Berliners partied together atop the Berlin Wall in front of the iconic city gate, which today is a photogenic symbol of united Germany.

Potsdamer Platz
Nowhere was the death strip as wide as on the former no-man's-land around Potsdamer Platz from which sprouted a new postmodern city quarter in the 1990s. A tiny section of the Berlin Wall serves as a reminder.

Checkpoint Charlie
Only diplomats and foreigners were allowed to use this border crossing. Weeks after the Wall was built, US and Soviet tanks faced off here in one of the hottest moments of the Cold War.

Tränenpalast
This modernist 1962 glass-and-steel border pavilion was dubbed 'Palace of Tears' because of the many tearful farewells that took place outside the building as East Germans and their western visitors had to say goodbye.

Bernauer Strasse

Chausseestr

Unter den Linden

Leipziger Str

Wall's demise at the ④ **Brandenburg Tor**, then marvel at the revival of ⑤ **Potsdamer Platz**, which was nothing but death-strip wasteland until the 1990s. The Wall's geopolitical significance is the focus at ⑥ **Checkpoint Charlie**, which saw some of the tensest moments of the Cold War. Wrap up with finding your favourite mural motif at the ⑦ **East Side Gallery**.

It's possible to explore these sights by using a combination of walking and public transport, but a bike ride is the best method for gaining a sense of the former Wall's erratic flow through the central city.

FAST FACTS

Beginning of construction 13 August 1961
Total length 155km
Height 3.6m
Weight of each segment 2.6 tonnes
Number of watchtowers 300

② ·····································

Remnants of the Wall ⟶

Mauerpark
Famous for its flea market and karaoke, this popular park actually occupies a converted section of death strip. A 30m segment of surviving Wall is now an official practice ground for budding graffiti artists.

Alexanderplatz

Alexanderstr

East Side Gallery
Paralleling the Spree for 1.3km, this is the longest Wall vestige. After its collapse, more than a hundred international artists expressed their feelings about this historic moment in a series of colourful murals.

⑦

Mitte

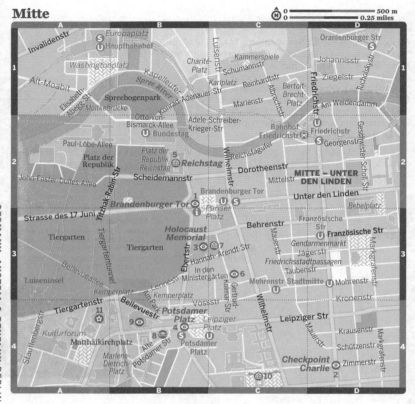

⊙ 0 ──── 500 m
0 ──── 0.25 miles

Mitte

★ **Checkpoint Charlie**   HISTORIC SITE
(Map p210; cnr Zimmerstrasse & Friedrichstrasse; ⊙24hr; Ⓤ Kochstrasse) FREE Checkpoint Charlie was the principal gateway for for-

eigners and diplomats between the two Berlins from 1961 to 1990. Unfortunately this potent symbol of the Cold War has degenerated into a tacky tourist trap, though a free open-air exhibit that illustrates milestones in Cold War history is one redeeming aspect.

★ **Gedenkstätte**
Berliner Mauer   MEMORIAL
(Berlin Wall Memorial; Map p212; ☎030-467 986 666; www.berliner-mauer-gedenkstaette.de; Bernauer Strasse btwn Schwedter Strasse & Gartenstrasse; ⊙visitor & documentation centre 10am-6pm Tue-Sun, open-air exhibit 8am-10pm daily; Ⓢ Nordbahnhof, Bernauer Strasse, Eberswalder Strasse) FREE For an insightful primer on the Berlin Wall, visit this outdoor memorial, which extends for 1.4km along Bernauer Strasse and integrates an original section of Wall, vestiges of the border installations and escape tunnels, a chapel and a monument. Multimedia stations, panels, excavations and

a Documentation Centre provide context and explain what the border fortifications looked like and how they shaped the everyday lives of people on both sides of it. There's a great view from the centre's viewing platform.

★ **East Side Gallery** LANDMARK
(Map p214; www.eastsidegallery-berlin.de; Mühlenstrasse btwn Oberbaumbrücke & Ostbahnhof; ⊙24hr; ⓤWarschauer Strasse, ⓢOstbahnhof, Warschauer Strasse) **FREE** The year was 1989. After 28 years, the Berlin Wall, that grim and grey divider of humanity, finally met its maker. Most of it was quickly dismantled, but along Mühlenstrasse, paralleling the Spree, a 1.3km stretch became the East Side Gallery, the world's largest open-air mural collection. In more than 100 paintings, dozens of international artists translated the era's global euphoria and optimism into a mix of political statements, drug-induced musings and truly artistic visions.

★ **Potsdamer Platz** AREA
(Map p210; Alte Potsdamer Strasse; ⊟200, ⓢPotsdamer Platz, ⓤPotsdamer Platz) The rebirth of the historic Potsdamer Platz was Europe's biggest building project of the 1990s, a showcase of urban renewal masterminded by such top international architects as Renzo Piano and Helmut Jahn. An entire city quarter sprouted on terrain once bifurcated by the Berlin Wall and today houses offices, theatres and cinemas, hotels, apartments and museums. Highlights include the glass-tented **Sony Center** (Map p210; Potsdamer Strasse; ⊟200, ⓤPotsdamer Platz, ⓢPotsdamer Platz) and the **Panoramapunkt** (Map p210; ☑030-2593 7080; www.panoramapunkt.de; Potsdamer Platz 1; adult/concession €7.50/6, without wait €11.50/9; ⊙10am-8pm Apr-Oct, to 6pm Nov-Mar; ⊟M41, 200, ⓢPotsdamer Platz, ⓤPotsdamer Platz) observation deck.

ℹ TOP BERLIN FREEBIES

It's no secret that you can get more bang for your euro in Berlin than in any other Western European capital. Better still, there are plenty of ways to stretch your budget even further by cashing in on some tip-top freebies:

Museums & Memorial Sites

Most sights related to WWII and Cold War history are free, including top draws like the **East Side Gallery**, the **Holocaust Memorial** (p204), **Gedenkstätte Berliner Mauer**, **Checkpoint Charlie** and the **Topography of Terror** (p213).

Tours

Alternative Berlin Tours (p213) and **New Berlin Tours** (p213) are English-language walking tour companies that advertise 'free' guided tours, although the guides actually depend on tips.

Karaoke

On Sunday afternoons in the warmer months, **Bearpit Karaoke** (Map p212; www.bearpitkaraoke.com; Amphitheatre Mauerpark; ⊙around 3-8pm Sun spring-autumn; ⊟M1, M10, 12, ⓤEberswalder Strasse) sees thousands of spectators cheering on crooners in the outdoor amphitheatre of the Mauerpark, which is also home to a famous **flea market** (also held on Sundays).

Classical concerts

At 1pm on Tuesdays from September to mid-June, the foyer of the **Berliner Philharmonie** (Map p210; ☑tickets 030-2548 8999; www.berliner-philharmoniker.de; Herbert-von-Karajan-Strasse 1; tickets €21-290; ⊟M29, M48, M85, 200, ⓢPotsdamer Platz, ⓤPotsdamer Platz) fills with music lovers for free lunchtime chamber-music concerts.

Jazz concerts

Jazz fans can bop gratis at **A-Trane** (☑030-313 2550; www.a-trane.de; Bleibtreustrasse 1; admission varies; ⊙8pm-1am Sun-Thu, to late Fri & Sat; ⓢSavignyplatz) on Mondays and at the late-night jam session after 12.30am on Saturday.

Prenzlauer Berg & Museumsinsel

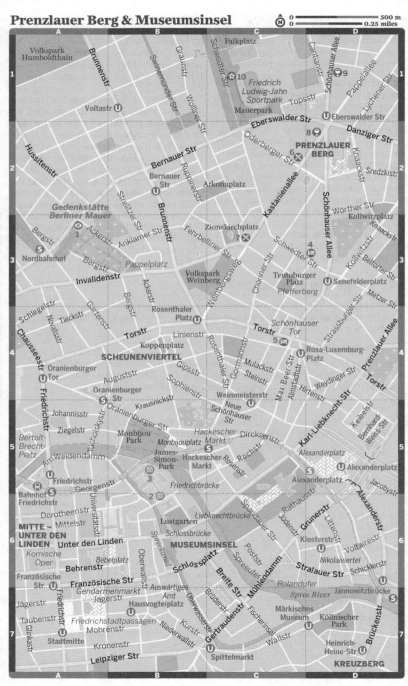

Prenzlauer Berg & Museumsinsel

Topographie des Terrors   MUSEUM

(Topography of Terror; Map p210; ☎030-2545 0950; www.topographie.de; Niederkirchner Strasse 8; ☺10am-8pm, grounds close at dusk or 8pm at the latest; ⓢPotsdamer Platz, ⓤPotsdamer Platz) **FREE** In the same spot where the most feared institutions of Nazi Germany (including the Gestapo headquarters and the SS central command) once stood, this compelling exhibit chronicles the stages of terror and persecution, puts a face on the perpetrators and details the impact these brutal institutions had on all of Europe. A second exhibit outside zeroes in on how life changed for Berlin and its people after the Nazis made it their capital.

★ Jüdisches Museum   MUSEUM

(Jewish Museum; Map p214; ☎030-2599 3300; www.jmberlin.de; Lindenstrasse 9-14; adult/concession €8/3, audioguide €3; ☺10am-8pm; ⓤHallesches Tor, Kochstrasse) In a landmark building by American-Polish architect Daniel Libeskind, Berlin's Jewish Museum offers a chronicle of the trials and triumphs in 2000 years of Jewish life in Germany. The exhibit smoothly navigates all major periods, from the Middle Ages via the Enlightenment to the community's post-1990 renaissance. Find out about Jewish cultural contributions, holiday traditions, the difficult road to emancipation, outstanding individuals (eg Moses Mendelssohn, Levi Strauss) and the fates of ordinary people.

★ Schloss Charlottenburg   PALACE

(☎030-320 910; www.spsg.de; Spandauer Damm 10-22; day passes to all 4 buildings adult/concession €17/13; ☺hours vary by building; Ⓟ; ⓠM45, 109, 309, ⓤRichard-Wagner-Platz, Sophie-Charlotte-Platz) Charlottenburg Palace is one of the few sites in Berlin that still reflects the one-time grandeur of the Hohenzollern clan that ruled the region from 1415 to 1918. Originally a petite summer retreat, it grew into an exquisite baroque pile with opulent private apartments, richly decorated festival halls, collections of precious porcelain and paintings by French 18th-century masters. It's lovely in fine weather when you can fold a stroll in the palace park into a day of peeking at royal treasures.

☞ Tours

Alternative Berlin Tours   WALKING

(☎0162 819 8264; www.alternativeberlin.com; tours €12-35) Not your run-of-the-mill tour company, this outfit runs tip-based subculture tours that get beneath the skin of the city, plus an excellent street-art tour and workshop, an alternative pub crawl, a craft beer tour and an eco-tour.

New Berlin Tours   WALKING

(www.newberlintours.com; adult/concession from €14/12; ☺free tour 10am, 11am, noon & 2pm) Entertaining and informative city spins by the pioneers of the donation-based 'free tour' and the pub crawl (€12). Also offers tours to Sachsenhausen concentration camp, themed tours (Red Berlin, Third Reich, Alternative Berlin) and a trip to Potsdam. Check the website for timings, prices and meeting points.

🛏 Sleeping

Wombat's Berlin   HOSTEL €

(Map p212; ☎030-8471 0820; www.wombats-hostels.com/berlin; Alte Schönhauser Strasse 2; dm €19-27, d €62-78; ❀@⑨; ⓤRosa-Luxemburg-Platz) Sociable and central, Wombat's gets hostelling right. From backpack-sized in-room lockers to individual reading lamps and a guest kitchen with dishwasher, the attention to detail here is impressive. Spacious and clean en-suite dorms are as much part of the deal as free linen and a welcome drink, best enjoyed with fellow party pilgrims at sunset on the rooftop.

Kreuzberg & Friedrichshain

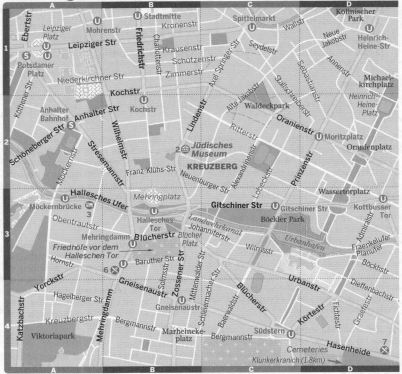

Kreuzberg & Friedrichshain

★ **Grand Hostel Berlin**　　　HOSTEL €
(Map p214; ☎030-2009 5450; www.grandhostel-berlin.de; Tempelhofer Ufer 14; dm €10-28, tw with/without bathroom from €49/38; ✿@✿; Ⓤ Möckernbrücke) Cocktails in the library bar? Check. Rooms with stucco-ornamented ceilings? Got 'em. Canal views? Yep. Ensconced in a fully renovated 1870s building, the 'five-star' Grand Hostel is one of Berlin's most supremely comfortable, convivial and atmospheric hostels. Private rooms are spacious and nicely furnished, and dorms come with freestanding quality beds and large lockers. Breakfast is €6.50.

★ **EastSeven Berlin Hostel**　　HOSTEL €
(Map p212; ☎030-9362 2240; www.eastseven.de; Schwedter Strasse 7; dm €21-33, d €70;

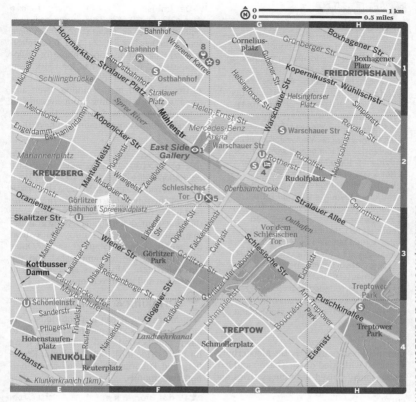

@ 🛜; (U) Senefelderplatz) An excellent choice for solo travellers, this small indie hostel has personable staff that go out of their way to make all feel welcome. Make new friends while chilling in the lounge or garden (hammocks!), firing up the barbecue or hanging out in the 24-hour kitchen. Brightly painted dorms feature comfy pine beds and lockers. Linen is free and breakfast €3.

★ Plus Berlin HOSTEL €

(Map p214; ☑ 030-311 698 820; www.plushostels. com/plusberlin; Warschauer Platz 6; dm/d from €19/90; 🅿 ❄ @ 🛜 ☂; (U) Warschauer Strasse, (S) Warschauer Strasse) A hostel with an indoor pool, steam room and yoga classes? Yep. Within stumbling distance of Berlin's best nightlife, Plus is a flashpacker favourite. There's a bar for easing into the night and a tranquil courtyard to soothe that hangover. Spacious dorms have four or six bunks,

desks and lockers, while private rooms have TV and air-con. All have en suites. Optional breakfast is €7.

✗ Eating

Berlin is a snacker's paradise with speedfeed shops, called *Imbiss*, serving all sorts of savoury fodder, from sausage-in-a-bun to *Döner Kebab* and pizza. Many bakeries serve sandwiches alongside pastries. For a local snack, try a ubiquitous *Currywurst* (slivered sausage drizzled with ketchup and curry powder).

★ Burgermeister BURGERS €

(Map p214; ☑ 030-2388 3840; www.burger-meister.de; Oberbaumstrasse 8; burgers €3.50-4.80; ⏰ 11am-3am Mon-Thu, to 4am Fri, noon-4am Sat, to 3am Sun; (U) Schlesisches Tor) It's green, ornate, a century old and...it used to be a toilet. Now it's a burger joint beneath the elevated U-Bahn tracks. Get in line for the

WORTH A TRIP

POTSDAM

Easily reached in half an hour from central Berlin, the former royal Prussian seat of Potsdam lures visitors to its splendid Unesco-recognised palaces and parks dreamed up by 18th-century King Friedrich II (Frederick the Great). Headlining the roll call of royal pads is **Schloss Sanssouci** (☑0331-969 4200; www.spsg.de; Maulbeerallee; adult/concession incl tour or audioguide €12/8; ⊙10am-5.30pm Tue-Sun Apr-Oct, to 5pm Nov & Dec, to 4.30 Jan-Mar; 🚌 614, 650, 695), a celebrated rococo palace and the king's favourite summer retreat. Standouts on the audioguided tour include the whimsically decorated concert hall, the intimate library and the domed Marble Hall. Admission is limited and by timed ticket only; book online (http://tickets.spsg.de) to avoid wait times and/or disappointment. The castle is surrounded by a sprawling park dotted with numerous other palaces, pavilions, fountains, statues and romantic corners.

plump all-beef patties (try the Meisterburger served with fried onions, bacon and barbecue sauce) paired with cheese fries and such homemade dips as peanut or mango curry.

Curry 36   GERMAN €

(Map p214; ☑030-2580 088 336; www.curry36. de; Mehringdamm 36; snacks €2-6; ⊙9am-5am; Ⓤ Mehringdamm) Day after day, night after night, a motley crowd – cops, cabbies, queens, office jockeys, savvy tourists etc – wait their turn at this top-ranked *Currywurst* snack shop that's been frying 'em up since 1981.

Masaniello   ITALIAN €

(Map p214; ☑030-692 6657; www.masaniello.de; Hasenheide 20; pizza €6-10; ⊙noon-midnight; Ⓤ Hermannplatz) Tables are almost too small for the wagon-wheel-sized certified Neapolitan pizzas tickled by wood fire at this old-timey pizzeria, whose spacious flowery terrace transports you to the boot on a balmy summer night. A vegan fave is the Pizza Contadina with aubergine, peppers, zucchini, mushrooms and artichokes. Fresh fish on Friday and Saturday.

W-Der Imbiss   FUSION €

(Map p212; ☑030-4435 2206; www.w-derimbiss. de; Kastanienallee 49; dishes €5-12; ⊙noon-10pm Sun-Thu, to 11pm Fri & Sat; 🖋; 🚊M1, Ⓤ Rosenthaler Platz) The self-described home of 'indo-mexi-cal-ital' fusion, W has for years been delighting fans with its signature naan pizza freshly baked in the tandoor oven and decorated with anything from avocado to smoked salmon. The fish tacos, thali curry spread and tandoori salmon also have their fans.

Habba Habba   MIDDLE EASTERN €

(Map p212; ☑030-3674 5726; www.habba-habba. de; Kastanienallee 15; dishes €4.50-10; ⊙11am-11pm Mon, Wed & Sun; 🖋; 🚊M1, 12, Ⓤ Eberswalder Strasse) This tiny *Imbiss* (snack bar) makes the best wraps in town for our money, especially the one stuffed with tangy pomegranate-marinated chicken and nutty buckwheat dressed in a minty yoghurt sauce. Other faves include the halloumi salad and the coriander kofta. All dishes are available in vegetarian and vegan versions.

🍷 Drinking & Nightlife

With no curfew, Berlin is a notoriously late city, where bars stay packed from dusk to dawn and beyond, and some clubs don't hit their stride until 4am. Neukölln, Kreuzberg and Friedrichshain are all primo bar-hopping grounds.

⭐ Prater Biergarten   BEER GARDEN

(Map p212; ☑030-448 5688; www.pratergarten. de; Kastanienallee 7-9; snacks €2.50-6; ⊙noon-late Apr-Sep, weather permitting; Ⓤ Eberswalder Strasse) Berlin's oldest beer garden has seen beer-soaked nights since 1837 and is still a charismatic spot for guzzling a custom-brewed Prater Pilsner beneath the ancient chestnut trees (self-service). Kids can romp around the small play area.

Klunkerkranich   BAR

(www.klunkerkranich.de; Karl-Marx-Strasse 66; ⊙10am-2am Mon-Sat, from noon Sun, weather permitting; 🛜; Ⓤ Rathaus Neukölln) During the warmer months, this club-garden-bar combo is mostly a fab place for day-drinking and chilling to local DJs or bands up on the rooftop parking deck of the Neukölln Arcaden shopping mall. It also does breakfast, light lunches and tapas. Check the website – these folks come up with new ideas all the time (gardening workshops anyone?).

To get up here, take the lifts just inside the 'Bibliothek/Post' entrance on Karl-Marx-Strasse to the 5th floor.

Zum Starken August PUB
(Map p212; ☑ 030-2520 9020; www.zumstarken august.de; Schönhauser Allee 56; ⊗ 5pm-2.30am Sun-Thu, to 5am Fri & Sat; ☑ M1, M10, Ⓤ Eberswalder Strasse) Part circus, part burlesque bar, this vibrant venue dressed in Victorian-era exuberance is a fun and friendly addition to the Prenzlauer Berg pub culture. Join the unpretentious, international crowd over cocktails and craft beers while being entertained with drag-hosted bingo, burlesque divas, wicked cabaret or the hilarious 'porno karaoke'.

★ **Berghain/Panorama Bar** CLUB
(Map p214; www.berghain.de; Am Wriezener Bahnhof; ⊗ midnight-late Fri-Mon; Ⓢ Ostbahnhof) Only world-class spinmasters heat up this hedonistic bass-junkie hellhole inside a labyrinthine ex–power plant. Hard-edged minimal techno dominates the ex–turbine hall (Berghain) while house dominates at Panorama Bar, one floor up. Strict door, no cameras allowed. Check the website for information about midweek concerts and record-release parties at the main venue and the adjacent **Kantine am Berghain** (Map p214; ☑ 030-2936 0210; Am Wriezener Bahnhof; admission varies; ⊗ hours vary).

ⓘ **Information**

Berlin Tourist Info – Brandenburg Gate (Map p210; ☑ 030-250 023; www.visitberlin.de; Brandenburger Tor, south wing, Pariser Platz; ⊗ 9.30am-7pm Apr-Oct, to 6pm Nov-Mar; Ⓢ Brandenburger Tor, Ⓤ Brandenburger Tor) Official tourist office. Additional branches are at the airports, the Hauptbahnhof (main train station), the TV Tower and near Zoo Station. See website for details.

ⓘ **Getting There & Away**

Until the opening of Berlin's new central airport (scheduled for late 2020), flights continue to land at the city's Tegel and Schönefeld airports.

Most long-haul buses arrive at the **Zentraler Omnibusbahnhof** (ZOB; ☑ 030-3010 0175; www.iob-berlin.de; Masurenallee 4-6; Ⓢ Messe/ICC Nord, Ⓤ Kaiserdamm) in far western Berlin. The U2 U-Bahn line links to the centre from Kaiserdamm station, while S41 and S42 S-Bahn trains leaving from Messe Süd/ICC station are handy for such districts as Friedrichshain and Neukölln.

Berlin's **Hauptbahnhof** (Main Train Station; www.berliner-hbf.de; Europaplatz, Washingtonplatz; Ⓢ Hauptbahnhof, Ⓤ Hauptbahnhof) is near the Reichstag in the city centre. From here, the U-Bahn, S-Bahn, trams and buses provide links to all parts of town.

ⓘ **Getting Around**

TO/FROM THE AIRPORT

Tegel TXL bus runs to Alexanderplatz (Tariff AB, 40 minutes) via Hauptbahnhof every 10 minutes. The closest U-Bahn station is Jakob-Kaiser-Platz served by bus 109 and X9.
Schönefeld Airport-Express trains (denoted RE7 and RB14 in timetables) go to central Berlin twice hourly (Tariff ABC, 20 to 30 minutes). S-Bahn S9 runs every 20 minutes and is handy for Friedrichshain or Prenzlauer Berg.

PUBLIC TRANSPORT

One ticket is valid on all forms of public transport, including the U-Bahn (underground or subway), S-Bahn (light rail), buses, trams and ferries. Plan routes at www.bvg.de.

Most rides require a Tariff AB ticket, which is valid for two hours (interruptions and transfers allowed, but not return trips). Tickets are available from bus drivers, vending machines at U- and S-Bahn stations and aboard trams, and at station offices. Expect to pay cash (change given) and be sure to validate (stamp) your ticket or risk a €60 fine during spot-checks.

Dresden

POP 512,000

There are few city silhouettes more striking than Dresden's. The classic view from the Elbe's northern bank takes in spires, towers and domes belonging to palaces, churches and stately buildings, and indeed it's hard to believe that the city was all but wiped off the map by Allied bombings in 1945.

◉ **Sights**

Dresden straddles the Elbe River, with the attraction-studded Altstadt (old town) in the south and the Neustadt (new town) pub and student quarter to the north.

Frauenkirche CHURCH
(☑ 0351-6560 6100; www.frauenkirche-dresden. de; Neumarkt; audio guide €2.50, cupola adult/student €8/5; ⊗ 10am-noon & 1-6pm Mon-Fri, weekend hours vary) The domed Frauenkirche – Dresden's most beloved symbol – has literally risen from the city's ashes. The original graced its skyline for two centuries before collapsing after the February 1945 bombing,

Dresden

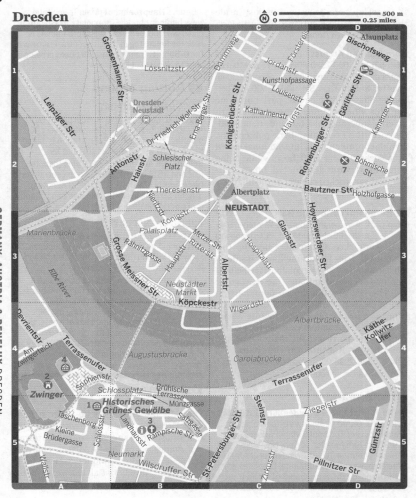

▲ N 0 ━━━━━ 500 m
0 ━━━━━ 0.25 miles

and was rebuilt from a pile of rubble between 1994 and 2005. A spitting image of the original, it may not bear the gravitas of age but that only slightly detracts from its festive beauty inside and out. The altar, reassembled from nearly 2000 fragments, is especially striking.

★ **Zwinger**   PALACE
(☑ 0351-4914 2000; www.der-dresdner-zwinger. de; Theaterplatz 1; adult/concession €10/7.50; ☺ 6am-10pm Apr-Oct, to 8pm Nov-Mar) FREE A collaboration between the architect Matthäus Pöppelmann and the sculptor

Balthasar Permoser, the Zwinger was built between 1710 and 1728 on the orders of Augustus the Strong, who, having returned from seeing Louis XIV's palace at Versailles, wanted something similar for himself. Primarily a party palace for royals, the Zwinger has ornate portals that lead into the vast fountain-studded courtyard, which is framed by buildings lavishly ornamented with evocative sculpture. Today it houses three superb museums within its baroque walls.

Atop the western pavilion stands a tense-looking Atlas. Opposite him is a cutesy

Dresden

◎ Top Sights

1 Historisches Grünes Gewölbe.............A5
2 Zwinger A4

◎ Sights

3 Frauenkirche B5
4 Semperoper A4

🛏 Sleeping

5 Lollis Homestay D1

✖ Eating

6 Cafe Continental.................................. D1
7 Raskolnikoff...D2

carillon of 40 Meissen porcelain bells, which emit a tinkle every 15 minutes. Entry to the magnificent courtyard is free, but all three museums are ticketed. The **Gemäldegalerie Alte Meister** (Old Masters Gallery) and **Porzellansammlung** (Porcelain Collection) are unmissable, while the historic scientific instruments (globes, clocks, telescopes etc) at the **Mathematisch-Physikalischer Salon** are perhaps more for the scientifically minded.

★**Historisches
Grünes Gewölbe**   MUSEUM
(Historic Green Vault; ☑ 0351-4914 2000; www.skd.museum; Residenzschloss; €12; ◎10am-6pm Wed-Mon) The Historic Green Vault displays some 3000 precious items in the same fashion as during the time of August der Starke, namely on shelves and tables without glass protection in a series of increasingly lavish rooms. Admission is by timed ticket only, and only a limited number of visitors per hour may pass through the 'dust lock'. Get advance tickets online or by phone, since

only 40% are sold at the palace box office for same-day admission.

Semperoper   HISTORIC BUILDING
(☑0351-320 7360; www.semperoper-erleben. de; Theaterplatz 2; tour adult/concession €11/7; ◎hours vary) One of Germany's most famous opera houses, the Semperoper opened in 1841 and has hosted premieres of famous works by Richard Strauss, Carl Maria von Weber and Richard Wagner. Guided 45-minute tours operate almost daily (the 3pm tour is in English); exact times depend on the rehearsal and performance schedule. Buy advance tickets online to skip the queue.

🛏 Sleeping & Eating

The Neustadt has oodles of cafes and restaurants, especially along Königsstrasse and the streets north of Albertplatz. The latter is also the centre of Dresden's nightlife. Altstadt restaurants are more tourist-geared and pricier.

Lollis Homestay   HOSTEL €
(☑0351-810 8458; www.lollishome.de; Görlitzer Strasse 34; dm/s/d from €13/30/40, linen €2, breakfast €5; @🤏) This is a textbook backpacker hostel: friendly, communicative, casual and with neatly designed themed rooms (Cinema, Desert, Giants), including a rather gimmicky double where you live out that *Good Bye, Lenin!* vibe by bedding down in a real GDR-era Trabi car. Bikes, tea and coffee are welcome freebies, and the communal room and kitchen are conducive to meeting fellow travellers.

Cafe Continental   INTERNATIONAL €€
(☑0351-272 1722; www.cafe-continental-dresden. de; Görlitzer Strasse 1; dishes €6-20; ◎9am-1pm

---

DRESDEN & WWII

Between 13 and 15 February 1945, British and American planes unleashed 3900 tonnes of explosives on Dresden in four huge air raids. Bombs and incendiary shells whipped up a mammoth firestorm, and ashes rained down on villages 35km away. When the blazes had died down and the dust settled, tens of thousands of Dresdners had lost their lives and 20 sq km of this once-elegant baroque city lay in smouldering ruins.

Historians still argue over whether this constituted a war crime committed by the Allies on an innocent civilian population. Some claim that with the Red Army at the gates of Berlin, the war was effectively won, and the Allies gained little military advantage from the destruction of Dresden. Others have said that as the last urban centre in the east of the country left intact, Dresden could have provided shelter for German troops returning from the east and was a viable target.

Sun-Thu, to 3am Fri & Sat; 🛜) If the greenly lit openings behind the bar remind you of aquariums, you've hit the nail on the head, for buzzy 'Conti' was a pet shop back in GDR days. Today it's a great place to hit no matter the hour for anything from cappuccino and cocktails to homemade cakes or a full meal. Breakfast is served until 4pm.

★**Raskolnikoff** INTERNATIONAL €€
(📞0351-804 5706; www.raskolnikoff.de; Böhmische Strasse 34; mains €10-15; ⊙11am-10.30pm Mon-Sat, from 9am Sun) An artist squat before the Wall came down, Raskolnikoff now brims with grown-up artsy-bohemian flair, especially in the sweet little garden at the back, complete with bizarre water feature. The seasonally calibrated menu showcases the fruits of the surrounding land in globally inspired dishes, and the beer is brewed locally. Breakfast is served until 2pm, with an excellent brunch (€14.90) on Sundays.

ℹ️ Information

Tourist Office – Frauenkirche (📞0351-501 501; www.dresden.de; QF Passage, Neumarkt 2; ⊙10am-7pm Mon-Fri, to 6pm Sat, to 3pm Sun) Go to the basement of the shopping mall to find the city's most central tourist office. Helpful English-speaking staff can give you advice, book rooms and tours, rent out audioguides and sell the excellent-value Dresden Cards.

ℹ️ Getting There & Away

Fast trains make the trip to Dresden from Berlin-Hauptbahnhof in two hours (€40) and Leipzig in 1¼ hours (€24.50).

Leipzig

POP 532,000

'Hypezig!' cry the papers. 'The New Berlin', says just about everybody. Yes, Leipzig is Saxony's coolest city, a playground for young creatives who have been displaced even by the fast-gentrifying German capital. But it's also a city of enormous history, a trade-fair mecca and solidly in the sights of classical music lovers due to its intrinsic connection to the lives and work of Bach, Mendelssohn and Wagner.

⊙ Sights

The partly pedestrianised city centre is crisscrossed by historic shopping arcades, including the classic **Mädlerpassage**.

★**Nikolaikirche** CHURCH
(Church of St Nicholas; www.nikolaikirche.de; Nikolaikirchhof 3; ⊙10am-6pm Mon-Sat, to 4pm Sun) This church has Romanesque and Gothic roots, but since 1797 has sported a striking neoclassical interior with palm-like pillars and cream-coloured pews. The design is certainly gorgeous, but the church is most famous for playing a key role in the nonviolent movement that led to the downfall of the East German government. As early as 1982 it hosted 'peace prayers' every Monday at 5pm (still held today), which over time inspired and empowered local citizens to confront the injustices plaguing their country.

Stasi Museum MUSEUM
(📞0341-961 2443; www.runde-ecke-leipzig.de; Dittrichring 24; ⊙10am-6pm) FREE In the GDR the walls had ears, as is chillingly documented in this exhibit in the former Leipzig headquarters of the East German secret police (the Stasi), a building known as the Runde Ecke (Round Corner). English-language audioguides (€4) aid in understanding the all-German displays on propaganda, preposterous disguises, cunning surveillance devices, recruitment (even among children), scent storage and other chilling machinations that reveal the GDR's all-out zeal when it came to controlling, manipulating and repressing its own people.

★**Museum der Bildenden Künste** MUSEUM
(📞0341-216 990; www.mdbk.de; Katharinenstrasse 10; adult/concession €10/7, audio guide €2; ⊙10am-6pm Tue & Thu-Sun, noon-8pm Wed) This imposing modernist glass cube is the home of Leipzig's fine arts museum and its world-class collection of paintings from the 15th century to today, including works by Caspar David Friedrich, Cranach, Munch and Monet. Highlights include rooms dedicated to native sons Max Beckmann, Max Klinger and Neo Rauch. Exhibits are playfully juxtaposed and range from sculpture and installation to religious art. The collection is enormous, so set aside at least two hours to do it justice.

Thomaskirche CHURCH
(📞0341-222 240; www.thomaskirche.org; Thomaskirchhof 18; tower €2; ⊙church 9am-6pm, tower 1pm, 2pm & 4.30pm Sat, 2pm & 3pm Sun Apr-Nov) Johann Sebastian Bach worked as a cantor in the Thomaskirche from 1723 until his

Central Leipzig

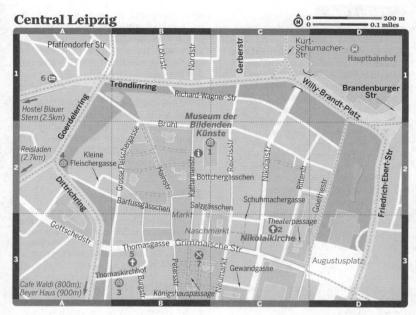

death in 1750, and his remains lie buried beneath a bronze plate in front of the altar. The Thomanerchor, once led by Bach, has been going strong since 1212 and now includes 100 boys aged eight to 18. The church tower can be climbed, though the real reason to come here is to absorb the great man's legacy, often played on the church's giant organ.

Bach-Museum Leipzig MUSEUM
(☎0341-913 7202; www.bachmuseumleipzig.de; Thomaskirchhof 16; adult/concession/child under 16yr €8/6/free; ◷10am-6pm Tue-Sun) This interactive museum does more than tell you about the life and accomplishments of Johann Sebastian Bach. Learn how to date a Bach manuscript, listen to baroque instruments or treat your ears to any composition he ever wrote. The 'treasure room' downstairs displays rare original manuscripts.

🛏 Sleeping

Hostel Blauer Stern HOSTEL €
(☎0341-4927 6166; www.hostelblauerstern.de; Lindenauer Markt 20; dm/s/d €18/25/35; 🛜) If you're interested in exploring Leipzig's alternative scene, then this is a great option, in the western district of Plagwitz, a fast up-and-coming, young and arty slice of town.

The thoughtfully decorated rooms all have an East German retro style, and big weekly discounts can make them a steal. Take tram 7 or 15 from Hauptbahnhof.

Hostel Sleepy Lion HOSTEL €
(☎0341-993 9480; www.hostel-leipzig.de; Jacobstrasse 1; dm/d/apt from €14/46/62, linen €2.50, breakfast €4; @🛜) This top-rated hostel gets our thumbs up with its clean and cheerfully painted en-suite rooms, a super-central location and clued-in staff. Every budget can be catered for in dorms sleeping four to 10, as well as private rooms and spacious 4th-floor

WORTH A TRIP

DACHAU

Officially called the **KZ-Gedenkstätte Dachau** (Dachau Concentration Camp Memorial Site; ☑ 08131-669 970; www.kz-gedenkstaette-dachau.de; Peter-Roth-Strasse 2a, Dachau; ☺ 9am-5pm) **FREE**, this was the Nazis' first concentration camp, built by Heinrich Himmler in March 1933 to house political prisoners. All in all, it 'processed' more than 200,000 inmates, killing at least 43,000, and is now a haunting memorial. Expect to spend two to three hours here to fully absorb the exhibits.

The S2 makes the trip from Munich Hauptbahnhof to Dachau train station in 20 minutes from where bus 726 (direction Saubachsiedlung) goes to the camp. You'll need a two-zone ticket (€5.60).

apartments with killer views. The kitchen is very basic, however, and not really suitable for self-caterers.

✖ Eating & Drinking

In the city centre, party activity focuses on the boisterous 'Drallewatsch' pub strip on Barfussgässchen and the more genteel theatre district around Gottschedstrasse. Younger crowds gravitate towards Karl-Liebknecht-Strasse (aka Südmeile) south the centre.

★ Auerbachs Keller   GERMAN €€€
(☑ 0341-216 100; www.auerbachs-keller-leipzig.de; Mädlerpassage, Grimmaische Strasse 2-4; mains Keller €16-28, Weinstuben €33-35; ☺ Keller noon-11pm daily, Weinstuben 6-11pm Mon-Sat) Founded in 1525, Auerbachs Keller is one of Germany's best-known restaurants. It's cosy and touristy, but the food's actually quite good and the setting memorable. There are two sections: the vaulted Grosser Keller for hearty Saxonian dishes and the four historic rooms of the Historische Weinstuben for upsmarket German fare. Reservations highly advised.

Cafe Waldi   BAR
(☑ 0341-462 5667; www.cafewaldi.de; Petersssteinweg 10; ☺ 11.30am-late Mon-Fri, from 9am Sat & Sun; ☜) Despite its great-grandma's-living-room look – complete with big sofas, cuckoo clocks and mounted antlers – Waldi is an

up-to-the-minute hang-out where you can eat breakfast until 4pm, fuel up on coffee and a light meal, or nurse cocktails and pints until the wee hours. On weekends, DJs rock the upstairs area with house, indie and hip-hop.

Beyerhaus   PUB
(Ernst-Schneller-Strasse 6; ☺ 7pm-2am) Just off the Karli, this large but extremely cosy pub is popular with a studenty, alternative crowd who come here to drink beer under the two enormous glass chandeliers and to enjoy the odd live musical performances. Friendly fun.

ℹ Information

Tourist Office (☑ 0341-710 4260; www.leipzig.travel; Katharinenstrasse 8; ☺ 10am-6pm Mon-Fri, to 4pm Sat, to 3pm Sun) Room referrals, ticket sales, maps and general information. Also sells the Leipzig Card (one/three days €11.90/23.50).

ℹ Getting There & Away

Deutsche Bahn has frequent daily services to Frankfurt (3¾ hours), Dresden (1¼ hours) and Berlin (1¼ hours), among others.

Munich
POP 1.38 MILLION

If you're looking for Alpine clichés, they're all here, but Munich also has plenty of unexpected cards down its dirndl. Its walkable centre retains a small-town air but holds some world-class sights, especially art galleries and museums. Throw in royal Bavarian heritage, an entire suburb of Olympic legacy and a kitbag of dark tourism, and it's clear why southern Germany's metropolis is such a favourite among those who seek out the past but like to hit the town once they're done.

⊙ Sights

Munich's major sights cluster around the Altstadt, with the main museum district just north of the Residenz.

Marienplatz   SQUARE
(Ⓢ Marienplatz; Ⓤ Marienplatz) The epicentral heart and soul of the Altstadt, Marienplatz is a popular gathering spot and packs a lot of personality into a compact frame. It's anchored by the **Mariensäule** (Mary's Column), built in 1638 to celebrate victory over Swedish forces during the Thirty

Years' War. This is the busiest spot in all Munich, with throngs of tourists swarming across its expanse from early morning till late at night.

Munich Residenz — PALACE

(☎089-290 671; www.residenz-muenchen.de; Max-Joseph-Platz 3; Museum & Schatzkammer each adult/concession/under 18 €7/6/free, combination ticket €11/9/free; ☉9am-6pm Apr–mid-Oct, 10am-5pm mid-Oct–Mar, last entry 1hr before closing) Generations of Bavarian rulers expanded a medieval fortress into this vast and palatial compound that served as their primary residence and seat of government from 1508 to 1918. Today it's an Aladdin's cave of fanciful rooms and collections through the ages that can be seen on an audio-guided tour of what is called the Residenzmuseum. Allow at least two hours to see everything at a gallop.

Englischer Garten — PARK

(ⓊUniversität) The sprawling English Garden is among Europe's biggest city parks – it even rivals London's Hyde Park and New York's Central Park for size – and is a popular playground for locals and visitors alike. Stretching north from Prinzregentenstrasse for about 5km, it was commissioned by Elector Karl Theodor in 1789 and designed by Benjamin Thompson, an American-born scientist working as an adviser to the Bavarian government.

Viktualienmarkt — MARKET

(☉Mon-Fri & morning Sat; ⓊMarienplatz, ⓈMarienplatz) Fresh fruit and vegetables, piles of artisanal cheeses, tubs of exotic olives, hams and jams, chanterelles and truffles – Viktualienmarkt is a feast of flavours and one of central Europe's finest gourmet markets.

Alte Pinakothek — MUSEUM

(☎089-238 0516; www.pinakothek.de; Barer Strasse 27; adult/child €4/free, Sun €1, audioguide €4.50; ☉10am-8pm Tue, to 6pm Wed-Sun; 🚌Pinakotheken, 🚊Pinakotheken) Munich's main repository of Old European Masters is crammed with all the major players that decorated canvases between the 14th and 18th centuries. This neoclassical temple was masterminded by Leo von Klenze and is a delicacy even if you can't tell your Rembrandt from your Rubens. The collection is world famous for its exceptional quality and depth, especially when it comes to German masters.

Neue Pinakothek — MUSEUM

(☎089-2380 5195; www.pinakothek.de; Barer Strasse 29; adult/child €7/free, Sun €1; ☉10am-6pm Thu-Mon, to 8pm Wed; 🚌Pinakotheken, 🚊Pinakotheken) The Neue Pinakothek harbours a well-respected collection of 19th- and early-20th-century paintings and sculpture, from rococo to *Jugendstil* (art nouveau). All the world-famous household names get wall space here, including crowd-pleasing French artists such as Monet, Cézanne and Degas as well as Van Gogh, whose boldly pigmented *Sunflowers* (1888) radiates cheer.

BMW Museum — MUSEUM

(www.bmw-welt.de; Am Olympiapark 2; adult/concession €10/7; ☉10am-6pm Tue-Sun; ⓊOlympiazentrum) This silver, bowl-shaped museum comprises seven themed 'houses' that examine the development of BMW's product line and include sections on motorcycles and motor racing. Even if you can't tell a head gasket from a crankshaft, the interior design – with its curvy retro feel, futuristic bridges, squares and huge backlit wall screens – is reason enough to visit.

The museum is linked to two more architecturally stunning buildings: the BMW headquarters (closed to the public) and the **BMW Welt showroom** (BMW World; ☎089-125 016 001; Am Olympiapark 1; tours adult/child €7/5; ☉7.30am-midnight Mon-Sat, from 9am Sun) FREE.

DON'T MISS

OKTOBERFEST

Hordes come to Munich for Oktoberfest (www.oktoberfest.de), running the 15 days before the first Sunday in October. Reserve accommodation well ahead and go early in the day so you can grab a seat in one of the hangar-sized beer tents spread across the Theresienwiese grounds, about 1km southwest of the Hauptbahnhof. While there is no entrance fee, those €11 1L steins of beer (called Maß) add up fast. Although its origins are in the marriage celebrations of Crown Prince Ludwig in 1810, there's nothing regal about this beery bacchanal now: expect mobs, expect to meet new and drunken friends, and expect decorum to vanish as night sets in and you'll have a blast.

Central Munich

N
0   500 m
0   0.25 miles

NEUHAUSEN

MAXVORSTADT

ALTSTADT

Englischer Garten

Eisbach Creek

Königinstr

Kaulbachstr

Schellingstr

Geschwister-Scholl-Platz

Universität

Schönfeldstr

Ludwigstr

Von-der-Tann-Str

Galeriestr

Hofgarten

Prinzregentenstr

Hofgartenstr

Franz-Josef-Str-Ring

Karl-Scharnagl-Ring

Lehel

Thomas-Wimmer-Ring

Maximilianstr

Marstallplatz

Max-Joseph-Platz

Theatinerstr

Odeonsplatz

Amalienstr

Türkenstr

Barer Str

Theresienstr

Hessstr

Augustenstr

Gabelsbergerstr

Karolinenplatz

Brienner Str

Oskar-von-Miller-Ring

Jägerstr

Maximiliansplatz

Lenbachplatz

Pfandnerstr

Promenadeplatz

Maffeistr

Löwengrube

Frauenplatz

Neuhauser Str

Kaufinger Str

Herzogspitalstr

Josephspitalstr

Sendlinger Str

Marienplatz

Petersplatz

Rindermarkt

Dreifaltigkeits Platz

Isartor

Neuturmstr

Maximilianstr

Lehel

Leherchelstr

Thierschst

Mariannen Platz

Karlsplatz

Karlstr

Arcisstr

Luisenstr

Theresienstr

Dachauer Str

Seidlstr

Marsstr

Hirtenstr

Arnulfstr

Elisenstr

Alter Botanischer Garten

Sonnenstr

Schützenstr

Adolf-Kolping-Str

Sonnenstr

Schillerstr

Schwanthalerstr

Landwehrstr

Senefelderstr

Hauptbahnhof

Paul-Heyse-Str

St-Paul's Str

Bayerstr

Theresienwiese

Schwanthalerstr

Schleissheimer Str

Stiglmaierplatz

Dachauer Str

BMW Museum (2.9km)

Nymphenburger Str

Blutenburgstr

Marsstr

Karlstr

Erzgiessereistr

Mailingerstr

Lothstr

Linprunstr

Hackerbrücke

Zirkus-Krone-Str

Wredestr

Arnulfstr

Zentraler Omnibusbahnhof

Schloss Nymphenburg (3.6km)

Landsberger Str

Westendstr

Parkstr

Schiesssstätterstr

Schiessstätterstr

Karlsplatz

Sonnenstr

Map markers

2
10
5
14
6
1
4 3
7
12
8
13
11
9
1

Central Munich

🛏 Sleeping

Wombats City Hostel Munich HOSTEL €

(☑089-5998 9180; www.wombats-hostels.com; Senefelderstrasse 1; dm/d from €25/95; P@奈; 🚇Hauptbahnhof, Ⓤ Hauptbahnhof) Munich's top hostel is a professionally run affair with a whopping 300 dorm beds plus private rooms. Dorms are painted in cheerful pastels and outfitted with wooden floors, en-suite facilities, sturdy lockers and comfy pine bunks, all in a central location near the train station. A free welcome drink awaits in the bar. Buffet breakfast costs €4.50.

Meininger's HOSTEL, HOTEL €

(☑089-5499 8023; www.meininger-hostels.de; Landsbergerstrasse 20; dm/s/d without breakfast from €30/50/70; 奈; 🚇Holzapfelstrasse) About 800m west of the Hauptbahnhof, this energetic hostel-hotel has basic, clean, bright rooms with big dorms divided into two for a bit of privacy. Room rates vary wildly depending on the date, events taking place in Munich, and occupancy. Breakfast is an extra €6.90; bike hire costs from €8 per day.

🍴 Eating & Drinking

★**Augustiner Bräustuben** BEER HALL

(☑089-507 047; www.braeustuben.de; Landsberger Strasse 19; ⊙10am-midnight; 🚇Holzapfelstrasse) Depending on the wind, an aroma of hops envelops you as you approach this traditional beer hall inside the Augustiner brewery. The Bavarian fare is superb, especially the *Schweinshaxe* (pork knuckle). Due to the location the atmosphere in the evenings is slightly more authentic than that of its city-centre cousins, with fewer tourists at the long tables.

★ **Hofbräuhaus** BEER HALL
(☑089-2901 36100; www.hofbraeuhaus.de; Am Platzl 9; 1L beer €8.60, mains €10-19; ☺9am-midnight; ⛶Kammerspiele, Ⓢ Marienplatz, Ⓤ Marienplatz) Every visitor to Munich should make a pilgrimage to this mothership of all beer halls, if only once. Within this major tourist attraction you'll discover a range of spaces in which to do your Maß lifting: the horse chestnut–shaded garden, the main hall next to the oompah band, tables opposite the industrial-scale kitchen and quieter corners.

★ **Marais** CAFE €
(Parkstrasse 2; dishes €5-13; ☺8am-8pm Tue-Sat, 10am-6pm Sun; ☑; ⛶Holzapfelstrasse) Is it a junk shop, a cafe or a sewing shop? Well, Westend's oddest coffeehouse is in fact all three, and everything you see in this converted haberdashery – the knick-knacks, the cakes and the antique chair you're sitting on – is for sale.

ⓘ ROMANTIC ROAD COACH

Frankfurt and Munich are the most popular gateways for exploring the Romantic Road. The ideal way to travel is by car, though many foreign travellers prefer to take Deutsche Touring's Romantic Road Coach (www.romanticroadcoach.de), which runs daily in each direction between Frankfurt and Füssen (for Neuschwanstein) via Munich. The service operates between April and October and the entire journey takes around 12 hours. There's no charge for breaking the journey and continuing the next day. Tickets are available for the entire route or for short segments, and reservations are only necessary during peak-season weekends. Buy them online or from travel agents. **EurAide** (www.euraide. de; Desk 1, Reisezentrum, Hauptbahnhof; ☺10am-7pm Mon-Fri Mar-Apr & Aug-Dec, to 8pm May-Jul; ⛶Hauptbahnhof, Ⓤ Hauptbahnhof, Ⓢ Hauptbahnhof) in Munich or Reisezentrum offices in larger train stations.

Schmalznudel CAFE €
(Cafe Frischhut; Prälat-Zistl-Strasse 8; pastries €2; ☺8am-6pm; Ⓤ Marienplatz, Ⓢ Marienplatz) This incredibly popular institution serves just four traditional pastries, one of which, the *Schmalznudel* (an oily type of doughnut), gives the place its local nickname. Every baked goodie you munch here is crisp and fragrant, as they're always fresh off the hotplate. They're best eaten with a steaming pot of coffee on a winter's day.

Cafe an der Uni CAFE €
(Ludwigstrasse 24; snacks & mains €6-11; ☺8am-1am Mon-Fri, from 9am Sat & Sun; ☎☑; Ⓢ Universität) Anytime is a good time to be at charismatic CADU. Enjoy breakfast (served until a hangover-friendly 11.30pm!), a cup of java or a Helles in the lovely garden hidden by a wall from busy Ludwigstrasse.

ⓘ Information

Tourist Office - Hauptbahnhof (☑089-21 800; www.muenchen.de; Bahnhofplatz 2; ☺9am-8pm Mon-Sat, 10am-6pm Sun; ⛶Hauptbahnhof, Ⓤ Hauptbahnhof, Ⓢ Hauptbahnhof) Tourist information centre just outside the main train station.

ⓘ Getting There & Away

The hub for Flixbus and other coach operators is the **Zentraler Omnibusbahnhof** (Central Bus Station, ZOB; www.muenchen-zob.de; Arnulfstrasse 21; Ⓢ Hackerbrücke) next to the Hackerbrücke S-Bahn station.

Munich's Hauptbahnhof handles train services to all major destinations, domestic and abroad, including Berlin, Prague, Paris and Budapest.

Romantic Road

Stretching 400km from the vineyards of Würzburg to the foot of the Alps, the Romantic Road (Romantische Strasse) is by far the most popular of Germany's themed holiday routes. It passes through more than two dozen cities and towns, most famously Rothenburg ob der Tauber, and also takes in Schloss Neuschwanstein, Germany's most famous palace.

Füssen

POP 14,600

In the foothills of the Alps, Füssen itself is a charming town, although most visitors skip it and head straight to Schloss

Neuschwanstein and Hohenschwangau, the two most famous castles associated with 'Fairytale King' Ludwig II. You can see both on a long day trip from Munich.

⊙ Sights

★ Schloss Neuschwanstein
CASTLE

(☑ tickets 08362-930 830; www.neuschwanstein. de; Neuschwansteinstrasse 20; adult/concession €13/12, incl Hohenschwangau €25/23; ⊗ 9am-6pm Apr–mid-Oct, 10am-4pm mid-Oct–Mar) Appearing through the mountaintops like a mirage, Schloss Neuschwanstein was the model for Disney's *Sleeping Beauty* castle. King Ludwig II planned this fairy-tale pile himself, with the help of a stage designer rather than an architect. He envisioned it as a giant stage on which to recreate the world of Germanic mythology, inspired by the operatic works of his friend Richard Wagner. The most impressive room is the Sängersaal (Minstrels' Hall), whose frescos depict scenes from the opera *Tannhäuser*.

Built as a romantic medieval castle, work started in 1869 and, like so many of Ludwig's grand schemes, was never finished. For all the coffer-depleting sums spent on it, the king spent just over 170 days in residence.

Completed sections include Ludwig's *Tristan and Isolde*–themed bedroom, dominated by a huge Gothic-style bed crowned with intricately carved cathedral-like spires; a gaudy artificial grotto (another allusion to *Tannhäuser*); and the Byzantine-style Thronsaal (Throne Room) with an incredible mosaic floor containing over two million stones. The painting opposite the (throneless) throne platform depicts another castle dreamed up by Ludwig that was never built. Almost every window provides tour-halting views across the plain below.

The tour ends with a 20-minute film on the castle and its creator, and there's a reasonably priced cafe and the inevitable gift shops.

For the postcard view of Neuschwanstein and the plains beyond, walk 10 minutes up to Marienbrücke (Mary's Bridge), which spans the spectacular Pöllat Gorge over a waterfall just above the castle. It's said Ludwig enjoyed coming up here after dark to watch the candlelight radiating from the Sängersaal.

---

❶ CASTLE TICKETS

Schloss Neuschwanstein and Schloss Hohenschwangau can only be visited on guided tours (in German or English), which last about 35 minutes each (Hohenschwangau is first). Strictly timed tickets are available from the **Ticket Centre** (☑ 08362-930 830; www.hohenschwangau.de; Alpenseestrasse 12; ⊗ 8am-5pm Apr–mid-Oct, 9am-3pm mid-Oct–Mar) at the foot of the castles. In summer, come as early as 8am to ensure you get in that day. Enough time is left between tours for the steep 30- to 40-minute walk between the castles.

Schloss Hohenschwangau
CASTLE

(☑ 08362-930 830; www.hohenschwangau.de; Alpseestrasse 30; adult/concession €13/12, incl Neuschwanstein €25/23; ⊗ 8am-5pm Apr–mid-Oct, 9am-3pm mid-Oct–Mar) King Ludwig II grew up at the sun-yellow Schloss Hohenschwangau and later enjoyed summers here until his death in 1886. His father, Maximilian II, built this palace in a neo-Gothic style atop 12th-century ruins left by Schwangau knights. Far less showy than Neuschwanstein, Hohenschwangau has a distinctly lived-in feel where every piece of furniture is a used original. After his father died, Ludwig's main alteration was having stars, illuminated with hidden oil lamps, painted on the ceiling of his bedroom.

❶ Getting There & Away

If you want to do the castles in a single day from Munich, you'll need to start early. The first train leaves Munich at 5.53am (€26.20; change in Buchloe), reaching Füssen at 7.52am. Otherwise, direct trains leave Munich once every two hours throughout the day.

Rothenburg ob der Tauber
POP 10,900

With its jumble of half-timbered houses enclosed by Germany's best-preserved ramparts, Rothenburg ob der Tauber lays on the medieval cuteness with a trowel. It's an essential stop on the Romantic Road but, alas, overcrowding can detract from its charm. Visit early or late in the day (or, ideally, stay overnight) to experience this historic wonderland sans crowds.

◎ Sights

Jakobskirche
CHURCH

(Church of St Jacob; Klingengasse 1; adult/concession €2.50/1.50; ☺9am-5.15pm Apr-Oct, shorter hours Nov-Mar) One of the few places of worship in Bavaria to charge admission, Rothenburg's Lutheran parish church was begun in the 14th century and finished in the 15th. The building sports some wonderfully aged stained-glass windows, but the top attraction is Tilman Riemenschneider's **Heilig Blut Altar** (Altar of the Holy Blood). The gilded cross above the main scene depicting the Last Supper incorporates Rothenburg's most treasured reliquary – a rock crystal capsule said to contain three drops of Christ's blood.

Mittelalterliches Kriminalmuseum
MUSEUM

(Medieval Crime & Punishment Museum; www.kriminalmuseum.eu; Burggasse 3; adult/concession €7/4; ☺10am-6pm May-Oct, 1-4pm Nov-Apr) Medieval implements of torture and punishment are on show at this gruesomely fascinating museum. Exhibits include chastity belts, masks of disgrace for gossips, a cage for cheating bakers, a neck brace for quarrelsome women and a beer-barrel pen for drunks. You can even snap a selfie in the stocks!

Rathausturm
HISTORIC BUILDING

(Town Hall Tower; Marktplatz; adult/concession €2/0.50; ☺9.30am-12.30pm & 1-5pm daily Apr-Oct, 10.30am-2pm & 2.30-6pm Sun-Thu, to 7pm Fri & Sat Dec, noon-3pm Sat & Sun Jan-Mar & Nov) The Rathaus on Marktplatz was begun in Gothic style in the 14th century and was completed during the Renaissance. Climb the 220 steps of the medieval town hall to the viewing platform of the Rathausturm to be rewarded with widescreen views of the Tauber.

🛏 Sleeping & Eating

Gasthof Butz
GERMAN €

(☑09861-2201; Kapellenplatz 4; mains €7-15; ☺11.30am-2pm & 6pm-9pm Fri-Wed; 🛜) For a quick, no-nonsense goulash, schnitzel or roast pork, lug your weary legs to this locally adored, family-run inn that is situated in a former brewery. In summer two flowery beer gardens beckon. It also has a dozen simply furnished rooms (double rooms €36 to €75).

Gasthof Goldener Greifen
FRANCONIAN €€

(☑09861-2281; www.gasthof-greifen-rothenburg.de; Obere Schmiedgasse 5; mains €8-17; ☺11.30am-10pm) Erstwhile home of Heinrich Toppler, one of Rothenburg's most famous medieval mayors (the dining room was his office), the 700-year-old Golden Griffin is the locals' choice in the touristy centre, serving a hearty menu of Franconian favourites in an austere semi-medieval setting and out back in the sunny and secluded garden.

ℹ Information

Tourist Office (☑09861-404 800; www.tourismus.rothenburg.de; Marktplatz 2; ☺9am-6pm Mon-Fri, 10am-5pm Sat & Sun May-Oct, 9am-5pm Mon-Fri, 10am-1pm Sat Nov-Apr) Helpful office offering free internet access.

ℹ Getting There & Away

The Romantic Road Coach pauses in town for 45 minutes. There are hourly trains to/from Steinach (15 minutes), a transfer point for services to Würzburg (€13.30,1¼ hours).

Würzburg

POP 133,800

Tucked in among river valleys lined with vineyards, Würzburg's crowning architectural glory is the Residenz, one of the finest baroque structures in Germany and a Unesco World Heritage site.

◎ Sights

★ Würzburg Residenz
PALACE

(www.residenz-wuerzburg.de; Balthasar-Neumann-Promenade; adult/concession/under 18yr €7.50/6.50/free; ☺9am-6pm Apr-Oct, 10am-4.30pm Nov-Mar, 45min English tours 11am & 3pm, plus 1.30 & 4.30pm Apr-Oct) The vast Unesco-listed Residenz, built by 18th-century architect Balthasar Neumann as the home of the local prince-bishops, is one of Germany's most important and beautiful baroque palaces. Top billing goes to the brilliant zigzagging **Treppenhaus** (staircase) lidded by what still is the world's largest fresco, a masterpiece by Giovanni Battista Tiepolo depicting allegories of the four then-known continents (Europe, Africa, America and Asia).

The structure was commissioned in 1720 by prince-bishop Johann Philipp Franz von Schönborn, who was unhappy with his old-fashioned digs up in Marienberg Fortress, and took almost 60 years to complete. Today the 360 rooms are home to govern-

BAMBERG

Off the major tourist routes, Bamberg is one of Germany's most delightful and authentic towns. It has a bevy of beautifully preserved historic buildings, palaces and churches in its Unesco-recognised **Altstadt**, a lively student population and its own style of beer, the *Rauchbier* (smoked beer). An easy side trip from Nuremberg or Würzburg, it's compact enough to explore on a leisurely wander. A key stop is the **Bamberger Dom** (www.erzbistum-bamberg.de; Domplatz; ⊘ 9.30am-6pm Apr-Oct, to 5pm Nov-Mar), the treasure-packed cathedral, famous for the life-size equestrian *Bamberger Reiter* (Bamberg Horseman) statue. Another insta-moment is delivered by the **Altes Rathaus** (Old Town Hall; Obere Brücke; adult/concession €4.50/4; ⊘ 9.30am-4.30pm Tue-Sun), the richly frescoed town hall – note the cherub's leg cheekily sticking out from its east facade. Trains run four times hourly from Nuremberg (€21, 40 to 60 minutes) and twice hourly from Würzburg (€20.70, one hour) .

ment institutions, university faculties and a museum, but the grandest 40 have been restored for visitors to admire.

Besides the Grand Staircase, feast your eyes on the ice-white stucco-adorned **Weisser Saal** (White Hall) before entering the **Kaisersaal** (Imperial Hall), canopied by yet another impressive Tiepolo fresco. Other stunners include the gilded stucco **Spiegelkabinett** (Mirror Hall), covered with mirror-like glass painted with figural, floral and animal motifs (accessible by tour only).

In the residence's south wing, the **Hofkirche** (Court Church) is another Neumann and Tiepolo co-production. Its marble columns, gold leaf and profusion of angels match the Residenz in splendour and proportions.

Entered via frilly wrought-iron gates, the **Hofgarten** (Court Garden; open until dusk, free) is a smooth blend of French- and English-style landscaping teeming with whimsical sculptures of children, mostly by court sculptor Peter Wagner. Concerts, festivals and special events take place here during the warmer months.

The complex also houses collections of antiques, paintings and drawings in the Martin-von-Wagner Museum (no relation to Peter) and, handily, a winery in the atmospheric cellar, the **Staatlicher Hofkeller Würzburg**, that is open for tours with tastings.

✖ Eating

Uni-Café   CAFE **€**
(Neubaustrasse 2; snacks €4-8; ⊘ 8am-1am Mon-Sat, from 9am Sun; 📶) A popular cafe strung over two levels, with a student-priced, daily-changing menu of burgers, baguettes and salads plus a buzzy bar and much full-mouthed and animated waffling.

Backöfele   FRANCONIAN **€€**
(📞 0931-590 59; www.backoefele.de; Ursulinergasse 2; mains €7-23; ⊘ noon-midnight Mon-Thu, to 1am Fri & Sat, to 11pm Sun) This old-timey warren has been serving hearty Franconian food for nearly 50 years. Find a table in the cobbled courtyard or one of four historic rooms, each candlelit and furnished with local flair. Featuring schnitzel, snails, bratwurst in wine, wine soup with cinnamon croutons, venison, boar and other local faves, the menu makes for mouth-watering reading. Bookings recommended.

ℹ Information

Tourist Office (📞 0931-372 398; www.wuerzburg.de; Marktplatz 9; ⊘ 10am-6pm Mon-Fri, to 3pm Sat, to 2pm Sun May-Oct, closed Sun and slightly shorter hours Nov-Apr)

ℹ Getting There & Away

The Romantic Road Coach stops next to the Hauptbahnhof and at the Residenzplatz. Würzburg is also linked by train and budget coach company Flixbus to numerous destinations across Germany.

Nuremberg

POP 510,600

Nuremberg (Nürnberg) woos visitors with its wonderfully restored medieval Altstadt, its grand castle and, in December, its magical *Christkindlmarkt* (Christmas market). The town played a key role during the Nazi years. It was here that the fanatical party rallies were held, the boycott of Jewish businesses began and the anti-Semitic Nuremberg Laws were enacted. After WWII the city was chosen as the site of the Nuremberg Trials of Nazi war criminals.

Nuremberg

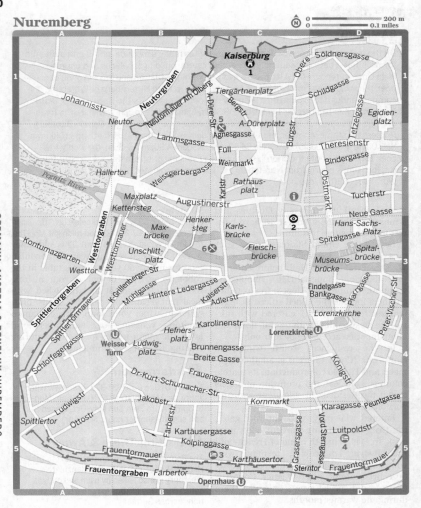

GERMANY, AUSTRIA & BENELUX NUREMBERG

⊙ Sights

The city centre is best explored on foot, but the Nazi-related sights are a tram ride away.

Hauptmarkt   SQUARE
(Hauptmarkt) This bustling square in the heart of the Altstadt is the site of daily markets as well as the famous *Christkindlsmarkt*. At the eastern end is the ornate Gothic **Frauenkirche** (church). Daily at noon crowds crane their necks to witness the clock's figures enact a spectacle called the *Männleinlaufen* (Little Men Dancing). Rising from the square like a Gothic spire

is the sculpture-festooned **Schöner Brunnen** (Beautiful Fountain). Touch the golden ring in the ornate wrought-iron gate for good luck.

★ **Kaiserburg** CASTLE

(Imperial Castle; ☑0911-244 6590; www.kaiserburg-nuernberg.de; Auf der Burg; adult/concession incl Sinwell Tower €7/6, Palas & Museum €5.50/4.50; ☉9am-6pm Apr-Sep, 10am-4pm Oct-Mar) This enormous castle complex above the Altstadt poignantly reflects Nuremberg's medieval might. The main attraction is a tour of the newly renovated residential wing (**Palas**) to see the lavish Knights' and Imperial Hall, a Romanesque double chapel and an exhibit on the inner workings of the Holy Roman Empire. This segues to the **Kaiserburg Museum**, which focuses on the castle's military and building history. Elsewhere, enjoy panoramic views from the **Sinwell Tower** or peer 48m down into the **Deep Well**.

Reichsparteitagsgelände HISTORIC SITE

(Luitpoldhain; ☑0911-231 7538; www.museen.nuernberg.de/dokuzentrum; Bayernstrasse 110; grounds free, Documentation Centre adult/concession incl audioguide €6/1.50; ☉grounds 24hr, Documentation Centre 9am-6pm Mon-Fri, 10am-6pm Sat & Sun) If you've ever wondered where the infamous black-and-white images of ecstatic Nazi supporters hailing their Führer were taken, it was here in Nuremberg. Much of the grounds were destroyed during Allied bombing raids, but enough remain to get a sense of the megalomania behind it, especially after visiting the excellent **Dokumentationszentrum** (Documentation Centre) served by tram 9 from the Hauptbahnhof.

Memorium
Nuremberg Trials MEMORIAL

(☑0911-3217 9372; www.memorium-nuremberg.de; Bärenschanzstrasse 72; adult/concession incl audioguide €6/1.50; ☉9am-6pm Mon & Wed-Fri, 10am-6pm Sat & Sun Apr-Oct, slightly shorter hours Nov-Mar) Göring, Hess, Speer and 21 other Nazi leaders were tried for crimes against peace and humanity by the Allies in **Schwurgerichtssaal 600** (Court Room 600) of this still-working courthouse. Today the room forms part of an engaging exhibit detailing the background, progression and impact of the trials using film, photographs, audiotape and even the original defendants' dock. To get here, take the U1 towards Bärenschanze and get off at Sielstrasse.

🛏 **Sleeping**

Five Reasons HOSTEL €

(☑0911-9928 6625; www.five-reasons.de; Frauentormauer 42; dm/d from €18/49; @☎) This crisp, 21st-century 90-bed hotel-hostel boasts spotless dorms, the trendiest hostel bathrooms you are ever likely to encounter, pre-made beds, card keys, a fully equipped kitchen, a small bar and very nice staff. Breakfast is around €5 extra depending on what option you choose. Overall a great place to lay your head in a very central location.

Probst-Garni Hotel PENSION €€

(☑0911-203 433; www.hotel-garni-probst.de; Luitpoldstrasse 9; s/d €54.50/72; ☎) A creaky lift from street level takes you up to this realistically priced, centrally located guesthouse, run for over 70 years by three generations of Probsts. The 33 gracefully old-fashioned rooms are multi-hued and high-ceilinged, but some are more renovated than others. Breakfast is an extra €6.50.

✕ **Eating**

Don't leave Nuremberg without trying its famous *Nürnberger Bratwürste* sausages.

Café am Trödelmarkt CAFE €

(Trödelmarkt 42; dishes €4-10; ☉9am-6pm Mon-Sat, 10am-6pm Sun) A gorgeous place on a sunny day, this multilevel waterfront cafe overlooks the covered Henkersteg bridge. It's especially popular for its continental breakfasts, and has fantastic cakes, as well as good blackboard lunchtime specials between 11am and 2pm.

★ **Albrecht Dürer Stube** FRANCONIAN €€

(☑0911-227 209; www.albrecht-duerer-stube.de; cnr Albrecht-Dürer-Strasse & Agnesgasse; mains €6-15.50; ☉6pm-midnight Mon-Sat plus 11.30am-2.30pm Fri & Sun) This unpretentious and intimate restaurant has a Dürer-inspired dining room, prettily laid tables, a ceramic stove keeping things toasty when they're not outside and a menu of Nuremberg sausages, steaks, sea fish, seasonal specials, Franconian wine and *Landbier* (regional beer). There aren't many tables so booking ahead at weekends is recommended.

ⓘ **Information**

Tourist Office - Hauptmarkt (☑0911-233 60; www.tourismus.nuernberg.de; Hauptmarkt 18; ☉9am-6pm Mon-Sat, 10am-4pm Sun) Hauptmarkt branch of the tourist office. Has extended hours during *Christkindlesmarkt*, which takes place on its doorstep.

ℹ Getting There & Away

Buses to destinations across Europe leave from the main bus station (ZOB) near the Hauptbahnhof, including an express coach to Prague (€54, 3½ hours, nine daily).

Heidelberg

POP 152,435

Germany's oldest and most famous university town is renowned for its lovely Altstadt, its plethora of pubs and its evocative half-ruined castle. Millions of visitors are drawn each year to this photogenic assemblage, thereby following in the footsteps of Mark Twain who kicked off his European travels in 1878 in Heidelberg, later recounting his bemused observations in *A Tramp Abroad*.

◉ Sights

Heidelberg's sites cluster in the Altstadt, about 2km east of the main train station (bus 32 or 38).

★ Schloss Heidelberg   CASTLE

(☑06221-658 880; www.schloss-heidelberg.de; adult/child incl Bergbahn €7/4, tours €5/2.50, audioguide €5; ⊙grounds 24hr, castle 8am-6pm, English tours hourly 11.15am-4.15pm Mon-Fri, 10.15am-4.15pm Sat & Sun Apr-Oct, reduced hours Nov-Mar) Towering over the Altstadt, Heidelberg's ruined Renaissance castle cuts a romantic figure, especially across the Neckar River when illuminated at night. Attractions include the world's largest wine cask and fabulous views. It's reached either via a steep, cobbled trail in about 10 minutes or by taking the Bergbahn (cogwheel train) from Kornmarkt station. The only way to see the less-than-scintillating interior is by tour, which can be safely skipped. After 6pm you can stroll the grounds for free.

Alte Brücke   BRIDGE

(Karl-Theodor-Brücke) Heidelberg's 200m-long 'old bridge', built in 1786, connects the Altstadt with the river's right bank and the **Schlangenweg** (Snake Path), whose switchbacks lead to the **Philosophenweg** (Philosophers' Walk; south bank of the Neckar River).

Next to the tower gate on the Altstadt side of the bridge, look for the brass sculpture of a monkey holding a mirror. It's the 1979 replacement of the 17th-century original sculpture.

Studentenkarzer   HISTORIC SITE

(Student Jail; ☑06221-5412 813; www.uni-heidelberg.de; Augustinergasse 2; adult/child incl Universitätsmuseum €3/2.50; ⊙10am-6pm Tue-Sun Apr-Oct, 10am-4pm Mon-Sat Nov-Mar) From 1823 to 1914, students convicted of misdeeds such as public inebriation, loud nocturnal singing, freeing the local pigs or duelling were sent to this student jail for at least 24 hours. Judging by the inventive wall graffiti, some found their stay highly amusing. Delinquents were let out to attend lectures or take exams. In certain circles, a stint in the Karzer was considered a rite of passage.

🛏 Sleeping

Steffis Hostel   HOSTEL €

(☑06221-778 2772; www.hostelheidelberg.de; Alte Eppelheimer Strasse 50; dm from €22, s/d/f without bathroom from €50/60/64; ⊙reception 8am-10pm; P@🖘) In a 19th-century tobacco factory a block north of the Hauptbahnhof, accessed via an industrial-size lift, Steffis offers bright, well-lit dorms and rooms (all with shared bathrooms), a colourful lounge that's great for meeting fellow travellers, a spacious kitchen and an old-school hostel vibe. Breakfast costs €3. Perks include tea, coffee and free bike rental.

🍴 Eating & Drinking

Die Kuh Die Lacht   BURGERS €

(www.diekuhdielacht.com; Hauptstrasse 133; mains €6.50-10; ⊙11.30am-10pm Mon-Thu, to 11pm Fri & Sat, noon-9pm Sun; 🖝) Since it opened in 2015, this sleek burger joint has been packed to the rafters. Its 18 different, all-natural burgers are handmade on the premises, with choices like chicken Caesar, barbecued beef and a Mexican burger with beans and corn, as well as veggie options including a tofu burger and a falafel burger. Sides include onion rings or fried bacon.

KulturBrauerei   MICROBREWERY

(www.heidelberger-kulturbrauerei.de; Leyergasse 6; ⊙7am-11pm) With its wood-plank floor, chairs from a Spanish monastery and black iron chandeliers, this brewpub is an atmospheric spot to quaff the house brews (including many seasonal specialities) in the enchanting beer garden. Soak them up with time-tested local dishes such as homemade sausages with cream cheese, radish and dark bread. It also has some lovely **hotel rooms** (☑06221-502 980; d €120-180; 🖘).

ⓘ Information

Tourist Office - Hauptbahnhof (☑ 06221-584 4444; www.heidelberg-marketing.de; Willy-Brandt-Platz 1; ⊙ 9am-7pm Mon-Sat, 10am-6pm Sun Apr-Oct, 9am-6pm Mon-Sat Nov-Mar) Right outside the main train station.

ⓘ Getting There & Away

Long-distance coaches stop outside the Hauptbahnhof, which has frequent direct trains to Munich, Frankfurt and other destinations.

Black Forest

The Black Forest (Schwarzwald) gets its name from its dark canopy of evergreens. It's a myth-shrouded land of misty hills, thick forest and cute villages, with youthful and vibrant Freiburg as its only major town.

Triberg

POP 5000

Cuckoo-clock capital, black forest–cake pilgrimage site and Germany's highest waterfall – Triberg is a torrent of Schwarzwald superlatives and often deluged by visitors.

⊙ Sights

★**Triberger Wasserfälle** WATERFALL
(adult/concession €5/4.50; ⊙ waterfalls lit until 10pm; ⚑) Niagara they ain't but Germany's highest waterfalls do exude their own wild romanticism. The Gutach River feeds the seven-tiered falls, which drop a total of 163m and are illuminated until 10pm. A paved trail accesses the cascades. Pick up a bag of peanuts at the ticket counter to feed the tribes of inquisitive red squirrels. Entry is cheaper in winter.

Weltgrösste Kuckucksuhr LANDMARK
(First World's Largest Cuckoo Clock; www.dold-urlaub.de; Untertalstrasse 28, Schonach; adult/child €2/1; ⊙ 10am-noon & 1-5pm Tue-Sun; ⚑) The 'world's oldest-largest cuckoo clock' kicked into gear in 1980 and took local clockmaker Joseph Dold three years to build by hand. A Dold family member is usually around to the explain the mechanism.

✗ Eating

Café Schäfer CAFE €
(☑ 07722-4465; www.cafe-schaefer-triberg.de; Hauptstrasse 33; cakes €3-4; ⊙ 9am-6pm Mon, Tue, Thu & Fri, 8am-6pm Sat, 11am-6pm Sun) Confectioner Claus Schäfer uses the original 1915 recipe for Black Forest gateau to prepare this sinful treat that layers chocolate cake perfumed with cherry brandy, whipped cream and sour cherries and wraps it all in more cream and shaved chocolate. Trust us, it's worth the calories.

ⓘ Getting There & Away

The Schwarzwaldbahn train line loops southeast to Konstanz (€23.50, 1½ hours, hourly), and northwest to Offenburg (€12.10, 46 minutes, hourly), from where you can connect to trains running to other cities.

Freiburg

POP 224,190

Sitting at the foot of the Black Forest's wooded slopes and vineyards, Freiburg is a sunny, cheerful university town whose medieval Altstadt is a story-book tableau of gabled town houses, cobblestone lanes and cafe-rimmed plazas. Party-loving students spice up the local nightlife and give Freiburg its relaxed air.

⊙ Sights

★**Freiburger Münster** CATHEDRAL
(Freiburg Minster; www.freiburgermuenster.info; Münsterplatz; tower adult/concession €2/1.50; ⊙ 10am-5pm Mon-Sat, 1-7pm Sun, tower 9.30am-5pm Mon-Sat, 1-5pm Sun) With its lacy spires, cheeky gargoyles and intricate entrance portal, Freiburg's 11th-century minster cuts an impressive figure above the central market square. It has dazzling kaleidoscopic stained-glass windows that were mostly financed by medieval guilds and a high altar with a masterful triptych by Dürer protégé Hans Baldung Grien. Square at the base, the **tower** becomes an octagon higher up and is crowned by a filigreed 116m-high spire. On clear days you can spy the Vosges Mountains in France.

Rathausplatz SQUARE
(Town Hall Square) Join locals relaxing in a cafe by the fountain in chestnut-shaded Rathausplatz, Freiburg's prettiest square. Pull out your camera to snap pictures of the ox-blood-red 16th-century **Altes Rathaus** (Old Town Hall) with the tourist office, the step-gabled 19th-century **Neues Rathaus** (New Town Hall) and the medieval **Martinskirche** with its modern interior.

Black Forest

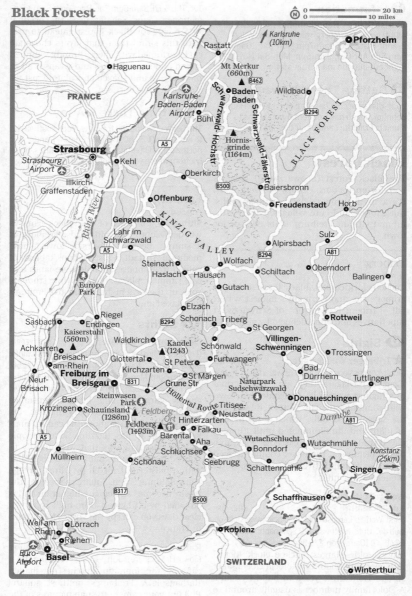

🛏 Sleeping

Black Forest Hostel HOSTEL €
(📞 0761-881 7870; www.blackforest-hostel.de; Kartäuserstrasse 33; dm €18-28, s/d €44/64, linen €4; ⊘ reception 7am-1am; @) Boho budget digs that have chilled-out common areas, a shared kitchen, bicycle rental, musical instruments and a ping-pong table. There is no wi-fi but you can check email using the hostel's internet terminals. It's situated a five-minute walk from the Freiburg town centre.

✕ Eating & Drinking

Markthalle MARKET €
(www.markthalle-freiburg.de; Martinsgasse 235; light meals €4-8; ☺ 8am-8pm Mon-Thu, to midnight Fri & Sat) Eat your way around the world – from curry to sushi, oysters to antipasti – at the food counters in this historic market hall, nicknamed 'Fressgässle'.

Schlappen PUB
(www.schlappen.com; Löwenstrasse 2; ☺ 11am-1am Mon-Wed, to 2am Thu, to 3am Fri & Sat, 3pm-1am Sun) In historic digs and crammed with antiques and vintage theatre posters, this rocking, friendly boozer has made the magic happen for generations of students. The drinks – a good array of beers, gins, absinthes and whiskies – are affordable and the terrace heaves in summer.

ℹ Information

Freiburg Tourist Office (📞 0761-388 1880; www.visit.freiburg.de; Rathausplatz 2-4; ☺ 8am-8pm Mon-Fri, 9.30am-5pm Sat, 10.30am-3.30pm Sun Jun-Sep, 8am-6pm Mon-Fri, 9.30am-2.30pm Sat, 10am-noon Sun Oct-May) Pick up the three-day WelcomeKarte (€26) at Freiburg's central tourist office.

ℹ Getting There & Away

Freiburg is a major transport hub in the southern Black Forest, with frequent rail and bus connections within the region and beyond.

Frankfurt am Main

POP 709,395
With its glinting skyscrapers, the business of Frankfurt on the Main may be business, but ths 'Mainhattan' is no buttoned-up metropolis, as you'll quickly discover in its cosy apple-wine taverns, fine museums and reconstructed medieval town square.

◉ Sights

★ Römerberg SQUARE
(Ⓢ Dom/Römer) The Römerberg is Frankfurt's old central square. Ornately gabled half-timbered buildings, reconstructed after WWII, give an idea of how beautiful the city's medieval core once was.

In the square's centre is the Gerechtigkeitsbrunnen (Fountain of Justice; Römerberg); in 1612, at the coronation of Matthias, the fountain ran with wine. The Römerberg is especially lovely as a backdrop for the

Christmas market (Weihnachtsmarkt; ☺ 10am-9pm Mon-Sat, 11am-9pm Sun late Nov-22 Dec).

★ Kaiserdom CATHEDRAL
(Imperial/Frankfurt Cathedral; www.dom-frankfurt.de; Domplatz 1; tower adult/child €3/1.5; ☺ church 9am-8pm Mon-Thu, 1pm-8pm Fri, 9am-8pm Sat & Sun, tower 9am-6pm Apr-Oct, 10am-5pm Thu-Mon Nov-Apr; Ⓢ Dom/Römer) Frankfurt's red-sandstone cathedral is dominated by a 95m-high Gothic tower, which can be climbed via 324 steps. Construction began in the 13th century; from 1356 to 1792 the Holy Roman Emperors were elected (and, after 1562, consecrated and crowned) in the Wahlkapelle at the end of the right aisle (look for the 'skull' altar). The cathedral was rebuilt both after an 1867 fire and after the bombings of 1944, which left it a burnt-out shell.

🛏 Sleeping & Eating

Five Elements HOSTEL €
(📞 069-2400 5885; www.5elementshostel.de; Moselstrasse 40; dm/s/d from €18/41/46; 🛜; 🚉 Hauptbahnhof) The location mightn't be Frankfurt's most salubrious, but once you're inside the turn-of-the-20th-century gabled building it's a sanctuary of parquet floors, boldly coloured walls and designer furniture. Facilities include a laundry and 24-hour bar with a billiard table; breakfast costs €4.50. A private apartment sleeping up to four people with a private bathroom and kitchen costs €426 per week.

★ Kleinmarkthalle MARKET €
(www.kleinmarkthalle.de; Hasengasse 5-7; ☺ 8am-6pm Mon-Fri, to 4pm Sat; Ⓢ Dom/Römer) 🍴 Aromatic stalls inside this bustling traditional market hall sell artisanal smoked sausages, cheeses, roasted nuts, breads, pretzels, loose-leaf teas, pastries, cakes and chocolates, as well as fruit, vegetables, spices, fresh Italian pasta, Greek olives, meat, poultry and, downstairs, fish. It's unmissable for picnickers or self-caterers, or anyone wanting to experience Frankfurt life. The upper-level wine bar opens out onto a terrace.

ℹ Information

Tourist Office - Hauptbahnhof (📞 069-2123 8800; www.frankfurt-tourismus.de; Main Hall, Hauptbahnhof; ☺ 8am-9pm Mon-Fri, 9am-6pm Sat & Sun; 🚉 Hauptbahnhof) At the main train station.

GERMANY, AUSTRIA & BENELUX FRANKFURT AM MAIN

Romantic Rhine Valley

Höhr-Grenzhausen

B42
B49

Koblenz
Festung Ehrenbreitstein
B261

Moselle River

Bad Ems

Lahn River

Nassau

Schloss Stolzenfels
B9
Lahnstein

Burg Lahneck

Rhens

RHINELAND-PALATINATE

Waldesch

Rhine River

B327

B260

Braubach
Marksburg

Filsen

Boppard

Kamp Bornhofen

B274

Buchholz

Burg Maus

Hunsrück

B274

A61

Emmelshausen

St Goarshausen
Burg Katz

St Goar

Burg Rheinfels

Loreley

Oberwesel
Sieben Jungfrauen Rocks

Schönburg

Kaub
Pfalzgrafstein

A61

Bacharach
Burg Stahleck
B42

Lorch

Niederheimbach

Burg Sooneck

Trechtingshausen

E50

Burg Reichenstein

Assmannshausen
Niederwald Monument
Eibingen

Burg Rheinstein
B9
Mäuseturm
Rüdesheim

Bingerbrück
Bingen

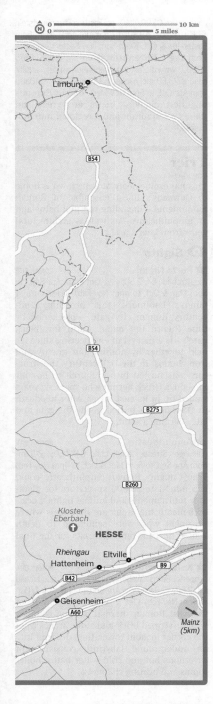

ℹ Getting There & Away

Frankfurt Airport (FRA; www.frankfurt-airport. com) is 12km southwest of town and linked to the centre by S-Bahn lines S8 and S9 shuttle (€4.35, 11 minutes) several times hourly. Note that Frankfurt-Hahn Airport (HHN; www. hahn-airport.de), served by Ryanair, is actually 125km west of Frankfurt.

The main bus station is at Mannheimer Strasse 15, on the south side of the main train station.

Frankfurt's super-busy Hauptbahnhof is about 1km west of the Altstadt.

The Romantic Rhine Valley

Between Koblenz and Mainz, the Rhine cuts deeply through the Rhenish slate mountains, a scenic stretch called Middle Rhine and nicknamed 'Romantic Rhine'. Forested hillsides cradle craggy cliffs and nearly vertical terraced vineyards. Idyllic villages pop up around each bend, their half-timbered houses and church steeples seemingly plucked from the world of fairy tales. High above the river, busy with barge traffic, are famous medieval castles – some ruined, some restored – all vestiges from a mysterious past.

Bacharach

One of the prettiest of the Rhine villages, tiny Bacharach conceals its considerable charms behind a 14th-century wall. Beyond the thick arched gateways awaits a beautiful medieval old town graced with half-timbered town houses. There's no shortage of atmospheric places to eat and sample the local vintages. For gorgeous views of village, vineyards and river, take a stroll atop the **medieval ramparts**. An especially scenic panorama unfolds from the **Postenturm**, a tower from where you can also espy the filigreed ruins of the **Wernerkapelle**, a medieval chapel, and the turrets of the 12th-century hilltop **Burg Stahleck**, a castle turned **youth hostel** (☑ 06743-1266; www.jugendherberge.de; Burg Stahleck; dm/s/d €22/34/56; ℗ @).

St Goar & St Goarshausen

These twin towns face each other across the Rhine. On the left bank, St Goar is lorded over by **Burg Rheinfels** (☑ 06741-7753; www. st-goar.de; Schlossberg 47; adult/child €5/2.50, guided mine tour €7/free; ☺ 9am-6pm late Mar-late Oct, 9am-5pm early-late Mar & late Oct–mid-Nov,

---

ℹ ROMANTIC RHINE IN A DAY

If you're short on time, it's possible to get a taste of the Romantic Rhine on a DIY day trip from Frankfurt. From Frankfurt Hauptbahnhof take a regional train to Rüdesheim (1¼ hours, several times hourly) and board one of the passenger ships run by **Köln-Düsseldorfer** (☑ 0221-208 8318; www.k-d.com) that link the Rhine villages on a set timetable from about Easter to October. Travel as far as St Goarshausen (two hours) from where hourly trains take you back to Frankfurt in another two hours.

---

guided mine tours by reservation). Once the mightiest fortress on the Rhine, it was built in 1245 by Count Dieter V of Katzenelnbogen as a base for his toll-collecting operations. The size of its labyrinthine ruins are astonishing.

A ferry links St Goar with St Goarshausen and the most fabled spot along the Romantic Rhine, the **Loreley Rock**. This vertical slab of slate owes its fame to a mythical maiden whose siren songs are said to have lured sailors to their death in the river's treacherous currents.

Braubach

Framed by forested hillsides, vineyards and Rhine-side rose gardens, the 1300-year-old town of Braubach, situated on the right bank, is centred on the small, half-timbered market square. High above are the dramatic towers, turrets and crenellations of the 700-year-old **Marksburg** (☑ 02627-206; www.marksburg.de; adult/child €7/5; ⊘ 10am-5pm mid-Mar–Oct, 11am-4pm Nov–mid-Mar), which – unique among the Rhine fortresses – was never destroyed.

Koblenz

Founded by the Romans, Koblenz sits at the confluence of the Rhine and Moselle Rivers, a point known as **Deutsches Eck** (German Corner) and dominated by a bombastic 19th-century statue of Kaiser Wilhelm I on horseback. On the right Rhine bank high above the town – and reached by an 850m-long **cable car** (☑ 0261-2016 5850; www.seilbahn-koblenz.de; Rheinstrasse 6; adult/

child return €9.90/4.40, incl Festung Ehrenbreitstein €13.80/6.20; ⊘ 9.30am-7pm Jul-Sep, 9.30am-6pm Easter-Jun & Oct, 10am-5pm Nov-Easter) – is the **Festung Ehrenbreitstein** (☑ 0261-6675 4000; www.diefestungehrenbreitstein.de; adult/child €7/3.50, incl cable car €13.80/6.20; ⊘ 10am-6pm Apr-Oct, to 5pm Nov-Mar), one of Europe's mightiest citadels. Views are great and there's a restaurant and a regional museum inside.

Trier

POP 106,544

This handsome, leafy Moselle town is home to Germany's finest ensemble of Roman monuments – including thermal baths and an amphitheatre – as well as architectural gems from later ages.

◉ Sights

★**Porta Nigra**   ROMAN SITE
(adult/child €4/2.50; ⊘ 9am-6pm Apr-Sep, to 5pm Mar & Oct, to 4pm Nov-Feb) Trier's most famous landmark, this brooding 2nd-century Roman city gate – blackened by time (hence the name, Latin for 'black gate') – is a marvel of engineering since it's held together by nothing but gravity and iron clamps. In the 11th century, the structure was turned into a church to honour Simeon, a Greek hermit who spent six years walled up in its east tower. After his death in 1134, he was buried inside the gate and later became a saint.

★**Amphitheatre**   ROMAN SITE
(Olewiger Strasse; adult/child €4/2.50; ⊘ 9am-6pm Apr-Sep, to 5pm Mar & Oct, to 4pm Nov-Feb) Trier's mighty Roman amphitheatre could accommodate 20,000 spectators for gladiator tournaments and animal fights. Located beneath the arena are dungeons where prisoners who were sentenced to death waited next to starving beasts for the final showdown.

★**Kaiserthermen**   ROMAN SITE
(Imperial Baths; Weberbachstrasse 41; adult/child €4/2.50; ⊘ 9am-6pm Apr-Sep, to 5pm Mar & Oct, to 4pm Nov-Feb) Get a sense of the layout of this vast Roman thermal bathing complex with its striped brick-and-stone arches from the corner lookout tower, then descend into an underground labyrinth consisting of cavernous hot and cold water baths, boiler rooms and heating channels.

★ Konstantin Basilika ROMAN SITE
(Constantine's Throne Room; ☑ 0651-9949 1200;
www.konstantin-basilika.de; Konstantinplatz 10;
☉ 10am-6pm Mon-Sat, 1-6pm Sun Apr-Oct, 10am-
noon & 2-4pm Tue-Sat, 1-3pm Sun Nov-Mar) `FREE`
Constructed around AD 310 as Constantine's
throne room, the brick-built basilica is now
an austere Protestant church. With built-to-
impress dimensions (some 67m long, 27m
wide and 33m high), it's the largest sin-
gle-room Roman structure still in existence.
Its organ, with 87 registers and 6500 pipes,
generates a seven-fold echo.

🛏 Sleeping & Drinking

Evergreen Hostel HOSTEL €
(☑ 0651-6998 7026, outside office hours 0157 8856
9594; www.evergreen-hostel.de; Gartenfeldstrasse
7; dm from €19, s/d from €44/56, without bathroom
from €40/50; ☉ reception 8-11am & 2-7pm May-
Oct, 9-11am & 3-6pm Nov-Apr; @🛜) This laid-
back indie hostel has a piano, well-equipped
self-catering kitchen and attractive, spacious
rooms, most with private bathrooms. Breakfast costs €8. Outside office hours, call ahead
to arrange your arrival.

de Winkel PUB
(☑ 0651-436 1878; www.de-winkel.de; Johan-
nisstrasse 25; ☉ 6pm-1am Tue-Thu, to 2am Fri &
Sat) Winny and Morris have presided over
this locally loved watering hole for years.
Drop by for a Pils and a bite, such as the
crispy chicken wings called 'Flieten' in Trier
dialect.

ⓘ Information

Tourist Office (☑ 0651-978 080; www.tri-
er-info.de; An der Porta Nigra; ☉ 9am-6pm
Mon-Sat, 10am-5pm Sun Mar-Dec, 10am-5pm
Mon-Sat Jan & Feb)

ⓘ Getting There & Away

Frequent direct train connections include Koblenz (€22.70, 1½ to two hours), Cologne (€33,
three hours) and Luxembourg (€17.90, one hour)
with onward connections to Paris.

Cologne
POP 1 MILLION
Cologne (Köln) offers lots of attractions, led
by its famous cathedral whose filigree twin
spires dominate the skyline. The city's museum landscape is especially strong when it
comes to art, but also has plenty in store for
fans of chocolate, sports and Roman history.

Its people are well known for their *joie de
vivre* and it's easy to have a good time right
along with them year-round in the beer halls
of the Altstadt.

⊙ Sights

★ Kölner Dom CATHEDRAL
(Cologne Cathedral; ☑ 0221-9258 4720; www.
koelner-dom.de; tower adult/concession €4/2;
☉ 6am-9pm May-Oct, to 7.30pm Nov-Apr, tower 9am-6pm May-Sep, to 5pm Mar, Apr & Oct, to
4pm Nov-Feb) Cologne's geographical and
spiritual heart – and its single-biggest tourist draw – is the magnificent Kölner Dom.
With its soaring twin spires, this is the Mt
Everest of cathedrals, jam-packed with art
and treasures. For an exercise fix, climb the
533 steps up the Dom's south tower to the
base of the steeple that dwarfed all buildings in Europe until Gustave Eiffel built a
certain tower in Paris. The underground
Domforum visitor centre is a good source
of info and tickets.

**★ Römisch-Germanisches
Museum** MUSEUM
(Roman Germanic Museum; ☑ 0221-2212 4438;
www.museenkoeln.de; Roncalliplatz 4; adult/con-
cession €9/5; ☉ 10am-5pm Tue-Sun) Sculptures
and ruins displayed outside the entrance
are merely the overture to a full symphony
of Roman artefacts found along the Rhine.
Highlights include the giant Poblicius tomb
(AD 30–40), the magnificent 3rd-century

`LOCAL KNOWLEDGE`

COLOGNE CARNIVAL

Carnival in Cologne is one of the best
parties in Europe and a thumb in the eye
of the German work ethic. It all starts
with *Weiberfastnacht,* the Thursday before Ash Wednesday, when women rule
the day (and do things like chop off the
ties of their male colleagues and boss-
es). The party continues through the
weekend, with more than 50 parades of
ingenious floats and wildly dressed luna-
tics dancing in the streets. By the time it
all comes to a head with the big parade
on Rosenmontag (Rose Monday), the
entire city has come unglued. Those still
capable of swaying and singing will live
it up one last time on Shrove Tuesday
before the curtain comes down on Ash
Wednesday.

Cologne

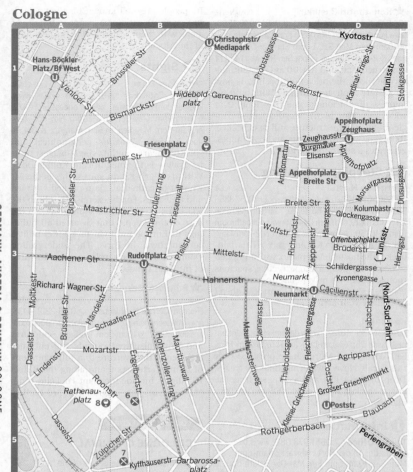

Dionysus mosaic, and astonishingly well-preserved glass items. Insight into daily Roman life is gained from toys, tweezers, lamps and jewellery, the designs of which have changed surprisingly little since Roman times.

Museum Ludwig
MUSEUM

(☎0221-2212 6165; www.museum-ludwig.de; Heinrich-Böll-Platz; adult/concession €13/8.50, more during special exhibits; ⊙10am-6pm Tue-Sun) A mecca of modern art, Museum Ludwig presents a tantalising mix of works from all major phases. Fans of German expres-sionism (Beckmann, Dix, Kirchner) will get their fill here as much as those with a penchant for Picasso, American pop art (Warhol, Lichtenstein) and Russian avant-garde painter Alexander Rodchenko. Rothko and Pollock are highlights of the abstract collection, while Gursky and Tillmanns are among the reasons the photography section is a must stop.

Schokoladenmuseum
MUSEUM

(Chocolate Museum; ☎0221-931 8880; www.schokoladenmuseum.de; Am Schokoladenmuseum 1a; adult/concession €11.50/7.50; ⊙10am-6pm

is a hostel as hostels should be: central, convivial and economical. A lounge gives way to clean, colourful rooms sleeping one to six people. There's lots of free stuff, including linen, internet access, lockers, city maps and guest kitchen. Some private rooms have their own bathrooms.

Engelbät EUROPEAN €
(☏ 0221-246 914; www.engelbaet.de; Engelbertstrasse 7; crepes €5-8.50; ⊙ 11am-midnight Sun-Thu, to 1am Fri & Sat) 🌱 This cosy restaurant-pub is famous for its habit-forming crêpes, which come in 40 varieties – sweet, meat or vegetarian. Also popular for weekend breakfast (served until 3pm). Outside of summer, there's often live jazz at night. The pavement tables are popular.

Freddy Schilling BURGERS €
(☏ 0221-1695 5515; www.freddyschilling.de; Kyffhäuserstrasse 34; burgers €6-10; ⊙ noon-10pm Sun-Tue, to 11pm Fri & Sat) A wholewheat bun provides a solid framework for the moist patties made with beef from happy cows and drizzled with Freddy's homemade 'special' sauce. Pair it with a side of Rosi's: small butter-and-rosemary-tossed potatoes.

🍷 Drinking & Nightlife

There are plenty of beer halls in the tourist-adored Altstadt, but for a more local vibe head to student-flavoured Zülpicher Viertel or the Belgisches Viertel, both in the city centre. Local breweries turn out a variety called *Kölsch*, which is served in skinny 200mL glasses.

Tue-Fri, 11am-7pm Sat & Sun, last entry 1hr before closing; 🅿) At this high-tech temple to the art of chocolate-making, exhibits on the origin of the 'elixir of the gods', as the Aztecs called it, and the cocoa-growing process are followed by a live-production factory tour and a stop at a chocolate fountain for a sample.

🛏 Sleeping & Eating

Station Hostel for Backpackers HOSTEL €
(☏ 0221-912 5301; www.hostel-cologne.de; Marzellenstrasse 44-56; dm €18-26, s/d from €35/52; @🅦) Located near the Hauptbahnhof, this

★ Päffgen
BEER HALL

(☑0221-135 461; www.paeffgen-koelsch.de; Friesenstrasse 64-66; mains €6-20; ☺10am-midnight Sun-Thu, to 12.30am Fri & Sat) Busy, loud and boisterous, Päffgen has been pouring *Kölsch* since 1883 and hasn't missed a step since. In summer you can enjoy the refreshing brew and local specialities (€1.10 to €10.70) beneath starry skies in the beer garden.

★ Biergarten Rathenauplatz
BEER GARDEN

(☑0221-801 7349; www.rathenauplatz.de; Rathenauplatz; ☺noon-11pm Apr-Sep) A large, leafy park has one of Cologne's best places for a drink: a community-run beer garden. Tables sprawl under huge, old trees, while simple snacks such as salads and very good *frikadelle* (spiced hamburger) issue forth from a cute little hut. Prices are cheap; beers come from nearby Hellers Brewery – try the organic lager. Proceeds help to maintain the park.

ⓘ Information

Tourist Office (☑0221-346 430; www.cologne-tourism.com; Kardinal-Höffner-Platz 1; ☺9am-8pm Mon-Sat, 10am-5pm Sun) Excellent; located near the cathedral. The app is well done.

ⓘ Getting There & Away

The central bus station is on Breslauer Platz, right behind the Hauptbahnhof (main train station), which has fast and frequent trains in all directions, including ICE trains leaving for Brussels to connect with the Eurostar for London or Paris.

Düsseldorf

POP 594,000

Düsseldorf dazzles with boundary-pushing architecture, zinging nightlife and a vibrant art scene. Although it's a hub of banking, advertising, fashion and telecommunications, all it takes is a couple of hours of partying in the boisterous pubs of the Altstadt (the historical quarter along the Rhine) to realise that locals have no problem letting their hair down once they slip out of those Boss jackets.

◎ Sights

K20 Grabbeplatz
MUSEUM

(☑0211-838 1204; Grabbeplatz 5; adult/child €12/2.50; ☺10am-6pm Tue-Fri, 11am-6pm Sat & Sun) A collection that spans the arc of 20th-century artistic vision gives the K20 an enviable edge in the art world. It encompasses major works by Picasso, Matisse and Mondrian, and more than 100 paintings

WORTH A TRIP

AACHEN

A spa town founded by the Romans, Aachen became the centre of early medieval Europe under the highly influential emperor Charlemagne, whose remains rest in the Aachener Dom, one of Germany's oldest and most stunning cathedrals. Aachen has tremendous amounts of character and makes for an easy and worthy day trip from Cologne or Düsseldorf or a handy overnight stop en route to adjacent Netherlands or Belgium.

It's impossible to overestimate the significance of Aachen's **cathedral** (☑0241-447 090; www.aachendom.de; Münsterplatz; ☺7am-7pm Apr-Dec, to 6pm Jan-Mar), which consists of an octagonal chapel with a colossal brass chandelier from the early 9th century and a Gothic choir that was added In 1414 and filled with such priceless treasures as a gold-plated altar-front depicting Christ's Passion and a jewel-encrusted gilded copper pulpit, both 1000 years old. Also here are Charlemagne's remains, which rest in an elaborate gilded shrine. The emperor's white marble throne in the upstairs gallery can only be seen on guided tours. It also served as the coronation throne of 30 German kings between 936 and 1531.

To deepen your knowledge about Charlemagne, Aachen and the early Middle Ages, stop by the **Centre Charlemagne** (☑0241-432 4956; www.centre-charlemagne.eu; Katschhof 1; adult/concession €6/3; ☺10am-5pm Tue-Sun).

Regional trains frequently head to Cologne (€17, one hour), Düsseldorf (€20.70, 1½ hours) and beyond.

Düsseldorf

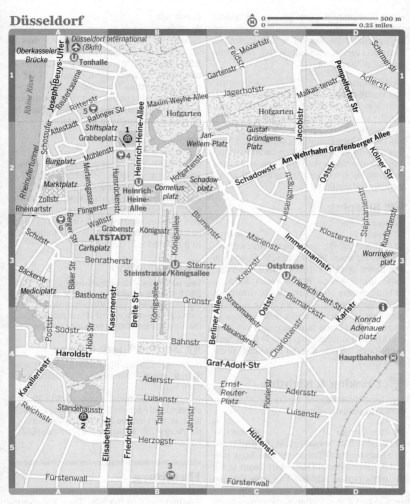

and drawings by Paul Klee. American artists represented include Jackson Pollock, Andy Warhol and Jasper Johns. Düsseldorf's own Joseph Beuys has a major presence as well.

K21 Ständehaus   MUSEUM
(☏ 0211-838 1204; Ständehausstrasse 1; adult/child €12/2.50; ☺ 10am-6pm Tue-Fri, 11am-6pm Sat & Sun) A stately 19th-century parliament building forms a fabulous dichotomy to the cutting-edge art of the K21 – a collection showcasing only works created after the 1980s. Large-scale film and

video installations and groups of works share space with site-specific rooms by an international cast of artists including Andreas Gursky, Candida Höfer, Bill Viola and Nam June Paik.

Medienhafen   ARCHITECTURE
(Am Handelshafen) This once-dead old harbour area has been reborn as the Medienhafen, an increasingly hip quarter filled with architecture, restaurants, bars, hotels and clubs. Once-crumbling warehouses have turned into high-tech office buildings and now rub shoulders with bold new structures designed by celebrated international architects, including Frank Gehry.

🛏 Sleeping

**Backpackers-
Düsseldorf**   HOSTEL €
(☑ 0211-302 0848; www.backpackers-duesseldorf.de; Fürstenwall 180; dm €19-25; ⊙ reception 8am-10pm; 🅿 @ 🛜) Düsseldorf's adorable indie hostel sleeps 60 in clean four- to 10-bed dorms outfitted with individual backpack-sized lockers. It's a low-key place with a kitchen and a relaxed lounge where cultural and language barriers melt quickly. The vending machine is filled with beer. Rates include a small breakfast; linen costs €3.

🍷 Drinking & Nightlife

The local beverage of choice is *Altbier,* a dark and semisweet beer.

★ Zum Uerige   BEER HALL
(☑ 0211-866 990; www.uerige.de; Berger Strasse 1; ⊙ 10am-midnight) This cavernous brew pub is the quintessential Düsseldorf haunt to try the city's typical *Altbier.* The suds flow so quickly from giant copper vats that the waiters – called *Köbes* – simply carry huge trays of brew and plonk down a glass whenever they spy an empty. Even on a cold day, the outside tables are alive with merriment.

ℹ CHEAP CRUISING

This maritime city offers a bewildering array of boat trips, but there's no need to book a pricey cruise to see the port. Instead, hop on one of the public ferries for the price of a public transport ticket (€3). The handiest line is ferry 62, which leaves from Landungsbrücken (pier 3) and travels west to Finkenwerder.

**Salon des
Amateurs**   LOUNGE
(☑ 0211-171 2830; www.salondesamateurs.de; Grabbeplatz 4; ⊙ 11.30am-1am Tue-Thu, to 5am Fri & Sat, to 6pm Sun) Tucked into the Kunsthalle, this tunnel-shaped cafe-lounge pulls off an artsy vibe without a single canvas. Museum-goers arrive in the afternoon for tea and a chat, while scenesters keep the bar and little dance floor hopping after dark.

**★ Stone Im
Ratinger Hof**   CLUB
(☑ 0211-210 7828; www.stone-club.de; Ratinger Strasse 10; cover varies; ⊙ 10pm-5am Fri & Sat) The venerable Ratinger Hof is the place for indie and alt sounds. Depending on the night, tousled boho types, skinny-jean emos and sneaker-wearing students thrash it out to everything from noise pop to indietronic to punk and roll.

ℹ Information

Tourist Office – Hauptbahnhof (☑ 0211-1720 2844; www.duesseldorf-tourismus.de; Immermannstrasse 65b; ⊙ 9.30am-7pm Mon-Fri, to 5pm Sat) The main tourist office, across from the train station; has an exchange window.

ℹ Getting There & Away

Düsseldorf's central bus station is on Worringer Strasse, about 250m north of the Hauptbahnhof main exit.

Regional trains travel to Cologne (€12.30, 30 minutes) and Aachen (€20.70, 1½ hours). Fast ICE train links include Berlin (€111, 4¼ hours), Hamburg (€82, 3½ hours) and Frankfurt (€82, 1½ hours).

Hamburg

POP 1.8 MILLION

Situated right on the Elbe River, Hamburg's maritime spirit infuses the entire city; from its stunning new Elbphilharmonie concert hall and placid villa-lined canals to the bold contemporary architecture in Hafencity to a bustling riverfront that's lined with fish kiosks, you always know you're near the water. (In)famous for its gloriously seedy Reeperbahn red-light district, Hamburg is also a mosaic of vibrant neighbourhoods that are awash with global eateries, indie boutiques and a distinctive live- and electronic-music scene that is a legacy from the time when the Beatles cut their teeth in the city's divey clubs.

◉ Sights

Elbphilharmonie ARTS CENTRE
(Elbe Philharmonic Hall; ☑040-3576 6666; www.
elbphilharmonie.de; Platz der Deutschen Einheit
4; ⑤Baumwall) A squat brown-brick former
warehouse at the far west of HafenCity is
the base for the architecturally bold Elbphilharmonie, a major concert hall and
performance space. Pritzker Prize–winning
Swiss architects Herzog & de Meuron were
responsible for the design, which captivates
with its details like the 1096 individually
curved glass panes.

Rathaus HISTORIC BUILDING
(☑040-428 3124; Rathausmarkt 1; tours adult/
under 14yr €5/free; ◷tours half-hourly 11am-
4pm Mon-Fri, 10am-5pm Sat, to 4pm Sun, English
tours depend on demand; ⑭Rathausmarkt, Jun-
gfernstieg, ⑤Jungfernstieg) With its spectacular coffered ceiling, Hamburg's baroque
Rathaus is one of Europe's most opulent,
and is renowned for its Emperor's Hall and
Great Hall. The 40-minute tours take in
only a fraction of this beehive of 647 rooms.
A good secret to know about is the inner
courtyard, where you can take a break from
exploring the Rathaus on comfy chairs with
tables.

North of here, you can wander through
the **Alsterarkaden**, the Renaissance-style
arcades sheltering shops and cafes alongside
a canal or 'fleet'.

★Hamburger Kunsthalle MUSEUM
(☑040-428 131 200; www.hamburger-kunsthalle.
de; Glockengiesserwall; adult/child €14/free, Thu
evening €8/free; ◷10am-6pm Tue, Wed & Fri-Sun,
to 9pm Thu; ⑭Hauptbahnhof-Nord) A treasure
trove of art from the Renaissance to the
present day, the Kunsthalle spans two buildings linked by an underground passage. The
main building houses works ranging from
medieval portraiture to 20th-century classics, such as Klee and Kokoschka. There's
also a memorable room of 19th-century
landscapes by Caspar David Friedrich. Its
stark white modern cube, the **Galerie der
Gegenwart**, showcases contemporary German artists.

🛏 Sleeping

★Superbude St Pauli HOTEL €
(☑040-807 915 820; www.superbude.de; Ju-
liusstrasse 1-7; r from €65; @🛜; ⑭Sternschan-
ze, ⑤Sternschanze) The young and forev-
er-young mix and mingle without a shred of

HAMBURG'S FAMOUS FISH MARKET

Here's the perfect excuse to stay up
all Saturday night. Every Sunday in
the wee hours, some 70,000 locals
and visitors descend upon the famous
Fischmarkt in St Pauli. The market
has been running since 1703, and its
undisputed stars are the boisterous
Marktschreier (market criers) who
hawk their wares at full volume. Live
bands also entertainingly crank out
cover versions of ancient German pop
songs in the adjoining Fischauktion-
shalle (Fish Auction Hall).

prejudice at this rocking design hotel-hostel
combo that's all about living, laughing, partying and, yes, even sleeping well. All rooms
have comfy beds and sleek private baths,
breakfast is served until noon and there's
even a 'rock star suite' with an Astra beer as
a pillow treat.

Schanzenstern Altona PENSION €
(☑040-3991 9191; www.schanzenstern.
com; Kleine Rainstrasse 24-26; dm/s/d from
€20/50/75, apt from €83; ⊛@🛜; ⑭Altona) A
mix of families and slightly more grown-up
backpackers inhabit these sparkling rooms
(with private bathrooms), and self-catering
apartments. Staff are wired into what's happening around Hamburg. Dorms have two
to seven beds. There is another property in
St Pauli.

🍴 Eating

The Schanzenviertel (U-Bahn to Feldstrasse
or Schanzenstern) swarms with cheap eateries; try Schulterblatt for Portuguese outlets
or Susannenstrasse for Asian and Turkish. St
Georg's Lange Reihe (U-Bahn to Hauptbahnhof) offers many characterful eating spots
to suit every budget.

**★Fischbrötchenbude
Brücke 10** SEAFOOD €
(☑040-3339 9339; www.bruecke-10.de; Landungsbrücken, Pier 10; sandwiches €3-9.50; ◷10am-
10pm; ⑤Landungsbrücken, ⑭Landungsbrücken)
There are a gazillion fish sandwich vendors
in Hamburg, but we're going to stick our
neck out and say that this vibrant, clean and
contemporary outpost makes the best. Try a

Hamburg

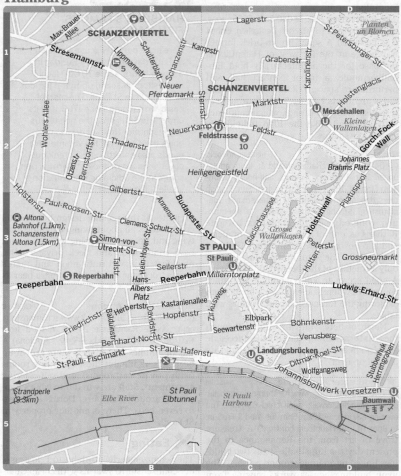

Hamburg

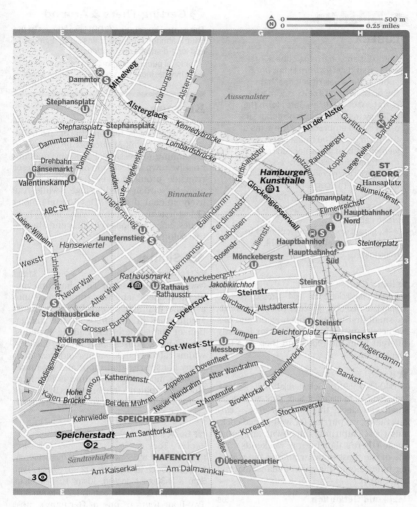

classic *Bismarck* (pickled herring) or *Matjes* (brined), or treat yourself to a bulging shrimp sandwich. Lovely tables outside.

Café Koppel VEGETARIAN €
(☏040-249 235; www.cafe-koppel.de; Lange Reihe 66; mains €5-10; ⊙10am-11pm; ☏; ⑤Hauptbahnhof) Set back from busy Lange Reihe in the gallery Koppel 66, this vegie cafe is a refined oasis (with a summer garden). The menu could be an ad for the fertile fields of northern Germany, as there are baked goods, salads, soups and much more made with fresh seasonal ingredients.

Drinking & Nightlife

No discussion of Hamburg is complete without mentioning St Pauli, home to one of Europe's most (in)famous red-light districts. Sex shops, table-dance bars and strip clubs still line its main drag, the Reeperbahn, and side streets, but prostitution has declined dramatically, being concentrated mainly on gated Herbertstrasse (no women or under-18s allowed). St Pauli is Hamburg's main nightlife district, drawing people of all ages and walks of life to live-music and dance clubs, chic bars and theatres.

WORTH A TRIP

LÜBECK

Compact and charming Lübeck makes for a great day trip from Hamburg. Looking like a pair of witches' hats, the pointed towers of its landmark **Holstentor** (Holsten Gate) form the gateway to its historic centre that sits on an island embraced by the arms of the Trave River. The Unesco-recognised web of cobbled lanes flanked by gabled merchants' homes and spired churches is an enduring reminder of Lübeck's role as the one-time capital of the medieval Hanseatic League trading power. Today the city enjoys fame as Germany's marzipan capital.

Regional train services connect to Hamburg twice every hour (€14, 45 minutes).

★ Indra Club   CLUB

(www.indramusikclub.com; 64 Grosse Freiheit; ⊙9pm-late Wed-Sun; ⓡReeperbahn) The Beatles' small first venue is open again and has live acts many nights. The interior is vastly different from the 1960s and there is a fine beer garden.

★ Katze   COCKTAIL BAR

(☑040-5577 5910; Schulterblatt 88; ⊙1pm-3am Mon-Sat, to midnight Sun; ⓢSternschanze) Small and sleek, this 'kitty' (*Katze* = cat) gets the crowd purring for well-priced cocktails (best caipirinhas in town) and great music (there's dancing on weekends). It's one of the most popular among the watering holes along this main Schanzenviertel booze strip.

Uebel und Gefährlich   CLUB

(☑040-3179 3610; www.uebelundgefaehrlich.com; Feldstrasse 66; ⓢFeldstrasse) DJ sets, live music and parties rock this soundproof WWII bunker. Doors open around 7pm weekdays but as late as midnight on Friday and Saturday.

ⓘ Information

Tourist Information Hauptbahnhof (☑040-3005 1701; www.hamburg-travel.com; Hauptbahnhof, near Kirchenallee exit; ⊙9am-7pm Mon-Sat, 10am-6pm Sun; ⓢHauptbahnhof, ⓡHauptbahnhof) Busy all the time.

ⓘ Getting There & Around

The central bus station (ZOB) is southeast of the Hauptbahnhof. Frequent trains serve regional and long-distance destinations.

For local public transport information, go to www.hvv.de. Most trips require a Zone A ticket.

Bremen

POP 546,450

This little city is big on charm, from the statue of Grimm's *Musicians of Bremen* to a stunning expressionist laneway and impressive town hall. On top of that, the Weser riverside promenade is a relaxing bistro-and-beer-garden–lined refuge, while the lively student district ('Das Viertel') along Ostertorsteinweg teems with indie boutiques, cafes, art-house cinemas and alternative cultural venues.

⊙ Sights

Böttcherstrasse   STREET

(www.boettcherstrasse.de) The charming medieval coopers' lane was transformed into a prime example of mostly expressionist architecture in the 1920s at the instigation of coffee merchant Ludwig Roselius. Its red-brick houses sport unique facades, whimsical fountains, statues and a carillon; many house artesanal shops and art museums. Its most striking feature is Bernhard Hoetger's golden **Lichtbringer** (Bringer of Light) relief that keeps an eye on the north entrance.

★ Beck's Brewery
Factory Tour   BREWERY

(☑0421-5094 5555; www.becks.de/besucherzentrum; Am Deich 18/19; tours €12.90; ⊙tours 1pm, 3pm & 4.30pm Mon-Wed, 10am, 11.30am, 1pm, 3pm, 4.30pm & 6pm Thu-Sat; ⓐ1, 2, 3 to Am Brill) Two-hour tours of one of Germany's most internationally famous breweries must be booked online. The 3pm tour is also in English. Minimum age 16. Meet at the brewery's visitor centre.

🛏 Sleeping & Eating

Townside Hostel Bremen   HOSTEL €

(☑0421-780 15; www.townside.de; Am Dobben 62; dm from €15, s/d from €32/46; ⓟ�{🖥}; ⓐ2, 3, 10 to Sielwall) This bright, professionally run hostel is right in the middle of Bremen's nightlife quarter and handy to Werder Bremen's stadium. Breakfast costs €5.50. Take tram 10 from Hauptbahnhof to Humboldtstrasse or tram 2 or 3 to Sielwall.

Engel Weincafe CAFE €
(☎0421-6964 2390; www.engelweincafe-bremen.de; Ostertorsteinweg 31; dishes €4.50-15.60; ☻9am-1am Mon-Fri, from 10am Sat & Sun; ☜☒; ☐2, 6 to Wulwesstrasse) Exuding the nostalgic vibe of a former pharmacy, this popular hang-out gets a good crowd no matter where the hand is on the clock. Come for breakfast, a hot lunch special, crispy *Flammekuche* (French pizza), carpaccio or pasta, or just some cheese and a glass of wine.

🍷 Drinking & Nightlife

★**Lila Eule** LIVE MUSIC
(www.lilaeule.de; Bernhardstrasse 10; ☻from 8pm; ☐2, 6 to Wulwesstrasse) A decade or more is a long time to be a hot tip, but this gem off Sielwall has pulled it off. A student crowd gathers here for parties and events, but it's also a very alternative place to watch the Werder Bremen football team; most Werder matches are shown here. Thursday night is the legendary student bash.

❶ Information

Hauptbahnhof Tourist Office (☎0421-308 0010; www.bremen-tourism.de; Hauptbahnhof; ☻9am-6.30pm Mon-Fri, 9.30am-5pm Sat & Sun; ☜) Handily located at the main train station.

❶ Getting There & Away

Long-distance services depart from and arrive at the central bus station (ZOB) on Breitenweg in front of the Hauptbahnhof. Frequent trains leave for Hamburg several times hourly (from €23, one hour).

Germany Survival Guide

❶ Directory A–Z

ACCOMMODATION

Reservations are a good idea, especially between June and September and around major holidays, festivals, trade shows and events.

LGBT TRAVELLERS

Germany is a magnet for *schwule* (gay) and *lesbische* (lesbian) travellers, with the rainbow flag flying especially proudly in Berlin and Cologne, and with sizeable communities in Hamburg, Frankfurt and Munich.

MONEY

ATMs are widely available in cities and towns but rarely in villages. Cash is king almost everywhere; credit cards are not widely accepted.

Restaurant bills include a *Bedienung* (service charge), but most people add 5% or 10%, unless service was awful.

OPENING HOURS

Typical opening hours may vary seasonally and between cities and villages.

Bars 6pm to 1am

Cafes 8am to 8pm

Clubs 11pm to early morning hours

Malls and supermarkets 9.30am to 8pm Monday to Saturday

Restaurants 11am to 11pm (food service often stops at 9pm in rural areas)

PUBLIC HOLIDAYS

Neujahrstag (New Year's Day) 1 January

Ostern (Easter) March/April; Good Friday, Easter Sunday and Easter Monday

Christi Himmelfahrt (Ascension Day) Forty days after Easter

Maifeiertag/Tag der Arbeit (Labour Day) 1 May

Pfingsten (Whit/Pentecost Sunday & Monday) Fifty days after Easter

Tag der Deutschen Einheit (Day of German Unity) 3 October

Weihnachten (Christmas) 25 & 26 December

❶ Getting There & Around

AIR

Frankfurt and Munich are the main gateways for transcontinental flights, but Hamburg, Düsseldorf and Berlin also get a good share of the traffic. Budget airlines also hit numerous regional airports.

---

❶ PRICE RANGES

Sleeping price ranges refer to the cost of a double room with private bathroom:

€ less than €80

€€ €80–160

€€€ more than €160

Eating price ranges are for the cost of a main course:

€ less than €8

€€ €8–18

€€€ more than €18

BUS

Exploring Germany by coach easy, inexpensive and popular. Buses are modern, clean, comfortable and air-conditioned. Flixbus (www.flixbus.com) is the dominant company for domestic and European services.

FERRY

Germany's main ferry ports with services running to Scandinavia and the Baltic are Kiel and Travemünde (near Lübeck) and Rostock and Sassnitz (on Rügen Island). Check www.ferrysavers.com or www.directferries.com for details.

TRAIN

➜ Most train services are run by Deutsche Bahn (DB; www.bahn.com) with a number of routes operated by private companies but integrated into the DB network as far as ticketing and timetables.

➜ Of the several train types, ICE trains are the fastest and most comfortable. IC trains (EC if they cross borders) are almost as fast but older. Regional Express (RE) and Regionalbahn (RB) trains are regional. S-Bahn are suburban trains operating in large cities and conurbations.

➜ Buy tickets online (www.bahn.com) or at stations from vending machines or a *Reisezentrum* (ticket office).

➜ Eurail and Interrail passes are valid on all trains.

BELGIUM

Brussels

POP 1.2 MILLION

Belgium's fascinating capital, and the administrative capital of the EU, Brussels is historic yet hip, bureaucratic yet bizarre, self-confident yet unshowy, and multicultural to its roots. All this plays out in a cityscape that swings from majestic to quirky to rundown and back again. Organic art nouveau facades face off against 1960s concrete developments, and regal 19th-century mansions contrast with the brutal glass of the EU's Gotham City. This whole maelstrom swirls out from Brussels' medieval core, where the Grand Place is surely one of the world's most beautiful squares.

One constant is the enviable quality of everyday life, with a cafe and bar scene that never gets old.

⊙ Sights

Grand Place   SQUARE
(Ⓜ Gare Centrale) Brussels' magnificent Grand Place is one of the world's most unforgettable urban ensembles. Oddly hidden, the enclosed cobblestone square is only revealed as you enter on foot from one of six narrow side alleys: Rue des Harengs is the best first approach. The focal point is the spired 15th-century city hall, but each of the antique guildhalls (mostly 1697–1705) has a charm of its own. Most are unashamed exhibitionists, with fine baroque gables, gilded statues and elaborate guild symbols.

★ Église Notre-Dame du Sablon   CHURCH
(Rue de la Régence; ⊙ 9am-6.30pm Mon-Fri, 10am-6.30pm Sat & Sun; Ⓜ Porte de Namur) The Sablon's large, flamboyantly Gothic church started life as the 1304 archers' guild chapel. A century later it had to be massively enlarged to cope with droves of pilgrims attracted by the supposed healing powers of its Madonna statue. The statue was procured in 1348 by means of an audacious theft from an Antwerp church – apparently by a vision-motivated husband-and-wife team in a rowing boat. It has long since gone, but a boat behind the pulpit commemorates the curious affair.

Manneken Pis   MONUMENT
(cnr Rue de l'Étuve & Rue du Chêne; Ⓜ Gare Centrale) Rue Charles Buls – Brussels' most unashamedly touristy shopping street, lined with chocolate and trinket shops – leads the hordes three blocks from the Grand Place to the Manneken Pis. This fountain-statue of a little boy taking a leak is comically tiny and a perversely perfect national symbol for surreal Belgium. Most of the time the statue's nakedness is hidden beneath a costume relevant to an anniversary, national day or local event: his ever-growing wardrobe is partly displayed at the **Maison du Roi** (Musée de la Ville de Bruxelles; Grand Place; Ⓜ Gare Centrale).

Musées Royaux des Beaux-Arts   GALLERY
(Royal Museums of Fine Arts; ☎ 02-508 32 11; www.fine-arts-museum.be; Rue de la Régence 3; adult/6-25yr/BrusselsCard €8/2/free, with Magritte Museum €13; ⊙ 10am-5pm Tue-Fri, 11am-6pm Sat &

Sun; Ⓜ Gare Centrale, Parc) This prestigious museum incorporates the Musée d'Art Ancien (ancient art); the Musée d'Art Moderne (modern art), with works by surrealist Paul Delvaux and fauvist Rik Wouters; and the purpose-built Musée Magritte. The 15th-century Flemish Primitives are wonderfully represented in the Musée d'Art Ancien: there's Rogier Van der Weyden's *Pietà* with its hallucinatory sky, Hans Memling's refined portraits, and the richly textured *Madonna With Saints* by the Master of the Legend of St Lucy.

Musée Magritte   MUSEUM

(Ⓙ 02-508 32 11; www.musee-magritte-museum.be; Rue de la Régence 3; adult/under 26yr/BrusselsCard €8/2/free; ⊙ 10am-5pm Tue-Fri, 11am-6pm Sat & Sun; Ⓜ Gare Centrale, Parc) The beautifully presented Magritte Museum holds the world's largest collection of the surrealist pioneer's paintings and drawings. Watch his style develop from colourful Braque-style cubism in 1920 through a Dali-esque phase and a late-1940s period of Kandinsky-like brushwork to his trademark bowler hats of the 1960s. Regular screenings of a 50-minute documentary provide insights into the artist's unconventional conventional life.

Atomium   MONUMENT

(Ⓙ 02-475 47 75; www.atomium.be; Av de l'Atomium; adult/teen/child €15/8/free; ⊙ 10am-6pm; Ⓜ Heysel, ⊟ 51) The space-age Atomium looms 102m over north Brussels' suburbia, resembling a steel alien from a '60s Hollywood movie. It consists of nine house-sized metallic balls linked by steel tube-columns containing escalators and lifts. The balls are arranged like a school chemistry set to represent iron atoms in their crystal lattice... except these are 165 billion times bigger. It was built as a symbol of postwar progress for the 1958 World's Fair and became an architectural icon, receiving a makeover in 2006.

🛏 Sleeping

★ Captaincy Guesthouse   HOSTEL €

(Ⓙ 0496 59 93 79; www.thecaptaincybrussels.be; Quai à la Chaux 8; dm €34-50, d €90; Ⓜ Ste-Catherine) This is an idiosyncratic, warmly friendly venture, housed in a 17th-century mansion with a hip Ste-Catherine location and a mix of dorms (some mixed sex) and rooms. A generous €7.50 breakfast is served in the spacious living area. The wooden attic housing an en-suite four-bed female dorm has a fabulous boutique-hotel feel, and the attic double is a winner too.

HI Hostel
John Bruegel   HOSTEL €

(Ⓙ 02-511 04 36; www.jeugdherbergen.be/en/brussels; Rue du St-Esprit 2; dm/tw adult €23.90/64, youth €21.60/60; ⊙ lockout 10am-2pm, curfew 1am-7am; ⊛@🛜; Ⓜ Louise) Superbly central but somewhat institutional with limited communal space. The attic singles are a cut above singles at other hostels. Internet costs €2 per hour, and lockers €1.50. There's a 10% discount for HI members. Free wi-fi.

DON'T MISS

WATERLOO

Tourists have been swarming to Waterloo ever since Napoleon's 1815 defeat, a seminal event in European history.

Inaugurated for the 2015 bicentenary, **Memorial 1815** (Ⓙ 02-385 19 12; www.waterloo1815.be; Rte du Lion, Hameau du Lion; adult/child €16/13, with Wellington & Napoleon headquarters museums €20/16; ⊙ 9.30am-6.30pm Apr-Sep, to 5.30pm Oct-Mar) is a showpiece underground museum and visitor centre at the main battlefield site known as Hameau du Lion (Lion Hamlet). There's a detailed audioguide and some enjoyable technological effects, as well as an impressive 3D film that sticks you right into the middle of the cavalry charges. Tickets include admission to various other battlefield attractions, including **Butte du Lion**, a memorial hill from which you can survey the terrain, and the restored **Hougoumont** farmhouse that played a key part in the battle.

TEC bus W runs every 30 minutes from Ave Fonsny at Brussels-Midi to Braine-l'Alleud train station, passing through Waterloo town and stopping near Hameau du Lion (€3.20). The tourist office in Waterloo town rents bicycles.

NETHERLANDS, BELGIUM & LUXEMBOURG AT A GLANCE

Don't Miss

Amsterdam The Dutch capital is a watery wonderland. Amsterdam made its fortune in maritime trade, and its Canal Ring was constructed during the city's Golden Age. Stroll alongside the canals and check out the narrow, gabled houses and thousands of houseboats; relax on a canal-side café (pub) terrace; or, better still, go for a ride.

Brussels The Belgian capital's heart beats in the Grand Place – the most theatrically beautiful medieval square in Europe. It is ringed by gold-trimmed, gabled guildhouses and flanked by the 15th-century Gothic town hall.

Luxembourg City No it's not just banks and Eurocrats. Wealthy Luxembourg City is one of Europe's most underestimated capitals, with a fine range of museums and galleries and a brilliant dining scene. But most impressive is the town centre's spectacular setting, straddling a deep-cut river gorge whose defences were the settlement's original raison d'être.

Rotterdam The world's best architects compete here for commissions that result in eye-popping, one-of-a-kind designs, such as a 'vertical city', a forest of cube houses, a pencil-shaped residential tower and an ethereal 'cloud-like' building housing the city's history museum.

Bruges Laced with canals and full of evocative step-gabled houses, Bruges is the ultimate picture-postcard tourist destination. The Groeningemuseum is hard to beat, offering a potted history of Belgian art, with an outstanding selection of works by the Flemish Primitives.

Itineraries

One Week

Start your trip in lively **Amsterdam**. Visit the big museums, relax in Vondelpark, discover the foodie De Pijp neighbourhood and hang out with the locals at a brown café. Drop by **Delft**, Vermeer's charming hometown, before plunging on to hip and happening **Rotterdam**, with its fab street art, edgy architecture and lively party scene. Continue south into Belgium where your first stop should be cosmopolitan **Antwerp**, which is not only the home town of baroque painter Pieter Paul Rubens but also has great fashion, party and art scenes.

Two Weeks

Antwerp is a great warm-up for **Brussels**, home to one of the world's most beautiful squares, seductive chocolate shops, wonderful cafes, great galleries, fine museums and art nouveau buildings. From here turn west to magical **Ghent**, whose intimate medieval core is complemented by a lively student vibe and some wonderful museums. A hop, skip and jump away, **Bruges** is considered one of Europe's most romantic getaways thanks to its medieval architecture and endless canalside charm. Wrap up your sojourn by pondering the heartbreaking futility of WWI in **Flanders'** fields and meticulously rebuilt **Ypres**.

Essential Food & Drink

Vlaamse frites Fries made from whole potatoes and smothered in mayonnaise, ketchup, curry sauce, garlic sauce or other gloppy toppings.

Kroketten Croquettes – crumbed, deep-fried dough balls with various fillings.

Mosselen/moules Steaming cauldrons of in-the-shell mussels, typically cooked in white wine and served with a mountain of *frites* (fries).

Judd mat gaardebounen Luxembourg's national dish: smoked pork neck in a thick, cream-based sauce with chunks of potato and broad beans.

Chicon au gratin Belgian endive rolled in ham and cooked in a cheese/béchamel sauce.

Rijstafel (rice table) Indonesian import features an array of spicy and savoury dishes such as braised beef, pork satay and ribs; served with rice.

Getting Around

Train A comprehensive network means that service is fast, distances are short and trains are frequent.

Car An easy option good for visiting regions with minimal public transport. In cities, however, cars can be encumbrance and parking expensive. Drive on the right.

Bus Cheaper and slower than trains but useful for remote villages that aren't serviced by trains.

Bicycle Short- and long-distance bike routes lace the region. All but the smallest train stations have bike-rental shops, as do most towns and all cities.

When to Go
Amsterdam

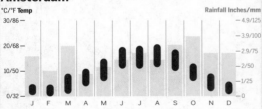

Jun–Aug Everything is open, the weather is balmy, crowds and prices peak - book ahead.

Apr & May, Sep & Oct Most sights open, few crowds, moderate prices, weather can be wet and cold.

Nov–Mar Many sights outside major cities close, no crowds, weather is chilly and/or snowy, deals abound.

Arriving in Benelux

Schiphol International Airport (Amsterdam) Trains from the airport serve many destinations around the country, often directly, including Amsterdam Centraal Station (€4.10; every 10 minutes or so from 6am to 12.30am). A taxi to central Amsterdam costs approximately €47.

Brussels Airport Several trains an hour run to central Brussels (€8.50, 20 minutes) and two to Leuven (€8.80, 15 minutes).

Luxembourg Airport Luxembourg's international airport. Flights mostly limited to European hops. EasyJet links to/from London Gatwick.

Top Phrases

Hello. Dag./Bonjour.

Goodbye. Dag./Au revoir.

Please. Alstublieft./S'il vous plaît.

Thank you. Dank u./Merci.

Yes/No. Jan./Nee. & Oui./Non.

Resources

Netherlands Tourism Board (www.holland.com)

Visit Wallonia (www.belgiumtheplaceto.be)

Visit Luxembourg (www.visitluxembourg.com)

Set Your Budget

➡ Dorm bed including breakfast: €20–35

➡ Daily meal special: €9–14

➡ Train ticket: €10

➡ Short-hop city bike hire: €2

Central Brussels

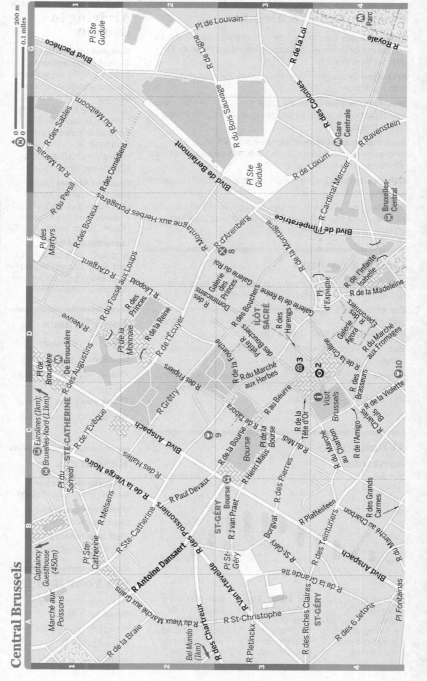

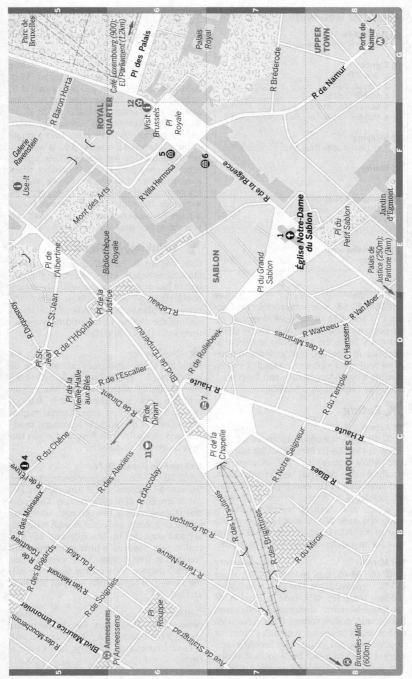

5

6

7

8

A

B

C

D

E

F

G

Parc de
Bruxelles

Pl des Palais

Palais
Royal

UPPER
TOWN

Porte de
Namur

R Baron Horta

R Bréderode

R de Namur

Café Luxembourg (900);
EU Parliament (1.2km)

ROYAL
QUARTER

12

Visit
Brussels

Pl
Royale

Galerie
Ravenstein

Use-It

5

6

R de la Régence

Jardin
d'Egmont

Mont des Arts

R Villa Hermosa

Pl du
Petit Sablon

Église Notre-Dame
du Sablon

1

Pl de
l'Albertine

Bibliothèque
Royale

SABLON

Pl du Grand
Sablon

Palais de
Justice (250m);
Pantone (1km)

R St-Jean

R Dubbing

Pl de la
Justice

R Lebeau

R Van Moer

R de l'Hôpital

R des Minimes

R Watteeu

R C Hanssens

Pl St-
Jean

Blvd de l'Empereur

R de Rollebeek

R du Temple

R de l'Escalier

R Haute

Pl de la
Vieille Halle
aux Blés

R de Dinant

7

Pl de
Dinant

R Haute

MAROLLES

R du Chêne

Pl de la
Chapelle

R Notre Seigneur

R Blaes

4

R de l'Étuve

11

R des Alexiens

R d'Accolay

R des Ursulines

R du Miroir

R des Moineaux

R du Poingon

R des Brigittines

R de
Bogards

R van Helmont

R du Midi

R Terre-Neuve

l'Goutière

R de Soignies

R des Moucherons

Blvd Maurice Lemonnier

Anneessens

Pl
Anneessens

Pl
Rouppe

Ave de Stalingrad

Bruxelles-Midi
(600m)

Central Brussels

★**Pantone**   HOTEL €€
(☎02-541 48 98; www.pantonehotel.com; Place Loix 1; d from €59; Ⓜ Hotel des Monnaies) An eye-popping array of Pantone colours greets you here, from the turquoise pushbike at reception to moulded-plastic chairs to lime-green bedrooms – all with refreshing swaths of white too. Modern, stylish and functional, as well as surprisingly affordable.

🍴 Eating

★**Arcadi**   BRASSERIE €
(☎02-511 33 43; Rue d'Arenberg 1b; mains €10-15; ⊗8am-11.45pm Tue-Fri, from 7.30am Sat, from 9am Sun; Ⓜ Gare Centrale) The jars of preserves, beautiful cakes and fruit tarts of this classic and charming bistro entice plenty of Brussels residents, as do well-priced meals such as lasagne and steak, all served nonstop by courteous staff. With a nice location on the edge of the Galeries St-Hubert, this is a great spot for an indulgent, creamy hot chocolate.

Bel Mundo   BRASSERIE €
(☎02-669 08 45; Quai du Hainaut 41-43; mains €10-15; ⊗noon-2.30pm Mon-Wed, noon-2.30pm & 6-9pm Thu & Fri; ☒51/Porte de Flandre) 🌿 As Brussels' most sustainable restaurant, Bel Mundo makes scrumptious, affordable dishes using seasonal vegetables from its organic backyard garden and unsold supermarket items in a bid for zero food waste. The furniture is made of recycled pallets, crafted in the carpentry workshop, and the friendly staff were previously unemployed long term. Expect soups, seasonal salads and pasta dishes.

Cafe Luxembourg   CAFE €
(☎02-721 57 15; www.cafeluxembourg.be; Place du Luxembourg 10; lunch €10-15, brunch €14-17; ⊗8am-1am Mon & Tue, 8am-3am Wed-Fri, 10am-3am Sat, 11am-midnight Sun; ☒12, 21, 22, 27, 34, 38, 64, 80, 95/Luxembourg) Among a leather and copper interior, this cafe offers a range of quinoa-based superbowls and other market-fresh nibbles for lunch. Their terrace gets seriously packed on Thursdays when loose-tied Eurocrats sip after-work Wasatinis (vodka with wasabi) and craft beers. On weekends, the wallet-friendly brunch boasts a killer banana-raspberry French toast, velvety scrambled eggs and fresh pressed juices.

🍷 Drinking & Nightlife

Cafe culture is one of Brussels' greatest attractions.Nearly every street in the city centre has at least one marvellously atmospheric cafe. Styles vary from showy art-nouveau places and medieval survivors around the Bourse to hip and heaving options in St-Géry and Ixelles.

★**Goupil le Fol**   BAR
(☎02-511 13 96; www.goupillefol.com; Rue de la Violette 22; ⊗4pm-2am; Ⓜ Gare Centrale) Overwhelming weirdness hits you as you acid-trip your way through this sensory overload of rambling passageways, ragged old sofas and inexplicable beverages mostly based on madly fruit-flavoured wines (no beer is served). Unmissable.

La Fleur en Papier Doré   CAFE
(☎02-511 16 59; www.goudblommekeinpapier.be; Rue des Alexiens 53; ⊗11am-midnight Tue-Sat, to 7pm Sun; ☒Bruxelles Central) The nicotine-stained walls of this tiny cafe, adored by artists and locals, are covered with writings, art and scribbles by Magritte and his surrealist pals, some of which were reputedly traded for free drinks. 'Ceci n'est pas un musée', quips a sign on the door reminding visitors to buy a drink and not just look around.

Celtica   BAR
(www.celticpubs.com/celtica; Rue de Marché aux Poulets 55; ☒Bourse) Lewd, loud, central and – most importantly – cheap: just €1 for a beer.

ℹ️ Information

Use-It (☑️ 02-218 39 06; www.brussels.use-it. travel; Galerie Ravenstein 17; ⊘10am-6pm Mon-Sat; 🛜; Ⓜ Gare Central) A meeting place for young travellers, with free coffee and tea and a list of live-music events written up by the door. It does a free alternative city tour at 2pm on Monday, with an emphasis on social history and nightlife. The printed material is first rate, with a quirky city map, a guide for wheelchair users and a beer pamphlet.

Visit Brussels (☑️ 02-513 89 40; www.visit. brussels; Hôtel de Ville, Grand Place; ⊘9am-6pm; 🖼️ Bourse) Visit Brussels has stacks of city-specific information as well as handy fold-out guides (independently researched) to the best shops, restaurants and pubs in town. The Rue Royale (☑️ 02-513 89 40; www.visit.brussels; Rue Royale 2; ⊘9am-6pm Mon-Fri, from 10am Sat & Sun; Ⓜ Parc) office is much less crowded than the Grand Place one. Here you'll also find the Arsène50 (www.arsene50.be; ⊘12.30pm-5pm; Ⓜ Parc) desk, which provides great discounts for cultural events.

ℹ️ Getting There & Away

Eurolines operates bus services to London, Amsterdam, Paris and other international destinations from Bruxelles-Nord.

Bruxelles-Midi is the main station for international rail connections: the Eurostar, TGV and Thalys high-speed trains (with prebooking compulsory) only stop here. Most other mainline trains stop in quick succession at Bruxelles-Midi, Bruxelles-Central and, except for Amsterdam trains, also at Bruxelles-Nord.

ℹ️ Getting Around

Brussels' bus, tram and metro system is run by STIB/MIVB (www.stib.de) and operates from about 6am to midnight. On Friday and Saturday, Noctis night buses run on 17 routes twice hourly from midnight to 3am, most starting from Place de Brouckère.

Antwerp

POP 503,200

Belgium's second city and biggest port, Antwerp (Antwerpen/Anvers in Dutch/French) is the country's capital of cool and magnet for fashion moguls, clubbers, art lovers and diamond dealers. The home of 16th-century baroque superstar painter Pieter Paul Rubens, it retains an intriguing medieval heart with cafe-filled cobbled lanes, a riverside fortress and a truly impressive cathedral.

BEER, BARS & STUDENTS: LEUVEN

Lively Leuven (Louvain in French), some 25km east of Brussels, is synonymous with beers, bars and students. More than half of the population (nearly 55,000) is enrolled in KU Leuven, the largest and oldest university in the Low Countries. Leuven is the home base of Stella Artois (www.breweryvisits.com; Aarschotsesteenweg 22; adult/concession €8.50/7.50; ⊘9am-9pm Tue-Sat), which runs brewery tours. If you prefer to sample the suds, head to the picturesque town centre. Oude Markt in particular is wall-to-wall with cafe-bars that buzz until the wee hours. To keep your brain in balance, pick up cheap Asian food, pizza and snacks, on pedestrianised Parijsstraat, Tiensestraat or Naamsestraat.

Leuven's train station is about 800m east of the centre and served by trains from Brussels five times hourly (€5.30, 30 minutes).

⊙ Sights

★ Grote Markt   SQUARE

As with every great Flemish city, Antwerp's medieval heart is a classic Grote Markt (Market Sq). Here the triangular, pedestrianised space features the voluptuous, baroque Brabo Fountain depicting Antwerp's giant-killing, hand-throwing legend. Flanked on two sides by very photogenic guildhalls, the square is dominated by an impressive Italo-Flemish Renaissance-style stadhuis (Town Hall), completed in 1565.

★ Onze-Lieve-Vrouwekathedraal   CATHEDRAL

(☑️ 03-213 99 51; www.dekathedraal.be; Handschoenmarkt; adult/reduced €6/4; ⊘10am-5pm Mon-Fri, to 3pm Sat, 1-4pm Sun) Belgium's finest Gothic cathedral was 169 years in the making (1352–1521). Wherever you wander in Antwerp, its gracious, 123m-high spire has a habit of popping unexpectedly into view and it rarely fails to prompt a gasp of awe. The sight is particularly well framed when looking up Pelgrimstraat in the afternoon light.

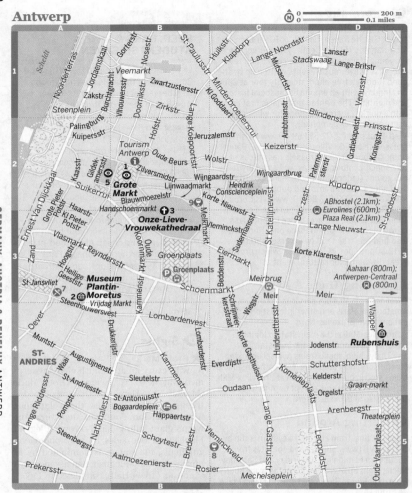

★**Rubenshuis** MUSEUM
(📞03-201 15 55; www.rubenshuis.be; Wapper 9-11; adult/concession €8/6, audioguide €3; ⊙10am-5pm Tue-Sun) The 1611 building was built as home and studio by celebrated painter Pieter Paul Rubens. Rescued from ruins in 1937, and extensively and sensitively restored, the building is a delightfully indulgent one, with baroque portico, rear facade and exquisite formal garden. The furniture all dates from Rubens' era, although it's not part of the original decor. Fourteen Rubens canvases are displayed, along with some wonderful period ephem-

era, such as the metal frame of a ruff collar and a linen press.

★**Museum Plantin-Moretus** HISTORIC BUILDING
(📞03-221 14 50; www.museumplantinmoretus.be; Vrijdag Markt 22; adult/reduced/child €8/6/free; ⊙10am-5pm Tue-Sun) Giving a museum Unesco World Heritage status might seem odd – until you've seen this astonishing, recently renovated place. Once home to the world's first industrial printing works, it's been a museum since 1876. The medieval building and 1622 courtyard garden alone would be

Antwerp

worth a visit, but the world's oldest printing press, priceless manuscripts and original type sets make for a giddy experience indeed. Other highlights include the 1640 library, a bookshop dating from 1700 and rooms lined with gilt leather.

🛏 Sleeping

ABhostel HOSTEL €
(☎0473 57 01 66; www.abhostel.com; Kattenberg 110; dm/tw €20/47; ☺reception noon-3pm & 6-8pm; 🕾; 🚊10, 24 to Drink) This adorable, brightly decorated and family-run hostel has lots of little added extras. Its Borgerhout setting is 20 minutes' walk east of Antwerpen-Centraal station. Across the street is the brilliantly unpretentious local pub **Plaza Real** (www.plazareal.be; Kattenberg 89; ☺from 8pm Wed-Sun; 🚊10, 24 to Drink), owned by a member of Antwerp band dEUS, and there are lots of cheap ethnic eats nearby too.

Pulcinella HOSTEL €
(☎03-234 03 14; www.jeugdherbergen.be; Bogaardeplein 1; dm €29, tw €64; @🕾) This giant, tailor-made HI hostel is hard to beat for its Fashion District location and cool modernist decor. It's a little cheaper for HI members and under-30s; breakfast is included.

🍴 Eating

Cheap dining is the thing north and east of Antwerpen-Centraal station: on the decidedly unglamorous Van Arteveldestraat alone you'll find African, Himalayan, Filipino, Thai and Indian cafes all within a block.

LOA INTERNATIONAL, FAST FOOD €
(☎03-291 64 85; www.loa.be; Hoogstraat 77; dishes €8-12; ☺noon-10pm Mon, Wed & Thu, to 11pm Fri & Sat, to 10pm Sun) International 'street food' – *pad thai,* Moroccan pancakes, tortillas, croquettes – are made with love and care in this bright cafe. There's complimentary mint tea to sip with your meal and front-row seats onto the square.

Aahaar INDIAN, VEGAN €
(www.aahaar.com; Lange Herentalsestraat 23; buffet €10; ☺noon-3pm & 5.30-9.30pm Mon-Fri, 1-9.30pm Sat & Sun; 🥄) An unpretentious little place that's well known for its vegan and vegetarian Jain-Indian food. No menu, just an eat-all-you-like buffet with five mains, two sweets and rice.

🍷 Drinking & Nightlife

To sound like a local, stride into a pub and ask for a *bolleke*. It means a 'little bowl' (ie glass) of De Koninck, the city's favourite ale.

Bierhuis Kulminator PUB
(☎03-232 45 38; Vleminckveld 32; ☺4pm-11.30pm Tue-Sat, from 8pm Mon) A classic beer pub boasting 800 mostly Belgian brews, including notably rare 'vintage' bottles laid down to mature for several years like fine wine.

Pelikaan BROWN CAFE
(Melkmarkt 14; ☺9am-1am Mon-Thu, to 3am Fri, 10am-3am Sat, to midnight Sun) A lively, inexpensive brown *café* (pub) with summer street-seating spilling out towards the cathedral.

ℹ Information

Tourism Antwerp (☎03-232 01 03; www.visitantwerpen.be; Grote Markt 13; ☺10am-5pm) Tourism Antwerp has a large, central office with helpful staff – pick up maps, buy tram/bus passes and book tickets here. There is also a booth on the ground floor of Antwerpen-Centraal station.

ℹ Getting There & Away

Eurolines (☎03-233 86 62; www.eurolines.com; Van Stralenstraat 8; ☺9am-6pm Mon-Fri, to 3.30pm Sat) buses start from near its office.

From gorgeous **Antwerpen-Centraal** (Koningin Astridplein 27) station, high-speed Fyra and Thalys trains head to Amsterdam via Rotterdam and Schiphol Airport. To reach the Netherlands without reservations or high-speed supplements, take the hourly local service to Rosendaal, then change.

Ghent

POP 247,500

Ghent (Gent in Dutch, Gand in French) is one of Europe's great discoveries – small enough to feel cosy but big enough to stay vibrant. It has enough medieval frivolity to create a spectacle, but retains a gritty industrial edge that keeps things 'real'. Tourists remain surprisingly thin on the ground, yet with its fabulous canalside architecture, wealth of quirky bars and some of Belgium's most fascinating museums, this is a city you really won't want to miss.

⊙ Sights

Ghent's magnificent medieval core comprises three interconnected squares, dominated by the towers and spires of the Belfort and two imposing, if dour, churches. Directly west, the canal is lined with medieval-styled buildings curving around to the pretty Patershol district.

★ Patershol   AREA

Dotted with half-hidden restaurants, enchanting Patershol is a web of twisting cobbled lanes whose old-world houses were once home to leather tradesmen and to the

Ghent Centre

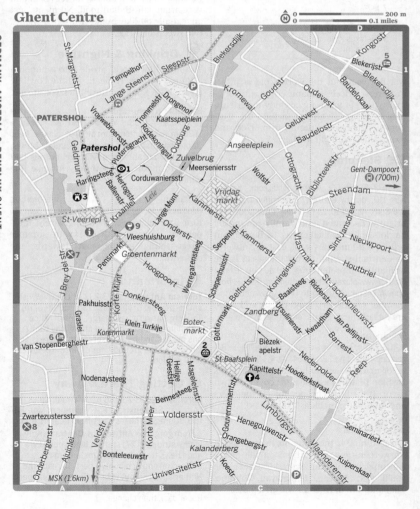

Carmelite Fathers (Paters), hence the name. An aimless wander here is one of the city's great pleasures; the low-key restaurants and bars make it a popular hang-out for students.

St-Baafskathedraal
CATHEDRAL

(www.sintbaafskathedraal.be; St-Baafsplein; ☉8.30am-6pm Mon-Sat, 10am-6pm Sun Apr-Oct, to 5pm Nov-Mar) St-Baafs cathedral's towering interior has some fine stained glass and an unusual combination of brick vaulting with stone tracery. A €0.20 leaflet guides you round the cathedral's numerous art treasures, including a big original Rubens opposite the stairway that leads down into the partly muralled crypts. However, most visitors come to see just one magnificent work – the Van Eycks' 1432 Flemish Primitive masterpiece, *The Adoration of the Mystic Lamb* (adult/child/audioguide €4/1.50/1).

Gravensteen
CASTLE

(www.gravensteen.stad.gent; St-Veerleplein; adult/concession/child €10/6/free; ☉10am-6pm Apr-Oct, 9am-5pm Nov-Mar) The counts of Flanders' quintessential 12th-century stone castle comes complete with moat, turrets and arrow slits. It's all the more remarkable considering that during the 19th century the site was converted into a cotton mill. Meticulously restored since, the interior sports the odd suit of armour, a guillotine and torture devices. The relative lack of furnishings is compensated by a hand-held 45-minute movie guide, which sets a tongue-in-cheek historical costumed drama in the rooms, prison pit and battlements.

If you just want a photo of the castle, there's a great viewpoint on St-Widostraat.

Belfort
HISTORIC BUILDING

(☎09-375 31 61; www.belfortgent.be; Botermarkt; adult/concession/child €8/2.70/free; ☉10am-6pm) Ghent's soaring, Unesco-listed, 14th-century belfry is topped by a large dragon. That's a weathervane not a fire breather, and it's become something of a city mascot. You'll meet two previous dragon incarnations on the climb to the top (mostly by lift), but other than some bell-making exhibits, the real attraction is the view. Enter through the Lakenhalle, Ghent's cloth hall that was left half-built in 1445 and only completed in 1903.

★MSK
GALLERY

(Museum voor Schone Kunsten; ☎09-323 67 00; www.mskgent.be; Citadelpark; adult/youth/child €8/2/free; ☉9.30am-5.30pm Tue-Fri, 10am-6pm Sat & Sun) Styled like a Greek temple, this superb 1903 fine-art gallery introduces a veritable A–Z of great Belgian and Low Countries' painters from the 14th to mid-20th centuries. Highlights include a happy family of coffins by Magritte, Luminist canvases by Emile Claus, and Pieter Breughel the Younger's 1621 *Dorpsadvocaat*, featuring a village lawyer oozing with arrogance. English-language explanation cards are available in each room.

🛏 Sleeping

★Uppelink
HOSTEL €

(☎09-279 44 77; www.hosteluppelink.com; Sint-Michielsplein 21; dm €19-35) Within a classic step-gabled canalside house, the show-stopping attraction at this super-central new hostel is the unbeatable view of Ghent's main towers from the breakfast room and from the biggest, cheapest dorms. Smaller rooms have little view, if any.

Hostel 47
HOSTEL €

(☎0478 71 28 27; www.hostel47.com; Blekerijstraat 47-51; dm €27-30, d/tr €72/€99; ☞) Unusually calm yet pretty central, this inviting hostel has revamped a high-ceilinged historic house with virginal white walls, spacious bunk rooms and designer fittings. Free lockers and cursory breakfast with Nespresso coffee; no bar.

GERMANY, AUSTRIA & BENELUX GHENT

BELGIAN BREWS

No other country has a brewing tradition as richly diverse as that of Belgium, with beers ranging from pleasant pale lagers to wild, wine-like Flemish reds and lambics. But its the 'angels and demons' that draw the connoisseurs: these big bold brews often derive from monastery recipes and conjure the diabolical with names like Forbidden Fruit, Judas and Duvel (devil). The most famous of all, six Trappist beers, are still brewed in active abbeys. With alcohol levels coming in at between 7% and 11% alcohol by volume, such brews are designed to be sipped slowly and savoured, certainly not chugged by the pint. For that, you have the standard Belgian lagers, notably Jupiler, Maes and Stella Artois – what you'll get at any *café* (pub/bar) if you just ask for a *pintje/bière* – which perhaps can't rival their German or Czech counterparts, but are deliciously drinkable none the less.

✕ Eating & Drinking

There's fast food around Korenmarkt and great-value Turkish options along Sleepstraat. Numerous vegetarian and organic choices feature on the tourist office's free *Veggieplan Gent* map.

't Oud Clooster CAFE €
(☑ 09-233 78 02; www.toudclooster.be; Zwartezusterstraat 5; mains €15-21; ☺ 11.45am-2.30pm & 6-10.30pm Mon-Fri, 11.45am-2.30pm & 5.30-10.30pm Sat, 5.30-9.30pm Sun) Mostly candle-lit at night, this atmospheric double-level 'pratcafe' is built into sections of what was long ago a nunnery, hence the sprinkling of religious statues and cherub lamp-holders. Well-priced *café* food is presented with unexpected style.

Brooderie BAKERY €
(☑ 09-225 06 23; Jan Breydelstraat 8; mains €9-16; ☺ 8.45am-6pm Wed-Sun) A rustic bakery and tearoom serving lunches, breakfasts, soups and savoury snacks. It also has simple, colourful B&B rooms with shared bathrooms (from €60).

★ 't Dreupelkot BAR
(☑ 09-224 21 20; www.dreupelkot.be; Groentenmarkt 12; ☺ 11am-1.30am Mon-Thu, to 2am Fri, 2pm-2am Sat & Sun) A traditional *jenever* bar, serving 100 Belgian concoctions – including the owner's homemade prune and raisin versions – and one north French. Traditionally *jenever* is made from grain and malt and packs a punch at 40% proof. The bare brick and tiled interior is warmly atmospheric.

ℹ Information

Ghent Tourist Office (☑ 09-266 56 60; https://visit.gent.be; Oude Vismijn, St-Veerleplein 5; ☺ 10am-6pm) Very helpful for free maps and accommodation bookings.

ℹ Getting There & Away

Eurolines buses depart from Gent-Dampoort Bus Station.

Gent-Dampoort, 1km west of the old city, is the handiest train station for such destinations as Antwerp, Bruges and Brussels.

Bruges

POP 117,000

If you set out to design a fairy-tale medieval town, it would be hard to improve on central Bruges (Brugge in Dutch). Cobbled lanes and dreamy canals link market squares lined with towers, historic churches and old whitewashed almshouses. To avoid the crush of tourists in the centre, especially in summer, stay overnight or visit midweek.

◉ Sights

Brugge is an ambler's dream, its sights sprinkled within leisurely walking distance around its compact centre. The train station sits about 1.5km south of the central square (Markt); buses shuttle regularly between the two, but it's a lovely walk via Minnewater.

Belfort HISTORIC BUILDING
(Belfry; adult/child €12/10; ☺ 9.30am-6pm) Towering 83m above the square like a gigantic medieval rocket is the fabulous 13th-century belfort. There's relatively little to see inside, but it's worth the mildly claustrophobic 366-step climb for the fine views. Look out through wide-gauge chicken wire for panoramas across the spires and red-tiled rooftops towards the wind turbines and giant cranes of Zeebrugge. Visitor numbers are limited to 70 at once, which can cause queues at peak times.

Bruges

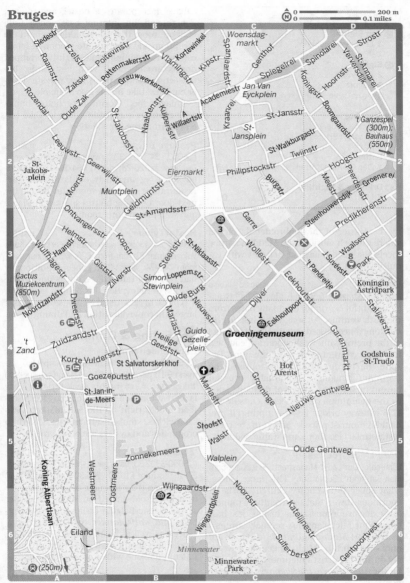

★ **Groeningemuseum**　　　GALLERY
(☎ 050-44 87 11; www.museabrugge.be; Dijver 12; adult/concession €12/10; ⊙ 9.30am-5pm Tue-Sun) Bruges' most celebrated art gallery boasts an astonishingly rich collection whose strengths are in superb Flemish Primitive and Renaissance works, depicting the conspicuous wealth of the city with glitteringly realistic artistry. In room 2 are meditative works including Jan Van Eyck's 1436 radiant masterpiece *Madonna with Canon George Van der Paele* (1436) and the *Madonna*

GERMANY, AUSTRIA & BENELUX BRUGES

by the Master of the Embroidered Foliage, where the rich fabric of the Madonna's robe meets the 'real' foliage at her feet with exquisite detail.

Begijnhof HISTORIC BUILDING
(Wijngaardstraat; ⊙ 6.30am-6.30pm) FREE Bruges' delightful *begijnhof* originally dates from the 13th century. Although the last *begijn* has long since passed away, today residents of the pretty, whitewashed garden complex include a convent of Benedictine nuns. Despite the hordes of summer tourists, the *begijnhof* remains a remarkably tranquil haven. In spring, a carpet of daffodils adds to the quaintness of the scene. Outside the 1776 gateway bridge lies a tempting, if predictably tourist-priced, array of terraced restaurants, lace shops and waffle peddlers.

Onze-Lieve-Vrouwekerk CHURCH
(Church of Our Lady; Mariastraat; ⊙ 9.30am-5pm Mon-Sat, from 1.30pm Sun) This large, somewhat sober 13th-century church sports an enormous tower that's currently 'wrapped' for extensive renovation. Inside, it's best known for Michelangelo's serenely contemplative 1504 *Madonna and Child* statue, the only such work by Michelangelo to leave Italy during the artist's lifetime; look out also for the *Adoration of the Shepherds* by Pieter Pourbus.

🛏 Sleeping

Bauhaus HOSTEL €
(St Christopher's Hostel; ☑ 050-34 10 93; www.bauhaus.be; Langestraat 145; dm €21-31, d €67-97; @ 🔊) One of Belgium's most popular hangouts for young travellers, this backpacker 'village' incorporates a hostel, apartments, a nightclub, an internet cafe and a little chill-out room that's well hidden behind the reception, and a laundrette section at Langestraat 145. Simple and slightly cramped dorms are operated with key cards; hotel-section double rooms have private shower cubicles; bike hire is also available.

Smarter 'pod' dorms have better bunks with curtains and reading lamps. Take bus 6 or 16 from the train station.

Passage Bruges HOSTEL €
(☑ 050 34 02 32; www.passagebruges.com; Dweersstraat 26-28; d/tr/q €64/96/128) Located above an invitingly old-fashioned cafe-restaurant is a recently renovated hostel; the next-door building houses spartan but large and well-priced hotel rooms.

Hostel Lybeer HOSTEL €
(☑ 050 33 43 55; www.hostellybeer.com; Korte Vulderssstraat 31; dm from €26, s/d without bathroom €42/74; @ 🔊) The Lybeer traditionally had plenty of tatty edges, but is now in the process of renovation. It's handily central in a typical Bruges terraced house and has a large and convivial sitting and dining room.

🍴 Eating & Drinking

Den Gouden Karpel SEAFOOD €
(☑ 050-33 33 89; www.dengoudenkarpel.be; Vismarkt 9-11; dishes from €4; ⊙ 11am-6pm Tue-Sat) Takeaway or eat in, this sleek little *café*/bar is a great location for a jumpingly fresh seafood lunch, right by the fish market. Crab sandwiches, smoked salmon salads, shrimp croquettes and oysters are on the menu.

't Ganzespel BELGIAN €
(☑ 050-33 12 33; www.ganzespel.be; Ganzenstraat 37; mains from €10.50; ⊙ 6.30-10pm Sat & Sun) Providing a truly intimate eating experience in a lovely old gabled building, the owner serves classic Belgian dishes such as meatballs and *kalfsblanket* (veal in a creamy sauce), as well as pasta dishes. Upstairs are three idiosyncratic B&B guest rooms (double €55 to €85), one with a musical shower.

L'Estaminet PUB
(☑ 050-33 09 16; Park 5; beer/snacks/pastas from €1.80/6/8; ⊙ noon-2am Tue, Wed & Sun, 5pm-2am Thu, noon-4am Fri & Sat) With its dark timber beams, low lighting, convivial clatter and park setting, L'Estaminet scarcely seems to have changed since it opened in 1900. It's primarily a drinking spot, but also serves time-honoured dishes such as spaghetti

bolognese with a baked cheese crust (€10). Summer sees its loyal local following flow out onto the front terrace.

❶ Information

Tourist Office (In&Uit Brugge; ☑ 050-44 46 46; www.visitbruges.be; 't Zand 34; ⊗10am-5pm Mon-Sat, 10am-2pm Sun)

❶ Getting There & Away

Eurolines has buses to London departing at 5.30pm from the bus station, but tickets must be booked by phone, online or in Ghent.

Bruges' train station is 1.5km south of the Markt.

Ypres

POP 35,100

Only the hardest of hearts are unmoved by historic Ypres (Ieper in Dutch). In WWI some 300,000 Allied soldiers died in the 'Salient', a bow-shaped bulge that formed the front line around town. Ypres remained unoccupied by German forces, but was utterly flattened by bombardment. Incredibly, after the war the beautiful medieval core was convincingly rebuilt and the restored Ypres Lakenhalle is today one of the most spectacular buildings in Belgium. Most tourism still revolves around WWI and related themes, and the Salient remains dotted with cemeteries, memorials, bunkers and war museums.

◉ Sights

★ **In Flanders Fields**   MUSEUM
(☑ 057-23 92 20; www.inflandersfields.be; Lakenhalle, Grote Markt 34; adult/under 26yr/child €9/5/4; ⊗10am-6pm Apr–mid-Nov, to 5pm Tue-Sun mid-Nov–Mar) No museum gives a more balanced yet moving and user-friendly introduction to WWI history. It's a multi-sensory experience combining soundscapes, videos, well-chosen exhibits and interactive learning stations at which you 'become' a character and follow his/her progress through the wartime period. An electronic 'identity' bracelet activates certain displays.

Lakenhalle   HISTORIC BUILDING
(Cloth Hall; Grote Markt 34) Dominating the Grote Markt, the enormous reconstructed Lakenhalle is one of Belgium's most impressive buildings. Its 70m-high belfry has the vague appearance of a medieval Big Ben. The original version was completed in 1304 beside the Ieperslee, a river that, now covered over, once allowed ships to sail right up to the Lakenhalle to unload their cargoes of wool. These were stored beneath the high gables of the 1st floor, where you'll find the unmissable In Flanders Fields Museum.

GERMANY, AUSTRIA & BENELUX YPRES

WORTH A TRIP

WWI SITES OF YPRES SALIENT

Many WWI sites are in rural locations that are awkward to reach without a car or tour bus. But the following are all within 600m of Ypres–Roeselare bus routes 94 and 95 (once or twice hourly weekdays, five daily weekends), so could be visited en route between Ypres and Bruges.

In central Zonnebeke village, a lake-fronted mansion hosts a tourist office, cafe and the Memorial **Museum Passchendaele 1917** (www.passchendaele.be; Ieperstraat 5; €10.50; ⊗9am-6pm Feb–mid-Dec; ▯94), a particularly polished WWI museum charting local battle progressions with plenty of multilingual commentaries. The big attraction here is descending into its multi-room 'trench experience' with low-lit, wooden-clad subterranean bunk rooms and a soundtrack.

Probably the most visited Salient site, **Tyne Cot** (⊗24hr, visitor centre 10am-6pm Feb-Nov; ▯94) is the world's biggest British Commonwealth war cemetery, with 11,956 graves. A huge semicircular wall commemorates another 34,857 lost-in-action soldiers. The name Tyne Cot was coined by Northumberland Fusiliers who fancied that German bunkers on the hillside here looked like Tyneside cottages. Two such dumpy concrete bunkers sit amid the graves.

The area's main German WWI cemetery, the **Deutscher Soldatenfriedhof** sits amid oak trees and trios of squat, mossy crosses. Some 44,000 corpses are grouped together here, surveyed by four eerie silhouette statues. Entering takes you through a black concrete 'tunnel' that clanks and hisses with distant war sounds, while four short video montages commemorate the tragedy of war.

OFF THE BEATEN TRACK

CHÂTEAU DE BOUILLON

In Belgium's far southeastern corner, **Château de Bouillon** (☎061-46 62 57; www.bouillon-initiative.be; Rue du Château; adult/child €7/5; ⊙10am-6.30pm Jul & Aug, 10am-5pm or 6pm Mar-Jun & Sep-Nov, see website for winter opening; P ♿) is Belgium's finest feudal castle, slouching like a great grey dragon high on a central rocky ridge. Accessed by two stone bridges between crags, it harks back to 988, but is especially associated with Crusader knight Godefroid (Godefroy) de Bouillon, whose name you'll hear a lot in these parts. The super-atmospheric castle still offers everything you might wish for – dank dripping passageways tunnelling into the hillside, musty half-lit cell rooms, rough-hewn stairwells and many an eerie nook and cranny to discover.

To reach Bouillon, train to Libramont (direct services from Brussels-Midi and Luxembourg City), then take bus 8 (€3.20, 45 minutes, roughly hourly weekdays, two-hourly weekends).

👉 Tours

Over the Top   BUS
(☎057-42 43 20; www.overthetoptours.be; Meensestraat 41; tours €40; ⊙tours 9am-1.30pm & 2-5.30pm) A WWI specialist bookshop towards the Menin Gate offers twice-daily, half-day guided minibus tours of the Ypres Salient; the north salient tour is in the morning, the south in the afternoon.

British Grenadier   BUS
(☎057-21 46 57; www.salienttours.be; Meensestraat 5; standard tour €40; ⊙10am-1.30pm) Offers three different Ypres tours, with morning and afternoon departures for various sites on the Salient. It also offers full-day tours (€110) around the Somme region and/or Vimy Ridge.

🛏 Sleeping & Eating

B&B Ter Thuyne   B&B €€
(☎057-36 00 42; www.terthuyne.be; Gustave de Stuersstraat 19; s/d from €80/95; @) Three comfortable rooms that are luminously bright and scrupulously clean, but not overly fashion-conscious.

't Leedvermaak   BISTRO €
(☎057-21 63 85; Korte Meersstraat 2; mains €7-17; ⊙5-11pm Tue-Thu & Sat, 11am-2pm & 5-11pm Fri & Sun) Low-key theatrically themed bistro serving fair-priced pasta, veggie dishes and tapas.

ℹ Information

Tourist Office (☎057-23 92 20; www.toerismeieper.be; Lakenhalle; ⊙9am-6pm Mon-Fri, 10am-6pm Sat & Sun Apr–mid-Nov, to 5pm mid-Nov–Mar) Tourist office for Ypres and surrounds with an extensive bookshop.

ℹ Getting There & Away

Most buses leave from the train station and also pick up in Grote Markt. For Bruges, take bus 94 or 95 to Roeselare, then swap to a train.

There are at least hourly train services to Brussels.

Mons

POP 93,400

Mons (Bergen in Dutch), in French-speaking Wallonia, has a characterful medieval centre climbing up a hill and a fine Grand Place along with a handful of entertaining modern museums.

👁 Sights

★Mons Memorial Museum   MUSEUM

(☎065-40 53 20; www.monsmemorialmuseum.mons.be; Blvd Dolez 51; adult/child €9/2; ⊙10am-6pm Tue-Sun) A superb new museum, this extensive display mostly covers Mons' experience of the two world wars, though the constant sieges of this town's turbulent history are also mentioned. It gets the balance just right between military history, personal testimony of civilians and soldiers, and thought-provoking items on display. Some seriously good visuals make the to-and-fro (and stuck for years in the mud) of WWI instantly comprehensible, and there's an animated 3D film on the legend of the Angels of Mons.

Musée du Doudou   MUSEUM
(☎065-40 53 18; www.museedudoudou.mons.be; Jardin du Mayeur; adult/child €9/6; ⊙10am-6pm Tue-Sun) Head through the Hôtel de Ville on the Grand Place to reach this museum, dedicated to Mons' riotous **Ducasse festival** (www.doudou.mons.be). All aspects of this curious event, as well as background on St

George, Ste Waudru and dragons, are covered in entertaining interactive fashion, and there are interesting cultural musings on the festival's changing nature over time. During the audiovisual, showing the climactic Lumeçon battle, you can almost smell the beer and sweat. There's audio content in French, Dutch and English.

🛏 Sleeping & Eating

Auberge de Jeunesse HOSTEL €
(☎ 065-87 55 70; www.lesaubergesdejeunesse. be; Rampe du Château 2; dm/d/q €27/70/116; P@❖) Just before the base of the belfry, this modern, well-equipped HI hostel has an attractive tiered design making good use of the sloping terrain. Worth booking ahead. Prices drop significantly in quieter months. Rates are €2 less per person for those 26 and under; 10% HI discount.

La Vie est Belle BELGIAN €
(☎ 065-56 58 45; Rue d'Havré 39; mains €8-18; ☻ noon-midnight Sun-Wed, to 1am Thu, to 2am Fri & Sat) This family-style restaurant is superb value for home-style Belgian food that's filling rather than gourmet (think meatballs, mashed potatoes, rabbit or mussels). The naive puppet models adorning the decorative mirrors add character.

ℹ Information

Maison du Tourisme (☎ 065-33 55 80; www. visitmons.be; Grand Place 27; ☻ 9am-5.30pm daily; ❖) On the main square, with lots of booklets and information, and bike rental.

ℹ Getting There & Away

Mons' train station and neighbouring TEC bus station are located 700m west of the Grand Place.

Belgium Survival Guide

ℹ Directory A–Z

ACCOMMODATION
Availability varies markedly by season and area. May to September occupancy is very high (especially at weekends) in Bruges, for example.

LGBT TRAVELLERS
Attitudes to homosexuality are pretty laid-back in both Belgium and Luxembourg.

MONEY
Credit cards are widely accepted and ATMs ubiquitous.

Tipping is not required for taxis, restaurants or bars, though some locals round up a bill.

OPENING HOURS
Many sights close on Monday. Restaurants normally close one full day per week. Opening hours for shops, bars and cafes vary widely.

Banks 8.30am to 3.30pm or later Monday to Friday, some also Saturday morning

Bars 10am to 1am, but hours very flexible

Restaurants noon to 2.30pm and 7pm to 9.30pm

Shops 10am to 6.30pm Monday to Saturday, sometimes closed for an hour at lunchtime

PUBLIC HOLIDAYS

New Year's Day 1 January

Easter Monday March/April

Labour Day 1 May

Iris Day 8 May (Brussels region only)

Ascension Day 39 days after Easter Sunday (always a Thursday)

Pentecost Monday 50 days after Easter Sunday

Luxembourg National Day 23 June (Luxembourg only)

Flemish Community Day 11 July (Flanders only)

Belgium National Day 21 July (Belgium only)

Assumption Day 15 August

Francophone Community Day 27 September (Wallonia only)

All Saints' Day 1 November

Armistice Day 11 November (Belgium only)

Christmas Day 25 December

> ### ℹ PRICE RANGES FOR BELGIUM & LUXEMBOURG
>
> Sleeping price ranges are for the cost of a double room with private bathroom in high season:
>
> **€** less than €60
>
> **€€** €60–140
>
> **€€€** more than €140
>
> Eating price ranges are for the cost of a main course:
>
> **€** less than €15
>
> **€€** €15–25
>
> **€€€** more than €25

VIANDEN

Palace, citadel, fortified cathedral? At first glance it's hard to tell just what it is towering so grandly amid the mists and wooded hills above historic Vianden. In fact it's a vast slate-roofed **castle complex** (☑83 41 08; www.castle-vianden.lu; adult/child €7/2; ☺10am-4pm Nov-Feb, to 5pm Mar & Oct, to 6pm Apr-Sep) whose impregnable white stone walls glow golden in the evening's floodlights, creating one of Luxembourg's most photogenic scenes. Walkways in the bowels of the edifice display different layers of occupation, from Roman onwards. There's not much info in English, so grab an audioguide (€2).

From Luxembourg City, bus or train it to Diekirch or Ettelbrück from where bus 570 leaves half-hourly for Vianden.

ⓘ Getting There & Around

AIR

Brussels is the major airport and is pretty well connected. Charleroi airport is a budget hub.

BUS

Useful Eurolines bus routes include London–Brussels (seven to eight hours), London–Bruges/Ghent (six to seven hours), Paris–Brussels (four hours), Amsterdam–Brussels (three to four hours) and Berlin–Brussels (10 hours).

Within Belgium, the train is normally more convenient, but the route planner at www.belgianrail.be gives useful bus suggestions where that's the logical choice.

TRAIN

➡ Belgium is served from most of northern Europe, with high-speed links running regularly between major cities, and easy connections to the broader French, Dutch and German networks.

➡ Thalys (www.thalys.com) operates high-speed trains from Brussels to Cologne (1¾ hours, five daily), Paris (82 minutes, 16 daily) and Amsterdam via Rotterdam (110 minutes, 11 daily).

➡ Eurostar (www.eurostar.com) runs Brussels Midi–Lille–London (two hours) seven to 10 times daily.

➡ Deutsche Bahn (www.bahn.com) has ICE trains running Brussels Midi–Aachen–Frankfurt (three hours, four daily) via Cologne (1¾ hours) and Frankfurt airport.

➡ SNCF (http://voyages-sncf.com), the French rail operator, runs TGV trains Bruxelles Midi–Paris CDG Airport (1½ hours) and direct to several other French cities.

➡ There's a comprehensive domestic network. Belgian trains are run by **SNCB** (Belgian Railways; ☑ 02-528 28 28; www.belgianrail.be (domestic trains)).

LUXEMBOURG

Luxembourg City

POP 111,300

If you thought that the Grand Duchy's capital was nothing more than banks and EU offices, you'll be delighted at discovering the attractive reality. The Unesco-listed Old Town is one of Europe's most scenic capitals, thanks largely to its unusual setting, draped across the deep gorges of the Alzette and Pétrusse rivers. It's full of weird spaces, tunnels, and surprising nooks to explore. Good museums and a great dining scene makes this a top city to visit. It's worth visiting on a weekend, when hotel prices drop and on-street parking is free.

◉ Sights

The Old Town counterpoints some fine old buildings with modern museums and an offering of high-end restaurants. The picturesque Grund area lies riverside, way below at the base of a dramatic fortified escarpment.

★**Chemin de la Corniche**　　　　AREA
This pedestrian promenade has been hailed as 'Europe's most beautiful balcony'. It winds along the course of the 17th-century city ramparts with views across the river canyon towards the hefty fortifications of the Wenzelsmauer (Wenceslas Wall). The rampart-top walk continues along Blvd Victor Thorn to the Dräi Tier (Triple Gate) tower.

★**Bock Casemates**　　　　FORTRESS
(www.lcto.lu; Montée de Clausen; adult/child €6/3; ☺10am-5.30pm mid-Feb–Mar & Oct–early Nov, 10am-8.30pm Apr-Sep) Beneath the Montée de Clausen, the clifftop site of Count Sigefroi's once-mighty fort, the Bock Casemates are a picturesque, atmospheric honeycomb of rock galleries and passages – yes, kids will

Luxembourg City

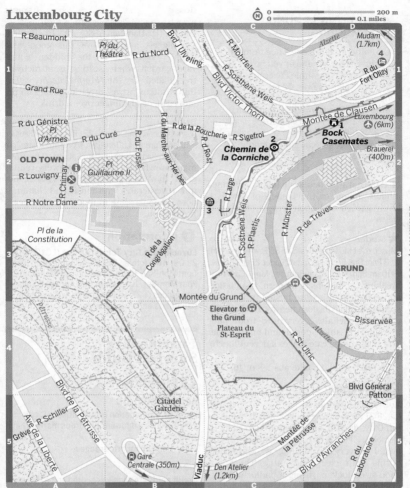

love it – initially carved by the Spaniards between 1737 and 1746. Over the years the casemates have housed everything from garrisons to bakeries to slaughterhouses; during WWI and WWII they sheltered 35,000 locals.

★ **Musée d'Histoire
de la Ville de Luxembourg**   MUSEUM
(Luxembourg City History Museum; ☑ 47 96 45 00; www.mhvl.lu; 14 Rue du St-Esprit; adult/under 21 yr €5/free; ⊙ 10am-6pm Tue, Wed & Fri-Sun, to 8pm Thu) This remarkably engrossing and interactive museum hides within a series

GETTING AROUND LUXEMBOURG

Luxembourg has a one-price domestic ticket system. Wherever you go by public transport within Luxembourg the price is the same: €2 for up to two hours, or €4 for the day. With the **Luxembourg Card** (www.visitluxembourg.com; 1-/2-/3-day adult €13/20/28, family €28/48/68) it's entirely free, as is entry to many sights located throughout the country.

of 17th-century houses, including a former 'holiday home' of the Bishop of Orval. A lovely garden and open terrace offer great views.

★Mudam GALLERY
(Musée d'Art Moderne; ☎45 37 85 1; www.mudam.lu; 3 Parc Dräi Eechelen; adult/under 21 yr €8/free; ⏱10am-8pm Wed, 10am-6pm Thu-Mon) Groundbreaking exhibitions of modern, installation and experiential art are hosted in this airy architectural icon designed by IM Pei. The collection includes everything from photography to fashion, design and multimedia. The glass-roofed cafe makes a decent lunch/snack spot.

To reach Mudam, take bus 1, 8 or 16.

Sleeping

Auberge de Jeunesse HOSTEL €
(☎26 27 66 650; www.youthhostels.lu; 5 Rue du Fort Olisy; dm €25, €3 per person discount for HI members; P❄@📶) This state-of-the-art hostel has very comfortable, sex-segregated dorms with electronic entry. There are good-sized lockers (bring a padlock), laundry facilities and masses of space, including a great terrace from which to admire views to the old city. En-suite dorms cost €1 more.

Eating & Drinking

For characterful dining options, hunt around in the alleys nicknamed 'Ilôt Gourmand' behind the Royal Palace. Inexpensive Asian food can be found near the train station.

Á la Soupe CAFE €
(www.alasoupe.net; 9 Rue Chimay; breakfast €3.50-7, soup €4.90-7.30; ⏱10am-7pm Mon-Fri, 10am-6pm Sat) Central and minimally stylish soup station serving Moroccan and detox soups, as well as classic chicken.

Bosso ALSATIAN €
(www.bosso.lu; 7 Bisserwée; mains €9-17; ⏱5.30-1am Tue-Thu, 11am-1am Fri-Sun; 📶) In summer, the biggest attraction of this good-value Grund restaurant is the hidden courtyard garden where seating is attractively tree-shaded. Try the *flammeküeche,* wafer-thin Alsatian 'pizzas', or various takes on potato rösti, or just linger over a drink.

Brauerei BAR
(www.bigbeercompany.lu; 12 Rives de Clausen; ⏱10am-2pm & 4.30pm-1am Mon-Thu, 10am-2pm & 4.30pm-3am Fri, 10am-3am Sat; 📶) The huge main brewhall of a former brewery retains giant flywheels and brewing vessels. but now reverberates with music and chatter. It does a popular line in food, and the beer is pretty good.

Information

Luxembourg City Tourist Office (LCTO; ☎22 28 09; www.lcto.lu; Place Guillaume II; ⏱9am-6pm Mon-Sat, 10am-6pm Sun Oct-Mar, 9am-7pm Mon-Sat, 10am-6pm Sun Apr-Nov) Sells city guides (€2), and has maps, walking-tour pamphlets and event guides.

Luxembourg Survival Guide

Directory A–Z

ACCOMMODATION

Hotel accommodation in Luxembourg City is very expensive midweek but drops markedly at weekends.

See Belgium for price ranges.

MONEY

Credit cards are widely accepted and ATMs are prevalent.

Getting There & Away

BUS

Long-distance buses pick up from a variety of central points. Several routes head into Germany and France, where you can connect with local networks. Consult timetables at www.mobiliteit.lu.

TRAIN

Trains are run by CFL (www.cfl.lu), with good connections all through northern Europe. The Gare Centrale station is 1km south of the old city.

THE NETHERLANDS

Amsterdam

POP 848,948

The free-spirited Dutch capital is one of Europe's great cities with liberal roots going back to the 17th century – the 'Golden Age' – when the Netherlands was at the forefront of European art and trade. Meandering canals lined by tilting gabled houses form an atmospheric backdrop for Amsterdam's treasure-packed museums, vintage-filled shops, and hyper-creative design, drinking and dining scenes. Amsterdam's world-class museums draw millions of visitors each year. The art collections take pride of place – you can't walk a kilometre without bumping into a Van Gogh, Rembrandt or Mondrian masterpiece.The dance-music scene thrives, with big-name DJs spinning at clubs around town. Amsterdam's classical venues put on a full slate of shows. Famously hedonistic diversions include the Red Light District's carnival of vice.

⊙ Sights

Amsterdam's Unesco-listed Canal Ring is a sight in itself, but the city is also home to over 60 museums. Several blockbusters conveniently congregate at Museumplein, adjacent to the oasis-like Vondelpark, while other unmissable sights like the Anne Frank Huis are also central.

★ Rijksmuseum   MUSEUM

(National Museum; Map p274; ☑ 020-674 70 00; www.rijksmuseum.nl; Museumstraat 1; adult/child €17.50/free, audio guide €5; ⊗ 9am-5pm; ⊜ 2/5 Rijksmuseum) The Rijksmuseum is among the world's finest art museums, packing works by local heroes Rembrandt, Vermeer and Van Gogh as well as 7500 other masterpieces over 1.5km of galleries. To avoid the biggest crowds, come before 10am or after 3pm. Prebook tickets online, which provides fast-track entry.

Start on the 2nd floor, with the astounding Golden Age works. Intimate paintings by Vermeer and de Hooch allow insight into everyday life in the 17th century, while Rembrandt's *The Night Watch* (1642) takes pride of place.

★ Van Gogh Museum   MUSEUM

(Map p274; ☑ 020-570 52 00; www.vangoghmuseum.com; Museumplein 6; adult/child €18/free, audio guide €5/3; ⊗ 9am-7pm Sun-Thu, to 9pm Sat mid-Jul–Aug, to 6pm Sat-Thu Sep–mid-Jul, to 5pm Jan-Mar, to 10pm Fri; ⊜ 2/3/5/12 Van Baerlestraat) It's a moving experience to visit this museum, which traces Van Gogh's life and development via the world's largest collection of his work, both familiar paintings and wonderful little-known pieces. It's fascinating to see his work change from tentative beginnings to giddily bright sunflowers, and on to his frenzy of creative brilliance towards the end of his life. There are also paintings by contemporaries Gauguin, Toulouse-Lautrec, Monet and Bernard.

★ Anne Frank Huis   MUSEUM

(Map p272; ☑ 020-556 71 05; www.annefrank.org; Prinsengracht 263-267; adult/child €9/4.50; ⊗ 9am-10pm Apr-Oct, 9am-7pm Sun-Fri, to 9pm Sat Nov-Mar; ⊜ 13/14/17 Westermarkt) The Anne Frank Huis draws more than one million visitors annually. With Anne's melancholy bedroom and her actual diary – sitting alone in its glass case, filled with sunnily optimistic writing tempered by quiet despair – it's a powerful experience. Choose a timeslot and prepurchase tickets online to minimise the queues. Only online-ticket holders are admitted before 3.30pm. Ongoing renovations include a new Westermarkt entrance and extensions to the museum, but the house will remain open.

★ Museum het Rembrandthuis   MUSEUM

(Rembrandt House Museum; Map p272; ☑ 020-520 04 00; www.rembrandthuis.nl; Jodenbreestraat 4; adult/child €13/4; ⊗ 10am-6pm; ⊜ 9/14 Waterlooplein) This museum is housed in Rembrandt's former home, where the master painter spent his most successful years, painting big commission such as *The Night Watch* and running the Netherlands' largest painting studio. It wasn't to last, however: his work fell out of fashion, he had some expensive relationship problems and bankruptcy came a-knocking. The inventory drawn up when he had to leave the house is the reason that curators have been able to refurnish the house so faithfully.

★ Hermitage Amsterdam   MUSEUM

(Map p272; ☑ 020-530 74 88; www.hermitage.nl; Amstel 51; single exhibitions adult/child €17.50/free, all exhibitions adult/child €25/free; ⊗ 10am-5pm; Ⓜ Waterlooplein, ⊜ 9/14 Waterlooplein) There have long been links between Russia and the Netherlands – Tsar Peter the Great

Central Amsterdam

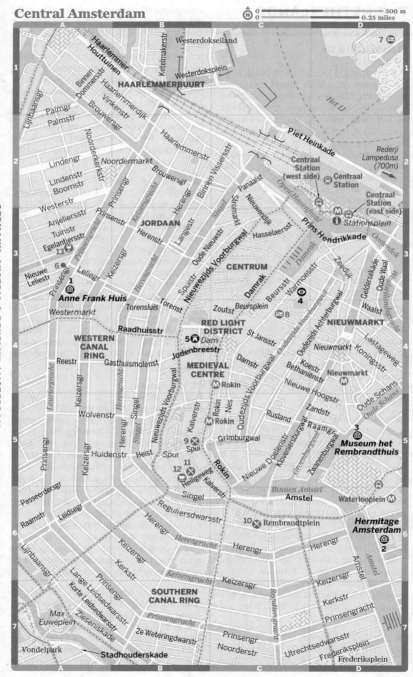

Central Amsterdam

learned shipbuilding here in 1697 – hence this branch of St Petersburg's State Hermitage Museum. Blockbuster temporary exhibitions show works from the Hermitage's vast treasure trove, while the permanent **Portrait Gallery of the Golden Age** has formal group portraits of the 17th-century Dutch A-list; the Outsider Gallery also has temporary shows. I Amsterdam and Museum cards allow free entrance or a discount, depending on the exhibition.

★**Vondelpark** PARK
(Map p274; www.hetvondelpark.net; 2 Amstelveenseweg) A private park for the wealthy until 1953, Vondelpark now occupies a special place in Amsterdam's heart. It's a magical escape, but also supplies a busy social scene, encompassing cycle pathways, pristine lawns, ponds with swans, quaint cafes, footbridges and winding footpaths. On a sunny day, an open-air party atmosphere ensues when tourists, lovers, cyclists, in-line skaters, pram-pushing parents, cartwheeling children, football-kicking teenagers, spliff-sharing friends and champagne-swilling picnickers all come out to play.

★**Royal Palace** PALACE
(Koninklijk Paleis; Map p272; 020-522 61 61; www.paleisamsterdam.nl; Dam; adult/child €10/free; 10am-5pm; 4/9/16/24 Dam) Opened as a town hall in 1655, this resplendent building became a palace in the 19th century. The interiors gleam, especially the marble work – at its best in a floor inlaid with maps of the world in the great *burgerzaal* (citizens' hall) at the heart of the building. Pick up a free audioguide at the desk when you enter; it explains everything you see in vivid detail. King Willem-Alexander uses the palace only for ceremonies; check for periodic closures.

★**Albert Cuypmarkt** MARKET
(Map p274; www.albertcuyp-markt.amsterdam; Albert Cuypstraat, btwn Ferdinand Bolstraat & Van Woustraat; 9.30am-5pm Mon-Sat; 16/24 Albert Cuypstraat) Some 260 stalls fill the Albert Cuypmarkt, Amsterdam's largest and busiest market. Vendors loudly tout their array of gadgets, homewares, flowers, fruit, vegetables, herbs and spices. Many sell clothes and other goods too, and they're often cheaper than anywhere else. Snack vendors tempt passers-by with raw-herring sandwiches, *frites* (fries), *poffertjes* (tiny Dutch pancakes dusted with icing sugar) and caramel syrup–filled *stroopwafels*. If you have room after all that, the surrounding area teems with cosy *cafés* (pubs) and eateries.

★**Heineken Experience** BREWERY
(Map p274; 020-523 92 22; https://tickets. heinekenexperience.com; Stadhouderskade 78; adult/child self-guided tour €18/12.50, VIP guided tour €49, Rock the City ticket €25; 10.30am-7.30pm Mon-Thu, to 9pm Fri-Sun; 16/24 Stadhouderskade) On the site of the company's old brewery, Heineken's self-guided 'Experience' provides an entertaining overview of the brewing process, with a multimedia exhibit where you 'become' a beer by getting shaken up, sprayed with water and subjected to heat. Prebooking tickets online saves adults €2 and, crucially, allows you to skip the ticket queues. Guided 2½-hour VIP tours end with a five-beer tasting and cheese pairing. Great-value Rock the City tickets include a 45-minute canal cruise to A'DAM Tower.

🏃 Activities & Tours

★**Rederij Lampedusa** BOATING
(www.rederijlampedusa.nl; canal tour 1-2hr €17, VIP tours by donation; canal tours Sat & Sun, VIP tours Fri fortnightly May-Sep; 26

GERMANY, AUSTRIA & BENELUX AMSTERDAM

Southern Canal Ring

Southern Canal Ring

◎ Top Sights
1 Heineken Experience	F1
2 Rijksmuseum	E1
3 Van Gogh Museum	E1

◎ Sights
4 Albert Cuypmarkt	G2
5 Vondelpark	C1

🛏 Sleeping
6 Cocomama	H1
7 Collector	D2

🍴 Eating
8 Braai BBQ Bar	A2

Muziekgebouw) Take a canal-boat tour or a sunset trip around Amsterdam harbour in former refugee boats, brought from Lampedusa by Dutch founder Tuen. The tours are full of heart and offer a fascinating insight, not only into stories of contemporary migration, but also of how immigration shaped Amsterdam's history – especially the canal tour. Both leave from next to Mediamatic.

Those Dam Boat Guys   CRUISE
(Map p272; ☏ 06 1885 5219; www.thosedamboat-guys.com; tours €25; ⊙11am, 1pm, 3pm, 5pm & 7pm Mar-Sep; 🚊13/14/17 Westermarkt) Here's your least touristy canal-cruise option. The guys offer cheeky small tours (maximum 10 people) on electric boats. Feel free to bring food, beer, smoking material and whatever else you want for the 90-minute jaunt. Departure is from Cafe Wester (Nieuwe Leliestraat 2). Blankets and rain ponchos are provided.

**Prostitution Information Centre
Red Light District Tour**   WALKING
(Map p272; www.pic-amsterdam.com; Enge Kerksteeg 3; tours €17.50; ⊙5pm Wed, Fri & Sat; 🚊4/9/16/24 Dam) The nonprofit **Prostitution Information Centre** (PIC; Map p272; ☏020-420 73 28; ⊙noon-5pm Wed-Fri, to 7pm Sat) offers insightful 90-minute tours of the Red Light District, where guides explain the details of how the business works and take you into a Red Light room. Profits go to the centre; reservations are not necessary.

🛏 Sleeping

Book ahead for the summer months and weekends year-round.

★**Cocomama**   HOSTEL €
(Map p274; ☏020-627 24 54; www.cocomama-hostel.com; Westeinde 18; d €107-212, 6-/4-bed dm €39/44, min 2-night stay; @ 🛜; 🚊4/25 Stad-

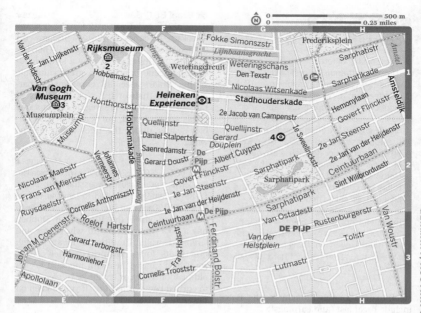

houderskade) Once a high-end brothel, this boutique hostel's doubles and dorms are light, bright and decorated with flair, with white walls and quirky designer Delftware or windmill themes. Amenities are way above typical hostel standard, with en suite bathrooms, in-room wi-fi, a relaxing back garden, a well-equipped kitchen, a book exchange and a super-comfy lounge for movie nights. Breakfast is included.

★ **ClinkNOORD** HOSTEL €

(Map p272; ☎020-214 97 30; www.clinkhostels.com; Badhuiskade 3; dm €17-50, s/d from €90/125; ❊ ☞; ☲ Buiksloterweg) Clink is a designer hostel chain with other branches in London, and here occupies a 1920s laboratory on the IJ riverbank by the ferry terminal – a free, five-minute ferry ride from Centraal Station (ferries run 24/7). Dorms are done up in minimalist-industrial style, with four to 16 beds and en suite facilities.

St Christopher's at the Winston HOSTEL, HOTEL €

(Map p272; ☎020-623 13 80; www.st-christophers.co.uk; Warmoesstraat 129; dm/d from €52/145; @ ☞; ☲ 4/9/16/24 Dam) This place hops 24/7 with rock-and-roll rooms, a busy **nightclub** (Map p272; www.winston.nl; ☺9pm-4am Sun-Thu, to 5am Fri & Sat) with live bands nightly, a bar

and restaurant, a beer garden and a smoking deck downstairs. En suite dorms sleep up to eight. Local artists were given free rein on the rooms, with super-edgy (entirely stainless

LOCAL EAT STREETS

Jan Pieter Heijestraat Sociable spots keep popping up on this artery between Vondelpark and De Hallen cultural complex.

Amstelveenseweg Loads of international options along the western edge of Vondelpark.

Utrechtsestraat Chock-a-block with cafes where cool young Amsterdammers hang out; in the Southern Canal Ring.

Haarlemmerstraat and Haarlemmerdijk Adjoining streets spanning the Western Canal Ring and Jordaan that burst with trendy spots.

2e Tuindwarsstraat Cosy restaurants, including many Italian spots, congregate on and around this narrow Jordaan backstreet.

LOCAL KNOWLEDGE

COFFEESHOP VS CAFE

There's a big difference between a *café* (pub) or *koffiehuis* (espresso bar) and a coffeeshop. Open to anyone over 18, a coffeeshop may serve coffee (never alcohol), but its focus is cannabis and hash. Ironically, cannabis is not technically legal in the Netherlands, but the purchase and possession of up to 5g of marijuana or hashish is allowed. Most cannabis products sold in the Netherlands used to be imported, but today the country has high-grade home produce: so-called *nederwiet*, which is particularly strong. If you're in the market for pot, do ask coffeeshop staff for advice on what and how to consume, and heed it, even if nothing happens after an hour. Don't ask for hard (illegal) drugs.

steel) to questionably raunchy results. Rates include breakfast (and earplugs!).

★ **Collector** B&B €€
(Map p274; ☑ 020-673 67 79; www.the-collector. nl; De Lairessestraat 46; r from €105-125; @ ⏏; ☐ 5/16/24 Museumplein) This lovely B&B has immaculate rooms with large windows and leafy outlooks, plus each is furnished with its own museum-style displays of clocks, wooden clogs and ice skates that the owner, Karel, collects. Each room has balcony access and a TV. Karel stocks the kitchen for guests to prepare breakfast at their leisure (the eggs come from his hens in the garden).

✖ Eating

★ **Vleminckx** FAST FOOD €
(Map p272; http://vleminckxdesausmeester. nl; Voetboogstraat 33; fries €3-5, sauces €0.70; ⏱ noon-7pm Sun & Mon, 11am-7pm Tue, Wed, Fri & Sat, to 8pm Thu; ☐ 1/2/5 Koningsplein) Frying up *frites* (fries) since 1887, Amsterdam's best *friterie* has been based at this hole-in-the-wall takeaway shack near the Spui since 1957. The standard order of perfectly cooked crispy, fluffy *frites* is smothered in mayonnaise, though its 28 sauces also include apple, green pepper, ketchup, peanut, sambal and mustard. Queues almost always stretch way down the block, but they move fast.

★ **Braai BBQ Bar** BARBECUE €
(Map p274; www.braaiamsterdam.nl; Schinkelhavenkade 1; dishes €6-12; ⏱ 4-9.30pm; ☐ 1 Overtoomsesluis) Once a *haringhuis* (herring stand), this tiny place is now a street-food-style barbecue bar, with a great canalside setting. Braai's speciality is marinated, barbecued ribs (half or full rack) and roasted sausages, but there are veggie options too. Cards are preferred, but it accepts cash. Tables scatter under the trees alongside the water.

★ **Van Dobben** DUTCH €
(Map p272; ☑ 020-624 42 00; www.eetsalonvandobben.nl; Korte Reguliersdwarsstraat 5-9; dishes €3-8; ⏱ 10am-9pm Mon-Wed, to 1am Thu, to 2am Fri & Sat, 10.30am-8pm Sun; ☐ 4/9/14 Rembrandtplein) Open since the 1940s, Van Dobben has a cool diner feel, with white tiles and siren-red walls. Traditional meaty Dutch fare is its forte: low-priced, finely sliced roast-beef sandwiches with mustard are an old-fashioned joy, or try the *pekelvlees* (akin to corned beef) or *halfom* (if you're keen on *pekelvlees* mixed with liver).

★ **Gartine** CAFE €
(Map p272; ☑ 020-320 41 32; www.gartine.nl; Taksteeg 7; dishes €6-12, high tea €17-25; ⏱ 10am-6pm Wed-Sat; ☑; ☐ 4/9/14/16/24 Spui/Rokin) 🌿 Gartine is magical, from its covert location in an alley off busy Kalverstraat to its mismatched antique tableware and its sublime breakfast pastries, sandwiches and salads (made from produce grown in its garden plot and eggs from its chickens). The sweet-and-savoury high tea, from 2pm to 5pm, is a treat.

🍷 Drinking & Nightlife

In addition to the Medieval Centre and Red Light District, party hotspots include Rembrandtplein and Leidseplein, both awash with bars, clubs, pubs and coffeeshops.

★ **'t Smalle** BROWN CAFE
(Map p272; www.t-smalle.nl; Egelantiersgracht 12; ⏱ 10am-1am Sun-Thu, to 2am Fri & Sat; ☐ 13/14/17 Westermarkt) Dating back to 1786 as a *jenever* (Dutch gin) distillery and tasting house, and restored during the 1970s with antique porcelain beer pumps and lead-framed windows, locals' favourite 't Smalle is one of Amsterdam's most charming *bruin cafés* (pubs). Dock your boat right by the pretty stone terrace, which is wonderfully convivial by day and impossibly romantic at night.

GERMANY, AUSTRIA & BENELUX AMSTERDAM

★ **Amsterdam Roest**   BEER GARDEN
(www.amsterdamroest.nl; Jacob Bontiusplaats 1;
⊘noon-1am Sun-Thu, to 3pm Fri & Sat; 🚃22 Wittenburgergracht) This is one of those 'only in Amsterdam' places, and well worth the trip. Once-derelict shipyards now host an epically cool artist collective–bar-restaurant, Amsterdam Roest (Dutch for 'Rust'), with a canalside terrace, mammoth playground of ropes and tyres, hammocks, street art, a sandy beach in summer and bonfires in winter.

Dampkring   COFFEESHOP
(Map p272; http://dampkring-coffeeshop-amsterdam.nl; Handboogstraat 29; ⊘8am-1am; 🚬; 🚃1/2/5 Koningsplein) With an interior that resembles a larger-than-life lava lamp, Dampkring is famed for having one of Amsterdam's most comprehensive coffeeshop menus, with details about aroma, taste and effect. Its name references the ring of the earth's atmosphere where smaller items combust.

★ **Warehouse Elementenstraat**   CLUB
(www.elementenstraat.nl; Elementenstraat 25; ⊘hours vary; 🚬; 🚃748 Contactweg, Ⓜ Isolatorweg) In an industrial estate at Sloterdijk, this warehouse's four enormous halls with phenomenal lighting and sound systems accommodate up to 2500 clubbers, who come from all over Europe and beyond to dance to house, techno and other EDM styles 24 hours. Check the online agenda ahead of time, as events often sell out. Door tickets are cash only.

❶ Information

I Amsterdam Visitor Centre (Map p272; ☏020-702 60 00; www.iamsterdam.com; Stationsplein 10; ⊘9am-5pm Mon-Sat; 🚃1/2/4/5/9/13/16/17/24 Centraal Station) Located outside Centraal Station, this office can help with just about anything: it sells the I Amsterdam discount card; theatre and museum tickets; a good city map (€2.50); cycling maps; and public-transit passes – the GVB (www.gvb.nl; ⊘7am-9pm Mon-Fri, 8am-9pm Sat & Sun) transport office is attached. Queues can be long; be sure to take a number when you walk in.

❶ Getting There & Away

Most major airlines serve Schiphol airport, 18km southwest of the city centre.

Buses operated by Eurolines and FlixBus connect Amsterdam with all major European capitals and numerous smaller destinations. Eurolines buses use **Duivendrecht train station** (Stationsplein 3, Duivendrecht), 7.5km southeast of the centre, while Flixbus services are based at **Sloterdijk train station** (Ⓜ Sloterdijk) west of the city centre.

Centraal Station in the city centre has extensive train services to the rest of the country and major European cities.

❶ Getting Around

To/From the Airport Trains to Centraal Station leave every few minutes, take 15 minutes and cost €5.20.Bike The locals' main mode of getting around. Rental companies are all over town; bikes cost about €12 per day.

Bike The locals' main mode of getting around. Rental companies are all over town; bikes cost about €12 per day.

Public Transport Walking and trams are handy for the centre; bus, ferry and metro primarily serve outer districts. Tickets are not sold on board. Buy a disposable OV-chipkaart (www.ov-chipkaart.nl; one hour, €2.90) or a day pass (one to seven days €7.50 to €34) from GVB ticket offices or visitor centres and wave them at the pink machine upon entering and deboarding.

Delft
POP 101,600

Compact and charming, Delft makes a perfect Dutch day trip. Founded around 1100, and renowned for its blue-and-white ceramics, it maintains tangible links to its romantic past despite the pressures of

---

OFF THE BEATEN TRACK

TULIPS IN SPRING

One of the Netherlands' top attractions, **Keukenhof** (www.keukenhof.nl; Stationsweg 166; adult/child €18/8, parking €6; ⊘8am-7.30pm late Mar–mid-May, last entry 6pm), 1km west of Lisse, is the world's largest bulb-flower garden. It attracts around 1.4 million visitors during its eight-week season, which coincides with the transient blooms on fields of multi-coloured tulips, daffodils and hyacinths. Book ahead online to ensure a place. Special buses link Keukenhof with Amsterdam's Schiphol Airport and Leiden's Centraal Station.

modernisation and tourist hordes. Many of the canalside vistas could be scenes from the work of Delft-born Golden Age painter Johannes Vermeer.

⊙ Sights

Delft is best seen on foot: almost all the interesting sights lie within a 1km radius of the vast Markt.

★ Oude Kerk
CHURCH

(Old Church; Heilige Geestkerkhof 25; adult/child incl Nieuwe Kerk €5/1, Nieuwe Kerk tower additional €4/2, combination ticket €8/2.50; ⊙9am-6pm Mon-Sat Apr-Oct, 11am-4pm Mon-Fri, 10am-5pm Sat Nov-Jan, 10am-5pm Mon-Sat Feb & Mar) The Gothic Oude Kerk, founded in 1246, is a surreal sight: its 75m-high tower leans nearly 2m from the vertical due to subsidence caused by its canal location, hence its nickname Scheve Jan ('Leaning Jan'). One of the tombs that is situated inside the church belongs to painter Johannes Vermeer.

★ Nieuwe Kerk
CHURCH

(New Church; Markt 80; adult/child incl Oude Kerk €5/1, Nieuwe Kerk tower additional €4/2, combination ticket €8/2.50; ⊙9am-6pm Mon-Sat Apr-Oct, 11am-4pm Mon-Fri, 10am-5pm Sat Nov-Jan, 10am-5pm Mon-Sat Feb & Mar) Construction of Delft's Nieuwe Kerk began in 1381; the church was finally completed in 1655. Amazing views extend from the 108.75m-high tower: after climbing its 376 narrow, spiralling steps you can see as far as Rotterdam and Den Haag on a clear day. It's the resting place of William of Orange (William the Silent), in a mausoleum designed by Hendrick de Keyser. Children under five are not permitted to climb the tower.

★ Vermeer Centrum Delft
MUSEUM

(www.vermeerdelft.nl; Voldersgracht 21; adult/child €9/free; ⊙10am-5pm) As the place where Vermeer was born, lived and worked, Delft is 'Vermeer Central' to many art-history and Dutch Masters enthusiasts. Along with viewing life-size images of Vermeer's oeuvre, you can tour a replica of his studio, which reveals the way the artist approached the use of light and colour in his craft. A 'Vermeer's World' exhibit offers insight into his environment and upbringing, while temporary exhibits show how his work continues to inspire other artists.

De Candelaer
FACTORY

(☑015-213 18 48; www.candelaer.nl; Kerkstraat 13; ⊙9:30-5pm Mon-Sat) FREE The most central and modest Delftware outfit is de Candelaer, just off the Markt. Owned by a fourth-generation potter, it offers 20-minute guided tours.

🛏 Sleeping

Hostel Delft
HOSTEL €

(☑06 1649 6621; www.hosteldelft.nl; Voldersgracht 17a; ⊙dm from €22; 🛜) In the heart of town a block from the Markt, this 2015-opened independent hostel has roof terraces, a self-catering kitchen and a cosy lounge. Its 43 beds are spread across en suite dorms sleeping between four and 16, with secure lockers.

✕ Eating & Drinking

Stads-Koffyhuis
CAFE €

(www.stads-koffyhuis.nl; Oude Delft 133; dinner mains €13-15, sandwiches €6.95-9, pancakes €8-13; ⊙9am-8pm Mon-Fri, to 6pm Sat, 11am-6pm Sun Apr-Sep, 9am-7pm Mon-Fri, to 6pm Sat Oct-Mar) The most coveted seats at this delightful cafe are on the terrace, aboard a barge moored out front. Tuck into award-winning bread rolls, with fillings such as aged artisanal Gouda with apple sauce, mustard, fresh figs and walnuts, or house-speciality pancakes, while admiring possibly the best view of the Oude Kerk, just ahead at the end of the canal.

De Oude Jan
BROWN CAFE

(Heilige Geestkerkhof 4; ⊙11am-1am Mon, to 5am Tue-Thu & Sun, 11am-2am Fri, 10am-2am Sat) Student-friendly hours and frequent live bands taking to the umbrella-shaded courtyard's outdoor stage (the timber-lined café interior's too small) make this one of Delft's most popular hang-outs. It's on Delft's oldest square, situated opposite the Oude Kerk.

ⓘ Information

Tourist Office (☑015-215 40 51; www.delft.nl; Kerkstraat 3; ⊙11am-3pm Sun & Mon, 10am-4pm Tue-Sat) Sells excellent walking-tour brochures.

ⓘ Getting There & Away

Delft has regular train links to such destinations as Amsterdam (€14.20, one hour) and Rotterdam (€4.40, 15 minutes).

Rotterdam

POP 616,000

Futuristic architecture, fantastic street art and museums plus a surge of drinking, dining and nightlife venues have turned Rotterdam into one of Europe's most dynamic cities. The Netherlands' second-largest metropolis has a diverse, multiethnic community, an absorbing maritime tradition centred on Europe's busiest port, and a wealth of top-class museums.

◎ Sights & Activities

★ Museum Boijmans van Beuningen
MUSEUM

(www.boijmans.nl; Museumpark 18-20; adult/child €17.50/8.75; ⊙11am-5pm Tue-Sun) Among Europe's finest museums, the Museum Boijmans van Beuningen has a permanent collection spanning all eras of Dutch and European art, including superb Old Masters. Among the highlights are *The Marriage Feast at Cana* by Hieronymus Bosch, the *Three Maries at the Open Sepulchre* by Van Eyck, the minutely detailed *Tower of Babel* by Pieter Brueghel the Elder, and *Portrait of Titus* and *Man in a Red Cap* by Rembrandt.

Het Nieuwe Instituut
MUSEUM

(☑010-440 12 00; www.hetnieuweinstituut.nl; Museumpark 25; adult/child €10/free; ⊙11am-5pm Tue, Wed & Fri-Sun, to 9pm Thu) With one side surrounded by a green moat and new garden, and the other comprising a sweeping flow of brick along Rochussenstraat, the Het Nieuwe Instituut is striking. It's a merger of the Netherlands Architecture Institute, the Netherlands Institute for Design and Fashion, and e-culture institute Virtueel Platform, presenting exhibitions on architecture, design, digital culture and fashion.

Witte de With Centre for Contemporary Art
MUSEUM

(☑010-411 01 44; www.wdw.nl; Witte de Withstraat 50; adult/child €6/3; ⊙11am-6pm Tue-Thu, Sat & Sun, to 9pm Fri) Founded in 1990, the Witte de With Centre for Contemporary Art has its finger on the pulse of breaking developments in contemporary art worldwide. Its experimental exhibitions, installations and events have a laser-sharp social and political focus, and it has a reputation as a launch pad for up-and-coming talent. It closes between exhibitions while new works are being set up, so check ahead to be sure it's open.

🛏 Sleeping & Eating

★ King Kong Hostel
HOSTEL €

(☑010-818 87 78; www.kingkonghostel.com; Witte de Withstraat 74; dm/d/q from €17.50/70/97; @🛜) Outdoor benches made from salvaged timbers and garden hoses by Sander Bokkinga sit outside King Kong, a design haven on Rotterdam's coolest street. Artist-designed rooms and dorms are filled with vintage and industrial furniture; fab features include hammocks, lockers equipped with device-charging points, a gourmet self-catering kitchen, roof garden and barbecue area, and Netflix.

★ Fenix Food Factory
MARKET €

(www.fenixfoodfactory.nl; Veerlaan 19d; ⊙10am-7pm Tue-Thu, to 8pm Fri, to 6pm Sat, noon-6pm

---

LOCAL KNOWLEDGE

ROTTERDAM'S ARCHITECTURAL JEWELS

Rotterdam is a veritable open-air gallery of modern, postmodern and contemporary architecture. Here are a few of our faves:

De Rotterdam (www.derotterdam.nl; Wilhelminakade 177) Glitzy 'vertical city' designed by native son Rem Koolhaas and completed in 2013.

Overblaak Development (Overblaak) Designed by Piet Blom from 1978 to 1984, this complex is marked by a pencil-shaped tower, De Kolk, and a 'forest' of 45-degree-tilted, cube-shaped apartments on hexagonal pylons.

Van Nelle Fabriek (Van Nelle Factory; www.vannellefabriek.com; Van Nelleweg 1) This industrial glass palace built as a coffee, tea and tobacco factory between 1925 and 1931 enjoys Unesco World Heritage status.

Witte Huis (White House; Wijnhaven 3) Europe's first skyscraper, this 11-storey art-nouveau tower was designed by Willem Molenbroek in 1897-98.

Rotterdam

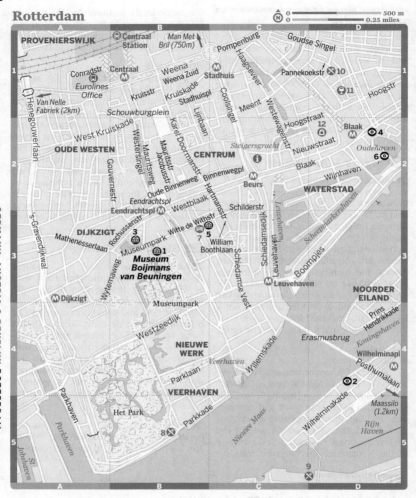

GERMANY, AUSTRIA & BENELUX ROTTERDAM

Sun, individual stall hours vary) 🍴 Almost everything in this vast former warehouse is made locally and sold by separate vendors making their mark on the food scene. They include Booij Kaasmakers (cheese), Cider Cider (cider), Jordy's Bakery (bread and baked goods), Stielman Koffiebranders (coffee roasters), Kaapse Brouwers (craft beer) and Rechtstreex (locally grown fruit and veggies).

★ Tante Nel
FAST FOOD €
(www.tante-nel.com; Pannekoekstraat 53a; dishes €2.25-13.50; ⏱ noon-10pm Mon-Sat, to 9pm Sun) New-generation Tante Nel is as tiny as a traditional *frites* (fries) stand but decked out with a stunning Dutch-design painted brick interior and marquee-style canopied terrace for savouring its organic, hand-cut fries (topped by nine different sauces), along with house-speciality milkshakes, beer, wine and 13 different gins.

De Ballentent
CAFE €
(www.deballentent.nl; Parkkade 1; mains €7-16.50; ⏱ 9am-11pm) Rotterdam's best waterfront pub-*café* is also a great spot for a meal. Dine on one of two terraces or inside. Mussels, schnitzels and more line the menu, but the real speciality here are *bals,* huge homemade meatloafy meatballs. Plain ones are tremendous, but go for the house style with a piquant sauce of fresh peppers, mushrooms and more. Waiters and customers alike enjoy a good laugh.

🍷 Drinking & Nightlife

★ Bokaal
BAR
(www.bokaalrotterdam.nl; Nieuwemarkt 11; ⏱ 11am-1am Mon-Thu, to 2am Fri & Sat) In a *bokaal* (trophy) location at the heart of the enclave around pedestrian Nieuwmarkt and Pannekoekstraat locally dubbed 'Soho Rotterdam', Bokaal's spectacularly designed bar has butcher-shop tiling, raw concrete floors, an oak bar and a huge all-day-sun terrace. Beer (craft and Trappist) is its speciality, with nine on tap and more than 80 in bottles, along with charcuterie and cheese.

Man Met Bril
COFFEE
(www.manmetbrilkoffie.nl; Vijverhofstraat 70; ⏱ 8am-5pm Mon-Fri, 9pm-6pm Sat-Sun; 🚋4) With a huge industrial-sized coffee roaster and stacks of imported beans in hessian sacks, Man Met Bril feels like a working warehouse. However, as the home of Rotter-

FOOD HALL FRENZY

Markthal Rotterdam (https://markthal.klepierre.nl/; Nieuwstraat; ⏱ 10am-8pm Mon-Thu & Sat, to 9pm Fri, noon-6pm Sun), the Netherlands' first indoor food market, opened in 2014. Its inverted-U-shaped design is truly striking, with glass-walled apartments arcing over the food hall's 40m-high fruit- and vegetable-muralled ceiling. It's a great place to stock up on a tantalising array of produce and prepared food and drinks.

dam's only coffee roasters, it is also one of the best places in the city to get your caffeine fix. Expect expertly prepared brews, flaky pastries and light lunches as well.

ℹ Information

Tourist Office (☎ 010-790 01 85; www.rotterdam.info; Coolsingel 114; ⏱ 9.30am-6pm; 📶) Main tourist office.

ℹ Getting There & Away

The **Eurolines** (☎ 0888 076 17 00; Conradstraat 16; ⏱ 9am-6pm Mon-Fri, 9.30am-5.30 Sat) office is in the Groothandelsgebouw by Centraal Station.

Rotterdam's stunning Centraal Station has direct train services to Amsterdam (from €14.80, 70 minutes), Brussels and Paris and is also a Eurostar stop en route to London.

Maastricht
POP 122,397

Spanish and Roman ruins, sophisticated food and drink, French and Belgian twists in the architecture, a shrugging off of the shackles of Dutch restraint – are we still in the Netherlands? The people are irreverent, there are hordes of university students and the streets are steeped in history. Maastricht is a lively and energetic place, with appeal and allure out of proportion to its size.

👁 Sights

Maastricht's delights dot a compact area on both sides of the Maas river. The Vrijthof, an expansive square surrounded by grand cafes, museums and a pair of magnificent churches, is a focal point.

GERMANY, AUSTRIA & BENELUX MAASTRICHT

★Sint Servaasbasiliek CHURCH
(www.sintservaas.nl; Keizer Karelplein 3; basilica free, treasury adult/child €4.50/free; ☉10am-5pm Mon-Sat, from 12.30pm Sun) Built around the shrine of St Servatius, the first bishop of Maastricht, the basilica presents an architectural pastiche dating from 1000. Its beautiful curved brick apse and towers dominate the Vrijthof. The **Treasury** is filled with medieval gold artwork. Be sure to duck around the back to the serene cloister garden.

★Bonnefantenmuseum MUSEUM
(☑043-329 01 90; www.bonnefanten.nl; Ave Cèramique 250; adult/child €12.50/free; ☉11am-5pm Tue-Sun) Maastricht's star museum, in the Ceramique district east of the Maas, is easily recognisable by its rocket-shaped tower. Designed by the Italian Aldo Rossi, the distinctive E-shaped structure displays early European painting and sculpture on the 1st floor and contemporary works by Limburg artists on the next, linked by a dramatic sweep of stairs. The dome of the tower is reserved for large-scale installations.

Fort Sint Pieter FORTRESS
(☑043-325 21 21; www.maastrichtunderground.nl; Luikerweg 71; fort tour adult/child €6.75/5.30, combination tour €10.40/8; ☉English tour 12.30pm) Looming atop a marlstone hill with commanding views of the Maas, the five-sided Fort Sint Pieter formed the city's southern defence and is linked to a network of underground tunnels. It's been fully restored to its original 1701 appearance. Visit is by guided tour only, which can be combined with a tunnel tour. Purchase tickets at the visitor centre below the fort. It's a 2km walk south of Maastricht, or take bus 7 and get off at 'Mergelweg'.

🛏 Sleeping

Stayokay Maastricht HOSTEL €
(☑750 17 90; www.stayokay.com/maastricht; Maasboulevard 101; dm €21-41, d €53-96; @🛜) A terrace right on the Maas highlights this stunner of a hostel with 199 beds in dorms and private rooms. It's 1km south of the centre.

🍴 Eating & Drinking

Maastricht has a thriving cafe scene and most serve food. The east side of the Vrijthof harbours an almost endless row of options.

★Bisschopsmolen BAKERY €
(www.bisschopsmolen.nl; Stenebrug 3; vlaai €2.40, baguette sandwiches €6; ☉9am-6pm Tue-Sat, 10am-5pm Sun) A working 7th-century water wheel powers a vintage flour mill that supplies its adjoining bakery. Spelt loaves and *vlaai* (seasonal fruit pies) come direct from the ovens out back. You can dine on-site at the cafe, and, if it's not busy, self-tour the mill and see how flour's been made for aeons.

Marres Kitchen MEDITERRANEAN €
(www.marres.org; Capucijnenstraat 98; mains €18-24) Adjunct to a gallery for contemporary art, the kitchen here is run by a Syrian who previously resided in Tuscany, and dishes span the Mediterranean spectrum. Facing a lush garden, the small dining hall consists of long tables conducive to interaction. Start your noshing from an array of Mideast appetizers.

★Take One BROWN CAFE
(www.takeonebiercafe.nl; Rechtstraat 28; ☉4pm-2am Thu-Mon) This narrow, eccentric 1930s tavern has well over 100 beers from the most obscure parts of the Benelux. It's run by a husband-and-wife team who help you select the beer most appropriate to your taste. The Bink Blonde is sweet, tangy and very good.

ℹ Information

Tourist Office (VVV; ☑043-325 21 21; www.vvvmaastricht.nl; Kleine Straat 1; ☉10am-6pm Mon-Sat, 11am-5pm Sun May-Oct, 10am-6pm Mon-Fri, 10am-5pm Sat, 11am-5pm Sun Nov-Apr) In the 15th-century Dinghuis; cycling tours offered.

ℹ Getting There & Away

The bus station is to the right as you exit the train station. Eurolines has buses to/from Brussels. Interliner has hourly buses to/from Aachen (in Germany).

Trains to Amsterdam (€25, 2½ hours) leave twice an hour. Getting to Brussels and Cologne requires a change in Liège.

Netherlands Survival Guide

ℹ Directory A–Z

ACCOMMODATION

Always book accommodation ahead, especially during high season.

MONEY

ATMs are widely available. Credit cards are accepted in most hotels but not all restaurants. Non-European credit cards are sometimes rejected.

> **ⓘ PRICE RANGES**
>
> The following price ranges refer to a double room with bathroom in high season:
>
> € less than €100
>
> €€ €100–180
>
> €€€ more than €180
>
> The following price ranges refer to a main course:
>
> € less than €12
>
> €€ €12–25
>
> €€€ more than €25

In restaurants, round up, or tip 5% to 10%.

OPENING HOURS

Hours can vary by season and often decrease during the low season.

Cafés and bars Open noon (exact hours vary); most close 1am Sunday to Thursday, 3am Friday and Saturday

Museums 10am to 5pm daily, some close Monday

Restaurants Lunch 11am to 2.30pm, dinner 6 to 10pm

Shops 10am or noon to 6pm Tuesday to Friday, 10am to 5pm Saturday and Sunday, noon or 1pm to 5pm or 6pm Monday (if at all)

PUBLIC HOLIDAYS

Nieuwjaarsdag (New Year's Day) Parties and fireworks galore

Goede Vrijdag Good Friday

Eerste & Tweede Paasdag Easter Sunday and Monday

Koningsdag (King's Day) 27 April (26 April if the 27th is a Sunday)

Bevrijdingsdag (Liberation Day) 5 May. Not a universal holiday: government workers have the day off, but almost everyone else has to work.

Hemelvaartsdag (Ascension Day) Fortieth day after Easter Sunday

Eerste & Tweede Pinksterdag (Whit Sunday & Monday; Pentecost) Fiftieth and 51st day after Easter Sunday.

Eerste & Tweede Kerstdag (Christmas Day & Boxing Day) 25 and 26 December

 Getting There & Around

AIR

Huge Schiphol airport (AMS; www.schiphol.nl) is the Netherlands' main international airport, but smaller ones in Rotterdam and The Hague also serve more than 40 European destinations.

BUS

Eurolines (www.eurolines.com) serves the Netherlands' major cities.

LOCAL TRANSPORT

Local transport tickets are smart cards called OV-chipkaart (www.ov-chipkaart.nl). Either purchase a reusable OV-chipkaart at a local transport-information office or a disposable one when you board a bus or tram.

TRAIN

Train connections are excellent. Amsterdam is linked to Cologne, Brussels, Paris and London by high-speed trains. All Eurail and Inter-Rail passes are valid on the Dutch national train service (www.ns.nl).

AUSTRIA

Vienna

POP 1,766,750

Few cities in the world waltz so effortlessly between the present and the past like Vienna. Baroque streetscapes and imperial palaces set the stage for artistic and musical masterpieces alongside a traditional coffeehouse culture and vibrant epicurean and design scenes.

But Vienna is also one of Europe's most dynamic urban spaces. Provocative contemporary art hides behind striking basalt facades, design stores sidle up to old-world confectioners, and Austro-Asian fusion restaurants stand alongside traditional *Beisl* (small taverns).

Throw in the mass of green space within the confines of the city limits and the 'blue' Danube (Donau) cutting a path east of the historical centre, and this is a capital that is distinctly Austrian.

⊙ Sights

Vienna's magnificent series of boulevards, the Ringstrasse, encircles the Innere Stadt, with many of the city's most famous sights situated on or within it. Just outside the Ringstrasse is the exceptional MuseumsQuartier, while attractions further afield include the sumptuous palaces Schloss Schönbrunn and Schloss Belvedere, and the woodlands and meadows of the Prater, topped by Vienna's iconic Riesenrad (Ferris wheel).

AUSTRIA AT A GLANCE

Don't Miss

Vienna The capital's imperial palaces are striking, from the monumentally graceful Hofburg, home of the treasury's imperial crowns, to the 1441-room Schloss Schönbrunn, a Unesco World Heritage site, and baroque Schloss Belvedere. The latter two are both set in exquisite gardens.

Salzburg Mozart's spiritual home may have been Vienna, but it was in Salzburg where the 18th-century superstar lived, loved and composed. Stunning views of the baroque old town unfold from the Festung Hohensalzburg, Europe's best-preserved fortress

Grossglockner Road Hairpin bends: 36. Length: 48km. Average slope gradient: 9%. Highest viewpoint: Edelweiss Spitze (2571m). Grossglockner Road is one of Europe's greatest drives and the showpiece of Hohe Tauern National Park.

Innsbruck Set against an impressive backdrop of the Nordkette Alps, Tyrol's capital is the kind of place where at one moment you may be celebrating cultural achievement in elegant state apartments or the Gothic Hofkirche, and the next whizzing up into the Alps inside Zaha Zadid's futuristic funicular or heading out for the ski pistes.

Salzkammergut With its sparkling alpine lakes, the lake district is one of Austria's finest regions for peeling off the city clothing and washing away the dust of travel in swimmable waters. The Hallstätter See, set at the foot of the abrupt and monumentally rugged Dachstein Mountains, is one spectacular place to enjoy the lakes.

Itineraries

One Week

This itinerary is Austria in a nutshell, winging you from Vienna's opulent palaces and coffee houses to the vine-stitched Wachau Valley, and west to the Alps around Salzburg and Innsbruck. In **Vienna**, devote a couple of cultural days to swanning around Habsburg palaces, world-class galleries hung with Klimts and sumptuous coffee houses. A breezy hour's train ride west and you're in the heart of wine country and on the Danube in the picture-book **Wachau**. Linger for a day or two to lap up the castles, abbeys and local rieslings.

Two Weeks

Swing west now to the **Salzkammergut**, where cinematic mountain backdrops rim lakes of bluest blue. Base yourself in ludicrously pretty **Hallstatt** for peak-gazing swims. From here, head west to **Salzburg** for a feast of baroque art, palaces, Mozart and more. Comb the back alleys and clamber up to the Festung Hohensalzburg, the castle to outpomp all castles. Finish up in **Innsbruck** with a dose of culture, hiking, skiing – whatever takes your fancy.

285

Essential Experiences

Skiing in the Alps Cross-country or back-country, downhill or glacier; whatever your ski style, Austria has a piste with your name on it.

Cafe culture in Vienna The capital has a coffee house for every mood and occasion. Indulge, talk, read and dream; just as Trotsky and Freud, Hundertwasser and Warhol once did.

Salzburg Festival No country can outshine Austria when it comes to classical music. And there's always a reason to celebrate that great heritage, especially at the much-lauded Salzburg Festival, held late July to August.

Wine tasting in Heurigen If you see an evergreen branch hanging on a door on Vienna's outskirts and Burgenland you've probably stumbled across a Heuriger. Pull up a chair in one of these cosy wine taverns to taste the crisp white Grüner Veltliner and spicy Blaufränkisch wines.

Getting Around

Public transport is excellent for reaching even remote regions, but it takes longer. Most provinces have an integrated transport system offering day passes covering regional zones for both bus and train travel.

Car Small towns and even small cities often have limited or no car-hire services, so reserve ahead from major cities.

Train and bus Austria's national railway system is integrated with the Postbus bus services. Plan your route using the ÖBB or Postbus websites.

Bicycle Separate bike tracks are common in cities, and long-distance tracks and routes also run along many of the major valleys such as the Danube, Enns and Mur.

When to Go
Vienna

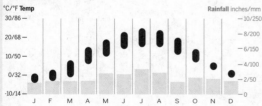

Jun–Sep High season peaks in July and August. In lake areas, the peak is June to September.

Apr–May & Oct The weather's changeable, the lakes are chilly and the hiking is excellent.

Nov–Mar Many sights are closed. High season for skiing is mid-December to March.

Arriving in Austria

Vienna International Airport The City Airport Train (CAT) runs to Wien-Mitte every 30 minutes from 5.36am to 11.06pm and takes 16 minutes. A single/return costs €11/17. Vienna Airport Lines buses run every 30 minutes 24/7; it's 20 minutes to Schwedenplatz (central Vienna). A single costs €8.

Salzburg Airport Buses 2, 8 and 27 (€2, 19 minutes) depart from outside the terminal roughly every 10 to 15 minutes and make several central stops near the Altstadt; buses 2 and 27 terminate at the Hauptbahnhof. Services operate roughly from 5.30am to 11pm.

Top Phrases

Hello. Guten Tag.

Goodbye. Auf Wiedersehen.

Yes./No. Ja./Nein.

Thank you. Danke.

Please. Bitte.

Resources

Embassy of Austria (www.austria.org)

Österreich Werbung (www.austria.info)

Tiscover (www.tiscover.com)

Set Your Budget

➡ Dorm beds or cheap doubles: about €25 per person

➡ Self-catering or lunch specials: €6–12

➡ Cheap museums: €4

Central Vienna

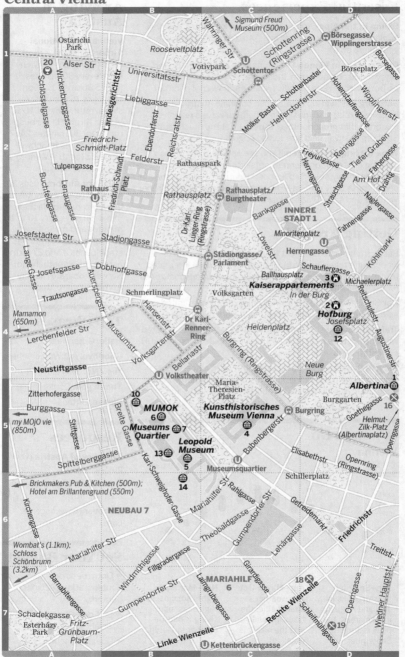

Sigmund Freud Museum (500m)

Börsegasse/Wipplingerstrasse

Ostarichi Park

20

Alser Str

Rooseveltplatz

Schlösselgasse

Wickenburggasse

Universitätsstr

Votivpark

Schottenring (Ringstrasse)

Börseplatz

Schottentor

Börsegasse

Wipplingerstr

Landesgerichtstr

Liebiggasse

Mölker Bastei

Schottenbastei

Helferstorferstr

Hohenstaufengasse

Friedrich-Schmidt-Platz

Felderstr

Ebendorferstr

Reichsratstr

Rathauspark

Freyungasse

Herrengasse

Renngasse

Tiefer Graben

Färbergasse

Drahtg

Tulpengasse

Buchfeldgasse

Lenaugasse

Rathaus

Friedrich-Schmidt-Platz

Rathausplatz

Dr-Karl-Lueger-Ring (Ringstrasse)

Rathausplatz/Burgtheater

Bankgasse

Am Hof

Strauchgasse

Naglergasse

INNERE STADT 1

Fahnengasse

Kohlmarkt

Josefstädter Str

Stadiongasse

Lange Gasse

Josefsgasse

Doblhoffgasse

Stadiongasse/Parlament

Lowelstr

Minoritenplatz

Herrengasse

Reitschulstr

Trautsongasse

Auerspergstr

Schmerlingplatz

Volksgarten

Ballhausplatz

Schauflergasse

3

Kaiserappartements

In der Burg

Michaelerplatz

Mamamon (650m)

Lerchenfelder Str

Museumstr

Hansenstr

Dr Karl-Renner-Ring

Burgring (Ringstrasse)

Heldenplatz

2

Hofburg

Josefsplatz

12

Augustinerstr

Neustiftgasse

Volksgartenstr

Bellariastr

Volkstheater

Maria-Theresien-Platz

Neue Burg

Albertina

1

Zitterhofergasse

Breite Gasse

10

MUMOK

6

Kunsthistorisches Museum Vienna

4

Burgring

Burggarten

Goethegasse

16

Burggasse

my MOjO vie (850m)

Stiftgasse

Museums Quartier

7

Leopold Museum

5

Babenbergerstr

Museumsquartier

Helmut-Zilk-Platz (Albertinaplatz)

Opernring (Ringstrasse)

Spittelberggasse

13

14

Elisabethstr

Schillerplatz

Opernring

Brickmakers Pub & Kitchen (500m); Hotel am Brillantengrund (550m)

Karl-Schweighofer-Gasse

Mariahilfer Str

Rahlgasse

Getreidemarkt

Friedrichstr

NEUBAU 7

Theobaldgasse

Gumpendorfer Str

Lehárgasse

Wombat's (1.1km); Schloss Schönbrunn (3.2km)

Kirchengasse

Mariahilfer Str

Windmühlgasse

Filgradergasse

MARIAHILF 6

Girardigasse

Laimgrubengasse

Rechte Wienzeile

18

Treitlstr

Wiedner Hauptstr

Schadekgasse

Barnabitengasse

Gumpendorfer Str

Esterházy Park

Fritz-Grünbaum-Platz

Linke Wienzeile

Kettenbrückengasse

Schleifmühlgasse

Opergasse

19

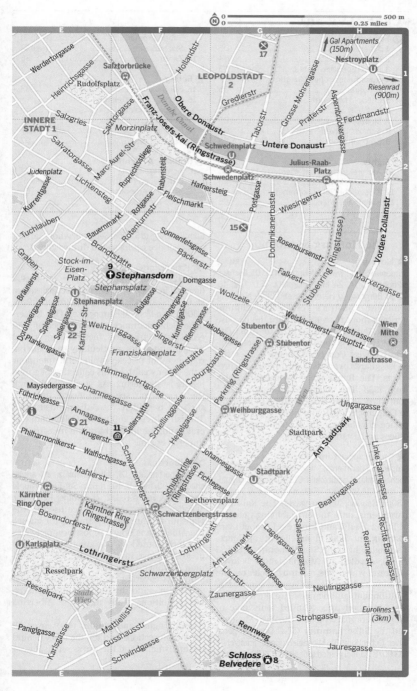

Central Vienna

◉ The Hofburg & Around

★ Hofburg
PALACE

(Imperial Palace; www.hofburg-wien.at; 01, Michaelerkuppel; 🚋1A, 2A Michaelerplatz, 🚆D, 1, 2, 46, 49, 71 Burgring, Ⓤ Herrengasse) FREE Nothing symbolises Austria's resplendent cultural heritage more than its Hofburg, home base of the Habsburgs from 1273 to 1918. The oldest section is the 13th-century **Schweizerhof** (Swiss Courtyard), named after the Swiss guards who used to protect its precincts. The Renaissance **Swiss gate** dates from 1553. The courtyard adjoins a larger courtyard, **In der Burg**, with a monument to Emperor Franz II adorning its centre. The palace now houses the Austrian president's offices and a raft of museums.

★ Kaiserappartements
PALACE

(Imperial Apartments; www.hofburg-wien.at; 01, Michaelerplatz; adult/child €13.90/8.20, incl guided tour €16.90/9.70; ⊙9am-6pm Jul & Aug, to 5.30pm Sep-Jun; Ⓤ Herrengasse) The Kaiserappartements, once the official living quarters of Franz Josef I and Empress Elisabeth, are dazzling in their chandelier-lit opulence. The highlight is the **Sisi Museum** (📞01-533 75 70), devoted to Austria's most beloved empress, which has a strong focus on the clothing and jewellery of Austria's monarch. Multilingual audioguides are included in the admission price. Guided tours take in the Kaiserappartements, the Sisi Museum and the **Silberkammer** (Silver Depot, Imperial Silver Collection; 01, Michaelerkuppel; adult/child €13.90/8.20, incl guided tour €16.90/9.70; ⊙9am-

6pm Jul & Aug, to 5.30pm Sep-Jun), whose largest silver service caters to 140 dinner guests.

★ Kaiserliche Schatzkammer
MUSEUM

(Imperial Treasury; www.kaiserliche-schatzkammer.at; 01, Schweizerhof; adult/child €12/free; ⊙9am-5.30pm Wed-Mon; Ⓤ Herrengasse) The Kaiserliche Schatzkammer contains secular and ecclesiastical treasures, including devotional images and altars, particularly from the baroque era, of priceless value and splendour – the sheer wealth of this collection of crown jewels is staggering. As you walk through the rooms you see magnificent treasures such as a golden rose, diamond-studded Turkish sabres, a 2680-carat Colombian emerald and, the highlight of the treasury, the imperial crown.

★ Albertina
GALLERY

(www.albertina.at; 01, Albertinaplatz 3; adult/child €12.90/free; ⊙10am-6pm Sat-Tue & Thu, to 9pm Wed & Fri; 🚆D, 1, 2, 71 Kärntner Ring/Oper, Ⓤ Karlsplatz, Stephansplatz) Once used as the Habsburgs' imperial apartments for guests, the Albertina is now a repository for what's regularly touted as the greatest collection of graphic art in the world. The permanent Batliner Collection – with over 100 paintings covering the period from Monet to Picasso – and the high quality of changing exhibitions really make the Albertina worthwhile.

Multilingual audioguides (€4) cover all exhibition sections and tell the story behind the apartments and the works on display.

◉ Stephansdom & the Historic Centre

★ Stephansdom   CATHEDRAL

(St Stephen's Cathedral; 🎧 tours 01-515 523 054; www.stephanskirche.at; 01, Stephansplatz; adult/child €6/2.50; ⊘ public visits 9-11.30am & 1-4.30pm Mon-Sat, 1-4.30pm Sun; Ⓤ Stephansplatz) Vienna's Gothic masterpiece Stephansdom – or Steffl (Little Stephan), as it's ironically nicknamed – is Vienna's pride and joy. A church has stood here since the 12th century, and reminders of this are the Romanesque **Riesentor** (Giant Gate) and **Heidentürme**. From the exterior, the first thing that will strike you is the glorious tiled roof, with its dazzling row of chevrons and Austrian eagle. Inside, the magnificent Gothic stone pulpit presides over the main nave, fashioned in 1515 by Anton Pilgrim.

★ Haus der Musik   MUSEUM

(www.hausdermusik.com; 01, Seilerstätte 30; adult/child €13/6, with Mozarthaus Vienna €18/8; ⊘ 10am-10pm; 🚃 D, 1, 2, 71, Ⓤ Karlsplatz) The Haus der Musik explains the world of sound and music to adults and children alike in an amusing and interactive way (in English and German). Exhibits are spread over four floors and cover how sound is created, from Vienna's Philharmonic Orchestra to street noises. The staircase between floors acts as a piano; its glassed-in ground-floor courtyard hosts musical events. Admission is discounted after 8pm. The nearest tram stop is Kärntner Ring/Oper.

◉ Museum District & Neubau

★ MuseumsQuartier   MUSEUM

(Museum Quarter; MQ; www.mqw.at; 07, Museumsplatz; ⊘ information & ticket centre 10am-7pm; Ⓤ Museumsquartier, Volkstheater) The MuseumsQuartier is a remarkable ensemble of museums, cafes, restaurants and bars inside former imperial stables designed by Fischer von Erlach. This breeding ground of Viennese cultural life is the perfect place to hang out and watch or meet people on warm evenings. With over 60,000 sq metres of exhibition space – including the Leopold Museum, MUMOK, **Kunsthalle** (Arts Hall; 🎧 01-521 890; www.kunsthallewien.at; adult/child €8/free; ⊘ 11am-7pm Fri-Wed, to 9pm Thu), **Architekturzentrum** (Vienna Architecture Centre; 🎧 01-522 31 15; www.azw.at; exhibition prices vary, library admission free; ⊘ architecture centre

10am-7pm, library 10am-5.30pm Mon, Wed & Fri, to 7pm Sat & Sun) and **Zoom** (🎧 01-524 79 08; www.kindermuseum.at; exhibition adult/child €4/free, activities child €4-6, accompanying adult free; ⊘ 12.45-5pm Tue-Sun Jul & Aug, 8.30am-4pm Tue-Fri, 9.45am-4pm Sat & Sun Sep-Jun, activity times vary) – the complex is one of the world's most ambitious cultural hubs.

If you're planning on visiting several museums, combined tickets are available from the **MQ Point** (🎧 01-523 58 81-17 31; www.mqpoint.at; ⊘ 10am-7pm). The **MQ Kombi Ticket** (€32) includes entry into every museum (Zoom only has a reduction) and a 30% discount on performances in the Tanzquartier Wien; the **MQ Art Ticket** (€26) gives admission into the Leopold Museum, MUMOK, Kunsthalle and reduced entry into Zoom, plus a 30% discount on the Tanzquartier Wien.

★ Leopold Museum   MUSEUM

(www.leopoldmuseum.org; 07, Museumsplatz 1; adult/child €13/8; ⊘ 10am-6pm Fri-Wed, to 9pm Thu Jun-Aug, 10am-6pm Wed & Fri-Mon, to 9pm Thu Sep-May; Ⓤ Volkstheater, Museumsquartier) Part of the MuseumsQuartier, the Leopold Museum is named after ophthalmologist

---

DON'T MISS

THE KISS

A masterpiece of total art, **Schloss Belvedere** (www.belvedere.at; adult/child Oberes Belvedere €15/free, Unteres Belvedere €11/free, combined ticket €22/free; ⊘ 9am-6pm Sat-Thu, to 9pm Fri; 🚃 D, 71 Schwarzenbergplatz, Ⓤ Taubstummengasse, Südtiroler Platz) is one of the world's finest baroque palaces. Designed by Johann Lukas von Hildebrandt (1668–1745), it was built for the brilliant military strategist Prince Eugene of Savoy, conqueror of the Turks in 1718. Its sumptuously frescoed halls brim with artworks by Egon Schiele, Oskar Kokoschka and Gustav Klimt, including the latter's super-famous painting *The Kiss* (1908), the pinnacle of Viennese art nouveau. It's the star exhibit in the **Oberes Belvedere**, the first of the palace's two buildings. The lavish **Unteres Belvedere** (Lower Belvedere), with its richly frescoed Marmorsaal (Marble Hall), sits at the end of sculpture-dotted gardens.

A BIRD'S-EYE VIEW

One of Vienna's most visible icons is the **Riesenrad** (www.wienerriesenrad.com; 02, Prater 90; adult/child €10/4.50; ⊗9am-11.45pm, shorter hours in winter; 🚼; Ⓤ Praterstern), a 65m-high Ferris wheel built in 1897 and the key attraction of the **Prater**, a large city park encompassing meadows, woodlands and an amusement park. It takes about 20 minutes to complete the circle, giving you ample time to snap fantastic shots of the city spread out at your feet.

Rudolf Leopold, who, after buying his first Egon Schiele for a song as a young student in 1950, amassed a huge private collection of mainly 19th-century and modernist Austrian artworks. In 1994 he sold the lot – 5266 paintings – to the Austrian government for €160 million (individually, the paintings would have made him €574 million), and the Leopold Museum was born. **Café Leopold** (www.cafeleopold.wien; ⊗9.30am-1am Mon-Fri, to midnight Sat & Sun; 🛜) is located on the top floor.

★ MUMOK   GALLERY

(Museum Moderner Kunst; Museum of Modern Art; www.mumok.at; 07, Museumsplatz 1; adult/child €12/free; ⊗2pm-7pm Mon, 10am-7pm Tue, Wed & Fri-Sun, 10am-9pm Thu; 🚃 49 Volkstheater, Ⓤ Volkstheater, Museumsquartier) The dark basalt edifice and sharp corners of the Museum Moderner Kunst are a complete contrast to the MuseumsQuartier's historical sleeve. Inside, MUMOK contains Vienna's finest collection of 20th-century art, centred on fluxus, nouveau realism, pop art and photo-realism. The best of expressionism, cubism, minimalism and Viennese Actionism is represented in a collection of 9000 works that are rotated and exhibited by theme – but note that sometimes all this Actionism is packed away to make room for temporary exhibitions.

★ Kunsthistorisches
Museum Vienna   MUSEUM

(KHM, Museum of Art History; www.khm.at; 01, Maria-Theresien-Platz; adult/child incl Neue Burg museums €15/free; ⊗10am-6pm Fri-Wed, to 9pm Thu Jun-Aug, closed Mon Sep-May; Ⓤ Museumsquartier, Volkstheater) One of the unforgettable experiences of any trip to Vienna is a visit to the Kunsthistorisches Museum Vienna, brimming with works by Europe's finest painters, sculptors and artisans. Occupying a neoclassical building as sumptuous as the art it contains, the museum takes you on a time-travel treasure hunt from Classical Rome to Egypt and the Renaissance. If your time's limited, skip straight to the **Picture Gallery**, where you'll want to dedicate at least an hour or two to Old Masters.

◉ Hietzing

★ Schloss Schönbrunn   PALACE

(www.schoenbrunn.at; 13, Schönbrunner Schlossstrasse 47; adult/child Imperial Tour €14.20/10.50, Grand Tour €17.50/11.50, Grand Tour with guide €20.50/13; ⊗8am-6.30pm Jul & Aug, to 5.30pm Sep, Oct & Apr-Jun, to 5pm Nov-Mar; Ⓤ Hietzing) The Habsburgs' overwhelmingly opulent summer palace is now a Unesco World Heritage site. Of the palace's 1441 rooms, 40 are open to the public; the Imperial Tour takes you into 26 of these, including the private apartments of Franz Josef and Sisi, while the Grand Tour covers all 40 and includes the precious 18th-century interiors from the time of Maria Theresia. These mandatory tours are done with an audioguide or, for an additional charge, a tour guide.

Because of the popularity of the palace, tickets are stamped with a departure time and there may be a gap of one hour or more, so buy your ticket straight away and then explore the **gardens** (⊗6.30am-dusk) **FREE**, or book and buy for a specific time online.

Klimt Villa   MUSEUM

(www.klimtvilla.at; 13, Feldmühlgasse 11; adult/child €10/5; ⊗10am-6pm Thu-Sat Apr-Dec; 🚃58) The Klimt Villa, which opened to the public in September 2012 following a complete makeover, immerses you in the sensual world of Vienna's most famous Secessionist. Set in landscaped grounds in a leafy corner of Hietzing, the 1920s neo-baroque villa was built on and around the site of the original rustic studio, the artist's last, where he worked from 1911 to 1918.

🛏 Sleeping

★ my MOjO vie   HOSTEL €

(📱0676-551 11 55; www.mymojovie.at; 07, Kaiserstrasse 77; dm €25, d/tr/q with private bathroom €80/100/120, s/d/tr/q with shared bathroom €44/60/80/100; @🛜; Ⓤ Burggasse-Stadthalle) An old-fashioned cage lift rattles up to these design-focused backpacker digs. Everything you could wish for is here – well-equipped dorms with two power points per bed, a self-catering kitchen, netbooks for surfing, guidebooks for browsing and musical instruments for your own jam session. There's no air-con, but fans are available in summer.

Wombat's
HOSTEL €

(☑01-897 23 36; www.wombats-hostels.com; 15, Mariahilfer Strasse 137; dm €18-23, s €34, d €68; P @ 🛜; Ⓤ Westbahnhof) For a dash of Aussie charm in Vienna, Wombat's is where savvy backpackers gravitate. The interior is a rainbow of colours, common areas include a bar, pool tables, music and comfy leather sofas, and the modern dorms have en suites. The relaxed staff hand you a drink and a useful city map on arrival, and bike hire can be arranged.

Hotel am Brillantengrund
HOTEL €

(☑01-523 36 62; www.brillantengrund.com; 07, Bandgasse 4; s/d/tr/q from €59/69/89/109; @ 🛜; Ⓤ Westbahnstrasse/Zieglergasse, Ⓤ Zieglergasse) In a lemon-yellow building set around a sociable courtyard strewn with potted palms, this community linchpin works with local artists and hosts regular exhibitions, along with DJs, live music and other events such as pop-up markets and shops. Parquet-floored rooms are simple but decorated with vintage furniture, which variously incorporate local artworks, funky wallpapers and retro light fittings. Breakfast included.

Gal Apartments
APARTMENT €

(☑0650 561 19 42; www.apartmentsvienna. net; 02, Grosse Mohrengasse 29; apt d/tr/q €98/120/149; @ 🛜; Ⓤ Nestroyplatz, Taborstrasse) For a superb home away from home, check into these roomy apartments smack in the action of up-and-coming Leopoldstadt. Occupying a renovated Biedermeier house, the apartments are dressed in modern furniture and *Jugendstil*-inspired paintings. It's a short walk to the Karmelitermarkt, the Prater and the Augarten, and the subway whips you to the centre of town in less than 10 minutes.

🍴 Eating

Self-caterers can stock up at central Hofer, Billa and Spar supermarkets. Some have delis that make sandwiches to order. *Würstelstände* (sausage stands) are great for a cheap bite on the run.

★ Naschmarkt
MARKET €

(06, Linke & Rechte Wienzeile; ⊙ 6am-7.30pm Mon-Fri, to 6pm Sat; Ⓤ Karlsplatz, Kettenbrückengasse) Vienna's aromatic Naschmarkt unfurls over 500m along Linke Wienzeile between the U4 stops of Kettenbrückengasse and Karlsplatz. The western (Kettengasse) end has all sorts of meats, fruit and vegetables (including exotic varieties), spices, wines, cheeses, olives, Indian and Middle Eastern specialities and fabulous kebab and falafel stands. Altogether there are 123 fixed stalls, including a slew of sit-down restaurants.

★ Vollpension
CAFE €

(www.vollpension.wien; 04, Schleifmühlgasse 16; dishes €4.60-8.90; ⊙ 9am-10pm Tue-Sat, to 8pm Sun; 🖊; 🚌 1, 62 Wien Paulanergasse) This white-painted brick space with mismatched vintage furniture, tasselled lampshades and portraits on the walls is run by 15 *omas* (grandmas) and *opas* (grandpas) along with their families, with more than 200 cakes in their collective repertoire. Breakfast, such as avocado and feta on pumpernickel bread, is served until 4pm; lunch dishes include a vegan goulash with potato and tofu.

LOCAL KNOWLEDGE

DRINKING & EATING LIKE A LOCAL

Vienna's legendary *Kaffeehäuser* (coffee houses) are hotspots for people-watching, daydreaming, chatting and browsing the news. Most serve light meals alongside mouth-watering cakes, such as the famous *Sacher Torte*, an iced-chocolate cake with apricot jam.

To locals, the coffee houses are like 'living rooms', especially in winter when cosy wood-panelled *Beisln* (bistro pubs) and wine bars (many with candlelit vaulted cellars) are also favourite places to escape the chill.

When the weather warms up, everything spills outdoors to the *Schanigärten*. Unlike Gastgärten (beer gardens), Schanigärten set up on public property such as pavements and sometimes parking areas and squares. *Heurigen* (wine taverns) at vineyards within the greater city limits are also wonderful places to experience the local wines as well as hearty Viennese hospitality.

★**Mamamon** THAI €
(☎01-942 31 55; www.mamamonthaikitchen.com; 08, Albertgasse 15; mains €7-9.50; ⏲11.30am-9.30pm Mon-Fri, noon-9.30pm Sat; Ⓤ Josefstädter Strasse, Rathaus) Owner Piano, who named her restaurant for her mum Mon, has spiced up Vienna's burgeoning Southeast Asian food scene with a menu of southern Thai flavours, street-style decor and an indie soundtrack. On mild nights, a young, happy crowd spills out into the courtyard, while single diners pull up a stool at the large communal table or window seats within.

★**Bitzinger Würstelstand am Albertinaplatz** STREET FOOD €
(www.bitzinger-wien.at; 01, Albertinaplatz; sausages €3.50-4.40; ⏲8am-4am; 🚊Kärntner Ring/Oper, Ⓤ Karlsplatz, Stephansplatz) Behind the Staatsoper, Vienna's best sausage stand has cult status. Bitzinger offers the contrasting spectacle of ladies and gents dressed to the nines, sipping beer, wine (from €2.30) or Joseph Perrier Champagne (€19.90 for 0.2L) while tucking into sausages at outdoor tables or the heated counter after performances. Mustard (€0.40) comes in *süss* (sweet, ie mild) or *scharf* (fiercely hot).

Harvest VEGAN €
(☎0676 492 77 90; www.harvest-bistrot.at; 02, Karmeliterplatz 1; mains €10-12, brunch €15.50, lunch €8.80; ⏲10am-midnight Wed-Sun; 📝; 🚊Karmeliterplatz (Taborstrasse), Ⓤ Nestroyplatz) A bubble of bohemian warmth, Harvest swears by seasonality in its super-healthy vegetarian and vegan dishes, swinging from lentil, pear, walnut and smoked tofu salad to coconutty vegetable curries. Candles, soft lamp light and mismatched vintage furniture set the scene, and there's a terrace for summer dining. Alt Wien roasted coffee, homemade cakes and weekend brunches round out the picture.

Beim Czaak BISTRO €€
(☎01-513 72 15; www.czaak.com; 01, Postgasse 15; mains €11-18.90; ⏲4-11.30pm Mon-Sat; 🚊1, 2, Ⓤ Schwedenplatz) In business since 1926, Beim Czaak retains a genuine and relatively simple interior, entered via the restaurant's tree-shaded, ivy-clad courtyard garden. Classic Viennese meat dishes dominate the menu, with long-time favourites including schnitzels (gluten-free variations available), *Tafelspitz* (boiled prime beef), beef goulash with bacon and shredded dumplings, and fried Styrian chicken. Midweek lunch menus cost €9.90.

🍷 Drinking & Nightlife

Pulsating bars cluster north and south of the Naschmarkt, around Spittelberg and along the Gürtel (mainly near the U-Bahn U6 stops of Josefstädter Strasse and Nussdorfer Strasse).

★**Kruger's American Bar** BAR
(www.krugers.at; 01, Krugerstrasse 5; ⏲6pm-3am Mon-Thu, to 4am Fri & Sat, 7pm-2am Sun; 🚊D, 1, 2, 71, Ⓤ Stephansplatz) Retaining some of its original decor from the 1920s and '30s, this

WORTH A TRIP

THE DANUBE VALLEY

The Danube, which enters Lower Austria from the west near Ybbs and exits in the east near Bratislava, Slovakia's capital, carves a picturesque path through hills and fields.

Austria's most spectacular section of the river is the stretch between **Krems an der Donau** with its atmospheric historical centre and gallery-dotted **Kunstmeile** (Art Mile; www.kunstmeile.at), and **Melk**, dominated by a spectacular abbey fortress called **Stift Melk** (Benedictine Abbey of Melk; www.stiftmelk.at; Abt Berthold Dietmayr Strasse 1; adult/child €11/6, with guided tour €13/8; ⏲9am-4.30pm, tours 10.55am & 2.55pm Apr-Oct, tours only 11am & 2pm Nov-Mar) . The landscape here – known as Wachau and a Unesco World Heritage site – is characterised by vineyards, forested slopes, wine-producing villages and imposing fortresses at nearly every bend. Art lovers will enjoy the town of **Linz** with its exceptional **Lentos** (www.lentos.at; Ernst-Koref-Promenade 1; adult/child €8/4.50, guided tours €3; ⏲10am-6pm Tue, Wed & Fri-Sun, 10am-9pm Thu) contemporary art museum and digital-savvy **Ars Electronica Center** (www.aec.at; Ars-Electronica-Strasse 1; adult/child €9.50/7.50; ⏲9am-5pm Tue, Wed & Fri, 9am-7pm Thu, 10am-6pm Sat & Sun).

Contact **Tourismusverband Wachau Nibelungengau** (☎02713-300 60 60; www.wachau.at; Schlossgasse 3, Spitz an der Donau; ⏲9am-4.30pm Mon-Thu, to 2.30pm Fri) for comprehensive information on the Wachau and surrounding area.

dimly lit, wood-panelled American-style bar is a legend in Vienna, furnished with leather Chesterfield sofas and playing a soundtrack of Frank Sinatra, Dean Martin and the like. The drinks list runs to 71 pages; there's a separate cigar and smoker's lounge. Tram to Kärntner Ring/Oper.

★ **Achtundzwanzig** WINE BAR
(www.achtundzwanzig.at; 08, Schlösslegasse 28; ⊙ 4pm-1am Mon-Thu, to 2am Fri, 7pm-2am Sat; 🚋 5, 43, 44, Ⓤ Schottentor) Austrian wine fans with a rock-and-roll sensibility will feel like they've found heaven at this black-daubed *vinothek* (wine bar) that vibes casual but takes its wines super seriously. Wines by the glass are all sourced from small producers – many of them are organic or minimal-intervention and friends of the owners – and are well priced at under €4 a glass.

★ **Brickmakers Pub & Kitchen** CRAFT BEER
(📞 01-997 44 14; www.brickmakers.at; 07, Ziegler-gasse 42; ⊙ 4pm-2am Mon-Fri, 10am-2am Sat, 10am-1am Sun; Ⓤ Zieglergasse) British rac-ing-green metro tiles, a mosaic floor and a soundtrack of disco, hip-hop, funk and soul set the scene for brilliant craft beers and ci-ders: there are 30 on tap at any one time and over 150 by the bottle. Pop-ups take over the kitchen, and at lunch and dinner guest chefs cook anything from gourmet fish and chips to barbecue-smoked beef brisket.

★ **Loos American Bar** COCKTAIL BAR
(www.loosbar.at; 01, Kärntner Durchgang 10; ⊙ noon-4am Sun-Wed, to 5am Thu-Sat; Ⓤ Stephansplatz) Loos is *the* spot in the In-nere Stadt for a classic cocktail such as its signature dry martini, expertly whipped up by talented mixologists. Designed by Ad-olf Loos in 1908, this tiny 27-sq-metre box (seating just 20 or so patrons) is bedecked from head to toe in onyx and polished brass, with mirrored walls that make it appear far larger.

ⓘ Information

Tourist Info Wien (📞 01-245 55; www.wien.info; 01, Albertinaplatz; ⊙ 9am-7pm; 🛜; 🚋 D, 1, 2, 71 Kärntner Ring/Oper, Ⓤ Stephansplatz) Vienna's main tourist office has free maps and racks of brochures.

ⓘ Getting There & Away

Vienna International Airport (VIE; 📞 01-700 722 233; www.viennaairport.com; 🛜), 20km

ⓘ WORTH THE CASH

The **Vienna Card** (www.wienkarte.at/en; 48/72hr €22/25) gives you unlimited travel plus discounts at selected muse-ums, attractions, cafes and shops. Buy it at hotels and tourist offices.

southwest of the city centre, has good connec-tions worldwide.

Eurolines (📞 01-798 29 00; www.eurolines.at; 03, Erdbergstrasse 200; ⊙ office 6.30am-9pm; Ⓤ Erdberg)' main terminal is at the U3 U-Bahn station Erdberg, but some buses stop at the U6 and U1 U-Bahn and train station Praterst-ern, and at Südtiroler Platz by the main train station.

Vienna's main train station, Wien Hauptbahn-hof, is 3km south of Stephansdom and handles domestic and international trains. For timeta-bles and fares, see www.oebb.at.

ⓘ Getting Around

TO/FROM THE AIRPORT
The **City Airport Train** (CAT; www.cityairport-train.com; single/return €12/21) links the airport and centre every 30 minutes between 6am and 11.30pm (€11, 15 minutes). The S-Bahn (S7) does the same journey (single €4.40) but in 25 minutes between 4.45am and 12.15am.

BICYCLE
Citybike Wien (Vienna City Bike; www.city-bikewien.at; 1st/2nd/3rd hr free/€1/2, per hr thereafter €4) is a city-run shared-bike pro-gram, with bike stands scattered throughout the city.

PUBLIC TRANSPORT
Vienna's comprehensive and unified public transport network is one of the most efficient in Europe. Flat-fare tickets are valid for trains, trams, buses, the underground (U-Bahn) and the S-Bahn regional trains. Tickets and passes can be purchased at U-Bahn stations and on trams and buses, in a Tabakladen (Trafik; tobacco kiosk) and from a few staffed ticket offices.

Graz

POP 265,780

Austria's second-largest city, Graz is a re-laxed, appealing place bristling with leafy green parkland, a sea of red rooftops and a narrow, fast-flowing river. A beautiful bluff – connected to the centre by steps, a funic-ular and a glass lift – is the city's signature

GERMANY, AUSTRIA & BENELUX GRAZ

Graz

attribute. Architecturally, Graz hints at nearby Italy with its Renaissance courtyards and baroque palaces. That said, there's a youthful energy here too, with a handful of edgily modern buildings, a vibrant arts scene and great nightlife.

⊙ Sights

Graz's most compelling sights can comfortably be seen in a day or two and are easily accessible by foot or a quick tram ride. Most local museums are under the umbrella of the Universalmuseum Joanneum. A 24-hour ticket costs €13/4.50 for adults/ children.

★ **Schlossberg**   VIEWPOINT
(1hr ticket for lift or funicular €2.20, lift adult/child €1.40/0.90; 🚋 4, 5 Schlossbergplatz) **FREE** Rising to 473m, Schlossberg is the site of the original fortress where Graz was founded and is marked by the city's most visible

icon – the **Uhrturm** (Clock Tower; 🚠4, 5 Schlossplatz/Murinsel (for lift)) `FREE`. Its wooded slopes can be reached by a number of bucolic and strenuous paths, but also by lift or Schlossbergbahn funicular. It's a brief walk or take tram 4 or 5 to Schlossplatz/Murinsel for the lift.

★ Kunsthaus Graz   GALLERY

(www.kunsthausgraz.at; Lendkai 1; adult/child €9.50/3.50; ⊙10am-5pm Tue-Sun; 🚌1, 3, 6, 7 Südtiroler Platz) Designed by British architects Peter Cook and Colin Fournier, this world-class contemporary-art space is known as the 'friendly alien' by locals. The building is signature Cook, a photovoltaic-skinned, sexy biomorphic blob that is at once completely at odds with its pristine historic surroundings but also sitting rather lyrically within in it as well. Exhibitions change every three to four months.

Neue Galerie Graz   GALLERY

(www.museum-joanneum.at; Joanneumsviertel; adult/child €9.50/3.50; ⊙10am-5pm Tue-Sun; 🚌1, 3, 4, 5, 6, 7 Hauptplatz) The Neue Galerie is the crowning glory of the three museums inside the Joanneumsviertel complex. The stunning collection on level 0 is the highlight. Though not enormous, it showcases vibrant works by painters such as Ernst Christian Moser, Ferdinand Georg Waldmüller and Johann Nepomuk Passini. Egon Schiele is also represented here.

Schloss Eggenberg   PALACE

(www.museum-joanneum.at; Eggenberger Allee 90; adult/child €13/5.50; ⊙tours hourly 10am-4pm, except 1pm Tue-Sun late Mar-Oct, exhibitions 10am-5pm Wed-Sun; 🚌1 Schloss Eggenberg) Graz' elegant palace was created for the Eggenberg dynasty in 1625 by Giovanni Pietro de Pomis (1565–1633) at the request of Johann Ulrich (1568–1634). Admission is on a highly worthwhile guided tour during which you learn about the idiosyncrasies of each room, the stories told by the frescoes and about the Eggenberg family itself.

🛏 Sleeping

Hotel Daniel   HOTEL €

(🖉0316-71 10 80; www.hoteldaniel.com; Europaplatz 1; d €69-350; 🅿🌀@🖥; 🚌1, 3, 6, 7 Hauptbahnhof) The Daniel's rooms are well designed and super simple, and while its small 'smart' rooms scrape into budget territory, it also now offers the exclusive loft cube on the roof if you're looking for something out of the ordinary. The lobby area is a lot of fun: a great space to work or just hang out.

🍴 Eating & Drinking

Cheap eats abound near Universität Graz, particularly on Halbärthgasse, Zinzendorfgasse and Harrachgasse. Stock up for a picnic at the farmers markets situated on **Kaiser-Josef-Platz** (⊙6am-1pm Mon-Sat; 🚌1, 7 Kaiser-Josef-Platz) and **Lendplatz** (⊙6am-1pm Mon-Sat; 🚌1, 3, 6, 7 Südtiroler Platz). For fast-food joints, hit Hauptplatz and Jakominiplatz.

Kunsthauscafé   INTERNATIONAL €

(🖉0316-71 49 57; www.kunsthauscafe.co.at; Südtirolerplatz 2; mains €6-16.50; ⊙9am-11pm Mon-Thu, to 1am Fri & Sat, to 8pm Sun) A happy, young crowd fills the long tables here for a menu that incorporates burgers (from big beef to goats cheese), vaguely Mexican dishes, main-sized salads and the house special 'Styrian Sandwich', a combination of crispy pork belly, creamy sauerkraut and horseradish. It's very, very loud, but fun if you're in the mood.

★ Promenade   CAFE

(http://promenade.aiola.at; Erzherzog-Johann-Allee 1; ⊙9am-1am Mon-Thu, to 2am Fri & Sat, to midnight Sun; 🚌30 Schauspielhaus) Delightful Promenade is a Graz institution. Recently refurbished by the people behind the legendary **Aiola** (www.aiola.at; Schlossberg 2; pasta €14.50-16.50, mains €19.50-27.50; ⊙9am-midnight; 🖥; 🚠4, 5 Schlossbergplatz/Murinsel (for lift)), it's a pretty, modern take on the traditional coffee house. On a tree-lined avenue in the Stadtpark, it's the perfect place for weekend breakfasts – eggs or savoury plates – or for an afternoon spritz and a few of the smart little tapas-style dishes.

ℹ Information

Graz Tourismus (🖉0316-807 50; www.graztourismus.at; Herrengasse 16; ⊙10am-5pm Jan-Mar & Nov, to 6pm Apr-Oct & Dec; 🖥; 🚌1, 3, 4, 5, 6, 7 Hauptplatz) Graz' main tourist office, with loads of free information on the city and helpful and knowledgeable staff.

ℹ Getting There & Away

Six direct ÖBB buses daily (€28.60, two hours) leave for Klagenfurt from the Hauptbahnhof.

Services to Vienna depart hourly while five trains daily go to Salzburg. International connections include Zagreb (Croatia), Ljubljana (Slovenia) and Budapest (Hungary).

Klagenfurt

POP 95,450

With its captivating location on Wörthersee lake and Renaissance looks, Klagenfurt has a distinct Mediterranean feel. As capital to the southern state of Carinthia, it makes a handy base for exploring lakeside villages and elegant medieval towns to the north. At the city's western limit is the wide green space of Europapark, along with Austria's largest bathing complex.

◉ Sights

Boating and swimming in the lake are usually possible May to September. Summertime operas, ballets and pop concerts take place on an offshore stage on Wörthersee during the summer-long **Wörthersee Festspiele**.

Bendediktinermarkt MARKET
(Fruit & Vegetable Market; Benediktinerplatz) Produce and flower stalls fill this pretty market square on Thursday and Saturday mornings. During the rest of the week, there are great restaurant stalls to lunch in or grab coffee or wine.

Dragon Fountain MONUMENT
Neuer Platz, Klagenfurt's central square, is dominated by the 16th-century Dragon Fountain, the emblem of the city. The blank-eyed, wriggling statue is modelled on the *Lindwurm* (dragon) of legend, which is said to have resided in a swamp here long ago, devouring cattle and virgins.

🛏 Sleeping & Eating

★**Das Domizil** APARTMENT €€
(☑ 0664 843 30 50; www.das-domizil.at; Bahnhofstrasse 51; apt €78; P 🛜) This large, light and sweetly decorated apartment is in a grand 19th-century building just beyond the ring of the historic centre. It's extremely well equipped with a full kitchen, laundry facilities and lots of space. Owner Ingo Dietrich is a friendly and fashionable young local who is generous with his insider tips and time. Courtyard parking is €12 per day extra.

Bierhaus zum Augustin PUB FOOD €€
(www.gut-essen-trinken.at; Pfarrhofgasse 2; mains €9.50-18; ⊙ 11am-midnight Mon-Sat) *Beisl* (bistro pub) Bierhaus zum Augustin is one of Klagenfurt's liveliest haunts for imbibers, with a particularly warm traditional pub atmosphere. There's a cobbled courtyard at the back for alfresco eating. The menu is as Carinthian as can be, with bar snacks of rye spread with a spicy meat paste, the delightful 'beer sandwich' or a trio of beef, brawn and aspic.

★**Lendhafencafe** BAR
(www.lendhafencafe.at; Villacher Strasse 18; ⊙ 9am-1pm & 6pm-midnight Tue-Sat) This wonderfully rambling bar-cafe has a lovely outlook over the Lend Canal, along with a delightful ivy-clad internal courtyard. You can occasionally chance upon concerts and spill out to the pavillion downstairs where there is a range of edgy cultural events and parties.

ℹ Information

Tourist Office (☑ 0463-287 4630; www.visit-klagenfurt.at; Neuer Platz 1, Rathaus; ⊙ 9am-5pm Mon-Fri, 10am-3pm Sat) Sells Kärnten Cards and books accommodation.

ℹ Getting There & Away

Postbus services depart outside the Hauptbahnhof with direct buses to Graz (€27.50, two hours). At least four daily buses to Venice via Villach (€28, 4¼ hours)

There are direct trains to Vienna (€52.60, 3¾ hours) and Salzburg (€41.25, three hours). For Graz, change in Leoben or Bruck an der Mur. Trains to western Austria, Italy, Slovenia and Germany go via Villach.

Salzburg

POP 146,631

The joke 'If it's baroque, don't fix it' is a perfect maxim for Salzburg: the storybook Old Town burrowed below steep hills looks much as it did when Mozart lived here 250 years ago. Beyond the city's two biggest money-spinners – Mozart and *The Sound of Music* – hides a city with a burgeoning arts scene, wonderful food, manicured parks, quiet side streets where classical music wafts from open windows, and concert halls that uphold musical tradition 365 days a year.

◉ Sights

Salzburg's trophy sights huddle in the pedestrianised Altstadt, which straddles both banks of the Salzach River but centres largely on the left bank.

★**Festung Hohensalzburg** FORT
(www.salzburg-burgen.at; Mönchsberg 34; adult/child/family €9.40/5.40/20.90, incl funicular

€12.20/7/27.10; ⊙ 9.30am-5pm Oct-Apr, 9am-7pm May-Sep) Salzburg's most visible icon is this mighty, 900-year-old clifftop fortress, one of the biggest and best preserved in Europe. It's easy to spend half a day up here, roaming the ramparts for far-reaching views over the city's spires, the Salzach River and the mountains. The fortress is a steep 15-minute jaunt from the centre or a speedy ride up in the glass **Festungsbahn funicular** (Festungsgasse 4; one way/return adult €6.90/8.60, child €3.70/4.70; ⊙ 9am-8pm, shorter hours in winter).

Residenzplatz   SQUARE
With its horse-drawn carriages, palace and street entertainers, this stately baroque square is the Salzburg of a thousand postcards. Its centrepiece is the **Residenzbrunnen**, an enormous marble fountain. The plaza is the late-16th-century vision of Prince-Archbishop Wolf Dietrich von Raitenau who, inspired by Rome, enlisted Italian architect Vincenzo Scamozzi to design it.

★ Residenz   PALACE
(www.domquartier.at; Residenzplatz 1; DomQuartier ticket adult/child €12/5; ⊙ 10am-5pm Wed-Mon Sep-Jun, 10am-5pm Thu-Tue, to 8pm Wed Jul & Aug) The crowning glory of Salzburg's new DomQuartier, the Residenz is where the prince-archbishops held court until Salzburg became part of the Habsburg Empire in the 19th century. An audio-guide tour takes in the exuberant **state rooms**, lavishly adorned with tapestries, stucco and frescoes by Johann Michael Rottmayr. The 3rd floor is given over to the **Residenzgalerie**, where the focus is on Flemish and Dutch masters. Must-sees include Rubens' *Allegory on Emperor Charles V* and Rembrandt's chiaroscuro *Old Woman Praying*.

Dom   CATHEDRAL
(Cathedral; www.salzburger-dom.at; Domplatz; ⊙ 8am-7pm Mon-Sat, from 1pm Sun May-Sep, shorter hours Oct-Apr) Gracefully crowned by a bulbous copper dome and twin spires, the Dom stands out as a masterpiece of baroque art. Bronze portals symbolising faith, hope and charity lead into the cathedral. In the nave, both the intricate stucco and Arsenio Mascagni's ceiling frescoes recounting the Passion of Christ guide the eye to the polychrome dome.

Mozart's Geburtshaus   MUSEUM
(Mozart's Birthplace; www.mozarteum.at; Getreidegasse 9; adult/child €11/3.50; ⊙ 8.30am-7pm Jul & Aug, 9am-5.30pm Sep-Jun) Wolfgang Amadeus Mozart, Salzburg's most famous son, was born in this bright-yellow town house in 1756 and spent the first 17 years of his life here. Today's museum harbours a collection of instruments, documents and portraits. Highlights include the mini-violin he played as a toddler, plus a lock of his hair and buttons from his jacket. In one room, Mozart is shown as a holy babe beneath a neon-blue halo – we'll leave you to draw your own analogies.

WORTH A TRIP

HITLER'S MOUNTAIN EYRIE

Back across the border in Germany, Berchtesgaden makes for an easy and rewarding day trip from Salzburg. Framed by six formidable mountain ranges and home to Germany's second-highest mountain, the Watzmann (2713m), its dreamy, fir-lined valleys are a filled with gurgling streams and peaceful Alpine villages.

Alas, Berchtesgaden's history is also indelibly tainted by the Nazi period. In 1933 the area became the second seat of Nazi power after Berlin, a dark period that's given the full historical treatment at the excellent **Dokumentation Obersalzberg** (☑ 08652-94 79 60; www.obersalzberg.de; Salzbergstrasse 41, Obersalzberg; adult/concession €3/free, audioguide €2; ⊙ 9am-5pm daily Apr-Oct, 10am-3pm Tue-Sun Nov-Mar, last entry 1hr before closing).

The biggest dark tourism attraction, though, is the **Eagle's Nest** (Kehlsteinhaus; ☑ 08652-29 69; www.kehlsteinhaus.de; Obersalzberg; tour €30.50; ⊙ buses 8.30am-4.50pm mid-May–Oct), a mountaintop retreat for Hitler on his 50th birthday. It took some 3000 workers only two years to carve the precipitous 6km-long mountain road, cut a 124m-long tunnel and a brass-panelled lift through the rock, and build the lodge itself (now a restaurant). It can only be reached by special shuttle bus from the Kehlsteinhaus bus station, a short walk from the Dokumentation Obersalzberg.

To get to either, take the hourly 45-minute trip on bus 840 from Salzburg Hauptbahnhof to Berchtesgaden Hauptbahnhof and then local bus 838.

Salzburg

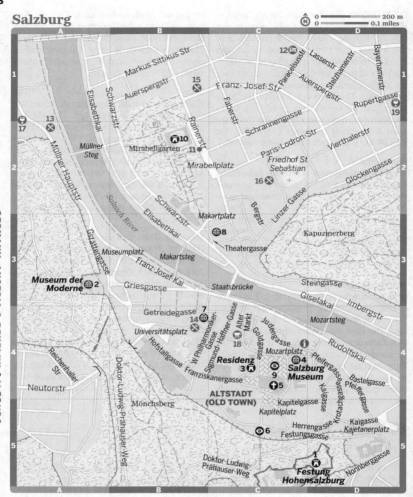

Mozart-Wohnhaus MUSEUM
(Mozart's Residence; www.mozarteum.at; Makartplatz 8; adult/child €11/3.50; ☺8.30am-7pm Jul & Aug, 9am-5.30pm Sep-Jun) Tired of the cramped living conditions on Getreidegasse, the Mozart family moved to this more spacious abode in 1773, where a prolific Wolfgang composed works such as the *Shepherd King* (K208) and *Idomeneo* (K366). Emanuel Schikaneder, a close friend of Mozart and the librettist of *The Magic Flute*, was a regular guest here. An audioguide accompanies your visit, serenading you with opera excerpts. Alongside family portraits and documents, you'll find Mozart's original fortepiano.

★**Salzburg Museum** MUSEUM
(www.salzburgmuseum.at; Mozartplatz 1; adult/child €8.50/3; ☺9am-5pm Tue-Sun;) Housed in the baroque Neue Residenz palace, this flagship museum takes you on a fascinating romp through Salzburg past and present. Ornate rooms showcase everything from Roman excavations to royal portraits. There are free guided tours at 6pm every Thursday.

Salzburg

★**Museum der Moderne**   GALLERY
(www.museumdermoderne.at;   Mönchsberg 32;
adult/child €8/6;   ⊙10am-6pm Tue-Sun, to 8pm
Wed; 🅿) Straddling Mönchsberg's cliffs, this
contemporary glass-and-marble oblong of a
gallery stands in stark contrast to the fortress,
and shows first-rate temporary exhibitions
of 20th- and 21st-century art. The works of
Alberto Giacometti, Dieter Roth, Emil Nolde
and John Cage have previously been featured.
There's a free guided tour of the gallery at
6.30pm every Wednesday. The **Mönchsberg
Lift** (Gstättengasse 13; one way/return €2.40/3.70,
incl gallery entry €9.10/9.70;   ⊙8am-11pm Jul & Aug,
8am-7pm Mon, to 9pm Tue-Sun Sep-Jun) whizzes
up to the gallery year-round.

Schloss Mirabell   PALACE
(Mirabellplatz 4;   ⊙Marble Hall 8am-4pm Mon,
Wed & Thu, from 1pm Tue & Fri, gardens 6am-dusk)
FREE Prince-Archbishop Wolf Dietrich built
this splendid palace in 1606 to impress his
beloved mistress Salome Alt. It must have
done the trick because she went on to bear
the archbishop some 15 children (sources
disagree on the exact number – poor Wolf
was presumably too distracted by spiritual
matters to keep count). Johann Lukas von
Hildebrandt, of Schloss Belvedere fame, remodelled the palace in baroque style in 1721.
The lavish interior, replete with stucco, marble and frescoes, is free to visit.

☞ Tours

Fräulein Maria's Bicycle Tours   CYCLING
(www.mariasbicycletours.com;   Mirabellplatz
4;   adult/child €30/18;   ⊙9.30am Apr-Oct, plus
4.30pm Jun-Aug; 🅿) Belt out *The Sound of
Music* faves as you pedal on one of these

jolly 3½-hour bike tours, taking in locations
from the film including the Mirabellgarten,
Stift Nonnberg, Schloss Leopoldskron and
Hellbrunn. No advance booking is neces-
sary; just turn up at the meeting point on
Mirabellplatz.

🛏 Sleeping

★**Haus Ballwein**   GUESTHOUSE €
(📞0662-82 40 29; www.haus-ballwein.at; Mooss-
trasse 69a;   s €55-65, d €72-85, tr €85-90, q €90-
100; 🅿🛜) With its bright, pine-filled rooms,
mountain views, free bike hire and garden,
this place is big on charm. The largest, quietest rooms face the back and have balconies
and kitchenettes. It's a 10-minute trundle
from the *Altstadt;* take bus 21 to Gsenger-
weg. Breakfast is a wholesome spread of
fresh rolls, eggs, fruit, muesli and cold cuts.

Yoho Salzburg   HOSTEL €
(📞0662-87 96 49; www.yoho.at; Paracelsusstrasse
9;   dm €20-26, d €70-88; @🛜) Free wi-fi, secure lockers, comfy bunks, plenty of cheap
beer and good-value schnitzels – what more
could a backpacker ask for? Except, perhaps, a merry sing-along with *The Sound of
Music* screened daily (yes, *every* day). The
friendly crew can arrange tours, adventure
sports such as rafting and canyoning, and
bike hire.

🍴 Eating

Grünmarkt   MARKET €
(Green Market; Universitätsplatz;   ⊙7am-7pm Mon-
Fri, to 3pm Sat) A one-stop picnic shop on one
of Salzburg's grandest squares, for regional cheese, ham, fruit, bread and gigantic
pretzels.

Heart of Joy
CAFE €

(✎0662-89 07 73; www.heartofjoy.at; Franz-Josef-Strasse 3; lunch €8.30-10.40, snacks & light meals €5.50-6.50; ⏰8am-7pm Mon-Thu, to 8.30pm Fri-Sun; 🛜✎) This Ayurveda-inspired cafe has an all-vegetarian, part-vegan and mostly organic menu. It does great bagels, salads, homemade cakes (including gluten-free ones), juices and creative breakfasts, plus specials such as homemade pumpkin risotto with parmesan and quinoa-filled aubergines with cashew-coriander dip.

Ludwig
BURGERS €

(✎0662-87 25 00; www.ludwig-burger.at; Linzer Gasse 39; burgers €7.40-13.60; ⏰11am-10pm Tue-Fri, from 9am Sat & Sun; ✎) Gourmet burger joints are all the rage in Austria at the moment and this hip newcomer fits the bill nicely, with its burgers made from organic, regional ingredients, which go well with hand-cut fries and homemade lemonade and shakes. It also rustles up superfood salads and vegan nut-mushroom-herb burgers. An open kitchen is the centrepiece of the slick, monochrome interior.

Bärenwirt
AUSTRIAN €€

(✎0662-42 24 04; www.baerenwirt-salzburg.at; Müllner Hauptstrasse 8; mains €12-20; ⏰11am-11pm) Sizzling and stirring since 1663, Bärenwirt is Austrian through and through. Go for hearty *Bierbraten* (beer roast) with dumplings, locally caught trout or organic wild-boar *Bratwurst*. A tiled oven warms the woody, hunting-lodge-style interior in winter, while the river-facing terrace is a summer crowd-puller. The restaurant is 500m north of Museumplatz.

🍷 Drinking & Nightlife

Bars are concentrated along both banks of the Salzach and some of the most upbeat around Gstättengasse. Rudolfskai can be on the rough side of rowdy at weekends.

★ Augustiner Bräustübl
BREWERY

(www.augustinerbier.at; Auginergasse 4-6; ⏰3-11pm Mon-Fri, from 2.30pm Sat & Sun) Who says monks can't enjoy themselves? Since 1621, this cheery, monastery-run brewery has been serving potent homebrews in beer steins in the vaulted hall and beneath the chestnut trees in the 1000-seat beer garden. Get your tankard filled at the foyer pump and visit the snack stands for hearty, beer-swigging grub like *Stelzen* (ham hock), pork belly and giant pretzels.

Die Weisse
PUB

(www.dieweisse.at; Rupertgasse 10; ⏰pub 10am-2am Mon-Sat, bar from 5pm) The cavernous brewpub of the Salzburger Weissbierbrauerei, this is the place to guzzle cloudy wheat beers in the wood-floored pub and the shady beer garden out back. DJs work the decks in Sudwerk bar, especially at the monthly Almrausch when locals party in skimpy *Dirndls* and strapping Lederhosen.

Café Tomaselli
CAFE

(www.tomaselli.at; Alter Markt 9; ⏰7am-7pm Mon-Sat, from 8am Sun) Going strong since 1705, this marble and wood-panelled cafe is a former Mozart haunt. It's famous for having Salzburg's flakiest strudels, best *Einspänner* (coffee with whipped cream) and grumpiest waiters.

❶ Information

Tourist Office (✎0662-88 98 73 30; www.salzburg.info; Mozartplatz 5; ⏰9am-6pm Apr-Sep, 9am-6pm Mon-Sat Oct-Mar) Helpful tourist office with a ticket-booking service (www.salzburgticket.com) located in the same building.

❶ Getting There & Away

Buses depart from just outside the Hauptbahnhof on Südtiroler Platz. For timetables and fares, see www.svv-info.at and www.postbus.at.

Train services leave frequently for Vienna (€51.90, three hours), Linz (€26, 1¼ hours), Klagenfurt (€39.50, three hours), Innsbruck (€45.50, two hours) and Munich (€30.70, 1½ to two hours).

Salzkammergut

A wonderland of glassy blue lakes and craggy peaks, Austria's Lake District is a long-time favourite holiday destination. The peaceful lakes attract scores of visitors who come to boat, fish, swim or just laze on the shore.

Bad Ischl is the region's transport hub, but Hallstatt is its true jewel. For info visit **Salzkammergut Touristik** (✎06132-24 00 00; www.salzkammergut.co.at; Götzstrasse 12; ⏰9am-6pm Mon-Sat Sep-Jun, 9am-6pm daily Jul & Aug).

The **Salzkammergut Card** (€4.90, available May to October) provides up to 30% discounts on sights, ferries, cable cars and some buses.

Hallstatt

POP 790

With pastel-hued homes, swans and towering mountains on either side of the glassy green Hallstätter lake, Hallstatt looks like some kind of greeting card for tranquillity, at least outside the tourist-deluged summer months. The town's beauty and prosperity stems from the area's huge salt deposits that have been mined and processed since the late second millennium BC.

◉ Sights & Activities

Salzwelten MINE
(☑06132-200 24 00; www.salzwelten.at; Salzbergstrasse 21; funicular return & tour adult/child/family €30/15/63; ⊙9.30am-4.30pm Apr-Sep, to 2.30pm Oct & Nov) The fascinating *Salzbergwerk* (salt mine) is situated high above Hallstatt on **Salzberg** (Salt Mountain) and is the lake's major cultural attraction. The bilingual German-English tour details how salt is formed and the history of mining, and takes visitors down into the depths on miners' slides – the largest is 60m (on which you can get your photo taken).

The **Hallstätter Hochtal** (Hallstatt High Valley) near the mine was also an Iron Age burial ground. An audioguide, available from the base station of the funicular, takes you through the numbered stations and explains the site and rituals of burial.

The **funicular** (single/return adult €9/16, child €4.50/8; ⊙9am-6pm Apr-Sep, to 4pm Oct & Nov) is the easiest way up to the mountain station, from where the mine is 15 minutes' walk; a switchback trail takes about 40 minutes to walk. Another option is to take the steps behind the Beinhaus and follow the trail until it joins the picturesque **Soleleitungsweg**; go left and follow the very steep trail past the waterfall and up steps. It's a tough climb, and not really for children.

🛏 Sleeping & Eating

Bräugasthof am Hallstätter See GUESTHOUSE €€
(☑06134-82 21; www.brauhaus-lobisser.com; Seestrasse 120; s/d/tr €65/105/155) A central, friendly guesthouse with comfortable rooms decked out in light wood.

Balthazar im Rudolfsturm AUSTRIAN €€
(Rudolfsturm; mains €10.50-20; ⊙10am-4pm) Balthazar is situated 855m above Hallstatt and has the most spectacular terrace in the region. The menu is Austrian comfort food and the service is charming, but you're here for the gobsmacking views. It's best accessed by the funicular.

ℹ Information

Tourist Office (☑05950-95 30; www.dachstein-salzkammergut.at; Seestrasse 99; ⊙8.30am-5pm Mon-Fri, 9am-3pm Sat & Sun Nov-Apr, 8.30am-6pm Mon-Fri, 9am-3pm Sat & Sun May-Oct) Turn left from the ferry to reach this office. It stocks a free leisure map of lakeside towns, and hiking and cycling trails.

ℹ Getting There & Away

Hallstatt train station is across the lake from the village, and boat services coincide with train arrivals (€2.40, 10 minutes, last ferry to Hallstatt Markt 6.50pm). About a dozen trains daily connect Hallstatt and Bad Ischl (€3.80, 25 minutes).

Tyrol

With converging mountain ranges behind lofty pastures and tranquil meadows, Tyrol (also Tirol) captures a quintessential Alpine panoramic view. Occupying a central position is Innsbruck, the region's jewel, while in the northeast and southwest are superb ski resorts. In the southeast, separated somewhat from the main state since part of South Tyrol was ceded to Italy at the end of WWI, lies the protected natural landscape of the Hohe Tauern National Park, an Alpine wonderland of 3000m peaks, including the country's highest, the Grossglockner (3798m).

Innsbruck

POP 124,580

Tyrol's capital is a sight to behold. The mountains are so close that within 25 minutes it's possible to travel from the heart of the city to over 2000m above sea level. Summer and winter outdoor activities abound, and it's understandable why some visitors only take a peek at Innsbruck proper before heading for the hills. But to do so is a shame, for Innsbruck is in many ways Austria in microcosm: its late-medieval Altstadt is picture-book stuff, presided over by a grand royal palace and baroque cathedral, and its nightlife vibrant and student-driven.

Innsbruck

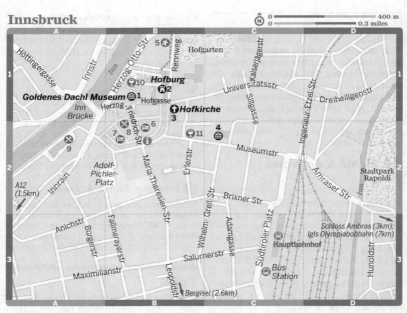

Innsbruck

◎ Sights

★ Hofburg
PALACE

(Imperial Palace; www.hofburg-innsbruck.at; Rennweg 1; adult/child €9/free; ⊙9am-5pm) Grabbing attention with its pearly white facade and cupolas, the Hofburg was built as a castle for Archduke Sigmund the Rich in the 15th century, expanded by Emperor Maximilian I in the 16th century and given a baroque makeover by Empress Maria Theresia in the 18th century. The centrepiece of the lavish rococo state apartments is the 31m-long **Riesensaal** (Giant's Hall).

★ Hofkirche
CHURCH

(www.tiroler-landesmuseum.at; Universitätstrasse 2; adult/child €7/free; ⊙9am-5pm Mon-Sat, from 12.30pm Sun) Innsbruck's pride and joy is the Gothic Hofkirche, one of Europe's finest royal court churches. It was commissioned in 1553 by Ferdinand I, who enlisted top artists of the age such as Albrecht Dürer, Alexander Colin and Peter Vischer the Elder. Top billing goes to the empty **sarcophagus of Emperor Maximilian I** (1459–1519), a masterpiece of German Renaissance sculpture, elaborately carved from black marble.

★ Goldenes Dachl Museum
MUSEUM

(Golden Roof Museum; Herzog-Friedrich-Strasse 15; adult/child €4.80/2.40; ⊙10am-5pm daily May-Sep, 10am-5pm Tue-Sun Oct & Dec-Apr) Innsbruck's golden wonder and most distinctive landmark is this Gothic oriel, built for Holy

Roman Emperor Maximilian I (1459–1519), lavishly festooned with murals and glittering with 2657 fire-gilt copper tiles. It is most impressive from the exterior, but the museum is worth a look – especially if you have the Innsbruck Card – with an audioguide whisking you through the history. Keep an eye out for the grotesque tournament helmets designed to resemble the Turks of the rival Ottoman Empire.

★ **Schloss Ambras** PALACE
(www.schlossambras-innsbruck.at; Schlossstrasse 20; palace adult/child €10/free, gardens free; ⊘ palace 10am-5pm, gardens 6am-8pm; 🚗) Picturesquely perched on a hill and set among beautiful gardens, this Renaissance pile was acquired in 1564 by Archduke Ferdinand II, then ruler of Tyrol, who transformed it from a fortress into a palace. Don't miss the centrepiece **Spanische Saal** (Spanish Hall), the dazzling **Armour Collection** and the gallery's Velázquez and Van Dyck originals.

★ **Tiroler Landesmuseum Ferdinandeum** MUSEUM
(☎ 0512-594 89; www.tiroler-landesmuseum.at; Museumstrasse 15; adult/child €11/free; ⊘ 9am-5pm Tue-Sun) This treasure-trove of Tyrolean history and art moves from Bronze Age artefacts to the original reliefs used to design the Goldenes Dachl. Alongside brooding Dutch masterpieces of the Rembrandt ilk, the gallery displays an astounding collection of Austrian art including Gothic altarpieces,

a handful of Klimt and Kokoschka paintings, and some shocking Viennese Actionist works.

Bergisel VIEWPOINT
(www.bergisel.info; adult/child €9.50/4.50; ⊘ 9am-6pm daily Jun-Oct, 10am-5pm Wed-Mon Nov-May) Rising above Innsbruck like a celestial staircase, this glass-and-steel ski jump was designed by much-lauded Iraqi architect Zaha Hadid. It's 455 steps or a two-minute funicular ride to the 50m-high **viewing platform**, with a breathtaking panorama of the Nordkette range, Inntal and Innsbruck. Tram 1 trundles here from central Innsbruck.

From May to July, fans pile in to see athletes train, while preparations step up a gear in January for the World Cup Four Hills Tournament.

🏃 **Activities**

Nordkettenbahnen FUNICULAR
(www.nordkette.com; single/return to Hungerburg €5.40/9, to Seegrube €18.60/31.10, to Hafelekar €20.70/34.50; ⊘ Hungerburg 7.15am-7.15pm Mon-Fri, 8am-7.15pm Sat & Sun, Seegrube 8.30am-5.30pm daily, Hafelekar 9am-5pm daily) Zaha Hadid's space-age funicular runs every 15 minutes, whizzing you from the Congress Centre to the slopes in no time. Walking trails head off in all directions from **Hungerburg** and **Seegrube**. For more of a challenge, there is a downhill track for mountain bikers and two fixed-rope routes (Klettersteige) for climbers.

OFF THE BEATEN TRACK

HOHE TAUERN NATIONAL PARK

The Hohe Tauern National Park straddles Tyrol, Carinthia and Salzburgerland and is one of Europe's largest nature reserves (1786 sq km). It is lorded over by the 3798m hump of **Grossglockner**, Austria's highest peak.

A stupendous feat of 1930s engineering, the 48km **Grossglockner Road** (www.grossglockner.at; day ticket car/motorbike €36/26; ⊘ 6am-8pm May, 5am-9.30pm Jun-Aug, 6am-7.30pm Sep-Oct) swings giddily around 36 switchbacks, passing jewel-coloured lakes, forested slopes and above-the-clouds glaciers from Bruck in Salzburgerland to Heiligenblut in Carinthia. The route is doable by bus, though it's a time-consuming option. Bus 5002 runs frequently between Lienz and Heiligenblut on weekdays (€8.70, one hour), less frequently at weekends. From late June to late September, four buses run from Monday to Friday, and three at weekends between Heiligenblut and Kaiser-Franz-Josefs-Höhe (€5.90, 32 minutes).

A real crash-bang spectacle, the 380m-high, three-tier **Krimmler Wasserfälle** (Krimml Falls; ☎ 06564-72 12; www.wasserfaelle-krimml.at; adult/child incl WasserWelten Krimml €9.20/4.60; ⊘ 9am-5pm May-Oct), Europe's highest waterfall, is the thunderous centrepiece of the tiny village of Krimml. The **Wasserfallweg** (Waterfall Trail), which starts at the ticket office and weaves gently uphill through mixed forest, has numerous viewpoints with photogenic close-ups of the falls.

Olympiabobbahn
ADVENTURE SPORTS

(☑0512-338 382 21; www.olympiaworld.at; Heilwasserweg, Igls; €30; ⊙5-8pm daily Dec-Mar, 4-6pm Wed-Fri Jul & Aug) For a minute in the life of an Olympic bobsleigh racer, you can't beat the Olympiabobbahn, built for the 1976 Winter Olympics. Zipping around 10 curves and picking up speeds of up to 100km/h, the bob run is 800m of pure hair-raising action. You can join a professional bobsled driver in winter or summer; call ahead for the exact times. To reach it, take Bus J from the Landesmuseum to Igls Olympiaexpress.

🛏 Sleeping

Nepomuk's
HOSTEL €

(☑0512-584 118; www.nepomuks.at; Kiebachgasse 16; dm/d from €24/58; 🛜) Could this be backpacker heaven? Nepomuk's sure comes close, with its Altstadt location, well-stocked kitchen and high-ceilinged dorms with homely touches like CD players. The delicious breakfast in attached Cafe Munding, with homemade pastries, jam and fresh-roasted coffee, gets your day off to a grand start.

★ Hotel Weisses Kreuz
HISTORIC HOTEL €€

(☑0512-594 79; www.weisseskreuz.at; Herzog-Friedrich-Strasse 31; s/d from €80/119, with shared bathroom from €42/77; 🅿@🛜) Beneath the arcades, this atmospheric Altstadt hotel has played host to guests for 500 years, including a 13-year-old Mozart. With its wood-panelled parlours, antiques and twisting staircase, the hotel oozes history with every creaking beam. Rooms are supremely comfortable, staff charming and breakfast is a lavish spread.

🍴 Eating

Markthalle
MARKET €

(www.markthalle-innsbruck.at; Herzog-Siegmund-Ufer 1-3; ⊙7am-6.30pm Mon-Fri, to 1pm Sat) Fresh-baked bread, Tyrolean cheese, organic fruit, smoked ham and salami – it's all under one roof at this riverside covered market.

★ Die Wilderin
AUSTRIAN €€

(☑0512-562 728; www.diewilderin.at; Seilergasse 5; mains €9.50-20; ⊙5pm-midnight Tue-Sun) 🌿 Take a gastronomic walk on the wild side at this modern-day hunter-gatherer of a restaurant, where chefs take pride in local sourcing and using top-notch farm-fresh and foraged ingredients. The menu sings of the seasons, be it asparagus, game, strawberries or winter veg. The vibe is urbane and relaxed.

Drinking & Nightlife

Besides a glut of bars in the Altstadt, a string of bars huddles under the railway arches on Ingenieur-Etzel-Strasse, otherwise known as the Viaduktbögen.

Moustache
BAR

(www.cafe-moustache.at; Herzog-Otto-Strasse 8; ⊙11am-2am Tue-Sun; 🛜) Playing Spot-the-Moustache (Einstein, Charlie Chaplin and co) is the preferred pastime at this retro bolthole, with table football and a terrace overlooking pretty Domplatz. They knock up a mean pisco sour.

Tribaun
CRAFT BEER

(www.tribaun.com; Museumstrasse 5; ⊙5pm-2am Mon-Thu, to 3.30am Fri & Sat) This cracking new bar taps into craft-beer culture, with a wide variety of brews – from stouts and porters to IPA, sour, amber, honey and red ales. The easygoing vibe and fun-loving crew add to its appeal. For more insight, hook onto a 90-minute, seven-beer tasting (€19).

❶ Information

Innsbruck Information (☑0512-53 56-0, 0512-59 850; www.innsbruck.info; Burggraben 3; ⊙9am-6pm) Main tourist office with truckloads of info on the city and surrounds, including skiing and walking.

❶ Getting There & Away

The **bus station** is at the southern end of the Hauptbahnhof; its ticket office is located within the station.

Train services depart several times daily for Salzburg, Kitzbühel, Lienz and Munich.

Kitzbühel

POP 8135

One of Austria's top ski resorts, Kitzbühel began life in the 16th century as a silver- and copper-mining town, and today preserves a charming car-free medieval centre and a reputation as a fashionable and prosperous winter resort renowned for the excellence of its 170km of groomed slopes.

🏃 Activities

Hahnenkammbahn
CABLE CAR

(Hahnenkamm Cable Car; adult/child return €25.50/8.60) This cable car whisks you up to the summit of 1712m Hahnenkamm, a magnet for hikers and downhill bikers in summer and hard-core skiers – many attempting the mythical Streif race – in winter.

Kitzbüheler Hornbahn   CABLE CAR

(Kitzbüheler Horn Cable Car; adult/child return €25.50/8.90) Hitching a ride on this cable car brings you to the Alpine Flower Garden. Hiking and mountain-biking trails fan out from the summit. A panoramic pick is the 2.4km Karstweg circuit, which affords impressive glimpses of the surrounding karst landscape. In winter Kitzbüheler Horn is a magnet for beginners, with gentle cruising on sunny slopes.

🛏 Sleeping & Eating

Snowbunny's Hostel   HOSTEL €

(📞 067 6794 0233; www.snowbunnys.co.uk; Bichlstrasse 30; dm €24-38, d €66-96; @🛜) This friendly, laid-back hostel is a bunny-hop from the slopes. Dorms are fine, if a tad dark; breakfast is DIY-style in the kitchen. There's a TV lounge, a ski storage room and cats to stroke.

Huberbräu Stüberl   AUSTRIAN €€

(📞 05356-656 77; Vorderstadt 18; mains €9-18; ⊗ 8am-11.45pm Mon-Fri, from 9am Sat & Sun) An old-world Tyrolean haunt with vaults and pine benches, this tavern favours substantial portions of Austrian classics, such as schnitzel, goulash and dumplings, cooked to perfection.

ℹ Information

Tourist Office (📞 666 60; www.kitzbuehel. com; Hinterstadt 18; ⊗ 8.30am-6pm Mon-Fri, 9am-6pm Sat, 10am-noon & 4-6pm Sun) The central tourist office has loads of info in English and a 24-hour accommodation board.

ℹ Getting There & Away

The main train station is 1km north of central Vorderstadt. Trains run frequently to Innsbruck (€15.80, 1¼ hours) and Salzburg (€30.30, 2½ hours).

Austria Survival Guide

ℹ Directory A–Z

ACCOMMODATION

➡ Book ahead for weekends and any time during the high seasons: July and August, and December to April (in ski resorts).

➡ Some hostels and rock-bottom digs have an *Etagendusche* (communal shower).

➡ You will often see signs advertising 'Privatzimmer' (private room) or 'Zimmer Frei'

(room free). These are rooms in private houses and cheap, although the level of service varies.

➡ In mountain resorts, high-season prices can be up to double the prices charged in the low season (May and November, which fall between the summer and winter).

➡ Some resorts issue a *Gästekarte* (guest card) when you stay overnight, offering discounts on things such as cable cars and admission.

INTERNET RESOURCES

Austrian Hotelreservation (www.austrian-hotelreservation.at) Find hotels Austria-wide by theme and/or destination.

Austrian National Tourist Office (www. austria.info)

LGBT TRAVELLERS

Vienna is reasonably tolerant towards gays and lesbians, more so than the rest of the country.

MONEY

ATMs are widely available. Most hotels and mid-range to high-end restaurants accept Maestro direct debit and Visa and MasterCard credit cards. An approximate 10% tip is expected in restaurants.

OPENING HOURS

Cafes Usually 7am or 8am to 11pm or midnight; some traditional cafes close at 7pm or 8pm

Pubs & bars Close anywhere between midnight and about 4am

Restaurants Generally 11am to 2.30pm or 3pm and 6pm to 11pm or midnight; kitchens may close an hour earlier in the evening

Shops 9am to 6.30pm Monday to Friday (often to 9pm Thursday or Friday in cities); from 9am to 5pm Saturday

PUBLIC HOLIDAYS

New Year's Day (Neujahr) 1 January

Epiphany (Heilige Drei Könige) 6 January

ℹ PRICE RANGES

Accommodation prices listed refer to a double room with private bathroom, including breakfast:

€ less than €80

€€ €80–200

€€€ more than €200

Eating price ranges are for the cost of a two-course meal, excluding drinks:

€ less than €80

€€ €80–200

€€€ more than €200

Easter Sunday and Monday (Ostersonntag & Ostermontag) March/April Labour Day (Tag der Arbeit) 1 May

Whit Sunday and Monday (Pfingstsonntag & Pfingstmontag) 6th Monday after Easter

Ascension Day (Christi Himmelfahrt) 6th Thursday after Easter

Corpus Christi (Fronleichnam) 2nd Thursday after Whitsunday

Assumption (Maria Himmelfahrt) 15 August

National Day (Nationalfeiertag) 26 October

All Saints' Day (Allerheiligen) 1 November

Immaculate Conception (Mariä Empfängnis) 8 December

Christmas Day (Christfest) 25 December

St Stephen's Day (Stephanitag) 26 December

ⓘ Getting There & Away

AIR

Vienna is the main transport hub for Austria, but Graz, Linz, Klagenfurt, Salzburg and Innsbruck all receive international flights. Flights to these cities are often a cheaper option than those to the capital, as are flights to Airport Letisko (Bratislava Airport, Slovakia), which is only 60km east of Vienna.

LAND
Bus

Travelling by bus is a cheap but less comfortable way to reach Austria from other European coun-

tries. Options include Eurolines, Busabout and ÖBB Intercity Bus.

Train

Austria benefits from its central location within Europe by having excellent rail connections to all important destinations. For timetables and tickets, visit the website of **ÖBB** (Österreichische Bundesbahnen; Austrian Federal Railways; ☑ 24hr hotline 05-17 17; www.oebb.at), which also shows Postbus services.

RIVER

Hydrofoils run to Bratislava (Slovakia) and Budapest (Hungary) from Vienna; slower boats cruise the Danube between the capital and Passau. The **Danube Tourist Commission** (www.danube-river.org) has a country-by-country list of operators and agents who can book tours.

ⓘ Getting Around

Austria's national railway system is integrated with the Postbus services, which really come into their own in the less accessible mountainous regions. Buses are fairly reliable, and usually depart from outside train stations. Plan your route using the **ÖBB** or **Postbus** (☑ 24hr hotline 0810 22 23 33; www.postbus.at) websites.

Reservations are usually unnecessary. On buses, it's possible to buy tickets in advance on some routes, but on others you can only buy tickets from the drivers.

France & Switzerland

Best Places to Eat

➡ 59 Faubourg St-Denis (p318)

➡ Holybelly 5 (p319)

➡ Breizh Café (p336)

➡ Daniel et Dénise (p344)

➡ Magasin Général (p346)

➡ La Grillade Gourmande (p341)

Best Places to Sleep

➡ Generator Hostel (p318)

➡ Cosmos Hôtel (p318)

➡ Le Colbert (p350)

➡ Nice Pebbles

➡ Hotel Anne de Bretagne (p337)

Why Go?

Historic cities crammed with architectural icons and opulence, storybook villages, vine-stitched valleys and Alpine landscapes so hallucinatorily beautiful they must be seen to be believed. Travelling through this sophisticated wedge of Western Europe is a kaleidoscope of top-of-the-world landscapes and sensory experiences.

Visiting France is about lapping up French *art de vivre* between celebrity sights. Think wine, food and excessive *dégustation* (tasting), indulged in, as required by local etiquette, at a delicious escargot-slow pace.

Moving east, across Europe's largest alpine lake shared by France and Switzerland, is a picture-perfect country that has seduced since Grand Tour days. The only tricky part about Switzerland is deciding where to snap that perfect selfie – at edgy urbanite Zürich, chocolate-box Bern, adventure-sports hub Innsbruck or Italianate lake-laced Ticino?

Fast Facts

Capitals Paris (France), Bern (Switzerland)

Emergency ☑ 112 (France), ☑ 117 (Switzerland)

Currency Euro (€; France), Swiss franc (CHF or Sfr; Switzerland)

Languages French (France), French, German, Italian, Romanesch (Switzerland)

Visas Not required for stays of up to 90 days (or at all for EU citizens); some nationalities need a Schengen visa.

Mobile phones European and Australian phones work, but only American cells with 900 and 1800 Mhz are compatible; slip in a local SIM card to call with a cheaper local number.

Time zone Central European Time (GMT/UTC plus one hour)

France & Switzerland Highlights

1 Paris Enjoying a whirlwind romance with one of the world's greatest cities. (p310)

2 Mont St-Michel Following pilgrims to this ancient island abbey. (p334)

3 Loire Valley Reliving the Renaissance in royal châteaux. (p336)

4 French Riviera corniches Motoring along a trio of coastal cliffhangers near Nice. (p350)

5 **Lake Geneva** Admiring Mont Blanc and live the good life ashore Europe's largest alpine lake. (p358)

6 **Matterhorn** Pandering to every last topographic need of this iconic peak in uber-cool Zermatt. (p366)

7 **Zürich** Shopping, partying and kicking back with wild lake swimming in this Swiss ode to urban innovation. (p372)

FRANCE

Paris

POP 2.2 MILLION

Paris' monument-lined boulevards, museums, classical bistros and boutiques are enhanced by a new wave of multimedia galleries, creative wine bars, design shops and tech start-ups.

◉ Sights

◉ Left Bank

★ Eiffel Tower   LANDMARK
(Map p316; ☑ 08 92 70 12 39; www.toureiffel.paris; Champ de Mars, 5 av Anatole France, 7e; adult/child lift to top €25/6.30, lift to 2nd fl €16/4, stairs to 2nd fl €10/2.50; ☺ lifts & stairs 9am-12.45am mid-Jun–Aug, lifts 9.30am-11.45pm, stairs 9.30am-6.30pm Sep–mid-Jun; Ⓜ Bir Hakeim or RER Champ de Mars–Tour Eiffel) No one could imagine Paris today without it. But Gustave Eiffel only constructed this elegant, 320m-tall signature spire as a temporary exhibit for the 1889 World's Fair. Luckily, the art nouveau tower's popularity assured its survival. Prebook online to avoid painfully long ticket queues.

Lifts ascend to the tower's three floors; change lifts on the 2nd floor for the final ascent to the top. Energetic visitors can climb as far as the 2nd floor via the south pillar's 704 stairs (no prebooking).

★ Musée du Quai Branly   MUSEUM
(Map p316; ☑ 01 56 61 70 00; www.quaibranly.fr; 37 quai Branly, 7e; adult/child €10/free; ☺ 11am-7pm Tue, Wed & Sun, 11am-9pm Thu-Sat; Ⓜ Alma Marceau or RER Pont de l'Alma) A tribute to the diversity of human culture, Musée du Quai Branly's highly inspiring overview of indigenous and folk art spans four main sections – Oceania, Asia, Africa and the Americas. An impressive array of masks, carvings, weapons, jewellery and more make up the body of the rich collection, displayed in a refreshingly unorthodox interior without rooms or high walls. Look out for excellent temporary exhibitions and performances.

★ Hôtel des Invalides   MONUMENT, MUSEUM
(Map p316; www.musee-armee.fr; 129 rue de Grenelle, 7e; adult/child €12/free; ☺ 10am-6pm; Ⓜ Varenne, La Tour Maubourg) Flanked by the 500m-long Esplanade des Invalides lawns,

Hôtel des Invalides was built in the 1670s by Louis XIV to house 4000 *invalides* (disabled war veterans). On 14 July 1789, a mob broke into the building and seized 32,000 rifles before heading on to the prison at Bastille and the start of the French Revolution.

Admission includes entry to all Hôtel des Invalides sights (temporary exhibitions cost extra). Hours for individual sites can vary – check the website for updates.

★ Musée Rodin   MUSEUM, GARDEN
(Map p316; ☑ 01 44 18 61 10; www.musee-rodin.fr; 79 rue de Varenne, 7e; adult/child €10/free, garden only €4/free; ☺ 10am-5.45pm Tue-Sun; Ⓜ Varenne or Invalides) Sculptor, painter, sketcher, engraver and collector Auguste Rodin donated his entire collection to the French state in 1908 on the proviso that they dedicate his former workshop and showroom, the beautiful 1730 Hôtel Biron, to displaying his works. They're now installed not only in the magnificently restored mansion itself, but also in its rose-filled garden – one of the most peaceful places in central Paris and a wonderful spot to contemplate his famous work *The Thinker*. Prepurchase tickets online to avoid queuing.

Église St-Germain des Prés   CHURCH
(Map p324; ☑ 01 55 42 81 18; www.eglise-saintgermaindespres.fr; 3 place St-Germain des Prés, 6e; ☺ 9am-7.45pm; Ⓜ St-Germain des Prés) Paris' oldest standing church, the Romanesque St Germanus of the Fields, was built in the 11th century on the site of a 6th-century abbey and was the main place of worship in Paris until the arrival of Notre Dame. It's since been altered many times. The oldest part, Chapelle de St-Symphorien is to the right as you enter; St Germanus (496–576), the first bishop of Paris, is believed to be buried there.

★ Jardin du Luxembourg   PARK
(Map p324; www.senat.fr/visite/jardin; ☺ hours vary; Ⓜ Mabillon, St-Sulpice, Rennes, Notre Dame des Champs, RER Luxembourg) This inner-city oasis of formal terraces, chestnut groves and lush lawns has a special place in Parisians' hearts. Napoléon dedicated the 23 gracefully laid-out hectares of the Luxembourg Gardens to the children of Paris, and many residents spent their childhood prodding 1920s wooden sailboats (Map p324; sailboat rental per 30min €4; ☺ 11am-6pm Apr-Oct; Ⓜ Notre Dame des Champs, RER Luxembourg) with long sticks on the octagonal Grand Bassin pond,

watching puppets perform puppet shows at the **Théâtre du Luxembourg** (Map p324; 01 43 29 50 97; www.marionnettesduluxembourg.fr; tickets €6.40; ⊙ Wed, Sat & Sun, daily during school holidays; Ⓜ Notre Dame des Champs), and riding the *carrousel* (merry-go-round) or **ponies** (Map p324; 06 07 32 53 95; www.animaponey.com; 600m/900m pony ride €6/8.50; ⊙ 3-6pm Wed, Sat, Sun & school holidays; Ⓜ Notre Dames des Champs, RER Luxembourg).

★ **Musée d'Orsay** MUSEUM
(Map p316; 01 40 49 48 14; www.musee-orsay.fr; 1 rue de la Légion d'Honneur, 7e; adult/child €12/free; ⊙ 9.30am-6pm Tue, Wed & Fri-Sun, to 9.45pm Thu; Ⓜ Assemblée Nationale, RER Musée d'Orsay) The home of France's national collection from the impressionist, postimpressionist and art nouveau movements spanning from 1848 to 1914 is the glorious former Gare d'Orsay railway station – itself an art-nouveau showpiece – where a roll-call of masters and their world-famous works are on display.

Top of every visitor's must-see list is the painting collection, centred on the world's largest collection of impressionist and postimpressionist art. Allow ample time to swoon over masterpieces by Manet, Monet, Cézanne, Renoir, Degas, Pissarro and Van Gogh.

Panthéon MAUSOLEUM
(Map p324; 01 44 32 18 00; www.paris-pantheon.fr; place du Panthéon, 5e; adult/child €9/free; ⊙ 10am-6.30pm Apr-Sep, to 6pm Oct-Mar; Ⓜ Maubert-Mutualité or RER Luxembourg) The Panthéon's stately neoclassical dome is a Parisian skyline icon and its vast interior is an architectural masterpiece: originally an abbey church dedicated to Ste Geneviève and now a mausoleum, it has served since 1791 as the resting place of some of France's greatest thinkers, including Voltaire, Rousseau, Braille and Hugo. A copy of Foucault's pendulum, first hung from the dome in 1851 to demonstrate the rotation of the earth, takes pride of place.

Musée National du Moyen Âge MUSEUM
(Map p324; 01 53 73 78 16; www.musee-moyenage.fr; 6 place Paul Painlevé, 5e; adult/child €8/free; ⊙ 9.15am-5.45pm Wed-Mon; Ⓜ Cluny–La Sorbonne) Undergoing renovation until late 2020, the National Museum of the Middle Ages is considered one of Paris' top small museums. It showcases a series of sublime treasures, from medieval statuary, stained glass and objets d'art to its celebrated series of tapestries, *The Lady with the Unicorn*

(1500). Other highlights include ornate 15th-century mansion Hôtel de Cluny and the *frigidarium* (cold room) of an enormous Roman-era bathhouse.

Institut du Monde Arabe MUSEUM
(Arab World Institute; Map p324; 01 40 51 38 38; www.imarabe.org; 1 place Mohammed V, 5e; adult/child €8/4; ⊙ 10am-6pm Tue-Fri, to 7pm Sat & Sun; Ⓜ Jussieu) The Arab World Institute was jointly founded by France and 18 Middle Eastern and North African nations in 1980, with the aim of promoting cross-cultural dialogue. It hosts temporary exhibitions and a fascinating museum of Arabic culture and history (4th to 7th floors). The stunning building, designed by French architect Jean Nouvel, was inspired by latticed-wood windows *(mashrabiya)* traditional to Arabic architecture: thousands of modern-day photo-electrically sensitive apertures cover its sparkling glass facade.

Les Catacombes CEMETERY
(Map p316; 01 43 22 47 63; www.catacombes.paris.fr; 1 av Colonel Henri Roi-Tanguy, 14e; adult/child €13/free, online booking incl audioguide €29/5; ⊙ 10am-8.30pm Tue-Sun; Ⓜ Denfert Rochereau) Paris' most macabre sight is its underground tunnels lined with skulls and bones. In 1785 it was decided to rectify the hygiene problems of Paris' overflowing cemeteries by exhuming the bones and storing them in disused quarry tunnels and the Catacombes were created in 1810.

After descending 20m (via 130 narrow, dizzying spiral steps), follow dark, subterranean passages to the ossuary (1.5km in all). Exit via a minimalist all-white 'transition space' with gift shop onto 21bis av René Coty, 14e. Buy tickets in advance online to avoid queueing.

⭐ FRANCE AT A GLANCE

Don't Miss

Eiffel Tower More than six million people visit Paris' iconic tower annually; ascend the twinkling tower after dark and sip champagne at the top.

Mont St-Michel The play of tides on this abbey-island in Normandy is magical and mysterious. Make your way barefoot across rippled sand to feel the immense history.

Champagne Visit world-famous Champagne houses in Reims and Épernay, then hit the open road through rolling vineyards and drop-dead-gorgeous villages. Taste bubbles with passionate, small-scale winemakers.

Chamonix action Winter playground to the rich, famous and not-so-famous, this iconic ski resort in the French Alps has something for everyone, buzzing après-ski included.

Dune du Pilat Europe's largest sand dune is a 'mountain' that has to be staggered up – and romped down at speed. Nearby beaches have some of the Atlantic Coast's finest surf

Itineraries

One Week

For a taste of quintessential France at its biggest and boldest, follow this two-week 'best of' itinerary. No place screams 'France!' more than **Paris**. Spend two days in the capital, allowing time for cafe lounging, bistro lunches and waterside strolls along the Seine and Canal St-Martin. If grandiose architecture rocks your boat, consider a day trip to the country's grandest chateau at **Versailles**. On day three, enjoy Renaissance royalty in Blois, Amboise and Chambord in the **Loire Valley**. Or spend two days in **Normandy**, marvelling at the Bayeux tapestry, sea-splashed **Mont St-Michel** and – should modern history be your passion – the **D-Day landing beaches**.

Two Weeks

Day five, zoom south along the Atlantic Coast to **Bordeaux**, one of France's most dynamic cities with fantastic museums, edgy dining and seriously fine wine. The staggering **Dune du Pilat** is an easy trip from here. On the third day, drive three hours to Roman **Nîmes**, the **Pont du Gard** and **Avignon** with its famous summertime arts festival. Finish on the French Riviera with a casino flutter in Grace Kelly's **Monaco**, a port-side aperitif in Brigitte Bardot's **St-Tropez** and a stroll through Matisse's **Nice**. Don't miss a scenic cruise along Nice's trio of cliffhanger *corniches* (coastal roads).

Essential Food & Drink

Baguette French simplicity at its finest: buy a crunchy baguette from the local *boulangerie* (bakery), fill it with a creamy Camembert cheese, pâté and *cornichons* (mini gherkins), or a few slices of rosette de Lyon or other salami and, *voila* – picnic perfection! The sweet-toothed can do it the French-kid way – with a slab of milk chocolate inside.

Macarons No sweeter way to end a gourmet picnic, most famously from Ladurée in Paris.

Fruit Big juicy black cherries from Apt,and peaches, apricots and tomatoes from the Rhône Valley, Provence and the Riviera.

Provençal olives or peppers Marinated and stuffed with a multitude of edible sins from market stands.

Champagne from Reims and biscuit roses.

Getting Around

Transport in France is comfortable, quick, usually reliable and reasonably priced.

Train Run by the state-owned SNCF, France's rail network is truly first-class, with extensive coverage of the country and frequent departures.

Car Meander away from cities and large towns (where a car is hard to park) and a car comes into its own. Cars can be hired at airports and train stations. Drive on the right. Be aware of France's potentially hazardous 'priority to the right' rule.

Bus Cheaper and slower than trains. Useful for more remote villages that aren't serviced by trains.

Bicycle Certain regions – the Loire Valley, the Lubéron in Provence and Burgundy – have dedicated cycling paths.

When to Go

Paris

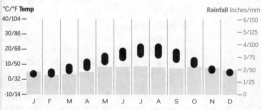

Jul & Aug	Apr–Jun & Sep	Oct–Mar
Queues at big sights and on the road, especially August.	Spring is idyllic, with warm temperatures, flowers and local produce.	Prices can be 50% lower than in high season. Sights and restaurants open fewer days and shorter hours.

Arriving in France

Aéroport de Charles de Gaulle (Paris) RER trains, buses and night buses to the city centre €6 to €17; taxi €50 to €55, 15% higher evenings and Sundays.

Aéroport d'Orly (Paris) Orlyval then RER trains, buses and night buses to the city centre €8.70 to €13.25; T7 tram to Villejuif–Louis Aragon then metro to centre (€3.80); taxi €30 to €35, 15% higher evenings and Sundays.

Top Phrases

Hello. Bonjour.

Goodbye. Au revoir.

Excuse me. Excusez-moi.

Sorry. Pardon.

You're welcome. De rien.

Resources

France.fr (www.france.fr)

France 24 (www.france24. com/en/france)

Paris by Mouth (www. parisbymouth.com)

French Word-a-Day (http:// french-word-a-day.typepad. com)

Set Your Budget

➡ Dorm bed: €18–30

➡ Double room in a budget hotel: €90

➡ Admission to many attractions first Sunday of month: free

➡ Lunch menus (set meals): less than €20

⊙ The Islands

Paris' geographic and spiritual heart is here in the Seine, on inner-city islands Île de la Cité, dominated by Notre Dame, and serene eatery-clad Île St-Louis.

★ Cathédrale
Notre Dame de Paris   CATHEDRAL

(Map p324; ☎ 01 42 34 56 10, towers 01 53 10 07 00; www.notredamedeparis.fr; 6 Parvis Notre Dame – place Jean-Paul-II, 4e; cathedral free, adult/child towers €10/free, treasury €5/3; ⊙ cathedral 7.45am-6.45pm Mon-Fri, to 7.15pm Sat & Sun, towers 10am-6.30pm Sun-Thu, 10am-11pm Fri & Sat Jul & Aug, 10am-6.30pm Apr-Jun & Sep, 10am-5.30pm Oct-Mar, treasury 9.45am-5.30pm; Ⓜ Cité) Paris' most visited unticketed site, with upwards of 14 million visitors per year, is a masterpiece of French Gothic architecture. The focus of Catholic Paris for seven centuries, its vast interior accommodates 6000 worshippers.

Highlights include its three spectacular rose windows, treasury and bell towers which can be climbed. From the North Tower, 400-odd steps spiral to the top of the western facade, where you'll find yourself face-to-face with frightening gargoyles and a spectacular view of Paris.

Sainte-Chapelle   CHAPEL

(Map p324; ☎ 01 53 40 60 80, concerts 01 42 77 65 65; www.sainte-chapelle.fr; 8 bd du Palais, 1er; adult/child €10/free, joint ticket with Conciergerie €15; ⊙ 9am-7pm Apr-Sep, to 5pm Oct-Mar; Ⓜ Cité) Try to save Sainte-Chapelle for a sunny day, when Paris' oldest, finest stained glass is

---

DON'T MISS

JE T'AIME ...

Few visitors can resist a selfie in front of Montmartre's 'I Love You' wall, a public artwork created in a small park by artists Frédéric Baron and Claire Kito in the year 2000. Made from dark-blue enamel tiles, the striking **Le Mur des Je t'aime** (Map p321; www.lesjetaime. com; Sq Jehan Rictus, place des Abbesses ,18e; ⊙ 8am-9.30pm Mon-Fri, from 9am Sat & Sun mid-May–Aug, shorter hours Sep–mid-May; Ⓜ Abbesses) mural features the immortal phrase 'I love you' 311 times in 250 different languages. The red fragments, if joined together, would form a heart.

---

at its dazzling best. Enshrined within the Palais de Justice (Law Courts), this gemlike Holy Chapel is Paris' most exquisite Gothic monument. It was completed in 1248, just six years after the first stone was laid, and was conceived by Louis IX to house his personal collection of holy relics, including the famous Holy Crown (now in Notre Dame).

⊙ Right Bank

★ Musée du Louvre   MUSEUM

(Map p324; ☎ 01 40 20 53 17; www.louvre.fr; rue de Rivoli & quai des Tuileries, 1er; adult/child €15/free; ⊙ 9am-6pm Mon, Thu, Sat & Sun, to 9.45pm Wed & Fri; Ⓜ Palais Royal–Musée du Louvre) It isn't until you're standing in the vast courtyard of the Louvre, with sunlight shimmering through the glass pyramid and crowds milling about beneath the museum's ornate facade, that you can truly say you've been to Paris. Holding tens of thousands of works of art – from Mesopotamian, Egyptian and Greek antiquities to masterpieces by artists such as da Vinci (including his incomparable *Mona Lisa*), Michelangelo and Rembrandt – it's no surprise that this is one of the world's most visited museums. See also p322.

Jardin des Tuileries   PARK

(Map p316; rue de Rivoli, 1er; ⊙ 7am-9pm Apr–late Sep, 7.30am-7.30pm late Sep–Mar; Ⓜ Tuileries, Concorde) Filled with fountains, ponds and sculptures, the formal 28-hectare Tuileries Garden, which begins just west of the Jardin du Carrousel, was laid out in its present form in 1664 by André Le Nôtre, architect of the gardens at Versailles. The Tuileries soon became the most fashionable spot in Paris for parading about in one's finery. It now forms part of the Banks of the Seine Unesco World Heritage site.

★ Basilique du
Sacré-Cœur   BASILICA

(Map p321; ☎ 01 53 41 89 00; www.sacre-coeur-montmartre.com; Parvis du Sacré-Cœur; basilica free, dome adult/child €6/4, cash only; ⊙ basilica 6am-10.30pm, dome 8.30am-8pm May-Sep, 9am-5pm Oct-Apr; Ⓜ Anvers, Abbesses) Begun in 1875 in the wake of the Franco-Prussian War and the chaos of the Paris Commune, Sacré-Cœur is a symbol of the former struggle between the conservative Catholic old guard and the secular, republican radicals. It was finally consecrated in 1919, standing in contrast to the bohemian lifestyle that surrounded it. The view over

ART ATTACK

Paris' refreshingly low-key **Musée Marmotan Monet** (Map p316; ☑ 01 44 96 50 33; www.marmottan.fr; 2 rue Louis Boilly, 16e; adult/child €11/7.50; ☺ 10am-6pm Tue, Wed & Fri-Sun, to 9pm Thu; Ⓜ La Muette) showcases the world's largest collection of works by impressionist painter Claude Monet (1840–1926) – about 100 – as well as paintings by Gauguin, Sisley, Pissarro, Renoir, Degas, Manet and Morisot. It also contains an important collection of French, English, Italian and Flemish illuminations from the 13th to 16th centuries.

If Asian art is more your cup of tea, make a beeline for another largely unsung art museum: the **Musée Guimet des Arts Asiatiques** (Map p316; ☑ 01 56 52 53 00; www.guimet.fr; 6 place d'Iéna, 16e; adult/child €8.50/free; ☺ 10am-6pm Wed-Mon; Ⓜ Iéna) squirrels away France's foremost collection of Asian art, ranging from 1st-century Gandhara Buddhas from Afghanistan and Pakistan to later Central Asian, Chinese and Japanese Buddhist sculptures and art works.

Paris from its parvis is breathtaking. Avoid walking up the steep hill by using a regular metro ticket aboard the **funicular** (www.ratp.fr; place St-Pierre, 18e; ☺ 6am-12.45am; Ⓜ Anvers, Abbesses) to the **upper station** (rue du Cardinal Dubois, 18e; Ⓜ Abbesses).

★ Musée National Picasso
MUSEUM

(Map p324; ☑ 01 85 56 00 36; www.museepicassoparis.fr; 5 rue de Thorigny, 3e; adult/child €12.50/free; ☺ 10.30am-6pm Tue-Fri, from 9.30am Sat & Sun; Ⓜ Chemin Vert, St-Paul) One of Paris' most treasured art collections is showcased inside the mid-17th-century Hôtel Salé, an exquisite private mansion owned by the city since 1964. The Musée National Picasso is a staggering art museum devoted to Spanish artist Pablo Picasso (1881–1973), who spent much of his life living and working in Paris. The collection includes more than 5000 drawings, engravings, paintings, ceramic works and sculptures by the *grand maître* (great master), although they're not all displayed at the same time.

★ Centre Pompidou
MUSEUM

(Map p324; ☑ 01 44 78 12 33; www.centrepompidou.fr; place Georges Pompidou, 4e; museum, exhibitions & panorama adult/child €14/free, panorama ticket only €5/free; ☺ 11am-9pm Wed-Mon, temporary exhibits to 11pm Thu; Ⓜ Rambuteau) Renowned for its radical architectural statement, the 1977-opened Centre Pompidou brings together galleries and cutting-edge exhibitions, hands-on workshops, dance performances, cinemas and other entertainment venues, with street performers and fanciful fountains outside. The **Musée National d'Art Moderne**, France's national collection of art dating from 1905 onward, is the main draw; a fraction of its 100,000-plus

pieces – including fauvist, cubist, surrealist, pop-art and contemporary works – is on display. Don't miss the spectacular Parisian panorama from the rooftop.

Cimetière du Père Lachaise
CEMETERY

(Map p316; ☑ 01 55 25 82 10; www.pere-lachaise.com; 16 rue du Repos & 8 bd de Ménilmontant, 20e; ☺ 8am-6pm Mon-Fri, from 8.30am Sat, from 9am Sun mid-Mar–Oct, shorter hours Nov–mid-Mar; Ⓜ Père Lachaise, Gambetta) Opened in 1804, Père Lachaise is today the world's most visited cemetery. Its 70,000 ornate tombs of the rich and famous form a verdant, 44-hectare sculpture garden. The most visited are those of 1960s rock star Jim Morrison (division 6) and Oscar Wilde (division 89). Pick up cemetery maps at the **conservation office** (Bureaux de la Conservation; Map p316; ☺ 8.30am-12.30pm & 2-5pm Mon-Fri) near the main bd de Ménilmontant entrance. Other notables buried here include composer Chopin, playwright Molière, poet Apollinaire, and writers Balzac, Proust, Gertrude Stein and Colette.

★ Arc de Triomphe
LANDMARK

(Map p316; www.paris-arc-de-triomphe.fr; place Charles de Gaulle, 8e; viewing platform adult/child €12/free; ☺ 10am-11pm Apr-Sep, to 10.30pm Oct-Mar; Ⓜ Charles de Gaulle–Étoile) If anything rivals the Eiffel Tower (p310) as the symbol of Paris, it's this magnificent 1836 monument to Napoléon's victory at Austerlitz (1805), which he commissioned the following year. The intricately sculpted triumphal arch stands sentinel in the centre of the Étoile (Star) roundabout. From the viewing platform on top of the arch (50m up via 284 steps and well worth the climb) you can see the dozen avenues.

FRANCE & SWITZERLAND PARIS

Greater Paris

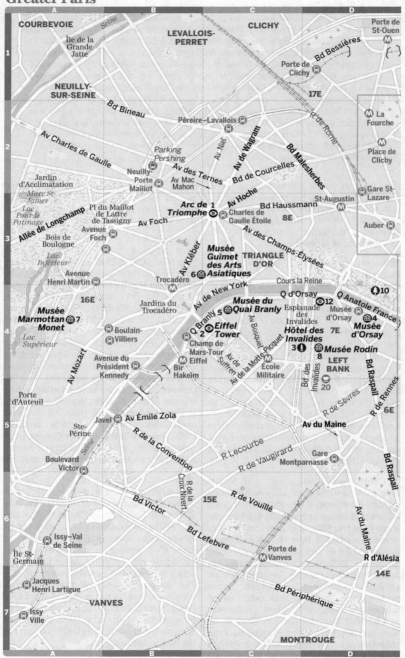

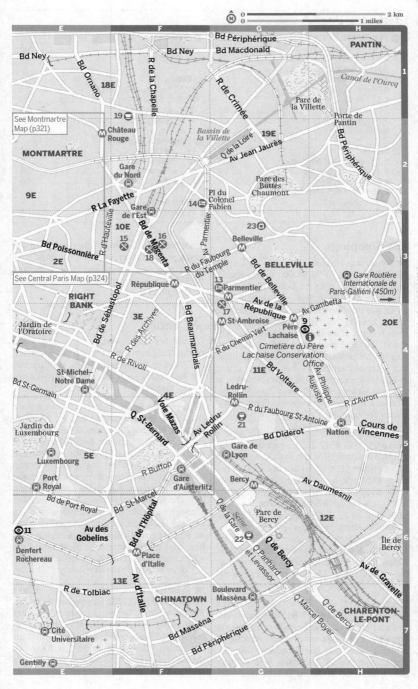

Greater Paris

🛏 Sleeping

★ Generator Hostel   HOSTEL €
(Map p316; ☑ 01 70 98 84 00; www.generator-hostels.com; 9-11 place du Colonel Fabien, 10e; dm/d from €33/92; ✱ @ 🛜; Ⓜ Colonel Fabien) From the 9th-floor rooftop bar overlooking Sacré-Cœur to the stylish ground-floor cafe-restaurant and vaulted basement bar-club styled like a Paris metro station, and su-percool bathrooms with 'I love you' tiling, this ultra-contemporary hostel near Canal St-Martin is sharp. Dorms have USB sockets and free lockers, and the best doubles have fabulous terraces with views. Female-only dorms are available.

Hôtel Eldorado   HOTEL €
(Map p321; ☑ 01 45 22 35 21; www.eldoradohotel. fr; 18 rue des Dames, 17e; d from €100, with shared bathroom from €65; 🛜; Ⓜ Place de Clichy) Bohemian Eldorado is a welcoming, reasonably well-run hotel with 33 colourfully decorated rooms above the **Bistro des Dames** (Map p321; ☑ 01 45 22 13 42; mains €16-24; ⊘noon-2.30pm & 7-11pm), with a private garden. Rooms facing the back can be quite noisy as they look out onto the restaurant terrace, which stays open until 2am – earplugs may be a good idea. Cheaper-category rooms have washbasins only. Breakfast costs €12.

Cosmos Hôtel   HOTEL €
(Map p316; ☑ 01 43 57 25 88; www.cosmos-ho-tel-paris.com; 35 rue Jean-Pierre Timbaud, 11e; s/d from €67/72; 🛜; Ⓜ Parmentier, Goncourt) Cheap, brilliant value and just footsteps from the nightlife of rue JPT, Cosmos is a shining star with retro style on the budget-hotel scene that, unlike most other hotels in the same price bracket, has been treated to a thoroughly modern makeover this century. Breakfast is basic but is also budget priced, costing just €8.

Baby cots are available on request.

🍴 Eating

On the Left Bank, cheap-eat student spots riddle the Latin Quarter. Across the river, Le Marais is the premier foodie destination; rue Rosiers, 4e, is lined with cheap eateries (many kosher).

52 Faubourg St-Denis   CAFE, BISTRO €
(Map p316; www.faubourgstdenis.com; 52 rue du Faubourg St-Denis, 10e; mains €17-20; ⊘kitchen noon-2.30pm & 7-11pm, bar 8am-midnight, closed Aug; 🛜; Ⓜ Château d'Eau) With its polished concrete floors, stone walls and exposed ducting, this contemporary neighbourhood cafe-restaurant is a brilliant space to hang out throughout the day, from breakfast through to lunch, dinner and drinks. Creative cuisine might include tuna sashimi salad with beetroot jelly, egg-yolk ravioli with ham and mushrooms or lamb-shoulder pie with cinnamon fig jus. No reservations.

Coffee is from Parisian roastery Coutume.

★ Breizh Café   CRÊPES €
(Map p324; ☑ 01 42 72 13 77; www.breizhcafe.com; 109 rue Vieille du Temple, 3e; crêpes & galettes €6.80-18.80; ⊘11.30am-11pm Mon-Sat, to 10pm Sun; Ⓜ St-Sébastien–Froissart) Everything at the Breizh ('Breton' in Breton) is 100% authentic, including its organic-flour crêpes and *galettes* that top many Parisians' lists

for the best in the city. Other specialities include Cancale oysters and 20 types of cider. Tables are limited and there's often a wait; book ahead or try its deli, **L'Épicerie** (Map p324; ☑ 01 42 71 39 44; 111 rue Vieille du Temple, 3e; ⏱11.30am-10pm), next door.

Holybelly 5
CAFE €

(Map p316; www.holybellycafe.com; 5 rue Lucien Sampaix, 10e; dishes €6.50-16.50; ⏱9am-5pm; ⏶🖉; Ⓜ Jacques Bonsergent) Light-filled Holybelly's regulars never tire of its outstanding coffee, cuisine and service. Sarah Mouchot's breakfast pancakes (with eggs, bacon, bourbon butter and maple syrup) and chia-seed porridge are legendary, while her lunch menu features everything from beetroot gnocchi to slow-cooked pork belly with sweet potato purée. Wash them down with a Bloody Mary or Deck & Donahue beer. No reservations.

Café Pinson
CAFE, VEGETARIAN €

(Map p324; ☑ 09 83 82 53 53; www.cafepinson.fr; 6 rue du Forez, 3e; 2-course lunch menus €17.50, mains €13.50-14.50, Sunday brunch €27; ⏱9am-10pm Mon-Fri, from 10am Sat, noon-6pm Sun; ⏶🖉; Ⓜ Filles du Calvaire) ⬧ Tucked down a narrow Haut Marais side street, this stylish cafe with an interior by celebrity designer Dorothée Meilichzon sees a fashionable lunchtime crowd flock for its organic vegetarian and vegan dishes such as beetroot-stuffed squash with vegetable crumble and chia pudding with cranberry sauce. Freshly squeezed juices are excellent, as is Sunday brunch (noon and 2.30pm).

L'Avant Comptoir de la Mer
SEAFOOD €

(Map p324; ☑ 01 42 38 47 55; www.hotel-paris-relais-saint-germain.com; 3 Carrefour de l'Odéon, 6e; tapas €5-25, oysters per six €17; ⏱noon-11pm; Ⓜ Odéon) One of Yves Camdeborde's stunning line-up of St-Germain hors d'oeuvre bars – alongside **Le Comptoir** (Map p324; ☑ 01 44 27 07 97; 9 Carrefour de l'Odéon, 6e; lunch mains €14-30, dinner menu €60; ⏱noon-6pm & 8.30-11.30pm Mon-Fri, noon-11pm Sat & Sun; Ⓜ Odéon), **L'Avant Comptoir de la Terre** (Map p324; 3 Carrefour de l'Odéon, 6e; tapas €5-10; ⏱noon-11pm; Ⓜ Odéon) and **L'Avant Comptoir du Marché** (Map p324; 15 rue Lobineau, 6e; tapas €3.50-20; ⏱noon-11pm; Ⓜ Mabillon) – serves succulent Cap Ferret oysters (straight, Bloody Mary–style or with chipolata sausages), herring tartine, cauliflower and trout roe, blood-orange razor clams, roasted scallops and salmon croquettes, complemented by fantastic artisan bread, hand-churned flavoured butters, sea salt and Kalamata olives.

Chez Alain Miam Miam
SANDWICHES, CRÊPES €

(Map p324; www.facebook.com/ChezAlainMiamMiam; Marché des Enfants Rouges, 39 rue de Bretagne & 33bis rue Charlot, 3e; dishes €3-9.50; ⏱9am-3.30pm Wed-Fri, to 5.30pm Sat, to 3pm Sun, closed Aug; 🖉; Ⓜ Filles du Calvaire) Weave your way through the makeshift kitchens inside **Marché des Enfants Rouges** (Map p324; ⏱8.30am-1pm & 4-7.30pm Tue-Sat, 8.30am-2pm Sun, individual stall hours vary) to find Alain, a retired baker sporting T-shirts with attitude, whose passion, humour and food are legendary. Watch him prepare you a monster sandwich or *galette* (savoury crêpe) on a sizzling griddle from a fresh, organic ingredients – grated fennel, smoked air-dried beef, avocado, sesame salt and prized honeys.

★ Shakespeare & Company Café
CAFE

(Map p324; ☑ 01 43 25 95 95; www.shakespeareandcompany.com; 2 rue St-Julien le Pauvre, 5e; ⏱9.30am-7pm Mon-Fri, to 8pm Sat & Sun; ⏶; Ⓜ St-Michel) ⬧ Instant history was made when this literary-inspired cafe opened in

FRANCE & SWITZERLAND PARIS

DON'T MISS

GLORIOUSLY GLUTEN-FREE

In a city known for its bakeries, it's only right there's **Chambelland** (Map p316; ☑ 01 43 55 07 30; www.chambelland.com; 14 rue Ternaux, 11e; lunch menus €10-12, pastries €2.50-5.50; ⏱9am-8pm Tue-Sat, to 6pm Sun; Ⓜ Parmentier) – a 100% gluten-free bakery in the Marais with serious breads to die for. Using rice and buckwheat flour milled at the bakery's own mill in southern France, this pioneering bakery creates exquisite cakes and pastries as well as sourdough loaves and brioches peppered with nuts, seeds, chocolate and fruit.

Stop for lunch at one of the handful of formica tables in this relaxed space, strewn with sacks of rice flour and books. There is always a salad (summer) or homemade soup (winter), served with a designer chunk of crunchy focaccia, perhaps of brown linseed-laced loaf. Or grab a sandwich – to eat in or take away.

2015 adjacent to magical bookshop **Shakespeare & Company** (Map p324; ☑01 43 25 40 93; 37 rue de la Bûcherie, 5e; ⊕10am-10pm), designed from long-lost sketches to fulfil a dream of late bookshop founder George Whitman from the 1960s. Organic chai tea, turbo-power juices and specialist coffee by Parisian roaster Café Lomi marry with soups, salads, bagels and pastries by Bob's Bake Shop, of **Bob's Juice Bar** (Map p316; ☑09 50 06 36 18; www.bobsjuicebar.com; 15 rue Lucien Sampaix, 10e; dishes €3.50-6, pastries €1.75-3; ⊕8am-3pm Mon-Fri, 8.30am-4pm Sat; ☑; Ⓜ Jacques Bonsergent).

★ **Café de la Nouvelle Mairie**   CAFE €
(Map p324; ☑01 44 07 04 41; 19 rue des Fossés St-Jacques, 5e; mains €10-20; ⊕8am-midnight Mon-Fri, kitchen noon-2.30pm & 8-10.30pm Mon-Thu, 8-10pm Fri; Ⓜ Cardinal Lemoine) Shhhh…just around the corner from the Panthéon (p311) but hidden away on a small, fountained square, this hybrid cafe-restaurant and wine bar is a tip-top neighbourhood secret, serving blackboard-chalked natural wines by the glass and delicious seasonal bistro fare from oysters and ribs (à la française) to grilled lamb sausage over lentils. It takes reservations for dinner but not lunch – arrive early.

Drinking & Nightlife

For the French, drinking and eating go together like wine and cheese, and the line between a cafe, *salon de thé* (tearoom), bistro, brasserie, bar, and even *bar à vins*

(wine bar) is blurred. It costs more to sit at a table than to stand at the counter, more on a fancy square than a backstreet, and more in the 8e than in the 18e. After 10pm many cafes charge a pricier *tarif de nuit* (night rate).

★ **Coutume Café**   COFFEE
(Map p316; ☑01 45 51 50 47; www.coutumecafe. com; 47 rue de Babylone, 7e; ⊕8.30am-5.30pm Mon-Fri, 9am-6pm Sat & Sun; ☎; Ⓜ St-François Xavier) ☞ The Parisian coffee revolution is thanks in no small part to Coutume, artisanal roaster of premium beans for scores of establishments around town. Its flagship cafe – a bright, light-filled, postindustrial space – is ground zero for innovative preparation methods including cold extraction and siphon brews. Couple some of Paris' finest coffee with a tasty, seasonal cuisine and the place is always packed out.

Be it porridge and fruit or pancakes for *petit dej* (breakfast), a bowl of homemade soup and tartine laden with fresh veggies or weekend brunch (€12), Coutume is an excellent spot to eat all day too.

★ **Le Baron Rouge**   WINE BAR
(Map p316; ☑01 43 43 14 32; www.lebaronrouge. net; 1 rue Théophile Roussel, 12e; ⊕5-10pm Mon, 10am-2pm & 5-10pm Tue-Fri, 10am-10pm Sat, 10am-4pm Sun; Ⓜ Ledru-Rollin) Just about the ultimate Parisian wine-bar experience, this wonderfully unpretentious local meeting place where everyone is welcome has barrels stacked against the bottle-lined walls and serves cheese, charcuterie and oysters in

---

DON'T MISS

SENSATIONAL COFFEE

Coffee has always been Parisians' drink of choice to kick-start the day and, thanks to an ongoing coffee revolution spear-headed by urban roasteries such as **Belleville Brûlerie** (Map p316; ☑09 83 75 60 80; http://cafesbelleville.com; 10 rue Pradier, 19e; ⊕11.30am-6.30pm Sat; Ⓜ Pyrénées), **Coutume** (p320) and **Café Lomi** (Map p316; ☑09 80 39 56 24; www.lomi.paris; 3ter rue Marcadet, 18e; ⊕8am-6pm Mon-Fri, 10am-7pm Sat & Sun; Ⓜ Marcadet–Poissonniers), Paris now has a bevy of *nouvelle génération* coffee shops and craft roasters.

Parisian pioneer and boutique-roaster **La Caféothèque** (Map p324; ☑01 53 01 83 84; www.lacafeotheque.com; 52 rue de l'Hôtel de Ville, 4e; ⊕8.30am-7.30pm Mon-Fri, from noon Sat & Sun; ☎; Ⓜ Pont Marie, St-Paul) by the Seine in the 4e arrondissement was among the first to open. Others include **Telescope** (Map p324; ☑01 42 61 33 14; 5 rue Villedo, 1er; ⊕8.30am-5pm Mon-Fri; Ⓜ Pyramides) near the Louvre and **Loustic** (Map p324; www. cafeloustic.com; 40 rue Chapon, 3e; ⊕8.30am-6pm Mon-Fri, from 9.30am Sat, from 10am Sun; ☎; Ⓜ Arts et Métiers), **Fondation Café** (Map p324; www.facebook.com/fondationcafe; 16 rue Dupetit Thouars, 3e; ⊕8am-6pm Mon-Fri, from 9am Sat & Sun; Ⓜ Temple) and **Boot Café** (Map p324; 19 rue du Pont aux Choux, 3e; ⊕10am-6pm; ☎; Ⓜ St-Sébastien–Froissart) in the trendy Marais.

Montmartre

season. It's especially busy on Sunday after the Marché d'Aligre wraps up. For a small deposit, you can fill up 1L bottles straight from the barrel for under €5.

Le Mary Céleste   COCKTAIL BAR
(Map p324; www.quixotic-projects.com/venue/mary-celeste; 1 rue Commines, 3e; ⊙6pm-2am, kitchen 7-11.30pm; M Filles du Calvaire) Snag a stool at the central circular bar at this uber-popular brick-and-timber-floored cocktail bar or reserve one of a handful of tables online. Innovative cocktails such as Ahha Kapehna (grappa, absinthe, beetroot, fennel

Montmartre

The Louvre

A HALF-DAY TOUR

Successfully visiting the Louvre is a fine art. Its complex labyrinth of galleries and staircases spiralling three wings and four floors renders discovery a snakes-and-ladders experience. Initiate yourself with this three-hour itinerary – a playful mix of *Mona Lisa*–obvious and up-to-the-minute unexpected.

Arriving in the newly renovated **❶ Hall Napoléon** beneath IM Pei's glass pyramid, pick up colour-coded floor plans at an information stand, then ride the escalator up to the Sully Wing and swap passport or credit card for a multimedia guide (there are limited descriptions in the galleries) at the wing entrance.

The Louvre is as much about spectacular architecture as masterful art. To appreciate this, zip up and down Sully's Escalier Henri II to admire **❷ Venus de Milo**, then up parallel Escalier Henri IV to the palatial displays in **❸ Cour Khorsabad**. Cross Room 1 to find the escalator up to the 1st floor and the opulent **❹ Napoleon III apartments**. Next traverse 25 consecutive galleries (thank you, floor plan!) to flip conventional contemplation on its head with Cy Twombly's **❺ The Ceiling**, and the hypnotic **❻ Winged Victory of Samothrace sculpture**, which brazenly insists on being admired from all angles. End with the impossibly famous **❼ The Raft of the Medusa**, **❽ Mona Lisa** and **❾ Virgin & Child**.

TOP TIPS

➡ Don't even consider entering the Louvre's maze of galleries without a floor plan, free from the information desk in the Hall Napoléon.

➡ The Denon Wing is always packed; visit on late nights (Wednesday or Friday) or trade Denon in for the notably quieter Richelieu Wing.

➡ Tickets to the Louvre are valid for the whole day, meaning that you can nip out for lunch.

Napoleon III Apartments
1st Floor, Richelieu
Napoleon III's gorgeous gilt apartments were built from 1854 to 1861, featuring an over-the-top decor of gold leaf, stucco and crystal chandeliers that reaches a dizzying climax in the Grand Salon and State Dining Room.

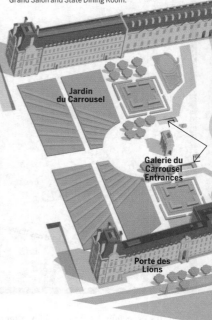

Jardin du Carrousel

Galerie du Carrousel Entrances

Porte des Lions

LOUVRE AUDITORIUM

Classical-music concerts are staged several times a week at the Louvre Auditorium (off the main entrance hall). Don't miss the Thursday lunchtime concerts featuring emerging composers and musicians. The season runs from September to April or May, depending on the concert series.

Mona Lisa
Room 6, 1st Floor, Denon
No smile is as enigmatic or bewitching as hers. Da Vinci's diminutive *La Joconde* hangs opposite the largest painting in the Louvre – sumptuous, fellow Italian Renaissance artwork *The Wedding at Cana*.

The Raft of the Medusa
Room 77, 1st Floor, Denon
Decipher the politics behind French romanticism in Théodore Géricault's *Raft of the Medusa*.

Cour Khorsabad
Ground Floor, Richelieu
Time travel with a pair of winged human-headed bulls to view some of the world's oldest Mesopotamian art. **DETOUR»** Night-lit statues in Cour Puget.

The Ceiling
Room 32, 1st Floor, Sully
Admire the blue shock of Cy Twombly's 400-sq-metre contemporary ceiling fresco – the Louvre's latest, daring commission. **DETOUR»** *The Braque Ceiling*, Room 33.

Rue de Rivoli Entrance

SULLY WING

Cour Khorsabad

③

Cour Puget

Cour Marly

④

RICHELIEU WING

Cour Carrée

⑤

Cour Napoléon

①

Pyramid Main Entrance

②

Inverted Pyramid

⑥

Cour Visconti

⑦ ⑧

⑨

DENON WING

Pont des Arts

Pont du Carrousel

Venus de Milo
Room 16, Ground Floor, Sully
No one knows who sculpted this seductively realistic goddess from Greek antiquity. Naked to the hips, she is a Hellenistic masterpiece.

Winged Victory of Samothrace
Escalier Daru, 1st Floor, Sully
Draw breath at the aggressive dynamism of this headless, handless Hellenistic goddess. **DETOUR»** The razzle-dazzle of the Apollo Gallery's crown jewels.

Virgin & Child
Grande Galerie, 1st Floor, Denon
In the spirit of artistic devotion save the Louvre's most famous gallery for last: a feast of Virgin-and-child paintings by Da Vinci, Raphael, Domenico Ghirlandaio, Giovanni Bellini and Francesco Botticini.

Central Paris

FRANCE & SWITZERLAND PARIS

500 m
0.25 miles

R de la Pierre Levée

Bd Jules Ferry
Bd Richard Lenoir
Bd Voltaire
31
11E
R Alphonse Baudin
St-Sébastien Froissart
Bd Richard Lenoir
Bréguet Sabin
R Daval
Bastille

Av de la République
Oberkampf
R Amelot
Chemin Vert
Bd Beaumarchais

Pl de la République
République
10E
Bd du Temple
R Béranger
Filles du Calvaire
26
R de Poitou
21
R St-Claude
Jardin St-Gilles Grand Veneur
R St-Gilles
R des Tournelles
Pl du Marché Ste-Catherine
R des Tournelles

Bd St-Martin
R Meslay
R Notre Dame de Nazareth
R de Turbigo
Temple
R Dupetit Thouars
24
16
22
R de Bretagne
R de Saintonge
R de Poitou
19
R Ste-Anastase
5 Musée National Picasso
R de Béarn
R du Pas de la Mule

R Vertbois
R Réaumur
Sq du Temple
R Perrée
3E
20
R Charlot
R de Turenne
14
Jardin de l'Hôtel Salé
R Barbette
R des Francs Bourgeois
R des Rosiers
R du Roi de Sicile
R de Rivoli
R Pavée
4E

Arts et Métiers
R des Gravilliers
R du Temple
R Pastourelle
R des Quatre Fils
R des Archives
LE MARAIS
R des Blancs Manteaux
R Vieille du Temple
R Ste-Croix de la Bretonnerie
25
R François Miron
R de Fourcy
R François Miron

Sq Emile Chautemps
R Beaubourg
R de Montmorency
R Michel le Comte
R Rambuteau
R St-Merri
Hôtel de Ville
R de la Verrerie
Q de l'Hôtel de Ville
Pont Louis-Philippe

Réaumur Sébastopol
R St-Martin
Bd de Sébastopol
Pl Georges Pompidou
Centre Pompidou 12
R du Renard
R St-Martin
Pl de l'Hôtel de Ville
Châtelet
Pont d'Arcole

St-Denis
R St-Sauveur
R Greneta
R de Turbigo
Les Halles
Rambuteau
R Berger
Pl Joachim du Bellay
Sq de la Tour St-Jacques
Châtelet
Pont au Change
Pont Notre Dame
Q de Gesvres
Pont de la Corse
Pont de l'Horloge

Sentier
2E
R de Réaumur
R du Caire
R d'Aboukir
Étienne Marcel
R Montorgueil
R Étienne Marcel
Les Halles
R Jean-Jacques Rousseau
Pl René Cassin
R Rambuteau
R Berger
Châtelet
Jean Lantier
Pont au Change
Q de la Mégisserie
Île de la Cité
R de la Cité
R de Lutèce
11
Bd du Palais

29
Pyramides
R des Petits Champs
R Vivienne
R de Richelieu
Pl des Victoires
R Croix des Petits Champs
1ER
R St-Honoré
R du Louvre
R de Rivoli
Louvre Rivoli
Pont Neuf
Q du Louvre
Pont Neuf
Q de l'Horloge
Île de la Cité
Q de l'Horloge
Q des Orfèvres
R de Savoie
R de la Cité

Paris Convention & Visitors Bureau
Av de l'Opéra
R de Richelieu
Pl du Palais Royal
Palais Royal – Musée du Louvre
Jardin du Palais Royal
RIGHT BANK
Pl du Palais Royal
Jardin de l'Oratoire
R de l'Oratoire
Q du Louvre
Sq du Vert Galant
Q de Conti
Q des Grands Augustins
R de Nesle
R Dauphine
R de Guénégaud

Jardin des Tuileries
Palais Royal – Musée
Pl du Carrousel
Cour Napoléon
4 Musée du Louvre
Pl du Palais Royal
Jardin de l'Infante
Q François Mitterrand
Pont des Arts
Q de Conti
Q Malaquais
R Mazarine
R de Seine
École des Beaux-Arts
R Bonaparte
6
R Jacob
R des Sts-Pères
7E
Pont du Carrousel
Seine

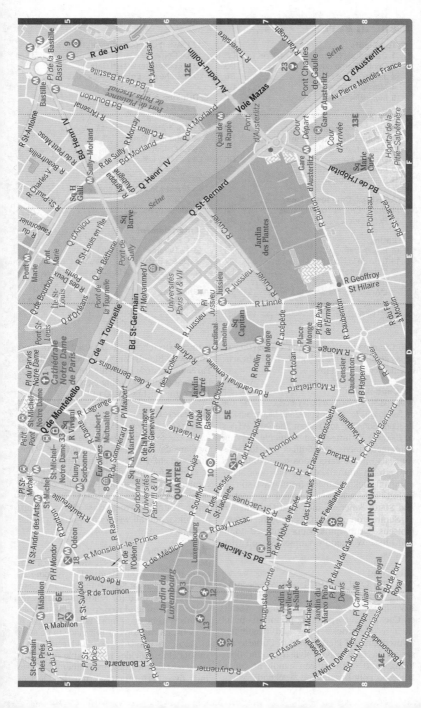

Central Paris

and Champagne) are the perfect partner to tapas-style 'small plates' (grilled duck hearts, devilled eggs) to share.

★ Candelaria   COCKTAIL BAR

(Map p324; www.quixotic-projects.com; 52 rue de Saintonge, 3e; ☺ bar 6pm-2am, taqueria noon-10.30pm Sun-Wed, to 11.30pm Thu-Sat; Ⓜ Filles du Calvaire) A lime-green *taqueria* serving homemade tacos, quesadillas and tostadas conceals one of Paris' coolest cocktail bars through an unmarked internal door. Phenomenal cocktails made from agave spirits, including mezcal, are inspired by Central and South America, such as a Guatemalan El Sombrerón (tequila, vermouth, bitters, hibiscus syrup, pink-pepper-infused tonic and lime). Weekend evenings kick off with DJ sets.

Lockwood   COCKTAIL BAR

(Map p324; ☏ 01 77 32 97 21; www.lockwoodparis. com; 73 rue d'Aboukir, 2e; ☺ 6pm-2am Mon-Fri, 10am-4pm & 6pm-2am Sat, 10am-4pm Sun; Ⓜ Sentier) Cocktails incorporating premium spirits such as Hendrick's rose- and cucumber-infused gin and Pierre Ferrand Curaçao are served in Lockwood's stylish ground-floor lounge and subterranean candle-lit cellar. It's especially buzzing on weekends, when

brunch stretches out between 10am and 4pm, with Bloody Marys, coffee brewed with Parisian-roasted Belleville Brûlerie (p320) beans and fare including eggs Benedict and Florentine (dishes €8.50 to €13).

★ Concrete   CLUB

(Map p324; www.concreteparis.fr; 69 Port de la Rapée, 12e; ☺ Thu-Sun; Ⓜ Gare de Lyon) Moored by Gare de Lyon on a barge on the Seine, this wild-child club with two dance floors is famed for introducing an 'after-hours' element to Paris' somewhat staid clubbing scene, with the country's first 24-hour licence. Watch for world-class electro DJ appearances and all-weekend events on social media.

★ Le Batofar   CLUB

(Map p316; ☏ 01 53 60 37 85; www.batofar.fr; opposite 11 quai François Mauriac, 13e; ☺ 6pm-7am Wed-Sat, to midnight Sun-Tue; Ⓜ Quai de la Gare, Bibliothèque) Closed for renovation when we visited, this much-loved, red-metal tugboat promises to be even more fabulous when it reopens. Its rooftop bar is a place to be seen in summer; it has a respected restaurant; and its club provides memorable underwater acoustics for edgy, experimental music and live performances (mostly electro-oriented but hip hop, new wave, rock, punk and jazz too).

☆ Entertainment

Paris' top listings entertainment guide, L'Officiel des Spectacles (www.offi.fr; €1), is published in French but is easy to navigate. It's available from news stands on Wednesday. Online, surf Paris Nightlife (www.parisnightlife.fr).

Buy concert, theatre, cultural and sporting event tickets from **Fnac** (☑08 92 68 36 22; www.fnactickets.com). On the day of performance, theatre, opera and ballet tickets are sold for half price (plus €3 commission) at **Kiosque Théâtre Madeleine** (Map p321; www.kiosqueculture.com; opposite 15 place de la Madeleine, 8e; ⊙12.30-7.30pm Tue-Sat, to 3.45pm Sun; Ⓜ Madeleine).

Opéra Bastille   OPERA

(Map p324; ☑international calls 01 71 25 24 23, within France 08 92 89 90 90; www.operadeparis.fr; 2-6 place de la Bastille, 12e; ⊙box office 11.30am-6.30pm Mon-Sat, 1hr prior to performances Sun; Ⓜ Bastille) Paris' premier opera hall, Opéra Bastille's 2745-seat main auditorium also stages ballet and classical concerts. Online tickets go on sale up to three weeks before telephone or box-office sales (from noon on Wednesdays; online flash sales offer significant discounts). Standing-only tickets (*places débouts; €5*) are available 90 minutes before performances. French-language 90-minute **guided tours** take you backstage.

Significant discounts are available for those aged under 28.

★ Café Universel   JAZZ, BLUES

(Map p324; ☑01 43 25 74 20; www.facebook.com/cafeuniverseljazzbar; 267 rue St-Jacques, 5e; ⊙8.30pm-1.30am Tue-Sat; 🛜; Ⓜ Censier Daubenton or RER Port Royal) Café Universel hosts a brilliant array of live concerts with everything from bebop and Latin sounds to vocal jazz sessions. Plenty of freedom is given to young producers and artists, and its convivial relaxed atmosphere attracts a mix of students and jazz lovers. Concerts are free, but tip the artists when they pass the hat around.

Le Bataclan   LIVE MUSIC

(Map p324; ☑01 43 14 00 30; www.bataclan.fr; 50 bd Voltaire, 11e; Ⓜ Oberkampf, Filles du Calvaire) Built in 1864, intimate concert, theatre and dance hall Le Bataclan was Maurice Cheva-

lier's debut venue in 1910. The 1497-capacity venue reopened with a concert by Sting on 12 November 2016, almost a year to the day following the tragic 13 November 2015 terrorist attacks that took place here, and once again hosts French and international rock and pop legends.

ⓘ Information

Paris Convention & Visitors Bureau (Paris Office de Tourisme; Map p324; ☑01 49 52 42 63; www.parisinfo.com; 29 rue de Rivoli, 4e; ⊙9am-7pm; 🛜; Ⓜ Hôtel de Ville) This is the main branch of the Paris Convention & Visitors Bureau.

ⓘ Getting There & Away

AIR

There are three main airports in Paris:

Aéroport de Charles de Gaulle (CDG; ☑01 70 36 39 50; www.parisaeroport.fr) Most international airlines fly to CDG, 28km northeast of central Paris.

Aéroport d'Orly Located 19km south of Paris but not as frequently used by international airlines.

Aéroport de Beauvais (BVA; ☑08 92 68 20 66; www.aeroportbeauvais.com) Not really in Paris at all (it's 75km north); used by some low-cost carriers.

BUS

Eurolines (Map p324; ☑08 92 89 90 91; www.eurolines.fr; 55 rue St-Jacques, 5e; ⊙9.30am-6.30pm Mon-Fri, 10am-1pm & 2-5pm Sat; Ⓜ Cluny-La Sorbonne) connects all major European capitals to Paris' international bus terminal, **Gare Routière Internationale de Paris-Galliéni** (28 av du Général de Gaulle, Bagnolet; Ⓜ Galliéni). The terminal is in the eastern suburb of Bagnolet; it's about a 15-minute metro ride to the more central République station.

Major European bus company Flixbus (www.flixbus.com) uses western **Parking Pershing** (Map p316; 16-24 bd Pershing, 17e; Ⓜ Porte Maillot).

TRAIN

Paris has six major train stations serving both national and international destinations. For mainline train information, check SNCF (www.oui.sncf).

ⓘ Getting Around

TO/FROM THE AIRPORT

Charles de Gaulle Airport Trains (RER), buses and night buses to the city centre cost €6 to €21; taxis cost €50 to €55 (15% higher evenings and Sundays).

CHÂTEAU DE VERSAILLES

Amid magnificently landscaped formal gardens, this splendid and enormous **palace** (☑ 01 30 83 78 00; www.chateauversailles.fr; place d'Armes; adult/child passport ticket incl estate-wide access €20/free, with musical events €27/free, palace €18/free except during musical events; ⊙ 9am-6.30pm Tue-Sun Apr-Oct, to 5.30pm Tue-Sun Nov-Mar; Ⓜ RER Versailles-Château–Rive Gauche) was built in the mid-17th century during the reign of Louis XIV. To project the absolute power of the French monarchy, which was then at the height of its glory, the *Roi Soleil* (Sun King) transformed his father's hunting lodge into what is now France's most famous palace. Since its construction the château has undergone relatively few alterations, though almost all the interior furnishings disappeared during the Revolution and many of the rooms were rebuilt by Louis-Philippe (r 1830–48).

To reduce queue time, pre-purchase tickets on the château's website and head straight to Entrance A. Arrive early morning and avoid Tuesday, Saturday and Sunday (its busiest days).

The easiest way to get to/from Versailles is aboard RER line C5 (€4.45, 40 minutes, every 15 minutes) from Paris' Left Bank RER stations to Versailles-Château–Rive Gauche, 700m southeast of the château.

Orly Airport Trains (Orlyval then RER), buses and night buses to the city centre cost €6.25 to €13.25; T7 tram to Villejuif-Louis Aragon then take the metro to the city centre (€3.60); taxis cost €30 to €35 (15% higher evenings and Sundays).

Beauvais Airport Shuttle buses cost €17 (or €15.90 purchased in advance online at www.aeroportparisbeauvais.com) to Porte Maillot then take the metro (€1.90).

BICYCLE

The **Vélib'** (☑ 01 76 49 12 34; www.velib-metropole.fr; day/week subscription for up to 5 people €5/15, standard bike hire up to 30/60min free/€1, electric bike €1/2) bike share scheme puts more than 20,000 bikes – some electric - at the disposal of Parisians and visitors for getting around the city. There are some 1400 stations throughout the city, each with 20 to 70 bike stands.

BOAT

Batobus (www.batobus.com; adult/child 1-day pass €17/8, 2-day pass €19/10; ⊙ 10am-9.30pm late Apr-Aug, shorter hours Sep-late Apr) runs glassed-in trimarans that dock every 20 to 25 minutes at nine small piers along the Seine. Buy tickets online, at ferry stops or at tourist offices.

PUBLIC TRANSPORT

Paris' public transit system is operated by the RATP (www.ratp.fr). RATP tickets are valid on the 14-line metro, RER (underground suburban train line with five lines within the city limits), buses, trams and the Montmartre funicular. A single ticket/carnet of 10 costs €1.90/14.90.

Lille

POP 236,381

Thanks to the Eurostar and the TGV, Lille makes an easy, environmentally sustainable weekend destination from London, Paris or Brussels. Highlights include an attractive old town with a strong Flemish accent, renowned art museums, stylish shopping, excellent dining options and a cutting-edge, student-driven nightlife scene.

◉ Sights

The **Lille City Pass** (€25/35/45 per 24/48/72 hr) covers museum admission and unlimited use of public transport; buy it online at http://en.lilletourism.com.

★ Palais des
Beaux Arts   MUSEUM

(Fine Arts Museum; ☑ 03 20 06 78 00; www.pba-lille.fr; place de la République; adult/child €7/4; ⊙ 2-6pm Mon, 10am-6pm Wed-Sun; Ⓜ République Beaux-Arts) Inaugurated in 1892, Lille's illustrious Fine Arts Museum claims France's second-largest collection after Paris' Musée du Louvre. Its cache of sublime 15th- to 20th-century paintings include works by Rubens, Van Dyck and Manet. Exquisite porcelain and faience (pottery), much of it of local provenance, is on the ground floor, while in the basement you'll find classical archaeology, medieval statuary and 18th-century scale models of the fortified cities of northern France and Belgium.

Musée d'Art Moderne, d'Art Contemporain et d'Art Brut – LaM MUSEUM

(📞 03 20 19 68 68; www.musee-lam.fr; 1 allée du Musée, Villeneuve-d'Ascq; adult/child €7/5, 1st Sun of month free; ⏰ museum 10am-6pm Tue-Sun, sculpture park 9am-6pm Tue-Sun) Colourful, playful and just plain weird works of modern and contemporary art by masters such as Braque, Calder, Léger, Miró, Modigliani and Picasso are the big draw at this renowned museum and sculpture park in the Lille suburb of Villeneuve-d'Ascq, 9km east of Gare Lille-Europe. Take metro line 1 to Pont de Bois, then bus L4 six stops to 'LaM'.

⭐ La Piscine Musée d'Art et d'Industrie GALLERY

(📞 03 20 69 23 60; www.roubaix-lapiscine.com; 23 rue de l'Espérance, Roubaix; ⏰ 11am-6pm Tue-Thu, 11am-8pm Fri, 1-6pm Sat & Sun; Ⓜ Gare Jean Lebas) An art deco municipal swimming pool built between 1927 and 1932 is now an innovative museum showcasing fine arts (paintings, sculptures, drawings) and applied arts (furniture, textiles, fashion) in a delightfully watery environment: the pool is still filled and sculptures are reflected in the water. Reopening in autumn 2018 with a new wing and 2000 sq metres of additional exhibition space; check the website for updated entry prices. It's 12km northeast of Gare Lille-Europe in Roubaix.

🍴 Eating & Drinking

Dining hot spots in Vieux Lille include rue de Gand, home to small, moderately priced French and Flemish restaurants, and rue de la Monnaie and its side streets, alleys and courtyards. Grab drinks al fresco on rue Masséna, rue Solférino, place du Général de Gaulle and place du Théâtre.

⭐ Meert PASTRIES €

(📞 03 20 57 07 44; www.meert.fr; 27 rue Esquermoise; waffles & pastries €3-7.60, tearoom dishes €4.50-11.50, restaurant mains €26-32; ⏰ shop 2-7.30pm Mon, 9.30am-7.30pm Tue-Fri, 9am-7.30pm Sat, 9am-7pm Sun, tearoom 2-7pm Mon, 9.30am-10pm Tue-Fri, 9am-10pm Sat, 9am-6.30pm Sun, restaurant noon-2.30pm & 7.30-10pm Tue-Sat, 11am-2pm Sun; 🛜; Ⓜ Rihour) Famed for its *gaufres* (waffles) made with Madagascar vanilla, Meert has served kings, viceroys and generals since 1761. The sumptuous chocolate shop's coffered ceiling, painted wooden panels, wrought-iron balcony and mosaic floor date from 1839. Its *salon de thé* (tearoom) is a delightful spot for a morning Ar-

abica or a mid-afternoon tea. Also here is a French gourmet restaurant.

Restaurant dishes might include roast pigeon with potato mousse or spinach, kale and Brussels sprouts crumble.

🎉 Festivals & Events

On the first weekend in September, Lille's entire city centre – 200km of footpaths – is transformed into the **Braderie de Lille** (www.braderie-de-lille.fr), billed as the world's largest flea market. It runs nonstop – yes, all night long – from 2pm on Saturday to 11pm on Sunday, when street sweepers emerge to tackle the mounds of mussel shells and old *frites* (French fries) left behind by the merrymakers.

ℹ️ Information

Tourist Office (📞 03 59 57 94 00; www.lilletourism.com; 3 rue du Palais Rihour; ⏰ 9.30am-1pm & 2-6pm Mon-Sat, 10am-12.30pm & 1.15-4.30pm Sun; Ⓜ Rihour)

ℹ️ Getting There & Around

Aéroport de Lille (LIL; www.lille.aeroport.fr; rte de L'Aéroport, Lesquin) is situated 11km southeast of the centre. It's linked to destinations around France and southern Europe by a variety of low-cost carriers. To get to/from the city centre (Gare Lille-Europe), you can take a shuttle bus (return €8, 20 minutes, hourly).

Lille has two train stations: **Gare Lille-Flandres** (🛜; Ⓜ Gare Lille-Flandres) for regional services and Paris' Gare du Nord (€29 to €68, one hour, 16 to 24 daily), and ultra-modern **Gare Lille-Europe** (🛜; Ⓜ Gare Lille-Europe) for all other trains, including Eurostars to London and TGVs/Eurostars to Brussels-Midi (€30, 35 minutes, at least a dozen daily).

WORTH A TRIP

LILLE DAYTRIPPER: LOUVRE-LENS

Long known for its black slag heaps, the former coal-mining town of Lens, 40km southwest of Lille, today squirrels away a northern branch of Paris' Louvre art museum. The **Louvre-Lens** (📞 03 21 18 62 62; www.louvrelens.fr; 99 rue Paul Bert; temporary exhibitions adult/child €10/5; ⏰ 10am-6pm Wed-Mon) **FREE** showcases hundreds of treasures from Paris' Musée du Louvre in state-of-the-art exhibition spaces. Hourly trains link Lille-Flandres and Lens (€8.30, 45 minutes).

Versailles

A DAY IN COURT

Visiting Versailles – even just the State Apartments – may seem overwhelming at first, but think of it as a house where people ate, drank, worked, slept and conspired and you'll be on the right path.

Some two decades into his long reign, Louis XIV began turning his father's hunting lodge into a palace large enough to house his entire court (to keep closer tabs on the 6000-strong army of courtiers). Sparing no expense, the Sun King employed the greatest artists and craftspeople of the day and by 1682 he'd created the most extravagant dormitory in history.

The royal schedule was as accurate and predictable as a Swiss watch. By following this itinerary of rooms you can recreate the king's day, starting with the ❶ **King's Bedchamber** and the ❷ **Queen's Bedchamber**, where the royal couple was roused at about the same time. The royal procession then leads through the ❸ **Hall of Mirrors** to the ❹ **Royal Chapel** for morning Mass and returns to the ❺ **Council Chamber** for late-morning meetings with ministers. After lunch the king might ride or hunt or visit the ❻ **King's Library**. Later he could join courtesans for an 'apartment evening' starting from the ❼ **Hercules Drawing Room** or play billiards in the ❽ **Diana Drawing Room** before supping at 10pm.

VERSAILLES BY NUMBERS

Rooms 700 (11 hectares of roof)

Windows 2153

Staircases 67

Gardens and parks 800 hectares

Trees 200,000

Fountains 50 (with 620 nozzles)

Paintings 6300 (measuring 11km laid end to end)

Statues and sculptures 2100

Objets d'art and furnishings 5000

Visitors 5.3 million per year

Queen's Bedchamber
Chambre de la Reine
The queen's life was on constant public display and even the births of her children were watched by crowds of spectators in her own bedchamber. DETOUR » The Guardroom, with a dozen armed men at the ready.

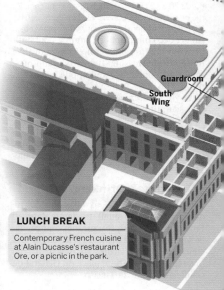

Guardroom

South Wing

LUNCH BREAK

Contemporary French cuisine at Alain Ducasse's restaurant Ore, or a picnic in the park.

Hercules Drawing Room
Salon d'Hercule
This salon, with its stunning ceiling fresco of the strong man, gave way to the State Apartments, which were open to courtiers three nights a week. DETOUR» Apollo Drawing Room, used for formal audiences and as a throne room.

Hall of Mirrors
Galerie des Glaces
The solid-silver candelabra and furnishings in this extravagant hall, devoted to Louis XIV's successes in war, were melted down in 1689 to pay for yet another conflict. **DETOUR»** The antithetical Peace Drawing Room, adjacent.

King's Bedchamber
Chambre du Roi
The king's daily life was anything but private and even his *lever* (rising) at 8am and *coucher* (retiring) at 11.30pm would be witnessed by up to 150 sycophantic courtiers.

Council Chamber
Cabinet du Conseil
This chamber, with carved medallions evoking the king's work, is where the monarch met his various ministers (state, finance, religion etc) depending on the days of the week.

King's Library
Bibliothèque du Roi
The last resident, bibliophile Louis XVI, loved geography and his copy of *The Travels of James Cook* (in English, which he read fluently) is still on the shelf here.

Diana Drawing Room
Salon de Diane
With walls and ceiling covered in frescoes devoted to the mythical huntress, this room contained a large billiard table reserved for Louis XIV, a keen player.

Royal Chapel
Chapelle Royale
This two-storey chapel (with gallery for the royals and important courtiers, and the ground floor for the B-list) was dedicated to St Louis, patron of French monarchs. **DETOUR»** The sumptuous Royal Opera.

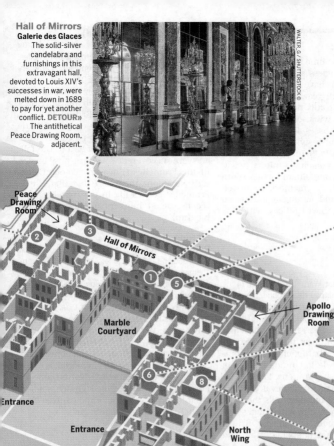

Peace Drawing Room

Hall of Mirrors

Marble Courtyard

Apollo Drawing Room

Entrance

Entrance

North Wing

To Royal Opera

WALTER.G / SHUTTERSTOCK ©

COIATO / BUDGET TRAVEL ©

SAVVY SIGHTSEEING

Avoid Versailles on Monday (closed), Tuesday (Paris' museums close, so visitors flock here) and Sunday, the busiest day. Also, book tickets online so you don't have to queue.

The Somme

The Battle of the Somme has become a symbol of the meaningless slaughter of WWI, and its killing fields have since become sites of pilgrimage. Each year, thousands of visitors follow the **Circuit du Souvenir** (Remembrance Trail; www.somme-battlefields.com). Convenient bases for exploring the area include Flemish-styled **Arras** (www.explore arras.com), 50km south of Lille, and former Picardy capital **Amiens** (www.amiens-tour isme.com), 60km further south again. Battlefields and memorials are relatively scattered and joining a tour is an excellent option – tourist offices help book tours.

👁 Sights

★ Historial de la Grande Guerre
MUSEUM

(Museum of the Great War; ☑ 03 22 83 14 18; www.historial.org; Château de Péronne, place André Audinot, Péronne; adult/child incl audioguide €9/4.50; ⊙ 9.30am-6pm Apr-Oct, to 5pm Thu-Tue Nov–mid-Dec & late Jan-Mar) For historical and cultural context, the best place to begin a visit to the Somme battlefields is the outstanding Historial de la Grande Guerre in Péronne, 60km east of Amiens. Located inside the town's fortified medieval château, this award-winning museum tells the story of the war chronologically, with equal space given to the German, French and British perspectives on what happened, how and why.

Beaumont-Hamel Newfoundland Memorial
MEMORIAL

(☑ 03 22 76 70 86; www.veterans.gc.ca; rue de l'Église, Beaumont-Hamel; ⊙ visitor centre noon-6pm Mon, 10am-6pm Tue-Sun Apr-Sep, 11am-5pm Mon, 9am-5pm Tue-Sun Oct-Mar) FREE This evocative memorial preserves part of the Western Front in the state it was in at fighting's end. The zigzag trench system, which still fills with mud in winter, is clearly visible, as are countless shell craters and the remains of barbed-wire barriers. Canadian students based at the Welcome Centre, which resembles a Newfoundland fisher's house, give free guided tours on the hour (except from mid-December to mid-January). It's 9km north of Albert; follow the signs that point to the 'Memorial Terre-neuvien'.

Fromelles (Pheasant Wood) Cemetery & Museum
CEMETERY, MUSEUM

(☑ 03 59 61 15 14; www.musee-bataille-fromelles.fr; 2 rue de la Basse Ville, Fromelles; cemetery free, museum adult/child €6.50/4; ⊙ cemetery 24hr, museum 9.30am-5.30pm Wed-Mon early Mar–mid-Jan) The death toll was horrific – 1917 Australians and 519 Britons killed in just one day of fighting – yet the Battle of Fromelles was largely forgotten until 2008, when the remains of 250 of the fallen were discovered. They are now buried in the Fromelles (Pheasant Wood) Cemetery. Next door, the Musée de la Bataille de Fromelles evokes life in the trenches with reconstructed bunkers, photographs and biographies.

★ Ring of Remembrance
MEMORIAL

(L'Anneau de la Mémoire; www.lens14-18.com; chemin du Mont de Lorette, Ablain-St-Nazaire; ⊙ 8.30am-11pm Apr-Nov, to 8pm Dec-Mar) FREE It's hard not to be overwhelmed by the waste and folly of the Western Front as you walk past panel after panel engraved with 579,606 tiny names: WWI dead from both sides who are listed in strict alphabetical order, without reference to nationality, rank or religion. Across the road from the memorial, is a vast French military cemetery, Notre-Dame de Lorette; 6000 unidentified French soldiers are interred in the base of the Lantern Tower (1921). It's 13km west of Lens.

Vimy Ridge Canadian National Historic Site
MEMORIAL

(☑ 03 21 50 68 68; www.cheminsdememoire.gouv.fr; chemins des Canadiens, Vimy; ⊙ memorial site 24hr, visitor centre 10am-6pm May-Oct, 9am-5pm Nov-Apr) FREE After the war, the French attempted to erase signs of battle and return northern France to agriculture and normalcy. Conversely, the Canadians remembered their fallen by preserving part of the crater-pocked battlefield as it was when the guns fell silent. The resulting chilling, eerie moonscape of Vimy, 11km north of Arras, is a poignant place to comprehend the hell of the Western Front. During visitor centre opening hours, bilingual Canadian students lead free guided tours of reconstructed tunnels and trenches.

ℹ Information

Tourist offices in **Amiens** (☑ 03 22 71 60 50; www.visit-amiens.com; 23 place Notre Dame;

9.30am-6.30pm Mon-Sat, 10am-noon & 2-5pm Sun Apr-Sep, 9.30am-6pm Mon-Sat, 10am-noon & 2-5pm Sun Oct-Mar; 🛜) and **Arras** (☑ 03 21 51 26 95; www.explorearras.com; place des Héros; ⊙ 9am-6.30pm Mon-Sat, 10am-1pm & 2.30-6.30pm Sun early Apr–mid-Sep, shorter hours mid-Sep–early Apr; 🛜) provide information on the area.

Péronne Tourist Office (☑ 03 22 84 42 38; www.hautesomme-tourisme.com; 16 place André Audinot, Péronne; ⊙ 9.30am-12.30pm & 1.30-6.30pm Mon-Sat, 10am-noon & 2-5pm Sun Jul & Aug, 9am-12.30pm & 2-6pm Mon-Fri, 9am-noon & 2-6pm Sat Apr-Jun, Sep & Oct, shorter hour Nov-Mar) Has excellent English brochures on the battlefields. Situated 100m up the hill from the Historial de la Grande Guerre.

Albert Tourist Office (☑ 03 22 75 16 42; www.tourisme-paysducoquelicot.com; 9 rue Gambetta, Albert; ⊙ 9am-12.30pm & 1.30-6.30pm Mon-Fri, 9am-12.30pm & 2-6.30pm Sat, 9am-1pm Sun May-Aug, 9am-12.30pm & 1.30-5pm Mon-Fri, 9am-noon & 2-5pm Sat Sep-Apr) Abundant information on the battlefields. Also rents out bicycles.

Normandy

Famous for cows, cider and Camembert, this largely rural region (www.normandie-tourisme.fr) is one of France's most traditional – and most visited thanks to a trio of world-renowned sights.

Bayeux

POP 14,305

Bayeux has become famous throughout the English-speaking world thanks to a 68.3m-long piece of painstakingly embroidered cloth: the 11th-century Bayeux Tapestry. With its delightful, flowery city centre crammed with 13th- to 18th-century buildings and a fine Norman Gothic cathedral, the town is a wonderful spot for soaking up authentic Norman atmosphere.

◉ Sights

A 'triple ticket' that is good for all three of Bayeux' outstanding municipal museums costs €15/13.50 for an adult/child (€12/10 for two museums).

★ **Bayeux Tapestry**　　　　MUSEUM
(☑ 02 31 51 25 50; www.bayeuxmuseum.com; 15bis rue de Nesmond; adult/child incl audioguide €9.50/5; ⊙ 9.30am-12.30pm & 2-5.30pm Mon-Sat, 10am-1pm & 2-5.30pm Sun Feb, Mar, Nov & Dec, to 6pm Apr-Jun, Sep & Oct, 9am-7pm Mon-Sat, 9am-1pm & 2-6pm Sun Jul & Aug, closed Jan) The world's most celebrated embroidery depicts the conquest of England by William the Conqueror in 1066 from an unashamedly Norman perspective. Commissioned by Bishop Odo of Bayeux, William's half-brother, for the opening of Bayeux' cathedral in 1077, the well-preserved cartoon strip tells

FRANCE & SWITZERLAND NORMANDY

WORTH A TRIP

D-DAY BEACHES

Code-named 'Operation Overlord', the D-Day landings were the largest seaborne invasion in history. Early on 6 June 1944, Allied troops stormed 80km of beaches north of Bayeux, code-named (from west to east) Utah, Omaha, Gold, Juno and Sword. The landings on D-Day – called Jour J in French – ultimately led to the liberation of Europe from Nazi occupation.

The most brutal fighting on D-Day took place 15km northwest of Bayeux along the 7km-long stretch of coastline now known as **Omaha Beach**, today a peaceful stretch of fine golden sand partly lined with sand dunes and summer homes. **Circuit de la Plage d'Omaha**, a trail marked with a yellow stripe, is a self-guided tour along the beach, surveyed from a bluff above by the huge **Normandy American Cemetery & Memorial** (☑ 02 31 51 62 00; www.abmc.gov; Colleville-sur-Mer; ⊙ 9am-6pm mid-Apr–mid-Sep, to 5pm mid-Sep–mid-Apr) FREE.

Caen's high-tech, hugely impressive **Le Mémorial – Un Musée pur la Paix** (Memorial – A Museum for Peace; ☑ 02 31 06 06 44; www.memorial-caen.fr; esplanade Général Eisenhower; adult/child €19.80/17.50, family pass €51; ⊙ 9am-7pm Apr-Sep, 9.30am-6pm Oct-Dec, 9am-6pm Feb-Mar, closed 3 weeks in Jan, shut most Mon in Nov & Dec) is one of Europe's premier WWII museums. Book online for the excellent year-round minibus tours it organises. Bayeux tourist office handles reservations for other guided minibus tours – an excellent way to get a sense of the D-Day beaches and their place in history.

the dramatic, bloody tale with verve and vividness as well as some astonishing artistry. What is particularly incredible is both its length – nearly 70m long – and fine attention to detail.

★ **Musée d'Art et d'Histoire Baron Gérard** MUSEUM
(MAHB; ☑ 02 31 92 14 21; www.bayeuxmuseum.com; 37 rue du Bienvenu; adult/child €7.50/5; ☺ 9.30am-6.30pm May-Sep, 10am-12.30pm & 2-6pm Oct-Apr, closed 3 weeks in Jan) Make sure you drop by this museum – one of France's most gorgeously presented provincial museums – where exhibitions cover everything from Gallo-Roman archaeology through medieval art to paintings from the Renaissance and on to the 20th century, including a fine work by Gustave Caillebotte. Other highlights include impossibly fine local lace and Bayeux-made porcelain. The museum is housed in the former bishop's palace.

A joint ticket for admission to the Musée d'Art et d'Histoire Baron Gérard and either the Bayeux Tapestry or the Musée Mémorial de la Bataille de Normandie is €12 (or €15 for all three).

Musée Mémorial de la Bataille de Normandie MUSEUM
(Battle of Normandy Memorial Museum; ☑ 02 31 51 46 90; www.bayeuxmuseum.com; bd Fabien Ware; adult/child €7.50/5; ☺ 9.30am-6.30pm May-Sep, 10am-12.30pm & 2-6pm Oct-Apr, closed 3 weeks in Jan) Using well-chosen photos, personal accounts, dioramas and wartime objects, this first-rate museum offers an excellent introduction to the Battle of Normandy. The 25-minute film is screened in both French and English. A selection of hardware – tanks and artillery pieces – is displayed outside.

A joint ticket for admission to Musée Mémorial de la Bataille de Normandie and Musée d'Art et d'Histoire Baron Gérard or the Bayeux Tapestry is €12 (or €15 for all three).

✗ Eating

Bayeux is very well supplied with good restaurants, across all budgets. Local specialities to keep an eye out for include *cochon de Bayeux* (a local heritage pig breed). Near the tourist office, along rue St-Jean and rue St-Martin, there is a variety food shops and cheap eateries.

★ **La Reine Mathilde** PASTRIES €
(☑ 02 31 92 00 59; 47 rue St-Martin; cakes from €2.50; ☺ 9am-7.30pm Tue-Sun) With a vast acreage of glass in its windows and set with white-painted cast-iron chairs, this sumptuously decorated patisserie and *salon de thé* (tearoom), ideal for a sweet breakfast or a relaxing cup of afternoon tea, hasn't changed much since it was built in 1898. Size up the sweet offerings on display and tuck in.

❶ Information

Tourist Office (☑ 02 31 51 28 28; www.bayeux-bessin-tourisme.com; Pont St-Jean; ☺ 9am-7pm Mon-Sat, 10am-1pm & 2-6pm Sun Jul & Aug, shorter hours rest of year)

❶ Getting There & Away

Trains link Bayeux train station, 1km southeast of the cathedral, with Caen (€8, 20 minutes, hourly), from where there are connections to Paris' Gare St-Lazare and Rouen.

Mont St-Michel

On a rocky island opposite the coastal town of Pontorson, connected to the mainland by a narrow causeway, the sky-scraping turrets of **Abbaye du Mont St-Michel** (☑ 02 33 89 80 00; www.abbaye-mont-saint-michel.fr/en; adult/child incl guided tour €10/free; ☺ 9am-7pm May-Aug, 9.30am-6pm Sep-Apr, last entry 1hr before closing) provide one of France's iconic sights. The surrounding bay is infamous for its fast-rising tides: at low tide, the Mont is surrounded by bare sand for miles around; at high tide, just six hours later, the bay is submerged.

From the **tourist office** (☑ 02 33 60 14 30; www.ot-montsaintmichel.com; bd Avancée, Corps de Garde des Bourgeois; ☺ 9.30am-7pm Jul & Aug, to 6.30pm Mon-Sat, 9.30am-12.30pm & 1.30-6pm Sun Apr, May, Jun & Sep, shorter hours rest of year; ☎) at the foot of Mont St-Michel, a cobbled street winds up to the **Église Abbatiale** (Abbey Church), incorporating elements of both Norman and Gothic architecture.

Pontorson, 7km south of the La Caserne parking area, is linked with Bayeux (one hour 45 minutes, three daily) by train and with La Caserne by bus. To get to/from the Mont from La Caserne, walk the 2.5km, rent a bicycle from Hôtel Mercure or hop aboard a free shuttle bus. For more details on getting to Mont St-Michel, see www.bienvenueaumontsaintmichel.com.

Brittany

Brittany, with its wild coastline, thick legend-laced forests and the eeriest stone circles this side of Stonehenge, is for explorers. It's a land of prehistoric mysticism, proud tradition and culinary wealth, where Breton culture (and cider) is fiercely celebrated.

Quimper

POP 66,979

Small enough to feel like a village – with its slanted half-timbered houses and narrow cobbled streets – and large enough to buzz as the troubadour of Breton culture, Quimper (pronounced kam-pair) is the thriving capital of Finistère (meaning 'land's end'). At the centre of the city is Quimper's Gothic **Cathédrale St-Corentin** (place St-Corentin; ⊙8.30am-noon & 1.30-6.30pm Mon-Sat, 8.30am-noon & 2-6.30pm Sun); the neighbouring **Musée Départemental Breton** (☑02 98 95 21 60; http://musee-breton.finistere. fr; 1 rue du Roi Gradlon; adult/child €5/free, free weekends Oct-Jun; ⊙10am-7pm mid-Jun–mid-Sep, 9.30am-5.30pm Tue-Fri, 2-5.30pm Sat & Sun

mid-Sep–mid-Jun) showcases Breton history, crafts and archaeology in a former bishop's palace.

As a bastion of Breton culture, Quimper has some exceptional crêperies, all centred on, fittingly, place au Beurre. Covered market **Halles St-François** (www.halles-cornouaille.com; 16 quai du Stéïr; ⊙7am-7.30pm Mon-Sat, to 1pm Sun) has a slew of salad and sandwich options. Find hipsters listening to traditional Breton music over a Breton Coreff or a Telenn Du beer at **Le Ceili** (☑02 98 95 17 61; www.facebook.com/Ceili.Pub; 4 rue Aristide Briand; ⊙11am-1am Mon-Sat, from 5pm Sun).

The **tourist office** (☑02 98 53 04 05; www. quimper-tourisme.bzh; 8 rue Élie Fréron; ⊙9am-7pm Mon-Sat, 10am-12.45pm & 3-5.45pm Sun Jul & Aug, shorter hours rest of year; ☎) has accommodation lists, although Quimper has a chronic shortage of inexpensive sleeping options.

Frequent trains serve Paris' Gare Montparnasse (€45 to €108, 4¾ hours).

St-Malo

POP 47,670

The enthralling mast-filled port of fortified St-Malo is inextricably tied up with the deep

---

OFF THE BEATEN TRACK

MORBIHAN MEGALITHS

Predating Stonehenge by around 100 years, Carnac (Garnag in Breton) safeguards the world's greatest concentration of megalithic sites. There are no fewer than 3000 of these upright stones, erected between 5000 and 3500 BC.

One kilometre north of **Carnac-Ville** a vast array of monoliths are set up in several distinct alignments, all visible from the road. The best way to appreciate the sheer numbers of stones is to walk or cycle between the **Ménec** and **Kerlescan** groups, with menhirs almost continuously in view. Between June and September seven buses a day run between the two sites, as well as Carnac-Ville and Carnac-Plage. **A Bicyclette** (☑02 97 52 75 08; www.velocarnac.com; 93bis av des Druides, Carnac-Plage; bicycle per day from €10, buggy per hour from €8) near the beach rents bikes.

Near the stones, the **Maison des Mégalithes** (☑02 97 52 29 81; www.menhirs-carnac. fr; rte des Alignements, D196; tour adult/child €9/5; ⊙9.30am-7pm Jul & Aug, 9.30am-6pm Sep, Apr & Jun, 10am-1pm & 2-5pm Oct-Mar) explores the history of the site and offers guided visits. Due to severe erosion the sites are fenced off to allow the vegetation to regenerate. From October to March you can wander freely through parts – the Maison des Mégalithes has maps of what's open.

For background, visit Carnac's **Musée de Préhistoire** (☑02 97 52 22 04; www. museedecarnac.fr; 10 place de la Chapelle, Carnac-Ville; adult/child €6/3; ⊙10am-6.30pm Jul & Aug, 10am-12.30pm & 2-6pm Wed-Mon Apr-Jun & Sep, shorter hours Oct-Mar). Later, head 8km north for the ultimate eco-escape at **Dihan** (☑02 97 56 88 27; www.dihan-evasion. org; Kerganiet, Ploëmel; tent/treehouse from €65/90) 🌿, a secluded guesthouse in a leafy dell outside Ploëmel (follow the black signs from the village). Run by fun-loving Myriam and Arno Le Masle, the farmhouse and barn house several guest rooms and the grounds shelter yurts, bubble tents and tree houses. Guests can fire up the barbecue and dine beneath a pergola.

DON'T MISS

OYSTER FEAST

Tucked into the curve of a shimmering shell-shaped bay, the idyllic little fishing port of **Cancale**, 14km east of St-Malo, is famed for its offshore *parcs à huîtres* (oyster beds) that stretch for kilometres around the surrounding coastline. There's no real beach, but the waterfront is a relaxing place to stroll and soak up the atmosphere, and sampling freshly shucked oysters at fishermen stalls clustered by the Pointe des Crolles lighthouse is one of France's most memorable seafood experiences. End with a scenic drive or hike to **Pointe du Grouin**, a stunning headland and a nature reserve 7km north of town.

briny blue: the town became a key harbour during the 17th and 18th centuries, functioning as a base for merchant ships and government-sanctioned privateers. These days it's a busy cross-Channel ferry port and summertime getaway.

👁 Sights

Exploring the tangle of streets in the walled city of St-Malo, known as **Intra-Muros** ('within the walls') is a highlight of a visit to Brittany – walking on top of the sturdy 17th-century ramparts (1.8km) ensnaring the city affords great views.

★ Château de St-Malo   CASTLE
(place Chateaubriand; ⊙10am-12.30pm & 2-6pm Apr-Sep, 10am-noon & 2-6pm Tue-Sun Oct-Mar) Château de St-Malo was built by the dukes of Brittany in the 15th and 16th centuries, and is now the home of the **Musée d'Histoire de St-Malo** (☎02 99 40 71 57; www.ville-saint-malo.fr/culture/les-musees; place Chateaubriand, Château de St-Malo; adult/child €6/3; ⊙10am-12.30pm & 2-6pm Apr-Sep, 10am-noon & 2-6pm Tue-Sun Oct-Mar), which examines the life and history of the city, while the lookout tower offers eye-popping views of the old city.

Île du Grand Bé &
Fort du Petit Bé   ISLAND, CASTLE
(☎06 08 27 51 20; fort guided tours adult/child €6/4; ⊙fort by reservation, depending on tides & weather) At low tide, cross the beach to walk out via Porte des Bés to Île du Grand Bé, the rocky islet where the great St-Malo-born, 18th-century writer Chateaubriand is buried. About 100m beyond Grand Bé is the privately owned, Vauban-built, 17th-century Fort du Petit Bé. Once the tide rushes in, the causeway remains impassable for about six hours; check tide times with the **tourist office** (☎08 25 13 52 00; www.saint-malo-tourisme.com; esplanade St-Vincent; ⊙9am-7.30pm Mon-Sat, 10am-7pm Sun Jul & Aug, shorter hours rest of year; ☎) so you don't get trapped on the island.

The owner runs 30-minute guided tours in French; leaflets are available in English.

🍴 Eating

Breizh Café   CRÊPES €
(☎02 99 56 96 08; www.breizhcafe.com; 6 rue de l'Orme; crêpes €10-15, menu €15.80; ⊙noon-2pm & 7-10pm Wed-Sun) This will be one of your most memorable meals in Brittany, from the delicious menu at this international name to the excellent service. The creative chef combines traditional Breton ingredients and *galette* and crêpe styles with Japanese flavours, textures and presentation, where seaweed and delightful seasonal pickles meet local ham, organic eggs and roast duck.

★ Bistro Autour du Beurre   BISTRO €€
(☎02 23 18 25 81; www.lebeurrebordier.com; 7 rue de l'Orme; 3-course weekday lunch menu €22, mains €19-26; ⊙noon-2pm & 7-10pm Tue-Sat Jul & Aug, noon-2pm Tue & Wed, plus 7-10pm Thu-Sat Sep-Oct, Apr & Jun, noon-2pm Tue-Thu, plus 7-10pm Fri & Sat Nov-Mar) This casual bistro showcases the cheeses and butters handmade by the world-famous Jean-Yves Bordier; you'll find his **shop** (☎02 99 40 88 79; 9 rue de l'Orme; ⊙9am-1pm & 3.30-7.30pm Mon-Sat, 9am-1pm Sun Jul & Aug, closed Mon Sep-Jun) next door. At the bistro, the butter sampler and bottomless bread basket are just the start to creative, local meals that change with the seasons.

ℹ Getting There & Away

Brittany Ferries (www.brittany-ferries.com) sails between St-Malo and Portsmouth; Condor Ferries (www.condorferries.co.uk) runs to/from Poole via Jersey or Guernsey.

TGV train services serve Paris' Gare Montparnasse (€62 to €107.70, 3½ hours, three daily).

The Loire Valley

If it's French splendour you seek, stop off in the Loire Valley. Poised on the crucial frontier between northern and southern France, and just a short ride from Paris. This fertile river valley – an enormous Unesco World Heritage site – is where France's kings and queens, princes and nobles had the most fabulous *châteaux* (castles) built.

Blois

POP 48,287

Towering above the northern bank of the Loire, Blois' royal château, one-time feudal seat of the powerful counts of Blois, offers a great introduction to some key periods in French history and architecture.

⊙ Sights

★ Château Royal de Blois   CHATEAU
(☏ 02 54 90 33 33; www.chateaudeblois.fr; place du Château; adult/child €12/6.50, audioguide €4; ☉ 9am-6.30pm or 7pm Apr-Oct, 10am-5pm Nov-Mar) Seven French kings lived in Blois' royal château, whose four grand wings were built during four distinct periods in French architecture: Gothic (13th century), Flamboyant Gothic (1498–1501), early Renaissance (1515–20) and classical (1630s). You can easily spend a half-day immersing yourself in the château's dramatic and bloody history and its extraordinary architecture. In July and August there are free tours in English (at 10.30am, 1.15pm and 3pm).

★ Maison de la Magie   MUSEUM
(☏ 02 54 90 33 33; www.maisondelamagie.fr; 1 place du Château; adult/child €10/6.50; ☉ 10am-

ⓘ COMBO TICKET

Save money with a *billet jumelé* (combo ticket; adult/child €19.50/10.50) covering admission to both chateau and Maison de la Magie; buy at either sight.

12.30pm & 2-6.30pm Apr-Aug & mid-Oct–early Nov, 2-6.30pm daily plus 10am-12.30pm Sat & Sun 1st 2 weeks Sep; ⊕) This museum of magic occupies the one-time home of watchmaker, inventor and conjurer Jean Eugène Robert-Houdin (1805–71), after whom the American magician Harry Houdini named himself. Dragons emerge roaring from the windows every half-hour, while inside the museum has exhibits on Houdin and the history of magic, displays of optical trickery, and several daily magic shows.

🛏 Sleeping & Eating

Hôtel Anne de Bretagne   HOTEL €
(☏ 02 54 78 05 38; www.hotelannedebretagne.com; 31 av du Dr Jean Laigret; s/d/tr/q €60/69/76/95, winter s/d €45/55; ☉ reception 7am-11pm; ℗ ⊛) This ivy-covered hotel, in a great location midway between the train station and the château, has friendly staff, a cosy piano-equipped *salon* and 29 brightly coloured rooms with bold bedspreads. A packed three-course picnic lunch costs €11.50. Rents out bicycles (€16) and has free enclosed bike parking.

FRANCE & SWITZERLAND THE LOIRE VALLEY

DON'T MISS

CHATEAUX DAY-TRIPPER

The peaceful, verdant countryside around the former royal seat of Blois is home to some of France's finest châteaux.

One of the crowning achievements of French Renaissance architecture, the **Château de Chambord** (☏ info 02 54 50 40 00, tour & show reservations 02 54 50 50 40; www.chambord. org; adult/child €13/free, parking distant/near €4/6; ☉ 9am-6pm Apr-Oct, to 5pm Nov-Mar; ⊕) – with 426 rooms, 282 fireplaces and 77 staircases – is the largest, grandest and most visited château in the Loire Valley. Begun in 1519 by François I (r 1515–47) as a weekend hunting retreat, it quickly grew into one of the most ambitious – and expensive – building projects ever undertaken by a French monarch. A French-style **formal garden** opened in 2017.

Perhaps the Loire's most elegantly proportioned château, **Château de Cheverny** (☏ 02 54 79 96 29; www.chateau-cheverny.fr; av du Château; château & gardens adult/child €11.50/8.20; ☉ 9.15am-6.30pm Apr-Sep, 10am-5pm Oct-Mar) represents the zenith of French classical architecture: a perfect blend of symmetry, geometry and aesthetic order. Inside are some of the most sumptuous and elegantly furnished rooms anywhere in the Loire Valley, virtually unchanged for generations because the de Vibraye family has lived here, almost continuously, ever since the château's construction in the early 1600s by Jacques Hurault, an attendant to Louis XII.

DON'T MISS

TOURAINE CHÂTEAUX

Often dubbed the 'Garden of France', the Touraine region is known for its rich food, famously pure French accent and glorious châteaux.

Spanning the languid Cher River atop a supremely graceful arched bridge, **Château de Chenonceau** (☑ 02 47 23 90 07; www.chenonceau.com; adult/child €14/11, with audioguide €18/14.50; ☺ 9am-6.30pm or later Apr-Oct, to 5pm or 6pm Nov-Mar) is one of France's most elegant châteaux. Its formal gardens, architecture, richly furnished interiors and fascinating history shaped by a series of powerful women are all inspirational.

Six exquisite landscaped gardens – some of France's finest – are the main draw of **Château de Villandry** (☑ 02 47 50 02 09; www.chateauvillandry.com; 3 rue Principale; château & gardens adult/child €11/7, gardens only €7/5, cheaper Dec-Feb, audioguide €4; ☺ 9am-5pm or 6.30pm year-round, château interior closed mid-Nov–late Dec & early Jan-early Feb). Visit when the gardens are blooming, between April and October; midsummer is most spectacular.

For pure romance, head to moat-ringed **Château d'Azay-le-Rideau** (☑ 02 47 45 42 04; www.azay-le-rideau.fr; adult/child €10.50/free, audioguide €3; ☺ 9.30am-11pm Jul & Aug, to 6pm Apr-Jun & Sep, 10am-5.15pm Oct-Mar), built in the early 1500s on a natural island in the middle of the Indre River. Don't miss the open, Italian-style loggia staircase overlooking the central courtyard, decorated with the salamanders and ermines of François I and Queen Claude.

Le Coup de Fourchette BISTRO €
(☑ 02 54 55 00 24; 15 quai de la Saussaye; menus weekday lunch €14-25, weekend & dinner €19-30; ☺ noon-2pm Tue-Thu, noon-2pm & 7-9.30pm Fri & Sat; 🕸) Simple, delectable French *cuisine maison* (home cooking) is dished up with a smile in this mod eatery with a terrace. Offers some of Blois' best cheaper eats.

ℹ️ Information

Tourist Office (☑ 02 54 90 41 41; www.blois-chambord.co.uk; 6 rue de la Voûte du Château; ☺ 9am-7pm Apr-Sep, 10am-12.30pm & 2-5pm Mon-Sat, plus Sun school holidays, Oct-Mar)

ℹ️ Getting There & Away

The tourist office has a brochure detailing public-transport options to nearby châteaux and can give you current timetables on shuttle buses operated by **Route 41** (☑ 02 54 58 55 44; www.remi-centrevaldeloire.fr) to Chambord and Cheverny.

From **Blois-Chambord train station** (av Dr Jean Laigret) there are regular trains to Amboise (€7.20, 15 minutes) and Paris Gare d'Austerlitz (€29.40, 1½ hours).

Amboise

POP 13,790

Elegant Amboise, childhood home of Charles VIII and final resting place of the incomparable Leonardo da Vinci, is gor-

geously situated on the southern bank of the Loire, guarded by a towering château. It's an upmarket place to stay – visit as a day trip from Blois.

⊙ Sights

★**Château Royal d'Amboise** CHATEAU
(☑ 02 47 57 00 98; www.chateau-amboise.com; place Michel Debré; adult/child €11.70/7.80, incl audioguide €15.70/10.80; ☺ 9am-5.45pm Dec-Feb, to btwn 6.30pm & 8pm Mar-Nov, last entry 1hr before closing) Perched atop a rocky escarpment above town, Amboise's castle was a favoured retreat for all of France's Valois and Bourbon kings. Only a few of the château's original structures survive, but you can still visit the furnished Logis (Lodge) – Gothic except for the top half of one wing, which is Renaissance – and the Flamboyant Gothic Chapelle St-Hubert (1493), where Leonardo da Vinci's presumed remains have been buried since 1863. The ramparts afford thrilling views of the town and river.

★**Le Clos Lucé** HISTORIC BUILDING
(☑ 02 47 57 00 73; www.vinci-closluce.com; 2 rue du Clos Lucé; adult/child €15.50/11, mid-Nov–Feb €13.50/10.50; ☺ 9am-7pm or 8pm Feb-Oct, 9am or 10am-6pm Nov-Jan, last entry 1hr before closing; 🕸) It was at the invitation of François I that Leonardo da Vinci (1452–1519), aged 64, took up residence in this grand manor house, built in 1471. An admirer of the

Italian Renaissance, the French monarch named Da Vinci 'first painter, engineer and king's architect', and the Italian spent his time here sketching, tinkering and dreaming up ingenious contraptions.

✗ Eating

★ Sunday Food Market MARKET €
(quai du Général de Gaulle; ☺ 8am-1pm Sun, small market 8am-1pm Fri) Voted France's *marché préféré* (favourite market) a few years back, this riverfront extravaganza, 400m southwest of the château, hosts 200 to 300 stalls selling both edibles and durables. Worth timing your visit around.

❶ Information

Tourist Office (☑ 02 47 57 09 28; www.amboise-valdeloire.co.uk; quai du Général de Gaulle; ☺ 9am or 10am-6pm or 7pm Mon-Sat, 10am-1pm & 2-5pm Sun Apr-Oct, 10am-12.30pm & 2-5pm Mon-Sat Nov-Mar; 🛜)

❶ Getting There & Away

Touraine Fil Vert (☑ 02 47 31 14 00; www.remi-centrevaldeloire.fr; all destinations €2.40) bus line C links Amboise with Chenonceau (€2.40, 18 minutes, one or two daily Monday to Saturday).

From the **train station** (bd Gambetta), 1.5km north of the château, services include Blois (€7.20, 15 minutes, 16 to 25 daily) and Paris Gare d'Austerlitz (€28.10 to €38.60, 1¾ hours, four direct daily).

Champagne

Called Campania meaning (plain) in Roman times, the wealthy agricultural region of Champagne is synonymous these days with its world-famous bubbly. Touring its cellars is a must, as is a scenic motor along the region's most celebrated vineyards along the self-drive Champagne Route (www.tourisme-en-champagne.com) .

Reims

POP 186,971

Along with Épernay, Reims is the most important centre of Champagne production, and a fine base for exploring the Montagne de Reims Champagne Route. Over the course of a millennium (from 816 to 1825), some 34 sovereigns kicked off their reigns in Reims' famed cathedral. Reconstructed after both WWI and WWII, the city – whose name is pronounced something like 'rance' – is endowed with handsome pedestrian boulevards, art deco cafes and lively nightlife.

◉ Sights

The **Reims City Pass** (€22/32/42 for 1/2/3 days), available at the tourist office, covers admission to most museums, plus a free city tour, unlimited public transport and discounts at various Champagne houses.

★ Cathédrale Notre Dame CATHEDRAL
(☑ 03 26 47 81 79; www.cathedrale-reims.fr; 2 place du Cardinal Luçon; tower adult/child €8/free, incl Palais du Tau €11/free; ☺ 7.30am-7.30pm, tower tours 10am, 11am & 2-5pm Tue-Sat, 2-5pm Sun May-Aug, 10am, 11am & 2-4pm Sat, 2-4pm Sun Sep, Oct & mid-Mar–Apr) Imagine the extravagance of a French royal coronation. The focal point of such pomposity was Reims' resplendent Gothic cathedral, begun in 1211 on a site occupied by churches since the 5th century. The interior is a rainbow of stained-glass windows; the finest are the western façade's great rose window, the north transept's rose window and the vivid Chagall creations (1974) in the central axial chapel. The **tourist office** (☑ 03 26 77 45 00; www.reims-tourisme.com; 6 rue Rockefeller; ☺ 10am-5pm Mon-Sat, 10am-12.30pm & 1.30-5pm Sun; 🛜) rents audioguides for self-paced tours.

Basilique St-Rémi BASILICA
(place du Chanoine Ladame; ☺ 9am-7pm) This 121m-long former Benedictine abbey church, a Unesco World Heritage Site, mixes Romanesque elements from the mid-11th century (the worn but stunning nave and transept) with early Gothic features from the latter half of the 12th century (the choir, with a large triforium gallery and, way up top, tiny clerestory windows). Next door is the **Musée St-Rémi** (http://musees-reims.fr; 53 rue Simon; adult/child €5/free; ☺ 10am-noon & 2-6pm Tue-Sun).

★ Palais du Tau MUSEUM
(www.palais-du-tau.fr; 2 place du Cardinal Luçon; adult/child €8/free, incl cathedral tower €11/free; ☺ 9.30am-6.30pm Tue-Sun May–mid-Sep, 9.30am-12.30pm & 2-5.30pm Tue-Sun mid-Sep–Apr) A Unesco World Heritage site, this lavish former archbishop's residence, redesigned in neoclassical style between 1671 and 1710, was where French princes stayed before their coronations – and where they threw

DON'T MISS

TASTING CHAMPAGNE

The musty caves (cellars) of the 10 Reims-based Champagne houses can be visited on guided tours that end with tastings. Cellar temperatures hover at 10°C , so it's a good idea to bring warm clothes.

The headquarters of **Taittinger** (📞 03 26 85 45 35; https://cellars-booking. taittinger.fr; 9 place St-Niçaise; tours €19-55; ⊙ tours 10am-4.30pm) is an excellent place to come for a clear, straightforward presentation on how Champagne is actually made – there's no claptrap about 'the Champagne mystique' here. Parts of the cellars occupy 4th-century Roman stone quarries; other bits were excavated by 13th-century Benedictine monks. No need to reserve. it's 1.5km southeast of Reims centre; take the Citadine 1 or 2 bus to the St-Niçaise or Salines stops.

sumptuous banquets afterwards. Now a museum, it displays truly exceptional statuary, liturgical objects and tapestries from the cathedral, some in the impressive, Gothic-style **Salle de Tau** (Great Hall). Treasures worth seeking out include the 9th-century talisman of Charlemagne and St Remi's golden, gem-encrusted chalice, which dates from the 12th century.

🛏 Sleeping & Eating

Hôtel Azur   B&B €

(📞 03 26 47 43 39; www.hotel-azur-reims.com; 9 rue des Ecrevées; s €55-85, d €79-109, tr €109, q €119; 🅿🛜) Slip down a side street in the heart of Reims to reach this petite B&B, which extends a heartfelt welcome. Rooms are cheerfully painted and immaculately kept, and breakfast is served on the garden patio when the sun's out. There's no lift, so be prepared to lug your bags.

à l'ère du temps   CRÊPES €

(📞 03 26 06 16 88; www.aleredutemps.com; 123 av de Laon; lunch menus €9.90, mains €7-14; ⊙ noon-2pm & 7-9.30pm Tue-Sat) A short stroll north of place de la République brings you to this sweet and simple crêperie. It does a roaring trade in homemade crêpes, *galettes* (savoury buckwheat crêpes) and gourmet salads.

ℹ Getting There & Away

From Reims train station direct trains run to/ from Épernay (€7, 20 to 42 minutes). For Paris Gare de l'Est (€28.50 to €48.50, 46 to 60 minutes), change trains at Champagne-Ardenne TGV train station, 8km from Reims.

Épernay

POP 23,732

Prosperous Épernay, 25km south of Reims, is the self-proclaimed *capitale du Champagne*. Beneath the town's streets, some 200 million bottles of Champagne are slowly being aged in 110km of cellars.

◉ Sights & Activities

Numerous *maisons de Champagne* offer informative and engaging cellar tours, followed by a *dégustation* (tasting) and a visit to the factory-outlet shop. The **tourist office** (📞 03 26 53 33 00; www.ot-epernay.fr; 7 av de Champagne; ⊙ 9am-12.30pm & 1.30-7pm Mon-Sat, 10.30am-1pm & 2-4.30pm Sun mid-Apr–mid-Oct, 9.30am-12.30pm & 1.30-5.30pm Mon-Sat mid-Oct–mid-Apr; 🛜) can point you in the right direction.

Avenue de Champagne   STREET

Épernay's handsome av de Champagne fizzes with *maisons de champagne* (Champagne houses). The boulevard is lined with mansions and neoclassical villas, rebuilt after WWI. Peek through wrought-iron gates at Moët's private **Hôtel Chandon**, an early-19th-century pavilion-style residence set in landscaped gardens, which counts Wagner among its famous past guests. The haunted-looking **Château Perrier**, a redbrick mansion built in 1854 in neo–Louis XIII style, is aptly placed at number 13! It's set to open as a new Champagne museum in 2019.

★ Moët & Chandon   WINE

(📞 03 26 51 20 20; www.moet.com; 20 av de Champagne; 1½hr tour with tasting €25-40, 10-17yr €10; ⊙ tours 9.30-11.30am & 2-4.30pm) Flying the Moët, French, European and Russian flags, this prestigious *maison* is the world's biggest producer of Champagne. It has frequent 90-minute tours that are among the region's most impressive, offering a peek at part of its 28km labyrinth of *caves* (cellars).

Villa Bissinger
WINE

(📞 03 26 55 78 78; www.villabissinger.com; 15 rue Jeanson, Ay) You can taste Champagne anywhere, but you might get more out of a two-hour workshop at Villa Bissinger, home to the International Institute for the Wines of Champagne. Besides covering the basics like names, producers, grape varieties and characteristics, the workshop includes a tasting of four different Champagnes. The institute is in Ay, 3.5km northeast of Épernay.

Workshops (€25) are held the first Saturday of the month in French only; arrange visits in English (two people from €150) in advance by email.

🍴 Eating & Drinking

Épernay's main eat street is rue Gambetta and adjacent place de la République.

Covered Market
MARKET €

(Halle St-Thibault; rue Gallice; ⊙ 7am-12.30pm Wed & Sat) Picnic treats galore.

★ La Grillade Gourmande
FRENCH €€

(📞 03 26 55 44 22; www.lagrilladegourmande. com; 16 rue de Reims; lunch menus €21, dinner menus €33-59, mains €20-26; ⊙ noon-1.45pm & 7.30-9.30pm Tue-Sat) This chic, red-walled, art-slung bistro is an inviting spot to try char-grilled meats and dishes rich in texture and flavour, such as crayfish pan-fried in Champagne and lamb cooked in rosemary and honey until meltingly tender. Diners spill out onto the covered terrace in the warm months. Both the presentation and service are flawless.

★ C. Comme
WINE BAR

(📞 03 26 32 09 55; www.c-comme.fr; 8 rue Gambetta; 2-/4-/6-glass Champagne tasting €13/26.60/37.50; ⊙ 10am-8pm Mon, Tue & Thu, 3-8pm Wed, 10am-midnight Fri & Sat) The downstairs cellar has a stash of 400 different varieties of Champagne; sample them in the softly lit bar-bistro upstairs. Accompany with a tasting plate of regional cheese, charcuterie and *rillettes* (pork pâté). We love the funky bottle-top tables and relaxed ambience.

ℹ️ Getting There & Away

From Épernay there are direct trains to/from Reims (€7.20, 24 to 37 minutes, 14 daily) and Paris Gare de l'Est (€24.20 to €44.10, 1¼ hours to 2¾ hours, eight daily).

Lyon
POP 514,707

France's third-largest city offers urban explorers a wealth of enticing experiences: outstanding museums, a dynamic cultural life, busy clubbing and drinking scenes, a thriving university, fantastic shopping and superb cuisine.

⊙ Sights

Over two millennia ago, the Romans built the city of Lugdunum on the slopes of **Fourvière**, on the Saône's western bank. Footpaths and a less-taxing funicular wind uphill from the Unesco-protected old town, **Vieux Lyon**.

Basilique Notre Dame de Fourvière
CHURCH

(📞 04 78 25 13 01; www.fourviere.org; place de Fourvière, 5e; rooftop tour adult/child €10/5; ⊙ basilica 7am-7pm, tours 9am-12.30pm & 2-6pm Mon-Fri, 9am-12.30pm & 2-4.45pm Sat, 2-4.45pm Sun Apr-Nov; 🚠 Fourvière) Crowning the hill, with stunning city panoramas from its terrace, this superb example of late-19th-century French ecclesiastical architecture is lined with magnificent mosaics. From April to November, free 30-minute discovery visits take in the main features of the basilica and crypt; otherwise, 90-minute rooftop tours ('Visite Insolite') climax on the stone-sculpted roof. Reserve tickets in advance online for the latter.

Cathédrale St-Jean-Baptiste
CATHEDRAL

(www.cathedrale-lyon.fr; place St-Jean, 5e; ⊙ cathedral 8.15am-7.45pm Mon-Fri, 8am-7pm Sat & Sun, treasury 9.30am-noon & 2-6pm Tue-Sat; Ⓜ Vieux Lyon) Lyon's partly Romanesque cathedral

---

ℹ️ CENT SAVER

The **Lyon City Card** (www.lyoncity card.com; 1/2/3 days €25/35/45) offers free admission to every Lyon museum, the roof of Basilique Notre Dame de Fourvière, guided city tours, Guignol puppet shows and river excursions (April to October). It also includes unlimited city-wide public transport. Save 10% by booking online and presenting your confirmation number at the tourist office.

Lyon

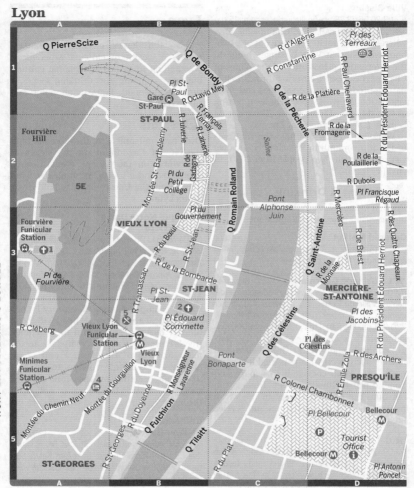

was built between the late 11th and early 16th centuries. The portals of its Flamboyant Gothic facade, completed in 1480 (and recently renovated), are decorated with 280 square stone medallions. Inside, the highlight is the astronomical clock in the north transept.

A small but impressive collection of sacred artworks (including 17th-century Flemish tapestries and a striking 10th-century carved ivory chest from the Byzantine era) is housed in the adjoining treasury. During the Fête des Lumières, the cathedral plays a starring role, with vivid projections lighting up the main facade.

Musée des Beaux-Arts MUSEUM
(☑ 04 72 10 17 40; www.mba-lyon.fr; 20 place des Terreaux, 1er; adult/child €8/free; ☺ 10am-6pm Wed, Thu & Sat-Mon, 10.30am-6pm Fri; Ⓜ Hôtel de Ville) This stunning and eminently manageable museum showcases France's finest collection of sculptures and paintings outside of Paris from antiquity onwards. Highlights include works by Rodin, Monet and Picasso. Pick up a free audioguide and be sure to stop for a drink or meal on the delightful stone

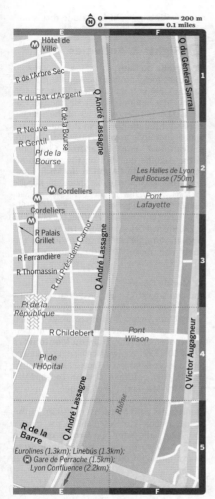

ties, and death in different civilisations) and a fabulous array of temporary exhibitions are housed in a futuristic, steel-and-glass structure, set on a concrete base on the water's edge.

🛏 Sleeping

Auberge de Jeunesse du Vieux Lyon
HOSTEL €

(☎ 04 78 15 05 50; www.hifrance.org; 41-45 montée du Chemin Neuf, 5e; dm incl breakfast €20-27; ⊙ reception 7am-1pm, 2-8pm & 9pm-1am; @ 🛜; Ⓜ Vieux Lyon, 🚡 Minimes) Stunning city views unfold from the terrace of Lyon's HI affiliated hostel, and from many of the (mostly four- and six-bed) dorms. Bike parking and kitchen facilities are available, and there's an on-site bar. Try for a dorm with city views. To avoid the tiring 10-minute climb from Vieux Lyon metro station, take the funicular to Minimes station and walk downhill.

🍴 Eating

Eatery-lined streets include cobbled rue Mercière and rue des Marronniers in the 2e (metro Bellecour), and rue du Garet, rue Neuve and rue Verdi (metro Hôtel de Ville) near the opera house.

★ Les Halles de Lyon Paul Bocuse
MARKET €

(☎ 04 78 62 39 33; www.hallespaulbocuse.lyon.fr; 102 cours Lafayette, 3e; ⊙ 7am-10.30pm Tue-Sat, to 4.30pm Sun; Ⓜ Part-Dieu) Lyon's famed indoor food market has nearly five-dozen stalls selling countless gourmet delights. Pick up a round of runny St Marcellin from legendary cheesemonger Mère Richard, and a knobbly Jésus de Lyon from Charcuterie Sibilia. Or enjoy a sit-down lunch of local produce, especially enjoyable on Sundays when local families congregate for shellfish and white-wine brunches.

terrace off its cafe-restaurant or take time out in its tranquil cloister garden.

Musée des Confluences
MUSEUM

(☎ 04 28 38 12 12; www.museedesconfluences.fr; 86 quai Perrache, 6e; adult/child €9/free; ⊙ 11am-7pm Tue, Wed & Fri, to 10pm Thu, 10am-7pm Sat & Sun; 🚋 T1) Lying at the confluence of the Rhône and Saône rivers, this ambitious science and humanities museum is the crowning glory of Lyon's newest neighbourhood, the Confluence. Four permanent exhibitions (exploring the origins of the universe, humankind's place in the living world, socie-

FRANCE & SWITZERLAND LYON

DON'T MISS

DRINKS AFLOAT

Along quai Victor Augagneur on the Rhône's left bank, a string of *péniches* (barges with on board bars) serve drinks from mid-afternoon onwards, with many of them rocking until the wee hours with DJs and/or live bands. To study your options, stroll the quayside between Pont Lafayette and Pont de la Guillotière.

★ **Daniel et Denise** BOUCHON **€€**
(✆04 78 42 24 62; www.danieletdenise.fr; 36 rue Tramassac, 5e; mains €17-29, 2-course lunch menu €21, dinner menus €33-51; ☉noon-2pm & 7.30-9.30pm Tue-Sat; Ⓜ Vieux Lyon) One of Vieux Lyon's most dependable and traditional eateries, this classic spot is run by award-winning chef Joseph Viola. Come here for elaborate variations on traditional Lyonnais themes.

You'll also find branches of Daniel et Denise in Croix Rousse and across the Rhône in the *troisieme*.

❶ Information

Tourist Office (✆04 72 77 69 69; www. lyon-france.com; place Bellecour, 2e; ☉9am-6pm; 🐾; Ⓜ Bellecour)

❶ Getting There & Around

Lyon-St-Exupéry Airport (www.lyonaeroports. com), 25km east of the city, is linked to the Part-Dieu train station by the Rhônexpress tramway in less than 30 minutes.

Lyon has two main-line train stations with direct TGV services: **Gare de la Part-Dieu** (place Charles Béraudier, 3e; Ⓜ Part-Dieu) and **Gare de Perrache** (cours de Verdun Rambaud, 2e; Ⓜ Perrache). Frequent TGV services include Marseille (€49.80 to €73, 1¾ hours) and Paris (€97 to €105, two hours).

Buses, trams, the metro and funicular linking Vieux Lyon to Fourvière are operated by TCL (www.tcl.fr). A ticket costs €1.80. Sail to/from the Confluence district aboard a Le Vaporetto river boat.

Chamonix

POP 9399

With the sheer white heights of the Mont Blanc massif as its sensational backdrop, the Chamonix Valley shows the Alps at their most dramatic. At its heart is the iconic town, a mountaineering mecca and top ski resort with bags of high-altitude thrills and a pumping après-ski scene.

◉ Sights & Activities

★ **Aiguille du Midi** VIEWPOINT
The great rocky fang of the Aiguille du Midi (3842m), rising from the Mont Blanc massif, is one of Chamonix' most distinctive features. The 360-degree views of the French, Swiss and Italian Alps from the summit are (quite literally) breathtaking. Year-round, you can float via cable car from Chamonix to the Aiguille du Midi on the vertiginous **Téléphérique de l'Aiguille du Midi** (www. compagniedumontblanc.co.uk; place de l'Aiguille du Midi; adult/child return to Aiguille du Midi €61.50/52.30, to Plan de l'Aiguille €32.50/27.60; ☉1st ascent btwn 6.30am & 8.10am, last btwn 4pm & 5.30pm, mid-Dec–early Nov). Dress warmly, even in summer temperatures at the top rarely rise above -10°C (in winter prepare for -25°C).

★ **Mer de Glace** GLACIER
France's largest glacier, the 200m-deep 'Sea of Ice', flows 7km down the northern side of Mont Blanc, scarred with crevasses formed by the immense pressure of its 90m-per-year movement. The **Train du Montenvers** (✆04 50 53 22 75; www.montblancnaturalresort. com; 35 place de la Mer de Glace; adult/child return €32.50/27.60; ☉10am-4.30pm late Dec–mid-Mar, to 5pm mid-Mar–Apr), a picturesque, 5km-long cog railway opened in 1909, links Gare du Montenvers with Montenvers (1913m), from where a cable car descends to the glacier and, 420 stairs later, the **Grotte de Glace** FREE. Also worth a visit is the **Glaciorium**, an exhibition on the formation (and future) of glaciers.

SkyWay Monte Bianco CABLE CAR
(www.montebianco.com; Pointe Helbronner; single/return €37/49; ☉6.30am-4.30pm Jul & Aug, 8.30am-4pm Sep–mid-Nov & Dec-May, 7.30am-4.20pm Jun) This spectacular, international cable car links France with Italy, from Pointe Helbronner to Courmayeur in the Val d'Aosta. The cars rotate a full 360 degrees, affording peerless views of Mont Blanc, the Matterhorn and Gran Paradiso. To get there, take the Aiguille du Midi and **Télécabine Panoramique Mont Blanc** (✆04 50 53 22 75; www.montblancnaturalresort.com; Aiguille du Midi; adult/child return from Chamonix €89/75.70; ☉7.30am-4.30pm Jul & Aug, 8am-4pm Jun, 9am-3.30pm Sep) cable cars.

✕ Eating & Drinking

In the centre, riverside rue des Moulins buzzes with après-ski joints serving food as well as booze into the wee hours; favourites include 'Australian' dive bar **Bar'd Up** (123 rue des Moulins; ⊘3pm-late) with live music.

Crèmerie du Glacier FRENCH €
(☑04 50 54 07 52; www.lacremerieduglacier. fr; 766 chemin de la Glacière; lunch menus €17-22, fondues €15-20; ⊘noon-2pm & 7-9pm mid-Dec–mid-May & late Jun–mid-Sep, closed Wed in winter) A wooden forest chalet is the setting for Chef Claudy's *croûte aux fromages* (bread drenched in a secret white-wine sauce, topped with cheese and baked) and other cheesy Savoyard delights including *gratin d'oeufs* (creamy baked eggs) and half a dozen kinds of fondue (the best with forest mushrooms). Reserve by phone and follow the signpost from the roundabout near the bridge at the southern entrance to Argentière.

MBC MICROBREWERY
(Micro Brasserie de Chamonix; ☑04 50 53 61 59; www.mbchx.com; 350 rte du Bouchet; ⊘4pm-2am Mon-Fri, 10am-2am Sat & Sun) This Canadian-run microbrewery is one of Chamonix' most unpretentious and gregarious watering holes, pouring its own locally made blonde, stout, pale ale, German-style wheat beer and mystery beer of the month. Soaking it up is a menu of huge burgers, poutine and vegetarian choices. Eclectic live music (usually from 9pm) could mean anything from soul to hard rock. Enormously satisfying.

Closes at 1am outside ski season.

ℹ Information

Tourist Office (☑04 50 53 00 24; www. chamonix.com; 85 place du Triangle de l'Amitié; ⊘9am-7pm mid-Jun–mid-Sep & mid-Dec-Apr, 9am-12.30pm & 2-6pm rest of year, closed Sun Oct & Nov; ⊛)

ℹ Getting There & Away

From Chamonix **bus station** (☑04 50 53 01 15; 234 av Courmayeur, Chamonix Sud; ⊘ticket 8am-noon & 1.15-6.30pm in winter, shorter hours rest of year) in Chamonix Sud there are regular services to/from Geneva in Switzerland (operated by Starshipper) and Courmayeur in Italy (run by Savda).

The Mont Blanc Express narrow-gauge train trundles from St-Gervais-Le Fayet station, 23km west of Chamonix, to Martigny in Switzerland, stopping in Chamonix (45 minutes) en route. From St-Gervais-Le Fayet, there are trains to major French cities.

Bordeaux

POP 250,776

The southern city of Bordeaux is exciting, vibrant and spirited. Half the city is Unesco-listed, making it the largest urban World Heritage site, and its pedestrian streets and squares buzz with students feasting on the city's barista-run coffee shops, super-food food trucks, exceptional dining scene and fine wine from its many surrounding vineyards. *Santé!*

⊙ Sights

★**Cathédrale St-André** CATHEDRAL
(☑05 56 44 67 29; www.cathedrale-bordeaux. fr; place Jean Moulin; ⊘2-7pm Mon, 10am-noon & 2-6pm Tue-Sun) FREE The Cathédrale St-André, a Unesco World Heritage Site prior to the city's classification, lords over the city. The cathedral's oldest section dates from 1096; most of what you see today was built in the 13th and 14th centuries. Enjoy exceptional masonry carvings in the north portal.

Even more imposing than the cathedral itself is the gargoyled, 50m-high Gothic belfry, **Tour Pey Berland** (☑05 56 81 26 25; www. pey-berland.fr; place Pey-Berland; adult/child €6/ free; ⊘10am-1.15pm & 2-6pm Tue-Sun Jun-Sep, 10am-12.30pm & 2-5.30pm Tue-Sun Oct-May), erected between 1440 and 1466.

★**La Cité du Vin** MUSEUM
(☑05 56 16 20 20; www.laciteduvin.com; 134-150 Quai de Bacalan, 1 Esplanade de Pontac; adult/child €20/free; ⊘10am-7pm Apr-Aug, shorter hours rest of year) The complex world of wine is explored in depth at ground-breaking La Cité du Vin, a stunning piece of contemporary architecture resembling a wine decanter on the banks of the River Garonne. The curvaceous gold building glitters in the sun and

> ## ℹ CENT SAVER
>
> Consider investing in a Bordeaux City Pass (www.bordeauxcitypass.com). A one-/two-/three-day card costs €29/39/43 and covers admission to many museums and monuments, unlimited public transport and various other discounts. The tourist office sells it.

its 3000 sq metres of exhibits are equally sensory and sensational. Digital guides lead visitors around 20 themed sections covering everything from vine cultivation, grape varieties and wine production to ancient wine trade, 21st-century wine trends and celebrated personalities.

★ **Miroir d'Eau** FOUNTAIN
(Water Mirror; place de la Bourse; ◷ 10am-10pm summer) FREE A fountain of sorts, the Miroir d'Eau is the world's largest reflecting pool. Covering an area of 3450 sq metres of black granite on the quayside opposite the imposing Palais de la Bourse, the 'water mirror' provides hours of entertainment on warm sunny days when the reflections in its thin slick of water – drained and refilled every half-hour – are stunning. Every 23 minutes a dense fog-like vapour is ejected for three minutes to add to the fun (and photo opportunities).

✗ Eating & Drinking

Iconic addresses mingle with new openings in the tasty tangle of pedestrian streets around place du Parlement; place St-Pierre is perfect for cheaper eats alfresco. North along the river, quai des Chartons is laced with waterfront restaurants and bars. Student pubs, coffee shops and wine bars pepper rue St-James.

★ **Magasin Général** INTERNATIONAL €
(☑ 05 56 77 88 35; www.magasingeneral.camp; 87 quai des Queyries; mains €10-20; ◷ 8am-6pm Mon, to 7pm Tue & Wed, to midnight Thu & Fri, 8.30am-midnight Sat, 8.30am-6pm Sun; 🛜) Follow the hip crowd across the river to this huge industrial hangar on the right bank, France's biggest and best organ-

ic restaurant with a gargantuan terrace complete with vintage sofa seating, ping-pong table and table football. Everything here, from vegan burgers and superfood salads to smoothies, pizzas, wine and French bistro fare, is *bio* (organic) and sourced locally. Sunday brunch is a bottomless feast.

Find the restaurant in a former military barracks, abandoned in 2005 and since transformed into the green creative hub known as Darwin.

Seasons INTERNATIONAL €
(www.seasonsfoodtruck.fr; mains €5-7, menus €8-10) This retro food truck – a French-manufactured Citroën HY – is worth tracking down; the week's schedule is on its website. Sydney chef Tristan and savvy sous-chef Margot cook up homemade health-busting cuisine using local seasonal produce: think homemade wraps, muffins with creative toppings (the coriander- and date-laced marinated pork is outstanding), vitamin-packed soups and salads.

❶ Information

Tourist Office (☑ 05 56 00 66 00; www. bordeaux-tourisme.com; 12 cours du 30 Juillet; ◷ 9am-6.30pm Mon-Sat, to 5pm Sun)

❶ Getting There & Around

Hourly shuttle buses (€8, 30 minutes) link **Aéroport de Bordeaux** (Bordeaux Airport; ☑ Information 05 56 34 50 50; www.bordeaux. aeroport.fr; Mérignac) with the city centre, 10km southeast.

There are regular trains to/from Paris Gare Montparnasse (€36 to €98, two hours, at least 16 daily) and dozens of other French cities from central train station, **Gare St-Jean** (Cours de la Marne).

PARTY TIME

Hip hop, rock, indie pop, psych blues rock, punk and hardcore are among the varied sounds that blast out of **I.Boat** (☑ 05 56 10 48 37; www.iboat.eu; quai Armand Lalande, Bassins à Flot 1; ◷ 7.30pm-6am), a fun nightclub and concert venue aboard a decommissioned ferry moored in the increasingly trendy, industrial Bassins à Flot district in the north of Bordeaux. Live music starts at 7pm, with DJ sets kicking in on the club dance floor from 11.30pm.

Provence

Provence conjures up images of rolling lavender fields, blue skies, gorgeous villages, wonderful food and superb wine. It certainly delivers on all those fronts, but it's not just worth visiting for its good looks – dig a little deeper to find extraordinary art, culture and a party vibe.

Marseille

POP 861,600

Marseille grows on you with its fusion of cultures, souk-like markets, vibrant millen-

DUNE DU PILAT

This colossal sand dune, 60km south of Bordeaux and 4km from the small seaside resort town of Pyla-sur-Mer, stretches from the mouth of the Bassin d'Arcachon southwards for 2.7km. Already Europe's largest, the dune is growing eastwards by 1.5m a year – it has swallowed trees, a road junction and even a hotel, so local lore claims.

The view from the top – approximately 115m above sea level – is magnificent. To the west you see the sandy shoals at the mouth of the **Bassin d'Arcachon**, including **Cap Ferret** and the **Banc d'Arguin** bird reserve where up to 6000 pairs of Sandwich terns nest each spring.

Although an easy day trip from Bordeaux (the dune is 8km from Arcachon train station, with local bus line 1 linking the two), the dune area is an enjoyable place to kick back for a while. For a splurge to remember, head downhill into Pyla-sur-Mer after the dune for a stylish drink with big dune view at fashionable **La Co(o)rniche** (☑ 05 56 22 72 11; www.lacoorniche-pyla.com; 46 av Louis Gaume; 2-/3-course lunch menu €58/63, seafood platters €40-85). A swag of seasonal campgrounds are listed at www.bassin-arcachon.com.

nia-old port and *corniches* (coastal roads) along rocky inlets and sun-baked beaches. Founded by Greek settlers who came ashore here around 600 BC, this is France's second-largest city.

⊙ Sights & Activities

Marseille is a natural launch-pad for exploring the nearby **Parc National des Calanques** (www. calanques-parcnational.fr), a 20km stretch of high, rocky promontories rising from brilliant-turquoise Mediterranean waters.. Several boat tours depart from the old port.

★ Vieux Port   PORT
(Old Port; Ⓜ Vieux Port) Ships have docked for millennia at Marseille's birthplace, the vibrant Vieux Port. The main commercial docks were transferred to the Joliette area in the 1840s, but the old port remains a thriving harbour for fishing boats, pleasure yachts and tourist boats. Guarded by the forts **St-Jean** (Ⓜ Vieux Port) and **St-Nicolas** (1 bd Charles Livon; 🚌 83), both sides of the port are dotted with bars, brasseries and cafes, with more to be found around place Thiars and cours Honoré d'Estienne d'Orves, where the action continues until late.

★ Basilique Notre Dame
de la Garde   BASILICA
(Montée de la Bonne Mère; ☑ 04 91 13 40 80; www. notredamedelagarde.com; rue Fort du Sanctuaire; ⊙ 7am-8pm Apr-Sep, to 7pm Oct-Mar; 🚌 60) Occupying Marseille's highest point, La Garde (154m), this opulent 19th-century Romano-Byzantine basilica is Marseille's most-visited icon. Built on the foundations of a 16th-century fort, as an enlargement of a 13th-century chapel, the basilica is ornamented with coloured marble, superb Byzantine-style mosaics, and murals depicting ships sailing under the protection of La Bonne Mère ('The Good Mother'). The campanile supports a 9.7m-tall gilded statue of said Mother on a 12m-high pedestal, and the hilltop gives 360-degree panoramas of the city.

The basilica is a steep 1km walk from the Vieux Port; alternatively, take bus 60, or the tourist train.

★ Musée des Civilisations de
l'Europe et de la Méditerranée   MUSEUM
(MuCEM, Museum of European & Mediterranean Civilisations; ☑ 04 84 35 13 13; www.mucem.org; 7 promenade Robert Laffont; adult/child incl exhibitions €9.50/free; ⊙ 10am-8pm Wed-Mon Jul & Aug, 11am-7pm Wed-Mon May-Jun & Sep-Oct, 11am-6pm Wed-Mon Nov-Apr; 🚻; Ⓜ Vieux Port|Joliette) The icon of modern Marseille, this stunning museum explores the history, culture and civilisation of the Mediterranean region through anthropological exhibits, rotating art exhibitions and film. The collection sits in a bold, contemporary building designed by Algerian-born, Marseille-educated architect Rudy Ricciotti. It is linked by a vertigo-inducing footbridge to the 13th-century Fort St-Jean, from which there are stupendous views of the Vieux Port and the surrounding sea. The fort grounds and their gardens are free to explore.

FRANCE & SWITZERLAND PROVENCE

★ **Le Panier**　　　　　　AREA

(Ⓜ Vieux Port) 'The Basket' is Marseille's oldest quarter – site of the original Greek settlement and nicknamed for its steep streets and buildings. Its close, village-like feel, artsy ambience, cool hidden squares and sun-baked cafes make it a delight to explore. Rebuilt after destruction in WWII, its mishmash of lanes hide artisan shops, *ateliers* (workshops), and terraced houses strung with drying washing. Its centrepiece is **La Vieille Charité** (☑ 04 91 14 58 80; www. vieille-charite-marseille.com; 2 rue de la Charité; museums adult/child €6/3; ⊙ 10am-6pm Tue-Sun mid-Sep–mid-May, longer hours in summer; Ⓜ Joliette).

🛌 Sleeping & Eating

The Vieux Port and surrounding pedestrian streets teem with cafe terraces, but choose carefully. For international cuisine, try cours Julien and the nearby rue des Trois Mages.

★ **Vertigo Vieux-Port**　　　HOSTEL €

(☑ 04 91 54 42 95; www.hotelvertigo.fr; 38 rue Fort Notre Dame; dm/tw €26/76; 🛜; Ⓜ Vieux Port) This award-winning hostel shows a swanky sleep is possible for those who are on a shoestring budget – for your euro you can expect breakfast, murals by local artists, vintage furniture, stripped wooden floors and original architectural details such as exposed wooden beams and stone arches. All rooms have their own modern bathrooms, and there are lockers, a good kitchen and a TV lounge.

LOCAL KNOWLEDGE

A DIFFERENT SOUVENIR

Pick up your very own travelling set of handmade boules (with matching carry bag), plus plenty of other souvenirs relating to France's iconic game at **Maison de la Boule** (☑ 04 88 44 39 44; www.museedelaboule.com; 4 place des 13 Cantons; ⊙ 10am-7pm Mon-Sat, to 6pm Sun; 🚊 49; Ⓜ Vieux Port). There's also a little museum exploring the history of the sport, including the curious figure of Fanny. Tradition dictates if you lose a game 13-nil, you must kiss her bare bum cheeks.

**Pizzeria
La Bonne Mère**　　　　　PIZZA €

(☑ 04 91 58 22 05; www.pizzeria-labonnemere.fr; 16 rue Fort du Sanctuaire; pizza €12-13; ⊙ 6-10pm Tue-Thu, 11am-2pm & 6-10pm Fri-Sat; 🚊 57, 60) Reservations are essential at this fantastic pizzeria in the lee of Basilique Notre-Dame de la Garde. La Bonne Mère uses only the freshest organic and imported ingredients and the creamiest mozzarella, strewing them on hand-spun dough that proves for 24 hours before crisping to perfection in its wood-fired oven.

**Les Buffets du
Vieux Port**　　　　　　FRENCH €€

(☑ 04 13 20 11 32; www.lesbuffetsduvieuxport. com; 158 quai du Port; menu adult/child €24/13; ⊙ noon-3pm & 7.30-10.30pm Feb-Dec; ♿; Ⓜ Vieux Port) This is no ordinary all-you-can-eat: a sleek modern dining room spreads around a buffet overflowing with Italian, Spanish and (above all) Provençal starters, mains, salads and desserts. Charcuterie, cheese, seafood, bouillabaisse, mussels, roast joints, fresh fruit and pastries – it's all here and it's all good. Portside tables go fast, but there's plenty of room inside.

ⓘ Information

Tourist Office (☑ 08 26 50 05 00, box office 04 91 13 89 16; www.marseille-tourisme.com; 11 La Canebière; ⊙ 9am-6pm; Ⓜ Vieux Port)

ⓘ Getting There & Around

Navette Marseille (www.lepilote.com; one-way/return €8.30/14; ⊙ 4.30am-11.30pm) buses (€8.30, every 15 to 20 minutes) shuttle between **Aéroport Marseille-Provence** (Aéroport Marseille-Marignane; MRS; ☑ 08 20 81 14 14; www.marseille.aeroport.fr), 25km northwest, and the central train station **Gare St-Charles** (☑ 04 91 08 16 40; www.rtm.fr; rue Jacques Bory; Ⓜ Gare St-Charles SNCF) in town.

SNCM has regular ferries from Marseille's **passenger ferry terminal** (Marseille Fos; www. marseille-port.fr; Quai de la Joliette; Ⓜ Joliette) to Corsica and Sardinia, plus long-distance routes to Algeria and Tunisia.

Buses to/from Aix-en-Provence depart from the **bus station** (Gare Routière; ☑ 04 91 08 16 40; www.rtm.fr; 3 rue Honnorat; Ⓜ Gare St-Charles), on the northern side of the train station.

For local transport information in and around Marseille, see www.lepilote.com.

PONT DU GARD

An icon of Roman France, this extraordinary three-tiered **aqueduct** (☑ 04 66 37 50 99; www.pontdugard.fr; adult/child €8.50/6, Pass Aqueduc incl guided visit of topmost tier €11.50/6; ⊙ 9am-11pm Jul & Aug, to 10pm Jun & Sep, to 9pm May, to 8pm Apr & Oct, to 6pm Nov-Mar), 45km southwest of Avignon, was once part of a 50km-long system of channels built around 19 BC to transport up to 20,000 cu metres of water per day from Uzès to Nîmes. The scale is huge: the bridge is 48.8m high, 275m long and graced with 35 precision-built arches.

You can walk across the tiers for panoramic views over the Gard River, but the best perspective on the bridge is from downstream, along the 1.4km **Mémoires de Garrigue** walking trail. In summer, paddle downstream here by canoe from **Collias** (several companies here rent out single and tandem canoes) and bring a picnic to join the sun-frolicking hordes cliff-jumping and beach-lounging in the shade of one of the world's most magnificent Roman monuments. Does life get any better?

Avignon

POP 94,087

For 70-odd years of the early 1300s, graceful Avignon served as the centre of the Roman Catholic world, hence the lively student town's impressive legacy of ecclesiastical architecture, most notably the World Heritage–listed Palais des Papes. Avignon's performing arts festival in July is iconic, and a myriad of affordable bistros, bars and cafes lace its medieval streets ensnared within a 4.3km ring of superbly preserved ramparts. Students love the place.

◉ Sights

⭐ **Palais des Papes**   PALACE
(Papal Palace; ☑ tickets 04 32 74 32 74; www. palais-des-papes.com; place du Palais; adult/ child €12/10, with Pont St-Bénezet €14.50/11.50; ⊙ 9am-8pm Jul, to 8.30pm Aug, shorter hours Sep-Jun) The largest Gothic palace ever built, the Palais des Papes was erected by Pope Clement V, who abandoned Rome in 1309 in the wake of violent disorder after his election. Its immense scale illustrates the medieval might of the Roman Catholic church.

Ringed by 3m-thick walls, its cavernous halls, chapels and antechambers are largely bare today – but tickets now include tablet 'Histopads' revealing VR representations of how the building would have looked in all its papal pomp.

⭐ **Pont St-Bénezet**   BRIDGE
(☑ tickets 04 32 74 32 74; bd de la Ligne; adult/child 24hr ticket €5/4, with Palais des Papes €14.50/11.50;

⊙ 9am-8pm Jul, to 8.30pm Aug, shorter hours Sep-Jun) Legend says Pastor Bénezet (a former shepherd) had three visions urging him to build a bridge across the Rhône. Completed in 1185, the 900m-long bridge linked Avignon with Villeneuve-lès-Avignon. It was rebuilt several times before all but four of its 22 spans were washed away in the 1600s, leaving the far side marooned in the middle of the Rhône. There are fine (and free) views from Rocher des Doms park, Pont Édouard Daladier, and Île de la Barthelasse's chemin des Berges.

⭐ **Musée du Petit Palais**   MUSEUM
(☑ 04 90 86 44 58; www.petit-palais.org; place du Palais; adult/child €6/free; ⊙ 10am-1pm & 2-6pm Wed-Mon) The archbishops' palace during the 14th and 15th centuries now houses outstanding collections of primitive, pre-Rennaissance, 13th- to 16th-century Italian religious paintings by artists including Botticelli, Carpaccio and Giovanni di Paolo – the most famous is Botticelli's *La Vierge et l'Enfant* (1470).

✯ Festivals & Events

Hundreds of artists take to the stage and streets during the world-famous **Festival d'Avignon** (☑ box office 04 90 14 14 14; www. festival-avignon.com; ⊙ Jul) and fringe **Festival Off** (www.avignonleoff.com; ⊙ Jul).

🛏 Sleeping

Avignon, with a wide range of good-value hotels and B&Bs, is an excellent place to base yourself for Provence explorations.

THE PINE CONE TRAIN

Chugging between the mountains and the sea, the **Train des Pignes** (Pine Cone Train; www.trainprovence.com; single/return €24.10/48.20; 🚇1 to Libération) is one of Provence's most picturesque train rides. The 151km-long track between Nice and Digne-les-Bains rises to 1000m for breathtaking views as it passes through Haute-Provence's scarcely populated backcountry. Break en route for a picnic lunch and meander through historic lanes and medieval citadel in enchanting **Entrevaux**.

Le Colbert   HOTEL €

(📞04 90 86 20 20; www.lecolbert-hotel.com; 7 rue Agricol Perdiguier; s €78-134, d €93-149; ⊙ Apr-Oct; 🛜) One of several hotels on a shaded side-street off rue de la République, this pleasant, old-fashioned hotel has 15 rooms decked out in art posters and zingy shades of yellow, terracotta and tangerine. Rooms are fairly standard, but it's the sweet interior patio that sells it – with a palm tree and a tinkling fountain, it's a dreamy setting for breakfast.

✖ Eating & Drinking

Chic yet laid-back Avignon is awash with tree-shaded squares buzzing with cafe life. Favourites include place Crillon, place Pie and place des Corps Saints. Students favour the many bars on rue de la Verrerie.

Le Barrio   BISTRO €

(📞04 90 27 00 45; 13 rue des Infirmières; 2-course weekday lunch €14.90, mains €10-20; ⊙11am-2.30pm & 7-10pm Tue-Sat) In the town's studenty quarter near elegant place des Carmes, this no-fuss hangout is ideal for solid, unpretentious grub like stir-fries, crusted cod, burgers and hotpots. It attracts a young crowd – note the vintage vinyl hanging on the walls and shabby-chic tables – and there's a choice of inside or outside dining. Head here for a laid-back lunch.

ⓘ Information

Tourist Office (📞04 32 74 32 74; www. avignon-tourisme.com; 41 cours Jean Jaurès; ⊙9am-6pm Mon-Sat, 10am-5pm Sun Apr-Oct, shorter hours Nov-Mar)

ⓘ Getting There & Away

Avignon has two stations: **Gare Avignon TGV** (Courtine), 4km southwest, and **Gare Avignon Centre** (42 bd St-Roch), linked by local shuttle train (€1.70, five minutes). Destinations served by TGV include Paris Gare du Lyon (€54 to €121, 2½ hours), Marseille (€15 to €27.50, 35 minutes) and Nice (€62, four hours).

French Riviera

With its glistening seas and picture-postcard beaches, the sun-rich French Riviera (Côte d'Azur in French) is the A-lister place to frolic on the sand. It has been a favourite getaway for the European jet set since Victorian times.

Nice

POP 347,636

Riviera queen Nice is what good living is all about – shimmering shores, the very best of Mediterranean food, a unique historical heritage, free museums, a charming Old Town and exceptional art.

◉ Sights

★**Vieux Nice**   HISTORIC SITE

(🚇1 to Opéra-Vieille Ville or Cathédrale-Vieille Ville) Getting lost among the dark, narrow, winding alleyways of Nice's old town is a highlight. The layout has barely changed since the 1700s, and it's now packed with delis, restaurants, boutiques and bars, but the centrepiece remains **cours Saleya**: a massive market square that's permanently thronging in summer. The **food market** (⊙6am-1.30pm Tue-Sun) is perfect for fresh produce and foodie souvenirs, while the **flower market** (⊙6am-5.30pm Tue-Sat, 6.30am-1.30pm Sun) is worth visiting just for the colours and fragrances. A **flea market** (Marché à la Brocante; cours Saleya; ⊙7am-6pm Mon) is held on Monday.

★**Promenade des Anglais**   ARCHITECTURE

(🚌8, 52, 62) The most famous stretch of seafront in Nice – if not France – is this vast paved promenade, which gets its name from the English expat patrons who paid for it in 1822. It runs for the whole 4km sweep of the Baie des Anges with a dedicated lane for cyclists and skaters; if you fancy joining them, you can rent skates, scooters and bikes from **Roller Station** (📞04 93 62 99 05; www.roller-

Nice

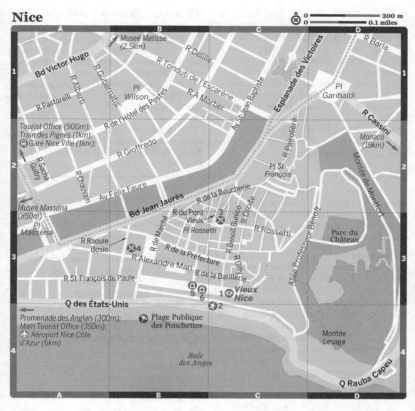

N 0 ———— 200 m
  0 ———— 0.1 miles

Musée Matisse
(2.5km)

Bd Victor Hugo

R Delille

R Tonduti de l'Escarène

Pl Wilson

R A Mortier

Esplanade des Victoires

R Barla

Pl Garibaldi

R Cassini

R Pastorelli

R Alberti

R Gubernatis

Av St Jean Baptiste

R Pairolière

Monaco
(19km)

Tourist Office (900m);
Train des Pignes (1km);
Gare Nice Ville (1km);

R de l'Hôtel des Postes

R Giofreddo

R Sacha Guitry

R Chauvain

Av Félix Faure

Pl St-François

Montée de Montfort

Musée Masséna
(850m);
Pl Masséna

Bd Jean Jaurès

R du Pont Vieux

R de la Boucherie

R Droite

R Rossetti

Parc du Château

R Raoule Bosio

R de Marché

R de la Préfecture

Pl Rossetti

R Benoît Bunico

R Giling

Allée Professeur Bénoît

R Alexandre Mari

R de la Barillerie

R St-François de Paule

Vieux Nice

Q des États-Unis

Promenade des Anglais (300m);
Main Tourist Office (350m);
Aéroport Nice Côte
d'Azur (6km)

Plage Publique
des Ponchettes

Montée
Lesage

Baie
des Anges

Q Rauba Capeu

station.fr; 49 quai des États-Unis; skates, boards
& scooters per hour/day €5/12, bicycles €5/15;
⊙9am-8pm Jul & Aug, 10am-7pm May, Jun, Sep &
Oct, to 6pm Nov-Apr).

★ **Musée Masséna**　　　　　　　MUSEUM
(☐04 93 91 19 10; 65 rue de France; museum
pass 24hr/7 days €10/20; ⊙10am-6pm Wed-Mon
late-Jun–mid-Oct, from 11am rest of year; ☐8, 52,
62 to Congrès/Promenade) Originally built as
a holiday home for Prince Victor d'Essling
(the grandson of one of Napoléon's favourite generals, Maréchal Massena), this lavish belle-époque building is another of the
city's iconic architectural landmarks. Built
between 1898 and 1901 in grand neoclassical style with an Italianate twist, it's now a
fascinating museum dedicated to the history
of the Riviera – taking in everything from
holidaying monarchs to expat Americans,
the boom of tourism and the enduring importance of Carnival.

Nice

★ **Musée Matisse**　　　　　　　　GALLERY
(☐04 93 81 08 08; www.musee-matisse-nice.
org; 164 av des Arènes de Cimiez; museum pass
24hr/7 days €10/20; ⊙10am-6pm Wed-Mon late
Jun–mid-Oct, from 11am rest of year; ☐15, 17, 20
or 22 to Arènes/Musée Matisse) This museum,
2km north of the city centre in the leafy

Cimiez quarter, houses a fascinating assortment of works by Matisse, including oil paintings, drawings, sculptures, tapestries and Matisse's famous paper cut-outs. The permanent collection is displayed in a red-ochre 17th-century Genoese villa in an olive grove. Temporary exhibitions are in the futuristic basement building. Matisse is buried in the **Monastère Notre Dame de Cimiez** (place du Monastère; ⊙8.30am-12.30pm & 2.30-6.30pm; ☐15, 17, 20 or 22 to Arènes/Musée Matisse) cemetery, across the park from the museum.

✖ Eating

To lunch with locals, grab a pew in the midday sun on one of the many place Garibaldi cafe terraces. Otherwise, Vieux Nice is stuffed with dining, drinking and dancing options.

La Merenda FRENCH €
(www.lamerenda.net; 4 rue Raoul Bosio; mains €15-23; ⊙noon-2pm & 7-10pm Mon-Fri) Simple, solid Niçois cuisine – stockfish, calf tripe à la Niçoise with *panisse* (chunky, pan-fried sticks of chickpea batter) and the like – by former Michelin-starred chef Dominique Le Stanc draws the crowds to this pocket-sized bistro where diners rub shoulders, literally. The tiny open kitchen stands proudly at the back of the room, and the equally small menu is chalked on the board.

No phone, no credit cards. Seatings are at noon and 1.15pm for lunch, and 7pm and 9pm for dinner; reserve ahead in person.

Fenocchio ICE CREAM €
(☑04 93 80 72 52; www.fenocchio.fr; 2 place Rossetti; 1/2 scoops €2.50/4; ⊙9am-midnight Mar-Nov) There's no shortage of ice-cream sellers in the old town, but this *maître glacier* (master ice-cream maker) has been king of the scoops since 1966. The array of flavours is mind-boggling – olive, tomato, fig, beer, lavender and violet to name a few. Dither too long over the 70-plus flavours and you'll never make it to the front of the queue.

ℹ Information

Tourist Office (☑04 92 14 46 14; www.nicetourisme.com; 5 Promenade des Anglais; ⊙9am-7pm daily Jun-Sep, to 6pm Mon-Sat Oct-May; ☎; ☐8, 52, 62 to Massenet)

ℹ Getting There & Around

Buses 98 and 99 link **Nice Côte d'Azur Airport** (☑08 20 42 33 33; www.nice.aeroport.fr; ☎; ☐98, 99, ☐2) with Promenade des Anglais and Nice train station respectively (€6, 35 minutes, every 20 minutes).

Bus 100 goes to Menton (1½ hours) and Monaco (40 minutes); bus 200 serves Cannes (1½ hours). Tickets cost a flat €1.50 (€10 for a carnet of 10).

From Nice's train station, 1.2km north of the beach, there are frequent services to Cannes (€6.10, 40 minutes) and Monaco (€3.50, 25 minutes).

Cannes

POP 74,673

Cannes' celebrity film festival only lasts for two weeks in May, but the buzz and glitz linger all year thanks to celebs who flock here year-round to pose on the steps of the Palais des Festivals and give the credit card a workout in the designer boutiques, beaches and palace hotels of the Riviera's most glam seafront. Budget accommodation is scarce – visit for the day from Nice, a 40-minute train ride away.

◉ Sights & Activities

Book guided tours (€4, 1½ hours) of La Croisette's famous, bunker-like Palais des Festivals at the tourist office.

★ La Croisette ARCHITECTURE
The multi-starred hotels and couture shops lining the iconic bd de la Croisette (aka La Croisette) may be the preserve of the rich and famous, but anyone can enjoy strolling the palm-shaded promenade – a favourite pastime among Cannois at night, when it twinkles with bright lights. Views of the Baie de Cannes and nearby Estérel mountains are beautiful, and seafront hotel palaces dazzle in all their stunning art deco glory.

Îles de Lérins ISLAND
Although just 20 minutes away by boat, these tranquil islands feel far from the madding crowd. **Île Ste-Marguerite**, where the mysterious Man in the Iron Mask was incarcerated during the late 17th century, is known for its bone-white beaches, eucalyptus groves and small marine museum. Tiny **Île St-Honorat** has been a monastery since the 5th century; you can visit the church and small chapels and stroll through the monks' vineyards.

Boats leave Cannes from quai des Îles on the western side of the harbour. **Trans Côte d'Azur** (☑04 92 98 71 30; www.transcote-azur.com; quai Max Laubeuf), **Riviera Lines** (☑04 92 98 71 31; www.riviera-lines.com; quai Max Laubeuf) and **Horizon** (☑04 92 98 71 36; www.horizon-lerins.com; quai Laubeuf) all run ferries to Île Ste-Marguerite and **Planaria** (☑04 92 98 71 38; www.cannes-ilesdelerins.com; quai Max Laubeuf) covers Île St-Honorat.

✖ Eating & Drinking

To find the best culinary deals, avoid the chi-chi beach restaurants and head to the tangle of streets around Cannes' atmospheric food market, **Marché Forville** (11 rue du Marché Forville; ◷7.30am-1pm Tue-Fri, to 2pm Sat & Sun).

Bars around the **Carré d'Or** (Golden Sq) – bordered by rue Commandant André, rue des Frères Pradignac, rue du Batéguier and rue du Dr Gérard Monod – are young, trendy and busy.

★ Bobo Bistro   MEDITERRANEAN €€
(☑04 93 99 97 33; www.facebook.com/BoboBistroCannes; 21 rue du Commandant André; pizzas €14-20, mains €18-31; ◷noon-3pm & 7-11pm) Predictably, it's a 'bobo' (bourgeois bohemian) crowd that gathers at this achingly cool bistro in Cannes' fashionable Carré d'Or. Decor is stylishly retro, with attention-grabbing objets d'art including a tableau of dozens of spindles of coloured yarn. Cuisine is local, seasonal and invariably organic: artichoke salad, tuna carpaccio with passion fruit, roasted cod with mash *fait masion* (homemade).

❶ Information

Tourist Office (☑04 92 99 84 22; www.cannes-destination.fr; 1 bd de la Croisette; ◷9am-7pm Mar-Oct, to 8pm Jul & Aug, 10am-6pm Nov-Feb; 🛜)

❶ Getting There & Away

Cannes' gleaming white train station is well connected with other towns along the coast, including Nice (€6.10, 40 minutes, every 15 minutes), Marseille (€32.40 to €38, two hours, half-hourly) and Monaco (€10, one hour, at least twice hourly).

St-Tropez

POP 4441

In the soft autumn or winter light, it's hard to believe the pretty terracotta fishing vil-

FAST FOOD CANNES-STYLE

For a tasty lunch with sensational views, grab a seafront pew at **PhilCat** (☑04 93 38 43 42; promenade de la Pantiéro; sandwiches & salads €3.50-5.50; ◷7am-7pm mid-Mar–Oct; 🖉), a prefab cabin with plastic tables and chairs on the waterfront. Phillipe and Catherine cook up giant salads, toasted panini and the best *pan bagna* (€5; a gargantuan bun filled with tuna, onion, red pepper, lettuce and tomato, and dripping in olive oil) on the Riviera. The 'super' version (€5.30) throws anchovies into the mix.

lage of St-Tropez is a stop on the Riviera celebrity circuit. It seems far removed from its glitzy siblings further up the coast, but come spring or summer, it's a different world: the population increases tenfold, prices triple and fun-seekers pile in to party till dawn.

◉ Sights & Activities

For St-Tropez' fabled beach scene, head to **Plage de Pampelonne**, a glorious 9km stretch of golden sand peppered with A-lister beach bars and restaurants.

Vieux Port   PORT
Yachts line the harbour (as their uniformed crews diligently scrub them) and visitors stroll the quays at the picturesque old port. In front of the sable-coloured townhouses, the **Bailli de Suffren statue** (quai Suffren) of a 17th-century naval hero cast from a 19th-century cannon, peers out to sea. Duck beneath the archway, next to the tourist office, to uncover St-Tropez' daily morning fish market, on place aux Herbes.

★ La Ponche   HISTORIC SITE
Shrug off the hustle of the port in St-Tropez's historic fishing quarter, La Ponche, located northeast of the Vieux Port. From the southern end of quai Frédéric Mistral, place Garrezio sprawls east from 10th-century **Tour Suffren** to place de l'Hôtel de Ville. From here, rue Guichard leads southeast to iconic **Église de St-Tropez** (Eglise Notre Dame de l'Assomption; rue Commandant Guichard). Follow rue du Portail Neuf south to **Chapelle de la Miséricorde** (1-5 rue de la Miséricorde; ◷10am-6pm).

★ Musée de l'Annonciade
GALLERY

(☑ 04 94 17 84 10; www.saint-tropez.fr/fr/culture/musee-de-lannonciade; place Grammont; adult/child €6/free; ◷ 10am-6pm daily mid-Jun–Sep, Tue-Sun Oct–mid-Jun) In a gracefully converted 16th-century chapel, this small but famous museum showcases an impressive collection of modern art infused with that legendary Côte d'Azur light. Pointillist Paul Signac bought a house in St-Tropez in 1892 and introduced other artists to the area. The museum's collection includes his *St-Tropez, Le Quai* (1899) and *St-Tropez, Coucher de Soleil au Bois de Pins* (1896). Vuillard, Bonnard and Maurice Denis (the self-named 'Nabis' group) have a room to themselves.

Place des Lices
SQUARE

St-Tropez' legendary and very charming central square is studded with plane trees, cafes and *pétanque* players. Simply sitting on a cafe terrace watching the world go by or jostling with the crowds at its twice-weekly market (◷ 8am-1pm Tue & Sat) extravaganza, jam-packed with everything from fruit and veg to antique mirrors and sandals, is an integral part of the St-Tropez experience.

Place des Lices has seen artists and intellectuals fraternising for decades here, most frequently in the famous Café des Arts, now simply called Le Café (☑ 04 94 97 44 69; www.lecafe.fr; Traverse des Lices; 2-course lunch menu €18, mains €22-29; ◷ 8am-11pm) – and not to be confused with the newer, green-canopied Café des Arts on the corner of the square. Aspiring *pétanque* players can borrow a set from the bar.

🛏 Sleeping & Eating

This is no shoestring destination, although campgrounds do sit southeast along Plage de Pampelonne.

Hôtel Lou Cagnard
HOTEL €€

(☑ 04 94 97 04 24; www.hotel-lou-cagnard.com; 30 av Paul Roussel; r from €95; ◷ Apr-Oct; P ❋ 🛜) This old-school hotel stands in stark contrast to most of the swanky hotels around St-Tropez. Located in an old house shaded by lemon and fig trees, its 18 rooms are unashamedly frilly and floral, but some have garden patios, and the lovely jasmine-scented garden and welcoming family feel make it a home away from home. The cheapest rooms share toilets.

La Pesquière
SEAFOOD €

(☑ 04 94 97 05 92; http://pesquiere.mazagran.free.fr; 1 rue des Remparts; menus adult/child €29/14; ◷ 9am-midnight late Mar-Oct) It's no surprise this old-fashioned place survives in restless, modish St Tropez: since 1962 the one family has made an art of buying the day's freshest catch – whether that be dourade, red mullet, bass or prawns – and cooking it to simple perfection. Locals love it, as do visitors, and you feel you've had your money's worth.

ℹ Information

Tourist Office (☑ 08 92 68 48 28; www.sainttropeztourisme.com; quai Jean Jaurès; ◷ 9.30am-1.30pm & 3-7.30pm Jul & Aug, 9.30am-12.30pm & 2-7pm Apr-Jun, Sep & Oct, to 6pm Mon-Sat Nov-Mar)

ℹ Getting There & Away

During high season, avoid horrendous four-hour traffic bottlenecks on the one road into St-Tropez (or €40 parking, impossible to find) by parking in **Port Grimaud** or **Ste-Maxime** and taking a **Les Bateaux Verts** (☑ 04 94 49 29 39; www.bateauxverts.com; 7 quai Jean Jaurès) shuttle boat.

By train, the most convenient station is in St-Raphaël, served by bus or **Les Bateaux de St-Raphaël** (☑ 04 94 95 17 46; www.bateaux-saintraphael.com; ◷ Apr-late Nov) boats in high season.

Monaco
POP 37,550

Squeezed into just 200 hectares, this glitzy, glam principality is the world's second-smallest country (the Vatican is smaller) and a notorious tax haven. With its dramatic coastal location, celebrity yachts, skyscrapers and iconic Formula 1 Grand Prix, Monaco is truly beguiling.

Skip Monaco's outlandish accommodation prices by visiting for the day from Nice. Include Monaco's country code (377) when calling Monaco from outside the principality.

⊙ Sights & Activities

★ Le Rocher
HISTORIC SITE

Monaco Ville, also called Le Rocher, is the only part of Monaco to have retained its original old town, complete with small, windy medieval lanes. The old town thrusts skywards on a pistol-shaped rock, its strate-

Monaco

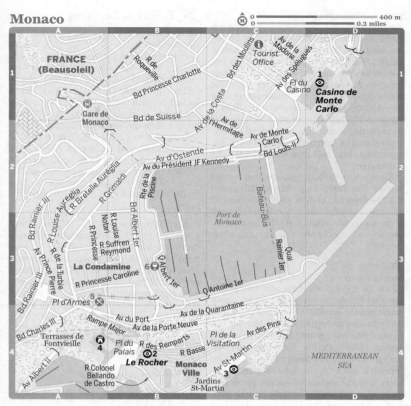

gic location overlooking the sea that became the stronghold of the Grimaldi dynasty. There are various staircases up to Le Rocher; the best route up is via Rampe Major, which starts from place d'Armes near the port.

Palais Princier de Monaco PALACE

(☑ 93 25 18 31; www.palais.mc; place du Palais; adult/child €8/4, incl car museum €11.50/5, incl Oceanographic Museum €19/11; ☺ 10am-6pm Apr-Jun & Sep–mid-Oct, to 7pm Jul & Aug) Built as a fortress atop Le Rocher in the 13th century, this palace is the private residence of the Grimaldi family. It is protected by the blue-helmeted, white-socked Carabiniers du Prince; changing of the guard takes place daily at 11.55am, when crowds gather outside the gates to watch.

Most of the palace is off limits, but you can get a glimpse of royal life on a tour of the

Monaco

◎ Top Sights
1 Casino de Monte Carlo	D1
2 Le Rocher	B4

◎ Sights
3 Musée Océanographique de Monaco	C4
4 Palais Princier de Monaco	A4

⊗ Eating
5 Marché de la Condamine	A3

◎ Drinking & Nightlife
6 Brasserie de Monaco	B3

glittering **state apartments**, where you can see some of the lavish furniture and priceless artworks collected by the family over the centuries. It's a good idea to buy tickets online in advance to avoid queuing.

Musée Océanographique de Monaco
AQUARIUM

(☑ 93 15 36 00; www.oceano.mc; av St-Martin; adult/child high season €16/12, low season €11/7; ⏰ 9.30am-8pm Jul & Aug, 10am-7pm Apr-Jun & Sep, to 6pm Oct-Mar) Stuck dramatically to the edge of a cliff since 1910, the world-renowned Musée Océanographique de Monaco, founded by Prince Albert I (1848–1922), is a stunner. Its centrepiece is its aquarium, that has a 6m-deep lagoon where sharks and marine predators are separated from colourful tropical fishes by a coral reef.

Upstairs, two huge colonnaded rooms retrace the history of oceanography and marine biology (as well as Prince Albert's valuable contribution to the field) through a photographic exhibition, old equipment, numerous specimens and interactive displays.

★ Casino de Monte Carlo
CASINO

(☑ 98 06 21 21; www.casinomontecarlo.com; place du Casino; morning visit incl audioguide adult/child Oct-Apr €14/10, May-Sep €17/12; salons ordinaires gaming Oct-Apr €14, May-Sep €17; ⏰ visits 9am-1pm, gaming 2pm-late) Peeping inside Monte Carlo's legendary marble-and-gold casino is a Monaco essential. The building, open to visitors every morning, including the exclusive *salons privés,* is Europe's most lavish example of belle époque architecture. Prince Charles III spearheaded the casino's development and in 1866, three years after its inauguration, the name 'Monte Carlo' – Ligurian for 'Mount Charles' – in honour of the prince – was coined. To gamble here, visit after 2pm (when a strict over-18s-only admission rule kicks in).

> ### ⓘ SLEEPING PRICE RANGES
>
> Price ranges listed refer to a double room in high season, with private bathroom, excluding breakfast unless otherwise noted.
>
> € less than €90 (less than €130 in Paris)
>
> €€ €90–190 (€130–250 in Paris)
>
> €€€ more than €190 (more than €250 in Paris)

✖ Eating & Drinking

★ Marché de la Condamine
MARKET €

(www.facebook.com/marche.condamine; 15 place d'Armes; ⏰ 7am-3pm Mon-Sat, to 2pm Sun) For tasty, excellent-value fare around shared tables, hit Monaco's fabulous food court, tucked beneath the arches behind the open-air place d'Armes market. Rock-bottom budget faves include fresh pasta from **Maison des Pâtes** (☑ 93 50 95 77; pasta €6.40-12; ⏰ 7am-3.30pm) and traditional Niçois *socca* from **Chez Roger** (☑ 93 50 80 20; socca €3; ⏰ 10am-3pm); there's also pizza and seafood from Le Comptoir, truffle cuisine from Truffle Bistrot, a deli, a cafe, a cheesemonger and more.

Brasserie de Monaco
MICROBREWERY

(☑ 97 98 51 20; www.facebook.com/brasseriedemonacomc; 36 rte de la Piscine; ⏰ noon-2am) Having Monaco's only microbrewery gives this bar down by La Condamine a useful USP, and its organic lagers and ales pack the punters in. Inside it's all chrome, steel and big-screen TVs, and live sports and DJs keep the weekends extra busy. For a more chilled experience, head for the portside patio out the front. Happy hour's from 6pm to 8pm.

ⓘ Information

Tourist Office (☑ 92 16 61 16; www.visitmonaco.com; 2a bd des Moulins; ⏰ 9am-7pm Mon-Sat, 11am-1pm Sun)

ⓘ Getting There & Away

Train services run about every 20 minutes to Nice (€3.50, 25 minutes).

France Survival Guide

ⓘ Directory A–Z

ACCOMMODATION

Many tourist offices make room reservations, for free or a fee of €5; many only do so if you stop by in person.

For charm, welcome and good value, it's hard to beat a *chambre d'hôte* (B&B). Pick up *chambre d'hôte* listings at tourist offices or find one online to suit.

To prevent outbreaks of bed bugs, sleeping bags are not permitted in almost all hostels.

INTERNET RESOURCES

France.fr (www.france.fr) Official country website.

France 24 (www.france24.com/en/france) French news in English.

Paris by Mouth (https://parisbymouth.com) Dining and drinking in Paris.

MONEY

Credit cards issued in France have embedded chips – you have to type in a PIN to make a purchase. Some places (eg 24-hour petrol stations, autoroute toll machines and city bike-share pay machines like Paris' Vélib) won't accept a card without a chip; pay in cash.

In Paris and major cities, *bureaux de change* (exchange bureaus) are fast and easy, open long hours and offer competitive exchange rates.

Restaurant and bar prices always include a 15% service charge, but locals still tend to leave a small 'extra' tip (around 10%) for the waitstaff.

OPENING HOURS

Banks 9am to noon and 2pm to 5pm Monday to Friday or Tuesday to Saturday

Bars 7pm to1am

Cafes 7am to 11pm

Clubs 10pm to 3am, to 4am or 5am Thursday to Saturday

Restaurants Noon to 2.30pm and 7pm to 11pm six days a week

Shops 10am to noon and 2pm to 7pm Monday to Saturday

PUBLIC HOLIDAYS

New Year's Day 1 January

Easter Sunday & Monday Late March/April

May Day 1 May

Victoire 1945 8 May

Ascension Thursday May; on the 40th day after Easter

Pentecost/Whit Sunday & Whit Monday Mid-May to mid-June; on the seventh Sunday after Easter

Bastille Day/National Day 14 July

Assumption Day 15 August

All Saints' Day 1 November

Remembrance Day 11 November

Christmas Day 25 December

SMOKING

Smoking is illegal in all indoor public spaces, including restaurants and pubs (though, of course, smokers still light up on the terraces outside).

 EATING PRICE RANGES

Price indicators refer to the average cost of a two-course meal, be it an *entrée* (starter) and *plat* (main course) or main and dessert, or a two- or three-course *menu* (set meal at a fixed price).

€ less than €20

€€ €20–40

€€€ more than €40

TELEPHONE

➨ Area codes do not exist in France.

➨ The country code for France is 33. When calling France from abroad, drop the initial '0' from the 10-digit telephone number.

➨ To call abroad from France, use the international access code 00.

➨ Buy prepaid SIM cards from a French provider such as Orange, SFR, Bouygues and Free Mobile.

➨ French mobile telephone numbers begin with 06 or 07.

➨ Save up to 60% on the normal international rate by buying a prepaid Ticket Téléphone (phonecard) from tobacconists or online at www.topengo.fr.

VISAS

For up-to-date details on visa requirements, check the **Ministry of Foreign Affairs** (Map p316; www.diplomatie.gouv.fr; 37 quai d'Orsay, 7e, Paris; Ⓜ Assemblée Nationale).

Getting There & Away

AIR

International airports include the following; there are many smaller ones serving European destinations.

Aéroport de Charles de Gaulle (p327)

Aéroport Marseille-Provence (p348)

Aéroport Nice Côte d'Azur (p352)

 DINING ON THE CHEAP

➨ Daily *formules* or *menus* (*prix-fixe* menus) typically include two- to four-course meals. In some cases, particularly at market-driven neobistros, there is no *carte* (menu).

➨ Lunch *menus* are often a fantastic deal and allow you to enjoy *haute cuisine* at very affordable prices.

FRANCE & SWITZERLAND FRANCE SURVIVAL GUIDE

LAND

Car & Motorcycle

A right-hand-drive vehicle brought to France from the UK or Ireland must have deflectors affixed to the headlights to avoid dazzling on-coming traffic.

Departing from the UK, **Eurotunnel Le Shuttle** (☑ in France 08 10 63 03 04, in UK 08443 35 35 35; www.eurotunnel.com) trains whisk bicycles, motorcycles, cars and coaches in 35 minutes from Folkestone through the Channel Tunnel to Coquelles, 5km southwest of Calais. Shuttles run 24 hours a day, with up to three departures an hour during peak periods. The earlier you book, the less you pay. Fares for a car, including passengers, start at UK£30/€37.

Train

Rail services – including **Eurostar** (☑ in France 08 92 35 35 39, in UK 08432 186 186; www. eurostar.com) services to/from the UK – link France with virtually every country through Europe.

➡ Book tickets and get train information from Rail Europe (www.raileurope.com). In the UK contact Railteam (www.railteam.co.uk) for train service information.

➡ In France, ticketing is handled by SNCF (https://en.oui.sncf); internet bookings are possible, but SNCF won't post tickets outside France.

SEA

Regular ferries travel to France from the UK, Ireland and Italy. To get the best fares, check Ferry Savers.

➡ Brittany Ferries (www.brittany-ferries.co.uk) Links between England/Ireland and Brittany and Normandy.

➡ Condor Ferries (www.condorferries.co.uk) Ferries from England to/from Brittany and Normandy.

➡ P&O Ferries (www.poferries.com) Ferry services running between England and northern France.

❶ Getting Around

BICYCLE

The Loire Valley and Provence beg two-wheel exploration and have dedicated cycling paths, some along canal towpaths or between fruit orchards and vineyards.

Online see Voies Vertes (www.voiesvertes.com).

BUS

Cheaper and slower than trains, they're useful for more remote villages that aren't serviced by trains.

CAR & MOTORCYCLE

Meander away from cities and large towns (where a car is hard to park) and a car comes into its own.

➡ Cars can be hired at airports and train stations.

➡ Drive on the right. Be aware of France's potentially hazardous 'priority to the right' rule.

➡ You have to pay to use France's well-serviced *autoroutes* (highways, motorways); calculate tolls at www.autoroutes.fr.

➡ Bison Futé (www.bison-fute.equipement. gouv.fr) is an excellent source of information about traffic conditions.

TRAIN

Run by the state-owned SNCF, France's rail network is truly first-class, with extensive service coverage of the country and frequent departures.

Check timetable and fare information on www. oui.sncf.

SWITZERLAND

Geneva

POP 198,072 / ELEV 375M

Like the swans that frolic on its eponymous Alpine lake (Europe's largest), Geneva (Genève) is a rare bird. Slick, cosmopolitan and constantly perceived as the Swiss capital (it isn't – that's Bern), the people of Switzerland's second-largest city chatter in almost every language on streets that are paved with plush hotels, banks,

---

Geneva

◎ Top Sights
1	Cathédrale St-Pierre	B5
2	Jet d'Eau	D3
3	Musée International de la Réforme	B5
4	Vieille Ville	B6

◎ Sights
5	Maison de Rousseau et de la Littérature	B5
	Site Archéologique de la Cathédrale St-Pierre	(see 1)

◆ Activities, Courses & Tours
6	Bains des Pâquis	D2

✖ Eating
7	Buvette des Bains	D2

luxury jewellers and chocolate shops. The United Nations, the International Committee of the Red Cross, the World Health Organization, the World Trade Organization and 200-odd governmental and nongovernmental international organisations are all situated here.

◉ Sights

★ Jet d'Eau   FOUNTAIN

(Quai Gustave-Ador) When landing in Geneva by plane, this lakeside fountain is your first dramatic glimpse of the city below. The 140m-tall structure shoots up water

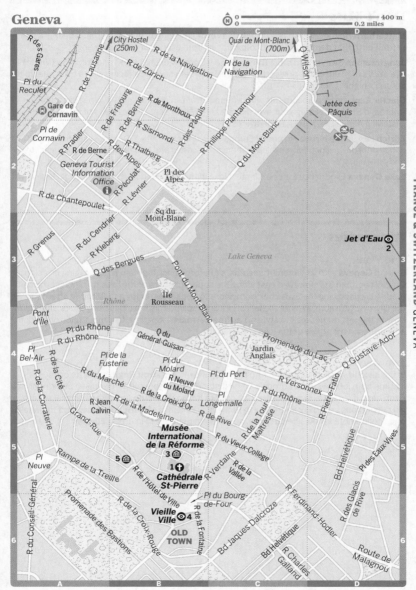

Geneva

☆ SWITZERLAND AT A GLANCE

Don't Miss

Matterhorn No mountain has as much natural magnetism as this charismatic peak – a beauty from birth that demands to be photographed from every last infuriating angle.

Jungfraujoch Switzerland's 'big three' – Eiger (Ogre), Mönch (Monk) and Jungfrau (Virgin) – rise above the 19th-century resort of Grindelwald. Set your pulse racing with a train ride up to Europe's highest station (3454m).

Glacier Express Hop aboard this world-famous train linking the glitzy Alpine resorts of Zermatt and St Moritz. Bring your own picnic to enjoy over sensational views of green peaks, glistening Alpine lakes and glacial ravines.

Zürich Lap up the hip vibe in one of Europe's most liveable cities. Drink in waterfront bars, dance until dawn, shop for recycled fashion accessories and boogie at Europe's largest street party in August.

Lake Geneva Experience Europe's largest lake in the chic, French-speaking city of Geneva.

Itineraries

One Week

Start in **Geneva** with its vibrant museums, signature pencil fountain and engaging lakeside life. On day two, take the slow road east along the southern shore of the lake in France or the fast road (A1) shadowing the Swiss northern shore to **Lausanne**. Enjoy a fascinating afternoon in the Olympic Museum, explore the lakeshore and dip into this fun city's bridge bars after dark. Devote the rest of the week to stylish, car-free **Zermatt**, launch pad for mountains of outdoor adventures in the shade of the iconic Matterhorn.

Two Weeks

In the second week, dive straight into the magnificent **Jungfrau Region** with its once-in-a-lifetime train journey up to Europe's highest station; base yourself in Interlaken or Grindelwald. From here, it's a toss-up between a trip south to Italianate **Ticino** for shimmering lake life in glitzy gorgeous Locarno or a trip north to the art-rich cities of **Bern** and **Basel**. End the week on a mellow note in lakeside **Lucerne**, or join the hipster party in urban **Zürich**.

Swiss Outdoors

Zermatt Holy grail of mountaineering where rock climbers can get to grips with the 4000ers and measure up to the Matterhorn; world-class winter skiing and summer hiking too.

Interlaken High-adreneline, adventure sports hub for all manner of Alpine activities.

Grindelwald Stunning hikes through wildflower-strewn meandows; climbing, canyoning and heart-stopping bungee jumping in the Gletscherschlucht too.

Adventure Park Swing from the tree tops at Switzerland's largest rope park, with stunning views of the thundering Rheinfall to boot.

Lake Lucerne and Lake Geneva Two beautiful lakes from which to savour Switzerland's majestic scenery.

Getting Around

Switzerland's fully integrated public-transport system is among the world's most efficient. However, travel is expensive and visitors planning to use intercity routes should consider investing in a Swiss travel pass. For timetables and tickets, head to www.sbb.ch.

Bicycle Switzerland is well equipped for cyclists. Many cities have free-bike-hire schemes. Bicycle and e-bike rental is usually available at stations.

Bus Filling the gaps in more remote areas, Switzerland's post-bus service is synchronised with train arrivals.

Car Handy for remote regions where public transport is minimal.

Train Swiss trains run like a dream. Numerous discount-giving travel cards and tickets are available.

When to Go

Geneva

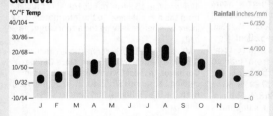

°C/°F **Temp** Rainfall inches/mm

| **Jul, Aug & Dec–Apr** Summertime walking and biking; winter skiing. | **Apr–Jun & Sep** Idyllic: warm temperatures, springtime flowers and local produce. | **Oct–Mar** Prices can be 50% lower than in high season. Sights and restaurants open shorter hours. |

Arriving in Switzerland

Zürich Airport Up to nine SBB (www.sbb.ch) trains run hourly to Hauptbahnhof from 5am to midnight; taxis cost around Sfr60 to the centre.

Geneva Airport SBB trains run at least every 10 minutes to Gare de Cornavin; taxis charge Sfr35 to Sfr50 to the centre.

Top Phrases

French, German, Italian and Romansch are all spoken in Switzerland.

Hello. Bonjour. (French) Grüezi. (German) Buongiorno. (Italian)

Goodbye. Au revoir. (French) Auf Wiedersehen. (German) Arrivederci .(Italian)

Please. S'il vous plaît. (French) Bitte. (German), Per favore. (Italian)

Thank you. Merci. (French) Danke. (German) Grazie (Italian)

Resources

My Switzerland (www.myswitzerland.com)

Swiss Info (www.swissinfo.ch)

Set Your Budget

➡ Dorm bed: Sfr30–60

➡ Double room in a budget hotel: Sfr100

➡ Lunch out; self-catering after dark: from Sfr25

➡ Public transport: free with a *Gästekarte* (visitors' card), issued by your accommodation.

with an incredible force (200km/h, 1360 horsepower) to create the sky-high plume, which is kissed by a rainbow on sunny days. At any one time, 7 tonnes of water are in the air, much of which sprays spectators standing on the pier beneath. Two or three times a year it is illuminated in pink, blue or another colour to mark a humanitarian occasion.

Quai du Mont-Blanc   WATERFRONT
Flowers, statues, outdoor art exhibitions and views of Mont Blanc (on clear days only) abound on this picturesque northern lakeshore promenade, which leads past the **Bains des Pâquis** (☑022 732 29 74; www.bains-des-paquis.ch; Quai du Mont-Blanc 30; pools adult/child Sfr2/1, sauna, hammam & Turkish bath Sfr20; ⊙9am-9.30pm Mon-Sat, from 8pm Sun), where the *Genevois* have frolicked in the sun since 1872, to **Parc de la Perle du Lac**, a city park where Romans built ornate thermal baths. Further north, the peacock-studded lawns of **Parc de l'Ariana** ensnare the UN and Geneva's pretty **Conservatoire et Jardin Botaniques** (Conservatory & Botanical Gardens; ☑022 418 51 00; www.ville-ge.ch/cjb/index_en.php; Chemin de l'Impératrice 1; ⊙8am-5pm Nov-Apr, to 7.30pm Apr-Nov) FREE.

★ **Vieille Ville**   AREA
(Old Town) A stroll around Geneva's beautiful Old Town is a must. Its main street, the Grand-Rue, shelters the **Maison de Rousseau et de la Literature** (☑022 310 10 28; www.m-r-l.ch; Grand-Rue 40; adult/child Sfr5/3; ⊙11am-5.30pm Tue-Sun) at No 40, where the 18th-century philosopher was born. Nearby, the part-Romanesque, part-Gothic **Cathédrale St-Pierre** (www.cathedrale-geneve.ch; Cour de St-Pierre; towers adult/child Sfr5/2; ⊙9.30am-6.30pm Mon-Sat, noon-6.30pm Sun Jun-Sep, 10am-5.30pm Mon-Sat, noon-5.30pm Sun Oct-May) is where Protestant John Calvin preached from 1536 to 1564. Situated beneath the cathedral is the **Site Archéologique** (☑022 310 29 29; www.site-archeologique.ch; adult/child Sfr8/4; ⊙10am-5pm), an interactive space that safeguards fine 4th-century mosaics as well as a 5th-century baptismal font. You can trace John Calvin's life in the neighbouring **Musée International de la Réforme** (Museum of the Reformation; ☑022 310 24 31; www.mir.ch; Rue du Cloître 4; adult/child Sfr13/6; ⊙10am-5pm Tue-Sun).

🛏 Sleeping & Eating

Geneva flaunts ethnic cuisines galore. If it's local and traditional you're after, dip into a cheese fondue or platter of pan-fried *filets de perche* (perch fillets), a simple Lake Geneva speciality.

City Hostel   HOSTEL €
(☑022 901 15 00; www.cityhostel.ch; Rue de Ferrier 2; dm Sfr33-36, s Sfr65-73, tw Sfr79-95; ⊙reception 7.30am-noon & 1pm-midnight; 🅿@🛜) This clean, well-organised hostel near the train station feels more like a hotel than a hostel. Breakfast (Sfr6) is served in a nearby cafe and parking costs Sfr12 to Sfr15 per night.

★ **Buvette des Bains**   CAFETERIA €
(☑022 738 16 16; www.bains-des-paquis.ch; Quai du Mont-Blanc 30, Bains des Pâquis; mains Sfr14-23; ⊙7am-10.30pm; 🅿🍴) Meet Genevans at this earthy beach bar – rough and hip around the edges – at the Bains des Pâquis lakeside pool and sauna complex. Grab breakfast, a salad or the *plat du jour* (dish of the day), or dip into a *fondue au crémant* (sparkling-wine fondue). Dining is self-service on trays and al fresco in summer.

🛈 Information

Geneva Tourist Information Office (☑022 909 70 00; www.geneve.com; Rue du Mont-Blanc 18; ⊙10am-6pm Mon, 9am-6pm Tue-Sat, 10am-4pm Sun)

🛈 Getting There & Around

Regular trains (six minutes) and bus No 10 to Rive (30 minutes, four to nine hourly) link **Aéroport de Genève** with the centre of town, 4km away. Grab a free public transport ticket from the machine next to the information desk in arrivals before leaving the airport luggage hall.

More-or-less-hourly connections run from Geneva's central train station, **Gare CFF de Cornavin**, to most Swiss towns and cities including Lausanne (Sfr22.40, 35 to 50 minutes), Bern (Sfr50, 1¾ hours) and Zürich (Sfr87, 2¾ hours).

Lausanne

POP 146.372

French-speaking Lausanne is known for its upbeat vibe, enviable lakeside location (vistas are more dramatic than Geneva's) and party-hearty student population – EPFL,

Lausanne

0 — 400 m
0 — 0.2 miles

Av A.Vinet
Av de Beaulieu
R St Roch
R.Pré du Marché
R du Valentin
R de la Borde
Rte du Signal
Bois de Sauvabelin
R du Bugnon

R du Tunnel
Place du Tunnel

Pl de la Madeleine
R de la Tour
R de l'Ale
R Neuve
R Cité-Devant
R Louis Auguste-Curtat
R.Dr.César-Roux

Musée Cantonal des Beaux Arts 2
4
R Pierre Viret
Pl de la Cathédrale 1

R des Terreaux
R de Genève
R du Grand Pont
Pl de la Riponne
Riponne
Cathédrale de Notre Dame
R St-Martin

Pont Chauderon
Voie du Chariot
FLON
Pl Pépinet
R Mercerie
R Centrale
Bessières
R Caroline

Av Jules Gonin
Pl de l'Europe
Pl Centrale
R Pépinet
6
R Enning
R Marterey
Ours

Montbenon
Flon
Rue Pépinet 5
R du Bourg

Av Louis-Ruchonnet
R du Grand-Chêne
Pl St François
Av B Constant
Av Mon Repos

R du Petit-Chêne
Gare
R du Midi
Av du Théâtre
Av Villamont
Av Bellefontaine

Chemin des Epinettes
Pl de la Gare
Av Sainte-Luce
R Beau-Séjour

Av du Mont d'Or
Av W Fraisse
Av du Rond Point
Lausanne Tourisme (Gare)
Train Station
Av de la Gare
R Beau-Séjour

Crêt de Montriond
Bd de Grancy
Av Juste-Olivier

Botanical Gardens
Grancy
Av Dapples

Chemin de Bellerive
Jordils
Av de Cour
Av d'Ouchy

Av de la Harpe
Délices
Av de l'Elysée
Av de Montchoisi

OUCHY
3

Av de Rhodanie
Chemin de Beau-Rivage
Ouchy
Quai de Belgique

Quai des Savoyards
Pl de la Navigation
Pl du Port
Quai d'Ouchy

Compagnie Générale de Navigation
Quai J-P Delamuraz
Port d'Ouchy
Lake Geneva

Lausanne

◉ **Top Sights**
1 Cathédrale de Notre Dame C2
2 Musée Cantonal des Beaux Arts C2

◉ **Sights**
3 Olympic Museum................................. C6
4 Palais de Rumine C2

✖ **Eating**
5 Eat Me...C3
6 Holy Cow..C3
7 Holy Cow..B2

Lausanne's science and technology university, is Europe's version of Boston's MIT. Districts to explore include the Gothic Old Town, chi-chi lakeside Ouchy, and urban-hip Flon, a warehouse district of bars and boutiques.

◉ Sights

★**Cathédrale
de Notre Dame**   CATHEDRAL
(☑021 316 71 60; www.cath-vd.ch/cvd_parish/
notre-dame; Pl de la Cathédrale; ⊙9am-7pm Apr-
Sep, to 5.30pm Oct-Mar) Lausanne's Gothic cathedral, Switzerland's finest, stands proudly at the heart of the Old Town. Raised in the 12th and 13th centuries on the site of earlier, humbler churches, it lacks the lightness of French Gothic buildings but is remarkable nonetheless. Pope Gregory X, in the presence of Rudolph of Habsburg (the Holy Roman Emperor) and an impressive following of European cardinals and bishops, consecrated the church in 1275.

★**Musée Cantonal
des Beaux Arts**   MUSEUM
(MCB-A; ☑021 316 34 45; www.mcba.ch; Pl de la Riponne 6; adult/child Sfr10/free, 1st Sat of month free; ⊙11am-6pm Tue-Thu, to 5pm Fri-Sun) The **Palais de Rumine** (☑021 316 33 10; http://musees.vd.ch/palais-de-rumine/accueil/; ⊙11am-6pm Tue-Thu, to 5pm Fri-Sun) FREE, where the

BRIDGE BARS

Where there's a bridge, there's a bar. At least that's how it works in artsy Lausanne where the monumental arches of its bridges shelter the city's most happening summertime bars.

Treaty of Lausanne was signed in 1923, safeguards the city's Fine Arts museum, though in 2019, it will be relocating to Plateforme10. Works by Swiss and foreign artists, ranging from Ancient Egyptian art to Cubism, are displayed, but the core of the collection is made up of works by landscape painter Louis Ducros (1748–1810). During temporary exhibitions (many with free admission), the permanent collection is often closed.

Olympic Museum   MUSEUM
(Musée Olympique; ☑021 621 65 11; www.olympic.
org/museum; Quai d'Ouchy 1; adult/child Sfr18/10;
⊙9am-6pm daily May–mid-Oct, 10am-6pm Tue-
Sun mid-Oct–Apr; P 🖼) Musée Olympique is easily Lausanne's most lavish museum and an essential stop for sports buffs (and children). State-of-the-art installations recount the Olympic story from its inception to the present day through video, interactive displays, memorabilia and temporary themed exhibitions. Other attractions include the tiered landscaped gardens, site-specific sculptural works and a fabulous cafe that has champion lake views from out on its terrace.

🛏 Sleeping & Eating

When checking in at your accommodation, pick up a Lausanne Transport Card, which gives you unlimited use of public transport for the duration of your stay.

**SYHA Lausanne
Jeunotel**   HOSTEL €
(☑021 626 02 22; www.youthhostel.ch/lausanne;
Chemin du Bois-de-Vaux 36; 4-bed dm Sfr43, s/d
from Sfr105/130; P 🛜) 🏊 A stone's throw from Lake Geneva, near the offices of the International Olympic Committee, this Swiss YHA (SYHA) is classed as a 'top' level hostel for its smartly renovated rooms, 24-hour reception and pleasant location nestled among parkland just a stone's throw from the lake. A breakfast buffet is included in the rate and daily lunches and dinners are available (Sfr17.50).

★**Eat Me**   TAPAS €
(☑021 311 76 59; www.eat-me.ch; Rue Pépinet 3;
small plates Sfr10-20; ⊙noon-2pm & 5pm-mid-
night Tue-Sat; 🛜🍴) Eat Me's tagline of 'The world on small plates' will give you an idea of what this fun, immensely popular and downright delicious resto-bar is all about: global tapas, basically, with everything from

THE GLACIER EXPRESS

Marketed as the world's slowest express train, the Glacier Express (www.glacierex-press.ch; adult/child one-way St Moritz–Zermatt Sfr153/76.50, obligatory seat reservation summer/winter Sfr33/13, on-board 3-course lunch Sfr45; ☺3 trains daily May-Oct, 1 daily mid-Dec–Feb) is one of Europe's legendary train journeys. It starts and ends in two of Switzerland's oldest, glitziest mountain resorts – Zermatt and St Moritz – and the Alpine scenery is truly magnificent in parts. But a ticket is not cheap, and to avoid disappointment it pays to know the nuts and bolts of this long mountain train ride, 290km in distance.

➡ Check the weather forecast: ride the *Glacier Express* on a grey, cloudy day and you'll definitely feel you've been taken for a ride. Beneath a clear blue sky is the *only* way to do it.

➡ Don't assume it is hard-core mountain porn for the duration of the journey: the views in the 191 tunnels the train passes through are not particularly wonderful, for starters.

➡ The complete trip takes almost eight hours. If you're travelling with children or can't bear the thought of sitting all day watching mountain scenery that risks becoming monotonous, opt for just a section of the journey: the best bit is the one-hour ride from Disentis to Andermatt, across the Oberalp Pass (2033m) – the highest point of the journey in every way. The celebrity six-arch, 65m-high Landwasser Viaduct, pictured on almost every feature advertising the *Glacier Express,* dazzles passengers during the 50km leg between Chur and Filisur.

➡ Windows in the stylish panoramic carriages are sealed and can't be opened, making it tricky to take good photographs or film. If photography or video is the reason you're aboard, ditch the direct glamour train for regional express SBB trains along the same route – they're cheaper, no reservations are required, and they have windows that open, opportunities to mingle with locals and time to stretch your legs when changing trains.

➡ The southern side of the train is said to have the better views.

baby burgers (sliders) to electric sashim-iviche (Sichuan sashimi à la *ceviche*!) and shrimp lollipops. Everything is well priced and it's just downright fun. Bring your friends!

★ **Holy Cow**   BURGERS **€**
(☑ 021 312 24 04; www.holycow.ch; Rue Chene-au-de-Bourg 17; burger with chips & drink Sfr14-26; ☺11am-11pm; 🖭) A Lausanne success story, with branches in Geneva, Zürich and France, its burgers (beef, chicken or veggie) feature local ingredients, creative toppings and witty names. Grab an artisanal beer, sit at a shared wooden table, and wait for your burger and fab fries to arrive in a straw basket. A second outlet can be found at Rue des Terreaux.

ℹ Information

Lausanne Tourisme (☑ 021 613 73 73; www.lausanne-tourisme.ch; Pl de la Gare 9; ☺9am-7pm)

ℹ Getting There & Away

CGN (www.cgn.ch; Quai Jean-Pascal Delamu-raz; leisure cruises from Sfr25) runs passenger boats (no car ferries) from Ouchy to destinations around Lake Geneva (including France). To hop on and off as you please, buy a one-day pass (adult/child Sfr64/32) covering unlimited lake travel. Destinations include Montreux (Sfr27, 1½ hours, up to six daily) and Geneva (Sfr45, 3½ to four hours, up to five daily).

You can travel by train to and from Geneva (Sfr22.40, 35 to 50 minutes, up to six hourly), Geneva Airport (Sfr27, 45 to 50 minutes, up to four hourly) and Bern (Sfr33, 65 to 70 minutes, one or two hourly).

Valais

This is Matterhorn country, an intoxicating land that seduces the toughest of critics with its endless panoramic vistas and breathtaking views. Switzerland's 10 highest mountains rise to the sky here, while snow fiends get high in top European resort Zermatt.

Zermatt

POP 5760 / ELEVATION 1605M

Since the mid-19th century, Zermatt has starred as one of Switzerland's glitziest resorts. Today it attracts intrepid mountaineers and hikers, skiers and boarders, all spellbound by the scenery and the Matterhorn (4478m) – an unfathomable monolith synonymous with Switzerland that you simply can't quite stop looking at.

◉ Sights & Activities

An essential stop in activity planning is the **Snow & Alpine Center** (Snow & Alpine Center; ☑ 027 966 24 66; www.zermatters.ch; Bahnhofstrasse 58; ⊙ 8am-noon & 3-7pm Dec-Apr, 9am-noon & 3-7pm Jul-Sep), home to Zermatt's ski school and mountain guides. In winter buy **lift passes** here (Sfr79/430 for a one-day/one-week pass excluding Cervinia, Sfr92/494 including Cervinia).

★ **Matterhorn
Glacier Paradise** CABLE CAR
(www.matterhornparadise.ch; Schluhmattstrasse; adult/child return Sfr100/50; ⊙ 8.30am-4.20pm) Views from Zermatt's cable cars are all remarkable, but the Matterhorn Glacier Paradise is the icing on the cake. Ride Europe's highest-altitude cable car to 3883m and gawp at 14 glaciers and 38 mountain peaks over 4000m from the **Panoramic Platform** (only open in good weather). Don't miss the **Glacier Palace**, an ice palace complete with glittering ice sculptures and an ice slide to swoosh down bum first. End with some exhilarating **snow tubing** outside in the snowy surrounds.

★ **Gornergratbahn** RAILWAY
(www.gornergrat.ch; Bahnhofplatz 7; adult/child round trip Sfr94/47; ⊙ 7am-7.15pm) Europe's highest cogwheel railway has climbed through stunning scenery to **Gornergrat** (3089m) – a 30-minute journey – since 1898. On the way up, sit on the right-hand side of the train to gaze at the Matterhorn. Tickets allow you to get on and off en route; there are restaurants at Riffelalp (2211m) and Riffelberg (2582m). In summer an extra train runs once a week at sunrise and sunset – the most spectacular trips of all.

⊨ Sleeping & Eating

★ **Hotel Bahnhof** HOTEL €
(☑ 027 967 24 06; www.hotelbahnhof.com; Bahnhofstrasse; dm Sfr35-50, s/d from Sfr80/120;

⊙ closed May–mid-Jun & mid-Oct–Nov; 🛜) Opposite the train station, these budget digs have comfy beds, spotless bathrooms and family-perfect rooms for four. Dorms are cosy and there's a stylish lounge with armchairs to flop in and books to read. No breakfast, but feel free to prepare your own in the snazzy, open-plan kitchen. Ski storage room, lockers and laundry are available.

★ **Bayard Metzgerei** SWISS €
(☑ 027 967 22 66; www.metzgerei-bayard.ch; Bahnhofstrasse 9; sausage Sfr6; ⊙ noon-6.30pm Jul-Sep, 4-6.30pm Dec-Mar) Join the line for a street-grilled sausage (pork, veal or beef) and chunk of bread to down with a beer on the hop – or at a bar stool with the sparrows in the alley – of this first-class butcher's shop.

ℹ Information

Tourist Office (☑ 027 966 81 00; www.zermatt.ch; Bahnhofplatz 5; ⊙ 8.30am-6pm; 🛜)

ℹ Getting There & Around

Zermatt is car-free. Motorists have to park in the **Matterhorn Terminal Täsch** (☑ 027 967 12 14; www.matterhornterminal.ch; Täsch; per 24hr Sfr15.50) and ride the Zermatt Shuttle train (return adult/child Sfr16.80/8.40, 12 minutes, every 20 minutes from 6am to 9.40pm) the last 5km up to Zermatt. Täsch is 31km south of Visp.

Mittelland & Bernese Oberland

At first glance it may seem funny that this flat, unassuming 'middle ground', as its straight-talking name states, should have Switzerland's delightfully languid and laid-back capital at its heart. Moving south, nature works on an epic scale in the Bernese Oberland where the Swiss Alps make hearts skip a beat.

Bern

POP 141,762

One of the planet's most underrated capitals, riverside Bern seduces and surprises at every turn. Its museums are excellent, its drinking scene dynamic and its locals happy to switch from their famously lilting dialect to textbook French, High German or English – which all goes to show that there's more to Bern than bureaucracy. Its 15th-century Old Town, with striking Gothic cathedral, is definitely worthy of its Unesco World Heritage site status.

◎ Sights & Activities

★ Berner Altstadt   AREA
(Bern Old Town) Bern's flag-bedecked medieval centre has 6km of covered arcades and cellar shops and bars descending from the streets. After a devastating fire in 1405, the wooden city was rebuilt in today's sandstone. Bern's clock tower, **Zytglogge** (Marktgasse), is a focal point; crowds congregate to watch its revolving figures twirl at four minutes before the hour, after which the actual chimes begin. Tours enter the tower to see the clock mechanism from May to October; contact the tourist office for details.

★ Zentrum Paul Klee   MUSEUM
(📞 031 359 01 01; www.zpk.org; Monument im Fruchtland 3; adult/child Sfr20/7; ⊙10am-5pm Tue-Sun) Bern's answer to the Guggenheim, Renzo Piano's architecturally bold, 150m-long wave-like edifice houses an exhibition space that showcases rotating works from Paul Klee's prodigious and often playful career. Interactive computer displays and audio guides help interpret the Swiss-born artist's work. Next door, the fun-packed **Kindermuseum Creaviva** (📞 031 359 01 61; www.creaviva-zpk.org; Monument im Fruchtland 3; ⊙10am-5pm Tue-Sun; ♦) [FREE] lets kids experiment with hands-on art projects or create original artwork with the atelier's materials during the weekend **Five Franc Studio** (www.creaviva-zpk.org/5-franc-studio; Zentrum Paul Klee; Sfr5; ⊙10am-4.30pm Sat & Sun; ♦). Bus 12 runs from Bubenbergplatz direct to the museum.

★ Museum für
Kommunikation   MUSEUM
(Museum of Communication; 📞 031 357 55 55; www.mfk.ch; Helvetiastrasse 16; adult/child Sfr15/5; ⊙10am-5pm Tue-Sun) Fresh from extensive renovation and expansion, Bern's Museum of Communication reopened its doors in August 2017. Occupying almost 2000 sq metres of exhibition space, it has cutting-edge interactive stations that explore the hows and whys of human communications with a focus on the role technology plays in our interactions with each other. Expect engaging, hands-on, high-tech interactive exhibits complemented by the museum's fabulous

COCKTAIL SPLURGE

When the fancy strikes, join beautiful people hob-nobbing over cocktails alongside historic stained-glass windows at **Kornhauskeller** (📞 031 327 72 72; www.bindella.ch; Kornhausplatz 18; mains Sfr24-58; ⊙11.45am-2.30pm & 6pm-12.30am), a stunning cellar restaurant serving Mediterranean cuisine beneath vaulted frescoed arches at Bern's ornate former granary. Next door, at its neighbouring cafe, punters lunch in the sun on Bern's best pavement terrace.

original collection of retro phones and computers.

✗ Eating & Drinking

Look for interesting cafes and bistros scattered amid the arcades on Old Town streets including Zeughausgasse, Rathausgasse, Marktgasse and Kramgasse.

★ Terrasse & Casa   SWISS €€
(📞 031 350 50 01; www.schwellenmaetteli.ch; Dalmaziquai 11; mains Sfr20-64; ⊙Terrasse 9am-12.30am Mon-Sat, 10am-11.30pm Sun, Casa noon-2.30pm & 6-11.30pm Mon-Fri, 6-11.30pm Sat, noon-11pm Sun) Dubbed 'Bern's Riviera', this twinset of eateries enjoys a blissful Aareside setting. Terrasse is a glass shoebox with wooden decking over the water, sunloungers overlooking a weir (illuminated at night) and comfy sofa seating, perfect for lingering over Sunday brunch, a drink, or midweek two-course lunch specials (Sfr25). Next door, Casa serves Italian delicacies in a cosy, country-style house.

Altes Tramdepot   SWISS €€
(📞 031 368 14 15; www.altestramdepot.ch; Grosser Muristalden 6, Am Bärengraben; mains Sfr18-46; ⊙11am-12.30am Mon-Fri, from 10am Sat & Sun) At this cavernous microbrewery, Swiss specialities compete against wok-cooked stir-fries for your affection, and the microbrews go down a treat – sample three different varieties for Sfr10.90, four for Sfr14.60, or five for Sfr18.20.

ℹ Information

Tourist Office (📞 031 328 12 12; www.bern.com; Bahnhofplatz 10a; ⊙9am-7pm Mon-Sat, to 6pm Sun)

❶ Getting There & Away

Trains run at least hourly to Geneva (Sfr51, 1¾ hours), Basel (Sfr41, 55 minutes), Interlaken Ost (Sfr29, 55 minutes) and Zürich (Sfr51, 55 minutes to 1½ hours).

Interlaken

POP 5692 / ELEV 570M

Once Interlaken made the Victorians swoon with mountain vistas from the chandelier-lit confines of grand hotels; today it makes daredevils scream with adrenaline-loaded adventures. Straddling the glacier-fed Lakes Thun and Brienz and capped by the pearly white peaks of Eiger, Mönch and Jungfrau, the town is the gateway to Switzerland's fabled Jungfrau region and the country's hottest adventure destination bar none.

◎ Sights & Activities

Switzerland is the world's second-biggest adventure-sports centre and Interlaken is its busiest hub.

Harder Kulm   MOUNTAIN

(www.jungfrau.ch/harderkulm; adult/child Sfr16/8) For far-reaching views to the 4000m giants, take the eight-minute funicular ride to 1322m Harder Kulm. Many hiking paths begin here, and the vertigo-free can enjoy the panorama from the Zweiseensteg (Two Lake Bridge) jutting out above the valley. The wildlife park near the valley station is home to Alpine critters, including marmots and ibex.

Bernatone Alphornbau   WORKSHOP

(☑ 079 840 38 10; www.bernatone.ch; Im Holz, Habkern; ⊙ 10am-noon & 1.30-5pm Mon-Fri; ♿) It doesn't get more Swiss than the alphorn,

---

DON'T MISS

INTERLAKEN FOR FREE

Explore Interlaken with a fun and insightful two-hour guided walking tour with a local. Tours depart at 6pm daily April to September, and at 11am on Monday, Wednesday and Saturday October to March. The meeting point is at **Backpackers Villa Sonnenhof**. The tour is free of charge, but tips to your guide are, of course, appreciated. For more details, consult www.interlaken freetour.com.

---

that fabulous-looking instrument often played by bearded Alpine men with ruddy cheeks and a good set of lungs at summer folk festivals. Call ahead and you can visit the workshop of master alphorn craftsman Heinz Tschiemer. A genuine alphorn, which takes around 60 days to make, will set you back around Sfr3000 but smaller instruments are also available for purchase. From Interlaken West, take bus 106 to Haberkern (18 minutes).

🛏 Sleeping & Eating

Höheweg and Hauptstrasse are the go-to streets for cafes and restaurants, many with al fresco seating in summer.

Backpackers Villa
Sonnenhof   HOSTEL €

(☑ 033 826 71 71; www.villa.ch; Alpenstrasse 16; dm Sfr40-47, d Sfr110-148; 🅿 🛜) Repeatedly voted one of Europe's best hostels, Sonnenhof is a slick, ecofriendly combination of ultramodern chalet and elegant art nouveau villa. Dorms are immaculate, and some have balconies with Jungfrau views. There's also a relaxed lounge, a well-equipped kitchen, a kids' playroom and a vast backyard for mountain gazing. Special family rates are available.

★ The Verandah   SWISS €€

(☑ 033 822 75 75; Höheweg 139, Hotel Royal-St Georges; mains Sfr21-38; ⊙ 6-10pm) This restaurant at Hotel Royal-St Georges is a winning combination of old-school elegance and contemporary style, with its stucco trimmings and slick bistro seating. The menu has riffs on Swiss food, with well-prepared classics such as fondue and rösti, grilled fish and meats.

❶ Information

Tourist Office (☑ 033 826 53 00; www.interlakentourism.ch; Marktgasse 1; ⊙ 8am-7pm Mon-Fri, to 5pm Sat, 10am-4pm Sun Jul & Aug, shorter hours Sep-Jun)

❶ Getting There & Away

There are two train stations: Interlaken West is situated slightly closer to the centre and is a stop for trains that are departing for Bern (Sfr28, one hour). Interlaken Ost is the railway hub for all lines, including the scenic ones that travel up into the Jungfrau region and the lovely GoldenPass Line that goes to Lucerne (Sfr32, two hours).

Grindelwald

POP 3740 / ELEV 1034M

Grindelwald's sublime natural assets are film-set stuff – the chiselled features of the Eiger's north face, the glinting tongues of Oberer and Unterer Glaciers and the crown-like peak of Wetterhorn will make you stare, swoon and lunge for your camera. Skiers and hikers cottoned onto its charms in the late 19th century, which makes it one of Switzerland's oldest resorts, and it has lost none of its appeal over the decades, with geranium-studded Alpine chalets and verdant pastures set against an Oscar-worthy backdrop.

🏃 Activities

★ Kleine Scheidegg Walk   HIKING
One of the region's most stunning day hikes is the 15km trek from Grindelwald Grund to Wengen via Kleine Scheidegg, which heads up through wildflower-freckled meadows to skirt below the Eiger's north face and reach Kleine Scheidegg, granting arresting views of the 'Big Three': Eiger (3970m), Mönch (4107m) and Jungfrau (4158m). Allow around 5½ to six hours to complete the walk.

Grindelwald Sports   ADVENTURE SPORTS
(📞 033 854 12 80; www.grindelwaldsports.ch; Dorfstrasse 103; ⏰ 8.30am-7pm) Situated opposite the tourist office, this outfit arranges mountain climbing, ski and snowboard instruction and the heart-stopping canyon swing and bungee jumping in the **Gletscherschlucht** (Glacier Gorge; adult/child Sfr19/10; ⏰ 9.30am-6pm Sat-Thu, to 10pm Fri). It also houses a cosy cafe and sells walking guides.

🛏 Sleeping & Eating

Bars, restaurants, bakeries and supermarkets line central Dorfstrasse.

★ Gletschergarten   HISTORIC HOTEL €€
(📞 033 853 17 21; www.hotel-gletschergarten.ch; Obere Gletscherstrasse 1; s Sfr130-170, d Sfr230-320; 🅿🛜) The sweet Breitenstein family makes you feel at home in their rustic timber chalet that is brimming with heirlooms from landscape paintings to snapshots of Elsbeth's grandfather who had 12 children (those were the days...). Decked out in pine and flowery fabrics, the rooms have balconies that are facing Unterer Gletscher at

JUNGFRAUJOCH

Two million people a year make the once-in-a-lifetime trip to **Jungfraujoch** (www.jungfrau.ch; return Interlaken Ost–Jungfraujoch Sfr210.80, Kleine Scheidegg–Jungfraujoch Sfr128; ⏰ trains 8am-6.43pm May-Sep, shorter hours rest of year), Europe's highest train station at 3454m. The train that chugs up from Kleine Scheidegg ramps up the drama as it delves into Eiger's icy heart to emerge at the Sphinx meteorological station. At the summit, sensational views of the Aletsch Glacier and a never-ending ripple of Alpine peaks unfold. Besides the staggering panorama, there's an Ice Palace and Snow Fun Park to explore. Warm clothing and sturdy shoes are essential.

the front and Wetterhorn (best for sunset) at the back.

★ Cafe 3692   CAFE €
(📞 033 853 16 54; www.cafe3692.ch; Terrassenweg 61; snacks & light meals Sfr7-25; ⏰ 8.30am-6pm Sun-Tue, to midnight Fri & Sat) Run by dream duo Myriam and Bruno, Cafe 3692 is a delight. Bruno is a talented carpenter and has let his imagination run riot – a gnarled apple tree is an eye-catching artwork, a mine-cart trolley cleverly transforms into a grill, and the ceiling is a wave of woodwork. Garden herbs and Grindelwald-sourced ingredients are knocked up into tasty specials.

ℹ Information

Tourist Office (📞 033 854 12 12; www.grindelwald.ch; Dorfstrasse 110; ⏰ 8am-6pm Mon-Fri, 9am-6pm Sat & Sun; 🛜)

ℹ Getting There & Away

Hourly trains depart for Grindelwald (Sfr11.40, 33 minutes) from Interlaken Ost station; sit in the back half of the train.

Lucerne

POP 80,500 / ELEV 435M

Recipe for a gorgeous Swiss city: take a cobalt lake ringed by mountains of myth, add a well-preserved medieval Altstadt (Old Town) and a reputation for making beautiful

DON'T MISS

CROSS-BORDER SIGHTSEEING

Showcasing the works of the adjoining, eponymous high-end furniture manufacturer, **Vitra Campus** (☎ +49 7621 702 3500; www.vitra.com/en-hu/campus; Charles-Eames-Strasse 1, Weil am Rhein; Vitra Campus adult/child €17/15, Design Museum only €11/9, 1/2hr tours €7/14; ⏲10am-6pm) comprises the dazzling **Vitra Design Museum** (of Guggenheim Bilbao architect Frank Gehry fame), **Vitra Haus** and **Vitra Schaudepot** (both by Herzog & de Meuron). Highlights of the ever-expanding bevy of installations by cutting-edge architects and designers include Carsten Höller's whimsical, corkscrewing 30m-high **Vitra Slide**.

The campus is just across the German border in Weil am Rhein. Take tram 8 from Basel SBB station, Barfüsserplatz or Claraplatz to the terminus at Weil am Rhein Bahnhof/Zentrum, or walk the **Rehberger-Weg**.

music, then sprinkle with covered bridges, sunny plazas, candy-coloured houses and waterfront promenades. Lucerne in central Switzerland is stunning, and deservedly popular since the likes of Goethe, Queen Victoria and Wagner savoured her views in the 19th century.

Sights & Activities

Lake Lucerne boat trips depart from the quays around Bahnhofplatz and Europaplatz. The **Lucerne Museum Card** (www.luzern.com/en/museum-card; 2-day card Sfr36) can save you money if you plan to visit multiple museums.

Old Town HISTORIC SITE

(Altstadt) The medieval Old Town, with its ancient rampart walls and towers, 15th-century buildings with painted facades and two covered bridges, is fascinating. **Kapellbrücke** (Chapel Bridge), dating from 1333, is Lucerne's best-known landmark. It's famous for its distinctive water tower and the spectacular 1993 fire that nearly destroyed it. Look for the 17th-century pictorial panels under the roof. The Dance of Death panels under the roofline of **Spreuerbrücke** (Spreuer Bridge; btwn Kasernenplatz & Mühlenplatz) are a tad dark and dour.

★ **Sammlung Rosengart** MUSEUM

(☎ 041 220 16 60; www.rosengart.ch; Pilatusstrasse 10; adult/child Sfr18/10; ⏲10am-6pm) Lucerne's blockbuster cultural attraction is the Sammlung Rosengart, occupying a graceful neoclassical pile in the heart of town. It showcases the outstanding stash of Angela Rosengart, a Swiss art dealer and close friend of Picasso. Alongside works by the great Spanish master are paintings and sketches by Klee, Cézanne, Renoir, Chagall, Kandinsky, Miró, Matisse, Modigliani and Monet, among others. Complementing this collection are some 200 photographs by David Douglas Duncan documenting the last 17 years of Picasso's life.

Sleeping & Eating

Wander the Old Town for countless cafes and restaurants, especially along Rathausquai and Unter der Egg on the north side of the river.

★ **Schlössli Hotel & Restaurant** HOTEL €

(☎ 041 377 14 72; www.schloesslimeggen.ch; Luzernerstrasse 4, Meggen; s/d Sfr80/100; P 📶) This very friendly hotel in Meggen, 6km east of Lucerne, is a find if you are on a budget. Rooms are simple but spotless, there's free parking and wi-fi, and it's only 10 minutes to Lucerne train station on bus 24 (Sfr4.10). Its **Schlössli** restaurant serves everything from pizzas and salads to Swiss staples.

★ **Wirtshaus Galliker** SWISS €€

(☎ 041 240 10 02; Schützenstrasse 1; mains from Sfr21; ⏲11.30am-2pm & 6-8.30pm Tue-Sat) Passionately run by the Galliker family for over four generations, this old-style, wood-panelled tavern attracts a lively bunch of regulars. Motherly waitresses dish up Lucerne soul food – rösti, *Chögalipaschtetli* (veal pastry pie) and the like – that is batten-the-hatches filling.

Information

Tourist Office (☎ 041 227 17 17; www.luzern.com; Zentralstrasse 5; ⏲8.30am-7pm Mon-Fri, 9am-7pm Sat, 9am-5pm Sun May-Oct, shorter hours Nov-Apr)

ⓘ Getting There & Away

Frequent trains connect Lucerne to Interlaken Ost (Sfr33, 1¾ hours), Bern (Sfr40, one to 1½ hours), Lugano (Sfr61, two hours) and Zürich (Sfr26, 45 to 60 minutes).

Basel

POP 176,117 / ELEV 273M

Tucked up against the French and German borders in Switzerland's northwest corner, multicultural Basel straddles the majestic Rhine. Art and architecture lovers flock here each year for the world-famous ART Basel festival and the city's wealth of galleries, museums and iconic buildings. Its Altstadt (Old Town) is picture book-enchanting.

⊙ Sights & Activities

Swimming or floating down the rushing Rhine and sunbathing on its banks are popular summer pastimes. You can purchase a 'Wickelfisch' at Basel Tourismus (p372) offices and local boutiques – it's a watertight plastic 'fish' to put your clothes in to keep them dry as you whoosh down the river!

★**Kunstmuseum Basel**   MUSEUM

(Museum of Fine Arts; ☑061 206 62 62; www. kunstmuseumbasel.ch; St Alban-Graben 16; adult/student/child Sfr16/8/free; ⊙10am-6pm Tue, Wed & Fri-Sun, to 8pm Thu; ℗) Housing the most comprehensive collection of public art in Switzerland, this superb fine arts museum reopened in mid-2016 after updates to the existing galleries (Hauptbau) and construction of a new modernist wing (Neubau). It houses the world's largest collection of Holbeins and a substantial collection of Renaissance and impressionist works among its thousands of pieces. The entrance price includes admission to the permanent collection – surcharges are applicable for visiting exhibits. Guided tours (from Sfr5) are available.

★**Fondation Beyeler**   MUSEUM

(☑061 645 97 00; www.fondationbeyeler.ch; Baselstrasse 101, Riehen; adult/under 25yr Sfr25/free; ⊙10am-6pm Thu-Tue, to 8pm Wed; ℗) This astounding private-turned-public collection, assembled by former art dealers Hildy and Ernst Beyeler, is housed in a long, low, light-filled, open-plan building designed by Italian architect Renzo Piano. The varied exhibits juxtapose 19th- and 20th-century works by Picasso and Rothko against sculptures by Miró and Max Ernst and tribal figures from Oceania; there are also regular visiting exhibitions. Take tram 6 to Riehen from Barfüsserplatz or Marktplatz.

★**Museum Jean Tinguely**   MUSEUM

(☑061 681 93 20; www.tinguely.ch; Paul Sacher-Anlage 2; adult/student/child Sfr18/12/free; ⊙11am-6pm Tue-Sun; ℗) Built by the leading Ticino architect Mario Botta, this museum showcases the playful, mischievous and downright wacky artistic concoctions of sculptor-turned-mad-scientist Jean Tinguely. Buttons next to some of Tinguely's 'kinetic' sculptures allow visitors to set them in motion. It's great fun to watch them rattle, shake and twirl, with springs, feathers and wheels radiating at every angle, or to hear the haunting musical sounds that are produced by the gigantic *Méta-Harmonies* on the upper floor. Catch bus 31 from Claraplatz.

FRANCE & SWITZERLAND BASEL

OFF THE BEATEN TRACK

RHEINFALL

Ensnared in wispy spray, the thunderous **Rheinfall** (Rhine Falls; www.rheinfall.ch) in Schloss Laufen am Rheinfall might not give Niagara much competition in height (23m), width (150m) or even flow of water (700 cu metre per second in summer), but Europe's largest plain waterfall is a real crash-bang spectacle nonetheless.

Trails thread up and along its shore, with viewpoints providing abundant photo ops. Or ride the panoramic lift down to the Känzeli viewing platform at neighbouring medieval castle, **Schloss Laufen** (www.schlosslaufen.ch; adult/child Sfr5/3; ⊙8am-7pm Jun-Aug, shorter hours rest of year). For an above-the-treetops perspective of the falls, hit **Adventure Park** (www.ap-rheinfall.ch; Nohlstrasse; adult/child Sfr40/26; ⊙10am-7pm Apr-Oct; 🖪), one of Switzerland's biggest rope parks, with routes graded according to difficulty. From Schloss Laufen am Rheinfall train station, walk up the hill to the falls and castle.

ℹ WHAT'S ON

To see what's on, pick up a copy of *Züritipp* (www.zueritipp.ch), which comes out on Thursdays with the *TagesAnzeiger* newspaper. Also look for the bi-monthly city guide *Zürich In Your Pocket* (www.inyourpocket.com/zurich).

🛏 Sleeping & Eating

⭐ **Basel Backpack**   HOSTEL €

(☑061 333 00 37; www.baselbackpack.ch; Dornacherstrasse 192; 4-/8-bed dm Sfr39/31, s/d from Sfr75/89; ⊜@🛜) Converted from a factory, this independent hostel has friendly staff, bright and roomy four- and eight-bed dorms and a selection of smart, simply stylish single and deluxe double rooms. Other perks include bike rental (Sfr20 per day), breakfast (Sfr8), a bar, guest kitchen and laundry (Sf4) and two convivial lounges.

⭐ **Volkshaus Basel**   BRASSERIE, BAR €€

(☑061 690 93 10; www.volkshaus-basel.ch/en; Rebgasse 12-14; mains Sfr28-60; ⊗restaurant noon-2pm & 6-10pm Mon-Sat, bar 10am-midnight Mon-Wed, to 1am Thu-Sat) This stylish Herzog & de Meuron–designed venue is part resto-bar, part gallery and part performance space. For relaxed dining, head for the atmospheric beer garden in a cobblestoned courtyard decorated with columns, vine-clad walls and light-draped rows of trees. The menu ranges from brasserie classics (*steak frites*) to more innovative offerings (house-pickled wild salmon with mustard, dill and beetroot).

ℹ Information

Pop into **Basel Tourismus (Bahnhof)** (☑061 268 68 68; www.basel.com; Centralbahnstrasse 10; ⊗8-6pm Mon-Fri, 9am-5pm Sat, 9am-3pm

DON'T MISS

STREET PARADE

This techno celebration (www.streetparade.com) in the middle of August has established itself as one of Europe's largest and wildest street parties since its first festive outing in 1992.

Sun) or **Basel Tourismus (Stadtcasino)** (☑061 268 68 68; www.basel.com; Steinenberg 14; ⊗9am-6.30pm Mon-Fri, to 5pm Sat, 10am-3pm Sun) to pick up a BaselCard (Sfr20/30 for 24/48 hours) for a bunch of value-adds, including one free city walking tour and ferry crossing, and half-price tickets to all museums within the city limits.

ℹ Getting There & Away

Basel has two main train stations: Swiss/French train station **SBB Bahnhof** to the south, and the German train station **BBF Bahnhof** in the north.

Two or three trains an hour run from SBB Bahnhof to Geneva (Sfr77, 2¾ hours). At least four, mostly direct, leave every hour for Zürich (Sfr34, 55 minutes to 1¼ hours). There's also fast TGV service to Paris (Sfr142, three hours) every other hour.

Zürich

POP 396,955

Culturally vibrant, efficiently run and attractively set at the meeting of river and lake, Swiss German-speaking Zürich is regularly recognised as one of the world's most liveable cities. It is also Switzerland's largest and wealthiest metropolis, with an evocative Old Town, vibrant nightlife, and a gritty, postindustrial edge that always surprises.

⊙ Sights & Activities

The city spreads around the northwest end of Zürichsee (Lake Zürich), from where the Limmat River runs further north still, splitting the medieval city centre in two. The majority of Zürich's big-hitters cluster in and around the medieval centre, but the edgy **Züri-West** neighbourhood also has some terrific galleries.

⭐ **Fraumünster**   CHURCH

(www.fraumuenster.ch/en; Münsterhof; Sfr5 incl audioguide; ⊗10am-6pm Mar-Oct, to 5pm Nov-Feb; 🚋6, 7, 10, 11, 14 to Paradeplatz) This 13th-century church is renowned for its stunning stained-glass windows, designed by the Russian-Jewish master Marc Chagall (1887–1985), who executed the series of five windows in the choir stalls in 1971 and the rose window in the southern transept in 1978. The rose window in the northern transept was created by Augusto Giacometti in 1945. Admission includes a multilingual audioguide.

★ **Kunsthaus** MUSEUM

(☑ 044 253 84 84; www.kunsthaus.ch; Heimplatz 1; adult/child Sfr16/free, Wed free; ⊙ 10am-8pm Wed & Thu, to 6pm Tue & Fri-Sun; ☑ 5, 8, 9, 10 to Kunsthaus) Zürich's impressive fine-arts gallery boasts a rich collection of largely European art. It stretches from the Middle Ages through a mix of Old Masters to Alberto Giacometti stick figures, Monet and Van Gogh masterpieces, Rodin sculptures, and other 19th- and 20th-century art. Swiss Rail and Museum Passes don't provide free admission to the gallery but the Zürich-Card does.

Letten SWIMMING

(☑ 044 362 92 00; Lettensteg 10; ☑ 3, 4, 6, 10, 11, 13, 15, 17 to Limmatplatz) FREE North of the train station on the eastern bank of the Limmat (just south of Kornhausbrücke), this is where Züri-West trendsetters swim, dive off bridges, skateboard, play volleyball, or just drink at the riverside bars and chat on the grass and concrete steps.

🛏 Sleeping & Eating

Tasty dining and drinking options pepper the narrow streets of the Niederdorf quarter on the river's east bank. The bulk of the more animated drinking dens are in Züri-West, especially along Langstrasse in Kreis 4 and Hardstrasse in Kreis 5.

City Backpacker HOSTEL €

(☑ 044 251 90 15; www.city-backpacker.ch; Niederdorfstrasse 5; dm/s/d Sfr37/77/118; ⊙ reception closed noon-3pm; @ ⬛ ⬛; ☑ 2, 4, 15 to Rathaus) Attractively situated in the Old Town, this private hostel with a youthful party vibe is friendly and well equipped, if a trifle cramped. In summer, you can overcome the claustrophobia by hanging out on the rooftop terrace. Be prepared for a climb, as the reception area and hostel rooms are located up several flights of stairs, and there's no lift.

★ **Haus Hiltl** VEGETARIAN €

(☑ 044 227 70 00; www.hiltl.ch; Sihlstrasse 28; per 100g Sfr4.90, mains Sfr25-35; ⊙ 6am-midnight Mon-Sat, 8am-midnight Sun; ☑; ☑ 4, 6, 7, 10, 11, 13, 14, 15, 17 to Rennweg) Guinness-certified as the world's oldest vegetarian restaurant (established 1898), Hiltl proffers an astounding smorgasbord of meatless delights, from Indian and Thai curries to Mediterranean grilled veggies, plus salads and desserts. You can opt for the buffet (charged per

100g) or for more substantial mains. Sit in the informal cafe or the spiffier adjoining restaurant. Good-value takeaway service is also available.

★ **Frau Gerolds Garten** BAR

(www.fraugerold.ch; Geroldstrasse 23/23a; ⊙ bar-restaurant 11am-midnight Mon-Sat, noon-10pm Sun Apr-Sep, 6pm-midnight Mon-Sat Oct-Mar, market & shops 11am-7pm Mon-Fri, to 6pm Sat year-round; ☑; ⑤ Hardbrücke) Hmm, where to start? The wine bar? The margarita bar? The gin bar? Whichever poison you choose, this wildly popular focal point of Zürich's summer drinking scene is pure unadulterated fun and one of the best grown-up playgrounds in Europe.

ⓘ Information

Tourist Office (☑ 044 215 40 00, hotel reservations 044 215 40 40; www.zuerich. com; Hauptbahnhof; ⊙ 8am-8.30pm Mon-Sat, 8.30am to 6.30pm Sun May-Oct, 8.30am-7pm Mon-Sat, 9am-6pm Sun Nov-Apr)

ⓘ Getting There & Around

Up to nine trains an hour connect Zürich airport, 9km north of the centre, with the Hauptbahnhof between around 5am and midnight (Sfr6.80, 10 to 13 minutes).

Direct train services run to Stuttgart (Sfr63, three hours), Munich (Sfr96, 4¼ hours), Innsbruck (Sfr76, 3½ hours) and other international destinations, plus there are regular direct train departures to most major Swiss towns.

A single-trip ticket on buses, trams, the S-Bahn and river boats run by ZVV (www.zvv. ch) costs Sfr2.70; a 24-hour city pass costs Sfr8.80.

Ticino

Switzerland meets Italy: in Ticino the summer air is rich and hot, peacock-proud posers propel their scooters in and out of traffic, then there's the Italian gelato, Italian pizza, Italian architecture and Italian language.

Locarno

POP 15,968

With its palm trees and much-hyped 2300 hours of sunshine a year, Switzerland's near-Mediterranean, lowest-altitude town is quite special. Strung along the northern end of Lago Maggiore, Locarno proffers a pretty Renaissance Old Town, a renowned music and film summer festival and outdoor action galore. Navigazione Lago Maggiore (www.navigazionelaghi.it) operates boats that run across the entire lake.

⊙ Sights & Activities

Old Town HISTORIC SITE

You can feel just how close you are to Italy when exploring Locarno's hilly Città Vecchia (Old Town), an appealing jumble of piazzas, arcades, churches and tall, shuttered Lombard houses in ice-cream colours. At its centre sits the **Piazza Grande**, with narrow lanes threading off in all directions, while the **Castello Visconteo** (Piazza Castello; adult/child Sfr7/free; ⊙10am-noon & 2-5pm Tue-Sun Apr-Oct) guards its southwestern fringes.

★ Santuario della Madonna del Sasso CHURCH

(www.madonnadelsasso.org; Via Santuario 2; ⊙7.30am-6pm) Overlooking the town, this sanctuary was built after the Virgin Mary supposedly appeared in a vision to a monk, Bartolomeo d'Ivrea, in 1480. There's a highly adorned church and several rather rough, near-life-size statue groups (including one of the *Last Supper*) in niches on the stairway. The best-known painting in the church is *La fuga in egitto* (Flight to Egypt), painted in 1522 by Bramantino.

A **funicular** (one way/return adult Sfr4.80/7.20, child Sfr2.20/3.60; ⊙8am-10pm May, Jun & Sep, to midnight Jul & Aug, to 9pm Apr & Oct, to 7.30pm Nov-Mar) runs every 15 minutes from the town centre past the sanctuary to Orselina, but a more scenic, pilgrim-style approach is the 20-minute walk up the chapel-lined Via Crucis (take Via al Sasso off Via Cappuccini).

ⓘ Information

Tourist Office (☑084 809 10 91; www.ascona-locarno.com; Piazza Stazione; ⊙9am-6pm Mon-Fri, 10am-6pm Sat, 10am-1.30pm & 2.30-5pm Sun)

ⓘ Getting There & Away

Hourly trains run direct to/from Brig (Sfr56, 2¾ hours), passing through Italy (bring your passport; change trains at Domodossola). Most trains to/from Zürich (Sfr64, 2¼ hours) go via Bellinzona. There are twice-hourly train connections from Lugano (Sfr15.20, 58 minutes).

Switzerland Survival Guide

ⓘ Directory A–Z

ACCOMMODATION

⇒ Switzerland sports traditional and creative accommodation in every price range. Some budget hotels have cheaper rooms with shared toilet and shower.

⇒ Hotel rates usually include breakfast.

⇒ Experience Swiss farm life in summer with **Agrotourismus Schweiz** (☑031 359 50 30; www.agrotourismus.ch): pay Sfr20 to Sfr30 to sleep on straw in their hay barns or lofts (bring your own sleeping bag and pocket torch).

⇒ Rates in cities and towns stay constant most of the year. In mountain resorts prices are seasonal (and can fall by 50% or more outside high season).

⇒ High season is July to August, plus Christmas and mid-February to Easter in mountain resorts.

ELECTRICITY

The electrical current in Switzerland is 230V, 50Hz. Swiss sockets are recessed, three-holed, hexagonally shaped and incompatible with many plugs from abroad.

INTERNET RESOURCES

My Switzerland (www.myswitzerland.com) Swiss tourism.

ch.ch (www.ch.ch) Swiss authorities online.

ⓘ SLEEPING PRICE RANGES

The following price ranges refer to a double room with a private bathroom, except in hostels or where otherwise specified. Quoted rates are for high season and include breakfast, unless otherwise noted.

€ less than Sfr170

€€ Sfr170–350

€€€ more than Sfr350

Swiss Info (www.swissinfo.ch) Swiss news and current affairs.

Lonely Planet (www.lonelyplanet.com/switzerland) Destination information, hotel bookings, traveller forum and more.

SBB (www.sbb.ch) Swiss Federal Railways.

MONEY

➡ Swiss francs are divided into 100 centimes (*Rappen* in German-speaking Switzerland). There are notes for 10, 20, 50, 100, 200 and 1000 francs, and coins for 5, 10, 20 and 50 centimes, as well as for one, two and five francs.

➡ Businesses throughout Switzerland, including most hotels and some restaurants and souvenir shops, will accept payment in euros.

➡ ATMs are at every airport and most train stations and on every second street corner in towns and cities; Visa, MasterCard and Amex are widely accepted.

➡ Not all shops, hotels or restaurants accept credit cards. EuroCard/MasterCard and Visa are the most popular.

OPENING HOURS

Each Swiss canton currently decides how long shops and businesses can stay open. With the exception of convenience stores at 24-hour service stations and shops at airports and train stations, businesses shut completely on Sunday. High-season opening hours appear in listings for sights and attractions; hours are almost always shorter during low season.

Banks 8.30am to 4.30pm Monday to Friday

Museums 10am to 5pm, many close Monday and stay open late Thursday

Restaurants noon to 2.30pm and 6pm to 9.30pm; most close one or two days per week

Shops 10am to 6pm Monday to Friday, to 4pm Saturday

PUBLIC HOLIDAYS

Some cantons observe their own special holidays and religious days, eg 2 January, Labour Day (1 May), Corpus Christi, Assumption (15 August) and All Saints' Day (1 November).

New Year's Day 1 January

Good Friday March/April

Easter Sunday and Monday March/April

Ascension Day 40th day after Easter

Whit Sunday and Monday (Pentecost) 7th week after Easter

National Day 1 August

Christmas Day 25 December

St Stephen's Day 26 December

TELEPHONE

➡ Area codes do not exist in Switzerland. Numbers in a particular city or town share the

 EATING PRICE RANGES

The following price ranges refer to a main course.

€ less than Sfr25

€€ Sfr25–Sfr50

€€€ more than Sfr50

same three-digit prefix (Bern 031, Geneva 022 etc) that must always be dialled, even when calling locally.

➡ The country code for Switzerland is 41. When calling Switzerland from abroad, drop the initial zero from the local telephone number.

➡ To call abroad from Switzerland, use the international access code 00.

➡ Buy prepaid SIM cards online from Mobile Zone (www.mobilezone.ch).

➡ Swiss mobile telephone numbers begin with 076, 078 or 079.

➡ Save money on the normal international rate by buying a prepaid Swisscom card worth Sfr10 to Sfr100.

VISAS

For up-to-date details on visa requirements, go to www.sem.admin.ch.

Visas are not required for passport holders from the UK, the EU, Ireland, the USA, Canada, Australia, New Zealand, Norway and Iceland.

Getting There & Away

AIR

International airports, with flights to many European capitals as well as some in Africa, Asia and North America:

Geneva Airport (p362)

Zürich Airport (p373)

EuroAirport (MLH or BSL; ☑ +33 3 89 90 31 11; www.euroairport.com) (Basel)

LAND
Train

Switzerland is a hub of train connections to the rest of the Continent. Zürich is the busiest international terminus, with trains to Munich and Vienna, from where there are extensive onward connections to cities in Eastern Europe.

➡ Numerous TGV trains daily connect Paris to Geneva (three hours), Lausanne (3¾ hours), Basel (three hours) and Zürich (four hours).

➡ Nearly all connections from Italy pass through Milan before branching off to Zürich, Lucerne, Bern or Lausanne.

➡ Most connections from Germany pass through Zürich or Basel.

ℹ ONE-STOP SHOP

The **Swiss Travel System** (www.swiss travelsystem.co.uk) is an interconnected web of trains, boats, cable cars and postal buses that puts almost the entire country within easy car-free reach – and, naturally, with its famous precision you can set your watch by it.

➡ Swiss Federal Railways accepts internet bookings but does not post tickets outside of Switzerland; print off an e-ticket or save it on your smartphone.

ℹ Getting Around

Swiss public transport is an efficient, fully integrated and comprehensive system, incorporating rains, buses, boats and funiculars. However, travel is expensive and visitors planning to use inter-city routes should consider investing in a Swiss travel pass.

PASSES & DISCOUNTS
For extensive travel within Switzerland, various national travel passes (www.swiss-pass.ch) generally offer better savings than Eurail or InterRail passes. Check online for details.

BICYCLE
Switzerland is well equipped for cyclists. Many cities have free-bike-hire schemes. Bicycle and e-bike rental is usually available at train stations.

BOAT
Ferries and steamers link towns and cities on many lakes, including Geneva, Lucerne, Lugano and Zürich.

BUS
Filling the gaps in more remote areas, Switzerland's **Postbus** (www.postauto.ch) service is synchronised with train arrivals.

CAR & MOTORCYCLE
➡ The Swiss drive on the right-hand side of the road.

➡ Headlights must be on at all times.

➡ The blood alcohol content (BAC) limit is 0.05%.

➡ The speed limit is 50km/h in towns, 80km/h on main roads outside towns, 100km/h on single-lane freeways and 120km/h on dual-lane freeways.

➡ There's an annual charge of Sfr40 (www. vignette.ch) to use Swiss freeways and semi-freeways. Buy the required windscreen sticker at the border (in cash, including euros), at Swiss petrol stations and Swiss tourist offices abroad.

➡ In winter equip your car with winter tyres and snow chains. Some Alpine mountain passes are closed from November to May.

TRAIN
➡ The Swiss Federal Railway (www.sbb.ch) is abbreviated to SBB in German, CFF in French and FFS in Italian. Swiss trains have power points for laptops and wi-fi hotspots.

➡ Seat reservations (Sfr5) are advisable for longer journeys in high season.

➡ The SBB smartphone app is an excellent resource and can be used to store your tickets electronically.

➡ European rail passes such as Eurail and Interrail passes are valid on Swiss national railways.

Spain & Portugal

Best Places to Stay

➜ Casa Gràcia (p408)

➜ Lisbon Destination Hostel (p449)

➜ Russafa Youth Hostel (p423)

➜ Bed and Be (p431)

➜ La Banda (p427)

Best Places to Eat

➜ El Celler de Can Roca (p412)

➜ Mercado de San Miguel (p386)

➜ La Cuchara de San Telmo (p393)

➜ Mercado da Ribeira (p449)

➜ Suculent (p409)

Why Go?

Beyond the Pyrenees is another Europe, a diverse and magical land surrounded by sea and with cultures all of its own. It is scenically spectacular, with a staggering array of beaches, national parks and mountains, and a turbulent history has left a majestic range of architecture, from Roman remains to noble cathedrals, and from Moorish palaces to Modernista gems and landmark modern buildings.

Some of the continent's best food is produced here: Portugal's excellent fish is famed, while Spain's legendary tapas culture is just one aspect of a country enthusiastically dedicated to sociable eating and drinking. The nightlife is superb, but adjust your body clock: when midnight strikes, things are often just beginning. Whether you're showing off your dance moves at a superclub, trying the astonishing variety of local wines or listening to fado's soulful strains or flamenco's anguished energy, many of your best moments in the region will come after dark.

Fast Facts

Capitals Madrid (Spain), Lisbon (Portugal)

Emergency ☑ 112

Currency Euro (€)

Languages Spanish, Portuguese, Catalan, Basque, Galician, Aranese

Time zones Central European (Spain; UTC/GMT plus one hour); Western European (Portugal; UTC/GMT)

Country codes ☑ 34 (Spain), ☑ 351 (Portugal)

Population 49 million (Spain), 11 million (Portugal)

Spain & Portugal Highlights

1 Barcelona
Admiring the genius of Gaudí and wallowing in cultural riches and a glorious food culture. (p402)

2 Mallorca
Enjoying the Mediterranean sunshine on the blessed Balearic beaches. (p413)

3 Madrid Spending your days in some of Europe's best galleries, and nights amid its best nightlife. (p380)

4 Toledo
Discovering Spain's multicultural past and staggering architectural legacy. (p390)

5 Granada
Exploring the exquisite Alhambra and wandering the Albayzín's twisting lanes. (p431)

6 Seville Admiring the architecture and enjoying the party atmosphere. (p425)

7 Lisbon Following the sound of fado spilling from the lamplit lanes of the Alfama. (p443)

8 Porto Sampling velvety ports at riverside wine lodges in the World Heritage-listed centre. (p463)

9 Santiago de Compostela
Joining the pilgrims making their way to the magnificent cathedral. (p400)

10 San Sebastián
Eating your way through the peninsula's foodie capital. (p392)

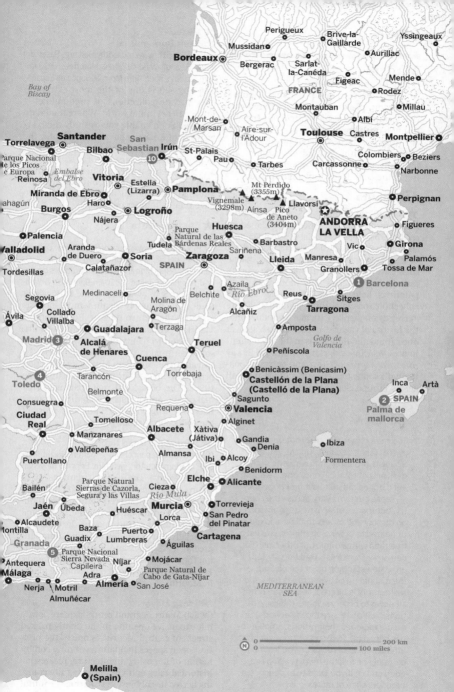

SPAIN

Madrid

POP 3.17 MILLION / ELEV 667M

No city on earth is more alive than Madrid, a beguiling place whose sheer energy carries a simple message: *madrileños* (people from Madrid) know how to live. Explore the old streets of the centre, relax in the plazas, soak up the culture in Madrid's excellent art museums, and spend at least one night taking in the city's legendary nightlife scene.

👁 Sights

★ Museo del Prado   MUSEUM

(www.museodelprado.es; Paseo del Prado; adult/child €15/free, 6-8pm Mon-Sat & 5-7pm Sun free, audio guide €3.50, admission plus official guidebook €24; ⏰10am-8pm Mon-Sat, to 7pm Sun; Ⓜ Banco de España) Welcome to one of the world's premier art galleries. The more than 7000 paintings held in the Museo del Prado's collection (of which only around 1500 are currently on display) are like a window onto the historical vagaries of the Spanish soul, at once grand and imperious in the royal paintings of Velázquez, darkly tumultuous in *Las pinturas negras* of Goya, and outward looking with sophisticated works of art from all across Europe. See also p388.

TAPAS

Too many travellers miss out on the joys of tapas because, unless you speak Spanish, ordering can seem one of the dark arts of Spanish etiquette. Fear not – it's not as difficult as it first appears.

Tapas customs vary across the country, but there's often a mixture of tapas on display and others that are cooked or heated to order. Sometimes you get a free tapa with a drink, but otherwise you can order from a list. Traditionally tapas are eaten standing up at the bar, but the distinction between tapas bars and restaurants is blurred, so you can often sit down to order *raciones* (literally 'rations'; full-plate-size tapas servings) or *media raciones* (half-rations; smaller tapas servings). Remember, however, that after a couple of *raciones* you'll almost certainly be full; the *media ración* is a good choice if you want to experience a broader range of tastes.

★ Museo Thyssen-Bornemisza   MUSEUM

(☎ 902 760511; www.museothyssen.org; Paseo del Prado 8; adult/child €12/free, Mon free; ⏰10am-7pm Tue-Sun, noon-4pm Mon; Ⓜ Banco de España) The Thyssen is one of the most extraordinary private collections of predominantly European art in the world. Where the Prado or Reina Sofía enable you to study the body of work of a particular artist in depth, the Thyssen is the place to immerse yourself in a breathtaking breadth of artistic styles. Most of the big names are here, sometimes with just a single painting, but the Thyssen's gift to Madrid and the art-loving public is to have them all under one roof.

★ Centro de Arte Reina Sofía   MUSEUM

(☎ 91 774 10 00; www.museoreinasofia.es; Calle de Santa Isabel 52; adult/concession €10/free, 1.30-7pm Sun, 7-9pm Mon & Wed-Sat free, tickets cheaper if purchased online; ⏰10am-9pm Mon & Wed-Sat, to 7pm Sun; Ⓜ Atocha) Home to Picasso's *Guernica,* arguably Spain's most famous artwork, the Centro de Arte Reina Sofía is Madrid's premier collection of modern art. In addition to plenty of paintings by Picasso, other major drawcards are works by Salvador Dalí and Joan Miró. The collection principally spans the 20th century up to the 1980s. The occasional non-Spaniard artist makes an appearance (including Francis Bacon's *Lying Figure;* 1966), but most of the collection is strictly peninsular.

★ Parque del Buen Retiro   GARDENS

(Plaza de la Independencia; ⏰6am-midnight May-Sep, to 10pm Oct-Apr; Ⓜ Retiro, Príncipe de Vergara, Ibiza, Atocha) The glorious gardens of El Retiro are as beautiful as any you'll find in a European city. Littered with marble monuments, landscaped lawns, the occasional elegant building (the Palacio de Cristal is especially worth seeking out) and abundant greenery, it's quiet and contemplative during the week but comes to life on weekends. Put simply, this is one of our favourite places in Madrid.

★ Plaza Mayor   SQUARE

(Ⓜ Sol) Madrid's grand central square, a rare but expansive opening in the tightly packed streets of central Madrid, is one of the prettiest open spaces in Spain, a winning combination of imposing architecture, picaresque historical tales and vibrant street life coursing across its cobblestones. At once beautiful in its own right and a reference point for so many Madrid days, it also hosts the city's main tourist office, a Christmas market in December and arches leading to laneways out into the labyrinth.

★ **Palacio Real**   PALACE
(☑ 91 454 88 00; www.patrimonionacional.es; Calle de Bailén; adult/concession €11/6, guide/audioguide €4/3, EU citizens free last 2hr Mon-Thu; ⊙ 10am-8pm Apr-Sep, to 6pm Oct-Mar; M Ópera) Spain's lavish Palacio Real is a jewel box of a palace, although it's used only occasionally for royal ceremonies; the royal family moved to the modest Palacio de la Zarzuela years ago.

When the *alcázar* burned down on Christmas Day 1734, Felipe V, the first of the Bourbon kings, decided to build a palace that would dwarf all its European counterparts. Felipe died before the palace was finished, which is perhaps why the Italianate baroque colossus has a mere 2800 rooms, just one-quarter of the original plan.

★ **Ermita de San Antonio de la Florida**   GALLERY
(Panteón de Goya; ☑ 91 542 07 22; www.sanantoniodelaflorida.es; Glorieta de San Antonio de la Florida 5; ⊙ 9.30am-8pm Tue-Sun, hours vary Jul & Aug; M Príncipe Pío) **FREE** The frescoed ceilings of the recently restored Ermita de San Antonio de la Florida are one of Madrid's most surprising secrets. The southern of the two small chapels is one of the few places to see Goya's work in its original setting, as painted by the master in 1798 on the request of Carlos IV. It's simply breathtaking.

🛏 Sleeping

★ **Hostal Main Street Madrid**   HOSTAL $
(☑ 91 548 18 78; www.mainstreetmadrid.com; 5th fl, Gran Vía 50; r from €55; ❋ 🕏; M Callao, Santo Domingo) Excellent service is what travellers rave about here, but the rooms – modern and cool in soothing greys – are also some of the best *hostal* rooms you'll find anywhere in central Madrid. It's an excellent package and not surprisingly it's often full, so book well in advance.

Hostal Madrid   HOSTAL, APARTMENT $
(☑ 91 522 00 60; www.hostal-madrid.info; Calle de Esparteros 6; s €35-75, d €45-115, d apt €45-150; ❋ 🕏; M Sol) The 24 rooms at this well-run *hostal* have exposed brickwork, updated bathrooms and a look that puts many three-star hotels to shame. It also has terrific apartments (ageing in varying stages of

gracefulness and ranging in size from 33 sq metres to 200 sq metres) that have kitchens, their own sitting area and bathroom.

Mola! Hostel   HOSTEL $
(☑ 663 62 41 43; www.molahostel.com; Calle de Atocha 16; dm €15-20, d from €53; ❋ @ 🕏; M Sol, Tirso de Molina) This sparkling new hostel overlooking the Plaza de Jacinto Benavente in the heart of town is a terrific deal. Rooms are colourful, warmly decorated and well sized, and dorms (with four to 10 beds) are rather stylish. It's a friendly place where the staff are eager to connect you with other travellers and for you to make the most of your time in Madrid.

🍴 Eating

Madrid has transformed itself into one of Europe's culinary capitals, not least because the city has long been a magnet for people (and cuisines) from all over Spain. Travel from one Spanish village to the next and you'll quickly learn that each has its own speciality; travel to Madrid and you'll find them all.

★ **Casa Revuelta**   TAPAS $
(☑ 91 366 33 32; Calle de Latoneros 3; tapas from €3; ⊙ 10.30am-4pm & 7-11pm Tue-Sat, 10.30am-4pm Sun, closed Aug; M Sol, La Latina) Casa Revuelta puts out some of Madrid's finest tapas of *bacalao* (cod) bar none – unlike elsewhere, *tajadas de bacalao* don't have bones in them and slide down the throat with the greatest of ease. Early on a Sunday afternoon, as the Rastro crowd gathers here, it's filled to the rafters. Other specialities include *torreznos* (bacon bits) and *callos* (tripe).

★ **Casa Julio**   SPANISH $
(☑ 91 522 72 74; Calle de la Madera 37; 6/12 croquetas €6/12; ⊙ 1-3.30pm & 6.30-11pm Mon-Sat

 **SPAIN AT A GLANCE**

Don't Miss Spain

Barcelona One of Europe's most alluring destinations – days in Barcelona are spent wandering the cobblestone lanes of the Gothic quarter, basking on Mediterranean beaches or marvelling at Gaudí masterpieces. By night, the city is a whirl of vintage cocktail bars, gilded music halls, innovative eateries and dance-loving clubs, with the party extending well into the night.

Madrid nightlife Madrid is not the only European city with nightlife, but few can match its intensity and street clamour. As Ernest Hemingway said, 'Nobody goes to bed in Madrid until they have killed the night'.

Alhambra The palace complex of Granada's Alhambra is close to architectural perfection. It is perhaps the most refined example of Islamic art anywhere in the world, not to mention the most enduring symbol of 800 years of Moorish rule in what was known as Al-Andalus.

Pintxos in San Sebastián Chefs here have turned bar snacks into an art form. Sometimes called 'high cuisine in miniature', pintxos (Basque tapas) are piles of flavour; as you step into any bar in central San Sebastián, the choice lined up along the counter will leave you gasping. In short, this is Spain's most memorable eating experience.

Seville Nowhere is as quintessentially Spanish as Seville, a city of capricious moods and soulful secrets, which has played a pivotal role in the evolution of flamenco, bullfighting, baroque art and Mudéjar architecture.

Itineraries

One Week

So many Spanish trails begin in **Barcelona**, Spain's second-biggest city and one of the coolest places on earth. Explore the architecture and sample the food, before catching the train down the coast to **Valencia** for a dose of paella, nightlife and the 21st-century wonders of the Ciudad de las Artes y las Ciencias. A fast train whisks you inland to the capital, mighty **Madrid**, for the irresistible street energy, the pretty plazas and one of the richest concentrations of art museums on the planet.

Two Weeks

Another week gives you time to explore the south. Yet another fast train takes you deep into Andalucía, with **Córdoba** your entry point into this wonderful corner of Spain; the most obvious highlight is its 8th-century Mezquita. From Córdoba it's a short hop to fabulous **Seville**. But we've saved the best until last: **Granada** boasts the extraordinary Alhambra, its soulful alter ego the Albayzín, and an eating and drinking scene that embraces Spanish culinary culture in all its variety.

Essential Food & Drink

Tapas or pintxos Possibly the world's most ingenious form of snacking. Madrid's La Latina *barrio* (district), Zaragoza's El Tubo and most Andalucían cities offer rich pickings, but a *pintxo* (Basque tapas) crawl in San Sebastián's Parte Vieja is one of life's most memorable gastronomic experiences.

Chocolate con churros These deep-fried doughnut strips dipped in thick hot chocolate are a Spanish favourite for breakfast, afternoon tea or at dawn on your way home from a night out.

Bocadillos Rolls filled with *jamón* (cured ham) or other cured meats, cheese or (in Madrid) deep-fried calamari.

Pa amb tomaquet Bread rubbed with tomato, olive oil and garlic – a staple in Catalonia and elsewhere.

Getting Around

Spain's public transport system is one of the best in Europe, with a fast, supermodern train system, an extensive domestic air network, a well-maintained road network, and buses that connect villages in the country's remotest corners.

Train Extremely efficient rail network, from slow intercity regional trains to some of the fastest trains on the planet. More routes are added to the network every year.

Car Vast network of motorways radiating out from Madrid to all corners of the country are shadowed by smaller but often more picturesque minor roads.

Bus The workhorses of the Spanish roads, from slick express services to stop-everywhere village-to-village buses.

When to Go

Madrid

°C/°F Temp | Rainfall Inches/mm

Mar–May, Sep & Oct A good time to travel: mild, clear weather and smaller crowds. Easter week very busy.

Jun–Aug High season on the coast; accommodation books out and prices increase by up to 50%.

Nov–Feb Cold in central Spain, rain in the north, mild in the south.

Arriving in Spain

Adolfo Suárez Madrid-Barajas Airport (Madrid)
The Metro (€4.50 to €5, 30 minutes to the centre) runs from 6.05am to 1.30am; the Exprés Aeropuerto bus (30 to 40 minutes, €5) runs 24 hours between the airport and Puerta de Atocha train station or Plaza de Cibeles. Minibuses or taxis are €30.

El Prat Airport (Barcelona)
Buses cost €5.90 and run from 6.10am to 1.05am; it's 30 to 40 minutes to the centre. Trains (€4.10, 25 to 30 minutes to the centre) run from 5.42am to 11.38pm. Taxis cost €30.

Top Phrases

Hello. Hola.

Goodbye. Hasta luego.

Excuse me. Perdón.

Thank you. Gracias.

You're welcome. De nada.

Resources

Fiestas.net (www.fiestas.net) Festivals around the country.

Turespaña (www.spain.info) Spanish tourist office's site.

Renfe (www.renfe.com) Spain's rail network.

Set Your Budget

➡ Dorm bed: €20–30

➡ Double room in *hostal* (budget hotel): €50–65 (€60–75 in Madrid, Barcelona and the Balearics)

➡ Self-catering and lunch *menú del día* (set menu): €10–15

Central Madrid

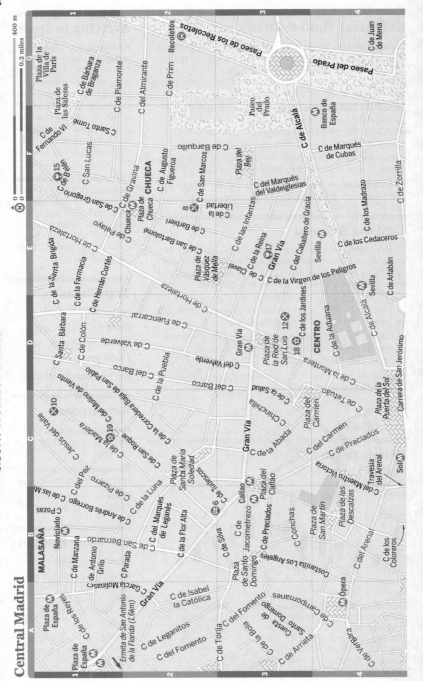

SPAIN & PORTUGAL MADRID

400 m
0.2 miles

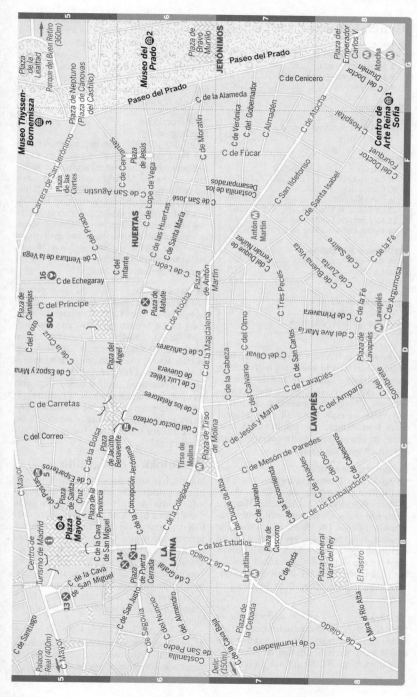

SPAIN & PORTUGAL MADRID

Central Madrid

Sep-Jul; M Tribunal) A citywide poll for the best *croquetas* in Madrid would see half of those polled voting for Casa Julio and the remainder not doing so only because they haven't been yet. They're that good that celebrities and mere mortals from all over Madrid come here sample the traditional *jamón* (ham) variety or more creative versions such as spinach with gorgonzola.

La Gloria de Montera   SPANISH $
(☑ 915 23 44 07; www.grupandilana.com; Calle del Caballero de Gracia 10; mains €8-14; ⊙ 1.15-11.30pm; M Gran Vía) La Gloria de Montera combines classy decor with eminently reasonable prices. The food isn't especially creative, but the tastes are fresh and the surroundings sophisticated. You'll get a good initiation into Spanish cooking without paying over the odds. It doesn't take reservations, so turn up early or be prepared to wait.

★Bazaar   MODERN SPANISH $
(☑ 91 523 39 05; www.restaurantbazaar.com; Calle de la Libertad 21; mains €7.50-13; ⊙ 1.15-4pm & 8.30-11.30pm Sun-Wed, 1.15-4pm & 8.15pm-midnight Thu-Sat; 🛜; M Chueca) Bazaar's popularity among the well-heeled Chueca set shows no sign of abating. Its pristine white interior design, with theatre-style lighting and wall-length windows, may draw a crowd that looks like it's stepped out of the pages of *¡Hola!* magazine, but the food is extremely well priced and innovative, and the atmosphere is casual.

★Mercado de San Miguel   TAPAS $$
(☑ 91 542 49 36; www.mercadodesanmiguel. es; Plaza de San Miguel; tapas from €1.50; ⊙ 10am-midnight Sun-Wed, to 2am Thu-Sat; M Sol) This is one of Madrid's oldest and most beautiful markets, set within early 20th-century glass walls and offering an inviting space strewn with tables. You can order tapas and sometimes more substantial plates at most of the counter-bars, and everything here (from caviar to chocolate) is as tempting as the market is alive. It's one of our favourite experiences in Madrid.

★Casa Alberto   TAPAS $$
(☑ 91 429 93 56; www.casaalberto.es; Calle de las Huertas 18; tapas €3.25-10, raciones €7-16.50, mains €16-19; ⊙ restaurant 1.30-4pm & 8pm-midnight Tue-Sat, 1.30-4pm Sun, bar noon-1.30am Tue-Sat, 12.30-4pm Sun, closed Sun Jul & Aug; M Antón Martín) One of the most atmospheric old *tabernas* (taverns) of Madrid, Casa Alberto has been around since 1827 and occupies a building where Cervantes is said to have written one of his books. The secret to its staying power is vermouth on tap, excellent tapas at the bar and fine sit-down meals.

🍷 Drinking & Nightlife

Madrid has more bars than any other city in the world – six, in fact, for every 100 inhabitants, so wherever you are in town, there'll be a bar close by. But bars are only half the story. On any night in Madrid, fdrinks, tapas and wines segue easily into cocktail bars and the nightclubs that have brought such renown to Madrid as the unrivalled scene of all-night fiestas. Don't expect dance clubs or *discotecas* (nightclubs) to get going until after 1am at the earliest. Standard entry fee is €12, which usually includes the first drink.

The area around Sol is the epicentre of Madrid's night-time action, while Malasaña and Chueca to the north of here are all-night neighbourhoods with great options.

ÁVILA

Ávila's old city, just over an hour from Madrid and a good day trip, is surrounded by imposing city walls comprising eight monumental gates, 88 watchtowers and more than 2500 turrets. It's one of the best-preserved medieval bastions in Spain. Two sections of the **walls** (www.murralladeavila.com; adult/child under 12yr €5/free; ☉10am-8pm Apr-Oct, to 6pm Nov-Mar; 🖼️) can be climbed – a 300m stretch that can be accessed from just inside the Puerta del Alcázar, and a longer (1300m) stretch from Puerta de los Leales that runs the length of the old city's northern perimeter. The admission price includes a multilingual audioguide.

Also worth a visit, Ávila's 12th-century **cathedral** (📞920 21 16 41; Plaza de la Catedral; admission incl audio guide €5; ☉10am-7pm Mon-Fri, 10am-8pm Sat, noon-6.30pm Sun Apr-Sep, 10am-5pm Mon-Fri, 10am-6pm Sat, noon-5pm Sun Oct-Mar) is both a house of worship and an ingenious fortress: its granite apse forms the central bulwark in the historic city walls. The Gothic-style facade conceals a magnificent interior with an exquisite early-16th-century altar frieze showing the life of Jesus, plus Renaissance-era carved choir stalls and a museum with an El Greco painting and a splendid silver monstrance by Juan de Arfe.

There are train services to Madrid (from €12.25, 1¼ to two hours), Salamanca (from €12.25, 1¼ hours) and elsewhere. Buses run to Salamanca (€7.95, 1½ hours, five daily) and Madrid (€11, 1½ hours).

★**La Venencia** BAR
(📞91 429 73 13; Calle de Echegaray 7; ☉12.30-3.30pm & 7.30pm-1.30am; Ⓜ Sol, Sevilla) La Venencia is a *barrio* classic, with *manzanilla* (chamomile-coloured sherry) from Sanlúcar and sherry from Jeréz poured straight from the dusty wooden barrels, accompanied by a small selection of tapas with an Andalucian bent. There's no music and no flashy decorations; here it's all about you, your *fino* (sherry) and your friends.

★**Café Belén** BAR
(📞91 308 27 47; www.elcafebelen.com; Calle de Belén 5; ☉3.30pm-3am Tue-Thu, to 3.30am Fri & Sat, to midnight Sun; 🖼️; Ⓜ Chueca) Café Belén is cool in all the right places – lounge and chill-out music, dim lighting, a great range of drinks (the mojitos are especially good) and a low-key crowd that's the height of casual sophistication. It's one of our preferred Chueca watering holes.

★**Museo Chicote** COCKTAIL BAR
(📞91 532 67 37; www.grupomercadodelareina.com/en/museo-chicote-en; Gran Vía 12; ☉7pm-3am Mon-Thu, to 4am Fri & Sat, 4pm-1am Sun; Ⓜ Gran Vía) With its 1930s-era interior, this place is a Madrid landmark, and its founder is said to have invented more than 100 cocktails, which the likes of Ernest Hemingway, Ava Gardner, Grace Kelly, Sophia Loren and Frank Sinatra have all enjoyed at one time or another.

☆ Entertainment

★**Estadio Santiago Bernabéu** FOOTBALL
(📞902 324 324; www.realmadrid.com; Av de Concha Espina 1; tickets from €40; Ⓜ Santiago Bernabéu) Watching Real Madrid play is one of football's greatest experiences, but tickets are difficult to find. Tickets can be purchased online, by phone or in person from the ticket office at Gate 42 on Av de Concha Espina; turn up early in the week before a scheduled game. Numerous online ticketing agencies also sell tickets. Otherwise, you'll need to take a risk with scalpers.

★**Teatro Flamenco Madrid** FLAMENCO
(📞911 59 20 05; www.teatroflamencomadrid.com; Calle del Pez 10; adult/student & senior/child €25/16/12; ☉6.45pm & 8.15pm; Ⓜ Noviciado) This excellent new flamenco venue is a terrific deal. With a focus on quality flamenco (dance, song and guitar) rather than the more formal meal-and-floor-show package of the *tablaos*, and with a mixed crowd of locals and tourists, this place generates a great atmosphere most nights for the hour-long show. Prices are also a notch below what you'll pay elsewhere.

★**Sala El Sol** LIVE MUSIC
(📞91 532 64 90; www.elsolmad.com; Calle de los Jardines 3; admission incl drink €10, concert tickets €6-30; ☉midnight-5.30am Tue-Sat Jul-Sep; Ⓜ Gran Vía) Madrid institutions don't come

Museo del Prado

PLAN OF ATTACK

Begin on the 1st floor with ❶ **Las meninas** by Velázquez. Although it alone is worth the entry price, it's a fine introduction to the 17th-century golden age of Spanish art; nearby are more of Velázquez' royal paintings and works by Zurbarán and Murillo. While on the 1st floor, seek out Goya's ❷ **La maja vestida and La maja desnuda**, with more of Goya's early works in neighbouring rooms. Downstairs at the southern end of the Prado, Goya's anger is evident in the searing ❸ **El dos de mayo and El tres de mayo**, and the torment of Goya's later years finds expression in the adjacent rooms with his ❹ **Las pinturas negras** (the Black Paintings). Also on the lower floor, Hieronymus Bosch's weird and wonderful ❺ **The Garden of Earthly Delights** is one of the Prado's signature masterpieces. Returning to the 1st floor, El Greco's ❻ **Adoration of the Shepherds**, is an extraordinary work, as is Peter Paul Rubens' ❼ **Las tres gracias** which forms the centrepiece of the Prado's gathering of Flemish masters. (Note: this painting may be moved to the 2nd floor.) A detour to the 2nd floor takes in some lesser-known Goyas, but finish in the ❽ **Edificio Jerónimos** with a visit to the cloisters and the outstanding bookshop.

TOP TIPS

➡ Purchase your ticket online (www.museodelprado.es) and avoid the queues.

➡ Best time to visit is as soon after opening time as possible.

➡ The website (www.museodelprado.es/coleccion/que-ver/) has self-guided tours for one- to three-hour visits.

➡ Nearby are Museo Thyssen-Bornemisza and Centro de Arte Reina Sofía. Together they form an extraordinary trio of galleries.

Las meninas (Velázquez)
This masterpiece depicts Velázquez and the Infanta Margarita. According to some experts, the images of the king and queen appear in mirrors behind Velázquez.

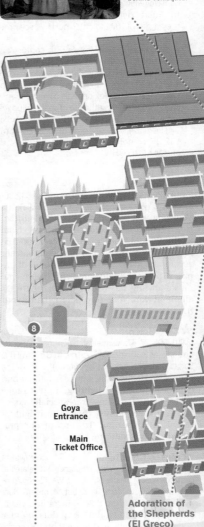

Goya Entrance

Main Ticket Office

Edificio Jerónimos
Opened in 2007, this state-of-the-art extension has rotating exhibitions of Prado masterpieces held in storage for decades for lack of wall space, and stunning 2nd-floor granite cloisters that date back to 1672.

Adoration of the Shepherds (El Greco)
There's an ecstatic quality to this intense painting. El Greco's distorted rendering of bodily forms came to characterise much of his later work.

Las tres gracias (Rubens)

A late Rubens masterpiece, *The Three Graces* is a classical and masterly expression of Rubens' preoccupation with sensuality, here portraying Aglaia, Euphrosyne and Thalia, the daughters of Zeus.

La maja vestida & La maja desnuda (Goya)

These enigmatic works scandalised early 19th-century Madrid society, fuelling the rumour mill as to the woman's identity and drawing the ire of the Spanish Inquisition.

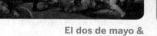

Edificio Villanueva

El dos de mayo & El tres de mayo (Goya)

Few paintings evoke a city's sense of self quite like Goya's portrayal of Madrid's valiant but ultimately unsuccessful uprising against French rule in 1808.

Las pinturas negras (Goya)

Las pinturas negras are Goya's darkest works. *Saturno devorando a su hijo* evokes a writhing mass of tortured humanity, while *La romería de San Isidro* and *El aquelarre* are profoundly unsettling.

Information Counter & Audioguides **Gift Shop**   **Cafeteria**

Ónimos Entrance (Main Entrance)

Murillo Entrance

Velázquez Entrance

The Garden of Earthly Delights (Bosch)

A fantastical painting in triptych form, this overwhelming work depicts the Garden of Eden and what the Prado describes as 'the lugubrious precincts of Hell' in exquisitely bizarre detail.

any more beloved than the terrific Sala El Sol. It opened in 1979, just in time for *la movida madrileña* (the Madrid scene), and quickly established itself as a leading stage for all the icons of the era, such as Nacha Pop and Alaska y los Pegamoides.

ℹ Information

Centro de Turismo de Madrid (☑ 010, 91 578 78 10; www.esmadrid.com; Plaza Mayor 27; ⊙ 9.30am-8.30pm; Ⓜ Sol) The Madrid government's Centro de Turismo is fantastic. Housed in the Real Casa de la Panadería on the northern side of the Plaza Mayor, it allows access to its outstanding website and city database, and offers free downloads of the metro map to your mobile; staff are also helpful.

ℹ Getting There & Away

Madrid's **Barajas Airport** (☑ 902 404 704; www.aena.es; Ⓜ Aeropuerto T1, T2 & T3, Aeropuerto T4) is one of Europe's busiest and is served by almost 100 airlines.

Within Spain, Madrid is the hub of the country's outstanding bus and train network.

Estación Sur de Autobuses (☑ 91 468 42 00; Calle de Méndez Álvaro 83; Ⓜ Méndez Álvaro), just south of the M-30 ring road, is the city's principal bus station.

Madrid's main train station, the **Puerta de Atocha** (www.renfe.es; Av de la Ciudad de Barcelona; Ⓜ Atocha Renfe), is at the southern edge of the city centre. This is where most international, national and local *cercanías* arrive, including many high-speed AVE services. North of the city centre, **Estación de Chamartín** (☑ 902 432343; Paseo de la Castellana; Ⓜ Chamartín) has numerous long-distance rail services, especially those to/from northern Spain. This is also where long-haul international trains arrive from Paris and Lisbon.

ℹ Getting Around

The easiest way into town from the airport is line 8 of the metro. A single ticket costs €4.50 including the €3 airport supplement.

Ten-trip Metrobús tickets cost €12.20 and are valid for journeys on Madrid's metro and bus network. Tickets can be bought from most newspaper kiosks and *estancos* (tobacconists), as well as in metro stations.

Metro The quickest and easiest way to get around. Runs 6.05am to 1.30am.

Bus There's an extensive network but careful planning is needed to make the most of over 200 routes. Runs 6.30am to 11.30pm.

Taxi Cheap fares by European standards; plentiful.

Walking A compact city centre makes walking a good option, but it's hillier than first appears.

Around Madrid

Toledo

POP 85,593

Dramatically sited atop a gorge overlooking the Río Tajo, Toledo was known as the 'city of three cultures' in the Middle Ages, a place where – legend has it – Christian, Muslim and Jewish communities peacefully coexisted. Rediscovering the vestiges of this unique cultural synthesis remains modern Toledo's most compelling attraction. Horseshoe-arched mosques, Sephardic synagogues and one of Spain's finest Gothic cathedrals cram into its dense historical core. Toledo's other forte is art, in particular the haunting canvases of El Greco, the influential, difficult-to-classify painter with whom the city is synonymous.

⊙ Sights

★**Catedral de Toledo**　　　CATHEDRAL
(☑ 925 22 22 41; www.catedralprimada.es; Plaza del Ayuntamiento; adult/child €12.50/free, incl Museo de Textiles y Orfebrería admission; ⊙ 10am-6pm Mon-Sat, 2-6pm Sun) Toledo's illustrious main church ranks among the top 10 cathedrals in Spain. An impressive example of medieval Gothic architecture, its humongous interior is full of the classic characteristics of the style, rose windows, flying buttresses, ribbed vaults and pointed arches among them. The cathedral's sacristy is a veritable art gallery of old masters, with works by Velázquez, Goya and – of course – El Greco.

★**Sinagoga del Tránsito**　SYNAGOGUE, MUSEUM
(☑ 925 22 36 65; http://museosefardi.mcu.es; Calle Samuel Leví; adult/child €3/1.50, after 2pm Sat & all day Sun free; ⊙ 9.30am-7.30pm Tue-Sat Mar-Oct, to 6pm Tue-Sat Nov-Feb, 10am-3pm Sun year-round) This magnificent synagogue was built in 1355 by special permission from Pedro I and now houses the **Museo Sefardí** (⊙ 9.30am-6pm Mon-Sat, 10am-3pm Sun). The vast main prayer hall has been expertly restored and the Mudéjar decoration and intricately carved pine ceiling are striking. Exhibits provide an insight into the history of Jewish culture in Spain, and include archaeological finds, a memorial garden, costumes and ceremonial artefacts.

Alcázar　　　　FORTRESS
(Museo del Ejército; ☑ 925 22 30 38; Calle Alféreces Provisionales; adult/child €5/free, Sun free; ⊙ 10am-5pm Thu-Tue) At the highest point in the city

Toledo

looms the forebidding Alcázar. Rebuilt under Franco, it has bween reopened as a vast military museum. The usual displays of uniforms and medals are here, but the best part is the exhaustive historical section, with an in-depth overview of the nation's history in Spanish and English. The exhibition is epic in scale but like a well-run marathon, it's worth the physical (and mental) investment.

🛏 Sleeping

Oasis Backpackers Hostel　　　　HOSTEL $
(☎925 22 76 50; www.hostelsoasis.com; Calle de las Cadenas 5; dm €18, d €34-44; @ 🛜) One of four Oasis hostels in Spain, this hostel sparkles with what have become the chain's glowing hallmarks: laid-back but refreshingly well-organised service and an atmosphere that is fun without ever being loud or obnoxious. There are private rooms if you're not up for a dorm-share, and lots of free information on city attractions.

Hotel Santa Isabel　　　　　　　HOTEL $
(☎925 25 31 20; www.hotelsantaisabeltoledo.es; Calle de Santa Isabel 24; s/d €40/50; 🛜) Providing a safe, economical base to stay in Toledo, the Santa Isabel is clean, central and friendly. It's encased in an old noble house with simple rooms set around two courtyards. Several have cathedral views and there's a charming rooftop terrace, accessed by a spiral staircase.

🍴 Eating & Drinking

Bar Ludeña　　　　　　　　　　SPANISH $
(☎925 22 33 84; Plaza de Magdalena 10; mains €8-12; ⏱10.30am-4.30pm & 8-11.30pm) Despite its

Toledo

◉ Top Sights
1 Catedral de Toledo	B2
2 Sinagoga del Tránsito	A2

◉ Sights
3 Alcázar	C2
Museo Sefardí	(see 2)

🛏 Sleeping
4 Hotel Santa Isabel	B2
5 Oasis Backpackers Hostel	B1

🍴 Eating
6 Bar Ludeña	C1

🍷 Drinking & Nightlife
7 Libro Taberna El Internacional	B2

central location close to Toledo's main tourist thoroughfare, Ludeña retains a wholesome local image courtesy of the flock of regulars who – despite the tourist infiltration – still frequent it. Join them as they prop up the bar with a *caña* (beer) and a plate of the Toledano speciality, *carcamusa* (pork and vegetable stew). Alternatively grab a pew on the delightful shady terrace.

★**Libro Taberna El Internacional**　BAR, CAFE
(☎925 67 27 65; www.facebook.com/librotabernatoledo; Calle de la Ciudad 15; ⏱8pm-1.30am Tue-Thu, noon-1.30am Fri & Sat, noon-4pm Sun) If you think Toledo is more touristy than trendy, you haven't dipped your hipster detector into the cool confines of El Internacional, a purveyor of slow food, spray-painted tables, overflowing bookcases, rescued 1970s armchairs and, of course, beards.

ℹ️ Information

Main Tourist Office (☎ 925 25 40 30; www.toledo-turismo.com; Plaza Consistorio 1; ⏰ 10am-6pm) Located virtually across from the cathedral, this office could not be more central. It has an excellent free map and plenty of 'what's on' type of information.

ℹ️ Getting There & Away

From Toledo's bus station, buses depart for Madrid's Plaza Elíptica every half-hour (from €5.50, one hour to 1¾ hours). High-speed AVE trains run every hour to Madrid (€13, 30 minutes).

El Escorial

The imposing palace and monastery complex of **San Lorenzo de El Escorial** (☎ 91 890 78 18; www.patrimonionacional.es; adult/concession €10/5, guide/audioguide €4/3, EU citizens free last three hours Wed & Thu; ⏰ 10am-8pm Apr-Sep, to 6pm Oct-Mar, closed Mon) is an impressive place, rising up from the foothills of the mountains that shelter Madrid from the north and west. Built in the 16th century by King Felipe II, it became a symbol of Spanish imperial power. The project included a monastic centre, a decadent royal palace and a mausoleum for Felipe's parents, Carlos I and Isabel. Architect Juan de Herrera oversaw the works. The Escorial imposes by its sheer size; within, its sombre basilica, galleries and rooms are a treasure chest of Spanish and European art.

A few dozen Renfe C8 *cercanías* make the trip daily from Madrid's Atocha or Chamartín train station to El Escorial (€1.50, one hour).

San Sebastián

POP 186,100

San Sebastián (Basque: Donostia) is a city filled with people who love to indulge – and with Michelin stars apparently falling from the heavens onto its restaurants, not to mention an unmatched *pintxo* (tapas) culture, San Sebastián frequently tops lists of the world's best places to eat.

👁 Sights

San Telmo Museoa　　　　　MUSEUM
(☎ 943 48 15 80; www.santelmomuseoa.com; Plaza Zuloaga 1; adult/student/child €6/3/free; ⏰ 10am-8pm Tue-Sun) One of the best museums in the Basque Country, the San Telmo Museoa has a thought-provoking collection that explores Basque history and culture in all its complexity. Exhibitions are spread between a restored convent dating from the 16th century, and a cutting-edge newer wing that blends into its plant-lined backdrop of Mount Urgull. The collection ranges from historical artefacts to bold fusions of contemporary art. San Telmo also stages some outstanding temporary exhibitions.

⭐ **Playa de la Concha**　　　　　BEACH
(Paseo de la Concha) Fulfilling almost every idea of how a perfect city beach should be formed, Playa de la Concha (and its westerly extension, Playa de Ondarreta), is easily among the best city beaches in Europe. Throughout the long summer months a fiesta atmosphere prevails, with thousands of tanned and toned bodies spread across the sands. The swimming is almost always safe.

⭐ **Aquarium**　　　　　AQUARIUM
(www.aquariumss.com; Plaza Carlos Blasco de Imaz 1; adult/child €13/6.50; ⏰ 10am-9pm Jul & Aug, 10am-8pm Mon-Fri, 10am-9pm Sat & Sun Easter-Jun & Sep, 10am-7pm Mon-Fri, to 8pm Sat & Sun Oct-Easter) Fear for your life as huge sharks bear down from behind glass panes, or gaze in disbelief at tripped-out fluoro jellyfish. The highlights of a visit to the city's excellent aquarium are the cinema-screen-sized deep-ocean and coral-reef exhibits and the long tunnel, around which swim monsters of the deep. The aquarium also contains a maritime museum section. Allow at least 1½ hours for a visit.

🛌 Sleeping

Prices are high and availability in peak season is very tight. Budget *pensiones* (small private hotels) cluster in the old town.

Pensión Amaiur　　　BOUTIQUE HOTEL **$$**
(☎ 943 42 96 54; www.pensionamaiur.com; Calle de 31 de Agosto 44; d with/without bathroom from €75/60; @🤖) A top-notch guesthouse in a prime old-town location, Amaiur has bright floral wallpapers and bathrooms tiled in Andalucían blue and white. The best rooms are those that overlook the main street, where you can sit on a little balcony and be completely enveloped in blushing red flowers. Some rooms share bathrooms. Guest kitchen and free snacks add to the value.

🍴 Eating

A Fuego Negro　　　　　BASQUE **$**
(www.afuegonegro.com; Calle 31 de Agosto 31; pintxos from €2.50; ⏰ noon-4pm & 7-11.30pm) Dark,

San Sebastián

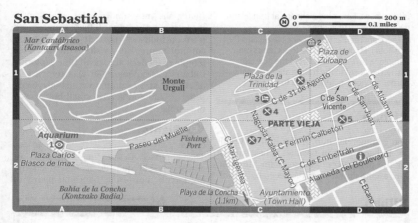

theatrical and anything but traditional, A Fuego Negro is one of the leading designers of arty *pintxos*. Everything here is a surprise: expect olives stuffed with a burst of vermouth, mini Kobe beef burgers on a tomato bun, and codfish with pureed cauliflower curry.

Bar Borda Berri PINTXOS **$$**
(📋 943 43 03 42; Calle Fermín Calbetón 12; pintxos from €2.50; ⊙ 12.30-3.30pm & 7.30-11pm Tue-Sat, 12.30-3.30pm Sun) The uber-popular Bar Borda Berri is a *pintxos* bar that really lives up to the hype. Amid mustard-coloured walls hung with old photos and strands of garlic, hungry diners crowd in for house specials like braised veal cheeks in wine, mushroom and *idiazabal* (a sheep cheese) risotto and decadent octopus.

★La Cuchara de San Telmo BASQUE **$$**
(📋 043 44 16 55; www.lacucharadesantelmo. com; Calle de 31 de Agosto 28; pintxos from €2.50; ⊙ 7.30-11pm Tue, 12.30-3.30pm & 7.30-11pm Wed-Sun) This bustling, always packed bar offers miniature *nueva cocina vasca* (Basque nouvelle cuisine) from a supremely creative kitchen. Unlike many San Sebastián bars, this one doesn't have any *pintxos* laid out on the bar top; instead you must order from the blackboard menu behind the counter.

★La Fábrica BASQUE **$$**
(📋 943 43 21 10; www.restaurantelafabrica.es; Calle del Puerto 17; mains €15-20, menús from €29; ⊙ 1-4pm & 7.30-11.30pm Mon-Fri, 1-3.30pm & 8-11.30pm Sat & Sun) The red-brick interior walls and white tablecloths lend an air of class to this

San Sebastián

restaurant, whose modern takes on Basque classics have been making waves with San Sebastián locals in recent years. La Fábrica only works with multicourse *menús*, which means you'll get to sample various delicacies like wild mushroom ravioli with foie gras cream or venison in red wine sauce.

🛈 Information

Oficina de Turismo (📋 943 48 11 66; www. sansebastianturismo.com; Alameda del Boulevard 8; ⊙ 9am-8pm Mon-Sat, 10am-7pm Sun Jul-Sep, 9am-7pm Mon-Sat, 10am-2pm Sun Oct-May) This friendly office offers comprehensive information on the city and the Basque Country in general.

🛈 Getting There & Away

Trains run from the station, just across the river from the centre, to Madrid (from €29, 5½ hours) and Barcelona (from €39, six hours) among other places. For France, change at Irún/Hendaye for French mainline services.

There are regular bus services to Bilbao (€9, one hour), Madrid (€37, five to six hours) and Pamplona (€8, one hour) from the new bus station adjacent to the train station. Cross-border services include buses to Biarritz.

Bilbao

POP 345,200

The commercial hub of the Basque Country, Bilbao (Bilbo in Basque) is best known for the magnificent Guggenheim Museum. An architectural masterpiece by Frank Gehry, the museum was the catalyst of a turnaround that saw Bilbao transformed from an industrial port city into a vibrant cultural centre. After visiting this must-see temple to modern art, spend time exploring Bilbao's Casco Viejo (Old Quarter), a grid of elegant streets dotted with shops, cafes, *pintxos* bars and several small but worthy museums.

◉ Sights

Casco Viejo   OLD TOWN
The compact Casco Viejo, Bilbao's atmospheric old quarter, is full of charming streets, boisterous bars and plenty of

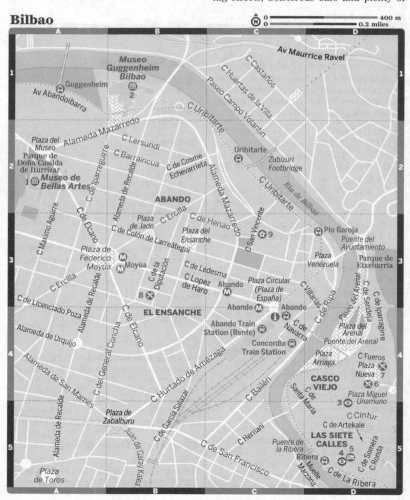

Bilbao

SPAIN & PORTUGAL BILBAO

quirky and independent shops. At the heart of the Casco are Bilbao's original seven streets, **Las Siete Calles**, which date from the 1400s.

★Museo
Guggenheim Bilbao   GALLERY
(📞944 35 90 16; www.guggenheim-bilbao.es; Avenida Abandoibarra 2; adult/student/child from €16/9/free; ⊙10am-8pm, closed Mon Sep-Jun) Shimmering titanium Museo Guggenheim Bilbao is one of modern architecture's most iconic buildings. It played a major role in helping to lift Bilbao out of its post-industrial depression and into the 21st century – and with sensation. It sparked the city's inspired regeneration, stimulated further development and placed Bilbao firmly in the international art and tourism spotlight.

★Museo de
Bellas Artes   GALLERY
(📞944 39 60 60; www.museobilbao.com; Plaza del Museo 2; adult/student/child €9/7/free, free 10am-3pm Wed & 3-8pm Sun; ⊙10am-8pm Wed-Mon) The Museo de Bellas Artes houses a compelling collection that includes everything from Gothic sculptures to 20th-century pop art. There are three main subcollections: classical art, with works by Murillo, Zurbarán, El Greco, Goya and van Dyck; contemporary art, featuring works by Gauguin, Francis Bacon and Anthony Caro; and Basque art, with works of the great sculptors Jorge Oteiza and Eduardo Chillida, and strong paintings by the likes of Ignacio Zuloaga and Juan de Echevarría.

Bilbao

⊙ **Top Sights**

🛏 Sleeping

Numerous cheap *pensiones* dot the old town.

Quartier Bilbao   HOSTEL $
(📞944 97 88 00; www.quartierbilbao.com; Calle Artekale 15; dm/d with shared bathroom from €18/55; 🛜) In a great location in the old town, this new hostel has much to recommend it, including modern, well-maintained facilities and helpful staff. It's spread over several floors of a six-storey building, and the attractive common areas are good places to meet other travellers.

✖ Eating & Drinking

★La Viña del Ensanche   PINTXOS $
(📞944 15 56 15; www.lavinadelensanche.com; Calle de la Diputación 10; small plates €5-15, menú €30; ⊙8.30am-11pm Mon-Fri, noon-1am Sat) Set with old-fashioned wood-panelled walls and framed postcards written by adoring fans over the years, La Viña del Ensanche maintains a reputation as one of Bilbao's best eating spots – no small achievement for a place that has been in business since 1927. Mouth-watering morsels of ham, tender octopus and crispy asparagus tempura are just a few of the many temptations.

Gure Toki   PINTXOS $
(Plaza Nueva 12; pintxos from €2.50; ⊙10am-11.30pm Mon-Sat, to 4pm Sun) One of the best *pintxo* bars in Casco Viejo, this popular place serves creative and outstandingly good bites, including tender mini-steak burgers, *bacalao* (codfish) with creamy pil pil and various goat cheese-topped delicacies.

Café-Bar Bilbao   PINTXOS $
(Plaza Nueva 6; pintxos from €2.50; ⊙7am-11pm Mon-Fri, 9am-11.30pm Sat, 10am-3pm Sun) This delightful choice on Bilbao's most food-centric plaza is all cool blue southern tiles and warm northern atmosphere, with a superb array of *pintxos*. Grab a table out the front, beside slender palm trees, and watch the world stroll past.

☆ Entertainment

★Kafe Antzokia   LIVE MUSIC
(📞944 24 46 25; www.kafeantzokia.com; Calle San Vicente 2) This is the vibrant heart of contemporary Basque Bilbao, featuring international rock, blues and reggae, as well as the cream of Basque rock-pop. Weekend concerts run from 10pm to 1am, followed

SPAIN & PORTUGAL BILBAO

DON'T MISS

LOS SANFERMINES

Immortalised by Ernest Hemingway in *The Sun Also Rises*, Pamplona (Iruña in Basque) is home of the wild Sanfermines festival, which features among astonishing general revelry – it's one of Spain's most vibrant fiestas – a daily *encierro* (running of the bulls). The festival is held from 6 to 14 July, when Pamplona is overrun with thrill-seekers, curious onlookers and, yes, bulls. The *encierro* begins at 8am, when bulls are let loose from the Coralillos Santo Domingo and run an 825m course to the bullring. Animal rights groups oppose bullrunning as a cruel tradition, and the participating bulls will almost certainly all be killed in the afternoon bullfight. The anti-bullfighting demonstration, the Running of the Nudes, takes place two days before the first bullrun. Accommodation for Los Sanfermines is priced through the roof and should be booked way in advance. There are frequent bus connections from Bilbao and San Sebastián though, which many partygoers opt for.

by DJs until 5am. During the day it's a cafe, restaurant and cultural centre all rolled into one and hosts frequent exciting events.

ℹ️ Information

Main Tourist Office (📞 944 79 57 60; www.bilbaoturismo.net; Plaza Circular 1; ⏰ 9am-9pm; 🛜) The very helpful main branch of the tourist office is near the Abando train station.

ℹ️ Getting There & Around

A number of European airlines, including budget choices, serve Bilbao's airport.

Bilbao's main bus station, Termibus, has departures to Barcelona (€36 to €52, seven to eight hours), Madrid (€32 to €43, 4¾ hours) and San Sebastián (€9, 1¼ hours) among other departures.

The very central train station has services to Barcelona (from €27, 6¾ hours) and Madrid (from €27, five to seven hours) among other destinations.

A metro and tram service with convenient stops make getting around central Bilbao a breeze.

Burgos

POP 176,608 / ELEV 859M

The extraordinary Gothic cathedral of Burgos is one of Spain's glittering jewels of religious architecture – it looms large over the city and skyline. Conservative Burgos seems to embody all the stereotypes of a north-central Spanish town, with sombre greystone architecture, the fortifying cuisine of the high *meseta* (plateau) and a climate of extremes. But this is a city that rewards deeper exploration.

👁️ Sights

⭐ **Catedral**   CATHEDRAL
(📞 947 20 47 12; www.catedraldeburgos.es; Plaza del Rey Fernando; adult/under 14yr incl audio guide €7/2, from 4.30pm Tue free; ⏰ 9.30am-7.30pm Apr-Sep, to 6.30pm Oct-Mar) This Unesco World Heritage–listed cathedral, once a former modest Romanesque church, is a masterpiece. Work began on a grander scale in 1221; remarkably, within 40 years most of the French Gothic structure had been completed. You can enter from Plaza de Santa María for free for access to the **Capilla del Santísimo Cristo**, with its much-revered 13th-century crucifix, and the **Capilla de Santa Tecla**, with its extraordinary ceiling. However, we recommend that you visit the cathedral in its entirety.

⭐ **Museo de la Evolución Humana** MUSEUM
(MEH; 📞 902 02 42 46; www.museoevolucionhumana.com; Paseo Sierra de Atapuerca; adult/concession/child €6/4/free, 4.30-8pm Tue & Thu free; ⏰ 10am-2.30pm & 4.30-8pm Tue-Fri, 10am-8pm Sat & Sun) This exceptional museum just across the river from the old quarter is a marvellously told story of human evolution. The basement exhibitions on **Atapuerca** (📞 902 02 42 46; www.atapuerca.org; guided tours in Spanish €6; ⏰ tours by appointment), an archaeological site north of Burgos where a 2007 discovery of Europe's oldest human fossil remains was made, are stunning; the displays on Charles Darwin and the extraordinary 'Human Evolution' section in the centre of the ground floor are simply outstanding. Even if you've no prior interest in the subject, don't miss it.

🛏️ Sleeping & Eating

⭐ **Rimbombín**   HOSTAL $
(📞 947 26 12 00; www.rimbombin.com; Calle Sombrería 6; d/tr/apt from €60/70/110; ❄️🛜)

Opened in 2013, this 'urban *hostal*' has an upbeat, contemporary feel – its slick white furnishings and decor are matched with light-pine beams and modular furniture. Three of the rooms have balconies overlooking the pedestrianised street. Conveniently, it's in the heart of Burgos' compact tapas district. The apartment is excellent value for longer stays, with the same chic modern look and two bedrooms.

★**Cervecería Morito**   TAPAS $
(☑ 947 26 75 55; Calle de Diego Porcelos 1; tapas/raciones from €4/6; �---12.30-3.30pm & 7-11.30pm) Cervecería Morito is the undisputed king of Burgos tapas bars and as such it's always crowded. A typical order is *alpargata* (lashings of cured ham served with bread, tomato and olive oil) or the *revueltos Capricho de Burgos* (scrambled eggs served with potatoes, blood sausage, red peppers, baby eels and mushrooms) – the latter is a meal in itself.

ℹ Information

Oficina de Turismo de Burgos (☑ 947 28 88 74; www.aytoburgos.es/turismo; Plaza de Santa María; ☺9am-8pm daily Jun-Sep, 9.30am-2pm & 4-7pm Mon-Sat, 9.30am-5pm Sun Oct-May) Pick up its 24-hour, 48-hour and 72-hour guides to Burgos. These helpful itinerary suggestions can also be downloaded as PDFs from its website. Ask about its guided visits of the town.

ℹ Getting There & Around

Regular buses run to Madrid (from €12,25, three hours, up to 20 daily), Bilbao (€6.25 to €13.30, two hours, eight daily) and León (from €5.20, two hours, three daily).

The train station is a considerable hike northeast of the town centre – bus 2 (€1.30) connects the train station with Plaza de España. Destinations include Madrid (from €25.85, 2½ to 4½ hours, six daily), Bilbao (from €13.85, three hours, four daily), León (from €9.90, two hours, four daily) and Salamanca (from €14.40, 2½ hours, seven daily).

Salamanca

POP 144,949 / ELEV 802M

Whether floodlit by night or bathed in late afternoon light, there's something magical about Salamanca. This is a city of rare beauty, awash with golden sandstone overlaid with ochre-tinted Latin inscriptions – an extraordinary virtuosity of plateresque

and Renaissance styles. The monumental highlights are many, with the exceptional Plaza Mayor (illuminated to stunning effect at night) an unforgettable highlight. But this is also Castilla's liveliest city, home to a massive Spanish and international student population that throngs the streets at night and provides the city with so much of its vitality.

◉ Sights

★**Plaza Mayor**   SQUARE
Built between 1729 and 1755, Salamanca's exceptional grand square is widely considered to be Spain's most beautiful central plaza. The square is particularly memorable at night when illuminated (until midnight) to magical effect. Designed by Alberto Churriguera, it's a remarkably harmonious and controlled baroque display. The medallions placed around the square bear the busts of famous figures.

★**Catedral Nueva**   CATHEDRAL
(☑ 923 21 74 76; www.catedralsalamanca.org; Plaza de Anaya; adult/child incl audio guide & Catedral Vieja €4.75/3; ☺10am-8pm Apr-Sep, 10am-6pm Oct-Mar) The tower of this late-Gothic cathedral lords over the city centre, its compelling churrigueresque (an ornate style of baroque architecture) dome visible from almost every angle. The interior is similarly impressive, with elaborate choir stalls, main chapel and retrochoir, much of it courtesy of the prolific José Churriguera. The ceilings are also exceptional, along with the Renaissance doorways – particularly the **Puerta del Nacimiento** on the western face, which stands out as one of several miracles worked in the city's native sandstone.

★**Catedral Vieja**   CATHEDRAL
(☑ 923 28 10 45; www.catedralsalamanca.org; Plaza de Anaya; adult/child incl audio guide & Catedral Nueva €4.75/3; ☺10am-8pm Apr-Sep, 10am-6pm Oct-Mar) The Catedral Nueva's largely Romanesque predecessor, the Catedral Vieja is adorned with an exquisite 15th-century **altarpiece**, one of the finest outside Italy. Its 53 panels depict scenes from the lives of Christ and Mary and are topped by a haunting representation of the Final Judgement. The cloister was largely ruined in an earthquake in 1755, but the **Capilla de Anaya** houses an extravagant alabaster sepulchre and one of Europe's oldest organs, a Mudéjar work of art from the 16th century.

Salamanca

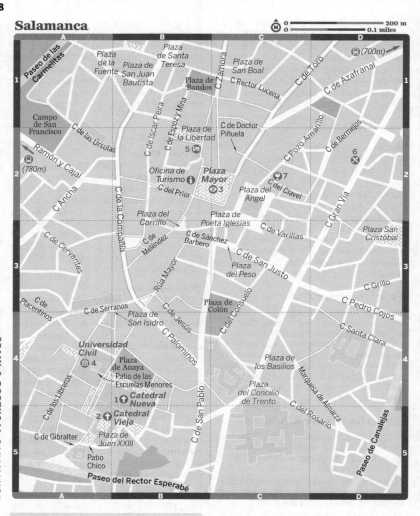

Salamanca

◎ Top Sights

◎ Sleeping

◎ Eating

◎ Drinking & Nightlife

★ **Universidad Civil**   HISTORIC BUILDING
(📞923 29 44 00, ext 1150; www.salamanca.es;
Calle de los Libreros; adult/concession €10/5, audio
guide €2; ⏰10am-6.30pm Mon-Sat, 10am-1.30pm
Sun) Founded initially as the Estudio General in 1218, the university reached the peak
of its renown in the 15th and 16th centuries.
The visual feast of the entrance facade is a
tapestry in sandstone, bursting with images of mythical heroes, religious scenes and
coats of arms. It's dominated by busts of
Fernando and Isabel. Behind the facade, the
highlight of an otherwise-modest collection

of rooms lies upstairs: the extraordinary **university library**, the oldest in Europe.

🛏 Sleeping

Hostal Concejo   HOSTAL **$**
(☑ 923 21 47 37; www.hconcejo.com; Plaza de la Libertad 1; s €28-50, d €37-70; P ❄ 🛜) A cut above the average *hostal*, the stylish Concejo has polished-wood floors, tasteful furnishings, light-filled rooms and a superb central location. Try to snag one of the corner rooms, such as number 104, which has a traditional, glassed-in balcony, complete with a table, chairs and people-watching views.

✗ Eating & Drinking

★**La Cocina de Toño**   TAPAS **$$**
(☑ 923 26 39 77; www.lacocinadetoño.es; Calle Gran Via 20; tapas from €2, menú €17-38, mains €18-23; ☉ noon-4.30pm & 8-11.30pm Tue-Sat, noon-4.30pm Sun; 🛜) This place owes its loyal following to its creative *pinchos* (tapas-like snacks) and half-servings of dishes such as escalope of foie gras with roast apple and passionfruit gelatin. The restaurant serves more traditional fare as befits the decor, but the bar is one of Salamanca's gastronomic stars. Slightly removed from the old city, it draws a predominantly Spanish crowd.

★**Tío Vivo**   BAR
(☑ 923 215 768; www.tiovivosalamanca.com; Calle del Clavel 3-5; ☉ 3.30pm-late) Sip drinks by flickering candlelight to a background of '80s music, enjoying the whimsical decor of carousel horses and oddball antiquities. There's live music Tuesday to Thursday from midnight, sometimes with a €5 cover charge.

❶ Information

Oficina de Turismo (☑ 923 21 83 42; www.salamanca.es; Plaza Mayor 32; ☉ 9am-2pm & 4.30-8pm Mon-Fri, 10am-8pm Sat, 10am-2pm Sun Easter–mid-Oct, 9am-2pm & 4-6.30pm Mon-Fri, 10am-6.30pm Sat, 10am-2pm Sun mid-Oct–Easter) The regional tourist office shares its space with the municipal office on Plaza Mayor. An audio city guide (www.audioguiasalamanca.es) is available.

❶ Getting There & Away

The bus and train stations are a 10- and 15-minute walk, respectively, from Plaza Mayor.

Buses include the following destinations: Madrid (regular/express €17/24.50, 2½ to three

hours, hourly), Ávila (€7.95, 1½ hours, five daily), Segovia (€16, 2½ hours, four daily) and Valladolid (€9.20, 1½ hours, eight daily).

Regular trains depart to Madrid's Chamartín station (from €16, 1½ to four hours), Ávila (€12.25, 1¼ hour) and Valladolid (from €10.45, 1½ hours).

León

POP 126,192 / ELEV 837M

León is a wonderful city, combining stunning historical architecture with an irresistible energy. Its standout attraction is the cathedral, one of the most beautiful in Spain, but there's so much more to see and do here. By day you'll encounter a city with its roots firmly planted in the soil of northern Castilla, with its grand monuments, loyal Catholic heritage and a role as an important staging post along the Camino de Santiago. By night León is taken over by its large student population, who provide it with a deep-into-the-night soundtrack of revelry that floods the narrow streets and plazas of the picturesque old quarter, the Barrio Húmedo. It's a fabulous mix.

◎ Sights

★**Catedral**   CATHEDRAL
(☑ 987 87 57 70; www.catedraldeleon.org; Plaza de Regia; adult/concession/under 12yr €6/5/free, combined ticket with Claustro & Museo Catedralicio-Diocesano €9/8/free; ☉ 9.30am-1.30pm & 4-8pm Mon-Fri, 9.30am-noon & 2-6pm Sat, 9.30-11am & 2-8pm Sun Jun-Sep, 9.30am-1.30pm & 4-7pm Mon-Sat, 9.30am-2pm Sun Oct-May) León's 13th-century cathedral, with its soaring towers, flying buttresses and breathtaking interior, is the city's spiritual heart. Whether spotlit by night or bathed in glorious northern sunshine, the cathedral, arguably Spain's premier Gothic masterpiece, exudes a glorious, almost luminous quality. The show-stopping facade has a radiant rose window, three richly sculpted doorways and two muscular towers. The main entrance is lorded over by a scene of the Last Supper, while an extraordinary gallery of *vidrieras* (stained-glass windows) awaits you inside.

★**Panteón Real**   HISTORIC BUILDING
(www.turismoleon.org; Plaza de San Isidoro; adult/child €5/free; ☉ 10am-2pm & 4-7pm Mon-Sat, 10am-2pm Sun) Attached to the **Real Basílica de San Isidoro** (☑ 987 87 61 61; ☉ 7.30am-11pm) **FREE**, the stunning Panteón Real houses royal sarcophagi, which rest

ASTURIAS & THE PICOS DE EUROPA

Asturias, a Celtic province of cider, green valleys, industry and super cold-water beaches, is an enticing, hospitable place to explore for a few days, starting in its main cities Oviedo and Gijón. The jagged Picos de Europa in its southeast is some of the finest walking country in Spain. They comprise three limestone massifs (the highest peak rises 2648m). The 647-sq-km **Parque Nacional de los Picos de Europa** (www. picosdeeuropa.com) covers all three massifs and is Spain's second-biggest national park. There are numerous places to stay and eat all over the mountains. Getting here and around by bus can be slow-going but the Picos are accessible from Santander and Oviedo (the latter is easier) by bus.

with quiet dignity beneath a canopy of some of the finest Romanesque frescos in Spain. Colourful motifs of biblical scenes drench the vaults and arches of this extraordinary hall, held aloft by marble columns with intricately carved capitals. The pantheon also houses a small **museum** where you can admire the shrine of San Isidoro, a mummified finger of the saint and other treasures.

🛏 Sleeping & Eating

The most atmospheric part of town for restaurants is the old town. You can easily fill up on tapas here – free with every drink. A good place to start is Plaza de San Martín, while on the other side of Calle Ancha, Plaza de Torres de Omaña is the epicentre of another good zone.

Pensión Blanca B&B PENSIÓN $
(☎987 25 19 91; www.pensionblanca.com; Calle de Villafranca 2; d/tr €45/60, s/d without bathroom €30/40; 🛜) A cut above your average *pensión* and easily one of the best budget choices in León, Pensión Blanca has attractive, brightly coloured rooms in a good location about halfway between the bus and train stations and the cathedral; the latter is a 10-minute walk away, along the main shopping street.

La Trébede TAPAS $
(☎637 25 91 97; Plaza de Torres de Omaña; tapas from €2.50, raciones from €7; ⊙noon-4pm & 8pm-midnight Mon-Sat) As good for tapas (try the croquettes) as for first drinks (wines by the glass start at €1.50), La Trébede is always full. The interior decor is eclectic – deer's antlers, historic wirelesses and the scales of justice – and the sign outside declaring 350km to Santiago may just prompt you to abandon the Camino and stay a little longer.

Racimo de Oro TAPAS $$
(☎987 21 47 67; www.racimodeoro.com; Plaza de San Martín 8; raciones from €7, mains €12-19; ⊙1-5pm & 8pm-12.30am) A lovely brick-lined interior provides an appealing backdrop for this wildly popular tapas bar and restaurant, which is arguably the pick of the choices around Plaza de San Martín. The food is predominantly from Castilla y León's north, such as cured meats, strong cheeses and roasted red peppers.

ℹ Information

Oficina de Turismo de León (☎987 87 83 27; www.turismoleon.org; Plaza de San Marcelo 1; ⊙9am-8pm) Information on the city and surrounding region.

ℹ Getting There & Away

Buses depart to Madrid (€24, 3½ hours, eight daily), Burgos (€5 to €15.50, two hours, three daily) and Valladolid (€11.30, two hours, nine daily).

The AVE fast train services run to/from Madrid (from €27, 2¼ hours), although there are cheaper and slower train services. Other destinations include Burgos (from €9.90, two hours).

Santiago de Compostela
POP 79,800

Locals say the arcaded, stone streets of Santiago de Compostela – the final stop on the epic Camino de Santiago pilgrimage trail – are at their most beautiful in the rain, when the Old Town glistens. Most would agree, however, that it's hard to catch Santiago in a bad pose. Whether you're wandering the streets of the Old Town, nibbling on tapas in the taverns, or gazing down at the rooftops from atop the cathedral, Santiago seduces.

Santiago de Compostela

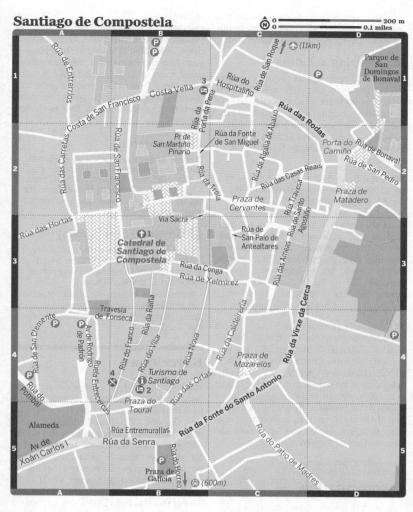

◉ Sights

★ Catedral de Santiago de Compostela

CATHEDRAL

(http://catedraldesantiago.es; Praza do Obradoiro; ⊙7am-8.30pm) The grand heart of Santiago, the cathedral soars above the city in a splendid jumble of spires and sculpture. Built piecemeal over several centuries, its beauty is a mix of the original Romanesque structure (constructed between 1075 and 1211) and later Gothic and baroque flourishes. The tomb of Santiago beneath the main altar is a magnet for all who come here. The cathedral's artistic high point is the Pórtico de la Gloria inside the west entrance, featuring 200 masterly Romanesque sculptures.

🛏 Sleeping & Eating

Central Santiago is packed with eateries and most do their job pretty well. The many lining Rúa do Franco cater chiefly to a not particularly discriminating tourist market, and you'll find the most enticing options elsewhere. Don't leave Santiago without trying a *tarta de Santiago,* the city's famed almond cake.

★ Hostal Suso   HOSTAL $
(☎981 58 66 11; www.hostalsuso.com; Rúa do Vilar 65; r €48-65; ❄@🛜) Stacked above a convenient cafe (with excellent-value breakfasts), the friendly, family-run, 14-room Suso received a full makeover in 2016 and boasts immaculate, thoughtfully designed rooms in appealing greys and whites, with up-to-date bathrooms and firm beds. It's very good for the price. Everything is thoroughly soundproofed too – the street outside is traffic-free but can get quite celebratory in summer.

★ Café-Jardin Costa Vella   CAFE $
(www.costavella.com; Rúa da Porta da Pena 17; breakfast €2.70-4.50; ⊗8am-11pm; 🛜) The garden cafe of **Hotel Costa Vella** (☎981 56 95 30; s €50-60, d €55-97; ❄@🛜) is the most delightful spot for breakfast (or a drink later in the day), with its fountain, a scattering of statuary and beautiful flowering fruit trees. And if the weather takes a Santiago-esque rainy turn, you can still enjoy it from the glass pavilion or the *galería.*

OFF THE BEATEN TRACK

AROUND GALICIA

Galicia's dramatic Atlantic coastline is one of Spain's best-kept secrets, with wild and precipitous cliffs and isolated fishing villages. The lively port city of A Coruña has a lovely city beach and fabulous seafood (a recurring Galician theme). It's also the gateway to the stirring landscapes of the Costa da Morte and Rías Altas; the latter's highlight among many is probably Cabo Ortegal. Inland Galicia is also worth exploring, especially the old town of Lugo, surrounded by what many consider to be the world's best preserved Roman walls.

Mesón O 42   GALICIAN $$
(www.universomilongas.com; Rúa do Franco 42; raciones €6-16; ⊗noon-4pm & 7.30pm-midnight, closed Tue Nov-Mar) Probably the best place on busy Rúa do Franco for a reliably well-prepared range of Galician and other Spanish favourites – beef sirloin, *pulpo á feira* with potatoes, steamed cockles, goat's cheese and dried-fruit salad. Generous free tapas with drinks.

ℹ Information

Turismo de Santiago (☎981 55 51 29; www.santiagoturismo.com; Rúa do Vilar 63; ⊗9am-9pm Apr-Oct, 9am-7pm Mon-Fri, 9am-2pm & 4-7pm Sat & Sun Nov-Mar) The very efficient city tourist office. Its website is a multilingual mine of information.

ℹ Getting There & Away

The bus station is 1.5km northeast of the centre. Destinations include León (€30, six hours), Madrid (€20 to €67, eight hours) and Porto, Portugal (€27 to €34, 3¼ hours).

The train station is about a kilometre south of the old town. High-speed AVE services to/from Madrid (currently €36, 5¼ hours) were due to start in 2018.

Barcelona
POP 1,621,090

Barcelona is one of Europe's coolest cities. Despite two millennia of history, it's a forward-thinking place, always on the cutting edge of art, design and cuisine. Whether you explore its medieval palaces and plazas, admire the Modernista masterpieces, shop for designer fashions along its bustling boulevards, sample its exciting nightlife or soak up the sun on the beaches, you'll find it hard not to fall in love with this vibrant city. And as much as Barcelona is a visual feast, it will also lead you into culinary temptation. Anything from traditional Catalan cooking to the latest in avant-garde new Spanish cuisine will have your appetite in overdrive.

⊙ Sights

★ La Rambla   STREET
(Map p410; Ⓜ Catalunya, Liceu, Drassanes) Barcelona's most famous street is both a tourist magnet and a window into Catalan culture, with cultural centres, theatres and intriguing architecture. Flanked by plane trees, the middle section of La Rambla is a broad pedestrian boulevard, crowded until the wee

hours with a wide cross-section of society. The horrific terrorist attacks in 2017 did little to diminish its popularity; neither with the tourists, nor with the hawkers, buskers, pavement artists, mimes and living statues.

★ **Mercat de la Boqueria** MARKET
(Map p410; ☑ 93 318 20 17; www.boqueria.info; La Rambla 91; ☺ 8am-8.30pm Mon-Sat; Ⓜ Liceu) Mercat de la Boqueria is possibly La Rambla's most interesting building, not so much for its Modernista-influenced design (it was actually built over a long period, from 1840 to 1914, on the site of the former St Joseph Monastery), but for the action of the food market within.

★ **La Catedral** CATHEDRAL
(Map p410; ☑ 93 342 82 62; www.catedralbcn.org; Plaça de la Seu; donation entrance €7, choir €3, roof €3; ☺ 8am-12.45pm & 5.45-7.30pm Mon-Fri, 8am-8pm Sat & Sun, entry by donation 1-5.30pm Mon,1-5pm Sat, 2-5pm Sun; Ⓜ Jaume I) Barcelona's central place of worship presents a magnificent image. The richly decorated main facade, dotted with gargoyles and the stone intricacies you would expect of northern European Gothic, sets it quite apart from other churches in Barcelona. The facade was actually added in 1870, although the rest of the building was built between 1298 and 1460. The other facades are sparse in decoration, and the octagonal, flat-roofed towers are a clear reminder that, even here, Catalan Gothic architectural principles prevailed.

★ **Museu Picasso** MUSEUM
(Map p410; ☑ 93 256 30 00; www.museupicasso. bcn.cat; Carrer de Montcada 15-23; adult/concession/under 16yr all collections €14/7.50/free, permanent collection €11/7/free, temporary exhibitions varies, 6-9.30pm Thu & 1st Sun of month free; ☺ 9am-7pm Tue-Sun, to 9.30pm Thu; Ⓜ Jaume I) The setting alone, in five contiguous medieval stone mansions, makes the Museu Picasso unique (and worth the probable queues). The pretty courtyards, galleries and staircases preserved in the first three of these buildings are as delightful as the collection inside.

★ **La Sagrada Família** CHURCH
(Map p406; ☑ 93 208 04 14; www.sagradafamilia. org; Carrer de Mallorca 401; adult/child €15/free; ☺ 9am-8pm Apr-Sep, to 7pm Mar & Oct, to 6pm Nov-Feb; Ⓜ Sagrada Família) If you have time for only one sightseeing outing, this should be it. La Sagrada Família inspires awe by its sheer verticality, and in the manner of the medieval cathedrals it emulates, it's still under construction. Work began in 1882 and is hoped (perhaps optimistically) to be completed in 2026, a century after the Gaudí's death. Unfinished it may be, but it attracts around 2.8 million visitors a year and is the most visited monument in Spain.

★ **Casa Batlló** ARCHITECTURE
(Map p406; ☑ 93 216 03 06; www.casabatllo.es; Passeig de Gràcia 43; adult/child €28/free; ☺ 9am-9pm, last admission 8pm; Ⓜ Passeig de Gràcia) One of the strangest residential buildings in Europe, this is Gaudí at his hallucinatory best. The facade, sprinkled with bits of blue, mauve and green tiles and studded with wave-shaped window frames and balconies, rises to an uneven blue-tiled roof with a solitary tower.

★ **La Pedrera** ARCHITECTURE
(Casa Milà; Map p406; ☑ 902 202138; www. lapedrera.com; Passeig de Gràcia 92; adult/child €25/15; ☺ 9am-8.30pm Mar-Oct, 9am-6.30pm Nov-Feb; Ⓜ Diagonal) This madcap Gaudí masterpiece was built in 1905–10 as a combined apartment and office block. Formally called Casa Milà, after the businessman who commissioned it, it is better known as La Pedrera (the Quarry) because of its uneven grey stone facade, which ripples around the corner of Carrer de Provença.

★ **Park Güell** PARK
(☑ 93 409 18 31; www.parkguell.cat; Carrer d'Olot 7; adult/child €8/5.60; ☺ 8am-9.30pm May-Aug, to 8.30pm Apr, Sep & Oct, to 6.30pm Dec-Mar; ☒ 24, 92, Ⓜ Lesseps, Vallcarca) North of Gràcia, Unesco-listed Park Güell is where Gaudí turned his hand to landscape gardening. It's a strange, enchanting place where his passion for natural forms really took flight and the artificial almost seems more natural than the natural.

The park is extremely popular, receiving an estimated four million visitors a year. Access is limited to a certain number of people every half-hour, and it's wise to book ahead online (you'll also save a euro on the admission fee).

★ **MACBA** ARTS CENTRE
(Museu d'Art Contemporani de Barcelona; Map p406; ☑ 93 412 08 10; www.macba.cat; Plaça dels Àngels 1; adult/concession/child under 14yr €10/8/free; ☺ 11am-7.30pm Mon & Wed-Fri, 10am-9pm Sat, 10am-3pm Sun & holidays; Ⓜ Universitat) Designed by Richard Meier and opened in

La Sagrada Família

A TIMELINE

1882 Construction begins on a neo-Gothic church designed by Francisco de Paula del Villar y Lozano.

1883 Antoni Gaudí takes over as chief architect and plans a far more ambitious church to hold 13,000 faithful.

1926 Gaudí dies; work continues under Domènec Sugrañes i Gras. Much of the **apse ❶** and **Nativity Facade ❷** is complete.

1930 Bell towers ❸ of the Nativity Facade completed.

1936 Construction is interrupted by Spanish Civil War; anarchists destroy Gaudí's plans.

1939–40 Architect Francesc de Paula Quintana i Vidal restores the crypt and meticulously reassembles many of Gaudí's lost models, some of which can be seen in the **museum ❹**.

1976 Passion Facade ❺ completed.

1986–2006 Sculptor Josep Subirachs adds sculptural details to the Passion Facade including the panels telling the story of Christ's last days, amid much criticism for employing a style far removed from what was thought typical of Gaudí.

2000 Central nave vault ❻ completed.

2010 Church completely roofed over; Pope Benedict XVI consecrates the church; work begins on a high-speed rail tunnel that will pass beneath the church's **Glory Facade ❼**.

2020s–40s Projected completion date.

TOP TIPS

➡ The best light through the stained-glass windows of the Passion Facade bursts into the heart of the church in the late afternoon.

➡ Visit at opening time on weekdays to avoid the worst of the crowds.

➡ Head up the Nativity Facade bell towers for the views, as long queues generally await at the Passion Facade towers.

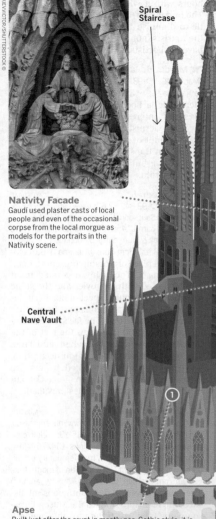

Spiral Staircase

Nativity Facade
Gaudí used plaster casts of local people and even of the occasional corpse from the local morgue as models for the portraits in the Nativity scene.

Central Nave Vault

KIEVVICTOR/SHUTTERSTOCK ©

Apse
Built just after the crypt in mostly neo-Gothic style, it is capped by pinnacles that show a hint of the genius that Gaudí would later deploy in the rest of the church.

STEFAN CIOATA/GETTY IMAGES ©

Bell Towers
The towers of the three facades will represent the 12 Apostles. Eight are completed. Lifts whisk visitors up one tower of the Nativity and Passion Facades (the latter gets longer queues) for fine views.

NIKADA/GETTY IMAGES ©

Completed Church
Along with the Glory Facade and its four towers, six other towers remain to be completed. They will represent the four Evangelists, the Virgin Mary and, soaring above them all over the transept, a 170m colossus symbolising Christ.

Glory Facade
This will be the most fanciful facade of all, with a narthex boasting 16 hyperboloid lanterns topped by cones that will look something like an organ made of melting ice cream.

Museu Gaudí
Jammed with old photos, drawings and restored plaster models that bring Gaudí's ambitions to life, the museum also houses an extraordinarily complex plumb-line device he used to calculate his constructions.

Escoles de Gaudí

Crypt
The first completed part of the church, the crypt is in largely neo-Gothic style and lies under the transept. Gaudí's burial place here can be seen from the Museu Gaudí.

FOTOKON/SHUTTERSTOCK ©

Passion Facade
See the story of Christ's last days from Last Supper to burial in an S-shaped sequence from bottom to top of the facade. Check out the cryptogram in which the numbers always add up to 33, Christ's age at his death.

YURY DMITRIENKO/SHUTTERSTOCK ©

Barcelona

1 km
0.5 miles

SANT MARTÍ

EL CLOT

CAMP DE L'ARPA

Clot

Encants

LA DRETA DE L'EIXAMPLE

Glòries

Plaça de les Glòries Catalanes

Av Meridiana

Plaça de les Arts

C dels Almogàvers

C de Pamplona

Bogatell

C de Zamora

C de Joan Miró

Parc de Carles I

Ciutadella Vila Olímpica

C de la Marina

C de Wellington

Pompeu Fabra

C de Universitat

Parc de la Ciutadella

Cascada

Pg de Pujades

Pg de

C del Comerç

Arc de Triomf

C d'Ali Bei

EL FORT PIENC

C de Nàpols

C de Sardenya

C de la Marina

Monumental

C de Padilla

C de Cartagena

C de Sant Pau / Dos de Maig

C de València

C de la Independència

C del Dos de Maig

GRÀCIA

EL GUINARDÓ

Alfons X

C de Lepant

C de la Marina

C de Sardenya

C de Sicília

C de Nàpols

C de Roger de Flor

C de l'Indústria

C de Sant Antoni Maria Claret

Sagrada Família

La Sagrada Família

SAGRADA FAMÍLIA

Av Diagonal

C del Consell de Cent

C de Mallorca

C del Rosselló

C de Còrsega

Verdaguer

Plaça de Mossèn Jacint Verdaguer

L'EIXAMPLE

Plaça de Tetuan

Tetuan

C d'Ausiàs Marc

C de Casp

C de la Diputació

Pg de Sant Joan

Girona

C del Bruc

C de Girona

C de Roger de Llúria

C de Pau Claris

Urquinaona

Catalunya

Plaça de Joan Carles I

Passeig de Gràcia

Casa Batlló

La Pedrera

Provença

Diagonal

C d'Aragó

C de la Marina

Pg de Sant Joan

Pg de Gràcia

C de Bailèn

C de Sardenya

C del Rosselló

C de Còrsega

Joanic

Verdaguer

Plaça del Diamant

Fontana

C de Verdi

C del Robí

C de l'Or

C de Sant Lluís

Plaça de la Virreina

C de Cal'Alegre de Dalt

C de l'Escorial

C de Martí

C de Sant Salvador

Travessera de Dalt

EL CARMEL

Park Güell (200m)

Vallcarca

Av de l'Hospital Militar

Plaça de Lesseps

Lesseps

SANT GERVASI DE CASSOLES

Av Tibidabo

C de Balmes

C de Muntaner

Ronda del General Mitre

Muntaner

Via Augusta

La Bonanova

Pàdua

Sant Gervasi

C de Vallirana

C de Saragossa

Plaça de la Torre

Molina

C d'Alfons XII

C de Tavern

C d'Amigó

C de Calvet

Av Diagonal

C de Balmes

C de Bori i Fontestà

Camp Nou (2km)

Travessera de les Corts

C de Loreto

C de Viladomat

C de Londres

C de París

C de Còrsega

C d'Aribau

C d'Enric Granados

C de Muntaner

C de Casanova

Hospital Clínic

C de València

C d'Enric Granados

C de Balmes

C d'Enric Granados

Travessera de Gràcia

Plaça de Raspall

Gràcia

Gran de Gràcia

Via Augusta

C de Tuset

C d'Aribau

C de Madrazo

C dels Madrazo

Plaça de Joan Carles I

C d'Aragó

C de Provença

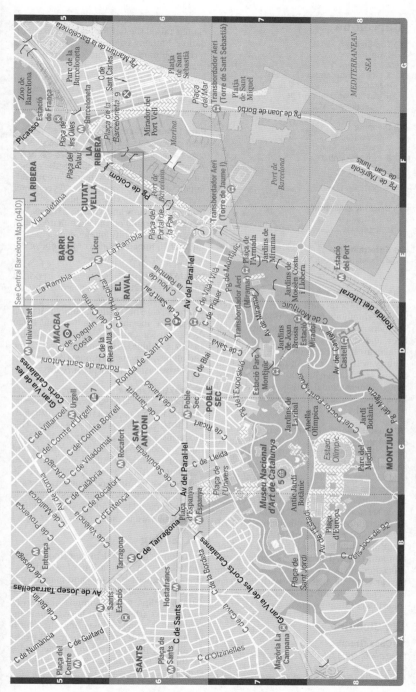

SPAIN & PORTUGAL BARCELONA

Barcelona

1995, MACBA has become the city's foremost contemporary art centre, with captivating exhibitions for the serious art lover. The permanent collection is on the ground floor and dedicates itself to Spanish and Catalan art from the second half of the 20th century, with works by Antoni Tàpies, Joan Brossa and Miquel Barceló, among others, though international artists, such as Paul Klee, Bruce Nauman and John Cage, are also represented.

★**Museu Nacional d'Art de Catalunya**   MUSEUM

(MNAC; Map p406; ☑ 93 622 03 76; www.museunacional.cat; Mirador del Palau Nacional; adult/child €12/free, after 3pm Sat & 1st Sun of month free, rooftop viewpoint only €2; ☉ 10am-8pm Tue-Sat, to 3pm Sun May-Sep, to 6pm Tue-Sat Oct-Apr; ☐ 55, Ⓜ Espanya) From across the city, the bombastic neobaroque silhouette of the Palau Nacional can be seen on the slopes of Montjuïc. Built for the 1929 World Exhibition and restored in 2005, it houses a vast collection of mostly Catalan art spanning the early Middle Ages to the early 20th century. The high point is the collection of extraordinary Romanesque frescoes.

🛏 Sleeping

★**Casa Gràcia**   HOSTEL $
(Map p406; ☑ 93 174 05 28; www.casagraciabcn.com; Passeig de Gràcia 116; dm/s/d/tr/apt from €31/106/120/147/194; ✷@ 🛜; Ⓜ Diagonal) A

hostel with a difference, the hip Casa Gràcia has raised the bar for budget accommodation. Enticing common spaces include a terrace, library nook and artistically decorated lounge as well as a fully equipped kitchen – not to mention a restaurant and DJ-fuelled bar. Dorms aside, there are private rooms and apartments with their own terraces.

Pars Tailor's Hostel   HOSTEL $
(Map p406; ☑ 93 250 56 84; www.parshostels.com; Carrer de Sepúlveda 146; dm €25-33; ✷🛜; Ⓜ Urgell) Decorated like a mid-20th-century tailor's shop, with rooms themed around different fabrics, this popular hostel's common areas have old sewing machines, lovingly framed brassieres and vintage fixtures. You can shoot a round on the old billiards table, hang out in the comfy lounge, cook a meal in the well-equipped kitchen, or join one of the activities on offer.

Pensió 2000   PENSION $
(Map p410; ☑ 93 310 74 66; www.pensio2000.com; Carrer de Sant Pere més Alt 6; d €70-80; ✷🛜; Ⓜ Urquinaona) This 1st-floor, family-run place is opposite the anything-but-simple Palau de la Música Catalana. Seven reasonably spacious doubles have mosaic-tiled floors, and all have private bathrooms. You can eat your breakfast in the little courtyard.

★**Praktik Rambla**   BOUTIQUE HOTEL $$
(Map p406; ☑ 93 343 66 90; www.hotelpraktikrambla.com; Rambla de Catalunya 27; s/d/tr from €119/140/165; ✷🛜; Ⓜ Passeig de Gràcia) This Modernista gem hides a gorgeous little boutique number. While the high ceilings and most of the original tile floors have been maintained, the 43 rooms have bold ceramics, spot lighting and contemporary art. There's a chilled reading area and deck-style lounge terrace. The handy location on a tree-lined boulevard is another plus.

🍽 Eating

Barcelona has a celebrated food scene fuelled by a combination of world-class chefs, imaginative recipes and magnificent ingredients fresh from farms and the sea. Catalan culinary masterminds like Ferran Adrià and Carles Abellan have become international icons, reinventing the world of haute cuisine, while classic old-world Catalan recipes continue to earn accolades in dining rooms and tapas bars across the city.

La Cova Fumada
TAPAS **$**

(Map p406; ☑ 93 221 40 61; Carrer del Baluard 56; tapas €4-12; ☉ 9am-3.15pm Mon-Wed, 9am-3.15pm & 6-8.15pm Thu & Fri, 9am-1pm Sat; Ⓜ Barceloneta) There's no sign and the setting is decidedly downmarket, but this tiny, buzzing family-run tapas spot always packs in a crowd. The secret? Mouthwatering *pulpo* (octopus), calamari, sardines, *bombas* (meat and potato croquettes served with alioli) and grilled *carxofes* (artichokes) cooked in the open kitchen. Everything is amazingly fresh.

Bormuth
TAPAS **$**

(Map p410; ☑ 93 310 21 86; Carrer del Rec 31; tapas €4-10; ☉ noon-1.30am Sun-Thu, to 2.30am Fri & Sat; ☏; Ⓜ Jaume I) Bormuth has tapped into the vogue for old-school tapas with modern-day service and decor, and serves all the old favourites – *patatas bravas, ensaladilla* (Russian salad) and tortilla – along with some less predictable and superbly prepared numbers (try the chargrilled red pepper with black pudding).

Can Culleretes
CATALAN **$$**

(Map p410; ☑ 93 317 30 22; www.culleretes.com; Carrer d'en Quintana 5; mains €10-18; ☉ 1.30-3.45pm & 8-10.45pm Tue-Sat, 1.30-3.45pm Sun; ☏; Ⓜ Liceu) Founded in 1786, Barcelona's oldest restaurant is still going strong, with tourists and locals flocking here to enjoy its rambling interior, old-fashioned tile-filled decor and enormous helpings of traditional Catalan food, including fresh seafood and sticky stews. From Tuesday to Friday there is a fixed lunch menu for €14.50.

★ La Vinateria del Call
SPANISH **$$**

(Map p410; ☑ 93 302 60 92; www.lavinateriadelcall.com; Carrer de Sant Domènec del Call 9; raciones €7-12; ☉ 7.30pm-1am; ☏; Ⓜ Jaume I) In a magical setting in the former Jewish quarter, this tiny jewel box of a restaurant serves up tasty Iberian dishes including Galician octopus, cider-cooked chorizo and the Catalan *escalivada* (roasted peppers, aubergine and onions) with anchovies. Portions are small and made for sharing, and there's a good and affordable selection of wines.

Suculent
CATALAN **$$$**

(Map p410; ☑ 93 443 65 79; www.suculent.com; Rambla del Raval 43; tasting menus €45-75; ☉ 1-4pm & 8-11.30pm Wed-Sun; ☏; Ⓜ Liceu) Celebrity chef Carles Abellan adds to his stable with this old-style bistro, which showcases the best of Catalan cuisine. From the cod brandade to the oxtail stew with truffled sweet potato, only the best ingredients are used. There is no à la carte, just four different tasting menus to choose from.

🍷 Drinking & Nightlife

Barcelona is a nightlife-lovers' town, with an enticing school taverns, stylish lounges and kaleidoscopic nightclubs where the party continues until daybreak. For something a little more sedate, the city's atmospheric cafes and teahouses make a fine retreat when the skies turn grey.

★ La Confitería
BAR

(Map p406; ☑ 93 140 54 35; Carrer de Sant Pau 128; ☉ 7pm-2.30am Mon-Thu, 6pm-3am Fri & Sat, 5pm-2.30am Sun; ☏; Ⓜ Paral·lel) This is a trip into the 19th century. Until the 1980s it was a confectioner's shop, and although the original cabinets are now lined with booze, the look of the place barely changed with its conversion. A recent refurb of the back room is similarly sympathetic, and the vibe these days is lively cocktail bar.

★ Rabipelao
COCKTAIL BAR

(Map p406; ☑ 93 182 50 35; www.elrabipelao.com; Carrer del Torrent d'En Vidalet 22; ☉ 7pm-1.30am Sun-Thu, to 3am Fri & Sat, 1-4.30pm Sun; Ⓜ Joanic) An anchor of Gràcia's nightlife, Rabipelao is a celebratory space with a shiny disco ball and DJs spinning salsa beats. A silent film plays in one corner beyond the red velvety wallpaper-covered walls and there's a richly hued mural above the bar. Tropical cocktails like mojitos and caipirinhas pair with South American snacks such as *arepas* (meat-filled cornbread patties) and ceviche (fish cured in citrus).

Marula Café
BAR

(Map p410; ☑ 93 318 76 90; www.marulacafe.com; Carrer dels Escudellers 49; cover up to €10; ☉ 11pm-5am Mon-Thu & Sun, 11.30pm-6am Fri, 9.30pm-6am Sat; Ⓜ Liceu) A fantastic find situated right in the heart of the Barri Gòtic, Marula will transport you back to the 1970s and the best in funk and soul. James Brown fans will think they've died and gone to heaven. It's not, however, a mono-thematic place and DJs slip in other tunes, from breakbeat to house. Samba and other Brazilian dance sounds also penetrate here.

Central Barcelona

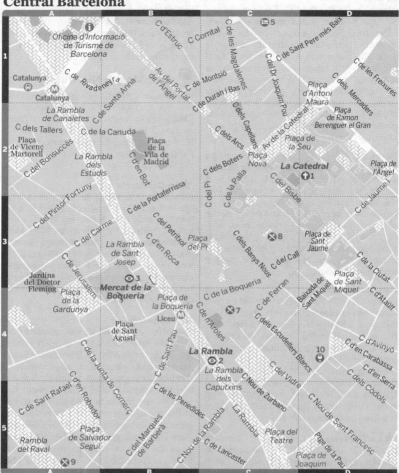

☆ Entertainment

Camp Nou FOOTBALL
(☎902 189900; www.fcbarcelona.com; Carrer d'Arístides Maillol; Ⓜ Palau Reial) The stadium of Camp Nou ('New Field' in Catalan) is home to the Futbol Club Barcelona. Attending a game is an unforgettable experience; the season runs from September to May. Alternatively, get a taste of all the excitement at the **Camp Nou Experience** (Gate 9, Avinguda de Joan XXIII; adult/child €25/20; ⊙9.30am-7.30pm Apr-Sep, 10am-6.30pm Mon-Sat, to 2.30pm Sun Oct-Mar; Ⓜ Palau Reial), which includes a tour of the stadium.

★ Palau de la Música Catalana CLASSICAL MUSIC
(Map p406; ☎93 295 72 00; www.palaumusica.cat; Carrer de Palau de la Música 4-6; tickets from €18; ⊙box office 9.30am-9pm Mon-Sat, 10am-3pm Sun; Ⓜ Urquinaona) A feast for the eyes, this Modernista confection is also the city's most traditional venue for classical and choral music, although it has a wide-ranging program, including flamenco, pop and – particularly – jazz. Just being here for a performance is an experience. In the foyer, its tiled pillars all a-glitter, sip a pre-concert tipple.

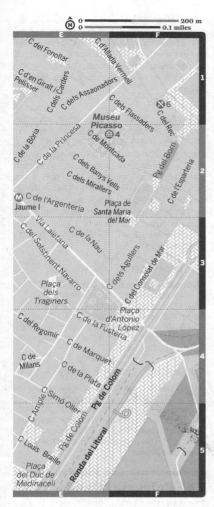

Europe. Some budget carriers use Girona and Reus airports (buses link Barcelona to both).

Long-distance trains arrive in **Estació Sants**, about 2.5km west of La Rambla. There are direct overnight trains from Paris, Geneva, Milan and Zürich. Fast train connections to Madrid run 18 times daily, some taking under three hours.

Long-haul buses arrive in **Estació del Nord**. A plethora of companies services different parts of Spain; many come under the umbrella of **Alsa** (✆ 902 422242; www.alsa.es). Eurolines and other operators service various European cities.

ⓘ Getting Around

From the airport, frequent buses make the 35-minute run into town (€5.90) from 6am to 1am.

The excellent metro can get you most places around town, with buses and trams filling in the gaps. Targeta T-10 (10-ride passes; €10.20) are the best value; otherwise it's €2.15 per ride.

Girona
POP 94,300

Northern Catalonia's largest city is a jewellery box of museums, galleries and Gothic churches, strung around a tangle of cobbled lanes and medieval walls. Reflections of Modernista mansions shimmer in the Riu Onyar, which demarcates the historic centre on its right bank from the gleaming commercial centre on the left.

◎ Sights

★ **Catedral de Girona**　　CATHEDRAL
(www.catedraldegirona.org; Plaça de la Catedral; adult/student incl Basílica de Sant Feliu €7/5; ⊙10am-7.30pm Jul & Aug, to 6.30pm Apr-Jun, Sep &

ⓘ Information

Oficina d'Informació de Turisme de Barcelona (Map p410; ✆ 93 285 38 34; www.barcelonaturisme.com; Plaça de Catalunya 17-S, underground; ⊙8.30am-9pm; Ⓜ Catalunya) Provides maps, sights information, tours, concert and events tickets, and last-minute accommodation.

ⓘ Getting There & Away

After Madrid, Barcelona is Spain's busiest international transport hub. A host of airlines, including many budget carriers, fly directly to **Barcelona airport** (✆ 902 404704; www.aena.es) from around

SPAIN & PORTUGAL GIRONA

Oct, to 5.30pm Nov–Mar) Towering over a flight of 86 steps rising from Plaça de la Catedral, Girona's imposing cathedral is far more ancient than its billowing baroque facade suggests. Built over an old Roman forum, parts of its foundations date from the 5th century. Today, 14th-century Gothic styling – added over an 11th-century Romanesque church – dominates, though a double-columned Romanesque **cloister** dates from the 12th century. With the world's second-widest Gothic nave, it's a formidable sight to explore, but audio guides are provided.

★**Museu d'Història dels Jueus**   MUSEUM
(www.girona.cat/call; Carrer de la Força 8; adult/child €4/free; ☉10am-8pm Mon-Sat & 10am-2pm Sun Jul & Aug, 10am-2pm Mon & Sun, 10am-6pm Tue-Sat Sep–Jun) Until 1492, Girona was home to Catalonia's second most important medieval Jewish community (after Barcelona), and one of the country's finest Jewish quarters. This excellent museum takes pride in Girona's Jewish heritage, without shying away from less salubrious aspects such as Inquisition persecution and forced conversions. You also see a rare 11th-century *miqvé* (ritual bath) and a 13th-century Jewish house.

🛏 Sleeping & Eating

Pensió Viladomat   PENSION $
(☑972 20 31 76; www.pensioviladomat.cat; Carrer dels Ciutadans 5; d/tr €53/72, s/d without bath-

room €24/42; ⊚) One of the nicest of the cheaper *pensiones* (small private hotels) that are dotted around the southern end of the old town, Pensió Viladomat has simple, modernised, well-maintained rooms, some of which have a balcony, and a friendly welcome.

Nu   CATALAN $$
(☑972 22 52 30; www.nurestaurant.cat; Carrer dels Abeuradors 4; mains €14-20; ☉8.15-10.30pm Mon, 1.15-3.30pm & 8.15-10.30pm Tue-Sat; ⊚) Sleek and confident, this beautiful, contemporary old-town spot has innovative, top-notch plates prepared in view by a friendly team. Catalan-Asian flavour fusions keep things exciting: sample red-tuna sashimi with soy, beef tenderloin in Iberian-ham sauce, or squid-ink rice with poached egg. Considering the high level of culinary quality, it's excellent value.

ℹ Information

Oficina de Turisme de Girona (☑972 22 65 75; www.girona.cat/turisme; Rambla de la Llibertat 1; ☉9am-8pm Mon-Fri, 9am-2pm & 4-8pm Sat Apr-Oct, 9am-7pm Mon-Fri, 9am-2pm & 3-7pm Sat Nov-Mar, 9am-2pm Sun year round) Multilingual and helpful tourist information spot by the river.

ℹ Getting There & Away

Girona is on the train line between Barcelona (€10 to €31, 40 minutes to 1¼ hours, at least half-hourly), Figueres (€4.10 to €6.90, 30 to 40 minutes, at least half-hourly) and Portbou, on the French border (€6.15 to €8.25, one hour, 11 to 15 daily). There are several through trains to France and beyond.

SPLURGE

Ever-changing avant-garde takes on Catalan dishes have catapulted **El Celler de Can Roca** (☑972 22 21 57; www.cellercanroca.com; Carrer Can Sunyer 48; degustation menus €180-205; ☉12.30-2pm Tue, 12.30-2pm & 8-9.30pm Wed-Sat, closed late Dec–mid-Jan & 10 days late Aug) to global fame. Holding three Michelin stars, it was named the best restaurant in the world in 2015 by The World's 50 Best. Each year brings new innovations, from molecular gastronomy and multi-sensory food-art interplay to sci-fi dessert trolleys, all with mama's home-cooking as the core inspiration.

Run by the three Girona-born Roca brothers, El Celler is set in a refurbished country house, 2km northwest of central Girona. Book online 11 months in advance or join the standby list.

The Balearic Islands

The Balearic Islands (Illes Balears in Catalan) adorn the glittering Mediterranean waters off Spain's eastern coastline. Beach tourism destinations par excellence, each of the islands has a quite distinct identity and they have managed to retain much of their individual character and beauty. All boast beaches second to none in the Med, but each offers reasons for exploring inland, too.

ℹ Getting There & Around

In summer, charter and regular flights converge on Palma de Mallorca and Ibiza from all over Europe.

Ferries are the other main way of getting to and between the islands. Barcelona, Dénia, Gandia and Valencia are the principal mainland ports. Check www.directferries.com for all routes. Ferry service operators include the following:

Trasmediterránea (☎902 454645; www. trasmediterranea.es)

Baleària (☎902 16 01 80; www.balearia.com)

Mallorca

The sunny, warm hues of the medieval heart of Palma de Mallorca, the archipelago's capital, make a great introduction to the islands. The northwest coast, dominated by the Serra de Tramuntana mountain range, is a beautiful region of olive groves, pine forests and ochre villages, with a spectacularly rugged coastline. Most of Mallorca's best beaches are on the north and east coasts, and although many have been swallowed up

DON'T MISS

ON THE DALÍ TRAIL

Figueres and the lovely seaside town of Cadaqués, easily accessible by train and bus respectively from Girona, have two excellent attractions intimately connected with the master artist and showman Salvador Dalí.

by tourist developments, you can still find the occasional exception.

PALMA DE MALLORCA
POP 400,578

Nestled in the crook of the Badia de Palma, Mallorca's capital is among the most agreeable of all Mediterranean towns. Shaped and defined by the sea and backed by not-so-distant mountains, it is a city of open horizons, oft-blue skies and a festive nature.

Mallorca

Alhambra

A TIMELINE

900 The first reference to *al-qala'a al-hamra* (the Red Castle) atop Granada's Sabika Hill.

1237 Founder of the Nasrid dynasty, Mohammed I, moves his court to Granada. Threatened by belligerent Christian armies he builds a new defensive fort, the ① **Alcazaba**.

1302–09 Designed as a summer palace-cum-country estate for Granada's foppish rulers, the bucolic ② **Generalife** is begun by Mohammed III.

1333–54 Yusuf I initiates the construction of the ③ **Palacios Nazaríes**, still considered the highpoint of Islamic culture in Europe.

1350–60 Up goes the ④ **Palacio de Comares**, taking Nasrid lavishness to a whole new level.

1362–91 The second coming of Mohammed V ushers in even greater architectural brilliance, exemplified by the construction of the ⑤ **Patio de los Leones**.

1527 The Christians add the ⑥ **Palacio de Carlos V**. Inspired Renaissance palace or incongruous crime against Moorish art? You decide.

1829 The languishing, half-forgotten Alhambra is 'rediscovered' by American writer Washington Irving during a protracted sleep-over.

1954 The Generalife gardens are extended southwards to accommodate an outdoor theatre.

TOP TIPS

➡ Reserve tickets either by phoning 858 95 36 16 or online http://alhambra-patronato.es

➡ http://alhambra-patronato.es'You can visit the general areas of the palace free of charge any time by entering through the Puerta de la Justicia.

➡ Two fine hotels are housed on the grounds if you wish to stay over: Parador de Granada (pricey) and Hotel América (more economical).

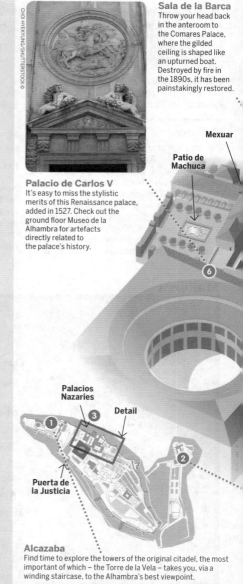

Sala de la Barca
Throw your head back in the anteroom to the Comares Palace, where the gilded ceiling is shaped like an upturned boat. Destroyed by fire in the 1890s, it has been painstakingly restored.

CHO HYEKYUNG/SHUTTERSTOCK ©

Palacio de Carlos V
It's easy to miss the stylistic merits of this Renaissance palace, added in 1527. Check out the ground floor Museo de la Alhambra for artefacts directly related to the palace's history.

Mexuar

Patio de Machuca

Palacios Nazaríes

Detail

Puerta de la Justicia

Alcazaba
Find time to explore the towers of the original citadel, the most important of which – the Torre de la Vela – takes you, via a winding staircase, to the Alhambra's best viewpoint.

EMPERORCOSAR/SHUTTERSTOCK ©

Palacio de Comares

The neck-ache continues in the largest room in the Comares Palace, renowned for its rich geometric ceiling. A negotiating room for the emirs, the Salón de los Embajadores is a masterpiece of Moorish design.

Patio de los Arrayanes

If only you could linger longer beside the rows of *arrayanes* (myrtle bushes) that border this calming rectangular pool. Shaded porticos with seven harmonious arches invite further contemplation.

Salón de los Embajadores

④

Patio de los Arrayanes

Baños Reales

Washington Irving Apartments

Sala de Dos Hermanas

Focus on the *dos hermanas* – two marble slabs either side of the fountain – before enjoying the intricate cupola embellished with 5000 tiny moulded stalactites. Poetic calligraphy decorates the walls.

Patio de la Lindaraja

⑤

Sala de los Reyes

Patio del Partal

Sala de los Abencerrajes

Jardines del Partal

Palacio del Partal

Generalife

A coda to most people's visits, the 'architect's garden' is no afterthought. While Nasrid in origin, the horticulture is relatively new: the pools and arcades were added in the early 20th century.

Patio de los Leones

Count the 12 lions sculpted from marble, holding up a gurgling fountain. Then pan back and take in the delicate columns and arches built to signify an Islamic vision of paradise.

◉ Sights

★ Catedral de Mallorca
CATHEDRAL

(La Seu; www.catedraldemallorca.org; Carrer del Palau Reial 9; adult/child €7/free; ⊙10am-6.15pm Mon-Fri Jun-Sep, to 5.15pm Apr, May & Oct, to 3.15pm Nov-Mar, 10am-2.15pm Sat year-round) Palma's vast cathedral ('La Seu' in Catalan) is the city's major architectural landmark. Aside from its sheer scale and undoubted beauty, its stunning interior features, designed by Antoni Gaudí and renowned contemporary artist Miquel Barceló, make this unlike any cathedral elsewhere in the world. The awesome structure is predominantly Gothic, apart from the main facade, which is startling, quite beautiful and completely mongrel.

★ Palau de l'Almudaina
PALACE

(https://entradas.patrimonionacional.es; Carrer del Palau Reial; adult/child €7/4, audio guide €3, guided tour €4; ⊙10am-8pm Tue-Sun Apr-Sep, to 6pm Oct-Mar) Originally an Islamic fort, this mighty construction opposite the cathedral was converted into a residence for the Mallorcan monarchs at the end of the 13th century. The King of Spain resides here still, at least symbolically. The royal family are rarely in residence, except for the occasional ceremony, as they prefer to spend summer in the Palau Marivent (in Cala Major). At other times you can wander through a series of cavernous stone-walled rooms that have been lavishly decorated.

★ Es Baluard
GALLERY

(Museu d'Art Modern i Contemporani; ☑971 90 82 00; www.esbaluard.org; Plaça de Porta de Santa Catalina 10; adult/temporary exhibitions/child €6/4/free; ⊙10am-8pm Tue-Sat, to 3pm Sun) Built with flair and innovation into the shell of the Renaissance-era seaward walls, this contemporary art gallery is one of the finest on the island. Its temporary exhibitions are worth viewing, but the permanent collection – works by Miró, Barceló and Picasso – give the gallery its cachet. Entry on Fridays is by donation, and anyone turning up on a bike, on any day, is charged just €2.

★ Museu Fundación Juan March
GALLERY

(☑97 171 35 15; www.march.es; Carrer de Sant Miquel 11; ⊙10am-6.30pm Mon-Fri, 10.30am-2pm Sat) FREE The 17th-century Can Gallard del Canya, a 17th-century mansion overlaid with minor Modernist touches, now houses a small but significant collection of painting and sculpture. The permanent exhibits – some 80 pieces held by the Fundación Juan March –

constitute a veritable who's who of contemporary Spanish art, including Miró, Picasso, fellow cubist Juan Gris, Dalí, and the sculptors Eduardo Chillida and Julio González.

🛏 Sleeping & Eating

Hostal Apuntadores
HOTEL $

(☑971 71 34 91; www.palma-hostales.com; Carrer dels Apuntadors 8; s/d €50/55; ❄@🛜) Just off the main drag (bring earplugs, or ask for a quieter rear room), this unfussy spot makes up for smallish rooms and lumpy beds with balconies overlooking Plaça de la Reina (in some rooms) lots of sunlight and a rooftop terrace with cathedral views. Drinks and breakfast are available from the cafe.

Bar Bodega Morey
TAPAS $

(☑634 673351; Carrer d'en Morei 4; tapas €3; ⊙7.30am-4.30pm Mon-Fri) As Palma's food evolution races ahead, and the tourist dollars keep pouring in, it's reassuring to find places still giving the locals what they've long loved, at very decent prices.This whitewashed, timber-floored hole-in-the-wall just deals in classics – tortilla, *albondigas* (meatballs), *pulpo* (octopus) – but nails them without fuss. Great for a coffee or draught beer, too.

Restaurant Celler Sa Premsa
MALLORCAN $

(☑971 72 35 29; www.cellersapremsa.com; Plaça del Bisbe Berenguer de Palou 8; mains €9-14, menús €14; ⊙12.30-4pm & 7.30-11.30pm Mon-Sat Sep-Jun, Mon-Fri Jul & Aug) A visit to this local institution, going strong since 1958, is almost obligatory. It's a cavernous tavern filled with huge old wine barrels and faded bullfighting posters – you find plenty of these places in the Mallorcan interior but they're a dying breed here in Palma. Mallorcan specialities dominate the menu.

ℹ Information

Consell de Mallorca Tourist Office (☑971 17 39 90; www.infomallorca.net; Plaça de la Reina 2; ⊙8.30am-6pm Mon-Fri, to 3pm Sat; 🛜) Covers the whole island.

Municipal Tourist Office (☑902 102365; www.infomallorca.net; Plaça d'Espanya; ⊙9am-8pm) In one of the railway buildings off Plaça d'Espanya.

AROUND MALLORCA

Mallorca's northwestern coast is a world away from the high-rise tourism on the other side of the island. Dominated by the Serra de Tramuntana, it's a beautiful region of olive groves, pine forests and small

Menorca

10 km
5 miles

Barcelona
(256km)

Palma de
Mallorca (187km);
Ibiza (282km);
Valencia (417km)

Cap de
Favàritx
Cala Presili
Platja d'en Tortuga
Illa
d'en Colom
Es Grau
Cala
Mesquida
Golden Farm Cap Negre
Collingwood House
Es Freus
Fortalesa de la Mola
Castell San Felipe
Cala de
Sant Esteve
Fort
Sant Marlborough
Platja de
Punta Prima

Parc Natural
S'Albufera
d'es Grau

Maó
Es Castell
Bodegas
Binifadet
Sant
Lluís

ME7

ME5

ME6

Far de
Cavalleria
Ecomuseu Cap
de Cavalleria
Cap de
Cavalleria
Cala
Pregonda
Platja
Cavalleria

Fornells
Platges de
Fornells

ME15

Cala en
Culderrer

Monte
El Toro
(357m)

Alaior

Talatí
de Dalt
Sant
Climent
Llucmaçanes
Aeropuerto
de Menorca
Cap de
Binidalí
Binibèquer

Cala de
Binidalí

ME1

Torralba
d'en Salord

Torre d'en
Galmés

Cala'n
Porter

Cales
Coves

Es Canutells
Cova
d'en
Xoroi

Es Mercadal

ME16
ME18
Es Migjorn
Gran

ME20

Son Bou

Ferreries

ME22

Cala
Mitjana
Cala
Galdana
Cala
Macarella
Arenal de
Son
Saura
Cala es
Talaier
Cala
Turqueta

Cap
Gros
Cala
d'Algaiarens

Cala
Morell

Naveta des
Tudons

Son
Catlar

Santandria
Cala en
Bosc
Platja de
Son Xoriguer

Ciutadella

Cala Blanca

Cap
d'Artrutx

Cala Ratjada (41km);
Port d'Alcúdia (63km)

FORMENTERA

If Ibiza is the party queen, her little sister, Formentera (population 12,120), is the shy, natural beauty, who prefers barefoot beach strolls by starlight to all-night raving in superclubs. Dangling off the south coast of Ibiza, a mere half an hour away by fast ferry, this 20km-long island is a place of lazy days spent lounging on some of Europe's (dare we say the world's?) most ravishing beaches.

Nowhere is the lure of the sea more powerful in the Balearics than here, where enticing, frost-white slivers of sand are smoothed by water in unbelievable shades of azure, turquoise and lapis lazuli that will have you itching to leap in the moment you step off the boat. Ask people what they've done for the week here and watch them shrug their shoulders, shake the last sand out of their shoes, grin and reply: 'Nothing, it was awesome.'

villages with shuttered stone buildings. There are a couple of highlights for drivers: the hair-raising road down to the small port of Sa Calobra, and the amazing trip along the peninsula leading to the island's northern tip, Cap Formentor.

Menorca

Renowned for its pristine beaches and archaeological sites, tranquil Menorca was declared a Biosphere Reserve by Unesco in 1993.

Maó absorbs most of the tourist traffic. North of Maó, a drive across a lunar landscape leads to the lighthouse at Cap de Favàritx. South of the cape stretch some fine sandy bays and beaches, including Cala Presili and Platja d'en Tortuga, reachable on foot. Ciutadella, with its smaller harbour and historic buildings, has a more distinctly Spanish feel to it and is the more attractive of the island's two main towns. A narrow country road leads south of Ciutadella (follow the 'Platges' sign from the *ronda*, or ring road) and then forks twice to reach some of the island's loveliest beaches: (from west to east) Arenal de Son Saura, Cala en Turqueta, Es Talaier, Cala Macarelleta and

Cala Macarella. As with most beaches, you'll need your own transport. In the centre of the island, the 357m-high Monte Toro has great views; on a clear day you can see Mallorca. On the northern coast, the picturesque town of Fornells is on a large bay popular with windsurfers. The ports in both Maó and Ciutadella are lined with bars and restaurants.

Ibiza

Ibiza (Eivissa in Catalan) is an island of extremes. Its formidable party reputation is completely justified, with some of the world's greatest clubs attracting hedonists from across the world. The interior and northeast of the island, however, are another world. Peaceful country drives, hilly green territory, a sprinkling of mostly laid-back beaches and coves, and some wonderful inland accommodation and eateries are light years from the ecstasy-fuelled madness of the clubs that dominate the west.

IBIZA TOWN
POP 49,320

Ibiza's capital is a vivacious, enchanting town with a captivating whitewashed old quarter topped by a cathedral. It's also a focal point for some of the island's best cafes, bars and clubs.

⊙ Sights

★ **Dalt Vila**   OLD TOWN
Its formidable, floodlit, 16th-century bastions visible from across southern Ibiza, Dalt Vila is a fortified hilltop first settled by the Phoenicans and later occupied by a roster of subsequent civilisations. Tranquil and atmospheric, many of its cobbled lanes are accessible only on foot. It's mostly a residential area, but contains moody medieval mansions and several key cultural sights. Enter via the **Portal de Ses Taules** gateway and wind your way uphill: all lanes lead to the cathedral-topped summit.

🛏 Sleeping & Eating

Many of Ibiza City's hotels and *hostales* are closed in the low season and heavily booked between April and October. Make sure you book ahead.

★ **Comidas Bar San Juan**   SPANISH $
(📞 971 31 16 03; Carrer de Guillem de Montgrí 8; mains €7-11; ⏰ 1-3.30pm & 8.30-11pm Mon-Sat)

Ibiza

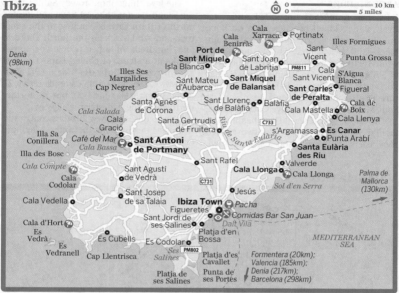

More traditional than trendy, this popular family-run operation, with two small dining rooms, harks back to the days before Ibiza became a byword for glam. It offers outstanding value, with fish dishes and steaks for around €10, plus omelettes, salads, croquettes, cheese platters and other local favourites. No reservations, so arrive early and expect to share your table.

🍷 Drinking & Nightlife

Sa Penya is the nightlife centre. Dozens of bars keep the port area jumping from sunset until the early hours. Alternatively, various bars at Platja d'en Bossa combine sounds, sand and sea with sangria and other tipples. After they wind down, you can continue at one of the island's world-famous nightclubs.

★ Pacha
CLUB
(www.pachaibiza.com; Avinguda 8 d'Agost; admission from €20; ⊗ midnight-6.30am May-Sep) Going strong since 1973, Pacha is Ibiza's original megaclub and the islanders' party venue of choice. It's built around the shell of a farmhouse, boasting a multilevel main dance floor, a Funky Room (for soul and disco beats), a huge VIP section and myriad other places to dance or lounge.

ℹ Information

Oficina d'Informació Turística (☑ 971 30 19 00; http://ibiza.travel; Avinguda de Santa Eulària; ⊗ 9am-8pm Mon-Sat, to 3pm Sun, reduced hours mid-Oct–Apr) Island-wide and Ibiza Town info. Next to the Formentera ferry terminal.

CLUBBING IN IBIZA

From late May to the end of September, the west of the island is one big, nonstop dance party from sunset to sunrise and back again. The major clubs operate nightly from around midnight to 6am from mid-May or June to early October. Theme nights, fancy-dress parties and foam parties are regular features. Entertainment Ibiza-style doesn't come cheaply. Admission can cost anything from €20 to €65 (mixed drinks and cocktails then go for around €10 to €15).

Taxis are notorious for overcharging clubbers so use the **Discobus** (www.discobus.es; ⊗ midnight-6am Jun-Sep), which does an all-night whirl of the major clubs, bars and hotels.

AROUND IBIZA

Ibiza has numerous unspoiled and relatively undeveloped beaches. Cala de Boix, on the northeastern coast, is the only black-sand beach that is on the island, while further north are the lovely beaches of S'Aigua Blanca. On the north coast near Portinatx, Cala Xarraca is located in a picturesque, secluded bay, and near Port de Sant Miquel is the attractive Cala Benirrás. In the southwest, Cala d'Hort has a spectacular setting that overlooks two rugged rock islets, Es Verda and Es Verdranell.

The best thing about rowdy Sant Antoni, the island's second-biggest town and located north of Ibiza City, is heading to the small rock-and-sand strip on the north shore to join hundreds of other people for sunset drinks at a string of chilled bars. The best known remains **Café del Mar** (☑971 80 37 58; www.cafedelmaribiza.es; Carrer de Lepant 27; ◷5pm-midnight May–mid-Oct), but it's further north along the pedestrian walkway.

Local buses (www.ibizabus.com) run to most destinations between May and October.

Valencia City

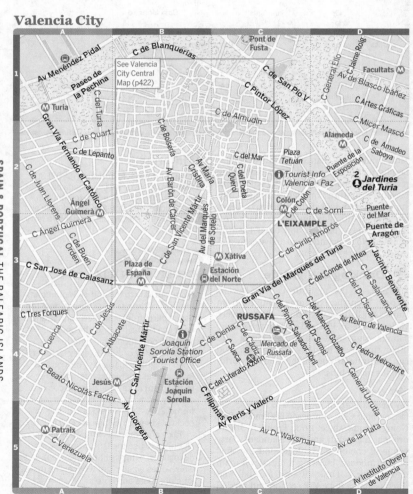

Valencia

POP 790,200

Spain's third-largest city is a magnificent place, content for Madrid and Barcelona to grab the headlines while it gets on with being a wonderfully liveable city with thriving cultural, eating and nightlife scenes. Never afraid to innovate, Valencia diverted its flood-prone river to the outskirts of town and converted the former riverbed into a superb green ribbon of park winding right through the city. On it are the strik-

ingly futuristic buildings of the Ciudad de las Artes y las Ciencias, designed by local boy Santiago Calatrava. The city also has great museums and a large, characterful old quarter. Valencia, surrounded by its *huerta,* a fertile fruit-and-veg farmland, is famous as the home of rice dishes like paella but its buzzy dining scene offers plenty more besides.

◉ Sights

★**La Lonja** HISTORIC BUILDING
(Map p422; ☑ 962 08 41 53; www.valencia.es; Calle de la Lonja; adult/child €2/1, Sun free; ☺ 10am-7pm Mon-Sat, to 2pm Sun) This splendid building, a Unesco World Heritage site, was originally Valencia's silk and commodity exchange, built in the late 15th century when the city was booming. It's one of Spain's finest examples of a civil Gothic building. Two main structures flank a citrus-studded courtyard: the magnificent Sala de Contratación, a cathedral of commerce with soaring twisted pillars, and the Consulado del Mar, where a maritime tribunal sat. The top floor boasts a stunning coffered ceiling brought here from another building.

Mercado Central MARKET
(Map p422; ☑ 963 82 91 00; www.mercadocentralvalencia.es; Plaza del Mercado; ☺ 7.30am-3pm Mon-Sat) Valencia's vast Modernista covered market, constructed in 1928, is a swirl of

SPAIN & PORTUGAL VALENCIA

Valencia City Central

smells, movement and colour. Spectacular seafood counters display cephalopods galore and numerous fish species, meat stalls groan under the weight of sausages and giant steaks, while the fruit and vegetables, many produced locally in Valencia's *huerta*, are of special quality. A tapas bar lets you sip wine and enjoy the atmosphere.

★ **Catedral de Valencia** CATHEDRAL
(Map p422; ☎ 963 91 81 27; www.catedraldevalencia.es; Plaza de la Virgen; adult/child incl

audio guide €7/5.50; ⊙10am-6.30pm Mon-Sat, 2-6.30pm Sun Jun-Sep, to 5.30pm Oct-May, closed Sun Nov-Feb) Valencia's cathedral was built over a mosque after the 1238 reconquest. Its low, wide, brick-vaulted triple nave is mostly Gothic, with neoclassical side chapels. Highlights include its **museum**, rich Italianate frescoes above the altarpiece, a pair of Goyas in the Capilla de San Francisco de Borja, and...ta-da...in the flamboyant Gothic Capilla del Santo Cáliz, what's claimed to be the Holy Grail from which Christ sipped during the Last Supper. It's a Roman-era agate cup, later modified, so at least the date is right.

⭐**Jardines del Turia** PARK
(Map p420; 🌐) Stretching the length of Río Turia's former course, this 9km-long green lung is a fabulous mix of playing fields, cycling, jogging and walking paths, lawns and playgrounds. Because it curves around the eastern part of the city, it's also a pleasant way of getting around. See Lilliputian kids scrambling over a magnificent, ever-patient **Gulliver** (Map p420; ⊙10am-8pm Sep-Jun, 10am-2pm & 5-9pm Jul & Aug; 🌐; 🚌19, 95) south of the Palau de la Música.

⭐**Ciudad de las Artes
y las Ciencias** ARCHITECTURE
(City of Arts & Sciences; Map p420; 📞961 97 46 86; www.cac.es; Avenida del Profesor López Piñero; 🌐) This aesthetically stunning complex occupies a massive 350,000-sq-metre swath of the old Turia riverbed. It's occupied by a series of spectacular buildings that are mostly the work of world-famous, local-

ly born architect Santiago Calatrava. The principal buildings are a majestic **opera house** (Map p420; 📞tours 672 062523; www.lesarts.com; Avenida del Professor López Piñero 1; guided visit adult/child €10.60/8.10; ⊙guided visits 10.45am, noon & 1.30pm daily, plus 3.45pm & 5pm Mon-Sat), a **science museum** (Map p420; 📞961 97 47 86; www.cac.es; Ciudad de las Artes y las Ciencias; adult/child €8/6.20, with Hemisfèric €12.60/9.60; ⊙10am-6pm or 7pm mid-Sep–Jun, 10am-9pm Jul–mid-Sep; 🌐), a **3D cinema** (Map p420; 📞961 97 46 86; www.cac.es; sessions adult/child €8.80/6.85, with Museo de las Ciencias Príncipe Felipe €12.60/9.60; ⊙from 10am) and an **aquarium** (Map p420; 📞960 47 06 47; www.oceanografic.org; Camino de las Moreras; adult/child €29.10/21.85, audio guide €3.70, combined ticket with Hemisfèric & Museo de las Ciencias Príncipe Felipe €37.40/28.40; ⊙10am-6pm Sun-Fri, 10am-8pm Sat mid-Sep–mid-Jun, 10am-8pm mid-Jun–mid-Jul & early Sep, 10am-midnight mid-Jul–Aug; 🌐). Calatrava is a controversial figure for many Valencians, who complain about the expense and various design flaws. Nevertheless, if your taxes weren't involved, it's awe-inspiring and pleasingly family oriented.

🛏 Sleeping

⭐**Russafa Youth Hostel** HOSTEL $
(Map p420; 📞963 31 31 40; www.russafayouth-hostel.com; Carrer del Padre Perera 5; dm €18-20, s without bathroom €30, d without bathroom €40-54; @🌐) You'll feel instantly at home in this super-welcoming, cute hostel set over various floors of a venerable building in the heart of vibrant Russafa. It's all beds, rather than bunks, and with a maximum of three to a room, there's no crowding. Sweet rooms and spotless bathrooms make for a mighty easy stay.

⭐**Hostal Antigua
Morellana** HOSTAL $$
(Map p422; 📞963 91 57 73; www.hostalam.com; Calle En Bou 2; s/d €55/65; ❄@🌐) This friendly, family-run, 18-room spot occupies a renovated 18th-century *posada* (where wealthier merchants bringing produce to market would spend the night) and has cosy, good-sized rooms, many with balconies. It's kept extremely shipshape by the house-proud owners and there are loads of great features, including memory-foam mattresses, handsome fabrics and lounge with coffee. Higher floors have more natural light. Great value.

LAS FALLAS

The exuberant, anarchic swirl of **Las Fallas de San José** (www.fallas.com; ☉Mar) is a must if you're visiting Spain in mid-March.

The *fallas* themselves are huge sculptures of papier mâché on wood built by teams of local artists. Round-the-clock festivities include street parties, paella-cooking competitions, parades, open-air concerts and free firework displays. After midnight on the final day each *falla* goes up in flames – backed by yet more fireworks.

✖ Eating

In the centre there are numerous traditional options, as well as trendy tapas choices. The main eating zones are the Barrio del Carmen, L'Eixample and, above all, the vibrant tapas-packed streets of Russafa.

La Pilareta   TAPAS $
(Bar Pilar; Map p422; ☑963 91 04 97; www.barlapilareta.es; Calle del Moro Zeit 13; mussels €7.10; ☉noon-midnight) Earthy, century-old and barely changed, La Pilareta is great for hearty tapas and *clóchinas* (small, juicy local mussels), available between May and August. For the rest of the year it serves *mejillones* (mussels), which are altogether fatter if less tasty. A platterful comes in a spicy broth that you scoop up with a spare shell. It's got atmosphere in spades.

Copenhagen   VEGETARIAN $
(Map p420; ☑963 28 99 28; www.grupocopenhagen.com; Calle del Literato Azorín 8; dishes €8-12; ☉1.30-4pm & 8.30-11.30pm Thu-Mon, 1.30-4pm Tue & Wed; ☎🌱) Bright and lively, the buzz from this popular vegetarian restaurant seems to spread a contagion of good cheer all along the street. It does a very toothsome soy burger as well as top homemade pasta, but the truth is it's all pretty tasty.

★Navarro   VALENCIAN $$
(Map p422; ☑963 52 96 23; www.restaurantenavarro.com; Calle del Arzobispo Mayoral 5; rices €14-17, set menu €22; ☉1.30-4pm Mon-Fri, 1.30-4pm & 8.30-11pm Sat; ☎) A byword in the city for decades for its quality rice dishes, Navarro is run by the grandkids of the original founders and it offers plenty of choice, outdoor seating and a set menu, including one of the rices as a main.

☆ Entertainment

★Jimmy Glass   LIVE MUSIC
(Map p422; www.jimmyglassjazz.net; Calle Baja 28; ☉8pm-2.30am Mon-Thu, 9pm-3.30am Fri & Sat; ☎) Atmospheric Jimmy Glass is just what a jazz bar should be, with dim lighting and high-octane cocktails. It has four live performances a week, many of them free, and also runs an annual jazz festival in October/November that attracts some top musicians. At other times it plays tracks from the owner's vast CD collection. Tapas are available Thursday to Saturday.

ℹ Information

City tourist offices include the following:

Ayuntamiento Tourist Office (Map p422; ☑963 52 49 08; www.visitvalencia.com; Plaza del Ayuntamiento 1; ☉9am-6.50pm Mon-Sat, 10am-1.50pm Sun) In the town hall

Paz Tourist Office (Map p420; ☑963 98 64 22; www.visitvalencia.com; Calle de la Paz 48; ☉9am-6.50pm Mon-Sat, 10am-1.50pm Sun; ☎)

Joaquín Sorolla Station Tourist Office (Map p420; ☑963 80 36 23; www.visitvalencia.com; Valencia Joaquín Sorolla; ☉10am-5.50pm Mon-Fri, to 2.50pm Sat & Sun) At the fast train station.

ℹ Getting There & Around

Valencia's **bus station** (Map p420; ☑963 46 62 66; Avenida Menéndez Pidal) is beside the riverbed. Bus 8 connects it to Plaza del Ayuntamiento. There are very regular buses to/from Madrid (€30 to €36, four hours) and Barcelona (€29 to €36, four to five hours).

Trains run to Barcelona (€29 to €45, 3¼ to five hours) and Madrid (€27 to €73, 1¾ to seven hours). Fast trains run from the Valencia Joaquín Sorolla station, 800m south of the old town. Some slow trains still use Estación del Norte, between it and the old town.

Andalucía

Images of Andalucía are so potent, so quintessentially Spanish that it's sometimes difficult not to feel a sense of déjà vu. It's almost as if you've already been there in your dreams: a solemn Easter parade, an ebullient spring festival, exotic nights in the Alhambra. In the stark light of day, the picture is no less compelling.

Seville

POP 690,570

Some cities have looks, other cities have personality. The *sevillanos* – lucky devils – get both, courtesy of their flamboyant, charismatic, ever-evolving Andalucian metropolis founded, according to myth, 3000 years ago by the Greek god Hercules. Drenched for most of the year in spirit-enriching sunlight, this is a city of feelings as much as sights, with different seasons prompting vastly contrasting moods: solemn for Semana Santa, flirtatious for the spring fiesta and soporific for the gasping heat of summer.

◉ Sights & Activities

Seville's medieval *judería* (Jewish quarter), east of the cathedral and Alcázar, is today a tangle of atmospheric, winding streets and lovely plant-decked plazas perfumed with orange blossom. Among its most characteristic plazas is Plaza de Santa Cruz, which gives the *barrio* (district) its name. Nearby, Plaza de Doña Elvira is perhaps the most romantic small square in Andalucía, especially in the evening.

★ Catedral & Giralda   CATHEDRAL

(🖉954 21 49 71; www.catedraldesevilla.es; Plaza del Triunfo; adult/child €9/free, rooftop tours €15; ⏰11am-3.30pm Mon, to 5pm Tue-Sat, 2.30-6pm Sun) Seville's immense cathedral is awe-inspiring in its scale and majesty. The world's largest Gothic cathedral, it was built between 1434 and 1517 over the remains of what had previously been the city's main mosque. Highlights include the Giralda, the mighty bell tower which incorporates the mosque's original minaret, the monu-mental tomb of Christopher Columbus, and the Capilla Mayor with an astonishing gold altarpiece.

★ Real Alcázar   PALACE

(🖉954 50 23 24; www.alcazarsevilla.org; Plaza del Triunfo; adult/child €9.50/free; ⏰9.30am-7pm Apr-Sep, to 5pm Oct-Mar) A magnificent marriage of Christian and Mudéjar architecture, Seville's Unesco-listed palace complex is a breathtaking spectacle. The site, which was originally developed as a fort in 913, has been revamped many times over the 11 centuries of its existence, most spectacularly in the 14th century when King Pedro added the sumptuous Palacio de Don Pedro, still today the Alcázar's crown jewel. More recently, the Alcázar featured as a location for the *Game of Thrones* TV series.

Archivo de Indias   MUSEUM

(🖉954 50 05 28; Calle Santo Tomás; ⏰9.30am-5pm Mon-Sat, 10am-2pm Sun) FREE Occupying a former merchant's exchange on the western side of Plaza del Triunfo, the Archivo de Indias provides a fascinating insight into Spain's colonial history. The archive, established in 1785 to house documents and maps relating to Spain's American empire, is vast, boasting 7km of shelves, 43,000 documents, and 80 million pages dating from 1492 to the end of the empire in the 19th century. Most documents are filed away but you can examine some fascinating letters and hand-drawn maps.

★ Hospital de los Venerables Sacerdotes   MUSEUM

(🖉954 56 26 96; www.focus.abengoa.es; Plaza de los Venerables 8; adult/child €8/4, 1st Thu of month to 2pm free; ⏰10am-2pm Thu-Sat

SPAIN & PORTUGAL ANDALUCÍA

PAELLA & MORE

There's something life-affirming about eating a proper Spanish paella, cheerily yellow like the sun and bursting with intriguing morsels. It seems to promise warm days and fine company. But there's more to this most Valencian of dishes than meets the eye. Traditional Valencian rices – always eaten for lunch by locals, never dinner – can have almost any ingredients, varying by region and season. The base always includes short-grain rice, garlic, olive oil and saffron. Paella should be cooked in a large shallow pan to enable maximum contact with flavour. And for the final touch of authenticity, the grains on the bottom (and only those) should have a crunchy, savoury crust known as the *socarrat*. Restaurants should take around 20 minutes or more to prepare a rice dish – beware if they don't – so expect to wait. Though rice dishes are usually for a minimum of two, many places will do one for a solo diner if asked. Paella has all the liquid evaporated, *meloso* rices are wet, and *caldoso* rices come with liquid.

Seville

N 0 —————— 200 m
0 —————— 0.1 miles

summer, to 6pm Thu-Sat rest of year) This gem of a museum, housed in a former hospice for ageing priests, is one of Seville's most rewarding attractions to visit. The artistic highlight is the Focus Abengoa Foundation's collection of 17th-century paintings in the Centro Velázquez. It's not a big collection but each work is a masterpiece of its genre – highlights include Diego Velázquez' *Santa Rufina* and *Inmaculada Concepción*, and a sharply vivid portrait of *Santa Catalina* painted by Bartolomé Murillo.

Casa de Pilatos
HISTORIC BUILDING

(☏954 22 52 98; www.fundacionmedinaceli.org; Plaza de Pilatos; ground fl €8, whole house €10; ⊙9am-7pm Apr-Oct, to 6pm Nov-Mar) The haunting Casa de Pilatos, which is still occupied by the ducal Medinaceli family, is one of the city's most glorious mansions. Originally dating from the late 15th century, it incorporates a wonderful mixture of Mudéjar, Gothic and Renaissance decor, with some beautiful tilework and *artesonados* (ceilings of interlaced beams with decorative insertions). The overall effect is like a mini-Alcázar.

Seville

★ **Metropol Parasol**   LANDMARK
(📞 606 635214; www.metropolsevilla.com; Plaza de la Encarnación; €3; ⊙ 10am-10.30pm Sun-Thu, to 11pm Fri & Sat) Since opening in 2011, the opinion-dividing Metropol Parasol, known locally as *las setas* (the mushrooms), has become something of a city icon. Designed as a giant sunshade by German architect Jürgen Mayer-Hermann, it's said to be the world's largest wooden structure, and it's certainly a formidable sight with its 30m-high mushroom-like pillars and undulating honeycombed roof. Lifts run up from the basement to the top where you can enjoy killer city views from a winding walkway.

Museo de Bellas Artes   MUSEUM
(Fine Arts Museum; 📞 955 54 29 42; www.museodebellasartesdesevilla.es; Plaza del Museo 9; EU citizens/other free/€1.50; ⊙ 9am-8pm Tue-Sat, to 3pm Sun mid-Sep–mid-Jun, 9am-3pm Tue-Sun mid-Jun–mid-Sep) Housed in the beautiful former Convento de la Merced, Seville's Fine Arts Museum provides an elegant showcase for a comprehensive collection of Spanish and Sevillan paintings and sculptures. Works date from the 15th to 20th centuries, but the onus is very much on brooding religious paintings from the city's 17th-century *Siglo de Oro* (Golden Age).

★ **Plaza de España**   SQUARE
(Avenida de Portugal, Parque de María Luisa) This bombastic plaza in the Parque de María Luisa was the most grandiose of the building projects completed for the 1929 Exposición Iberoamericana. A huge brick-and-tile confection, it's all very over the top, but it's undeniably impressive with its fountains, mini-canals and Venetian-style bridges. A series of gaudy tile pictures depict maps and historical scenes from each Spanish province.

You can hire row boats to ply the canals (€6 for 35 minutes).

🎭 Festivals & Events

Semana Santa   RELIGIOUS
(www.semana-santa.org; ⊙ Mar/Apr) Seville's Holy Week celebrations are legendary. Every day from Palm Sunday to Easter Sunday, large, life-size *pasos* (sculptural representations of events from Christ's Passion) are solemnly carried from the city's churches to the cathedral, accompanied by processions of marching *nazarenos* (penitents).

Feria de Abril   FERIA
(www.turismosevilla.org; ⊙ Apr) The largest and most colourful of all Andalucía's *ferias* (fairs), Seville's week-long spring fair is held in the second half of the month (sometimes edging into May) on El Real de la Feria, in the Los Remedios area west of the Río Guadalquivir.

For six nights, *sevillanos* dress up in elaborate finery, parade around in horse-drawn carriages, eat, drink and dance till dawn.

🛏 Sleeping

★ **La Banda**   HOSTEL $
(📞 955 22 81 18; www.labandahostel.com; Calle Dos de Mayo 16; dm €18-38; 🅰🛜) Run by a young, energetic crew, this Arenal hostel ticks all the boxes. Its mixed dorms are clean and tidily furnished, communal areas are relaxed and inviting, and best of all, it has a great rooftop bar. Evening meals are available at 9pm and a weekly program of events ensures there's always something going on.

Pensión San Pancracio   PENSION $
(📞 954 41 31 04; Plaza de las Cruces 9; tr €75, q €85-90, with shared bathroom s €25, d €30-40, tr €45.50, q €85-90; 🅰🛜) A cheap-as-chips budget option in Santa Cruz, this old, rambling family house has plenty of room options (all cheap) and a pleasant flower-bedizened patio-lobby. Don't expect frills,

FLAMENCO

Seville is arguably Spain's flamenco capital and you're most likely to catch a spontaneous atmosphere (of unpredictable quality) in one of the bars staging regular nights of flamenco with no admission fee. The *soleá*, flamenco's truest *cante jondo* (deep song), was first concocted in Triana; head here to find some of the more authentic clubs.

just friendly staff and basic, spartan rooms. Note that only the triples and quads with private bathrooms have air-con; all other rooms have fans.

✕ Eating

Seville produces Andalucía's most inventive tapas – end of story – and, if you're not enamoured with the new culinary alchemists, there are plenty of decent salt-of-the-earth tapas bars too.

Bodega Santa Cruz TAPAS **$**
(☑954 21 86 18; Calle Rodrigo Caro 1; tapas €2; ⊙8am-midnight) This is as old-school as it gets, a perennially busy bar staffed by gruff waiters and frequented by locals and visitors alike. Its fiercely traditional tapas are best enjoyed al fresco with a cold beer as you watch the passing armies of Santa Cruz tourists traipse past.

★**La Brunilda** TAPAS **$**
(☑954 22 04 81; www.labrunildatapas.com; Calle Galera 5; tapas €3.20-7.50; ⊙1-4pm & 8.30-11.30pm Tue-Sat, 1-4pm Sun) A regular fixture on lists of Seville's best tapas joints, this backstreet Arenal bar is at the forefront of the city's new wave of gourmet eateries. The look is modern-casual with big blue doors, brick arches and plain wooden tables and the food is imaginative and good-looking. The word is out, though, so arrive promptly or expect to queue.

★**Bar-Restaurante Eslava** FUSION, ANDALUCIAN **$$**
(☑954 90 65 68; www.espacioeslava.com; Calle Eslava 3; tapas €2.90-4.20, restaurant mains €15-22; ⊙bar 1-4.30pm & 7.30-11.30pm Tue-Sat, 1.30-4.30pm Sun, restaurant 1.30-4pm & 9-11.30pm Tue-Sat, 1.30-4pm Sun) A hit with locals and savvy visitors, much-lauded Eslava shirks the traditional tilework and bullfighting posters of tapas-bar lore in favour of a simple blue

space and a menu of creative contemporary dishes. Standouts include slow-cooked egg served on a mushroom cake, and memorable pork ribs in a honey and rosemary glaze. Expect crowds and a buzzing atmosphere.

★**Mamarracha** TAPAS **$$**
(☑955 12 39 11; www.mamarracha.es; Calle Hernando Colón 1-3; tapas €2.20-8, mains €6.50-16; ⊙1.30pm-midnight) Ideal for a lunch after a morning visit to the cathedral, this is a fine example of the modern tapas bars that Seville so excels at. Its interior is a handsome mix of blond wood, bare cement surfaces and exposed ducts, while its menu reveals some adventurous combos, including a terrific foie gras and orange dish.

☕ Drinking & Entertainment

In summer dozens of *terrazas de verano* (summer terraces; temporary, open-air, late-night bars), many of them with live music and plenty of room to dance, spring up along both banks of the river. Classic spots include drinks on the banks of the Río Guadalquivir in Triana (the wall along Calle del Betis forms a fantastic makeshift bar), Plaza de la Alfalfa (cocktail and dive bars), the Barrio de Santa Cruz and the Alameda de Hércules. The latter is the hub for young *sevillanos* and the city's gay nightlife.

★**El Viajero Sedentario** CAFE
(☑677 535512; www.elviajerosedentario.jimdo.com; Alameda de Hércules 77; ⊙9am-2pm & 6pm-2am) With its bright murals, shady courtyard and tiny book-stacked interior, this boho book cafe is a lovely place to hang out. From breakfast to the early hours people stop by, and it's not uncommon to find people dancing to low-key jazz tunes on sultry summer nights.

★**Casa de la Memoria** FLAMENCO
(☑954 56 06 70; www.casadelamemoria.es; Calle Cuna 6; adult/child €18/10; ⊙10.30am-10.30pm, shows 6pm & 9pm) Housed in the old stables of the **Palacio de la Condesa de Lebrija** (☑954 22 78 02; www.palaciodelebrija.com; Calle Cuna 8; ground fl €6, whole bldg €9, ground fl free 10am & 11am Mon; ⊙10.30am-7.30pm Mon-Fri, 10am-2pm & 4-6pm Sat, to 2pm Sun Sep-Jun, 10am-3pm Mon-Fri, to 2pm Sat Jul & Aug), this cultural centre stages authentic, highly charged flamenco shows. On nightly, they are perennially popular; as space is limited, you'll need to reserve tickets a day or so in advance by calling or visiting the venue.

Casa Anselma   FLAMENCO
(Calle Pagés del Corro 49; ⊙ 11.45pm-late Mon-Sat)
True, the music is often more folkloric than
flamenco, but this characterful Triana spot
is the antithesis of a touristy flamenco *tab-lao*, with cheek-to-jowl crowds, zero amplifi-
cation and spontaneous outbreaks of danc-
ing. Beware: there's no sign of life until the
doors open at around 11.45pm.

❶ Information

Tourist Office (☑ 954 21 00 05; www.turismo-
sevilla.org; Plaza del Triunfo 1; ⊙ 9am-7.30pm
Mon-Fri, 9.30am-7.30pm Sat & Sun) Central
office with information on Seville city, Sevilla
province and the Andalucía region.

❶ Getting There & Away

Seville's **airport** (Aeropuerto de Sevilla; ☑ 902
404 704; www.aena.es; A4, Km 532) has a fair
range of international and domestic flights.

Estación de Autobuses Plaza de Armas is
Seville's main bus station, with links including
Málaga (€18.50 to €23.50, 2¾ hours, seven
daily), Granada (€23 to €29, three hours,
eight daily), Córdoba (€12, two hours, seven
daily) and Madrid. Eurolines has international
services to Germany, Belgium, France and
beyond.

Seville's **Estación Santa Justa** is 1.5km northeast of the centre. High-speed AVE trains go to/
from Madrid (€60, 2½ to 3¼ hours, 14 daily) and
Córdoba (from €21, 45 minutes to 1¼ hours, 25
daily). Slower trains head to Cádiz (€16 to €23,
1¾ hours, 13 daily), Granada (€30, 3½ hours,
four daily) and Málaga (€24 to €44, two to 2½
hours, 10 daily).

❶ Getting Around

Central Seville is relatively compact and is best
explored on foot. Getting around by bike is also
an option – the city is flat and bike lanes are
ubiquitous. Driving is not recommended in the
city centre.

Public transport comprises buses, trams and
a metro. Buses are the most useful for getting
around the main visitor areas.

Córdoba

POP 294,300

One building alone is enough to put Córdoba high on any traveller's itinerary: the
mesmerising multiarched Mezquita. One of
the world's greatest Islamic buildings, it's a
symbol of the worldly and sophisticated Islamic culture that flourished here more than
a millennium ago when Córdoba was the
capital of Islamic Spain, and Western Eu-

rope's biggest and most cultured city. Once
here, you'll find there's much more to this
city: Córdoba is a great place for exploring
on foot or by bicycle, staying and eating well
in old buildings centred on verdant patios,
diving into old wine bars, and feeling millennia of history at every turn.

◉ Sights & Activities

★ **Mezquita**   MOSQUE, CATHEDRAL
(Mosque; ☑ 957 47 05 12; www.mezquita-catedral-
decordoba.es; Calle Cardenal Herrero; adult/child
€10/5, 8.30-9.30am Mon-Sat free; ⊙ 8.30-9.30am
& 10am-7pm Mon-Sat & 8.30-11.30am & 3-7pm Sun
Mar-Oct, 8.30-9.30am & 10am-6pm Mon-Sat &
8.30-11.30am & 3-6pm Sun Nov-Feb) It's impossible to overemphasise the beauty of Córdoba's great mosque, with its remarkably serene (despite tourist crowds) and spacious
interior. One of the world's greatest works
of Islamic architecture, the Mezquita hints,
with all its lustrous decoration, at a refined
age when Muslims, Jews and Christians
lived side by side and enriched their city
with a heady interaction of diverse, vibrant
cultures.

Arab chronicles recount how Abd ar-Rahman I purchased half of the Visigothic
church of San Vicente for the Muslim community's Friday prayers, and then, in AD
784, bought the other half on which to erect
a new mosque. Three later extensions nearly quintupled the size of Abd ar-Rahman I's
mosque and brought it to the form you see
today – with one major alteration: a Christian cathedral plonked right in the middle
of the mosque in the 16th century.

★ **Palacio de Viana**   MUSEUM
(www.palaciodeviana.com; Plaza de Don Gome 2;
whole house/patios €8/5; ⊙ 10am-7pm Tue-Sat &
to 3pm Sun Sep-Jun, 9am-3pm Tue-Sun Jul & Aug) A
stunning Renaissance palace with 12 beautiful, plant-filled patios, the Viana Palace is
a particular delight to visit in spring. Occupied by the aristocratic Marqueses de Viana until 1980, the large building is packed
with art and antiques. You can just walk
round the lovely patios and garden with a
self-guiding leaflet, or take a guided tour of
the rooms as well. It's an 800m walk northeast from Plaza de las Tendillas.

★ **Alcázar de los
Reyes Cristianos**   FORTRESS
(Fortress of the Christian Monarchs; ☑ 957 42
01 51; www.alcazardelosreyescristianos.cordoba.
es; Campo Santo de Los Mártires; adult/student/

SPAIN & PORTUGAL ANDALUCÍA

Córdoba

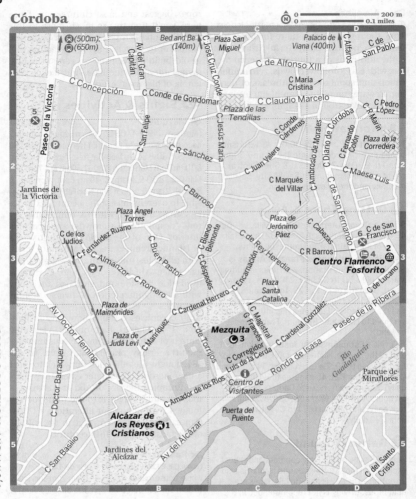

N 0 ——— 200 m
0 ——— 0.1 miles

Córdoba

◎ Top Sights
1	Alcázar de los Reyes Cristianos	B5
2	Centro Flamenco Fosforito	D3
3	Mezquita	C4

🛏 Sleeping
4	Hotel Maestre	D3

🍴 Eating
5	Mercado Victoria	A2
6	Taberna Sociedad de Plateros	D3

🍷 Drinking & Nightlife
7	Bodega Guzmán	A3

child €4.50/2.25/free; ⊙ 8.30am-3pm Tue-Sat & to 2.30pm Sun mid-Jun–mid-Sep, 8.30am-8.45pm Tue-Fri, to 4.30pm Sat & to 2.30pm Sun mid-Sep–mid-Jun; 🚻) Built under Castilian rule in the 13th and 14th centuries on the remains of a Moorish predecessor, this fort-cum-palace was where the Catholic Monarchs, Fernando and Isabel, made their first acquaintance with Columbus in 1486. One hall displays some remarkable Roman mosaics, dug up from Plaza de la Corredera in the 1950s. The Alcázar's terraced gardens – full of fish ponds, fountains, orange trees and flowers – are a delight to stroll around.

★ **Centro Flamenco Fosforito**   MUSEUM
(Posada del Potro; ☑957 47 68 29; www.cent-
roflamencofosforito.cordoba.es; Plaza del Potro;
⊙8.30am-3pm Tue-Sun mid-Jun–mid-Sep, 8.30am-
7.30pm Tue-Fri 8.30am-2.30pm Sat & Sun mid-Sep–
mid-Jun) FREE Possibly the best flamenco museum in Andalucía, the Fosforito centre has
exhibits, film and information panels in English and Spanish telling you the history of the
guitar and all the flamenco greats. Touch-
screen videos demonstrate the important
techniques of flamenco song, guitar, dance
and percussion – you can test your skill at
beating out the *compás* (rhythm) of different
palos (song forms). Regular free live flamenco performances are held here, too, often at
noon on Sundays (listed on the website).

🛏 Sleeping

★ **Bed and Be**   HOSTEL $
(☑661 420733; www.bedandbe.com; Calle José
Cruz Conde 22; incl breakfast dm €17-35, s €30-
50, d €49-80; ❋🛜) 𝒫 An exceptional hostel
option 300m north of Plaza de las Tendillas.
Staff are clued up about what's on in Córdoba, and there's a social event every evening –
often a drink on the roof followed by a bar
or tapas tour. The shared-bathroom private
rooms and four- or eight-bunk dorms are
all super-clean and as gleaming white as a
pueblo blanco.

Hotel Maestre   HOTEL $
(☑957 47 24 10; www.hotelmaestre.com; Calle
Romero Barros 4-6; s €25-55, d €38-90; ℙ❋🛜)
Within easy reach of the Mezquita and some
good restaurants, the Maestre is welcoming,
efficiently run and well priced. Rooms are
medium-sized and fairly plain, but clean
and comfy. The three patios, and walls full of
art, add light and colour, and there's parking
(€10) right on the spot.

🍴 Eating & Drinking

Córdoba's signature dish is *salmorejo,* a
delicious, thick, chilled soup of blended tomatoes, garlic, bread, lemon, vinegar and
olive oil, sprinkled with hard-boiled egg and
strips of ham. Along with *rabo de toro* (bull's
tail stew), it appears on every menu. Don't
miss the strong white wines from nearby
Montilla and Moriles.

★ **Mercado Victoria**   FOOD HALL $
(http://mercadovictoria.com; Paseo de la Victoria;
items €2-19; ⊙10am-midnight Sun-Thu, 10am-
2pm Fri & Sat) The Mercado Victoria is, yes,

a food court – but an unusually classy one,
with almost everything, from Argentine empanadas and Mexican burritos to sushi and
classic Spanish seafood and grilled meats,
prepared fresh before your eyes. The setting
is special too – a 19th-century wrought-iron-
and-glass pavilion in the Victoria gardens
just west of the old city.

Taberna Sociedad de Plateros   ANDALUCIAN $
(☑957 47 00 42; Calle de San Francisco 6; tapas €2.25-2.50, raciones €5-12; ⊙noon-4pm &
8pm-midnight Tue-Sat, noon-4pm Sun; 🛜) Run by
the silversmiths' guild, this well-loved traditional bar-cum-restaurant serves a selection
of generous tapas and *raciones* (full plates
of tapas items) in its light, glass-roofed patio. The seafood selection is particularly
good, highlighted by such items as *gambas
rebozados* (battered shrimps) and *salpicón
de mariscos* (shellfish salad), but there's a
good choice of meat, fish, eggs, salads and
other dishes too.

Bodega Guzmán   WINE BAR
(Calle de los Judíos 7; ⊙noon-4pm & 8.30-11.30pm
Fri-Wed) This atmospheric, somewhat cavern-
like Judería drinking spot, frequented by
both locals and tourists, is bedecked with
bullfighting memorabilia and dispenses
Montilla wine from three giant barrels behind the bar: don't leave without trying
some *amargoso* (bitter).

❶ Information

Centro de Visitantes (Visitors Centre; ☑902
201774; www.turismodecordoba.org; Plaza del
Triunfo; ⊙9am-7pm Mon-Fri, 9.30am-2.15pm
Sat & Sun) The main tourist information centre,
with an exhibit on Córdoba's history, and some
Roman and Visigothic remains downstairs.

❶ Getting There & Away

Córdoba's train station is 1.2km northwest of
central Plaza de las Tendillas. Destinations
include Granada (€36, 2¾ hours), Madrid (€33
to €63, 1¾ to two hours) and Seville (€14 to €30,
45 to 80 minutes).

Buses run from behind the train station to
Granada (€15, 2¾ hours), Madrid (€17, five
hours), Málaga (€12, three hours), Seville (€12,
two hours) and more.

Granada

POP 234,758 / ELEV 738M
Granada's eight centuries as a Muslim capital are symbolised in its keynote attraction,
the remarkable Alhambra, one of the most

Granada

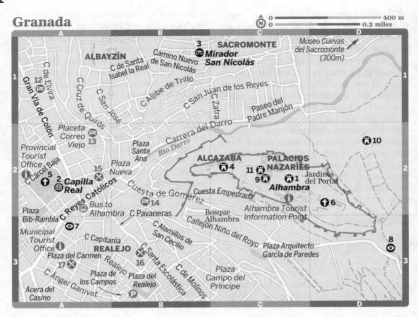

Granada

◎ Top Sights

◎ Sights

◉ Sleeping

◉ Eating

graceful architectural achievements in the Muslim world. Islam was never completely expunged here, and today it seems more present than ever in the shops, restaurants, tearooms and mosque of a growing North African community in and around the maze of the Albayzín. The tapas bars fill to bursting, while flamenco dives resound to the heart-wrenching tones of the south.

◉ Sights

Most major sights are an easy walk within the city centre, and there are buses for when the hills wear you out. Rectangular Plaza Nueva is Granada's main nexus. The Albayzín sits on a hill immediately to the north and is roughly demarcated by Gran Via de Colón and the Río Darro. The Alhambra lies on a separate hill on the opposite side of the Darro.

★ Alhambra   ISLAMIC PALACE
(☎ 958 02 79 71, tickets 858 95 36 16; http://alhambra-patronato.es; adult/12-15yr/under 12yr €14/8/free, Generalife & Alcazaba adult/under 12yr €7/free; ⏰ 8.30am-8pm Apr–mid-Oct, to 6pm mid-Oct–Mar, night visits 10-11.30pm Tue-Sat Apr–mid-Oct, 8-9.30pm Fri & Sat mid-Oct–Mar) The Alhambra is Granada's – and Europe's – love letter to Moorish culture. Set against a backdrop of brooding Sierra Nevada peaks, this fortified palace complex started life as a walled citadel before going on to become the opulent seat of Granada's Nasrid emirs. Their showpiece palaces, the 14th-century Palacios Naz-

aríes, are among the finest Islamic buildings in Europe and, together with the gorgeous Generalife gardens, form the Alhambra's great headline act.

The Alhambra is Spain's most visited tourist attraction, drawing almost 2.5 million visitors a year. To ease your visit, it pays to book ahead and know the ropes.

You can **buy tickets** (☑858 95 36 16; https://tickets.alhambra-patronato.es) from two hours to three months in advance, online, by phone or at the Alhambra ticket office. Depending on the number of tickets reserved in advance, a limited number of same-day tickets are available at the ticket office. These sell out quickly, so get in early.

If you've booked a ticket, you can either print it yourself, or pick it up at the ticket office located at the **Alhambra Entrance Pavilion** (☑958 02 79 71; http://alhambra-patronato.es) or the **Corral del Carbón** (Calle Mariana Pineda; ⊙9am-8pm) where there's a ticket machine.

By foot, walk up the Cuesta de Gomérez from Plaza Nueva through the woods to the Puerta de la Justicia. Enter here if you already have your ticket, otherwise continue to the ticket office.

Bus C3 runs to the ticket office from a **bus stop** just off Plaza Isabel la Católica. See also p414.

➡ Alcazaba

Occupying the western tip of the Alhambra are the martial ramparts and towers of the Alcazaba, the site's original 13th-century citadel. The Torre de la Vela (Watchtower) is famous as the tower where the cross and banners of the Reconquista were raised in January 1492. A winding staircase leads to the top where you can enjoy sweeping views over Granada's rooftops.

➡ Palacios Nazaríes

(Nasrid Palaces) This is the stunning centrepiece of the Alhambra, with perfectly proportioned rooms and courtyards, intricately moulded stucco walls, beautiful tiling, fine carved wooden ceilings and elaborate stalactite-like *muqarnas* vaulting, all worked in mesmerising, symbolic, geometrical patterns. Arabic inscriptions proliferate in the stucco work.

Admission to the *palacios* (included in the Alhambra ticket) is strictly controlled. When you buy your ticket, you'll be given a time to enter. Once inside, you can stay as long as you like.

EXPLORING THE ALBAYZÍN

On the hill facing the Alhambra across the Darro valley, Granada's old Muslim quarter (the Albayzín) is a place for aimless wandering; you'll get lost regularly whatever map you're using. The cobblestone streets are lined with signature only-in-Granada *cármenes* (large mansions with walled gardens, from the Arabic *karm* for garden). The Albayzín survived as the Muslim quarter for several decades after the Christian conquest in 1492.

Bus C1 runs circular routes from Plaza Nueva around the Albayzín about every eight minutes, from 7am to 11pm.

The palace was originally divided into three main areas: the **Mexuar**, the administrative and public part of the complex; the **Palacio de Comares**, the emir's official residence; and the **Palacio de los Leones**, his private quarters.

Entrance is through the Mexuar, a 14th-century room used as a ministerial council chamber and antechamber for those awaiting audiences with the emir. The public would have gone no further.

From the Mexuar you pass into the **Patio del Cuarto Dorado**, a courtyard where the emirs gave audiences, with the Cuarto Dorado (Golden Room) on the left. Opposite the Cuarto Dorado is the entrance to the Palacio de Comares through a beautiful facade of glazed tiles, stucco and carved wood. Built for Emir Yusuf I, the Palacio de Comares served as his official residence. It's set around the lovely **Patio de los Arrayanes** (Patio of the Myrtles) with its rectangular pool.

Inside the northern Torre de Comares (Comares Tower), the **Sala de la Barca** (Hall of the Blessing) leads into the **Salón de los Embajadores** (Chamber of the Ambassadors), where the emirs would have conducted negotiations with Christian emissaries. This room's marvellous domed marquetry ceiling contains more than 8000 cedar pieces in a pattern of stars representing the seven heavens of Islam.

The Patio de los Arrayanes leads into the **Palacio de los Leones** (Palace of the Lions), built in the second half of the 14th century under Muhammad V. The palace rooms surround the famous **Patio de los Leones** (Lion Courtyard), with its marble fountain

SACROMONTE

Sacromonte, the primarily *gitano* (Roma) neighbourhood northeast of the Albayzín, is renowned for its flamenco traditions, drawing tourists to nightclubs and aficionados to music schools. But it still feels like the fringes of the city, literally and figuratively, as the homes dug out of the hillside alternate between flashy and highly extemporaneous, despite some of the caves having been established since the 14th century.

The area is good for a stroll – though solo women should avoid the uninhabited areas – yielding great views (especially from an ad hoc cafe on Vereda de Enmedio). For some insight into the area, the **Museo Cuevas del Sacromonte** (🗷 958 21 51 20; www.sacromontegranada.com; Barranco de los Negros; ☉ 10am-8pm mid-Mar–mid-Oct, to 6pm mid-Oct–mid-Mar) provides an excellent display of local folk art. This wide-ranging ethnographic and environmental museum and arts centre is set in large herb gardens and hosts art exhibitions, as well as flamenco and films.

channelling water through the mouths of 12 marble lions. Of the four halls around the patio, the southern **Sala de los Abencerrajes** is the most spectacular. Boasting a mesmerising octagonal stalactite ceiling, this is the legendary site of the murders of the noble Abencerraj family, whose leader, the story goes, dared to dally with Zoraya, Abu al-Hasan's favourite concubine.

On the northern side of the patio is the richly decorated **Sala de Dos Hermanas** (Hall of Two Sisters), probably named after the slabs of white marble flanking its fountain. It features a fantastic muqarnas dome with a central star and 5000 tiny cells, reminiscent of the constellations. This may have been the room of the emir's favourite paramour. At its far end, the tile-trimmed **Mirador de Daraxa** (Daraxa lookout) was a lovely place for palace denizens to look onto the garden below.

From the Sala de Dos Hermanas a passage leads through the **Estancias del Emperador** (Emperor's Chambers), built for Carlos I in the 1520s, and later used by the American author Washington Irving. From here, descend to the Patio de la Reja (Patio of the Grille) and Patio de Lindaraja before emerging into the **Jardines del Partal,** an area of terraced gardens.

➡ Palacio de Carlos V

This huge Renaissance palace clashes spectacularly with the style of its surroundings on the Alhambra. Its main (western) facade features three porticoes divided by pairs of fluted columns, with bas-relief battle carvings at their feet. The building is square but contains a two-tiered circular courtyard with 32 columns. This circle inside a square is the only Spanish example of a Renaissance ground plan symbolising the unity of earth and heaven.

➡ Palacio del Generalife

This whitewashed country house served as the sultan's summer palace on the Alhambra. In the Generalife gardens, it boasts a series of delightful courtyards – in the second one, the trunk of a 700-year-old cypress tree suggests the delicate shade that once would have graced the area.

Catedral de Granada CATHEDRAL
(🗷 958 22 29 59; www.catedraldegranada.com; Plaza de las Pasiegas; adult/reduced €5/3.50; ☉ 10am-6.30pm Mon-Sat, 3-6pm Sun) From street level it's difficult to appreciate the immensity of Granada's cavernous cathedral. It's too boxed in by other buildings to stand out, but it's nonetheless a monumental work of architecture. Built atop the city's former mosque, it was originally intended to be Gothic in appearance but over the two centuries of its construction (1523–1704) it underwent major modifications. Most notably, architect Diego de Siloé changed its layout to a Renaissance style, and Alonso Cano added a magnificent 17th-century baroque facade.

★ **Capilla Real** HISTORIC BUILDING
(Royal Chapel; 🗷 958 22 78 48; www.capillareal-granada.com; Calle Oficios; adult/student/child €5/3.50/free; ☉ 10.15am-6.30pm Mon-Sat, 11am-6.30pm Sun) The Royal Chapel is the last resting place of Spain's Reyes Católicos (Catholic Monarchs), Isabel I de Castilla (1451–1504) and Fernando II de Aragón (1452–1516), who commissioned the elaborate Isabelline-Gothic-style mausoleum that was to house them. It wasn't completed until 1517, hence their interment in the Alhambra's

Convento de San Francisco (www.parador. es; Calle Real de la Alhambra) until 1521.

Their monumental marble tombs (and those of their heirs) lie in the chancel behind a gilded wrought-iron screen, created by Bartolomé de Jaén in 1520.

★ Mirador San Nicolás   VIEWPOINT
(Plaza de San Nicolás) This is the place for those classic sunset shots of the Alhambra sprawled along a wooded hilltop with the dark Sierra Nevada mountains looming in the background. It's a well-known spot, accessible via Callejón de San Cecilio, so expect crowds of camera-toting tourists, students and buskers. It's also a haunt of pickpockets and bag-snatchers, so keep your wits about you as you enjoy the views.

🛏 Sleeping

Oasis Backpackers' Hostel   HOSTEL $
(📞 958 21 58 48; https://hostelsoasis.com/grana-da-hostels/oasis-granada; Placeta Correo Viejo 3; dm €11-23; ❈ @ 🛜 🏊) Offering budget digs in a bohemian quarter, the friendly Oasis is seconds away from the *teterías* (teahouses) and bars on Calle Elvira. The first in what is now a chain of Oasis hostels, it has beds in six-to 10-person dorms, both mixed and women only, and a long list of facilities including a fully equipped kitchen and a rooftop terrace.

Hostal Arteaga   HOSTAL $
(📞 958 20 88 41; www.hostalarteaga.es; Calle Arteaga 3; s €25-50, d €30-60; ❈ @ 🛜) Basic, value-for-money digs in a convenient central location just off Gran Vía de Colón are what you get at this friendly old-school *hostal*. The rooms leave little lasting impression but do the job well enough with their laminate floors, functional furniture and ceramic-tiled bathrooms.

Pensión Landázuri   PENSION $
(📞 958 22 14 06; www.hostallandazuri.com; Cuesta de Gomérez 24; s €28-39, d €38-59) On an attractive street snaking up from Plaza Nueva, this modest family-run outfit boasts simple, no-frills rooms, a terrace with Alhambra (p432) views, and an all-day cafe. Cheaper rates are available for rooms with shared bathrooms.

🍴 Eating

Granada is a bastion of the fantastic practice of free tapas with every drink. Place your drink order at the bar and, hey presto, a plate will magically appear with a gener-

ous portion of something delicious-looking on it. Order another drink and another plate will materialise. The process is repeated with every round you buy – and each time the tapa gets better. As Spanish bars serve only small glasses of beer (*cañas* measure just 250ml) it is perfectly easy to fill up on free tapas over an enjoyable evening without getting totally inebriated. Indeed, some people 'crawl' from bar to bar getting a drink and free tapa in each place. Packed shoulder-to-shoulder with tapas institutions, Calle de Elvira and Calle Navas are good places for bar crawls. If you're hungry you can always order an extra plate or two to soak up the *cervezas*.

Bodegas Castañeda   TAPAS $
(📞 958 21 54 64; Calle Almireceros 1; tapas €2-5; ⏱ 11.30am-4.30pm & 7.30pm-1.30am) Eating becomes a contact sport at this traditional tapas bar where crowds of hungry punters jostle for food under hanging hams. Don't expect any experimental nonsense here, just classic tapas (and *raciones*) served lightning-fast with booze poured from big wall-mounted casks.

Los Diamantes   TAPAS, SEAFOOD $$
(www.barlosdiamantes.com; Calle Navas 26; raciones €10-14; ⏱ 12.30-4.30pm & 8.30pm-midnight) A Granada institution, this scruffy old-school joint is one of the best eateries on bar-lined Calle Navas. Always busy, it's generally standing room only but the seafood – the first tapa comes free with your drink – is excellent and there's usually a wonderfully sociable vibe.

SPAIN & PORTUGAL ANDALUCÍA

DON'T MISS

THE TEAHOUSES OF GRANADA

Granada's *teterías* (teahouses) have proliferated in recent years, but there's still something exotic and dandyish about their dark atmospheric interiors, stuffed with lace veils, stucco, low cushioned seats and an invariably bohemian clientele. Most offer a long list of aromatic teas along with sticky Arabic sweets. Some serve up music and more substantial snacks and many still permit their customers to indulge in the *cachimba* (shisha pipe). Narrow Calle Calderería Nueva is Granada's classic 'tetería street'.

Hicuri Art Restaurant VEGAN $
(☑858 98 74 73; www.restaurantehicuriartvegan.
com; Plaza de los Girones 3; mains €7.50-10, menú
del día €13.80; ☺11am-11pm Mon-Fri, noon-11pm
Sat, to 4.30pm Jul & Aug; ☑) Granada's leading
graffiti artist, El Niño de las Pinturas, has
been let loose inside Hicuri, creating a psychedelic backdrop to the vegan food served
at this friendly, laid-back restaurant. Zingy
salads, tofu and curried seitan provide welcome alternatives to the traditional meat
dishes that dominate so many city menus.

☻ Drinking & Nightlife

The best street for drinking is the rather
scruffy Calle de Elvira, but other chilled bars
line Río Darro at the base of the Albayzín
and Calle Navas. Just north of Plaza de Trin-
idad is a bunch of cool hipster-ish bars.

❶ Information

Information is available at various offices in
town:
Municipal Tourist Office (☑958 24 82 80;
www.granadatur.com; Plaza del Carmen 9;
☺9am-8pm Mon-Sat, to 2pm Sun) The official
city tourist office.
Alhambra Tourist Information Point (☑958
02 79 71; www.granadatur.com; Calle Real de
la Alhambra Granada, Alhambra; ☺8.30am-
8.30pm) Up in the Alhambra.
Provincial Tourist Office (☑958 24 71 28;
www.turgranada.es; Cárcel Baja 3; ☺9am-
8pm Mon-Fri, 10am-7pm Sat, 10am-3pm Sun)
Information on Granada Province.

❶ Getting There & Around

Granada's **bus station** (☑958 18 54 80; Avenida
Juan Pablo II; ☺6.30am-1.30am) is 3km northwest of the city centre. Take city bus SN1 for the
centre. Destinations include Córdoba (€15, 2¾
hours), Málaga (€12, 1½ hours), Madrid (€25, six
hours) and Seville (€23, three hours).

The **train station** (☑958 27 12 72; Avenida de
Andaluces) is 1.5km northwest of the centre, off
Avenida de la Constitución. For the centre, walk
straight ahead to Avenida de la Constitución and
turn right to pick up the LAC bus to Gran Vía de
Colón. Destinations include Madrid (€30 to 40,
four hours), Barcelona (€59, seven to 11 hours),
Córdoba (€36, 2½ hours) and Seville (€30, three
hours).

Cádiz

POP 118.920

You could write several weighty tomes about
Cádiz and still fall miles short of nailing its
essence. Old age accounts for much of the
complexity. Cádiz is generally considered to
be the oldest continuously inhabited settlement in Europe, founded as Gadir by the
Phoenicians in about 1100 BC. Now well into
its fourth millennium, the ancient centre,
surrounded almost entirely by water, is a romantic jumble of sinuous streets where Atlantic waves crash against eroded sea walls,
salty beaches teem with sun-worshippers,
and cheerful taverns echo with the sounds
of cawing gulls and frying fish.

◉ Sights & Activities

★**Museo de Cádiz** MUSEUM
(www.museosdeandalucia.es; Plaza de Mina; €1.50,
EU citizens free; ☺9am-3pm Tue-Sun mid-Jun–mid-
Sep, 9am-8pm Tue-Sat, to 3pm Sun mid-Sep–mid-
Jun) Admittedly a little dusty, the Museo de
Cádiz is the province's top museum. Stars of
the ground-floor archaeology section are two
Phoenician marble sarcophagi carved in human likeness, along with lots of headless Roman statues and a giant marble 2nd-century
Emperor Trajan (with head) from Bolonia's
Baelo Claudia (☑956 10 67 96; www.museos-
deandalucia.es; €1.50, EU citizens free; ☺9am-3pm
Tue-Sun mid-Jun–mid-Sep, 9am-8pm Tue-Sat, to
3pm Sun Apr–mid-Jun, 9am-6pm Tue-Sat, to 3pm
Sun mid-Sep–Mar) ruins. Upstairs, the excellent fine-art collection displays Spanish art
from the 18th to early 20th centuries, including 18 superb 17th-century canvases of saints,
angels and monks by Francisco de Zurbarán.

Playa de la Victoria BEACH
Often overshadowed by the city's historical
riches, Cádiz' beaches are Copacabana-like
in their size, vibe and beauty. This fine, wide
strip of Atlantic sand, with summer beach
bars, starts 1km south of the Puerta de Tierra
and stretches 4km back along the peninsula.

✦ Festivals & Events

Carnaval CARNIVAL
(www.turismo.cadiz.es; ☺Feb) No other Spanish
city celebrates Carnaval with as much spirit, dedication and humour as Cádiz. Here
it becomes a 10-day singing, dancing and
drinking fancy-dress street party spanning
two February weekends. The fun, fuelled by
huge amounts of alcohol, is irresistible.

☐ Sleeping & Eating

Casa Caracol HOSTEL $
(☑956 26 11 66; www.casacaracolcadiz.com; Calle
Suárez de Salazar 4; incl breakfast dm €22-28, d
€43-55, with shared bathroom €40-50; ☎) ☑

Cádiz

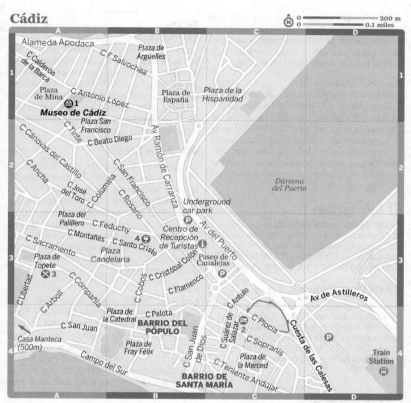

Mellow Casa Caracol is Cádiz' original old-town backpacker hostel. Cheery as only Cádiz can be, it has colourful, contemporary, locker-equipped dorms for four, six or seven, a sociable communal kitchen, and a roof terrace with hammocks, along with three private doubles (one a duplex-style affair with bathroom). Other perks include home-cooked dinners, yoga, and bike and surfboard rental. No lift.

★ Casa Manteca
TAPAS **$**

(☑ 956 21 36 03; www.facebook.com/tabernamanteca; Calle Corralón de los Carros 66; tapas €2.50; ⊘ noon-4pm & 8.30pm-12.30am, may close Sun & Mon evenings Nov-Mar) The hub of the Barrio de la Viña's Carnaval fun, with every inch of its walls covered in flamenco, bullfighting and Carnaval paraphernalia, always-busy Casa Manteca is full of old tapas faves. Ask the chatty waiters for a tapa of mussels or *chicharrones* (pressed pork dressed with a

Cádiz

◎ **Top Sights**
1 Museo de Cádiz.....................................A1

⬤ **Sleeping**
2 Casa Caracol...C4

✴ **Eating**
3 Freiduría Las Flores.............................A3

◉ **Drinking & Nightlife**
4 Taberna La Manzanilla........................B3

squeeze of lemon), and it'll fly across the bar on waxed paper.

Freiduría Las Flores
SEAFOOD, TAPAS **$**

(☑ 956 22 61 12; Plaza de Topete 4; tapas €1.50, raciones €5-12; ⊘ noon-4pm & 7.30pm-midnight) Cádiz' addiction to fried fish reaches new heights at this packed-out spot. If it comes from the sea, it's been fried and dished up at Las Flores as a tapa, *media ración* (larger tapas serving) or *ración* (full-plate serving), or fish-and-chips style in improvised paper cups. If you can't choose, try a *surtido* (mixed fry-up). Don't count on a table.

Taberna La Manzanilla WINE BAR
(www.lamanzanilladecadiz.com; Calle Feduchy 19; ◷ 11am-3.30pm & 7-10.30pm Mon-Fri, 11am-3.30pm Sat & Sun; ❷) Family-run since the 1930s, La Manzanilla is a gloriously time-warped sherry tavern decked with bullfighting posters, on a spot once occupied by a pharmacy. The speciality, of course, is *manzanilla* from the giant oak barrel. Keep an eye out for tastings and other events.

ⓘ Information

Centro de Recepción de Turistas (☎ 956 24 10 01; www.turismo.cadiz.es; Paseo de Canalejas; ◷ 9am-7pm Mon-Fri, to 5pm Sat & Sun Jul-Sep, 8.30am-6.30pm Mon-Fri, 9am-5pm Sat & Sun Oct-Jun) Near the bus and train stations.

ⓘ Getting There & Away

Buses run regularly to Seville (€13, 1¾ hours), Málaga (€28, 4½ hours), Tarifa (€10, 1¾ hours) and other destinations. From the nearby train station are services to Seville (€16 to €22, 1¾ hours, 15 daily) and Madrid (€74, 4½ hours, three to four daily) among others.

WORTH A TRIP

MOROCCO
....

At once African and Arab, and looming large across the Straits of Gibraltar across from Tarifa, Morocco is an exciting detour from your Western European journey. The country's attractions are endless, from the fascinating souqs and medieval architecture of Marrakesh and Fès to the Atlantic charms of Asilah and Essaouira, and from the High Atlas and Rif Mountains to the soulful sand dunes of the Sahara.

Several ferry services zip from southern Spain across to Morocco, including a fast **ferry** (☎ 956 68 18 30; www.frs.es; Avenida de Andalucía 16; adult/child/car/motorcycle 1 way €41/15/136/33) from Tarifa that makes a day-trip an easy prospect. For further information, refer to shop.lonelyplanet.com to purchase Lonely Planet's *Morocco* guide.

Tarifa

POP 13,680

Tarifa's tip-of-Spain location, where the Mediterranean and the Atlantic meet, gives it a different climate and character from the rest of Andalucía. Stiff Atlantic winds draw in surfers, windsurfers and kitesurfers who, in turn, lend this ancient yet deceptively small settlement a refreshingly laid-back international vibe.

⚡ Activities

Tarifa's legendary winds have turned the town into one of Europe's premier windsurfing and kitesurfing destinations. The most popular strip is along the coast between Tarifa and Punta Paloma, 10km northwest. Over 30 places offer equipment hire and classes, from beginner to expert. The best months are May, June and September, but bear in mind that the choppy seas aren't always beginner's territory.

FIRMM WHALE WATCHING
(☎ 956 62 70 08; www.firmm.org; Calle Pedro Cortés 4; 2hr tours adult/child €30/20; ◷ 10am-7pm Easter-Oct) ◢ Among Tarifa's dozens of whale-watching outfits, not-for-profit FIRMM is a good option. Its primary purpose is to study the whales and record data, and this gives rise to environmentally sensitive two- or three-hour tours and week-long whale-watching courses.

🛏 Sleeping & Eating

⭐ **Hostal África** HOSTAL $
(☎ 956 68 02 20; www.hostalafrica.com; Calle María Antonia Toledo 12; s €40-55, d €55-80, tr €80-110; ◷ Mar-Nov; ❷) This mellow, revamped 19th-century house within Tarifa's old town is one of the Costa de la Luz' (and Cádiz province's) best *hostales* (budget hotels). Full of potted plants and sky-blue-and-white arches, it's run by hospitable, on-the-ball owners, and the 13 all-different rooms (including one triple) sparkle with bright colours. Enjoy the lovely roof terrace, with its loungey cabana and Africa views.

N°6 TAPAS $
(☎ 671 237941; www.facebook.com/No6CocinaSencilla; Calle Colón 6; tapas €2.50-3.50, mains €6.50-14; ◷ 7.30pm-12.30am Mon-Thu, 1-4pm & 7.30pm-12.30am Fri-Sun Mar-Nov; ❷) All stone walls, tall tables and cheery staff, this zestful newcomer prides itself on its *cocina*

sencilla (simple cooking), but there's nothing plain about its imaginative Spanish-international creations and modern-rustic setting. Tapas, chalked up on the board, might include ricotta ravioli, curried chicken and sweet-potato fries; mains wander from Argentine chorizo to carrot-and-mozzarella salad served with a goji-berry vinaigrette.

ⓘ Getting There & Away

Buses run regularly to Cádiz (€10, 1½ hours), Málaga (€17, 2¾ hours) and Seville (€20, three hours).

Málaga

POP 569,000

Málaga – worlds away from the adjoining Costa del Sol – is a historic and culturally rich provincial capital that has long lived in the shadow of the iconic Andalucian cities of Granada, Córdoba and Seville. Yet, it has rapidly emerged as the province's city of culture with its so-called 'mile of art' being compared to Madrid, and its dynamism and fine dining reminiscent of Barcelona. The tastefully restored historic centre is a delight.

⊙ Sights

★ **Museo Picasso Málaga**　　MUSEUM
(☏952 12 76 00; www.museopicassomalaga.org; Calle San Agustín 8; €7, incl temporary exhibition €10; ☺10am-8pm Jul & Aug, to 7pm Mar, Jun, Sep & Oct, to 6pm Nov-Feb) This unmissable museum in the city of Picasso's birth provides a solid overview of the great master and his work, although, surprisingly, it only came to fruition in 2003 after over 50 years of planning. The 200-plus works in the collection were donated and loaned to the museum by Christine Ruiz-Picasso (wife of Paul, Picasso's eldest son) and Bernard Ruiz-Picasso (Picasso's grandson) and catalogue the artist's sparkling career with a few notable gaps (the 'blue' and 'rose' periods are largely missing).

★ **Alcazaba**　　CASTLE
(☏630 932987; www.malagaturismo.com; Calle Alcazabilla; €2.20, incl Castillo de Gibralfaro €3.55; ☺9.30am-8pm Tue-Sun) No time to visit Granada's Alhambra? Then Málaga's Alcazaba can provide a taster. The entrance is next to the **Roman amphitheatre** (☏951 50 11 15; Calle Alcazabilla 8; ☺10am-8pm) **FREE**, from where a meandering path climbs amid lush greenery: crimson bougainvillea, lofty palms, fragrant jasmine bushes and rows of orange trees. Extensively restored, this palace-fortress dates from the 11th-century Moorish period; the caliphal horseshoe arches, courtyards and bubbling fountains are evocative of this influential period in Málaga's history.

Museo Carmen Thyssen　　MUSEUM
(www.carmenthyssenmalaga.org; Calle Compañía 10; €6, incl temporary exhibition €9; ☺10am-8pm Tue-Sun) Located in an aesthetically renovated 16th-century palace in the heart of the city's former Moorish quarter, this extensive collection concentrates on 19th-century Spanish and Andalucian art by painters such as Joaquín Sorolla y Bastida and Ignacio Zuloaga.

✦ Festivals & Events

Feria de Málaga　　FAIR
(☺mid-Aug) Málaga's nine-day feria, launched by a huge fireworks display, is the most ebullient of Andalucía's summer fairs. It resembles an exuberant Rio-style street party, with plenty of flamenco and *fino* (dry and straw-coloured sherry); head for the city centre to be in the thick of it. At night, festivities switch to large fairgrounds and nightly rock and flamenco shows at Cortijo de Torres, 3km southwest of the city centre; special buses run from all over the city.

⨳ Sleeping

★ **Dulces Dreams**　　HOSTEL $
(☏951 35 78 69; www.dulcesdreamshostel.com; Plaza de los Mártires 6; r incl breakfast €45-60; ❊⧠) Managed by an enthusiastic young team, the rooms at Dulces (sweet) Dreams are, appropriately, named after desserts; 'Cupcake' is a good choice, with a terrace overlooking the imposing red-brick church across the way. This is an older building, so there's no lift and the rooms vary in size, but they're bright and whimsically decorated, using recycled materials as much as possible.

✕ Eating & Drinking

★ **El Mesón de Cervantes**　　TAPAS, ARGENTINE $$
(☏952 21 62 74; www.elmesondecervantes.com; Calle Álamos 11; media raciones €4.50-8, raciones €9-16; ☺7pm-midnight Wed-Mon) Cervantes started as a humble tapas bar run by expat Argentine Gabriel Spatz but has now expanded into four bar-restaurants (each with a slightly different bent), all within a block of each other. This one is the HQ, where pretty much everything

Málaga

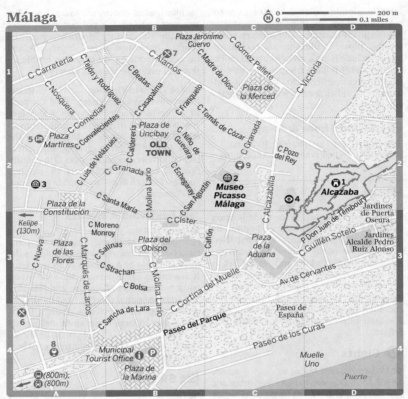

Málaga

200 m
0.1 miles

Málaga

◎ Top Sights
1 Alcazaba	D2
2 Museo Picasso Málaga	C2

◎ Sights
3 Museo Carmen Thyssen	A2
4 Roman Amphitheatre	C2

◎ Sleeping
5 Dulces Dreams	A2

◎ Eating
6 Casa Aranda	A4
7 El Mesón de Cervantes	B1

◎ Drinking & Nightlife
8 Antigua Casa de Guardia	A4
9 Bodegas El Pimpi	C2

on the menu is a show-stopper – lamb stew with couscous, pumpkin and mushroom risotto, and, boy, the grilled octopus!

Casa Aranda CAFE $
(www.casa-aranda.net; Calle Herrería del Rey; churro €0.45; ⊙8am-3pm Mon-Sat; 🖼) Casa Aranda is in a narrow alleyway next to the market and, since 1932, has been *the* place in town to enjoy chocolate and churros (tubular-shaped doughnuts). The cafe has taken over the whole street, with several outlets overseen by an army of mainly elderly, white-shirted waiters who welcome everyone like an old friend (and most are).

Antigua Casa de Guardia BAR
(www.antiguacasadeguardia.net; Alameda Principal 18; ⊙10am-10pm Mon-Sat, 11am-3pm Sun) This atmospheric tavern dates from 1840 and is the oldest bar in Málaga. The peeling custard-coloured paintwork, black-and-white photographs of local boy Picasso and elderly bar staff look fittingly antique. Try the dark brown, sherry-like *seco* (dry) Málaga wine or the romantically named *lágrima tranañejo* (very old tear).

Bodegas El Pimpi
BAR

(www.elpimpi.com; Calle Granada 62; ⊙noon-2am Mon-Fri, to 3am Sat & Sun; 🛜) This rambling bar is an institution in this town. The interior encompasses a warren of rooms, and there's a courtyard and open terrace overlooking the Roman amphitheatre (p439). Walls are decorated with historic feria posters and photos of visitors past, while the enormous barrels are signed by more well-known passers-by, including Tony Blair and Antonio Banderas. Tapas and meals are also available.

★ Kelipe
FLAMENCO

(📞692 829885; www.kelipe.net; Muro de Puerta Nueva 10; €25; ⊙shows 9.30pm Thu-Sat) There are many flamenco clubs springing up all over Andalucía, but few are as soul-stirring as Kelipe. Not only are the musicianship and dancing of the highest calibre but the talented performers also create an intimate feel and a genuine connection with the audience.

ℹ Information

Municipal Tourist Office (📞951 92 60 20; www.malagaturismo.com; Plaza de la Marina; ⊙9am-8pm Mar-Sep, to 6pm Oct-Feb) Offers a range of city maps and booklets. It also operates information kiosks at the Alcazaba entrance (Calle Alcazabilla), at the main train station (Explanada de la Estación), on Plaza de la Merced and on the eastern beaches (El Palo and La Malagueta).

ℹ Getting There & Away

Málaga's airport is one of Spain's busiest, with budget connections from all over Europe. The airport is connected by train to central Málaga.

The bus station has links to all major cities in Spain, including Cádiz (€27, four hours), Córdoba (€12, three hours), Granada (€12, two hours), Madrid (€45, nine hours) and Seville (€19, 2¾ hours).

Train services include Córdoba (€27.50, one hour, 18 daily), Seville (€24, 2¾ hours, 11 daily) and Madrid (€80, 2½ hours, 17 daily). Note that for Córdoba and Seville the daily schedule includes faster trains at roughly double the cost.

Ronda

POP 34,400

Perched on an inland plateau riven by the 100m fissure of El Tajo gorge, Ronda is Málaga province's most spectacular town. It has a superbly dramatic location, and owes its name ('surrounded' by mountains) to the encircling Serranía de Ronda.

⊙ Sights

Puente Nuevo
BRIDGE

(New Bridge; €2; ⊙10am-6pm Mon-Fri, to 3pm Sat & Sun) Straddling the dramatic gorge and the Río Guadalevín (Deep River) is Ronda's most recognisable sight, the towering Puente Nuevo, so named not because it's particularly new (building started in 1759) but because it's newer than the **Puente Viejo** (Old Bridge). It's best viewed from the Camino de los Molinos, which runs along the bottom of the gorge. The bridge separates the old and new towns.

Casa del Rey Moro
GARDENS

(House of the Moorish King; Calle Santo Domingo 17; adult/child €5/3; ⊙10am-7pm) Several landscaped terraces give access to La Mina, an Islamic stairway of more than 300 steps cut into the rock all the way down to the river at the bottom of the gorge. These steps enabled Ronda to maintain water supplies when it was under attack. It was also the point where Christian troops forced entry in 1485. The steps are not well lit and are steep and wet in places. Take care.

🛏 Sleeping & Eating

Hotel San Francisco
HOTEL $$

(📞952 87 32 99; www.hotelsanfrancisco-ronda.com; Calle María Cabrera 18; r incl breakfast €64-75; ❄) This is possibly the best budget option in Ronda, offering a warm welcome. Once

ANDALUCÍA'S QUIETEST BEACHES

The coast east of Almería in eastern Andalucía is perhaps the last section of Spain's Mediterranean coast where you can have a beach to yourself. This is Spain's sunniest region – even in late March it can be warm enough to strip off and take in the rays. The best thing about the region is the wonderful coastline and semidesert scenery of the Cabo de Gata promontory. All along the 50km coast from El Cabo de Gata village to Agua Amarga, some of the most beautiful and empty beaches on the Mediterranean alternate with precipitous cliffs and scattered villages. The main village is laid-back San José, with excellent beaches nearby, such as Playa de los Genoveses and Playa de Mónsul.

a humble *hostal* (family-run budget hotel), it has been refurbished and upgraded to the status of hotel, with facilities to match – including wheelchair access.

Casa María ANDALUCIAN $
(📱951 083 663; Plaza Ruedo Alameda 27; menú €20; ⊗ noon-3.30pm & 7.30-10.30pm Thu-Tue; 🛗) Walk straight through Ronda's old town and out of the **Carlos V gate** and the crowds mysteriously melt away, leaving just you and a few locals propping up the bar at Casa María. Lap it up. Set menus include dishes featuring the likes of steak, scallops, salmon, cod and asparagus.

ℹ️ Information

Tourist Office (www.turismoderonda.es; Paseo de Blas Infante; ⊗ 10am-6pm Mon-Fri, to 7pm Sat, to 2.30pm Sun) Helpful staff with a wealth of information on the town and region.

ℹ️ Getting There & Away

Slow buses reach Ronda from Málaga, Seville and Cádiz. Trains run to Málaga, Córdoba, Madrid and Granada, as well as to Seville with a change in Bobadilla or Antequera.

Spain Survival Guide

ℹ️ Directory A–Z

ACCOMMODATION

At the budget end of the market, places listing accommodation use all sorts of overlapping names to describe themselves. *Pensiones*, *hospedajes* and *casas de huéspedes* all offer simple, cheap rooms, often with shared bathroom.

ℹ️ PRICE RANGES

The following price ranges refer to a double room with private bathroom:

€ less than €65

€€ €65–140

€€€ more than €140

The price ranges for Madrid and Barcelona are inevitably higher:

€ less than €75

€€ €75–200

€€€ more than €200

Hostales are a step up from *pensiones* and operate as simple, small hotels – you'll find them everywhere across the country

Spain has official youth hostels – *albergues juveniles* – as well as backpackers' hostels dotted around the country. These are often the cheapest places for lone travellers, but two people can usually get a better double room elsewhere for a similar price.

DISCOUNT CARDS

Many cities offer a special card that includes entry to attractions, public transport, a city bus tour and restaurant discounts. Typically, you need to do lots of sightseeing to save money with it.

LGBT TRAVELLERS

Spain has become perhaps the most gay-friendly country in southern Europe.

Lesbians and gay men generally keep a fairly low profile, but are quite open in the cities. Madrid, Barcelona, Sitges and Ibiza have particularly lively gay and lesbian scenes. Sitges is a major destination on the international gay party circuit; gay participants take a leading role in the wild **Carnaval** (www.carnavaldesitges.com), which is held there in February/March.

MONEY

ATMs are plentiful. Cards are widely accepted, but not as widely as in most of Europe – carry cash for cheaper restaurants and all bars.

Tipping is always optional in Spain. In restaurants, Spaniards leave small change, and others up to 5%, which is considered generous. Tipping in bars is rare.

OPENING HOURS

Banks 8.30am to 2pm Monday to Friday; some also open 4pm to 7pm Thursday and 9am to 1pm Saturday

Central post offices 8.30am to 9.30pm Monday to Friday, 8.30am to 2pm Saturday (most other branches 8.30am to 2.30pm Monday to Friday, 9.30am to 1pm Saturday)

Nightclubs Midnight or 1am to 5am or 6am

Restaurants Lunch 1pm to 4pm, dinner 8.30pm to 11pm or midnight

Shops 10am-2pm and 4.30-7.30pm or 5-8pm Monday to Friday or Saturday; big supermarkets and department stores generally open 10am-10pm Monday to Saturday

PUBLIC HOLIDAYS

There are at least 14 official holidays a year – some observed nationwide, some locally. When a holiday falls close to a weekend, Spaniards like to make a *puente* (bridge), meaning they take the intervening day off too. Here are the national holidays:

Año Nuevo (New Year's Day) 1 January
Viernes Santo (Good Friday) March/April
Fiesta del Trabajo (Labour Day) 1 May
La Asunción (Feast of the Assumption) 15 August
Fiesta Nacional de España (National Day) 12 October
La Inmaculada Concepción (Feast of the Immaculate Conception) 8 December
Navidad (Christmas) 25 December

Regional governments set five holidays and local councils two more. Common dates include the following:

Epifanía (Epiphany) or **Día de los Reyes Magos** (Three Kings' Day) 6 January
Jueves Santo (Good Thursday) March/April; not observed in Catalonia and Valencia.
Corpus Christi June. This is the Thursday after the eighth Sunday after Easter Sunday.
Día de Santiago Apóstol (Feast of St James the Apostle) 25 July
Día de Todos los Santos (All Saints Day) 1 November
Día de la Constitución (Constitution Day) 6 December

TELEPHONE

Local SIM cards with call and data packages are widely available. Spanish landline and mobile numbers have nine digits, with no separate area code.

International dialling code ⏺ 00
Country code ⏺ 34

❶ Getting There & Away

AIR

There are direct flights to Spain from most European countries, as well as North America, South America, Africa, the Middle East and Asia.

BUS

Apart from shorter cross-border services, Eurolines (www.eurolines.com) is the main operator of international bus services to Spain from most of Europe and Morocco. Other bus services connect Portugal and Spain, including three daily bus services between Lisbon and Madrid.

BOAT

Regular car ferries and hydrofoils run to and from Morocco, and there are ferry links to the UK, Italy, the Canary Islands and Algeria. Check www.directferries.com for a run down of routes.

TRAIN

The principal rail crossings into Spain pierce the Franco-Spanish frontier along the Mediterranean coast and via the Basque Country. From Portugal, the main train line runs from Lisbon across Extremadura to Madrid. In addition to the rail services connecting Spain with France and Portugal, there are direct train services that run between Zürich and Barcelona (via Bern, Geneva, Perpignan and Girona), and between Milan and Barcelona (via Turin, Perpignan and Girona).

❶ Getting Around

Spain has an extensive network of internal flights, many operated by budget airlines like Vueling and Ryanair.

The bus network is fast, cheap and comfortable. Alsa (www.alsa.es) is one of the main operators.

Renfe (www.renfe.com) is the main rail operator, and runs a wide network, which includes speedy but pricy AVE trains. Book ahead online for discounts.

Ferries and hydrofoils link Barcelona, Valencia, Gandia and Dénia with the Balearic Islands. There are also services to Spain's North African enclaves of Ceuta and Melilla.

PORTUGAL

Lisbon

POP 547,700 (2.7 MILLION IN URBAN AREA)

Spread across steep hillsides that overlook the Rio Tejo, Lisbon has captivated visitors for centuries. Windswept vistas reveal the city in all its beauty: Roman and Moorish ruins, white-domed cathedrals and grand plazas lined with sun-drenched cafes. The real delight of discovery, though, is delving into the narrow cobblestone lanes.

◎ Sights

At the riverfront is the grand Praça do Comércio. Behind it march the pedestrian-filled streets of Baixa (lower) district, up to Praça da Figueira and Praça Dom Pedro IV (aka Rossio). From Baixa it's a steep climb west, through swanky shopping district Chiado, into the narrow streets of nightlife-haven Bairro Alto. Eastwards from the Baixa it's another climb to Castelo de São Jorge and the Moorish, labyrinthine Alfama district around it. The World Heritage sites

PORTUGAL AT A GLANCE

Don't Miss Portugal

The Alfama This Lisbon district, with its labyrinthine alleyways, hidden courtyards and curving, shadow-filled lanes, is a magical place in which to lose all sense of direction and delve into the soul of the city. You'll pass breadbox-sized grocers, brilliantly tiled buildings and cosy taverns filled with easy-going chatter, accompanied by the scent of chargrilled sardines and the mournful rhythms of fado drifting in the breeze.

Sintra Resembling an illustration from a fairy tale, Sintra is sprinkled with stone-walled taverns and has a whitewashed palace looming over it. Forested hillsides form the backdrop to the village's storybook setting, with imposing castles, mystical gardens, strange mansions and centuries-old monasteries hidden among the woodlands.

Porto Laced with narrow pedestrian laneways, romantic Porto is blessed with baroque churches, epic theatres and sprawling plazas. Its Ribeira district – a Unesco World Heritage site – is just a short walk across a landmark bridge from centuries-old port wineries in Vila Nova de Gaia, where you can sip one of the world's great sweet wines.

Beaches of the Algarve Along Portugal's south coast, the Algarve is home to a wildly varied coastline. There are sandy islands reachable only by boat, dramatic cliff-backed shores, rarely visited rugged beaches and people-packed sands near buzzing nightlife.

Alcobaça, Batalha and Tomar These medieval Christian monuments – all Unesco World Heritage sites – constitute one of Portugal's greatest national treasures. Each has its own magic.

Itineraries

One Week
Start in **Lisbon**, spending two days exploring the city's enchanting neighbourhoods. On day three, head to nearby **Sintra**, for quaint village life amid woodlands and palaces. Head north, spending a day in **Tomar**, a sleepy river town that's home to the staggering Convento de Cristo, then a night or two in the venerable university town of **Coimbra** Spend your last days in **Porto**, Lisbon's rival in beauty.

Two Weeks
Follow the same itinerary but before heading to Tomar, hit the Alentejo to explore fascinating **Évora** and its nearby megaliths.From there, head to beach- and nightlife-loving **Lagos**. Keep going west until you hit laid-back **Sagres**, where you can visit its dramatically sited fort, surf good waves and contemplate the endless horizon at the cliffs near town. Go north back to Lisbon and resume the one-week itinerary.

Essential Food & Drink

Pastel de nata Custard tart, ideally served warm and dusted with cinnamon.

Travesseira A rolled puff pastry filled with almond-and-egg-yolk custard. Find them in Sintra.

Tinned fish Sardines, mackerel and tuna served with bread, olives and other accompaniments.

Francesinha Porto's favourite hangover snack is a thick open-faced sandwich covered in melted cheese.

Marzipan In the Algarve, this very sweet almond-infused confection is a local favourite.

Grilled chicken Rotisserie chicken is an art form in Portugal. Spice it up with *piri-piri* (hot sauce).

Bifana A bread roll served with a slice of fried pork inside. They're best in the Alentejo.

Getting Around

Transport in Portugal is reasonably priced, quick and efficient.

Train Extremely affordable, with a decent network between major towns from north to south. Visit **Comboios de Portugal** (☑ 707 210 220; www.cp.pt) for schedules and prices.

Car Useful for visiting small villages, national parks and other regions with minimal public transport. Cars can be hired in major towns and cities. Drive on the right.

Bus Cheaper and slower than trains. Useful for more remote villages that aren't serviced by trains. Infrequent service on weekends.

When to Go

Lisbon

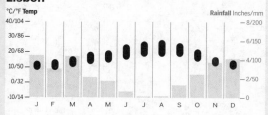

Apr–Jun Spring wildflowers and mild days are ideal for outdoor activities. Lively June festivals.

Jul–Aug Accommodation prices increase by 30%; big crowds in the Algarve and coastal resorts.

Sep–Nov Colder ocean temperatures; crowds and prices reduce.

Arriving in Portugal

Aeroporto de Lisboa (Lisbon) Metro trains allow convenient access to downtown (€1.90, 20 minutes to the centre, frequent departures from 6.30am to 1am). The AeroBus (€3.50) departs every 20 minutes from 7am to 11pm, while a taxi to the centre will cost around €15 and take 15 minutes.

Aeroporto Francisco Sá Carneiro (Porto) Metro trains run to the city centre (€2.45) and take about 45 minutes. A taxi will cost €20 to €25 and take around 30 to 60 minutes.

Top Phrases

Hello. Olá.

Goodbye. Adeus.

Please. Por favor.

Thank you. Obrigado. (m) / Obrigada. (f)

Sorry. Desculpe.

Resources

Portugal Tourism (www.visitportugal.com) Portugal's official tourism site.

Portugal News (www.theportugalnews.com) The latest news in Portugal.

Wines of Portugal (www.winesofportugal.info) Overview of Portugal's wines.

Set Your Budget

➡ Dorm bed: €15–22

➡ Basic hotel room for two: from €30

➡ Lunch special at a family-run restaurant: €7–9

Central Lisbon

200 m
0.1 miles

Museu Calouste Gulbenkian - Coleção do Fundador (2.8km)

Parque Eduardo VII

Elevador da Lavra

R das Portas de Santo Antão

Cç de Santano

Cç do Monte

R dos Lagares

Cç de Sto André

Lg das Olarias

R do Terreirinho

R dos Cavaleiros

R do Arco da Graça

R de São Lazaro

Martim Moniz

R da Palma

Lg Martim Moniz

R do Arco do Marquês do Alegrete

R da Mouraria

R do São Pedro Martir

Tram 28/Largo Martim Moniz

Castelo de São Jorge

CASTELO

Esplanada do Castelo

Costa do Castelo

Cç Marquês de Tancos

Lg Adelino Amaro da Costa

R da Madalena

R dos Fanqueiros

BAIXA

R de Santa Justa

R da Assunção

R dos Condes de Monsanto

R de São Domingos

Lg de São Domingos

R Barros Queirós

Tv Nova de São Domingos

Rossio
Pç da Figueira

ROSSIO

Pç Dom Pedro IV (Rossio)

R do Carmo

R 1 de Dezembro

Convento do Carmo & Museu Arqueológico

R da Trindade

R do Duque

R da Condessa

R da Oliveira

R Nova da Trindade

Estação do Rossio (Rossio Train Station)

R das Taipas

R do Regedor

R do Jardim do Regedor

Pç dos Restauradores

Restauradores

Ask Me Lisboa

Av da Liberdade

R da Glória

Elevador da Glória

R Dom Pedro V

R Luísa Todi

Tv de São Pedro

R do Teixeira

R da Água da Flor

Tv da Boa Hora

BAIRRO ALTO

Lg Trindade Coelho

R da Misericórdia

R das Gáveas

R do Norte

R do Diário de Notícias

R da Barroca

R da Atalaia

R da Rosa

Tv da Queimada

R Luz Soriano

Tv dos Fiéis de Deus

1 Castelo de São Jorge
2 Convento do Carmo & Museu Arqueológico
3 Av da Liberdade
4
6
7

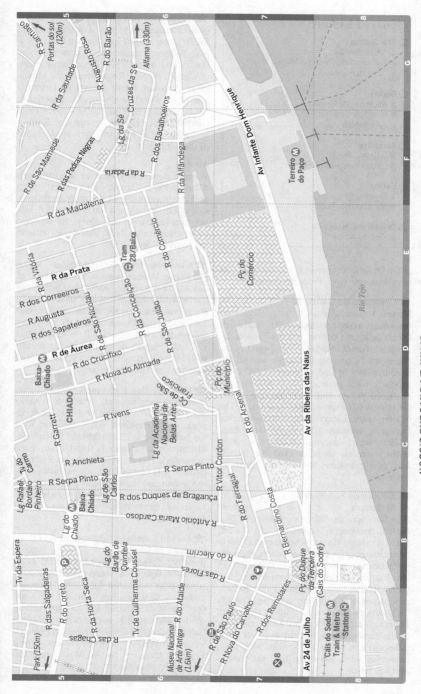

R. S. Ssantiago
Portas do sol (120m)
R. da Saudade
R. Augusto Rosa
R. do Barão
Alfama (330m)
Cruzes da Sé
R. dos Bacalhoeiros
Lg da Sé
R. da Padaria
R. de São Mamede
R. das Pedras Negras
R. da Alfândega
Av Infante Dom Henrique
R. da Madalena
Terreiro do Paço M
R. do Comércio
R. da Vitória
Tram 28/Baixa
R. da Prata
R. do Comércio
Pç do Comércio
R dos Correeiros
R Augusta
R da Conceição
R de São Nicolau
R dos Sapateiros
R de São Julião
R de Áurea
R do Crucifixo
Rio Tejo
Baixa-Chiado M
R Nova do Almada
Pç do Município
CHIADO
R Garrett
R Ivens
Cç de São Francisco
R do Arsenal
Av da Ribeira das Naus
Lg da Academia Nacional de Belas Artes
R Anchieta
R Serpa Pinto
R Serpa Pinto
R Vitor Cordon
Lg Rafael Bordalo Pinheiro
Tv do Carmo
R de São Carlos
R do Ferragial
Baixa-Chiado M
R dos Duques de Bragança
R Antonio Maria Cardoso
R Bernardino Costa
Lg do Chiado
Pç do Duque da Terceira (Cais do Sodré)
Tv da Espera
Lg do Barão de Quintela
R do Alecrim
R das Salgadeiras
R do Loreto
R das Flores
R da Horta Seca
9
Park (150m)
R das Chagas
Tv de Guilherme Coussel
R do Atalde
Museu Nacional de Arte Antiga (1.6km)
R de São Paulo
5
R dos Remolares
Cais do Sodré Train & Metro Station
R Nova do Carvalho
8
Av 24 de Julho

Central Lisbon

of Belém lie further west along the river – an easy tram ride from Praça do Comércio.

★**Convento do Carmo & Museu Arqueológico**　RUINS
(www.museuarqueologicodocarmo.pt; Largo do Carmo; adult/child €4/free; ⊙10am-7pm Mon-Sat Jun-Sep, to 6pm Oct-May) Soaring above Lisbon, the skeletal Convento do Carmo was all but devoured by the 1755 earthquake and that's precisely what makes it so captivating. Its shattered pillars and wishbone-like arches are completely exposed to the elements. The Museu Arqueológico shelters archaeological treasures, such as 4th-century sarcophagi, griffin-covered column fragments, 16th-century *azulejo* (hand-painted tile) panels and two gruesome 16th-century Peruvian mummies.

Miradouro de São Pedro de Alcântara　VIEWPOINT
(Rua São Pedro de Alcântara; ⊙viewpoint 24hr, kiosk 10am-midnight Sun-Wed, to 2am Thu-Sat) Hitch a ride on vintage **Ascensor da Glória** (www.carris.pt/pt/ascensores-e-elevador; Praça dos Restauradores; return €3.70; ⊙7.15am-11.55pm Mon-Thu, to 12.25am Fri, 8.45am-12.25am Sat, 9.15am-11.55pm Sun) from Praça dos Restauradores, or huff your way up steep Calçada da Glória to this terrific hilltop viewpoint. Fountains and Greek busts add a regal air to the surroundings, and the open-air kiosk doles out wine, beer and snacks, which you can enjoy while taking in the castle views and live music.

★**Castelo de São Jorge**　CASTLE
(www.castelodesaojorge.pt; adult/student/child €8.50/5/free; ⊙9am-9pm Mar-Oct, to 6pm Nov-Feb) Towering dramatically above Lisbon, the mid-11th-century hilltop fortifications of Castelo de São Jorge sneak into almost every snapshot. Roam its snaking ramparts and pine-shaded courtyards for superlative views over the city's red rooftops to the river. Guided tours daily (in Portuguese, English and Spanish) at 1pm and 5pm are included in the admission price.

Alfama　AREA
Wander down (to save your legs) through Alfama's steep, narrow, cobblestoned streets and catch a glimpse of the more traditional side of Lisbon before it too is gentrified. Linger in a backstreet cafe along the way and experience some local bonhomie without the tourist gloss.

★**Museu Nacional de Arte Antiga**　MUSEUM
(Ancient Art Museum; www.museudearteantiga.pt; Rua das Janelas Verdes; adult/child €6/free, with themed exhibitions €10/free, free Sun until 2pm for Portuguese citizens/residents only; ⊙10am-6pm Tue-Sun) Set in a lemon-fronted, 17th-century palace, the Museu Nacional de Arte Antiga is Lapa's biggest draw. It presents a star-studded collection of European and Asian paintings and decorative arts.

★**Mosteiro dos Jerónimos**　MONASTERY
(www.mosteirojeronimos.pt; Praça do Império; adult/child €10/5, free Sun until 2pm for Portuguese citizens/residents only; ⊙10am-6.30pm Tue-Sun Jun-Sep, to 5.30pm Oct-May) Belém's undisputed heart-stealer is this Unesco-listed monastery. The *mosteiro* is the stuff of pure fantasy; a fusion of Diogo de Boitaca's creative vision and the spice and pepper dosh of Manuel I, who commissioned it to trumpet Vasco da Gama's discovery of a sea route to India in 1498.

★**Museu Calouste Gulbenkian – Coleção do Fundador**　MUSEUM
(Founder's Collection; www.gulbenkian.pt; Av de Berna 45A; Coleção do Fundador/Coleção Moderna combo ticket adult/child €11.50/free, temporary exhibitions €3-6, Sun free from 2pm; ⊙10am-6pm Wed-Mon) Famous for its outstanding quality and breadth, the world-class Museu Calouste Gulbenkian showcases an epic collection of Western and Eastern art – from Egyptian treasures to Old Master and Impressionist paintings.

🛏 Sleeping

Lisbon Calling
HOSTEL $

(☑213 432 381; www.lisboncalling.net; Rua de São Paulo 126, 3rd fl; dm from €20, d with/without bathroom from €60/53; @ 🖥) This fashionable, unsigned backpacker favourite near Santa Catarina features original frescoes, *azulejos* and hardwood floors – all lovingly restored by friendly Portuguese owners. The bright, spacious dorms and a brick-vaulted kitchen are easy on the eyes, but the private rooms – specifically room 1812 – will floor you: boutique-hotel-level dens of style and comfort that thunderously out-punch their price point.

Lisbon Destination Hostel
HOSTEL $

(☑213 466 457; www.destinationhostels.com; Rossio train station, 2nd fl; dm €25, s/d without bathroom from €36/54, d from €107; @ 🖥) Housed in Lisbon's loveliest train station, this world-class hostel has a glass ceiling lighting the spacious plant-filled common area. Rooms are crisp and well-kept, and there are loads of activities (bar crawls, beach day trips, etc). Facilities include a shared kitchen, game consoles, movie room (with popcorn) and 24-hour self-service bar. Breakfast is top-notch with crêpes and fresh fruit.

🍴 Eating

⭐Mercado da Ribeira
MARKET $

(www.timeoutmarket.com; Av 24 de Julho; ⊙10am-midnight Sun-Wed, to 2am Thu-Sat, traditional market 6am-2pm Mon-Sat; 🖥) Doing trade in fresh fruit and veg, fish and flowers since 1892, this oriental-dome-topped market hall is the word on everyone's lips since *Time Out* transformed half of it into a gourmet food court in 2014. Now it's like Lisbon in microcosm, with everything from Garrafeira Nacional wines to Conserveira de Lisboa fish, Arcádia chocolate and Santini gelato.

⭐Gelataria Nannarella
GELATO $

(www.facebook.com/gelaterianannarella; Rua Nova da Piedade 68; small/medium/large €2.50/3/3.50; ⊙noon-10pm) This is where you'll get Lisbon's best gelato. Seatless Nannarella is squeezed into little more than a doorway, where Roman transplant Constanza Ventura churns out some 25 perfect, spatula-slabbed flavours of traditional gelato and sorbet daily to anxious lines of *lisboêtas*. Nailing both consistency and flavour, this sweet, sweet stuff from which heaven is made seemingly emerges straight from Ventura's kitchen.

Frangasqueira Nacional
PORTUGUESE $

(www.facebook.com/frangasqueira; Rua da Imprensa Nacional 116; chicken/ribs per kg €10.60/13; ⊙6-10pm Tue, noon-2.30pm & 6-10pm Wed-Fri, noon-3pm & 6pm-2am Sat & Sun) This takeaway-only grill does splendid chicken, ribs, crioula sausage and turkey kebabs along with house-cut potato chips and spiced olives that all make for a wondrously carnivorous picnic in nearby Jardim do Príncipe Real.

⭐Ti-Natércia
PORTUGUESE $

(☑218 862 133; Rua Escola Gerais 54; mains €5-12; ⊙7pm-midnight Tue-Fri, noon-3pm & 7pm-midnight Sat) A decade in and a legend in the making, 'Aunt' Natércia and her downright delicious Portuguese home cooking is a tough ticket: there are but a mere six tables and they fill up fast. She'll talk your ear off (and doesn't mince words!) while you devour her excellent take on the classics. Reservations essential (and cash only).

Antiga Confeitaria de Belém
PASTRIES $

(Pastéis de Belém; www.pasteisdebelem.pt; Rua de Belém 84-92; pastries from €1.10; ⊙8am-11pm Oct-Jun, to midnight Jul-Sep) Since 1837, this patisserie has been transporting locals to sugar-coated nirvana with heavenly *pastéis de belém*. The pastry nests are filled with custard, baked at 200ºC for that perfect golden crust, then lightly dusted with cinnamon. Admire *azulejos* (hand-painted tiles) in the vaulted rooms or devour a still-warm tart at the counter and try to guess the secret ingredient. Go early midweek to avoid nasty lines.

Decadente
PORTUGUESE $$

(☑213 461 381; www.thedecadente.pt; Rua de São Pedro de Alcântara 81; mains €9-16; ⊙noon-midnight Sun-Wed, to 1am Thu, to 2am Fri & Sat; 🖥) This beautifully designed restaurant inside a boutique hotel overlooking the stunning São Pedro de Alcântara lookout, with touches of industrial chic, geometric artwork and an enticing back patio, serves inventive dishes showcasing high-end Portuguese ingredients at excellent prices. The changing three-course lunch menu (€10) is first-rate. Start with creative cocktails in the front bar.

🍷 Drinking & Entertainment

Alfama and Graça are perfect for a relaxed drink with a view, while Bairro Alto is like a student at a house party: wasted on cheap booze, flirty and everybody's friend. At dusk, the nocturnal hedonist rears its head with bars trying to out-decibel each other, hash-peddlers lurking in the shadows and kamikaze taxi drivers forcing kerbside sippers to leap aside.

★**Pensão Amor**   BAR
(www.pensaoamor.pt; Rua do Alecrím 19; ☺2pm-3am Sun-Wed, to 4am Thu-Sat) Set inside a former brothel, this cheeky bar pays homage to its passion-filled past with colourful wall murals, a library of erotic-tinged works, and a small stage where you can sometimes catch burlesque shows. The Museu Erótico de Lisboa (MEL) was on the way at time of research.

★**Park**   BAR
(www.facebook.com/parklisboaofficial; Calçada do Combro 58; ☺1pm-2am Tue-Sat, to 8pm Sun; ☎) If only all multistorey car parks were like this... Take the liftto the 5th floor, and head up and around to the top, which has been transformed into one of Lisbon's hippest rooftop bars, with sweeping views reaching right down to the Tejo and over the bell towers of Santa Catarina Church.

Portas do Sol   BAR
(www.portasdosol.pt; Largo das Portas do Sol; ☺10am-1am Sun-Thu, to 2am Fri & Sat; ☎) Near one of Lisbon's iconic viewpoints, this spacious sun-drenched terrace has a mix of sofas and white patio furniture, where you can sip cocktails while taking in magnificent river views. DJs bring animation to the darkly lit industrial interior on weekends.

ℹ Information

Ask Me Lisboa (☎213 463 314; www.askmelisboa.com; Praça dos Restauradores, Palácio Foz; ☺9am-8pm) The largest and most helpful tourist office in the city faces Praça dos Restauradaures inside the Palácio Foz. Staff dole out maps and information, book accommodation and reserve rental cars.

ℹ Getting There & Away

Situated around 6km north of the centre, the ultramodern **Aeroporto de Lisboa** (Lisbon Airport; ☎218 413 500; Alameda das Comunidades Portuguesas) operates direct flights to major international hubs.

Lisbon's main long-distance bus terminal is **Sete Rios** (Praça General Humberto Delgado, Rua das Laranjeiras), adjacent to both Jardim Zoológico metro station and Sete Rios train station. The big carriers, Rede Expressos and Eva, run frequent services to almost every major town. **Internorte** (☎707 200 512; www.intercentro.pt; Av Dom João II, Gare do Oriente; ☺9am-6pm) runs coaches to destinations all over Europe. The other major terminal is the **Gare do Oriente** (Oriente Station; Av Dom João II), concentrating on services to the north and Spain and beyond.

Lisbon has several major train stations. **Santa Apolónia** is the terminal for trains from northern and central Portugal. **Gare do Oriente** is Lisbon's biggest station. Trains to the Alentejo and the Algarve originate from here. Note that all of Santa Apolónia's services also stop here.

ℹ Getting Around

Carris (☎213 500 115; www.carris.pt) operates all transport in Lisbon proper except the metro. Individual tickets on board cost €1.85 (buses and trams).

The **metro** (☎213 500 115; www.metrolisboa.pt; single/day ticket €1.45/6.30; ☺6.30am-1am) is useful for short hops and to reach the Gare do Oriente and nearby Parque das Nações.

Around Lisbon

Sintra
POP 26,000
With its rippling mountains, dewy forests exotic gardens and glittering palaces, Sintra is like a page torn from a fairy tale. Its Unesco World Heritage–listed centre, Sintra-Vila, is dotted with pastel-hued manors folded into luxuriant hills that roll down to the blue Atlantic. It's the must-do day trip from Lisbon. Go early in the day midweek to escape the worst of the crowds.

◉ Sights

★**Palácio Nacional de Sintra**   PALACE
(www.parquesdesintra.pt; Largo Rainha Dona Amélia; adult/child €10/8.50; ☺9.30am-7pm) The star of Sintra-Vila is this palace, with its iconic twin conical chimneys and lavish interior. The whimsical interior is a mix of Moorish and Manueline styles, with arabesque courtyards, barley-twist columns and 15th- and 16th-century geometric *azulejos* that figure among Portugal's oldest.

★**Quinta da Regaleira**   NOTABLE BUILDING, GARDENS
(www.regaleira.pt; Rua Barbosa du Bocage; adult/child €6/4, tours €12/8; ☺9.30am-7pm Apr-Sep, to 5pm Oct-Mar) This magical villa and gardens is a neo-Manueline extravaganza, dreamed up by Italian opera-set designer Luigi Manini, under the orders of Brazilian coffee tycoon António Carvalho Monteiro, aka 'Monteiro

dos Milhões' ('Moneybags Monteiro'). The villa is surprisingly homely inside, despite its ferociously carved fireplaces, frescoes and Venetian-glass mosaics. Keep an eye out for mythological and Knights Templar symbols.

★ **Castelo dos Mouros** CASTLE
(www.parquesdesintra.pt; adult/child €8/6.50; ⊙9.30am-8pm) Soaring 412m above sea level, this mist-enshrouded ruined castle looms high above the surrounding forest. When the clouds peel away, the vistas over Sintra's palace-dotted hills and dales, across to the glittering Atlantic are – like the climb – breathtaking. The 10th-century Moorish castle's dizzying ramparts stretch across the mountain ridges and past moss-clad boulders the size of small buses.

🛏 Sleeping

★ **Moon Hill Hostel** HOSTEL **$**
(☑219 243 755; www.moonhillhostel.com; Rua Guilherme Gomes Fernandes 19; dm €19-22, d with/without bathroom €75/55; ✴@🛜) 🅿 This design-forward, minimalist newcomer easily outshines the Sintra competition. Whether you book a boutique-hotel-level private room, with colourful reclaimed-wood headboards and wall-covering photos of enchanting Sintra forest scenes (go for 10 or 14 for Pena National Palace views, and 12 or 13 for Moorish castle views) or a four-bed mixed dorm (with lockers), you are sleeping in high style.

ⓘ Information

Ask Me Sintra (☑219 231 157; www.visitlisboa. com; Praça da República 23; ⊙9.30am-6pm), near the centre of Sintra-Vila, is a helpful multilingual office with expert insight into Sintra and the surrounding areas. There's also a **train station branch** (☑211 932 545; www.visitlisboa.com; Sintra train station; ⊙10am-noon & 2.30-6pm), often overrun by those arriving by rail.

ⓘ Getting There & Away

Trains (€2.20, 40 minutes) run every 15 minutes (hourly at weekends) between Sintra and Lisbon's Rossio station. From Sintra station, it's a pleasant 1km walk (or short bus ride) into the village. Regular buses head from Sintra to Cascais (€4.15, one hour).

Cascais
POP 35,000
Cascais rocketed from sleepy fishing village to much-loved summertime playground of wave-frolicking *lisboêtas* after King Luís I went for a dip in 1870. Its trio of golden bays attracts sun-worshipping holidaymakers, who come to splash in the ice-cold Atlantic. Don't expect to get much sand to yourself at the weekend, though.

◉ Sights & Activities

Cascais' sandy bays – Praia da Conceição, Praia da Rainha and Praia da Ribeira – are fine for a sunbake or a tingly Atlantic dip, but there's not much towel space in summer.

The best beach is wild, windswept Praia do Guincho, 9km northwest, a mecca to surfers and windsurfers with massive crashing rollers, powder-soft sands, fresh seafood and magical sunsets.

FADO

Infused by Moorish song and the ditties of homesick sailors, bluesy, bittersweet fado encapsulates the Lisbon psyche like nothing else. Ask 10 *lisboêtas* to explain it and each will give a different version. This is because fado is deeply personal and explanations hinge on the mood of the moment. Recurring themes are love, destiny, death and the omnipresent *saudade* or 'nostalgic longing'; a kind of musical soap opera.

Though a *fadista* (singer of fado) is traditionally accompanied by a classical and 12-string Portuguese guitar, many new-generation stars such as Mariza, Ana Moura and Joana Amendoeira are putting their own spin on the genre, giving it a twist of Cuban *son* or a dash of Argentine tango.

At Bairro Alto's touristy, folksy performances, you'll only be skating the surface. For authentic fado, go to where it was born – Alfama. While wandering the narrow lanes by night you'll be serenaded by mournful ballads.

There's usually a minimum cover of €15 to €25, and as food is often mediocre, it's worth asking if you can just order a bottle of wine. Book ahead at weekends. If you prefer a spontaneous approach, seek out *fado vadio* where anyone can – and does – have a warble.

You will find **Moana Surf School** (☑964 449 436; www.moanasurfschool.com; Estrada do Abano, Praia do Guincho; private lesson per hr €50, group lesson €30, 4-lesson course €85) at Wave Center, which is located next door to Bar do Gunicho.

🛏 Sleeping & Eating

Perfect Spot
Lisbon   HOSTEL $
(☑924 058 645; www.perfectspot-lisbon.com; Av de Sintra 354; dm/d/tr from €22/60/75; P🛜) New parents Jon and Rita run this lovely hostel – perfect for families in addition to surfers and climbers – in a large home just

a smidgen outside the tourist zone. Spacious rooms and dorms are themed with unique art, but the real coup is the closed-in garden, a supreme hang space with day beds and a barbecue lounge.

★**Bar do Guincho**   PORTUGUESE $$
(www.bardoguincho.pt; Estrada do Abano, Praia do Guincho; mains €8.50-17.50; ⊘noon-7pm Sun & Tue-Thu, noon-11.45pm Fri-Sat, later hours Jul & Aug; 🛜) Sweeping the awards for the most dramatic location in Cascais, the good-time Bar do Guincho bar-restaurant sits tucked behind a craggy ridge located on the northern end of Guincho. Looking out from the

The Algarve

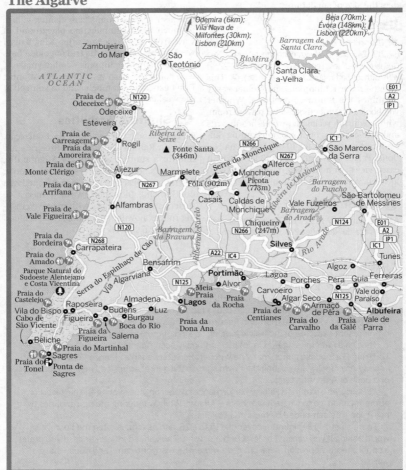

sand, you would never know it's there, but it is – and it is packed! Revellers rake in the beach-friendly burgers, seafood and salads washed down with cold *cerveja* (beer). Grab some refreshments and settle in for the afternoon.

ℹ Information

Ask Me Cascais (Turismo; ☏ 912 034 214; www.visitcascais.com; Largo Cidade Vitória; ☺9am-8pm summer, to 6pm winter) This tourist information centre as a handy map, events guide *(What's in Cascais)* and is helpful to an extent.

ℹ Getting There & Away

Bus 417 goes about hourly from Cascais to Sintra (€4.10, 40 minutes).

Trains run from Lisbon's Cais do Sodré station to Cascais (€2.15, 40 minutes, every 20 to 30 minutes).

The Algarve

The Algarve, Portugal's premier holiday destination, is alluring. Coastal Algarve receives a great deal of exposure for its breathtaking cliffs, golden beaches, scalloped bays and beautiful sandy islands. But

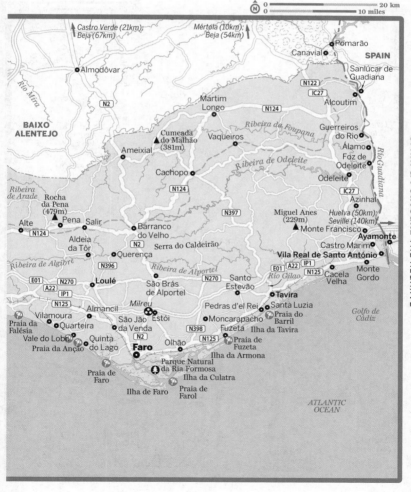

the letter 'S' (which stands for sun, surf and sand) is only one letter in the Algarvian alphabet, as there are also plenty of activities, beach bars (and discos), castles (both sandy and real), diving, entertainment and fun...

Faro

POP 50,000

The Algarve's capital has a more distinctly Portuguese feel than most of the country's beach resort towns. Many visitors only pass through this underrated city, which is a pity as it makes for an enjoyable stopover. It offers an attractive marina, well-maintained parks and plazas, and a historic old town that is full of pedestrian lanes and outdoor cafes. Its student population of 8000 ensures that there is a happening nightlife.

◉ Sights & Activities

Igreja da Misericórdia   CHURCH
(Praça Dom Francisco Gomes) The 16th-century Igreja da Misericórdia, opposite the Arco da Vila, was originally built in Manueline (Portuguese late Gothic) style but is now nearly all baroque after the destruction of the 1755 earthquake.

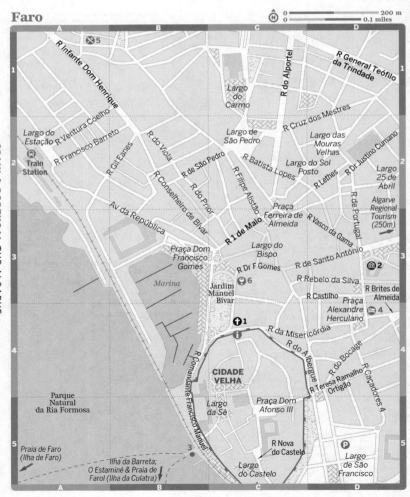

Faro

SPAIN & PORTUGAL THE ALGARVE

Museu Regional do Algarve
MUSEUM

(🖉289 289 893; Praça da Liberdade; adult/concession €1.50/1; ⊙10am-1.30pm & 2.30-6pm Mon-Fri) Three of the four halls at this worthwhile museum house exhibitions on rural life in the Algarve. This includes mock-ups of 19th-century shops and rooms, a real fishing boat, some impressively woven creations in wicker, bamboo and palm leaves, and lots of rag rugs and fishing nets. The fourth hall is always given over to a temporary show on a folksy local theme.

★ Animaris
BOATING

(🖉918 779 155, 917 811 856; www.animaris.pt) Runs trips to Ilha da Barreta (Ilha Deserta). Boats (€10 to €15 return) leave from southeast of the marina, in front of the Cidade Velha (Old Town) walls. There's a ticket kiosk by the marina. The same company runs one-hour year-round boat trips (€40) through Parque Natural da Ria Formosa. Boats leave from the pier next to Arco da Porta Nova.

Animaris also runs eco-friendly restaurant Estaminé on Ilha da Barreta, and it is the only company to operate year-round, providing stable employment for locals – another reason to go with it.

🛌 Sleeping

★ Casa d'Alagoa
HOSTEL $

(🖉289 813 252; www.farohostel.com; Praça Alexandre Herculano 27; dm not incl breakfast €21-30, d €68; 🛜) Housed in a renovated mansion on a pretty square, this commendable budget option has all the elements of today's sophisticated hostel: it's funky, laid-back and cool (and clean!). There's a range of spacious dorms, a great lounge and an upstairs terrace, plus a communal kitchen...but hey, why do you need it when dinner is on offer? Bike rental also available.

🍴 Eating & Drinking

Chefe Branco
PORTUGUESE $

(Rua de Loulé 9; mains €4.50-13.50; ⊙noon-midnight) A fabulous local spot that has an appealing street-side seating and a slightly tacky but cosy interior. The delightful staff serve honest, homestyle fare including rabbit, goat and seafood dishes. The half portions are the biggest this side of the Rio Tejo. Finish with an excellent Algarvian dessert.

★ Columbus Bar
BAR

(www.barcolumbus.pt; Praça Dom Francisco Gomes 13; ⊙noon-4am; 🛜) Definitely the place to be, this popular central place has a street-side terrace in the heart of town and an attractive brick-vaulted interior. The bar staff do a fine job mixing cocktails, and there's a pleasing range of spirits. Gets lively from around 11pm.

ℹ️ Information

Turismo (www.visitalgarve.pt; Rua da Misericórdia 8; ⊙9.30am-1pm & 2-5.30pm) Busy but efficient office with friendly staff.

ℹ️ Getting There & Away

Faro's airport has many domestic flights as well as dozens of flights from airports around Western Europe, many with budget and charter airlines.

Bus services run to Seville in Spain (€20, 3½ hours, four daily) and to Lisbon (€20, five hours, at least hourly).

There are three direct trains from Lisbon daily (€21.20 to €22.20, 3¾ hours) and connections to Porto. Locally, destinations include Lagos (€5.90, two hours, hourly).

Lagos

POP 22,000

As far as touristy towns go, Lagos (*lah-goosh*) has got the lot. It lies along the bank of the Rio Bensafrim, with 16th-century walls enclosing the old town's pretty, cobbled lanes and picturesque piazzas and churches. Beyond these lies a modern, but not overly unattractive, sprawl. The town's good restaurants and range of fabulous beaches nearby add to the allure. With every activity under the sun (literally) on offer, plus a pumping nightlife, it's not surprising that people of all ages are drawn here.

Lagos

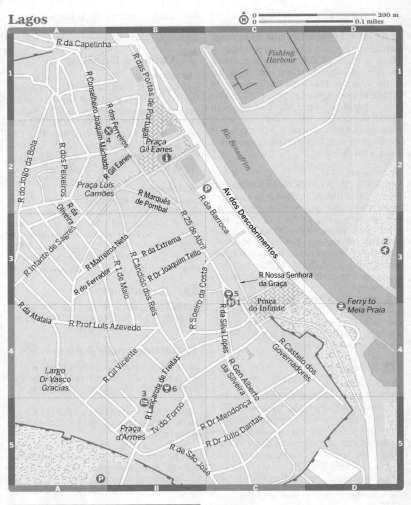

SPAIN & PORTUGAL THE ALGARVE

🏃 Activities

Numerous operators offer special guided tours on boat trips and dolphin-watching excursions.

Meia Praia   BEACH
Meia Praia, the vast expanse of sand to the east of town, has outlets offering sailboard rental and waterskiing lessons, plus several laid-back restaurants and beach bars. An informal **boat service** (€0.50; ☺ Apr-Oct) shuttles back and forth from the waterfront in Lagos.

Lagos Surf Center   SURFING
(☑ 282 764 734; www.lagossurfcenter.com; Rua da Silva Lopes 31; 1-/3-/5-day courses €60/165/250) Will help you catch a wave and head to where there are suitable swells. Children must be accompanied by a family member over 14 years of age. It also rents out wetsuits (€5 per day) and boards (€15 to €25) and offers beach kayaking and paddle-boarding trips.

🛏 Sleeping & Eating

Pousada da Juventude   HOSTEL $
(☑ 282 761 970; www.pousadasjuventude.pt; Rua Lançarote de Freitas 50; dm/d €14/43; @ 🛜) This well-run hostel is a good place to meet other travellers and is in a lively, central bar street. It's brutally basic and slightly worn in places, thanks to its popularity, but there's a kitchen and a pleasantly sunny courtyard to chill in. Reception is very helpful and open 24 hours.

★ A Forja   PORTUGUESE $$
(☑ 282 768 588; Rua dos Ferreiros 17; mains €8-17.50; ⊙ noon-3pm & 6.30-10pm Sun-Fri) Like an Italian trattoria, this buzzing *adega tipica* pulls in the crowds – locals, tourists and expats – for its hearty, top-quality traditional food served in a bustling environment at great prices. Plates of the day are always reliable, as are the simply prepared fish dishes.

🍸 Drinking & Nightlife

Dozens of bars – party palaces and local beer stops – litter the streets of Lagos, with some of the Algarve's most diverse and most clichéd drinking holes on hand. These gather plenty of surfers, backpackers and younger party animals. They are generally open until the wee hours of the morning, and a few are open during the day.

Meia Praia has some beachfront gems just seconds from sun, swimming and sand, some with weekend live music.

★ Bon Vivant   BAR
(www.bonvivantbarinlagos.com; Rua 25 de Abril 105; ⊙ 2pm-4am; 🛜) This long-standing central bar is far classier than some of the nearby options, takes some care over its mainly R&B music and makes an effort to keep patrons entertained. Spread across several levels with various terraces, Bon Vivant shakes up some great cocktails and is pretty hot once it gets going (usually late). Look out for the bartenders' juggling feats.

Garden   BEER GARDEN
(Rua Lançarote de Freitas 29; ⊙ 1pm-midnight; 🛜) This appealingly decorated beer garden makes a great spot to lounge around on a sunny afternoon with a beer or cocktail. Once you smell the barbecuing meat, you might decide to stay for a meal, too. To find it, look for the kissing-snails mural on the outside wall.

ℹ Information

Turismo (☑ 282 763 031; www.visitalgarve.pt; Praça Gil Eanes; ⊙ 9.30am-1pm & 2.30-6pm) The very helpful staff offer excellent maps and leaflets.

ℹ Getting There & Away

Bus services include Lisbon (€20, four hours, 10 expresses daily) and Sagres (€3.85, one hour, roughly hourly).

Lagos is at the western end of the Algarve train line, and has services to Faro (€7.30, 1¾ hours, nine daily) and, with a change, Lisbon (€22.70, four hours, five daily).

Sagres
POP 1900

Overlooking some of the Algarve's most dramatic scenery, the small, elongated village of Sagres has an end-of-the-world feel with its sea-carved cliffs and empty, wind-whipped fortress high above the ocean. It has a laid-back vibe, and simple, cheery cafes and bars. It's especially popular, particularly in the last decade, with the surfing crowd.

👁 Sights & Activities

There are four good beaches a short drive or long walk from Sagres: **Praia da Mareta**, just below the town; lovely **Praia do Martinhal** to the east; **Praia do Tonel** on the other side of the Ponta de Sagres, and especially good for surfing; and the isolated **Praia de Beliche**, on the way to Cabo de São Vicente.

Fortaleza de Sagres   FORT
(☑ 282 620 140; adult/child €3/1.60; ⊙ 9.30am-8pm May-Sep, to 5.30pm Oct-Apr) Blank, hulking and forbidding, Sagres' fortress offers breathtaking views over the sheer cliffs, and all along the coast to Cabo de São Vicente. According to legend, this is where Prince Henry the Navigator established his navigation school and primed the early Portuguese explorers. It's quite a large site, so allow at least an hour to see everything.

SPAIN & PORTUGAL THE ALGARVE

WORTH A TRIP

WALKING THE ALGARVE

If you like a good walk, by far the best way to appreciate the magnificent landscapes of the inland Algarve is to hike part (or all) of the 300km **Via Algarviana** (www.viaalgarviana.org) that crosses the region from northeast to southwest. Some of the most beautiful sections are around Monchique, where splendid vistas open up as you climb through cork groves to the Algarve's highest hilltops.

Download route information on the website; grabbing the GPS points is also a good idea, as signposting isn't always clear. The official Via Algarviana route booklet (€7) is available from the Algarve Tourist Association's tourist offices.

The best two-day taster of the trail is to stay in Monchique, walk up to Picota and back one day, and up to Fóia and back the next.

Cabo de São Vicente   LANDMARK
(🕐 lighthouse complex 10am-6pm Tue-Sun Apr-Sep, to 5pm Oct-Mar) Five kilometres from Sagres, Europe's southwesternmost point is a barren headland, the last piece of home that Portuguese sailors once saw as they launched into the unknown. It's a spectacular spot: at sunset you can almost hear the hissing as the sun hits the sea. A red lighthouse houses the small but excellent **Museu dos Faróis** (adult/child €1.50/1), showcasing Sagres' role in Portugal's maritime history.

★ Mar Ilimitado   BOATING
(📞 916 832 625; www.marilimitado.com; Porto da Baleeira) 🐚 Mar Ilimitado, a team of marine biologists, offers a variety of highly recommended, ecologically sound boat trips, from dolphin spotting (€35, 1½ hours) and seabird watching (€45, 2½ hours) to excursions up to Cabo de São Vicente (€25, one hour).

✕ Eating & Drinking

Dromedário   BAR
(📞 282 624 219; Rua Comandante Matoso; 🕐 10am-late; 🛜) Sagres' original cafe-bar, Dromedário is still going strong (it's been here for well over 30 years). There's good food (try the burgers), karaoke and 'mixology', aka creative cocktails. The spacious, mildly Moorish-themed interior is a cool spot to hang out after a day on the waves.

Pau de Pita   CAFE
(Rua Comandante Matoso; 🕐 10am-3am; 🛜) The funkiest of its neighbours in the bar strip (at least in terms of its design), this place has great salads, crêpes and juices (€4 to €10), all enjoyed to a chilled-out soundtrack. At night, it mixes decent drinks and is as lively as any of the other bars, with a good post-surfing vibe.

ℹ Getting There & Away

Buses come from Lagos (€3.85, one hour, around 12 daily). On weekends there are fewer services.

Évora

POP 49,000

One of Portugal's most beautifully preserved medieval towns, Évora is an enchanting place to delve into the past. Inside the 14th-century walls, Évora's narrow, winding lanes lead to striking architectural works: an elaborate medieval cathedral and cloisters; the cinematic columns of the Templo Romano (near the intriguing Roman baths); and a picturesque town square, once the site of some rather gruesome episodes courtesy of the Inquisition. Aside from its historic and aesthetic virtues, Évora is also a lively university town, and its many attractive restaurants serve up hearty Alentejan cuisine.

◉ Sights

Sé   CATHEDRAL
(Largo do Marquês de Marialva; €2, with cloister & towers €3.50, with museum €4.50; 🕐 9am-5pm) Guarded by a pair of rose granite towers, Évora's fortress-like medieval cathedral has fabulous cloisters and a museum jam-packed with ecclesiastical treasures. It was begun around 1186, during the reign of Sancho I, Afonso Henriques' son; there was probably a mosque here before. It was completed about 60 years later. The flags of Vasco da Gama's ships were blessed here in 1497.

★ Templo Romano   RUINS
(Temple of Diana; Largo do Conde de Vila Flor) Once part of the Roman Forum, the remains of this temple, dating from the 2nd or early 3rd century, provide a heady slice of drama right in town. It's among the best-preserved Roman monuments in Portugal, and probably on the Iberian Peninsula. Though it's commonly referred to as the Temple of Diana, there's no consensus about the deity to

which it was dedicated, and some archaeologists believe it may have been dedicated to Julius Caesar.

★ Capela dos Ossos CATACOMB

(Chapel of Bones; Praça 1 de Maio; ⊘ 9am-12.50pm & 2.30-5.45pm) One of Évora's most popular sights is also one of its most chilling. The walls and columns of this mesmerising *memento mori* (reminder of death) are lined with the bones and skulls of some 5000 people. This was the solution found by three 17th-century Franciscan monks for the overflowing graveyards of churches and monasteries.

🛏 Sleeping & Eating

Évora Inn HOSTEL $

(☎ 266 744 500; www.evorainn.com; Rua da República 11; s/d/ste from €35/40/45; 🛜) This friendly nine-room guesthouse in a 120-year-old building brings a serious dose of style to Évora. Pop art adorns the rooms and corridors, along with eye-catching wallpaper, modular chairs, a bold colour scheme and unusual features (including a telescope in the Mirante room up top). Rooms are bright, if a bit boxy, and staff have loads of great tips on discovering the hidden gems of Évora.

★ Salsa Verde VEGETARIAN $

(☎ 266 743 210; www.salsa-verde.org; Rua do Raimundo 93A; small plate €4.95, per kg €14.40; ⊘ noon-3pm & 7-9.30pm Mon-Fri, noon-3pm Sat; 🛜🍴) Vegetarians (and Portuguese pigs) will be thankful for this veggie-popping paradise. Pedro, the owner, gives a wonderful twist to traditional Alentejan dishes such as the famous bread dish, *migas*, prepared with mushrooms. Low-playing bossa nova and a cheerful airy design make a fine complement to the dishes – all made from fresh, locally sourced products (organic when possible).

ℹ️ Information

Turismo (☎ 266 777 071; www.cm-evora. pt; Praça do Giraldo 73; ⊘ 9am-7pm Apr-Oct, 9am-6pm Mon-Fri, 10am-2pm & 3-6pm Sat & Sun Nov-Mar) This helpful, central tourist office offers a great town map.

ℹ️ Getting There & Away

The **bus station** is just west of the walled centre. Destinations include Coimbra (€18.50, 4½ hours), Faro (€17.50, four hours) and Lisbon (€12.50, 1½ to two hours).

The **train station** is outside the walls, 600m south of the *jardim público* (public garden). There are daily trains to/from Lisbon (€12.20, 1½ hours, four daily), Lagos (€26.30, 4½ to five hours, three daily) and Faro (€25.30, four to five hours, two daily).

Óbidos

POP 3100

Surrounded by a classic crenellated wall, Óbidos' gorgeous historic centre is a labyrinth of cobblestoned streets and flower-bedecked, whitewashed houses livened up with dashes of yellow and blue paint. It's a delightful place to pass an afternoon, but there are plenty of reasons to stay overnight.

⊙ Sights

Castelo, Walls & Aqueduct HISTORIC SITE

FREE You can walk around the unprotected muro (wall) for uplifting views over the town and surrounding countryside. The walls date from Moorish times (later restored), but the castelo (castle) itself is one of Dom Dinis' 13th-century creations. It's a stern edifice, with lots of towers, battlements and big gates. Converted into a palace in the 16th century (some Manueline touches add levity), it's now a deluxe **pousada** (☎ 210 407 630; www.pousadas.pt; d/ste from €170/275; ❄🛜).

The impressive 3km-long aqueduct, southeast of the main gate, dates from the 16th century.

Igreja de Santa Maria CHURCH

(Praça de Santa Maria; ⊘ 9.30am-12.30pm & 2.30-7pm summer, to 5pm winter) The town's elegant main church, near the northern end of Rua Direita, stands out for its interior, with a wonderful painted ceiling and walls done up in beautiful blue-and-white 17th-century *azulejos* (hand-painted tiles). Paintings by the renowned 17th-century painter Josefa de Óbidos are to the right of the altar. There's a fine 16th-century Renaissance tomb on the left, probably carved by French sculptor Nicolas Chanterène.

🛏 Sleeping & Eating

Hostel Argonauta HOSTEL $

(☎ 963 824 178, 262 958 088; www.hostelargonauta.com; Rua Adelaide Ribeirete 14; dm/d €23/46; 🛜) In a pretty spot just outside the walls, this feels more like a friend's place than a hostel. Run with good cheer, it has an arty, colourful dorm with wood-stove heating and beds as well as bunks; there's also a cute double with a great view.

Senhor da Pedra
PORTUGUESE $

(Largo do Santuário; mains €6-9; ⊙ 11.30am-10pm Mon-Sat, 11am-4pm Sun) Behind the striking church of Senhor da Pedra below town, this simple white-tiled eatery (the one on the right as you look at the row of restaurants) is a recommended place to try low-priced authentic Portuguese cuisine. It's a classic affair with mum in the kitchen, and dad on the tables. Don't expect fast service.

ℹ️ Information

Turismo (📞 262 959 231; www.obidos.pt; ⊙ 9.30am-7.30pm summer, to 6pm winter) Just outside Porta da Vila, near the bus stop, with helpful multilingual staff offering town brochures and maps in five languages.

ℹ️ Getting There & Away

There are at least six daily trains to Lisbon (€8.45 to €9.30, 2½ hours) mostly via connections at Mira Sintra-Meleças station on the suburban Lisbon line. It's a pretty but uphill walk to town.

Buses run hourly to Lisbon (€8.15, one hour) on weekdays, plus five on Saturday and Sunday.

Nazaré
POP 10,500

With a warren of narrow, cobbled lanes running down to a wide, cliff-backed beach, Nazaré is a picturesque coastal resort. The sands are packed in summer; for a different perspective, take the funicular up to Promontório do Sítio, where picture-postcard coastal views unfold from the cliffs.

Nazaré has hit the headlines in recent years for the monster waves that roll in just north of town and the record-breaking feats of the gutsy surfers that ride them.

👁️ Sights & Activities

Promontório do Sítio
HISTORIC SITE

Until the 18th century the sea covered the present-day site of Nazaré; locals lived at this clifftop area 110m above the beach. Today this tourist-filled promontory is popular for its tremendous views, the lighthouse and its religious associations. From Rua do Elevador, north of the *turismo*, an ascensor climbs up the hill to Promontório do Sítio; it's nice to walk back down, escaping the

crowds of trinket-sellers. There are plenty of places to stay and eat up on the cliff top too.

🎭 Festivals & Events

Carnaval
MARDI GRAS

One of Portugal's brashest Mardi Gras celebrations, held in February, with lots of costumed parades and general irreverence. Many people dress up and the nights go loud and long.

🛏️ Sleeping & Eating

⭐ Lab Hostel
HOSTEL $

(www.labhostel.pt; Rua de Rio Maior 4; dm €27-28, d €75-81; 🛜) One of Portugal's band of growing 'glostels' (glamorous hostels), this just about takes the cake with its stylish, clean design, attention to detail and some of the whitest, brightest and cleanest rooms around. There's a female dorm and a family room, and breakfast is included. Prices here are for August only (they're reduced at other times).

⭐ A Tasquinha
SEAFOOD $

(📞 262 551 945; Rua Adrião Batalha 54; mains €7-11; ⊙ noon-3pm & 7-10.30pm Tue-Sun) This exceptionally friendly family affair has been running for 50-plus years, serving high-quality seafood in a pair of snug but pretty tiled dining rooms. Expect queues on summer nights.

ℹ️ Information

Turismo (📞 262 561 194; www.cm-nazare.pt; Avenida Vieira Giumarães, Edifício do Mercado Municipal; ⊙ 9.30am-1pm & 2.30-6pm Oct-Apr, 9.30am-1pm & 2.30-7pm May, Jun & Sep, 9am-8pm Jul & Aug) In the front offices of the food market. Helpful, multilingual staff.

ℹ️ Getting There & Away

Regular buses serve surrounding towns as well as Lisbon (€11, 1¾ hours).

Coimbra
POP 101,455

The medieval capital of Portugal for over a hundred years, and site of the country's greatest university, Coimbra's atmospheric, beautiful historic core cascades down a hillside in a lovely setting on the east bank of the Rio Mondego. If you visit during the academic year, you'll be sure to feel the university's influence. Students throng bars and cafes; posters advertise talks on everything from genetics to genocide; and graffiti scrawled outside *repúblicas* (communal student dwellings) address the political issues of the day.

◉ Sights

★ Universidade de Coimbra
UNIVERSITY

(☎ 239 242 744; www.uc.pt/en/informacaopara/visit/paco; adult/student €12/9, tower €1; ☺ 9am-7pm Mar-Oct, 9.30am-1pm & 2-5.30pm Nov-Apr) The city's high point, the university nucleus, consists of a series of remarkable 16th- to 18th-century buildings, all set within and around the vast Páteo das Escolas ('patio' or courtyard). These include the **Paço das Escolas (Royal Palace), clock tower, Prisão Acadêmica (prison), Capela de São Miguel (chapel)** (Universidade de Coimbra; ☺ 9am-7pm Mar-Oct, 9.30am-1pm & 2-5.30pm Nov-Apr) and **Biblioteca Joanina (library)** (João V Library; ☎ 239 242 744; Universidade de Coimbra; ☺ 9am-7pm Mar-Oct, 9.30am-1pm & 2-5.30pm Nov-Apr). Visitors to the library are admitted in small groups every 20 minutes. Buy your ticket at the university's visitor centre near the Porta Férrea. With the exception of the library, you can enter and explore on your own, or head off with a knowledgeable university tour guide on one of three different tours (€12.50/15/20). These take place daily at 11am and 3pm.

★ Museu Nacional de Machado de Castro
MUSEUM

(☎ 239 853 070; www.museumachadocastro.pt; Largo Dr José Rodrigues; adult/child €6/3, cryptoportico only €3, with audio guide €7.50; ☺ 2pm-6pm Tue, 10am-6pm Wed-Sun) This great museum is a highlight of central Portugal. It's built over the Roman forum, the remains of which can be seen and cover several levels. Part of the visit here takes you down to the vaulted, spooky and immensely

---

WORTH A TRIP

THE MONASTERY CIRCUIT

Three extraordinary monasteries are in fairly close proximity in central Portugal and make very rewarding visits from the coast or on the way between the country's south and north.

Mosteiro de Santa Maria de Alcobaça (☎ 262 505 120; www.mosteiroalcobaca.pt; €6, with Tomar & Batalha €15, church free; ☺ 9am-7pm Apr-Sep, 9am-6pm Oct-Mar) One of Iberia's great monasteries, this utterly dominates the town of Alcobaça. Hiding behind the imposing baroque facade lies a high, austere, monkish church with a forest of unadorned 12th-century arches. But make sure you visit the rest too: the atmospheric refectory, vast dormitory and other spaces bring back the Cistercian life, which apparently wasn't quite as austere here as it should have been.

Batalha (☎ 244 765 497; www.mosteirobatalha.pt; €6, with Alcobaça & Tomar €15, church free; ☺ 9am-6.30pm Apr-Sep, 9am-6pm Oct-Mar) This extraordinary abbey nearby was built to commemorate the 1385 Battle of Aljubarrota (fought just south of here). Most of the monument was completed by 1434 in Flamboyant Gothic style, but Manueline exuberance steals the show, thanks to additions made in the 15th and 16th centuries.

Convento de Cristo (www.conventocristo.pt; Rua Castelo dos Templários; adult/under 12yr €6/free, with Alcobaça & Batalha €15; ☺ 9am-6.30pm Jun-Sep, 9am-5.30pm Oct-May) The larger town of Tomar is dominated from above by this monastery. Wrapped in splendour and mystery, the Knights Templar held enormous power in Portugal from the 12th to 16th centuries, and largely bankrolled the Age of Discoveries. Their headquarters sit on wooded slopes above the town and enclosed within 12th-century walls. The monastery is a stony expression of magnificence, founded in 1160 by Gualdim Pais, Grand Master of the Templars. It has chapels, cloisters and choirs in diverging styles, added over the centuries by successive kings and Grand Masters. The Charola, an extraordinary 16-sided Templar church, thought to be in imitation of the Church of the Holy Sepulchre in Jerusalem, dominates the complex.

Batalha and Alcobaça are easily accessible by bus from each other and from Nazaré, while Tomar is reachable via a change from either.

Central Coimbra

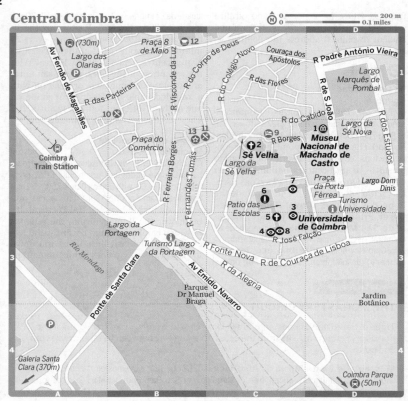

atmospheric galleries of the cryptoportico that allowed the forum to be level on such a hilly site. The artistic collection is wide-ranging and superb. The route starts with sculpture, from the architectural (column capitals) through Gothic religious sculpture and so on.

★ **Sé Velha** CATHEDRAL
(Old Cathedral; ☑ 239 825 273; www.sevelha-coimbra.org; Largo da Sé Velha, Rua do Norte 4; €2.50; ◷10am-6pm Mon-Fri, to 6.30pm Sat, 11am-5pm Sun) Coimbra's stunning 12th-century cathedral is one of Portugal's finest examples of Romanesque architecture. The main portal and facade are exceptionally striking. Its crenellated exterior and narrow, slit-like lower windows serve as reminders of the nation's embattled early days, when the Moors were still a threat. These buildings were designed to be useful as fortresses in times of trouble.

🛏 Sleeping & Eating

★ **Serenata Hostel** HOSTEL $
(☑ 239 853 130; www.serenatahostel.com; Largo da Sé Velha 21; dm/d without bathroom €15/39, d/f with bathroom €49/69; 🛜) In the pretty heart of the (noisy at night) old town, this noble building with an intriguingly varied history has been converted to a fabulous hostel, chock-full of modern comforts and facilities while maintaining a period feel in keeping with this historic zone. Great lounge areas, a cute, secluded sun terrace, spacious dorms and a modern kitchen complete a very happy picture.

Adega Paço dos Condes PORTUGUESE $
(☑ 239 825 605; Rua do Paço do Conde 1; mains €5-10; ◷11am-10pm Mon-Sat) Usually crowded with students and Coimbra locals, this straightforward family-run grill, with its retro sign out the front, is one of the city's best budget eateries. It's like something from a

Central Coimbra

◉ Top Sights

bygone era: prices are great and there's a long list of daily specials, which are usually your best way forward.

★**Tapas Nas Costas** TAPAS **$$**
(☑ 239 157 425; www.tapasnascostas.pt; Rua Quebra Costas 19; tapas €3.50-6.60; ☺ 11am-midnight Tue-Sat, to 4pm Sun) *The* hotspot about town at the time of research, this sophisticated joint delivers delicious tapas. Decor is stylish, as are the gourmet-style goodies, such as *ovo com alheira de caça e grelos* (sausage with turnip greens and egg; €5.60). What are 'small-to-medium' sized servings for Portuguese are possibly 'normal' for anyone else, so share plates are a satisfying experience.

🍷 Drinking & Entertainment

★**Café Santa Cruz** CAFE
(☑ 239 833 617; www.cafesantacruz.com; Praça 8 de Maio; ☺ 7am-midnight) One of Portugal's most atmospheric cafes, where the elderly statesmen meet for their daily cuppas, Santa Cruz is set in a dramatically beautiful high-vaulted former chapel, with stained-glass windows and graceful stone arches. The terrace grants lovely views of Praça 8 de Maio. Don't miss the *crúzios,* award-winning, egg- and almond-based conventual cakes for which the cafe is famous.

★**Galeria Santa Clara** BAR
(☑ 239 441 657; www.galeriasantaclara.com; Rua António Augusto Gonçalves 67; ☺ 1pm-2am Mon-Thu, to 3am Fri & Sat) Arty tea room by day and chilled-out bar by night, this terrific place across the Mondego has good art on the walls, a series of sunny rooms and a fine terrace. It's got a great indoor-outdoor vibe and can feel like a party in a private house when things get going.

★**Fado ao Centro** FADO
(☑ 239 837 060; www.fadoaocentro.com; Rua Quebra Costas 7; show incl drink €10) At the bottom of the old town, this friendly fado centre is a good place to introduce yourself to the genre. There's a performance every evening at 6pm. Shows include explanations, in Portuguese and English, about the history of Coimbra fado and the meaning of each song.

ⓘ Information

Turismo Largo da Portagem (☑ 239 488 120; www.turismodecoimbra.pt; Largo da Portagem; ☺ 9am-6pm Mon-Fri, 9am-1pm & 2-5.30pm Sat & Sun mid-Sep–mid-Jun, 9am-8pm Mon-Fri, 9am-6pm Sat & Sun mid-Jun–mid-Sep) By the bridge, in the centre of things.

Turismo Universidade (☑ 239 834 158; www.turismodecoimbra.pt; Praça da Porta Férrea; ☺ 9am-6pm mid-Mar–Oct, 9am-5.30pm Mon-Fri, 10am-4pm Sat & Sun Nov–mid-Mar) Adjacent to the Universidade de Coimbra ticket desk, just outside the Porta Férrea.

ⓘ Getting There & Away

From the rather grim **bus station** (Av Fernão de Magalhães), a 15-minute walk northwest of the centre, there are at least a dozen buses daily to Lisbon (€14.50, 2½ hours) and Porto (€12, 1½ hours), with almost as many to Braga (€14, 2¾ hours) and Faro (€27, six to nine hours).

Long-distance trains stop at **Coimbra B** station, north of the city. Cross the platform for quick, free connections to more-central **Coimbra A** (called just 'Coimbra' on timetables).

Coimbra is linked by regular Alfa Pendular (AP) and intercidade (IC) trains to Lisbon (AP/IC €22.80/19.20, 1¾/two hours) and Porto (€16.70/13.20, one/1¼ hours).

Porto

POP 237,600

From across the Rio Douro at sunset, romantic Porto looks like a pop-up town: a colourful tumbledown dream with medieval relics, soaring bell towers, extravagant

SPAIN & PORTUGAL PORTO

Porto

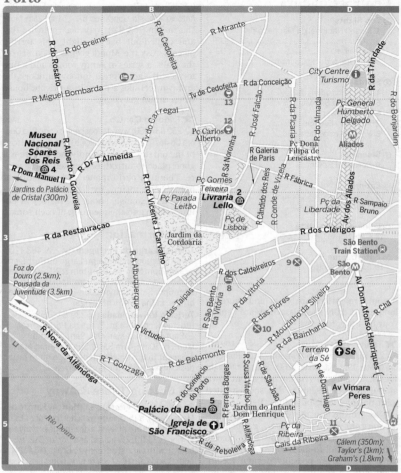

baroque churches and stately beaux-arts buildings piled on top of one another, illuminated by streaming shafts of sun. If you squint you might be able to make out the open windows, the narrow lanes and the staircases zigzagging to nowhere. Porto is a lively walkable city with chatter in the air and a tangible sense of history, and its old-world riverfront district is a remarkable World Heritage site. Across the water twinkle the neon signs of Vila Nova de Gaia, the headquarters of the major port wine manufacturers.

Sights

The Ribeira district – Porto's riverfront nucleus – is a remarkable window into the history of the city. Along the riverside promenade, *barcos rabelos* (the traditional boats that are used to ferry port wine down the Douro River) bob beneath the shadow of the photogenic Ponte de Dom Luís I. From here you have a fine perspective of the port-wine lodges across the river in Vila Nova de Gaia. It's also packed with flocks of tourists.

★**Palácio da Bolsa**　　HISTORIC BUILDING
(Stock Exchange; www.palaciodabolsa.com; Rua Ferreira Borges; tours adult/child €9/5.50; ⊙9am-6.30pm Apr-Oct, 9am-12.30pm & 2-5.30pm Nov-Mar) This splendid neoclassical monument (built from 1842 to 1910) honours Porto's past and present money merchants. Just past the entrance is the glass-domed **Pátio das Nações** (Hall of Nations), where the exchange once operated. But this pales in comparison with rooms deeper inside; to visit these, join one of the half-hour guided tours, which set off every 30 minutes.

★**Sé**　　CATHEDRAL
(Terreiro da Sé; cloisters adult/student €3/2; ⊙9am-7pm Apr-Oct, to 6pm Nov-Mar) From Praça da Ribeira rises a tangle of medieval alleys and stairways that eventually reach the hulking, hilltop fortress of the cathedral. Founded in the 12th century, it was largely rebuilt a century later and then extensively altered during the 18th century. However, you can still make out the church's Romanesque origins in the barrel-vaulted nave. Inside, a rose window and a 14th-century Gothic cloister also remain from its early days.

★**Mercado do Bolhão**　　MARKET
(Rua Formosa; ⊙7am-5pm Mon-Fri, to 1pm Sat) The 19th-century, wrought-iron Mercado do Bolhão does a brisk trade in fresh produce, including cheeses, olives, smoked meats, sausages, breads and more. At its lively best on Friday and Saturday mornings,

★**Igreja de São Francisco**　　CHURCH
(Praça Infante Dom Henrique; adult/child €6/5; ⊙9am-8pm Jul-Sep, to 7pm Mar-Jun & Oct, to 5.30pm Nov-Feb) Sitting on Praça Infante Dom Henrique, Igreja de São Francisco looks from the outside to be an austerely Gothic church, but inside it hides one of Portugal's most dazzling displays of baroque finery. Hardly a centimetre escapes unsmothered, as otherworldly cherubs and sober monks are drowned by nearly 100kg of gold leaf. If you see only one church in Porto, make it this one.

OFF THE BEATEN TRACK

SERRA DA ESTRELA

The forested Serra da Estrela has a raw natural beauty and offers some of the country's best hiking. This is Portugal's highest mainland mountain range (1993m), and the source of two great rivers: Rio Mondego and Rio Zêzere. The town of Manteigas makes a great base for hiking and exploring the area (plus skiing in winter). The main park office here provides details of popular walks in the Parque Natural da Serra da Estrela – some of which leave from town or just outside it. A solid budget option in town is **Pensão Estrela** (☑275 981 288; Rua Doutor Sobral 5; s/d from €25/32; ☎). This recommended mother-and-son team in the heart of the village offers very clean, comfortable heated rooms with good bathrooms at a great price. Two weekday buses connect Manteigas with Guarda, which is easily reached by bus from Porto, Coimbra and other major towns.

the market is also sprinkled with inexpensive stalls where you can eat fish so fresh it was probably swimming in the Atlantic that morning, or taste or sample local wines and cheeses.

★ **Livraria Lello**   HISTORIC BUILDING
(www.livrarialello.pt; Rua das Carmelitas 144; €4; ☺10am-7.30pm Mon-Fri, 10am-7pm Sat, 11am-7pm Sun; ☒) It's ostensibly a bookshop, but even if you're not after books, don't miss this exquisite 1906 neo-Gothic confection, with its lavishly carved plaster resembling wood and stained-glass skylight. Feels magical? Its intricately wrought, curiously twisting staircase was supposedly the inspiration for the one in the Harry Potter books, which JK Rowling partly wrote in Porto while working here as an English teacher from 1991 to 1993.

★ **Museu Nacional Soares dos Reis**   MUSEUM
(www.museusoaresdosreis.pt; Rua Dom Manuel II 44; adult/child €5/free; ☺10am-6pm Tue-Sun) Porto's best art museum presents a stellar collection ranging from Neolithic carvings to Portugal's take on modernism, all housed in the formidable Palácio das Carrancas.

★ **Jardins do Palácio de Cristal**   GARDENS
(Rua Dom Manuel II; ☺8am-9pm Apr-Sep, to 7pm Oct-Mar; ☒) Sitting atop a bluff, this gorgeous botanical garden is one of Porto's best-loved escapes, with lawns interwoven with sun-dappled paths and dotted with fountains, sculptures, giant magnolias, camellias, cypress and olive trees. It's actually a mosaic of small gardens that open up little by little as you wander – as do the stunning views of the city and Rio Douro.

🛏 Sleeping

★ **Gallery Hostel**   HOSTEL $
(☑224 964 313; www.gallery-hostel.com; Rua Miguel Bombarda 222; dm/d/tr/q from €22/64/80/96; ☒☎) A true travellers' hub, this hostel-gallery has clean and cosy dorms and doubles, a sunny, glass-enclosed back patio, a grassy terrace, a cinema room, a shared kitchen and a bar-music room. Throw in its free walking tours, homemade dinners on request, port-wine tastings and concerts, and you'll see why it's booked up so often – reserve ahead.

Poets Inn   B&B $
(☑223 324 209; www.thepoetsinn.com; Rua dos Caldeireiros 261; d €40-70, apt €80-90; ☎) This laid-back B&B has a central but tucked-away location. Decorated by local artists, each of the doubles has a theme and some have fine city views. Most rooms share a bathroom. There's also a garden complete with hammock, a guest kitchen and a lounge with DVDs, plus a decent breakfast included in the price.

🍽 Eating

★ **A Sandeira**   SANDWICHES $
(☑223 216 471; www.asandeira.pt; Rua dos Caldeireiros 85; sandwiches €4.90, lunch menu €5; ☺9am-midnight Mon-Sat; ☎) Charming, boho-flavoured and lit by fairy lights, A Sandeira is a great bolt hole for an inexpensive lunch. Chipper staff bring to the table creative salads such as smoked ham, rocket, avocado and walnuts, and Porto's best sandwiches (eg olive, feta, tomato and basil). The lunch menu – including soup, a salad or a sandwich, and a drink – is a steal.

Casinha São João   TAPAS $
(☑220 197 889, 914 237 742; Cais da Ribeira 9; petiscos €3.50-12; ☺noon-midnight Tue-Sun) With tables gathered under stone arches and big river views from the terrace, this is a truly

charming place for drinks and *petiscos* (Portuguese tapas). The welcome is warm and the kitchen serves simple and tasty dishes that are perfect for sharing – from grilled prawns to *feijoada* (bean stew), *rojões* (strips of seasoned pork loin) and clams in white wine and coriander.

★ **Cantina 32**   PORTUGUESE **$$**
(☑ 222 039 069; www.cantina32.com; Rua das Flores 32; petiscos €3.50-20; ◑ 12.30-3pm & 6.30-10.30pm Mon-Sat; ☜) Industrial-chic meets boho at this delightfully laid-back haunt, with its walls of polished concrete, mismatched crockery, verdant plants, and vintage knick-knacks ranging from a bicycle to an old typewriter. The menu is just as informal – *petiscos* such as *pica-pau* steak (bite-sized pieces of steak in a garlic-white-wine sauce), quail egg croquettes, and cheesecake served in a flower pot reveal a pinch of creativity.

🍷 Drinking & Nightlife

Nightlife rules in central Porto with some eclectic bar-gallery spaces leading the way. It's worth exploring the narrow cobblestone streets just north of Rua das Carmelitas, which become an all-out street party (especially Rua Galeria de Paris, Cândido dos Reis and Conde de Vizela) on warm summer nights and on weekends throughout the year. Down by the water, the open-air bar scene on Praça da Ribeira is great for drinks with a view.

★ **Museu d'Avó**   BAR
(Travessa de Cedofeita 54; ◑ 8pm-4am Mon-Sat) The name translates as 'Grandmother's Museum' and indeed it's a gorgeous rambling attic of a bar, crammed with cabinets, old clocks, *azulejos* (hand-painted tiles) and gramophones, with curios hanging from its rafters. Lanterns and candles illuminate young *tripeiros* (Porto residents) locked in animated conversation as the house beats spin. If you get the late-night munchies, it also whips up tasty *petiscos* (€2 to €8).

★ **Aduela**   BAR
(Rua das Oliveiras 36; ◑ 3pm-2am Mon, 10am-2am Tue-Thu, to 4am Fri & Sat, 3pm-midnight Sun) Retro and hip but not self-consciously so, chilled Aduela bathes in the nostalgic orange glow of its glass lights, which illuminate the green walls and mishmash of vintage furnishings. Once a sewing machine warehouse, today it's where friends gather to converse over wine and appetising *petiscos* (€3 to €8).

ℹ Information

City Centre Turismo (☑ 300 501 920; www.visitporto.travel; Rua Clube dos Fenianos 25; ◑ 9am-8pm May-Oct, to 7pm Nov-Apr, to 9pm Aug) The main city *turismo* has a detailed city map, a transport map and the *Agenda do Porto* cultural calendar, among other printed materials.

SPAIN & PORTUGAL PORTO

DON'T MISS

VILA NOVA DA GAIA

While technically its own municipality, Vila Nova de Gaia ('Gaia') sits just across the Rio Douro from Porto and is woven into the city's fabric both by a series of stunning bridges and by its shared history of port-wine making. Since the mid-18th century, port-wine bottlers and exporters have been obliged to maintain their 'lodges' – basically dressed-up warehouses – here. Today some 30 of these lodges line the steep riverbank.

From Porto's Ribeira district, a short walk across Ponte de Dom Luís I lands you on Gaia's inviting riverside promenade. Lined with beautiful *barcos rabelos* – flat-bottomed boats specially designed to carry wine down the Douro's once-dangerous rapids – the promenade offers grandstand views of Porto's historic centre.

Most people come here to taste the tipple, of course, and about 17 lodges oblige them. Tourist offices keep a list of lodges and opening times. **Taylor's** (☑ 223 742 800; www.taylor.pt; Rua do Choupelo 250; tours incl tasting adult/child €12/6; ◑ 10am-6pm), **Cálem** (☑ 916 113 451; www.calem.pt; Av Diogo Leite 344; tours incl tasting €12; ◑ 10am-7pm May-Oct, to 6pm Nov-Apr) and **Graham's** (☑ 223 776 492, 223 776 490; grahams@grahamsportlodge.com; Rua do Agro 141; tours incl tasting from €15; ◑ 9.30am-6pm Apr-Oct, to 5.30pm Nov-Mar) offer some of the best tours.

❶ Getting There & Away

The airport, 19km northwest of the centre, is served from many European cities and is used by budget airlines.

There's no central bus terminal, but there are frequent services to nearly everywhere in the country, including Lisbon (€20, 3½ hours) and Braga (€6, 1¼ hours). Eurolines serves much of Europe from here.

Long-distance rail services start at **Campanhã** station, which is 3km east of the centre. Most urbano, regional and interregional (IR) trains depart from the stunning indoor-outdoor **São Bento** station, though all these lines also pass through Campanhã. Direct intercity trains head to Lisbon (€24.30, three hours, hourly) via Coimbra. There are also trains north to Vigo in Spain.

❶ Getting Around

An extensive bus network and newish metro system provide easy service around town. Porto's trams used to be one of its delights. Only three lines remain but they're very scenic.

For maximum convenience, Porto's transport system offers the rechargeable Andante Card (www.linhandante.com), allowing smooth movement between tram, metro, funicular and many bus lines.

Braga

POP 136,885

Portugal's third-largest city is an elegant town laced with ancient narrow lanes strewn with plazas and a splendid array of baroque churches. The constant chiming of bells is a reminder of Braga's age-old devotion to the spiritual world. But don't come expecting piety alone: Braga's upmarket old centre is packed with lively cafes and trim boutiques, some excellent restaurants, and low-key bars catering to students from the Universidade do Minho.

◉ Sights

★ **Sé** CATHEDRAL

(www.se-braga.pt; Rua Dom Paio Mendes; ⊙9.30am-12.30pm & 2.30-6.30pm high season, to 5.30pm low season) Braga's extraordinary cathedral, the oldest in Portugal, was begun when the archdiocese was restored in 1070 and completed in the following century. It's a rambling complex made up of differing styles, and architecture buffs could spend half a day happily distinguishing the Ro-

manesque bones from Manueline musculature and baroque frippery.

⨶ Sleeping & Eating

★ **Collector's Hostel** HOSTEL $

(☑253 048 124; www.collectorshostel.com; Rua Francisco Sanches 42; dm €17-20, s/d €27/40) A lovely hostel, lovingly run by two well-travelled women who met in Paris (one of whom was born in the hostel's living room), restored the family house and all the furniture inside, and turned the three floors into a cosy hideaway where guests feel like they're in their grandparents' home, with a twist.

★ **Livraria Centésima Página** CAFE $

(Avenida Central 118-120; snacks €2.60-4.90; ⊙9am-7.30pm Mon-Sat) Tucked inside Centésima Página, an absolutely splendid bookshop with foreign-language titles, this charming cafe serves a rotating selection of tasty quiches along with salads and desserts, and has outdoor tables in the pleasantly rustic garden. Its lunch specials are a steal.

❶ Information

Turismo (☑253 262 550; www.cm-braga.pt; Avenida da Liberdade 1; ⊙9am-1pm & 2pm-6.30pm Mon-Fri, to 6pm Sat & Sun) Braga's helpful tourist office is in an art-deco-style building facing the fountain.

❶ Getting There & Away

There are bus services all over northern Portugal and to other major towns, including Lisbon (€21, 4½ hours) and Porto (€4.80, one hour).

Braga is within Porto's *suburbano* network, which means commuter trains travel every hour or so from Porto (€3.10, about one hour). Useful long-distance trains include Coimbra (€19.80, 2¼ hours, five to seven daily) and Lisbon (€31, four hours, two to four daily).

Parque Nacional da Peneda-Gerês

Spread across four impressive granite massifs, this vast park encompasses boulder-strewn peaks, precipitous valleys, gorse-clad moorlands and forests of oak and pine. It also shelters more than 100 granite villages that, in many ways, have changed little since Portugal's founding in the 12th century. For nature lovers, the stunning scenery

Parque Nacional da Peneda-Gerês

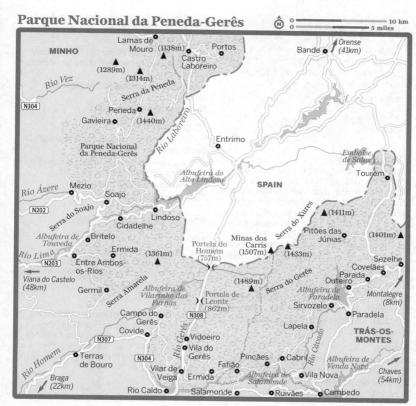

here is unmatched in Portugal for camping, hiking and other outdoor adventures. The park's main centre is at Vila do Gerês, a sleepy, hot-springs village.

There are trails and footpaths through the park, some between villages with accommodation. Leaflets detailing these are available from the park offices. Day hikes around Vila do Gerês are popular. An adventurous option is the old Roman road from Mata do Albergaria (10km up-valley from Vila do Gerês), past the Vilarinho das Furnas reservoir to Campo do Gerês.

Gerês has plenty of *pensões* (guesthouses), though in summer you may find some are block-booked for spa patients and other visitors. Outside July and August, prices plummet.

Between four and seven buses daily run from Braga to Gerês (€4.25 1½ hours).

Portugal Survival Guide

ℹ Directory A–Z

ACCOMMODATION

There's an excellent range of good-value accommodation in Portugal. Budget places provide some of Western Europe's cheapest rooms. For a local experience, stay in a *pensão* or *residencial*. These are small, often family-run places, and some are set in historic buildings. Amenities range from simple to luxury. Portugal has a growing network of hostels, with stylish, award-winning options in both Lisbon and Porto.

DISCOUNT CARDS

Lisbon and Porto offer a card that includes entry to attractions, public transport, a city bus tour and restaurant discounts. Typically, you need to do lots of sightseeing to save money with it.

🛈 PRICE RANGES

The following price ranges refer to a double room with bathroom in high season. Unless otherwise stated breakfast is included in the price.

€ less than €60

€€ €60–120

€€€ more than €120

LGBT TRAVELLERS

In 2010 Portugal legalised gay marriage, becoming the sixth European country to do so. Most Portuguese profess a laissez-faire attitude about same-sex couples, although how out you can be depends on where you are in Portugal. In Lisbon, Porto and the Algarve, acceptance has increased, whereas in most other areas, same-sex couples can be met with incomprehension.

Lisbon has the country's best gay and lesbian network and nightlife.

MONEY

Credit cards are accepted at smarter hotels and restaurants and in larger towns, but aren't much use to pay for things in the budget arena or in rural outposts.

Tipping

Restaurants Not necessary in cheaper places, where you can round up, otherwise 5% to 10%.

Bars Not expected unless table service is provided.

OPENING HOURS

Restaurants noon to 3pm and 7pm to 10pm

Cafes 9am to 7pm

Shops 9.30am to noon & 2pm to 7pm Monday to Friday, 10am to 1pm Saturday

Bars 7pm to 2am

Nightclubs 11pm to 4am Thursday to Saturday

Malls 10am to 10pm

Banks 8.30am to 3pm Monday to Friday

PUBLIC HOLIDAYS

New Year's Day 1 January

Carnaval Tuesday February/March; the day before Ash Wednesday

Good Friday March/April

Liberty Day 25 April; celebrating the 1974 revolution

Labour Day 1 May

Corpus Christi May/June; ninth Thursday after Easter

Portugal Day 10 June; also known as Camões and Communities Day

Feast of the Assumption 15 August

Republic Day 5 October; commemorating the 1910 declaration of the Portuguese Republic

All Saints' Day 1 November

Independence Day 1 December; commemorating the 1640 restoration of independence from Spain

Feast of the Immaculate Conception 8 December

Christmas Day 25 December

TELEPHONE

Local SIM cards with call and data packages are widely available.

Portuguese landline and mobile numbers have nine digits, with no separate area code.

International dialling code 00

Country code 351

🛈 Getting There & Away

AIR

Most international flights arrive in Lisbon, though Porto and Faro also have some. For more information, including live arrival and departure schedules, see www.ana.pt.

BUS

The major long-distance carriers that serve European destinations are Busabout (www.busabout.com) and Eurolines (www.eurolines.com). From Spain, there's also daily service from Madrid to Lisbon and Porto, and from Seville to Faro and Lisbon.

TRAIN

From Spain, the Sud-Expresso heads from the French border across to Portugal, continuing to Coimbra and Lisbon; change at Pampilhosa for Porto. From Madrid, the Talgo Lusitânia heads to Lisbon. A faster Madrid–Lisbon route is in the planning stages. There's also a train from Vigo in Spain's northwest to Porto.

🛈 Getting Around

A host of small private bus operators, most amalgamated into regional companies, runs a dense network of services across the country. Among the largest are **Rede Expressos** (707 223 344; www.rede-expressos.pt), **Rodonorte** (259 340 710; www.rodonorte.pt) and the Algarve line Eva Transportes (www.eva-bus.com). It's a reliable, cheap way to travel.

Portugal has an extensive railroad network, making for a scenic way of travelling between destinations; see www.cp.pt. Classes are:

Regional (R) Slow, stop everywhere.

Interregional (IR) Reasonably fast.

Intercidade (IC) Rápido or express trains.

Alfa Pendular Deluxe Marginally faster than express and much pricier.

Italy, Greece & Turkey

Best Activities

➡ Row Venice (p478)

➡ Cinque Terre (p494)

➡ Meteora (p538)

➡ Hamam (p561)

➡ Ihlara Valley (p576)

Best Ruins

➡ Colosseum (p495)

➡ Pantheon (p501)

➡ Acroplis (p527)

➡ Ancient Delphi (p536)

➡ Ancient Akrotiri (p539)

Why Go?

Travelling southeast is like riding the crest of culture. Everything becomes tangibly more intense, from the food to the sights and scenery, and that passionate zest for life that's woven throughout it all. The region is a cultural parade. See dervishes whirling; visit monasteries hewn out of rock or built atop soaring pinnacles; get pampered in a Turkish bath; paddle down Venice's canals; lose yourself in Rhodes' walled, medieval city; and gaze up, spellbound by the Sistine Chapel. Dig into the freshest pasta, relish the tangiest local cheeses and savour the most aromatic pastries. Visit vineyards in Italy, drink ouzo with locals in Greek villages and experience Turkey's teahouses. When you're satiated, witness history first-hand: sights like Pompeii, the Acropolis and Ephesus are merely the sprinkles on the gelato. And as if this weren't enough to lure you, it's all ringed by bewitching turquoise waters, silky soft sand and sunset-coloured cliffs. Prepare yourself: the southeast is boundless and magnetic.

Fast Facts

Capitals Rome (Italy), Athens (Greece), Ankara (Turkey)

Country code ☑39 (Italy), ☑30 (Greece), ☑90 (Turkey)

Currency euro (€, Italy, Greece), lira (₺, Turkey)

Visas Not required for EU citizens or for stays of up to 90 days for many nationals (Italy, Greece). Required for many nationals and available online at www.evisa.gov.tr (Turkey)

Time zones GMT/UTC plus two hours (Italy), GMT/UTC plus three hours (Greece, Turkey)

Hello *Ciao* (Italian), *Yasas* (Greek), *Merhaba* (Turkish)

Italy, Greece & Turkey Highlights

❶ Venice Taking in gorgeous Venetian architecure from a gondola. (p474)

❷ Florence Exploring the streets of this Renaissance time capsule. (p487)

❸ Rome Haunting sights, awe-inspiring art and must-see sights. (p495)

❹ Corfu Beautiful architecure, a colourful history and fantastic cuisine. (p519)

❺ Athens Ancient and contemporary come together, from the Acropolis to museums and atmospheric bars. (p527)

❻ Santorini Being mesmerised by this island's

ROMANIA

BUCHAREST

N 0 ——— 400 km
0 ——— 200 miles

CRIMEA

BULGARIA

SOFIA

İstanbul
10

Thessaloniki

Çanakkale

TURKEY

ANKARA

Cappadocia

Bergama

Konya

İzmir
Selçuk
Ephesus 9

Delphi

5 Athens

Antalya
8

Mycenae
Epidavros
Nafplio

Bodrum

Marmaris

Fethiye

Sparta

Gythio

6 Santorini

7
Rhodes

CYPRUS

Olymbos

Hania   Iraklio

Crete

volcanic caldera and its world-famous sunsets. (p539)

7 **Rhodes** Losing yourself within the city's Old Town and then heading for sandy beaches. (p542)

8 **Antalya** Strolling lanes between Ottoman mansions in the shadow of the snowcapped Bey Mountains. (p550)

9 **Ephesus** Fulfilling your toga-loaded daydreams in one

of the world's best surviving Graeco-Roman cities. (p557)

10 **İstanbul** Taking in the minaret-studded skyline, along with the city's stately mosques and opulent palaces. (p558)

ITALY

Venice

POP 76,650

A city of marble palaces built atop 117 small islands in a shallow lagoon, Venice (Venezia) is hauntingly beautiful. At every turn you're assailed by unforgettable images: tiny bridges arching over limpid canals; chintzy gondolas sliding past working barges; towers and distant domes silhouetted against the watery horizon. Its celebrated sights are legion, and its labyrinthine alleyways exude a unique, almost eerie atmosphere, redolent of cloaked passions and dark secrets. Parts of the Cannaregio, Dorsoduro and Castello *sestieri* (districts) rarely see many tourists, and you can lose yourself for hours in the lanes between the Accademia and train station. Many of the city's treasures date from its time as a powerful medieval republic known as La Serenissima.

⊙ Sights

★ Basilica di San Marco   CATHEDRAL

(St Mark's Basilica; Map p482; ✆ 041 270 83 11; www.basilicasanmarco.it; Piazza San Marco; ⊙9.45am-5pm Mon-Sat, 2-5pm Sun summer, to 4pm Sun winter; 🚊San Marco) FREE With a profusion of domes and over 8000 sq metres of luminous mosaics, Venice's cathedral is an unforgettable sight. It was founded in the 9th century to house the corpse of St Mark after wily Venetian merchants smuggled it out of Egypt in a barrel of pork fat. When the original building burnt down in 932 Venice rebuilt the basilica in its own cosmopolitan image, with Byzantine domes, a Greek cross layout and walls that are clad in marble from Syria, Egypt and Palestine.

VENETIAN GLASS

Venetians have been working in crystal and glass since the 10th century. Trade secrets were so closely guarded that any glass worker who left the city was considered guilty of treason. Today, along Murano's Fondamenta dei Vetrai, centuries of tradition are upheld by Davide Penso, Nason Moretti and Marina and Susanna Sent.

★ Gallerie dell'Accademia   GALLERY

(Map p482; ✆ 041 520 03 45; www.gallerieaccademia.org; Campo della Carità 1050, Dorsoduro; adult/reduced €12/6, 1st Sun of month free; ⊙8.15am-2pm Mon, to 7.15pm Tue-Sun; 🚊Accademia) Venice's historic gallery traces the development of Venetian art from the 14th to 18th centuries, with works by Bellini, Titian, Tintoretto, Veronese and Canaletto, among others. The former Santa Maria della Carità convent complex housing the collection maintained its serene composure for centuries until Napoleon installed his haul of Venetian art trophies here in 1807. Since then there's been non-stop visual drama on its walls.

★ Palazzo Ducale   MUSEUM

(Ducal Palace; Map p482; ✆ 041 271 59 11; www.palazzoducale.visitmuve.it; Piazzetta San Marco 1; adult/reduced incl Museo Correr €20/13, with Museum Pass free; ⊙8.30am-7pm Apr-Oct, to 5.30pm Nov-Mar; 🚊San Zaccaria) Holding pride of place on the waterfront, this pretty Gothic confection is an unlikely setting for the political and administrative seat of a great republic, but an exquisitely Venetian one. Beyond its dainty colonnades and geometrically patterned facade of white Istrian stone and pale pink Veronese marble lie grand rooms of state, the Doge's private apartments and a large complex of council chambers, courts and prisons.

Scuola Grande di San Rocco   MUSEUM

(Map p482; ✆ 041 523 48 64; www.scuolagrandesanrocco.it; Campo San Rocco 3052, San Polo; adult/reduced €10/8; ⊙9.30am-5.30pm; 🚊San Tomà) Everyone wanted the commission to paint this building dedicated to the patron saint of the plague-stricken, so Tintoretto cheated: instead of producing sketches like rival Veronese, he gifted a splendid ceiling panel of patron St Roch, knowing it couldn't be refused, or matched by other artists. The artist documents Mary's life story in the assembly hall, and both Old and New Testament scenes in the Sala Grande Superiore upstairs.

Museo Correr   MUSEUM

(Map p482; ✆ 041 240 52 11; www.correr.visitmuve.it; Piazza San Marco 52; adult/reduced incl Palazzo Ducale €20/13, with Museum Pass free; ⊙10am-7pm Apr-Oct, to 5pm Nov-Mar; 🚊San Marco) Napoleon pulled down an ancient church to build his royal digs over Piazza San Marco and then filled them with the riches of the

Greater Venice

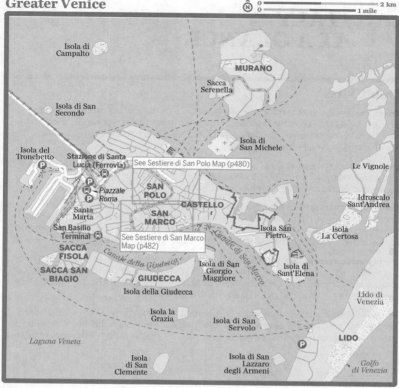

doges while taking some of Venice's finest heirlooms to France as trophies. When Austria set up shop, Empress Sissi remodelled the palace, adding ceiling frescoes, silk cladding and brocade curtains. It's now open to the public and full of many of Venice's reclaimed treasures, including ancient maps, statues, cameos and four centuries of artistic masterpieces.

**Peggy Guggenheim
Collection**   MUSEUM
(Map p482; ☏ 041 240 54 11; www.guggenheim-venice.it; Palazzo Venier dei Leoni 704, Dorsoduro; adult/reduced €15/9; ⊙10am-6pm Wed-Mon; ☻Accademia) After losing her father on the *Titanic,* heiress Peggy Guggenheim became one of the great collectors of the 20th century. Her palatial canalside home, Palazzo Venier dei Leoni, showcases her stockpile of surrealist, futurist and abstract expressionist art with works by up to 200 artists,

including her ex-husband Max Ernst, Jackson Pollock (among her many rumoured lovers), Picasso and Salvador Dalí.

---

❶ DISCOUNT PASSES

Access some of Venice's finest masterpieces in 16 churches with a Chorus Pass. It costs €12/8 (adult/student); otherwise, admission to these individual churches costs €3. Passes are for sale at church ticket booths; proceeds support restoration and maintenance of churches throughout Venice (excludes I Frari).

The San Marco Pack (adult/reduced €20/13), which covers four museums around Piazza San Marco (Palazzo Ducale, Museo Correr, Museo Archeologico Nazionale and Biblioteca Nazionale Marciana) and is vailable from any civic museum and the tourist office.

ITALY AT A GLANCE

Don't Miss

Rome Western Europe's first superpower, Rome became the spiritual centrepiece of the Christian world and is now the repository of over two millennia of European art and architecture. From the Pantheon and the Colosseum to Michelangelo's Sistine Chapel, there's simply too much to see in one visit.

Venice An Escher-esque maze of skinny streets and waterways, Venice straddles the middle ground between reality and sheer fantasy. This is a city of ethereal winter fogs, fairy-tale domes and Gothic arches fit for the set of an opera.

Cuisine It might look like a boot, but food-obsessed Italy feels more like a decadently stuffed Christmas stocking. From delicate tagliatelle al ragu to velvety cannoli, every bite feels like a revelation. While Italy's culinary soul might be earthy and rustic, it's equally ingenious and sophisticated. Expect some of the world's top fine-dining destinations.

Mighty masterpieces Many of the pivotal movements in Western art were forged in Italy by a red-carpet roll call of artists including Giotto, da Vinci, Michelangelo, Botticelli, Bernini, Caravaggio and Carracci. Find the best in Rome's Museo e Galleria Borghese and Vatican Museums, Florence's Uffizi and Venice's Gallerie dell'Accademia.

Pompeii Frozen in its death throes, the time-warped ruins of Pompeii hurtle you 2000 years into the past. With your eye on ominous Mt Vesuvius, wander through chariot-grooved Roman streets, lavishly frescoed villas and bathhouses, markets, theatres and even an ancient brothel.

Itineraries

One Week
A perfect introduction to Italy, this easy tour ticks off some of the country's most seductive sights, including the world's most beautiful lagoon city, Renaissance masterpieces and stunning hillside villages amid dramatic seaside scenery. A trip to Italy without a stop in **Venice** would be criminal. Begin with three unforgettable days in this iconic city. Check off musts like the mosaic-encrusted Basilica di San Marco and art-slung Gallerie dell'Accademia, then live like a true Venetian, noshing on the city's famous *cicheti* (Venetian tapas) and toasting with a Veneto *prosecco* (sparkling wine). From Venice, hop a train to **Cinque Terre** to stay in villages from the Middle Ages chiselled into seemingly impregnable cliffsides along the deep blue Mediterranean.

Two Weeks
Follow the one week itinerary and then tear yourself away from your village haven for Renaissance **Florence**. Drop in on Michelangelo's *David* at the Galleria dell'Accademia and pick your favourite Botticelli at the Galleria degli Uffizi. Head south for three days in mighty **Rome**, visiting blockbuster sights like the Colosseum and Sistine Chapel with market grazing, boutique-hopping and late-night revelry.

Essential Food & Drink

Antipasto misto Mixed antipasto; a platter of morsels including anything from olive *fritte* (fried olives) and *prosciutto e melone* (cured ham and cantaloupe) to *friarielli con peperoncino* (Neapolitan broccoli with chilli).

Formaggi Try parmigiano reggiano, a nutty hard cheese produced in the northern provinces; pungent gorgonzola, a washed-rind, blue-veined cheese; and mozzarella, a chewy, silky cheese best eaten the day it's made.

Gelato Ice cream made using only seasonal ingredients like pistachios, almonds or strawberries. In the height of summer, try *grattacheca*: crushed ice topped with fruit and syrup.

Digestivo Digestifs are post-dinner drinks, including *grappa*, a potent grape-derived pomace brandy. Another popular digestivo is *amaro*. Literally translating as 'bitter', this dark, bittersweet liqueur is prepared from herbs, roots and flowers.

Getting Around

Train Reasonably priced, with extensive coverage and frequent departures.

Car Handy for travelling at your own pace, or for visiting regions with minimal public transport.

Bus Cheaper and slower than trains. Useful for more remote villages not serviced by trains.

Air An extensive network of internal flights. Alitalia is the main domestic carrier, and budget airlines also operate countrywide.

Bicycle Cycling is very popular in Italy. Bikes can be wheeled onto many regional trains and most ferries also allow free bicycle passage. Available for hire in most Italian towns.

When to Go

Rome

°C/°F Temp
40/104 —
30/86 —
20/68 —
10/50 —
0/32 —
-10/14 —

Rainfall inches/mm
— 6/150
— 4/100
— 2/50
— 0

J F M A M J J A S O N D

Jul–Aug Expect long queues at all the big sights. Prices rocket during high season.

Apr–June & Sep–Oct Good deals on accommodation. Spring is best for festivals while autumn has warm weather.

Nov–Mar Prices can drop 30%. Many sights and hotels closed. Cultural events happen in large cities.

Arriving in Italy

Leonardo da Vinci Airport (Rome) The express train (€14) takes 30 minutes and runs between 6.23am and 11.23pm. Buses (€6) take an hour and run between 5am and 12.30am; night services run at 1.15am, 2.15am and 3.30am. Taxis (set fare €48) complete the journey in 45 to 60 minutes.

Marco Polo Airport (Venice) The ferry (€15) takes 45 to 90 minutes and runs between 6.15am and 1.15am. Buses (€8) take 30 minutes and run between 5.20am and 12.50am. Water taxis (from €110) take 30 minutes.

Top Phrases

Hello. Buongiorno.

Goodbye. Arrivederci.

Please. Per favore.

Thank you. Grazie.

How much is it? Quant'è?

Resources

Agriturismi (www.agriturismi.it) Guide to farm accommodation.

ENIT (www.italia.it) Official Italian-government tourism website.

The Local (www.thelocal.it) English-language news from Italy.

Set Your Budget

➤ Dorm bed: €20–35

➤ Double room in a budget hotel: €60–130

➤ Pizza or pasta: €6–12

➤ Admission to many state museums is free on Sundays

I Frari   CHURCH

(Basilica di Santa Maria Gloriosa dei Frari; Map p482; ☑ 041 272 86 18; www.basilicadeifrari.it; Campo dei Frari 3072, San Polo; adult/reduced €3/1.50; ⊙ 9am-6pm Mon-Sat, 1-6pm Sun; ⚑ San Tomà) A soaring Gothic church, I Frari's assets include marquetry choir stalls, Canova's pyramid mausoleum, Bellini's achingly sweet *Madonna with Child* triptych in the sacristy, and Longhena's creepy Doge Pesaro funereal monument. Upstaging them all, however, is the small altarpiece. This is Titian's 1518 *Assunta* (Assumption), in which a radiant red-cloaked Madonna reaches heavenward, steps onto a cloud and escapes this mortal coil. Titian himself – lost to the plague in 1576 at the age 94 – is buried near his celebrated masterpiece.

Chiesa di San Giorgio Maggiore   CHURCH

(☑ 041 522 78 27; www.abbaziasangiorgio.it; Isola di San Giorgio Maggiore; bell tower adult/reduced €6/4; ⊙ 8.30am-6pm; ⚑ San Giorgio Maggiore) **FREE** Solar eclipses are only marginally more dazzling than Palladio's white Istrian stone facade at this abbey church. Begun in 1565 and completed in 1610, it owes more to ancient Roman temples than the bombastic baroque of Palladio's day. Inside, ceilings billow over a generous nave, with high windows distributing filtered sunshine. Two of Tintoretto's masterworks flank the altar, and a lift whisks visitors up the 60m-high bell tower for stirring panoramas – a great alternative to queuing at San Marco's *campanile*.

★ Basilica di Santa Maria della Salute   BASILICA

(La Salute; Map p482; www.basilicasalutevenezia.it; Campo della Salute 1b, Dorsoduro; basilica free, sacristy adult/reduced €4/2; ⊙ basilica 9.30am-noon & 3-5.30pm, sacristry 10am-noon & 3-5pm Mon-Sat, 3-5pm Sun; ⚑ Salute) Guarding the entrance to the Grand Canal, this 17th-century domed church was commissioned by Venice's plague survivors as thanks for their salvation. Baldassare Longhena's uplifting design is an engineering feat that defies simple logic; in fact, the church is said to have mystical curative properties. Titian eluded the plague until age 94, leaving 12 key paintings in the basilica's art-slung sacristy.

☞ Tours

Row Venice   BOATING

(☑ 347 7250637; www.rowvenice.org; Fondamenta Gasparo Contarini; 90min lessons 1-2 people €85, 3/4 people €120/140; ⚑ Orto) The next best thing to walking on water: rowing a traditional *batellina coda di gambero* (shrimp-tailed boat) standing up like gondoliers do. Tours must be pre-booked and commence at the wooden gate of the Sacca Misericordia boat marina.

Walks of Italy   CULTURAL TOUR

(☑ 069 480 4888; www.walksofitaly.com/venice-tours; tours per person €56-137) Highly professional walking tours exploring every nook and cranny of Venice from a three-hour tour of the Doge's palace to a Rialto food tour with food and wine tastings and an after-hours tour of the Basilica di San Marco. Top-notch guides make these some of the best tours in Venice.

Monica Cesarato   CULTURAL

(www.monicacesarato.com; tours €35) With her mesmerising storytelling skills, Monica's tours are a whirlwind of cultural, social and epicurean information punctuated by generous glugs of wine and excellent plates of *cicheti* (Venetian tapas). She's so persuasive that she's even been known to mop up a plate of octopus. Kids will love her cleverly conceived ghost tours, full of grisly murders and plague deaths. Snacks along the way are paid for separately.

✦ Festivals & Events

La Biennale di Venezia   ART

(www.labiennale.org; Giardini della Biennale; ⊙ mid-May–Nov; ⚑ Giardini Biennale) Europe's premier arts showcase since 1907 is something of a misnomer: the Biennale is now held every

---

THE GHETTO

In medieval times, Cannaregio housed a getto (foundry). But it was as the designated Jewish quarter from the 16th to 19th centuries that the word acquired a whole new meaning. In accordance with the Venetian Republic's 1516 decree, Jewish lenders, doctors and clothing merchants were allowed to attend to Venice's commercial interests by day, while at night and on Christian holidays they were locked into the gated island of the Ghetto Nuovo (New Foundry). Catch a ferry to Guglie to visit.

year, but the spotlight alternates between art (odd-numbered years) and architecture (even-numbered years). Running alongside the two main events are annual showcases of dance, theatre, cinema and music.

Regata Storica
CULTURAL
(www.regatastoricavenezia.it; ⊙ Sep) Sixteenth-century costumes, eight-oared gondolas and ceremonial barques feature in this historical procession (usually held in early September) along the Grand Canal, which re-enacts the arrival of the Queen of Cyprus and precedes gondola races.

Venice Glass Week
ART
(www.theveniceglassweek.com; ⊙ Sep) Celebrating over a thousand years of alchemy and artisanship the newly inaugurated Venice Glass Week showcases Venetian glassworking skills in exhibitions, workshops and seminars. Guided tours at usually off-limit working furnaces are a highlight.

🛏 Sleeping

★ Le Terese
B&B €
(☏ 041 523 17 28; www.leterese.com; Campiello Tron 1902, Dorsoduro; d €80-100; ☕; 🚊 San Basilio) Join architectural duo Antonella and Mauro in their 18th-century granary on the Rio Terese for a dose of local living. There are just two rooms overlooking the canal and both are furnished in understated style with comfortable beds, Persian rugs and modernist furniture. The large, marble-tiled bathroom is shared, which just adds to the home-away-from-home feeling.

B&B San Marco
B&B €
(☏ 041 522 75 89; www.realvenice.it; Fondamente San Giorgio dei Schiavoni 3385l; r with/without bathroom €135/105; ☀; 🚊 San Zaccaria) Alice and Marco welcome you warmly to their home overlooking Carpaccio's frescoed Scuola Dalmata. The 3rd-floor apartment (no lift), with its parquet floors and large windows, is furnished with family antiques and offers photogenic views over the terracotta rooftops and canals. The hosts live upstairs, so they're always on hand with great recommendations.

Generator
HOSTEL €
(☏ 041 877 82 88; www.generatorhostels.com; Fondamenta de la Croce 86, Giudecca; dm/r from €35/155; ❄@☕; 🚊 Zitelle) Generator rocks a sharp, contemporary interior including a fabulous kooky-kitsch bar-restaurant with

THE TIDE IS HIGH

The alarm from 16 sirens throughout the city is a warning that acqua alta (high tide) is expected to reach the city within two to four hours. Venetians aren't often surprised: most monitor Venice's Centro Maree 48-hour tidal forecast at www.comune.venezia.it for high-tide warnings between November and April. When alarms sound, it's a non-emergency situation principally affecting low-lying areas. One tone signals a tide up to 110cm above normal, barely warranting a pause in happy-hour conversation. With two tones, you might want your welly boots and with four, shops close early and flood barriers are slung across doorsteps. Within five hours, the tide usually ebbs, clearing the lagoon of extra silt and maintaining the balance of its waters.

crazy wallpaper, Murano chandeliers and a pool table. Try to score a bunk up to the window – you might even wake up to a San Marco view. Sheets, blanket and a pillow are provided; breakfast is an additional €4.50.

★ Locanda Ca' Le Vele
B&B €€
(Map p480; ☏ 041 241 39 60; www.locandalevele.com; Calle de le Vele 3969; r/ste from €130/183; ❄☕; 🚊 Ca' d'Oro) The lane may be quiet and the house might look demure but inside it's Venetian glam all the way. The six guestrooms are a surprisingly stylish riot of terrazzo floors, damask furnishings, Murano glass sconces and ornate gilded beds with busy covers. Pay a little extra for a canal view.

🍴 Eating

Garden islands and lagoon aquaculture yield speciality produce and seafood you won't find elsewhere, with tantalising traces of ancient spice routes. The city knows how to put on a royal spread, as France's King Henry III once found out when faced with 1200 dishes and 200 bonbons. Today such feasts are available in miniature with *cicheti* (Venetian tapas). Local specialities include *risi e bisi* (pea soup thickened with rice) and *sarde in saor* (fried sardines marinated in vinegar and onions), along with Veneto's signature bubbly, *prosecco*.

Sestiere di San Polo

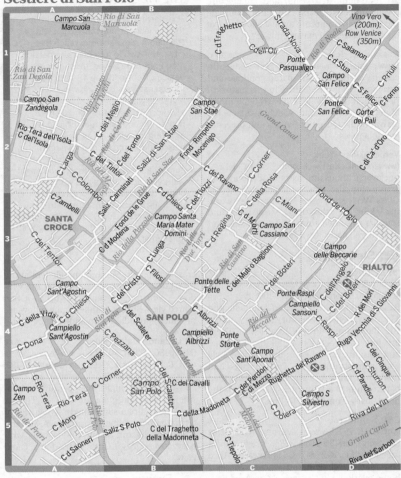

Map: Sestiere di San Polo

★ **All'Arco**   VENETIAN €

(Map p480; ☎ 041 520 56 66; Calle dell'Ochialer 436, San Polo; cicheti from €2; ⊗ 8am-2.30pm Mon, Tue & Sat, to 7pm Wed-Fri summer, 8am-2.30pm Mon-Sat winter; 🚤 Rialto-Mercato) Search out this authentic neighbourhood *osteria* for the best *cicheti* in town. Armed with ingredients from the nearby Rialto Market, father-son team Francesco and Matteo serve miniature masterpieces such as *cannocchia* (mantis shrimp) with pumpkin and roe, and *otrega crudo* (raw butterfish) with mint-and-olive-oil marinade. Even with copious *prosecco*, hardly any meal here tops €20.

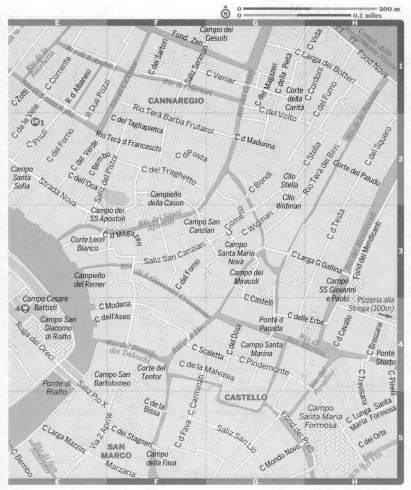

★ **Dai Zemei** VENETIAN **€**

(Map p480; ☎ 041 520 85 96; www.ostariadaizemei.it; Ruga Vecchia San Giovanni 1045, San Polo; cicheti from €1.50; ☺ 8.30am-8.30pm Mon-Sat, 9am-7pm Sun; ⛴ San Silvestro) Running this closet-sized *cicheti* counter are *zemei* (twins) Franco and Giovanni, who serve loyal regulars small meals with plenty of imagination: gorgonzola lavished with *peperoncino* (chilli) marmalade, duck breast drizzled with truffle oil, or chicory paired with leek and marinated anchovies. It's a gourmet bargain for inspired bites and impeccable wines.

ℹ **NAVIGATING VENICE**

Venice is not an easy place to navigate and even with a map you're bound to get lost. The main area of interest lies between Santa Lucia train station (signposted as the Ferrovia) and Piazza San Marco (St Mark's Sq). The path between the two is a good 40- to 50-minute walk. It also helps to know that the city is divided into six *sestieri* (districts): Cannaregio, Castello, San Marco, Dorsoduro, San Polo and Santa Croce.

Sestiere di San Marco

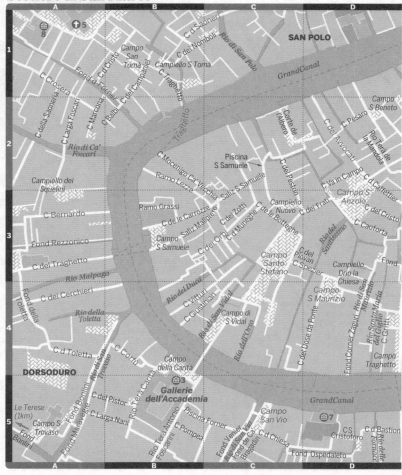

★ **Pasticceria Dal Mas**　　　BAKERY €
(📞 041 71 51 01; www.dalmaspasticceria.it; Rio Terà Lista di Spagna 150; pastries €1.30-6.50; ⊙ 7am-9pm; 🚶; 🚊 Ferrovia) Our favourite Venetian bakery-cafe sparkles with mirrors, marble and metal trim, providing a fitting casket for the precious pastries displayed within. Despite the perpetual morning crush, the efficient team dispenses top-notch coffee and *cornetti* (croissants) with admirable equanimity. Come mid-morning for mouth-watering, still-warm quiches. The hot chocolate is also exceptional – hardly surprising given its sister chocolate shop next door.

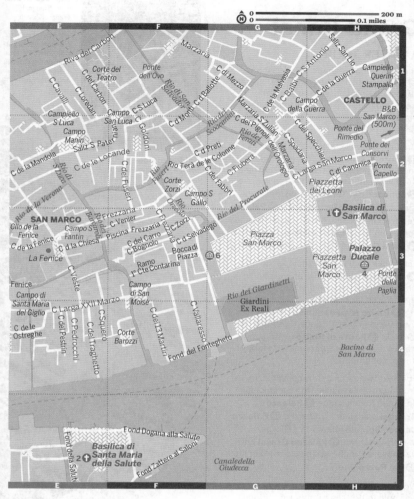

Pizzeria alla Strega PIZZA €

(☑041 528 64 97; www.facebook.com/alla.stre ga.venezia; Barbaria de le Tole 6418; pizzas €8-9, cicheti platters €14-23; ☺noon-2.45pm & 6.45-10pm Thu-Tue; 🚢Ospedale) This hugely popular pizzeria and *cichetteria* has been feeding locals for years. Although best known as a pizza parlour, you can also enjoy a wide range of hearty salads and bar snacks: the famous Venetian *cicheti*. A large platter consists of typical dishes such as *baccalà* (cod), *sarde in saor* (marinated sardines) and polenta.

ⓘ GONDOLA RIDES FOR A SONG

Ditch those €80 gondola rides for the cheap thrill of standing on the *traghetto* (public gondola) as you cross the Grand Canal (€2 per ride). If you simply must hop on a gondola, Tu.Ri.Ve (www.turive. it) offers budget-conscious rides at €32 a pop. That's worth singing about.

Grand Canal

A WATER TOUR

The 3.5km route of vaporetto (passenger ferry) No 1, which passes some 50 palazzi (mansions), six churches and scene-stealing backdrops featured in four James Bond films, is public transport at its most glamorous.

The Grand Canal starts with controversy: ❶ **Ponte di Calatrava** a luminous glass-and-steel bridge that cost triple the original €4 million estimate. Ahead are castle-like ❷ **Fondaco dei Turchi**, the historic Turkish trading-house; Renaissance ❸ **Palazzo Vendramin**, housing the city's casino; and double-arcaded ❹ **Ca' Pesaro**. Don't miss ❺ **Ca' d'Oro**, a 1430 filigree Gothic marvel.

Points of Venetian pride include the ❻ **Pescaria**, built in 1907 on the site where fishmongers have been slinging lagoon crab for 600 years, and neighbouring ❼ **Rialto Market** stalls, overflowing with island-grown produce. Cost overruns for 1592 ❽ **Ponte di Rialto** rival Calatrava's, but its marble splendour stands the test of time.

The next two canal bends could cause architectural whiplash, with Sanmicheli-designed Renaissance ❾ **Palazzo Grimani** and Mauro Codussi's ❿ **Palazzo Corner-Spinelli** followed by Giorgio Masari-designed ⓫ **Palazzo Grassi** and Baldassare Longhena's baroque jewel box, ⓬ **Ca' Rezzonico**.

Wooden ⓭ **Ponte dell'Accademia** was built in 1930 as a temporary bridge, but the beloved landmark remains. Stone lions flank the ⓮ **Peggy Guggenheim Collection**, where the American heiress collected ideas, lovers and art. You can't miss the dramatic dome of Longhena's ⓯ **Chiesa di Santa Maria della Salute** or ⓰ **Punta della Dogana**, Venice's triangular customs warehouse reinvented as a contemporary art showcase. The Grand Canal's grand finale is pink Gothic ⓱ **Palazzo Ducale** and its adjoining ⓲ **Ponte dei Sospiri**.

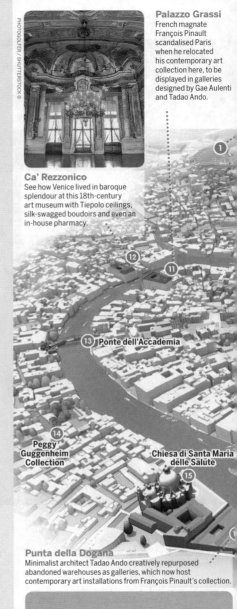

Palazzo Grassi
French magnate François Pinault scandalised Paris when he relocated his contemporary art collection here, to be displayed in galleries designed by Gae Aulenti and Tadao Ando.

Ca' Rezzonico
See how Venice lived in baroque splendour at this 18th-century art museum with Tiepolo ceilings, silk-swagged boudoirs and even an in-house pharmacy.

Ponte dell'Accademia

Peggy Guggenheim Collection

Chiesa di Santa Maria delle Salute

Punta della Dogana
Minimalist architect Tadao Ando creatively repurposed abandoned warehouses as galleries, which now host contemporary art installations from François Pinault's collection.

Ponte di Calatrava
With its starkly streamlined fish-fin shape, the 2008 bridge was the first to be built over the Grand Canal in 75 years.

Fondaco dei Turchi
Recognisable by its double colonnade, watchtowers, and dugout canoe parked at the Museo di Storia Naturale's ground-floor loggia.

Ca' d'Oro
Behind the triple Gothic arcades are priceless masterpieces: Titians looted by Napoleon, a rare Mantegna and semiprecious stone mosaic floors.

② ③ **Palazzo Vendramin**

④ ⑤

⑥ **Pescaria**

⑦ **Rialto Market**

Palazzo Grimani
⑨

⑩ **Palazzo Corner-Spinelli**

⑧ **Ponte di Rialto**

Ponte dei Sospiri
⑱

Palazzo Ducale ⑰

Ponte di Rialto
Antonio da Ponte beat out Palladio for the commission of this bridge, but construction costs spiralled to 250,000 Venetian ducats – about €19 million today.

Ca' Pesaro
Originally designed by Baldassare Longhena, this palazzo was bequeathed to the city in 1898 to house the Galleria d'Arte Moderna and Museo d'Arte Orientale.

🍷 Drinking & Entertainment

★**Al Mercà**   WINE BAR
(Map p480; ☎346 8340660; Campo Cesare Battisti 213, San Polo; ⏱10am-2.30pm & 6-8pm Mon-Thu, to 9.30pm Fri & Sat; ☗Rialto-Mercato) Discerning drinkers throng to this cupboard-sized counter on a Rialto Market square to sip on top-notch *prosecco* and DOC (Denominazione de Origine Controllata) wines by the glass (from €3). Edibles usually include meatballs and mini *panini* (€1.50), proudly made using super-fresh ingredients.

★**Vino Vero**   WINE BAR
(☎041 275 00 44; www.facebook.com/vinoverovenezia; Fondamenta de la Misericordia 2497; ⏱11am-midnight Tue-Sun, from 6pm Mon; ☗San Marcuola) Lining the exposed-brick walls of this superior wine bar are interesting small-production wines, including a great selection of natural and biodynamic labels. However it's the *cicheti* that really lifts this place beyond the ordinary, with arguably the most mouth-watering display of continually replenished, fresh *crostini* (open-face sandwiches) in the entire city. In the evenings the crowd spills out onto the canal.

ℹ Information

Marco Polo Airport Tourist Office (☎041 24 24; www.veneziaunica.it; Arrivals Hall, Marco Polo Airport; ⏱8.30am-7pm) Multilingual tourist information is available at the airport tourist information office. It can help with information on transport to the city and offers a city map for €3.

Vènezia Unica (☎041 24 24; www.veneziaunica.it) The provider of tourist information services in Venice, including ticketing for public transport, museums, churches, theatres and events. It also provides information and assistance in arranging various tours and guides.

ℹ Getting There & Away

Marco Polo Airport (VCE) Located on the mainland 12km from Venice, east of Mestre. Alilaguna operates a ferry service (€15) to Venice from the airport ferry dock (an eight-minute walk from the terminal); expect it to take 45 to 90 minutes to reach most destinations. Water taxis to Venice from airport docks cost from €110, or from €25 for shared taxis with up to 10 passengers. ATVO buses (€8) depart from the airport every 30 minutes from 7.50am to 12.20am, and reach Venice's Piazzale Roma within 20 to 30 minutes, traffic permitting.

Piazzale Roma This car park is the only point within central Venice accessible by car or bus. *Vaporetto* (water-bus) lines to destinations throughout the city depart from Piazzale Roma docks.

Stazione Santa Lucia Venice's train station. *Vaporetto* lines depart from Ferrovia (Station) docks to all parts of Venice. There is also a handy water-taxi stand just out the front if you are heavily laden.

Stazione Venezia Mestre Mestre's mainland train station; transfer here to Stazione Santa Lucia.

ℹ Getting Around

Vaporetto Venice's main public transport. Single rides cost €7.50; for frequent use, get a timed pass for unlimited travel within a set period (one-/two-/three-/seven-day passes cost €20/30/40/60). Tickets and passes are available dockside from ACTV ticket booths and ticket vending machines, or from tobacconists.

Gondola Daytime rates run to €80 for 30 minutes (six passengers maximum) or €100 for 35 minutes from 7pm to 8am, not including songs (negotiated separately) or tips.

Traghetto Locals use this daytime public gondola service (€2) to cross the Grand Canal between bridges.

Water taxi Sleek teak boats offer taxi services for €15 plus €2 per minute, plus €5 for pre-booked services and extra for night-time, luggage and large groups. Ensure the meter is working when boarding.

Florence

POP 377.650

Return time and again and you still won't see it all. Surprisingly small as it is, this riverside city looms large on the world's 'must-sees' list. The cradle of the Renaissance and of tourist masses that flock here to feast on world-class art, Florence (Firenze) is magnetic, romantic and busy. Its urban fabric has hardly changed since the Renaissance, its narrow streets evoke a thousand tales, and its food and wine are so wonderful the tag 'Fiorentina' has become an international label of quality assurance.

Fashion designers parade on Via de' Tornabuoni. Gucci was born here, as was Roberto Cavalli, who, like many a smart Florentine these days, hangs out in wine-rich hills around Florence. After a while in this absorbing city, you might want to do the same.

◎ Sights

★ **Duomo**   CATHEDRAL

(Cattedrale di Santa Maria del Fiore; ☑ 055 230 28 85; www.ilgrandemuseodelduomo.it; Piazza del Duomo; ⊙ 10am-5pm Mon-Wed & Fri, to 4.30pm Thu, to 4.45pm Sat, 1.30-4.45pm Sun) **FREE** Florence's

Duomo is the city's most iconic landmark. Capped by Filippo Brunelleschi's red-tiled **cupola** (Brunelleschi's Dome; adult/reduced incl cupola, baptistry, campanile, crypt & museum €15/3; ⊙ 8.30am-7pm Mon-Fri, to 5pm Sat, 1-4pm Sun), it's a staggering construction whose breathtaking pink, white and green marble facade and graceful *campanile* (bell tower) dominate the Renaissance cityscape. Sienese architect Arnolfo di Cambio began work on it in 1296, but construction took almost 150 years and it wasn't consecrated until 1436. In the echoing interior, look out for frescoes by Vasari and Zuccari and up to 44 stained-glass windows.

★ **Galleria degli Uffizi**   GALLERY

(Uffizi Gallery; ☑ 055 29 48 83; www.uffizi.it; Piazzale degli Uffizi 6; adult/reduced €20/10, combined ticket with Palazzo Pitti & Giardino di Boboli €38/21; ⊙ 8.15am-6.50pm Tue-Sun) Home to the world's greatest collection of Italian Renaissance art, Florence's premier gallery occupies the vast U-shaped Palazzo degli Uffizi, built between 1560 and 1580 to house government offices. The collection, bequeathed to the city by the Medici family in 1743 on condition that it never leave

---

DON'T MISS

PALAZZO VECCHIO TOURS

To get the most out of one of Florence's most dynamic, well-thought-out museums, join one of its excellent guided tours that take you into parts of the building otherwise inaccessible; many are in English. You need a valid museum ticket in addition to the guided-tour ticket.

The best of the adult bunch is the 'Secret Passages' tour (adult/reduced €4/2, 1¼ hours, twice daily), which leads small groups along the secret staircase built between the palace's super-thick walls in 1342 as an escape route for French Duke of Athens Walter de Brienne, who seized the palace and nominated himself Lord of Florence, only to be sent packing back to France by the Florentines a year later. It follows this staircase to the Tesoretto (Treasury) of Cosimo I – a tiny room no larger than a cupboard for his private collection – and the equally intimate, sumptuous Studiolo (Study) of his introverted, alchemy-mad son Francesco I. The tour ends in the palace roof above the Salone dei Cinquecento, where you can see the huge wooden trusses supporting Vasari's ornate ceiling.

The 'Invitation to the Court' tour (adult/child €4/2, 1¼ hours), open to visitors aged eight years and upwards, ushers in actors dressed in Renaissance costume. A sumptuously attired Eleonora of Toledo, clearly shocked by the casual attire of today's children, has been known to give advice about proper grooming for young ladies, and Cosimo I is happy to lay down the law about the proper age for a Medici to take on duties as a cardinal.

There are also story-telling sessions for children and hands-on fresco and panel painting workshops (adult/child €4/2, 1¼ hours). Reserve tours and workshops in advance by telephone (055 276 82 24, 055 276 85 58), email (info@muse.comune.fi.it) or directly at the ticket desk of Palazzo Vecchio.

Florence

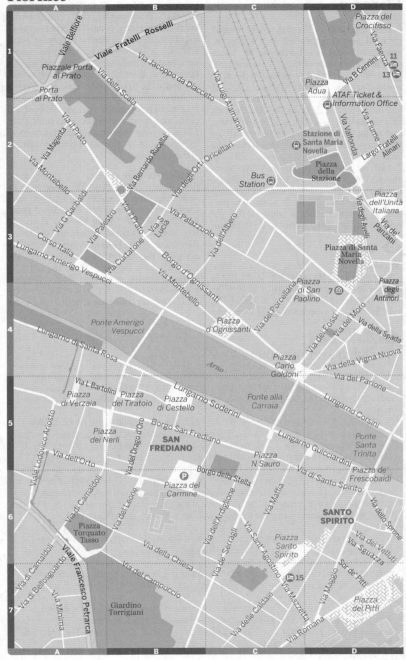

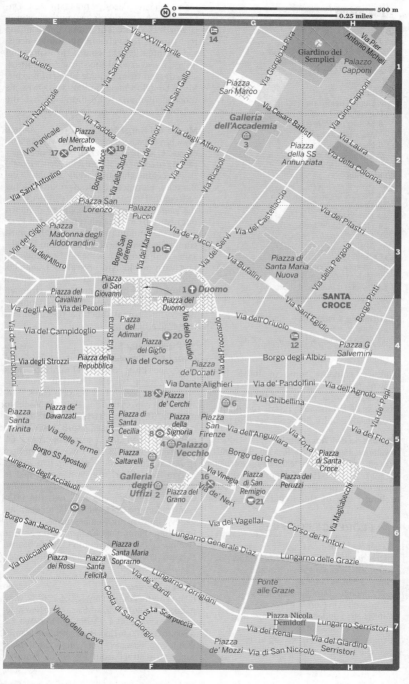

Florence

Florence, contains some of Italy's best-known paintings, including Piero della Francesco's profile portaits of the Duke and Duchess of Urbino and rooms full of masterpieces by Sandro Botticelli. See also p496.

★ **Galleria dell'Accademia**　　　GALLERY
(www.firenzemusei.it; Via Ricasoli 60; adult/reduced €8/4, incl temporary exhibition €12.50/6.25; ⏱ 8.15am-6.50pm Tue-Sun) A queue marks the door to this gallery, built to house one of the Renaissance's most

ⓘ FLORENCE FOR FREE

To cut costs, visit on the first Sunday of the month, when admission to state museums, including the Uffizi and Galleria dell'Accademia, is free. Free admission to state-run galleries and cultural sites in Florence is available to youths aged under 18 and seniors over 65. Those entitled to reduced admission usually include EU citizens aged between 18 and 25 years.

iconic masterpieces, Michelangelo's *David*. But the world's most famous statue is worth the wait. The subtle detail of the real thing – the veins in his sinewy arms, the leg muscles, the change in expression as you move around the statue – *is* impressive. Carved from a single block of marble, Michelangelo's most famous work was his most challenging – he didn't choose the marble himself and it was veined.

Museo del Bargello　　　MUSEUM
(www.bargellomusei.beniculturali.it; Via del Proconsolo 4; adult/reduced €8/4; ⏱ 8.15am-1.50pm, closed 2nd & 4th Sun, 1st, 3rd & 5th Mon of month) It was behind the stark walls of Palazzo del Bargello, Florence's earliest public building redecorated in neo-Gothic style in 1845, that the *podestà* (governing magistrate) meted out justice from the 13th century until 1502. Today the building safeguards Italy's most comprehensive collection of Tuscan Renaissance sculpture with some of Michelangelo's best early works and several by Donatello. Michelangelo was just 21 when a cardinal commissioned him to create the drunken grape-adorned *Bacchus* (1496–97). Unfortunately the cardinal didn't like the result and sold it to a banker.

★ **Piazza della Signoria**　　　PIAZZA
(Piazza della Signoria) The hub of local life since the 13th century, Florentines flock here to meet friends and chat over early-evening *aperitivi* at historic cafes. Presiding over everything is **Palazzo Vecchio** (☑ 055 276 85 58, 055 27 68 22; www.musefirenze.it; adult/reduced museum €10/8, tower €10/8, museum & tower €14/12, archaeological tour €4, combination ticket €18/16; ⏱ museum 9am-11pm Fri-Wed, to 2pm Thu Apr-Sep, 9am-7pm Fri-Wed, to 2pm Thu Oct-Mar, tower 9am-9pm Fri-Wed, to 2pm Thu Apr-Sep, 10am-5pm Fri-Wed, to 2pm Thu Oct-Mar), Florence's city hall, and the 14th-century **Loggia dei Lanzi** FREE, an open-air gallery showcasing Renaissance sculptures, including Giambologna's *Rape of the Sabine Women* (c 1583), Benvenuto Cellini's bronze *Perseus* (1554) and Agnolo Gaddi's *Seven Virtues* (1384–89).

Museo Novecento　　　MUSEUM
(Museum of the 20th Century; ☑ 055 28 61 32; www.museonovecento.it; Piazza di Santa Maria Novella 10; adult/reduced €8.50/4; ⏱ 9am-7pm Mon-Wed, Sat & Sun, to 2pm Thu, to 11pm Fri summer, 9am-6pm Fri-Wed, to 2pm Thu winter) Don't allow the Renaissance to distract from Florence's fantastic

modern art museum in a 13th-century *palazzo* (mansion) previously used as a pilgrim shelter, hospital and school. A well-articulated itinerary guides visitors through modern Italian painting and sculpture from the early 20th century to the late 1980s. Installation art makes effective use of the outside space located on the 1st-floor loggia. Fashion and theatre get a nod on the 2nd floor, and the itinerary ends with a 20-minute cinematic montage of the best films that were set in Florence.

Ponte Vecchio BRIDGE
Dating from 1345, Ponte Vecchio was the only Florentine bridge to survive destruction at the hands of retreating German forces in 1944. Above the jewellers' shops on the eastern side, the **Corridoio Vasariano** (Vasari Corridor) is a 16th-century passageway between the Uffizi and Palazzo Pitti that runs around, rather than through, the medieval **Torre dei Mannelli** at the bridge's southern end. The first documentation of a stone bridge here, at the narrowest crossing point along the entire length of the Arno, dates from 972.

🛏 Sleeping

⭐ **Academy Hostel** HOSTEL €
(☑ 055 239 86 65; www.academyhostel.eu; Via Ricasoli 9; dm €32-45, d €80-100; ✳ @ 🛜) This classy 13-room hostel – definitely not a party hostel – is situated on the 1st floor of Baron Ricasoli's 17th-century *palazzo*. The inviting lobby, with books to browse and computers to surf, was once a theatre and is a comfy spot to chill on the sofa over TV or a DVD. Dorms sport four, five or six beds, high moulded ceilings and brightly coloured lockers.

⭐ **Hotel Dalí** HOTEL €
(☑ 055 234 07 06; www.hoteldali.com; Via dell'Oriuolo 17; d €90, s/d without bathroom €40/70, apt from €95; ℗ 🛜) A warm welcome from hosts Marco and Samanta awaits at this lovely small hotel. A stone's throw from the Duomo, it has 10 sunny rooms, some overlooking a leafy inner courtyard, decorated in a low-key modern way and equipped with kettles, coffee and tea. No breakfast, but – miraculous for downtown Florence – free parking in the rear courtyard.

WHO'S THAT BLOKE?

Name *David*.

Occupation World's most famous sculpture.

Vital statistics Height: 516cm tall; weight: 19 tonnes of mediocre-quality pearly white marble from the Fantiscritti quarries in Carrara.

Commissioned In 1501 by the Opera del Duomo for the cathedral, but subsequently placed in front of the Palazzo Vecchio on Piazza della Signoria, where it stayed until 1873.

Outstanding features (a) His expression, which, from the left profile, appears serene, Zen and boy-like, and from the right, concentrated, manly and highly charged in anticipation of the gargantuan Goliath he is about to slay; (b) the sense of counterbalanced weight rippling through his body, from the tension in his right hip on which he leans to his taut left arm.

Why the small penis? In classical art a large or even normal-sized packet was not deemed elegant, hence the daintier size.

And the big head and hands? *David* was designed to stand up high on a cathedral buttress in the apse, from where his head and hands would have appeared in perfect proportion.

Beauty treatments Body scrub with hydrochloric acid (1843); clay and cellulose pulp 'mud pack' and bathe in distilled water (2004).

Occupational hazards Over the centuries he's been struck by lightning, attacked by rioters and had his toes bashed with a hammer. The two pale white lines visible on his lower left arm is where his arm got broken during the 1527 revolt when the Medici were kicked out of Florence.

ITALY, GREECE & TURKEY FLORENCE

LESSER-KNOWN GEMS

When the Uffizi, *David* and Ponte Vecchio crowds get too much, flee to one of Florence's faintly lesser-known gems: Palazzo Strozzi (blockbuster art exhibitions), Museo del Bargello (early Michelangelos), Chiesa di Orsanmichele (medieval statuary), Biblioteca Laurenziana Medicea (Michelangelo staircase), Museo Marino Marini (Rucellai Chapel) and Chiesa di Santa Trinita (frescoes).

Hotel Marine
HOTEL €

(☑ 055 26 42 51; www.hotelmarineflorence.com; Via Faenza 56; d/tr/q €100/120/140; ☎) Run by the same team as **Hotel Azzi** (Locanda degli Artisti; ☑ 055 21 38 06; www.hotelazzi.com; Via Faenza 56/88r; d/tr/q €120/140/160; ✳☎) on the ground floor (the two hotels even share the same reception), 2nd-floor Marine is tip-top value for those on a budget. Its 15 rooms are plain but spotlessly clean and decently sized. The star attraction is breakfast on the summer terrace with dreamy rooftop views, including the Duomo, Capelle Medicee and Palazzo Vecchio.

★ Hotel Orto de' Medici
HOTEL €€

(☑ 055 48 34 27; www.ortodeimedici.it; Via San Gallo 30; d from €174; ✳@☎) This three-star hotel in San Marco redefines elegance with its majestic ceilings, chic oyster-grey colour scheme and contemporary furnishings, set off to perfection by the historic *palazzo* in which it languishes. Hunt down the odd remaining 19th-century fresco, and don't miss the garden with lemon trees in terracotta pots and rambling ivy. To splurge, go for a room with its own flowery terrace.

★ Hotel Palazzo Guadagni
HOTEL €€

(☑ 055 265 83 76; www.palazzoguadagni.com; Piazza Santo Spirito 9; d €150-220, tr/q €265/310; ✳☎) This romantic hotel overlooking Florence's liveliest summertime square is legendary – Zeffirelli shot scenes from *Tea with Mussolini* here. Housed in an artfully revamped Renaissance palace, it has 15 spacious if old-fashioned rooms and an impossibly romantic loggia terrace with wicker chairs and predictably dreamy views.

Eating

★ Trattoria Mario
TUSCAN €

(☑ 055 21 85 50; www.trattoria-mario.com; Via Rosina 2; meals €25; ⏰ noon-3.30pm Mon-Sat, closed 3 weeks Aug; ✳) Arrive by noon to ensure a stool around a shared table at this noisy, busy, brilliant trattoria – a legend that retains its soul (and allure with locals) despite being in every guidebook. Charming Fabio, whose grandfather opened the place in 1953, is front of house while big brother Romeo and nephew Francesco cook with speed in the kitchen. No advance reservations; no credit cards.

★ Osteria Il Buongustai
OSTERIA €

(☑ 055 29 13 04; Via dei Cerchi 15r; meals €15-20; ⏰ 8am-4pm Mon-Fri, to 11pm Sat) Run with breathtaking speed and grace by Laura and Lucia, this place is unmissable. Lunchtimes heave with locals who work nearby and savvy students who flock here to fill up on tasty Tuscan home cooking at a snip of other restaurant prices. The place is brilliantly no frills – expect to share a table and pay in cash; no credit cards.

★ Mercato Centrale
FOOD HALL €

(☑ 055 239 97 98; www.mercatocentrale.it; Piazza del Mercato Centrale 4; dishes €7-15; ⏰ 10am-midnight; ☎) Wander the maze of stalls rammed with fresh produce at Florence's oldest and largest food market, on the ground floor of a fantastic iron-and-glass structure designed by architect Giuseppe Mengoni in 1874. Head to the 1st floor's buzzing, thoroughly contemporary food hall with dedicated bookshop, cookery school and artisan stalls cooking steaks, burgers, tripe *panini*, vegetarian dishes, pizza, gelato, pastries and pasta.

★ All'Antico Vinaio
OSTERIA €

(☑ 055 238 27 23; www.allanticovinaio.com; Via de' Neri 65r; tasting platters €10-30; ⏰ 10am-4pm & 6-11pm Tue-Sat, noon-3.30pm Sun) The crowd spills out the door of this noisy Florentine thoroughbred. Push your way to the tables at the back to taste cheese and salami in situ (reservations recommended). Or join the queue at the deli counter for a well-stuffed focaccia wrapped in waxed paper to take away – the quality is outstanding. Pour yourself a glass of wine while you wait.

🍷 Drinking & Nightlife

★ Ditta Artigianale
CAFE, BAR

(☑ 055 274 15 41; www.dittaartigianale.it; Via de' Neri 32r; ⊙8am-10pm Sun-Thu, 8am-midnight Fri, 9.30am-midnight Sat; 🛜) With industrial decor and welcoming laid-back vibe, this ingenious coffee roastery and gin bar is a perfect place to hang at any time of day. The creation of three-times Italian barista champion Francesco Sanapo, it's famed for its first-class coffee and outstanding gin cocktails. If you're yearning a flat white, cold brew tonic or cappuccino made with almond, soy or coconut milk, come here.

Coquinarius
WINE BAR

(www.coquinarius.com; Via delle Oche 11r; ⊙12.30-3pm & 6.30-10.30pm Wed-Mon) With its old stone vaults, scrubbed wooden tables and refreshingly modern air, this *enoteca* run by the dynamic Nicolas is spacious and stylish. The wine list features bags of Tuscan greats and unknowns, and outstanding crostini and *carpacci* (cold sliced meats) ensure you don't leave hungry. The ravioli stuffed with silky *burrata* cheese and smothered in pistachio pesto is particularly outstanding.

ℹ️ Information

Airport Tourist Office (☑ 055 31 58 74; www.firenzeturismo.it; Florence Airport, Via del Termine 11; ⊙9am-7pm Mon-Sat, to 2pm Sun)

Firenze Musei (Florence Museums; www.firenzemusei.it) Official ticketing website for Florence's state-run museums, including the Uffizi and Accademia.

ℹ️ Getting There & Away

AIR

Also known as Amerigo Vespucci or Peretola airport, **Florence airport** (Aeroporto Amerigo Vespucci; ☑ 055 3 06 15, 055 306 18 30; www.aeroporto.firenze.it; Via del Termine 11) is 5km

northwest of the city centre and is served by both domestic and European flights. ATAF operates a Volainbus shuttle (single/return €6/10, 30 minutes) between Florence airport and Florence bus station every 30 minutes between 6am and 8.30pm, then hourly from 8.30pm until 11.30pm. A taxi between Florence airport and the city centre costs a flat rate of €20 (€24 on Sundays and holidays, and €25.30 between 10pm and 6am).

The city's other handy airport is **Pisa International Airport** (Galileo Galilei Airport; ☑ 050 84 93 00; www.pisa-airport.com) in Pisa, 80km west of Florence, with flights to most major European cities. Daily buses are operated by Autostradale (www.airportbusexpress.it; single/return €7.50/13.50, 80 minutes, hourly) between Pisa International Airport and the bus stops near Florence's Stazione di Santa Maria Novella. Buy tickets online, on board and at the Pisa Airport Information Desk. Regular trains link Florence's Stazione di Santa Maria Novella with Pisa's central train station, Pisa Centrale (€9.70, 1½ hours, at least hourly from 4.30am to 10.25pm), with fully automated, super-speedy PisaMover trains (€2.70, five minutes, every five minutes from 6am to midnight) continuing to Pisa International Airport.

BUS

Services from the **SITA bus station** (Autostazione Busitalia-Sita Nord; ☑ 800 373760; Via Santa Caterina da Siena 17r; ⊙5.30am-8.30pm Mon-Sat, 6am-8pm Sun), just west of Piazza della Stazione, are limited; the train is better.

TRAIN

Florence's central train station is **Stazione di Santa Maria Novella** (Piazza della Stazione). The **left-luggage counter** (Deposito Bagagliamano; 1st 5hr €6, then per hour €0.90; ⊙6am-11pm) is on platform 16. Tickets for all trains are sold in the main ticketing hall, but skip the permanently long queue by buying tickets from the touch-screen automatic ticket-vending machines; machines have an English option and accept cash and credit cards.

ℹ️ SHORT ON TIME?

In July, August and other busy periods such as Easter, unbelievably long queues are a fact of life at Florence's key museums – if you haven't prebooked your ticket, you could well end up standing in line queuing for four hours or so.

For a fee of €3 per ticket (€4 for the Uffizi and Galleria dell'Accademia), tickets to nine *musei statali* (state museums) can be reserved, including the Uffizi, Galleria dell'Accademia (where *David* lives), Palazzo Pitti, Museo del Bargello and the Medicean chapels (Cappelle Medicee). In reality, the only museums where prebooking is vital are the Uffizi and Accademia – to organise your ticket, go online or call **Firenze Musei**, with ticketing desks at the **Uffizi** (p487; Door 3) and **Palazzo Pitti** (Piazza dei Pitti; ⊙8.15am-6.05pm summer, reduced hours winter).

WORTH A TRIP

CINQUE TERRE

Set amid some of the most dramatic coastal scenery on the planet, these five ingeniously constructed fishing villages – Monterosso al Mare, Vernazza, Corniglia, Manarola and Riomaggiore – can bolster the most jaded of spirits. A Unesco World Heritage site since 1997, Cinque Terre isn't the undiscovered Eden it once was but, frankly, who cares? Sinuous paths traverse seemingly impregnable cliffsides, while a 19th-century railway line cut through a series of coastal tunnels ferries the footsore from village to village. Thankfully cars were banned over a decade ago.

Rooted in antiquity, Cinque Terre's five villages date from the early medieval period and while much of this fetching vernacular architecture remains, Cinque Terre's unique historical draw is the steeply terraced cliffs bisected by a complicated system of fields and gardens that have been hacked, chiselled, shaped and layered over the course of nearly two millennia. The extensive *muretti* (low stone walls) can be compared to the Great Wall of China in their grandeur and scope.

Each of Cinque Terre's villages is associated with a sanctuary perched high on the cliffsides above the azure Mediterranean. Reaching these religious retreats used to be part of a hefty Catholic penance, but these days the walks through terraced vineyards and across view-splayed cliffs are a heavenly reward in themselves

Since flash floods in 2011, many of Cinque Terre's walking paths have been in a delicate state and prone to periodic or permanent closure. However, Cinque Terre has a whole network of spectacular trails and you can still plan a decent village-to-village hike by choosing from any of 30 numbered paths. Check ahead for the most up-to-date trail information at www.parconazionale5terre.it/Esentieri-outdoor.php.

Sleeping & Eating

Ostello 5 Terre (☏0187 92 00 39; www.hostel5terre.com; Via Riccobaldi 21; dm/d/f €28/80/120; ⊘closed mid-Jan–mid-Feb; @☏) Manarola's hostel sits at the top of the village next to the Chiesa di San Lorenzo. It has single-sex, six-bed dorms, each with its own bathroom and great views, and several double and family rooms. It has its own bright and stylish little restaurant and a terrace for evening drinks.

3 Passi dal Mare (www.vernazzani5terre.it/it/camere-corniglia; Via Fieschi 204; s/d €70/90; ☏) Four appealingly simple, rustic rooms all have spectacular views, including the single room, and two have terraces. Private bathrooms are new, if basic, and breakfast is taken in the town's best bar, **La Scuna** (☏347 7997527; Via Fieschi 185; ⊘9am-1am late-March–Nov). A rare find.

Getting There & Around

Cinque Terre is sandwiched between Genoa (accessible by regular train services from Venice) and La Spezia (reached by regular train services from Florence). Between 6.30am and 10pm, one to three trains an hour trundle along the coast between Genoa and La Spezia, stopping at each of the Cinque Terre's villages. In summer the Golfo Paradiso SNC runs boats to the Cinque Terre from Genoa (one way/return €21/36).

Easily the best way to get around Cinque Terre is with a Cinque Terre card, including unlimited use of walking paths and electric village buses, as well as cultural exhibitions. The basic one-/two-day card for those aged over four years costs €7.50/14.50. With unlimited train trips between the towns, the card costs €12/23. Cards are sold at all Cinque Terre park information offices and Cinque Terre's train stations. For those not interested in hiking, an all-day train ticket between villages is also good value at €4.

From late March to October, La Spezia–based Consorzio Marittimo Turistico Cinque Terre Golfo dei Poeti runs daily shuttle boats between all of the Cinque Terre villages (except Corniglia), costing €5 to €12 one way, €18 including all stops, or €25 for an all-day unlimited ticket.

Florence is on the Rome–Milan line. Services include the following:

DESTINATION	COST (€)	DURATION
Milan	54-64	1¾hr-2hr
Pisa	8.40	45min-1hr
Rome	45-55	1¾-4¼hr
Venice	49-54	2hr

ℹ Getting Around

Florence is small and best navigated on foot, with most major sights within easy walking distance. There are bicycles for rent and an efficient network of buses and trams. Unless you're mad, forget a car.

Buses and electric minibuses run by public transport company ATAF serve the city. Most buses start/terminate at the ATAF bus stops opposite the southeastern exit of Stazione di Santa Maria Novella. Tickets valid for 90 minutes (no return journeys) cost €1.20 (€2 on board – drivers don't give change!) and are sold at kiosks, tobacconists and at the **ATAF ticket & information office** (☑ 800 424500, 199 104245; www.ataf.net; Stazione di Santa Maria Novella, Piazza della Stazione; ◷ 6.45am-8pm Mon-Sat) inside the main ticketing hall at Santa Maria Novella train station. A travel pass valid for one/three/seven days is €5/12/18. Upon boarding, time-stamp your ticket (punch on board) or risk an on-the-spot €50 fine. One tramline is up and running; two more are in the pipeline. Trams use the same tickets as buses.

Rome

POP 2.86 MILLION

Even in this country of exquisite cities, Rome is special. Pulsating, seductive and utterly disarming, the Italian capital is an epic, monumental metropolis. They say a lifetime's not enough *(Roma, non basta unavita)*, but even on a short visit you'll be swept off your feet by its artistic and architectural masterpieces, its operatic piazzas, romantic corners and cobbled lanes. Yet while history reverberates all around, modern life is lived to the full – and it's this intoxicating mix of past and present, of style and urban grit, that makes Rome such a compelling place.

⊙ Sights

⊙ Ancient Rome

★**Colosseum** AMPHITHEATRE
(Colosseo; Map p502; ☑ 06 3996 7700; www.coopculture.it; Piazza del Colosseo; adult/reduced incl Roman Forum & Palatino €12/7.50; ◷ 8.30am-1hr before sunset; Ⓜ Colosseo) Rome's great gladiatorial arena is the most thrilling of the city's ancient sights. Inaugurated in AD 80, the 50,000-seat Colosseum, also known as the Flavian Amphitheatre, was clad in travertine and covered by a huge canvas awning held aloft by 240 masts. Inside, tiered seating encircled the arena, itself built over an underground complex (the hypogeum) where animals were caged and stage sets prepared. Games involved gladiators fighting wild animals or each other.

★**Capitoline Museums** MUSEUM
(Musei Capitolini; Map p502; ☑ 06 06 08; www.museicapitolini.org; Piazza del Campidoglio 1; adult/reduced €11.50/9.50; ◷ 9.30am-7.30pm, last admission 6.30pm; ☐ Piazza Venezia) Dating from 1471, the Capitoline Museums are the world's oldest public museums. Their collection of classical sculpture is one of Italy's finest, including crowd-pleasers such as the iconic *Lupa Capitolina* (Capitoline Wolf), a sculpture of Romulus and Remus under a wolf, and the *Galata morente* (Dying Gaul), a moving depiction of a dying warrior. There's also a formidable picture gallery with masterpieces by the likes of Titian, Tintoretto, Rubens and Caravaggio.

ITALY, GREECE & TURKEY ROME

ℹ VATICAN MUSEUMS: TOP TIPS

➡ The museums are free on the last Sunday of the month.

➡ Exhibits are not well labelled, so consider hiring an audio guide (€7) or buying the *Guide to the Vatican Museums and City* (€14).

➡ To avoid queues book tickets online (http://biglietteriamusei.vatican.va/musei/tickets/do; plus €4 booking fee).

➡ Time your visit to minimise waiting: Tuesdays and Thursdays are quietest; Wednesday mornings are good as everyone is at the Pope's weekly audience; afternoon is better than morning; and avoid Mondays when many other museums are shut.

➡ Check the museums' website for details of tours and visitor packages.

The Uffizi

JOURNEY INTO THE RENAISSANCE

Navigating the Uffizi's chronologically-ordered art collection is straightforward enough: knowing which of the 1500-odd masterpieces to view before gallery fatigue strikes is not. Swap coat and bag (travel light) for floor plan and audioguide on the ground floor, then meet 16th-century Tuscany head-on with a walk up the *palazzo's* magnificent bust-lined staircase (skip the lift – the Uffizi is as much about masterly architecture as art).

Allow four hours for this journey into the High Renaissance. At the top of the staircase, on the 2nd floor, show your ticket, turn left and pause to admire the full length of the first corridor sweeping south towards the Arno river. Then duck left into room 2 to witness first steps in Tuscan art – shimmering altarpieces by ❶ **Giotto** et al. Journey through medieval art to room 9 and ❷ **Piero della Francesca's** impossibly famous portrait, then break in the corridor with playful ❸ **ceiling art**. After Renaissance heavyweight ❹ **Botticelli**, meander past the Tribuna (potential detour) and enjoy the daylight streaming in through the vast windows and panorama of the ❺ **riverside second corridor**. Lap up soul-stirring views of the Arno, crossed by Ponte Vecchio and its echo of four bridges drifting towards the Apuane Alps on the horizon. Then saunter into the third corridor, pausing between rooms 25 and 34 to ponder the entrance to the enigmatic Vasari Corridor. End with High Renaissance maestro Michelangelo in the ❻ **San Marco sculpture garden** and with ❼ **Doni Tondo**.

Giotto's Madonna
Room 2
Draw breath at the shy blush and curvaceous breast of Giotto's humanised Virgin (*Le Maestà di Ognissanti;* 1310) – so feminine compared with those of Duccio and Cimabue painted just 25 years before.

Portraits of the Duke & Duchess of Urbino
Room 9
Revel in realism's voyage with these uncompromising, warts-and-all portraits (1472–75) by Piero della Francesca. No larger than A3 size, they originally slotted into a portable, hinged frame that folded like a book.

Start of Vasari Corridor (linking the Palazzo Vecchio with the Uffizi and Palazzo Pitti)

Entrance to 2nd Floor Gallery

Palazzo Vecchio

Piazza della Signoria

Grotesque Ceiling Frescoes
First Corridor
Take time to study the make-believe monsters and most unexpected of burlesques (spot the arrow-shooting satyr outside room 15) waltzing across this eastern corridor's fabulous frescoed ceiling (1581).

The Genius of Botticelli
Room 10–14
The miniature form of *The Discovery of the Body of Holofernes* (c 1470) makes Botticelli's early Renaissance masterpiece all the more impressive. Don't miss the artist watching you in *Adoration of the Magi* (1475), oddly hidden in Room 15.

View of the Arno
Indulge in intoxicating city views from this short glassed-in corridor – an architectural masterpiece. Near the top of the hill, spot one of 73 outer towers built to defend Florence and its 15 city gates below.

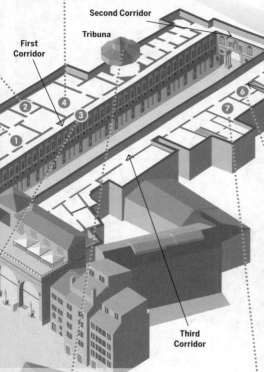

Second Corridor

Tribuna

First Corridor

Arno River

Entrance to Vasari Corridor

Third Corridor

San Marco sculpture garden
Room 34
A 13-year-old Michelangelo studied classical sculpture as an apprentice at Lorenzo de Medici's sculpture school in San Marco. Admire relief-sculpted sarcophagi that had such a massive influence on this artist.

VALUE LUNCHBOX

Try the Uffizi rooftop cafe or – better value – gourmet *panini* at 'Ino (www.ino-firenze.com; Via dei Georgofili 3-7r).

Tribuna
No room in the Uffizi is so tiny or so exquisite. It was created in 1851 as a 'treasure chest' for Grand Duke Francesco and in the days of the Grand Tour, the Medici Venus here was a tour highlight.

MATTER OF FACT
The Uffizi collection spans the 13th to 18th centuries, but its 15th- and 16th-century Renaissance works are second to none.

Doni Tondo
Room 35
The creator of *David*, Michelangelo, was essentially a sculptor and no painting expresses this better than *Doni Tondo* (1506–08). Mary's muscular arms against a backdrop of curvaceous nudes are practically 3D in their shapeliness.

Greater Rome

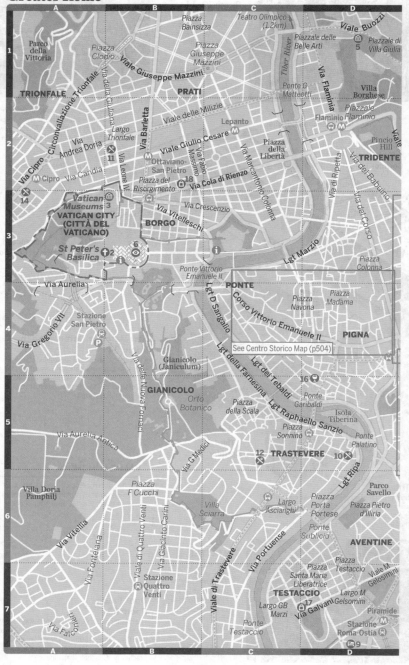

Parco della Vittoria

TRIONFALE

Piazza Clodio

Piazza Bainsizza

Teatro Olimpico (1.2km)

Viale Buozzi

Piazzale delle Belle Arti

Piazzale di Villa Giulia

Piazza Giuseppe Mazzini

Viale Giuseppe Mazzini

PRATI

Tiber River

Ponte G Matteotti

Via Flaminia

Villa Borghese

Via della Giuliana

Circonvallazione Trionfale

Via Cipro

Via Andrea Doria

Largo Trionfale

Viale delle Milizie

Via Barletta

Lepanto

Viale Giulio Cesare

Piazza della Libertà

Via Marcantonio Colonna

Piazzale Flaminio

Flaminio

TRIDENTE

Via del Babuino

Via del Corso

Via di Ripetta

Via Candia

Via Leone IV

Ottaviano-San Pietro

Via Fabio Massimo

Piazza del Risorgimento

Via Cola di Rienzo

Via Crescenzio

Vatican Museums

VATICAN CITY (CITTÀ DEL VATICANO)

BORGO

Via Vitelleschi

Lgt Marzio

Piazza Colonna

St Peter's Basilica

Via Aurelia

Ponte Vittorio Emanuele II

PONTE

Lgt D Sangallo

Corso Vittorio Emanuele II

Piazza Navona

Piazza Madama

PIGNA

Stazione San Pietro

Via Gregorio VII

Lgt della Farnesina

Lgt dei Tebaldi

See Centro Storico Map (p504)

Gianicolo (Janiculum)

GIANICOLO

Orto Botanico

Via della Nuova Fornaci

Piazza della Scala

Lgt Raphaello Sanzio

Ponte Garibaldi

Isola Tiberina

Via Aurelia Antica

Via G Medici

Piazza Sonnino

TRASTEVERE

Ponte Palatino

Lgt Ripa

Villa Doria Pamphilj

Piazza F Cucchi

Villa Sciarra

Largo Ascianghi

Piazza Porta Portese

Piazza Pietro d'Illiria

Parco Savello

Via Vitellia

Viale di Quattro Venti

Via Giacinto Carini

Ponte Sublicio

Via Portuense

AVENTINE

Via Fontelana

Viale di Trastevere

Stazione Quattro Venti

Piazza Santa Maria Liberatrice

TESTACCIO

Piazza Testaccio

Largo M Gelsomini

Viale M Gelosimini

Via Fal

Largo GB Marzi

Via Galvani

Ponte Testaccio

Piramide

Stazione Roma-Ostia

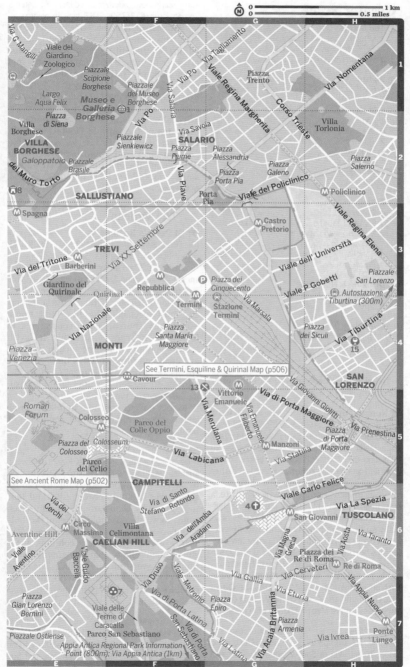

Greater Rome

Ticket prices increase when a temporary exhibition is on.

★ **Roman Forum**   ARCHAEOLOGICAL SITE
(Foro Romano; Map p502; ☏ 06 3996 7700; www. coopculture.it; Largo della Salara Vecchia, Piazza di Santa Maria Nova; adult/reduced incl Colosseum & Palatino €12/7.50; ☺ 8.30am-1hr before sunset; 🚇 Via dei Fori Imperiali) An impressive – if rather confusing – sprawl of ruins, the Roman Forum was ancient Rome's showpiece centre, a grandiose district of temples, basilicas and vibrant public spaces. The site, which was originally an Etruscan burial ground, was first developed in the 7th century BC, growing over time to become the social, political and commercial hub of the Roman empire. Landmark sights include the **Arco di Settimio Severo** (Arch of Septimius Severus; Map p502), the **Curia** (Map p502) and the **Casa delle Vestali** (House of the Vestal Virgins; Map p502). See also p508.

★ **Palatino**   ARCHAEOLOGICAL SITE
(Palatine Hill; Map p502; ☏ 06 3996 7700; www. coopculture.it; Via di San Gregorio 30, Piazza di Santa Maria Nova; adult/reduced incl Colosseum & Roman Forum €12/7.50; ☺ 8.30am-1hr before sunset; 🚇 Colosseo) Sandwiched between the Roman Forum and the Circo Massimo, the Palatino (Palatine Hill) is an atmospheric area of towering pine trees, majestic ruins and memorable views. It was here that Romulus supposedly founded the city in 753 BC and Rome's emperors lived in unabashed luxury. Look out for the **stadio** (Map p502; Via di San Gregorio 30, Palatino; 🚇 Colosseo) (stadium), the ruins of the **Domus Flavia** (Map p502; Via di San Gregorio 30, Palatino; 🚇 Colosseo) (imperial palace), and grandstand views over the Roman Forum from the **Orti Farnesiani** (Map p502; Via di San Gregorio 30, Palatino; 🚇 Colosseo).

◉ The Vatican

★ **St Peter's Basilica**   BASILICA
(Basilica di San Pietro; Map p498; ☏ 06 6988 3731; www.vatican.va; St Peter's Square; ☺ 7am-7pm summer, to 6.30pm winter; 🚇 Piazza del Risorgimento, 🚇 Ottaviano-San Pietro) FREE In this city of outstanding churches, none can hold a candle to St Peter's, Italy's largest, richest and most spectacular basilica. Built atop a 4th-century church, it was consecrated in 1626 after 120 years' construction. Its lavish interior contains many spectacular works of art, including three of Italy's most celebrated masterpieces: Michelangelo's *Pietà*, his soaring dome, and Bernini's 29m-high baldachin over the papal altar.

Expect queues and note that strict dress codes are enforced (no shorts, miniskirts or bare shoulders).

St Peter's Square   PIAZZA
(Piazza San Pietro; Map p498; 🚇 Piazza del Risorgimento, 🚇 Ottaviano-San Pietro) Overlooked by St Peter's Basilica, the Vatican's central square was laid out between 1656 and 1667 to a design by Gian Lorenzo Bernini. Seen from above, it resembles a giant keyhole with two semicircular colonnades, each consisting of four rows of Doric columns, encircling a giant ellipse that straightens out to funnel believers into the basilica. The effect was deliberate – Bernini described the colonnades as representing 'the motherly arms of the church'.

★ **Vatican Museums**   MUSEUM
(Musei Vaticani; Map p498; ☏ 06 6988 4676; www. museivaticani.va; Viale Vaticano; adult/reduced €17/8; ☺ 9am-6pm Mon-Sat, 9am-2pm last Sun

of month, last entry 2hr before close; ☒ Piazza del Risorgimento, Ⓜ Ottaviano-San Pietro) Founded by Pope Julius II in the early 16th century and enlarged by successive pontiffs, the Vatican Museums boast one of the world's greatest art collections. Exhibits, which are displayed along about 7km of halls and corridors, range from Egyptian mummies and Etruscan bronzes to ancient busts, old masters and modern paintings. Highlights include the spectacular collection of classical statuary in the **Museo Pio-Clementino**, a suite of rooms frescoed by Raphael, and the Michelangelo-painted **Sistine Chapel**.

◉ Historic Centre

★ Pantheon
CHURCH

(Map p504; www.pantheonroma.com; Piazza della Rotonda; €2; ⊙ 8.30am-7.15pm Mon-Sat, 9am-5.45pm Sun; ☒ Largo di Torre Argentina) A striking 2000-year-old temple, now a church, the Pantheon is the best preserved of Rome's ancient monuments and one of the most influential buildings in the Western world. Built by Hadrian over Marcus Agrippa's earlier 27 BC temple, it has stood since around AD 125, and although its greying, pockmarked exterior looks its age, it's still a unique and exhilarating experience to pass through its vast bronze doors and gaze up at the largest unreinforced concrete dome ever built.

DON'T MISS

CAMPO DE' FIORI

Noisy, colourful **'Il Campo'** (Map p504; ☒ Corso Vittorio Emanuele II) is a major focus of Roman life: by day it hosts one of Rome's best-known markets, while at night it morphs into a raucous open-air pub as drinkers spill out from its many bars and eateries. For centuries the square was the site of public executions, and it was here that philosopher Giordano Bruno was burned for heresy in 1600. The spot is marked by a sinister statue of the hooded monk, which was created by Ettore Ferrari in 1889.

★ Piazza Navona
PIAZZA

(Map p504; ☒ Corso del Rinascimento) With its showy fountains, baroque *palazzi* and colourful cast of street artists, hawkers and tourists, Piazza Navona is central Rome's elegant showcase square. Built over the 1st-century **Stadio di Domiziano** (Domitian's Stadium; Map p504; ☎ 06 6880 5311; www.stadio domiziano.com; Via di Tor Sanguigna 3; adult/reduced €8/6; ⊙ 10am-7pm Sun-Fri, to 8pm Sat), it was paved over in the 15th century and for almost 300 years hosted the city's main market. Its grand centrepiece is Bernini's **Fontana dei Quattro Fiumi** (Fountain of the Four Rivers; Map p504), a flamboyant fountain

FINER DETAILS

The jewel in the Vatican crown, the *Cappella Sistina* (Sistine Chapel) is home to two of the world's most famous works of art – Michelangelo's ceiling frescoes and his *Giudizio Universale* (Last Judgment).

The central focus of the painting is the figure of Christ, near the top. Around him, in a kind of vortex, the souls of the dead are torn from their graves to face his judgment. The saved get to stay up in heaven (the throng of bodies in the upper right quadrant), while the damned are sent down to face the demons in hell (in the bottom right).

An interesting point to note is the striking amount of ultramarine blue in this painting. At the time, this colour was made from the hugely expensive stone lapis lazuli. But as it was the pope who was paying for all the paint Michelangelo had no qualms about applying it in generous measure. In contrast, he didn't use any in his ceiling frescoes because he had to pay for all his own materials on that job.

Look in the bottom right-hand corner and you'll see a nude figure with a snake around him. This is Minos, judge of the underworld, with the face of Biagio de Cesena, the papal master of ceremonies and one of Michelangelo's loudest critics. Look closer and you'll see that he also has donkey ears and that the snake wrapped around him is actually biting him on his crown jewels.

Further up the painting, just beneath Christ, is the bald, beefy figure of St Bartholomew holding his own flayed skin. The face painted in the skin is said to be a self-portrait of Michelangelo, its anguished look reflecting the artist's tormented faith.

Ancient Rome

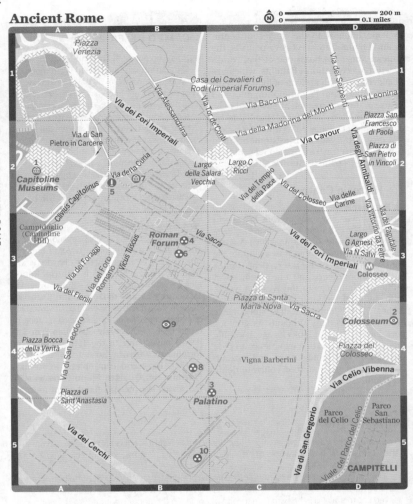

N 0 _____ 200 m
0 _____ 0.1 miles

Ancient Rome

featuring an Egyptian obelisk and muscular personifications of the rivers Nile, Ganges, Danube and Plate.

★ **Piazza di Spagna &**
the Spanish Steps PIAZZA
(Map p506; Ⓜ Spagna) A magnet for visitors since the 18th century, the Spanish Steps (Scalinata della Trinità dei Monti) provide a perfect people-watching perch. The 135 gleaming steps rise from Piazza di Spagna to the landmark **Chiesa della Trinità dei Monti** (Map p506; ☎ 06 679 41 79; Piazza Trinità

dei Monti 3; ☉7.30am-7pm Tue-Thu, noon-7pm Fri, 10am-5pm Sat & Sun; Ⓜ Spagna).

Piazza di Spagna was named after the Spanish Embassy to the Holy See, although the staircase, designed by the Italian Francesco de Sanctis, was built in 1725 with money bequeathed by a French diplomat.

★ Trevi Fountain
FOUNTAIN

(Fontana di Trevi; Map p506; Piazza di Trevi; Ⓜ Barberini) The Fontana di Trevi, scene of movie star Anita Ekberg's dip in *La Dolce Vita*, is a flamboyant baroque ensemble of mythical figures and wild horses taking up the entire side of the 17th-century Palazzo Poli. After a Fendi-sponsored restoration finished in 2015, the fountain gleams brighter than it has for years. The tradition is to toss a coin into the water, thus ensuring that you'll return to Rome – on average about €3000 is thrown in every day.

Villa Medici
PALACE

(Map p498; ☏06 676 13 11; www.villamedici.it; Viale Trinità dei Monti 1; 1½hr guided tour adult/reduced €12/6; ☉ticket office 9.30am-7pm Tue-Sun; Ⓜ Spagna) This sumptuous Renaissance palace was built for Cardinal Ricci da Montepulciano in 1540, but Ferdinando de' Medici bought it in 1576. It remained in Medici hands until 1801, when Napoleon acquired it for the French Academy. Guided tours take in the wonderful landscaped gardens, the cardinal's painted apartments, and incredible views over Rome – tours in English depart at 11am and 3.30pm. Note the pieces of ancient Roman sculpture from the Ara Pacis embedded in the villa's walls.

★ Galleria Doria Pamphilj
GALLERY

(Map p504; ☏06 679 73 23; www.doriapamphilj.it; Via del Corso 305; adult/reduced €12/8; ☉9am-7pm, last entry 6pm; ☒ Via del Corso) Hidden behind the grimy grey exterior of Palazzo Doria Pamphilj, this wonderful gallery boasts one of Rome's richest private art collections, with works by Raphael, Tintoretto, Titian, Caravaggio, Bernini and Velázquez, as well as several Flemish masters. Masterpieces abound, but the undisputed star is Velázquez' portrait of an implacable Pope Innocent X, who grumbled that the depiction was 'too real'. For a comparison, check out Gian Lorenzo Bernini's sculptural interpretation of the same subject.

⊙ Villa Borghese

Accessible from Piazzale Flaminio, Pincio Hill and the top of Via Vittorio Veneto, Villa Borghese is Rome's best-known park.

★ Museo e Galleria Borghese
MUSEUM

(Map p498; ☏06 3 28 10; http://galleriaborghese.beniculturali.it; Piazzale del Museo Borghese 5; adult/child €15/8.50; ☉9am-7pm Tue-Sun; ☒ Via Pinciana) If you only have time for one art gallery in Rome, make it this one. Housing what's often referred to as the 'queen of all private art collections', it boasts paintings by Caravaggio, Raphael and Titian, plus some sensational sculptures by Bernini. Highlights abound, but look for Bernini's *Ratto di Proserpina* (Rape of Proserpina) and Canova's *Venere vincitrice* (Venus Victrix).

To limit numbers, visitors are admitted at two-hourly intervals, so you'll need to prebook tickets and get an entry time.

Museo Nazionale Etrusco di Villa Giulia
MUSEUM

(Map p498; ☏06 322 65 71; www.villagiulia.beniculturali.it; Piazzale di Villa Giulia; adult/reduced €8/4; ☉9am-8pm Tue-Sun; ☒ Via delle Belle Arti) Pope Julius III's 16th-century villa provides the charming setting for Italy's finest collection of Etruscan and pre-Roman treasures. Exhibits, many of which came from tombs in the surrounding Lazio region, range from bronze figurines and black *bucchero* tableware to temple decorations, terracotta vases

---

ⓘ ROMA PASS

The Roma Pass (www.romapass.it) comes in two forms:

72 hours (€38.50) Provides free admission to two museums or sites, as well as reduced entry to extra sites, unlimited city transport, and discounted entry to other exhibitions and events.

48 hours (€28) Gives free admission to one museum or site, and then as per the 72-hour pass. They're available online, from tourist information points or participating museums.

Note that EU citizens aged between 18 and 25 generally qualify for a discount at most galleries and museums, while those under 18 and over 65 often get in free. In both cases you'll need proof of your age, ideally a passport or ID card.

Centro Storico

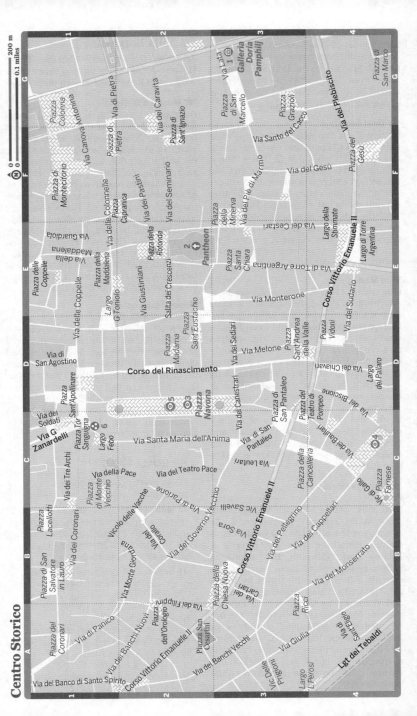

Centro Storico

and a dazzling display of sophisticated jewellery.

Must-sees include a polychrome terracotta statue of Apollo from a temple in Veio, and the 6th-century-BC *Sarcofago degli Sposi* (Sarcophagus of the Betrothed), found in 1881 in Cerveteri.

⊙ San Giovanni

Basilica di San Giovanni in Laterano　BASILICA

(Map p498; Piazza di San Giovanni in Laterano 4; basilica free, cloister €3; ⊙7am-6.30pm, cloister 9am-6pm; M San Giovanni) For a thousand years this monumental cathedral was the most important church in Christendom. Commissioned by Emperor Constantine and consecrated in AD 324, it was the first Christian basilica built in the city and, until the late 14th century, was the pope's main place of worship. It's still Rome's official cathedral and the pope's seat as the bishop of Rome.

Terme di Caracalla　ARCHAEOLOGICAL SITE

(Map p498; ☎06 3996 7700; www.coopculture. it; Viale delle Terme di Caracalla 52; adult/reduced €8/4; ⊙9am-1hr before sunset Tue-Sun, 9am-2pm Mon; ☐Viale delle Terme di Caracalla) The remains of the emperor Caracalla's bathhouse complex are among Rome's most awe-inspiring ruins. Inaugurated in AD 216, the original 10-hectare site, which comprised baths, gyms, libraries, shops and gardens, was used by up to 8000 people daily.

Most of the ruins are what's left of the central bathhouse. This was a huge rectangular edifice bookended by two *palestre* (gyms) and centred on a *frigidarium* (cold room), where bathers would stop after the warmer *tepidarium* and dome-capped *caldarium* (hot room).

🛏 Sleeping

★ **Beehive**　HOSTEL €

(Map p506; ☎06 4470 4553; www.the-beehive. com; Via Marghera 8; dm €35-40, d without bathroom €80, s/d/tr €70/100/120; ⊙reception 7am-11pm; ❋ 🕱; M Termini) 🖉 More boutique chic than backpacker dive, the Beehive is a small and stylish hostel with a glorious summer garden. Dynamic American owners Linda and Steve exude energy and organise cooking classes, storytelling evenings, weekly hostel dinners around a shared table, pop-up dinners with chefs, and so on. Pick from a spotless eight-bed dorm (mixed), a four-bed female dorm, or private rooms with ceiling fan and honey-based soap.

★ **Generator Hostel**　HOSTEL €

(Map p506; ☎06 492 330; https://generatorhostels.com; Via Principe Amedeo 257; dm €17-70, d €50-200; ❋ @ 🕱; M Vittorio Emanuele) Hostelling just got a whole lot smarter in Rome thanks to this designer hostel which, quite frankly, is more uber-cool hotel in mood – 72% of the 174 beds here occupy bright white private rooms with sharp bathrooms, and dorms max out at four beds. Check in at the

---

A SLICE OF ROME

Remarkably, pizza was only introduced to Rome post-WWII, by southern immigrants. It caught on. Every Roman's favourite casual (and cheap) meal is the gloriously simple pizza, with Rome's signature wafer-thin bases, covered in fresh, bubbling toppings, slapped down on tables by waiters on a mission. Pizzerias often only open in the evening, as their wood-fired ovens take a while to get going. Most Romans will precede their pizza with a starter of bruschetta or fritti (mixed fried foods, such as zucchini flowers, potato, olives etc) and wash it all down with beer. Pizza menus are traditionally divided into pizza rosso ('red' pizza meaning with tomato sauce) and pizza bianco ('white' pizza with no tomato sauce, traditionally simply sprinkled with rosemary, salt and olive oil). For a snack on the run, Rome's pizza al taglio (by the slice) places are hard to beat, with toppings loaded atop thin, crispy, light-as-air, slow-risen bread that verge on the divine.

Termini, Esquiline & Quirinal

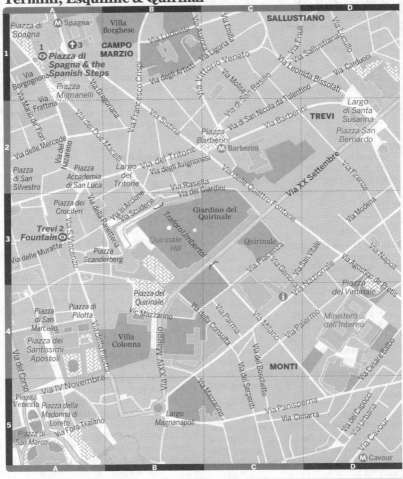

Termini, Esquiline & Quirinal

zinc-topped bar, linger over a cappuccino in the stylish lounge, or chill on the sensational rooftop lounge.

★ Yellow Hostel HOSTEL €
(Map p506; ☑ 06 446 35 54; www.the-yellow.com; Via Palestro 51; dm €20-35, d €90-120, q €100-150;

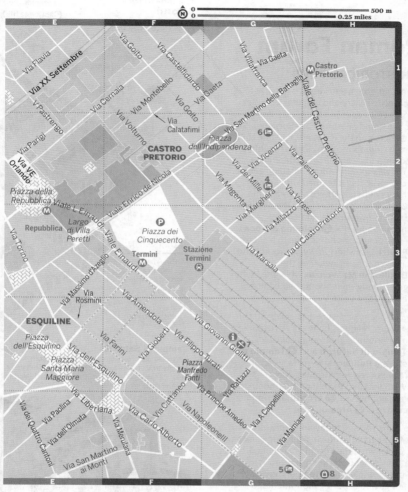

❀@🛜; Ⓜ Castro Pretorio) This sharp, 300-bed party hostel, with designer dorms, play area sporting comfy beanbags, escape room and kitchen you'd actually want to hang out in, is rapidly colonising the entire street – aka the 'Yellow Square' – with its top-notch facilities aimed squarely at young travellers.

⭐ **Althea Inn**   B&B €
(Map p498; 📞 06 9893 2666, 339 4353717; www.altheainn.com; Via dei Conciatori 9; d €120; ❀🛜; Ⓜ Piramide) In a workaday apartment block near the Aurelian Walls, this friendly B&B offers superb value for money and easy access to Testaccio's bars, clubs and restau-rants. Its spacious, light-filled rooms sport a modish look with white walls and tasteful modern furniture, and each has its own small terrace.

🍴 Eating

⭐ **Panella**   BAKERY, CAFE €
(Map p498; 📞 06 487 24 35; www.panellaroma.com; Via Merulana 54; meals €7-15; ⏰ 7am-11pm Mon-Thu & Sun, to midnight Fri & Sat; Ⓜ Vittorio Emanuele) Pure heaven for foodies, this enticing bakery is littered with well-used trays of freshly baked pastries loaded with confec-tioner's custard, wild-cherry fruit tartlets,

Roman Forum

A HISTORICAL TOUR

In ancient times, a forum was a market place, civic centre and religious complex all rolled into one, and the greatest of all was the Roman Forum (Foro Romano). Situated between the Palatino (Palatine Hill), ancient Rome's most exclusive neighbourhood, and the Campidoglio (Capitoline Hill), it was the city's busy, bustling centre. On any given day it teemed with activity. Senators debated affairs of state in the **1 Curia**, shoppers thronged the squares and traffic-free streets and crowds gathered under the **2 Colonna di Foca** to listen to politicians holding forth from the **2 Rostri**. Elsewhere, lawyers worked the courts in basilicas including the **3 Basilica di Massenzio**, while the Vestal Virgins quietly went about their business in the **4 Casa delle Vestali**.

Special occasions were also celebrated in the Forum: religious holidays were marked with ceremonies at temples such as **5 Tempio di Saturno** and **6 Tempio di Castore e Polluce**, and military victories were honoured with dramatic processions up Via Sacra and the building of monumental arches like **7 Arco di Settimio Severo** and **8 Arco di Tito**.

The ruins you see today are impressive but they can be confusing without a clear picture of what the Forum once looked like. This spread shows the Forum in its heyday, complete with temples, civic buildings and towering monuments to heroes of the Roman Empire.

TOP TIPS

➡ Get grandstand views of the Forum from the Palatino and Campidoglio.

➡ Visit first thing in the morning or late afternoon; crowds are worst between 11am and 2pm.

➡ In summer it gets hot in the Forum and there's little shade, so take a hat and plenty of water.

Colonna di Foca & Rostri
The free-standing, 13.5m-high Column of Phocus is the Forum's youngest monument, dating to AD 608. Behind it, the Rostri provided a suitably grandiose platform for pontificating public speakers.

Campidoglio (Capitoline Hill)

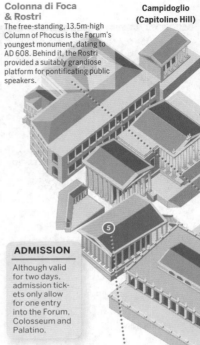

ADMISSION

Although valid for two days, admission tickets only allow for one entry into the Forum, Colosseum and Palatino.

Tempio di Saturno
Ancient Rome's Fort Knox, the Temple of Saturn was the city treasury. In Caesar's day it housed 13 tonnes of gold, 114 tonnes of silver and 30 million sestertii worth of silver coins.

IASCIC/SHUTTERSTOCK©

VIACHESLAV LOPATIN/SHUTTERSTOCK©

Tempio di Castore e Polluce
Only three columns of the Temple of Castor and Pollux remain. The temple was dedicated to the Heavenly Twins after they supposedly led the Romans to victory over the Latin League in 496 BC.

Arco di Settimio Severo

One of the Forum's signature monuments, this imposing triumphal arch commemorates the military victories of Septimius Severus. Relief panels depict his campaigns against the Parthians.

Curia

This big barn-like building was the official seat of the Roman Senate. Most of what you see is a reconstruction, but the interior marble floor dates to the 3rd-century reign of Diocletian.

Basilica di Massenzio

Marvel at the scale of this vast 4th-century basilica. In its original form the central hall was divided into enormous naves; now only part of the northern nave survives.

JULIUS CAESAR

Julius Caesar was cremated on the site where the Tempio di Giulio Cesare now stands.

Via Sacra

Tempio di Giulio Cesare

Arco di Tito

Said to be the inspiration for the Arc de Triomphe in Paris, the well-preserved Arch of Titus was built by the emperor Domitian to honour his elder brother Titus.

Casa delle Vestali

White statues line the grassy atrium of what was once the luxurious 50-room home of the Vestal Virgins. The virgins played an important role in Roman religion, serving the goddess Vesta.

Tragedy in Pompeii

24 AUGUST AD 79

8am Buildings including the **❶ Terme Suburbane** and the **❷ Foro** are still undergoing repair after an earthquake in AD 63 caused significant damage to the city. Despite violent earth tremors overnight, residents have little idea of the catastrophe that lies ahead.

Midday Peckish locals pour into the **❸ Thermopolium di Vetutius Placidus**. The lustful slip into the **❹ Lupanare**, and gladiators practise for the evening's planned games at the **❺ Anfiteatro**. A massive boom heralds the eruption. Shocked onlookers witness a dark cloud of volcanic matter shoot some 14km above the crater.

3pm–5pm Lapilli (burning pumice stone) rains down on Pompeii. Terrified locals begin to flee; others take shelter. Within two hours, the plume is 25km high and the sky has darkened. Roofs collapse under the weight of the debris, burying those inside.

25 AUGUST AD 79

Midnight Mudflows bury the town of Herculaneum. Lapilli and ash continue to rain down on Pompeii, bursting through buildings and suffocating those taking refuge within.

4am–8am Ash and gas avalanches hit Herculaneum. Subsequent surges smother Pompeii, killing all remaining residents, including those in the **❻ Orto dei Fuggiaschi**. The volcanic 'blanket' will safeguard frescoed treasures like the **❼ Casa del Menandro** and **❽ Villa dei Misteri** for almost two millennia.

TOP TIPS

➡ Visit in the afternoon.
➡ Allow three hours.
➡ Wear comfortable shoes and a hat.
➡ Bring drinking water.
➡ Don't use flash photography.

VIACHESLAV LOPATIN / SHUTTERSTOCK ©

Terme Suburbane
The *laconicum* (sauna), *caldarium* (hot bath) and large, heated swimming pool weren't the only sources of heat here; scan the walls of this suburban bathhouse for some of the city's raunchiest frescoes.

Villa di Diomede

Casa del Poeta Tragico

Porta Ercolano

Casa del Fauno

Basilica

Tempio di Apollo

Porta Marina

Terme del Foro

Macellum

Teatro Grande

Quadriportico dei Teatri

Porta di Stabia

Teatro Piccolo

Foro
An ancient Times Square of sorts, the forum sits at the intersection of Pompeii's main streets and was closed to traffic in the 1st century AD. The plinths on the southern edge featured statues of the imperial family.

PHODEY / GETTY IMAGES ©

Villa dei Misteri
Home to the world-famous *Dionysiac Frieze* fresco. Other highlights at this villa include *trompe l'oeil* wall decorations in the *cubiculum* (bedroom) and Egyptian-themed artwork in the *tablinum* (reception).

Lupanare
The prostitutes at this brothel were often slaves of Greek or Asian origin. Mattresses once covered the stone beds and the names engraved in the walls are possibly those of the workers and their clients.

POROJNICU STELIAN / SHUTTERSTOCK ©

Thermopolium di Vetutius Placidus
The counter at this ancient snack bar once held urns filled with hot food. The *lararium* (house-hold shrine) on the back wall depicts Dionysus (the god of wine) and Mercury (the god of profit and commerce).

asa dei Vettii

Porta del Vesuvio

EYEWITNESS ACCOUNT

Pliny the Younger (AD 61–c 112) gives a gripping, first-hand account of the catastrophe in his letters to Tacitus (AD 56–117).

Porta di Nola

Casa della Venere in Conchiglia

Porta di Sarno

③

⑦

Grande Palestra

⑤

Tempio di Iside

Orto dei Fuggiaschi
The Garden of the Fugitives showcases the plaster moulds of 13 locals seeking refuge during Vesuvius' eruption – the largest number of victims found in any one area. The huddled bodies make for a moving scene.

Anfiteatro
Magistrates, local senators and the games' sponsors and organisers enjoyed front-row seating at this veteran amphitheatre, home to gladiatorial battles and the odd riot. The parapet circling the stadium featured paintings of com-bat, victory celebrations and hunting scenes.

Casa del Menandro
This dwelling most likely belonged to the family of Poppaea Sabina, Nero's second wife. A room to the left of the atrium features Trojan War paintings and a polychrome mosaic of pygmies rowing down the Nile.

EDELLA / GETTY IMAGES ©

WDJ / GETTY IMAGES ©

WORTH A TRIP

POPMEII

POMPEII

The ghostly **Ruins of Pompeii** (☑081 857 53 47; www.pompeiisites.org; entrances at Porta Marina, Piazza Esedra & Piazza Anfiteatro; adult/reduced €13/7.50, incl Herculaneum €22/12; ⊙9am-7.30pm, last entry 6pm Apr-Oct, to 5pm, last entry 3.30pm Nov-Mar) (Pompei in Italian) make for one of the world's most engrossing archaeological experiences. Much of the site's value lies in the fact that the town wasn't simply blown away by Vesuvius in AD 79 but buried under a layer of lapilli (burning fragments of pumice stone). The result is a remarkably well-preserved slice of ancient life, where visitors can walk down Roman streets and snoop around millennia-old houses, temples, shops, cafes, amphitheatres, and even a brothel. The origins of Pompeii are uncertain, but it seems likely that it was founded in the 7th century BC by the Campanian Oscans. Over the next seven centuries, the city fell to the Greeks and the Samnites before becoming a Roman colony in 80 BC. In AD 62, a mere 17 years before Vesuvius erupted, the city was struck by a major earthquake. Damage was widespread and much of the city's 20,000-strong population was evacuated. Fortunately, many had not returned by the time Vesuvius blew, but 2000 men, women and children perished nevertheless. After its catastrophic demise, Pompeii receded from the public eye until 1594, when the architect Domenico Fontana stumbled across the ruins while digging a canal. Exploration proper, however, didn't begin until 1748. Of Pompeii's original 66 hectares, 44 have now been excavated. Of course that doesn't mean you'll have unhindered access to every inch of the Unesco-listed site – expect to come across areas cordoned off for no apparent reason, a noticeable lack of clear signs, and the odd stray dog. Audio guides are a sensible investment (€8, cash only) and a good guidebook will also help – try Pompeii, published by Electa Napoli. Maintenance work is ongoing, but progress is beset by political, financial and bureaucratic problems.

Getting There & Away

To reach the *scavi* (ruins) by Circumvesuviana train (€2.80 from Naples, €2.40 from Sorrento), alight at Pompei-Scavi-Villa dei Misteri station, beside the main entrance at Porta Marina.

Regional trains (www.trenitalia.com) stop at Pompei station in the centre of the modern town. From mid-April to mid-October, tourist train Campania Express runs four times daily between Naples (Porta Nolana and Piazza Garibaldi Circumvesuviana stations) and Sorrento, stopping at Ercolano-Scavi and Pompei-Scavi-Villa dei Misteri en route. One-day return tickets from Naples to Pompeii (€11) or from Sorrento to Pompeii (€7) can be purchased at the stations or online at www.eavsrl.it.

---

pizza al taglio, arancini and focaccia – the smell alone is heavenly. Grab a bar stool between shelves of gourmet groceries inside or congratulate yourself on scoring a table on the flowery, sun-flooded terrace – one of Rome's loveliest.

★Pizzarium   PIZZA €

(Map p498; ☑06 3974 5416; Via della Meloria 43; pizza slices €5; ⊙11am-10pm Mon-Sat, noon-10pm Sun; MCipro-Musei Vaticani) When a pizza joint is packed at lunchtime on a wet winter's day, you know it's something special. Pizzarium, the takeaway of Gabriele Bonci, Rome's acclaimed pizza king, serves Rome's best sliced pizza, bar none. Scissor-cut squares of soft, springy base are topped with original combinations of seasonal ingredients and served on paper trays for immediate consumption.

Also worth trying are the freshly fried *supplì* (risotto balls).

★Da Enzo   TRATTORIA €€

(Map p498; ☑06 581 22 60; www.daenzoal29. com; Via dei Vascellari 29; meals €30; ⊙12.30-3pm & 7.30-11pm Mon-Sat; 🚊Viale di Trastevere, 🚊Viale di Trastevere) Vintage buttermilk walls, red-checked tablecloths and a traditional menu featuring all the Roman classics: what makes this staunchly traditional trattoria exceptional is its careful sourcing of local, quality products, many from nearby farms in Lazio. The seasonal, deep-fried Jewish artichokes and the *pasta cacio e pepe* (cheese-and-black-pepper pasta) in particular are among the best in Rome.

Mercato Centrale
FOOD HALL €

(Map p506; www.mercatocentrale.it/roma; Stazione Termini, Via Giolitti 36; snacks/meals from €3/10; ⊗8am-midnight; 🛜; Ⓜ Termini) A gourmet oasis for hungry travellers at Stazione Termini (p514), this dazzling three-storey food hall is the latest project of Florence's savvy Umberto Montano. You'll find bread, pastries, cakes, burgers, pasta, truffles, pizza and a whole lot more beneath towering vaulted 1930s ceilings, plus some of the city's most prized producers, including Gabriele Bonci (bread, focaccia, pizza) and Marcella Bianchi (vegetarian).

★Fatamorgana
GELATO €

(Map p498; 📞06 3751 9093; www.gelateriafatamorgana.it; Via Leone IV 52; gelato €2.50-5; ⊗noon-11pm summer, to 9pm winter; Ⓜ Ottaviano-San Pietro) The Prati branch of Rome's hit gelateria chain. As well as all the classic flavours there are some wonderfully left-field creations, including a strange but delicious *basilico, miele e noci* (basil, honey and hazelnuts).

🍷 Drinking & Nightlife

★Open Baladin
CRAFT BEER

(Map p498; 📞06 683 89 89; www.openbaladinroma.it; Via degli Specchi 6; ⊗noon-2am; 🛜; 🚌 Via Arenula) For some years, this cool, modern pub near Campo de' Fiori has been a leading light in Rome's craft-beer scene, and with more than 40 beers on tap and up to 100 bottled brews (many from Italian artisanal microbreweries) it's still a top place for a pint. There's also a decent food menu with *panini,* gourmet burgers and daily specials.

★Co.So
COCKTAIL BAR

(📞06 4543 5428; Via Braccio da Montone 80; ⊗7pm-3am Mon-Sat; 🚌 Via Prenestina) The chicest bar in Pigneto, tiny Co.So (meaning 'Cocktails & Social') was founded by Massimo D'Addezio (a former master mixologist at Hotel de Russie) and is hipster to the hilt. Think Carbonara Sour cocktails (with pork-fat-infused vodka), bubblewrap coasters, and popcorn and M&M bar snacks.

★Il Sori
WINE BAR

(Map p498; 📞393 4318681; www.ilsori.it; Via dei Volsci 51; ⊗6pm-2am Mon-Sat; 🚌 Via Tiburtina) Every last salami slice and chunk of cheese has been carefully selected from Italy's finest artisanal and small producers at this gourmet wine bar and *bottega* (shop), an unexpected pearl for dedicated foodies in San Lorenzo. Interesting and unusual wine tastings, theme nights, 'meet the producer' soirées and other events cap off what's already a memorable drinking (and dining) experience.

★Spirito
COCKTAIL BAR

(📞327 2983900; www.club-spirito.com; Via Fanfulla da Lodi 53; ⊗7.30pm-3.30am Wed-Mon; 🚌 Via Prenestina) A fashionable address only for those in the know, Spirito is spirited away behind a simple white door at the back of a sandwich shop in edgy Pigneto. This New Yorker Prohibition–style speakeasy has expertly mixed craft cocktails (around €10), gourmet food, live music and shows, roulette at the bar and a fun-loving crowd.

TO MARKET, TO MARKET...

Rome's well-stocked delis and fresh-produce markets are a fabulous feature of the city's foodscape. Most neighbourhoods have a few local delis and their own daily food market, operating from around 7am to 1.30pm, Monday to Saturday.

Rome's most famous markets include the following:

Nuovo Mercato Esquilino (Map p506; Via Filippo Turati 160; ⊗5am-3pm Mon, Wed & Thu, to 5pm Tue, Fri & Sat; Ⓜ Vittorio Emanuele) Cheap and the best place to find exotic herbs and spices.

Piazza dell' Unità (Map p498; Piazza dell' Unità 53; ⊗6.30am-7.30pm Mon-Sat; 🚌 Piazza del Risorgimento) Near the Vatican; perfect for stocking up for a picnic.

Nuovo Mercato di Testaccio (Map p498; entrances Via Galvani, Via Beniamino Franklin, Via Volta, Via Manuzio, Via Ghiberti; ⊗7am-3.30pm Mon-Sat; 🚌 Via Marmorata) A purpose-built site crammed with enticing stalls, including many serving gourmet 'fast food' to go.

Mercato di Piazza San Cosimato (Map p498; Piazza San Cosimato; ⊗7am-2pm Mon-Sat; 🚌 Viale di Trastevere, 🚌 Viale di Trastevere) Trastevere's neighbourhood market, at least a century old and still the biz for fresh, locally sourced foodstuffs.

ⓘ STOP, THIEF!

The greatest risk visitors face in Rome is from pickpockets and thieves. Pickpockets go where the tourists go, so watch out around the most touristed and crowded areas, such as the Colosseum, Piazza di Spagna, St Peter's Sq and Stazione Termini. Note that thieves prey on disoriented travellers at the bus stops around Termini, fresh in from airports. Crowded public transport is another hot spot – the 64 Vatican bus is notorious. If travelling on the metro, try to use the end carriages, which are usually less busy.

A money belt with your essentials (passport, cash, credit cards) is a good idea. However, to avoid delving into it in public, carry a wallet with a day's cash. Don't flaunt expensive goods. If you're carrying a bag or camera, wear the strap across your body and away from the road – moped thieves can swipe a bag and be gone in seconds. Be careful when you sit down at a streetside table – never drape your bag over an empty chair by the road or put it where you can't see it.

A common method is for one thief to distract you while their assistant makes away with your purse. Beware of gangs of kids or others demanding attention. If you notice that you've been targeted, either take evasive action or shout *va via!* ('go away!') in a loud, angry voice. Remember also that some of the best pickpockets are well dressed.

In case of theft or loss, always report the incident to the police within 24 hours and ask for a statement.

ⓘ Information

Turismo Roma (www.turismoroma.it; ⓘ) Rome's official tourist website has comprehensive information about sights, accommodation, and city transport, as well as itineraries and up-to-date listings.

There are tourist information points at Fiumicino and Ciampino airports, and locations across the city including **Stazione Termini** (Map p506; ☑ 06 06 08; www.turismoroma. it; Via Giovanni Giolitti 34; ⊘ 8am-6.45pm; Ⓜ Termini), **Via Nazionale** (Map p506; ☑ 06 06 08; www.turismoroma.it; Via Nazionale 184; ⊘ 9.30am-7pm; Ⓠ Via Nazionale) and **Castel Sant'Angelo** (Map p498; Piazza Pia; ⊘ 9.30am-7pm summer, 8.30am-6pm winter; Ⓠ Piazza Pia). For information about the Vatican, contact the **Ufficio Pellegrini e Turisti** (Map p498; ☑ 06 6988 1662; St Peter's Square; ⊘ 8.30am-6.30pm Mon-Sat; Ⓠ Piazza del Risorgimento, Ⓜ Ottaviano-San Pietro).

ⓘ Getting There & Away

AIR

Rome's main international airport, **Leonardo da Vinci** (Fiumicino; ☑ 06 6 59 51; www.adr.it/fiumicino), is 30km west of the city. The easiest way to get into town is by train, but there are also buses, private shuttle and the following train services.

Leonardo Express (www.trenitalia.com; one way €14) Runs to/from Stazione Termini. Departures from the airport every 30 minutes between 6.23am and 11.23pm, and from Termini between 5.35am and 10.35pm. Journey time is 30 minutes.

FL1 (www.trenitalia.com; one way €8) Connects to Trastevere, Ostiense and Tiburtina stations, but not Termini. Departures from the airport every 15 minutes (half-hourly on Sundays and public holidays) between 5.57am and 10.42pm, and from Tiburtina every 15 minutes between 5.01am and 7.31pm, then half-hourly to 10.01pm.

BUS

Long-distance national and international buses use **Autostazione Tiburtina** (Tibus; Largo Guido Mazzoni; Ⓜ Tiburtina).

From the bus station, cross under the overpass for the Tiburtina train station, where you can pick up metro line B and connect with Termini for onward buses, trains and metro line A.

TRAIN

Rome's main station and principal transport hub is **Stazione Termini** (www.romatermini. com; Piazza dei Cinquecento; Ⓜ Termini). It has regular connections to other European countries, all major Italian cities and many smaller towns.

Train information is available from the Customer Service area on the main concourse to the left of the ticket desks. Alternatively, check www.trenitalia.com or phone 892021.

From Termini, you can connect with the metro or take a bus from Piazza dei Cinquecento out front. Taxis are outside the main entrance/exit.

ⓘ Getting Around

Public Transport includes buses, trams, metro and a suburban train network. The main hub is Stazione Termini. Tickets, which come in various forms, are valid for all forms of transport. Children under 10 years travel free.

Metro The metro is quicker than surface transport but the network is limited. There are two main lines, A (orange) and B (blue), which cross at Stazione Termini. Trains run between 5.30am and 11.30pm (to 1.30am on Fridays and Saturdays).

Buses Most routes pass through Stazione Termini. Buses run from approximately 5.30am until midnight, with limited services throughout the night.

Foot Walking is the best way of getting around the *centro storico* (historic centre).

Italy Survival Guide

ⓘ Directory A–Z

BARGAINING

Gentle haggling is common at markets in Italy. Haggling in stores is generally unacceptable, although some good-humoured bargaining at smaller artisan or craft shops in southern Italy is not unusual if you are making multiple purchases.

DISCOUNT CARDS

Free admission to many art galleries and cultural sites is available to those under 18 and over 65 years old; and visitors aged between 18 and 25 often qualify for a discount. In some cases, these discounts only apply to EU citizens.

In many places around Italy, you can also save money by purchasing a *biglietto cumulativo*, a ticket that allows admission to a number of associated sights for less than the combined cost of separate admission fees.

ELECTRICITY

Electricity in Italy conforms to the European standard of 220V to 230V, with a frequency of 50Hz. Wall outlets typically accommodate plugs with two or three round pins (the latter grounded, the former not).

EMBASSIES & CONSULATES

For foreign embassies and consulates in Italy not listed here, look under 'Ambasciate' or 'Consolati' in the telephone directory.

Australian Embassy (☏ 06 85 27 21, emergencies 800 877790; www.italy.embassy.gov.au; Via Antonio Bosio 5, Rome; ⊕9am-5pm Mon-Fri; 🚇Via Nomentana)

Canadian Embassy (☏ 06 8 5444 2911; www.canadainternational.gc.ca/italy-italie; Via Zara 30, Rome; ⊕9am-noon Mon-Fri; 🚇Via Nomentana)

New Zealand Embassy (☏ 06 853 75 01; www.mfat.govt.nz/en/countries-and-regions/europe/italy/new-zealand-embassy; Via Clitunno 44, Rome; ⊕8.30am-12.30pm & 1.30-5pm Mon-Fri; 🚇Corso Trieste)

UK Embassy (☏ 06 4220 0001; www.ukinitaly.fco.gov.uk; Via XX Settembre 80a, Rome)

US Embassy (☏ 06 4 67 41; www.italy.usembassy.gov; Via Vittorio Veneto 121, Rome)

EMERGENCY & IMPORTANT NUMBERS

From outside Italy, dial your international access code, Italy's country code (39) then the number (including the '0').

Italy country code	☑39
International access code	☑00
Ambulance	☑118
Police	☑112, ☑113
Fire	☑115

ETIQUETTE

Italy is a surprisingly formal society; the following tips will help avoid awkward moments.

Greetings Shake hands and say *buongiorno* (good day) or *buona sera* (good evening) to strangers; kiss both cheeks and say *come stai* (how are you) to friends. Use *lei* (you) in polite company; use *tu* (you) with friends and children. Only use first names if invited.

Asking for help Say *mi scusi* (excuse me) to attract attention; and use *permesso* (permission) when you want to pass someone in a crowded space.

Religion Dress modestly (cover shoulders, torsos and thighs) and show respect when visiting religious sites.

GAY & LESBIAN TRAVELLERS

Homosexuality is legal (over the age of 16) and even widely accepted, but Italy is notably conservative in its attitudes, largely keeping in line with those of the Vatican. Overt displays of affection by homosexual couples can attract a negative response, especially in smaller towns. There are gay venues in Rome and a handful in

---

> ### ⓘ SLEEPING PRICE RANGES
>
> The following price ranges refer to a double room with private bathroom (breakfast included) in high season.
>
> **€** under €110
>
> **€€** €110-200
>
> **€€€** over €200

Florence. Online resources include the following Italian-language websites:

Arcigay (www.arcigay.it) Bologna-based national organisation for the LGBTI community.

Circolo Mario Mieli (www.mariomieli.org) Rome-based cultural centre that organises debates, cultural events and social functions, including Gay Pride.

Coordinamento Lesbiche Italiano (CLR; www.clrbp.it) The national organisation for lesbians, holding regular conferences and literary evenings.

Gay.it (www.gay.it) Website featuring LGBT news, feature articles and gossip.

Pride (www.prideonline.it) Culture, politics, travel and health with an LGBT focus.

LEGAL MATTERS

Drugs & Alcohol

➜ If you're caught with what the police deem to be a dealable quantity of hard or soft drugs, you risk prison sentences of between two and 20 years.

➜ The legal limit for blood-alcohol when driving is 0.05% and random breath tests do occur.

Police

The Italian police force is divided into three main bodies: the *polizia*, who wear navy-blue jackets; the *carabinieri*, in a black uniform with a red stripe; and the grey-clad *guardia di finanza* (fiscal police), responsible for fighting tax evasion and drug smuggling. If you run into trouble, you're most likely to end up dealing with the *polizia* or *carabinieri*. To contact the police in an emergency, dial 112 or 113.

 EATING PRICE RANGES

The following price ranges refer to a meal of two courses (antipasto/*primo* and *secondo*), a glass of house wine, and *coperto* (cover charge) for one person.

€ under €25

€€ €25-45

€€€ over €45

These figures represent a halfway point between expensive cities such as Milan and Venice and the considerably cheaper towns across the south. Indeed, a restaurant rated as midrange in rural Sicily might be considered dirt cheap in Milan. Note that most eating establishments add *coperto* of around €2 to €3. Some also include a service charge (*servizio*) of 10% to 15%.

MONEY

ATMs are widespread in Italy. Major credit cards are widely accepted, but some smaller shops, trattorias and hotels might not take them.

Visa, MasterCard, Eurocard, Cirrus and Eurocheques are widely accepted. Amex is also recognised, although it's less common than Visa or MasterCard.

ATMs are everywhere, but be aware of transaction fees. Some ATMs in Italy reject foreign cards. If this happens, try a few before assuming your card is the problem.

Tipping

Tipping is not generally expected nor demanded in Italy as it is in some other countries. This said, a discretionary tip for good service is appreciated in some circumstances. Use the following table as a guide.

PLACE	SUGGESTED TIP
Restaurant	10% restaurants if service charge (*servizio*) not included
Bar	€0.10–0.20 if drinking at bar, 10% for table service
Taxi	Round up to the nearest euro

OPENING HOURS

Opening hours vary throughout the year. We've provided high-season opening hours, which will generally decrease in the shoulder and low seasons. 'Summer' times generally refer to the period from April to September or October, while 'winter' times generally run from October or November to March.

Banks 8.30am to 1.30pm and 2.45pm to 4.30pm Monday to Friday

Restaurants noon to 3pm and 7.30pm to 11pm or midnight

Cafes 7.30am to 8pm, sometimes until 1am or 2am

Bars and clubs 10pm to 4am or 5am

Shops 9am to1pm and 4pm to 8pm Monday to Saturday, some also open Sunday

PUBLIC HOLIDAYS

Most Italians take their annual holiday in August, with the busiest period occurring around 15 August, known locally as Ferragosto. As a result, many businesses and shops close for at least part of that month. Settimana Santa (Easter Holy Week) is another busy holiday period for Italians.

National public holidays include the following:

Capodanno (New Year's Day) 1 January

Epifania (Epiphany) 6 January

Pasquetta (Easter Monday) March/April

Giorno della Liberazione (Liberation Day) 25 April

Festa del Lavoro (Labour Day) 1 May

Festa della Repubblica (Republic Day) 2 June

Ferragosto (Feast of the Assumption) 15 August

Festa di Ognisanti (All Saints' Day) 1 November

Festa dell'Immacolata Concezione (Feast of the Immaculate Conception) 8 December

Natale (Christmas Day) 25 December

Festa di Santo Stefano (Boxing Day) 26 December

TELEPHONE

→ Italian telephone area codes all begin with 0 and consist of up to four digits. The area code is followed by anything from four to eight digits. The area code is an integral part of the telephone number and must always be dialled, even when calling from next door.

→ Mobile-phone numbers begin with a three-digit starting with a 3.

→ Toll-free (free-phone) numbers are known as *numeri verdi* and usually start with ☑ 800.

→ To call Italy from abroad, call your international access number, then Italy's country code (☑ 39) and then the area code of the location you want, including the leading ☑ 0.

→ To call abroad from Italy dial ☑ 00, then the country and area codes, followed by the telephone number.

→ To make a reverse-charge (collect) international call from a public telephone, dial ☑ 170. All phone operators speak English.

Mobile Phones

→ Italian mobile phones operate on the GSM 900/1800 network, which is compatible with the rest of Europe and Australia but not always with the North American GSM or CDMA systems – check with your service provider.

→ The cheapest way of using your mobile is to buy a prepaid *(prepagato)* Italian SIM card. TIM (www.tim.it), Wind (www.wind.it), Vodafone (www.vodafone.it) and Tre (www.tre.it) all offer SIM cards and have retail outlets in most Italian cities and towns. All SIM cards must be registered in Italy, so make sure you have a passport or ID card with you when you buy one.

TIME

→ Italy is one hour ahead of GMT. When it is noon in London, it is 1pm in Italy.

→ Italy operates on a 24-hour clock.

TOURIST INFORMATION

Provincial and local offices deal directly with the public and most will respond to written and telephone requests for information. Staff can usually provide a city map, lists of hotels and information on the major sights. In larger towns and major tourist areas, English is generally spoken, along with other languages.

Main offices are generally open Monday to Friday; some also open on weekends, especially in urban areas or during peak summer season. Affiliated information booths (eg at train stations and airports) may keep slightly different hours.

TRAVEL WITH CHILDREN

To get the most out of exploring as a family, plan ahead.

Cities in Italy are second to none in extraordinary sights and experiences, and with the aid of audio guides, smart-phone apps and some inventive guided tours, parents can find kid-appeal in almost every museum and monument. Discounted admission for children is available at most attractions, although there is no fixed rule as to how much – or not – children pay. State-run museums and archaeological sites usually offer free entry to EU citizens under the age of 18. Otherwise, museums and monuments offer a reduced admission fee (generally half the adult price) for children, usually from the ages of 6 to 18. Many offer money-saving family tickets covering admission for two adults and two children or more.

In cities and towns countrywide, family and four-person rooms can be hard to find and should be booked in advance. Increasingly, boutique B&Bs offer family rooms and/or self-catering apartments suited to families with young children..

When travelling by train, reserve seats where possible to avoid finding yourselves standing. You can hire car seats for infants and children from most car-rental firms, but you should always book them in advance.

Children are welcomed in most eateries, especially in casual trattorias and osterie. A *menù bambini* (children's menu) is fairly common. It's also acceptable to order a *mezzo piatto* (half-portion) or a simple plate of pasta with butter or olive oil and Parmesan. Italian families eat late. Few restaurants open their doors before 7.30pm or 8pm, making pizzerias – many open early – more appealing for families with younger children. High chairs are occasionally available; if your toddler absolutely needs to be strapped in, bring your own portable cloth seat.

Baby requirements are easily met (except on Sundays when most shops are closed). Pharmacies and supermarkets sell baby formula, nappies (diapers), ready-made baby food and sterilising solutions. Fresh cow's milk is sold in cartons in supermarkets and in bars with a 'Latteria' sign.

For more information and ideas about travelling with children in Italy, visit the superb Italy-focused website www.italiakids.com.

VISAS

EU citizens do not need a visa to enter Italy. Nationals of some other countries, including Australia, Canada, Israel, Japan, New Zealand, Switzerland and the USA, do not need a tourist visa for stays in Italy of up to 90 days. To check the visa requirements for your country, see the website www.schengenvisainfo.com/tourist-schengen-visa.

ⓘ Getting There & Away

AIR

Italy's main intercontinental gateways are Rome's **Leonardo da Vinci airport** (p514) (www.adr.it/fiumicino) and Milan's **Malpensa airport** (MXP; ☑ 02 23 23 23; www.milanomalpensa-airport.com; ⓡ Malpensa Express) (www.milanomalpensa-airport.com). Both are served by nonstop flights from around the world. Venice's **Marco Polo airport** (www.veniceairport.it) is also served by a handful of intercontinental flights.

Intra-European flights serve plenty of other Italian cities; the leading mainstream carriers include Alitalia, Air France, British Airways, Lufthansa and KLM.

Cut-rate airlines, led by Ryanair and easyJet, fly from a growing number of European cities to more than two dozen Italian destinations, typically landing in smaller airports such as Rome's Ciampino (www.adr.it/ciampino).

BUS

Buses are the cheapest overland transport option to Italy, but services are less frequent, less comfortable and significantly slower than the train.

Eurolines (www.eurolines.com) is a consortium of coach companies with offices throughout Europe. Italy-bound buses head to Rome, Florence, Venice and other Italian cities. It offers a bus pass valid for 15/30 days that costs €320/425 (reduced €270/350) in high season and €225/340 (reduced €195/265) in low season. This pass allows unlimited travel between 47 European cities, including Milan, Venice, Florence and Rome.

TRAIN

Regular trains on two western lines connect Italy with France (one along the coast and the other from Turin into the French Alps). Trains from Milan head north into Switzerland and on towards the Benelux countries. Further east, two main lines head for the main cities in Central and Eastern Europe. Those crossing the Brenner Pass go to Innsbruck, Stuttgart and Munich.

Those crossing at Tarvisio proceed to Vienna, Salzburg and Prague. The main international train line to Slovenia crosses near Trieste.

Depending on distances covered, rail can be highly competitive with air travel. Those travelling from neighbouring countries to northern Italy will find it is frequently more comfortable, less expensive and only marginally more time-consuming than flying.

Those who are travelling longer distances (say, from London, Spain, northern Germany or Eastern Europe) will doubtless find flying cheaper and quicker. Bear in mind, however, that the train is a much greener way to go – a trip by rail can contribute up to 10 times less carbon dioxide emissions per person than the same trip by air.

Voyages-sncf (http://uk.voyages-sncf.com) is an online booking service for rail journeys across Europe.

SEA

Multiple ferry companies connect Italy with countries throughout the Mediterranean. Many routes only operate in summer, when ticket prices also rise. Prices for vehicles vary according to their size.

The helpful website www.directferries.co.uk allows you to search routes and compare prices between the numerous international ferry companies servicing Italy. Another useful resource for ferries from Italy to Greece is www.ferries.gr. You'll find services from Bari and Brindisi to Corfu.

ⓘ Getting Around

AIR

Italy offers an extensive network of internal flights. The privatised national airline, Alitalia, is the main domestic carrier, with numerous low-cost airlines also operating across the country. Useful search engines for comparing multiple carriers' fares (including those of cut-price airlines) are www.skyscanner.com, www.kayak.com and www.azfly.it. Airport taxes are factored into the price of your ticket.

BUS

Routes Everything from meandering local routes to fast, reliable InterCity connections is provided by numerous bus companies.
Timetables and tickets These are available on bus-company websites and from local tourist offices. Tickets are generally competitively priced with the train and are often the only way to get to smaller towns. In larger cities most of the InterCity bus companies have ticket offices or sell tickets through agencies. In villages and even some good-sized towns, tickets are sold in bars or on the bus.

Advance booking Generally not required, but advisable for overnight or long-haul trips in high season.

LOCAL TRANSPORT

Major cities all have good transport systems, including bus and underground-train networks. In Venice, the main public transport option is *vaporetti* (small passenger ferries).

Bus & Metro

➡ Cities and towns of any size have an efficient *urbano* (urban) and *extraurbano* (suburban) bus system. Services are generally limited on Sundays and holidays.

➡ Purchase bus and metro tickets before boarding and validate them once on board. Passengers with unvalidated tickets are subject to a fine (between €50 and €110). Buy tickets from a *tabaccaio* (tobacconist's shop), newsstands, ticket booths or dispensing machines at bus and metro stations. Tickets usually cost around €1 to €2. Many cities offer good-value 24-hour or daily tourist tickets.

Taxi

➡ You can catch a taxi at the ranks outside most train and bus stations, or simply telephone for a radio taxi. Radio taxi meters start running from when you've called rather than when you're picked up.

➡ Charges vary somewhat from one region to another. Most short city journeys cost between €10 and €15. Generally, no more than four people are allowed in one taxi.

TRAIN

Trains in Italy are convenient and relatively cheap compared with other European countries. The better train categories are fast and comfortable.

Trenitalia (☎ 892021; www.trenitalia.com) is the national train system that runs most services. Train tickets must be stamped in the green machines (usually found at the head of rail platforms) just before boarding. Failure to do so usually results in fines.

Italy operates several types of trains:

Regionale/interregionale Slow and cheap, stopping at all or most stations.

InterCity (IC) Faster services operating between major cities. Their international counterparts are called Eurocity (EC).

Alta Velocità (AV) State-of-the-art, high-velocity trains, including Frecciarossa, Frecciargento, Frecciabianca and Italo trains, with speeds of up to 300km/hr and connections to the major cities. More expensive than InterCity express trains, but journey times are cut by almost half.

GREECE

Corfu

POP 102,070

Still recognisable as the idyllic refuge where the shipwrecked Odysseus was soothed and sent on his way home, Corfu, or Kerkyra (ker-kih-rah) in Greek, continues to welcome weary travellers with its lush scenery, bountiful produce and pristine beaches.

Since it was first settled by the Corcyrans in the 8th century, Corfuhas been an object of desire for both its untamed beauty and strategic position in the Mediterranean. It was a seat of European learning in the early days of modern Greece and Corfiots remain fiercely proud of their intellectual and artistic roots, a legacy visible from its fine museums and cultural life.

Corfu is large enough to make it possible to escape the crowds. Venture across cypress-studded hills to find vertiginous villages in the fertile interior, and sandy coves lapped by cobalt-blue waters.

🛈 Getting There & Away

AIR

Corfu's **airport** (☎ 26610 89600; www.corfu-airport.com) is about 2km southwest of the town centre. There are regular flights to Athens (€65, one hour) from where you can connect to the rest of Greece

Both EasyJet (www.easyjet.com) and Ryanair (www.ryanair.com) offer direct flights in summer between Corfu and the UK, and several other European destinations, while British Airways (www.ba.com) also flies from the UK to Corfu. Between May and September, many charter flights come from northern Europe and the UK.

BOAT

Ferries depart from Neo Limani (New Port), west of Corfu Town's Old Town. Ticket agencies line Ethnikis Antistaseos in Corfu Town, facing the Neo Limani. As well as services to neighbouring islands, there are sailings to Bari (€60, eight hours, two weekly) and Ancona (€85, 14½ hours, one to two daily) in Italy, and Igoumenitsa on the Greek mainland, where you can pick up other connections.

BUS

Green Buses (www.greenbuses.gr) goes to Athens (€48, 8½ hours, three daily, from Monday to Thursday; one via Lefkimmi), Thessaloniki (€38.50, eight hours, twice daily) and Larisa (€30.40, 5½ hours, daily).

GREECE AT A GLANCE

Don't Miss

The Acropolis You will be mesmerised by its beauty, history and sheer size. Beyond the Parthenon, you can find quieter spots such as the exquisite Temple of Athena Nike and the Theatre of Dionysos. Nearby, the Acropolis Museum showcases the surviving treasures of the Acropolis.

Meteora Soaring pillars of rock jut heavenward, a handful complete with monasteries perched on their summits. Built as early as the 14th century, these were home to hermit monks fleeing persecution. Today this spectacular stone forest beckons pilgrims and rock climbers from around the world.

Santorini sunsets There's more to Santorini than sunsets, but this remarkable island, shaped by the fire of prehistoric eruptions, has made the celebratory sunset its own. On summer evenings, the clifftop towns of Fira and Oia are packed with visitors awed by the vast blood-red canvas of the cliff face as the sun struts its stuff.

Rhodes' Old Town Get lost meandering down twisting, cobbled alleyways with soaring archways. Explore the ancient Knights' Quarter, the old Jewish Quarter and the Hora (Turkish Quarter). Hear traditional live music in tiny tavernas, dine on fresh seafood and wander atop the city's walls, with the sea on one side and a bird's-eye view into this living museum.

Corfu Stroll past Byzantine fortresses, neoclassical 19th-century British buildings, Parisian-style arcades, Orthodox church towers and the narrow, sun-dappled streets of the Venetian Old Town. Beyond the town, Corfu is lush green mountains, rolling countryside and dramatic coastlines. And if the architecture and scenery aren't enough, come to enjoy the Italian-influenced food.

Itineraries

10 Days

Here's a mixed bag of the country's top sights, most beautiful beaches, cultural highs, contemporary cities and laid-back island life. Begin on **Corfu**, spending a couple of days wandering through the amazing blend of Italian, French and British architecture in Corfu's Old Town, indulging in gourmet cuisine, exploring picturesque coastal villages and lounging on sandy beaches. Corfu is also great for windsurfing, or biking in the mountainous interior. From Corfu, head to **Athens**, visiting grand ancient sites and museums. Dive into the markets, contemporary-art scene and award-winning restaurants. Head north to **Ancient Delphi**, former home of the mysterious Delphic oracle. Your last stop is the monasteries of **Meteora**, perched high on narrow pinnacles of rock.

Two Weeks

Following your visit to Meteora, return to Athens and hop a ferry to spectacular **Santorini** to watch the sun sink from the dramatic cliffs of its volcanic caldera. Visit the fascinating Minoan site and black sand beaches. Catch a flight to **Rhodes**. Spend a couple of days exploring the atmospheric, walled medieval Old Town and checking out its burgeoning nightlife. Visit some of the surrounding beaches and stunning Byzantine chapels.

Essential Food & Drink

Mezedhes These small dishes (or appetisers) are often shared. Classics include *tzatziki* (yoghurt, cucumber and garlic dip), *melidzanosalata* (aubergine dip), *taramasalata* (fish roe dip), *fava* (split-pea puree with lemon juice) and *saganaki* (fried cheese).

Greek salad This ubiquitous salad (*horiatiki* or 'village salad') is made of tomatoes, cucumber, onions, feta and olives.

Cheese Apart from feta, local cheeses include *graviera* (a nutty, mild Gruyere-like sheep's-milk cheese), *kaseri* (similar to provolone), *myzithra* (ricotta-like whey cheese) and *manouri* (creamy soft cheese from the north).

Grills Greeks are masterful with grilled and spit-roasted meats. *Souvlaki* comes in many forms, from cubes of grilled meat on a skewer to pitta-wrapped snacks

Getting Around

Air Domestic flights are abundant and significantly cut down travel time. In high season, flights fill up fast so book ahead.

Boat Ferries link the islands to each other and the mainland, including catamarans, modern ferries and boats with cabins. Schedules can be unreliable. In high season book ahead.

Bus Generally air-conditioned and frequent, buses are a good way to travel between major cities.

Car Rentals are reasonably priced and found on all but the tiniest islands. They give you the freedom to explore the islands, but you'll need a good dose of bravery and road smarts.

When to Go

Athens

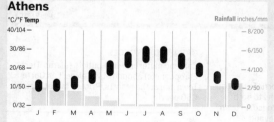

May–Aug Hotel prices can double. Both crowds and temperatures soar.

Apr, Sep & Oct Hotel prices can drop by 20%. Fewer internal flights and ferries. Crowds begin to thin.

Nov–Mar Many hotels, sights and restaurants shut down, especially on the islands. Hotel rates can drop by 50%.

Arriving in Greece

Eleftherios Venizelos International Airport (Athens) Express buses operate 24 hours between the airport, city centre and Piraeus. Half-hourly metro trains run between the city centre and the airport from 5.30am to 11.30pm. Taxis to the city centre cost €38 and take about 45 minutes.

Diagoras Airport (Rhodes) Buses run between the airport and Rhodes Town from 6.30am to 11.15pm (from 11.45am Sunday). Taxis from the airport to Rhodes Town cost around €30.

Top Phrases

Hello. Yia su.

Goodbye. Adio.

Please. Parakalo.

Thank you. Efkharisto.

How much is it? Posokani?

Resources

EOT (Greek National Tourist Organisation; www.gnto.gr)

Greek Travel Pages (www.gtp.gr)

Greece Is (www.greece-is.com)

Greece by a Greek (www.greecebyagreek.com)

Set Your Budget

➡ Dorm bed and domatio (Greek B&B): less than €60

➡ Meal at markets and street stalls: less than €15

➡ Many cities have joint sightseeing passes that greatly reduce entry fees.

Corfu

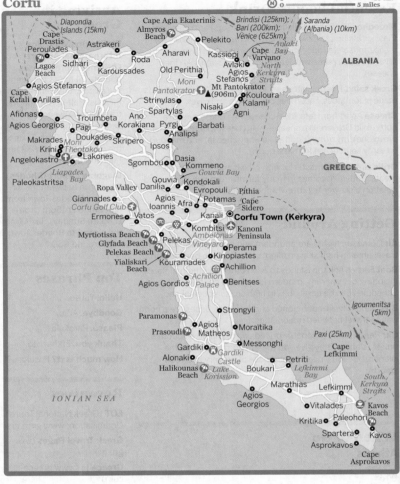

ⓘ Getting Around

TO/FROM THE AIRPORT

Taxis between the airport and Corfu Town cost around €12, while local bus 15 runs to both Plateia G Theotoki (Plateia San Rocco) in town and the Neo Limani (New Port) beyond.

BUS

Long-distance Green Buses radiate out from Corfu Town's **long-distance bus station** (☎ 26610 28900; www.greenbuses.gr; I Theotoki, Corfu Town) in the New Town. Fares cost €1.50 to €4.80; services are reduced on Saturday, and may be non-existent on Sundays and holidays.

CAR & MOTORCYCLE

Car- and motorbike-hire outlets (Alamo, Hertz, Europcar etc) abound at the airport, in Corfu Town and at the resorts. Prices start at around €50 per day.

Corfu Town

Imbued with Venetian grace and elegance, historic Corfu Town (also known as Kerkyra) leaves you spellbound from the moment you wander its tangle of cobbled streets. Encounter majestic architecture like the splendid Liston arcade, high-class museums and no fewer than 39 churches. The name

Corfu, meaning 'peaks', refers to its twin hills topped by massive fortresses built to withstand Ottoman sieges. The day bustles with cruise passengers and day trippers; come evening, everyone settles down to enjoy some off the region's top restaurants.

⊙ Sights

★ Palaio Frourio   FORTRESS
(Old Fort; ☑ 26610 48310; adult/concession €6/3; ⊗8am-8pm Apr-Oct, 8.30am-3pm Nov-Mar) The rocky headland that juts east from Corfu Town is topped by the Venetian-built 14th-century Palaio Frourio. Before that, already enclosed within massive stone walls, it cradled the entire Byzantine city. A solitary bridge crosses its seawater moat.

Only parts of this huge site, which also holds later structures from the British era, are accessible to visitors; wander up to the lighthouse on the larger of the two hills for superb views, or down to reach small gravelly beaches.

★ Corfu Museum of Asian Art   MUSEUM
(☑ 26610 30443; www.matk.gr; Palace of St Michael & St George; adult/child €6/3; ⊗8am-8pm) Home to stunning artefacts ranging from prehistoric bronzes to works in onyx and ivory, this excellent museum occupies the central portions of the Palace of St Michael & St George. One gallery provides a chronological overview of Chinese ceramics, while showcasing remarkable jade carvings and snuff bottles. The India section opens with Alexander the Great, 'When Greece Met India', and displays fascinating Graeco-Buddhist figures, including a blue-grey schist Buddha. A new Japanese section incorporates magnificent samurai armour, Noh masks and superb woodblock prints.

Antivouniotissa Museum   MUSEUM
(Byzantine Museum; ☑ 26610 38313; www.antivouniotissamuseum.gr; off Arseniou; adult/child €4/€2; ⊗8.30am-3pm Tue-Sun) Home to an outstanding collection of Byzantine and post-Byzantine icons and artefacts, the exquisite, timber-roofed Church of Our Lady of Antivouniotissa doubles as both church and museum. It stands atop a short, broad stairway that climbs from shore-front Arseniou, and frames views out towards the wooded Vidos island.

Mon Repos Estate   PARK
(Kanoni Peninsula; ⊗7.30am-7.30pm May-Oct, to 5pm Nov-Apr) **FREE** This park-like wooded estate 2km around the bay south of the Old Town was the site of Corfu's most important ancient settlement, Palaeopolis. More recently, in 1921, the secluded neoclassical villa that now holds the Museum of Palaeopolis was the birthplace of Prince Philip of Greece, who was to marry Britain's Queen Elizabeth II. Footpaths lead through the woods to ancient ruins, including sanctuaries to Hera and Apollo, and a more complete Doric temple atop a small coastal cliff.

🛏 Sleeping

★ Bella Venezia   BOUTIQUE HOTEL €€
(☑ 26610 46500; www.bellaveneziahotel.com; N Zambeli 4; s/d incl breakfast from €120/135; 🕸🛜) From the instant you enter this neoclassical villa, set in a peaceful central street, you'll be seduced by its pure old-world charm. Previously both a bank and a girls' school, it features an elegant lobby decked in candelabras, with velvet chairs and a grand piano. The plush, high-ceilinged rooms (some with balconies) have fine city views, while the garden breakfast room is delightful.

Folies Corfu   HOTEL €€
(☑ 26610 49300; www.foliescorfu.com; s/d €68/81; 🕸🛜) Bright, self-catering studios and one- or two-bedroom apartments, all with balconies or terraces, are arrayed around a lush garden pool in a residential neighbourhood. It's well priced thanks to the away-from-it-all location, 2km west of the New Town – a half-hour walk from the centre. Breakfast costs €5 extra.

✗ Eating

★ Pane & Souvlaki   GRILL €
(☑ 26610 20100; www.panesouvlaki.com; Guilford 77; mains €5-9; ⊗noon-1am) Arguably the Old Town's best budget option, with outdoor tables on the Town Hall square, this quick-fire restaurant does exactly what its name suggests, serving up three skewers of chicken or pork with chunky chips, dipping sauce and warm pitta in individual metal trays.

★ Starenio   BAKERY €
(☑ 26610 47370; Guilford 59; sweets & pastries from €2; ⊗8.30am-11pm Mon-Sat) A magical little bakery, dripping with bougainvillea, where in-the-know locals linger at little tables on the sloping pedestrian street to savour cakes, coffee, pastries, and delicious fresh pies with vegetarian fillings such as mushrooms or nettles.

Corfu Old Town

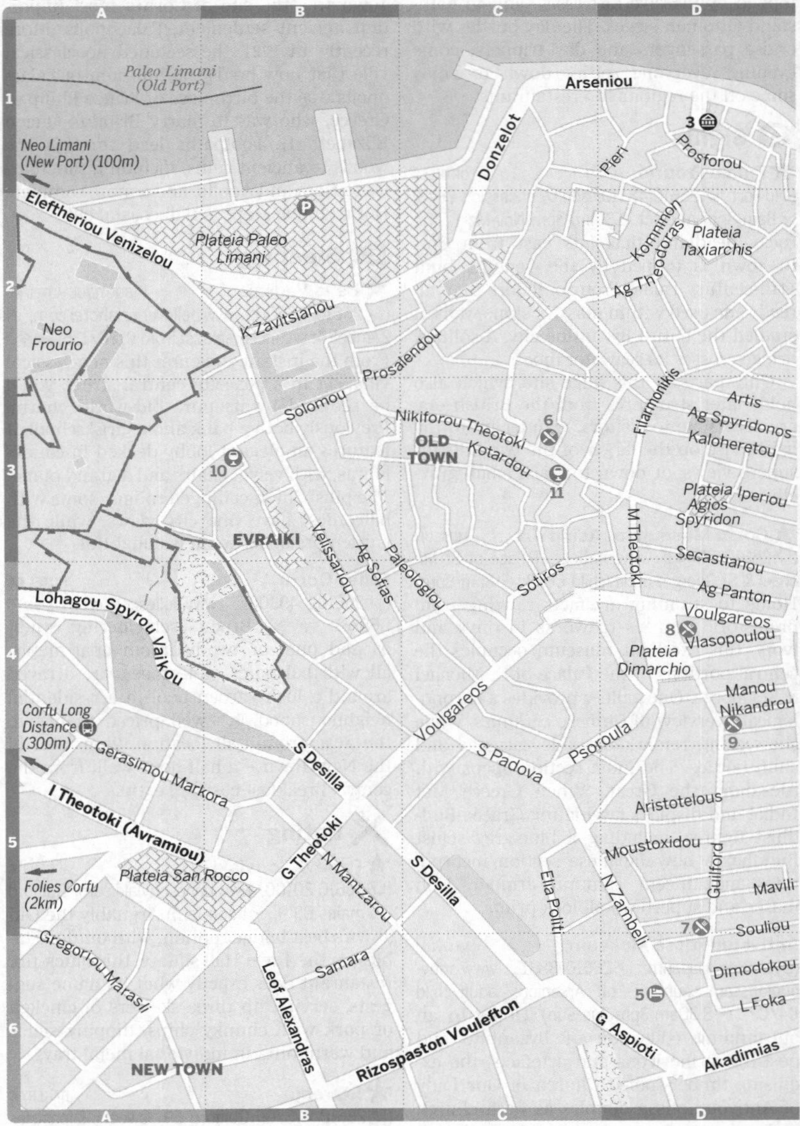

Estiatorio Bellissimo GREEK €€
(☎26610 41112; Plateia Limonia; mains €8-18; ⏲10am-midnight) The Old Town district holds few nicer spots for an al fresco evening than this casual but stylish restaurant that spreads out across a peaceful pedestrian square. As well as steaks and seafood on the menu, it also has on offer some Corfiot specialities, such as *pastitsadha kokora* – chicken that is cooked in a red sauce, 'with a lot of cheese' – plus various crepes and a selection of salads.

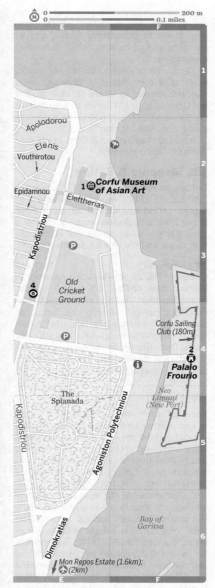

and pizza. Leave room for the silky-smooth panna cotta, so fresh it will make your taste buds sing.

🍷 Drinking & Nightlife

Perhaps the best place to kick-start the evening is on the stylish Liston arcade, where Corfiots go to see and be seen; after that, the choices are legion. Corfu Town also has a lively cultural life.

★ **Firi Firi – The Beer House**   BAR
(☎ 26610 33953; www.facebook.com/FiriFiriCorfu; Solomou 1; ⊙ 6pm-2am; 🛜) Sample local and imported beers, either inside the custard-coloured villa at the foot of the steps leading up to the New Fortress, or at the terraced tables beside the neighbouring church; if you find it hard to leave, it grills up some decent dishes, too.

★ **Mikro Café**   BAR
(☎ 26610 31009; www.mikrocafe.com; N Theotoki 42) Whether your favoured beverage is coffee, wine or beer, the Old Town holds no finer spot for drinking and people-watching than the delightful, multilevel vine-shaded terrace of the convivial 'little cafe'.

ⓘ Information

All Ways Travel (☎ 26610 33955; www.allways travel.com.gr; Plateia G Theotoki 34) Helpful English-speaking staff in the New Town's main square.
Aperghi Travel (☎ 26610 48713; www. aperghitravel.gr; I Polyla 1) Handles tours and

Il Vesuvio   ITALIAN €€
(☎ 26610 21284; Guilford 16; mains €9-18; ⊙ noon-late; 🛜) A classy Italian place, with outdoor tables on both sides of the pedestrian street, that's won awards for its moreish homemade gnocchi, cannelloni

ⓘ EXPLORING CORFU

All sorts of tours can help you explore in and around Corfu Town, whether on foot with **Corfu Walking Tours** (☑ 6980140160; www.corfuwalkingtours. com), by bus with **Corfu Sightseeing** (www.corfusightseeing.gr; €15), or in the toy-train and horse-drawn carriage tours that start from the Spianada.

The entire island has excellent walking. **The Corfu Trail** (www. thecorfutrail.com) traverses the island from north to south and takes between eight and 12 days to complete. You can organise a trip through **Aperghi Travel** (p525), or simply arrange a day's guided hiking with **Corfu Walks & Hikes** (www.walking-corfu.blogspot.co.uk).

accommodation, especially for walkers on the Corfu Trail (www.corfutrail.com).

Municipal Tourist Kiosk (Spianada; ⊙ 9am-4pm Mon-Sat Jun-Sep) Helps with accommodation, transport and things to do around Corfu.

Pachis Travel (☑ 26610 28298; www.pachis-travel.com; Guilford 7; ⊙ 9am-2.30pm & 5.30-9pm Mon-Sat) Busy little agency that's useful for hotels, ferry and plane tickets, and excursions to Paxi.

South of Corfu Town

The coast road south from Corfu Town leads to well-signposted Achillion Palace near the village of Gastouri.

Further south, beyond the popular but uninspiring beach resorts of **Moraïtika** and **Messonghi**, the coastal road winds through sun-dappled woods, passing prettier and much less developed little coves. Tiny **Boukari** cradles an attractive little harbour, while the fishing port of **Petriti**, where the road finally turns away from the shoreline, holds a row of welcoming seafood tavernas. Nearing the southern tip of Corfu, **Lefkimmi** is an elongated little town where everyday life simply carries on as usual, untroubled by visitors.

◉ Sights

Achillion Palace　　　　HISTORIC BUILDING
(☑ 26610 56210; www.achillion-corfu.gr; Gastouri; €8; ⊙ 8am-8pm Apr-Oct, to 4pm Nov-Mar) Set atop a steep coastal hill 12km south of Corfu Town, the Achillion Palace was built during the 1890s as the summer palace of Austria's empress Elizabeth, the niece of King Otto of Greece. The palace's two principal features are its intricately decorated central staircase, rising in geometrical flights, and its sweeping garden terraces, which command eye-popping views.

There's surprisingly little to see inside, other than mementoes of Elizabeth, who was assassinated in Genoa in 1898, and of the German kaiser Wilhelm II, who bought the palace in 1907 and added the namesake statue of Achilles Triumphant.

Bus N-10 runs to the Achillion from Corfu Town (€1.70, 20 minutes).

🛏 Sleeping & Eating

Golden Sunset Hotel　　　　HOTEL **€€**
(☑ 26620 51853; www.goldensunsetcorfu.gr; Boukari; s/d incl breakfast €50/65; ❄) A family-run hotel at a glorious curve in the coast road. Each of its 16 rooms enjoys magnificent views, and there's a terraced restaurant.

★ Klimataria　　　　TAVERNA **€€**
(☑ 26610 71201; www.klimataria-restaurant.gr; Benitses; mains €8-15; ⊙ 6.30-11.30pm Mon-Sat, noon-4.30pm Sun) This tiny, old-fashioned taverna, in a custard-coloured villa facing the main road, is worth a pilgrimage in its own right – every dish is delicious and superbly fresh, from the tender octopus or various mezedhes (appetisers) to the feta and olive oil. Call for reservations in summer.

West Coast

Some of Corfu's prettiest countryside, villages and beaches line the west coast. The scenic and popular resort area **Paleokastritsa**, 23km northwest of Corfu Town, stretches for nearly 3km through a series of small, picturesque bays. Craggy mountains swathed in cypress and olive trees tower above. The real treat comes at the resort's end, where an exquisite little beach is said to be where the weary Odysseus washed ashore. Boat trips from the little jetty here include **Paradise Sunset** (☑ 6972276442; Paleokastritsa; per person €10-20) cruises to nearby grottoes and the glass-bottomed **Yellow Submarine** (☑ 6977409246; www.yellowsubmarine.gr; Paleokastritsa; €10; ⊙ 10am-6pm, night cruises 9pm).

Set amid splendid gardens on the rocky promontory above, an easy 10-minute walk from the beach, the **Moni Theotokou** (Paleokastritsa; ⊙ 7am-1pm & 3-8pm) FREE monastery dates back to the 13th century, and is home to an interesting little **museum** (⊙ Apr-Oct) FREE and a shop selling oils and herbs.

A circuitous hike or drive west from Paleokastritsa will take you along a high winding road through the unspoiled villages of **Lakones** and **Krini**.

🛏 Sleeping & Eating

★ Levant Hotel   HOTEL €€

(📞 26610 94230; www.levantcorfu.com; Pelekas village; s/d incl breakfast €80/100; ☺ May–mid-Oct; P ❄ 🐾 🛜 ♨) A creamy neoclassical hotel, up in the gods just below the Kaiser's Throne, with pastel-blue rooms, wooden floors, belle époque lights and balconies. Throw in a refined restaurant serving shrimp, risotto and *stifadho* (stew) on a terrace with sublime sunset views. Tempted?

★ Elia Restaurant   TAVERNA €

(📞 6982316598; www.eliamirtiotissa.com; Myrtiotissa; mains €7-14; ☺ noon-late May-Oct) An irresistible taverna, perched above the track down to breathtaking Myrtiotissa Beach, serving an enticing menu of Corfiot specialities and much-needed cold drinks.

Athens

POP 3.1 MILLION

With equal measures of grunge and grace, Athens is a heady mix of history and edginess. Cultural and social life plays out amid, around and within ancient landmarks, with the magnificent Acropolis visible from almost every part of the city. Although individuals have endured difficult circumstances since the start of the economic crisis in 2009, the city is on the rise with a lively urban bustle, a crackling energy in the art scene and first-rate museums. At the end of the day, Athenians know how to unwind, especially in open-air restaurants and bars where they linger for hours.

👁 Sights

★ Acropolis   HISTORIC SITE

(📞 210 321 4172; http://odysseus.culture.gr; adult/concession/child €20/10/free; ☺ 8am-8pm May-Sep, reduced hours in winter, last entry 30min before closing; Ⓜ Akropoli) The Acropolis is the most important ancient site in the Western world. Crowned by the Parthenon, it stands sentinel over Athens, visible from almost everywhere within the city. Its monuments and sanctuaries of white Pentelic marble gleam in the midday sun and gradually take on a honey hue as the sun sinks, while at night they stand brilliantly illuminated above the city. A glimpse of this magnificent sight cannot fail to exalt your spirit.

★ Acropolis Museum   MUSEUM

(📞 210 900 0900; www.theacropolismuseum.gr; Dionysiou Areopagitou 15, Makrygianni; adult/child €5/free; ☺ 8am-4pm Mon, to 8pm Tue-Sun, to 10pm Fri Apr-Oct, 9am-5pm Mon-Thu, to 10pm Fri, to 8pm Sat & Sun Nov-Mar; Ⓜ Akropoli) This dazzling modernist museum at the foot of the Acropolis' southern slope showcases its surviving treasures still in Greek possession. While the collection covers the Archaic and Roman periods, the emphasis is on the Acropolis of the 5th century BC, considered the apotheosis of Greece's artistic achievement. The museum cleverly reveals layers of history, floating over ruins with the Acropolis visible below, showing the masterpieces in context. The surprisingly good-value restaurant has superb views; there's also a fine museum shop.

★ Ancient Agora   HISTORIC SITE

(📞 210 321 0185; http://odysseus.culture.gr; Adrianou 24, Monastiraki; adult/student/child €8/4/free, with Acropolis pass free; ☺ 8am-8pm daily May-Oct, to 3pm Nov-Apr; Ⓜ Monastiraki) The Agora was ancient Athens' heart, the lively hub of administrative, commercial, political and social activity. Socrates expounded his philosophy here, and in AD 49 St Paul came here to win converts to Christianity. The site today is a lush respite, with the grand **Temple of Hephaistos**, a good **museum** and the late-10th-century Byzantine **Church of the**

ⓘ COMBINED TICKETS & OPENING HOURS

➧ A €30 unified ticket covers entry to the Acropolis and Athens' other main ancient sites: Ancient Agora, Roman Agora, Hadrian's Library, Kerameikos, the Temple of Olympian Zeus and Aristotle's Lyceum. The ticket is valid for five days and can be purchased at any of the included sites.

➧ For museums, a €15 ticket covers the National Archaeological Museum, the Byzantine & Christian Museum, the Epigraphic Museum and the Numismatic Museum. It's valid for three days.

➧ Be sure to double-check hours before making a special trip. Box offices close 15 to 30 minutes before the sites close. Check www.culture.gr for free-admission holidays.

Central Athens

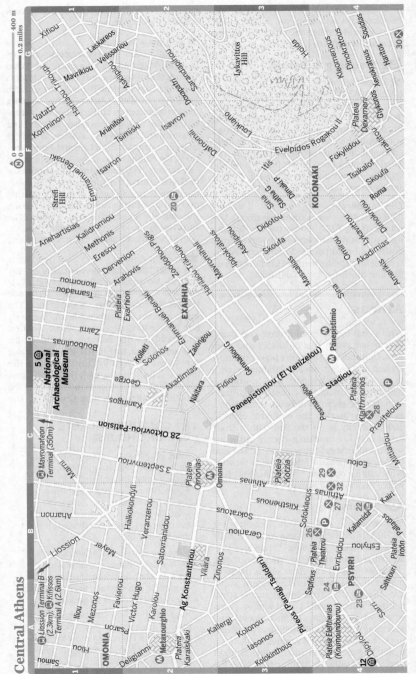

400 m
0.2 miles

OMONIA

EXARHIA

KOLONAKI

PSYRRI

Lykavittos Hill

Strefi Hill

National Archaeological Museum

Metaxourghio

Omonia

Panepistimio

Stadiou

28 Oktovriou-Patision

Panepistimiou (El Venizelou)

Plateia Omonias

Plateia Exarhion

Plateia Kotzia

Plateia Theatrou

Plateia Karaiskaki

Plateia Klafthmonos

Plateia Dexameni

Plateia Iroon

Plateia Eleftherias (Koumoundourou)

Pireos (Panagi Tsaldari)

Ag Konstantinou

Mavromateon Terminal (350m)

Liossion Terminal B (2.3km); Kifissos Terminal A (2.6km)

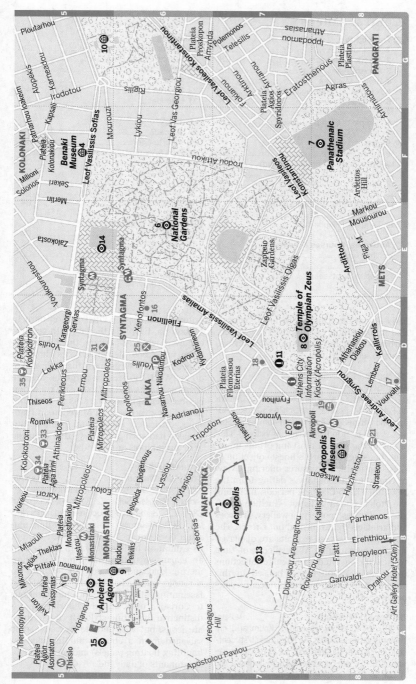

Ploutarhou

Alopekis
Patriarhou Ioakeim
Kapsali – Karneadou
Irodotou

10

Plateia Proskopon
Polemonos
Amynda
Telesilis

Plateia
Athanasias
Ippodamou

PANGRATI

Plateia
Plastira

KOLONAKI

Milioni
Solonos
Sekeri
Plateia
Kolonakiou

Benaki
Museum
4

Leof Vasilissis Sofias

Plateia Proskopon

Leof Vas Georgiou

Riglis

Mourouzi

Lykiou

Leof Vasileos Konstantinou

Plateia
Agios
Spyridonos
Eratosthenous

Agras

Arrianou
Fokianou
Ardittou Hill

Athanasiou
Diakou

METS

Merlin

Zaloskosta

Voukourestiou

14

Syntagma

M Syntagma

National
Gardens
6

Zappeio
Gardens

Leof Vasilissis Olgas

Markou
Mousourou

Piga M

Ardittou

7

Panathenaic
Stadium

Leof Vasileos Konstantinou

Leof Vasilissis Amalias

35

Plateia
Kolokotroni

Voulis

Lekka

Karageorgi Servias

Xenofontos

16

Filellinon

SYNTAGMA

31

25

Voulis

Kodrou

Kydathineon

Nikis

Plateia
Filomousou
Eterias

Frynihou

18

11

8 Temple of
Olympian Zeus

Athens City
Information
Kiosk (Acropolis)

Lembesi

Kallirrois

17

Vourvahi

Leof Andreas Syngrou

Perikleous

Ermou

Romvis

33

Kolokotroni

34

Plateia
Agia Irini Athinaidos

Voreou

Karori

Mitropoleos

Plateia
Mitropoleos

Apollonos

Navarhou Nikodimou

Adrianou

Tripodon

Thespidos

Vyronos

EOT

Akropoli

M Akropoli

19

Acropolis
Museum
2

Mitseon

Hatzihristou

21

Straton

Thiseos

PLAKA

Apollonos

Pelopida

Diogenous

Lyssiou

Epikolou

Prytaniou

Parthenos

Erehthiou →

Propyleon

Miaouli

Agias Theklas

Pittaki

Plateia
Monastirakiou

Itestou

Kladou

Pelikilis

MONASTIRAKI

Normanou

Theorias

1

Acropolis

13

Dionysiou Areopagitou

Rovertou Galli

Kallisperi

Fratti

Garivaldi

Drakou

Art Gallery Hotel (50m) →

Mikonos

Plateia
Avissynias

Adrianou

3

Ancient
Agora

36

15

9

Thissio

Plateia
Agion
Asomaton

Thermopylon

Avilion

Plateia
Agion
Asomaton

Areopagus
Hill

Apostolou Pavlou

Central Athens

Holy Apostles, trimmed in brick patterns that mimic Arabic calligraphy. The greenery harbours birds and lizards. Allow about two hours to see everything.

★ National Archaeological Museum
MUSEUM

(☏ 213 214 4800; www.namuseum.gr; 28 Oktovriou-Patision 44, Exarhia; adult/child €10/free; ⊗ 1-8pm Mon, 8am-8pm Tue-Fri, 9am-4pm Sat & Sun; 🚌 2, 3, 4, 5 or 11 to Polytechnio, Ⓜ Viktoria) This is one of the world's most important museums, housing the world's finest collection of Greek antiquities. Treasures offering a view of Greek art and history – dating from the Neolithic era to Classical periods, including the Ptolemaic era in Egypt – include exquisite sculptures, pottery, jewellery, frescoes and artefacts found throughout Greece. The beautifully presented exhibits are displayed mainly thematically. Allow plenty of time to view the vast and spectacular collections (more than 11,000 items) housed in this enormous (8000-sq-metre) 19th-century neoclassical building.

★ Benaki Museum
MUSEUM

(☏ 210 367 1000; www.benaki.gr; Koumbari 1, cnr Leoforos Vasilissis Sofias, Kolonaki; adult/student/child €9/7/free, Thu free, pass to all Benaki museums €20; ⊗ 9am-5pm Wed & Fri, to midnight Thu & Sat, to 3pm Sun; Ⓜ Syntagma, Evangelismos)

Antonis Benakis, a politician's son born in Alexandria, Egypt, in the late 19th century, endowed what is perhaps the finest museum in Greece. Its three floors showcase impeccable treasures from the Bronze Age up to WWII. Especially gorgeous are the Byzantine icons and the extensive collection of Greek regional costumes, as well as complete sitting rooms from Macedonian mansions, intricately carved and painted. But Benakis had such a good eye that even the agricultural tools are splendid.

Byzantine & Christian Museum
MUSEUM

(☏ 213 213 9500; www.byzantinemuseum.gr; Leoforos Vasilissis Sofias 22, Kolonaki; adult/child €8/free; ⊗ 8am-8pm Apr-Oct, reduced hours Nov-Mar; Ⓜ Evangelismos) This outstanding museum does not look like much at first, but its exhibition halls lead one to the next in an expansive underground maze of glimmering gold and mosaics. The exhibits go chronologically, charting the gradual and fascinating shift from ancient traditions to Christian ones, and the flourishing of a distinctive Byzantine style. Of course there are icons, but also delicate frescoes (some salvaged from a church and installed on haunting floating panels) and more personal remnants of daily life.

Museum of Islamic Art
MUSEUM

(☑210 325 1311; www.benaki.gr; Agion Asomaton 22, Keramikos; adult/student/child €9/7/free; ☺10am-6pm Thu-Sun; Ⓜ Thissio) While not particularly large, this museum houses one of the world's most significant collections of Islamic art. Four floors of a mansion display, in ascending chronological order, exceptionally beautiful weaving, jewellery, porcelain, even a marble-floored reception room from 17th-century Cairo mansion. It's all arranged for maximum dazzling impact, with informative signage. In the basement, part of Athens' ancient Themistoklean wall is exposed, and the top floor has a small cafe with a view of Kerameikos.

★ Temple of Olympian Zeus
TEMPLE

(Olympieio; ☑210 922 6330; http://odysseus.culture.gr; Leoforos Vasilissis Olgas, Syntagma; adult/student/child €6/3/free, with Acropolis pass free; ☺8am-3pm Oct-Apr, to 8pm May-Sep, final admission 30min before closing; Ⓜ Akropoli, Syntagma) A can't-miss on two counts: it's a marvellous temple, the largest in Greece, and it's smack in the centre of Athens. The temple is impressive for the sheer size of its 104 Corinthian columns (17m high with a base diameter of 1.7m), of which 15 remain – the fallen column was blown down in a gale in 1852.

Panathenaic Stadium
HISTORIC SITE

(☑210 752 2984; www.panathenaicstadium.gr; Leoforos Vasileos Konstantinou, Pangrati; adult/student/child €5/2.50/free; ☺8am-7pm Mar-Oct, to 5pm Nov-Feb; 🚍2, 4, 11 to Stadio, Ⓜ Akropoli, 🚇 Zappeio) As an actual site to visit, this ancient-turned-modern stadium – built in the 4th century BC, and restored for the first modern Olympic games in 1896 – will be most interesting to sports fans who can imagine the roar of the millennia-old crowds. A ticket gets you an audio tour, admission to a tiny exhibit on the modern Olympics and the opportunity to take your photo on a winners' pedestal. The stadium was first used as a venue for the Panathenaic athletic contests, and it's said that at Hadrian's inauguration in AD 120, a thousand wild animals were sacrificed in the arena. Later, the seats were rebuilt in Pentelic marble by Herodes Atticus.

Parliament &
Changing of the Guard
NOTABLE BUILDING

(Plateia Syntagmatos; Ⓜ Syntagma) `FREE` In front of the parliament building, the traditionally costumed *evzones* (guards) of the Tomb of the Unknown Soldier change every hour on the hour. On Sunday at 11am, a whole platoon marches down Vasilissis Sofias to the tomb, accompanied by a band.

☞ Tours

Three main companies – CHAT (☑210 323 0827; www.chatours.gr; Xenofontos 9, Syntagma; 5hr tour €68; Ⓜ Syntagma), GO Tours (☑210 921 9555; www.gotours.com.gr; Kallirrois 12, Makrygianni; Ⓜ Akropoli) and Hop In Sightseeing (☑210 428 5500; www.hopin.com; Leoforos Vasilissis Amalias 44, Makrygianni; ☺6.30am-10pm; Ⓜ Akropoli) – run almost identical air-conditioned city coach tours, as well as excursions to nearby sights. Hotels act as booking agents and often offer discounts.

This Is My Athens (http://myathens.thisisathens.org) is an excellent city-run program that pairs you with a volunteer local to show you around for two hours. You must book online 72 hours ahead.

☆☆ Festivals

Athens & Epidaurus Festival
PERFORMING ARTS

(Hellenic Festival; ☑210 928 2900; www.greekfestival.gr; ☺Jun-Aug) The ancient Theatre of Epidavros (adult/concession €12/6; ☺8am-8pm Apr-Aug, reduced hrs rest or year) and Athens' Odeon of Herodes Atticus (☑210 324 1807; Ⓜ Akropoli) are the headline venues for Greece's annual cultural festival, running since 1955 and featuring a top line-up of local and international music, dance and theatre.

⌨ Sleeping

★ Athens Backpackers
HOSTEL €

(☑210 922 4044; www.backpackers.gr; Makri 12, Makrygianni; dm incl breakfast €24-30; ❄@🛜; Ⓜ Akropoli) The popular rooftop bar with cheap drinks and Acropolis views is a major draw at this modern and friendly Australian-run backpacker favourite. There's a barbecue grill in the courtyard, a well-stocked kitchen and a busy social scene. Spotless dorms with private bathrooms and lockers have bedding, but towel use costs €2. Management also runs well-priced nearby Athens Studios (☑210 923 5811; www.athensstudios.gr; Veïkou 3a, Makrygianni; apt incl breakfast €105; @🛜; Ⓜ Akropoli).

★ City Circus
HOSTEL €

(☑213 023 7244; www.citycircus.gr; Sarri 16, Psyrri; dm incl breakfast €27-31.50; s/d from €36/72;

😊✳@🛜; MThissio, Monastiraki) It's not the cheapest hostel going, but with its jaunty style and helpful staff, City Circus does lift the spirit more than most ultrabudget lodgings. Its bright, well-designed rooms have modern bathrooms; some have kitchens. Book on its website for free breakfast at the chic bistro downstairs.

★ **Athens Quinta Hostel**　　HOSTEL €

(📋213 030 5322; www.facebook.com/athensquinta; Methonis 13, Exarhia; dm €25; 🛜; MPanepistimio) Set in an old mansion, complete with velvet sofas and patterned tile floors, this friendly place is pleasantly homey and a nice change from slicker, busier hostels. There's a nice backyard for lounging. The location in cool Exarhia is a plus for neighbourhood vibe, but it is far from the main sights.

Cecil　　HOTEL €

(📋210 321 7079; www.cecilhotel.gr; Athinas 39, Monastiraki; s/d/tr/q incl breakfast from €69/77/125/140; ✳@🛜; MMonastiraki) This charming old hotel on busy Athinas has beautiful high, moulded ceilings, polished timber floors and an original cage-style lift. The simple rooms are tastefully furnished, but don't have fridges. Two connecting rooms with a shared bathroom are ideal for families.

Evripides　　HOTEL €

(📋210 321 2301; www.evripideshotel.gr; Evripidou 79, Psyrri; s/d incl breakfast €63/81; ✳@🛜; MMonastiraki, Omonia, Thissio) An excellent and clean 62-room budget hotel situated on a somewhat divey block. Most rooms have a little balcony, and all have mini-fridges – handy for longer stays. Book early, and you might score a room with an Acropolis view and bigger balcony, for only a tiny bit more. Failing that, everyone can enjoy the view from the rooftop breakfast terrace and bar.

STREET FOOD

From vendors selling *koulouria* (fresh pretzel-style bread) and grilled corn or chestnuts to the raft of fast-food offerings, there's no shortage of snacks on the run in Athens. You can't go wrong with *tiropites* (cheese pies) or Greece's favourite savoury snack, souvlaki, which packs more punch for €2.50 than anything else.

✗ Eating

★ **Oikeio**　　MEDITERRANEAN €

(📋210 725 9216; Ploutarhou 15, Kolonaki; mains €8-12; ⊙12.30pm-midnight Mon-Thu, to 1am Fri & Sat, to 6pm Sun; MEvangelismos) With excellent home-style cooking, this modern taverna lives up to its name (meaning 'homey'). It's decorated like a cosy bistro, and tables on the footpath allow people-watching without the normal Kolonaki bill. Pastas, salads and international fare are tasty, but try the daily *mayirefta* (ready-cooked meals), such as the excellent stuffed zucchini. Book ahead on weekends.

★ **Diporto Agoras**　　TAVERNA €

(📋210 321 1463; cnr Theatrou & Sokratous; plates €5-7; ⊙7am-7pm Mon-Sat, closed 1-20 Aug; MOmonia, Monastiraki) This quirky old taverna is an Athens dining gem. There's no signage – two doors lead to a rustic cellar where there's no menu, just a few dishes that haven't changed in years. The house speciality is *revythia* (chickpeas), usually followed by grilled fish and paired with wine from one of the giant barrels lining the wall.

Avocado　　VEGETARIAN €

(📋210 323 7878; www.avocadoathens.com; Nikis 30, Plaka; mains €8-13; ⊙noon-11pm Mon-Fri, 11am-11pm Sat, noon-7pm Sun; 🛜🥢; MSyntagma) This excellent, popular cafe offers a full array of vegan, gluten-free and organic treats – a rarity in Greece. Next to an organic market, and with a tiny front patio, here you can enjoy everything from sandwiches to quinoa with aubergine or mixed-veg coconut curry. Juices and mango lassis are all made on the spot.

★ **Kalderimi**　　TAVERNA €

(📋210 331 0049; Plateia Agion Theodoron, cnr Skouleniou, Monastiraki; mains €6-8; ⊙11am-8pm Mon-Sat; 🛜; MPanepistimio) Look behind the Church of Agii Theodori for this taverna offering Greek food at its most authentic. Everything is freshly cooked and delicious: you can't go wrong. Hand-painted tables edge a pedestrian street, providing for a feeling of peace in one of the busiest parts of the city. (It helps that it closes just before nearby bars get rolling.)

Tzitzikas kai Mermigas　　MEZEDHES €

(📋210 324 7607; www.tzitzikasmermigas.gr; Mitropoleos 12-14, Syntagma; mezedhes €6-12; ⊙noon-11pm; MSyntagma) Greek merchandise lines the walls of this cheery, modern

> **WORTH A TRIP**
>
> ## CAPE SOUNION
>
> The Ancient Greeks knew how to choose a site for a temple. At Cape Sounion, 70km south of Athens, the **Temple of Poseidon** (☎22920 39363; http://odysseus.culture.gr; adult/child €8/4; ☉9am-sunset) stands on a craggy spur that plunges 65m to the sea. Built in 444 BC – same year as the Parthenon – of marble from nearby Agrilesa, it is a vision of gleaming white Doric columns, of which 16 remain. Sailors in ancient times knew they were nearly home when they saw the first glimpse of white, and views from the temple are equally impressive. On a clear day you can see Kea, Kythnos and Serifos to the southeast, and Aegina and the Peloponnese to the west. The site also contains scant remains of a **propylaeum** (a fortified tower) and, on a lower hill to the northeast, a 6th-century **temple to Athena**.
>
> As with all major sites, it's best to visit first thing in the morning, or head there for sunset to enact Byron's lines from Don Juan: 'Place me on Sunium's marbled steep/ Where nothing save the waves and I/May hear our mutual murmurs sweep.' Byron was so impressed by Sounion that he carved his name on one of the columns (sadly, many other not-so-famous travellers followed suit).
>
> There is a decent cafe-restaurant at the site, and from the parking lot at the Athena temple, a steep path leads down to a small beach. KTEL runs frequent buses from the Mavromateon Terminal in Athens.

mezedhopoleio that sits smack in the middle of central Athens. It serves a tasty range of delicious and creative mezedhes (appetisers), such as honey-drizzled, bacon-wrapped Naxos cheese, to a bustling crowd of locals and tourists.

★ **Varvakios Agora**   MARKET €
(Athens Central Market; Athinas, btwn Sofokleous & Evripidou, Omonia; ☉7am-6pm Mon-Sat; Ⓜ Monastiraki, Panepistimio, Omonia) The streets around the colourful and bustling Varvakios Agora are a sensory delight. The **meat and fish market** fills the historic building on the eastern side, and the **fruit and vegetable market** is across the road. The meatmarket **tavernas** are an Athenian institution. Clients range from hungry market workers to elegant couples emerging from nightclubs in search of hangover-busting *patsas* (tripe soup).

 Drinking & Entertainment

The best central bars are around Kolokotroni St, north of Syntagma, and around Plateia Agia Irini in Monastiraki. Look especially at the ends of shopping arcades for old-style bars staffed with smart barkeeps and DJs.

Get off the metro at Keramikos and you'll be smack in the middle of the thriving Gazi scene. In Thisio, cafes along the pedestrian promenade Apostolou Pavlou have great Acropolis views; those along pedestrianised Iraklidon pack 'em in at night.

In summer much of the city's serious nightlife moves to glamorous, enormous seafront clubs radiating out from Glyfada. Many sit on the tram route, which runs to 2.30am on Friday and Saturday. If you book for dinner you don't pay cover; otherwise admission ranges from €10 to €20 and includes one drink. Glam up to get in.

★ **Tailor Made**   BAR
(☎213 004 9645; www.tailormade.gr; Plateia Agia Irini 2, Monastiraki; ☉8am-2am Mon-Thu, to 4am Fri & Sat, 9am-2am Sun; Ⓜ Monastiraki) Arguably the best third-wave coffee operation in Athens, with its own microroastery and hand-pressed teas, this place has outdoor tables alongside the flower market. At night it turns into a happening cocktail and wine bar. Menu includes homemade desserts (€5) and sandwiches (€6) too.

Tall's Toy   COCKTAIL BAR
(☎213 044 8864; www.facebook.com/tallstoybar; Karytsi 10, Syntagma; ☉noon-4am; Ⓜ Syntagma) With jewel-toned walls, old-fashioned wood fittings, open windows to the street and a usually chilled DJ, this is close to an ideal small downtown bar. The crowd is generally 30-something and older.

Dude   BAR
(☎210 322 7130; www.facebook.com/thedudebar; Kalamiotou 14, Monastiraki; ☉12.30pm-5am, to 6am Fri & Sat; Ⓜ Monastiraki) Exceptionally good music – obscure funk and soul that makes you feel like you're living a Quentin

REMBETIKA

Athens has some of the best *rembetika* (Greek blues) in intimate, evocative venues. Performances usually include both *rembetika* and *laïka* (urban popular music), start at around 11.30pm and do not have a cover charge, though drinks can be expensive. Most close May to September, so in summer try live-music tavernas around Plaka and Psyrri, or small bars in Exarhia.

Tarantino soundtrack – plays at this little bar on a pedestrian street. Moreover, the Dude abides till practically dawn.

 Shopping

Central Athens is one big shopping hub. The main (if generic) shopping street is pedestrianised Ermou, running from Syntagma to Monastiraki.

Monastiraki Flea Market　　　MARKET
(btwn Adrianou, Ifestou & Ermou, Monastiraki; ⏱daily May-Oct, Sun-Wed & Fri Nov-Apr; Ⓜ Monastiraki) What's touted as a day-in-day-out 'flea market' on Ifestou is now mostly souvenir shops, though there are still a few good artisans. The true flea market feel is on Plateia Avyssinias, where many of the *palaiopoleia* ('old-stuff sellers') are. For the best rummaging, come Sunday mornings, when many more dealers set up tables here, on Astiggos and across Ermou.

 Information

DANGERS & ANNOYANCES

➡ Stay aware of your surroundings at night, especially in streets around Omonia, where prostitutes and junkies gather, as well as by the Mavromateon bus terminal, as the adjacent park is a rather grim homeless encampment.

➡ Watch for pickpockets on the metro and at the markets.

➡ When taking taxis, ask the driver to use the meter or negotiate a price in advance. Ignore stories that the hotel you've chosen is closed or full: they're angling for a commission from another hotel.

➡ Bar scams are commonplace, particularly in Plaka and Syntagma. Beware the over-friendly!

➡ Strikes and demonstrations can disrupt public transport and close sights and shops (check http://livingingreece.gr/strikes).

EMERGENCY

SOS Doctors (☏ 210 821 1888, 1016; www.sosiatroi.gr; ⏱24hr) Pay service with English-speaking doctors who make house (or hotel) calls.

TOURIST INFORMATION

EOT (Greek National Tourism Organisation; ☏ 210 331 0347, 210 331 0716; www.visitgreece.gr; Dionysiou Areopagitou 18-20, Makrygianni; ⏱8am-8pm Mon-Fri, 10am-4pm Sat & Sun May-Sep, 9am-7pm Mon-Fri Oct-Apr; Ⓜ Akropoli) Free Athens map, transport information and *Athens and Attica* booklet. There's also a desk at **Athens Airport** (9am to 5pm Monday to Friday and 10am to 4pm Saturday).

Athens Airport Information Desk (⏱24hr) has Athens info, booklets and the free Athens Spotlighted discount card for restaurants and attractions. **Athens City Information Kiosk** (☏ 210 321 7116; www.thisisathens.org; Dionysiou Areopagitou & Leoforos Syngrou; ⏱9am-9pm May-Sep; Ⓜ Akropoli), at the Acropolis, has maps, transport information and all Athens info.

ⓘ Getting There & Away

AIR

Modern **Eleftherios Venizelos International Airport** (ATH; ☏ 210 353 0000; www.aia.gr), at Spata, 27km east of Athens, has all the modern conveniences.

BOAT

Most ferry, hydrofoil and high-speed catamaran services to the islands leave from Athens' massive port at Piraeus, southwest of Athens.

Purchase tickets online at **Greek Ferries** (☏ 28105 29000; www.greekferries.gr), over the phone or at booths on the quay next to each ferry. Travel agencies selling tickets also surround each port; there is no surcharge.

BUS

Athens has two main intercity (IC) KTEL bus stations, 5km and 7km to the north of Omonia. Pick up timetables at the tourist office, or look online.

Kifissos Terminal A (☏ 210 515 0025; Leoforos Kifisou 100, Peristeri; Ⓜ Agios Antonios) Buses to Thessaloniki, the Peloponnese, Ionian Islands and destinations in western Greece. Local bus 051 goes to central Athens (junction of Zinonos and Menandrou, near Omonia) every 20 minutes from 5am to midnight. Local bus X93 goes to/from the airport. Local bus 420 goes to/from Piraeus (junction of Akti Kondili and Thermopilon). Taxis to Syntagma cost €16 (€28 at night).

Liossion Terminal B (☏ 210 831 7153; Rikaki 6, Thymarakia; Ⓜ Agios Nikolaos, Attiki) Buses to central and northern Greece, such as Trikala (for Meteora) and Delphi. To get here, take the metro to Attiki and catch any local bus north on Liossion. Get off the bus at Liossion 260 (stop labelled 'Stathmos Iperastikon Leof'), backtrack to Gousiou and turn left. Taxis to Syntagma cost about €9 (€15 at night). Local bus X93 connects Kiffisos Bus Terminal A, Liossion Terminal B, and the Athens airport.

Mavromateon Terminal (⊡ 210 822 5148, 210 880 8000; www.ktelattikis.gr; cnr Leoforos Alexandras & 28 Oktovriou-Patision, Pedion Areos; ⊡ 2, 4, 5 or 11 to OTE, Ⓜ Viktoria) Buses for destinations in southern Attica leave from this station, about 250m north of the National Archaeological Museum.

TRAIN

Intercity (IC) trains to central and northern Greece depart from the central **Larisis train station** (Stathmos Larisis; ⊡ €1 per min 6am-11pm 14511; www.trainose.gr; Ⓜ Larissa Station), about 1km northwest of Plateia Omonias. For the Peloponnese, take the **suburban rail** (⊡ 14511; www.trainose.gr) to Kiato and change for a bus there.

At the time of research, Greece's train system was in a state of flux due to the financial crisis. Domestic schedules and fares should be confirmed online or at OSE. Tickets can be bought online.

ⓘ Getting Around

TO/FROM THE AIRPORT
Bus

Express buses operate 24 hours between the airport and the city centre, Piraeus and KTEL bus terminals. At the airport, buy tickets (€6; not valid for other forms of public transport) at the booth near the stops.

Plateia Syntagmatos Bus X95, one to 1½ hours, every 30 minutes, 24 hours. The Syntagma stop is on Othonos St.

Kifissos Terminal A Bus X93, one hour, every 30 minutes (60 minutes at night), 24 hours.

Piraeus Bus X96, 1½ hours, every 20 minutes, 24 hours. To Plateia Karaïskaki.

Metro

Metro line 3 goes to the airport. Some trains terminate early at Doukissis Plakentias; disembark and wait for the airport train (displayed on the train and platform screen). Trains run every 30 minutes, leaving Monastiraki between 5.50am and midnight, and the airport between 5.30am and 11.30pm.

Airport tickets costs €10 per adult or €18 return (return valid seven days). The fare for two/three or more passengers is €9/8 each, so purchase tickets together (same with suburban rail). Tickets are valid for all forms of public transport for 90 minutes (revalidate your ticket on final mode of transport).

Taxi

Fixed fares are posted. Expect €38/54 day/night (midnight to 5am) to the city centre, and €50/62 to Piraeus. It's around 30 to 45 minutes to the centre and an hour to Piraeus.

To prebook a taxi, contact Welcome Pickups (www.welcomepickups.com), at the same flat rate as regular taxis, with local English-speaking drivers.

PUBLIC TRANSPORT
Bus & Trolleybus

Local express buses, regular buses and electric trolleybuses operate every 15 minutes from 5am to midnight. The **OASA** (Athens Urban Transport Organisation; ⊡ 11185; www.oasa.gr; ◷ 6.30am-11.30pm Mon-Fri, from 7.30am Sat & Sun) website's trip planner shows routes

Metro

The metro works well and posted maps have clear icons and English translations. Trains operate from 5am to midnight, every four minutes during peak periods and every 10 minutes off-peak. On Friday and Saturday, lines 2 and 3 run till 2am. Get information at www.stasy.gr. All stations have wheelchair access.

TAXIS

Despite the many yellow taxis, it can be tricky getting one, especially during rush hour. Make sure the meter is on. Uber (www.uber.com) operates in Athens.

If a taxi picks you up while already carrying passengers, the fare is not shared: each person pays the fare on the meter minus any diversions to drop others (note what it's at when you get in). Short trips around central Athens cost about €5; there are surcharges for pickups at the airport and transport hubs, as well as holiday and night tariffs. Taxi services include

---

ⓘ PUBLIC TRANSPORT TICKETS

Tickets good for 90 minutes (€1.40) and a 24-hour/five-day travel pass (€4/10) are valid for all forms of public transport except for airport services. The three-day tourist ticket (€22) includes one return-trip airport ride. Children under six travel free; people under 18 and over 65 pay half-fare. Buy tickets in metro stations or transport kiosks or most *periptera* (kiosks). Validate the ticket in the machine as you board your transport of choice.

Athina 1 (☏ 210 921 0417, 210 921 2800; www.athens1.gr), **Enotita** (☏ 6980666720, 18388, 210 649 5099; www.athensradiotaxienotita.gr), Taxibeat and **Parthenon** (☏ 210 532 3300; www.radiotaxi-parthenon.gr).

Delphi

POP 2370

If the ancient Greeks hadn't chosen Delphi (from *delphis,* womb) as their navel of the Earth and built the Sanctuary of Apollo here, someone else would have thought of a good reason to make this eagle's-nest town a tourist attraction. Its cliff-side location is spectacular and, despite its overt commercialism and the constant passage of tour buses through the modern village, it still has a special feel. Ancient Delphi (and the adjoining village of Delphi) is 178km northwest of Athens.

◎ Sights

★**Ancient Delphi**   ARCHAEOLOGICAL SITE
(☏ 22650 82312; http://ancient-greece.org/history/delphi.html; combined ticket for site & museum adult/student/child, €12/6/free; ◷ 8am-8pm Apr-Oct, to 3pm Nov-Mar) Of all the archaeological sites in Greece, Ancient Delphi is the one with the most potent spirit of place. Built on the slopes of Mt Parnassos, overlooking the Gulf of Corinth and extending into a valley of olive trees, this World Heritage site's allure lies both in its stunning setting and its inspiring ruins.

★**Delphi Archaeological
Museum**   MUSEUM
(☏ 22650 82313; www.culture.gr; combined ticket for site & museum adult/student/child €12/6/free; ◷ 8am-8pm summer, to 2.45pm winter) From around the 8th century BC, Ancient Delphi managed to amass a considerable treasure trove, much of it reflected in its magnificent museum. Opinions vary about whether to visit the museum or the site (p536) first, where the sense of place is unmistakably powerful. On the other hand, the museum helps construct (or complete) an image of what the site must have looked like with its wealthy buildings, statues (remember, these were then painted in colour) and other valuable offerings.

🏃 Activities

Contact local and multilingual hiking expert Girogos Korodimo at **Trekking Hellas** (☏ 6981114041; www.trekking.gr; Arahova) in Arahova for guided treks around Parnassos, including the Korykeon Cave.

Korykeon Cave Walk   HIKING
The wonderful Korykeon Cave walk connects two ancient sites: the **Temple of Apollo** (Ancient Delphi) and Korykeon Cave, a sacred mountain cave-shrine for Pan, companion of nymphs. The cavern comprises a natural amphitheatre filled with stalactites and stalagmites. You can walk 80m inside (caution: it can be slippery). Many hikers hire a taxi in Delphi or Arahova to take

---

THE DELPHI ORACLE

The Delphic oracle was considered one of the most important religious (and political) sanctuaries in Greece. Worshippers flocked here from far and wide to consult the god Apollo on serious decisions. Apollo's instrument of communication was the Pythia, or priestess, usually an older woman, who sat on a tripod in the Temple of Apollo.

During visitations and consultations, the priestess chewed laurel leaves and entered a trance after inhaling vapours from a chasm below. Archaeologists believe this could have been ethylene wafting through a crack from a fault line (carried by water running underground). Her vapour-inspired, if somewhat vague, answers were spoken in tongue then 'translated' by the priests of Apollo. In fact, the oracle's reputation for infallibility may have rested with the often ambiguous or cryptic answers. Wars were fought, marriages sealed, leaders chosen and journeys begun on the strength of the oracle's visions. After all, the prophecies were the will of a god, so the oracle's reputation remained throughout antiquity.

Legend holds that one priestess suffered for her vagueness. When Alexander the Great visited, hoping to hear a prophecy that he would soon conquer the ancient world, the priestess refused direct comment, instead asking that he return later. Enraged, he dragged her by the hair out of the chamber until she screamed, 'Let go of me; you're unbeatable'. He quickly dropped her, saying, 'I have my answer'.

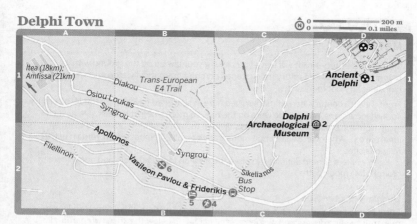

Delphi Town

ITALY, GREECE & TURKEY DELPHI

them about 2km from the cave entrance (around €30), and hike down to Delphi along the well-marked E4 path in about four hours.

**Delphi to Ancient
Kirra Walk** HIKING

The Delphi to Ancient Kirra hike meanders through shady olive groves – the largest continuous olive grove in Greece – and takes three to four hours to cover the 14km downhill trail. After lunch or a swim, return by bus (around €2) to Delphi. The E4 trailhead is marked 100m east of the Hotel Acropole.

🛏 Sleeping & Eating

★ Hotel Sibylla HOTEL €
(☎ 22650 82335; www.sibylla-hotel.gr; Vasileon Pavlou & Friderikis 9; s/d/tr €26/30/40; ❄ 🐾) A gem of a budget choice, cosy and central Sibylla has gracious and helpful owners along with eight light and tidy rooms, all with overhead fans and several with views across to the gulf. Book early.

★ Taverna Vakhos TAVERNA €€
(☎ 22650 83186; www.vakhos.com; Apollonos 31; mains €8-15; ⊙ noon-late; 🐾 ☕) Take the steps above the National Bank to this exceptional family taverna featuring traditional local fare and herbs gathered from the mountainside. Along with traditional *mayirefta* (ready-cooked meals) and hearty lamb and rooster recipes, Vakhos has an assortment of generous salads and veggie dishes ranging from *horta* (wild greens) to *trachanopita* (savoury pie of cracked wheat, zucchini and feta).

Delphi Town

ℹ Information

There is no tourist office, aside from a staffed exhibition space at the town hall. A useful website for information on the area is www.ancient-greece.org.

ℹ Getting There & Away

Buses (☎ 22650 82317; www.ktel-fokidas.gr; Vasileon Pavlou & Friderikis) depart from the eastern end of Vasileon Pavlou & Friderikis, next to the In Delphi restaurant, where tickets can be purchased between 9am and 8pm (the bus system's closing time). If you're taking an early bus, plan ahead and buy tickets the day before. The same especially applies in high season when buses fill up quickly. Travellers to Kalambaka/Meteora should find better connections via Lamia and Trikala, rather than Larissa.

METEORA

Meteora (meh-teh-o-rah) will leave you picking your jaw up off the ground with its magnificent late-14th-century monasteries perched dramatically atop enormous rocky pinnacles. Try not to miss it.

From the 11th century, hermit monks lived here in scattered caverns. By the 14th century, Turkish incursions into Greece were on the rise, so monks began to seek safe havens away from the bloodshed. The inaccessibility of the rocks of Meteora made them an ideal retreat. While there were once monasteries on all 24 pinnacles, six remain active religious sites.

Keen walkers should definitely explore the area on foot on the old and once-secret *monopatia* (monk paths).

Sights & Activities

Entry to each monastery is €3 and dress codes apply: no bare shoulders are allowed, men must wear trousers and women must wear skirts below the knee (wraparound skirts are generally provided at the entrances). Before planning your route, double-check days and opening hours. The six accessible monasteries are: **Moni Agias Triados** (Holy Trinity; ⊘ 9am-5pm Fri-Wed Apr-Oct, 9am-12.30pm & 3-5pm Fri-Tue Nov-Mar), **Moni Agias Varvaras Rousanou** (⊘ 9am-5.45pm Thu-Tue Apr-Oct, 9am-2pm Nov-Mar), **Moni Agiou Nikolaou** (Monastery of St Nikolaou Anapafsa; ⊘ 9am-3.30pm Sat-Thu Apr-Oct, 9am-2pm Nov-Mar), **Moni Agiou Stefanou** (St Stephen's; ⊘ 9am-1.30pm & 3.30-5.30pm Tue-Sun Apr-Oct, 9am-1pm & 3-5pm Tue-Sun Nov-Mar), **Moni Megalou Meteorou** (Grand Meteoron; ⊘ 9am-5pm Wed-Mon Apr-Oct, 9am-4pm Thu-Mon Nov-Mar) and **Moni Varlaam** (⊘ 9am-4pm Sat-Thu Apr-Oct, 9am-3pm Sat-Wed Nov-Mar).

Most of Meteora's tours and guided activities are run through the sharp crew at **Visit Meteora** (☑ 24320 23820; www.visitmeteora.travel; Patriarchou Dimitriou 2; ⊘ 8am-9pm). Guides are professional and very experienced. Guided activities-cum-tours include hiking and walking for the most part, and even rock climbing. The tours around Meteora are good value; most cost about €30 per person, including hotel pick-up and drop-off.

Sleeping & Eating

Doupiani House (☑ 24320 77555; www.doupianihouse.com; s/d/tr incl breakfast from €50/60/75; [P][⊛][@][☏]) The delightful Doupiani House has the lot: spotless, comfortable, tastefully decorated rooms with balconies or garden access. Its location – just outside the village – provides a window to Meteora, boasting one of the region's best panoramic views. There's a super breakfast on the terrace, birdsong and helpful hosts Toula and Thanasis.

Taverna Gardenia (☑ 6972700698; mains €7-11.50; ⊘ lunch & dinner; [⊛][☏]) Popular taverna for excellent *mousakas*, *yemista* (stuffed peppers and tomatoes) and other filling *mayirefta* (ready-cooked meals), along with great grilled and spit-roasted meats, which you can watch being prepared at the patio entrance. Just steps from the adjacent church square (Plateia Pavlou and Petrou).

Getting There & Around

From Athens, buses head north to Trikala (€29, five hours, six daily), where you can hop a bus to Kalambaka (€2.60, 30 minutes), Meteora's nearest village. Trains run between Athens and Kalambaka (regular/IC €23/290, seven/five hours, daily).

The main sealed road surrounding the entire Meteora complex of rocks and monasteries is about 15km in length. A bus (€1.80, 20 minutes) departs from Kalambaka and Kastraki at 9am and with the last bust returning at 5pm. That's enough time to explore at least three monasteries.

Santorini

POP 15,550

Santorini may well have conquered a corner of your imagination before you've even set eyes on it. With multicoloured cliffs soaring over 300m from a sea-drowned caldera, it rests in the middle of the indigo Aegean, looking like a giant slab of layered cake. Spooning the vast crater left by one of the biggest volcanic eruptions in history, the main island of Thira will take your breath away with its snow-drift of white Cycladic houses lining the cliff tops and, in places, spilling like icy cornices down the terraced rock. When the sun sets, the reflection on the buildings and the glow of the orange and red in the cliffs can be truly spectacular. Santorini is no secret and draws crowds for much of the year, yet it wears its tourism crown well.

◉ Sights

★ Museum of Prehistoric Thera
MUSEUM

(☑ 22860 22217; www.santorini.com/museums; Mitropoleos; adult/child €3/free; ⊙ 8.30am-3pm Wed-Mon) Opposite the bus station, this well-presented museum houses extraordinary finds excavated from Akrotiri and is all the more impressive when you realise just how old they are. Most remarkable is the glowing gold ibex figurine, dating from the 17th century BC and in mint condition. Also look for fossilised olive tree leaves from within the caldera, which date back to 60,000 BC.

★ Ancient Akrotiri
ARCHAEOLOGICAL SITE

(☑ 22860 81366; http://odysseus.culture.gr/h/3/eh351.jsp?obj_id=2410; adult/child €12/free; ⊙ 8am-8pm Apr-Oct, 8am-3pm Nov-Mar) In 1967, excavations uncovered an ancient Minoan city buried deep beneath volcanic ash from the catastrophic eruption of 1613 BC. Housed within a cool, protective structure, wooden walkways allow you to pass through the city. Peek inside three-storey buildings that survived, and see roads, drainage systems and stashes of pottery. The vibe of excitement still courses through the site, with continued excavations and discoveries. Guided tours are available (per person €10) and help to give context.

★ Art Space
GALLERY

(☑ 22860 32774; www.artspace-santorini.com; Exo Gonia; ⊙ 11am-sunset) FREE This unmissable, atmospheric gallery is on the way to Kamari, in Argyros Canava, one of the oldest wineries on the island. The atmospheric old wine caverns are hung with superb artworks, while sculptures transform lost corners and niches. The collection features some of Greece's finest modern artists. Winemaking is still in the owner's blood, and part of the complex produces some stellar vintages under the Art Space Wines label. Tastings (€5) enhance the experience.

★ Santorini Brewery Company
BREWERY

(☑ 22860 30268; www.santorinibrewingcompany.gr; ⊙ 11am-5pm Mon-Sat summer, shorter hr rest of year) The home of the island's in-demand Donkey beers (you may have seen the eye-catching logo on your travels) is well worth a stop. Sample the Yellow Donkey (golden ale), Red Donkey (amber ale), the Crazy Donkey (IPA) and the White Donkey (wheat with a touch of orange peel). All are unfiltered, unpasteurised and extremely palatable. There are free tastings, plus cool merchandise that makes a fun souvenir.

🏃 Activities

Walking

Walks in and around the capital, Fira, are spectacular, particularly heading north to Firostefani and Imerovigli along the caldera-edge pathway. This is about a 30-minute walk, one way.

If you want to keep walking, you can eventually reach Oia, but be aware that this is no small undertaking, and the trail beyond Imerovigli can be rough. It's about 9km in all, and a good three to four hours' walk one way. It's best not to undertake it in the heat of the day.

Beaches

Santorini's best beaches are on the east and south coasts. Sunbeds, beach bars and water sports operators are here to serve.

The long stretch of black sand, pebbles and pumice stones at **Perissa**, **Perivolos** and **Agios Georgios** is backed by bars, tavernas, hotels and shops and remains fairly relaxed.

Red (Kokkini) Beach, near Ancient Akrotiri in the south, has impressive red cliffs. Caïques from **Akrotiri Beach** can take you there and on to **White (Aspri)** and **Black (Mesa Pigadia) Beaches** for about €5 return.

Santorini (Thira)

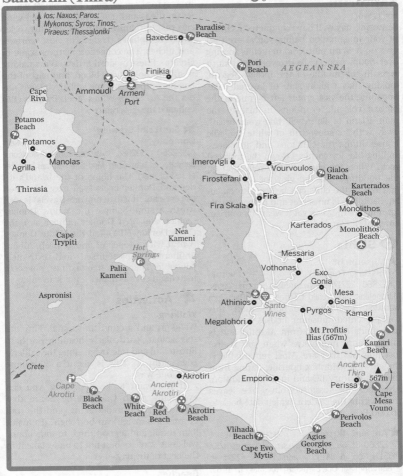

Vlihada, also on the south coast, has a beach backed by weirdly eroded cliffs as well as tavernas; it also has a photogenic fishing harbour.

Kamari is Santorini's best-developed resort, with a long beach of black sand. The beachfront road is dense with restaurants and bars, and things get extremely busy in high season. Boats connect Kamari with Perissa in summer.

Note: at times, Santorini's black-sand beaches become so hot that a sunlounge or mat is essential.

🛏 Sleeping

⭐ **Karterados Caveland Hostel**   HOSTEL €
(☎ 22860 22122; www.cave-land.com; Karterados; dm/d incl breakfast €25/90; ☺ Mar-Oct; ⓟ ❄ 🛜 🐾) This fabulous, chilled-out hostel is based in an old winery complex in Karterados about 2km from central Fira (see website for directions). Accommodation is in the big old wine caves, all of them with creative, colourful decor and good facilities. The surrounding garden is relaxing, and there are weekly barbecues, tennis courts, a swimming pool and yoga too.

★ **Stelios Place**   HOTEL €

(☎ 22860 81860; www.steliosplace.com; Perissa; d/tr/q €88/110/130; ❄@🖥🏊) This small, family-run hotel has a great position set back from the main drag in Perissa, one block from the beach. Well-equipped rooms sparkle with cleanliness, as does the swimming pool. Breakfast is available. Free airport or port transfers for those staying three nights or longer; note that off-peak rates fall to a bargain €35.

Villa Roussa   HOTEL €

(☎ 22860 23220; www.villaroussa.gr; Dekigala; s/d/tr from €80/100/120; 🅿❄🖥🏊) This place is all about location. Minutes from the caldera (without the prices to match) and seconds from the bus station (but thankfully out of earshot), it has fresh, immaculate rooms and helpful staff.

✗ Eating

★ **Theoni's Kitchen**   GREEK €

(☎ 22860 25680; www.theoniskitchen.com; Dekigala; mains from €7; ⏰noon-midnight) Theoni's isn't fancy and you won't be gazing out over the caldera, but this is the best 'mumma's kitchen' home-cooked Greek food you'll find, with smiling, friendly owners and good service. Expect decent-sized portions of Greek classics and daily specials that may well have you returning for more. The Greek salad here is exceptional.

Galini Cafe   CAFE €

(☎ 22860 22095; www.galinicafesantorini.com; mains €6-14; ⏰8am-midnight) Just as you reach Firostefani, this breezy cafe welcomes you with brightly coloured flowerpots and a hand-crafted school of fish swimming overhead. Chilled out and friendly, with unparalleled caldera views, it's a great place for breakfast or a light meal and cocktail at sunset. Gorgeous views.

Lolita's Gelato   ICE CREAM €

(☎ 22860 71279; www.lolitasgelato.com; cones €3-6) Situated near the bus station, Lolita's sells scoopfuls of homemade heaven, including classics like blueberry or pistachio, plus original flavours like rosewater and red pepper. Take a break while you wait for the bus.

Camille Stefani   GREEK €€

(☎ 22860 22762; www.camillestefani.com; mains €8-18; ⏰lunch & dinner) Going strong since the late '70s, this old-school rooftop restaurant has views across to the east coast. Its authentic, traditional atmosphere matches its meals. Dig into countless mezedhes like *saganaki* and stuffed vine leaves or opt for *mousakas,* chicken souvlaki or swordfish fillet. This place is as popular with locals as it is with tourists.

❶ Information

Dakoutros Travel (☎ 22860 22958; www.dakoutrostravel.gr; Fira; ⏰8.30am-10pm) Travel agency on the main street, just before Plateia Theotokopoulou. Ferry and air tickets sold; assistance with excursions, accommodation and transfers.

Information Kiosk (⏰9am-8pm Mon-Fri May-Sep) Seasonal information.

❶ Getting There & Around

AIR

Santorini Airport (JTR; ☎ 22860 28400; www.santoriniairport.com) has flights year-round to/from Athens (from €65, 45 minutes) with Olympic Air (www.olympicair.com) and Aegean Airlines (www.aegeanair.com). Seasonal European connections are plentiful, including easyJet from London, Rome, Geneva and Milan. Give yourself plenty of time when departing; the airport terminal can be mayhem.

BOAT

There are plenty of ferries each day to and from Piraeus and many Cyclades islands.

Thira's main port is Athinios. Buses (and taxis) meet all ferries. Accommodation providers can usually arrange transfers (to Fira per person is around €10).

> **DON'T MISS**
>
> ## OIA
>
> Perched on the northern tip of the island, the village of Oia (ee-ah) reflects the renaissance of Santorini after the devastating earthquake of 1956. Restoration work has whipped up its beauty and you will struggle to find a more stunning Cyclades village. Built on a steep slope of the caldera, many of its dwellings nestle in niches hewn into the volcanic rock.
>
> Not surprisingly, Oia draws enormous crowds. Try to visit in the morning or spend the night here. At sunset the town feels like a magnet for every traveller on the island.

BUS

There are frequent bus connections between Fira's bus station and the airport, located 5km east of Fira (€1.80, 20 minutes, 7am to 9pm). Most accommodation providers will arrange paid transfers.

KTEL Santorini Buses (☑ 22860 25404; http://ktel-santorini.gr) has a good website with schedules and prices. Tickets are purchased on the bus.

In summer buses leave Fira regularly for Oia, with more services pre-sunset (€1.80). There are also numerous daily departures for Akrotiri (€1.80), Kamari (€1.80), Perissa and Perivolos Beach (€2.40), and a few to Monolithos (€1.80).

Buses leave Fira for the port of Athinios (€2.30, 30 minutes) a half-dozen times per day, but it's wise to check times in advance. Buses for Fira meet all ferries, even late at night.

CAR

A car is the best way to explore the island during high season, when buses are intolerably overcrowded. Be very patient and cautious when driving – the narrow roads and heavy traffic, especially in and around Fira, can be a nightmare.

There are representatives of all the major international car-hire outfits, plus dozens of local operators in all tourist areas. A good local hire outfit is **Damigos Rent a Car** (☑ 22860 22048; www.santorini-carhire.com). You'll pay from around €50 per day for a car.

Rhodes

POP 115,000

By far the largest and historically the most important of the Dodecanese islands, Rhodes (ro-dos) abounds in beaches, wooded valleys and ancient history. Whether you arrive in search of buzzing nightlife, languid sun worshipping, diving in crystal-clear waters or to embark on a culture-vulture journey through past civilisations, it's all here. The atmospheric Old Town of Rhodes is a maze of cobbled streets that will spirit you back to the days of the Byzantine Empire and beyond. Further south is the picture-perfect town of Lindos, a soul-warming vista of sugar-cube houses spilling down to a turquoise bay.

ⓘ Getting There & Away

AIR

Diagoras Airport (RHO; ☑ 22410 88700; www.rhodes-airport.org) is near Paradisi on the west coast, 16km southwest of Rhodes Town. From there, **Aegean Airlines** (☑ 22410 98345; www.aegeanair.com; Diagoras Airport; ◷ 4.30am–9pm) and **Olympic Air** (☑ 22410 24571; www.olympicair.com; Ierou Lohou 9) fly to Athens and destinations throughout Greece, including several Dodecanese islands.

Taxis charge a set fare of around €25 to Rhodes Town, while buses connect the airport with Rhodes Town's Eastern Bus Terminal (25 minutes, €2.40) between 6.30am and 11.15pm daily.

BOAT

Rhodes is the main port in the Dodecanese. Two inter-island ferry operators operate from the Commercial Harbour, immediately outside the walls of Rhodes Old Town. **Dodekanisos Seaways** (☑ 22410 70590; www.12ne.gr; Afstralias 3, Rhodes Town) runs daily high-speed catamarans north up the chain, while **Blue Star Ferries** (☑ 22410 22461; www.bluestarferries.com; 111 Amerikis; ◷ 9am–8pm) provides slower and less frequent services. Tickets are available at the dock and from travel agents in Rhodes Town.

Getting To/From Turkey

Catamarans connect Rhodes' Commercial Harbour with Marmaris, Turkey (50 minutes), with two daily services in summer and two weekly in winter. Tickets cost €36 each way. Same-day returns cost €39, and longer-stay returns €70. For schedules and bookings, visit www.rhodes.marmarisinfo.com.

ⓘ Getting Around

BOAT

The quay at Mandraki Harbour is lined with excursion boats offering day trips to east-coast towns and beaches including Lindos.

Several islands can also be visited as day trips on Dodekanisos Seaways catamarans, departing from the Commercial Harbour. These include Symi and Kos (both daily), Halki and Tilos (both twice weekly), and Kastellorizo (once weekly).

BUS

Two bus terminals, a block apart in Rhodes Town, serve half the island each. There is regular transport across the island all week, with fewer services on Saturday and only a few on Sunday. Pick up schedules from the kiosks at either terminal, or from the EOT (Greek National Tourist Organisation) office.

The **Eastern Bus Terminal** (☑ 22410 27706; www.ktelrodou.gr) has frequent services to the airport (€2.40) and Kalithea Thermi (€2.20). From the **Western Bus Terminal** (☑ 22410 26300) there are services to East Coast beaches (€2.20 to €4) and Lindos (€5.20).

Rhodes Town

Rhodes Town is really two distinct and very different towns. The **Old Town** lies within but utterly apart from the New Town, sealed

Rhodes

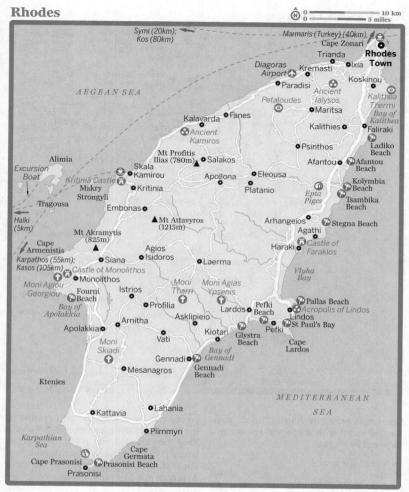

like a medieval time capsule behind a double ring of high walls and a deep moat. Nowhere else in the Dodecanese can boast so many layers of architectural history, with ruins and relics of the classical, medieval, Ottoman and Italian eras entangled in a mind-boggling maze of twisting alleys. Strolling its hauntingly pretty cobbled lanes, especially at night, is an experience no traveller should miss. The **New Town**, to the north, boasts upmarket shops and waterfront bars servicing the package crowd, along with the city's best beach, while bistros and bars lurk in the backstreets behind.

◉ Sights

A wander around Rhodes' Unesco World Heritage–listed Old Town is a must. It is reputedly the world's finest surviving example of medieval fortification, with 12m-thick walls. A mesh of Byzantine, Turkish and Latin architecture, the Old Town is divided into the Kollakio (the Knights' Quarter, where the Knights of St John lived during medieval times), the Hora and the Jewish Quarter. The **Knights' Quarter** is in the northern end of the Old Town and contains most of the medieval historical sights, while the **Hora**, often referred to as the Turkish

Rhodes Old Town

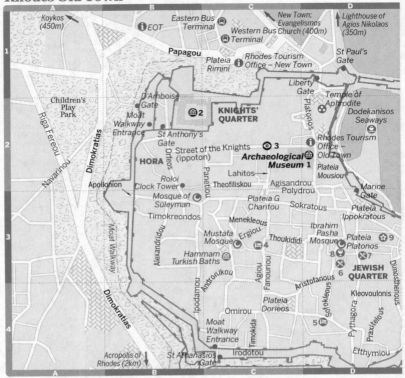

Quarter, is primarily Rhodes Town's commercial sector with shops and restaurants, thronged by tourists.

Palace of the Grand Master
HISTORIC BUILDING
(☑ 22413 65270, 22410 23359; €6; ⊙ 8am-8pm May-Oct, 8am-4pm Tue-Sun Nov-Apr) From the outside, the magnificent Palace of the Grand Master looks much as it did when erected by the Knights Hospitaller during the 14th century. During the 19th century, however, it was devastated by an explosion, so the interior as you see it today is an Italian reconstruction, completed in the '18th year of the Fascist Era' (1940). The dreary magisterial chambers upstairs hold haphazard looted artworks, so the most interesting section is the exhibit on ancient Rhodes downstairs.

Street of the Knights
HISTORIC SITE
(Ippoton; ⊙ 24hr) Austere and somewhat forbidding, the Street of the Knights (Ip-

poton) was home from the 14th century to the Knights Hospitaller who ruled Rhodes. They were divided into seven 'tongues', or languages, according to their birthplace – England, France, Germany, Italy, Aragon, Auvergne and Provence – each responsible for a specific section of the fortifications. As wall displays explain, the street holds an 'inn', or palace, for each tongue. Its modern appearance, though, owes much to Italian restorations during the 1930s.

★ Archaeological Museum
MUSEUM
(☑ 22413 65200; Plateia Mousiou; adult/child €8/free; ⊙ 9am-3pm Mon, 8am-8pm Tue-Fri, 8am-3pm Sat & Sun Apr-Oct, 9am-4pm Tue-Sat Nov-Mar) By far the best museum in the Dodecanese, this airy 15th-century former Knights' Hospital extends from its main building out into the beautiful gardens. Room after room holds magnificently preserved ancient treasures,

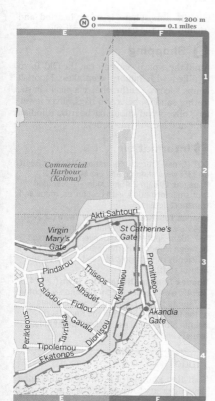

Rhodes Old Town

★ **Marco Polo Mansion**   BOUTIQUE HOTEL €€
(☏ 22410 25562; www.marcopolomansion.gr; Agiou Fanouriou 40; d incl breakfast €80-260; ☺ Apr-Oct; ❄ 🀫) With its stained-glass windows, dark-wood furniture, wood floors and raised beds, Marco Polo lovingly recreates an Ottoman ambience with verve and style, and is unlike anything in the Old Town. This former 15th-century pasha's house, complete with its own harem (now a magical suite), is like a journey back in time. Breakfast is served in the stunning flowering courtyard.

🍴 Eating

★ **Taverna Kostas**   GREEK €
(☏ 22410 26217; Pythagora 62; mains €7-10; ☺ 10am-late; ❄) Run by grandfather Kostas, this is not only the friendliest and best-value restaurant in the Old Town but also one of the best. Forget the bare lime-washed walls and simple decor; eating here is like taking a place at the table of a friend – indeed, regulars set their own places! Serves succulent octopus salad, calamari and sea bream.

Koykos   GREEK €
(☏ 22410 73022; http://koukosrodos.com; Mandilana 20-26; mains €3-10; ☺ breakfast, lunch & dinner; ❄ 🀫) This inviting complex, off a pedestrian shopping street, consists of several antique-filled rooms – a couple hold vintage jukeboxes – along with two bougainvillea-draped courtyards and a floral roof terrace. Best known for fabulous homemade pies, it also serves all the classic mezedhes (small

excavated from all over the island and ranging over 7000 years. Highlights include the exquisite 'Aphrodite Bathing' marble statue from the 1st century BC, a pavilion displaying wall-mounted mosaics, and a reconstructed burial site from 1700 BC that held not only a helmeted warrior but also his horse.

🛏 Sleeping

Minos Pension   PENSION €
(☏ 22410 31813; www.minospension.com; 5 Omirou St; d/ste €46/80; ❄ @ 🀫) Family-run Minos, perched beside a disused windmill on a quiet lane on the south side of the Old Town, has well-appointed, if slightly old-fashioned, studio rooms with gleaming kitchenettes and fridge. The compelling attraction, though, is the fabulous rooftop cafe, a lovely spot offering superb Old Town views. Downstairs there's a cosy communal lounge and book exchange.

DON'T MISS

KALITHEA THERMI

Italian architect Pietro Lombardi constructed opulent art deco spa, **Kalithea Thermi** (22410 65691; www.kalithea springs.gr; €3; ☺8am-8pm Apr-Oct, to 5pm Nov-Mar; ▦), on the site of ancient thermal springs in 1929. Its dazzling white-domed pavilions, pebble-mosaic courtyards and sweeping sea-view colonnades have appeared in movies such as Zorba the Greek and The Guns of Navarone, and have now been restored after years of neglect. In peak season its small sandy bathing beach and cafe get impossibly crowded.

Just 9km south of Rhodes Town, it can be reached by frequent buses from the eastern Bus Terminal (€2.20).

plates), plus meat and fish dishes, or you can drop in for a coffee or sandwich.

Nireas   SEAFOOD **€€**
(☎22410 21703; Sofokleous 45-47; mains €8-16; ☺lunch & dinner; ▣) Nireas' status as one of Rhodes' favourite seafood restaurants owes much to the sheer verve of genial owner Theo, from Symi – that and the beautifully prepared food, served beneath a vine-shaded canopy outside, or in the candlelit, lemon-walled interior. Be sure to sample the Symi shrimp, salted mackerel and, if you're in the mood, the 'Viagra' salad of small shellfish.

♫ Drinking & Entertainment

★**Raxati Cafe**   BAR
(☎22410 363651; Sofokleous 1-3; ☺10am-late; ☏) Overlooking stunning Ibrahim Pasha Mosque, this high-ceilinged, free-spirited bar and coffee house is as pretty as it is friendly. Its stone walls are peppered with vintage ad posters, there are recycled Singer sewing machine tables, and graceful chandeliers cast light across the stunning bar of glass spirit bottles. Snacks, cocktails, easy tunes and good conversation.

Cafe Chantant   LIVE MUSIC
(☎22410 32277; Dimokratou 3; ☺11pm-late Fri & Sat) Locals flock to sit at the long wooden tables here and listen to live traditional Greek music while drinking ouzo or beer. It's dark inside and you won't find snacks or nibbles,

but the atmosphere is warm-hearted and friendly and the band is always lively.

🛍 Shopping

Amid the typical souvenir tat, the Old Town is fillled with quality keepsakes: Moorish lamps, icons, anthracite classical busts, leather sandals, belts and bags, silver jewellery, olive wood chopping boards, Rhodian wine and local thyme honey.

ℹ Information

EOT (Greek Tourist Information Office; ☎22410 44335; www.ando.gr/eot; cnr Makariou & Papagou; ☺8am-2.45pm Mon-Fri) National tourism information, with brochures, maps and transport details.

Rhodes Tourism Office – New Town (☎22410 35495; www.rhodes.gr; Plateia Rimini; ☺7.30am-3pm Mon-Fri) Conveniently poised between Mandraki Harbour and the Old Town; efficiently run with lots of free brochures and helpful staff.

Rhodes Tourism Office – Old Town (☎22410 35945; www.rhodes.gr; cnr Platonos & Ippoton; ☺7am-3pm Mon-Fri) In an ancient building at the foot of the Street of the Knights, this helpful office supplies excellent street maps, leaflets and brochures.

Lindos

Your first glimpse of the ancient and unbelievably pretty town of Lindos is guaranteed to steal your breath away: the towering Acropolis radiant on the cypress-silvered hill, and the sugar-cube houses of the whitewashed town tumbling below it towards the aquamarine bay. Entering the town itself, you'll find yourself in a magical warren of hidden alleys, packed with the ornate houses of long-vanished sea captains that now hold appetising tavernas, effervescent bars and cool cafes. Pick your way past donkeys as you coax your calves up to the Acropolis and one of the finest views in Greece.

⊙ Sights

Two magnificent beaches line the crescent harbour that curves directly below the village. The larger, logically known as **Main Beach**, is a perfect swimming spot – sandy with shallow water – for kids. Follow a path north to the western tip of the bay to reach the smaller, taverna-fringed **Pallas Beach**. Don't swim near the jetty here, which is home to sea urchins.

Ten minutes' walk from town on the other, western, side of the Acropolis, sheltered St Paul's Bay is similarly caressed by turquoise waters.

★ **Acropolis of Lindos**　ARCHAEOLOGICAL SITE
(☑22413 65200; adult/concession/child €12/6/free; ⊘8am-7.40pm Tue-Fri, 8am-3pm Sat-Mon Apr-Oct, 8.30am-3pm Tue-Sun Nov-Mar) A steep footpath climbs the 116m-high rock above Lindos to reach the beautifully preserved Acropolis. First walled in the 6th century BC, the clifftop is now enclosed by battlements constructed by the Knights of St John. Once within, you're confronted by stunning ancient remains that include a **Temple to Athena Lindia** and a 20-columned **Hellenistic stoa**. Silhouetted against the deep blue sky, the stark white columns are dazzling, while the long-range coastal views are out of this world.

🛏 Sleeping & Eating

Electra Studios　PENSION €
(☑22440 31266; www.electra-studios.gr; studios €50; ⊘Apr-Oct; ❋🕙) A simple family-run pension, where the plain, but very pleasant, whitewashed rooms have varnished wooden twin beds, fridges and air-con. Some have balconies and there's also a lovely communal roof terrace overlooking a lemon grove and the sea.

Captain's House　CAFE €
(snacks €7; ⊘8am-midnight; ❋🕙) Soaked in Lyndian atmosphere, this nautically themed, 16th-century sea captain's house is perfect for a juice on your way down from the Acropolis. Grab a pew in the pebble-mosaic courtyard and ponder the fabulous carved stone reliefs.

★ **Calypso**　TAVERNA €€
(☑22440 32135; www.kalypsolindos.gr; mains €13; ⊘11am-midnight; ❋🕙) This former sea captain's residence with its beautiful stone relief is perfect for lunch or dinner on the roof terrace or inside. Sea bass, octopus, *makarounes* (homemade pasta served with fresh onions and melted local cheese) and grilled lamb chops are but a few of the delights. Try the 'Kalypso bread' with feta and tomato.

ℹ Information

Lindos Tourist Office (☑22440 31900; Plateia Eleftherias; ⊘9am-3pm) Small information kiosk at the entrance to central Lindos.

Greece Survival Guide

ℹ Directory A–Z

BARGAINING
Bargaining is acceptable in flea markets and markets, but elsewhere you are expected to pay the stated price.

CUSTOMS REGULATIONS
Import regulations for medicines are strict; if you are taking medication, make sure you get a statement from your doctor before you leave home. It is illegal, for instance, to take codeine into Greece without an accompanying doctor's certificate.

It is strictly forbidden to export antiquities (anything more than 100 years old) without an export permit. This crime is second only to drug smuggling in the penalties imposed. It is an offence to remove even the smallest article from an archaeological site.

DANGERS & ANNOYANCES
An unhealthy economy has led to an increase in pickpocketing; always be vigilant in busy bus stations, markets or on crowded streets.

Adulterated & Spiked Drinks
Adulterated drinks (known as *bombes*) are served in some bars and clubs in Athens and at resorts known for partying. These drinks are diluted with cheap illegal imports that leave you feeling worse for wear the next day.

At many of the party resorts catering to large budget-tour groups, spiked drinks are not uncommon; keep your hand over the top of your

---

ℹ SLEEPING PRICE RANGES

We have divided accommodation into budgets based on the rate for a double room in high season (May to August). Unless otherwise stated, all rooms have private bathroom facilities.

€ less than €60 (under €90 in Athens)

€€ €60–150 (€90–180 in Athens)

€€€ more than €150 (more than €180 in Athens)

For the Cyclades, the budgets are based on the rates in July and August. For Mykonos and Santorini only, the price ranges are as follows.

€ less than €100

€€ €100–250

€€€ more than €250

glass. More often than not, the perpetrators are foreign tourists rather than locals.

Tourist Police

The *touristikí astynomía* (tourist police) work in cooperation with the regular Greek police and are found in cities and popular tourist destinations. Each tourist police office has at least one member of staff who speaks English. If you need to report a theft or loss of passport, go to the tourist police first, and they will act as interpreters between you and the regular police.

EMBASSIES & CONSULATES

All foreign embassies in Greece are in Athens and its suburbs.

Australian Embassy (210 870 4000; www.greece.embassy.gov.au; 6th fl, Thon Bldg, cnr Leoforos Alexandras & Leoforos Kifisias, Ambelokipi)

Canadian Embassy (210 727 3400; www.greece.gc.ca; Ethnikis Antistaseos 48, Halandri)

French Embassy (210 339 1000; www.ambafrance-gr.org; Leoforos Vasilissis Sofias 7, Syntagma)

German Embassy (210 728 5111; www.athen.diplo.de; Dimitriou Karaoli 3, Kolonaki)

Irish Embassy (210 723 2771; www.embassyofireland.gr; Leoforos Vasileos Konstantinou 5-7, Pangrati)

Italian Embassy (210 361 7260; www.ambatene.esteri.it; Sekeri 2, Kolonaki)

Netherlands Embassy (210 725 4900; www.nederlandwereldwijd.nl/landen/griekenland; Leoforos Vasileos Konstantinou 5-7, Pangrati)

Turkish Embassy (210 726 3000; http://athens.emb.mfa.gov.tr; Vasileos Georgiou II 11, Syntagma) Has an additional branch in Athens (210 672 9830; Vasileos Pavlou 22, Psyhiko).

UK Embassy (210 727 2600; www.ukingreece.fco.gov.uk; Ploutarhou 1, Kolonaki)

US Embassy (210 721 2951; http://athens.usembassy.gov; 91 Vasilissis Sofias, Ilissia)

EMERGENCY & IMPORTANT NUMBERS

In Greece, the area code must be dialled, meaning you always dial the full 10-digit telephone number.

Country code	30
International access code	00
Ambulance	166
Highway rescue (ELPA)	104
Police	100
Tourist police	171

ETIQUETTE

Eating and dining Always accept an offer of a drink as it's a show of goodwill. Don't insist on paying if invited out; it insults your hosts. In restaurants, the pace of service might feel slow; dining is a drawn-out experience in Greece and it's impolite to rush waitstaff.

Photography In churches, avoid using a flash or photographing the main altar; this is considered taboo. At archaeological sites, you'll be stopped from using a tripod as this marks you as a professional and thereby requires special permission.

Places of worship If you plan to visit churches, carry a shawl or long sleeves and a long skirt or trousers to cover up in a show of respect. Some places will deny admission if you're showing too much skin.

Body language 'Yes' is a swing of the head and 'no' is a curt raising of the head or eyebrows, often accompanied by a 'ts' click-of-the-tongue sound.

INTERNET ACCESS

Free wi-fi is available in most cafes, restaurants and hotels. Some cities have free wi-fi zones in shopping and eating areas.

LGBT TRAVELLERS

In a country where the church still plays a prominent role in shaping society's views on issues such as sexuality, it comes as no surprise that homosexuality is generally frowned upon by many locals – especially outside major cities. While there is no legislation against homosexual activity, it pays to be discreet.

MONEY
ATMS

ATMs are found in every town large enough to support a bank and in almost all the tourist areas. Be aware that many ATMs on the islands can lose their connection for a day or two at a time, making it impossible for anyone (locals included) to withdraw money. It's useful to have a backup source of money.

Tipping

In restaurants a service charge is normally included in the bill, and while a tip is not expected (as it is in North America), it is always appreciated and should be left if the service has been good. Taxi drivers normally expect you to round up the fare.

OPENING HOURS

Always try to double-check opening hours before visiting. In summer, many shops in major tourist destinations are also open on Sunday. Hours decrease significantly in the shoulder and low seasons, when many places shut completely.

Banks 8am to 2.30pm Monday to Thursday, 8am to 2pm Friday

Bars 8pm to late

Cafes 10am to midnight

Clubs 10pm to 4am

Post offices 7.30am to 8pm Monday to Friday, 7.30am to 2pm Saturday (urban offices)

Restaurants 11am to 3pm and 7pm to 1am

Shops 8am to 3pm Monday, Wednesday and Saturday, 8am to 2.30pm and 5pm to 8.30pm Tuesday, Thursday and Friday

PUBLIC HOLIDAYS

All banks and shops and most museums and ancient sites close on public holidays.

Many sites (including the ancient sites in Athens) offer free entry on the first Sunday of the month, with the exception of July and August. You may also gain free entry on other locally celebrated holidays, although this varies across the country.

National public holidays:

New Year's Day 1 January

Epiphany 6 January

First Sunday in Lent February

Greek Independence Day 25 March

Good Friday March/April

Orthodox Easter Sunday 28 April 2019, 19 April 2020, 2 May 2021

May Day (Protomagia) 1 May

Whit Monday (Agiou Pnevmatos) 50 days after Easter Sunday

Feast of the Assumption 15 August

Ohi Day 28 October

Christmas Day 25 December

St Stephen's Day 26 December

TELEPHONE

The Greek telephone service is maintained by the public corporation known as OTE (pronounced o-*teh*). There are public telephones just about everywhere. The phones are easy to operate and can be used for local, long-distance and international calls. The 'i' at the top left of the push-button dialling panel brings up the operating instructions in English. Note that in Greece the area code must always be dialled when making a call (ie all Greek phone numbers are 10-digit).

All public phones use OTE phonecards (known as *telekarta*), not coins. These cards are widely available at *periptera* (street kiosks), corner shops and tourist shops. A local call costs around €0.30 for three minutes. There are also discount-card schemes with instructions in Greek and English; the talk time is enormous compared to the standard phonecard rates.

FOOD PRICE RANGES

The following price ranges refer to the average cost of a main course (not including service charges):

€ less than €10

€€ €10–20

€€€ more than €20

Mobile Phones

Local SIM cards can be used in European and Australian phones. Most other phones can be set to roaming. US and Canadian phones need to have a dual- or tri-band system.

There are several mobile service providers in Greece. Cosmote tends to have the best coverage in remote areas. All offer 2G connectivity and pay-as-you-talk services for which you can buy a rechargeable SIM card and have your own Greek mobile number. If you're buying a package, be sure to triple-check the fine print.

TRAVEL WITH CHILDREN

While Greece doesn't cater to kids in the way that some countries do – you won't find endless theme parks and children's menus here – children will be welcomed and included wherever you go. Greeks will generally make a fuss over your kids, who may find themselves receiving many small gifts and treats. Teach them a few Greek words and they will be made to feel even more appreciated.

Fresh milk is available in large towns and tourist areas, but harder to find on smaller islands. Supermarkets are the best place to look. Formula is available almost everywhere, as is heat-treated milk. Disposable nappies (diapers) are also available everywhere.

Travel on ferries, buses and trains is free for children under four. For those up to age 10 (ferries) or 12 (buses and trains) the fare is half. On domestic flights, you'll pay 10% of the adult fare to have a child under two sitting on your knee. Kids aged two to 12 travel for half-fare. If you plan to hire a car, it's wise to bring your own car seat or booster seat as rental agencies are not always reliable for these. If your kids aren't old enough to walk on their own for long, consider a sturdy carrying backpack; pushchairs (strollers) are a struggle in towns and villages with slippery cobblestones and high pavements.

VISAS

EU citizens do not need a visa to enter Greece. Nationals of some other countries, including Australia, Canada, Israel, Japan, New Zealand, Switzerland and the USA, do not need a tourist visa for stays of up to 90 days. To check the visa

requirements for your country, see www.
schengenvisainfo.com/tourist-schengen-visa.

❶ Getting There & Away

AIR

Greece has four main international airports that
take chartered and scheduled flights.

Eleftherios Venizelos International Airport
(p534) Athens' Eleftherios Venizelos International Airport lies near Spata, 27km east of
Athens. It has all the modern conveniences.

Nikos Kazantzakis International Airport
(HER; ☑ general 2810 397800, info 2810
397136; www.heraklion-airport.info) About 5km
east of Iraklio (Crete). Has a bank, an ATM, a
duty-free shop and a cafe-bar.

Diagoras Airport (p542) On the island of
Rhodes.

Makedonia International Airport (SKG;
☑ 2310 985 000; www.thessalonikiairport.
com) About 17km southeast of Thessaloniki.
Served by local bus 78 (half-hourly); a taxi
costs around €15 to €20.

LAND & SEA

You can now travel from London to Athens by
train and ferry in less than two days. By choosing to travel on the ground instead of the air,
you'll also be reducing your carbon footprint.

Train

The Greek railways organisation **OSE** (Organ-
ismos Sidirodromon Ellados; ☑ 14511; www.
trainose.gr) runs daily trains from Thessaloniki
to Sofia, Bulgaria, and to Belgrade, Serbia (via
Skopje, Republic of Macedonia), with a weekly
onward train to and from Budapest, Hungary.

Ferry

Ferries can get very crowded in summer. If you
want to take a vehicle across it's wise to make a
reservation beforehand. Please note that tickets
for all ferries to Turkey must be bought a day in
advance – and you will almost certainly be asked
to turn in your passport the night before the trip.
It will be returned the next day before you board
the boat. Port tax for departures to Turkey is
around €15.

❶ Getting Around

AIR

The vast majority of domestic mainland flights
are handled by the country's national carrier
Aegean Airlines (A3; ☑ 801 112 0000; www.
aegeanair.com) and its subsidiary, **Olympic Air**
(☑ 801 801 0101; www.olympicair.com). You'll
find offices wherever there are flights, as well as
in other major towns.

There are discounts for return tickets for travel between Monday and Thursday, and bigger

discounts for trips that include a Saturday night
away. Find full details and timetables on airline
websites.

The baggage allowance on domestic flights is
15kg, or 20kg if the domestic flight is part of an
international journey.

BOAT

Greece has an extensive network of ferries – the
only means of reaching many of the islands.
Schedules are often subject to delays due to
poor weather and industrial action, and prices
fluctuate regularly. In summer, ferries run regular services between all but the most out-of-the-
way destinations; however, services seriously
slow down in winter (and in some cases stop
completely).

BUS

The bus network is comprehensive. All long-
distance buses, on the mainland and the islands,
are operated by regional collectives known as
KTEL. Details of inter-urban buses throughout
Greece are available by dialling 14505. Bus fares
are fixed by the government and bus travel is
very reasonably priced. A journey costs approximately €5 per 100km.

CAR & MOTORCYCLE

No one who has travelled on Greece's roads will
be surprised to hear that the country's road
fatality rate is one of the highest in Europe. More
than a thousand people die on the roads every
year, with 10 times that number of people in-
jured. Overtaking is listed as the greatest cause
of accidents.

Heart-stopping moments aside, your own car
is a great way to explore off the beaten track. The
road network has improved enormously in recent years; many roads marked as dirt tracks on
older maps have now been asphalted and many
of the islands have very little traffic. There are
regular (if costly) car-ferry services to almost
all islands.

TURKEY

Antalya

POP 1.06 MILLION

Once seen simply as the gateway to the
Turkish Riviera, Antalya today is very much
a destination in its own right. Situated
smack on the Gulf of Antalya (Antalya Kör-
fezi), the largest Turkish city on the western Mediterranean coast is both classically
beautiful and stylishly modern. At its core
is the wonderfully preserved old city district
of Kaleiçi – literally 'within the castle'. The

old city wraps around a splendid Roman-era harbour with cliff-top views of hazy-blue silhouettes of the Beydağları (Bey Mountains). Just outside the central city is one of Turkey's finest museums.

☉ Sights

★ Antalya Museum
MUSEUM

(☏ 0242-238 5688; www.antalyamuzesi.gov.tr/en; Konyaaltı Caddesi; ₺20; ☺ 8am-7pm Apr-Oct, to 5pm Nov-Mar) Do not miss this comprehensive museum with exhibitions covering everything from the Stone and Bronze Ages to Byzantium. The Hall of Regional Excavations exhibits finds from ancient cities in Lycia (such as Patara and Xanthos) and Phrygia, while the Hall of Gods displays beautiful and evocative statues of 15 Olympian gods, many in excellent condition. Most of the statues were found at Perge, including the sublime Three Graces and the towering Dancing Woman dominating the first room.

★ Kaleiçi
HISTORIC SITE

Antalya's historic district is a sight in itself and you could happily spend an hour or so strolling the narrow lanes here while admiring the mix of finely restored and creakily dilapidated Ottoman-era architecture.

Roman Harbour
WATERFRONT

(İskele Caddesi) The Roman harbour at the base of Kaleiçi's slope was Antalya's lifeline from the 2nd century BC until late in the 20th century, when a new port was constructed about 12km to the west, at the far end of Konyaaltı Plajı. The harbour was restored during the 1980s and is now a marina for yachts and excursion boats. An **elevator** (Asansör) descends the cliff to the harbour from the western end of Cumhuriyet Meydanı.

🏃 Activities

Sefa Hamamı
HAMAM

(☏ 0532 526 9407, 0242-241 2321; www.sefahamam.com; Kocatepe Sokak 32; soak & steam ₺65, full hamam (soak, soap, scrub & steam) ₺100; ☺ 11am-8pm Mon-Sat) This atmospheric hamam retains much of its 13th-century Seljuk architecture. Men and women bathe separately, with mixed bathing also available.

🛏 Sleeping

Lazer Pension
PENSION €

(☏ 0242-242 7194; www.lazerpansiyon.com; Hesapçı Sokak 61; s/d/tr €15/23/32; ❄ ✳ 🛜) Recommended by Antalya regulars, this excellent no-frills option has spacious rooms with modern bathrooms, an upstairs terrace and a courtyard decorated with pot plants. Much care has been taken to ensure the rooms are shipshape, giving this old-town pension the edge on its competitors.

Sabah Pansiyon
PENSION €

(☏ 0242-247 5345, 0555 365 8376; www.sabahpansiyon.com; Hesapçı Sokak 60; s/d/tr €15/20/30, 2-bedroom self-catering apt €75-100; ❄ ✳ 🛜 ▣) The Sabah has long been the first port of call for travellers watching their kuruş, thanks to the Sabah brothers who run the show and organise transport and tours aplenty. Rooms vary in size but all are sweet, simple and superclean. The courtyard is prime territory for meeting other travellers and its onsite restaurant Yemenli turns out decent Turkish classics.

★ White Garden Pansion
PENSION €€

(☏ 0242-241 9115; www.whitegardenpansion.com; Hesapçı Geçidi 9; s/d €30/40, self-catering apt €95-140; ❄ ✳ @ 🛜 ▣) A positively delightful place to stay, combining quirky Ottoman character, modern rooms with an old-world veneer, and excellent service from Metin and team. The building itself is a fine restoration and the courtyard is particularly charming with its large pool. The breakfast also gets top marks.

🍴 Eating

A nearly endless assortment of cafes and restaurants is tucked in and around the Kaleiçi area. For cheap eating, walk east to the Dönerciler Çarşısı or north to the rooftop kebap places across the street from Kale Kapısı.

Dönerciler Çarşısı
KEBAP €

(Market of Döner Makers; İnönü Caddesi; mains ₺12-30; ☺ 11am-11pm) Its street sign says 'İnönü Caddesi' and the canopy of umbrellas has given it the nickname 'Şemsiye Sokak' (Umbrella St). Locals, however, refer to this pedestrianised lane and the gloomy arcade to the east as the Dönerciler Çarşısı. The entire street is devoted to kebap shops churning out grilled-meat dishes.

Yemenli
TURKISH €

(☏ 0242-247 5345; Hesapçı Sokak 60; mains ₺16.50-38; ☺ noon-11pm; 🛜) Tried-and-true Turkish favourites are served up by the team behind Sabah Pansiyon (and named after their Yemen-born grandfather) with

TURKEY AT A GLANCE

Don't Miss

İstanbul Board a commuter ferry and flit between Europe and Asia in under an hour. At sunset, the tapering minarets and Byzantine domes of the Old City are thrown into relief against a dusky pink sky – it's the city's most magical sight.

Ephesus Undoubtedly the most famous of Turkey's countless ancient sites, and considered the best-preserved ruins in the Mediterranean, Ephesus (Efes) is a powerful tribute to Greek artistry and Roman architectural prowess.

Hamams Experience the hamam experience – a soak and a scrub followed by a good (and optional) pummelling. After this cleansing ritual and cultural experience, the world (and your body) will never feel quite the same again; do leave time to relax with a çay (tea) afterwards.

Cappadocia This hard-set honeycomb landscape looks as if it were sculpted by a swarm of genius bees, the effects of erosion on rock formed of ash from megalithic volcanic eruptions. Humans have also left their mark here, in the Byzantine frescoes in rock-cut churches and in the bowels of complex underground cities.

Aya Sofya Even in mighty İstanbul, nothing beats the Church of the Divine Wisdom, which was for centuries the greatest church in Christendom. Gaze up at the floating dome where glittering mosaics depict biblical scenes and ancient figures.

Itineraries

One Week

Most first-time visitors to Turkey arrive with two ancient names on their lips: İstanbul and Ephesus. This journey across the Sea of Marmara and down the Aegean coast covers both. You'll need at least three days in **İstanbul** to even scrape the surface of its millennia of history. The top three sights are the Aya Sofya, Topkapı Palace and the Blue Mosque, but there's a sultan's treasury of other sights and activities, including a cruise up the Bosphorus, nightlife around İstiklal Caddesi, and the Grand Bazaar. From İstanbul, catch a bus or hop on the fast train to **Ankara**, the Turkish capital, with sights that give an insight into Turkish history, ancient and modern. Leave a couple of days to explore **Cappadocia**, based in a cave hotel in Göreme, the travellers' hang-out surrounded by valleys of fairy chimneys.

Two Weeks

From Cappadocia, head southwest to **Konya** with its magnificent mosques and the birthplace of the Whirling Dervishes. Carry on to **Antalya** for its Roman-Ottoman quarter against the backdrop of a jaw-dropping mountain range. Continue west to **Selçuk,** timing your visit to coincide with the sprawling Saturday market. This pleasantly rustic town is also the base for visiting your final stop, the glorious **Ephesus** (Efes), the best-preserved classical city in the eastern Mediterranean.

Essential Food & Drink

Simit Bread ring studded with sesame seeds; sold in bakeries and by street vendors.

Dolma Something stuffed with rice and/or meat. Try midye dolma: mussels stuffed with spiced rice.

Döner kebap Lamb cooked on a revolving upright skewer then thinly sliced and served in bread with salad and a sprinkling of sumac.

Gözleme Thin savoury pancakes filled with cheese, spinach, mushrooms or potato.

Ayvalık tost Toasted sandwich crammed with cheese, spicy sausage, pickles, tomatoes, ketchup, mayonnaise and anything else its creator can think of.

Tatlı(lar) Sweets; often baklava, stewed fruit or a milk-based pudding.

Türk kahve A thick and powerful brew, Turkish coffee is usually drunk in a couple of short sips.

Getting Around

Bus Generally efficient and good value, with frequent services between the major cities and tourist spots.

Air Turkey is a vast country and domestic flights are an affordable way of reducing travel time.

Train The growing network of high-speed services offers rapid routes across Anatolia, eg between İstanbul and Ankara.

Car A great way to explore rural areas, with rental operators in cities and airports. Drive on the right. Petrol is expensive.

Ferry Regular services cross the Sea of Marmara and link parts of the Aegean coast.

When to Go

İstanbul

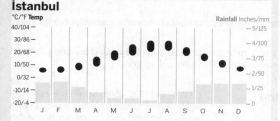

Jun–Aug Prices and temperatures highest. Expect crowds and book ahead.

May & Sep Smaller crowds, except during Kurban Bayramı holiday. Warm spring and autumn temperatures.

Oct–Apr Accommodation in tourist areas close or offer discounts. İstanbul's low season is November to mid-March.

Arriving in Turkey

Atatürk International Airport (İstanbul) Metro and tram to Sultanahmet (₺8, 6am to midnight, one hour); Havataş bus to Taksim Meydanı (₺11, 4am to 1am, 45 minutes); taxi to Sultanahmet (₺45, 35 minutes); taxi to Beyoğlu (₺55, 45 minutes).

Sabiha Gökçen International Airport (İstanbul) Havataş bus to Taksim Meydanı (₺14, 3.30am to 1am, 1½ hours), from where a funicular (₺4) and tram (₺4) travel to Sultanahmet (30 minutes); Havataş bus to Kadıköy (₺9, 4am to 1am, one hour); taxi to Sultanahmet (₺155, 1¼ hours) and Beyoğlu (₺140, one hour).

Top Phrases

Hello. Merhaba.

Goodbye. Hoşçakal.

Please. Lütfen.

Thank you. Teşekkür ederim.

How much is it? Ne kadar?

Resources

Go Turkey (www.goturkey-tourism.com)

Turkish Cultural Foundation (www.turkishculture.org)

All About Turkey (www.allaboutturkey.com)

Set Your Budget

➡ Dorm bed: €7–24

➡ Balık ekmek (fish kebap): ₺8–10

➡ Beer: ₺7–12

Kaleiçi District

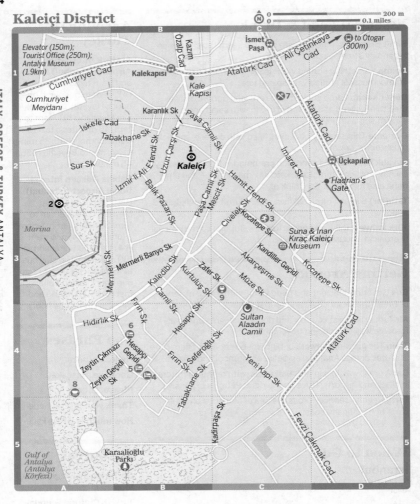

tables spilling out onto the street right in front of the hotel. Service is friendly and on the ball, and a large Efes is only ₺10.

🍷 Drinking & Nightlife

★ Castle Café
CAFE, BAR
(☎ 0242-248 6594; Hıdırlık Sokak 48/1; ⊗ 8am-11pm) This lively hang-out along the cliff edge is a local favourite, attracting a crowd of young Turks with its affordable drinks (300mL beer ₺11). Service can be slow, but the terrace's jaw-dropping views of the beaches and mountains west of town more than compensate, as does the well-priced menu (mains ₺14 to ₺24) featuring fish and chips and burgers.

Dem-Lik
BAR
(☎ 0242-247 1930; Zafer Sokak 6; ⊗ noon-midnight) This chilled-out garden bar-cafe, with tables scattered along stone walls and beneath shady fruit trees, is where Antalya's university crowd reshapes the world over ice-cold beers, while listening to Turkish troubadours perform live jazz, reggae, blues and more (on Wednesday, Friday and Saturday evenings). There's a menu of cheap pasta and other international dishes as well.

Kaleiçi District

ⓘ Information

Antalya Guide (www.antalyaguide.org) A comprehensive website with info on everything Antalya-related, from climate to cultural events.

Tourist Office (☏ 0242-241 1747; Cumhuriyet Caddesi; ⏱8am-6pm) This office with city maps and bochures is located at the back of a garden (signposted from the street), just after the Jandarma building. Minimal English spoken.

ⓘ Getting There & Away

Antalya's busy international airport is 10km east of the city centre. Low-cost carriers operate plentiful direct flights to European cities. Turkish Airlines (www.turkishairlines.com) and Pegasus Airlines (www.flypgs.com) both fly to domestic cities, including several daily flights to/from İstanbul.

The otogar (bus station) is 4km north of the centre with services to Denizli (₺40, four hours), Göreme (₺65, nine hours) and İstanbul (₺100, 11½ hours).

Antalya's AntRay tram is the simplest way to travel between downtown Antalya and the airport (40 minutes) or the bus station (20 minutes).

Selçuk

POP 35,960

Were it not for nearby Ephesus, Selçuk might be just another Turkish farming town, with its lively weekly markets and ploughs rusting away on side streets. That said, the gateway to Ephesus does have plenty of its own attractions, many topped with a picture-perfect stork's nest: Roman/Byzantine aqueduct arches, a lone pillar remaining from one of the Seven Wonders of the Ancient World, and the hilltop Byzantine ruins of the Basilica of St John and Ayasuluk Fortress.

◉ Sights

Ephesus Museum   MUSEUM
(☏ 0232-892 6010; Uğur Mumcu Sevgi Yolu Caddesi; ₺10; ⏱8am-6.30pm Apr-Oct, to 4.30pm Nov-Mar) An essential stop on every Ephesus itinerary, this small museum contains artefacts from the ancient city, including scales, jewellery and cosmetic boxes as well as coins, funerary goods and ancient statuary. Highlights include the famous phallic terracotta effigy of Bes in **room 2**, the huge statue of a resting warrior in **room 4** and the two extraordinary multibreasted marble statues of Artemis in **room 7**. The timelines on the walls are extremely useful for placing objects within their historical context.

Ayasuluk Fortress   FORTRESS
(Ayasuluk Kalesi; St Jean Caddesi; incl Basilica of St John ₺10; ⏱8am-6pm Apr-Oct, to 4pm Nov-Mar) Selçuk's crowning achievement is accessed on the same ticket as the Basilica of St John (p556), once the citadel's principal structure. Earlier and extensive excavations here, concluded in 1998 after a quarter century,

---

WORTH A TRIP

PRIENE, MILETUS & DIDYMA

Selçuk is a good base for visiting the superb ancient cities of **Priene** (₺5; ⏱8.30am-7pm Apr-Oct, to 5pm Nov-Mar), **Miletus** (Milet; ₺10, parking ₺4, audio guide ₺10; ⏱8.30am-7pm Apr-Oct, to 5pm Nov-Mar) and **Didyma** (₺10, audio guide ₺10; ⏱8.30am-7pm mid-May–mid-Sep, to 5pm mid-Sep–mid-May), all to the south. If you're pushed for time, a 'PMD' tour from Selçuk costs between €45 and €60.

Perched high on the craggy slopes of Mt Mykale, Priene has a beautiful windswept setting; Miletus boasts a spectacular theatre and Didyma hosts the stupendous Temple of Apollo.

Selçuk

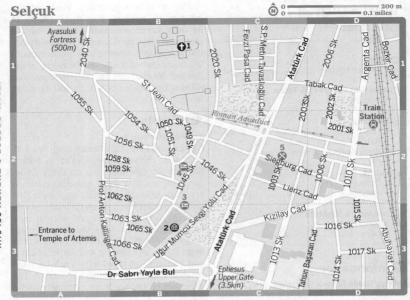

Selçuk

proved that there were castles on Ayasuluk Hill going back beyond the original Ephesian settlement to the Neolithic age. The fortress' partially restored remains, about 350m north of the church, date from Byzantine, Seljuk and Ottoman times and are well worth a visit.

Basilica of St John   CHURCH

(Aziz Yahya Kilisesi; St Jean Caddesi; incl Ayasuluk Fortress ₺10; ⊙8am-6pm Apr-Oct, to 4pm Nov-Mar) Despite a century of restoration, the once-great basilica built by Byzantine Emperor Justinian (r 527–565) remains a skeleton of its former self. Nonetheless, it is an atmospheric site with excellent hilltop views, and the best place in the area for a sunset photo. The information panels and scale model highlight the building's original grandeur, as do the marble steps and monumental gate.

🛏 Sleeping & Eating

★ Homeros Pension   PENSION €

(☑ 0535 310 7859, 0232-892 3995; www.homerospension.com; 1048 Sokak 3; s/d €15/28, with shared bathroom €10/17; ❄ 🛜) This long-time family-run favourite offers 10 rooms in two buildings. The decor features colourful hanging textiles and handcrafted furniture made by owner Derviş, a carpenter, antiques collector and ultra-welcoming host. Enjoy some of the best views in town on the roof terraces (one at each house). The six rooms in the newer (main) building are the nicest.

★ Boomerang Guesthouse   GUESTHOUSE €€

(☑ 0232-892 4879, 0534 055 4761; www.boomerangguesthouse.com; 1047 Sokak 10; dm/s/d/f €8/30/40/70, s/d with shared bathroom €20/30; ❄ @ 🛜) People keep coming back to this welcoming Turkish/Australian-Chinese operation to spend chilled-out evenings among the trees in the stone courtyard with its popular bar-restaurant. The best of the 10 rooms have balconies (ie Nos 13 and 14); all have kettles and fridges. The windowless basement dorm has 12 single beds, shares two bathrooms and has fans rather than air-con.

Ramazan Usta Gaziantep Kebap KEBAB €
(☑0232-892 8383; Siegburg Caddesi 11; kebaps ₺15-20; ⊘5-11pm Sun, Mon & Thu, 6pm-midnight Tue & Sat, 5pm-midnight Wed) A pocket-sized outpost of Turkey's southeast located in a pedestrianised street near the aqueduct, Master Ramazan's *kebapçı* (kebap eatery) serves the best meat dishes in town for some of the cheapest prices. It even serves beer. No wonder it's popular with locals and tourists alike.

DON'T MISS

EPHESUS

More than anywhere else, the Graeco-Roman world comes alive at Ephesus (Efes; www. ephesus.us; main site adult/child ₺40/free, Terraced Houses ₺20, parking ₺7.50; ⊘8am-6.30pm Apr-Oct, to 4.30pm Nov-Mar). After almost 150 years of excavation, the city's recovered and renovated structures have made Ephesus Europe's most complete classical metropolis – and that's with 82% of the city still to be unearthed.

As capital of Roman Asia Minor, Ephesus was a vibrant city of over 250,000 inhabitants. So important and wealthy was Ephesus that its Temple of Artemis (en route to present-day Selçuk) was the biggest on earth, and one of the Seven Wonders of the Ancient World.

There is a wealth of monuments to explore but don't miss the following:

Curetes Way Named for the demigods who helped Lena give birth to Artemis and Apollo, the Curetes Way was Ephesus' main thoroughfare, 210m long and lined with statuary, religious and civic buildings, and rows of shops selling incense, silk and other goods, workshops and even restaurants. Walking this street is the best way to understand Ephesian daily life.

Great Theatre Originally built under Hellenistic King Lysimachus, the Great Theatre was reconstructed by the Romans between AD 41 and 117 and it is thought St Paul preached here. However, they incorporated original design elements, including the ingenious shape of the *cavea* (seating area), part of which was under cover. Seating rows are pitched slightly steeper as they ascend, meaning that upper-row spectators still enjoyed good views and acoustics – useful, considering that the theatre could hold an estimated 25,000 people.

Library of Celsus This magnificent library dating from the early 2nd century AD, the best-known monument in Ephesus, has been extensively restored. Originally built as part of a complex, the library looks bigger than it actually is: the convex facade base heightens the central elements, while the middle columns and capitals are larger than those at the ends. Facade niches hold replica statues of the Four Virtues. From left to right, they are Sophia (Wisdom), Arete (Goodness), Ennoia (Thought) and Episteme (Knowledge).

Temple of Hadrian One of Ephesus' star attractions and second only to the Library of Celsus, this ornate, Corinthian-style temple honours Trajan's successor and originally had a wooden roof when completed in AD 138. Note its main arch; supported by a central keystone, this architectural marvel remains perfectly balanced, with no need for mortar. The temple's designers also covered it with intricate decorative details and patterns: Tyche, goddess of chance, adorns the first arch, while Medusa wards off evil spirits on the second.

Terraced Houses (₺20) The roofed complex here contains seven well-preserved Roman homes built on three terraces, which are well worth the extra visiting fee. As you ascend the stairs through the enclosure, detailed signs explain each structure's evolving use during different periods. Even if you aren't a history buff, the colourful mosaics, painted frescoes and marble provide breathtaking insight into the lost world of Ephesus and its aristocracy.

Dolmuşes serve the Lower Gate (₺2.50) every half-hour in summer, and hourly in winter. A taxi from Selçuk costs about ₺20, but it's also a pleasant 3.5km walk from town.

OLYMPOS & ÇIRALI

About 65km northeast of Demre, a road leads southeast from the main highway to the tiny hamlets of Olympos and Çıralı. A 7.5km section of the **Lycian Way** winds through the wild Mediterranean hills between the two villages.

Ancient Olympos is popular for its sand-and-shale **beach** with its tumble of seaside ruins and backpacker camp community. On the other side of the mountain, and over the narrow Ulupınar Stream, Çıralı is a holiday hamlet with dozens of hotels and pensions that may look like it was born yesterday but contains that most enigmatic of classical icons: the **eternal flame of the Chimaera**. Olympos devoutly worshipped Hephaestus (Vulcan), the god of fire.

Sleeping

Şaban Pension (☎0242-892 1265; www.sabanpansion.com; Yazırköyü, Olympos; incl half-board dm €9, bungalows s/d/tr €24/33/43, tree houses without bathroom s/d €19/24; P♿❄🛜) Our personal favourite, this is the place to lounge in a hammock in the orchard or on a wooden platform by the stream enjoying sociable owner Meral's home cooking. Şaban isn't a party spot; it's a tranquil getaway where relaxed conversations strike up around the bonfire at night. Accommodation is in charming cabins and tree houses.

Orange Motel (☎0242-825 7328; www.orangemotel.net; Yanartaş Yolu, Çıralı; s/d/tr €50/60/75, bungalows €70-90; P♿❄🛜) In the middle of an orange grove, the Orange feels like a farm despite its central location. Come here in spring and you'll never forget the overwhelming scent and buzz of bees. The garden is hung with hammocks, rooms are veritable wooden suites and there's a house travel agency. Breakfast features homemade orange and lemon marmalades and orange-blossom honey.

Getting There & Away

From the Olympos Junction, dolmuşes (₺6, 15 minutes) depart for Olympos every half-hour between 8am and 8pm from May to October. Returning, minibuses leave Olympos at 9am then every hour until 7pm. From October to April they generally run two-hourly, with the last minibus usually departing Olympos at 6pm.

Transport to Çıralı (₺6, 15 minutes) from the junction on the coastal highway is irregular; minibuses often don't depart until they are full, so you may wait some time. On average, there are departures every hour or so in summer, and one morning and one afternoon service in winter.

ℹ️ Getting There & Away

At least two buses head to İstanbul (₺90, nine hours) daily. For Antalya and other destinations along the Mediterranean coast, you usually have to change buses at Denizli (₺35, three hours)

İstanbul

POP 14.8 MILLION

This magical meeting place of East and West has more top-drawer attractions than it has minarets (and that's a lot). İstanbul's strategic location has attracted many marauding armies over the centuries. The fact that the city straddles two continents wasn't its only draw – it was also the final stage on the legendary Silk Road linking Asia with Europe. The resulting stately mosques, opulent palaces and elaborately decorated domed churches and crammed into the Old City quarter, while the hilly streets of Beyoğlu host state-of-the-art museums and art galleries, chic boutiques and funky cafes. Hop on a commuter ferry to cross between Europe and Asia. Haggle your heart out in the Grand Bazaar. Dine on aromatic Asian dishes, Italian classics or succulent kebaps. This marvelous metropolis is a showcase of Turkey at its most energetic, innovative and cosmopolitan.

👁️ Sights

⭐**Aya Sofya**   MUSEUM
(Hagia Sophia; Map p564; ☎0212-522 1750, 0212-522 0989; http://ayasofyamuzesi.gov.tr/en; Aya Sofya Meydanı 1; adult/child under 12yr ₺40/free;

⊗9am-6pm Tue-Sun mid-Apr–mid-Oct, to 4pm mid-Oct–mid-Apr; ⊠Sultanahmet) There are many important monuments in İstanbul, but this venerable structure – which was commissioned by the great Byzantine emperor Justinian, consecrated as a church in 537, converted to a mosque by Mehmet the Conqueror in 1453 and declared a museum by Atatürk in 1935 – surpasses the rest due to its innovative architectural form, rich history, religious importance and extraordinary beauty. See also p580.

★**Blue Mosque**　　　　　MOSQUE
(Sultanahmet Camii; Map p564; ☎0545 577 1899; www.bluemosque.co; Hippodrome; ⊗closed to non-worshippers during 6 daily prayer times; ⊠Sultanahmet) İstanbul's most photogenic building was the grand project of Sultan Ahmet I (r 1603–17), whose tomb is located on the north side of the site facing Sultanahmet Park. The mosque's wonderfully curvaceous exterior features a cascade of domes and six

> ### ⓘ MUSEUM PASS
>
> The **Museum Pass İstanbul** (http://www.muze.gov.tr/en/museum-card; ₺85) is valid for five days and offers significant savings on entry to the Old City's major sights. It sometimes allows you to bypass ticket queues too. Pick it up at any of the sights it covers.

slender minarets. Blue İznik tiles adorn the interior and give the building its unofficial but commonly used name.

★**Museum of Turkish & Islamic Arts**　　　　　MUSEUM
(Türk ve Islam Eserleri Müzesi; Map p564; www.tiem.gov.tr; Atmeydanı Caddesi 46, Hippodrome; adult/child under 12yr ₺25/free; ⊗9am-4.30pm Nov–mid-Apr, to 6.30pm mid-Apr–Oct; ⊠Sultanahmet) This Ottoman palace was built in 1524 for İbrahim Paşa, childhood friend,

ITALY, GREECE & TURKEY İSTANBUL

İstanbul

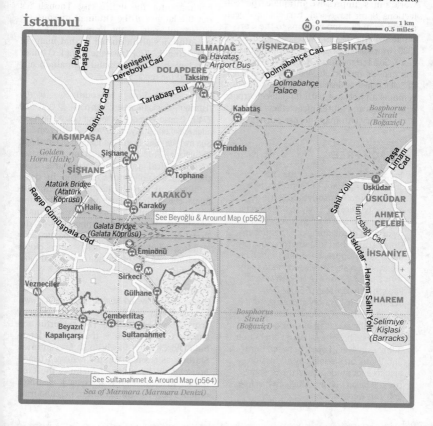

DON'T MISS

BOSPHORUS BOAT EXCURSION

İstanbul's soul is the Bosphorus. Don't miss seeing the city's iconic skyline and riverside views from the city's real highway aboard a Bosphorus excursion boat. Plenty of boats depart from Eminönü and stop at various points before turning around at Anadolu Kavağ (one way/return ₺15/25). Along the way you soak up sights such as the ornate Dolmabahçe Palace and majestically modern Bosphorus Bridge, along with plenty of lavish *yalıs* (seafront mansions).

brother-in-law and grand vizier of Süleyman the Magnificent. Recently renovated, it has a magnificent collection of artefacts, including exquisite calligraphy and one of the world's most impressive antique carpet collections. Some large-scale carpets have been moved from the upper rooms to the Carpet Museum (Halı Müzesi; Map p564; ☑ 0212-518 1330; www.halimuzesi.com; cnr Babıhümayun Caddesi & Soğukçeşme Sokak; ₺10; ⊙ 9am-6pm Tue-Sun mid-Apr–mid-Oct, to 4pm mid-Oct–mid-Apr; ⓢ Sultanahmet or Gülhane), but the collection remains a knockout with its palace carpets, prayer rugs and glittering artefacts such as a 17th-century Ottoman incense burner.

ⓘ FOR FREE

Topping the seven hills of the Old City and adorning many of its streets, İstanbul's Ottoman mosques are the jewels in the city's crown. Entry to these architectural wonders is open to everyone regardless of their religion. The *türbes* (tombs) attached to these mosques are often sumptuously decorated with İznik tiles and can also be visited; head to the Aya Sofya Tombs (Aya Sofya Müzesi Padişah Türbeleri; Map p564; ☑ 0212-522 1750; http://ayasofyamuzesi.gov.tr/en; Babıhümayun Caddesi; ⊙ 9am-5pm; ⓢ Sultanahmet) FREE to see some great examples. The Pera Museum offers free admission every Friday between 6pm and 10pm; on Wednesday admission is also free for students. On the Bosphorus, the Sakıp Sabancı Museum has free entry on Wednesdays.

★ **Topkapı Palace**   PALACE
(Topkapı Sarayı; Map p564; ☑ 0212-512 0480; www.topkapisarayi.gov.tr; Babıhümayun Caddesi; palace adult/child under 12yr ₺40/free, Harem adult/child under 6yr ₺25/free; ⊙ 9am-6.45pm Wed-Mon mid-Apr–Oct, to 4.45pm Nov–mid-Apr, last entry 45min before closing; ⓢ Sultanahmet) Topkapı is the subject of more colourful stories than most of the world's museums put together. Libidinous sultans, ambitious courtiers, beautiful concubines and scheming eunuchs lived and worked here between the 15th and 19th centuries when it was the court of the Ottoman empire. A visit to the palace's opulent pavilions, jewel-filled Treasury and sprawling Harem gives a fascinating glimpse into their lives.

★ **Süleymaniye Mosque**   MOSQUE
(Map p564; Professor Sıddık Sami Onar Caddesi; ⊙ dawn-dusk; Ⓜ Vezneciler) The Süleymaniye crowns one of İstanbul's seven hills and dominates the Golden Horn, providing a landmark for the entire city. Though it's not the largest of the Ottoman mosques, it is certainly one of the grandest and most beautiful. It's also unusual in that many of its original *külliye* (mosque complex) buildings have been retained and sympathetically adapted for reuse.

İstanbul Archaeology Museums   MUSEUM
(İstanbul Arkeoloji Müzeleri; Map p564; ☑ 0212-520 7740; Osman Hamdi Bey Yokuşu Sokak, Gülhane; adult/child under 12yr ₺20/free; ⊙ 9am-7pm Tue-Sun mid-Apr–Sep, 9am-4pm Tue-Sun Oct–mid-Apr; ⓢ Gülhane) This superb museum showcases archaeological and artistic treasures from the Topkapı collections. Housed in three buildings, its exhibits include ancient artefacts, classical statuary and an exhibition tracing İstanbul's history. There are many highlights, but the sarcophagi from the Royal Necropolis of Sidon are particularly striking. Note that the ticket office closes one hour before the museum's official closing time.

Grand Bazaar   MARKET
(Kapalı Çarşı, Covered Market; Map p564; www.kapalicarsi.org.tr; ⊙ 8.30am-7pm Mon-Sat, last entry 6pm; ⓢ Beyazıt Kapalıçarşı) The colourful and chaotic Grand Bazaar is the heart of İstanbul's Old City and has been so for centuries. Starting as a small vaulted *bedesten* (warehouse) built by order of Mehmet the Conqueror in 1461, it grew to cover a vast area as lanes between the *bedesten,* neighbouring

shops and *hans* (caravanserais) were roofed and the market assumed the sprawling, labyrinthine form that it retains today.

Basilica Cistern
HISTORIC SITE

(Yerebatan Sarnıçı; Map p564; ☎0212-512 1570; www.yerebatan.com; Yerebatan Caddesi; adult/child under 8yr ₺20/free; ⊙9am-6.30pm; 🚇Sultanahmet) This subterranean structure was commissioned by Emperor Justinian and built in 532. The largest surviving Byzantine cistern in İstanbul, it was constructed using 336 columns, many of which were salvaged from ruined temples and feature fine carved capitals. Its symmetry and sheer grandeur of conception are quite breathtaking, and its cavernous depths make a great retreat on summer days.

★Dolmabahçe Palace
PALACE

(Dolmabahçe Sarayı; ☎0212-327 2626; www.millisaraylar.gov.tr; Dolmabahçe Caddesi, Beşiktaş; adult/student/child Selâmlık ₺40/5/free, Harem ₺30/5/free, joint ticket ₺60/5/free; ⊙8.45am-4pm Tue, Wed & Fri-Sun; 🚇Kabataş) These days it's fashionable for architects and critics influenced by the less-is-more aesthetic of Bauhaus masters to sneer at buildings such as Dolmabahçe. However, the crowds that throng to this imperial pleasure palace with its neoclassical exterior and over-the-top interior clearly don't share that disdain,

flocking here to visit its Selâmlık (Ceremonial Suites), Harem and Veliaht Dairesi (Apartments of the Crown Prince). The latter houses the National Palaces Painting Museum (Milli Saraylar Resim Müzesi; ☎0212-236 9000; www.millisaraylar.gov.tr; Dolmabahçe Caddesi, Beşiktaş; adult/student/child ₺15/5/free; ⊙9am-4pm Tue, Wed & Fri-Sun; 🚇Akaretler, 🚇Kabataş), which can be visited on a Selâmlık or Harem ticket.

★İstanbul Modern
GALLERY

(İstanbul Modern Sanat Müzesi; Map p562; ☎0212-334 7300; www.istanbulmodern.org; Meclis-i Mebusan Caddesi, Tophane; adult/student/child under 12yr ₺25/14/free; ⊙10am-6pm Tue, Wed & Fri-Sun, to 8pm Thu; 🚇Tophane) This large, lavishly funded and innovative museum has an extensive collection of Turkish art and also stages a constantly changing and uniformly excellent program of mixed-media exhibitions by high-profile local and international artists. Its permanent home is next to the Bosphorus in Tophane, but the massive Galataport redevelopment project currently under way means that it will temporarily relocate to another site in Beyoğlu. Check the museum's website for up-to-date information.

Pera Museum
MUSEUM

(Pera Müzesi; Map p562; ☎0212-334 9900; www.peramuseum.org; Meşrutiyet Caddesi 65, Tepebaşı;

HAMAMS

Succumbing to a soapy scrub in a steamy hamam is one of the city's quintessential experiences.

The concept of the steam bath was passed from the Romans to the Byzantines and then on to the Turks. Until recent decades, many homes in İstanbul didn't have bathroom facilities, and due to Islam's emphasis on personal cleanliness, the community relied on the hundreds of hamams throughout the city, often as part of the *külliye* (mosque complex). Today, many carry on due to their roles as local meeting places.

The cheapest bath is the one you do yourself, having brought your own soap, shampoo and towel. But the real Turkish bath experience is to have an attendant wash, scrub and massage you. Our top three picks for sudsy relaxation after a long day of sightseeing:

Ayasofya Hürrem Sultan Hamamı (Map p564; ☎0212-517 3535; www.ayasofyahamami.com; Aya Sofya Meydanı 2; bath treatments €70-140, massages €40-75; ⊙8am-10pm; 🚇Sultanahmet) The most luxurious traditional bath experience in the Old City.

Kılıç Ali Paşa Hamamı (Map p562; ☎0212-393 8010; http://kilicalipasahamami.com; Hamam Sokak 1, off Kemeraltı Caddesi, Tophane; traditional hamam ritual ₺190; ⊙women 8am-4pm, men 4.30pm-midnight; 🚇Tophane) Meticulously restored and utterly enjoyable.

Çemberlitaş Hamamı (Map p564; ☎0212-522 7974; www.cemberlitashamami.com; Vezir Han Caddesi 8, Çemberlitaş; self-service ₺80, bath, scrub & soap massage ₺125; ⊙men 6am-midnight, women from 7.30am; 🚇Çemberlitaş) An architecturally splendid Ottoman hamam.

Beyoğlu & Around

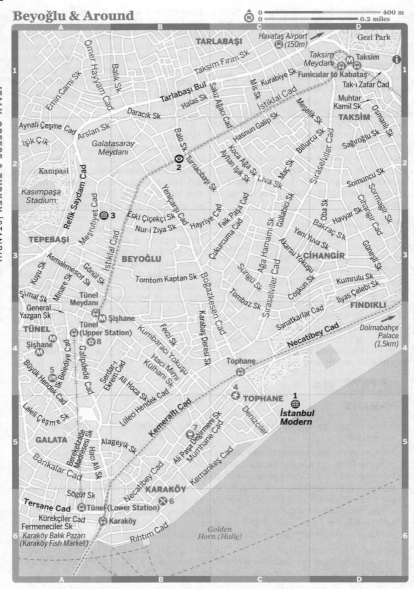

adult/student/child under 12yr ₺20/10/free; ⏰10am-7pm Tue-Thu & Sat, to 10pm Fri, noon-6pm Sun; Ⓜ Şişhane, 🚇 Tünel) There's plenty to see at this impressive museum, but its major draw is undoubtedly the 2nd-floor exhibition of paintings featuring Turkish Orien-

talist themes. Drawn from Suna and İnan Kıraç's world-class private collection, the works provide fascinating glimpses into the Ottoman world from the 17th to 20th centuries and include the most beloved painting in the Turkish canon – Osman Hamdi Bey's

Beyoğlu & Around

⊙ Top Sights
1 İstanbul Modern...................................C5

⊙ Sights
2 İstiklal Caddesi....................................B2
3 Pera Museum A3

⊕ Activities, Courses & Tours
4 Kılıç Ali Paşa Hamamı C5

⊟ Sleeping
5 Louis Appartements.............................A4

⊗ Eating
6 Karaköy Güllüoğlu B6

⊝ Drinking & Nightlife
7 Unter...B5

⊕ Entertainment
8 Galata Mevlevi Museum.......................A4

The Tortoise Trainer (1906). Other floors host high-profile temporary exhibitions (past exhibitions have showcased Warhol, de Chirico, Picasso and Botero).

⤳ Tours

★ Alternative City Tours   TOURS
(www.alternativecitytours.com; tour per group of up to 6 people €150 plus lunch) Having lived in İstanbul for many years, New York–born photographer Monica Fritz recently made the decision to share some of the many secrets she has learned about the city with fellow shutterbugs. Her informed and enjoyable tour portfolio covers the European and Asian shores and beyond, and she provides plenty of cultural and historical context.

★ Urban Adventures   CULTURAL
(☑0535 022 2003; www.urbanadventures.com; tours from €27) This highly professional outfit runs a number of cultural tours including a 3½-hour night tasting walk in Beyoğlu and a dinnertime visit to Small Projects İstanbul, an NGO working to support Syrian refugees in the city. All proceeds from the latter tour go to the charity.

✤ Festivals

İstanbul Music Festival   MUSIC
(http://muzik.iksv.org/en; ⊘Jun) The city's premier arts festival includes performances of opera, dance, orchestral concerts and cham-

ber recitals. Acts are often internationally renowned and the action takes place in June at atmosphere-laden venues such as **Aya İrini** (Hagia Eirene, Church of the Divine Peace; Map p564; ☑0212-512 0480; http://topkapisarayi.gov. tr; 1st Court, Topkapı Palace; adult/child under 6yr ₺20/free; ⊘9am-6.45pm Wed-Mon mid-Apr–Oct, to 4.45pm Nov–mid-Apr; ⓈSultanahmet) in Sultanahmet and the **Süreyya Opera House** (☑0216-346 1531; www.sureyyaoperasi.org; Gen Asim Gündüz (Bahariye) Caddesi 29; ⓈKadıköy) in Kadıköy.

İstanbul Biennial   ART
(http://bienal.iksv.org/en; ⊘mid-Sep–mid-Nov odd-numbered years) For the city's major visual-arts shindig, an international curator or panel of curators nominates a theme and puts together a cutting-edge program that is then exhibited in a variety of venues around town.

⊟ Sleeping

Hotel Nomade   BOUTIQUE HOTEL €
(Map p564; ☑0212-513 8173; www.hotelnomade. com; Ticarethane Sokak 15, Alemdar; s/d/tr from €50/55/60; Ⓟ⊛❉⊛@❅; ⓈSultanahmet) Designer style and budget pricing don't often go together, but the Nomade bucks the trend. Just a few steps off busy Divan Yolu, it offers simple rooms that some guests find too small – request the largest possible. Everyone loves the roof-terrace bar, though (smack-bang in front of Aya Sofya).

STREET SNACKING

Street vendors pound pavements across İstanbul, pushing carts laden with artfully arranged snacks to satisfy the appetites of commuters. You'll see these vendors next to ferry and bus stations, on busy streets and squares, and even on the city's bridges.

Some of their snacks are innocuous – freshly baked *simits* (bread rings studded with sesame seeds), golden roasted *mısır* (corn on the cob), refreshing chilled and peeled *salatalık* (cucumber) – but others are more confrontational for non-Turkish palates. These include *midye dolma* (stuffed mussels) and *kokoreç* (seasoned lamb or mutton intestines wrapped around a skewer and grilled over charcoal).

Sultanahmet & Around

HOCA GIYASETTİN

Sarı Beyazıt Cad
Vefa Cad
Oluk Sk
Şemsettin Sk
Namahrem Sk
Hayriye Hanım Sk
Kıble Çeşme Cad
Ragıp Gümüşpala Cad

SARIDEMİR

Prof Cemil Birsel Cad
Dökmeciler Hamamı Sk
Fetva Yokuşu
Mimar Sinan Cad

Süleymaniye Mosque
4

Şifahane Sk
Prof Sıddık Sami Onar Cad
Süleymaniye Cad

MOLLA HÜSREV

Kazlı Mescit Sk

SÜLEYMANİYE

Bozdoğan Kemeri Cad
Besim Ömer Paşa Cad

İstanbul University

Vezneciler Cad

Bakırcılar Cad

Sıyavuşpaşa Sk
Vasıf Çınar Cad

MERCAN

Havancı Sk
Nargileci Sk
Semaver Sk
Mercan Cad
Örücüler Hamamı Sk

Tahtakale Cad
Hasırcılar Cad

YENİ CAMİ MEYDANI

RÜSTEM PAŞA

Çiçek Pazarı Sk
Tahmis Sk
Yenicami Meydanı Sk

Reşadiye Cad

EMİNÖNÜ

Büyük Postane Cad
Aşir Efendi Cad

Sabuncu Hanı Sk
Yenicamii Cad

TAHTAKALE

Çakmakçılar Yokuşu

SURURİ

Hamideli Hoca Hanı Sk
Cemal Nadir Sk
Türkocağı Cad

Tarakçılar Cad
Sultan Mektep Sk
Bezciler Sk
Mengene Sk
Tasvir Sk
Şeref Efendi Sk
Nuruosmaniye Cad
Türbedar Sk
Bab-ı Ali Cad

Fabric
Fesçiler Cad
Carpets
9
Gold
Kalpakçılar Cad

NURUOSMANİYE

Tavuk Pazarı Sk

Kürkçüler Çarşısı

ÇEMBERLİTAŞ

Beyazıt Meydanı

BEYAZIT

Beyazıt Kapalıçarşı

17

Divan Yolu Cad

12

16

Ordu Cad

Çemberlitaş

Asma Kandil Sk
Divan-ı Ali Sk
Doğramacı Sk

EMİN SİNAN

Gedikpaşa Camii Sk
Emin Sinan Hamamı Sk

Derin Kuyu Sk
Abuhayat Sk
Soğanağa Camii Sk
Direkli Camii Sk
Yahya Paşa Sk
Tatlı Kuyu Sk
Molla Bey Sk
Gedikpaşa Cad

GEDİK PAŞA

Tüğcü Sk

Piyer Loti Cad
Dağhan Sk
Peykhane Cad
Klodfarer Cad
Dizdariye Çeşmesi Sk
Katip Sinan Camii Sk

Mabeyinçi Yokuşu
Saraç İshak Sk
TürkeliCad
Kumkapı Hanı Sk
Asmalı Han Sk

KUMKAPI

Mollataşı Cad
Arayıcı Sk
Ustad Sk
Sarayiçi Sk
Neviye Sk
Katip Sinan Sk
Özbekler Sk

KADIRGA

Çifte Gelinler Cad
Paye Sk
Kadırga Limanı Cad

Şarapnel Sk
Tavası Çeşme Sk
Telli Odalar Sk
Babayiğit Sk
Samsa Sk
Çapariz Sk
Işık Sk

ŞEHSUVAR

Alişan Sk

KÜÇÜK AYASOFYA

Kaleci Sk

Cinci Meydanı Sk

Kennedy Cad (Sahil Yolu)

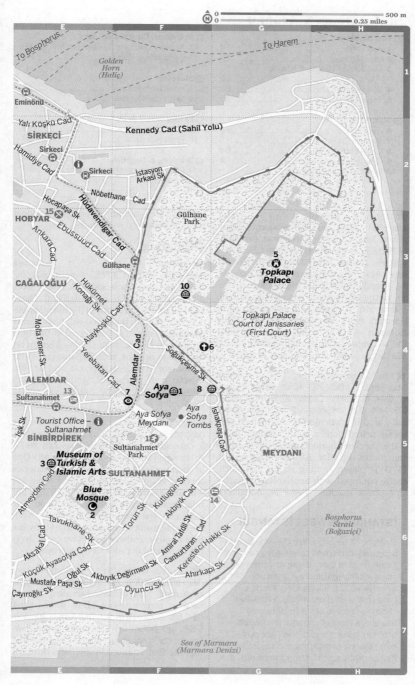

N

0   500 m
0   0.25 miles

To Bosphorus

Golden Horn (Haliç)

To Harem

Eminönü

Yalı Köşkü Cad

Kennedy Cad (Sahil Yolu)

SİRKECİ

Sirkeci

Hamidiye Cad

Sirkeci

İstasyon Arkası Sk

Nöbethane Cad

Hocapaşa Sk

Hüdavendigar Cad

HOBYAR

Ebussuud Cad

Ankara Cad

Gülhane

Gülhane Park

CAĞALOĞLU

Hükümet Konağı Sk

Alemdar Cad

Topkapı Palace
5

10

Topkapı Palace Court of Janissaries (First Court)

Molla Fenari Sk

Atayköşkü Cad

Yerebatan Cad

ALEMDAR

Soğukçeşme Sk

6

Sultanahmet

13

7

Aya Sofya
1

8

Işık Sk

Tourist Office – Sultanahmet

BİNBİRDİREK

Aya Sofya Meydanı

Aya Sofya Tombs

İstakpaşa Cad

MEYDANI

Museum of Turkish & Islamic Arts
3

Sultanahmet Park

1

SULTANAHMET

Atmeydanı Cad

Blue Mosque
2

Bosphorus Strait (Boğaziçi)

Kutlugün Sk

Torun Sk

Akbıyık Sk

14

Tavukhane Sk

Amiral Tafdil Sk

Cankurtaran Cad

Keresteci Hakkı Sk

Aksakal Cad

Küçük Ayasofya Cad

Oğul Sk

Akbıyık Değirmeni Sk

Ahırkapı Sk

Mustafa Paşa Sk

Çayıroğlu Sk

Oyuncu Sk

Sea of Marmara (Marmara Denizi)

Sultanahmet & Around

★ **Metropolis Hostel**   HOSTEL €
(Map p564; ☎0212-518 1822; www.metropolishostel.com; Terbıyık Sokak 24, Cankurtaran; dm €10-16, s €28, d €36, tw with shared bathroom €29; ⓟ⊛
❋@⑤; 🚇Sultanahmet) Located in a quiet street where a good night's sleep is assured, the friendly Metropolis offers four- to six-bed dorms, including a female-only en suite option with six beds and sweeping Sea of Marmara views. There are also small private rooms on offer. The rooftop terrace has a bar and sea views to equal many pricier hotels, and there's a busy entertainment program.

★ **Louis Appartements**   HOTEL €
(Map p562; ☎0212-293 4052; www.louis.com.
tr/galata; İlk Belediye Caddesi 10, Şişhane; d from €75; ⊛❋@⑤; Ⓜ Şişhane, 🚇Tünel) The tower suite at this meticulously maintained and keenly priced hotel near the Galata Tower is the knockout option among the 12 suites and rooms on offer. All have a large bed, TV/DVD player, ironing set-up and kitchenette equipped with appliances, including an espresso machine. Decor is understated

---

İSTANBUL, SWEET İSTANBUL

Turks don't usually finish their meal with a dessert, preferring to serve fruit as a finale. Most of them love a midafternoon sugar hit though, and will often pop into a *muhallebici* (milk pudding shop), *pastane* (patisserie) or *baklavacı* (baklava shop) for a piece of syrup-drenched baklava, a plate of chocolate-crowned profiteroles or a *fırın sütlaç* (rice pudding) tasting of milk, sugar and just a hint of exotic spices. Mmmmmmmm...

---

but pleasing; staff are helpful. An optional breakfast costs €6 per person.

❌ Eating

★ **Birecikli**   ANATOLIAN €
(Map p564; ☎0212-513 77 63; www.birecikli.com/
sirkeci; Hocapaşa Camii Sokak 2B, Sirkeci; pides ₺16-18, kebaps ₺12-33; ⊗9am-10.30pm) Those keen on robust flavours and the liberal application of chilli in their food will be instantly enamoured of the dishes served at this bustling eatery in Hocapaşa. Choose from an array of liver options, meat kebaps, pides and *lahmacun* (Arabic-style pizza), and be sure to start with a delicious *sarımsaklı Antep lahmacin* (thin, crispy Antep-style pizza). No alcohol.

Erol Lokantası   TURKISH €
(Map p564; ☎0212-511 0322; Çatal Çeşme Sokak 3, Cağaloğlu; soups ₺4.50-5.50, portions ₺9-22; ⊗11am-6pm Mon-Sat; ☑; 🚇Sultanahmet) One of Sultanahmet's last *lokantas* (eateries serving ready-made food), Erol wouldn't win any awards for its interior design but might for its warm welcome and food. The dishes in the bain-marie are made fresh every day using seasonal ingredients by the Erol family members, who have collectively put in several decades in the kitchen.

★ **Karaköy Güllüoğlu**   SWEETS, BÖREK €
(Map p562; ☎0212-293 0910; www.karakoygulluoglu.com; Katlı Otopark, Kemankeş Caddesi, Karaköy; portion baklava ₺11-19, portion börek ₺9-9.50; ⊗7am-11pm Sun-Thu, 8am-11.30pm Fri & Sat; ♠; 🚇Karaköy) This much-loved *baklavacı* (baklava shop) opened in 1949 and was the first İstanbul branch of a business

established in Gaziantep in the 1820s. There are other Güllüoğlu offshoots around town, but this remains the best. Pay for a *porsiyon* (portion) of whatever takes your fancy at the register, then order at the counters.

🍷 Drinking & Nightlife

★**Çorlulu Alipaşa
Nargile ve Çay Bahçesi** TEA GARDEN
(Map p564; Yeniçeriler Caddesi 35, Beyazıt; ⊙7am-midnight; 🚇Beyazıt-Kapalı Çarşı) Set in the vine-covered courtyard of the Çorlulu Ali Paşa Medrese, this nargile cafe near the Grand Bazaar is the most atmospheric in the Old City. Nargiles cost ₺25 and are best enjoyed with a glass of çay (tea; ₺2) or *Türk kahve* (Turkish coffee; ₺5).

★**Unter** BAR
(Map p562; ☎0212-244 5151; www.unter.com.tr; Kara Ali Kaptan Sokak 4, Karaköy; ⊙noon-midnight Tue-Thu, to 2am Fri, 9am-2am Sat, 9am-7pm Sun; 🖥; 🚇Tophane) This cafe, bar and restaurant hybrid epitomises the new Karaköy style: it's glam without trying too hard, and has a vaguely arty vibe. Ground-floor windows open to the street in fine weather, allowing the action to spill outside during busy periods. Waiters tend to shift tables and chairs after the dinner service on weekends, opening the floor and laneway for dancing.

🛈 Information

The Ministry of Culture & Tourism (www.turizm. gov.tr) currently operates three tourist information offices or booths in the city and has booths at both international airports.

Tourist Office – Atatürk International Airport (☎0212-465 3151; International Arrivals Hall, Atatürk International Airport; ⊙9am-9pm)

Tourist Office – Sabiha Gökçen International Airport (☎0216-588 8794; ⊙8am-7pm)

Tourist Office – Sirkeci Train Station (Map p564; ☎0212-511 5888; Sirkeci Gar, Ankara Caddesi, Sirkeci; ⊙9.30am-6pm mid-Apr–Sep, 9am-5.30pm Oct–mid-Apr; 🚇Sirkeci)

Tourist Office – Sultanahmet (Map p564; ☎0212-518 1802; Hippodrome, Sultanahmet; ⊙9.30am-6pm mid-Apr–Sep, 9am-5.30pm Oct–mid-Apr; 🚇Sultanahmet)

Tourist Office – Taksim (Map p562; ☎0212-233 0592; www.kulturturizm.gov.tr; Ground fl, Seyran Apartmanı, Mete Caddesi, Taksim; ⊙9.30am-6pm Mon-Sat mid-Apr–Sep, 9am-5.30pm Mon-Sat Oct–mid-Apr; Ⓜ Taksim)

🛈 GETTING INTO İSTANBUL FROM THE AIRPORTS

Havataş Airport Bus (☎444 2656; http://havatas.com) travels between the airports and Cumhuriyet Caddesi, just off Taksim Meydanı. Buses leave Atatürk (₺12, one hour) every 30 minutes between 4am and 1am. Its service between Sabiha Gökçen (₺15, 1½ hours) and Taksim leaves every 30 minutes between 4am and 1am – easily the cheapest way to get to the city from Sabiha Gökçen.

Metro Services run from Atatürk to Zeytinburnu, where you can connect with the tram to Sultanahmet (total one hour).

Shuttle Most hotels can book airport shuttles to/from both Atatürk (€25) and Sabiha Gökçen (€80). Check shuttle schedules at reception.

Taxi From Atatürk/Sabiha Gökçen to Sultanahmet costs around ₺50/175.

🛈 Getting There & Away

AIR

İstanbul's **Atatürk International Airport** (IST, Atatürk Havalimanı; ☎+90 444 9828; www. ataturkairport.com) is 23km west of Sultanahmet. Close by, the domestic terminal (İç Hatlar) is smaller but no less efficient.

Sabiha Gökçen International Airport (SAW, Sabiha Gökçen Havalimanı; ☎0216-588 8888; www.sgairport.com) is 50km east, on the Asian side of the city.

BUS

The **Büyük İstanbul Otogarı** (Big İstanbul Bus Station; ☎0212-658 0505; www.otogaristanbul. com) is the city's main bus station for both intercity and international routes. Often called simply 'the otogar' (bus station), it's located at Esenler in the municipality of Bayrampaşa, about 10km west of Sultanahmet. The metro service from Aksaray stops here (₺5; Otogar stop) on its way to the airport.

TRAIN

At the time of writing, the only international train services to/from İstanbul was the nightly İstanbul–Sofia Expressi, departing Halkali at 10.40pm daily. Ticket prices start at ₺120. Check Turkish State Railways (TCDD; www.tcdd. gov.tr) for updates.

🛈 Getting Around

Rechargable İstanbulkarts (travelcards) can be used on public transport city-wide. Purchase

WHIRLING DERVISHES

These sultans of spiritual spin known as the 'whirling dervishes' have been twirling their way to a higher plane ever since the 13th century and show no sign of slowing down.

There are a number of opportunities to see dervishes whirling in İstanbul. The best known of these is the weekly ceremony in the *semahane* (whirling dervish hall) in the **Galata Mevlevi Museum** (Galata Mevlevihanesi Müzesi; Map p562; www.galatamevlevihanesimuze-si.gov.tr; Galipdede Caddesi 15, Tünel; ₺70; ⊙ performances 5pm Sun; M Şişhane, 🚠 Tünel) in Tünel. Come early (preferably days ahead) to buy your ticket.

(₺10, including ₺4 credit) and recharge them at kiosks and machines at metro and tram stops, bus terminals and ferry docks. It reduces single fares from ₺5 to ₺2.60. If you're only using public transport for a few city journeys, *jetons* (single trip travel token; ₺5) can be purchased from machines at tram, metro and ferry docks.

BOAT

İstanbul's commuter ferries ply the Bosphorous between the city's European and Asian sides. Ferries for Üsküdar and the Bosphorus leave from Eminönü dock; ferries for the Princes' Islands depart from Kabataş (Adalar İskelesi dock). From Karaköy, ferries depart for Kadıköy on the Asian shore. Tickets are cheap (usually ₺5) and it's possible to use an İstanbulkart on most routes.

BUS

The bus system in İstanbul is extremely efficient, though traffic congestion in the city means that bus trips can be very long. Services run between 6.30am and 11pm. You must have an İstanbulkart before boarding.

METRO

The most useful metro service is the M1A Line connecting Aksaray with Atatürk Airport, stopping at 16 stations including the otogar (main bus station) along the way. Services leave every two to 10 minutes between 6am and midnight.

TAXI

İstanbul is full of yellow taxis, all of them with meters – insist that drivers use them. It costs around ₺20 to travel between Beyoğlu and Sultanahmet.

TRAM & FUNICULAR

A *tramvay* (tramway) service runs from Zeytinburnu (where it connects with the M1A Metro) to Kabataş (connecting with the funicular to-Taksim) via Sultanahmet, Eminönü and Karaköy (connecting with the funicular to Tünel). Trams run every five minutes from 6am to midnight. An antique tram rattles up and down İstiklal Caddesi between Tünel funicular station and Taksim Meydanı. The one-stop Tünel funicular between Karaköy and İstiklal Caddesi runs between 7am and 10.20pm. Another funicular runs from Kabataş (where it connects with the tram) up to the metro station at Taksim.

Ankara

POP 4.7 MILLION

Turkey's 'other' city may not have showy Ottoman palaces or regal facades, but Ankara thrums to a vivacious, youthful beat unmarred by the tug of history. The capital established by Atatürk boasts two of the country's most important sights; while the hilltop *hisar* (citadel) district is full of old-fashioned charm, and the cafe-crammed Kızılay neighbourhood is one of Turkey's hippest urban quarters.

◉ Sights

★**Museum of Anatolian Civilisations**   MUSEUM
(Anadolu Medeniyetleri Müzesi; ☎ 0312-324 3160; www.anadolumedeniyetlerimuzesi.gov.tr; Gözcü Sokak 2; ₺20; ⊙ 8.30am-7pm; M Ulus) The superb Museum of Anatolian Civilisations is the perfect introduction to the complex weave of Turkey's ancient past, with beautifully curated exhibits housing artefacts cherry-picked from just about every significant archaeological site in Anatolia.

The central hall houses reliefs and statuary, while the surrounding halls take you on a journey of staggering history from Palaeolithic, Neolithic, Chalcolithic, Bronze Age, Assyrian, Hittite, Phrygian, Urartian and Lydian periods. Downstairs is a collection of Roman artefacts unearthed at excavations in and around Ankara.

★**Anıt Kabir**   MONUMENT
(Atatürk Mausoleum & Museum; www.anitkabir. org; Gençlik Caddesi; audioguide ₺10; ⊙ 9am-5pm; M Anadolu) **FREE** The monumental mausoleum of Mustafa Kemal Atatürk (1881–1938), the founder of modern Turkey, sits high above the city with its abundance of marble and air of veneration. The tomb

itself actually makes up only a small part of this complex, which consists of **museums** and a **ceremonial courtyard**. For many Turks a visit is virtually a pilgrimage, and it's not unusual to see people visibly moved. Allow at least two hours in order to visit the whole site.

Citadel AREA
(Ankara Kalesi; Gözcü Sokak; Ⓜ Ulus) The imposing *hisar* (citadel) is the most interesting part of Ankara to poke about in. This well-preserved quarter of thick walls and intriguing winding streets took its present shape in the 9th century AD, when the Byzantine emperor Michael II constructed the outer ramparts. The inner walls date from the 7th century.

🛏 Sleeping

Book ahead, as many rooms are snapped up by business people. There are a number of budget and midrange hotels around Ulus Meydanı.

★ Deeps Hostel HOSTEL €
(✆ 0312-213 6338; www.deepshostelankara. com; Ataç 2 Sokak 46; dm/s/d without breakfast €12/17/25; ⊜ 🛜; Ⓜ Kızılay) At Ankara's best budget choice, friendly owner Şeyda has created a colourful, light-filled hostel with spacious dorms and small private rooms with squeaky-clean, modern shared bathrooms. It's all topped off by masses of advice and information, a fully equipped kitchen and a cute communal area downstairs where you can swap your Turkish travel tales.

★ Angora House Hotel HISTORIC HOTEL €€
(✆ 0312-309 8380; www.angorahouse.com.tr; Kale Kapısı Sokak 16; s/d/tr €30/55/75; ⊜ ❄ 🛜; Ⓜ Ulus) Be utterly charmed by this restored Ottoman house, which oozes subtle elegance at every turn. The six spacious rooms are infused with old-world atmosphere, featuring dark wood accents and colourful Turkish carpets, while the walled courtyard garden is the perfect retreat from the citadel streets. Delightfully helpful staff and a feast of a breakfast add to the appeal.

🍴 Eating

It's all about street stalls, hip bistros and cafe culture in Kızılay, where terraces line virtually every inch of space south of Ziya Gökalp Caddesi.

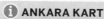

ⓘ ANKARA KART

If you're going to be kicking around the city for a couple of days it's worth investing ₺1 to get an **Ankara Kart** (rechargeable transport card; available at all metro station ticket counters and many kiosks around town), which gives you discounted fares of ₺2.45 on both the metro and bus system.

Mangal TURKISH €
(✆ 0312-466 2460; www.mangalkebap.com; Bestekar Sokak 78; mains ₺15-25; ⊗ 9am-10pm) For over 20 years this neighbourhood star has been churning out perfectly prepared pide and every kind of kebap or grilled meat you can think of, as well as many you can't. It's fairly smart, which makes the decent prices an unexpected surprise.

Balıkçıköy SEAFOOD €€
(✆ 0312-466 0450; Kırlangıç Sokak 3; mains ₺20-45; ⊗ noon-midnight) Ankara's favourite seafood restaurant. Take the waiter's recommendations for the cold meze, then take your pick of the fried and grilled fish – the fried whitebait is a favourite – all perfectly cooked and quick to the table. Book ahead to avoid disappointment.

🍷 Drinking & Nightlife

Kızılay is ripe for a night out with Ankara's student population – try Bayındır Sokak, between Sakarya and Tuna Caddesi. The tall, thin buildings pack in up to five floors of bars, cafes and *gazinos* (nightclubs). Many of the clubs offer live Turkish pop

GOAT OR RABBIT?

Can you tell the difference between a goat and a rabbit? It's not as easy as you think – or at least not if all you have to go on is the wool. One of the most popular misconceptions about Ankara's famous angora wool is that it comes from angora goats, a hardy breed believed to be descended from wild Himalayan goats. Not so: the soft, fluffy wool produced from these goats is correctly known as mohair. Angora wool in the strictest sense comes from angora rabbits, also local but much cuter and whose fur, weight for weight, was once worth as much as gold.

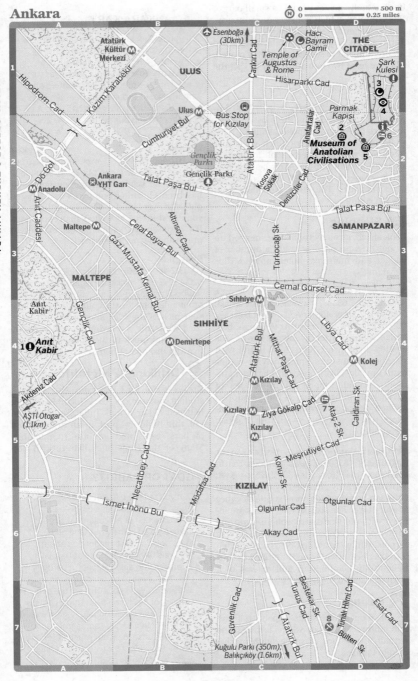

Ankara

0   500 m
0   0.25 miles

Atatürk Kültür Merkezi

ULUS

Esenboğa (30km)

Çankırı Cad

Hacı Bayram Camii

THE CITADEL

Temple of Augustus & Rome

Şark Kulesi

3

Hisarparkı Cad

4

Kazım Karabekir

Hipodrom Cad

Ulus

Bus Stop for Kızılay

Parmak Kapısı

2

Anafartalar Cad

6

Cumhuriyet Bul

Museum of Anatolian Civilisations

5

Dö Göt

Anadolu

Anıt Caddesi

Maltepe

Talat Paşa Bul

Gençlik Parkı

Gençlik Parkı

Ankara YHT Garı

Kosova Sokak

Denizciler Cad

Talat Paşa Bul

SAMANPAZARI

Celal Bayar Bul

Altınsoy Cad

Türkocağı Sk

MALTEPE

Gazi Mustafa Kemal Bul

Cemal Gürsel Cad

Anıt Kabir

Gençlik Cad

Sıhhiye

SIHHIYE

Libya Cad

1 Anıt Kabir

Demirtepe

Mithat Paşa Cad

Kolej

Akdeniz Cad

Atatürk Bul

Kızılay

Çaldıran Sk

AŞTİ Otogar (1.1km)

Kızılay

Ziya Gökalp Cad

Ataç 2 Sk

7

Kızılay

Meşrutiyet Cad

Konur Sk

KIZILAY

Necatibey Cad

Mudafaa Cad

Olgunlar Cad

Otgunlar Cad

Akay Cad

Ismet Inönü Bul

Güvenlik Cad

Atatürk Bul

Beştekar Sk

Tunus Cad

8

Tunalı Hilmi Cad

Bülten Sk

Esat Cad

Kuğulu Parkı (350m); Balıkçıköy (1.6km)

Ankara

music, and women travellers should feel OK in most of them.

ℹ Information

The Guide, available at the **Rahmi M Koç Industrial Museum** (📞 0312-309 6800; www.rmk-museum.org.tr; Depo Sokak 1; adult/student ₺8/4; ⏰10am-5pm Tue-Fri, to 7pm Sat & Sun; Ⓜ Ulus) and some bookshops, has listings for Ankara.

Tourist Office (📞 0312-310 3044; Kale Kapısı Sokak; ⏰10am-5pm; Ⓜ Ulus) Inside the Citadel. Gives out a decent free map of town and a pamphlet on Ankara's sights. There are also (usually unstaffed) branches at the AŞTİ otogar (Ankara Şehirlerarası Terminali İşletmesi; Mevlâna Bulvarı) and at the **train station**.

ℹ Getting There & Away

BUS

From Ankara's huge **AŞTİ otogar** (Ankara Şehirlerarası Terminali İşletmesi; Mevlâna Bulvarı), buses depart to all corners of Turkey day and night. Services to İstanbul (₺65 to ₺70, six hours) leave half-hourly. The AŞTİ is at the western end of Ankara's Ankaray Metro line, by far the easiest way to travel between the otogar and the centre. A taxi costs about ₺30 to the city centre and usually takes around 10 to 15 minutes.

TRAIN

Ankara's flash new **train station** (Ankara YHT Garı; www.tcdd.gov.tr; Celal Bayar Bulvarı) has high-speed train services with İstanbul Pendik (a suburb 25km east of central İstanbul; ₺70, four hours, eight trains daily), and Konya (₺30, two hours, 10 trains daily). Trains are fast, comfortable and efficient. Ticket queues can be long so it's best to buy tickets the day before travel or

buy online at www.tcdd.gov.tr. Maltepe, on the Ankaray line, is the nearest metro station.

ℹ Getting Around

BUS

Ankara has a good bus and dolmuş (minibus) network. Signs on the front and side of the vehicles are better guides than route numbers. Buses marked 'Ulus' and **'Çankaya'** run the length of Atatürk Bulvarı. Those marked 'Gar' go to the train station, and those marked 'AŞTİ' to the otogar.

Standard ₺4 tickets are available anywhere displaying an EGO Bilet sign (easiest purchased from metro station ticket booths), or buy an Ankara Kart (p569).

METRO

Ankara's underground train network is the easiest way to get between Ulus and Kızılay and the transport terminals. Tickets are available at all stations. Trains run from 6.15am to 11.45pm daily. A one-way fare costs ₺4, or ₺2.45 with the **Ankara Kart**. Tickets are available at all stations.

TAXI

Taxis are everywhere and they all have meters (built into the mirror). It costs about ₺20 to cross the centre during the day; charges rise at night.

Konya

The home of the whirling dervish orders is a bastion of Seljuk culture. The centre is dotted with imposing historic monument, topped off by the city's turquoise-domed Mevlâna Museum, one of Turkey's finest sights and most important centres of pilgrimage. It's worthwhile planning your Konya trip to be here on a Thursday evening when the *sema* ceremony is performed at the Mevlâna Museum.

◎ Sights

★**Mevlâna Museum**   MUSEUM
(📞 0332-351 1215; Asanlı Kışla Caddesi; audioguide ₺10; ⏰9am-6.30pm, to 5pm Nov-Apr; 🚇 Mevlâna) **FREE** For Muslims and non-Muslims alike, the main reason to come to Konya is to visit the Mevlâna Museum, the former lodge of the whirling dervishes and home to the tomb of Celaleddin Rumi (later known as Mevlâna), who we have to thank for giving the world the whirling dervishes. This is one of the biggest pilgrimage centres in Turkey, and the building's fluted dome of turquoise tiles is one of Turkey's most distinctive sights.

Konya

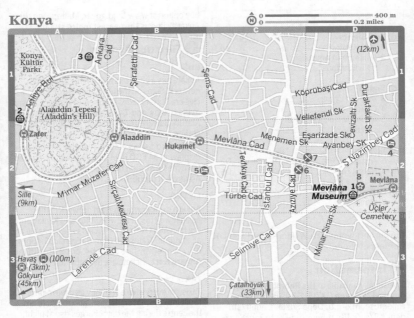

Konya

⊙ Top Sights
1 Mevlâna Museum.................................D2

⊙ Sights
2 Museum of Wooden Artefacts
   & Stone Carving..................................A1
3 Tile Museum..A1

🛏 Sleeping
4 Derviş Otel..D2
5 Ulusan Otel...B2

✕ Eating
6 Bolu Lokantası.....................................C2
7 Konya Mutfağı.....................................D2

🎭 Entertainment
8 Mevlâna Museum Whirling
   Dervish Performance.........................D2

★ **Tile Museum**   MUSEUM
(Karatay Medresesi Çini Müzesi; ☎0332-351 1914; Ankara Caddesi, just off Alaaddin Meydanı; ₺5; ☺9am-7pm, to 5pm Nov-Apr) Gorgeously restored, the interior central dome and walls of this former Seljuk theological school (1251) showcase some finely preserved blue-and-white Seljuk tilework. There is also an outstanding collection of ceramics on display including exhibits of the octagonal Seljuk tiles unearthed during excavations at Kubad Abad Palace on Lake Beyşehir. Emir Celaleddin Karatay, a Seljuk general, vizier and statesman who built the medrese (seminary), is buried in one of the corner rooms.

**Museum of Wooden Artefacts &
Stone Carving**   MUSEUM
(Tas ve Ahsap Eserler Müzesi; ☎0332-351 3204; Adliye Bulvarı; ₺5; ☺9am-7pm, to 5pm Nov-Apr) The İnce Minare Medresesi (Seminary of the Slender Minaret), now the Museum of Wooden Artefacts & Stone Carving, was built in 1264 for Seljuk vizier Sahip Ata. Inside, many of the carvings feature motifs similar to those used in tiles and ceramics. The Seljuks didn't heed Islam's traditional prohibition against human and animal images: there are images of birds (the Seljuk double-headed eagle, for example), humans, lions and leopards.

🛏 Sleeping

Ulusan Otel   HOTEL €
(☎0332-351 5004, 0532 488 2333; ulusanhotel@hotmail.com; Çarşi PTT Arkasi 4; s/d €10/20; ☺🛜) This is the pick of the Konya cheapies. The rooms may be totally basic, but they're bright and spotlessly clean. Shared bathrooms are immaculately kept (some rooms

have private bathrooms) and the communal area is full of homey knick-knacks.

⭐ **Derviş Otel** BOUTIQUE HOTEL €€
(📞 0332-350 0842; www.dervishotel.com; Güngör Sokak 7; r €50-60, f €100; ❄❄☎) This airy, light-filled, 200-year-old house has been converted into a rather wonderful boutique hotel. All of the seven spacious rooms have lovely soft colour schemes with local carpets covering the wooden floors, comfortable beds and modern bathrooms to boot. With enthusiastic management providing truly personal service this is a top-notch alternative to Konya's more anonymous hotels.

✗ Eating

⭐ **Bolu Lokantası** ANATOLIAN €
(📞 0332-352 4533; Aziziye Caddesi 27/B; etli ekmek & ayran ₺13; ☺10am-10pm) Konya's king of *etli ekmek* (the local version of pide), Bolu is tiny, basic and always crammed. There's no menu; just order *etli ekmek,* with a jug of *ayran* (yoghurt drink) to wash it down, squeeze over the lemon, sprinkle liberally with spice, then roll up the slices and eat with charred peppers. It's the best lunch in town.

Konya Mutfağı ANATOLIAN €
(📞 0332-350 4141; Mevlâna Caddesi 71; mains ₺15-27; ☺11.30am-11pm) Run by the *belediye* (town council), this restaurant offers up the regional tastes of Konya. It's a great place to sample *patlıcan közleme kebabı* (roasted eggplant, peppers and tomatoes topped with grilled lamb) and *tırıt* (a traditional wedding dish of bread, lamb and peppers topped with yoghurt and browned butter). Then cleanse your palate with a tamarind sherbet.

✗ Entertainment

⭐ **Mevlâna Museum Whirling Dervish Performance** LIVE PERFORMANCE
(Mevlâna Museum gardens, Aslanlı Kışla Caddesi, entry through east gate; ☺8.45pm Thu Jun-Sep) **FREE** In the summer months, the whirling dervishes perform the *sema* in the intimate setting of the Mevlâna Museum's outdoor theatre every Thursday night.

ⓘ Getting There & Away

Konya Airport (Konya Havalimanı; www.konya.dhmi.gov.tr; off Ankara Caddesi) is about 13km northeast of the city centre, with several flights daily to and from İstanbul. An airport shuttle-bus service (30 minutes) links the airport and central Konya.

The otogar is 7km north of the centre and connected by tram. There are frequent buses to all major destinations, including Ankara (₺35, four hours), İstanbul (₺85, 11½ hours) and Göreme (₺35, three hours).

The train station is 3km southwest of the centre. There are 10 high-speed train links between Konya and Ankara daily (₺30, two hours), and three to İstanbul's Pendik station (₺85, 4¼ hours) via Eskişehir (₺35, 1¾ hours).

ESSENTIAL TURKISH CUISINE

Kebaps and *köfte* (meatballs) in all their variations are the mainstay of restaurant meals. Look out particularly for the following:

Adana kebap Spicy *köfte* grilled on a skewer and served with onions, sumac, parsley, tomatoes and pide bread.

İskender kebap Döner kebap (spit-roasted lamb slices) on fresh pide and topped with savoury tomato sauce and browned butter.

Tokat kebap Lamb cubes grilled with potato, tomato, aubergine and garlic.

Meze is where Turkish cuisine really comes into its own. *Acılı ezme* (spicy tomato and onion paste), *fasulye pilaki* (white beans cooked with tomato paste and garlic) and *yapraksarma* (vine leaves stuffed with rice, herbs and pine nuts) are just a few of the myriad meze dishes on offer.

For quick cheap eats, try pide (Turkish pizza), *lahmacun* (Arabic-style pizza), *gözleme* (stuffed savoury crepe) and *börek* (filled pastries).

Popular non-kebap mains include *mantı* (Turkish ravioli), *saç kavurma* (stir-fried cubed meat dishes) and *güveç* (meat and vegetable stews cooked in a terracotta pot).

The national hot drink is *çay* (tea), served black in tulip-shaped glasses. The Turkish liquor of choice is *rakı*, a fiery aniseed drink similar to Greek ouzo; do as the Turks do and cut it by half with water. *Ayran* is a refreshing yoghurt drink made by whipping up yoghurt with water and salt, and is the perfect accompaniment to a kebap.

DON'T MISS

CAPPADOCIA FROM ABOVE

If you've never taken a flight in a hot-air balloon, Cappadocia is one of the best places in the world to try it. Flight conditions are especially favourable here, with balloons operating most mornings throughout the year. Seeing this area's remarkable landscape from above is a truly magical experience and many travellers judge it to be the highlight of their trip.

Be aware that, despite the aura of luxury that surrounds the hot-air ballooning industry, this is an adventure activity and is not without its risks. There have been several fatal ballooning accidents here over the past decade. It's your responsibility to check the credentials of your chosen operator carefully. The following agencies have good credentials.

Butterfly Balloons (☎0384-271 3010; www.butterflyballoons.com; Uzundere Caddesi 29; 1hr flight €140; ⊙9.30am-6pm)

Royal Balloon (☎0384-271 3300; www.royalballoon.com; Dutlu Sokak 9; 1hr flight €175; ⊙9.30am-5.30pm)

Cappadocia

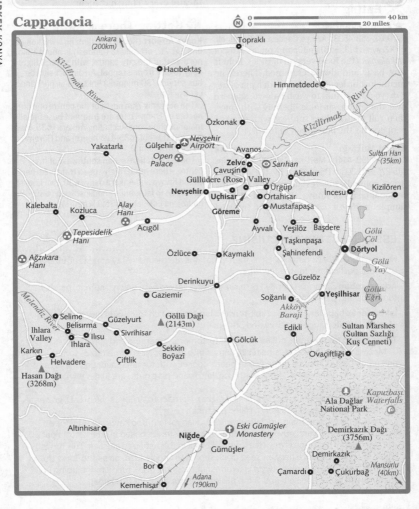

Cappadocia

As if plucked from a whimsical fairy tale and set down upon the stark Anatolian plains, Cappadocia is a geological oddity of honeycombed hills and towering boulders of otherworldly beauty. The fantastical topography is matched by the human history here. People have long utilised the region's soft stone, seeking shelter underground. Rock-hewn churches covered in Byzantine frescoes are secreted into cliffs, the villages are honeycombed out of hillsides and vast subterranean complexes, where early Christians once hid, are tunnelled under the ground.

Göreme

POP 2200

Surrounded by epic sweeps of moonscape valley, this remarkable honey-coloured village hollowed out of the hills may have long since grown beyond its farming-hamlet roots, but its charm has not diminished. Nearby, the Göreme Open-Air Museum is an all-in-one testament to Byzantine life, while if you wander out of town you'll find storybook landscapes and little-visited rock-cut churches at every turn. With its easygoing allure and stunning setting, it's no wonder Göreme continues to send travellers giddy.

◉ Sights & Activities

★ Göreme Open-Air Museum
HISTORIC SITE

(Göreme Açık Hava Müzesi; ☑0384-271 2167; Müze Caddesi; ₺30; ☉8.30am-7pm Apr-Nov, to 5pm Dec-Mar) One of Turkey's Unesco World Heritage sites, the Göreme Open-Air Museum is an essential stop on any Cappadocian itinerary and deserves a two-hour visit. First an important Byzantine monastic settlement that housed some 20 monks, then a pilgrimage site from the 17th century, this splendid cluster of monastic Byzantine artistry with its rock-cut churches, chapels and monasteries is 1km uphill from Göreme's centre.

Note that the museum's highlight – the Karanlık Kilise (Dark Church) – has an additional ₺10 entrance fee.

★ Güllüdere (Rose) Valley
AREA

FREE The trails that loop around Güllüdere Vadısı (Rose Valley) are easily accessible to all levels of walkers and provide some of the finest fairy chimney–strewn vistas in Cappadocia. As well as this, though, they hide fabulous, little-visited rock-cut churches boasting vibrant fresco fragments and intricate carvings hewn into the stone. If you only have time to hike through one valley in Cappadocia, this is the one to choose.

ITALY, GREECE & TURKEY CAPPADOCIA

GOING UNDERGROUND

Thought to have been carved out by the Hittites, the vast network of Cappadocia's underground cities was first mentioned by the ancient Greek historian Xenophon in his *Anabasis* (written in the 4th century BC).

During the 6th and 7th centuries, Byzantine Christians extended and enlarged the cities and used them as a means by which to escape persecution. If Persian or Arab armies were approaching, a series of beacons would be lit in warning – the message could travel from Jerusalem to Constantinople in hours. When it reached Cappadocia, the Christians would gather their belongings and relocate to the underground cities, hiding in the subterranean vaults for months at a time.

Some of the cities are remarkable in scale – it is thought that Derinkuyu and Kaymaklı housed about 10,000 and 3000 people respectively.

Around 37 underground cities have already been opened. There are at least 100 more, though the full extent of these subterranean refuges may never be known.

Touring the cities is like tackling an assault course for history buffs. Narrow walkways lead you into the depths of the earth, through stables with handles used to tether animals, churches with altars and baptism pools, walls with air-circulation holes, granaries with grindstones, and blackened kitchens with ovens. While it's a fascinating experience, be prepared for unpleasantly crowded and sometimes claustrophobic passages. Avoid visiting on weekends, when busloads of domestic tourists descend. Even if you don't normally like having a guide, it's worth having one: they can conjure up the details of life below the ground better than you can on your own.

WORTH A TRIP

HIKING THE IHLARA VALLEY

Southeast of Aksaray, the Ihlara Valley scythes through the stubbly fields and today is home to one of the prettiest strolls in the world. Once called Peristrema, the valley was a favourite retreat of Byzantine monks, who cut churches into the base of its towering cliffs.

Following the Melendiz River as it snakes between painted churches, piles of boulders and a sea of greenery ringing with birdsong and croaking frogs, is an unforgettable experience. The best times to visit are midweek in May (when spring blossoms abound) or September, when fewer people are about. There is an ATM in Ihlara village.

Ihlara Valley (Ihlara Vadısı; ₺20 incl Selime Monastery, Güzelyurt's Monastery Valley & Aksaray Museum; ⊗8am-6.30pm) Hiking the full trail between Ihlara village and Selime is a wonderfully bucolic day out. Most visitors come on a tour and only walk the short stretch with most of the churches, entering via the 360 steps of the **Ihlara Vadısı Turistik Tesisleri** (Ihlara Valley Tourist Facility) ticket booth and exiting at Belisırma. This means the rest of the path is blissfully serene, with farmers tilling their fields and shepherds grazing their flocks the only people you're likely to meet.

Other entrances are at **Ihlara village**, **Belisırma** and **Selime**. Including stops to visit the churches along the way, it takes about an hour to walk from Ihlara village to the Ihlara Vadısı Turistik Tesisleri stairs, 1½ hours to walk from there to Belisırma, and another hour to walk from Belisırma to Selime.

If you're planning to walk the entire trail, it's best to start early in the day, particularly in summer, when you'll need to take shelter from the fierce sun. Along the valley floor, signs mark the different churches.

Selime Monastery (Selime village; ₺20 incl Ihlara Valley, Güzelyurt's Monastery Valley & Aksaray Museum; ⊗8am-6pm) The monastery at Selime is an astonishing rock-cut structure incorporating a vast kitchen with a soaring chimney, three churches, stables with rock-carved feed troughs and other evidence of the troglodyte lifestyle.

Hot-Air Ballooning

Göreme is one of the best places in the world to go hot-air ballooning. Flight conditions are especially favourable here and seeing this remarkable landscape from above is a truly magical experience. Flights start from around ₺140. The Göreme-based ballooning agencies **Turkiye Balloons** (☑0384-271 3222; www.turkiyeballoons.com; Mezar Sokak 8; 1hr flight €140; ⊗9.30am-6pm), **Voyager Balloons** (☑0384-271 3030; www.voyagerballoons.com; Müze Caddesi 36/1; 1hr flight €140; ⊗9.30am-5pm), **Butterfly Balloons** (☑0384-271 3010; www.butterflyballoons.com; Uzundere Caddesi 29; 1hr flight €140; ⊗9.30am-6pm) and **Royal Balloon** (☑0384-271 3300; www.royalballoon.com; Dutlu Sokak 9; 1hr flight €175; ⊗9.30am-5.30pm) have good credentials.

Tours

Yama Tours   TOURS
(☑0384-271 2508; www.yamatours.com; Müze Caddesi 2; group tours north/south €29/34; ⊗9.30am-6pm) This popular backpacker-friendly travel agency runs daily Cappadocia North (Göreme Open-Air Museum, Paşabağı and Avanos) and South (Ihlara Valley and Derinkuyu Underground City) tours. They can also organise a bag full of other Cappadocia adventures and activities for you, including private trips to Hacıbektaş and Soğanlı that take in plenty of sights along the way, and three-day trips to Mt Nemrut.

Heritage Travel   TOURS
(☑0384-271 2687; www.turkishheritagetravel. com; Uzundere Caddesi; day tours per person cash/credit card €45/55; ⊗8.30am-5.30pm) This highly recommended local agency offers day-tour itineraries that differ from most operators in Cappadocia, including an 'Undiscovered Cappadocia' trip that visits Soğanlı, Mustafapaşa and Derinkuyu Underground City. It also offers private day trips for those with particular interests, including jeep safaris, tours to Hacıbektaş and a fresco trip exploring Cappadocia's Byzantine heritage.

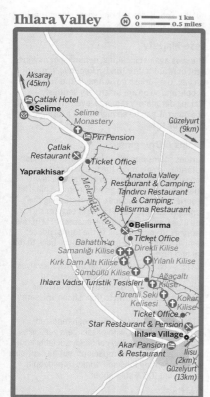

Ihlara Valley

0 — 1 km
0 — 0.5 miles

Aksaray
(45km)

Çatlak Hotel
Selime

Selime
Monastery

Güzelyurt
(9km)

Pirli Pension

Çatlak
Restaurant

Ticket Office

Yaprakhisar

Anatolia Valley
Restaurant & Camping;
Tandırcı Restaurant
& Camping;
Belisırma Restaurant

Belisırma

Ticket Office

Bahattin'in
Samanlığı Kilise
Kırk Dam Altı Kilise
Sümbüllü Kilise
Ihlara Vadısı Turistik Tesisleri

Direkli Kilise

Yılanlı Kilise

Ağaçaltı

Pürenli Seki
Kelisesi

Ticket Office

Kokar
Kilise

Star Restaurant & Pension

Ihlara Village

Akar Pansion
& Restaurant

Ilısu
(2km);
Güzelyurt
(13km)

ITALY, GREECE & TURKEY CAPPADOCIA

🛏 Sleeping

Dorm Cave
HOSTEL €

(☎0384-271 2770; www.travellerscave.com; Hafız Abdullah Efendi Sokak 4; dm/d €7/25, ste from €45; ➤🛜) Who needs to pay wads of cash to stay in a Cappadocian cave? This hostel offers three spacious cave-dorms that share small bathrooms across the courtyard and three petite private rooms upstairs. Next door, they've branched out with new comfortable suite-style rooms but if you're in that price range you're better off heading further up the hill for terrace views.

★ Kelebek Hotel
BOUTIQUE HOTEL €€

(☎0384-271 2531; www.kelebekhotel.com; Yavuz Sokak 31; s €44-56, d €55-70, fairy chimney s €56-84, d €70-105, s/d without bathroom €44/55, s/d ste from €68/85; P➤✳🛜🍴) Local guru Ali Yavuz leads a charming team at one of Göreme's original boutique hotels, which

has seen a travel industry virtually spring from beneath its stunning terraces. Exuding Anatolian inspiration at every turn, the rooms are spread over a labyrinth of stairs and balconies interconnecting two gorgeous stone houses, each with a fairy chimney protruding skyward.

🍴 Eating

Fırın Express
PIDE €

(☎0384-271 2266; Camı Sokak; pide ₺7-13; ⊙10am-10pm; 🛜🍴) Simply the best pide (Turkish-style pizza) in town is found in this local haunt. The cavernous wood oven fires up meat and vegetarian options and anything doused with egg. For a bargain feed we suggest the *patlıcanı* (aubergine) pide or *ıspınaklı kaşarlı* (spinach and cheese) pide and adding an *ayran* (yoghurt drink) to wash it down with.

★ Topdeck Cave Restaurant
ANATOLIAN €€

(☎0384-271 2474; Hafız Abdullah Efendi Sokak 15; mains ₺28-45; ⊙6-11pm) If it feels as though you're dining in a family home, it's because you are. Talented chef Mustafa (aka Topdeck) and his gracious clan have transformed an atmospheric cave room in their house into a cosy restaurant where the kids pitch in with the serving and diners dig into hearty helpings of Anatolian favourites with a spicy twist.

Göreme Market
MARKET

(⊙9am-4pm Wed) Pick up loads of fresh produce, locally made cheese and all sorts of other foodie delights at Göreme's weekly market.

ℹ Getting There & Away

AIR

Two airports serve central Cappadocia: **Kayseri Airport** (Kayseri Erkilet Havalimanı; ☎0352-337 5494; www.kayseri.dhmi.gov.tr; Kayseri Caddesi) and **Nevşehir Airport** (Nevşehir Kapadokya Havalimanı; ☎0384-421 4451; www.kapadokya. dhmi.gov.tr; Nevşehir Kapadokya Havaalanı Yolu, Gülşehir). Both have several flights daily to/from İstanbul.

Airport shuttle buses to Göreme from either airport must be pre-booked. All hotels can do this for you or book directly through **HeliosTransfer** (www.heliostransfer.com; Adnan Menderes Caddesi 24/A, Göreme; per passenger to/from either airport €8/10).

BUS

Most bus services from İstanbul and other western Turkey destinations travel to Cappadocia overnight. At Nevşehir, it's common for the bus to terminate there and passengers to transfer to a bus-company servis (shuttle bus) for the final 20-minute journey to Göreme. The major bus companies all have offices in Göreme otogar.

Turkey Survival Guide

❶ Directory A–Z

BARGAINING

Haggling is common in bazaars, as well as for out-of-season accommodation and long taxi journeys. In other instances, you're expected to pay the stated price.

DANGERS & ANNOYANCES

Although Turkey is by no means a dangerous country to visit, it's always wise to be a little cautious, especially if you're travelling alone.

Assaults

Sexual assaults have occurred against travellers of both sexes in hotels in central and eastern Anatolia. Make enquiries, check forums and try to do a little research in advance if you are travelling alone or heading off the beaten track.

Flies & Mosquitoes

In high summer, mosquitoes are troublesome even in İstanbul; they can make a stay along the coast a nightmare. Some hotel rooms come equipped with nets and/or plug-in bug-busters,

---

> ### ❶ SLEEPING PRICE RANGES
>
> Ranges are based on the cost of a double room in high season and include tax (KDV), an en suite bathroom and breakfast.
>
> #### İstanbul
>
> € less than €80
>
> €€ €80–180
>
> €€€ more than €180
>
> #### Rest of Turkey
>
> € less than €25
>
> €€ €26–60
>
> €€€ more than €60

---

but it's a good idea to bring some insect repellent and mosquito coils.

Lese-Majesty

The laws against insulting, defaming or making light of Atatürk, the Turkish Republic, the Turkish flag, the Turkish government, the Turkish people and so on are taken very seriously. Making derogatory remarks, even in the heat of a quarrel, can be enough to get a foreigner carted off to jail.

Scams & Druggings

Various scams operate in İstanbul. In the most notorious, single men (the usual target) are befriended, invited to a bar and, after a few drinks, presented with an astronomical bill. The proprietors can produce a menu showing the same prices. If you don't have enough cash, you'll be frogmarched to the nearest ATM. If this happens to you, report it to the tourist police; some travellers have taken the police back to the bar and received a refund.

A less common variation on this trick involves the traveller having their drink spiked and waking up in an unexpected place with their belongings, right down to their shoes, missing – or worse.

The spiking scam has also been reported on overnight trains, with passengers getting robbed. Turks are often genuinely sociable and generous travelling companions, but be cautious about accepting food and drinks from people you are not 100% sure about.

Traffic

As a pedestrian, note that some Turks are aggressive, dangerous drivers; 'right of way' doesn't compute with many motorists, despite the little green man on traffic lights. Give way to vehicles in all situations, even if you have to jump out of the way.

ELECTRICITY

➡ Electrical current is 230V AC, 50Hz.

➡ You can buy plug adaptors at electrical shops.

EMBASSIES & CONSULATES

Australian Embassy (☑ for initial appointment 0312-459 9500; www.turkey.embassy.gov.au; 7th fl, MNG Bldg, Uğur Mumcu Caddesi 88, Gaziosmanpaşa; ⊙8.30am-4.45pm Mon-Fri)

Canadian Embassy (☑ 0312-409 2700; http://turkey.gc.ca; Cinnah Caddesi 58, Çankaya; ⊙8am-noon & 12.30-4.45pm Mon-Thu, 8am-12.30pm Fri)

New Zealand Embassy (☑ 0312-446 3333; www.nzembassy.com/turkey; Kizkulesi Sokak 11, Gaziosmanpaşa; ⊙8.30am-5pm Mon-Fri)

UK Embassy (⌨ 0312-455 3344; www.gov.
uk/world/turkey; Şehit Ersan Caddesi 46a,
Çankaya; ⊙8.45am-5pm Mon-Fri)
US Embassy (⌨ for initial appointment 0312-
455 5555; https://tr.usembassy.gov; Atatürk
Bulvarı 110, Kavaklıdere; ⊙9am-4pm Mon-Fri)

EMERGENCY & IMPORTANT NUMBERS

Turkey country code	⌨90
International access code from Turkey	⌨00
Ambulance	⌨112
Fire	⌨110
Police	⌨155

ETIQUETTE

Religion Dress modestly and be quiet and respectful around mosques.

Restaurants Generally, whoever extended the invitation to eat together picks up the bill.

Alcohol Bars are common, but public drinking and inebriation are less acceptable away from tourist towns.

Greetings Turks value respect; greet or acknowledge people.

Language Learn a few Turkish phrases; it's immeasurably helpful and appreciated by Turks.

Relationships Do not be overly tactile with your partner in public; beware miscommunications with locals.

Politics Be tactful; criticising Turkish nationalism can land you in prison.

Shopping Visiting the bazaar, be prepared to haggle and drink tea with shopkeepers.

Queues Turks can be pushy in public situations; be assertive.

GAY & LESBIAN TRAVELLERS

Homosexuality is not a criminal offence in Turkey, but prejudice remains strong and there are sporadic reports of violence towards gay people – the message is discretion. İstanbul has a flourishing gay scene, as does Ankara.

BHN Mavi Tours (www.turkey-gay-travel.com) Gay-friendly İstanbul travel agent, with useful links on its website.

Kaos GL (www.kaosgl.com) Based in Ankara, the LGBT rights organisation publishes a gay-and-lesbian magazine and website with news and information in English.

Lambdaistanbul (www.lambdaistanbul. org) The Turkish branch of the International Lesbian, Gay, Bisexual, Trans and Intersexual Association.

LGBTI News Turkey (www.lgbtinewsturkey. com) News and links.

MONEY

➡ Turkey's currency is the Türk lirası (Turkish lira; ₺). The lira comes in notes of five, 10, 20, 50, 100 and 200, and coins of one, five, 10, 25 and 50 kuruş and one lira.

➡ ATMs are widely available.

➡ Visa and MasterCard are widely accepted by hotels, shops and restaurants, although often not by pensions and local restaurants outside the main tourist areas. You can also get cash advances on these cards. Amex is less commonly accepted outside top-end establishments.

Moneychangers

The Turkish lira is weak against Western currencies, and you will probably get a better exchange rate in Turkey than elsewhere. The lira is virtually worthless outside Turkey, so make sure you spend it all before leaving.

US dollars and euros are the easiest currencies to change. You'll get better rates at exchange offices, which often don't charge commission, than at banks. Turkey has no black market.

Tipping

Turkey is fairly European in its approach to tipping and you won't be pestered for baksheesh. Tipping is customary in restaurants, hotels and taxis; optional elsewhere.

Restaurants A few coins in budget eateries; 10% to 15% of the bill in midrange and top-end establishments.

Taxis Round up metered fares to the nearest 50 kuruş.

OPENING HOURS

The following are standard opening hours.

Tourist information 9am to 12.30pm and 1.30pm to 5pm Monday to Friday

Restaurants 11am to 10pm

Bars 4pm to late

Nightclubs 11pm to late

Shops 9am to 6pm Monday to Friday (longer in tourist areas and big cities – including weekend opening)

Government departments, offices and banks 8.30am tonoon and 1.30pm to 5pm Monday to Friday

---

ℹ **EATING PRICE RANGES**

Price ranges reflect the cost of a standard main-course dish.

€ less than ₺25

€€ ₺25–40

€€€ more than ₺40

MAJOR ISLAMIC HOLIDAYS

The rhythms of Islamic practice are tied to the lunar calendar, which is slightly shorter than its Gregorian equivalent, so the Muslim calendar begins around 11 days earlier each year. The following dates are approximate.

Islamic year	New Year	Prophet's Birthday	Start of Ramazan	Şeker Bayramı (After Ramazan finishes)	Kurban Bayramı
1440	20-21 Sep 2018	20-21 Nov 2018	16 May 2018	15-17 Jun 2018	21-24 Aug 2018
1441	31 Aug-1 Sep 2018	9-10 Nov 2019	6 May 2019	5-7 Jun 2019	11-14 Aug 2019
1442	19-20 Aug	28-29 Oct	23 Apr 2020	24-26 May 2020	31 July-3 Aug 2020

PUBLIC HOLIDAYS

As well as major Islamic holidays, the following are observed in Turkey:

New Year's Day (Yılbaşı) 1 January

National Sovereignty & Children's Day (Ulusal Egemenlik ve Çocuk Günü) 23 April

Labor & Solidarity Day (May Day) 1 May

Commemoration of Atatürk, Youth & Sports Day (Gençlik ve Spor Günü) 19 May

Democracy and National Solidarity Day 15 July

Victory Day (Zafer Bayramı) 30 August

Republic Day (Cumhuriyet Bayramı) 29 October

TELEPHONE

➡ Payphones require cards that can be bought at telephone centres or, for a small mark-up, at some shops.

➡ If you set up a roaming facility with your home phone provider, you should be able to connect your mobile to a network.

➡ SIM cards cost around ₺85 (including ₺30 in local call credit).

TRAVEL WITH CHILDREN

Your *çocuklar* (children) will be welcomed wherever they go. Your journey will be peppered with exclamations of *Maşallah* (glory be to God) and your children will be clutched into the adoring arms of strangers.

➡ Cots are increasingly common; many hotels will organise one with advance notice.

➡ Children's menus are uncommon outside tourist areas, but restaurants will often prepare special dishes for children.

➡ High chairs are by no means common, but increasingly widespread in tourist areas (apart from İstanbul).

➡ Public baby-changing facilities are rare.

➡ Breastfeeding in public is uncommon; it's best to do so in a private or discreet place.

➡ Free travel on public transport within cities, and discounts on longer journeys, are common for children.

➡ Dangerous drivers and uneven surfaces make using strollers an extreme sport.

➡ Pasteurised UHT milk is sold in cartons everywhere, but fresh milk is harder to find.

➡ Migros supermarkets have the best range of baby food.

➡ Most supermarkets stock formula (although it is very expensive) and vitamin-fortified rice cereal.

➡ Disposable *bebek bezi* (nappies or diapers) are readily available.

VISAS

➡ Nationals of countries including Denmark, Finland, France, Germany, Israel, Italy, Japan, New Zealand, Norway, Sweden and Switzerland don't need a visa to visit Turkey for a period of up to 90 days.

➡ Nationals of countries including Australia, Austria, Belgium, Canada, Ireland, the Netherlands, Norway, Portugal, Spain, the UK and USA need a visa, which must be purchased online at www.evisa.gov.tr before travelling.

➡ Most nationalities, including the above, are given a 90-day multiple-entry visa.

➡ In most cases, the 90-day visa stipulates 'per period 180 days'. This means you can spend three months in Turkey within a six-month period; when you leave after three months, you can't re-enter for three months.

➡ Visa fees cost US$15 to US$80, depending on nationality.

➡ Your passport must be valid for at least six months from the date that you enter the country.

WOMEN TRAVELLERS

Travelling in Turkey is straightforward for women, provided that you follow some simple guidelines.

➡ Outside tourist areas, the cheapest hotels are generally not suitable for women who are travelling alone. Stick with family-oriented midrange hotels.

➡ If there is a knock on your hotel door late at night, don't open it; in the morning, complain to the manager.

➡ Look at what local women are wearing. Cleavage and short skirts without leggings are a no-no everywhere except nightclubs in İstanbul and heavily touristed destinations along the coast.

➡ When you are travelling by taxi and dolmuş, try to avoid getting into the seat beside the driver, as this can be misinterpeted as a come-on.

❶ Getting There & Away

AIR
Airports

Atatürk International Airport (p567) İstanbul's main airport is in Yeşilköy, 23km west of Sultanahmet. The international terminal (Dış Hatlar) is polished and organised.

Sabiha Gökçen International Airport (p567) This airport on İstanbul's Asian side is popular with low-cost European airlines, but is not as conveniently located as Atatürk.

Antalya International Airport (Antalya Havalimanı; ☑ 0242-444 7423; www.aytport.com; Serik Caddesi) Receives flights from across Turkey and Europe.

Adnan Menderes Airport (☑ 444 9828; www.adnanmenderesairport.com; ☎) There are many flights to İzmir's Adnan Menderes Airport from European destinations.

Milas-Bodrum Airport (BJV; ☑ 444 9828; www.milas-bodrumairport.com) Receives flights from all over Europe, mostly with charter flights and budget airlines in summer, and from İstanbul and Ankara with the Turkish airlines.

Airlines

Turkish Airlines (☑ 1800-874 8875; www.turkishairlines.com), the national carrier, has extensive international and domestic networks, including budget subsidiaries **Sun Express** (☑ 444 0797; www.sunexpress.com) and **Anadolu Jet** (☑ 444 2538; www.anadolujet.com/tr). It is generally considered a safe airline, and its operational safety is certified by the International Air Transport Association (IATA).

LAND

There are direct bus services that run to İstanbul from Austria, Albania, Bulgaria, Germany, Greece, Hungary, Kosovo, the Republic of Macedonia, Romania and Slovenia. Major bus companies that operate these routes include **Metro Turizm** (☑ 0850-222 3455; www.metroturizm.com.tr) and **Ulusoy** (☑ 0850-811 1888; www.ulusoy.com.tr). Currently the only train route operating between Europe and İstanbul is the daily Bosfor/Balkan Ekspresi to Bucharest (Romania) and Sofia (Bulgaria). See **Turkish State Railways** (www.tcdd.gov.tr) for details.

SEA

Departure times and routes change between seasons, with fewer ferries generally running in the winter. Ferry lines (www.ferrylines.com) is a good starting point for information. The following is a list of ferry routes from Turkey:

Ayvalık–Lesvos, Greece (www.erturk.com.tr/en, www.jaletour.com)

Bodrum–Kos, Greece (www.bodrumexpresslines.com, www.bodrumferryboat.com, www.erturk.com.tr/en)

Bodrum–Rhodes, Greece (www.bodrumexpresslines.com, www.bodrumferryboat.com, www.erturk.com.tr/en, www.rhodesferry.com)

Marmaris–Rhodes, Greece (www.marmarisferry.com, www.rhodesferry.com)

Turgutreis–Kos, Greece (www.bodrumexpresslines.com, www.bodrumferryboat.com)

❶ Getting Around

BUS
➡ Turkey's intercity bus system is as good as any you'll find, with modern, comfortable coaches crossing the country at all hours and for very reasonable prices.

➡ Major companies with extensive networks include **Kamil Koç** (☑ 444 0562; www.kamilkoc.com.tr), Metro Turizm and Ulusoy.

➡ A town's otogar is often on the outskirts, but most bus companies provide a *servis* (free shuttle bus) to/from the centre.

➡ Local routes are usually operated by dolmuşes (minibuses), which might run to a timetable or set off when full.

CAR & MOTORCYCLE
➡ Turkey has the world's second-highest petrol prices. Petrol and diesel cost about ₺5.30 per litre.

➡ An international driving permit (IDP) is not obligatory, but handy if your driving licence is from a country likely to seem obscure to a Turkish police officer.

→ You must be at least 21 years of age to hire a car. Rental charges are similar to those in Europe.

→ You must have third-party insurance if you are bringing your own car into the country. Buying third-party insurance when you get to the border is a straightforward process (one month €80).

→ Road accidents claim about 10,000 lives in Turkey each year.

TRAIN

Train travel through Turkey is becoming increasingly popular as improvements are made, with high-speed lines such as İstanbul–Ankara appearing.

If you're on a budget, an overnight train journey is a great way to save accommodation costs.

InterRail, Balkan Flexipass and Eurodomino passes are valid on the Turkish railway network, but Eurail passes are not.

Balkans

Why Go?

The Balkans are an incredibly diverse and fast-changing slice of Europe, where the traces of the Habsburg and Ottoman Empires are never far away and the ancient and modern often coexist. Fabulous Croatia, famed for its island-studded coastline, as well as the walled city of Dubrovnik, is the most visited of the pack. But don't discount the magnificent mountain scenery of Slovenia and Montenegro, hip Serbia with its fortress cities and exuberant music festivals, Bosnia's rugged countryside and gorgeous Muslim-influenced old towns, or the sublime beaches and lakes of Albania and Macedonia. Travel here is a little rough around the edges compared with destinations further north and west, but few people visit the Balkans without leaving in awe, seduced by the hospitality and with their preconceptions smashed.

Best Places to Eat

➡ Male Madlene (p605)

➡ Konoba Školji (p633)

➡ Letna Bavča Kaneo (p655)

➡ Little Bay (p664)

Best Places to Sleep

➡ Isabegov Hamam Hotel (p619)

➡ Palazzo Drusko (p632)

➡ Hotel Mangalemi (p644)

➡ Villa Dihovo (p656)

➡ Savamala Bed & Breakfast (p664)

Fast Facts

Capitals Ljubljana (Slovenia), Zagreb (Croatia), Sarajevo (Bosnia and Hercegovina), Podgorica (Montenegro), Tirana (Albania), Skopje (Macedonia), Pristina (Kosovo), Belgrade (Serbia)

Currencies Convertible mark (KM; Bosnia & Hercegovina), dinar (DIN; Serbia), denar (MKD; Macedonia), euro (€; Kosovo, Montenegro, Slovenia), kuna (KN; Croatia), lekë (Albania)

Languages Albanian, Bosnian, Croatian, Macedonian, Montenegrin, Serbian, Slovene

Visas Not needed for EU, US, Canadian, Australian or New Zealand citizens

Time zones Central European Time; GMT/UTC plus one hour

Balkans Highlights

1 Ljubljana Strolling around Slovenia's tiny green capital. (p586)

2 Lake Bled Admiring the fairy-tale lake with the Julian Alps as a backdrop. (p592)

3 Split Exploring the mazelike Diocletian's Palace, the living soul of Dalmatia's great Adriatic port. (p605)

4 Sarajevo Experiencing the buzz of Baščaršija quarter's fascinating Ottoman-era alleyways. (p615)

5 Dubrovnik Circling the unforgettable city walls and marble streets in Croatia's most famous city. (p609)

6 **Kotor** Getting lost in the walled town wedged between mountains and bay. (p630)

7 **Berat** Travelling back in time in 'the town of a thousand windows'. (p643)

8 **Lake Ohrid** Taking a dip in the serene lake and roaming the old town. (p654)

9 **Belgrade** Soaking up Kalemegdan Citadel's history

and partying the night away on a river barge. (p658)

10 **Novi Sad** Feeling the laid-back vibe in the vibrant, creative city that hosts the famous EXIT festival. (p666)

SLOVENIA

Ljubljana

POP 278,800

Slovenia's capital and largest city also happens to be one of Europe's greenest and most liveable capitals. Car traffic is restricted in the centre, leaving the leafy banks of the emerald-green Ljubljanica River, which flows through the city's heart, free for pedestrians and cyclists. There's an active clubbing and cultural scene, and the museums, hotels and restaurants are among the best in the country.

◉ Sights

The easiest way to see Ljubljana is on foot. The oldest part of town, with the most important historical buildings and sights (including Ljubljana Castle), lies on the right (east) bank of the Ljubljanica River. The centre, which has the lion's share of the city's museums and galleries, is on the left (west) side of the river.

★ Ljubljana Castle   CASTLE

(Ljubljanski Grad; ☑ 01-306 42 93; www.ljubljanski-grad.si; Grajska Planota 1; adult/child incl funicular & castle attractions €10/7, castle attractions only €7.50/5.20; ⊙ castle 9am-11pm Jun-Sep, to 9pm Apr, May & Oct, 10am-8pm Jan-Mar & Nov, to 10pm Dec) Crowning a 375-metre-high hill east of the Old Town, the castle is an architectural mishmash, but most of it dates to the early 16th century when it was largely rebuilt after a devastating earthquake. It's free to ramble around the castle grounds, but you'll have to pay to enter the Watchtower, the Chapel of St George, to see the worthwhile Exhibition on Slovenian History, visit the new Puppet Theatre and take the Time Machine tour.

★ Prešernov Trg   SQUARE

The centrepiece of Ljubljana's wonderful architectural aesthetic is this marvellous square, a public space of understated elegance that not only serves as the link between the Center district and the Old Town but as the city's favourite meeting point. Taking pride of place is the **Prešeren monument** (Prešernov Trg) (1905) designed by Maks Fabiani and Ivan Zajc, and erected in honour of Slovenia's greatest poet, France Prešeren (1800–49). On the plinth are motifs from his poems.

Triple Bridge   BRIDGE

(Tromostovje; ⊙ 24h) Running south from the square to the Old Town is the much celebrated Triple Bridge. Originally called Špital (Hospital) Bridge, when it was built as a single span in 1842 it was nothing spectacular, but between 1929 and 1932 superstar architect Jože Plečnik added the two pedestrian side bridges, furnished all three with stone balustrades and lamps and forced a name change. Stairways on each of the side bridges lead down to the poplar-lined terraces along the Ljubljanica River.

★ National &
University Library   ARCHITECTURE

(Narodna in Univerzitetna Knjižnica, NUK; ☑ 01-200 12 09; www.nuk.uni-lj.si; Turjaška ulica 1; ⊙ 8am-8pm Mon-Fri, 9am-2pm Sat) This library is Jože Plečnik's masterpiece, completed in 1941. To appreciate this great man's philosophy, enter through the main door (note the horsehead doorknobs) on Turjaška ulica – you'll find yourself in near darkness, entombed in black marble. As you ascend the steps, you'll emerge into a colonnade suffused with light – the light of knowledge, according to the architect's plans.

National Gallery of Slovenia   MUSEUM

(☑ 01-241 54 18; www.ng-slo.si; Prešernova cesta 24; adult/child €7/3, 1st Sun of month free; ⊙ 10am-6pm Tue, Wed & Fri-Sun, to 8pm Thu) Slovenia's foremost assembly of fine art is housed over two floors both in an old building (1896) and a modern wing. It exhibits copies of medieval frescoes and wonderful Gothic statuary as well as Slovenian landscapes from the 17th to 19th centuries (check out works by Romantic painters Pavel Künl and Marko Pernhart). Other noteworthies: impressionists Jurij Šubic *(Before the Hunt)* and Rihard Jakopič *(Birches in Autumn)*, the pointillist Ivan Grohar *(Larch)* and Slovenia's most celebrated female painter, Ivana Kobilca *(Summer)*.

National Museum of Slovenia   MUSEUM

(Narodni Muzej Slovenije; ☑ 01-241 44 00; www.nms.si; Prešernova cesta 20; adult/student €6/4, with National Museum of Slovenia Metelkova or Slovenian Museum of Natural History €8.50/6, lapidarium free; ⊙ 10am-6pm, to 8pm Thu) Housed in a grand building from 1888 -- the same building as the Slovenian Museum of Natural History -- highlights include a highly embossed Vače situla, a Celtic pail from the 6th century BC unearthed in a town east of Ljubljana, and a Stone Age bone flute dis-

Slovenia

covered near Cerkno in western Slovenia in 1995. There are also examples of Roman jewellery found in 6th-century Slavic graves as well as a glass-enclosed Roman lapidarium (free entry) outside to the north.

🛏 Sleeping

⭐ Hostel Vrba
HOSTEL €

(📞 064 133 555; www.hostelvrba.si; Gradaška ulica 10; dm €11-17, d €35-65; @ 🛜) Definitely one of our favourite budget accommodations in Ljubljana, this nine-room hostel on the Gradiščica Canal is just opposite the bars and restaurants of delightful Trnovo. There are three doubles, dorms with four to eight beds, including a popular all-female dorm, hardwood floors, and an always warm welcome. Free bikes, too, in summer.

⭐ Hostel Tresor
HOSTEL €€

(📞 01-200 90 60; www.hostel-tresor.si; Čopova ulica 38; dm €11-15, d €38; ❄@🛜) This new 28-room hostel in the heart of Center is housed in a Secessionist-style former bank, and the money theme continues right into rooms named after currencies and financial aphorisms on the walls. Dorms have between four and 12 beds but are spacious. The communal areas (we love the atrium) are stunning; breakfast is served in the vaults.

⭐ Adora Hotel
HOTEL €€

(📞 082 057 240; www.adorahotel.si; Rožna ulica 7; s €115, d €125-155, apt €125-155; P❄@🛜) This small hotel located below Gornji trg is a welcome addition to accommodation options in Ljubljana's Old Town. The 10 rooms are small but fully equipped, with lovely hardwood floors and tasteful furnishings. The lovely breakfast room looks out onto a small garden, bikes are free for guests' use and the staff are overwhelmingly friendly and helpful.

SLOVENIA AT A GLANCE

Don't Miss

Climbing Mt Triglav The 2864m Mt Triglav (Three Heads) has been a source of inspiration and an object of devotion for Slovenes for more than a millennium. It's a challenging but accessible peak that just about anyone in decent shape can 'conquer' with an experienced guide. The reward is sheer exhilaration.

Ljubljana Slovenia's capital strikes that perfect yet elusive balance between size and quality of life. It's big enough to offer discoveries yet small enough to walk around at a leisurely pace. And no place in Slovenia waltzes through architecture so adroitly as the capital named 'beloved'.

Lake Bled This sky-blue lake in the Julian Alps seems to have been designed by the very god of tourism. But Bled offers more than just a picture-postcard church on a tiny island. There's a raucous adventure scene too, with diving, cycling, rafting and canyoning among other active pursuits.

Piran Slovenia was lucky to end up with one of the best-preserved medieval Venetian ports anywhere. Piran is never less than a constant delight. Enjoy fresh fish on the harbour, then wander the narrow streets and end up for drinks and people-watching in a glorious central square.

Postojna Cave The cave system at Postojna is Slovenia's biggest subterranean attraction. The caverns are a seemingly endless parade of crystal fancies – from frilly chandeliers and dripping spaghetti-like stalactites, to paper-thin sheets and stupendous stalagmites, all laid down over the centuries by the simple dripping of mineral-rich water.

Itineraries

One Week

This itinerary is ideal for first-time visitors wanting to experience the highlights of the country's alpine and coastal regions. Begin in the country's capital, **Ljubljana**, allowing a few days to take in the sights, restaurants and beautiful riverside setting. Next, head north to Lake Bled, for lakeside ambles and taking a *pletna* (gondola) to Bled Island. It's a popular approach for forays into **Triglav National Park** and scaling Mt Triglav.

Two Weeks

Continue northwest of Bled to Soča Valley and the activities centre of **Bovec** for white-water rafting trips on the Soča River. Then head back south to the amazing cave at **Postojna** and on to the coastal resorts of Piran and **Portorož**. If you're seeking romance, choose Piran; if it's sun and fun, Portorož is the centre of the action.

Essential Food & Drink

Žganci Slovenian dishes are often served with *žganci*, groats made from *ječmen* (barley) or *koruza* (corn) but usually *ajda* (buckwheat). A real rib-sticker is *ajdovi žganci z ocvirki, a* kind of dense buckwheat porridge with the savoury addition of *ocvirki* (pork crackling or scratchings).

Pršut Air-dried, thinly sliced ham from the Karst region that is related to Italian prosciutto.

Prekmurska gibanica A rich concoction of pastry filled with poppy seeds, walnuts, apples and cottage cheese and topped with cream.

Žganje This strong brandy is distilled from a variety of fruits. Common types are *slivovka* (made with plums), *češnjevec* (with cherries), *sadjevec* (with mixed fruit) and *brinjevec* (with juniper). A favourite type is *medica* (fruit brandy flavoured with honey).

Getting Around

Bicycle Cycling is a popular way of getting around and it's permitted on all roads except motorways. Larger towns and cities have dedicated bicycle lanes and traffic lights.

Bus Generally efficient and good value but very crowded on Friday afternoons and severely restricted on Sundays and holidays.

Car A great way to explore the countryside, with rental firms everywhere and the airport.

Train Cheaper but usually slower than buses (with the exception of intercity high-speed services). Getting from A to B often requires returning to Ljubljana.

When to Go

Ljubljana

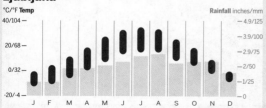

Jun–Aug Mostly sunny skies bring crowds to Ljubljana and the coast.

Apr & May, Sep & Oct Best time for hiking; September is good for climbing Mt Triglav and rafting is great by late May.

Nov–Mar Ski season; Christmas through New Year can be crowded.

Arriving in Slovenia

Jože Pučnik Airport (Ljubljana) Buses run to Ljubljana's train station hourly on weekdays (every two hours on weekends). Shuttle (€9) and taxi (around €40) services will transfer you to the centre in around half an hour.

Ljubljana train station and **Ljubljana bus station** are opposite one another north of the city centre, about a 500m walk from the Old Town. It's an easy walk, but should you need to take a taxi, nothing should cost more than €8.

Top Phrases

Hello. Zdravo.

Goodbye. Na svidenje.

Please. Prosim.

Thank you. Hvala.

How much is it? Koliko stane?

Resources

Slovenian Tourist Board (www.slovenia.info) Info on every conceivable sight and activity.

Slovenia Times (www.sloveniatimes.com) Website of the independent quarterly magazine.

City of Ljubljana (www.ljubljana.si/en) Comprehensive city hall information.

Set Your Budget

➡ Hostel dorm bed: €15–20

➡ Street food: €10

➡ Train and bus tickets: €10

➡ Bicycle rental: €15

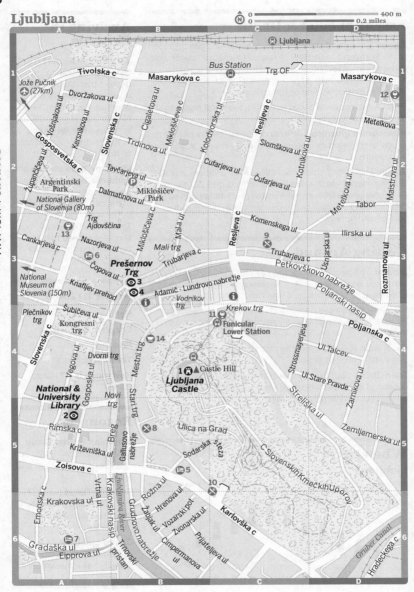

✕ Eating

 Druga Violina SLOVENIAN €

(☏ 082 052 506; www.facebook.com/drugaviolina/; Stari trg 21; mains €6-10; ⏱ 8am-midnight) Just opposite the Academy of Music, the 'Second Fiddle' is an extremely pleasant and afforda-

ble place for a meal in the Old Town. There are lots of very Slovenian dishes like *ajdova kaša z jurčki* (buckwheat groats with ceps) and *obara* (a thick stew of chicken and vegetables) on the menu. It's a social enterprise designed to help those with disabilities.

Ljubljana

Prince of Orange　　　ITALIAN €
(📞083 802 447; www.facebook.com/ThePrinceofOrange/; Komenskega ulica 30; dishes €5-10; ☺8am-5pm Mon-Fri) This bright, airy cafe serves outstanding homemade soups and bruschetta. Ask for some of the farmer's goat cheese and the link between the cafe and England's King William III (the sign on the wall is a clue). They offer a daily three-course lunch special and have a kids' playground.

Taverna Tatjana　　　SEAFOOD €€
(📞01-421 00 87; www.taverna-tatjana.si; Gornji trg 38; mains €10-25; ☺5pm-midnight Mon-Sat) This charming little tavern on the far end of Gornji trg specialises in fish and seafood (though there's some beef and foal on the menu too). Housed in several vaulted rooms of an atmospheric old townhouse with wooden ceiling beams, the fish is fresher than a spring shower.

🍷 Drinking & Nightlife

Ljubljana offers a dizzying array of drinking options. In summer, the banks of the Ljubljanica River transform into a long terrace and serve as the perfect people-watching spot. Most cafes also serve beer and wine, and many pubs and bars start the day out as cafes before morphing into nightspots after sundown.

⭐**Pritličje**　　　CAFE
(Ground Floor; 📞082 058 742; www.pritlicje.si; Mestni trg 2; ☺9am-1am Sun-Wed, to 3am Thu-Sat; 🛜) Ultra-inclusive cultural centre 'Ground Floor' offers something for everyone: cafe, bar, live music, cultural centre and comic-book shop. Events are scheduled almost nightly and the location next to the Town Hall, with good views across Mestni trg, couldn't be more perfect.

⭐**Klub Daktari**　　　BAR
(📞064 166 212; www.daktari.si; Krekov trg 7; ☺7.30am-1am Mon-Fri, 8am-1am Sat, 9am-midnight Sun) This rabbit-warren of a watering hole at the foot of the funicular to Ljubljana Castle is so chilled there's practically frost on the windows. The décor is retro-distressed, with shelves full of old books and a piano in the corner. More of a cultural centre than club, Daktari hosts live music sets and an eclectic mix of other cultural events.

Nebotičnik　　　CLUB
(📞040 233 078; www.neboticnik.si; 11th fl, Štefanova ul 1; ☺9am-1am Sun-Wed, to 3am Thu-Sat; 🛜) An elegant old cafe, its breathtaking terrace atop Ljubljana's famed art-deco Skyscraper (1933) and spectacular 360-degree views attract punters throughout the day, but Ljubljana's beau monde returns at night to party in the flashy club and lounge on the floor below — No 11.

Metelkova Mesto　　　CLUB
(Metelkova Town; www.metelkovamesto.org; Masarykova cesta 24) An ex-army garrison taken over by squatters in the 1990s and converted into a free-living commune is home to several clubs, bars and concert venues. It generally comes to life comes to life after 11pm daily in summer and on Friday and Saturday the rest of the year. While it's certainly not for the genteel, and the quality of the acts varies, there's usually a little of something for everyone.

ℹ Information

Ljubljana Tourist Information Centre (TIC; 📞01-306 12 15; www.visitljubljana.com; Adamič-Lundrovo nabrežje 2; ☺8am-9pm Jun-Sep, to 7pm Oct-May) Knowledgeable and enthusiastic staff dispense information, maps and useful literature and help with accommodation. Offers a range of interesting city and regional tours. Maintains an excellent website.
Slovenian Tourist Information Centre (STIC; 📞01-306 45 76; www.slovenia.info; Krekov trg 10; ☺8am-9pm daily Jun-Sep, 8am-7pm

DON'T MISS

POSTOJNA CAVE

The karst cave at **Postojna** (Postojnska Jama; ☑ 05-700 01 00; www.postojnska-jama.
eu; Jamska cesta 30; adult/child €25.80/15.50, with Predjama Castle €35.70/21.40; ☺ tours
hourly 9am-6pm Jul & Aug, 9am-5pm May-Jun & Sep, 10am, noon or 3pm Nov-Mar, 10am-noon
& 2-4pm Apr & Oct), one of the largest in the world, is among Slovenia's most popular
attractions, and its stalagmite and stalactite formations are unequalled anywhere. It's a
busy destination, with some 6000 visitors a day in August (rainy summer days bring the
biggest crowds). The amazing thing is how the large crowds at the entrance seem to get
swallowed whole by the size of the cave, and the tourist activity doesn't detract from the
wonder.

The jaw-dropping series of caverns, halls and passages (some 24km long and two
million years old) was hollowed out by the Pivka River, which enters a subterranean tunnel near the cave's entrance. Visitors get to see 5km of the cave on 1½-hour tours; 3.2km
of this is covered by a cool electric train. Postojna Cave has a constant temperature of
8°C to 10°C (46°F to 50°F) with a humidity of 95%, so a warm jacket and decent shoes
are advised.

Postojna is accessible by bus from Ljubljana (€6, one hour, hourly) or Piran (€8.30,
1¾ hours, four daily). It's also on a main rail line from Ljubljana (€5.80, one hour). In July
and August there is a free shuttle bus from the train station to the cave entrance.

Mon-Fri, 9am-5pm Sat & Sun Oct-May) Good
source of information for the rest of Slovenia,
with internet and bicycle rental also available.

❶ Getting There & Away

Buses to destinations both within Slovenia and
abroad leave from the **bus station**
(Avtobusna Postaja Ljubljana; ☑ 01-234 46 00;
www.ap-ljubljana.si; Trg Osvobodilne Fronte
4; ☺ 5am-10.30pm Mon-Fri, 5am-10pm Sat,
5.30am-10.30pm Sun) just next to the train
station. Next to the ticket windows are multilingual information phones and a touch-screen
computer. There's another touch-screen computer outside too.

Domestic and international trains arrive
at and depart from central Ljubljana's **train
station** (Železniška Postaja; ☑ 01-291 33 32;
www.slo-zeleznice.si; Trg Osvobodilne Fronte
6; ☺ 6am-10pm), where you'll find a separate
information centre on the way to the platforms.
Buy domestic tickets from windows 1 to 8 and
international ones from either window 9 or the
information centre.

Bled

POP 5120

Yes, it's every bit as lovely in real life. With
its emerald-green lake, picture-postcard
church on an islet, a medieval castle clinging to a rocky cliff and some of the highest
peaks of the Julian Alps and the Karavanke
as backdrops, Bled is Slovenia's most popular resort, drawing everyone from honey-
mooners lured by the over-the-top romantic

setting to backpackers, who come for the
hiking, biking, watersports and canyoning.

◉ Sights

★ **Lake Bled**   LAKE
(Blejsko jezero) Bled's greatest attraction is its
exquisite blue-green lake, measuring just
2km by 1.4km. The lake is lovely to behold
from almost any vantage point, and makes
a beautiful backdrop for the 6km walk along
the shore. Mild thermal springs warm the
water to a swimmable 26°C (79°F) from
June through August. The lake is naturally
the focus of the entire town: you can rent
boats, go diving or simply snap countless
photos.

★ **Bled Island**   ISLAND
(Blejski Otok; www.blejskiotok.si) Tiny, tear-
shaped Bled Island beckons from the shore.
There's the **Church of the Assumption** and
a small **museum**, but the real thrill is the
ride out by *pletna* (gondola). The *pletna* will
set you down on the south side at the monumental **South Staircase** (Južno Stopnišče),
built in 1655. The staircase comprises 99
steps – a local tradition is for the husband to
carry his new bride up them.

★ **Bled Castle**   CASTLE
(Blejski Grad; ☑ 04-572 97 82; www.blejski-grad.si;
Grajska cesta 25; adult/child €11/5; ☺ 8am-9pm
Jun-Aug, to 8pm Apr-May & Sep-Oct, to 6pm Nov-
Mar) Perched atop a steep cliff more than
100m above the lake, Bled Castle is how

most people imagine a medieval fortress to be, with towers, ramparts, moats and a terrace offering magnificent views. The castle houses a **museum collection** that traces the lake's history from earliest times to the development of Bled as a resort in the 19th century.

🛏️ Sleeping

Camping Bled — CAMPGROUND €
(☑02-512 22 00; www.camping-bled.com; Kidričeva cesta 10c; site from €19.80, glamping huts from €69; P@🛜) Bled's hugely popular, amenity-laden campground is in a rural valley at the western end of the lake, about 4km from the bus station. There's a rich array of family-friendly activities possible, and on-site are a restaurant and store.

Bledec Hostel — HOSTEL €
(☑04-574 52 50; www.bledec.si; Grajska cesta 17; dm €26-29, s/d €40/60; P@🛜) This well-organised HI-affiliated hostel in the shadow of the castle has 12 rooms of three to eight beds with attached bathrooms. It also has a bar, and an inexpensive restaurant (breakfast €5, dinner €10). Extra points for laundry room, and cheap bike hire.

★**Old Parish House** — GUESTHOUSE €€
(☑045 767 979; www.blejskiotok.si/hotel; Riklijeva cesta 22; s/d from €45/98; P🛜) In a privileged position, the Old Parish House (Stari Farovž) belonging to the Parish Church of St Martin has been newly transformed into a simple, welcoming guesthouse, with timber beams, hardwood floors and neutral, minimalist style. Pros include car parking, lake views, and waking to church bells.

🍴 Eating & Drinking

Slaščičarna Zima — CAFE €
(☑04-574 16 16; www.smon.si; Grajska cesta 3; kremna rezina €2.90; ⏰7.30am-9pm) Bled's culinary speciality is the delicious *kremna rezina*, also known as the *kremšnita*: it's a layer of vanilla custard topped with whipped cream and sandwiched between two layers of flaky pastry. While Šmon patisserie may not be its place of birth, it remains the best place in which to try it – retro decor and all.

Grajska Plaža — SLOVENIAN €€
(☑031 813 886; www.grajska-plaza.com; Veslaška promenada 11; mains €8-20; ⏰9am-11pm Jun–mid-Sep) Even the locals say that dining at this place feels like a summer holiday. It's built on a terrace over the Castle Lido and has a relaxed vibe, helpful service and an easy all-day menu that stretches from morning coffee to end-of-day cocktails. Meal options like grilled trout or octopus salad are generous and tasty.

BALKANS BLED

CLIMBING & RAFTING IN THE JULIAN ALPS

Bled is a popular jumping-off spot for exploring the nearby Triglav National Park and taking part in boundless adventure opportunities like climbing, canyoning and rafting.

Climbers will no doubt be tempted to scale the country's tallest peak: the 2864m-high Mt Triglav. It's a rite of passage for Slovenians and accessible to anyone who is reasonably fit and confident.

We strongly recommend hiring a guide for the ascent, even if you have some mountain-climbing experience under your belt. A local guide will know the trails and conditions.

Rafting and kayaking on the beautiful Soča River, northwest of Bled, provides all the adrenaline of a mountain climb, but has the added advantage of a cooling swim on a hot summer day. The rafting season lasts from April to October.

Rafting trips on the Soča over a distance of around 8km (1½ hours) usually cost from €35 to €40; longer trips may be possible when water levels are high. Prices include guiding, transport to/from the river, a neoprene suit, boots, life jacket, helmet and paddle. Wear a swimsuit and bring a towel.

The town of **Bovec** in the middle of the Soča Valley is the epicentre for rafting in these parts, but several agencies in Bled organise day-out-and-back excursions.

Outfitter **3glav Adventures** (☑041 683 184; www.3glav.com; Ljubljanska cesta 1; ⏰9am-noon & 4-7pm mid-Apr–Sep) offers both climbing and rafting trips, among other outdoor pursuits. For climbing, another useful contact is the **Alpine Association of Slovenia** (PZS; ☑01-434 56 80; www.pzs.si; Dvoržakova ulica 9, Ljubljana; ⏰9am-3pm Mon & Thu, 9am-5pm Wed, 9am-1pm Fri).

Bled

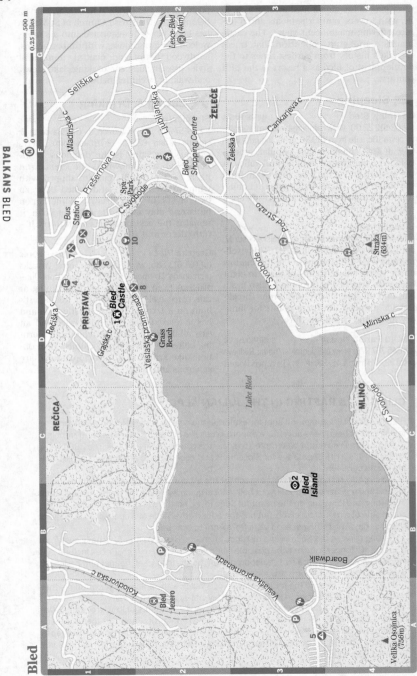

Bled

Gostilna Murka   SLOVENIAN €€
(☑ 04-574 33 40; www.gostilna-murka.com; Riklijeva cesta 9; mains €9-19; ⊙10am-10pm Mon-Fri, noon-11pm Sat & Sun) This traditional eatery set within a large, leafy garden may at first appear a bit theme-park-ish – but the food is super-authentic (lots of old-school national dishes) and the welcome warm. Offers good-value lunch specials for around €5.

Vila Prešeren   BAR
(☑ 04-575 25 10; www.vilapreseren.si; Veslaška promenada 14; ⊙7am-midnight Mon-Thu, to 1am Fri-Sun) A consummate all-rounder, this glamorous cafe-bar-restaurant-guesthouse sits in pole position on the lakeside promenade, with a huge terrace that's designed for people (and lake) watching. It morphs from coffees to cocktails and has a crowd-pleasing menu that helpfully flags dishes that bring you a taste of Bled, Slovenia or 'Ex Yu' (Yugoslavian).

ℹ Getting There & Away

Bled is well connected by bus; the **bus station** (Cesta Svobode 4) is a hub of activity at the lake's northeast. More than a dozen buses daily make the run to and from Ljubljana (€6.30, 80 to 90 minutes, 57km).

Bled has two train stations, though neither is close to the centre. The Lesce-Bled station, 4km east of Bled township on the road to Radovljica, is on the rail line to Ljubljana (€5.08 to €6.88, 40 to 60 minutes, 51km, up to 20 daily). Buses connect the station with Bled.

Piran

POP 3975

Picturesque Piran (Pirano in Italian), sitting pretty at the tip of a narrow peninsula, is everyone's favourite town on the Slovenian coast. Its Old Town – one of the best-preserved historical towns anywhere on the Adriatic – is a gem of Venetian Gothic architecture, but it can be a mob scene at the height of summer. In quieter times, it's hard not to fall instantly in love with the atmospheric winding alleyways, the sunsets and the seafood restaurants.

◎ Sights

⭐**Tartinijev Trg**   SQUARE
The much-photographed, pastel-toned Tartinijev Trg is a marble-paved square (oval-shaped, really) that was the inner harbour until it was filled in 1894. The statue of the nattily dressed gentleman in the centre is of native son, composer and violinist Giuseppe Tartini (1692–1770).

To the east is the 1818 Church of St Peter (Cerkev Sv Petra). Across from the church is Tartini House, the composer's birthplace.

⭐**Cathedral of St George**   CATHEDRAL
(Župnijska Cerkev Sv Jurija; www.zupnija-piran.si; Adamičeva ulica 2) A cobbled street leads from behind the Venetian House to Piran's hilltop cathedral, baptistery and bell tower. The cathedral was built in baroque style in the early 17th century, on the site of an earlier church from 1344.

The cathedral's doors are usually open and a metal grille allows you to see some of the richly ornate and newly restored interior, but full access is via the Parish Museum of St George (☑05-673 34 40; €1; ⊙9am-1pm & 5-7.30pm Mon-Fri, 9am-2pm & 5-8pm Sat, 11am-2pm & 5-8pm Sun), which includes the church's treasury and catacombs.

⭐**Sergej Mašera Maritime Museum**   MUSEUM
(☑05-671 00 40; www.pomorskimuzej.si; Cankarjevo nabrežje 3; adult/child €3.50/2.10; ⊙9am-noon & 5-9pm Tue-Sun Jul & Aug, 9am-5pm Tue-Sun Sep-Jun) Located in the 19th-century Gabrielli Palace on the waterfront, this museum's focus is the sea, with plenty of salty-dog stories relating to Slovenian seafaring. In the archaeological section, the 2000-year-old Roman amphorae beneath the glass floor are impressive. The antique model ships upstairs are very fine; other rooms are filled

with old figureheads and weapons, including some lethal-looking blunderbusses. The folk paintings are offerings placed by sailors on the altar of the pilgrimage church at Strunjan for protection against shipwreck.

🛏 Sleeping

Val Hostel HOSTEL €
(☑ 05-673 25 55; www.hostel-val.com; Gregorčičeva ulica 38a; per person €20-40; @ 🛜) Location is the winner here – this central hostel has 22 rooms (including a few singles) with shared bathrooms, and access to kitchenette and laundry.

★PachaMama GUESTHOUSE, APARTMENT €€
(☑ 059 183 495; www.pachamama.si; Trubarjeva 8; per person €30-40; ❀ 🛜) Built by travellers for travellers, this excellent new guesthouse ('PachaMama Pleasant Stay') sits just off Tartinijev trg and offers 12 simple, fresh rooms, decorated with timber and lots of travel photography. Cool private bathrooms and a 'secret garden' add appeal. There are also a handful of studios and family-sized apartments under the PachaMama umbrella, dotted around town and of an equally high standard.

★Max Piran B&B €€
(☑ 041 692 928; www.maxpiran.com; Ulica IX Korpusa 26; d €68-85; ❀ 🛜) Piran's most romantic accommodation has just six handsome, compact rooms, each bearing a woman's name rather than a number, in a delightful, coral-coloured, 18th-century townhouse. It's just down from the Cathedral of St George, and excellent value.

🍽 Eating & Drinking

Casa Nostromo SEAFOOD €€
(☑ 030 200 000; www.piranisin.com; Tomšičeva ul 24; mains €8-22; ⊙ 6pm-1am) Making a big splash (as it were) on the Piran culinary scene these days is decorated chef Gradimir Dimitrić's new eatery serving seafood and Istrian specialities.

Pirat SEAFOOD €€
(☑ 041 327 654; Župančičeva ulica 26; mains €8-18; ⊙ 11am-10pm) It's not the fanciest place in town but the atmosphere is top-notch and Rok and his crew do their best to ensure you have a good time. Seafood is king, from the fresh-fish carpaccio to pasta with lobster and grilled seabass filleted at the table. All nicely accompanied by local *malvazija* white wine.

Pri Mari MEDITERRANEAN €€
(☑ 05-673 47 35, 041 616 488; www.primari-piran.com; Dantejeva ulica 17; mains €8-22; ⊙ noon-4pm & 6-10pm Tue-Sun) This stylishly rustic and welcoming restaurant run by an Italian-Slovenian couple serves the most inventive Mediterranean and Slovenian dishes in town – lots of fish, a good selection of local wines. Space is restricted, so it pays to book ahead.

Mestna Kavarna BAR
(☑ 051 337 995; Tartinijev trg 3; ⊙ 8am-9pm Mon-Fri, to 10pm Sat, to 8pm Sun) A morning coffee or smoothie goes well with a strong dose of people-watching, and this cafe-bar on the main square delivers. By night, the orders turn to cocktails.

❶ Getting There & Away

The **bus station** (Dantejeva ulica) is south of the centre. Around three buses daily make the journey to Ljubljana (€12, three hours, 140km), via Postojna.

Slovenia Survival Guide

❶ Directory A–Z

ACCOMMODATION
➡ Accommodation tends to book up quickly in summer in Bled and along the coast, so try to reserve at least a few weeks in advance.

➡ Hotel rates vary seasonally, with July and August the peak season and September/October and May/June the shoulders.

➡ Slovenia has a growing stable of excellent hostels, especially in popular spots like Ljubljana and Bled.

➡ There's a *kamp* (camping ground) in virtually every corner of the country; seek out the Slovenian Tourist Board's *Camping in Slovenia* brochure. Some rent out inexpensive bungalows. Camping 'rough' is illegal.

INTERNET ACCESS
Virtually every hotel and hostel in the land offers wi-fi for guests' use, usually for free.

MONEY
➡ Slovenia uses the euro. Exchange cash at banks, post offices, tourist offices, travel agencies and private exchange offices.

➡ ATMs are ubiquitous throughout Slovenia.

➡ Credit cards, especially Visa, MasterCard and American Express, are widely accepted.

➡ When a gratuity is not included in your bill, which may or may not be the case, paying an extra 10% is customary.

OPENING HOURS

Banks 8.30am to 5pm Monday to Friday (lunch break 12.30pm to 2pm)

Museums 10am to 6pm Tuesday to Sunday, shorter hours in winter

Restaurants 11am to 10pm

Shops 8am to 7pm Monday to Friday, to 1pm Saturday

PUBLIC HOLIDAYS

New Year's holidays 1 and 2 January

Prešeren Day (Slovenian Culture Day) 8 February

Easter & Easter Monday March/April

Insurrection Day 27 April

Labour Day holidays 1 and 2 May

National Day 25 June

Assumption Day 15 August

Reformation Day 31 October

All Saints' Day 1 November

Christmas Day 25 December

Independence Day 26 December

TELEPHONE

➤ There are six area codes in Slovenia (01 to 05 and 07).

➤ Public telephones require a *telefonska kartica* or *telekartica* (telephone card) available at post offices and some news-stands.

➤ To call abroad from Slovenia, dial 00 followed by the country and area codes and then the number. Numbers beginning with 80 are toll-free.

➤ Slovenia uses GSM 900, which is compatible with the rest of Europe and Australia but not with the North American GSM 1900 or the Japanese system.

➤ Local SIM cards are available from providers SiMobil, Telekom Slovenija and Telemach.

ⓘ Getting There & Away

AIR

Slovenia's main international airport receiving regular scheduled flights is Ljubljana's **Jože Pučnik Airport** (Aerodrom Ljubljana; ☏04-206 19 81; www.lju-airport.si; Zgornji Brnik 130a, Brnik), 27km north of Ljubljana. In the arrivals hall there's a Slovenia Tourist Information Centre desk, several travel agencies and ATMs.

From its base at Brnik, the Slovenian flag-carrier, **Adria Airways** (☏01-369 10 10, 04-259 45 82; www.adria.si), serves more than 20 European destinations on regularly scheduled flights.

LAND

Slovenia is well connected by road and rail with its four neighbours: Italy, Austria, Hungary and Croatia. Bus and train timetables sometimes use Slovenian names for foreign cities.

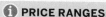

ⓘ PRICE RANGES

The following price ranges refer to a double room with en suite toilet and bath or shower, and include tax and breakfast.

€ less than €50

€€ €51–100

€€€ more than €100

The following price ranges refer to a two-course meal, including a drink, for one person. Many restaurants also offer an excellent-value set menu of two or even three courses at lunch.

€ less than €15

€€ €16–30

€€€ more than €31

Bus Most international buses arrive and depart from Ljubljana's bus station.

Train The **Slovenian Railways** (Slovenske Železnice, SŽ; ☏01-291 33 32; www.slo-zeleznice.si) network links up with the European railway network via Austria, Germany, Czech Republic (Prague), Croatia, Hungary (Budapest), Switzerland (Zürich) and Serbia (Belgrade).

ⓘ Getting Around

Bus These are generally efficient and good value but can be very crowded on Friday afternoons. Buy your ticket at the *avtobusna postaja* (bus station) or simply pay the driver as you board.

Train Cheaper but usually slower than buses (with the exception of intercity high-speed services); getting from A to B often requires returning to Ljubljana.

CROATIA

Zagreb

☏01 / POP 790,000

Zagreb has culture, arts, music, architecture, gastronomy and all the other things that make a quality capital city, so it's no surprise that the number of visitors has risen sharply in the last couple of years. Croatia's coastal attractions aside, Zagreb has finally been discovered as a popular city-break destination in its own right.

CROATIA AT A GLANCE

Don't Miss

Dubrovnik Croatia's most popular attraction, the extraordinary walled city of Dubrovnik, is a Unesco World Heritage site for good reason. Despite being relentlessly shelled in the 1990s during Croatia's Homeland War, its mighty walls, sturdy towers, medieval monasteries, baroque churches, graceful squares and fascinating residential quarters all look magnificent again.

Plitvice Lakes National Park A turquoise ribbon of lakes linked by gushing waterfalls in the forested heart of continental Croatia, Plitvice is an awe-inspiring sight. There are dozens of lakes – from 4km-long Kozjak to reed-fringed ponds – their startling colours a product of the karstic terrain.

Hvar Come high summer, there's no better place to dress up and get your groove on than Hvar Town. Gorgeous tanned people descend from their yachts in droves, rubbing shoulders with up-for-it backpackers at après-beach parties as the sun drops below the horizon.

Wining and dining in Istria *La dolce vita* reigns supreme in Istria, Croatia's top foodie destination. The seafood, truffles, wild asparagus and a rare breed of Istrian beef called *boškarin* all stand out, as do myriad regional specialities and award-winning olive oils and wines by small local producers. Slow food is a hit here: you can sample the ritual in Rovinj's restaurants.

Coffee in Zagreb Elevated to the status of ritual, having coffee in one of Zagreb's outdoor cafes is a must, involving hours of people-watching, gossiping and soul-searching, unhurried by waiters. Don't miss the Saturday morning *špica*, the coffee-drinking and people-watching ritual in the city centre that forms the peak of Zagreb's weekly social calendar.

Itineraries

One Week
The essential Croatian experience is a sunny trip along the Dalmatian coast exploring World Heritage Sites along the way. Start in exuberant **Split** with a couple of days of sightseeing and nightlife. Diocletian's Palace is a living part of this seafront city, a throbbing ancient quarter that's home to 220 historic buildings. Catch a ferry to Hvar Island whose chic capital, **Hvar Town**, offers an intriguing mix of European glamour and a raucous bar scene. Then hop over to the magnificent old town of **Dubrovnik**, ringed by mighty defensive walls and the sparkling blue Adriatic. Spend the next three days taking in its jaw-dropping sights.

Two Weeks
From Dubrovnik, head inland to spend a day exploring the dazzling natural wonderland of **Plitvice Lakes National Park**, with its verdant maze of turquoise lakes and cascading waterfalls. Push on north to Istria and set aside at least two days for the coast's showpiece resort town of **Rovinj**. Take a day to explore some of the 14 green islands that make up the Rovinj archipelago just offshore. Leave the final couple of days for the capital, **Zagreb**, and delve into its booming cafe culture, cutting-edge art scene, simmering nightlife and interesting museums.

Essential Outdoors

Windsurfing on Brač island Bol is a windsurfing hot spot, with most of the action taking place at the beaches west of the town centre. The *maestral* (strong, steady westerly wind) blows from April to October.

Cycling in Istria Cyclists shouldn't miss the Parenzana bike trail, which traverses three countries, Italy, Slovenia and Croatia. The Croatian stretch is 78km and has become a popular way to take in the highlights of Istria, especially in spring and autumn.

Hiking in Paklenica National Park Rising high above the Adriatic, the peaks of the Velebit Massif form a dramatic barrier between continental Croatia and the coast. The 95-sq-km Paklenica National Park contains some of the country's finest mountain scenery, and you can trek up two deep gorges.

Getting Around

Transport in Croatia is reasonably priced, quick and generally efficient.

Air A surprisingly extensive schedule of domestic flights, especially in summer.

Boat Extensive network of car ferries and faster catamarans all along the coast and the islands.

Bus Reasonably priced, with extensive coverage of the country and frequent departures.

Car Useful for travelling at your own pace, or for visiting regions with minimal public transport. Cars can be hired in every city or larger town. Drive on the right.

Train Less frequent and much slower than buses, with a limited network.

When to Go

Zagreb

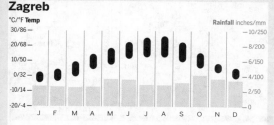

°C/°F Temp

30/86 —
20/68 —
10/50 —
0/32 —
-10/14 —
-20/-4 —

Rainfall inches/mm

— 10/250
— 8/200
— 6/150
— 4/100
— 2/50
— 0

J F M A M J J A S O N D

Jul & Aug Peak season brings the best weather, and Hvar Island gets the most sun. Prices are at their highest.

May–Jun & Sep The Adriatic is warm enough for swimming, the crowds are sparser and prices are lower.

Oct–Apr Christmas brings a buzz to Zagreb's streets, plus there's skiing too.

Arriving in Croatia

Zagreb Airport Croatia Airlines bus (30KN) leaves from the airport every half-hour or hour from about 4.30am to 8pm. Taxis to the centre cost between 110KN and 200KN (20 minutes).

Dubrovnik Airport Atlas runs the airport bus service (40KN, 30 minutes), timed around flights. Buses to Dubrovnik stop at the Pile Gate and the bus station. A taxi costs 250KN to 280KN.

Top Phrases

Hello. Dobar dan.

Goodbye. Zbogom.

Please. Molim.

Thank you. Hvala.

How much is it? Koliko stoji?

Resources

Croatian Tourism (www.croatia.hr) The best starting point to plan your holiday.

Parks of Croatia (www.parkovihrvatske.hr) Covers Croatia's national parks and nature parks.

Set Your Budget

➡ Dorm bed: 100–325KN

➡ Tent site for two: 100–360KN

➡ Meal in a local tavern: 60KN

➡ Bus, tram or train ticket: 10–150KN

Zagreb

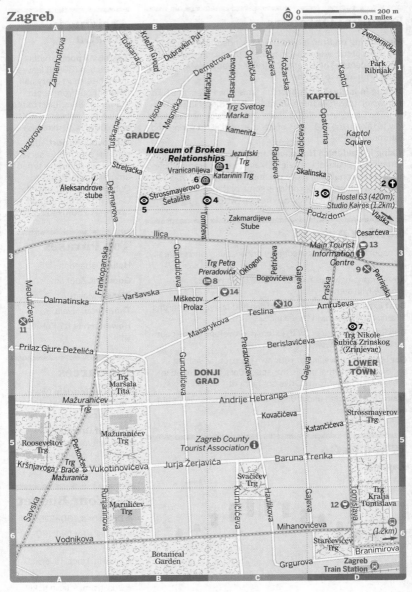

◉ Sights

As the oldest part of Zagreb, the Upper Town (also known as Gornji Grad), which includes the neighbourhoods of Gradec and Kaptol, has landmark buildings and churches from the earlier centuries of Zagreb's history. The Lower Town (also known as Donji Grad), which runs between the Upper Town and the train station, has the city's most interesting art museums and fine examples of 19th- and 20th-century architecture.

Zagreb

◎ Top Sights
1 Museum of Broken
    Relationships.................................C2

◎ Sights
2 Cathedral of the Assumption
   of the Blessed Virgin
   Mary..D2
3 Dolac Market...................................D2
4 Funicular Railway...........................C2
5 Grič Tunnel B2
6 Lotrščak Tower..............................C2
7 Zrinjevac..D4

ⓛ Sleeping
8 Shappy Hostel.................................C3

⊗ Eating
9 Mundoaka Street Food.....................D3
10 Vinodol...C4
11 Zrno...A4

◎ Drinking & Nightlife
12 Bacchus...D6
13 Johann Franck................................D3
14 Kino Europa....................................C3

★ Museum of Broken
Relationships   MUSEUM

(www.brokenships.com; Ćirilometodska 2; adult/
student 40/30KN; ◎9am-10.30pm Jun-Sep, to
9pm Oct-May) From romances that withered
to broken family connections, this wonderfully quirky museum explores the mementos
leftover after a relationship ends. Displayed
amid a string of all-white rooms are donations from around the globe, each with a
story attached. Exhibits range from hilarious
(the toaster someone nicked so their ex could
never make toast again), to heartbreaking
(the suicide note from somebody's mother).
In turns funny, poignant and moving, it's a
perfect summing up of the human condition.

Museum of Contemporary Art   MUSEUM
(Muzej Suvremene Umjetnosti; ☑01-60 52 700;
www.msu.hr; Avenija Dubrovnik 17; adult/concession
30/15KN; ◎11am-6pm Tue-Fri & Sun, to 8pm Sat)
Housed in a city icon designed by local star
architect Igor Franić, this museum displays
both solo and thematic group shows by Croatian and international artists in its 17,000 sq
metres. The permanent display, *Collection in
Motion,* showcases 620 edgy works by 240
artists, roughly half of whom are Croatian.
There's a packed year-round schedule of film,
theatre, concerts and performance art.

★ Mirogoj   CEMETERY
(Aleja Hermanna Bollea 27; ◎6am-8pm Apr-Oct,
7.30am-6pm Nov-Mar) A 10-minute ride north
of the city centre (or a 30-minute walk
through leafy streets) takes you to one of the
most beautiful cemeteries in Europe, sited at
the base of Mt Medvednica. It was designed
in 1876 by Austrian-born architect Herman
Bollé, who created numerous buildings
around Zagreb. The majestic arcade, topped
by a string of cupolas, looks like a fortress
from the outside, but feels calm and graceful
on the inside.

Dolac Market   MARKET
(off Trg Bana Jelačića; ◎open-air market 6.30am-
3pm Mon-Sat, to 1pm Sun, covered market 7am-2pm
Mon-Fri, 7am-3pm Sat, 7am-1pm Sun) Right in the
heart of the city, Zagreb's bustling fruit and
vegetable market has been trader-central
since the 1930s when the city authorities set
up a market space on the 'border' between
the Upper and Lower Towns. is Sellers from
all over Croatia descend here to hawk fresh
produce daily.

Zrinjevac   SQUARE
Officially called Trg Nikole Šubića Zrinskog
but lovingly known as Zrinjevac, this verdant square is a major hangout during sun-
shiny weekends and hosts pop-up cafe stalls
during the summer months. It's also a venue
for many festivals and events; most centred
around the ornate music pavilion which
dates from 1891.

Lotrščak Tower   HISTORIC BUILDING
(Kula Lotrščak; Strossmayerovo Šetalište 9; adult/
child 20/10KN; ◎9am-9pm Mon-Fri, 10am-5pm
Sat & Sun) This tower was built in the middle
of the 13th century in order to protect the
southern city gate. Normally you can enter and climb up to the top for a sweeping
360-degree view of the city but it was closed
for extensive restoration work in 2018, with
no date set for reopening. Directly across the
street, is the **funicular railway** (Tomiceva; one
way 4KN; ◎6.30am-10pm), constructed in 1888,
which connects the Lower and Upper Towns.

> ### ZAGREB GOES VEGIE
>
> In recent years, Zagreb, traditionally a
> carnivore-pleasing place, has woken up
> to the growing needs of vegetarians and
> vegans. Several dining options now exist
> for those who don't eat meat, including
> Zrno (p602)

Cathedral of the Assumption of the Blessed Virgin Mary   CHURCH

(Katedrala Marijina Uznešenja; Kaptol 31; ⊙10am-5pm Mon-Sat, 1-5pm Sun) This cathedral's twin spires – seemingly permanently under repair – soar over the city. Formerly known as St Stephen's, the cathedral's original Gothic structure has been transformed many times over but the sacristy still contains a cycle of **frescoes** dating from the 13th century. An earthquake in 1880 badly damaged the building and reconstruction in a neo-Gothic style began around the turn of the 20th century.

Grič Tunnel   TUNNEL

(⊙9am-9pm) **FREE** The mystery-laden Grič Tunnel that connects Mesnička and Radićeva streets opened to the public in the summer of 2016. Built in 1943 for use as a WWII air-raid shelter and rarely used since – except for the legendary rave party that took place here in 1993 – this 350m-long tunnel is now yours to cross.

🛏 Sleeping

Hostel 63   HOSTEL €

(☎01-55 20 557; www.hostel63.eu; Vlaška 63/7; dm/d/apt €22/65/75; ➌❄🐾) Everything is kept shipshape and squeaky clean at this grey-yellow-white themed hostel, run by helpful staff. Four-bed dorms are thought-

---

MARKET DAYS

Zagreb doesn't have many markets but those it does have are stellar. The weekend **antiques market** (Britanski trg; ⊙7am-2pm Sat, 7.30am-2.30pm Sun) on Britanski trg, for example, is one of central Zagreb's joys.

But to see a flea market that's unmatched in the whole of Croatia, you have to make it to **Hrelić** (⊙7am-3pm Wed, Sat & Sun). This humongous space is chock-full of eclectic items and quirky bric-a-brac. Don't miss it.

If you're into food, don't miss **Mali Plac s Tavana** (Little Market from the Attic; www.mali-plac.org; ⊙hours vary), a weekly gathering of small producers who hawk their wares in various locations around the city (see the website for the current schedule); you'll find anything from organic citrus fruits and sage honey to hemp oil and hummus, plus handcrafted natural cosmetics.

---

fully equipped with lockers, privacy-curtains and private bathrooms; there's even two dorms with two double bed bunks for couples. Breakfast is €4. It's quiet location, in a courtyard off the main road, means you'll get a good night's sleep.

Shappy Hostel   HOSTEL €

(☎01-48 30 483; www.hostel-shappy.com; Varšavska 8; dm 170KN, d from 550KN; 🅿➌❄ @🐾) This small hostel is a peaceful oasis tucked away in a courtyard. Private rooms are decked out with lashings of grey and white. Four-bed dorms (all sharing squeaky-clean bathrooms) are some of the most spacious in town. The sun-dappled terrace here is a relaxing hideaway for when you want to chill out.

★ Studio Kairos   B&B €€

(☎01-46 40 690; www.studio-kairos.com; Vlaška 92; s/d/tr/q from €36/50/65/70; ❄❄🐾) This adorable B&B in a street-level apartment has four well-appointed rooms decked out by theme – Writers', Crafts, Music and Granny's. The cosy common space, where a delicious breakfast is served, and the enthusiastic hosts, who are a fount of knowledge on all things Zagreb, adds to this place's intimate and homely appeal. Bikes are also available for rent.

🍴 Eating

Zrno   VEGETARIAN €

(www.zrnobiobistro.hr; Medulićeva 20; mains 59-75KN; ⊙noon-9.30pm Mon-Sat; ❄🍴) This contemporary 'bio-bistro' (as it dubs itself) is tucked away in a courtyard a 10-minute walk from the main square and serves dishes using ingredients from their own farm, from brown-rice gomoku to a daily 'makroplata' meal (macrobiotic platter of the day) and desserts like *crostata* (baked tart) with seasonal fruit.

Mundoaka Street Food   INTERNATIONAL €€

(☎01-78 88 777; www.facebook.com/mundoaka. streetfood; Petrinjska 2; mains 75-200KN; ⊙11am-11.30pm Mon-Thu, to midnight Fri & Sat; ❄🐾) The menu here traipses across the globe but is big on American classics – think NYC meatball sandwiches, burgers and BBQ sauce glazed ribs – while smaller dishes of veggie empanadas and *gyoza* (pan-fried dumplings) are great for grazers. It's often packed so it's a good idea to reserve ahead for dinner.

Vinodol

CROATIAN €€

(📞 01-48 11 427; www.vinodol-zg.hr; Teslina 10; mains 85-160KN; ⊙11.30am-midnight; 🌐) Giving central European fare a modern tweak, Vinodol is much-loved by locals. On warm days, eat on the covered patio (entered through an ivy-clad passageway off Teslina). Menu highlights include the succulent lamb or veal and potatoes cooked under *peka* (a domed baking lid) and the almond-crusted trout.

Drinking & Nightlife

In the Upper Town, the chic Tkalčićeva is throbbing with bars and cafes. With half a dozen bars and pavement cafes between Trg Petra Preradovića (known locally as Cvjetni trg) and Bogovićeva in the Lower Town, the scene on summer nights resembles a vast outdoor party. Things wind down by midnight though, and get quieter from mid-July to late August.

Johann Franck

CAFE

(www.johannfranck.hr; Trg Bana Jelačića 9; ⊙8am-2am Mon-Thu & Sun, 8am-4am Fri & Sat) Location, location, location. Named after Croatia's pioneer coffee roaster and the namesake coffee brand, everyone from fashionable young things to gossiping grandmas and museumed-out tourists pack out the front terrace and slick couch-filled ground floor here for coffee, cocktails and beer.

Kino Europa

CAFE

(Varšavska 3; ⊙8.30am-midnight Mon-Fri, to 2am Sat & Sun; 🖥) The front of Zagreb's oldest cinema (from the 1920s) houses a fun and funky cafe–wine bar–*grapperia* that attracts a diverse crowd in the evening. The coffee is decent, beers are 17-24KN and there's over 30 types of grappa for you to try. Service can be on the gruff side.

Bacchus

BAR

(Trg Kralja Tomislava 16; ⊙11am-midnight Mon-Fri, noon-midnight Sat) You'll be lucky if you score a table at Zagreb's funkiest courtyard garden, lush and hidden down a passageway behind an ornate door. In the evenings, you can often catch live jazz here.

ℹ Information

Main Tourist Information Centre (📞 information 0800 53 53, office 01-48 14 051; www.info-zagreb.hr; Trg Bana Jelačića 11; ⊙8.30am-8pm Mon-Fri, 9am-6pm Sat, 10am-4pm Sun) Organ-

ised and helpful with a wealth of free pamphlets and brochures as well as free city maps.

Zagreb County Tourist Association (📞01-48 73 665; www.tzzz.hr; Preradovićeva 42; ⊙8am-4pm Mon-Fri) Has tourist information and materials about attractions in Zagreb's surroundings, including wine roads and bike trails.

ℹ Getting There & Away

BUS

Zagreb's **bus station** (📞 060 313 333; www.akz.hr; Avenija M Držića 4) is 1km east of the train station. If you need to store bags, there's a **left-luggage office** (1-4 hr per hour 5KN, additional hours per hr 5KN; ⊙24hr). Trams 2 and 6 run from the bus station to the train station. Tram 6 goes to Trg Bana Jelačića.

Domestic destinations include Dubrovnik (191KN to 231KN, 9½ to 11 hours, nine to 12 daily), Rovinj (100KN to 195KN, four to six hours, 20 daily) and Split (115KN to 205KN, five to 8½ hours, 32 to 34 daily).

International destinations include Belgrade (230KN, six hours, six daily), Sarajevo (198KN, seven to eight hours, four to five daily) and Vienna (160KN to 247KN, five hours, 10 daily).

TRAIN

The **train station** (📞 060 333 444; www.hzpp.hr; Trg Kralja Tomislava 12) is in the southern part of the city centre. As you come out, you will see a series of parks and pavilions that are directly in front of you, which lead into the town centre.

Domestic trains head to Split (190KN to 208KN, five to seven hours, three to four daily). There are international departures to Belgrade (184KN, 6½ hours, two daily), Ljubljana (68KN, 2½ hours, five daily), Sarajevo (165KN, eight to 9½ hours, daily) and Vienna (549KN, six to seven hours, daily).

Rovinj

POP 14,300

Rovinj (Rovigno in Italian) is coastal Istria's star attraction. While it can get overrun with tourists in summer, it remains one of the last true Mediterranean fishing ports. Wooded hills and low-rise hotels surround the Old Town, which is webbed with steep cobbled streets and piazzas. The 14 green islands of the Rovinj archipelago make for a pleasant afternoon away; the most popular are Sveta Katarina and Crveni Otok (Red Island), also known as Sveti Andrija.

PLITVICE LAKES NATIONAL PARK

The absolute highlight of Croatia's Adriatic hinterland, this glorious expanse of forested hills and turquoise lakes is exquisitely scenic – so much so that in 1979 Unesco proclaimed the **park** (053-751 015; www.np-plitvicka-jezera.hr; adult/child Jul & Aug 250/110KN, Apr-Jun & Sep-Oct 150/80KN, Nov-Mar 55/35KN; 7am-8pm) a World Heritage site.

Sixteen crystalline lakes tumble into each other via a series of waterfalls and cascades, while clouds of butterflies drift above. It takes upwards of six hours to explore the 18km of wooden footbridges and pathways that snake around the edges of the rumbling water on foot, but you can slice two hours off by taking advantage of the park's free boats and buses (departing every 30 minutes from April to October).

While the park is beautiful year-round, spring and autumn are the best times to visit. In spring and early summer the falls are flush with water, while in autumn the changing leaves put on a colourful display. Winter is also spectacular, although snow can limit access and free park transport doesn't operate. If possible, avoid the peak months of July and August, when the falls reduce to a trickle, parking is problematic and the sheer volume of visitors can turn the walking tracks into a conga line.

◉ Sights

★ Church of St Euphemia
CHURCH

(Sveta Eufemija; Petra Stankovića; 10am-6pm Jun-Sep, to 4pm May, to 2pm Apr) FREE The town's showcase, this imposing church dominates the old town from its hilltop location in the middle of the peninsula. Built in 1736, it's the largest baroque building in Istria, reflecting the period during the 18th century when Rovinj was its most populous town. Inside, look for the marble **tomb of St Euphemia** behind the right-hand altar.

Batana House
MUSEUM

(www.batana.org; Pina Budicina 2; adult/concession 10/5KN; 10am-2pm & 7-11pm Jun-Sep, 10am-1pm & 4-6pm Oct-Dec & Mar-May) On the harbour, Batana House is a museum dedicated to the *batana,* a flat-bottomed fishing boat that stands as a symbol of Rovinj's seafaring and fishing traditions. The multimedia exhibits inside the 17th-century town house have interactive displays, excellent captions and audio with *bitinada,* which are typical fishers' songs. Check out the *spacio,* the ground-floor cellar where wine was kept, tasted and sold amid much socialising (open evenings on Tuesday and Thursday).

Grisia
STREET

Lined with galleries where local artists sell their work, this cobbled street leads uphill from behind the Balbi Arch to St Euphemia. The winding narrow backstreets that spread around Grisia are an attraction in themselves. Windows, balconies, portals and squares are a pleasant confusion of styles – Gothic, Renaissance, baroque and neoclassical. Notice the unique *fumaioli* (exterior chimneys), built during the population boom when entire families lived in a single room with a fireplace.

Punta Corrente Forest Park
PARK

(Zlatni Rt) Follow the waterfront on foot or by bike past Hotel Park to this verdant area, locally known as Zlatni Rt, about 1.5km south. Covered in oak and pine groves and boasting 10 species of cypress, the park was established in 1890 by Baron Hütterott, an Austrian admiral who kept a villa on Crveni Otok. You can swim off the rocks or just sit and admire the offshore islands.

🛏 Sleeping

Porton Biondi
CAMPGROUND €

(052-813 557; www.portonbiondirovinj.com; Aleja Porton Biondi 1; campsites per person/tent 57/50KN; Apr-Oct) This beachside camping ground, which sleeps 1200, is about 700m north of the old town. It has a restaurant, snack bar and, oddly enough, a massage service.

Roundabout Hostel
HOSTEL €

(052-817 387; www.roundabouthostel.com; Trg na Križu 6; dm from €21; P ✳ @ 🛜) This brand-new hostel, Rovinj's only real budget option, has smart, crisp rooms, bunks with individual reading lights and lockers. Reception is open 24 hours but there's no kitchen – however, the hostel does have its own cafe. It's located on the main roundabout as you come into Rovinj, hence the only downside – the distance into the old town (1.3km).

Villa Baron Gautsch GUESTHOUSE **€€**
(☐052-840 538; www.villabarongautsch.com; IM Ronjgova 7; s/d 294/454KN; ❄🐾) This German-owned *pansion* (guesthouse), on the leafy street leading up from Hotel Park, has 17 spick-and-span rooms, some with terraces and views of the sea and the old town. Breakfast is served on the small terrace out the back. It's cash (kuna) only and prices almost halve in low season.

✖ Eating

★ Male Madlene TAPAS **€€**
(☐052-815 905; Sv Križa 28; 5 courses finger food & wine 150KN; ☺11am-2pm & 6-11pm Jun-Sep) This adorable and popular spot is in the owner's tiny jumble sale of a living room hanging over the sea, where she serves creative finger food on market-fresh ingredients, based on old Italian recipes. Think tuna-filled zucchini, goat's-cheese-stuffed peppers and bite-size savoury pies and cakes. It has great Istrian wines by the glass. Reserve ahead, especially for evenings.

Kantinon SEAFOOD **€€**
(Alda Rismonda bb; mains 70-165KN; ☺noon-10pm Tue-Sun) Located right on the harbourside, this excellent eating choice is headed up by a stellar team – one of Croatia's best chefs and an equally amazing sommelier. The food is 100% Croatian, with ingredients as local and fresh as they get, plus lots of seafood based on old-fashioned fishers' recipes. The seafood stew with polenta is a real treat.

Maestral MEDITERRANEAN **€€**
(Vladimira Nazora bb; mains from 50-155KN; ☺11am-midnight Jun-Oct) Grab an alfresco table at this tavern on the sea edge for great views of the old town and well-prepared simple food that's priced just right. Its *ribarska pogača* (pizza-like pie with salted fish and veggies) is a winner. It's in an old stone house away from the tourist buzz – a wonderful place to watch the Adriatic sunset.

❶ Getting There & Away

The bus station is just to the southeast of the Old Town. There are daily services to Zagreb (109KN to 150KN, 3¼ to 5½ hours), Split (285KN, 11 hours) and Dubrovnik (402KN, 16 hours).

Split

POP 178,000

The second-largest city in Croatia, Split (Spalato in Italian) is a great place to see Dalmatian life as it's really lived. Always buzzing, this exuberant city has just the right balance of tradition and modernity. Step inside Diocletian's Palace (a Unesco World Heritage site and one of the world's most impressive Roman monuments) and you'll see dozens of bars, restaurants and shops thriving amid the atmospheric old walls where Split life has been humming along for thousands of years. To top it off, Split has a superb setting: its dramatic coastal mountains act as the perfect backdrop to the turquoise waters of the Adriatic.

◉ Sights

★ Diocletian's Palace HISTORIC SITE
Facing the harbour, Diocletian's Palace is one of the most imposing Roman ruins in existence and where you'll spend most of your time while in Split. Don't expect a palace though, nor a museum – this is the city's living heart, its labyrinthine streets packed with people, bars, shops and restaurants. Built as a military fortress, imperial residence and fortified town, the palace measures 215m from north to south and 180m east to west, altogether covering 38,700 sq metres.

Although the original structure has been added to continuously over the millennia, the alterations have only served to increase the allure of this fascinating site. The palace was built in the 4th century from lustrous white stone transported from the island of Brač, and construction lasted 10 years. Diocletian spared no expense, importing marble from Italy and Greece, and columns and sphinxes from Egypt.

Each wall has a gate at its centre, named after a metal: the north **Golden Gate** (Zlatna Vrata; Dioklecijanova bb) , the south **Bronze Gate** (Brončana Vrata; Obala hrvatskog narodnog preporoda bb), the east **Silver Gate** (Srebrna Vrata) and the west **Iron Gate** (Željezna Vrata). Between the eastern and western gates there's a straight road (Krešimirova; also known as Decumanus), which separates the imperial residence on the southern side, with its state rooms and temples, from the northern side, once used by soldiers and servants.

Central Split

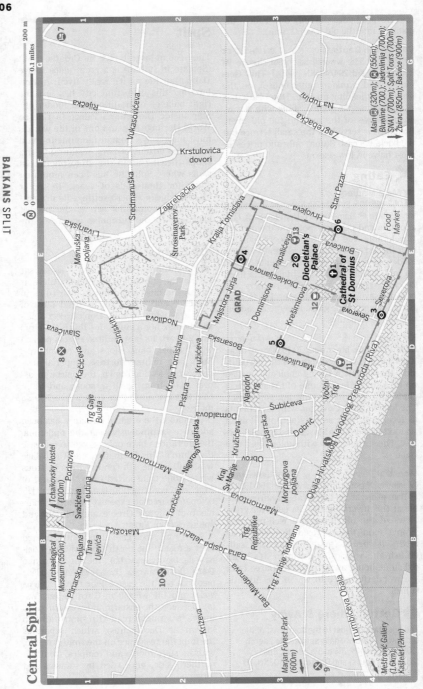

200 m
0.1 miles

Main (320m); (550m);
Blueline (700); Jadrolinija (700m);
SNAV (700m); Split Tours (700m);
Žbirac (850m); Bačvice (900m)

Food
Market

Stari Pazar

Hrvojeva

Buličeva

Diocletian's
Palace

13
Papalićeva
2

1

Cathedral of
St Domnius

Severova
3

Severova

12

Krešimirova

Dominisova

Dioklecijanova

4

GRAD

Majstora Juraja

Kralja Tomislava

Strossmayerov
Park

Zagrebačka

Na Tupini

Zagrebačka

Riječka

Krstulovića
dovori

Sredmanuška

Vukasovićeva

Livanjska

Manuška
poljana

Sinjskih

Nodilova

Bosanska

Kružićeva

Kralja Tomislava

Pistura

Domaldova

Narodni
Trg

Šubićeva

Dobrič

Vočni
Trg

Marulićeva

5

11

Obala Hrvatskog Narodnog Preporoda (Riva)

Slavićeva

Kačićeva

8

Trg Gaje
Bulata

Nigerova

Trogirska

Zadarska

Kružićeva

Obrov

Kraj
Sv. Marije

Marmontova

Morpugova
poljana

Marmontova

Tončićeva

Bana Josipa Jelačića

Trg
Republike

Trg Franje Tuđmana

Trumbićeva Obala

Ban Mladenova

Križeva

10

9

Plinarska

Poljana
Tina
Ujevića

Matošića

Teutina

Svačićeva

Porinova

Archaeological
Museum (550m)

Tchaikovsky Hostel
(100m)

Meštrović Gallery
(1.6km); Bačvice (2km)

Kaštelet (2km)

Marjan Forest Park
(600m)

7

6

Central Split

There are 220 buildings within the palace boundaries, home to about 3000 people. The narrow streets hide passageways and courtyards, some deserted and eerie, others thumping with music from bars and cafes, while the local residents hang out their washing overhead, kids play football amid the ancient walls, and grannies sit in their windows watching the action below.

★**Cathedral of St Domnius**   CHURCH
(Katedrala Sv Duje; Peristil; cathedral/belfry 35/20KN; ⊙8am-8pm Jun-Sep, 7am-noon & 5-7pm May & Oct, 7am-noon Nov-Apr) Split's octagonal cathedral is one of the best-preserved ancient Roman buildings standing today. It was built as a mausoleum for Diocletian, the last famous persecutor of the Christians, who was interred here in 311 AD. The Christians got the last laugh, destroying the emperor's sarcophagus and converting his tomb into a church in the 5th century, dedicated to one of his victims. Note that a ticket for the cathedral includes admission to its crypt, treasury and baptistery (Temple of Jupiter).

Archaeological Museum   MUSEUM
(Arheološki Muzej; ☎021-329 340; www.armus.hr; Zrinsko-Frankopanska 25; adult/concession 20/10KN; ⊙9am-2pm & 4-8pm Mon-Sat) A treasure trove of classical sculpture and mosaic is displayed at this excellent museum, a short walk north of the town centre. Most of the vast collection originated from the ancient Roman settlements of Split and neighbouring Salona (Solin), and there's also some Greek pottery from the island of Vis. There are displays of jewellery and coins, and a room filled with artefacts dating from the Paleolithic to the Iron Age.

Meštrović Gallery   GALLERY
(Galerija Meštrović; ☎021-340 800; www.mestrovic.hr; Šetalište Ivana Meštrovića 46; adult/child 40/20KN; ⊙9am-7pm Tue-Sun May-Sep, to 4pm Tue-Sat, 10am-3pm Sun Oct-Apr) At this stellar art museum, you'll see a comprehensive, well-arranged collection of works by Ivan Meštrović, Croatia's premier modern sculptor, who built the gallery as a personal residence in the 1930s. Although Meštrović intended to retire here, he emigrated to the USA soon after WWII. Admission includes entry to the nearby **Kaštelet** (Šetalište Ivana Meštrovića 39; admission incl in Meštrović Gallery ticket adult/child 40/20KN; ⊙9am-7pm Tue-Sun May-Sep), a fortress housing other Meštrović works.

Klis Fortress   CASTLE
(Tvrđava Klis; ☎021-240 578; www.tvrdavaklis.com; Klis bb; adult/child 40/15KN; ⊙9.30am-4pm) Controlling the valley leading into Split, this imposing fortress spreads along a limestone bluff, reaching 385m at its highest point. Its long and narrow form (304m by 53m) derives from constant extensions over the course of millennia. Inside, you can clamber all over the fortifications and visit the small museum, which has displays of swords and costumes and detailed information on the castle's brutal past.

🏃 **Activities**

Bačvice   SWIMMING
A flourishing beach life gives Split its aura of insouciance in summer, and sandy Bačvice is Split's most popular beach. Locals come here during the day to swim, sunbathe, drink coffee and play picigin; a younger crowd returns in the evening for the bars and clubs. There are showers and changing rooms at both ends of the beach.

Marjan Forest Park   WALKING
(Park šuma Marjan) Considered the lungs of the city, this hilly nature reserve offers trails through fragrant pine forests to scenic lookouts, medieval chapels and cave dwellings once inhabited by Christian hermits. For an afternoon away from the city buzz, consider taking a long walk through the park and descending to Kašjuni beach to cool off before catching the bus back.

HVAR ISLAND

Long, lean Hvar is Croatia's sunniest spot (2724 sunny hours each year) and its most luxurious beach destination. **Hvar Town** offers swanky hotels, elegant restaurants and a general sense that, if you care about seeing and being seen, this is the place to be. Rubbing shoulders with the posh yachties are hundreds of young partygoers, dancing on tables at the town's legendary beach bars. Looming high above the town and lit with a golden glow at night, the medieval castle has magnificent views over Hvar and the Pakleni Islands.

The northern coastal towns of **Stari Grad** and **Jelsa** are far more subdued and low-key, while Hvar's interior hides abandoned ancient hamlets, craggy peaks, vineyards and the lavender fields that the island is famous for. It's worth exploring on a day trip, as is the southern end of the island, which has some of Hvar's most beautiful and isolated coves.

Jadrolinija (☏ 021-773 433; www.jadrolinija.hr) has high-speed catamarans to Hvar Town from Split (55KN, 65 minutes, seven daily). From July to mid-September, there's also a daily catamaran to Hvar Town from Dubrovnik (190KN, four hours). **Kapetan Luka** (p609) has daily fast catamarans to Hvar Town from Dubrovnik (190KN, three hours) and Split (70KN, 65 minutes) from June to September.

🛏 Sleeping

Hostel Emanuel   HOSTEL €
(☏ 021-786 533; hostelemanuel@gmail.com; Tolstojeva 20; dm €29; ✱@🛜) Run by a friendly couple, this hip little hostel in a suburban apartment block has colourful contemporary interiors and a relaxed vibe. In the two dorms (one sleeping five, the other 10), each bunk has a large locker, curtains, a reading light and a power outlet.

Tchaikovsky Hostel   HOSTEL €
(☏ 021-317 124; www.tchaikovskyhostel.com; Čajkovskoga 4; dm 220-240KN; ✱@🛜) This four-dorm hostel in an apartment block in the neighbourhood of Špinut is run by a German-born Croat. Rooms are neat and tidy, with bunks featuring built-in shelves. Freebies include cereal, espresso and tea.

🍴 Eating

Makrovega   VEGETARIAN €
(☏ 021-394 440; www.makrovega.hr; Leština 2; mains 50-75KN; ⊙10am-8pm Mon-Fri, to 5pm Sat) Hidden away down a lane and behind a courtyard, this meat-free haven serves macrobiotic, vegetarian and some raw food. Think lots of seitan, tofu and tempeh, and excellent cakes.

Gušt   PIZZA €
(☏ 021-486 333; www.pizzeria-gust.hr; Slavićeva 1; pizzas 34-53KN; ⊙9am-11pm Mon-Sat) Split's diehard pizza fans swear by this joint – it's cheap and very local.

★Konoba Matejuška   DALMATIAN €€
(☏ 021-814 099; www.konobamatejuska.hr; Tomića Stine 3; mains 85-160KN; ⊙8am-11pm) This cosy, rustic tavern in an alleyway minutes from the seafront specialises in well-prepared seafood – as epitomised in its perfectly cooked fish platter for two. There are only four small tables outside and a couple of larger ones inside, so book ahead.

🍷 Drinking & Nightlife

Marcvs Marvlvs Spalatensis   WINE BAR
(www.facebook.com/marvlvs; Papalićeva 4; ⊙11am-11pm Mon-Thu, to midnight Fri & Sat; 🛜) Fittingly, the 15th-century Gothic home of the 'Dante of Croatia', Marko Marulić, now houses this wonderful little 'library jazz bar' – two small rooms crammed with books and frequented by ageless bohemians, tortured poets and wistful academics. Cheese, chess, cards and cigars are all on offer, and there's often live music.

Ghetto Club   BAR
(www.facebook.com/clubghetto; Dosud 10; ⊙4pm-midnight Sun-Thu, 5pm-1am Fri & Sat) Split's most bohemian and gay-friendly bar has ancient Roman walls, a large courtyard with a trickling fountain, a chandelier-festooned piano lounge and a small red-walled club space with poetry on the walls. The music is great and the atmosphere is friendly.

Luxor

CAFE

(www.lvxor.hr; Peristil; ⊙8am-midnight; 🛜) Touristy, yes, but this cafe-bar is a great place to have coffee and cake right in the ceremonial heart of Diocletian's Palace. Cushions are laid out on the steps and there's live music nightly.

ⓘ Information

Tourist Office (📞021-360 066; www.visitsplit. com; Obala hrvatskog narodnog preporoda 9; ⊙9am-4pm Mon-Fri, to 2pm Sat) Has info on Split and sells the Split Card (70KN), which offers free and reduced prices to Split attractions, plus discounts on car rental, restaurants, shops and theatres. You get the card for free if you're staying in Split more than three nights from October to May.

ⓘ Getting There & Away

BOAT

Jadrolinija (📞021-338 333; www.jadrolinija.hr; Gat Sv Duje bb) operates most of the ferries between Split and the islands, as well as overnight ferries to Ancona in Italy (from 300/450KN per person/car, 11 hours, three to four weekly).

BlueLine (📞021-223 299; www.blueline-ferries.com; ⊙Apr-Oct) has overnight car ferries to Ancona, stopping on Hvar on some days;

Split Tours (📞021-352 553; www.splittours.hr; Gat Sv Duje bb; ⊙closed Sat & Sun afternoon) handles its ticketing.

Kapetan Luka (Krilo; 📞021-645 476; www. krilo.hr) has a daily boat to Dubrovnik (190KN, 4¼ hours) from June to September, stopping on the islands of Mljet (130KN, three hours), Korčula (120KN, 1¾ hours), Hvar (70KN, 65 minutes) and Brač (40KN, 30 minutes).

SNAV (www.snav.it) has nightly ferries to/from Ancona (660KN, five hours) from April to October, some of which stop at Stari Grad on Hvar.

BUS

Advance bus tickets with seat reservations are recommended. Most buses leave from the **main bus station** (Autobusni Kolodvor Split; 📞060 327 777; www.ak-split.hr; Obala kneza Domagoja bb) beside the harbour, which has a **left-luggage office** (1st hour 5KN, additional hours 1.50KN; ⊙6am-10pm); destinations include Dubrovnik (130KN, 4½ hours, 21 daily), Pula (300KN, 10 hours, three daily) and Zagreb (130KN, five hours, at least hourly). Note that Split–Dubrovnik buses pass briefly through Bosnian territory, so keep your passport handy for border-crossing points.

TRAIN

Trains run to Split **train station** (📞021-338 525; www.hzpp.hr; Obala kneza Domagoja 9;

⊙6am-10pm) from Zagreb (112KN, six hours, five daily) and Knin (91KN, 1½ hours, five daily). There's also a direct train service that runs to Budapest (492KN) twice a week from June to September.

Dubrovnik

POP 42,600

Regardless of whether you are visiting Dubrovnik for the first time or the hundredth, the sense of awe never fails to descend when you set eyes on the beauty of the old town. Indeed it's hard to imagine anyone becoming jaded by the city's white limestone streets, baroque buildings and the endless shimmer of the Adriatic, or failing to be inspired by a walk along the ancient city walls that protected a civilised, sophisticated republic for centuries.

⊙ Sights

★**City Walls & Forts** FORT
(Gradske zidine; 📞020-638 800; www.citywalls-dubrovnik.hr; adult/child 70/30KN; ⊙8am-6.30pm Apr, May, Aug, Sep, to 7.30pm Jun & Jul, to 5.30pm Oct, 9am-3pm Nov-Mar) No visit to Dubrovnik would be complete without a walk around the spectacular city walls, the finest in the world and the city's main claim to fame. From the top, the view over the old town and the shimmering Adriatic is sublime. You can get a good handle on the extent of the shelling damage in the 1990s by gazing over the rooftops: those sporting bright new terracotta suffered damage and had to be replaced.

The first set of walls to enclose the city was built in the 9th century. In the middle of the 14th century the 1.5m-thick defences were fortified with 15 square forts. The threat of attacks from the Turks in the 15th century prompted the city to strengthen the existing forts and add new ones, so that the entire old town was contained within a stone barrier 2km long and up to 25m high. The walls are thicker on the land side – up to 6m – and range from 1.5m to 3m on the sea side.

The round **Minčeta Tower** (Tvrđava Minčeta; City Walls) protects the landward edge of the city from attack, the **Bokar Tower** (Tvrđava Bokar; City Walls) and **Fort Lawrence** (Tvrđava Lovrjenac; 📞020-638 800; incl city walls adult/child 70/30KN; ⊙8am-6.30pm Apr, May, Aug, Sep, to 7.30pm Jun & Jul, to 5.30pm Oct, 9am-3pm Nov-Mar) look west and out to sea, while

Dubrovnik

Villa Kraić (650m);
Way of the Cross
Walking Trail (750m)

Zagrebačka

Srednji Kono

Izmedu Vrta

Dura Pulića

Art Cafe (200m);
Lovrjenac Fort (350m);
Jadrolinija Ferry
Terminal (2.5km)

Branitelja Dubrovnika

Uz Posat

Put Iza Grada

Frana Supila

City Walls & Forts

Celestina Medovića

Od Sigurate

Palmotićeva

Antuninska

Nalješkovićeva

Kunićeva

Petrilovrijenci

Vetranićeva

Zamanjina

Dropčeva

Boškovićeva

Peline

Prijeko

War Photo Limited

Poljana
Paška
Miličevića

Garište

Zlatarićeva

Getaldićeva

Čubranovićeva

Dorđićeva

Široka

Placa (Stradun)

Izmedu Polača

Žudioska

Kovačka

Zlatarska

Za Rokom

Luža
Square

Lučarica

Pred Dvorom

Pužljiva

Na Andriji

Od šorte

Od Rupa

Od Domina

Sv Josipa

Nikole Božidarovića

Od Puča

C Zuzorić

Miha Pracata

M Kaboge

Dinka Ranjine

Uz Jezuite

Gundulićeva
Poljana

Držićeva
Poljana

Od Kaštela

Zvijezdićeva

Strossmayerova

Androvićeva

ADRIATIC
SEA

Od Margarite

Poljana
Rudera
Boškovića

Kneza Hvaša

Ilije Sarake

Pobijana

BALKANS DUBROVNIK

Fort Revelin (Trg Oružja) and Fort St John (Tvrđava sv Ivana; City Walls) guard the eastern approach and the Old Harbour.

There are entrances to the walls from near the Pile Gate, the Ploče Gate and the Maritime Museum. The Pile Gate entrance tends to be the busiest, and entering from the Ploče side has the added advantage of getting the steepest climbs out of the way first (you're required to walk in an anticlockwise direction). Don't underestimate how strenuous the wall walk can be, especially on a hot day. There's very little shelter

and the few vendors selling water on the route tend to be overpriced.

★**Rector's Palace** PALACE
(Knežev dvor; ☑ 020-321 497; www.dumus.hr; Pred Dvorom 3; single entrance 80KN, adult/child multimuseum pass 120/25KN; ⊙ 9am-6pm Apr-Oct, to 4pm Nov-Mar) Built in the late 15th century for the elected rector who governed Dubrovnik, this Gothic-Renaissance palace contains the rector's office, his private chambers, public halls, administrative offices and a dungeon. During his one-month term the rector was unable to leave the building without the

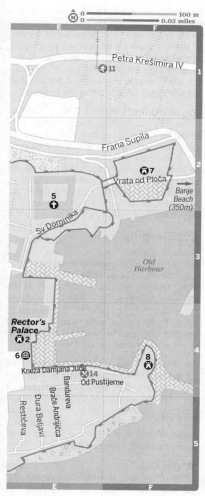

Dubrovnik

permission of the senate. Today the palace has been turned into the **Cultural History Museum**, with artfully restored rooms, portraits, coats of arms and coins, evoking the glorious history of Dubrovnik.

★**War Photo Limited**　　　　　GALLERY
(☎020-322 166; www.warphotoltd.com; Antuninska 6; adult/concession 50/40KN; ◎10am-10pm daily May-Sep, to 4pm Wed-Mon Apr & Oct) An immensely powerful experience, this gallery features intensely compelling exhibitions curated by New Zealand photojournalist Wade Goddard, who worked in the Balkans

in the 1990s. Its declared intention is to 'expose the myth of war...to let people see war as it is, raw, venal, frightening, by focusing on how war inflicts injustices on innocents and combatants alike'. There's a permanent exhibition on the upper floor devoted to the wars in Yugoslavia, but the changing exhibitions cover a multitude of conflicts.

★**Lokrum**　　　　　ISLAND
(www.lokrum.hr; ◎Apr-Nov) Lush Lokrum is a beautiful, forested island full of holm oaks, black ash, pines and olive trees, and an ideal escape from urban Dubrovnik. It's a popular swimming spot, although the beaches are rocky. To reach the nudist beach, head left from the ferry and follow the signs marked FKK; the rocks at the far end are Dubrovnik's de facto gay beach. Also popular is the small saltwater lake, which is known as the **Dead Sea**.

**Dulčić Masle
Pulitika Gallery**　　　　　GALLERY
(☎020-612 645; www.ugdubrovnik.hr; Držićeva poljana 1; adult/child multimuseum pass 120/25KN; ◎9am-8pm Tue-Sun) This small offshoot of the city's main gallery unites three friends

beyond the grave: local artists Ivo Dulčić, Antun Masle and Đuro Pulitika, who all came to the fore in the 1950s and 1960s. There's a permanent collection featuring the trio's work on the lower floor, while the upper gallery is given over to temporary exhibitions by current artists.

On the ground floor, Ronald Brown Memorial House honours the USA Secretary of Commerce who died tragically in a plane crash near Dubrovnik in 1996.

Dominican Monastery & Museum
CHRISTIAN MONASTERY

(Muzej Dominikanskog samostana; ☑ 020-321 423; dominikanci.muzej@gmail.com; Sv Dominika 4; 30KN; ⊙ 9am-6pm May-Oct, to 5pm Nov-Apr) This imposing structure is an architectural highlight, built in a transitional Gothic Renaissance style, and containing an impressive art collection. Constructed around the same time as the city walls in the 14th century, the stark exterior resembles a fortress more than a religious complex. The interior contains a graceful 15th-century **cloister** constructed by local artisans after the designs of the Florentine architect Maso di Bartolomeo.

Franciscan Monastery & Museum
CHRISTIAN MONASTERY

(Muzej Franjevačkog samostana; ☑ 020-321 410; Placa 2; adult 30KN; ⊙ 9am-6pm Mar-Oct, to 5pm Nov-Feb) Within this monastery's solid stone walls is a gorgeous mid-14th-century **cloister**, a historic **pharmacy** and a small **museum** with a collection of relics and liturgical objects, including chalices, paintings, gold jewellery and pharmacy items such as laboratory gear and medical books. The remains of artillery that pierced the monastery walls during the 1990s war have been saved, too.

🏃 Activities

Banje Beach
SWIMMING

(www.banjebeach.eu; Frana Supila 10) Banje Beach is the closest beach to the old town, just beyond the 17th-century Lazareti (a former quarantine station) outside Ploče Gate. Although many people rent lounge chairs and parasols from the beach club, there's no problem with just flinging a towel on the beach if you can find a space.

★ Cable Car
CABLE CAR

(Žičara; ☑ 020-414 355; www.dubrovnikcablecar. com; Petra Krešimira IV bb; adult/child return 140/60KN; ⊙ 9am-midnight Jun-Aug, to 10pm Sep, to 9pm May, to 8pm Apr & Oct, to 5pm Feb-Mar & Nov, to 4pm Dec & Jan) Dubrovnik's cable car whisks you from just north of the city walls to Mt Srđ in under four minutes. At the end of the line there's a stupendous perspective of the city from a lofty 405m, taking in the terracotta-tiled rooftops of the old town and the island of Lokrum, with the Adriatic and distant Elafiti Islands filling the horizon.

Way of the Cross Walking Trail
HIKING

(Križni Put; Jadranska) Filled with jaw-dropping views of the entire town and art reliefs illustrating the Stations of the Cross, the hike up the 418m Srđ hill takes roughly an hour. This free alternative to the cable-car ride starts nearby the eastern entrance to the Adriatic Motorway and runs up to the Fort Imperial on top. It's best done early in the morning or at sunset.

🛏 Sleeping

Hostel Angelina
HOSTEL €

(☑ 091 89 39 089; www.hostelangelinaoldtown-dubrovnik.com; Plovani skalini 17a; dm 290KN; ❋ 🛜) Hidden away in a quiet nook of the old town, this cute little hostel offers bunk rooms, a small guest kitchen and a bougainvillea-shaded terrace with memorable views over the rooftops. Plus you'll get a great glute workout every time you walk up the lane.

Apartments Silva
GUESTHOUSE €€

(☑ 098 244 639; Kardinala Stepinca 62; r/apt from €100/200; 🅿 ❋ 🛜) Lush Mediterranean foliage lines the terraces of this lovely hillside complex, a short hop up from the beach at Lapad. The rooms are comfortable and well priced, but best of all is the spacious top-floor apartment (sleeping five).

★ Villa Klaić
B&B €€

(☑ 091 73 84 673; www.villaklaic-dubrovnik.com; Šumetska 9; s/d from €80/120; 🅿 ❋ 🛜 🏊) Just off the main coast road, high above the old town, this outstanding guesthouse offers comfortable modern rooms and wonderful hospitality courtesy of the owner, Milo Klaić. Extras include a small swimming pool, continental breakfast, free pickups and free beer!

🍴 Eating

Barba
STREET FOOD €

(☑ 091 20 53 488; www.facebook.com/dubrovnik. barba; Boškovićeva 5; sandwiches from 39KN; ⊙ 10am-midnight) The pioneers of street food in Dubrovnik, Barba serve typical local ingredients in an untypical fashion, resulting in tasty quick bites such as fried oysters, shrimp and octopus burgers, or anchovy sandwiches. Eat in or take away.

Tutto Bene Fast Food   FAST FOOD €
(☑020-323 353; www.tuttobene-dubrovnik.com; Od Puča 7; mains 30-55KN; ⊙10am-11pm) As the name suggests, everything's good at Tutto Bene. Generously-sized kebabs, sumptuous pizza slices, delicious wraps, sandwiches and extra crispy fries can be savoured at the few tables indoors or on-the-go whilst sightseeing. Expect queues.

★Nishta   VEGETARIAN, VEGAN €€
(☑020-322 088; www.nishtarestaurant.com; Prijeko bb; mains 77-95KN; ⊙11.30am-10pm Mon-Sat; 🔊🖉) The popularity of this tiny old town eatery is testament not just to the paucity of options for vegetarians and vegans in Croatia, but to the imaginative food produced within. Alongside the expected curries, pastas and veggie burgers, the menu delivers more unusual options such as pasta-free zucchini 'spaghetti'. Reservations recommended. Kitchen closes at 10pm.

Konoba Ribar   DALMATIAN €€
(☑020-323 194; Kneza Damjana Jude bb; mains 77-122KN; ⊙10am-11pm; 🔊) Serving local food the way locals like it, at more or less local prices, this little family-run eatery is a blissfully untouristy choice. They don't attempt anything fancy or clever, just big serves of traditional favourites such as risotto and stuffed squid. It's set in a little lane pressed hard up against the city walls.

🍷 Drinking & Nightlife

Buža   BAR
(off Od Margarite; ⊙8am-2am) Finding this ramshackle bar-on-a-cliff feels like a real discovery as you duck and dive around the city walls and finally see the entrance tunnel. However, Buža's no secret – it gets insanely busy, especially around sunset. Wait for a space on one of the concrete platforms, grab a cool drink in a plastic cup and enjoy the vibe and views.

D'vino   WINE BAR
(☑020-321 230; www.dvino.net; Palmotićeva 4a; ⊙8am-late; 🔊) If you're interested in sampling top-notch Croatian wine, this convivial bar is the place to go. As well as a large and varied wine list, it offers tasting flights presented by cool and knowledgeable staff (three wines from 55KN) plus savoury breakfasts, snacks and platters.

Art Cafe   BAR
(☑020-311 097; www.facebook.com/ArtCafe Dubrovnik; Branitelja Dubrovnika 25; ⊙9am-2am; 🔊) Dubrovnik's most bohemian cafe-bar has seats constructed from bathtubs, tables made from washing-machine agitators, brightly coloured walls, funky music and terraces front and rear. A popular daytime coffee spot, Art fires up on weekend nights and delivers club-like parties.

ℹ Information

Pile Tourist Office (☑020-312 011; www.tzdubrovnik.hr; Brsalje 5; ⊙8am-7pm Mon-Sat, 9am-3pm Sun) The main tourist office, just outside the old town; dispenses maps, information and advice.

ℹ Getting There & Away

BOAT

From July to mid-September, there's a daily **Jadrolinija** (☑020-418 000; www.jadrolinija.hr; Obala Stjepana Radića 40; ⊙8am-4.30pm & 7-8pm Mon-Sat, 8-9.30am & 6-10pm Sun) catamaran to Hvar (190KN, four hours). From April to October, two to six car ferries per week travel between Dubrovnik and Bari, Italy (passenger/car from €44/59, 10 hours).

From June to September **Kapetan Luka** (Krilo; ☑021-645 476; www.krilo.hr) has a daily fast boat to/from Mljet (80KN, 1¼ hours), Korčula (120KN, 1¾ hours), Hvar (190KN, three hours), Brač (190KN, 3¾ hours) and Split (190KN, 4¼ hours).

BUS

Buses from **Dubrovnik Bus Station** (Autobusni kolodvor; ☑060 305 070; www.libertas dubrovnik.hr; Obala Pape Ivana Pavla II 44a; ⊙6am-9pm; 🔊) can be crowded, so book tickets in advance in summer. The station has a left-luggage office (5KN for the first hour, then 1.50KN per hour).

Split–Dubrovnik buses pass briefly through Bosnian territory, so keep your passport handy for border-crossing points.

Departure times are detailed at www.libertas dubrovnik.hr.

Croatia Survival Guide

ℹ Directory A–Z

ACCOMMODATION
➡ Croatia is traditionally seen as a summer destination and good places book out well in advance in July and August, when many establishments enforce minimum three-night stays

or a surcharge for shorter bookings (around 30%); some will insist on a seven-night minimum stay in the high season.

➡ Accommodation providers will handle travellers' registration with the local police, as required by Croatian authorities. The 'sojourn tax' (usually less than 10KN) is charged for every day you stay in Croatia. It's quite normal for this to be additional to the room rate you've been quoted.

➡ Private accommodation providers are an integral part of the local tourism industry and are often the best (and sometimes the only) option in more remote destinations. On top of that, many of the owners go out of their way to be hospitable and some even offer the option of eating with them, which is a great way to get to know the culture.

INTERNET ACCESS

Most cafes, restaurants and bars across Croatia have free wi-fi; just ask for the password. Hotels and private guesthouses are almost always equipped with wi-fi.

MONEY

➡ Croatia uses the kuna (KN). Each kuna is divided into 100 lipa.

➡ The kuna has a fixed exchange rate tied to the euro. However, to amass foreign currency, the government makes the kuna more expensive in summer when tourists visit. You'll get the best exchange rate from mid-September to mid-June.

➡ ATMs are widely available.

➡ Visa and MasterCard are widely accepted in hotels; Diners Club and American Express are less accepted. Many guesthouses, smaller restaurants and shops only take cash.

➡ Tipping is purely discretionary and generally only done in restaurants (up to 10%) and cafe-bars.

ⓘ PRICE RANGES

The following price ranges refer to a double room with a bathroom in July and August.

€ less than 450KN

€€ 450–800KN

€€€ more than 800KN

The following price ranges refer to a main course.

€ less than 70KN

€€ 70–120KN

€€€ more than 120KN

OPENING HOURS

Banks 8am or 9am to 8pm Monday to Friday, 7am to 1pm or 8am to 2pm Saturday

Bars and cafes 8am or 9am to midnight

Offices 8am to 4pm or 8.30am to 4.30pm Monday to Friday

Restaurants Noon to 11pm or midnight, closed Sunday out of peak season

Shops 8am to 8pm Monday to Friday, to 2pm or 3 pm Saturday

PUBLIC HOLIDAYS

New Year's Day 1 January

Epiphany 6 January

Easter Sunday & Monday March/April

Labour Day 1 May

Corpus Christi 60 days after Easter

Day of Antifascist Resistance 22 June

Statehood Day 25 June

Homeland Thanksgiving Day 5 August

Feast of the Assumption 15 August

Independence Day 8 October

All Saints' Day 1 November

Christmas 25 and 26 December

TELEPHONE

➡ To call from region to region within Croatia, start with the area code (with the initial zero); drop it when dialling within the same region.

➡ Phone numbers with the prefix 060 can be either free or charged at a premium rate, so watch out for the fine print.

➡ Phone numbers that begin with 09 are mobile phone numbers, calls to which are billed at a much higher rate than regular numbers.

➡ Users with unlocked phones can buy a local SIM card, which are easy to find. Otherwise you may be charged roaming rates.

ⓘ Getting There & Away

Getting to Croatia is becoming easier, with both budget and full-service airlines flying to various airports in summer. On top of this, buses and ferries also shepherd holidaymakers into the country.

AIR

Zagreb (☑ 01-45 62 170; www.zagreb-airport.hr), **Split** (Zračna Luka Split; ☑ 021-203 507; www.split-airport.hr; Cesta dr Franje Tuđmana 1270, Kaštel Štafilić, Kaštela) and **Dubrovnik** (DBV, Zračna luka Dubrovnik; ☑ 020-773 100; www.airport-dubrovnik.hr) airports welcome international flights year-round, with dozens of seasonal routes and charters added in summer.

Croatia Airlines (OU; ☑ 01-66 76 555; www.croatiaairlines.hr) is the national carrier; it's part of the Star Alliance.

LAND

Croatia has border crossings with Hungary, Slovenia, Bosnia and Hercegovina, Serbia and Montenegro. Zagreb is Croatia's main train hub.

SEA

Regular ferries connect Croatia with Italy. Split is the main hub, with overnight services to/from Ancona.

Blue Line (www.blueline-ferries.com)

Jadrolinija (www.jadrolinija.hr)

SNAV (www.snav.com)

Venezia Lines (www.venezialines.com)

ℹ Getting Around

Transport in Croatia is reasonably priced, quick and generally efficient.

Air A surprisingly extensive schedule of domestic flights, especially in summer.

Bus Reasonably priced, with extensive coverage of the country and frequent departures.

Boat There's an extensive network of car ferries and catamarans all along the coast and the islands.

Car Useful for travelling at your own pace, or for visiting regions with minimal public transport. Cars can be hired in every city or larger town. Drive on the right.

Train Less frequent and much slower than buses, with limited network, but generally more comfortable. For information about schedules, prices and services, contact **HŽPP** (☑ 01-37 82 583; www.hzpp.hr).

BOSNIA & HERCEGOVINA

Sarajevo

☑ 033 / POP 395,000

In the 1990s Sarajevo was besieged and on the edge of annihilation. Today its restored historic centre is full of welcoming cafes and good-value lodgings, the bullet holes largely plastered over on the city's curious architectural mixture of Ottoman, Yugoslav and Austro-Hungarian buildings.

The antique, stone-flagged alleys of Baščaršija give the delightful Old Town core a certain Turkish feel. Directly north and south, steep valley sides are fuzzed with red-roofed Bosnian houses and prickled with uncounted minarets, climbing towards green-topped mountain ridges. In winter, Bjelašnica and Jahorina offer some of Europe's best-value skiing, barely 30km away.

◉ Sights

The best way to really 'feel' the city is to stroll Old Sarajevo's pedestrian lanes and grand avenues, and climb the gently picturesque slopes of Bjelave and Vratnik for sweeping views. Seeking out key museums is likely to take you into modern, businesslike Novo Sarajevo, and beyond to park-filled Ilidža.

★ Baščaršija
AREA

Centred on what foreigners nickname Pigeon Sq, Baščaršija is the heart of old Sarajevo with pedestrians padding pale stone alleys and squares between lively (if tourist-centric) coppersmith alleys, grand Ottoman mosques, caravanserai-restaurants and lots of inviting little cafes and *ćevapi* serveries.

★ Sarajevo City Hall
ARCHITECTURE

(Vijećnica; www.nub.ba; adult/child 10/5KM; ⊘ 9am-6pm) Storybook neo-Moorish facades make the 1898 Vijećnica Sarajevo's most beautiful Austro-Hungarian–era building. Seriously damaged during the 1990s siege, it finally reopened in 2014 after laborious reconstruction. Its colourfully restored multiarched interior and stained-glass ceiling are superb. Your ticket also allows you to peruse the excellent *Sarajevo 1914-1981* exhibition in the octagonal basement. This gives well-explained potted histories of the city's various 20th-century periods, insights into fashion and music subcultures and revelations about Franz Ferdinand's love life.

National Museum
MUSEUM

(Zemaljski Muzej Bosne-i-Hercegovine; www.zemaljskimuzej.ba; Zmaja od Bosne 3; adult/child 6/3KM; ⊘ 10am-7pm Tue-Fri, to 2pm Sat & Sun) Bosnia's biggest and best-endowed museum of ancient and natural history is housed in an impressive, purpose-built quadrangle of neoclassical 1913 buildings. It's best known for housing the priceless Sarajevo Haggadah but there's much more to see. Highlights include Illyrian and Roman carvings, Frankish-style medieval swords, beautifully preserved 19th-century room interiors and meteorites among the extensive cabinets full of geological samples. Many explanatory panels have English translations.

★ Tunnel Museum
MUSEUM

(Tunel Spasa; www.tunelspasa.ba; Tuneli bb 1; adult/student 10/5KM; ⊘ 9am-5pm, last entry 4.30pm Apr-Oct, 9am-4pm, last entry 3.30pm Nov-Mar) The most visceral of Sarajevo's many 1990s

BOSNIA & HERCEGOVINA AT A GLANCE

Don't Miss

Stari Most, Mostar One of Bosnia's ultimate adrenaline rushes is jumping off Mostar's world-famous Old Bridge. In summer, young daredevils leap from the parapet of Stari Most, falling more than 20m into the freezing cold Neretva.The 16th-century stone arc was blown apart in 1993 during the Bosnian war but it has been magnificently rebuilt.

Baščaršija, Sarajevo Sarajevo's bustling old quarter, Baščaršija is a delightful warren of marble-flagged pedestrian courtyards and laneways full of Ottoman-era mosques, copper workshops, jewellery shops, caravanserai-cafes and inviting little restaurants. Start your explorations at the Sebilj, an 1891 ornamental gazebo-style water fountain on central 'Pigeon Sq'.

Rafting in western Bosnia The fast-flowing Una and Vrbas rivers offer some of the country's best rafting and kayaking, accessed from Bihać and Banja Luka respectively. The Una has gorgeous tree-shaded rapids and mossy waterfalls, while the Vrbas descends through a series of gorges and reservoir lakes.

Bjelašnica mountain Bosnia's second Olympic ski field rises above the Bjelašnica resort, around 30km south of Sarajevo, offering some of Europe's best-value skiing. An attraction here is floodlit night skiing and, in summer, the possibilities of exploring the magical mountain villages of Lukomir and Umoljani behind.

Hercegovinian wine The arid, Mediterranean landscape of Hercegovina region is famed for its homegrown wines and sun-packed fruits. Local *živalka* grapes yield dry yet fruit-filled whites, while suitably aged *blatina* and *vranac* reds can be velvety and complex. The Trebinje region produces some of Hercegovina's best wines, notably at Tvrdoš Monastery.

Itineraries

One Week

A week is enough to get a taste of the country's two key cities, their surroundings and turbulent histories. Spend the first couple of days in **Sarajevo**, soaking up the capital's vibrant cafe culture and remarkable mix of Turkish and Austrian historical influences. Join a free city walking tour on day one, and sign up for a war-survivors' tour for day two. Then jump on the bus to **Konjic** to visit Tito's nuclear bunker, and take a day trip to **Umoljani** and **Lukomir** mountain villages. Continue south to **Mostar** to admire its historic bridge and old town.

Two Weeks

Continue with the exploration of Hercegovina by visiting the glorious **Sutjeska National Park**, where you can spend a couple of days hiking and mountain biking. Make your way further north to **Višegrad**, with its majestic 16th-century bridge, soaring river canyons and Andrić-themed pseudo-antique inner city. Head back to Sarajevo and end the trip with a **rafting adventur**e in western Bosnia.

Essential Activities

Skiing Jahorina and Bjelašnica mountains rise directly behind Sarajevo, offering convenient access to bargain-value yet high-quality winter skiing. Another, lesser-known option is Vlašić mountain near Travnik in western Bosnia.

Rafting For a variety of rafting and canoeing experiences, the Una River near Bihać is hard to beat. The Vrbas River offers canyoning and wild river rafting by night, between Jajce and Banja Luka. The rapids reach terrifyingly difficult class V in April/May; rafting is more suitable for beginners in summer.

Hiking and mountain biking Many highland areas have mine-safe, marked trails. The splendid Sutjeska National Park in eastern Bosnia is one of the best places in the country to hike or mountain bike. Two of the most popular treks lead to Mt Maglić, Bosnia and Hercegovina's highest peak.

Getting Around

Bus Bus stations presell tickets. Between towns it's normally easy enough to wave down any bus en route. Advance reservations are sometimes necessary for overnight routes or at peak holiday times. The biggest companies, including Centrotrans (www.centrotrans.com) and Globtour (www.globtour.com), have online timetables and ticketing.

Car Bosnia and Hercegovina's winding roads are lightly trafficked and a delight for driving if you aren't in a hurry. And driving makes sense to reach the country's remoter areas and villages to where there is minimal public transport.

Train Trains are slower and far less frequent than buses but generally slightly cheaper. ŽFBH (www.zfbh.ba) has an online rail timetable search. Some lines are essentially dormant and the Sarajevo–Mostar track is under reconstruction.

When to Go

Sarajevo

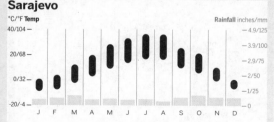

Apr–Jun You can beat the heat in Hercegovina, raft rivers, and see flowers blooming on the hiking trails.

Jul–Aug It gets sweaty and accommodation fills, but festivals keep things lively.

Mid-Jan–mid-Mar Skiing on Sarajevo's mountains gets cheaper after the New Year holidays.

Arriving in Bosnia & Hercegovina

Sarajevo International Airport (Sarajevo) Buses run roughly hourly (5km is €2.50, 30 minutes), last services at 9.10pm, 10.23pm and 11.40pm. Taxis should cost less than €10 to the old town.

Mostar Airport No public transport but taxis charge less than €5.

Istočno Sarajevo Bus Station Walk 400m then take trolleybus 103 to the old town (less than €1, 35 minutes).

Sarajevo Main Bus & Train Stations Take tram 1 to the old town (less than €1, 15 minutes).

Top Phrases

Hello. Dobar dan.

Goodbye. Zbogom.

Please. Molim.

Thank you. Hvala.

How much is it? Koliko je to?

Resources

Bosnia & Hercegovina Tourism (www.bhtourism.ba) Official tourism site.

Sarajevo Times (http://www.sarajevotimes.com) Comprehensive news site in English.

Set Your Budget

➡ Dorm bed: €8–15

➡ Ćevapi or burek: €3–5

➡ Prepurchased tram ticket: €0.80

➡ Intercity bus fare: €7–12

Central Sarajevo

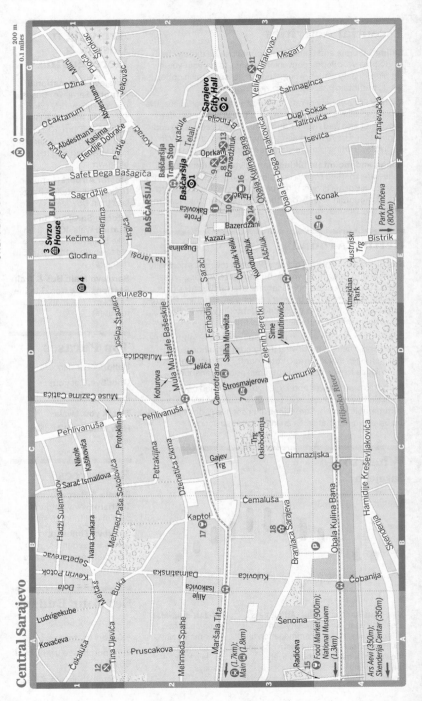

3 Svrzo House

4

12

Map scale: 200 m / 0.1 miles

Streets and labels (selection):

Šircokaj, Mlini, Pločča, Džina, Oćaktanum, Abdesthana, Kasima Efendije Dobrače, Plukša, Safet Bega Bašagiča, Sagrdžije, Čemerlina, Kečima, Glođina, Hrgiča, Na Varoš, Logavina, Josipa Štadlera, Mula Mustafe Bašeskije, Koturova, Mujabdiča, Muse Ćazime Čatića, Pehlivanuša, Protoklinica, Petrakijina, Nikole Kašikoviča, Sarač Ismailova, Hadži Sulemanov, Ivana Cankara, Sepatarevac, Kevrin Potok, Dola, Ludvigekube, Kovaćeva, Čekaluša, Tina Ujeviča, Mehmeda Spahe, Pruscakova, Mehmed Paše Sokoloviča, Dženetica čikma, Dalmatinska, Buka, Alije Isakoviča, Maršala Tita, Radiceva, Šenoina, Ćemaluša, Gajev Trg, Kaptol, Kulovića, Branilaca Sarajeva, Obala Kulina Bana, Čobanija, Hamidije Kreševljakoviča, Skenderija, Gimnazijska, Trg Oslobodenja, Ćumurija, Strosmajerova, Salina Muvekita, Zelenih Beretki, Sime Milutinoviča, Ferhadija, Jelića, Centrotrans, Bazerdžani, Kazazi, Ašćiluk, Kundurdžiluk, Ćurčiluk Veliki, Dugaljina, Sarači, Prote Bakoviča, Halači, Bravadžiluk, Oprkanj, Telali, Kračule, Kovač, Pathe, Abdesthana, Jetovać, B Fincija, Velika Alifakovac, Megara, Šahinaginca, Dugi Sokak, Taliroviča, Isevića, Franjevačka, Konak, Austriski Trg, Bistrik, Atmejdan Park, Park Prinčeva (800m), Obala Isa-bega Išhakoviča, Obala Kulina Bana, Miljacka River

Baščaršija Tram Stop

Baščaršija 1

BAŠČARŠIJA

BJELAVE

Sarajevo City Hall 2

Oprkanj 13, 9, 8, 16, 10, 14

Halač 16

5, **7**

6

11

17, **18**

15

Annotations: (1.7km); Main (1.8km); Food Market (900m); National Museum (1.3km); Ars Aevi (350m); Skenderija Centar (350m)

Central Sarajevo

war-experience 'attractions', this unmissable museum's centrepiece and raison d'être is a 25m section of the 1m wide, 1.6m high hand-dug tunnel under the airport runway. That acted as the city's lifeline to the outside world during the 1992–95 siege, when Sarajevo was virtually surrounded by hostile Serb forces.

Take tram 3 to Ilidža (35 minutes, 11km from Baščaršija), then switch to Kotorac-bound bus 12 (10 minutes). Get off at the last stop, walk across the Tilava bridge, then turn immediately left down Tuneli for 500m. The bus runs around twice hourly on weekdays but only every 90 minutes on Sundays, so it's often faster to walk from Ilidža (around 30 minutes). A group tour can prove cheaper than a taxi.

War Childhood Museum MUSEUM
(www.warchildhood.org; Logavina 32; adult/child 10/5KM; ◎11am-7pm) A fascinating new museum focusing on the experiences of children who grew up during the 1990s conflict. Poignantly personal items donated by former war children, such as diaries, drawings and ballet slippers, are displayed alongside written and video testimonies.

★**Svrzo House** MUSEUM
(Svrzina Kuća; ☑033-478740; www.muzejsarajeva.ba; Glođina 8; 3KM; ◎10am-6pm Mon-Fri, to 3pm Sat, closes early off-season) An oasis of white-washed walls, cobbled courtyards and partly vine-draped dark timbers, this 18th-century house-museum is brilliantly restored and appropriately furnished, helping visitors imagine Sarajevo life in eras past.

Ars Aevi GALLERY
(☑033-216927; info@arsaevi.ba; Skenderija Centar; adult/child 4/2KM; ◎10am-6pm) Many of the works in this thought-provoking contemporary art gallery were collected as donations for Bosnia after the 1990s conflict. They're displayed in a factory-esque interior of metal ducts and polished chipboard within the lumpy **Skenderija Centar** (www.skenderija.ba; Skenderija). A forbidding chain and padlock across the entry door are part of the art and do not necessarily mean the gallery is closed.

🛏 Sleeping

★**Seven Heavens** GUESTHOUSE €
(☑062-191508; 3rd fl, Štrossmayerova 3; dm/d €12/30) Three floors up in the grand mansion above the Monument Jazz Club, this boutique hostel/guesthouse has bathrooms that would put a five-star hotel to shame, shared by just three smart rooms and one spacious dorm.

Franz Ferdinand Hostel HOSTEL €
(☑033-238099; www.franzferdinandhostel.com; Jelića 4; dm 21-33KM, d 31-49KM; ✳@🛜) One of Sarajevo's most popular hostels, Franz Ferdinand uses giant sepia photos and a timeline floor to recall characters and scenes from Sarajevo's WWI history. The foyer walls are a-scribble with guest graffiti. Bunks have private power points and ample headroom, and the comfortably stylish kitchen-lounge is well designed for conversation between travellers.

★**Isabegov Hamam Hotel** HERITAGE HOTEL €€
(☑033-570050; www.isabegovhotel.com; Bistrik 1; s/d/q €90/100/140; ✳) After many years of restoration the classic 1462 Isabegov Hamam (bathhouse) reopened in 2015 with 15 hotel rooms designed to evoke the spirit

of the age with lashings of handcrafted dark-wood furniture, ornately carved bedsteads and tube-glass chandeliers.

Eating

Bravadžiluk
STREET FOOD €

(mains from 3KM) For inexpensive snack meals look along Bravadžiluk or nearby Kundurdžiluk: **Buregdžinica Bosna** (Bravadžulik; potato/cheese/meat pies per kg 8/10/12KM, meal portions 2-3.50KM; ⊙7am-midnight) is excellent for cheap, fresh *burek* sold by weight. Locals argue whether **Hodžić** (Sebilj Sq; čevapi small/large 3.50/7KM; ⊙7.30am-10pm), **Željo** (Kundurdžiluk 17 & 20; čevapi small/medium/large 3.5/7/10KM; ⊙8am-11pm) or **Mrkva** (www.mrkva.ba; Bravadžulik 15; čevapi small/large 3.5/7KM; ⊙8.30am-10pm) serves the best *ćevapi*, and there is plenty of attractively styled competition.

Food Market
INTERNATIONAL €

(top fl, SCC; mains 5-12KM; ❄🔊; 🚇1, 3 Marjin Dvor) With counterpointing interior foliage, grey metal girders and a giant chandelier, this adventurous restaurant has several cuisine-specific open kitchens and is built into the SCC's projecting spike behind Times Sq–style flashing info windows. Food choices include grilled asparagus on pasta, okonomiyaki, quesadillas, giant salads, avocado-filled croissant and curries of various Asian styles spiced according to your request.

★ Mala Kuhinja
FUSION €€

(📞061-144741; www.malakuhinja.ba; Tina Ujevića 13; mains 12-25KM; ⊙10am-11pm Mon-Sat; ❄🔊🍴) Run by former TV celebrity chefs, the novel concept here is to forget menus and simply ask you what you do/don't like. Spicy? Vegan? No problem. And armed with this knowledge the team makes culinary magic in the show-kitchen. Superb.

Inat Kuća
BOSNIAN €€

(Spite House; 📞033-447867; www.inatkuca.ba; Velika Alifakovac 1; mains 10-20KM; ⊙11am-10.30pm; ❄🔊) This Sarajevo institution occupies a classic Ottoman-era house that's a veritable museum piece with central stone water-trough, a case of antique guns and fine metal-filigree lanterns. A range of Bosnian specialities are served using pewter crockery at glass-topped display tables containing traditional local jewellery.

 Drinking & Nightlife

One of Sarajevo's delights is exploring its bars and cafes – the line between which can at times be rather blurred. For great coffee, cakes and ice cream there's a special concentration along and near Ferhadija. Increasing in popularity with the youth are cafes for smoking narghile (water pipes), tucked into the Old Town's former caravanserai courtyards.

★ Dekanter
WINE BAR

(📞033-263815; www.facebook.com/vinoteka.dekanter; Radićeva 4; ⊙10am-midnight Mon-Sat,

---

BOSNIA'S GREAT OUTDOORS

Sutjeska National Park Containing the nation's highest peak, Europe's oldest forest and some glorious canyon-land scenery, Sutjeska is a spectacular place to explore on foot or by mountain bike. The park has a network of trails, and you can arrange guides through reliable adventure-sports outfit **Encijan** (📞058-211150, 065-626588; www.pkencijan.com; Krajiška bb; ⊙9am-5pm Mon-Sat Apr-Oct), along with rafting on the Tara River at the park's fringes.

Lukomir Village Fabled Lukomir is the most remote of Sarajevo's highland villages, and was until recent times entirely without a road. Most of the houses are simple stone structures that you can survey from a knoll-top viewpoint near the edge of a toe-curlingly deep gorge. For a great day tour, drive to Umoljani, hike on to Lukomir and drive back; contact **Green Visions** (📞061-213278, 033-717290; www.greenvisions.ba; Trg Barcelone 3; ⊙9am-5pm Mon-Fri) for a guided tour.

Vrbas Canyons Between Jajce and Banja Luka in western Bosnia, the Vrbas River descends through a series of gorges and reservoir lakes that together form one of BiH's foremost adventure-sport playgrounds. **Kanjon Rafting Centre** (📞066-714169; www.guidelinebl.com; Karanovac; ⊙9am-6pm Apr-Oct) is a reliable, well-organised extreme-sports outfit offering guided canyoning (seasonal), hiking and top-class rafting. This is also a popular place for rock climbers.

OLD BOSNIAN TOWNS

Famous for the Unesco-listed 'bridge on the Drina' immortalised in Ivo Andrić's classic novel, eastern Bosnia's **Višegrad** has developed a niche tourist industry by building **Andrićgrad** (✆ 066-703722; www.andricgrad.com; ⏰ 24hr), a small mock-historical city core nominally celebrating the author. The surrounding deep-cut river canyons are most impressive seen from a boat chugging up the Drina from Serbia.

In western Bosnia, **Jajce** bills itself as Bosnia's 'Open Air Museum' and boasts impressive 21m-high waterfalls right in the town centre. The fortified old town climbs a steep rocky knoll to the powerful, ruined castle where Bosnia's medieval kings were once crowned. Surrounding mountains, lakes and canyons make Jajce a potentially useful exploration base.

The town of **Konjic** near Sarajevo has revived its small but pretty old town area and reconstructed its medieval bridge. It's also home to one of the most extraordinary remnants of the Cold War – a gigantic nuclear bunker, designed to keep Yugoslavia's President Tito safe from a 25-megaton blast. Visits only run a few times weekly and must be prebooked through a local agency.

Since 1998 **Banja Luka** has been one of Europe's least-known 'capitals' (of Bosnia's Serbian entity, the Republika Srpska). The city is lively more than lovely, but it's worth a visit for the splendid Unesco-listed **Ferhadija Mosque** (www.ferhadija.ba; Kralja Petra 42; ⏰ 10am-8pm). Built in 1579 and completely destroyed in 1993 during the Bosnian War, it's been meticulously reconstructed using 16th-century techniques.

from 6pm Sun; ☎) It's easy to sit for hours sampling from more than 100 local and world vintages in this glorious, low-lit wine bar decorated with bottles, chateau-boxes and swirling ceiling sculptures of intertwined wires.

★**Zlatna Ribica**   BAR
(✆ 033-836348; Kaptol 5; ⏰ 8am-late) Sedate and outwardly grand, this tiny and eccentric bar adds understated humour to a cosy treasure trove of antiques and kitsch, reflected in big art-nouveau mirrors.

★**Pink Houdini**   JAZZ
(www.facebook.com/jazzbluesclubpinkhoudini; Branilaca Sarajevo 31; ⏰ 24hr) One of Sarajevo's rare 24-hour drinking spots, this quirky basement jazz bar has a tree of guitars, a wacky-fiesta themed abstract ceiling sculpture and UV lighting that makes your gin-and-tonic luminescent. Romping live blues gigs start at 10.30pm on Wednesdays, Fridays and Sundays.

Kuća Sevdaha   CAFE
(Halači 5; ⏰ 10am-6pm Tue-Sun) Sit in the intimate fountain courtyard of an Ottoman-era building sipping Bosnian coffee, juniper sherbet, rose water or herb-tea infusions while nibbling local sweets. The experience is accompanied by the lilting wails of *sevdah* (traditional Bosnian music) – usually recorded, but a couple of times a month there are live performances too.

ℹ Information

Official Tourist Info Centre (Turistički Informativni Centar; ✆ 033-580999; www. sarajevo-tourism.com; Saraři 58; ⏰ 9am-8pm Mon-Fri, 10am-6pm Sat & Sun, varies seasonally) Helpful tourist information centre. Beware of commercial imitations.

ℹ Getting There & Away

BUS
Sarajevo's **main bus station** (✆ 033-213100; www.centrotrans.com; Put Života 8; ⏰ 6am-10pm) primarily serves locations in the country, Croatia and Western Europe. Many services to the Republika Srpska (RS) and Serbia leave from **East Sarajevo (Lukovica) Bus Station** (Autobuska Stanica Istočno Sarajevo; ✆ 057-317377; www.balkanexpress-is.com; Srpskih Vladara bb; ⏰ 6am-11.15pm). The latter lies way out in the suburb of Dobrijna, 400m beyond the western terminus stop of trolleybus 103 and bus 31E. To some destinations, buses leave from both stations. For Jajce (24.50KM, 3½ hours) take Banja Luka buses.

TRAIN
The only international rail service is to Zagreb, departing at 10.21am (56.10KM, 9½ hours via Banja Luka). Domestically there are Mostar trains at 7.15am and 6.57pm (2¾ hours).

Mostar

POP 105,800

At dusk, the lights of numerous millhouse restaurants twinkle across gushing streamlets. Narrow Kujundžiluk bustles joyously with trinket sellers. And in between, the Balkans' most celebrated bridge forms a majestic stone arc between reincarnated medieval towers. It's an enchanting scene. Do stay into the evening to see it without the summer hordes of day trippers. Indeed, stay longer to enjoy memorable attractions in the surrounding area as well as pondering the

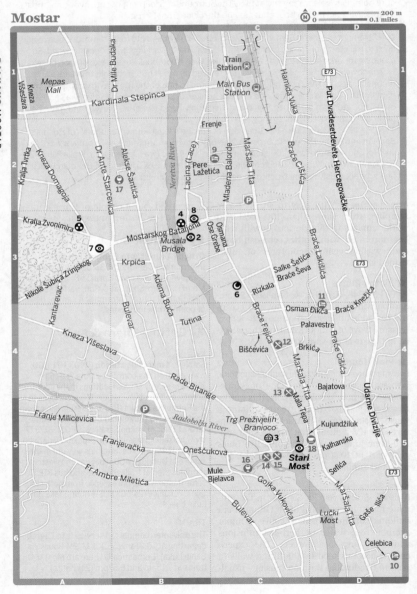

Mostar

city's darker side – beyond the cobbled lanes of the attractively restored Ottoman quarter are still-apparent scars of the 1990s conflict.

◉ Sights

★ Stari Most   BRIDGE

World-famous Stari Most (Old Bridge) is Mostar's indisputable visual focus. Its pale stone magnificently throws back the golden glow of sunset or the tasteful night-time floodlighting. The bridge's swooping arch was originally built between 1557 and 1566 on the orders of Suleyman the Magnificent. The current structure is a very convincing 21st-century rebuild following the bridge's 1990s bombardment during the civil war. Numerous well-positioned cafes and restaurants tempt you to sit and savour the splendidly restored scene.

The bridge has always been Mostar's raison d'être. The 16th-century stone version replaced a previous suspension bridge whose wobbling had terrified tradesmen as they gingerly crossed the fast-flowing Neretva River. An engineering marvel of its age, the new bridge had long been the 'old' bridge when, after 427 years, it was pounded into the river during a deliberate Croat artillery attack in November 1993. Depress-

ing footage of this sad moment is shown on many a video in Mostar. The laboriously reconstructed bridge reopened in 2004 and is now a Unesco World Heritage Site famed for its 'bridge divers'.

Hammam Museum   MUSEUM

(Džejvanbeg Bathhouse; Rad Bitange bb; adult/student 5/3KM; ⊘10am-6pm) This late-16th-century bathhouse has been attractively restored with whitewashed interior, bilingual panels explaining *hammam* (Turkish bath) culture and glass cabinets displaying associated traditional accoutrements.

Spanski Trg   HISTORIC SITE

In the early 1990s, Croat and Bosniak forces bombarded each other into the rubble across a 'front line' which ran along the Bulevar and Alekse Šantića St. Even now, several shell-pocked buildings remain in ruins around Spanski Trg, notably the triangular tower that was once Ljubljanska Banka (Snipers' Nest; Kralja Zvonimira bb) but is now a concrete skeleton plastered with graffiti.

Trg Musala   AREA

(Trg Musala) Trg Musala was once the heart of Austro-Hungarian Mostar. Today the square is a messy mishmash of architectural styles around a fountain garden. While the 1914 City Baths (Gradsko Kupatilo; www.orkamostar.ba; Trg Musala) building has been restored close to its original glory, the ruins of the once-splendid 1892 Hotel Neretva (Trg Musala) teeter on the verge of collapse with damage inflicted during the 1990s conflict.

Roznamedži Ibrahimefendi Mosque   MOSQUE

(Braće Fejića bb) This early-17th-century mosque was the only one to survive the 1993–95 shelling relatively unscathed. Its associated madrasa, demolished in 1960, has now also been rebuilt, its reincarnation hosting shops and a cafe.

🛏 Sleeping

Hostel Nina   HOSTEL €

(☏ 061-382743, 036-550820; www.hostelnina.ba; Čelebica 18; dm/s/d without bathroom €10/15/20; ✳@☎) This popular homestay-hostel is run by an obliging English-speaking lady whose husband is a war survivor and former bridge-jumper who pioneered and still runs regional Hercegovina day tours (€30) that just might end up with drinks at his Tabhana bar.

Hostel David HOSTEL €

(☑ 066-264173; www.hosteldavid.com; Pere Lažetića 6; dm €8.50-10; ☎) Hidden behind a high gate, this convivial place is given an unusual degree of charm by the palm tree and numerous flower boxes. It's on Mostar's hidden 'hostel street'.

★ Muslibegović House HISTORIC HOTEL €€

(☑ 036-551379; www.muslibegovichouse.com; Osman Đikća 41; s/d/ste €60/90/105; ⊙ museum 10am-6pm mid-Apr–mid-Oct; ❋ ☎) In summer, tourists pay 4KM to visit this beautiful, late-17th-century Ottoman courtyard house (extended in 1871). But it's also a charming boutique hotel. Room sizes and styles vary significantly, mixing excellent modern bathrooms with elements of traditional Bosnian, Turkish or even Moroccan design.

✖ Eating

Balkan 2 BOSNIAN €

(Mala Tepe; mains 4-12KM; ⊙ 6am-1am; ❋) Separated from the vegetable market by a trained curtain of vines, Balkan 2 fills an antique-style building with knick-knacks and, like **Balkan 1** (Aščinica Balkan; Braće Fejića 61; mains 3-7KM; ⊙ 8am-11pm), serves precooked stews, dolma and other homely Bosnian classics.

Šadrvan BALKAN €€

(☑ 061-891189; www.restoransadravan.ba; Jusovina 11; mains 10-25KM; ⊙ 9am-5pm; ☎) On a vine- and tree-shaded corner where the pedestrian lane from Stari Most divides, this delightful tourist favourite has tables set around a trickling fountain made of old Turkish-style metalwork. Obliging costumed waiters can help explain a menu that covers many bases and takes a stab at some vegetarian options. Meat-free *đuveč* (KM8) tastes like ratatouille on rice.

Hindin Han BALKAN €€

(☑ 036-581054; Jusovina bb; mains 10-18KM, seafood 14-24KM, ćevapi 7KM, wine per litre 15KM; ⊙ 11am-midnight; ☎) Hindin Han is a rebuilt historic mill-cottage building with several layers of summer terrace perched pleasantly above a side stream. Locals rate its food as better than most equivalent tourist restaurants. The stuffed squid we tried was perfectly cooked and generously garnished.

🍷 Drinking & Nightlife

Terasa CAFE

(Maršala Tita bb; coffee from 2KM; ⊙ hours vary) Half a dozen tables on an open-air perch-terrace survey Stari Most and the Old Town towers from photogenic yet unexpected angles. Enter beside MUM (Museum of Mostar & Herzegovina). Opening times are dependent on weather and temperature, not clocks.

OKC Abrašević BAR

(☑ 036-561107; www.okcabrasevic.org; Alekse Šantića 25; beer from 2.50KM; ⊙ 9am-11.45pm, to 1am concert nights) This understatedly intellectual two-level bar offers Mostar's most vibrantly alternative scene and has an attached venue for off-beat gigs. It's entered from an unlikely courtyard, the road-facing wall painted with a vast mural of a crouched figure.

Black Dog Pub PUB

(Crooked Bridge; beer/wine from 2/4KM; ⊙ 4pm-midnight) Old Mostar's best hostelry is a historic millhouse decked with flags and car number plates. It's about the only place you'll find draft ales from the local Oldbridz microbrewery (www.facebook.com/oldbridz. ale). Live bands play regularly midsummer, more rarely off season.

ℹ Getting There & Away

BUS

The **main bus station** (☑ 036-552025; Trg Ivana Krndelja) beside the train station has services to Sarajevo (20KM, 2½ hours, almost hourly), Kotor/Herceg Novi (68 to 60KM, 5½ to 6½ hours, 7am), Split (33KM to 37KM, three hours, five daily), Dubrovnik (40KM, 4½ hours, 7am, 10.15am and 1.50am), Zagreb (50KM to 52KM, 10 hours, five daily), Belgrade (60KM, 11 hours, 7.30am) and Vienna (106KM, 12 hours, 8.30am).

TRAIN

Trains to Sarajevo should leave morning and evening, but services were suspended at time of research pending track renewal.

Bosnia & Hercegovina Survival Guide

ℹ Directory A–Z

ACCOMMODATION

Accommodation costs are remarkably fair value by European standards. There's a good supply of midrange pensions, rental apartments and motels, plus hostels – many homestay-style – and a scattering of boutique and characterful properties. Business and five-star hotels are rare. High season generally means June to September. In Mostar and Sarajevo, rates rise 20% to 50% in summer and places fill up fast.

DANGERS & ANNOYANCES

Landmines and unexploded ordnance still affect 2.3% of Bosnia and Hercegovina's land area. **BHMAC** (www.bhmac.org) removes more every year with the aim of full clearance by 2019. However, progress was slowed by 2014 floods which added to the complexity of locating the last mines. For your safety, stick to asphalt and concrete surfaces or well-worn paths in affected areas, and avoid exploring war-damaged buildings.

INTERNET ACCESS

Almost all hotels and most cafes offer free wi-fi. Some towns have free wi-fi hotspots (including Jajce and Banja Luka).

MONEY

➤ Bosnia's convertible mark (KM or BAM) is divided into 100 fenig and tied to the euro at approximately €1 = 1.95KM.

➤ Though no longer officially sanctioned, many businesses still unblinkingly accept euros for minor purchases. Some even use a slightly customer-favourable 1:2 rate, though 10:19 is more common.

➤ ATMs accepting Visa and MasterCard are ubiquitous.

➤ It's normal to round up the bill and possibly add a bit extra. In swankier places you might want to be more generous, perhaps 5% or more, but there's no hard and fast rule.

OPENING HOURS

Banks 8am to 6pm Monday to Friday, 8.30am to 1.30pm Saturday

Bars and Clubs Most bars are cafes by day, some open at 8am and close 11pm or later. Pubs and clubs open later and, at weekends, might close at 3am.

Offices Typically 8am to 4pm Monday to Friday

Restaurants 7am to 10.30pm or last customer

Shops 8am to 6pm daily, many later

PUBLIC HOLIDAYS

New Year's Day 1 January
Independence Day 1 March
May Day 1 May
National Statehood Day 25 November
Additional holidays in the Federation:
Kurban Bajram (Islamic Feast of Sacrifice) 12 August 2019, 31 July 2020
Ramazanski Bajram (end of Ramadan) 5 June 2019, 24 May 2020
Catholic Easter 19 and 22 April 2019, 11 and 13 April 2020
Catholic Christmas 25 December

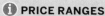

ⓘ PRICE RANGES

Except for hostels, the following price ranges refer to a double room with bathroom during high season. Unless otherwise stated, breakfast is included in the price.

€ less than 80KM
€€ 80–190KM
€€€ more than 190KM

The following price ranges refer to a main course.

€ less than 10KM
€€ 10–25KM
€€€ more than 25KM

Additional holidays in the Republika Srpska:
Orthodox Easter 22 and 29 April 2019, 17 and 20 April 2020
Orthodox Christmas 6 January

TELEPHONE

Buying a SIM card is straightforward and inexpensive, but you'll need a GSM telephone that is not locked to a home network. Mobile-phone companies BH Mobile (060, 061 and 062), HT/EroNet (063, 064) and M-Tel (065, 066) all have virtually nationwide coverage.

ⓘ Getting There & Away

AIR

The main gateway by air is **Sarajevo International Airport** (Aerodrom; www.sia.ba; Kurta Šchorka 36; ⊙5am-11pm). It's often worth comparing prices on flights to Dubrovnik, Split or Zagreb (Croatia), Belgrade (Serbia) or Podgorica (Montenegro), then connecting to Bosnia and Hercegovina overland.

LAND

Buses to Zagreb and/or Split (Croatia) run at least daily from most towns in the Federation. Some services to Herceg Novi (Montenegro) and Dubrovnik (Croatia) run in summer only. Buses run to several destinations in Serbia and/or Montenegro from many Republika Srpska towns. Buses to Vienna and Germany depart several times weekly from bigger Bosnia and Hercegovina cities.

The only international rail service links Sarajevo to Zagreb, daily, via Banja Luka.

ⓘ Getting Around

Bus stations pre-sell tickets. Between towns it's normally easy enough to wave down any bus en route. Advance reservations are sometimes necessary for overnight routes or at peak holiday times. The biggest company, **Centrotrans** (www.centrotrans.com; Ferhadija 16), has online timetables and ticketing.

Trains are slower and less frequent than buses, but generally slightly cheaper. ŽFBH (www.zfbh.ba) has an online rail timetable search. Some lines are essentially dormant and the Sarajevo–Mostar track is under reconstruction.

MONTENEGRO

Budva

POP 13,400

Budva is the poster child of Montenegrin tourism. Easily the country's most visited destination, it attracts hordes of holiday-makers intent on exploring its atmospheric Stari Grad (Old Town), sunning themselves on the bonny beaches of the Budva Riviera and partying until dawn; with scores of buzzy bars and clanging clubs, it's not nicknamed 'the Montenegrin Miami' for nothing.

◎ Sights

★ Stari Grad   HISTORIC SITE
Budva's best feature and star attraction is the Stari Grad (Old Town) – a mini-Dubrovnik with marbled streets and Venetian walls rising from the clear waters below. Much of it was ruined by two earthquakes in 1979 but it has since been completely rebuilt and now houses more shops, bars and restaurants than residences. At its seaward end, the Citadela offers striking views, a small museum and a library full of rare tomes and maps. In the square in front of the citadel is a cluster of interesting churches. Nearby is the entry to the **town walls** (admission €1.50).

★ Citadela   FORTRESS
(admission €2.50; ⊘9am-midnight May-Oct, to 5pm Nov-Apr) At the Stari Grad's seaward end, the old citadel offers striking views, a small museum and a library full of rare tomes and maps. It's thought to be built on the site of the Greek acropolis, but the present incarnation dates to the 19th century Austrian occupation. Its large terrace serves as the main stage of the annual Theatre City festival.

Sveti Nikola   ISLAND
Known locally as 'Hawaii', Sveti Nikola is Montenegro's largest island, stretching to nearly 2km. Fallow deer wander about on this uninhabited green spot, which is only a nautical mile away from Budva or Bečići Beach. Its rocky beaches make it a popular destination in summer when taxi boats regularly ferry sunseekers to and fro; those leaving from Slovenska Plaža charge about €3 per person each way (charter your own for €15 to €20).

Jaz Beach   BEACH
The blue waters and broad sands of Jaz Beach look spectacular when viewed from high up on the Tivat road. While it's not built-up like Budva and Bečići, the beach is still lined with loungers, sun umbrellas and noisy beach bars; head down the Budva end of the beach for a little more seclusion. If peace and privacy is what you're after, steer clear in mid-July, when Jaz is overrun by more than 100,000 merrymakers boogeying it up at the **Sea Dance Festival** (www.seadancefestival.me; ⊘mid-Jul).

🛏 Sleeping

★ Montenegro
Freedom Hostel   HOSTEL €
(📞 067-523 496; montenegrofreedom@gmail.com; Cara Dušana 21; dm/tw/d €18/50/66; ▣ 🛜) In a quieter section of the Old Town, this beloved, sociable hostel has tidy little rooms scattered between three buildings. The terraces and small courtyard are popular spots for impromptu guitar-led singalongs.

Montenegro Hostel   HOSTEL €
(📞 069-039 751; www.montenegrohostel.com; Vuka Karadžića 12; dm €9-20; r per person from €20; ▣ 🛜) With a right-in-the-thick-of-it Old Town location (pack earplugs), this colourful little hostel provides the perfect base for hitting the bars and beaches. Each floor has its own kitchen and bathroom, and there's a communal space at the top for fraternisation.

Sailor House   GUESTHOUSE €€
(www.sailor-house-guest-house-budva.bedspro. com; Vuka Karadžića 25; r from €50; ▣ 🛜) Come for the budget prices and great Old Town location, stay for the warm hospitality. The five cosy rooms are kept immaculate, and there's a shared kitchen for socialising. Bike rentals available. Online bookings only.

Budva

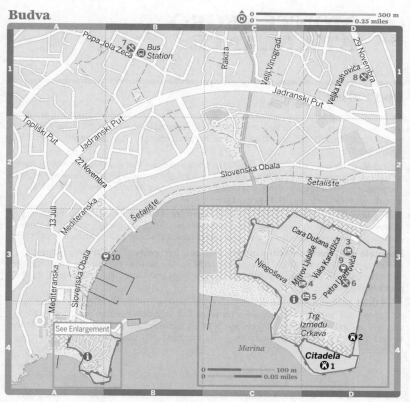

BALKANS BUDVA

Eating

Juice Bar CAFE €
(Vranjak 13; mains €3-10; ⊙9am-midnight) They
may serve delicious juices, smoothies and
shakes, but that's only part of the appeal of
this cosmopolitan cafe, set on a sunny Old
Town square. The crowd-pleasing menu
includes light breakfasts, salads, toasted
sandwiches, nachos, lasagne, cakes and
muffins.

Stari Ribar SEAFOOD, MONTENEGRIN €
(☑033-459 543; 29 Novembra 19; mains €4-10;
⊙7am-11pm) You'll be relieved to learn that
the name means Old Fisherman, not Old
Fish. This humble eatery sitiated in the
residential part of town serves grilled fish
(fresh, naturally) and meat dishes at local
prices.

MONTENEGRO AT A GLANCE

Don't Miss

Kotor Time-travel back to a Europe of moated walled towns with shadowy lanes and stone churches on every square. Kotor's lived-in Old Town seems to grow out of the sheer grey mountains surrounding it – as if they could at any point chose to squeeze the little town in a rocky embrace.

Njegoš Mausoleum On top of Mt Lovćen, the Black Mountain that gave Montenegro its name, is the final resting place for the 19th-century *vladika* (bishop-prince) Petar II Petrović Njegoš. The simple but affecting structure and monumental statuary do little to distract from the remarkable views over all of Old Montenegro.

Ostrog Monastery Set in a seemingly sheer mountain wall, this luminous white monastery is Montenegro's holiest site; whether you're a believer or not, it's an affecting place. The atmospheric cave chapels of the Upper Monastery have rock walls covered in centuries-old frescoes.

Mountain eyes, Durmitor National Park Reflecting the beauty of the Durmitor range's imposing grey peaks are 18 glacial lakes, known as *gorske oči* (mountain eyes). The largest and most beautiful is Black Lake, but more remote lakes await discovery further up along the park's hiking trails.

Stari Grad, Budva Budva's walled Old Town rises from the Adriatic like a miniature, less frantic Dubrovnik. There's an atmosphere of romance and a typically Mediterranean love of life palpable around every corner. While away the hours exploring the labyrinth of narrow cobbled streets,drinking in al fresco cafe-bars and being inspired by the gorgeous sea views from the Citadela.

Itineraries

One Week
This trip zigzags from the coast to Montenegro's heartland then back to the beaches, taking in some emblematic sights. Start in the bayside town of **Kotor**, filled with old churches and marbled squares, and spend a couple of days soaking up its lived-in vibe and climbing the ancient fortifications. Take a day trip to **Perast** to admire its baroque beauty and catch a boat to its two hugely picturesque islands. Go on a dazzling drive to the historic Montenegrin capital **Cetinje** through **Lovćen National Park**, stopping to visit the Njegoš Mausoleum on the way. After exploring Cetinje's museums and galleries, head up to the dramatic **Ostrog Monastery**.

Two Weeks
Carry on north to **Durmitor National Park** and base yourself in Žabljak. Allow plenty of time to enjoy the rugged mountain scenery and make sure you hike around the Black Lake or go for a rafting trip on the Tara River. Swing back south to the Adriatic coast and spend your last couple of days in buzzing **Budva**, exploring the walled Old Town, chilling out in bars and cafes and lazing on the sand.

Essential Food & Drink

Jagnjetina ispod sača In the northern mountains, the food is traditionally meat-heavy. A traditional method of cooking is *ispod sača*, where meat – usually *jagnjetina* (lamb) – and vegetables are roasted under a metal lid covered with hot coals.

Lignje na žaru The food on the coast is indistinguishable from Dalmatian cuisine. Grilled squid are a must-try, with crispy tentacles coated in garlic and olive oil.

Priganice The most typical Montenegrin sweet dish is *priganice* (fritters), served with honey, cheese and jam.

Rakija Many people distil their own *rakija* (akin to a very strong brandy). The most common variety in Montenegro is *loza*, made out of grapes, but it can be made from just about anything.

Getting Around

Bus Buses link all major towns and are affordable, reliable and reasonably comfortable.

Car While you can get to many places by bus, hiring a car will give you freedom to explore some of Montenegro's scenic back roads. Some of these are extremely narrow and cling to the sides of canyons, so it may not suit the inexperienced or faint-hearted.

Train Trains are cheap but the network is limited and many carriages are old and can get hot. The main line links Bar, Virpazar, Podgorica, Kolašin, Mojkovac and Bijelo Polje, and there's a second line from Podgorica to Danilovgrad and Nikšić.

When to Go

Podgorica

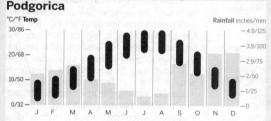

°C/°F **Temp**   **Rainfall** inches/mm

30/86												— 4.9/125
20/68												— 3.9/100
												— 2.9/75
10/50												— 2/50
												— 1/25
0/32												— 0
	J	F	M	A	M	J	J	A	S	O	N	D

Jul–Aug The warmest, busiest and most expensive time to visit.

May–Jun & Sep–Oct The best time to come, with plenty of sunshine and average water temperatures over 20°C.

Nov–Apr The ski season kicks in, with peak prices in Kolašin and Žabljak.

Arriving in Montenegro

Podgorica Airport Taxis charge an average €10 fare for the 9km to central Podgorica. There are no buses.

Tivat Airport Taxis charge €5 to €7 for the 3km to Tivat, €15 for Kotor and €20 for Budva. There are no buses.

Top Phrases

Hello. Dobar dan.

Goodbye. Zbogom.

Please. Molim.

Thank you. Hvala.

How much is it? Koliko košta?

Resources

Montenegrin National Tourist Organisation (www.montenegro.travel) Packed full of information, photos and some downloadable resources.

National Parks of Montenegro (www.nparkovi.me) All five national parks are covered, with information about activities and park fees.

Renome (www.renome. me) Montenegro's hugely interesting, in-depth cultural tourism magazine.

Set Your Budget

➡ Dorms or shared room in private accommodation: €11–18

➡ Pizza slice: €2.50

➡ Local beer: €1.70

Mercur MONTENEGRIN €€

(Katunska Trpeza; ☑ 067-570 483; Budva bus station; mains €3-12) Bus stations and top nosh are usually mutually exclusive territories, but this marvellous restaurant is the exception to the rule. For starters, it sits in a gorgeous green oasis populated by peacocks, deer and goats; there's also a playground. The menu is Montenegrin to the core, with superb grilled and baked (*ispod sač*) meats, spicy soups and local seafood. The prices are ridiculously low.

🍸 Drinking & Nightlife

Casper BAR

(www.facebook.com/casper.budva; Petra I Petrovića bb; ☺ 9am-2am; 🛜) Chill out under the pine tree in this picturesque Old Town cafe-bar. DJs kick off from July, spinning everything from soul to house. Casper hosts its own jazz festival in September.

Torch Beach Club BAR

(☑ 033-683 683; www.budvabeach.com; Slovenska Plaža; ☺ 8am-1am summer) It's totally scene-y, but Torch is a fun, over-the-top outdoor party palace that epitomises summertime Mediterranean madness. Pool parties, sun-lounge cocktails and light noshing are the order of the day; come sundown, DJs hit the decks and the carousing kicks off in earnest.

Top Hill CLUB

(www.tophill.me; Topliški Put; events €10-25; ☺ 11pm-5am Jul & Aug) The top cat of Montenegro's summer party scene attracts up to 5000 revellers to its open-air club atop Topliš Hill, offering them top-notch sound and lighting, sea views, big-name touring DJs and performances by local pop stars.

ℹ Information

Tourist Office (☑ 033-452 750; www.budva. travel; Njegoševa 28; ☺ 9am-9pm Mon-Sat, 5-9pm Sun Jun-Aug, 8am-8pm Mon-Sat Sep-May) Small but helpful office in the old town.

ℹ Getting There & Away

The **bus station** (☑ 033-456 000; Popa Jola Zeca bb) has frequent services to Herceg Novi (€6.50, 1¾ hours), Cetinje (€3.75, 40 minutes), Kotor (€3.75, 40 minutes) and Podgorica (€6.50, 1½ hours), and one daily to Žabljak (€16, five hours). International destinations include Belgrade (from €26, 11 hours, 15 daily) and Sarajevo (€22, 7½ hours, four daily).

Kotor

POP 5340

Wedged between brooding mountains and a moody corner of the bay, the achingly atmospheric Kotor is perfectly at one with its setting. Hemmed in by staunch walls snaking improbably up the surrounding slopes, the town is a medieval maze of museums, churches, cafe-strewn squares and Venetian palaces and pillories. It's a dramatic and delightful place where the past coexists with the present; its cobblestones ring with the sound of children racing to school in centuries-old buildings, lines of laundry flutter from wrought-iron balconies, and hundreds of cats loll in marble laneways. Come nightfall, Kotor's spectacularly lit-up walls glow as serenely as a halo; behind the bulwarks, the streets buzz with bars, live music and castle-top clubbing.

🅾 Sights & Activities

Town Walls FORTRESS

(€3; ☺ 24hr, fees apply 8am-8pm May-Sep) Kotor's fortifications started to head up St John's Hill in the 9th century and by the 14th century a protective loop was completed, which was added to right up until the 19th century. The energetic can make a 1200m ascent up the fortifications via 1350 steps to a height of 260m above sea level; the views from up here are glorious. There are entry points near the North Gate and behind Trg od Salate; avoid the heat of the day and bring lots of water.

Maritime Museum of Montenegro MUSEUM

(Pomorski muzej Crne Gore; www.museummaritimum.com; Trg Bokeljske Mornarice; adult/child €4/1; ☺ 8am-11pm Mon-Sat, 10am-4pm Sun Jul & Aug, 8am-6pm Mon-Sat, 9am-1pm Sun Apr-Jun & Sep, 9am-5pm Mon-Fri, 9am-noon Sat & Sun Oct-Mar) Kotor's proud history as a naval power is celebrated in three storeys of displays housed in a wonderful early-18th-century palace. An audio guide helps explain the collection of photographs, paintings, uniforms, exquisitely decorated weapons and models of ships.

St Tryphon's Cathedral CHURCH

(Katedrala Sv Tripuna; Trg Sv Tripuna; admission €2.50; ☺ 8am-7pm) Kotor's most impressive building, this Catholic cathedral was consecrated in the 12th century but reconstructed after several earthquakes. When the entire

Kotor

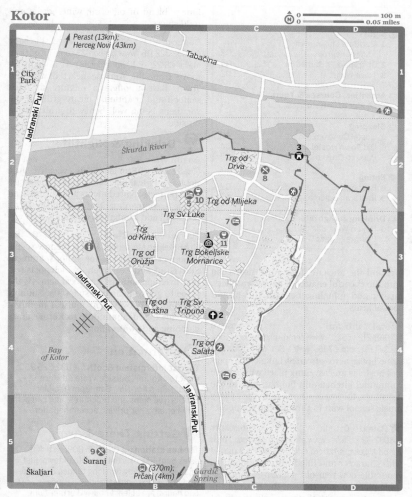

frontage was destroyed in 1667, the baroque bell towers were added; the left one remains unfinished. The cathedral's gently hued interior is a masterpiece of Romanesque architecture with slender Corinthian columns alternating with pillars of pink stone, thrusting upwards to support a series of vaulted roofs. Its gilded silver bas-relief altar screen is considered Kotor's most valuable treasure.

Ladder of Cattaro HIKING

FREE The truly vigorous can climb the ancient caravan trail known as the Ladder of Cattaro, which starts near the Škurda River and zigzags up the mountain to join the Coastal Mountain Traversal in Lovćen National Park. The usual requirements for water/sturdy shoes/strong lungs apply.

🛏 Sleeping

⭐ **Old Town Hostel** HOSTEL €

(☑ 032-325 317; www.hostel-kotor.me; near Trg od Salata; dm €12-17, d with/without bathroom €44/28, apt €74; 🕸🏠) If the ghosts of the Bisanti family had any concerns when their 13th-century palazzo was converted into a hostel, they must be overjoyed now. Sympathetic renovations have brought the place to

Kotor

life, and the ancient stone walls now echo with the cheerful chatter of happy travellers, mixing and mingling beneath the Bisanti coat of arms.

Hostel Centrum HOSTEL €
(🖉 068-212 552; www.centrumhostelkotor.com; Trg Sv Luke; dm €7-16; ❄ 🛜) Set up in an old stone house across from St Luke's, this spotless hostel is an easygoing place with a huge communal kitchen and bubbly staff. In the mornings, the sweet strains from the nearby music school waft in through the windows.

★ Palazzo Drusko GUESTHOUSE €€
(🖉 032-325 257; www.palazzodrusko.me; near Trg od Mlijeka; s/d from €40/80; ❄ 🛜) Loaded with character and filled with antiques, this venerable 600-year-old palazzo is a memorable place to stay, right in the heart of the old town. Thoughtful extras include a guest kitchen, 3D TVs and old-fashioned radios rigged to play Montenegrin music.

✗ Eating

Restoran Galerija MONTENEGRIN, SEAFOOD €€
(🖉 068-825 956; www.restorangalerija.com; Šuranj bb; mains €7-20; ⊙ 11am-11.30pm) This bustling place on the waterfront excels in both meat and seafood, as well as fast and attentive service (along the coast, you'll often find these things are mutually exclusive). Try the prawns or mixed seafood in buzara sauce, a deceptively simple – yet spectacularly sub-

lime – blend of olive oil, wine, garlic and mild spices.

Bastion MONTENEGRIN, SEAFOOD €€
(🖉 032-322 116; www.bastion123.com; Trg od Drva; mains €8-22; ⊙ 10am-midnight) At a slight remove from the frenetic heart of the Old Town, Bastion offers a mixture of fresh seafood and traditional meaty grills. If the weather's being well behaved, grab a table outside.

🍷 Drinking & Nightlife

Bokun Wine Bar WINE BAR
(Trg Sv Luke; ⊙ 8am-1am) This evocative little nook is an ideal place to sample local wines (and perfectly paired meats and cheeses), all to the accompaniment of live music (think jazz, soul and samba) on weekends.

Evergreen Jazz Club BAR
(Trg Bokeljske Mornarice) Jazz somehow seems a perfect soundtrack for Kotor's ambient Stari Grad, and Evergreen – which hosts regular live international and local acts – is the place to get your fingers snapping. Suitably mood-lit and covered in musical memorabilia, it's the ideal antidote to Kotor's crazy clubbing and *kafana* pop.

ⓘ Information

Tourist Information Booth (🖉 032-325 950; www.tokotor.me; outside Vrata od Mora; ⊙ 8am-8pm Apr-Nov, 8am-3pm Dec-Mar) Stocks free maps and brochures, and can help with contacts for private accommodation.

ⓘ Getting There & Away

The **bus station** (🖉 032-325 809; ⊙ ticket sales 6am-10pm) is to the south of town, just off the road leading to a long tunnel. Buses to Budva (€4, 55 minutes) and Podgorica (€7.50, two hours) are at least hourly. Further-flung destinations include Kolašin (€10.50, four hours), Dubrovnik (€14, two hours, six daily) and Belgrade (€30, 12 hours, seven daily).

A taxi to Tivat airport should cost €7 to €10.

Perast

POP 350

Looking like a chunk of Venice that has floated down the Adriatic and anchored itself onto the bay, Perast hums with melancholy memories of the days when it was rich and powerful. Despite having only one main street, this tiny town boasts 16 churches and 17 formerly grand palazzos. While some are just enigmatic ruins sprouting bougainvillea and wild fig, others are caught up in the whirlwind of renovation that has hit the town.

Sights

Perast's most famous landmark isn't on land at all: a peculiarly picturesque island with an equally peculiar history.

Gospa od Škrpjela ISLAND

(Our-Lady-of-the-Rock Island) This iconic island was artificially created (on 22 July 1452, to be precise) around a rock where an image of the Madonna was found; every year on that same day, the locals row over with stones to continue the task. The magnificent church was erected in 1630 and has sumptuous Venetian paintings, hundreds of silver votive tablets and a small museum (€1). The most unusual – and famous – exhibit is an embroidered icon of the Madonna and Child partly made with the hair of its maker.

Sveti Djordje ISLAND

(St George's Island) Sveti Djordje, rising from a natural reef, is the smaller of Perast's two islands. It houses a Benedictine monastery shaded by cypresses, and a large cemetery, earning it the local nickname 'Island of the Dead'. Legend has it that the island is cursed...but it looks pretty heavenly to us.

Sleeping & Eating

Bogišić Rooms and Apartments APARTMENT €

(☎067-440 062; www.bogisicroomsapartment.com; Obala Marka Martinovića bb; s €25, d without bathroom €42, apt €70; P ❄ ☎) This welcoming place offers great value for money. The rooms aren't massive, but they're comfortable, cute and right on the waterfront. The hosts have Montenegrin hospitality down pat; you'll want for naught here. The single room and two-bedroom apartment have kitchenettes.

★**Konoba Školji** SEAFOOD, MONTENEGRIN €€

(☎069-419 745; Obala Marka Martinovića bb; mains €7-17; ⏲11am-11pm) This cute, traditional waterfront restaurant is all about the thrill of the grill; fresh seafood and falling-off-the-bone meats are barbecued to perfection in full view of salivating diners. Thankfully, they're not shy with the portion sizes; the delightful/maddening smell of the cooking and the sea air will have you ravenous by the time your meal arrives.

Getting There & Away

There's no bus station, but buses to and from Kotor (€1.50, 25 minutes) stop at least every 30 minutes on the main road at the top of town. Water taxis zoom around Boka Bay during summer and call into all ports, including Perast.

Lovćen National Park

Siotiated directly behind Kotor is **Mt Lovćen** (1749m), the black mountain that gave Crna Gora (Montenegro) its name. This locale occupies a special place in the hearts of all Montenegrins. For most of its history it represented the entire nation – a rocky island of Slavic resistance in an Ottoman sea. A striking **mausoleum** (Njegošev Mauzolej; €3; ⏲8am-6pm) for Montenegro's most famous son, Petar II Petrović Njegoš, peers down from its heights, with views stretching as far as Albania and Croatia.

Two-thirds of the national park's 6220 hectares are covered in woods, particularly the black beech that gives it its moody complexion. Even the rockier tracts sprout wild herbs such as St John's wort, mint and sage. The park is home to various types of reptile, 85 species of butterfly and large mammals such as brown bears and wolves. The 200 avian species found here include regal birds of prey such as the peregrine falcon, golden eagle and imperial eagle.

The mountains are crossed with hiking paths and biking trails, which can be accessed from Kotor, Budva or Cetinje, and the Coastal Mountain Traversal runs straight through. If you're planning on hiking, come prepared: the temperature is on average 10ºC cooler than on the coast, and the weather is prone to sudden changes in summer.

The park's main hub is **Ivanova Korita**, near its centre, where there are a few eateries and accommodation providers. Here you'll also find the **National Park Visitor Centre** (www.nparkovi.me; Ivanova Korita;

WILD BEAUTY

'Wild Beauty', crows Montenegro's enduring tourism slogan, and indeed the marketing boffins are right to highlight the nation's extraordinary natural blessings. In the mountainous interior are pockets of virgin forest and large mammals, long since hunted out of existence on most of the continent, still hanging on – just.

9am-5pm), which rents bikes (€2 per hour) and offers accommodation in four-bed bungalows (€40). Informal camping is possible within the park (small/large tent €3/5, campervan €10), with additional charges for using established campgrounds (€10).

ⓘ Getting There & Away

If you're driving, the park (entry fee €2) can be approached from either Kotor (20km) or Cetinje (7km). Tour buses are the only buses that head into the park.

Cetinje

POP 16,700

Rising from a green vale surrounded by rough grey mountains, Cetinje is an odd mix of erstwhile capital and overgrown village, where single-storey cottages and stately mansions share the same street. The city was founded in 1482 by Ivan Crnojević, the ruler of the Zeta state, and was the capital of Montenegro until 1946, when it passed the baton to Titograd (now Podgorica).

◉ Sights

Cetinje is home to the country's most impressive collection of museums and galleries, known collectively as the National Museum of Montenegro. A joint ticket will get you into all of them or you can buy individual tickets. Some of the grandest buildings in town are former international embassies from Cetinje's days as Montenegro's royal capital.

Biljarda PALACE

(Njegoš Museum, Njegošev muzej; www.mn-museum.org; Dvorski Trg; adult/child €3/1.50; 9am-5pm Apr-Oct, to 4pm Mon-Fri Nov-Mar) This castle-like palace was the residence of Montenegro's favourite son, prince-bishop and poet Petar II Petrović Njegoš. It was built and financed by the Russians in 1838 and housed the nation's first billiard table (hence the name). The bottom floor is devoted to military costumes, photos of soldiers with outlandish moustaches and exquisitely decorated weapons. Upstairs are Njegoš' personal effects, including his bishop's cross and garments, documents, fabulous furniture and, of course, the famous billiard table.

History Museum MUSEUM

(Istorijski muzej; ☑ 041-230 310; www.mnmuseum.org; Novice Cerovića 7; adult/child €3/1.50; 9am-5pm Apr-Oct, to 4pm Mon-Fri Nov-Mar) Housed in the imposing former parliament building (1910), this fascinating museum follows a timeline from the Stone Age to 1955. There are few English signs but the enthusiastic staff will give you an overview. Bullet holes are a theme of some of the most interesting relics: there are three in the back of the tunic that Prince Danilo was wearing when assassinated; Prince Nikola's standard from the battle of Vučji Do has 396; while, in the communist section, there's a big gaping one in the skull of a fallen comrade.

King Nikola Museum PALACE

(Muzej kralja Nikole; www.mnmuseum.org; Dvorski Trg; adult/child €5/2.50; 9am-5pm Apr-Oct, to

DURMITOR NATIONAL PARK

The impossibly rugged and dramatic Durmitor is one of Montenegro's showpieces. Carved out by glaciers and underground streams, Durmitor stuns with dizzying canyons, glittering glacial lakes and nearly 50 limestone peaks soaring to over 2000m; the highest, **Bobotov Kuk**, hits 2523m. From December to March, Durmitor is a major ski resort, while in summer it's popular for hiking, rafting and other active pursuits.

The national park covers the Durmitor mountain range and a narrow branch heading east along the Tara River towards Mojkovac. It's home to 163 bird species, about 50 types of mammals and purportedly the greatest variety of butterflies in Europe. **Žabljak**, at the eastern edge of the range, is the gateway to Durmitor's mountain adventures. You'll find restaurants, hotels and a supermarket gathered around the car park that masquerades as Žabljak's main square. The **Žabljak tourist office** (☑ 052-361 802; www.tozabljak.com; Trg Durmitorskih ratnika, Žabljak; 7am-10pm mid-Jun–Sep, 8am-8pm Oct–mid-Jun) and the **National Park Visitors Centre** (☑ 052-360 228; www.nparkovi.me; 7am-5pm Mon-Fri, 10am-5pm Sat & Sun Jan & Jun–mid-Sep, 7am-3pm Mon-Fri mid-Sep–Dec & Feb-May) can help with thrill-seeking quests, and there are many private agencies based in Žabljak.

All of the approaches to Durmitor are spectacular. The bus station is at the southern edge of Žabljak, on the Šavnik road. Buses head to Nikšić (€5.50, six daily), Podgorica (€8.50, four daily) and Belgrade (€22, nine hours, two daily).

4pm Mon-Fri Nov-Mar) Entry to this stunning maroon-and-white palace (1871), home to the last sovereign of Montenegro, is by guided tour (you may need to wait for a group to form). Although looted during WWII, enough plush furnishings, stern portraits and taxidermied animals remain to capture the spirit of the court.

Montenegrin Art Gallery GALLERY
(Crnogorska galerija umjetnosti; www.mnmuseum.org; Novice Cerovića 7; adult/child €4/2; ⊙9am-5pm Apr-Oct, to 4pm Mon-Fri Nov-Mar) All of Montenegro's great artists are represented here, with the most famous (Milunović, Lubarda, Đurić etc) having their own separate spaces. There's a small collection of icons, the most important being the precious 9th-century Our Lady of Philermos, traditionally believed to be painted by St Luke himself. It's spectacularly presented in its own blue-lit 'chapel', but the Madonna's darkened face is only just visible behind its spectacular golden casing mounted with diamonds, rubies and sapphires.

Cetinje Monastery CHRISTIAN MONASTERY
(Cetinjski Manastir; ⊙8am-6pm) It's a case of four times lucky for the Cetinje Monastery, having been repeatedly destroyed during Ottoman attacks and rebuilt. This sturdy incarnation dates from 1786, with its only exterior ornamentation being the capitals of columns recycled from the original building, founded in 1484. The chapel to the right of the courtyard holds the monastery's proudest possessions: a shard of the True Cross (the pièce de résistance of many of Europe's churches) and the mummified right hand of St John the Baptist.

★ Lipa Cave CAVE
(Lipska Pećina; ☑ 067-003 040; www.lipa-cave.me; ⊙tours at 10am, 11.30, 1pm, 2.30pm and 4pm May-Oct) Cetinje may indeed be littered with old-time reminders of its days as Montenegro's capital city, but just 4km away lies an attraction that makes the town look positively modern. Millions of years old, Lipa Cave is one of the country's largest caves – and the only one open for organised visits – with 2.5km of passages and halls filled with stalactites, stalagmites and freaky natural pillars. Choose between basic, 45-minute tours (adult/child €7/5), a 100-minute 'adventure' tour (adult/child €20/10) or an 'extreme' exploration (fit adults only, €50).

DON'T MISS

OSTROG MONASTERY

Clinging improbably – miraculously? – to a cliff face 900m above the Zeta valley, the gleaming white Ostrog Monastery (1665) is a strangely affecting place that attracts up to one million visitors each year. A **guesthouse** (☑020-801 133; www.manastirostrog.com; dm €5) near the Lower Monastery offers tidy single-sex dorm rooms; in summer, sleeping mats are provided free to pilgrims in front of the Upper Monastery. There's no public transport but numerous tour buses (€20 to €30 for a day trip) head here from the coast. There's an Ostrog train station (€1.80, seven daily from Podgorica) way down at the bottom of the hill; it's about an hour's hike from there to the Lower Monastery.

BALKANS CETINJE

🛏 Sleeping & Eating

★ La Vecchia Casa B&B €
(☑067-629 660; www.lavecchiacasa.com; Vojvode Batrica 6; s/d/apt €20/30/36; P ✸ 🛜) With its gorgeous garden, traditional hospitality and pervading sense of tranquility, this remarkably renovated period house wouldn't be out of place in a quaint mountain village. Instead, it's right in the centre of Cetinje, offering a rural-feeling retreat with all of the historical capital's attractions, shops and restaurants a short stroll away. Clean, simple rooms retain a sense of the home's history; good-sized apartments have kitchens.

★ Kole MONTENEGRIN, EUROPEAN €€
(☑069-606 660; www.restaurantkole.me; Bul Crnogorskih Junaka 12; mains €4-15; ⊙7am-midnight) They serve omelettes and pasta at this snazzy modern eatery, but it are the local specialities that truly shine. Try the memorable Njeguški *ražanj*, smoky spit-roasted meat stuffed with *pršut* and cheese.

❶ Getting There & Away

Cetinje is on the main Budva–Podgorica highway and can also be reached by a glorious back road from Kotor via Lovćen National Park. The **bus station** (Trg Golootočkih Žrtava) has regular services from Herceg Novi (€7, 2½ hours), Budva (€4, 40 minutes), Kotor (€5, 1½ hours) and Podgorica (€3, 30 minutes).

Montenegro Survival Guide

ⓘ Directory A–Z

ACCOMMODATION

➡ Booking ahead in the summer – especially on the coast – is essential. Some places will require minimum stays in high season (often a three-day minimum).

➡ The cheapest options in any given town are almost always private rooms and apartment rentals, though recently some great hostels have sprung up, particularly in Kotor and Budva.

➡ Camping grounds are most common along the coast and near Žabljak, and some of the mountainous areas have cabin accommodation in 'ethno' and 'eco' villages or mountain huts.

➡ All visitors are required to pay a small nightly tourist tax (usually less than €1 per person per night), which is sometimes included in the quoted rate but more often added to the bill at the end.

INTERNET ACCESS

Most accommodation providers offer free wifi, although it may not always penetrate to every part of the building and can be limited to the reception area. Many bars and cafes also offer wifi. You'll find free wifi in Budva's Stari Grad and at other tourist hotspots in bigger cities.

MONEY

➡ Though it's not in the EU, Montenegro uses the euro (€).

➡ ATMs are widely available in all the main towns. They tend to dish out big notes, which can be hard to break.

ⓘ PRICE RANGES

The following price ranges refer to the cheapest option available for a double in the shoulder season (June and September).

€ less than €45

€€ €45–100

€€€ more than €100

Eating prices are based on the cost of the cheapest dish on the menu that could be considered a main meal.

€ up to €5

€€ €5–8

€€€ over €9

➡ Credit cards are accepted in larger hotels but aren't widely accepted elsewhere.

➡ Tipping isn't expected, although it's common to round up to the nearest euro.

OPENING HOURS

Montenegrins have a flexible approach to opening times.

Banks 8am to 5pm Monday to Friday, 8am to noon Saturday

Post offices 7am to 8pm Monday to Friday, sometimes Saturday; in smaller towns they may close midafternoon

Restaurants, cafes and bars 8am to midnight; cafe-bars may stay open until 2am or 3am

Shops 9am to 8pm; sometimes they close for a few hours in late afternoon

PUBLIC HOLIDAYS

New Year's Day 1 and 2 January

Orthodox Christmas 6, 7 and 8 January

Orthodox Good Friday & Easter Monday Usually April/May

Labour Day 1 May

Independence Day 21 May

Statehood Day 13 July

TELEPHONE

➡ Press the *i* button on public phones for dialling commands in English.

➡ The international access prefix is 00 or + from a mobile phone. Mobile numbers start with 06.

➡ Local SIM cards are a good idea if you're planning a longer stay. The main providers (T-Mobile, M:tel and Telenor) have storefronts in most towns. Many shopping centres have terminals where you can top up your prepay account. Mobile calls are expensive in Montenegro, but the main providers offer heavily discounted rates for calls within their networks.

ⓘ Getting There & Away

AIR

New routes – including those by low-cost carriers from the UK – are continually being added to Montenegro's two international airports, at **Podgorica** (TGD; ☎ 020-444 244; www.montenegroairports.com) and **Tivat** (TIV; ☎ 032-670 930; www.montenegroairports.com). Dubrovnik's airport is also very close to the border. **Montenegro Airlines** (https://montenegroairlines.com/) is the national carrier.

LAND

Montenegro borders five other states: Croatia, Bosnia and Hercegovina (BiH), Serbia, Kosovo and Albania. You can easily enter Montenegro from any of its neighbours.

There's a well-developed bus network linking Montenegro with the major cities of the former Yugoslavia and onwards to Western Europe and Turkey. At the border, guards will often enter the bus and collect passports for checking and stamping. They return them to the bus conductor, who will return them to you as the driver speeds off.

Montenegro's main train line starts at Bar and heads north through the middle of Montenegro and into Serbia. At least two trains go from Bar to Belgrade daily (€21, 11 hours). You'll find timetables on the website of **Montenegro Railways** (www.zpcg.me).

SEA

Montenegro Lines (www.montenegrolines.com) has boats from Bar to Bari, Italy, at least twice weekly from May to September (deck ticket €44 to €48, cabin €67 to €210, 10 hours); and from Bar to Ancona, Italy, at least weekly from July to August (deck €60, cabin €80 to €230, 16 hours). Cars cost €68 to €90, but are free for bookings for four cabin passengers.

ℹ Getting Around

Bus Buses link all major towns and are affordable, reliable and reasonably comfortable.

Car Hiring a car will give you freedom to explore some of Montenegro's scenic back roads. Some of these are extremely narrow and cling to the sides of canyons, so it may not suit the inexperienced or faint-hearted.

Train Trains are cheap, but the network is limited and many carriages are old and can get hot. The main line links Bar, Virpazar, Podgorica, Kolašin, Mojkovac and Bijelo Polje.

ALBANIA

Tirana

POP 835,000

Lively, colourful Tirana is the beating heart of Albania, where this tiny nation's hopes and dreams coalesce into a vibrant whirl of traffic, brash consumerism and unfettered fun. Trendy Blloku buzzes with the well-heeled and flush hanging out in bars and cafes, while the city's grand boulevards are lined with fascinating relics of its Ottoman, Italian and communist past – from delicate minarets to loud socialist murals. Add to this some excellent museums and you have a compelling list of reasons to visit.

◉ Sights

The centre of Tirana is the large Sheshi Skënderbej (Skanderbeg Sq). Running through the square is Tirana's main avenue, Blvd Zogu I, which south of the square becomes Blvd Dëshmorët e Kombit (Martyrs of the Nation Blvd). Most of the city's sights are within walking distance of the square.

★ Bunk'Art   MUSEUM

(☑068 4834 444, 067 2072 905; www.bunkart.al; Rr Fadil Deliu; 500 lekë; ⊙9am-4pm Wed-Sun) This fantastic conversion – from a massive cold war bunker on the outskirts of Tirana into a history and contemporary art museum – is Albania's most exciting new sight and easily a Tirana highlight. With almost 3000 sq metres of space underground spread over several floors, the bunker was built for Albania's political elite in the 1970s and remained a secret for much of its existence. Now it hosts exhibits that combine the modern history of Albania with pieces of contemporary art.

To get here from the centre of Tirana take a bus bound for Linza from outside the Palace of Culture on Sheshi Skënderbej, and ask the driver to let you out at Bunk'Art. It's located right next to the Dajti Express, so it makes sense to combine the two outings.

★ National Gallery of Arts   GALLERY

(Galeria Kombëtare e Arteve; www.galeriakombetare.gov.al/en/home/index.shtml; Blvd Dëshmorët e Kombit; adult/student 200/100 lekë; ⊙10am-6pm Wed-Sun) Tracing the relatively brief history of Albanian painting from the early 19th century to the present day, this beautiful space also has temporary exhibitions. Downstairs there's a small but interesting collection of 19th-century paintings depicting scenes from daily Albanian life, while upstairs the art takes on a political dimension with some truly fabulous examples of Albanian socialist realism. Don't miss the small collection of communist statues in storage behind the building, including two rarely seen statues of Uncle Joe Stalin himself.

★ National History Museum   MUSEUM

(Muzeu Historik Kombëtar; www.mhk.gov.al; Sheshi Skënderbej; adult/student 200/80 lekë; ⊙10am-6pm Tue-Sat, 9am-2pm Sun) The largest museum in Albania holds many of the country's

ALBANIA AT A GLANCE

Don't Miss

Accursed Mountains Join the hardy locals on the magical boat ride through stunning alpine scenery across the immense Lake Koman. For more of the dramatic Albanian Alps scenery, do the wonderful day trek between the isolated mountain hamlets of Valbona and Theth.

Berat Explore the Unesco World Heritage–listed museum town, known as the 'city of a thousand windows'. Its old quarters are lovely ensembles of whitewashed walls, tiled roofs and cobblestone roads, while inside the ancient hilltop castle walls there's a living, breathing neighbourhood.

Albanian riviera Catch some sun at one of the gorgeous beaches on the Albanian Riviera. Bunec is a lovely pebbly beach divided in two by a stream running down from the mountains; Gjipe is a gorgeous stretch of isolated white sand and rock backed by big cliffs; while Ksamil has three small, dreamy islands within swimming distance of shore.

Tirana Feast your eyes on the wild colour schemes and experience Blloku neighbourhood's cafe culture in the plucky Albanian capital. Contemplate Albania's paranoid, isolationist history in excellent bunkers-turned-museums that cast a light on Enver Hoxha's dictatorial regime.

Gjirokastra Take a trip to this traditional Albanian mountain town, defined by spectacular Ottoman-era mansions and impressive hilltop fortress. Wander the cobbled streets of the Old Town's bazaar with its stone- and wood-carving artisan shops, and descend into the giant Cold War bunker deep underneath the castle.

Itineraries

One Week

Spend a couple of days in lively, colourful **Tirana**, checking out the various excellent museums as well as the Blloku district's bars and cafes. On day three, make the three-hour trip to the evocative mountain town of **Berat** with striking Ottoman-era houses and a hilltop castle. Then head to **Gjirokastra**, another magical hillside town with spectacular Ottoman-era mansions and old bazaar, before returning to the capital.

Two Weeks

Following on from the first week's itinerary, travel north into Albania's incredible **Accursed Mountains**. Start in Shkodra, a pleasant lakeside town with an ancient fortress, from where you can get transport to **Koman** for the stunning three-hour ferry ride across Lake Koman to **Fierzë**. Continue the same day to the charming mountain village of **Valbona** for the night, before embarking on the five hour trek to **Theth**, another dramatically set village and then head back to Tirana to end the trip.

Essential Food & Drink

Byrek Pastry with cheese or meat.

Fergesë Tiranë Traditional Tirana dish of offal, eggs and tomatoes cooked in an earthenware pot.

Midhje Wild or farmed mussels, often served fried.

Paçë koke Sheep's head soup, usually served for breakfast.

Qofta Flat or cylindrical mince-meat rissoles.

Sufllaqë Doner kebab.

Tavë Meat baked with cheese and egg.

Raki Popular spirit made from grapes; the two main types are grape *raki* (the more common) and *mani* (mulberry) *raki*.

Getting Around

Bus Bus and *furgon* (privately run minibuses) are the main form of public transport in Albania. Fares are low, and you either pay the conductor on board or when you hop off, which can be anywhere along the route. Municipal buses operate in Tirana, Durrës, Shkodra, Berat, Korça and Vlora, and trips usually cost 30 lekë.

Car There's an excellent highway from Tirana to Kosovo, and the coastal route from the Montenegro border to Butrint, near Saranda, is in good condition. Apart from heavy traffic and bad drivers, car travel is generally hassle free. Off the main routes a 4WD is a good idea.

Train Trains are dirt cheap and travelling on them is an adventure. Daily passenger trains leave suburban Tirana for Durrës, Shkodra, Fier, Vlora, Elbasan and a few kilometres shy of Pogradec. Check timetables at the station in person, and buy your ticket 10 minutes before departure.

When to Go

Tirana

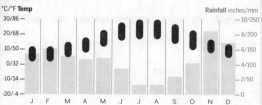

°C/°F Temp

Rainfall inches/mm

Jun Enjoy the perfect Mediterranean climate and deserted beaches.

Jul–Aug Albania's beaches may be packed, but this is a great time to explore the mountains.

Dec See features and shorts at the Tirana Film Festival, while the intrepid can snowshoe to Theth.

Arriving in Albania

Nënë Tereza International Airport The Rinas Express airport bus operates an on-the-hour service (7am to 6pm; 250 lekë one way). The going taxi rate is 2000 to 2500 lekë. The city centre is about 20 minutes' drive from the airport.

Train station Tirana's railway station was knocked down in 2013, and a new one is planned at the Casa Italia roundabout. Until the distant day when this station opens, all train services to Tirana go to the town of Vora, just outside the city on the way to Durrës. Taxis charge 500 to 600 lekë to the city centre.

Top Phrases

Hello. Tungjatjeta.

Goodbye. Mirupafshim.

Please. Ju lutem.

Thank you. Faleminderit.

How much is it? Sa kushton?

Resources

Visit Albania (www.albania.al) The offical portal of Albania's nascent tourist board.

Tirana Times (www.tirana times.com) Comprehensive Albanian news in English.

Set Your Budget

➡ Dorm bed: €15–20

➡ Double room in budget hotel: €25–40

➡ Cheap meal: €6–9

➡ Intercity *furgon* (minibus) ride: €2–7

Tirana

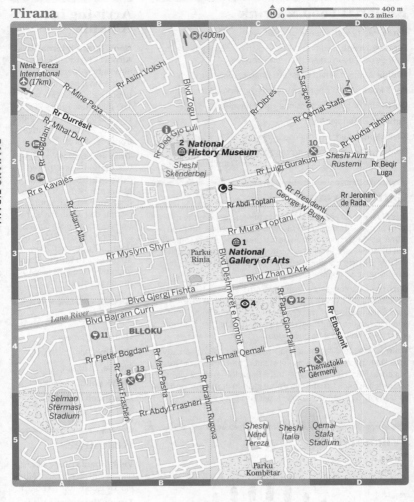

Tirana

◎ Top Sights
1 National Gallery of Arts	C3
2 National History Museum	B2

◎ Sights
3 Et'hem Bey Mosque	C2
4 Pyramid	C4

⌂ Sleeping
5 B&B Tirana Smile	A2
6 Tirana Backpacker Hostel	A2
7 Trip'n'Hostel	D1

⊗ Eating
8 Era	B4
9 New York Tirana Bagels	D4
10 Oda	D2

⊝ Drinking & Nightlife
11 Bunker 1944	A4
12 Komiteti Kafe Muzeum	C4
13 Radio	B4

archaeological treasures and a replica of Skanderbeg's massive sword (how he held it, rode his horse and fought at the same time is a mystery). The excellent collection is almost entirely signed in English and takes you chronologically from ancient Illyria to the postcommunist era. One highlight of the museum is a terrific exhibition of icons by Onufri, a renowned 16th-century Albanian master of colour.

Et'hem Bey Mosque
MOSQUE

(Sheshi Skënderbej; ⏲ 8am-11am) To one side of Sheshi Skënderbej, the 1789–1823 Et'hem Bey Mosque was spared destruction during the atheism campaign of the late 1960s because of its status as a cultural monument. Small and elegant, it's one of the oldest buildings left in the city. Take your shoes off to look inside at the beautifully painted dome.

Pyramid
NOTABLE BUILDING

(Blvd Dëshmorët e Kombit) Designed by Enver Hoxha's daughter and son-in-law and completed in 1988, this monstrously unattractive building was formerly the Enver Hoxha Museum and more recently a convention centre and nightclub. Today, covered in graffiti and surrounded by the encampments of Tirana's homeless, its once-white marble walls are now crumbling, but no decision on whether to demolish or restore it has yet been reached. It's sometimes open for temporary exhibits, for which it's a surprisingly great venue.

Mt Dajti National Park
NATIONAL PARK

Just 25km east of Tirana is Mt Dajti National Park (1611m). It is the most accessible mountain in the country, and many locals go there to escape the city rush and have a spit-roast lamb lunch. A sky-high, Austrian-made cable car, **Dajti Express** (⏲ 067 2084 471; www.dajtiekspres.com; €6; ⏲ 9am-9pm Wed-Mon, to 7pm Oct-Apr), takes 15 minutes to make the scenic trip to (almost) the top. Once there, you can avoid all the touts and their minibuses and take the opportunity to stroll through lovely, shady beech and pine forests.

To get to the Dajti Express departure point, take the public bus from outside Tirana's clock tower to Porcelan (30 lekë). From here, it's a 1.5km walk uphill, or you can wait for a free bus transfer (departures every 30 minutes, five minutes).

🛏 Sleeping

⭐ **Tirana Backpacker Hostel**
HOSTEL €

(⏲ 068 3113 451, 068 4682 353; www.tiranahostel.com; Rr e Bogdaneve 3; dm from €8, d €25, cabin per person €14; ❄@🛜) Albania's first-ever hostel goes from strength to strength and remains one of the best-value and most enthusiastically run places in the country. Housed in a charmingly decorated house, with a garden in which there are several cute cabins for those wanting more than a dorm room, the place is stylishly designed, excellently located and superfriendly.

⭐ **Trip'n'Hostel**
HOSTEL €

(⏲ 068 3048 905; www.tripnhostel.com; Rr Musa Maci 1; dm/d from €10/30; 🛜) Tirana's coolest hostel is on a small side street, housed in a design-conscious self-contained house with a leafy garden out the back, a bar, a kitchen and a cellar-like chill-out lounge downstairs. Dorms have handmade fixtures, curtains between beds for privacy and private lockable drawers, while there's also a roof terrace strewn with hammocks.

B&B Tirana Smile
HOTEL €€

(⏲ 04 2243 460, 068 4061 561; www.bbtiranasmile.com; Rr Bogdani; r incl breakfast €29; ❄🛜) Inside a residential building but doing a great job of hiding that fact, this small hotel has brightly decorated rooms, each individually colour coded and with plenty of light and space. It's all thoroughly modern and good value, with a central location and helpful staff.

> ### BUNKER LOVE
>
> On the hillsides, beaches and generally most surfaces in Albania, you will notice small concrete domes (often in groups of three) with rectangular slits. Meet the bunkers: Enver Hoxha's concrete legacy, built from 1950 to 1985. Weighing in at 5 tonnes of concrete and iron, these little mushrooms are almost impossible to destroy. They were built to repel an invasion and can resist full tank assault – a fact proved by their chief engineer, who vouched for his creation's strength by standing inside one while it was bombarded by a tank. The shell-shocked engineer emerged unscathed, and tens of thousands were built. Today, some are painted, one houses a tattoo artist, and some even house makeshift hostels.

OFF THE BEATEN TRACK

THE ACCURSED MOUNTAINS & THE KOMAN FERRY

The 'Accursed Mountains' offer some of Albania's most impressive scenery, and have exploded in recent years as a popular backpacker destination. You'll see a totally different side of the country here: that of blood feuds, deep tradition, extraordinary landscapes and fierce local pride. It's the undisputed highlight of any trip to Albania, and more remarkable to be so easily removed from modern life in the middle of 21st-century Europe. The two main villages with tourist infrastructure are **Theth** and **Valbona**, and a superb day hike links the two.

Another reason to head to this remote part of Albania is for the excellent three-hour ferry ride across Lake Koman, connecting the towns of **Koman** and **Fierzë**. The best way to experience the region is to make a loop beginning and ending in Shkodra, and taking in Koman, Fierzë, Valbona and Theth. To do this, arrange to have the morning 6.30am *furgon* (shared minibus) from Shkodra to Koman (600 lekë, two hours) pick you up at your hotel, which will get you to the departure point for the boats by 8.30am. There are two ferries daily (700 lekë, 2½ hours) in the summer months – both leave from Koman at 9am and arrive in Fierzë around 1pm. On arrival in Fierzë the boats are met by buses that will take you to Valbona (400 lekë, 15 minutes). Stay in Valbona for a night or two before doing the stunning day hike to Theth. After the hike you can stay for another night or two in Theth, before taking a *furgon* back to Shkodra.

 Eating

New York Tirana Bagels   CAFE €
(📱 069 540 7583; http://newyorktiranabagels.com; Rr Themistokli Gërmenji; bagels & sandwiches 80-300 lekë; ⏱ 7.30am-9.30pm; 🛜🅿) Believe it or not, Tirana is home to the Balkans' best bagels. Pick up one for breakfast from the aptly named New York Tirana Bagels, a cafe and social enterprise whose profits go towards supporting people in need.

Era   ALBANIAN, ITALIAN €€
(📱 04 225 7805; www.era.al; Rr Ismail Qemali; mains 400-900 lekë; ⏱ 11am-midnight; 🅿) This local institution serves traditional Albanian and Italian fare in the heart of Blloku. The inventive menu includes oven-baked veal and eggs, stuffed eggplant, pizza and pilau with chicken and pine nuts. Be warned: it's sometimes quite hard to get a seat as it's fearsomely popular, so you may have to wait. There's a second branch near the Stadium.

Oda   ALBANIAN €€
(Rr Luigj Gurakuqi; mains 350-650 lekë; ⏱ 11am-11pm Mon-Sat, from 1pm Sun; 🅿) This tourist favourite is stuffed full of traditional Albanian arts and crafts, and while its popularity with travellers means you won't feel like you've discovered a truly authentic slice of the country, the delicious menu and pleasant atmosphere make it well worth a visit. You can choose from two brightly lit dining rooms or an atmospheric terrace.

 Drinking & Nightlife

Tirana runs on caffeine during the day, switching to alcohol after nightfall. Popular places to get both are concentrated in the Blloku neighbourhood, where several streets have almost nothing but bars and cafes and become jam-packed at night. Nightlife in Tirana goes late, particularly in summer when the beautiful people are out until dawn.

★ Radio   BAR
(Rr Ismail Qemali 29/1; ⏱ 10am-3am; 🛜) Named for the owner's collection of antique Albanian radios, Radio is an eclectic dream with decor that includes vintage Albanian film posters and even a collection of communist-era propaganda books to read at the bar over a cocktail. It attracts a young, intellectual and alternative crowd. It's set back from the street, but it is well worth finding in otherwise rather mainstream Blloku.

Komiteti Kafe Muzeum   BAR
(📱 069 262 5514; Rr Fatmir Haxhiu; ⏱ 8am-midnight; 🛜) To get a sneak peak into life under Hoxha, pop into this quirky 'cafe-museum' (features various communist-era relics) for a coffee or one of 25 varieties of raki, the local fruit-based spirit.

Bunker 1944   BAR
(Rr Andon Zako Çajupi; ⏱ 5pm-1am Sun-Thu, 6pm-2am Fri & Sat) This former bunker is now a bohemian bolthole amid a sea of fairly pre-

dictable Blloku bars. Inside it's stuffed full of communist-era furniture and antiques/junk including homemade paintings, old vinyl, clocks and radios. There's a great selection of beers available, including IPA, London Porter and London Pride, and a friendly international crowd.

ℹ Getting There & Away

There is no official bus station in Tirana. Instead, there are a large number of bus stops around the city centre from which buses to specific destinations leave. Do check locally for the latest departure points.

Most international services depart from various parts of Blvd Zogu I, with multiple services to Skopje, Macedonia (€20, eight hours) and Pristina (via Prizren), Kosovo (€10, four hours) leaving from near the Tirana International Hotel, and services to Budva, Kotor and Podgorica in Montenegro (€15 to €25, four hours) leaving from in front of the **Tirana Tourist Information Centre** (📋 04-222 3313; www.tirana.gov.al; Rr Ded Gjo Luli; ⊘11am-5pm Mon-Fri, 9am-2pm Sat).

Departures to the south leave from Rr Myhedin Llegami near the corner with Blvd Gjergj Fishta. These include services to Berat (400 lekë, three hours, every 30 minutes until 6pm), Himara (1000 lekë, five hours, 1pm and 6pm), Saranda (1300 lekë, 6½ hours, roughly hourly 5am to midday) and Gjirokastra (1000 lekë, six hours, regular departures until midday, also at 2.30pm and 6.30pm).

Berat

POP 35,000

Berat weaves its own very special magic, and is easily a highlight of visiting Albania. Its most striking feature is the collection of white Ottoman houses climbing up the hill to its castle, earning it the title of 'town of a thousand windows' and helping it join Gjirokastra on the list of Unesco World Heritage sites in 2008. Its rugged mountain setting is particularly evocative when the clouds swirl around the tops of the minarets, or break up to show the icy top of Mt Tomorri.

◉ Sights

★ Kalaja
CASTLE
(100 lekë; ⊘24hr) The Kala neighbourhood inside the castle's walls still lives and breathes; if you walk around this busy, ancient neighbourhood for long enough you'll invariably stumble into someone's courtyard

thinking it's a church or ruin (no one seems to mind, though). In spring and summer the fragrance of camomile is in the air (and underfoot), and wildflowers burst from every gap between the stones, giving the entire sight a magical feel.

The highest point is occupied by the Inner Fortress, where ruined stairs lead to a Tolkienesque water reservoir. Views are spectacular in all directions, and guided tours are available from the entry gate for €10. It's a steep 10-minute walk up the hill from the centre of town.

★ Onufri Museum
GALLERY
(200 lekë; ⊘9am-7.30pm daily May-Sep, to 4pm Mon-Sat, to 2pm Sun Oct-Apr) The Onufri Museum is situated in the Kala quarter's biggest church, **Church of the Dormition of St Mary** (Kisha Fjetja e Shën Mërisë). The church itself dates from 1797 and was built on the foundations of an earlier 10th-century chapel. Today Onufri's spectacular 16th-century religious paintings are displayed along with the church's beautifully gilded 19th-century iconostasis. Don't miss the chapel behind the iconostasis, or its painted cupola, whose frescoes are now faded almost to invisibility.

Ethnographic Museum
MUSEUM
(200 lekë; ⊘8am-1pm & 4-7pm Tue-Sun May-Sep, 9am-1pm & 3-6pm Oct-Apr) On the steep hillside that leads up to the castle is this excellent museum, which is housed in an 18th-century Ottoman house that's as interesting as the exhibits. The ground floor has displays of traditional clothes and the tools used by silversmiths and weavers, while the upper storey has kitchens, bedrooms and guest rooms decked out in traditional style.

Mangalem Quarter
AREA
Down in the traditionally Muslim Mangalem quarter, there are three grand mosques. All are worth a visit and each has its own idiosyncratic design and history. The 16th-century Sultan's Mosque (Xhamia e Mbretit) is one of the oldest in Albania. The mosque on the town square is the 16th-century Lead Mosque (Xhamia e Plumbit). The 19th-century Bachelors' Mosque (Xhamia e Beqarëvet) is down by the Osumi River.

🛏 Sleeping & Eating

★ Berat Backpackers
HOSTEL €
(📋 069 7854 219; www.beratbackpackers.com; 295 Gorica; tent/dm/r €6/10/25; ⊘mid-Mar–Nov;

THE ALBANIAN RIVIERA

The Albanian Riviera was a revelation a decade or so ago, when backpackers discovered the last virgin stretch of the Mediterranean coast in Europe, flocking here in droves, setting up ad hoc campsites and exploring scores of little-known beaches. Since then, things have become significantly less pristine, with overdevelopment blighting many of the once-charming coastal villages. But worry not, while Dhërmi and Himara may be well and truly swarming, with a little persistence there are still spots to kick back and enjoy the empty beaches the region was once so famous for.

One such place is **Vuno**, a tiny hillside village above picturesque Jal Beach. Each summer Vuno's primary school is filled with blow-up beds and it becomes **Shkolla Hostel** (☑ 069 6515 588; www.tiranahostel.com/south-hostel; Vuno; tent €4, dm €7-9; ☺ May-Sep). What it lacks in infrastructure and privacy, it makes up for with its goat-bell soundtrack and evening campfire. **Jal** has two beaches: one has free camping while the other has a campground (2000 lekë including tent) set back from the sea. Fresh seafood is bountiful in Jal and there are plenty of beachside restaurants in summer.

@ ☎) This transformed traditional house in the Gorica quarter houses one of Albania's friendliest hostels. The vine-clad establishment contains a basement bar and restaurant, an alfresco drinking area and a relaxed atmosphere that money can't buy. There are two airy dorms with original ceilings, and four gorgeous, excellent-value double rooms with antique furnishings. Shaded camping area and cheap laundry also available.

★ **Hotel Mangalemi**　　HOTEL €€
(☑ 068 2323 238; www.mangalemihotel.com; Rr Mihail Komneno; s/d/tr from €25/35/50; P ✿ @ ☎) A true highlight of Berat is this gorgeous place inside two sprawling Ottoman houses where all the rooms are beautifully furnished in traditional Berati style and balconies give superb views. Its terrace restaurant (mains 400 lekë to 600 lekë; reserve on summer evenings) is the best place to eat in town and has great Albanian food with bonus views of Mt Tomorri.

It's on the left side of the cobblestone road leading to the castle.

★ **Lili Homemade Food**　　ALBANIAN €
(☑ 069 234 9362; mains 500-700 lekë; ☺ noon-9pm) This charming family home deep into the Mangalem Quarter underneath the castle is the setting for one of Berat's best restaurants. Lili speaks English and will invite you to take a table in his backyard where you can order a meal of traditional Berati cooking. We heartily recommend the *gjize ferges*, a delicious mash of tomato, garlic and cheese.

To get here, keep going down the narrow street beyond the **Hotel Osumi** (☑ 032 233 133; hotelosumi@gmail.com; Mangalem; s/d/tr incl breakfast €25/35/50; ✿ ☎), and you'll find the house signed on the right-hand side about 200m further on.

❶ Getting There & Away

The bus terminal is around 3km from the town centre on the main road to Tirana. To get there from the centre, ask locals to put you on a bus to 'Terminali Autobusave'. Bus services run to Tirana (400 lekë, three hours, half-hourly until 3pm). There are also buses to Vlora (300 lekë, two hours, hourly until 2pm), Durrës (300 lekë, two hours, six per day) and Saranda (1600 lekë, six hours, two daily at 8am and 2pm), one of which goes via Gjirokastra (1000 lekë, four hours, 8am).

Gjirokastra

POP 43,000

Defined by its castle, roads paved with chunky limestone and shale, imposing slate-roofed houses and views out to the Drina Valley, Gjirokastra is a magical hillside town described beautifully by Albania's most famous author, Ismail Kadare (b 1936), in *Chronicle in Stone*. There has been a settlement here for 2500 years, though these days it's the 600 'monumental' Ottoman-era houses in town that attract visitors. Far less touristy than Berat, the town is equally as charming and has several fascinating sights, as well as some excellent accommodation options.

⊙ Sights

★ Gjirokastra Castle   CASTLE
(200 lekë; ☺ 9am-7pm Apr-Sep, 9am-5pm Oct-Mar)
Gjirokastra's eerie hilltop castle is one of
the biggest in the Balkans and is definitely
worth the steep walk up from the Old Town.
The castle remains somewhat infamous due
to its use as a prison under the communists.
Inside there's an eerie collection of armoury,
two good museums, a recovered US Air
Force jet shot down during the communist
era, and a hilariously hard-to-use audiotour
that's included in your entry fee. The views
across the valley are simply superb.

★ Cold War Tunnel   TUNNEL
(200 lekë; ☺ 8am-4pm Mon-Fri, 10am-2pm Sat,
9am-3pm Sun) Gjirokastra's most interesting
sight in no way relates to its traditional architecture, but instead to its far more modern kind: this is a giant bunker built deep
under the castle for use by the local authorities during the full-scale invasion Hoxha
was so paranoid about. Built in secret during the 1960s, it has 80 rooms and its existence remained unknown to locals until the
1990s. Personal guided tours run from the
main square's tourist information booth.

★ Zekate House   HISTORIC BUILDING
(200 lekë; ☺ hours vary) This incredible
three-storey house dates from 1811 and has
twin towers and a double-arched facade. It's
fascinating to nose around the almost totally unchanged interiors of an Ottoman-era
home, especially the upstairs galleries,
which are the most impressive. The owners live next door and collect the payments;
to get here, follow the signs past the Hotel
Kalemi and keep zigzagging up the hill.

Gjirokastra Museum   MUSEUM
(Gjirokastra Castle; 200 lekë; ☺ 8am-noon & 4-7pm
Apr-Sep, 8am-4pm Wed-Sun Oct-Mar) This superb
new museum is a beautifully lit and presented, fully English-signed display on the long
and fascinating history of the town. Some
highlights include a 6th-century grave containing the skeletons of two small children,
as well as information on such luminaries
connected with Gjirokastra as Ali Pasha,
Lord Byron, Edward Lear and Enver Hoxha.

🛏 Sleeping & Eating

★ Gjirokastra Hotel   HOTEL €
(☑ 068 4099 669, 084 265 982; hhotelgjirokastra@
yahoo.com; Rr Sheazi Çomo; tw/d €35/40; ✳ 🛜) A

great option that combines modern facilities
with traditional touches, this lovely family-
run hotel inside a 300-year-old house has
rooms that boast huge balconies and gorgeously carved wooden ceilings. The suite
is gorgeous, with a long Ottoman style sofa,
original wooden doors and ceiling, and magnificent stone walls: it's an absolute bargain.

★ Stone City Hostel   HOSTEL €
(☑ 069 348 4271; www.stonecityhostel.com; Pazar;
incl breakfast dm €10-12, d €25-27; ☺ Apr-Oct; ✳ 🛜)
This brand new hostel is a fantastic conversion of an Old Town house, created and run
by Dutchman Walter. The attention to detail
and respect for traditional craftsmanship is
extremely heartening, with beautiful carved
wooden panels in all the rooms. Choose
between the dorm rooms with custom-
made bunks or the one double room, all of
which share spotless communal facilities.

Taverna Kuka   ALBANIAN €€
(Rr Astrit Karagjozi; mains 300-750 lekë; ☺ 9am-
1am Mon-Sat, from 10am Sun; 🛜) Just beyond
Gjirokastra's old mosque, this largely outdoor terrace restaurant has a wonderful
location and a menu full of delicious Albanian cooking, including *qofte* (meatballs),
Saranda mussels, pork pancetta and grilled
lamb. There's a surprisingly cool decor given
the rural Albanian setting and its terrace is
a firm local favourite on summer evenings.

❶ Getting There & Away

Buses stop at the ad hoc bus station just after the
Eida petrol station on the new town's main road.
Services include Tirana (1200 lekë, seven hours,
every one to two hours until 5pm), Saranda (300
lekë, one hour, hourly) and Berat (1000 lekë, four
hours, 9.15am and 3.45pm). A taxi between the
Old Town and the bus station is 300 lekë.

Albania Survival Guide

❶ Directory A–Z

ACCOMMODATION
Hotels and guesthouses are easily found
throughout Albania, as tourism continues to
grow and grow. You will almost never have
trouble finding a room for the night, though
seaside towns are often booked out in late July
and August. Homestays abound in Theth, while
the number of camping grounds is increasing;
you'll find them at Himara, Livadhi, Dhërmi and
Drymades. Most have hot showers and on-site
restaurants.

INTERNET ACCESS

Free wi-fi is ubiquitous in all but the most basic hotels. In larger towns many restaurants also offer free access.

MONEY

➡ The lekë is the official currency, though the euro is widely accepted; you'll get a better deal for things in general if you use lekë. Accommodation is generally quoted in euros but can be paid in either currency.

➡ ATMs can be found in all but the most rural of Albania's towns, and often dispense cash in both lekë and euros.

➡ Credit cards are accepted only in the larger hotels, shops and travel agencies, and few of these are outside Tirana.

➡ Tipping is appreciated in restaurants (10% is normal) and expected in fancier places. In cafes and bars it's polite to leave some change.

OPENING HOURS

Banks 9am to 3.30pm Monday to Friday
Cafes and bars 8am to midnight
Offices 8am to 5pm Monday to Friday
Restaurants 8am to midnight
Shops 8am to 7pm; siesta time can be any time between noon and 4pm

PUBLIC HOLIDAYS

New Year's Day 1 January
Summer Day 16 March
Nevruz 23 March
Catholic Easter March or April
Orthodox Easter March or April
May Day 1 May
Mother Teresa Day 19 October
Independence Day 28 November
Liberation Day 29 November
Christmas Day 25 December

ⓘ PRICE RANGES

The following price categories are based on the cost of a double room in high season.

€ less than €40

€€ €40–80

€€€ more than €80

The following price categories are based on the cost of a main course.

€ less than 300 lekë

€€ 300 – 600 lekë

€€€ more than 600 lekë

TELEPHONE

➡ Mobile phone coverage is excellent, though it's limited in very remote areas (most places have some form of connection including Theth).

➡ It's very straightforward to buy a SIM card with mobile data from any internet provider. Prepaid SIM cards cost around 500 lekë and include credit.

➡ Mobile numbers begin with 06. To call an Albanian mobile number from abroad, dial +355 then either 67, 68 or 69 (ie drop the 0).

ⓘ Getting There & Away

AIR

Nënë Tereza International Airport (Mother Teresa Airport; 04 2381 800; www.tirana-airport.com; Rinas) is a modern, well-run terminal 17km northwest of Tirana.

LAND

From Tirana, regular buses head to Pristina, Kosovo; to Skopje in Macedonia; to Ulcinj in Montenegro; and to Athens and Thessaloniki in Greece. *Furgons* (minibuses) and buses leave Shkodra for Montenegro, and buses head to Kosovo from Durrës. Buses travel to Greece from Albanian towns on the southern coast as well as from Tirana.

Travellers heading south from Croatia can pass through Montenegro to Shkodra (via Ulcinj), and loop through Albania before heading into Macedonia via Pogradec or Kosovo via the Lake Koman Ferry, or the new super-fast Albania–Kosovo highway.

There are no international train routes to/from Albania.

SEA

Two or three boats per day ply the route between Saranda and Corfu in Greece, and there are plenty of ferry companies making the journey to Italy from Vlora and Durrës. There are additional ferries from Vlora and Himara to Corfu in the summer.

ⓘ Getting Around

Bus and *furgon* (minibus) are the main form of public transport in Albania. Fares are low, and you either pay the conductor on board or when you hop off, which can be anywhere along the route. Municipal buses operate in Tirana, Durrës, Shkodra, Berat, Korça and Vlora, and trips usually cost 30 lekë.

Trains are dirt cheap and travelling on them is an adventure. Daily passenger trains leave suburban Tirana (the main train station in the city has been demolished and a new one is currently under construction) for Durrës, Shkodra,

Fier, Vlora, Elbasan and a few kilometres shy of Pogradec. Check timetables at the station in person, and buy your ticket 10 minutes before departure.

MACEDONIA

Skopje

POP 506,926

The Macedonian capital has become a thoroughly entertaining Balkan metropolis. In recent years, as a result of a controversial government project called 'Skopje 2014', the central riverside area of Skopje has hammered out the look of a set design for an ancient civilisation. Towering warrior statues gaze down on you and gleaming Italianate power buildings make visitors feel very small indeed. Marble-clad museums have mushroomed alongside hypnotic new mega-fountains.

But peel back the veneer and Skopje has a genuine historic core that warrants just as much attention as its new wonders. Ottoman- and Byzantine-era sights are focused around the city's delightful Čaršija (old Turkish bazaar), bordered by the 15th-century Kameni Most (Stone Bridge) and Tvrdina Kale Fortress – Skopje's guardian since the 5th century. The residential district of Debar Maalo, to the west of the city centre, is a very popular area for locals to eat, and has retained its local character more than the deeply altered city centre.

⊙ Sights

★ Čaršija   AREA
(Old Turkish Bazaar) Čaršija is the hillside Turkish old town of Skopje and evokes the city's Ottoman past with its winding lanes filled with teahouses, mosques, craftsmen's stores, and even good nightlife. It also boasts Skopje's best historic structures and a handful of museums, and is the first place any visitor should head. Čaršija runs from the Stone Bridge to the Bit Pazar, a big vegetable and household goods market. Expect to get pleasantly lost in its maze of narrow streets.

★ Archaeological Museum
of Macedonia   MUSEUM
(www.amm.org.mk; Bul Goce Delčev; adult/student & child 300/150MKD; ⊙10am-6pm Tue-Sun) All gleaming and shiny new, this supersized pile of Italianate-styled marble has been a giant receptacle for Skopje's recent splurge

BALKANS SKOPJE

WORTH A TRIP

MACEDONIA'S SACRED SIGHTS

In 1903, tiny **Kruševo** became home to a Macedonian Republic that was strangled by the Ottoman Empire just 10 days after being founded by revolutionaries. The country's first step towards sovereignty is commemorated with the **Ilinden Uprising Monument**, aka Makedonium (1974). Every aspect of the monument has symbolism and its presence is astonishing. The towering white form, with stained-glass windows, overlooks a circular field of concrete cannons and represents a 15th-century warrior mace – but looks more like an alien spacecraft. Buses to Kruševo run three times a day (390MKD, three hours) from Skopje.

Tetovo's surreal **Painted Mosque** (aka Pasha's Mosque) could be plucked right out of the illustrated pages of a fairy tale. First built in the 15th century, it was razed to the ground two centuries later in a great fire; the design and architectural form of today is a 19th-century folly and not an inch of exterior or interior is spared. The facade is a patchwork of rectangular panels worked in a fresco technique; inside, the decoration becomes floral, with geometric and arabesque ornamentation. Buses to Tetovo run every hour, if not more frequently, from Skopje and the journey takes 40 minutes to an hour.

The 13th-century **Treskavec Monastery** rises from Mt Zlato (1422m), a bare massif replete with impressive twisted rock formations. The monastery is half-ruined, though restoration work is slowly under way. Vivid frescoes, including a rare depiction of Christ as a boy, line the 14th-century Church of Sveta Bogorodica, built over a 6th-century basilica. Earlier Roman remains are inside, along with graves, inscriptions and monks' skulls. Treskavec is located 10km above Prilep and there's no public transport here; you'll need to drive.

MACEDONIA AT A GLANCE

Don't Miss

Ohrid's Old Town Explore Ohrid's seductive, lived-in historic quarter, right to the end of the boardwalk and pebble beach, and chill out in lake-front bars. Climb up the cobblestoned alleyways to the clifftop 13th-century Church of Sveti Jovan for sublime views over the ancient lake.

Skopje Bold new architecture in Macedonia's delightful capital will leave you wide-eyed. Dive into the winding lanes and craftsmen's stores of historic Čaršija (old Turkish bazaar) and marvel at the city's super-sized new riverside monuments and neoclassical facades.

Pelister National Park Eat your fill at food-focused guesthouses of Dihovo and Brajčino villages of this underrated national park, and walk it off the next day in its wooded environs and fresh alpine air. The signature hike is the full-day ascent to Mt Pelister and nearby mountain lakes nicknamed 'Pelister's Eyes'.

Mavrovo National Park Hike to Macedonia's highest peak, Mt Korab, go horse riding through Mavrovo's scenic mountain valleys, and take tea with the monks at the majestic Sveti Jovan Bigorski Monastery, teetering in the hills. The mountain hamlet of Galičnik is famed for its cheese making and a traditional summer wedding festival.

Tikveš wine region Sip and slurp your way through Macedonia's winery heartland, dotted with rolling vineyards, lakes, caves, gorges and churches. The region's shining star, Popova Kula winery, makes a wonderful base for appreciating the grapes.

Itineraries

One Week

Start with a couple of days in the capital **Skopje**, marvelling at the theatrical statues and visiting its old bazaar, museums and castle. Next, head southwest to charming **Ohrid** for some R&R and drinks by the spectacular lake and history lessons in its frescoed medieval churches. Complete the week with a couple of nights at a village guesthouse on the edge of **Pelister National Park** for hikes and excellent home cooking.

Two Weeks

Head north to **Mavrovo National Park** for some off-piste exploration. Stay in historic Janče village for superb Macedonian cuisine or Galičnik village for local cheese tastings and perhaps some horse riding, and visit the park's impressive and accessible Sveti Jovan Bigorski Monastery. Take a day trip to the **Tikveš wine region** for a wine-tasting tour, before returning to Skopje.

Essential Food & Drink

Šopska salata Served with just about every meal – tomatoes, onions and cucumbers topped with grated sirenje (white cheese).

Uviač Rolled chicken or pork wrapped in bacon, filled with melted yellow cheese.

Lukanci Homemade chorizo-like pork sausages, laced with paprika.

Tavče gravče Macedonian speciality of baked beans cooked with spices, onions and herbs and served in earthenware.

Pita A pie made of a coil of flaky pastry stuffed with various ingredients – usually local cheese and spinach or leek.

Vranec and **Temjanika** Macedonia's favourite red- and white-wine varietals.

Getting Around

Bus Skopje serves most domestic destinations. Larger buses are new and air-conditioned; *kombi* (minibuses) are usually not. Sunday is often the busiest day for inter-city bus travel among locals, so book ahead if you can.

Car Note that it's virtually impossible to hire a car with automatic transmission in Macedonia: it's manual-only here. There are occasional police checkpoints; make sure you have the correct documentation. Petrol stations are omnipresent except in very rural areas.

Train Domestic trains are reliable but slow. From Skopje, one train line runs to Negotino and another to Bitola via Veles and Prilep. A smaller line runs Skopje–Kičevo. Ohrid does not have a train station.

When to Go

Skopje

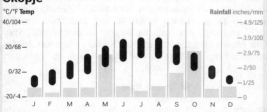

Jun–Aug Enjoy Ohrid's Summer Festival and dive into its 300m-deep ancient lake.

Sep–Oct Partake in Skopje's jazz festival or merrymaking at the Tikveš region's Kavadarci Wine Carnival.

Dec–Feb Ski Mavrovo, snuggle up beside fires in chalet-style lodges and experience Ohrid out of season.

Arriving in Macedonia

Skopje International Airport The Vardar Express bus runs to the city centre and its schedule is timed to coincide with flight arrivals. A taxi costs 1200MKD.

St Paul the Apostle Airport (Ohrid) Lies 10km north of Ohrid town. There is no public transport to and from the airport. Taxis charge a set rate of 500MKD to the city.

Skopje bus and train stations Located next to each other, a 10-minute walk east of the city centre.

Ohrid bus station A 1.5km schlep northeast of the Old Town; taxis to/from the station to the port area charge a set fare of 150MKD.

Top Phrases

Hello. Здраво.

Goodbye. Збогум.

Please. Молам.

Thank you. Благодарам.

How much is it? Која е цената?

Resources

Macedonia Timeless (www.macedonia-timeless.com) The country's official tourism website.

Municipality of Ohrid (http://ohrid.com.mk/) Official website with travel planning advice.

Set Your Budget

➡ Dorm bed: €10

➡ Beef kebab: 180MKD

➡ Skopje–Ohrid bus ticket: 500MKD

Skopje

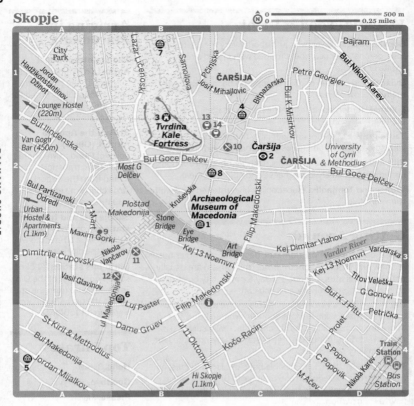

on government-led monuments to boost national pride. Inside, there are three floors displaying the cream of Macedonian archaeological excavations beneath the dazzle of hundreds of tiny lights. Highlights include Byzantine treasures; sophisticated 3D reconstructions of early Macedonian faces from skulls; a pint-sized replica of an early Christian basilica showing the life phases of mosaic conservation; and a Phoenician royal necropolis.

National Gallery of Macedonia

GALLERY

(Daut Paša Amam; www.nationalgallery.mk; Kruševska 1a; adult/student & child 50/20MKD; ⏰10am-6pm Tue-Sun Oct-Mar, to 9pm Apr-Sep) The Daut Paša Amam (1473) were once the largest Turkish baths outside of İstanbul and they make a magical setting for the permanent collection of Skopje's national art gallery, just by the entrance to the Čaršija (Old Turkish Bazaar). The seven restored rooms house mainly modern art and sculpture from Macedonia, brought to life by the sun piercing through the small star-shaped holes in the domed ceilings. Two other National Gallery sites (**Čifte Amam** (Bitpazarska; adult/student & child 50/20MKD; ⏰10am-6pm Tue-Sun Oct-Mar, to 9pm Apr-Sep) and **Mala Stanica** (www.nationalgallery.mk; Jordan Mijalkov 18; adult/student & child 50/20MKD; ⏰9am-9pm Apr-Sep, to 6pm Oct-Mar)) house rotating, temporary exhibitions.

★ Tvrdina Kale Fortress

FORTRESS

(Samoilova; ⏰7am-7pm) **FREE** Dominating the skyline of Skopje, this Game of Thrones–worthy 6th-century AD Byzantine (and later, Ottoman) fortress is an easy walk up from the Čaršija and its ramparts offer great views over the city and river. Inside the ruins, two mini museums were being built at the time of writing to house various archae-

Skopje

ological finds from neolithic to Ottoman times. This will be a welcome addition to the site, as there are no information boards at the fortress at present.

The entrance is up the hill on Samoilova inside a lovely park; opposite the gateway is a slightly unkempt path that leads across the hump of the hill to the **Museum of Contemporary Art**. En route, you'll get a stellar bird's-eye view of Skopje's futuristic, vortex-like Filip II sports arena in the valley below.

**Memorial House
of Mother Teresa**   MUSEUM
(☑ 02 3290 674; ul Makedonija 9; ⊙ 9am-8pm Mon-Fri, to 2pm Sat-Sun) **FREE** This extraordinary retro-futuristic memorial is the most unique church you'll see in Macedonia. Inside the building there's a small first-floor museum displaying memorabilia relating to the famed Catholic nun of Calcutta, born in Skopje in 1910. On the second floor there is a mind-boggling chapel, with glass walls wrought in filigree (a revered traditional craft of Skopje). Silhouettes of doves are worked into the filigree to symbolise peace, as a homage to Mother Teresa.

🛏 Sleeping

★ Urban Hostel &
Apartments   HOSTEL €
(☑ 02 6142 785; www.urbanhostel.com.mk; Adolf Ciborovski 22; dm/s/d €13/24/35, apt €35-70; ❄ 🌐) In a converted residential house with a sociable front garden for summer lounging, Urban is an excellent budget option on the outskirts of the leafy Debar Maalo neighbourhood, a 15-minute walk west of central Skopje. Decor is eclectic, with a fireplace for cosy winter nights and even a piano. The hostel's modern apartments, on the same road, are great value.

Lounge Hostel   HOSTEL €
(☑ 076 547 165; www.loungehostel.mk; 1st fl, Naum Naumovski Borče 80; dm €8-10, s/d €25/30; ❄ 🌐) A lovely large common area, orthopedic mattresses and bright, breezy balconies attached to every room (privates and dorms) are some of the highlights of this sociable retro-styled hostel with a view over the City Park. Staff are a little less clued up here than at some other hostels, but will bend over backwards to help make guests' lives easier.

Hi Skopje   HOSTEL €
(☑ 02 609 1242; www.hihostelskopje.com; Crniche 15; dm/d from €9/20) In a leafy, affluent suburb in the cool shade of Mt Vodno, this hostel's greatest assets are its garden and sprawling layout on different levels, which makes the hostel feel more spacious than many others in town. It's a 15-minute walk to Ploštad Makedonija from here (a 120MKD taxi from the bus/train stations), but the trade-off is a relaxing atmosphere.

The hostel has had a recent refresh: there's a comfy lounge area, communal kitchen, two six-bed dorms, an eight-bed dorm, and a couple of private rooms (shared bathrooms) that could work well for families. Plus lots of helpful leaflets and fliers in the reception area.

🍴 Eating

★ Kebapčilnica Destan   KEBAB €
(ul 104 6; set meal 180MKD; ⊙ 8am-11pm) Skopje's best beef kebabs, accompanied by seasoned grilled bread, peppers and a little raw onion, are served at this classic Čaršija place. There's no menu, everyone gets the same thing, but the terrace is usually full – that's how good it is. Ten stubby kebabs constitute a serious meat feast (180MKD); or you can ask for a half portion (120MKD).

Rock Kafana Rustikana
GRILL €

(☑ 02 72 561 450; off Dimitrije Čupovski; 140-300MKD; ☺ 8am-midnight Mon-Sat; 🐾) Just a block from the Ploštad but rocking a decidedly more local vibe, this humble bar-restaurant prides itself on good music, friendly service and simple dishes of grilled meats, sandwiches and inventive bar snacks such as zucchini with sour cream and garlic. Its setting amid an unkempt, mildly post-apocalyptic green space behind the Rekord Hostel only adds to its kooky charm.

Restaurant Pelister
INTERNATIONAL €€

(Ploštad Makedonija; mains 260-400MKD; ☺ 7am-midnight; 🐾) This cafe-restaurant is a real local fixture with a prime spot on Skopje's Ploštad and the feel of a Mitteleuropa grand cafe, attracting a diverse crowd. It's a good spot for coffee and people watching, and it also serves a vast array of decent pastas.

Drinking & Nightlife

Many of Skopje's bars double as cafes throughout the day. Mainstream bars fan out from Ploštad Makedonija and offer irresistible people-watching. Bars in the Čaršija are less manicured and more characterful; steep Teodosij Gologanov is the centre of the nightlife action. In summer, clubbers head to pop-up, open-air venues around Luna Park in the middle of City Park. Serious bars and clubs don't get going until after 10pm.

★Old Town Brewery
CRAFT BEER

(Gradište 1; ☺ 9am-midnight Sun-Thu, to 1am Fri & Sat; 🐾) The siren call of tasty craft beer sings to locals and tourists alike at Skopje's only microbrewery, which is justifiably popular for its Weiss beer, IPA, Golden Ale and dark beer – all brewed on-site and accompanied by a dependable menu of international pub grub. Its sunny terrace, sandwiched between the fortress walls and the Sveti Spas church, crowns its appeal.

Vinoteka Temov
WINE BAR

(Gradište 1a; ☺ 9am-midnight) Skopje's best wine bar, in a restored wooden building near Sveti Spas, is refined and atmospheric. Knowledgeable staff offer a vast wine list starring the cream of Macedonia's vineyards, though if you want to taste any of the better wines you'll need to buy a bottle as the glass selection is limited (as it is everywhere in Macedonia, unfortunately).

Van Gogh Bar
BAR

(☑ 02 3121 876; Mikhail Cokov 4; ☺ 8am-1am Mon-Fri, from 9am Sat & Sun) Whisky nights, cocktail nights, live-music nights... there's something going on every day of the week at Van Gogh, a poky bar with a lively local crew that spills onto the street. The bar is a haunt of local bikers, but all sorts of characters drink here and it's always good fun. It's close to the City Park, in Debar Maalo.

ℹ Information

Skopje Tourist Information Centre (Filip Makedonski; ☺ 8.30am-4.30pm Mon-Fri) Skopje's tourist information centre has maps available and a range of countrywide promotional literature. Note that the advertised opening hours are not kept.

ℹ Getting There & Away

BUS

Skopje's **bus station** (☑ 02 2466 313; www.sas.com.mk; bul Nikola Karev), with an ATM, exchange office and English-language info, adjoins the train station. Bus schedules are only available online in Macedonian.

There are numerous services to Ohrid (500MKD, three hours, 14 daily) and Bitola (480MKD, three hours, 11 daily). Most intercity buses are air-conditioned and are generally faster than trains, though more expensive. International services include Pristina (330, two hours, 14 daily), Belgrade (1400MKD, six to eight hours, 10 daily), Sofia (1040MKD, 5½ hours, five daily) and Thessaloniki (1300MKD, four hours, 6am and 5pm Monday, Wednesday and Friday).

TRAIN

The **train station** (Zheleznička Stanica; bul Kuzman Josifovski Pitu) serves local and international destinations. Disagreements with the Greek government have led to periodically suspended train routes to Greece; at the time of research the Skopje–Thessaloniki route involved a train to Gevgelija and then a bus across the border to Thessaloniki (760MKD, five hours, 4.45am daily). A train serves Belgrade (1430MKD, 10 hours, 10.19pm daily), and another heads for Pristina (three hours, 4.10pm daily) in Kosovo.

Ohrid

POP 55,750

Sublime Ohrid is Macedonia's most seductive destination, with an atmospheric old quarter cascading down a graceful hill, crammed full of beautiful churches and

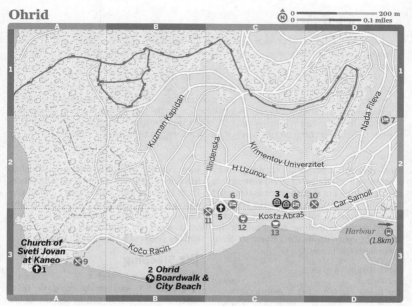

Ohrid

topped by the bones of a medieval castle. Its cobbled streets are flanked by traditional restaurants and lakeside cafes, but it's not a complete tourist circus just yet and still has a lived-in feel – particularly in the upper reaches of the Old Town. You can be skipping through historic monuments one minute and lying on a deck chair with your toes in the water the next – its location right on the edge of serene Lake Ohrid is hard to beat, and a lovely little town beach and boardwalk help make the most of its natural charms.

☉ Sights

★ Church of Sveti Jovan at Kaneo
CHURCH

(Kaneo; 100MKD; ☉9am-6pm) This stunning 13th-century church is set on a cliff over the lake, about a 15-minute walk west of Ohrid's port area, and is possibly Macedonia's most photographed structure. Peer down into the azure waters and you'll see why medieval monks found spiritual inspiration here. The small church has original frescoes behind the altar.

Little bobbing boats cluster beneath the church around the cliff base, waiting to whisk passengers back to the harbour (300MKD) if you don't fancy the walk.

Ohrid

☉ Top Sights
1 Church of Sveti Jovan at Kaneo..........A3
2 Ohrid Boardwalk & City Beach..........B3

☉ Sights
3 National Museum................................C2
4 National Workshop for Handmade Paper...........................C2
5 Sveta Sofija Cathedral C2

🛏 Sleeping
6 Jovanovic Guest House C2
7 Sunny Lake Hostel...............................D2
8 Villa Jovan..C2

🍴 Eating
9 Letna Bavča Kaneo............................A3
10 Restaurant Antiko.............................D2
11 Via Sacra..C3

🍷 Drinking & Nightlife
12 Jazz Inn..C3
13 Liquid..C3

★ Ohrid Boardwalk & City Beach
BEACH

Skimming the surface of the water along Ohrid's shore, snaking towards Kaneo fishing village and the town's most famous church, this over-water boardwalk propels

LAKE OHRID

Lake Ohrid's endemic trout (salmo letnica) is an endangered species and protected from fishing. Locals take the warning quite seriously these days and farm trout to put on their menus instead.

More broadly, the lake's growing popularity as a stop-off on the tourist circuit has become cause for concern among conservation groups. Plans have been drawn up to create a marina, artificial Mediterranean-style beaches and new apartments by draining an important marshland that acts as a natural filter to the lake. A local initiative called Ohrid SOS was set up in 2015 to help challenge the proposals, and the struggle to find a balance between commercial desires and conservation imperatives continues.

people towards a gorgeous outcrop of rocky beaches and a handful of small restaurants and bars. On a hot day, the area is thronged by bathers, drinkers and diners. The cool waters are translucent and inviting, the cliff-backed setting is sublime and strolling this stretch of coast up to the Church of Sveti Jovan is an Ohrid must.

Sveta Sofija
Cathedral
CHURCH

(Car Samoil; adult/student & child 100/30MKD; ⊙9am-7pm) Ohrid's grandest church, 11th-century Sveta Sofija is supported by columns and decorated with elaborate, if very faded, Byzantine frescoes, though they are well preserved and very vivid in the apse, still. Its superb acoustics mean it's often used for concerts. To one side of the church there's a peaceful, manicured garden providing a small oasis of green in the heart of the Old Town.

National Museum
MUSEUM

(Robev Family House Museum; Car Samoil 62; adult/student & child 100/50MKD; ⊙9am-3pm Tue-Sun) Ohrid's National Museum is housed over three floors of this remarkably well-preserved Old Town house, which dates to 1863 and was once owned by the Robev family of merchants. The creaking timbered building has just been renovated; on the top two floors displays include Roman archaeological finds, a 5th-century golden mask from Ohrid and local wood carving, while the ground floor is reserved for art exhibitions. Across the road the Urania Residence, a further part of the museum, has an ethnographic display.

National Workshop for
Handmade Paper
MUSEUM, SHOP

(Car Samoil 60; ⊙8.30am-9pm Mon-Sat, 9am-4pm Sun) FREE Here's a slightly random fact for you: Ohrid has been printing paper since the 16th century and this museum-cum-shop has one of only two copies of the Gutenberg Press in the world. Staff are on hand to give a demonstration of the paper-making process (in excellent English) and the teeny museum also sells handmade paper products such as pretty gift bags and notebooks.

🛏 Sleeping

★ Sunny Lake Hostel
HOSTEL €

(✆075 629 571; www.sunnylakehostel.mk; 11 Oktombri 15; dm €10-12, d €25 Jul-Sep, dm €8-9, d €22 Oct-Jun; ❋🛜) This excellent hostel is a bustling hub for backpackers stopping off in Ohrid. Space is a little cramped, but nobody cares because they have such a good time here. The common areas are a highlight: a snug upstairs terrace with lake views and a garden down below for beer drinking. Facilities include laundry, free breakfast, a kitchen, lockers and bike hire (per day €5).

★ Villa Jovan
HISTORIC HOTEL €

(✆076 236 606; vila.jovan@gmail.com; Car Samoli 44; s/d/ste €25/35/49; ❋🛜) There are nine rooms within this 1856 mansion in the heart of Ohrid's Old Town, and they're charmingly rustic with old-world furnishings and wooden beams. The rooms are a little on the small side but they're bright and have more character than anything else in town. Two of the rooms have quirky sunken baths and tiny sun-trap terraces.

★ Jovanovic
Guest House
GUESTHOUSE €€

(✆070 589 218; jovanovic.guesthouse@hotmail.com; Boro Sain 5; apt €40-65; ❋🛜) This property has two studio apartments, both of which sleep four, set in the heart of the Old Town. Each is well equipped and comes with a shady balcony. The apartment on the first floor is slightly bigger, but the top-floor apartment's balcony is more private and has one of the best views in town, right over the lake and Sveta Sofija Cathedral.

Eating

Via Sacra
PIZZA €

(☑ 075 440 654; www.viasacra.mk; Ilindenska 36; mains 160-350MKD; ⊗ 10am-midnight; 🛜) Pleasantly fusing the best of Italian and Macedonian fare, Via Sacra offers up crisp and tasty pizzas as well as a good selection of Macedonian national cooking and wines. Service is excellent and its location is a big draw too: facing the lovely Sveta Sofija Cathedral on a cobbled Old Town street. Breakfast is also served, a rarity in Ohrid.

★ Letna Bavča
Kaneo
SEAFOOD €€

(☑ 070 776 837; Kočo Racin 43; mains 220-370MKD; ⊗ 8am-midnight; 🛜) There are three terrace restaurants dipping their toes in the water at Kaneo and this one is marginally considered the best. A fry-up of *plasnica* (a diminutive fish commonly eaten fried in the Balkans; 190MKD), plus salad, feeds two cheaply, or try other Lake Ohrid specialities such as eel, carp or local lake fish *belvica* – the location doesn't come much better than this.

Restaurant Antiko
MACEDONIAN €€

(Car Samoil 30; mains 200-800MKD; ⊗ 11am-11pm) In an old Ohrid mansion in the middle of the Old Town, the famous Antiko has great traditional ambience and is a good place to try classic Macedonian dishes such as *tavče gravče* (beans cooked in spices and peppers), and top-quality Macedonian wines.

🍷 Drinking & Nightlife

Ohrid nightlife cranks up a notch or two in summer, when bars are busy every night and revellers spill onto the streets. The main area is along Kosta Abraš, where a strip of popular lakefront bar-cafes all have stellar views. Most drinking establishments double as cafes during the day.

★ Jazz Inn
BAR

(Kosta Abraš 74; ⊗ 9pm-1am) This unassuming little jazz-themed bar sways to a different rhythm to the strip of bars down on Ohrid's lakefront, with an alternative vibe, a different soundtrack and grungier clientele. Tucked down a cobbled backstreet away from the touristy hubbub, the low-lit interior has a speakeasy feel, though revellers can be found spilling out onto the road by midnight on weekends and throughout summer.

Liquid
CAFE

(Kosta Abraš 17; ⊗ 8am-1am; 🛜) Ohrid's most stylish lake-front bar is a relaxed chill-out place by day, serving coffee and drinks (no food). At night it morphs into the town's most lively bar with a beautiful crowd and pumping music. Its patio jutting into the lake has the best views and ambience on this strip. During the day this place is kid-friendly, too.

ℹ Getting There & Away

From the **bus station** (cnr 7 Noemvri & Klanoec), 1.5km from the centre, buses serve Skopje via Kičevo (490MKD, three hours, seven daily) or via Bitola (550MKD, five hours, two daily).

MAVROVO NATIONAL PARK

The gorges, pine forests, karst fields and waterfalls of Mavrovo National Park offer a breath of fresh air for visitors travelling between Skopje and Ohrid. Beautiful vistas abound, and the park is home to Macedonia's highest peak, Mt Korab (2764m). In summertime, it's glorious.

The atmospheric villages of **Galičnik** and **Janče**, separated by a mountain ridge, are both pretty spots with characterful guesthouses. **Macedonia Experience** (☑ 075 243 944; www.macedoniaexperience.com; ul Nikola Kljusev 3, Skopje) can arrange horse riding, bike riding and community tourism forays here from Skopje, often including food tastings. Mavrovo is also home to some of Macedonia's most revered cheese makers; the restaurant at **Hotel Tutto** (☑ 042 470 999; www.tutto.com.mk; Janče; s/d/t €30/50/60; P ❄ 🛜) is an excellent spot to try local cuisine with great views.

Without your own wheels, it's difficult to get around or do any hiking independently. Two buses a day run from Skopje to Mavrovo town Monday to Saturday (350MKD, 9.30am and 2.45pm).

International buses serve Belgrade (three daily but only one direct, 1790MKD, nine hours), Tirana (1000MKD, four hours, one daily) and Kotor (1530MKD, 8½ hours, one daily).

It's also possible to cross into Albania by taking the bus or a taxi to Sveti Naum, from where you can cross the border and take a taxi (€5, 6km) to Pogradeci.

Pelister National Park

Macedonia's oldest national park covers 171 sq km of the country's third-highest mountain range, the quartz-filled Baba massif. Eight peaks top 2000m, crowned by Mt Pelister (2601m). Two glacial lakes, known as 'Pelister's Eyes', sit at the top.

Pelister's 88 tree species include the rare five-leafed Molika pine. It also hosts endemic Pelagonia trout, deer, wolves, chamois, wild boars, bears and eagles.

The 830m-high mountainside hamlet of **Dihovo** is a charming spot, surrounded by thick pine forests and rushing mountain streams. The village is a popular base for walkers, with three guesthouses, a beekeeper, the icon-rich Church of Sveti Dimitrije (1830) and access to mountain paths, plus a waterfall to cool off in on hot summer days.

On the western edge of Pelister and within winking distance of Lake Prespa, the fresh mountain air and traditional rural architecture of **Brajčino** village make it an idyllic place to pitch up. There are five churches and a monastery in the leafy environs and a two- to three-hour, well-marked trail takes in all of them.

The **national park information centre** (☑ 047 237 010; www.park-pelister.com; ☺ 9am-3pm Tue-Sun) sells a detailed map of the park and its trails (120MKD) and has information on various routes and their starting points.

🛏 Sleeping & Eating

★ Vila Raskrsnica   BOUTIQUE HOTEL €
(☑ 047 482 322; vila.raskrsnica@gmail.com; Brajčino; d €40; P❋☜) It's worth detouring from the tourist trail between Skopje and Ohrid just to stay at this utterly lovely village hotel, which offers five rooms in a chalet-style house and lip-smacking country food. Rooms are relatively luxurious, with exposed stone walls and wooden floors, but it's the expansive mountain-backed garden, its rustic picnic tables and peeping view of Lake Prespa that make Raskrsnica so special.

★ Villa Dihovo   GUESTHOUSE €€
(☑ 070 544 744, 047 293 040; www.villadihovo. com; Dihovo; ☜) A remarkable guesthouse, Villa Dihovo comprises three traditionally decorated rooms in a historic house that's home to former professional footballer Petar Cvetkovski and family. There's a big, private flowering lawn and cosy living room with open fire place for winter. The only fixed prices are for the homemade wine, beer and *rakija* (fruit brandy); all else, room price included, is your choice.

ℹ Getting There & Away

Pelister is just 30 minutes away by car to Bitola, which is served by buses from Skopje (450MKD, 3¼ hours, hourly) and Ohrid (210MKD, 1¾ hours, four daily). A taxi from Bitola or Dihovo costs 360MKD one way.

Macedonia Survival Guide

ℹ Directory A–Z

ACCOMMODATION

The accommodation scene in Macedonia is slowly changing but, for now, many 'high-end' hotels feel dated and inexplicably expensive. Far better deals are at village guesthouses or city hostels; many also have a couple of private rooms and apartments. Be aware that 'apartment' usually just means a larger room rather than an actual apartment. It's well worth booking ahead for July and August.

INTERNET ACCESS

Wi-fi is widely available in restaurants, cafes, hotels and hostels – sometimes you just have to ask for the password; free wi-fi is not always advertised in food and drink venues. Some hotels have computers in common areas and even occasionally in guest rooms.

MONEY

➡ Macedonian currency is the denar (MKD). Euros are generally accepted – some hotels quote euro rates, but it's always possible (and usually beneficial) to pay in denar.

➡ ATMs are widespread in major towns, but surprisingly hard to find around Lake Ohrid except in Ohrid town itself.

➡ Credit cards can often be used in larger cities, but you can't really rely on them outside Skopje – most tourist businesses, including lower to midrange hotels, accept cash only.

➡ Macedonia doesn't have a tipping culture except at restaurants, where 10% is the norm.

KOSOVO

Europe's newest country, Kosovo is a fascinating land at the heart of the Balkans rewarding visitors with welcoming smiles, charming mountain towns, incredible hiking opportunities and Unesco-listed medieval Serbian monasteries – and that's just for starters. It's perfectly safe to travel here now, but despite this, Kosovo remains one of the last truly off-the-beaten-path destinations in Europe.

Kosovo declared independence from Serbia in 2008, and while it has been diplomatically recognised by 112 countries, there are still many nations that do not accept Kosovan independence, including Serbia. Do note that it's currently not possible to cross into Serbia from Kosovo, unless you entered Kosovo from Serbia first.

The capital **Pristina** is a fast-changing city that feels full of optimism and potential, even if its traffic-clogged streets and mismatched architectural styles don't make it an obviously attractive place. Kosovo's most atmospheric place is picturesque **Prizren**, with a mosque- and church-filled old town and an impressive fortress high above the town; it's also home to the famous Dokufest film festival each August. The town of Peja is a good base for exploring beautiful **Rugova Mountains**, which are becoming a popular destination for hikers and climbers. The 14th-century Serbian monasteries of **Gračanica** and **Visoki Dečani** are among Kosovo's absolute highlights and boast gorgeous ancient frescoes.

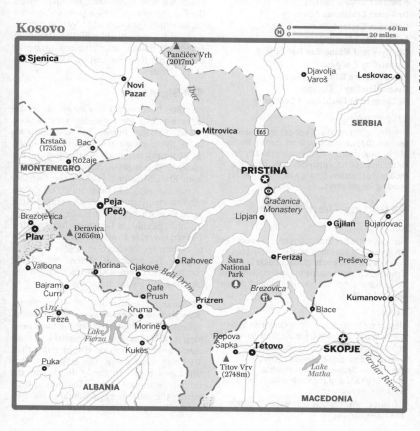

Kosovo

ℹ️ PRICE RANGES

The following price indicators are for a high-season double room.

€ less than €50

€€ €50–80

€€€ more than €80

The following prices are for a main meal.

€ less than 200MKD

€€ 200 – 350MKD

€€€ more than 350MKD

OPENING HOURS

Banks 7am to 5pm Monday to Friday

Cafes 8am to midnight

Museums Many close on Mondays

PUBLIC HOLIDAYS

New Year's Day 1 January

Orthodox Christmas 7 January

Orthodox Easter March/April/May

Labour Day 1 May

Sts Cyril and Methodius Day 24 May

Ilinden Day 2 August

Independence Day 8 September

Revolution Day 11 October

St Clement of Ohrid Day 8 December

TELEPHONE

Drop the initial zero in city codes and mobile prefixes (07) when calling from abroad. Within Macedonia, intercity calls require the city code; this is dropped for within-city calls. If using a mobile (cell) phone, buying a local SIM card is good for longer stays.

ℹ️ Getting There & Away

AIR

Flights from major European cities to Skopje and Ohrid airports have increased in the past few years. See the **Airports of Macedonia** (www.airports.com.mk) website for information about flying in and out of Macedonia, including timetables and carriers.

LAND

Macedonia borders four other countries: Albania, Bulgaria, Serbia and Kosovo. You can easily enter Macedonia from any of its neighbours.

International buses generally arrive and depart from Skopje or Ohrid. Pristina, Tirana, Sofia, Belgrade and Thessaloniki are the most common connections.

Trains connect Skopje to Pristina, Belgrade and Thessaloniki.

ℹ️ Getting Around

Skopje serves most domestic destinations. Larger buses are new and air-conditioned; *kombi* (minibuses) are usually not. During summer, pre-book for Ohrid.

SERBIA

Belgrade

POP 1.6 MILLION

Outspoken, adventurous, proud and audacious: Belgrade is not considered a 'pretty' capital, but its edginess and exuberance makes it one of the most happening cities in Europe. Its chaotic past unfolds before your eyes: socialist blocks are squeezed between art nouveau masterpieces, and remnants of the Habsburg legacy contrast with Ottoman relics. It's here where the Sava River meets the Danube, contemplative parkland nudges hectic urban sprawl, and old-world culture gives way to new-world nightlife. Deeper in Belgrade's bowels are museums guarding the cultural, religious and military heritage of the country.

⊙ Sights

Belgrade hustles and bustles along Terazije, crowned by the majestic Hotel Moskva. Grandiose coffee houses line Knez Mihailova, a lively pedestrian boulevard flanked by historical buildings all the way to the ancient Kalemegdan Citadel. Stretching from Knez Mihailova towards the Danube, Dorćol is a leafy, hip neighbourhood dotted with pavement cafes, boutiques and cocktail bars. Skadarlija, a cobblestoned strip east of Trg Republike, is Belgrade's Montmartre. The old riverside Savamala quarter has gone from ruin to resurrection and is the city's creative headquarters. Across the rivers' confluence, Zemun is known for its fish restaurants and quaint ambience.

★ **Kalemegdan Citadel**   FORTRESS
(Kalemegdanska tvrđava; www.beogradskatvrdjava.co.rs) FREE Some 115 battles have been fought over imposing, impressive Kalemegdan; the citadel was destroyed more than 40 times throughout the centuries. Fortifications began in Celtic times, and the Romans extended it onto the flood plains during the settlement of 'Singidunum', Belgrade's Roman name. Much of what stands

today is the product of 18th-century Austro-Hungarian and Turkish reconstructions. The fort's bloody history, discernible despite today's jolly cafes and funfairs, only makes Kalemegdan all the more fascinating.

Entering from Knez Mihailova, you first reach the Upper Town whose attractions include the Military Museum, Clock Tower, Ali Pasha's Turbeh, Roman Well and Victor Monument. In the Lower Town, which slopes down towards the river, look out for the Gunpowder Magazine, Ružica and Sveta Petka Churches, Old Turkish Bath and Nebojša Tower.

★ **Museum of Contemporary Art** MUSEUM
(☎011 3115 713; www.msub.org.rs; Ušće 10; 300DIN, free Wed; ☻10am-6pm Mon, Wed & Fri-Sun, 10am-10pm Thu) With its main building reopened after 10 years of major renovation, the Museum of Contemporary Art is back on the list of Belgrade's top cultural sights. A treasure trove of 20th-century art from the ex-Yugoslav cultural space, its massive collection is again on display in rotating exhibitions. The modernist building is surrounded by a sculpture park and has great views over the Sava river toward the Kalemegdan Citadel on the other bank.

★ **Museum of Yugoslavia** MUSEUM
(www.mij.rs; Botićeva 6; incl Maršal Tito's Grave 400DIN; ☻10am-8pm Tue-Sun May-Oct, to 6pm Nov-Apr) This must-visit museum houses an invaluable collection of more than 200,000 artefacts representing the fascinating, tumultuous history of Yugoslavia. Photographs, artworks, historical documents, films, weapons, priceless treasure; it's all here. It can be a lot to take in; English-speaking guides are available if booked in advance via email, or you can join a free tour on weekends (11am and noon).

Maršal Tito's Mausoleum (Kuća Cveća, House of Flowers; www.mij.rs; incl entry to Museum of Yugoslav History 400DIN; ☻10am-8pm Tue-Sun May-Oct, to 6pm Nov-Apr) is also on the museum grounds; admission is included in the ticket price.

★ **Nikola Tesla Museum** MUSEUM
(www.nikolateslamuseum.org; Krunska 51; admission incl guided tour in English 500DIN; ☻10am-8pm Tue-Sun) Meet the man on the 100DIN note at one of Belgrade's best museums, where you

---

DON'T MISS

GO WILD: TARA & DJERDAP NATIONAL PARKS

Serbia's cities offer fun, festivals, and possibly the nattiest nightlife in Europe. But if you need a breather, two spectacular national parks provide fresh-air fun in droves. Contact **Wild Serbia** (☎063 273 852; www.wildserbia.com; Birčaninova 120/I, Valjevo) for guided trips and outdoor adventures.

The sprawling Djerdap National Park (636 sq km) is home to the awe-inspiring Iron Gates gorge. Its formidable cliffs – some of which soar over 500m – dip and dive for 100km along the Danube on the border with Romania. The hulking **Golubac Fortress** and the ancient settlement of **Lepenski Vir** (www.lepenski-vir.org; adult/child 400/250DIN; ☻9am-8pm) are testimony to old-time tenacity. With marked paths and signposted viewpoints, Djerdap is an excellent hiking destination; the international EuroVelo 6 cycling path also runs through here. Boat tours through the gorge can be booked through **Serbian Adventures** (☎062 737 242; www.serbianadventures.com; ☻8am-5pm Mon-Fri, 9am-2pm Sat).

With forested slopes, dramatic ravines and jewel-like waterways, Tara National Park (220 sq km) is scenic Serbia at its best. Pressed up against Bosnia and Hercegovina, its main attraction is the **Drina River canyon**, the third-largest of its kind in the world. The emerald-green river offers ripper rafting; two artificial lakes (**Perućac** and **Zaovine**) are ideal for calm-water kayaking. Nearby is the **Šargan Eight** (Šarganska Osmica; ☎Mon-Fri 031 510 288, Sat & Sun 031 800 003; www.sarganskaosmica.rs; Mokra Gora; adult/child 600/300DIN; ☻twice daily Apr-Oct, once daily Dec-Feb) heritage railway, a 2½-hour journey with disorienting twists and tunnels, and the hilltop mini-village of **Drvengrad** (Küstendorf; www.mecavnik.info; Mećavnik hill, Mokra Gora; adult/child 250/100DIN; ☻7am-7pm) built by filmmaker Emir Kusturica for his movie Life is a Miracle.

SERBIA AT A GLANCE

Don't Miss

Kalemegdan Citadel, Belgrade Soak up the view over the Sava and Danube confluence at Belgrade's formidable fortress that once stood on the border between the Ottoman and Austro-Hungarian Empires. Explore the many historic monuments within its sturdy gates and toast the glorious sunset from the ramparts.

Novi Sad Join the thousands of party people for eclectic beats at the Petrovaradin Citadel during EXIT festival each July, splash on the Štrand beach and people-watch in outdoor cafes. This vibrant city is also the gateway to the Fruška Gora hills, studded with hushed monasteries and ancestral vineyards.

Tara National Park Go hiking and biking around the most scenic slice of Serbia or raft through the emerald-green Drina river canyon. On the park's outskirts, escape reality in the fantastical village of Drvengrad and on the winding, whimsical Šargan Eight narrow-gauge railway.

Djerdap National Park Join a boat cruise or go kayaking on the Danube through the awe-inspiring Iron Gates gorge. The hulking cliffs are guardians of the region's ancient history, whose remnants are the majestic Golubac Fortress and the Mesolithic settlement of Lepenski Vir.

Niš Get a crash course in Serbia's tumultuous past, from gorgeous Roman mosaics to a teetering tower of skulls, in the home town of Nišville Jazz Festival. Taste traditional Serbian cuisine in the *kafanas* of the cobblestoned Tinkers' Alley, where ubiquitous grilled meats rule the menus.

Itineraries

One Week

Revel in three days of historic, cultural and culinary exploration in **Belgrade**, allowing for at least one night of hitting the capital's legendary night spots. Carry on to the northern province of Vojvodina for another couple of days soaking up **Novi Sad's** laid-back, creative spirit in its many cafes and galleries, and roaming around the massive Petrovaradin Citadel.

Two Weeks

See more of the Vojvodina plains by heading north to the Hungarian border to admire the art nouveau architecture of **Subotica**. Next, explore southern Serbia's mountainous scenery and historic heritage. Slice southwest to **Tara National Park** for a couple of days of rafting and kayaking on the Drina river, and hop aboard the Šargan Eight vintage railway, en route to Turkish-flavoured **Novi Pazar**. Alternatively, head southeast via **Djerdap National Park** for some cycling along the Danube and a boat cruise through the Iron Gates gorge, followed by *kafana* cuisine of jazzy **Niš**.

Essential Activities

Hiking Soak up Zlatibor mountain's scenery on marked hiking paths, or blaze your own trail across its grassy slopes.

Cycling Biking is an ideal way to take in the rolling Fruška Gora region's 16 monasteries and countless wineries.

Kayaking Dawdle down the Danube by kayak through the Iron Gates gorge of Djerdap National Park in Serbia's east.

Rafting and canyoning Tara National Park is a favourite all-rounder for al fresco adventure, from rafting and canyoning to mountain biking and trekking.

Horse riding The *salaši* (homesteads) of the Vojvodina province offer heavenly horse riding.

Skiing Blanketed in snow from November to May, it's all downhill at the upbeat, affordable Kopaonik ski resort.

Getting Around

Serbia is, for the most part, easy to get around. Public transport is extensive, but for remote areas renting a car is the best.

Bus Bus services to major destinations are extensive, though outside major hubs connections may be sporadic. In southern Serbia particularly, you may have to double back to larger towns. Buy tickets from the station or on board.

Car Car-hire companies have offices at Nikola Tesla Airport in Belgrade. Traffic police are everywhere. You must drive with your headlights on, even in the daytime. Drive on the right.

Train Serbian Railways (www.serbianrailways.com) links Belgrade, Novi Sad, Subotica, Niš and Užice in the west. Trains usually aren't as regular and reliable as buses, and can be very slow.

When to Go

Belgrade

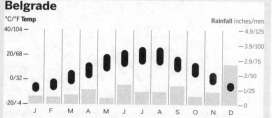

°C/°F **Temp**   Rainfall inches/mm

Apr Take a scenic ride on the Šargan Eight railway or cruise the Danube's Iron Gates gorge.

Jul & Aug Rock out at EXIT festival in Novi Sad and get jazzy at Nišville in Niš.

Dec–Mar Head to Tara or Kopaonik national parks for alpine adventure.

Arriving in Serbia

Belgrade Nikola Tesla Airport A taxi to central Belgrade (18km) should cost around 1800DIN. Head to the taxi information desk (near baggage claim area); they'll give you a taxi receipt with the name of your destination and the fare price. Buses (90DIN to 150DIN, half-hourly, 4.50am to midnight) and minibuses (300DIN, 5am to 3.50am) connect the airport to central Belgrade.

Novi Sad bus and train station The bus and train stations are next door to one another. Four stops on bus 4 will take you to the town centre.

Top Phrases

Hello. Dobar dan.

Goodbye. Zbogom.

Please. Molim.

Thank you. Hvala.

How much is it? Koliko košta?

Resources

National Tourism Organisation of Serbia (www.serbia.travel) Official tourism board's website.

Still in Belgrade (http://stillinbelgrade.com/) Independent online magazine covering Belgrade's contemporary culture.

Set Your Budget

➡ Dorm bed: 1200DIN

➡ City transport ticket: 90–150DIN

➡ Beer: 150DIN

Central Belgrade

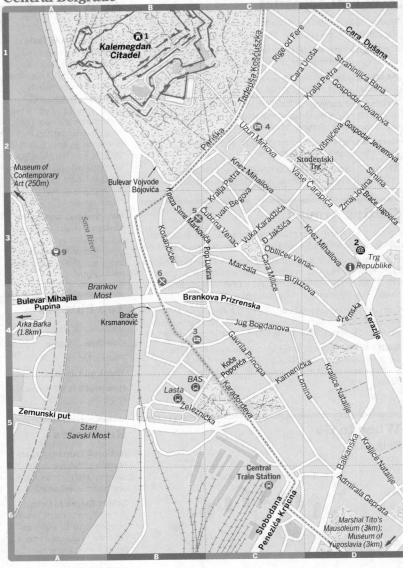

BALKANS BELGRADE

can release your inner nerd with some wondrously sci-fi-ish interactive elements. Tesla's ashes are kept here in a glowing, golden orb: debate has been raging for years between the museum (and its secular supporters) and the church as to whether the remains should be moved to Sveti Sava Temple.

National Museum
MUSEUM

(Narodni Muzej; www.narodnimuzej.rs; Trg Republike 1a; adult/child 200/100DIN; ⊙10am–5pm

slated for mid-2018; some of its collections are available for viewing in other museums around town.

Sveti Sava Temple CHURCH
(www.hramsvetogsave.com; Svetog Save; ⊘ 7am-7pm) Sveti Sava is the Balkans' biggest (and the world's second biggest) Orthodox church, a fact made entirely obvious when looking at the city skyline from a distance or standing under its dome. The church is built on the site where the Turks apparently burnt relics of St Sava. Work on the church interior (frequently interrupted by wars) continues today.

Topčider Park PARK
The vast Topčider (named after the Turkish word for cannons, as this is where the Turks cast their cannons for the 1521 attack on Belgrade) has been a favourite picnic area for Belgraders since the 19th century, when its gigantic sycamore tree was planted. It's home to the **Palace of Prince Miloš** (⏰ 011 266 0422; www.imus.org.rs; 200DIN; ⊘ 10am-8pm Tue-Sun Apr-Sep, 11am-4pm Tue-Sun Oct-Mar), the small Topčider Church and a restaurant. The park is south of the centre, next to the upmarket Dedinje neighbourhood; take tram 3 from the main railway station.

Ada Ciganlija BEACH
(www.adaciganlija.rs) In summertime, join the hordes of sea-starved locals (up to 250,000 a day) for sun and fun at this artificial island on the Sava. Cool down with a swim, kayak

Tue-Wed & Fri, noon-8pm Thu & Sat, 10am-2pm Sun) Trg Republike (Republic Sq), a meeting point and outdoor exhibition space, is home to the National Museum. Lack of funding for renovations has kept it mostly shuttered for over a decade, with reopening

or windsurf after a leap from the 55m bungee tower. Take bus 52 or 53 from Zeleni Venac.

🛏 Sleeping

YOLOstel
HOSTEL €

(☎ 064 141 9339; www.yolostel.rs; apt 6, 3rd fl, ul Uzun Mirkova 6; dm/d from €10/30; ❄ 🛜) This designer hostel enjoys an awesome location just a short stumble from Savamala. With custom-made furniture, quirky, gorgeous decor and a hip, refined air, this is not your usual backpacker flophouse.

Arka Barka
HOSTEL €

(☎ 064 925 3507; www.arkabarka.net; Bul Nikole Tesle bb; dm €15, r from €38; ❄ 🛜) Bobbing off Ušće Park, a mere stagger from the Danube barges, this 'floating house' offers sparkling rooms in 'wake-up!' colours, party nights, free bike use and fresh river breezes. It's a moderate walk, or a short ride on bus 15 or 84 from Zeleni Venac. Cash only.

⭐ Savamala Bed & Breakfast
B&B €€

(☎ 011 406 0264; www.savamalahotel.rs; Kraljevića Marka 6, Savamala; d from €50; ❄ 🛜) This brilliant B&B is all early 1900s charm out the front, nouveau-Savamala graffiti-murals out the back. As hip as you'd expect from its location in Belgrade's coolest quarter, the digs here are furnished with a mix of period furniture and the work of up-and-coming Belgrade designers. It's close to the city's main sights, and there are tons of happening bars and restaurants within staggering distance.

Smokvica Bed & Breakfast
B&B €€

(☎ 069 444 6403; www.smokvica.rs; Molerova 33; d from €40; ❄ 🛜) This ambient B&B offers eight good-sized rooms above one of Smokvica's famous garden cafes. The rooms are designer-vintage, spacious and comfortable; the big bathrooms have arguably the most powerful showers in the city. Smokvica's brilliant breakfasts alone are worth the stay.

🍴 Eating

⭐ To Je To
BALKAN €

(bul Despota Stefana 21; mains 220-700DIN; ⏲ 8am-midnight) The name means 'that's it', and in this case, they're talking about meat. Piles of the stuff, grilled in all its juicy glory, make up the menu here in the forms of Sarajevo-style *ćevapi* (spicy skinless sausages), turkey kebab, sweetbreads and more. It

serves home-made *sarma* (stuffed cabbage rolls) on the weekends. Cheap, scrumptious and highly recommended by the local community.

⭐ Gnezdo Organic
VEGETARIAN, VEGAN €€

(www.gnezdoorganic.rs; Karadjordjeva 43, Savamala; mains 850-1850DIN; ⏲ noon-midnight Tue-Sun; 🌱) This sweet little spot offers respite from Serbia's relentless menu of meat, stodge, meat and meat, with a menu chock-full of vegetarian, vegan and gluten-free treats (though carnivores do get a look-in, with some tasty steak and chicken dishes). Organic by name, organic by nature; even the wine list stays true to the theme. It's a welcoming nook, filled with like-minded locals and bubbly staff.

⭐ Little Bay
EUROPEAN €€

(www.littlebay.rs; Dositejeva 9a; mains 695-1590DIN; ⏲ 9am-1am) Little wonder locals and visitors have long been singing the praises of this gem: it's one of the most interesting dining experiences in Belgrade. Tuck yourself into a private opera box and let any of the meaty treats melt in your mouth as a live opera singer does wonderful things to your ears. It does a traditional English roast lunch (795DIN) on Sundays.

?
SERBIAN €€

(Znak Pitanja; Kralja Petra 6; mains 500-1150DIN; ⏲ 9am-1am) Belgrade's oldest *kafana* has been attracting the bohemian set since 1823 with dishes such as stuffed chicken and 'lamb under the iron pan'. Its quizzical name follows a dispute with the adjacent church, which objected to the boozy tavern – originally called 'By the Cathedral' – referring to a house of God.

🍷 Drinking & Nightlife

The once-derelict Savamala creative district is Belgrade's hip HQ, with bars, clubs and cultural centres that morph into achingly cool music venues come sundown. On the rough end of the otherwise genteel Skadarlija, the hotchpotch of bars and clubs in Cetinjska 15 is giving Savamala a run for its money. Belgrade is famous for its Sava and Danube river barge clubs, known collectively as *splavovi*. Most are open only in summer.

⭐ Blaznavac
BAR

(www.facebook.com/blaznavac; Kneginje Ljubice 18, Dorćol; ⏲ 9am-1am Sun-Thu, to 2am Fri & Sat)

Part cafe, part bar, part wonderfully wacko gallery, this pocket-sized place is one of the city's best spots for pre-drink drinks. Plastered in murals and quirky collectables, it's used as an exhibition space for young Belgrade artists; it also hosts live music and spoken-word events. Blaznavac's appeal isn't limited to nighttime jams and cocktails, it also makes a mean coffee, and is a great spot for a snack.

Dvorištance
BAR

(www.facebook.com/klub.dvoristance; Cetinjska 15; ⊙9am-1am Sun-Thu, to 2am Fri & Sat) Rainbow-bright cafe by day, absolute ripper of a bar/performance space by night, whimsical little Dvorištance is textbook Cetinjska 15. It regularly hosts live gigs and alternative/indie DJ parties.

★20/44
RIVER BARGE

(Savski kej bb, Sava River; ⊙9pm-5am Thu-Sat) Retro, run-down and loads of fun, this alternative splav is named for Belgrade's map co-ordinates. Open year-round.

★Kafana Pavle Korčagin
TAVERNA

(☑011 240 1980; www.kafanapavlekorcagin.rs; Ćirila i Metodija 2a; ⊙7.30am-1am Mon-Fri, 10am-1am Sat, 11am-11pm Sun) Raise a glass to Tito at this frantic, festive *kafana*. Lined with communist memorabilia and packed to the rafters with revellers and grinning accordionists, this table-thumping throwback fills up nightly; reserve a table via the website in advance.

Pržionica
CAFE

(Dobračina 59; ⊙8.30am-5.30pm Mon-Sat) If you're on a Lower Dorćol mission and in need of a caffeine fix, Pržionica is the place for you. Throughout its history this neighbourhood, with dozens of Jewish and Turkish stores, has had a special relationship with coffee. So it's no wonder that the tradition lives on in places like Pržionica, where excellent coffee blends go hand in hand with industrial design and friendly baristas.

ℹ Information

Tourist Organisation of Belgrade (☑011 263 5622; www.tob.rs; Trg Republike 5; ⊙9am-7pm) Helpful folk with a raft of brochures, city maps and all the info you could need.

ℹ Getting There & Away

AIR

Most international flights arrive in and depart from Belgrade's **Nikola Tesla Airport** (p670).

BUS

Belgrade has two adjacent bus stations, near the eastern banks of the Sava River: **BAS** (Central Bus Station; ☑011 263 6299; www.bas.rs; Železnička 4) and **Lasta** (☑011 334 8555, freecall 0800 334 334; www.lasta.rs; Železnička 2). Buses run from both to international and Serbian destinations. Sample daily destinations include Sarajevo (2585DIN, eight hours, three daily), Ljubljana (4300DIN, 7½ hours, two daily), Priština (3075DIN, seven hours, six daily) and Vienna (4430DIN, nine hours, two daily); frequent domestic services include Subotica (800DIN, three hours), Novi Sad (570DIN, one

---

WORTH A TRIP

SUBOTICA & NOVI PAZAR

Sugar-spun art nouveau marvels, a laid-back populace and a sprinkling of Serbian and Hungarian flavours make Subotica (10km from the Hungarian border) a worthy day trip or stopover. Once an important hub of the Austro-Hungarian Empire, the town attracted some of the region's most influential architects and artists; their excellently preserved handiwork is today the town's biggest drawcard. The unmissable eye candy includes the 1904 **Raichle Palace** (which now houses an art gallery), the 1910 **Town Hall**, the 1906 **City Museum** and the 1902 **Synagogue** (reopening for visitors after a long restoration in 2018).

Down south near the Montenegrin border, Novi Pazar is the cultural centre of the Raška/Sandžak region, with a large Muslim population. Turkish coffee, cuisine and customs abound, yet some idyllic and important Orthodox sights are in the vicinity: this was the heartland of the Serbian medieval state. The 16th-century **Altun Alem Mosque** is one of Serbia's oldest surviving Islamic buildings, while the small 4th-century **Church of St Peter** (3km from town) with a fascinating, photogenic cemetery, is the oldest intact church in the country. Around 14km west of town is the 13th-century, Unesco-listed **Sopoćani Monastery** whose frescoes are sublime examples of medieval art.

hour), Niš (1240DIN, three hours) and Novi Pazar (1470DIN, three hours).

TRAIN

The **central train station** (Savski Trg 2) has an information office on Platform 1, tourist information office, **exchange bureau** (☉ 6am-10pm) and **sales counter** (Savski Trg 2; ☉ 24hr).

Frequent trains go to Novi Sad (288DIN, 1½ hours, hourly), Subotica (560DIN, three hours, at least five daily) and Niš (784DIN, four hours, at least five daily). International destinations include Bar (2954DIN, 11½ hours, two daily), Budapest (1846DIN, eight hours, four daily) and Zagreb (2338DIN, seven hours, two daily). See www.serbianrailways.com for updated timetables and fares.

Novi Sad

POP 250,440

Novi Sad is a chipper town with all the spoils and none of the stress of the big smoke. Locals sprawl in pretty parks and outdoor cafes, and laneway bars pack out nightly. The looming Petrovaradin Citadel keeps a stern eye on proceedings, loosening its tie each July to host Serbia's famous EXIT festival.

Novi Sad's history as a vibrant, creative city continues today through its established galleries, alternative music scene and a liberal vibe. It is 2019's European Youth Capital, and in 2021 it will become the first non-EU city to spend a year with the prestigious title of the European Capital of Culture.

◉ Sights

★**Petrovaradin Citadel**　　FORTRESS
(Tvrdjava) Towering over the river on a 40m-high volcanic slab, this mighty citadel is aptly nicknamed 'Gibraltar on the Danube'. Constructed with slave labour between 1692 and 1780, its dungeons have held notable prisoners including Karađorđe (leader of the first uprising against the Turks and founder of a royal dynasty) and Tito. Have a good gawk at the iconic clock tower: the size of the minute and hour hands are reversed so far-flung fisherfolk can tell the time.

Within the citadel walls, a **museum** (Muzej Grada Novog Sada; ☏ 021-643 3145; www.museumns.rs; Petrovaradin Citadel; 150DIN; ☉ 9am-5pm Tue-Sun) offers insight into the site's history. The museum can also arrange tours (in English; 500DIN per person) of Petrovaradin's 16km of creepy, but cool, unlit underground tunnels known locally as *katakombe*.

Museum of Vojvodina　　MUSEUM
(Muzej Vojvodine; www.muzejvojvodine.org.rs; Dunavska 35-7; 200DIN; ☉ 9am-7pm Tue-Fri, 10am-6pm Sat & Sun) This worthwhile museum houses historical, archaeological and ethnological exhibits. Building 35 covers Vojvodinian history from Palaeolithic times to the late 19th century. Building 37 takes the story to 1945 with harrowing emphasis on WWI and WWII. The highlights include three gold-plated Roman helmets from the 4th century, excavated in Srem region situated not far from Novi Sad, and one of the city's first bicycles, dating from 1880.

★**Gallery of Matica Srpska**　　MUSEUM
(www.galerijamaticesrpske.rs; Trg Galerija 1; 100DIN; ☉ 10am-8pm Tue-Thu & Sat, to 10pm Fri, to 6pm Sat & Sun) First established in Pest (part of modern Budapest) in 1826 and moved to Novi Sad in 1864, this is one of Serbia's most important and long-standing cultural institutions. It's not a mere gallery, but rather a national treasure, with three floors covering priceless Serbian artworks from the 18th, 19th and 20th centuries in styles ranging from Byzantine to the baroque, with countless icons, portraits, landscapes and early graphic art (and more) in between.

Štrand　　BEACH
(50DIN) One of Europe's best by-the-Danube beaches, this 700m-long stretch morphs into a city of its own come summertime, with bars, stalls and all manner of recreational diversions attracting thousands of sun- and fun-seekers from across the globe. It's also the ultimate Novi Sad party venue, hosting everything from local punk gigs to EXIT raves.

It's also great for kids (watch them by the water: the currents here are strong), with playgrounds, trampolines and dozens of ice cream and fast-food stalls.

⌂ Sleeping

★**Varad Inn**　　HOSTEL €
(☏ 021 431 400; www.varadinn.com; Štrosmajerova 16, Petrovaradin; dm €10-13, r €30; ▣ ☏) Sitting in the shadow of Petrovaradin Fortress, this excellent budget option is housed in a gor-

geous yellow baroque-style building constructed in 1714. Completely renovated but making beautiful use of salvaged historical bits and bobs, the Varad Inn (get it?) has beautiful feel-at-home rooms (all with their own bathrooms, lockers and towels), a lovely garden cafe and communal kitchen.

★**Hostel Sova** HOSTEL €
(☎021 527 556; www.hostelsova.com; Ilije Ognjanovića 26; dm from €10, d €30; P🅟❄🛜) This cute spot is akin to a mini Novi Sad: super-friendly, attractive and given to laid-back socialising – and the odd *rakija* (fruit brandy) or two. It's perched above a deceptively quiet street that's just around the corner from buzzy Zmaj Jovina and a couple of minutes' stagger from the best bars in town.

★**Hotel Veliki** HOTEL €€
(☎021 4723 840; www.hotelvelikinovisad.com; Nikole Pašića 24; s/d €35/50, apt from €69; P❄🛜) Sitting atop an absolutely stupendous Vojvodinian restaurant of the same name, the Veliki ('Big') lives up to its name: some of the rooms are truly huge. Staff are delightful, and the location, around the corner from Zmaj Jovina, is top-notch. Bonus: free breakfast downstairs!

✖ **Eating & Drinking**

Laze Telečkog (a pedestrian side street off Zmaj Jovina) is lined with bars to suit every whim. During summer check out the bars along the Štrand, or catch a cab to Ribarsko Ostrvo to sample a *splav* (river-barge nightclub). The Chinese Quarter is lined with underground clubs, secret bars and squats. Hidden bars are also tucked away within the fortress walls.

Index House FAST FOOD €
(Mihajla Pupina 5; sandwiches from 120DIN; ⊙24hr) The locally famous Index Sandwich – an indulgent, sauce-laden spin on a ham-and-cheese sandwich – available for your munching pleasure, 24 hours a day.

Lazin Salaš SERBIAN €
(Laze Telečkog 5; mains 420-1300DIN; ⊙8am-3am) Replete with hay bales and knick-knackery, Lazin Salaš serves up great country-mouse cuisine on the most happening street in town. Don't be surprised if you find a violin in your ear; they love their *tamburaši* (musicians playing mandolin-like instruments) here.

★**Fish i Zeleniš** MEDITERRANEAN €€
(Fish and Greens; ☎021 452 002; www.fishizelenis.com; Skerlićeva 2; mains 690-1740DIN; ⊙noon-11pm; ✎) This bright, snug little nook serves up the finest vegetarian/pescatarian meals in northern Serbia (don't fret, meat-lovers – there's plenty here for you, too). Organic, locally sourced ingredients? Ambient? Ineffably delicious? Tick, tick, tick. A three-minute walk from Zmaj Jovina.

★**Martha's Pub** BAR
(Laze Telečkog 3; ⊙8am-3am) One of the best in a street of top bars, Martha's is a small, smokey and stupendously sociable den famous for its divine *medovača* (honey brandy). Crowbar yourself inside, or get there early to nab a table outside to watch the party people of Laze Telečkog romp by.

ℹ **Information**

Tourist Information Centre (www.novisad.travel; Jevrejska 10; ⊙7.30am-5pm Mon-Fri, 10am-3pm Sat) Ultra-helpful with maps and English info.

ℹ **Getting There & Away**

The **bus station** (Bul Jaše Tomića) has regular departures to Belgrade (570DIN, one hour, every 10 minutes) and Subotica (600DIN, 1½ hours), plus services to Užice (1230DIN, five hours) and Zlatibor (1330DIN, six hours).

Frequent trains leave the **train station** (Bul Jaše Tomića 4), next door to the bus station,for Belgrade (288DIN, 1½ hours) and Subotica (384DIN, 1½ hours). At least four trains go daily to Budapest (1479DIN, 6½ hours).

Niš

POP 183,000

Serbia's third-largest metropolis and home to acclaimed Nišville International Jazz Festival every August, Niš is a lively city of curious contrasts, where Roma in horse-drawn carriages trot alongside new cars, and posh cocktails are sipped in antiquated alleyways. Evidence of the city's long and tumultuous history are its significant Roman, Ottoman and WWII sights, but these days it's a buzzy kind of place, with a high number of university students, packed-out laneway bars and a happening live music scene.

◉ Sights

Niš Fortress
FORTRESS

(Niška tvrđava; Jadranska; ⊘24hr) Though its current incarnation was built by the Turks in the 18th century, there have been forts on this site since ancient Roman times. Today it's a sprawling recreational area with restaurants, cafes, market stalls and ample space for moseying, as well as the 16th-century **Bali-beg Mosque**. The fortress hosts the **Nišville International Jazz Festival** (www.nisville.com; ⊘Aug) each August and **Nišomnia** (www.facebook.com/festivalnisomnia; ⊘Sep), featuring rock and electro acts, in September. The city's main pedestrian boulevard, Obrenovićeva, stretches before the citadel.

Mediana
RUINS

(Bul Cara Konstantina; 150DIN; ⊘10am-5pm Tue-Fri, to 3pm Sat & Sun) Mediana is what remains of Constantine the Great's luxurious 4th-century Roman palace. The recently unveiled 1000 sq m of gorgeous mosaics are the highlight here; they were hidden from public view until protective renovations were completed in 2016. Digging has revealed a palace, a forum, a church and an expansive grain-storage area. There's not much in the way of signage, but knowledgeable staff are on hand to talk visitors through the complex.

Mediana is on the eastern outskirts of Niš and a short walk from Ćele Kula. Walk, catch a cab or take any bus marked 'Niška Banja' from the stop opposite the abandoned Ambassador Hotel.

Ćele Kula
MONUMENT

(Tower of Skulls; Bul Zoran Đinđić; 150DIN; ⊘9am-7pm Tue-Fri, to 5pm Sat & Sun) With Serbian defeat imminent at the 1809 Battle of Čegar, the Duke of Resava kamikazed towards the Turkish defenses, firing at their gunpowder stores, killing himself, 4000 of his men, and 10,000 Turks. The Turks triumphed regardless, and to deter future acts of rebellion, they beheaded, scalped and embedded the skulls of the dead Serbs in this tower. Only 58 of the initial 952 skulls remain. Contrary to Turkish intention, the tower serves as proud testament to Serbian resistance.

Red Cross
Concentration Camp
MUSEUM

(Crveni Krst; Bul 12 Februar; 150DIN; ⊘9am-4pm Tue-Fri, 10am-3pm Sat & Sun) One of the best-preserved Nazi camps in Europe, the deceptively named Red Cross held about 30,000 Serbs, Roma, Jews and Partisans during the German occupation of Serbia (1941-45). Harrowing displays tell their stories, and those of the prisoners who attempted to flee in the biggest ever breakout from a concentration camp. The English-speaking staff are happy to provide translations and explain the exhibits in depth. The camp is a short walk north of the Niš bus station.

⊨ Sleeping

Aurora Hostel
HOSTEL €

(☑018 214 642; www.aurorahostel.rs; Dr Petra Vučinića 16; dm/r from 990/1190DIN; ❄ ⊜) Set within a 19th-century former Turkish consulate, Aurora offers charm and comfort by the ladle-load. Though the building has been renovated, its wood-heavy interiors and hospitable host are redolent of a more gentle era. Rooms are spic, and there's a good communal kitchen and a lovely garden area for socialising.

Hotel
Panorama Lux
BOUTIQUE HOTEL €€

(☑018 561 214; www.panoramalux.co.rs; Svetolika Rankovica 51; d/ste from €38/49; P ❄ ⊜ ⊗) Set in a grand old home on a hill overlooking Niš, five minutes from the town centre, this hotel is true to its name, offering both panoramic views and luxury. It's a friendly, intimate place; there are just five rooms and three suites, all of which are beautifully decked out. The outdoor pool is a drawcard, as is the excellent attached restaurant; vegetarian options available.

Also runs a free airport shuttle for guests.

✗ Eating & Drinking

The cobblestoned Kopitareva (Tinkers' Alley) is chock-full of fast-paced bars and cafes. The fortress is another good spot for a tipple (or a nibble).

★ Kafana Galija
SERBIAN, GREEK €€

(www.kafanagalija.com; Nikole Pasica 35; mains 240-1700DIN; ⊘10am-midnight Mon-Thu, to 2am Fri & Sat, 11am-7pm Sun) The chefs here grill to thrill, with exceptional takes on classics, including spicy meat platters and barbecued seafood. The menu also features international favourites such as moussaka and homemade vine leaf rolls. Rouse yourself from your food coma by sticking around for the rollicking live music and associated crowd carousals.

 **Stara Srbija** SERBIAN €€
(Old Serbia; ☑ 018 521 902; www.starasrbija.com;
Trg Republike 12; mains 250-2000DIN; ☺ 9am-midnight Mon-Fri, to late Sat & Sun) Right at home in a restored 1876 house in the centre of Niš, this atmospheric spot serves up fantastic (and filling) traditional southern Serbian cuisine, including baked beans with smoked meat, and the divine chicken stuffed with prosciutto and *kajmak* (a spread somewhat akin to a salty clotted cheese).

Vespa Bar BAR
(www.vespabar.com; Trg Republike; ☺ 8am-midnight Mon-Thu, to 2am Fri-Sat, 9am-midnight Sun) There are literally Vespas coming out of the woodwork at this happy, happening bar in the centre of town. Chat with the friendly 'bikies' over beer (local and international) or something from the extensive cocktail list.

ℹ️ Information

Tourist Organisation of Niš (☑ 018 250 222; www.visitnis.com; Tvrđava; ☺ 7.30am-7pm Mon-Fri, 9am-1pm Sat) Helpful info within the citadel gates. There's another branch at Vožda Karađorđa 7 in the city centre.

ℹ️ Getting There & Away

The **bus station** (Bul 12 Februar) behind the fortress has frequent services to Belgrade (1240DIN, three hours) and three daily to Novi Pazar (1200DIN, four hours). From the **train station** (Dimitrija Tucovića), there are seven trains to Belgrade (784DIN, 4½ hours) and two to Sofia (730DIN, five hours).

Serbia Survival Guide

ℹ️ Directory A–Z

ACCOMMODATION

You'll find hotels and hostels in Serbia's cities and most towns. Private rooms and apartments offer superb value and can be organised through tourist offices. 'Wild' camping is possible outside national parks. In rural areas, look out for *etno sela* (traditional village accommodation); in Vojvodina, *salaši* (pastoral homesteads) and manor homes make for a memorable stay. **Rural Tourism Serbia** (www.selo.co.rs) can organise village sleepovers.

INTERNET ACCESS

Free wi-fi is available in most of the bigger city and town centres, and at almost every hotel or hostel. You may have to pay a small fee to con-

nect at cafes and bars, but it's generally on the house. Very rural areas may not have net access.

MONEY

→ Serbia's currency is the dinar (DIN).

→ ATMs are widespread and credit cards are accepted by established businesses.

→ Exchange offices *(menjačnica)* are on every street corner. Exchange machines accept euros, US dollars and British pounds.

→ Tipping is not obligatory, but always appreciated for good service.

OPENING HOURS

Banks 8am or 9am to 5pm Monday to Friday, 8am to 2pm Saturday

Bars 8am to midnight (later on weekends)

Restaurants 8am to midnight or 1am

Shops 8am to 6pm Monday to Friday, many open Saturday evenings

PUBLIC HOLIDAYS

New Year 1 and 2 January

Orthodox Christmas 7 January

National Statehood Day 15 and 16 February

Orthodox Easter April/May

Labour Day 1 and 2 May

Armistice Day 11 November

TELEPHONE

→ Press the *i* button on public phones for dialling commands in English. Long-distance calls can also be made from booths in post offices.

→ Local and international phonecards can be bought in post offices and tobacco kiosks.

→ Mobile-phone SIM cards (around 300DIN) and recharge cards can be purchased at supermarkets and kiosks. All mobile numbers in Serbia start with 06.

ℹ️ PRICE RANGES

The following price categories are based on the cost of a high-season double room. Although accommodation prices are often quoted in euros, you must pay in dinars.

€ less than 3000DIN

€€ 3000–7000DIN

€€€ more than 7000DIN

The following food price categories are based on the cost of a main course.

€ less than 600DIN

€€ 600–1000DIN

€€€ more than 1000DIN

❶ Getting There & Away

AIR

Belgrade's **Nikola Tesla Airport** (☎ 011 209 4444; www.beg.aero) handles most international flights. The airport website has a full list of airlines servicing Serbia. **Niš Constantine The Great Airport** (www.nis-airport.com) links Niš with countries including Italy, Germany, Slovakia and the Netherlands. The national carrier is **Air Serbia** (www.airserbia.com).

LAND

You can easily enter Serbia by land from Montenegro, Croatia, Bosnia and Hercegovina, Macedonia, Bulgaria, Romania and Hungary. Coming in via Kosovo can present difficulties. Because Serbia does not acknowledge crossing points into Kosovo as international border crossings, it may not be possible to enter Serbia from Kosovo unless you first entered Kosovo from Serbia. If you wish to enter Serbia from Kosovo, consider taking a route that transits another nearby country.

Bus services to both Western Europe and Turkey are well developed, with regular routes including Vienna, Sarajevo and Podgorica.

Bucharest, Budapest, Ljubljana, Moscow, Sofia and Zagreb are a train ride away. Heading north and west, most trains call in at Novi Sad and Subotica; heading east, they go via Niš. Several trips from Serbia offer a nice slice of scenery, such as the route to Bar on the Montenegrin coast. For more information, visit **Serbian Railways** (www.serbianrailways.com).

❶ Getting Around

Bus services are extensive, though outside major hubs connections can be sporadic. Reservations are only worthwhile for international buses and during festivals.

Trains usually aren't as regular and reliable as buses, and can be murderously slow, but they're a fun way to met locals and other travellers.

Central & Eastern Europe

Best Places to Eat

➜ Baczewski (p768)

➜ Maso a Kobliha (p682)

➜ Zeller Bistro (p715)

➜ Artist (p727)

➜ Shtastliveca (p750)

➜ Spotykach (p763)

Best Places to Drink

➜ Kofi (p698)

➜ Bunkier Café (p703)

➜ Linea / Closer to the Moon (p728)

➜ Closer (p763)

➜ Pravda Beer Theatre (p768)

Why Go?

Though the countries of Central and Eastern Europe emerged from communism more than a quarter-century ago, they still retain a feeling of the 'other' Europe – wilder, less refined and more remote than their cousins in the west. Medieval capitals like Prague, Kraków and Budapest number among the continent's most beautiful cities and belong on any first-timer's list. More exotic destinations such as Slovakia, Bulgaria and Romania boast rustic charm and extreme natural beauty. All are members of the European Union.

The situation changes as you move further east. The former Soviet countries of Belarus, Ukraine, Moldova and Georgia lie well off the beaten track for most travellers and will appeal mainly to adventurers. Eastern Ukraine remains embroiled in conflict, though the western parts of the country, particularly the majestic cities of Kyiv and Lviv, are peaceful. Mountainous Georgia is one of the most beautiful countries anywhere.

Fast Facts

Capitals Prague (Czech Republic), Warsaw (Poland), Bratislava (Slovakia), Budapest (Hungary), Bucharest (Romania), Chişinău (Moldova), Sofia (Bulgaria), Kyiv (Ukraine), Minsk (Belarus), Tbilisi (Georgia)

Currency Crown (Kč; Czech Republic), złoty (zł; Poland), euro (€; Slovakia), forint (ft; Hungary), lei (Romania), Moldovan lei (Moldova), lev (Bulgaria), hryvnya uah (Ukraine), Belarusian rouble (BR; Belarus), lari (GEL; Georgia)

Languages Czech (Czech Republic), Polish (Poland), Slovak (Slovakia), Hungarian (Hungary), Romanian (Romania), Moldovan and Russian (Moldova), Bulgarian (Bulgaria), Ukrainian and Russian (Ukraine), Belarusian and Russian (Belarus), Georgian (Georgia)

Visas Required for Belarus for stays longer than five days; other countries visa-free for most visitors for stays up to 90 days

COPENHAGEN
DENMARK

Liepāja
LATVIA
Rēzekne
Daugavpils
Šiauliai
LITHUANIA
Klaipēda
Curonian Spit
Vitsebsk
Kaliningrad
Kaunas
VILNIUS
RUSSIA
MINSK
Mahilieu
Koszalin
Gdańsk
Malbork
Suwałki
Hrodna
Nemunas
GERMANY
Szczecin
Olsztyn
BELARUS
Homel
BERLIN
Zielona
Góra
Poznań
Białystok
WARSAW
Brest
Chernihiv
POLAND
Łódź
Lublin
Wrocław
Ústi Nad
Labem
Kielce
Zamość
Kovel
Kyiv 8
Plzeň
Prague 1
Auschwitz-
Birkenau
Odra
Kraków
Przemyśl
Lviv
UKRAINE
CZECH
REPUBLIC
Kutná
Hora
3 2
Zakopane
Český
Krumlov
Brno
Olomouc
Vinnytsya
Trenčín
SLOVAKIA
Uzhhorod
VIENNA
BRATISLAVA
Košice
Danube
Chernivtsi
AUSTRIA
Győr
Eger
4 Budapest
Debrecen
Tisa
Bistrita
Suceava
CHIŞINĂU
Bovec
Bled
HUNGARY
Iaşi
7 Moldova
Trieste
LJUBLJANA
Pécs
Szeged
Cluj-Napoca
Transylvania
Ode
Piran
SLOVENIA
ZAGREB
5
Rijeka
CROATIA
Sava
Biertan
Pula
Banja Luka
Novi Sad
Timişoara
Sibiu
Bran
Braşov
Zadar
BOSNIA &
HERCEGOVINA
Belgrade
ROMANIA
Tulcea
SERBIA
Craiova
6
Constant
SARAJEVO
Bucharest
Split
Mostar
MONTENEGRO
Niš
Montana
Veliko
Târnovo
Varna
Dubrovnik
PODGORICA
PRISTINA
SOFIA
Kotor
KOSOVO
Plovdiv
BULGARIA
Kârdzhali
Burgas
Shkodra
SKOPJE
ALBANIA
MACEDONIA
ITALY
TIRANA
Ohrid
Berat
Korça

Central & Eastern Europe Highlights

❶ **Prague** Rambling around a 14th-century town core and crossing the continent's most beautiful bridge. (p674)

❷ **Kraków** Admiring the biggest medieval public square

in Europe situated right in the heart of Poland's historic capital. (p699)

❸ **Auschwitz-Birkenau** Bowing your head in remembrance of the more

than a million murdered here in WWII. (p704)

❹ **Budapest** Taking in the Danubian metropolis with a bowl of goulash and a soak in a thermal bath. (p707)

MOSCOW

RUSSIA

Don

Sumy

Kharkiv

Luhansk

Dnipropetrovsk

Donetsk

Kirovohrad

Zaporiyhzhya

Don

Kherson

CRIMEA

Simferopol

Yalta

TBILISI

YEREVAN

TURKEY

ANKARA

5 **Transylvania** Enjoying resplendent nature and historic churches in 'Dracula's' old stomping ground. (p729)

6 **Bucharest** Gawking at one of the world's biggest buildings

and absorbing Romania's energetic capital. (p722)

7 **Moldova** Raising a glass of wine and planting your flag of personal conquest in this little-visited land. (p736)

8 **Kyiv** Partying your way through Ukraine's capital, which seemingly overnight has become undeniably hip. (p757)

CZECH REPUBLIC

Prague

POP 1.3 MILLION

The Velvet Revolution that freed the Czechs from communism restored to Europe a gem of a city to stand beside Continental stalwarts such as Rome, Amsterdam and Paris. Not surprisingly, visitors from around the world have come in droves, and on a hot summer's day it can feel like you're sharing Charles Bridge with half of humanity. But even the crowds can't take away from the spectacle of a 14th-century stone bridge, a hilltop castle and a lovely, lazy river.

◉ Sights

◉ Prague Castle & Hradčany

Mighty Prague Castle is perched on a hilltop high above the Vltava River, with the attractive and peaceful residential area of Hradčany stretching westward to the Strahov Monastery.

★ Prague Castle   CASTLE

(Pražský hrad; Map p682; ☑224 372 423; www. hrad.cz; Hradčanské náměstí 1; grounds free, sights adult/concession Tour A & C 350/175Kc, Tour B 250/125Kč; ◎grounds 6am-10pm year-round, gardens 10am-6pm Apr-Oct, closed Nov-Mar, historic building 9am-5pm Apr-Oct, to 4pm Nov-Mar; ⓂMalostranská, ◻22) Prague Castle – Pražský hrad, or just *hrad* to Czechs – is Prague's most popular attraction. Looming above the Vltava's left bank, its serried ranks of spires, towers and palaces dominate the city centre like a fairy-tale fortress. Within its walls lies a varied and fascinating collection of histor-

ic buildings, museums and galleries that are home to some of the Czech Republic's greatest artistic and cultural treasures.

★ St Vitus Cathedral   CHURCH

(Katedrála sv Víta; Map p682; ☑257 531 622; www. katedralasvatehovita.cz; Third Courtyard, Prague Castle; admission incl with Prague Castle Tour A & B tickets; ◎9am-5pm Mon-Sat, noon-5pm Sun Apr-Oct, to 4pm Nov-Mar; ◻22) Built over a time span of almost 600 years, St Vitus is one of the most richly endowed cathedrals in central Europe. It is pivotal to the religious and cultural life of the Czech Republic, housing treasures that range from the 14th-century mosaic of the Last Judgement and the tombs of St Wenceslas and Charles IV, to the baroque silver tomb of St John of Nepomuck, the ornate Chapel of St Wenceslas, and art nouveau stained glass by Alfons Mucha.

Old Royal Palace   PALACE

(Starý královský palác; Map p682; admission with Prague Castle tour A & B tickets; ◎9am-5pm Apr-Oct, to 4pm Nov-Mar; ◻22) The Old Royal Palace is one of the oldest parts of Prague Castle, dating from 1135. It was originally used only by Czech princesses, but from the 13th to the 16th centuries it was the king's own palace. At its heart is the grand Vladislav Hall and the Bohemian Chancellery, scene of the famous Defenestration of Prague in 1618.

Lobkowicz Palace   MUSEUM

(Lobkovický palác; Map p682; ☑233 312 925; www.lobkowicz.com; Jiřská 3; adult/concession/ family 275/200/690Kč; ◎10am-6pm; ◻22) This 16th-century palace houses a private museum known as the Princely Collections, which includes priceless paintings, furniture and musical memorabilia. Your tour

---

PRAGUE'S JEWISH MUSEUM

The slice of Staré Město bounded by Kaprova, Dlouhá and Kozí streets is home to the remains of the once-thriving mini-town of Josefov, Prague's former Jewish ghetto. The **Prague Jewish museum** (Židovské muzeum Praha; ☑222 317 191; www.jewishmuseum.cz; Reservation Centre, Maiselova 38/15; ordinary ticket adult/child 300/200Kč, combined ticket incl entry to Old-New Synagogue 480/320Kč; ◎9am-6pm Sun-Fri Apr-Oct, to 4.30pm Nov-Mar; ⓂStaroměstská) encompasses half a dozen ancient synagogues, a ceremonial hall and former mortuary, and the powerful and melancholic Old Jewish Cemetery. These exhibits tell the often tragic and moving story of Prague's Jewish community, from the 16th-century creator of the Golem, Rabbi Loew, to the horrors of Nazi persecution.

An ordinary ticket gives admission to all six main monuments; a combined ticket includes the Old-New Synagogue as well. Completed around 1270, the Old-New Synagogue is Europe's oldest working synagogue and one of Prague's earliest Gothic buildings.

KARLŠTEJN CASTLE

Rising above the village of Karlštejn, 30km southwest of Prague and easily reachable by train, **Karlštejn Castle** (Hrad Karlštejn; ☑ tour booking 311 681 617; www.hradkarlstejn.cz; adult/child Tour 1 270/180Kč, Tour 2 300/200Kč, Tour 3 150/100Kč; ☺ 9am-6.30pm Jul & Aug, 9.30am-5.30pm Tue-Sun May, Jun & Sep, to 5pm Apr, to 4.30pm Oct, to 4pm Mar, reduced hours Sat & Sun only Dec-Feb) is rightly one of the top attractions in the Czech Republic. This fairytale medieval fortress is in such good shape that it wouldn't look out of place on Disney World's Main Street. Unfortunately, the crowds that throng its courtyards come in theme-park proportions too – in summer it's mobbed with visitors, ice-cream vendors and souvenir stalls.

Thankfully, the peaceful surrounding countryside offers views of Karlštejn's stunning exterior that rival anything you'll see on the inside. If at all possible, visit midweek or out of season, and avoid the queues at the castle ticket office by purchasing your tickets in advance via the link on the castle's website.

Karlštejn is easily reachable by frequent train service that leaves from Praha hlavní nádraží (Prague's main train station).

includes an audio guide dictated by owner William Lobkowicz and his family – this personal connection really brings the displays to life, and makes the palace one of the castle's most interesting attractions.

★ **Strahov Library** HISTORIC BUILDING
(Strahovská knihovna; ☑ 233 107 718; www.strahovskyklaster.cz; Strahovské nádvoří 1; adult/child 120/60Kč; ☺ 9am-noon & 1-5pm; 🚌 22) Strahov Library is the largest monastic library in the country, with two magnificent baroque halls dating from the 17th and 18th centuries. You can peek through the doors but, sadly, you can't go into the halls themselves – it was found that fluctuations in humidity caused by visitors' breath was endangering the frescoes. There's also a display of historical curiosities.

☉ Staré Město

Staré Město – meaning 'Old Town' – is the historic heart of medieval Prague, centred on one of Europe's most spectacular town squares (Old Town Square, or Staroměstské náměstí). The maze of cobbled streets and narrow alleys leading away from Old Town Square is perfect for exploring.

★ **Astronomical Clock** HISTORIC SITE
(Map p678; Staroměstské náměstí; ☺ chimes on the hour 9am-9pm; Ⓜ Staroměstská) Every hour, on the hour, crowds gather beneath the **Old Town Hall Tower** (Věž radnice; Map p678; ☑ 236 002 629; www.staromestskaradnicepraha.cz; adult/child 250/150Kč; ☺ 11am-10pm Mon, 9am-10pm Tue-Sun) to watch the Astronomical Clock in action. Despite a slightly underwhelming

performance that takes only 45 seconds, the clock is one of Europe's best-known tourist attractions, and a 'must-see' for visitors to Prague. After all, it's historic, photogenic and – if you take time to study it – rich in intriguing symbolism.

★ **Church of Our Lady Before Týn** CHURCH
(Kostel Panny Marie před Týnem; Map p678; ☑ 222 318 186; www.tyn.cz; Staroměstské náměstí; suggested donation 25Kč; ☺ 10am-1pm & 3-5pm Tue-Sat, 10am-noon Sun Mar-Dec; Ⓜ Staroměstská) Its distinctive twin Gothic spires make the Týn Church an unmistakable Old Town landmark. Like something out of a 15th-century – and probably slightly cruel – fairy tale, they loom over Old Town Square, decorated with a golden image of the Virgin Mary made in the 1620s from the melted-down Hussite chalice that previously adorned the church.

★ **Municipal House** HISTORIC BUILDING
(Obecní dům; Map p678; ☑ 222 002 101; www.obecnidum.cz; náměstí Republiky 5; guided tour adult/concession/child under 10yr 290/240Kč/free; ☺ public areas 7.30am-11pm, information centre 10am-8pm; Ⓜ Náměstí Republiky, 🚌 6, 8, 15, 26) Restored in the 1990s after decades of neglect, Prague's most exuberantly art-nouveau building is a labour of love, every detail of its design and decoration carefully considered, every painting and sculpture loaded with symbolism. The **restaurant** (Map p678; ☑ 222 002 770; www.francouzskarestaurace.cz; mains 695Kč; ☺ noon-11pm) and **cafe** (Map p678; ☑ 222 002 763; www.kavarnaod.cz; ☺ 7.30am-11pm; 🛈) here are like walk-in

CZECH REPUBLIC AT A GLANCE

Don't Miss

Prague Known as the 'City of a Hundred Spires', Prague is famed for Franz Kafka, the Velvet Revolution and its fine pubs. Unlike battle-scarred Warsaw or Berlin, Prague escaped WWII almost unscathed, and the city centre is a smorgasbord of stunning architecture. There's a maze of medieval lanes to explore, riverside parks, lively bars and beer gardens, jazz clubs, rock venues, museums and art galleries galore.

Czech beer 'Where beer is brewed, life is good', according to an old Czech proverb. Which means that life in the Czech Republic must be good indeed, as the country is awash in pubs and bars both large and small.

Český Krumlov None other than *National Geographic* has dubbed this former medieval stronghold one of the 'world's greatest places', and once you catch a glimpse of the rocky, rambling Renaissance castle (the second-biggest in the country, after Prague), with its mesmerising, multicoloured tower, you'll feel the appeal.

Brno The country's second-biggest city has a vibrant cafe and club scene that easily rivals Prague's, and Brno was a leading centre of experimental architecture in the early-20th century. The Unesco-protected Vila Tugendhat is considered a masterwork of functionalist design.

Kutná Hora This mining town once competed with Prague to be the most important town in Bohemia, growing rich on the silver ore that laced the rocks beneath it. Today it's an attractive town with several fascinating and unusual historical attractions, including a grimly fascinating chapel made up of human bones.

Itineraries

One Week

Three days is just enough time to take in the main attractions of **Prague** and add in a quick day trip. Spend the first two days ambling around the capital's atmospheric Old Town, as well as pretty Malá Strana, across the river, and majestic Prague Castle. Don't miss the city's Jewish Museum and be sure to take an early-morning stroll across Charles Bridge. The ideal day trip from Prague would be to **Kutná Hora** to see the town's spooky bone church at Sedlec Ossuary as well as the rest of the historic buildings there.

Two Weeks

After Prague and Kutná Hora, head south to the achingly picturesque Bohemian town of **Český Krumlov** to see the Renaissance Castle and pretty riverside setting. Spend the rest of your days in the eastern province of Moravia, with at least a day or two in the Moravian capital, **Brno**. The city has lively pubs and impressive historic architecture, including the early-modern masterpiece Vila Tugendhat. Note you'll have to book well in advance to tour the villa.

Essential Food & Drink

Beer The lifeblood of the Czech Republic, there are two main varieties: *světlé* (light) and *tmavy* (dark). The *světlé* is a golden lager-style beer with a crisp, hoppy flavour. Dark beers are sweeter.

Roast Pork The heart of Czech cooking is roast pork with dumplings and sauerkraut (*vepřové s knedlíky a kyselé zelí*).

Goulash A staple on every menu, *guláš* is a stew of cubed beef or pork, served with bread dumplings.

Svíčková It's hard to mess up marinated beef (*svíčková na smetaně*), served in a cream sauce and garnished with lemon and cranberries.

Becherovka The most distinctive of Czech spirits, a bitter-sweet concoction made in the spa town of Karlovy Vary.

Getting Around

Bus Highly affordable and useful for moving between major cities and destinations where train service is poor.

Car Useful for travelling at your own pace or for visiting regions with minimal public transport, though weekend traffic can be a nightmare. Cars can be hired in every major city. Drive on the right.

Train Similar to bus in terms of price and travel time, and convenient, with extensive coverage throughout the country and frequent departures. Buy tickets at train station ticket counters.

When to Go

Prague

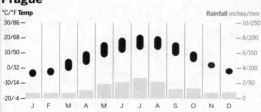

May The annual Prague Spring Festival makes this the capital's most popular month for visitors.

Sep Lovely strolling weather around the country.

Dec *Svařák* (mulled wine) and music at Christmas markets all across the land.

Arriving in Czech Republic

Václav Havel Airport Prague Buses to metro stations Nádraží Veleslavín (No 119) and Zličín (No 100) depart every 10 minutes from 4am to midnight from stops just outside the arrivals terminal (32Kč). A taxi to the city centre costs 600Kč.

Praha hlavní nádraží Prague's main train station is located in the city centre, a short walk from Wenceslas Sq and on metro line C (red); all international rail connections arrive here.

Top Phrases

Hello. Ahoj.

Goodbye. Na shledanou.

Please. Prosím.

Excuse me. Promiňte.

Cheers. Na zdraví!

Resources

CzechTourism (www.czechtourism.com)

Prague City Tourism (www.prague.eu)

Prague Events Calendar (www.pragueeventscalendar.com)

Transport Timetable (http://jizdnirady.idnes.cz)

Set Your Budget

➡ Dorm bed: €12

➡ Self-catering and lunch specials: €12

➡ Admission to major tourist attractions: €10

CENTRAL & EASTERN EUROPE CZECH REPUBLIC AT A GLANCE

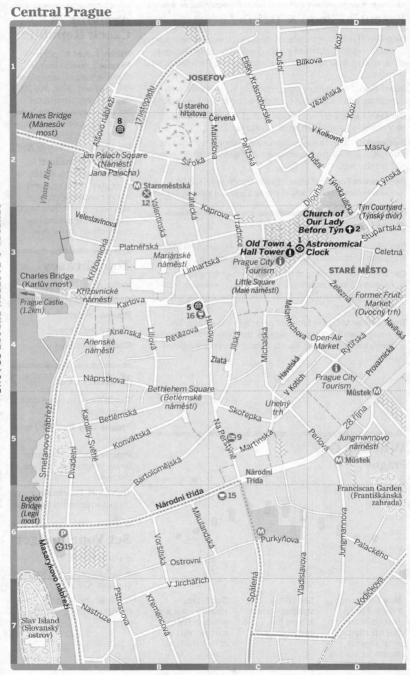

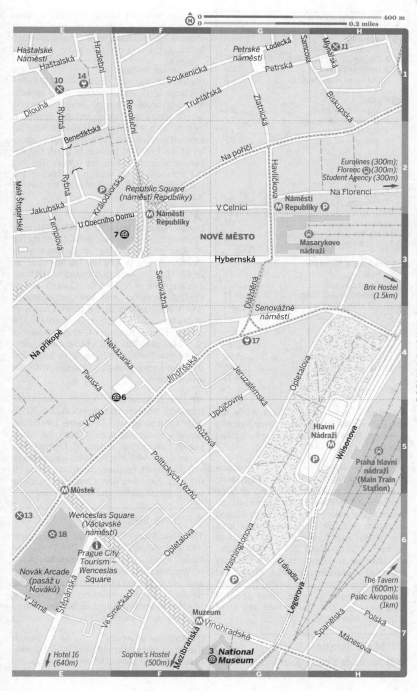

CENTRAL & EASTERN EUROPE PRAGUE

Central Prague

museums of art-nouveau design, while upstairs there are half a dozen sumptuously decorated halls that you can visit by guided tour.

★ **Apple Museum** MUSEUM
(Map p678; ☏ 774 414 775; www.applemuseum.com; Husova 21; adult/child 240/110Kč; ☉ 10am-10pm; Ⓜ Staroměstská) This shrine to all things Apple claims to be the world's biggest collection of Apple products, with at least one of everything made by the company between 1976 and 2012. Sleek white galleries showcase row upon row of beautifully displayed computers, laptops, iPods and iPhones like sacred reliquaries; highlights include the earliest Apple I and Apple II computers, an iPod 'family tree' and Steve Jobs's business cards.

◉ Malá Strana

Malá Strana (the 'Little Quarter') is a charming district of Renaissance palaces and gardens, with an idyllic riverside setting. Prague's scenic centrepiece, the 650-year-old Charles Bridge, links Malá Strana to Staré Město on the far side of the river.

★ **Charles Bridge** BRIDGE
(Karlův most; Map p682; ☉ 24hr; ☐ 2, 17, 18 to Karlovy lázně, 12, 15, 20, 22 to Malostranské náměstí) Strolling across Charles Bridge is everybody's favourite Prague activity. However, by 9am it's a 500m-long fairground, with an army of tourists squeezing through a gauntlet of hawkers and buskers beneath the impassive gaze of the baroque statues that line the parapets. If you want to experience the bridge at its most atmospheric, try to visit it at dawn.

★ **St Nicholas Church** CHURCH
(Kostel sv Mikuláše; Map p682; ☏ 257 534 215; www.stnicholas.cz; Malostranské náměstí 38; adult/child 70/50Kč; ☉ 9am-5pm Mar-Oct, to 4pm Nov-Jan, 9am-5pm Fri-Sun, to 4pm Mon-Thu Feb; ☐ 12, 15, 20, 22) Malá Strana is dominated by the huge green cupola of St Nicholas Church, one of Central Europe's finest baroque buildings. (Don't confuse it with the other Church of St Nicholas on Old Town Square.) On the ceiling, Johann Kracker's 1770 *Apotheosis of St Nicholas* is Europe's largest fresco (clever *trompe l'oeil* techniques have made the painting merge almost seamlessly with the architecture).

★ **John Lennon Wall** HISTORIC SITE
(Map p682; Velkopřevorské náměstí; ☐ 12, 15, 20, 22) After his murder on 8 December 1980, John Lennon became a pacifist hero for many young Czechs. An image of Lennon was painted on a wall in a secluded square opposite the French embassy (there is a niche on the wall that looks like a tombstone), along with political graffiti and Beatles lyrics.

◉ Nové Město

The 'New Town' – new in the 14th century, that is – wraps around the Old Town, and finds a focus in the broad, historic boulevard of Wenceslas Sq. Its sprawl of mostly 19th- and early 20th-century buildings encompasses important museums and galleries, impressive architecture and the city centre's main shopping streets.

★ **National Museum** MUSEUM
(Národní muzeum; Map p678; ☏ 224 497 111; www.nm.cz; Václavské náměstí 68; Ⓜ Muzeum) Looming above Wenceslas Square is the neo-

Renaissance bulk of the National Museum, designed in the 1880s by Josef Schulz as an architectural symbol of the Czech National Revival. Its magnificent interior is a shrine to the cultural, intellectual and scientific history of the Czech Republic. The museum's main building re-opened in 2018 after several years of renovation work.

★ **Mucha Museum** GALLERY
(Muchovo muzeum; Map p678; ☑ 224 216 415; www.mucha.cz; Panská 7; adult/child 240/160Kč; ☉ 10am-6pm; ☒ 3, 5, 6, 9, 14, 24) This fascinating (and busy) museum features the sensuous art-nouveau posters, paintings and decorative panels of Alfons Mucha (1860–1939), as well as many sketches, photographs and other memorabilia. The exhibits include countless artworks showing Mucha's trademark Slavic maidens with flowing hair and piercing blue eyes, bearing symbolic garlands and linden boughs.

★ **Vyšehrad Citadel** FORTRESS
(☑ 261 225 304; www.praha-vysehrad.cz; information centre at V pevnosti 159/5b; admission to grounds free; ☉ grounds 24hr; ☒ Vyšehrad) **FREE**
The Vyšehrad Citadel refers to the complex of buildings and structures atop Vyšehrad Hill that have played an important role in Czech history for over 1000 years as a royal residence, religious centre and military fortress. While most of the surviving structures date from the 18th century, the citadel is still viewed as the city's spiritual home. The sights are spread out over a wide area, with commanding views out over the Vltava and surrounding city.

🛏 Sleeping

★ **Brix Hostel** HOSTEL €
(☑ 222 742 700; www.brixhostel.com; Roháčova 15, Žižkov; dm/d from 250/540Kč; ☒; ☒ 133, 175, 207) Created by a group of friends who all previously worked in other hostels, this place benefits hugely from their experience – everything is focused on making your stay enjoyable, from the warm welcome to the custom-built bunks and clean, modern bathrooms. The hostel's own bar is open 24/7, and is a great place to make new acquaintances.

★ **Sophie's Hostel** HOSTEL €
(☑ 210 011 300; www.sophieshostel.com; Melounova 2; dm/d/apt from 380/1790/2300Kč; ☉☒@☒; ☒ IP Pavlova) This hostel makes a pleasant change from the usual charac-

terless backpacker hive. There's a touch of contemporary style here, with oak-veneer floors and stark, minimalist decor, along with neutral colours, chunky timber and quirky metal-framed beds – the place is famous for its 'designer' showers, with autographed glass screens and huge rainfall shower heads.

Ahoy! Hostel HOSTEL €
(Map p678; ☑ 773 004 003; www.ahoyhostel.com; Na Perštýně 10; dm/tw from 460/1220Kč; @☒; ☒ Národní Třída, ☒ 2, 9, 18, 22) No big signs or branding here, just an inconspicuous card by the blue door at No 10. But inside is a very pleasant, welcoming and peaceful hostel (definitely not for the party crowd), with eager-to-please staff, some self-consciously 'arty' decoration, clean and comfortable six- or eight-bed dorms, and a couple of private twin rooms. Ideal location too.

★ **Hotel 16** HOTEL €€
(☑ 224 920 636; www.hotel16.cz; Kateřinská 16; s/d from 2400/3500Kč; ☉☒@☒; ☒ 4, 6, 10, 16, 22) Hotel 16 is a friendly, family-run little place with just 14 rooms, tucked away in a very quiet corner of town where you're more likely to hear birdsong than traffic. The rooms vary in size and are simply but smartly furnished; the best, at the back, have views onto the peaceful terraced garden. Staff are superb, and can't do enough to help.

🍴 Eating

Traditional Czech cuisine can be heavy, built around meat (usually pork) and accompanied by bread dumplings, all washed down with copious quantities of beer. Most pubs also serve food.

★ **Mistral Café** BISTRO €
(Map p678; ☑ 222 317 737; www.mistralcafe.cz; Valentinská 11; mains 130-250Kč; ☉ 8am-11pm Mon-Fri, from 9am Sat & Sun; ☒☒; ☒ Staroměstská) Is this the coolest bistro in the Old Town? Pale stone, bleached birchwood and potted shrubs make for a clean, crisp, modern look, and the clientele of local students and office workers clearly appreciate the competitively priced, well-prepared food. Fish and chips in crumpled brown paper with lemon and black-pepper mayo – yum!

Lokál CZECH €
(Map p678; ☑ 734 283 874; www.lokal-dlouha. ambi.cz; Dlouhá 33; mains 115-235Kč; ☉ 11am-1am Mon-Sat, to midnight Sun; ☒; ☒ 6, 8, 15, 26) Who'd have thought it possible? A classic

Prague Castle

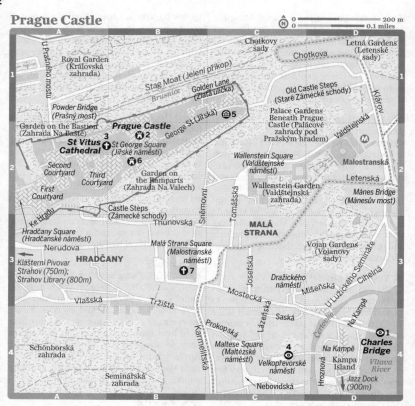

Prague Castle

Czech beer hall (albeit with slick modern styling); excellent *tankové pivo* (tanked Pilsner Urquell); a daily-changing menu of traditional Bohemian dishes; and smiling, efficient, friendly service! Top restaurant chain Ambiente has turned its hand to Czech cuisine, and the result has been so successful that the place is always busy, mostly with locals.

Maso a Kobliha GASTROPUB €
(Map p678; ☏ 224 815 056; www.masoakobliha. cz; Petrská 23; mains 185-210Kč; ◷ 11am-10pm Tue-Sat; ☏; ☒ 3, 8, 14, 24) ✿ Established by the British chef at Sansho, across the street, this pub-style eatery (and butcher shop; the name means 'Meat and Doughnuts') serves hearty pub-style food prepared using locally grown, seasonal, organic produce – it's famous for its Scotch eggs, beef shin pies and freshly made doughnuts filled with vanilla cream. All-day brunch at weekends.

Styl & Interier CAFE €
(Map p678; ☏ 222 543 128; www.stylainterier.cz/ kavarna; Vodičkova 35; mains 100-200Kč; ◷ 10am-10pm Mon-Sat, to 8pm Sun; ☏ ✦; ☒ 3, 5, 6, 9, 14, 24) A passage opposite the Vodičkova entrance to the Lucerna Palace leads to this secret retreat, a rustic cafe with a high-walled garden where local shoppers gather in wicker armchairs beneath the trees to enjoy coffee and cake, or a lunch of lasagne, quiche

and salad, or slow-cooked lamb with red wine gravy. Best to book a table.

The Tavern
BURGERS €

(www.eng.thetavern.cz; Chopinova 26, Vinohrady; burgers 180-230Kč; ⏱11.30am-10pm Mon-Fri, brunch from 11am Sat & Sun; 🗟; Ⓜ Jiřího z Poděbrad, 🚋11, 13) This cosy sit-down burger joint is the dream of a husband-and-wife team of American expats who wanted to create the perfect burger using organic products and free-range, grass-fed beef. Great pulled-pork sandwiches, fries and bourbon-based cocktails too. Reservations are taken (via the website) for dinner on Thursday, Friday and Saturday only.

🍷 Drinking & Nightlife

U Zlatého Tygra
PUB

(Map p678; 🗷222 221 111; www.uzlatehotygra.cz; Husova 17; ⏱3-11pm; Ⓜ Staroměstská) Novelist Bohumil Hrabal's favourite hostelry, the 'Golden Tiger' is one of the few Old Town drinking holes that has hung onto its soul – and its reasonable prices (45Kč per 0.45L of Pilsner Urquell), considering its location close to Old Town Square. A thick fog of cigarette smoke keeps many tourists away.

Klášterní Pivovar Strahov
BREWERY

(Strahov Monastery Brewery; 🗷233 353 155; www.klasterni-pivovar.cz; Strahovské nádvoří 301; ⏱10am-10pm; 🚋22) Dominated by two polished copper brewing kettles, this convivial little pub in Strahov Monastery serves up two varieties of its St Norbert beer – *tmavý* (dark), a rich, tarry brew with a creamy head, and *polotmavý* (amber), a full-bodied, hoppy lager; both cost 65Kč per 0.4L. There's also a strong (6.3% abv) IPA-style beer.

Vinohradský Pivovar
PUB

(🗷222 760 080; www.vinohradskypivovar.cz; Korunní 106, Vinohrady; ⏱11am-midnight; 🗟; 🚋10, 16) This popular and highly recommended neighbourhood pub and restaurant offers its own home-brewed lagers as well as a well-regarded IPA. There's seating on two levels and a large events room at the back for concerts and happenings. The restaurant features classic Czech pub dishes (like *Wienerschnitzel* and pork medallions) at reasonable prices (180Kč to 230Kč). Book in advance for an evening meal.

Bokovka
WINE BAR

(Map p678; 🗷731 492 046; www.bokovka.com; Dlouhá 37; ⏱5pm-1am Mon-Fri, from 3pm Sat; 🚋6, 8, 15, 26) Founded by a syndicate of oenophiles, including film directors Jan Hřebejk and David Ondříček, Bokovka has moved from its original New Town location to this hidden courtyard – look for the red wine droplet sign; the door is opposite it on the right. The crumbling, atmospheric cellar bar is a great place to sample the best of Czech wines.

★ Cross Club
CLUB

(🗷736 535 010; www.crossclub.cz; Plynární 23; admission free-200Kč; ⏱cafe 2pm-2am, club 6pm-5am Sun-Thu, to 7am Fri & Sat; 🗟; Ⓜ Nádraží Holešovice) An industrial club in every sense of the word: the setting in an industrial zone; the thumping music (both DJs and live acts); and the interior, an absolute must-see jumble of gadgets, shafts, cranks and pipes, many of which move and pulsate with light to the music. The program includes occasional live music, theatre performances and art happenings.

★ Vinograf
WINE BAR

(Map p678; 🗷214 214 681; www.vinograf.cz; Senovážné náměstí 23; ⏱11.30am-midnight Mon-Fri, 5pm-midnight Sat & Sun; 🗟; 🚋3, 5, 6, 9, 14, 24) With knowledgeable staff, a relaxed atmosphere and an off-the-beaten-track feel, this appealingly modern wine bar is a great place to discover Moravian wines. There's good finger food to accompany your wine, mostly cheese and charcuterie, with food and wine menus (in Czech and English) on big blackboards behind the bar. Very busy at weekends, when it's worth booking a table.

Cafe Louvre
CAFE

(Map p678; 🗷224 930 949; www.cafelouvre.cz; 1st fl, Národní třída 22; ⏱8am-11.30pm Mon-Fri, 9am-11.30pm Sat & Sun; 🚋2, 9, 18, 22) The French-style Cafe Louvre is arguably the most amenable of Prague's grand cafes, as popular today as it was in the early 1900s when it was frequented by the likes of Franz Kafka and Albert Einstein. The atmosphere is wonderfully olde-worlde, and it serves good food as well as coffee. Check out the billiard hall, and the ground-floor art gallery.

☆ Entertainment

Live Music

★ Palác Akropolis
LIVE MUSIC

(🗷296 330 913; www.palacakropolis.cz; Kubelíkova 27, Žižkov; tickets free-250Kč; ⏱club 7pm-5am; 🗟; 🚋5, 9, 15, 26) The Akropolis is a Prague institution, a smoky, labyrinthine, sticky-floored shrine to alternative music and drama. Its various performance spaces host a smorgasbord of musical and cultural events, from DJs to string quartets to Macedonian Roma bands to local rock gods to visiting talent – Marianne Faithfull, the Flaming Lips and the Strokes have all played here.

Jazz Dock JAZZ
(☑774 058 838; www.jazzdock.cz; Janáčkovo nábřeží 2, Smíchov; tickets 150-300Kč; ☉3pm-late Mon-Thu, from 1pm Fri-Sun Apr-Sep, 5pm-late Mon-Thu, from 3pm Fri-Sun Oct-Mar; ☎; Ⓜ Anděl, ☒9, 12, 15, 20) Most of Prague's jazz clubs are smoky cellar affairs, but this riverside club is a definite step up, with clean, modern decor and a decidedly romantic view out over the Vltava. It draws some of the best local talent and occasional international acts. Go early or book to get a good table. Shows normally begin at 7pm and 10pm.

Lucerna Music Bar LIVE MUSIC
(Map p678; ☑224 217 108; www.musicbar.cz; Palác Lucerna, Vodičkova 36; cover 100-500Kč; ☉hours vary; Ⓜ Můstek) Nostalgia reigns supreme at this atmospheric old theatre, now looking a little dog-eared. It hosts a hugely popular 1980s and '90s video party from 9pm every Friday and Saturday night, with crowds of young locals bopping along to Duran Duran and Gary Numan.

Performing Arts

National Theatre OPERA, BALLET
(Národní divadlo; Map p678; ☑224 901 448; www.narodni-divadlo.cz; Národní třída 2; tickets 100-1290Kč; ☉box offices 10am-6pm; ☒2, 9, 18, 22) The much-loved National Theatre provides a stage for traditional opera, drama and ballet by the likes of Smetana, Shakespeare and Tchaikovsky, sharing the program alongside more modern works by composers and playwrights such as Philip Glass and John Osborne. The box offices are in the Nový síň building next door, in the Kolowrat Palace (opposite the Estates Theatre) and at the State Opera.

Dvořák Hall CONCERT VENUE
(Dvořákova síň; Map p678; ☑227 059 227; www.ceskafilharmonie.cz; náměstí Jana Palacha 1, Rudolfinum; tickets 100-900Kč; ☉box office 10am-6pm Mon-Fri Sept-Jun, to 3pm Jul & Aug; Ⓜ Staroměstská) The Dvořák Hall in the neo-Renaissance **Rudolfinum** (Map p678; Alšovo nábřeží 12; ☒2, 17, 18) is home to the world-renowned Czech Philharmonic Or-chestra (Česká filharmonie). Sit back and be impressed by some of the best classical musicians in Prague.

Smetana Hall CLASSICAL MUSIC
(Smetanova síň; Map p678; ☑222 002 101; www.obecnidum.cz; náměstí Republiky 5, Municipal House; tickets 400-900Kč; ☉box office 10am-6pm; Ⓜ Náměstí Republiky) The Smetana Hall, centrepiece of the stunning Municipal House (p675), is the city's largest concert hall, with seating for 1200 beneath an art-nouveau glass dome. The stage is framed by sculptures representing the Vyšehrad legend (to the right) and Slavonic dances (to the left). This is the home venue of the Prague Symphony Orchestra (Symfonický orchestr hlavního města Prahy; www.fok.cz), and also stages performances of folk dance and music.

ℹ️ Information

Prague City Tourism (www.prague.eu; ☑221 714 714) branches are scattered around the town, including at both airport arrivals terminals at Václav Havel Airport Prague. Offices are good sources of maps and general information; they also sell Prague Card (www.praguecard.com) discount cards and can book guides and tours.

Prague City Tourism – Old Town Hall (Prague Welcome; Map p678; Staroměstské náměstí 5, Old Town Hall; ☉9am-7pm Mar-Dec, to 6pm Jan & Feb; Ⓜ Staroměstská) The busiest of the Prague City Tourism branches occupies the ground floor of the Old Town Hall.

Prague City Tourism – Rytířská (Prague Welcome; Map p678; Rytířská 12, Staré Město; ☉9am-7pm; Ⓜ Můstek) In addition to the usual services, such as handing out maps and advice, this office is a good place to buy tickets for various events around town.

Prague City Tourism – Wenceslas Square (Map p678; Václavské náměstí 42; ☉10am-6pm; Ⓜ Můstek, Muzeum) Handy tourist information kiosk on the busiest square in the city. Hands out free maps and advice.

ℹ️ Getting There & Away

See p691 for details on the main overland and air routes to Prague and the Czech Republic.

ℹ️ Getting Around

TO/FROM THE AIRPORT

From the airport, buy a full-price public transport ticket (32Kč) from the **Prague Public Transport Authority** (DPP; ☑296 191 817; www.dpp.cz; ☉7am-9pm) desk and take bus

119 (20 minutes; every 10 minutes from 4am to midnight) to the end station at metro line A, then continue by metro into the city centre (another 10 to 15 minutes; no new ticket needed).

There's also an Airport Express bus (AE, 60Kč, 35 minutes, every 30 minutes from 5am to 10pm) that runs to Praha hlavní nádraží (Prague's main train station), where you can connect to metro line C (buy ticket from driver; luggage goes free).

AAA Radio Taxi (☑14014, 222 333 222; www.aaataxi.cz) operates a 24-hour taxi service, charging around 500Kč to 600Kč to get to the centre of Prague.

PUBLIC TRANSPORT

Prague has an integrated metro, tram and bus network – tickets are valid on all types of transport, and for transfers between them. A basic ticket (32Kč) is good for 90 minutes – validate tickets once in yellow machines on trams and buses, and at the entrance to metro stations. Convenient one- and three-day passes are also available.

Bohemia

Beyond the apartment blocks of Prague's outer suburbs, the city gives way to the surprisingly green hinterland of Bohemia, a land of rolling hills, rich farmland and thick forests dotted with castles, chateaux and picturesque towns. Rural and rustic, yet mostly within two to three hours' drive of the capital, the Czech Republic's western province has for centuries provided an escape for generations of city-dwellers.

Kutná Hora

Enriched by the silver ore that veined the surrounding hills, the medieval city of Kutná Hora became the seat of Wenceslas II's royal mint in 1308, producing silver *groschen* that were then the hard currency of Central Europe. Boom-time Kutná Hora rivalled Prague in importance, but by the 16th century the mines began to run dry, and the town's demise was hastened by the Thirty Years' War and a devastating fire in 1770. The town became a Unesco World Heritage site in 1996, luring visitors with a smorgasbord of historic sights, including an eerie monastery crafted entirely from human bones. Most visitors come here as a day trip from Prague.

Sights

★ Sedlec Ossuary — CHURCH

(Kostnice; ☑information centre 326 551 049; www.ossuary.eu; Zámecká 127; adult/concession 90/60Kč; ☉8am-6pm Mon-Sat, 9am-6pm Sun Apr-Sep, 9am-5pm Mar & Oct, 9am-4pm Nov-Feb) When the Schwarzenbergs purchased Sedlec monastery (2.5km northeast of the town centre) in 1870 they allowed local woodcarver František Rint to get creative with the bones piled in the crypt (the remains of around 40,000 people), resulting in this remarkable 'bone church'. Garlands of skulls and femurs are strung from the vaulted ceiling like Addams Family Christmas decorations, while in the centre dangles a vast chandelier containing at least one of each bone in the human body.

★ Cathedral of St Barbara — CHURCH

(Chrám sv Barbora; ☑327 515 796; www.khfarnost.cz; Barborská; adult/concession 120/50Kč; ☉9am-6pm Apr-Oct, 10am-5pm Nov–mid-Jan & Mar, 10am-4pm mid-Jan–Feb) Kutná Hora's greatest monument is the Gothic Cathedral of St Barbara. Rivalling Prague's St Vitus in size and magnificence, its soaring nave culminates in elegant, six-petalled ribbed vaulting, and the ambulatory chapels preserve original 15th-century frescoes, some of them showing miners at work. Take a walk around the outside of the church; the terrace at the eastern end enjoys the finest view in town.

Czech Silver Museum — MUSEUM

(České muzeum stříbra; ☑327 512 159; www.cms-kh.cz; Barborská 28; adult/concession Tour 1 70/40Kč, Tour 2 130/90Kč, combined 150/100Kč; ☉10am-6pm Jul & Aug, 9am-6pm May, Jun & Sep, 9am-5pm Apr & Oct, 10am-4pm Nov, closed Mon year-round) Originally part of the town's fortifications, the Hrádek (Little Castle) was rebuilt in the 15th century as the residence of Jan Smíšek, administrator of the royal mines, who grew rich from silver mined illegally right under the building. It now houses the Czech Silver Museum. Visiting is by guided tour, which includes the chance to visit an ancient silver mine.

✗ Eating

Pivnice Dačický — PUB FOOD €€

(☑327 512 248; www.dacicky.com; Rakova 8; mains 160-350Kč; ☉11am-10pm Sun-Thu, to 11pm Fri & Sat; ☎⊛) Get some froth on your moustache at this old-fashioned, wood-panelled Bohemian beer hall, where you can dine on dumplings and choose from five draught beers including Pilsner Urquell, Primátor yeast beer and local Kutná Hora lager. Popular with coach parties so book ahead.

ⓘ Information

Kutná Hora Tourist Office (Informační centrum; ☎ 327 512 378; www.destinace.kutnahora.cz; Palackého náměstí 377; ◷ 9am-6pm Apr-Sep, 9am-5pm Mon-Fri, 10am-4pm Sat & Sun Oct-Mar) Books accommodation, rents bicycles (per day 220Kč; April to October only) and offers internet access (per minute 1Kč, minimum 15Kč).

ⓘ Getting There & Away

There are direct trains from Prague's main train station to Kutná Hora's main station every two hours (209Kč return, 55 minutes). It's a 10-minute walk from here to Sedlec Ossuary, and a further 2.5km (30 minutes) to the Old Town.

There are hourly buses that run on weekdays (three or four on Saturday) from Háje bus station on the southern edge of Prague to Kutná Hora (136Kč return, 1¾ hours); the train is a better bet.

Český Krumlov

POP 61,100

Český Krumlov, in Bohemia's deep south, is one of the most picturesque towns in Europe. It's a little like Prague in miniature – a Unesco World Heritage site with a stunning castle above the Vltava River, an old town square, Renaissance and baroque architecture, and hordes of tourists milling through the streets – but all on a smaller scale; you can walk from one side of town to the other in 20 minutes. There are plenty of lively bars and riverside picnic spots; in summer it's a popular hang-out for backpackers.

◉ Sights

★**Český Krumlov State Castle** CASTLE
(☎ 380 704 721; www.zamek-ceskykrumlov.eu; Zámek 59; adult/concession Tour 1 320/220Kč, Tour 2 240/170Kč, Theatre Tour 350/250Kč; ◷ 9am-5pm Tue-Sun Jun-Aug, to 4pm Apr, May, Sep & Oct) Český Krumlov's striking Renaissance castle, occupying a promontory high above the town, began life in the 13th century. It acquired its present appearance in the 16th to 18th centuries under the stewardship of the noble Rožmberk and Schwarzenberg families. The interiors are accessible by guided tour only, though you can stroll the grounds on your own.

Castle Museum & Tower MUSEUM, TOWER
(☎ 380 704 721; www.zamek-ceskykrumlov.eu; Zámek 59; museum adult/child 100/70Kč, tower 100/70Kč; ◷ 9am-5pm Jun-Aug, to 4pm Apr, May, Sep & Oct, to 3pm Tue-Sun Nov-Mar) Located within the castle complex, this small museum and adjoining tower is an ideal option if you don't have the time or energy for a full castle tour. Through a series of rooms, the museum traces the castle's history from its origins to the present day. Climb the tower for the perfect photo ops of the town below.

Egon Schiele Art Centrum MUSEUM
(☎ 380 704 011; www.schieleartcentrum.cz; Široká 71; adult/child under 6yr 180Kč/free; ◷ 10am-6pm Tue-Sun Apr-Dec) This excellent private gallery houses a small retrospective of the controversial Viennese painter Egon Schiele (1890–1918), who lived in Krumlov in 1911, and raised the ire of the townsfolk by hiring young girls as nude models. For this and other sins he was eventually driven out. The centre also houses interesting temporary exhibitions.

⌨ Sleeping

★**Krumlov House** HOSTEL €
(☎ 728 287 919; www.krumlovhostel.com; Rooseveltova 68; dm/d/tr 435/1035/1235Kč; ☻@☺) 🖉 Perched above the river, Krumlov House is friendly and comfortable, and has plenty of books, DVDs and local information to feed your inner wanderer. Accommodation is in a six-bed en suite dorm as well as private double and triple rooms or private, self-catered apartments. The owners are English-speaking and traveller-friendly.

★**Hotel Garni Myší Díra** HOTEL €€
(☎ 380 712 853; http://cz.ubytovani.ceskykrumlov-info.cz; Rooseveltova 28; d/tr 2497/3007Kč; P☺) This place has a superb location overlooking the river, and bright, spacious rooms with lots of pale wood and quirky handmade furniture; room No 12, with a huge corner bath and naughty decorations on the bed, is our favourite. Limited parking in front of the hotel costs 190Kč.

U Malého Vítka HOTEL €€
(☎ 380 711 925; www.vitekhotel.cz; Radnicni 27; s/d 1100/1700Kč; P☺) We like this small hotel in the heart of the Old Town. The simple room furnishings are of high-quality, hand-crafted wood, and each room is named

Český Krumlov

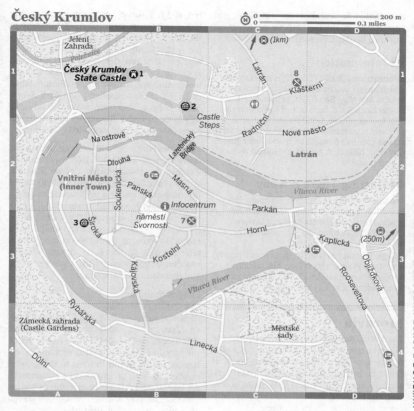

N 0 — 200 m
0 — 0.1 miles

Jelení Zahrada

Český Krumlov State Castle 1

2

Castle Steps

Na ostrově

Lazebnický Bridge

Dlouhá

Vnitřní Město (Inner Town)

Soukenická

Panská

6

Masná

Latrán

8
Klášterní

Radniční

Nové město

Latrán

Vltava River

3

Široká

Infocentrum

náměstí Svornosti

7

Parkán

Horní

Kaplická

(250m)

Kájovská

Kostelní

4

Rybářská

Zámecká zahrada (Castle Gardens)

Vltava River

Linecká

Městské sady

Rooseveltova

Obližáková

Dlní

5

after a traditional Czech fairy-tale character. The downstairs restaurant and cafe are very good too.

Eating

★ Nonna Gina   ITALIAN €
(☎ 380 717 187; www.pizzerianonnagina.wz.cz; Klášteriní 52; mains 100-200Kč; ⊙ 11am-11pm) Authentic Italian flavours from the Massaro family feature at this long-established pizzeria, where the quality of food and service knocks the socks off more expensive restaurants. Superb antipasti, great pizza and Italian wines at surprisingly low prices make for a memorable meal. Grab an outdoor table and pretend you're in Naples, or retreat to the snug and intimate upstairs dining room.

★ Krčma v Šatlavské   CZECH €€
(☎ 380 713 344; www.satlava.cz; Horní 157; mains 150-345Kč; ⊙ 11am-midnight) This medieval

barbecue cellar is hugely popular with visitors and your table mates are much more likely to be from Austria or China than from the town itself, but the grilled meats served up with gusto in a funky labyrinth illuminated by candles are excellent and perfectly in character with Český Krumlov. Advance booking is essential.

ℹ️ Information

Infocentrum (📞 380 704 622; www.ckrumlov. info; náměstí Svornosti 2; ⊙ 9am-7pm Jun-Aug, to 6pm Apr, May, Sep & Oct, to 5pm Nov-Mar, closed lunch Sat & Sun) One of the country's best tourist offices. Good source for transport and accommodation info, maps, internet access (per five minutes 5Kč) and audio guides (per hour 100Kč). A guide for disabled visitors is also available.

ℹ️ Getting There & Away

The train from Prague (275Kč, 3½ hours, four to six daily) requires a change in České Budějovice. There's regular train service between České Budějovice and Český Krumlov (51Kč, 45 minutes).

RegioJet coaches (200Kč, three hours, hourly) leave from Prague's Na Knížecí bus station at Anděl metro station (Line B). Book in advance for weekends or in July and August.

Moravia

The Czech Republic's easternmost province, Moravia is yin to Bohemia's yang. If Bohemians love beer, Moravians love wine. If Bohemia is towns and cities, Moravia is rolling hills and pretty landscapes. Once you've seen the best of Bohemia, head east for a different side of the Czech Republic.

Brno

POP 370,440

Among Czechs, Moravia's capital (and the country's second-biggest city) has a little bit of a dull rep: a likeable enough place where not much actually happens. The reality, though, is very different. Tens of thousands of students ensure lively cafe and club scenes that easily rival Prague's. Brno was one of the leading centres of experimental architecture in the early 20th century, and the Unesco-protected Vila Tugendhat is considered a masterwork of functionalist design.

◎ Sights

⭐ **Vila Tugendhat**   ARCHITECTURE
(Villa Tugendhat; 📞 515 511 015; www.tugendhat. eu; Černopolni 45; adult/concession basic tour 300/180Kč, extended tour 350/210Kč; ⊙ 10am-6pm Tue-Sun Mar-Dec, 9am-5pm Wed-Sun Jan & Feb; 🚊 3, 5, 9) Brno had a reputation in the 1920s as a centre for modern architecture in the Bauhaus style. Arguably the finest example is this family villa, designed by modern master Mies van der Rohe for Greta and Fritz Tugendhat in 1930. The house was the inspiration for British author Simon Mawer in his 2009 bestseller *The Glass Room*. Entry is by guided tour booked in advance by phone or email. Two tours are available: basic (one hour) and extended (1½ hours).

Old Town Hall   HISTORIC BUILDING
(Stará radnice; 📞 542 427 150; www.ticbrno.cz; Radnická 8; tower adult/concession 70/40Kč; ⊙ 10am-6pm; 🚊 4, 8, 9) No visit to Brno would be complete without a peek inside the city's medieval Old Town Hall, parts of which date back to the 13th century. The tourist office (p689) is here, plus oddities including a crocodile hanging from the ceiling (known affectionately as the Brno 'dragon') and a wooden wagon wheel with a unique story. You can also climb the tower.

**Labyrinth under
the Cabbage Market**   TUNNELS
(Brněnské podzemí; 📞 778 454 379; www.ticbrno. cz; Zelný trh 21; adult/concession 160/80Kč; ⊙ 9am-6pm Tue-Sun; 🚊 4, 8, 9) In recent years, the city has opened several sections of extensive underground tunnels to the general public. This tour takes around 40 minutes to explore several cellars situated 6m to 8m below the Cabbage Market, which has served as a food market for centuries. The cellars were built for two purposes: to store goods and to hide in during wars.

Capuchin Monastery   CEMETERY
(Kapucínský klášter; 📞 511 145 796; www.kapucini. cz; Kapucínské náměstí; adult/concession 70/35Kč; ⊙ 9am-noon & 1-6pm Mon-Sat, 11am-5pm Sun Apr-Oct, 10am-4pm Mon-Sat, 11am-4.30pm Sun Nov-Mar; 🚊 4, 8, 9) One of the city's leading attractions is this ghoulish cellar crypt that holds the mummified remains of several city noblemen from the 18th century. Apparently, the dry, well-ventilated crypt has the natural ability to turn dead bodies into mummies. Up to 150 cadavers were deposited here prior to 1784, the desiccated corpses including monks, abbots and local notables.

🛏️ Sleeping

⭐ **Hostel Mitte**   HOSTEL €
(📞 734 622 340; www.hostelmitte.com; Panská 22; dm 405Kč, s/d 930/1290Kč, all incl breakfast;

@ 📶; 🛏4, 8, 9) Set in the heart of the Old Town, this clean and stylish hostel smells and looks brand new. The rooms are named after famous Moravians (eg Milan Kundera) or famous events (Austerlitz) and decorated accordingly. There are six-bed dorms and private singles and doubles. Cute cafe on the ground floor.

Hotel Europa
HOTEL €€

(📞515 143 100; www.hotel-europa-brno.cz; třída kpt Jaroše 27; s/d 1249/1402Kč; P 🐕 📶; 🛏3, 5, 9) Set in a quiet neighbourhood a 10-minute walk from the city centre, this self-proclaimed 'art' hotel (presumably for the futuristic lobby furniture) offers clean and tastefully furnished modern rooms in a historic 19th-century building. Rooms come in 'standard' and more expensive 'superior', with the chief difference being size. There is free parking out the front and in the courtyard.

✗ Eating

Annapurna
INDIAN €

(📞774 995 122; www.indicka-restaurace-annapurna.cz; Josefská 14; mains 140-220Kč; ⊙10.30am-10.30pm Mon-Thu, to 11pm Fri, noon-11pm Sat, to 10.30pm Sun; 📷; 🛏1, 2, 4, 8, 9, 10, 12) The weekday lunch specials (110Kč for soup, main, rice and salad) are absolutely mobbed at this cramped space not far from the train station. People come for the very good Indian food and prompt service. It's less crowded at other times but still worth a trip for curries and lots of varied vegetarian dishes.

Bistro Franz
CZECH €€

(📞720 113 502; www.bistrofranz.cz; Veveří 14; mains 155-220Kč; ⊙8am-10pm Mon-Fri, 10am-10pm Sat, 10am-9pm Sun; 📶📷; 🛏1, 3, 9, 11, 12) Colourfully retro Bistro Franz is one of a new generation of restaurants that focuses on locally sourced, organic ingredients. The philosophy extends to the relatively simple menu of soups, baked chicken drumsticks, curried lentils and other student-friendly food. The wine is carefully chosen and the coffee is sustainably grown. Excellent choice for morning coffee and breakfast.

Drinking & Nightlife

Bar, Který Neexistuje
COCKTAIL BAR

(📞734 878 602; www.barkteryneexistuje.cz; Dvořákova 1; ⊙5pm-2am Sun-Tue, to 3am Wed & Thu, to 4am Fri & Sat; 📶; 🛏4, 8, 9) 'The bar that doesn't exist' boasts a long, beautiful bar backed by every bottle of booze imaginable. It anchors a row of popular, student-oriented bars along trendy Dvořákova. For a bar that 'doesn't exist', it gets quite crowded, so it's best to book ahead.

★ Cafe Podnebi
CAFE

(📞542 211 372; www.podnebi.cz; Údolní 5; ⊙8am-midnight Mon-Fri, from 9am Sat & Sun; 📶📷; 🛏4) This homey, student-oriented cafe is famous citywide for its excellent hot chocolate, but it also serves very good espresso drinks. There are plenty of baked goods and sweets to snack on. In summer the garden terrace is a hidden oasis, and there's a small play area for kids.

❶ Information

Tourist Information Centre (TIC Brno; 📞542 427 150; www.gotobrno.cz; Radnická 8, Old Town Hall; ⊙8.30am-6pm Mon-Fri, 9am-6pm Sat & Sun) Brno's main tourist office is located within the Old Town Hall complex. The office has loads of great information on the city in English, including events calendars and walking maps, and staff can help find accommodation. Lots of material on the city's rich architectural heritage is also available, as well as self-guided tours. There's a free computer for checking emails.

❶ Getting There & Away

Express trains to Brno depart Prague's main station, Praha hlavní nádraží, every couple of hours during the day (220Kč, three hours). Brno is a handy junction for onward train travel to Vienna (220Kč, two hours) and Bratislava (210Kč, 1½ hours).

Buses depart Prague's Florenc bus station hourly for Brno (200Kč, 2½ hours). Brno has two bus stations. Yellow RegioJet (Student Agency) buses use the small bus stop in front of the main train station, while most other buses use the Zvonařka bus station, located behind the train station.

Czech Republic Survival Guide

❶ Directory A–Z

ACCOMMODATION

The Czech Republic offers a wide range of accommodation options, from budget hostels and pensions to international chains and sharply styled boutique hotels.

➜ Prague, Brno and Český Krumlov all have backpacker-oriented hostels. Dorm bed prices vary according to the season, with the highest rates over holidays and in summer.

➡ The **Czech Youth Hostel Association** (www.czechhostels.com) is a handy website for scouting hostels and booking rooms.

➡ Campsites are normally open from May to September and charge from 60Kč to 120Kč per person. Camping on public land is prohibited.

MONEY

➡ Banks are the best places to exchange cash. They normally charge around a 2% commission with a 50Kč minimum.

➡ The easiest and cheapest way to carry money is in the form of a credit or debit card from your bank, which you can use to withdraw cash either from an ATM or over the counter in a bank.

➡ Avoid private exchange booths *(směnárna)* in the main tourist areas. They lure you in with attractive-looking exchange rates that quickly get eaten up in hidden fees.

OPENING HOURS

Banks 9am to 5pm Monday to Friday

Bars 11am to 1am Tuesday to Saturday; shorter hours Sunday and Monday.

Restaurants 11am to 11pm daily; many kitchens close by 10pm.

Shops 9am to 6pm Monday to Friday, 9am to 1pm Saturday (varies).

PUBLIC HOLIDAYS

New Year's Day 1 January

Easter Monday March/April

Labour Day 1 May

Liberation Day 8 May

Sts Cyril & Methodius Day 5 July

Jan Hus Day 6 July

Czech Statehood Day 28 September

Republic Day 28 October

Struggle for Freedom & Democracy Day 17 November

Christmas Eve 24 December

Christmas Day 25 December

St Stephen's Day 26 December

TELEPHONE

➡ All Czech telephone numbers, both landline and mobile (cell), have nine digits. There are no city or area codes, so to call any Czech number, simply dial the nine-digit number.

➡ To call abroad from the Czech Republic, dial the international access code (00), then the country code, then the area code (minus any initial zero) and the number. To dial the Czech Republic from abroad, dial your country's international access code, then 420 (the Czech Republic country code) and the unique nine-digit local number.

➡ Mobile phones use the GSM 900/1800 system. Czech SIM cards can be used in European and Australian mobile phones. Standard North American GSM1900 phones will not work, though dual-band GSM 1900/900 phones will.

Wi-fi

Nearly every hostel and hotel will have free wi-fi available. In addition, cafes, restaurants and bars will usually offer free wi-fi for customers.

WORTH A TRIP

SLOVAKIA

Right in the heart of Europe, Slovakia is a land of castles and mountains, occasionally interrupted by concrete sprawl. Now 25 years after Czechoslovakia's break-up, Slovakia has emerged as a self-assured, independent nation. Capital city Bratislava draws the most visitors, thanks to its excellent nightlife, resplendent old town and sheer ease of access from around Europe. Beyond Bratislava are countless gingerbread-style villages, a clear sign that modern Slovakia still reveres its folk traditions.

Start your exploration in **Bratislava**, where the city's charming Old Town (Staré Mesto) is filled with narrow pedestrian streets of pastel-coloured 18th-century buildings and myriad pavement cafes, all under the watchful gaze of the city's solemn castle.

From Bratislava, head north and east to the **High Tatras**, where you'll find true Alpine peaks, seemingly in the middle of nowhere. As you look upon the snow-strewn jagged mountains rising like an apparition east of Liptovský Mikuláš, you may think you're imagining things. But there they are indeed. The High Tatras are undoubtedly where adventure junkies head, though the mountains have a gentle side, too. Unwind in spa-and-lake getaway **Štrbské Pleso**, or make merry at the lesser-touristed eastern edge of the range, the **Belá Tatras**, where highlander folk culture comes to the fore.

Bratislava is well served by international rail, with frequent connections to Vienna (one hour, hourly), Prague (4¼ hours, six daily) and Budapest (2¾ hours, six daily). Rail is also the main way to get around Slovakia.

ℹ Getting There & Away

Prague sits at the heart of Europe and is well served by air, road and rail.

BORDER CROSSINGS

The Czech Republic has border crossings with Germany, Poland, Slovakia and Austria. These are all EU-member states within the EU's Schengen Zone, meaning there are no passport or customs checks, though international travellers are always expected to carry their passports.

AIR

Václav Havel Airport Prague (Prague Ruzyně International Airport; ☑ 220 111 888; www.prg.aero; K letišti 6, Ruzyně; ☎; 🚌 100, 119), 17km west of the city centre, is the main international gateway to the Czech Republic and the hub for the national carrier **Czech Airlines** (www.csa.com), which operates direct flights to Prague from many European cities.

The airport has two terminals: Terminal 1 for flights to/from non–Schengen Zone countries (including the UK, Ireland and countries outside Europe); Terminal 2 for flights to/from Schengen Zone countries (most EU nations plus Switzerland, Iceland and Norway).

LAND

Four-lane highways link points in both southern and eastern Germany to Prague, making driving in from here very easy. There are also good road connections with Poland, Austria and Slovakia.

Bus

Several bus companies offer coach services connecting Prague to cities around Europe. Nearly all international buses (and most domestic services) use the renovated and user-friendly **Florenc bus station** (ÚAN Praha Florenc; ☑ 900 144 444; www.florenc.cz; Křižíkova 2110/2b, Karlín; ☑ 5am-midnight; ☎; Ⓜ Florenc).

International bus operators include the excellent **RegioJet,** (☑ bus information 841 101 101, info 800 100 300; www.studentagency.cz; Křižíkova 2110/2b, ÚAN Praha Florenc; ☑ 5.30am-10.20pm) formerly known as Student Agency, and **Eurolines** (☑ 731 222 111; www.elines.cz; Křižíkova 2110/2b, ÚAN Praha Florenc; ☑ 6.30am-7pm; ☎; Ⓜ Florenc); both have offices at Florenc bus station, or you can buy tickets online.

Train

The Czech Republic is well integrated into European rail networks. **České dráhy** (ČD, Czech Rail; ☑ 221 111 122; www.cd.cz), the Czech state rail operator, sells tickets for international destinations.

For Prague, nearly all domestic and international trains arrive at **Praha hlavní nádraží** (Prague Main Train Station; ☑ 221 111 122; www.cd.cz; Wilsonova 8, Nové Město; ☑ 3.30am-12.30am; Ⓜ Hlavní nádraží), which is located on metro line C (red). Major international rail connections linking Prague to Bratislava, Vienna and Budapest also pass through Brno.

For outbound travel from Prague, buy tickets at ticket counters on the lower level of the main station.

ℹ Getting Around

The Czech Republic is well served by train and bus.

In Prague, most trains arrive at and depart from the main station, Praha hlavní nádraží. In other cities, train stations are generally located near the centre and within walking distance of sights and attractions.

Buses in Prague generally use the main Florenc bus station. RegioJet, formerly known as Student Agency, is a reliable domestic bus operator and runs regularly from Prague to Český Krumlov and Brno, among many other destinations.

ℹ **PRICE RANGES**

The following price ranges refer to the cost of a standard double room per night in high season.

€ less than 1600Kč

€€ 1600Kč to 3700Kč

€€€ more than 3700Kč

The following price ranges refer to the price of a main course at dinner:

€ less than 200Kč

€€ 200Kč to 500Kč

€€€ more than 500Kč

POLAND

Warsaw

POP 1.74 MILLION

Once you've travelled around Poland, you realise this: Warsaw is different. Rather than being centred on an old market square, the capital is spread across a broad area with diverse architecture: restored Gothic, communist concrete, modern glass and steel. Warsaw has suffered the worst history could throw at it, including virtual destruction at the end of World War II – and survived. As a result, it's a fascinating collection of neighbourhoods and landmarks.

POLAND AT A GLANCE

Don't Miss

Stately Kraków A unique atmosphere drifts through the attractive streets and squares of this former royal capital, with its heady blend of history and harmonious architecture. From the vast Rynek Główny, Europe's largest medieval market square, to the magnificent Wawel Castle on a hill above the Old Town, every part of the city is fascinating.

Warsaw's museums & palaces Poland's capital has an extravagantly dramatic history, and its best museums reflect that complex past. The city's darkest hour in the revolt against Nazi German rule is powerfully retold at the Warsaw Rising Museum, while Poland's long Jewish presence is related with energy at the Museum of the History of Polish Jews.

Malbork Castle Medieval monster mother ship of the Teutonic order, Gothic blockbuster Malbork Castle is a mountain of bricks held together by a lake of mortar. It was home to the all-powerful order's grand master and later to visiting Polish monarchs.

Nightlife in Kraków's Kazimierz Once a lively blend of both Jewish and Christian cultures, the western half of the Kraków district of Kazimierz has in recent years become one of the city's nightlife hubs. Hidden among its narrow streets and distressed facades are numerous small bars, ranging from grungy to glamorous.

Auschwitz-Birkenau This former extermination camp, established by the Nazi German military occupiers in 1941, is a grim reminder of part of one of history's greatest genocides, the killing of more than a million people here in the pursuit of Nazi ideology. Today it's a museum and memorial to the victims.

Itineraries

Three Days

An itinerary of three days allows for exploration of either Kraków or Warsaw, but not both. If you choose **Kraków**, on the first day, focus on the Old Town and don't miss the Rynek Underground museum and, naturally, towering St Mary's Basilica. For the second day, head up to historic Wawel Royal Castle and then go for a walk through atmospheric Kazimierz. For the third day, plan a side trip to the former Nazi German extermination camp at **Auschwitz-Birkenau**.

One Week

A full week allows for a more relaxed appreciation of both Kraków and **Warsaw**. After Kraków, spend most of the rest of your time in Poland's lively capital. Enjoy the fully reconstructed Old Town and stroll down elegant Nowy Świat. Leave at least a day for museum-hopping, particularly to the breathtaking Warsaw Rising Museum or newer attractions like the Chopin Museum and the Museum of the History of Polish Jews. For a longish day trip or overnight, consider a train journey to see **Malbork's** show-stoppingly massive castle.

Essential Food & Drink

Pierogi Tasty square-shaped dumplings made from dough and stuffed with anything from cottage cheese, potato and onion to minced meat, cabbage and fruit.

Kiełbasa What would a trip to Poland be without sampling the country's signature sausage? Kiełbasa is often served with brown bread and mustard.

Pork The main event is almost always *wieprzowina* (pork) and Poles have come up with delicious ways to prepare it: *golonka* is an oversized portion of pig's knuckle, served with horseradish and sauerkraut.

Barszcz We know this red-beetroot soup as 'borscht', but Poles eat it slightly differently. Here, it's served as a clear broth with a tiny meat-stuffed pastry.

Vodka Poles make some of the world's best and are not afraid to experiment.

Getting Around

Air The national carrier, LOT, operates a comprehensive network of domestic routes, though many flights travel via Warsaw and connections aren't always convenient.

Bus Polski Bus links big cities and can be faster than trains on some routes. Elsewhere, buses are useful for remote towns and villages that aren't serviced by trains.

Car Always handy for travelling at your own pace, but Polish highways can be narrow and crowded. Drive on the right.

Train Polish Rail/PKP Intercity trains offer an affordable and fast service between major cities. Slower trains run between cities and towns around the country. For an online timetable, see www.rozklad-pkp.pl.

When to Go
Warsaw

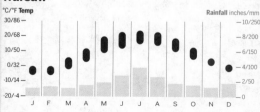

Jul & Aug Expect sunny skies, but always prepare for rain. Museums and other attractions are open for business.

Apr–Jun Spring is cool, but expect some sunny days too. Easter weekend can be very crowded; book in advance.

Nov–Mar Snow brings skiers to the southern resorts. Museums and castles in small towns may be closed.

Arriving in Poland

Frédéric Chopin Airport (Warsaw) The capital's main airport is also Poland's principal air gateway. Regular trains (4.40zł) take 20 minutes to get to Warszawa Centralna train station. Bus 175 (4.40zł) runs to the Old Town. A taxi costs 60zł and takes 20 to 30 minutes to the centre.

Warszawa Centralna. Warsaw's main train station is located in the city centre, a short walk from hotels and sights and easily accessible by tram from anywhere in the city.

Top Phrases

Hello. Cześć.

Goodbye. Do widzenia.

Excuse me. Przepraszam.

Thank you. Dziękuję.

Cheers! Na zdrowie!

Resources

Polish National Tourist Office (www.poland.travel)

Warsaw Voice (www.warsawvoice.pl)

Warsaw Tourist Information (www.warsawtour.pl)

InfoKraków (www.infokrakow.pl)

Set Your Budget

→ Hostel dorm room or low-cost guesthouse: 50zł

→ Meals in milk bars and self-catering: 40zł

→ Train or bus tickets: 30zł

→ Sundries: 10zł

CENTRAL & EASTERN EUROPE POLAND AT A GLANCE

Central Warsaw

N 0 _____ 500 m
0 _____ 0.25 miles

A | **B** | **C** | **D**

Museum of the History of Polish Jews (450m); Jewish Cemetery (2.5km)

Świętojerska

11
4

Warsaw Tourist Office

Długa

Wybrzeże Gdyńskie

Vistula

Miodowa

Świętojańska

7

Bugaj

Podwale

Jezuicka

Royal Castle

5

3

Al Solidarności

Senatorska

6

Generała Andersa

Długa

Bednarska

Furmańska

Dobra

Ratusz-Arsenał

Senatorska

Wierzbowa

Trębacka

Mollera

Krakowskie Przedmieście

Browarna

Elektoralna

Saxon Gardens

Plac Piłsudskiego

Plac Małachowskiego

Traugutta

Oboźna

Sewerynów

Dynasy

Warsaw Rising Museum (1.4km)

Grzybowska

Marszałkowska

Królewska

Kredytowa

Plac Dąbrowskiego

Czackiego

Nowy Świat

Chopin Museum

1

Plac Próżna Grzybowski

Zielna

15

Mazowiecka

Świętokrzyska

Nowy Świat - Uniwersytet

Tamka

Ordynacka

Okólnik

Twarda

10

Świętokrzyska

Moniuszki

14

Warecka

Plac Powstańców Warszawy

Kopernika

Foksal

Sienkiewicza

Jasna

Szpitalna

Górskiego

13

Nowy Świat

Złota

Zgoda

Chmielna

9

Smolna

Sienna

Złota

Emilii Plater

Palace of Culture & Science

2

Plac Defilad

Marszałkowska

8

12

Bracka

Warsaw Tourist Office

Centrum

Widok

Al Jerozolimskie

Warszawa Śródmieście Train Station

Al Jerozolimskie

Nowogrodzka

Książęca

Plac Trzech Krzyży

Warszawa Centralna Train Station

Żurawia

Wspólna

Hoża

Mokotowska

Al Ujazdowskie

Warszawa Zachodnia Terminal (2.2km)

Emilii Plater

Wspólna

Poznańska

Marszałkowska

Krucza

Wilcza

Wiejska

Niepodległoś

Hoża

Charlotte Chleb i Wino (550m); Plan B (550m); Stodoła (2km)

Łazienki Park (1.5km)

Central Warsaw

◎ Sights

Warsaw's Old Town (Stare Miasto) was rebuilt from rubble in the decades following World War II. Though it's a relatively recent reconstruction, it looks as though it's been there for centuries. Running south from Castle Sq to busy al Jerozolimskie is the stamping ground of Warsaw's students, shoppers and socialites.

◎ Old Town

★**Royal Castle**   CASTLE
(Zamek Królewski; ☑22 3555 170; www.zamek-krolewski.pl; Plac Zamkowy 4; adult/concession 30/20zł; ⊘10am-6pm Tue-Thu & Sat, to 8pm Fri, 11am-6pm Sun) This massive brick edifice, a copy of the original blown up by the Germans in WWII, began life as a wooden stronghold of the dukes of Mazovia in the 14th century. Its heyday came in the mid-17th century, when it became one of Europe's most splendid royal residences. It then served the Russian tsars and, in 1918, after Poland regained independence, became the residence of the president. Today it is filled with period furniture and works of art.

Plac Zamkowy   SQUARE
(Castle Square) A natural spot from which to start exploring the Old Town is triangular Castle Square. Attracting snap-happy tourists by the hundreds each day is the square's centrepiece, the Sigismund III Vasa Column (Kolumna Zygmunta III Wazy; M0560).

Barbican   FORTRESS
(Barbakan; ul Nowomiejska) Heading north out of the Old Town along ul Nowomiejska you'll soon see the red-brick Barbican, a semicircular defensive tower topped with a decorative Renaissance parapet. It was partially dismantled in the 19th century, but reconstructed after WWII, and is now a popular spot for buskers and art sellers.

◎ Royal Way

★**Chopin Museum**   MUSEUM
(☑22 441 6251; www.chopin.museum; ul Okólnik 1; adult/concession 22/13zł, Sun free; ⊘11am-8pm Tue-Sun) High-tech, multimedia museum within the baroque Ostrogski Palace, showcasing the work of the country's most famous composer. You're encouraged to take your time through four floors of displays, including stopping by the listening booths in the basement where you can browse Chopin's oeuvre to your heart's content. Limited visitation is allowed each hour; your best bet is to book your visit in advance by phone or email.

★**Łazienki Park**   GARDENS
(Park Łazienkowski; www.lazienki-krolewskie.pl; ul Agrykola 1; ⊘dawn-dusk) Pronounced wah-zhen-kee, this park is a beautiful place of manicured greens and wild patches. Its popularity extends to families, peacocks and fans of classical music, who come for the al fresco Chopin concerts on Sunday afternoons at noon and 4pm from mid-May through September. Once a hunting ground attached to Ujazdów Castle, Łazienki was acquired by King Stanisław August Poniatowski in 1764 and transformed into a splendid park complete with palace, amphitheatre, and various follies and other buildings.

St Anne's Church   CHURCH
(Kościół Św Anny; ul Krakowskie Przedmieście 68) Marking the start of the Royal Way, this is arguably the most ornate church in the city. It escaped major damage during WWII, which explains why it sports an original trompe l'oeil ceiling, a rococo high altar and a gorgeous organ. The facade is also baroque

in style, although there are neoclassical touches here and there.

◉ City Centre & Around

★ Palace of Culture & Science
HISTORIC BUILDING

(Pałac Kultury i Nauki; www.pkin.pl; Plac Defilad 1; observation terrace adult/concession 20/15zł; ⊙10am-8pm) Love it or hate it, every visitor to Warsaw should visit the iconic, socialist realist PKiN (as its full Polish name is abbreviated). This 'gift of friendship' from the Soviet Union was built in the early 1950s, and at 231m high remains the tallest building in Poland. It's home to a huge congress hall, theatres, a multiscreen cinema and museums. Take the high-speed lift to the 30th-floor (115m) observation terrace to take it all in.

★ Warsaw Rising Museum
MUSEUM

(Muzeum Powstania Warszawskiego; www.1944. pl; ul Grzybowska 79; adult/concession 20/16zł, Sun free; ⊙8am-6pm Mon, Wed & Fri, to 8pm Thu, 10am-6pm Sat & Sun; Ⓜ Rondo Daszyńskiego, 🚊 9, 22 or 24 along al Jerozolimskie) One of Warsaw's best, this museum traces the history of the city's heroic but doomed uprising against the German occupation in 1944 via three levels of interactive displays, photographs, film archives and personal accounts. The volume of material is overwhelming, but the museum does an excellent job of instilling in visitors a sense of the desperation residents felt in deciding to oppose the occupation by force, and of illustrating the dark consequences, including the Germans' destruction of the city in the aftermath.

★ Wilanów Palace
PALACE

(Pałac w Wilanowie; ☎22 544 2850; www.wilanow-palac.pl; ul Potockiego 10/16; adult/concession 20/15zł; ⊙9.30am-6pm Sat-Mon & Wed, to 4pm Tue, Thu & Fri mid-Apr–mid-Oct, 9.30am-4pm Wed-Mon mid-Oct–mid-Apr; 🚌116 or 180) Warsaw's top palace is Wilanów (vee-*lah*-noof), 6km south of Łazienki. It dates to 1677, when King Jan III Sobieski bought the land and turned an existing manor house into an Italian baroque villa fit for a royal summer residence (calling it in Italian 'villa nuova', from which the Polish name is derived). Wilanów changed hands several times over the centuries, and with every new owner it acquired a bit of baroque here and a touch of neoclassical there.

◉ Former Jewish District

★ Museum of the History of Polish Jews
MUSEUM

(Polin; ☎22 471 0301; www.polin.pl; ul Anielewicza 6; adult/concession 25/15zł, incl temporary exhibits 30/20zł; ⊙10am-6pm Mon, Thurs & Fri, to 8pm Wed, Sat & Sun; 🚊4, 15, 18 or 35 along ul Marszałkowska) This exceptional museum's permanent exhibition opened in late 2014. Impressive multimedia exhibits document 1000 years of Jewish history in Poland, from accounts of the earliest Jewish traders in the region through waves of mass migration, progress and pogroms, all the way to WWII and the destruction of Europe's largest Jewish community. It's worth booking online first, and you can hire an audioguide (10zł) to get the most out of the many rooms of displays, interactive maps, photos and videos.

Jewish Cemetery
CEMETERY

(Cmentarz Żydowski; ul Okopowa 49/51; adult/concession 10/5zł; ⊙10am-5pm Mon-Thu, 9am-1pm Fri, 9am-4pm Sun) Founded in 1806, Warsaw's main Jewish Cemetery incredibly suffered little during WWII and contains more than 150,000 tombstones, the largest collection of its kind in Europe. A notice near the entrance lists the graves of many eminent Polish Jews, including Ludwik Zamenhof, creator of the international artificial language Esperanto.

🛏 Sleeping

★ Oki Doki Hostel
HOSTEL €

(☎22 828 0122; www.okidoki.pl; Plac Dąbrowskiego 3; dm 38-70zł, d from 167zł; 🖻) Arguably Warsaw's most popular hostel, and certainly one of the best. Each of its bright, large rooms is individually named and decorated. Accommodation is in three- to eight-bed dorms, with a special three-bed dorm for women only. The owners are well travelled and know the needs of backpackers, providing a kitchen and a laundry service. Breakfast available (15zł).

★ Castle Inn
HOTEL €€

(☎22 425 0100; www.castleinn.pl; ul Świętojańska 2; s/d from 191/242zł; ❊🖻) Nicely decorated 'art hotel', housed in a 17th-century town house. All rooms overlook either Castle Sq or St John's Cathedral, and come in a range of playful styles. Our favourite would be No 121, 'Viktor', named for a reclusive street artist, complete with tasteful graffiti and a gorgeous castle view. Breakfast costs an extra 35zł.

Chmielna Guest House
GUESTHOUSE €€

(📞 22 828 1282; www.chmielnabb.pl; ul Chmielna 13; r 190-210zł; 🛜) Handily situated in the middle of a bustling shopping and restaurant zone, this sister property of New World Hostel offers a small number of comfortable budget rooms, some of which have shared bathrooms. Rooms are decked out in colourful contemporary decor, and there's a basic kitchen for guest use. Note that the rooms are on the 3rd floor.

Reception is located at **New World Street Hostel** (📞 22 828 1282; www.nws-hostel. pl; ul Nowy Świat 27; dm 37-64zł, r 169-189zł; 🛜).

Eating

★Mango
VEGAN €

(📞 535 533 629; www.mangovegan.pl; ul Bracka 20; mains 13-25zł; ⊗ 11am-10pm; 🛜 🖋) Mango is a stylish all-vegan eatery with a simple contemporary interior and pleasant outdoor seating. Excellent menu items range from veggie burgers to mango sticky rice. The 'Mango Plate' (Talerz Mango) of hummus,

---

WORTH A TRIP

MALBORK CASTLE

Malbork Castle (📞 tickets 556 470 978; www.zamek.malbork.pl; ul Starościńska 1; adult/concession 39.50/29.50zł; ⊗ 9am-7pm May-Sep, 10am-3pm Oct-Apr), northeast of Warsaw along the main train line to Gdańsk, is show-stoppingly massive. The Marienburg (Fortress of Mary) was originally built by the Teutonic Knights and was the headquarters of the order for almost 150 years. Its vast bulk is an apt embodiment of its weighty history. Visits are by audio headphone, which you pick up at the ticket office. Allow at least two hours to do the place justice.

The castle took shape in stages. First was the so-called High Castle, the formidable central bastion that was begun around 1276. When Malbork became the capital of the order in 1309, the fortress was expanded considerably. The Middle Castle was built to the side of the high one, followed by the Lower Castle still further along. The whole complex was encircled by three rings of defensive walls and strengthened with dungeons and towers. The castle eventually spread over 21 hectares, making it the largest fortress built anywhere in the Middle Ages.

The castle was seized by the Polish army in 1457, during the Thirteen Years' War, when the military power of the knights had started to erode. Malbork then became the residence of Polish kings visiting Pomerania, but from the Swedish invasions onwards it gradually went into decline. After the First Partition in 1772, the Prussians turned it into barracks, destroying much of the decoration and dismantling sections of no military use.

Despite sustaining damage during WWII, almost the entire complex has been preserved, and the castle today looks much as it did six centuries ago, dominating the town and the surrounding countryside. The best view is from the opposite side of the river (you can get there via the footbridge), especially in the late afternoon when the brick turns an intense red-brown in the setting sun.

The entrance to the complex is from the northern side, through what used to be the only way in. From the main gate, you walk over the drawbridge, then go through five iron-barred doors to the vast courtyard of the Middle Castle (Zamek Średni). On the western side (to your right) is the Grand Masters' Palace (Pałac Wielkich Mistrzów), which has some splendid interiors. Alongside is the Knights' Hall (Sala Rycerska), which is the largest chamber in the castle at 450 sq metres. The remarkable ceiling has its original palm vaulting preserved. The building on the opposite side of the courtyard houses a collection of armour and an excellent amber museum – the latter would be a major place of interest on its own, were it anywhere else.

The tour proceeds to the High Castle (Zamek Wysoki), over another drawbridge and through a gate (note the ornamented 1280 doorway) to a spectacular arcaded courtyard that has a reconstructed well in the middle.

Malbork sits on the busy Gdańsk–Warsaw railway route. The train station and bus terminal are at the eastern end of the town centre, 1km from the castle. Coming from Gdańsk by train, you'll catch a splendid view of the castle.

mango, falafel, eggplant, olives, sweet peppers and harissa paste served with pita bread is top value at 22zł.

★ Charlotte

Chleb i Wino FRENCH €

(www.bistrocharlotte.pl; al Wyzwolenia 18; mains 10-18zł; ⊙ 7am-midnight Mon-Thu, to 1am Fri, 9am-1am Sat, 9am-10pm Sun; 🗟) Dazzling French bakery and bistro facing Plac Zbawiciela. It dishes up tantalising croissants and pastries at the break of dawn, then transitions to big salads and crusty sandwiches through the lunch and dinner hours, and finally to wine on the terrace in the evening. Great value for money.

Bar Mleczny Pod

Barbakanem CAFETERIA €

(ul Mostowa 27; mains 7-10zł; ⊙ 8am-4pm Mon-Fri, 9am-5pm Sat; 🖉) In the Old Town, located just outside the Barbican, look for Bar Mleczny Pod Barbakanem, a staple that's been around for decades. Don't be put off by the faded exterior; this remains a popular place for lunch.

🍸 Drinking & Nightlife

★ Kofi CAFE

(ul Mińska 25; ⊙ 9am-5pm Mon-Fri; 🗟) If you're weary of the weak filtered coffee of Central Europe, you'll shed a happy tear when you enter this cool cafe within the sprawling Soho Factory compound in Praga. Excellent coffee is served in an atmospheric industrial interior, enhanced by the aroma of coffee beans being roasted on the premises.

Plan B BAR

(al Wyzwolenia 18; ⊙ 11am-late) Phenomenally popular, this upstairs bar on Plac Zbawiciela draws a mix of students and young office workers. Find some couch space and relax to smooth beats from regular DJs. On warm summer evenings the action spills out onto the street, giving the square the feel of a summer block party.

Cafe Blikle CAFE

(ul Nowy Świat 35; ⊙ 9am-10pm; 🗟) The mere fact that Blikle has survived two world wars and the challenges of communism makes it a household name locally. But what makes this legendary cafe truly famous is its doughnuts, for which people have been queuing up for generations. Enter its cake shop via the separate entrance to the right, and find out why.

☆ Entertainment

Tygmont LIVE MUSIC

(🖉 66 048 1890; www.tygmont.com.pl; ul Mazowiecka 6/8; ⊙ 9pm-late) Hosting both local and international acts, the live music here (occasionally including jazz) is both varied and plentiful. Concerts start around 10pm; it fills up early, so either reserve a table or turn up at opening time. Dinner is also available.

Stodoła LIVE MUSIC

(🖉 22 825 6031; www.stodola.pl; ul Batorego 10; ⊙ 9am-9pm Mon-Fri, to 2am Sat) Originally the canteen for builders of the Palace of Culture & Science, Stodoła is one of Warsaw's biggest and longest-running live music venues. A great place to catch touring bands.

Filharmonia

Narodowa CLASSICAL MUSIC

(National Philharmonic; 🖉 22 551 7130; www.filharmonia.pl; ul Jasna 5; ⊙ box office 10am-2pm & 3-7pm Mon-Sat) Home of the world-famous National Philharmonic Orchestra and Choir of Poland, founded in 1901, this venue has a concert hall (enter from ul Sienkiewicza 10) and a chamber-music hall (enter from ul Moniuszki 5), both of which stage regular concerts. The box office entrance is on ul Sienkiewicza.

ℹ Information

Warsaw Tourist Office (www.warsawtour.pl; Plac Defilad 1, enter from ul Emilii Plater; ⊙ 8am-7pm May-Jun, shorter hours rest of year; 🗟) The Palace of Culture & Science branch of Warsaw's official tourist information organisation is a central resource for maps and advice. The staff can also help with accommodation. There's no phone number, so visit in person or contact via email.

Also note the other helpful branches at the airport (www.warsawtour.pl; Terminal A, Warsaw Frédéric Chopin Airport, ul Żwirki i Wigury 1; ⊙ 9am-7pm Jan-Jun, shorter hours rest of year) and the Old Town (www.warsawtour.pl; Rynek Starego Miasta 19/21; ⊙ 9am-8pm May-Jun, shorter hours rest of year; 🗟).

ℹ Getting There & Away

The main airport, **Warsaw Frédéric Chopin Airport** (Lotnisko Chopina Warszawa; 🖉 22 650 4220; www.lotnisko-chopina.pl; ul Żwirki i Wigury 1), lies in the suburb of Okęcie, 10km south of the city centre; it handles most domestic and international flights. **Warsaw Modlin Airport** (🖉 223 15 1880; www.modlin

airport.pl; ul Generała Wiktora Thommée 1a), 35km north of Warsaw, handles some budget carriers, including Ryanair flights to and from the UK.

West of the city centre, **Warszawa Zachodnia bus terminal** (☏ 703 403 403; www. dworzeconline.pl; al Jerozolimskie 144; ☉ information & tickets 5.30am-10pm) handles the majority of international and domestic routes in and out of the city, run by various bus operators. Bus tickets are sold at the terminal. Polski Bus (www.polskibus.com) operates buses to cities across Poland and beyond from several stations, including the **Młociny bus station** (Dworzec Autobusowy Młociny; ul Kasprowicza 145) north of the city centre and the **Wilanowska bus station** (Dworzec Autobusowy Wilanowska; ul Puławska 145), south of the centre. Check the website.

Warsaw has several train stations, but the one most travellers use is **Warszawa Centralna** (Warsaw Central; www.pkp.pl; al Jerozolimskie 54; ☉24hr). You can travel by rail from Warsaw to every major Polish city and many other places in between; check the useful online timetable in English at www.rozklad-pkp.pl for details of times and fares.

ⓘ Getting Around

TO/FROM THE AIRPORT

Regular train services run between Warsaw Frédéric Chopin Airport and Warszawa Centralna stations every 30 minutes between about 5am and 10.30pm (4.40zł, 20 minutes).

Bus 175 (4.40zł, every 15 minutes, 5am to 11pm) runs from the airport, passing along ul Jerozolimiskie and ul Nowy Świat before terminating at Plac Piłsudskiego, within walking distance of the Old Town.

From Modlin Airport, the Modlin bus travels regularly between the airport and major landmarks, such as the Palace of Culture, along three different routes (33zł, 40 minutes, twice an hour).

PUBLIC TRANSPORT

Warsaw's integrated public-transport system is operated by **Zarząd Transportu Miejskiego** (Urban Transport Authority; ☏ 19 115; www.ztm. waw.pl) and consists of tram, bus and metro lines, all using the same ticketing system. Trams are especially handy for moving around the city's sprawling centre.

Kraków

POP 761,000

If you believe the legends, Kraków was founded on the defeat of a dragon, and it's true a mythical atmosphere permeates its attractive streets and squares. Wawel Castle is a major drawcard, while the Old Town contains soaring churches, impressive museums and the vast Rynek Główny, Europe's largest market square. However, there's more to the former royal capital than history and nightlife. As you walk through the Old Town, you'll sometimes find yourself overwhelmed by the harmony of a quiet back street – the 'just so' nature of the architecture and light.

◎ Sights

◉ Wawel Hill

South of Old Town, this hilltop location is enveloped in the heady atmosphere of Polish history perhaps more than any other site in the country. Its great castle was the seat of the kings for over 500 years from the early days of the Polish state.

★**Wawel Royal Castle**   CASTLE
(Zamek Królewski na Wawelu; ☏ Wawel Visitor Centre 12 422 5155; www.wawel.krakow.pl; Wawel Hill; grounds admission free, attractions priced separately; ☉ grounds 6am-dusk; 🚋6, 8, 10, 13, 18) As the political and cultural heart of Poland through the 16th century, Wawel Castle is a potent symbol of national identity. It's now a museum containing five separate sections: Crown Treasury & Armoury; State Rooms; Royal Private Apartments; Lost Wawel; and the Exhibition of Oriental Art. Each requires a separate ticket. Of the five, the State Rooms and Royal Private Apartments are most impressive.

The Renaissance palace you see today dates from the 16th century. An original, smaller residence was built in the early 11th century by King Bolesław I Chrobry. Kazimierz III Wielki (Casimir III the Great) turned it into a formidable Gothic castle, but when it burned down in 1499, Zygmunt I Stary (Sigismund I the Old; 1506–48) commissioned a new residence. Within 30 years, the current Italian-inspired palace was in place. Despite further extensions and alterations, the three-storey structure, complete with a courtyard arcaded on three sides, has been preserved to this day.

Repeatedly sacked and vandalised by the Swedish and Prussian armies, the castle was occupied in the 19th century by the Austrians, who intended to make Wawel a barracks, while moving the royal tombs elsewhere. They never got that far, but they did

Kraków – Old Town & Wawel

0 ——— 200 m
0 ——— 0.1 miles

KLEPARZ

Plac Matejki

Worcella

Pawia

13

8

Plac Kolejowy

Kraków Główny Train Station

Lubicz

(100m)

Bosacka

Opera Krakowska (500m)

Basztowa

Pijarska

Reformacka

Św Tomasza

17

Szczepańska

15 11

Rynek Główny

Jagiellońska

Szewska

9

6

20

5 7

16

Plac Mariacki

St Mary's Basilica 2

Mały Rynek

Sienna

Mikołajska

Florańska

Szpitalna

Plac Św Ducha

Św Marka

Sw Jana

Stawkowska

Św Tomasza

Św Krzyża

Westerplatte

Zamenhofa

Radziwiłłowska

Kopernika

Zyblikiewicza Librowszczyzna

Morsztynowska

gen Sołtyka

Kołłątaja

Blich

WESOŁA

18

Bracka

Grodzka

OLD TOWN

Stolarska

Planty

Dominikańska

Wielopole

Franciszkańska

Plac Wszystkich Świętych

Plac Dominikański

19

Poselska

Św Gertrudy

10

Sarego

Bogusławskiego

Dietla Dietla

Wrzesińska

Starowiślna

Siedleckiego

Trałowska

Straszewskiego

Plac Św Marii Magdaleny

Kanonicza

Grodzka

12

Św Idziego

Plac Na Groblach

Powiśle

Podzamcze

3

Wawel Cathedral

4

Wawel Royal Castle

Wawel Hill

Droga do Zamku

Bernardyńska

Sw Sebastiana

Podbrzezie

Św Sebastiana

Joselewicza

Brzozowa

Miodowa

Warszauera

Jakuba

Szeroka

Pharmacy under the Eagle (800m);
Schindler's Factory (1.2km)

Dajwór

Bartosza

Straszewskiego

Vistula

Smocza

Koletek

Sukiennicza

Orzeszkowej

Św Agnieszki

Stradomska

Dietla
Dietla

Meiselsa

14

Plac Nowy

Estery

Izaaka

Nowa

Józefa

Bożego Ciała

KAZIMIERZ

Waska

Józefa

1

Galicia Jewish Museum

Most Grunwaldzki

U Pana Cogito (800m)

Konopnickiej

Paulińska

Krakowska

Skałeczna

Augustiańska

Plac Wolnica

Św Wawrzyńca

Bocheńska

Mostowa

Gazowa

Podgórska

Skawińska

Trynitarska

Kraków – Old Town & Wawel

turn the royal kitchen and coach house into a military hospital and raze two churches. They also built a new ring of massive brick walls, largely ruining the original Gothic fortifications.

After Kraków was incorporated into re-established Poland after WWI, restoration work began and continued until the outbreak of WWII. The work was resumed after the war and has been able to recover a good deal of the castle's earlier external form and interior decoration.

★ Wawel Cathedral
CHURCH

(☑ 12 429 9515; www.katedra-wawelska.pl; Wawel 3, Wawel Hill; cathedral free, combined entry for crypts, bell tower & museum adult/concession 12/7zł; ⊘ 9am-5pm Mon-Sat, from 12.30pm Sun Apr-Oct, closes at 4pm Nov-Mar; ₪ 6, 8, 10, 13, 18) The Royal Cathedral has witnessed many coronations, funerals and burials of Poland's monarchs and strongmen over the centuries. This is the third church on this site, consecrated in 1364. The original was founded in the 11th century by King Bolesław I Chrobry and replaced with a Romanesque construction around 1140. When that burned down in 1305, only the Crypt of St Leonard survived. Highlights include the Holy Cross Chapel, Sigismund Chapel, Sigismund Bell, and the Crypt of St Leonard and Royal Crypts.

◎ Old Town

Kraków's atmospheric Old Town is packed with historical buildings and monuments, including several museums and many churches. It's been included on Unesco's World Heritage list since 1978, and is largely car-free.

★ St Mary's Basilica
CHURCH

(Basilica of the Assumption of Our Lady; ☑ 12 422 0521; www.mariacki.com; Plac Mariacki 5, Rynek Główny; adult/concession church 10/5zł, tower 15/10zł; ⊘ 11.30am-6pm Mon-Sat, 2-6pm Sun; ₪ 1, 6, 8, 13, 18) Overlooking Rynek Główny, this striking brick church, best known simply as St Mary's, is dominated by two towers of different heights. The first church here was built in the 1220s and following its destruction during a Tatar raid, construction of the basilica began. Tour the exquisite interior, with its remarkable carved wooden altarpiece, and in summer climb the tower for excellent views. Don't miss the hourly *hejnał* (bugle call) from the taller tower.

★ Rynek Underground
MUSEUM

(☑ 12 426 5060; www.podziemiarynku.com; Rynek Główny 1; adult/concession 19/16zł; ⊘ 10am-8pm Mon, to 4pm Tue, to 10pm Wed-Sun; ₪ 1, 6, 8, 13, 18) This fascinating attraction beneath the market square consists of an underground route through medieval market stalls and other long-forgotten chambers. The 'Middle Ages meets 21st century' experience is enhanced by holograms and audiovisual wizardry. Buy tickets at an office on the western side of the Cloth Hall (Sukiennice 21), where an electronic board shows tour times and tickets available. The entrance to the tunnels is on the northeastern end of the Cloth Hall.

Cloth Hall
HISTORIC BUILDING

(Sukiennice; www.mnk.pl; Rynek Główny 1/3; ₪ 1, 6, 8, 13, 18) FREE Dominating the middle of Rynek Główny, this building was once the centre of Kraków's medieval clothing trade. Created in the early 14th century when a roof was put over two rows of stalls, it was extended into a 108m-long Gothic structure, then rebuilt in Renaissance style after a 1555 fire; the arcades were a late-19th-century addition. The ground floor is now a busy trading centre for crafts and souvenirs; the upper floor houses the recently renovated **Gallery of 19th-Century Polish Painting**.

★**Collegium Maius**   HISTORIC BUILDING
(☑ 12 663 1521; www.maius.uj.edu.pl; ul Jagiellońska 15; adult/concession 16/12zł; ☺ 10am-2.20pm Mon-Fri, to 1.30pm Sat; ☐ 2, 13, 18, 20) The Collegium Maius, built as part of the Kraków Academy (now the Jagiellonian University), is the oldest surviving university building in Poland, and one of the best examples of 15th-century Gothic architecture in the city. It has a magnificent arcaded **courtyard** (7am-dusk) and a fascinating university collection. Visit is by guided tour only.

◉ Kazimierz & Podgórze

For much of its early history, the former mixed Jewish and Christian quarter of Kazimierz was an independent town with its own municipal charter and laws. Though the ethnic make-up of Kazimierz is now wholly different, the architecture gives hints of the past, with clearly distinguishable elements of what were Christian and Jewish areas.

The neighbourhood of Podgórze, across the river from Kazimierz, would pique the interest of very few travellers if it wasn't for the notorious role it played during WWII. It was here that the Germans herded some 16,000 Jews into a ghetto, centred on today's Plac Bohaterów Getta. Both ghetto and camp were chillingly recreated in the movie *Schindler's List*.

★**Schindler's Factory**   MUSEUM
(Fabryka Schindlera; ☑ 12 257 0096; www.mhk.pl; ul Lipowa 4; adult/concession 24/18zł, free Mon; ☺ 10am-4pm Mon, 9am-8pm Tue-Sun; ☐ 3, 9, 19, 24, 50) This impressive interactive museum covers the German occupation of Kraków in WWII. It's housed in the former enamel factory of Oskar Schindler, the Nazi industrialist who famously saved the lives of members of his Jewish labour force during the Holocaust. Well-organised, innovative exhibits tell the moving story of the city from 1939 to 1945.

★**Galicia Jewish Museum**   MUSEUM
(☑ 12 421 6842; www.galiciajewishmuseum.org; ul Dajwór 18; adult/concession 16/11zł; ☺ 10am-6pm;

☐ 3, 9, 19, 24, 50) This museum both commemorates Jewish victims of the Holocaust and celebrates the Jewish culture and history of the former Austro-Hungarian region of Galicia. It features an impressive photographic exhibition depicting modern-day remnants of southeastern Poland's once-thriving Jewish community, called 'Traces of Memory', along with video testimony of survivors and regular temporary exhibits. The museum also leads guided tours of the Jewish sites of Kazimierz. Call or email for details.

★**Pharmacy Under the Eagle**   MUSEUM
(Apteka Pod Orłem; ☑ 12 656 5625; www.mhk.pl; Plac Bohaterów Getta 18; adult/concession 11/9zł, free Mon; ☺ 9am-5pm Tue-Sun, 10am-2pm Mon; ☐ 3, 9, 19, 24, 50) On the south side of Plac Bohaterów Getta is this museum in a former pharmacy, which was run by the non-Jew Tadeusz Pankiewicz during the Nazi occupation. The interior has been restored to its wartime appearance and tells the story of the ghetto and the role of the pharmacy in its daily life.

◉ Outside the Centre

★**Wieliczka Salt Mine**   MUSEUM
(☑ 12 278 7302; www.kopalnia.pl; ul Daniłowicza 10; adult/concession 94/74zł; ☺ 7.30am-7.30pm Apr-Oct, 8am-5pm Nov-Mar) Some 14km southeast of Kraków, Wieliczka (vyeh-leech-kah) is famous for its deep salt mine. It's an eerie world of pits and chambers, and everything within its depths has been carved by hand from salt blocks. The mine has a labyrinth of tunnels, about 300km distributed over nine levels, the deepest being 327m underground. A section of the mine, some 22 chambers connected by galleries, from 64m to 135m below ground, is open to the public by guided tour, and it's a fascinating trip.

★**Kościuszko Mound**   MONUMENT
(Kopiec Kościuszki; ☑ 12 425 1116; www.kopieckosciuszki.pl; Al Waszyngtona 1; adult/concession 14/10zł; ☺ 9.30am-dusk; ☐ 1, 2, 6) The mound, dedicated to Polish (and American) military hero Tadeusz Kościuszko, was erected between 1820 and 1823, soon after the great man's death. The mound stands 34m high, and soil from the Polish and American battlefields where Kościuszko fought was placed here. The views over the city are spectacular. The memorial is located in the suburb of Zwierzyniec, just under 3km west of the Old Town.

🛏 Sleeping

★ Mundo Hostel
HOSTEL €

(☑ 12 422 6113; www.mundohostel.eu; ul Sarego 10; dm 60-65zł, d 170-190zł; @ 🛜; 🚌 6, 8, 10, 13, 18) Attractive, well-maintained hostel in a quiet courtyard location neatly placed between the Old Town and Kazimierz. Each room is decorated for a different country; for example, the Tibet room is decked out with colourful prayer flags. Barbecues take place in summer. There's a bright, fully equipped kitchen for do-it-yourself meals.

Greg & Tom Hostel
HOSTEL €

(☑ 12 422 4100; www.gregtomhostel.com; ul Pawia 12/7; dm/d 57/150zł; 🛜) This well-run hostel is spread over three locations, though all check-in is handled at the main branch on ul Pawia. The staff are friendly, the rooms are clean, and laundry facilities are included. On Tuesday and Saturday evenings, hot Polish dishes are served.

Hostel Flamingo
HOSTEL €

(☑ 12 422 0000; www.flamingo-hostel.com; ul Szewska 4; dm 47-65zł, d 158zł; 🛜; 🚌 2, 4, 14, 18, 20, 24) Highly rated hostel with an excellent central location, just a couple steps from the main square. Pluses – in addition to the expected amenities – include free breakfast, an in-house cafe and a cheeky attitude. Sleeping is in six- to 12-bed dorms plus a few private doubles.

U Pana Cogito
HOTEL €€

(☑ 12 269 7200; www.pcogito.pl; ul Bałuckiego 6; s/d/q 280/330/400zł; P ❈ @ 🛜; 🚌 11, 18, 22, 52) White and cream seem to be the colours of choice at this friendly 14-room hotel in a lovely mansion across the river and southwest of the centre. All rooms have big bathrooms and refrigerators, and for extra privacy, the one apartment has a separate entrance. The hotel also has its own restaurant, also done out in fresh, minimalist white.

🍴 Eating

★ Glonojad
VEGETARIAN €

(☑ 12 346 1677; www.glonojad.com; Plac Matejki 2; mains 10-16zł; ⊗ 8am-10pm Mon-Fri, 9am Sat & Sun; 🛜 🖉 🍴; 🚌 2, 4, 14, 19, 20, 24) Attractive and much-lauded, this vegetarian restaurant has a great view onto Plac Matejki, just north of the Barbican. The diverse menu has a variety of tasty dishes including samosas, curries, potato pancakes, burritos, gnocchi and soups. There's also an all-day breakfast menu, so there's no need to jump out of that hotel bed too early.

★ Charlotte Chleb i Wino
BAKERY €€

(☑ 600 807 880; www.bistrocharlotte.pl; Plac Szczepański 2; salads & sandwiches 10-20zł; ⊗ 7am-midnight Mon-Thu, to 1am Fri, 9am-1pm Sat, 9am-10pm Sun; 🛜; 🚌 2, 4, 14, 18, 20, 24) This is the Kraków branch of a popular Warsaw restaurant serving croissants, French breads, salads and sandwiches. The crowd on artsy Plac Szczepański is suitably stylish as they tuck into their croque monsieurs and sip from excellent but affordable French wines. The perfect stop for morning coffee.

Cupcake Corner
BAKERY €

(www.cupcakecorner.pl; ul Grodzka 60; cupcakes 7.50zł, ice cream 7zł-17zł, coffee 7zł-14zł; ⊗ 8am-9pm Mon-Sat, 9am-9pm Sun; 🛜 🖉 🍴; 🚌 Plac Wszystkich Świętych) This American-style bakery-cafe has really taken off, and now has four branches in the centre. Cupcakes come in to-die-for flavours, such as hazelnut crunch, red velvet and peanut-butter cup. Bagels, ice cream, coffee and brownies are also available in delicious flavours; pop out your laptop to get some work done, or sit in the window and people watch.

🍸 Drinking & Nightlife

★ Bunkier Cafe
CAFE

(☑ 12 431 0585; www.bunkiercafe.pl; Plac Szczepański 3a; ⊗ 9am-1am; 🛜; 🚌 2, 4, 14, 18, 20, 24) The 'Bunker' is a wonderful cafe with a positively enormous glassed-in terrace tacked onto the Bunkier Sztuki (Art Bunker), a cutting-edge gallery northwest of the Rynek. The garden space is heated in winter and seems to always have a buzz. Excellent coffee, non-filtered beers, and homemade lemonades, as well as light bites like burgers and salads. Enter from the Planty.

★ Café Camelot
CAFE

(☑ 12 421 0123; ul Św Tomasza 17; ⊗ 9am-midnight; 🚌 2, 4, 14, 19, 20, 24) For coffee and cake, try this genteel haven hidden around an obscure street corner in the Old Town. Its cosy rooms are cluttered with lace-covered candle-lit tables, and a quirky collection of wooden figurines featuring spiritual or folkloric scenes. Also a great choice for breakfasts and brunches.

Alchemia
CAFE

(☑ 12 421 2200; www.alchemia.com.pl; ul Estery 5; ⊗ 9am-late Tue-Sun, from 10am Mon; 🚌 3, 9, 19, 24,

WORTH A TRIP

AUSCHWITZ-BIRKENAU MEMORIAL & MUSEUM

The Nazi German–run **Auschwitz-Birkenau** (Auschwitz-Birkenau Miejsce Pamięci i Muzeum; ☑ guides 33 844 8100; www.auschwitz.org; ul Więźniów Oświęcimia 20; tours 50zł; ⊙ 7.30am-7pm Jun-Aug, to 6pm Apr-May & Sep, to 5pm Mar & Oct, to 4pm Feb, to 3pm Jan & Nov, to 2pm Dec) **FREE** concentration camp is synonymous with genocide and the Holocaust. More than a million Jews, and many Poles and Roma, were murdered here by the German occupiers during WWII. Both sections of the camp, base camp (Auschwitz I) and a much larger outlying camp at Birkenau (Auschwitz II), have been preserved and are open for visitors. It's essential to visit both to appreciate the extent and horror of the place.

From April to October it's compulsory to join a tour if you arrive between 10am and 3pm; book well ahead either via www.visit.auschwitz.org or by phone. English-language tours leave at numerous times throughout the day, generally most frequently between 11.30am and 1.30pm, when they operate half-hourly.

The Auschwitz extermination camp was established in April 1940 by the Germans in prewar Polish army barracks on the outskirts of Oświęcim. Auschwitz was originally intended for Polish political prisoners, but the camp was then adapted for the wholesale extermination of the Jews of Europe in fulfilment of Nazi ideology. For this purpose, the much larger camp at Birkenau (Brzezinka) was built 2km west of the original site in 1941 and 1942.

The museum's visitor centre is at the entrance to the Auschwitz site. Photography and filming are permitted throughout the camp without the use of a flash or stands.

Auschwitz

Auschwitz was only partially destroyed by the fleeing Germans, and many of the original brick buildings stand to this day as a bleak testament to the camp's history. Some 13 of the 30 surviving prison blocks now house museum exhibitions – either general, or dedicated to victims from particular countries or ethnic groups that lost people at Auschwitz.

From the visitor centre in the entrance building, you enter the barbed-wire encampment through the infamous gate, displaying the grimly cynical message in German: 'Arbeit Macht Frei' (Work Brings Freedom). The sign is in fact a replica, which replaced the original when it was stolen in 2009. Though it was recovered within a few days, it had been cut into pieces by the thieves and took 17 months to restore.

Birkenau (Auschwitz II)

It was actually at Birkenau, not Auschwitz, that most of the killing took place. Massive (175 hectares) and purpose-built for efficiency, the camp had more than 300 prison barracks – they were actually stables built for horses, but housed 300 people each. Birkenau had four huge gas chambers, complete with crematoria. Each could asphyxiate 2000 people at one time, and there were electric lifts to raise the bodies to the ovens.

Though much of Birkenau was destroyed by the retreating Germans, the size of the place, fenced off with long lines of barbed wire and watchtowers stretching almost as far as your eye can see, will give you some idea of the scale of the crime; climb the tower at the entrance gate to get the full effect.

Getting There

For most tourists, the jump-off point for Oświęcim is Kraków. Buses (1½ hours, hourly) can be a more convenient option than trains, as they generally drop you off in the car park opposite the entrance to Auschwitz. The alternative is catching a train from Kraków (1½ hours, hourly) to Oświęcim train station, then walking 1.5km to the museum entrance.

50) This Kazimierz venue exudes a shabby-is-the-new-cool look with rough-hewn wooden benches, candlelit tables and a companionable gloom. It hosts occasional live-music gigs and theatrical events through the week.

Klub Społem
CLUB

(☑12 421 79 79; www.pubspolem.pl/index.php; św Tomasza 4; ☉6pm-3am Sun-Tue, to 4am Wed & Thu, to 5am Fri & Sat; ⛎Teatr Bagatela) Just off plac Szczepańska is this deceptively large underground bar and club. With Communist throwback memorabilia covering the walls, and tunes of the '60s through to the '90s, Klub Społem is a cosy and fun find for a night of cheap beer and dancing. Look out for the DJ booth, housed in a disused van front.

Spokój
BAR

(☑501 652 478; www.spokoj.pl; ul Bracka 3; ☉10am-3am Mon-Fri, noon-3am Sat & Sun; ⛎Plac Wszystkich Świętych) Trendy young Krakowians populate this hidden retro bar. Surrounded by colourful '70s-style decor, mismatched furniture and a permeating orange hue, you'll soon find yourself settling into the low sofas and being transported back through the decades.

☆ Entertainment

★ Harris Piano Jazz Bar
JAZZ

(☑12 421 5741; www.harris.krakow.pl; Rynek Główny 28; ☉1pm-late Mon-Fri, from noon Sat & Sun; ⛎1, 6, 8, 13, 18) This lively jazz haunt is housed in an atmospheric, intimate cellar space right on the Rynek Główny. Harris hosts jazz and blues bands most nights of the week from around 9.30pm, but try to arrive an hour earlier to get a seat (or book in advance by phone). Wednesday nights see weekly (free) jam sessions.

Filharmonia Krakowska
CLASSICAL MUSIC

(Filharmonia im. Karola Szymanowskiego w Krakowie; ☑reservations 12 619 8722, tickets 12 619 8733; www.filharmonia.krakow.pl; ul Zwierzyniecka 1; ☉box office 9am-4pm Mon-Fri; ⛎1, 2, 6) Home to one of Poland's best orchestras. Tickets start at 25zł.

Opera Krakowska
OPERA

(☑12 296 6260; www.opera.krakow.pl; ul Lubicz 48; tickets 20-200zł; ☉10am-7pm Mon-Sat, and two hours before performances at box office; ⛎4, 10, 14, 20, 52) The Kraków Opera performs in the strikingly modern red building at the Mogilskie roundabout. The setting is decidedly 21st century, but the repertoire spans the ages, incorporating everything from Verdi to Bernstein.

ℹ Information

The official tourist information office, **InfoKraków** (www.infokrakow.pl), maintains branches around town, including at the **Cloth Hall** (☑12 354 2716; Cloth Hall, Rynek Główny 1/3; ☉9am-7pm May-Oct, to 5pm Nov-Apr; 🛜; ⛎1, 6, 8, 13, 18), **Kazimierz** (☑12 354 2728; ul Józefa 7; ☉9am-5pm; ⛎6, 8, 10, 13), **Old Town** (☑12 354 2725; www.infokrakow.pl; ul Św Jana 2; ☉9am-7pm; ⛎1, 6, 8, 13, 18) and the **Airport** (☑12 285 5341; www.infokrakow.pl; John Paul II International Airport, Balice; ☉9am-7pm). Expect cheerful service, loads of free maps and promotional materials, help in sorting out accommodation and transport, and a computer on hand (in some branches) for short-term web-surfing.

ℹ Getting There & Away

Air Kraków's **John Paul II International Airport** (KRK; ☑information 12 295 5800; www.krakowairport.pl; Kapitana Mieczysława Medweckiego 1, Balice; 🛜) is located in the town of Balice, about 15km west of the centre. The airport terminal hosts several car-hire desks, bank ATMs, and a branch of the InfoKraków tourist information office.

Bus Kraków's bus station is conveniently located next to the main train station on the fringe of the Old Town. Modern **Polski Bus** (www.polskibus.com) coaches depart from here to Warsaw (five hours, several daily); check fares and book tickets online.

Train Gleaming **Kraków Główny Train Station** (Dworzec Główny; ☑information 703 200 200; www.pkp.pl; Plac Dworcowy; ⛎2, 3, 4, 10, 14, 19, 24, 52), on the northeastern outskirts of the Old Town, handles all international trains and most domestic rail services. Hourly trains make the three-hour run to Warsaw (60zł). Popular international connections include Bratislava (seven hours, one daily), Budapest (10½ hours, one daily), Lviv (7½ to 9½ hours, two daily) and Prague (10 hours, one daily).

ℹ Getting Around

TO/FROM THE AIRPORT

Public buses 292 and 208 both run from the airport to Kraków's main bus station (and back) and require a 4zł ticket.

Trains depart once or twice an hour from 4am to 11.30pm between the airport and Kraków Główny (main) station. On exiting the airport terminal, take a free shuttle bus to a nearby station for the onward journey. Buy tickets (9zł) on board the train from a vending machine or the conductor. The trip takes about 20 minutes.

PUBLIC TRANSPORT

→ Kraków has an efficient network of buses and trams that run between 5am and 11pm. Trams are especially handy for moving between the Old Town and Kazimierz.

→ Two types of individual tickets are available: short-term tickets, which are valid for 20 minutes and are fine for short journeys, as well as normal 40-minute tickets. Both can be used interchangeably on buses and trams. You can also buy one-/two-/three-day passes for longer stays.

→ Buy tickets from machines located on board vehicles (have coins ready) or from news kiosks at important stops.

Poland Survival Guide

Directory A–Z

ACCOMMODATION

Poland has a wide choice of options to suit most budgets, including hotels, guesthouses, hostels, apartments and camping grounds.

→ Warsaw is the most expensive place to stay, followed by other large cities.

→ Prices are quoted in złoty, though some larger hotels may also quote rates in euros for guests' convenience.

→ The most popular lodging website for Polish hotels is Booking.com. Nearly all hotels, as well as pensions and even hostels, will have a listing on the site.

→ Hostel accommodation is abundant in Kraków. Expect amenities like shared kitchens, laundry facilities, a lounge and bar, and free wi-fi. **Hostels.com** (www.hostels.com) maintains an inventory of Polish hostels.

🛈 PRICE RANGES

Accommodation listings are grouped by price then ordered by preference. Prices listed are for an average double room in high season, with private bathroom and including breakfast.

€ less than 150zł

€€ 150–400zł

€€€ more than 400zł

The following price ranges refer to the cost of an average main-course item.

€ less than 20zł

€€ 20–40zł

€€€ more than 40zł

→ Poland has over 500 camping sites registered at the **Polish Federation of Camping & Caravanning** (☑ 22 810 6050; www.pfcc.eu).

MONEY

→ The Polish currency is the złoty, abbreviated as zł and pronounced *zwo-ti*. It is divided into 100 groszy, which are abbreviated to gr.

→ ATMs are ubiquitous in cities and towns, and even the smallest hamlet is likely to have at least one.

→ Change money at banks or *kantors* (private currency-exchange offices). Find these in town centres as well as travel agencies, train stations, post offices and department stores. Rates vary, so it's best to shop around.

→ In restaurants, tip 10% of the bill to reward good service. Leave the tip in the pouch the bill is delivered in or hand the money directly to the server.

OPENING HOURS

Banks 9am to 4pm Monday to Friday, 9am to 1pm Saturday

Offices 9am to 5pm Monday to Friday, 9am to 1pm Saturday

Post Offices 8am to 7pm Monday to Friday, 8am to 1pm Saturday (cities)

Restaurants 11am to 10pm daily

Shops 8am to 6pm Monday to Friday, 10am to 2pm Saturday

PUBLIC HOLIDAYS

New Year's Day 1 January

Epiphany 6 January

Easter Sunday March or April

Easter Monday March or April

State Holiday 1 May

Constitution Day 3 May

Pentecost Sunday Seventh Sunday after Easter

Corpus Christi Ninth Thursday after Easter

Assumption Day 15 August

All Saints' Day 1 November

Independence Day 11 November

Christmas 25 and 26 December

TELEPHONE

→ All Polish telephone numbers, whether landline or mobile (cell), have nine digits. Landlines are written 12 345 6789, with the first two numbers corresponding to the former city code. Mobile phone numbers are written 123 456 789.

→ To call abroad from Poland, dial the international access code (00), then the country code, then the area code (minus any initial zero) and the number.

→ To dial Poland from abroad, dial your country's international access code, then 48

(Poland's country code) and then the unique nine-digit local number.

➡ Poland uses the GSM 900/1800 network, which is compatible with the rest of Europe and Australia but not always with the North American GSM systems – check with your service provider.

➡ Prepaid SIM cards are readily available from telephone provider shop (GSM, Orange etc). Top-ups can be bought at phone shops, newspaper kiosks and even some ATMs.

WI-FI

Poland is well wired, and the majority of hotels offer some form of internet access (normally wi-fi) for you to log on to with your own laptop, smartphone or tablet.

ⓘ Getting There & Away

BORDER CROSSINGS

Poland shares long borders on its western and southern sides with EU members Germany, the Czech Republic and Slovakia. To the northeast is EU member Lithuania. To the north and east are Ukraine, Belarus and Russia's Kaliningrad enclave.

AIR

Most international flights to Poland arrive at Warsaw's **Frédéric Chopin Airport**. Warsaw has a second, smaller airport, **Warsaw Modlin Airport**, 35km north of the city, which handles budget flights. Other important international air gateways include the following:

Gdańsk Lech Wałęsa Airport (www.airport.gdansk.pl)

Katowice Airport (www.katowice-airport.com)

Kraków John Paul II International Airport (www.krakowairport.pl)

LAND

Poland has open borders (and plenty of rail and road crossings) on its western and southern frontiers with Germany, the Czech Republic and Slovakia. Crossings with Lithuania, on the northeastern end of the country, are also open, and you will normally not need to show a passport or undergo any border formalities.

It's a different story with Ukraine, Belarus and Kaliningrad. Visas are not required for most visitors to enter Ukraine, though the passport checks at the border may take a while. Entering Belarus and Russia will likely require visas and advance planning.

ⓘ Getting Around

BUS

Poland is easily accessible by bus. National **Polski Bus** (www.polskibus.com) service links big cities and can be faster than trains on some routes. Elsewhere, buses are useful for remote towns and villages that aren't serviced by trains.

TRAIN

Poland's train network is extensive and reasonably priced. Prices of Polish trains can vary greatly, even along the same lines. The **Express InterCity** trains (marked EIC) tend to be the most expensive, while trains marked TLK can be nearly as fast and much cheaper. Ask at ticket windows for the cheapest tickets available. For a handy train timetable, try Polish Rail's website: www.rozklad-pkp.pl.

HUNGARY

Budapest

POP 1.7 MILLION

Straddling the Danube River, with the Buda Hills to the west and sprawling Pest to the east, Budapest is a dazzling city. Its beauty is not all natural; humankind has played a role in shaping this pretty face too. Architecturally, the city is a treasure trove, with enough baroque, neoclassical, eclectic and art nouveau (or Secessionist) buildings to satisfy everyone.

⊙ Sights

⊙ Buda Hills

The hilly terrain lining the Danube's western bank is home to **Castle Hill** (Várhegy). This is the nerve centre of Budapest's history and the area is packed with many of the capital's most important museums and other attractions.

★ **Royal Palace**   PALACE

(Királyi Palota; Map p710; I Szent György tér; ▣ 16, 16A, 116) The former Royal Palace has been razed and rebuilt at least half a dozen times over the past seven centuries. Béla IV established a royal residence here in the mid-13th century, and subsequent kings added to the structure. The palace was levelled in the battle to rout the Turks in 1686; the Habsburgs rebuilt it but spent very little time here. Today the Royal Palace contains the Hungarian National Gallery (p710), the **Castle Museum** (Vármúzeum; Map p710; ☎1-487 8800; www.btm.hu; I Szent György tér 2, Bldg E; adult/concession 2000/1000Ft; ◷10am-6pm

HUNGARY AT A GLANCE

Don't Miss

Budapest's Castle Hill The city boasts architectural gems in spades, but the limestone plateau of Castle Hill towering over the Danube River's west bank is the Hungarian capital's most spectacular sight.

Budapest nightlife Alongside its age-old cafe culture and hallowed music halls, Budapest offers a magical blend of unique drinking holes, fantastic wine, home-grown firewaters and emerging craft beers, all served up with a warm Hungarian welcome. Distinctive are the *romkocsmák* (ruin bars) and *kertek* (gardens) that pop up in the warmer months.

Thermal baths With more than 300 thermal hot springs in public use across Hungary, it's not hard to find a place to take the waters. Some of the thermal baths, like the Rudas Baths in Budapest, date back to the 16th century. Increasingly popular are wellness spas and water parks, which draw different crowds.

Lake Balaton's northern shore Hungary's 'sea' (and Continental Europe's largest lake) is where people come to sun and swim in summertime. The quieter side of Lake Balaton mixes sizzling beaches and oodles of fun on the water with historic waterside towns like Keszthely and Balatonfüred.

Eger Beautifully preserved baroque architecture gives the town a relaxed, almost Mediterranean feel; it is flanked by two of northern Hungary's most beautiful ranges of hills (Bükk and Mátra), and is the home of some of Hungary's best wines.

Itineraries

Three Days

Focus mainly on **Budapest**. For the first day, head up to Castle Hill, taking in views from the Royal Palace. There are museums aplenty here. Spend the second day exploring the other side of the river, in Pest. Walk up leafy Andrássy út to Heroes' Square, past architectural gems like the Hungarian State Opera House. The absorbing House of Terror is also on Andrássy. Spend the third day at one of the city's thermal baths.

One Week

A few more days gives you time to stretch your legs and see some of the rest of the country. If it's hot, head to **Lake Balaton** for a dip in Hungary's little piece of the 'sea'. At other times in the year, the northeastern corner of the country calls. Here is where the foothills of the Carpathians begin, and the region is known for its forested hiking trails and traditional folk culture. The regional capital of **Eger** makes for an excellent base to explore and taste the region's wines.

Essential Food & Drink

Goulash The *sine qua non* of Hungarian cuisine is the thick beef soup *gulyás*, usually eaten as main course.

Fisherman's soup Hungarians love *leves* (soup), and one to look out for is *halászlé* (fisherman's soup), a bowl of fish stock, tomatoes, green peppers and paprika.

Paprika This red spice is essential to Hungarian cuisine. Not only is it used in preparing dishes, but it also appears on restaurant tables as a condiment.

Sweets Desserts include *Somlói galuska* (sponge cake with chocolate and whipped cream) and *Gundel palacsinta* (pancakes with chocolate and nuts).

Wine Hungarians love their wine and take it seriously. In summer spritzers of red or white wine mixed with mineral water are popular.

Getting Around

Boat From April to late October, the Budapest-based Mahart PassNave runs excursion boats on the Danube from Budapest to surrounding towns.

Bus Cheaper and often faster than trains. Useful for more remote destinations not served by trains.

Car Handy for exploring the wilder corners of Hungary. Drive on the right.

Train Reasonably priced, with extensive coverage of the country.

Menetred (www.menetrendek.hu) has links to all the timetables: bus, train, public transport and boat.

When to Go
Budapest

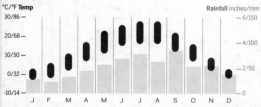

Apr & May Spring is glorious, though it can be pretty wet in May.

Jun–Sep Summer is warm, sunny and unusually long everywhere.

Oct–Mar Many sights reduce their hours sharply or close altogether. Prices are rock-bottom.

Arriving in Hungary

Ferenc Liszt International Airport (Budapest) Buses run round the clock from the airport to the Kőbánya-Kispest metro station. The airport shuttle does door-to-door drop-offs (around €22 to central Budapest), while taxis cost from around 5650Ft.

Keleti, Nyugati & Déli train stations (Budapest) All three stations are on metro lines of the same name; trams and/or night buses call when the metro is closed.

Top Phrases

Hello. Szervusz.

Goodbye. Viszlát.

Please. Kérem.

Thank you. Köszönöm.

Excuse me. Elnézést kérek.

Resources

Hungary Museums (www.museum.hu)

Hungarian National Tourist Office (www.gotohungary.com)

Tourinform (www.tourinform.hu)

Set Your Budget

➡ Dorm bed: 3000–6500Ft

➡ Meal at a cheap or self-service restaurant: 1500–2500Ft

➡ Ticket to national museum or other attraction: 700Ft

Buda

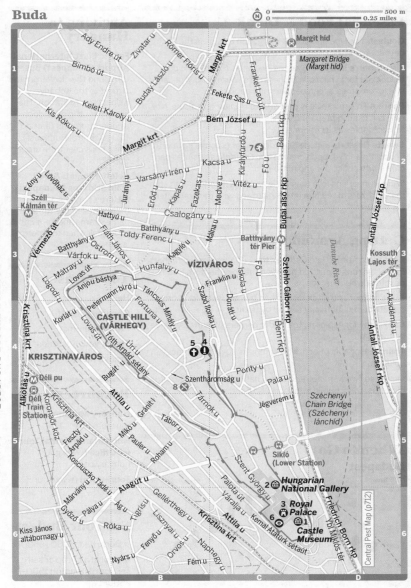

Tue-Sun Mar-Oct, to 4pm Nov-Feb; 🚌16, 16A, 116, 🚃19, 41), and the **National Széchenyi Library** (Országos Széchenyi Könyvtár; Map p710; ☎1-224 3700; www.oszk.hu; I Szent György tér 4-6, Bldg F; ⊗9am-8pm, stacks to 7pm Tue-Sat; 🚌16, 16A, 116).

⭐**Hungarian National Gallery** GALLERY
(Nemzeti Galéria; Map p710; ☎1-201 9082; www.mng.hu; I Szent György tér 2, Bldgs A-D; adult/concession 1800/900Ft, audio guide 800Ft; ⊗10am-6pm Tue-Sun; 🚌16, 16A, 116) The Hungarian National Gallery is an overwhelming

Buda

collection spread across four floors that traces Hungarian art from the 11th century to the present. The largest collections include medieval and Renaissance stonework, Gothic wooden sculptures and panel paintings, late Gothic winged altars, and late Renaissance and baroque art.

Matthias Church   CHURCH
(Mátyás templom; Map p710; ☑1-489 0716; www.matyas-templom.hu; I Szentháromság tér 2; adult/concession 1500/1000Ft; ⊗9am-5pm Mon-Fri, 9am-noon Sat, 1pm-5pm Sun; ☐16, 16A, 116) Parts of Matthias Church date back 500 years, notably the carvings above the southern entrance. But basically Matthias Church (so named because King Matthias Corvinus married Beatrix here in 1474) is a neo-Gothic confection designed by the architect Frigyes Schulek in 1896.

Fishermen's Bastion   MONUMENT
(Halászbástya; Map p710; I Szentháromság tér; adult/concession 800/400Ft; ⊗9am-8pm May-mid-Oct, to 7pm mid-Mar-Apr; ☐16, 16A, 116) The bastion, a neo-Gothic masquerade that looks medieval and offers some of the best views in Budapest, was built as a viewing platform in 1905 by Frigyes Schulek, the architect behind Matthias Church. Its name was taken from the medieval guild of fishermen responsible for defending this stretch of the castle wall. The seven gleaming white turrets represent the Magyar tribes that entered the Carpathian Basin in the late 9th century.

★**Citadella**   FORT
(Citadel; Map p712; ☐27) The Citadella is a fortress that never saw a battle. Built by the Habsburgs after the 1848–49 War of Independence to defend the city from further insurrection, the structure was obsolete by the time it was ready in 1851 due to the change in political climate. Today the fortress contains some big guns peeping through the loopholes, but the interior has now been closed to the public while its future is decided.

◎ Pest

The flat eastern bank of the Danube is where you begin to appreciate Budapest's size and

---

DON'T MISS

IN HOT WATER

Hungarians have been 'taking the waters' supplied by an estimated 300 thermal springs since togas were all the rage, and the practice really got a boost during the centuries-long Ottoman occupation (some baths retain their original Turkish appearance). These are the best and most visitor-friendly options in the capital:

Gellért Baths (Gellért gyógyfürdő; Map p712; ☑1-466 6166; www.gellertbath.hu; XI Kelenhegyi út 4, Danubius Hotel Gellért; incl locker/cabin Mon-Fri 5600/6000Ft, Sat & Sun 5800/6200Ft; ⊗6am-8pm; ☐7, 86, Ⓜ M4 Szent Gellért tér, ☐18, 19, 47, 49)

Rudas Baths (Rudas Gyógyfürdő; Map p712; ☑1-356 1322; www.rudasfurdo.hu; I Döbrentei tér 9; incl cabin Mon-Fri/Sat & Sun 3500/4000Ft, morning/night ticket 2800/5100Ft; ⊗men 6am-8pm Mon & Wed-Fri, women 6am-8pm Tue, mixed 10pm-4am Fri, 6am-8pm & 10pm-4am Sat, 6am-8pm Sun; ☐7, 86, ☐18, 19)

Széchenyi Baths (Széchenyi Gyógyfürdő; ☑1-363 3210; www.szechenyibath.hu; XIV Állatkerti körút 9-11; tickets incl locker/cabin Mon-Fri 5200/5700Ft, Sat & Sun 5400/5900Ft; ⊗6am-10pm; Ⓜ M1 Széchenyi fürdő)

Király Baths (Király Gyógyfürdő; Map p710; ☑1-202 3688; www.kiralyfurdo.hu; II Fő utca 84; daily tickets incl locker/cabin 2400/2700Ft; ⊗9am-9pm; ☐109, ☐4, 6, 19, 41)

Central Pest

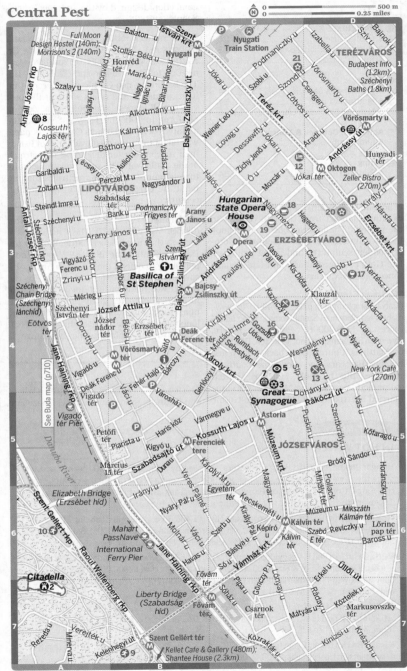

0 — 500 m
0 — 0.25 miles

Full Moon
Design Hostel (140m);
Morrison's 2 (140m)

Nyugati
Train Station

Budapest Info
(1.2km);
Széchenyi
Baths (1.8km)

TERÉZVÁROS

Nyugati pu

Szent István krt

Teréz krt

Vörösmarty u

Andrássy út

Hunyadi
tér

Oktogon

Zeller Bistro
(270m)

LIPÓTVÁROS

Kossuth
Lajos tér

Szabadság
tér

Hungarian
State Opera
House

ERZSÉBETVÁROS

Király
Harsfa u

Erzsébet krt

Arany
János u

Opera

Basilica of
St Stephen

Andrássy út

Bajcsy-
Zsilinszky út

Klauzál
tér

Klauzál u

New York Café
(270m)

Széchenyi
Chain Bridge
(Széchenyi
lánchíd)

Eötvös
tér

Deák
Ferenc tér

Vörösmarty
tér

Károly krt

Great
Synagogue

Rákóczi út

Astoria

JÓZSEFVÁROS

Danube River

Vigadó
tér Pier

Petőfi
tér

Kossuth Lajos u

Ferenciek
tere

Szabadsajtó út

Elizabeth Bridge
(Erzsébet híd)

Egyetem
tér

Kálvin tér

Mikszáth
Kálmán tér

Lőrinc
pap tér

Maháit
PassNave
International
Ferry Pier

Jane Hainling rkp

Raoul Wallenberg rkp

Citadella

Liberty Bridge
(Szabadság
híd)

Fővám
tér

Üllői út

Szent Gellért tér

Kellet Cafe & Gallery (480m);
Shantee House (2.3km)

Central Pest

urban character. You'll probably spend the bulk of your time here, which takes in the former Jewish quarter as well as high-heeled Andrássy út, the long, dramatic and très chic boulevard that slices through the area.

★ **Great Synagogue**   SYNAGOGUE
(Nagy Zsinagóga; Map p712; ☏ 1-462 0477; www. dohany-zsinagoga.hu; VII Dohány utca 2; adult/concession incl museum 4000/3000Ft; ⊙ 10am-8pm Sun-Thu, to 4pm Fri May-Sep, 10am-6pm Sun-Thu, to 4pm Fri Mar-Apr & Oct, 10am-4pm Sun-Thu, to 2pm Fri Nov-Feb; M M2 Astoria, ⊞ 47, 49) Budapest's stunning Great Synagogue is the largest Jewish house of worship in the world outside New York City. Built in 1859, the synagogue has both Romantic and Moorish architectural elements. Inside, is the Hungarian Jewish Museum & Archives. On the synagogue's north side, the **Holocaust Tree of Life Memorial** (Map p712; Raoul Wallenberg Memorial Park, opp VII Wesselényi utca 6; M M2 As-

toria, ⊞ 47, 49) presides over the mass graves of those murdered by the Nazis.

**Hungarian Jewish
Museum & Archives**   MUSEUM
(Magyar Zsidó Múzeum és Levéltár; Map p712; ☏ 1-343 6756; www.milev.hu; VII Dohány utca 2; incl in synagogue entry adult/concession 4000/3000Ft; ⊙ 10am-6pm Sun-Thu, to 4pm Fri Mar-Apr & Oct, 10am-8pm Sun-Thu, to 4pm Fri May-Sep, 10am-4pm Sun-Thu, to 2pm Fri Nov-Feb; M M2 Astoria, ⊞ 47, 49) Upstairs in an annexe of the Great Synagogue, this museum contains objects related to religious and everyday life, including 3rd-century Jewish headstones from Roman Pannonia discovered in 1792 in Nagykanizsa in southwestern Hungary, a vast amount of liturgical items in silver, and manuscripts, including a handwritten book of the local Burial Society from the late 18th century. Call ahead for guided tours (adult/concession 3700/2700Ft).

House of Terror   MUSEUM
(Terror Háza; Map p712; ☏ 1-374 2600; www.terrorhaza.hu; VI Andrássy út 60; adult/concession 3000/1500Ft; audioguide 1500Ft; ⊙ 10am-6pm Tue-Sun; M M1 Oktogon) The headquarters of the dreaded secret police is now the startling House of Terror, focusing on the crimes and atrocities of Hungary's fascist and Stalinist regimes in a permanent exhibition called Double Occupation. But the years after WWII leading up to the 1956 Uprising get the lion's share of the exhibition space (almost three-dozen spaces on three levels). The reconstructed prison cells in the basement and the Perpetrators' Gallery, featuring photographs of the turncoats, spies and torturers, are chilling.

★ **Hungarian State
Opera House**   NOTABLE BUILDING
(Magyar Állami Operaház; Map p712; ☏ 1-332 8197; www.operavisit.hu; VI Andrássy út 22; adult/concession 2490/2200Ft; ⊙ tours in English 2pm, 3pm & 4pm; M M1 Opera) The neo-Renaissance Hungarian State Opera House was designed by Miklós Ybl in 1884 and is among the most beautiful buildings in Budapest. Its facade is decorated with statues of muses and opera greats such as Puccini, Mozart, Liszt and Verdi, while its interior dazzles with marble columns, gilded vaulted ceilings, chandeliers and near-perfect acoustics. If you cannot attend a performance, join one of the three daily tours. Tickets are available from the souvenir shop inside the lobby.

LOCAL KNOWLEDGE

EAT, DRINK & BE MAGYAR

There is a lot more to Hungarian food than goulash, and it remains one of the most sophisticated styles of cooking in Europe. Magyars even go so far as to say there are three essential world cuisines: French, Chinese and their own.

That may be a bit of an exaggeration, but Hungary's reputation as a food centre dates largely from the late 19th century and the first half of the 20th, and despite a fallow period during the chilly days of communism is once again commanding attention. So too are the nation's world-renowned wines.

Parliament   HISTORIC BUILDING

(Országház; Map p712; ☑1-441 4904; www.hungarianparliament.com; V Kossuth Lajos tér 1-3; adult/student EU citizen 2000/1000Ft, non-EU citizen 5200/2600Ft; ⊙8am-6pm Mon-Fri, to 4pm Sat & Sun; ⓂM2 Kossuth Lajos tér, ⍗2) The Eclectic-style Parliament, designed by Imre Steindl and completed in 1902, has 691 sumptuously decorated rooms, but you'll only get to see several of these and other features on a guided tour of the North Wing: the Golden Staircase; the Domed Hall, where the **Crown of St Stephen**, the nation's most important national icon, is on display; the Grand Staircase and its wonderful landing; Loge Hall; and Congress Hall, where the House of Lords of the one-time bicameral assembly sat until 1944.

★**Basilica of
St Stephen**   CATHEDRAL

(Szent István Bazilika; Map p712; ☑1-338 2151, 06 30 703 6599; www.basilica.hu; V Szent István tér; requested donation 200Ft; ⊙9am-7pm Mon-Sat, 7.45am-7pm Sun; ⓂM3 Arany János utca) Budapest's neoclassical cathedral was built over half a century and completed in 1905. Much of the interruption during construction had to do with a fiasco in 1868 when the dome collapsed during a storm, and the structure had to be demolished and then rebuilt from the ground up. The basilica is rather dark and gloomy inside, but take a trip to the top of the **dome** for incredible views.

🛏 Sleeping

Accommodation in Budapest runs the gamut from hostels in converted flats and private rooms in far-flung housing estates to luxury guesthouses in the Buda Hills and five-star properties. The booking site **Hostelworld** (www.hostelworld.com) maintains a good list of Budapest hostels.

★**Shantee House**   HOSTEL €

(☑1-385 8946; www.backpackbudapest.hu; XI Takács Menyhért utca 33; beds in yurt €13.50, small/large dm from €10/16, d €32-52; Ⓟ@🛜; ⍗7, 7A, ⍗19, 49) Budapest's first hostel (originally known as the Back-Pack Guesthouse), the Shantee has added two floors to its colourfully painted suburban 'villa' in south Buda. It's all good and the fun (and sleeping bodies in high season) spills out into a lovely landscaped garden, with hammocks, a yurt and a gazebo. Two of the five doubles are en suite.

★**Hive Hostel**   HOSTEL €€

(Map p712; ☑06 30 826 6197; http://thehive.hu; VII Dob utca 19; dm €15-25, d €60-100; @🛜; ⓂM1/2/3 Deák Ferenc tér) This enormous and very central place with more than 50 rooms of all sizes and shapes over several levels is for the slightly better-heeled budget traveller. There's a big common area and kitchen and a wonderful rooftop bar that looks down on a courtyard with two large chestnut trees and a popular ruin garden. A wonderful place, with equally great staff.

**Home-Made
Hostel**   HOSTEL €

(Map p712; ☑06 30 200 4546, 1-302 2103; www.homemadehostel.com; VI Teréz körút 22; dm 3300-6500Ft, d 10000-16000Ft; @🛜; ⓂM1 Oktogon, ⍗4, 6) This homey, extremely welcoming hostel with 20 beds in four rooms has recycled tables hanging upside down from the ceiling and old valises under the beds that serve as lockers. The whole idea is to use forgotten objects from old Budapest homes in a new way. The old-style kitchen is museum quality. Dorms have four to eight beds.

**Full Moon
Design Hostel**   HOSTEL €€

(☑1-792 9045, 06 30 326 6888; www.fullmoonhostel.com; V Szent István tér 11; dm/d €13/60; Ⓟ✳🛜; ⍗4, 6) With oversized portraits of Joplin and Hendrix in the colourful lobby and an upbeat party atmosphere this is a hostel for the 21st century. There's a fabulous eat-off-the-floor kitchen, a huge breakfast bistro and generous-sized laundry. Dorms have between six and eight beds. Some of the candy-stripe doubles gaze down onto a courtyard and the popular club **Morrison's 2** (☑1-374 3329; www.morrisons2.hu; V Szent István körút 11; ☺5pm-6am; 🚊4, 6).

✕ Eating

The dining scene in Budapest has undergone a sea change in recent years. Hungarian food has 'lightened up', offering the same wonderfully earthy and spicy tastes but in less calorific dishes.

Kisharang   HUNGARIAN €
(Map p712; ☑1-269 3861; www.kisharang.hu; V Október 6 utca 17; mains 1000-2350Ft; ☺11.30am-8pm; 🚊15, 115) Centrally located 'Little Bell' is an *étkezde* (canteen serving simple Hungarian dishes) that's top of the list with students and staff of the nearby Central European University. The daily specials are something to look forward to and the retro decor is fun. *Főzelék* (370Ft to 490Ft), the traditional Hungarian way of preparing vegetables and sometimes served with meat, is always a good bet.

The daily menu is 990Ft.

★ Budavári Rétesvár   HUNGARIAN €
(Strudel Castle; Map p710; ☑06 70 408 8696; www.budavariretesvar.hu; I Balta köz 4; strudel 310Ft; ☺8am-8pm; 🚊16, 16A, 116) Strudel in all its permutations – from poppyseed with sour cherry to dill with cheese and cabbage – is available at this hole-in-the wall dispensary in a narrow alley of the Castle District.

★ Bors Gasztro Bár   SANDWICHES €
(Map p712; www.facebook.com/BorsGasztroBar; VII Kazinczy utca 10; soups 600Ft, baguettes 670-890Ft; ☺11.30am-9pm; 🖋; Ⓜ M2 Astoria) We love this thimble-sized place, not just for its hearty, imaginative soups (how about sweet potato with coconut or tiramisu?) but for its equally good grilled baguettes: try 'Bors Dog' (spicy sausage and cheese) or 'Brain Dead' (pig's brains are the main ingredient). It's not a sit-down kind of place; most chow down on the pavement outside.

★ Zeller Bistro   HUNGARIAN €€
(☑06 30 651 0880; Hercegprimas utca 18; mains 3600-4800Ft; ☺noon-midnight Tue-Sat; Ⓜ M1 Vörösmarty utca, 🚊4, 6) You'll receive a very warm welcome at this lovely candlelit cellar where the attentive staff serve food sourced largely from the owner's family and friends in the Lake Balaton area. The Hungarian home cooking includes some first-rate dishes such as grey beef, duck leg, oxtail and lamb's knuckle. Superb desserts too. Popular with both locals and expats; reservations are essential.

★ Kőleves   JEWISH €€
(Map p712; ☑06 20 213 5999; www.kolevesvendeglo.hu; VII Kazinczy utca 37-41; mains 2180-5180Ft; ☺8am-midnight Mon-Fri, from 9am Sat & Sun; 🖋; Ⓜ M1/2/3 Deák Ferenc tér) Always buzzy and lots of fun, the 'Stone Soup' attracts a young crowd with its Jewish-inspired (but not kosher) menu, lively decor, great service and reasonable prices. Good vegetarian choices. Breakfast (890Ft to 1250Ft) is served from 8am to 11.30am. The daily lunch is just 1250Ft, or 1100Ft for the vegetarian version.

WORTH A TRIP

LAKE BALATON

Extending roughly 80km like a skinny, lopsided paprika, at first glance Lake Balaton seems to simply be a happy, sunny expanse of opaque tourmaline-coloured water in which to play. But step beyond the beaches of Europe's biggest and shallowest body of water and you'll encounter vine-filled forested hills, a national park and a wild peninsula jutting out 4km, nearly cutting the lake in half. Oh, and did we mention Hungary's most famous porcelain producer and a hilltop fairy-tale fortress?

Still, the main pursuits for visitors to Lake Balaton are swimming, windsurfing, sailing, rowing, fishing, soaking in a thermal lake, and the recently introduced stand-up paddle-boarding. The 210km designated bike path around the lake is prime for cycling. Lake cruises offered by **Balaton Shipping Co** (Balatoni Hajózási Rt; ☑84-310 050; www.balatonihajozas.hu; Krúdy sétány 2, Siófok) leave from Keszthely, Tihany and Balatonfüred over the warmest months (June, July and August).

The high season is July and August, though the lake is swimmable (and crowds are much more manageable) in June and early September.

🍷 Drinking & Nightlife

In recent years, Budapest has gained a reputation as one of Europe's top nightlife destinations. Alongside its age-old cafe culture, it offers a magical blend of unique drinking holes, fantastic wine, homegrown fire waters and emerging craft beers.

★ New York Café   CAFE
(☑ 1-886 6167; www.newyorkcafe.hu; VII Erzsébet körút 9-11; ☺ 9am-midnight; Ⓜ M2 Blaha Lujza tér, 🚋 4, 6) Considered the most beautiful cafe in the world when it opened in 1894, this Renaissance-style place on the ground floor of the Boscolo Budapest Hotel has been the scene of many a literary gathering. Some say it lacks the warmth and erudite crowd of most traditional cafes but the opulence and history will impress.

It's a great place for breakfast (2400Ft to 7500Ft; 9am to noon).

Művész Kávéház   CAFE
(Map p712; ☑ 06 70 333 2116; www.muveszkave-haz.hu; VI Andrássy út 29; ☺ 8am-9pm Mon-Sat, from 9am Sun; Ⓜ M1 Opera) Almost opposite the Hungarian State Opera House, the Artist Coffeehouse is an interesting place to people-watch (especially from the shady terrace), though some say its cakes (550Ft to 890Ft) are not what they used to be (though presumably they're not thinking as far back as 1898, when the cafe opened).

★ Doblo   WINE BAR
(Map p712; www.budapestwine.com; VII Dob utca 20; ☺ 2pm-2am Sun-Wed, to 4am Thu-Sat; Ⓜ M1/2/3 Deák Ferenc tér) Brick-lined and candlelit, Doblo is where you go to taste Hungarian wines, with scores available by the 1.5cL (15mL) glass for 900Ft to 2150Ft. There's food too, such as meat and cheese platters.

★ Instant   CLUB
(Map p712; ☑ 06 70 638 5040; www.instant.co.hu; VII Akácfa utca 51; ☺ 4pm-6am; Ⓜ M1 Opera) We still love this 'ruin bar' situated on one of Pest's most vibrant nightlife strips and so do all our friends. It has 26 rooms, seven bars, seven stages and two gardens with underground DJs and dance parties. It's always heaving.

Kelet Cafe & Gallery   CAFE
(Kelet Kávézó és Galéria; ☑ 06 20 456 5507; www.facebook.com/keletkavezo; XI Bartók Béla út 29; ☺ 7.30am-11pm Mon-Fri, 9am-11pm Sat & Sun; Ⓜ M4 Móricz Zsigmond körtér, 🚋 18, 19, 47, 49)

This really cool cafe moonlights as a used-book exchange on the ground floor and a large, bright gallery with seating upstairs. There are foreign newspapers to read and soups (850Ft to 950Ft) and sandwiches (850Ft to 1100Ft) should you feel peckish. Try the super hot chocolate.

☆ Entertainment

★ Liszt Music Academy   CLASSICAL MUSIC
(Liszt Zeneakadémia; Map p712; ☑ 1-462 4600, box office 1-321 0690; www.zeneakademia.hu; VI Liszt Ferenc tér 8; ☺ box office 10am-6pm; Ⓜ M1 Oktogon, 🚋 4, 6) Performances at Budapest's most important concert hall are usually booked up at least a week in advance, but more expensive (though still affordable) last-minute tickets can sometimes be available. It's always worth checking.

Pótkulcs   LIVE MUSIC
(Map p712; ☑ 1-269 1050; www.potkulcs.hu; VI Csengery utca 65/b; ☺ 5pm-1.30am Sun-Wed, to 2.30am Thu-Sat; Ⓜ M3 Nyugati pályaudvar) The 'Spare Key' is a fine little drinking venue with a varied menu of live music most evenings and occasional *táncház* (Hungarian music and dance). The small central courtyard is a wonderful place to chill out in summer.

ℹ Information

Budapest Info (Map p712; ☑ 1-438 8080; www.budapestinfo.hu; V Sütő utca 2; ☺ 8am-8pm; Ⓜ M1/2/3 Deák Ferenc tér) Budapest Info is about the best single source of information about Budapest, but it can get hopelessly crowded in summer, and the staff are not very patient. Less crowded is the City Park branch (☑ 1-438 8080; www.budapestinfo.hu; Olof Palme sétány 5, City Ice Rink; ☺ 9am-7pm; Ⓜ M1 Hősök tere). There are also information desks in the arrivals sections of Ferenc Liszt International Airport.

ℹ Getting There & Away

Most people arrive in Budapest by air, but you can also get here from dozens of European cities by bus or train. You can even get to Budapest by Danube hydrofoil from Vienna. See p721 for international arrival and departure details.

Budapest's **Ferenc Liszt International Airport** (BUD; ☑ 1-296 7000; www.bud.hu) has two modern terminals side by side, 2A and 2B, 24km southeast of the city centre.

All international buses and domestic ones to/from western Hungary arrive at and depart from **Népliget bus station** (☑ 1-219 8086; IX Üllői út

131; Ⓜ M3 Népliget) in Pest. The international ticket office is upstairs. Eurolines (www.euro-lines.hu) is represented here, as is its Hungarian associate, **Volánbusz** (📱1-382 0888; www.volanbusz.hu).

MÁV (Magyar Államvasutak, Hungarian State Railways; 📱1-349 4949; www.mavcsoport.hu) links up with the European rail network in all directions. Most international trains (and domestic traffic to/from the north and northeast) arrive at **Keleti train station** (Keleti pályaudvar; VIII Kerepesi út 2-6; Ⓜ M2/M4 Keleti pályaudvar).

❶ Getting Around

TO/FROM THE AIRPORT

MiniBUD (📱1-550 0000; www.minibud.hu; one way from 2000Ft) is the airport's official shuttle bus service and runs regularly to the centre and back. Tickets are available at a clearly marked desk in the arrivals halls, though you may have to wait while the van fills up. You need to book your journey back to the airport at least 12 hours in advance.

The cheapest (and most time-consuming) way to get into the city centre is to take bus 200E (4am to midnight) – look for the stop on the footpath between terminals 2A and 2B – which terminates at the Kőbánya-Kispest metro station. From there take the M3 metro into the city centre.

PUBLIC TRANSPORT

Budapest has an extensive and reliable public transport network of buses, trams, trolleybuses and a metro. Most public transport runs from around 4am to about 11.15pm.

You must have a valid ticket (which you can buy at kiosks, news stands, metro entrances, machines and, in some cases, on the bus for an extra charge) or travel pass. Life will most likely be simpler if you opt for a pass, and you won't have to worry about validating your ticket each time you board. The most central place to buy them is the ticket office at the Deák Ferenc tér metro station, open from 6am to 11pm daily.

The basic fare for all forms of transport is 350Ft (3000Ft for a block of 10), allowing you to travel as far as you like on the same metro, bus, trolleybus or tram line without changing/transferring. A 'transfer ticket' allowing unlimited stations with one change within one hour costs 530Ft.

Northeastern Hungary

Hungary is mainly flat, though here in the northeastern part of the country, the foothills of the Carpathians begin. The region is known for its forested hiking trails, tradi-

tional folk culture and hilltop castle ruins. It's also known for its superb wine production. The region capital of Eger makes for an excellent base to explore and taste the grape.

Eger

POP 54,500

Filled with beautifully preserved baroque buildings, Eger (pronounced 'egg-air') is a jewellery box of a town with loads to see and do. Explore the bloody history of Turkish occupation and defeat at the hilltop castle, climb an original Ottoman minaret, listen to an organ performance at the colossal basilica, or relax in a renovated Turkish bath. Then spend time traipsing from cellar to cellar in the **Valley of Beautiful Women**, tasting the celebrated Eger Bull's Blood (Egri Bikavér) and other local wines from the cask.

◉ Sights & Activities

★**Eger Castle** FORTRESS
(Egri Vár; 📱36-312 744; www.egrivar.hu; Vár köz 1; castle grounds adult/child 850/425Ft, incl museum 1700/850Ft; ⊘ exhibits 10am-4pm Tue-Sun Nov-Mar, 10am-6pm daily Apr-Oct, castle grounds 8am-6pm Nov-Mar, to 10pm Apr-Oct) Climb up cobbled Vár köz from Tinódi Sebestyén tér to reach the castle, erected in the 13th century after the Mongol invasion. Models, drawings and artefacts like armour and Turkish uniforms in the **Castle History Exhibition**, on the 1st floor of the former Bishop's Palace (1470), painlessly explain the castle's story. On the eastern side of the complex are foundations of the 12th-century **St John's Cathedral**. Enter the **castle casemates** (Kazamata) hewn from solid rock via the nearby **Dark Gate**.

★**Minorite Church of St Anthony of Padua** CHURCH
(Páduai Szent Antal Minorita Templom; Dobó István tér 6; suggested donation 300Ft; ⊘ 9am-6pm) On the southern side of Eger's main square stands this church, built in 1771 by Bohemian architect Kilian Ignaz Dientzenhofer and one of the most glorious baroque buildings in the world. The altarpiece of the Virgin Mary and St Anthony of Padua is by Johann Lukas Kracker, the Bohemian painter who also created the fire-and-brimstone ceiling fresco in the Lyceum library (p718).

GEORGIA

From its green valleys spread with vineyards to its old churches and watchtowers perched in fantastic mountain scenery, Georgia (Saqartvelo) is one of the most beautiful countries on earth and a marvellous canvas for walkers, horse riders, cyclists, skiers, rafters and travellers of every kind. Equally special are its proud, high-spirited, cultured people: Georgia claims to be the birthplace of wine, and this is a place where guests are considered blessings and hospitality is the very stuff of life.

Tbilisi, the capital and usual first port of call for visitors, is redolent of an age-old Eurasian crossroads, with its winding lanes, balconied houses, leafy squares and handsome churches, all overlooked by the 17-centuries old Narikala Fortress. Neighbourhoods not far from the centre retain a village feel with narrow streets, small shops and community atmosphere. But this is also a country moving forward in the 21st century, with spectacular contemporary buildings, a minimal crime rate and ever-improving facilities for the visitors who are a growing part of its future.

The **Georgian National Tourism Administration** (www.georgia.travel) maintains an excellent website in English on tourist attractions and guidelines for visitors.

There are many small or medium-sized, midrange hotels with character in cities and towns around the country, and a handful of super-luxury top-end places, mainly located in big cities like Tbilisi. There are perhaps 50 travellers' hostels around Georgia (the majority in Tbilisi). They provide dormitory beds or bunks, sometimes a few private doubles, and shared bathrooms and kitchens.

Most travellers arrive by air to **Tbilisi's international airport** (www.tbilisiairport. com), located 15km east of the city centre. Direct flights head to/from more than 40 international destinations spread from Paris to China. There are also a few international bus connections, including daily service to/from Athens, İstanbul and Moscow.

Once in Georgia, *marshrutky* (minibuses) are the main transport option for moving around the country. Trains are mostly slower and less frequent than road transport.

★**Lyceum Library**   LIBRARY
(Liceumi Könyvtar; ☑36-520 400 ext 2214; Eszterházy tér 1, Lyceum; adult/child 1000/500Ft; ⊗9.30am-1.30pm Tue-Sun Mar & Apr, 9.30am-3.30pm Tue-Sun May-Sep, by appointment Oct-Feb) This awesome 60,000-volume all-wood library on the 1st floor of the Lyceum's south wing contains hundreds of priceless manuscripts, medical codices and incunabula. The *trompe l'oeil* ceiling fresco painted by Bohemian artist Johann Lukas Kracker in 1778 depicts the Counter-Reformation's Council of Trent (1545–63), with a lightning bolt setting heretical manuscripts ablaze. It was Eger's – and its archbishop's – response to the Enlightenment and the Reformation.

Minaret   ISLAMIC SITE
(☑06 70 202 4353; www.minareteger.hu; Knézich Károly utca; 300Ft; ⊗10am-6pm Apr-Sep, 10am-5pm Oct-Mar) This 40m-high minaret, topped incongruously with a cross, is one of the few reminders of the Ottoman occupation of Eger. Nonclaustrophobes can brave the 97 narrow spiral steps to the top for the awesome view.

★**Valley of the Beautiful Women**   WINE
(Szépasszony-völgy Hétvége) More than two dozen cellars are carved into rock at the evocatively named Valley of the Beautiful Women, where wine tasting is popular. Try ruby-red Bull's Blood or any of the whites: *leányka*, *olaszrizling* and *hárslevelű* from nearby Debrő. The choice of wine cellars can be a bit daunting so walk around and have a look yourself. The valley is a little over 1km southwest across Rte 25 and off Király utca.

🛏 Sleeping

Agria Retur Vendégház   GUESTHOUSE €
(☑36-416 650; www.returvendeghaz.hu; Knézich Károly utca 18; s/d/tr 4200/7400/10,600Ft; @🛜) You couldn't receive a warmer welcome than the one you'll get at this guesthouse near the minaret. Walking up three flights of stairs, you enter a cheery communal kitchen/eating area central to four mansard rooms. Out the back is a huge garden with tables and a barbecue at your disposal. Just read the fan mail on the wall.

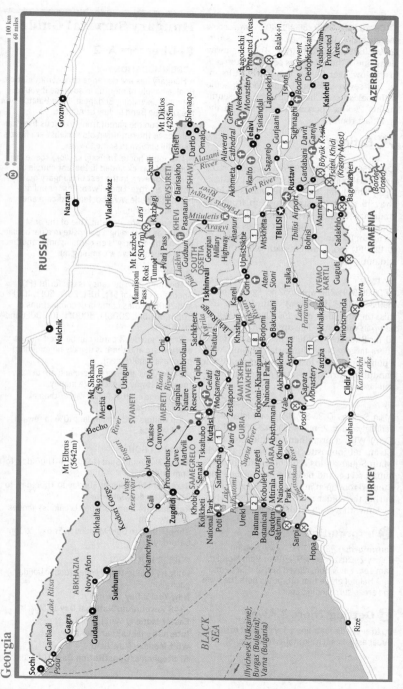

Georgia

RUSSIA

AZERBAIJAN

ARMENIA

TURKEY

BLACK SEA

ABKHAZIA

SVANETI

RACHA

IMERETI

SAMEGRELO

GURIA

ADJARA

SAMTSKHE-JAVAKHETI

KVEMO KARTLI

SOUTH OSSETIA

KHEVSURETI

PSHAVI

KHEVI

TUSHETI

KAKHETI

Sochi
Gantiadi
Gagra
Gudauta
Psou
Lake Ritsa
Novy Afon
Sukhumi
Ochamchyra
Chkhalta
Kodori Gorge
Gali
Zugdidi
Khobi
Kolkheti National Park
Poti
Ureki
Kobuleti
Batumi
Batumi Botanical Garden
Mtirala National Park
Sarpi
Hopa
Rize

Nalchik
Nazran
Vladikavkaz
Grozny

Mt Elbrus (5642m)
Mt Shkhara (5193m)
Mestia
Ushguli
Becho
Ivari
Enguri River
Jvari Reservoir
Okatse Canyon
Martvili
Prometheus Cave
Oni
Ambrolauri
Tqibuli
Chiatura
Sachkhere
Satsphlia Nature Reserve
Gelati
Motsameta
Kutaisi
Vani
Zestaponi
Samtredia
Senaki
Tskaltubo
Ozurgeti
Lake Paliastomi
Supsa River

Mamisoni Pass
Mt Kazbek (5047m)
Roki Tunnel
Larsi
Kazbegi
Jvari Pass
Pasanauri
Gudauri
Liakhvi
Didi
Tskhinvali
Georgian Military Highway
Ananuri
Mtiuletis
Aragvi
Pshavis Aragvi River
Akhmeta
Barisakho
Shatili
Shenaqo
Omalo
Dartlo
Mt Diklos (4285m)
Alazani River
Alaverdi Cathedral
Gremi
Nekresi
Lagodekhi Protected Areas
Lagodekhi
Tsnori
Balak÷n
Ikalto
Telavi
Tsinandali
Sagarejo
Gurjaani
Sighnaghi
Bodbe Convent
Dedoplistskaro
Vashlovani Protected Area

Khashuri
Gori
Ateni Sioni
Uplistsikhe
Mtskheta
TBILISI
Tbilisi Airport
Rustavi
Gardabani
Davit Gareja
Tsiteli Khidi (Krasny Most)
Marneuli
Bolnisi
Sadakhlo
Guguti
Bavra
Böyük Kəsik
Bağratashen

Kvira Range
Likhi Range
Kareli
Bakuriani
Borjomi
Borjomi-Kharagauli National Park
Tsalka
Lake Paravani
Akhalkalaki
Ninotsminda
Çıldır
Karitsakhi Lake
Ardahan
Abastumani
Akhaltsikhe
Vale
Posof
Sapara Monastery
Aspindza
Vardzia
Khulo

Ivari

Dobó Vendégház   GUESTHOUSE **€€**
(☑06 20 442 3849, 36-421 407; www.dobov-endeghaz.hu; Dobó István utca 19; s/d/tr 12,000/16,800/24,000Ft; ☏) Tucked away along one of the old town's pedestrian streets just below Eger Castle, this lovely little hotel has seven spick-and-span rooms, some with balconies. Check out the museum-quality Zsolnay porcelain collection in the breakfast room.

✗ Eating

Il Padrino   PIZZA **€**
(☑36-786 040, 06 20 547 9959; www.padrinopizza.hu; Fazola Henrik utca 1; pizza 990-2190Ft; ☺11am-10pm) This little hole in the wall is hidden away in a narrow street just up from the landmark former Neoclassical Synagogue. It's worth a look though as it serves the best premium Italian pizza in Eger. Salads (990Ft to 1290Ft) too. Limited seating both inside and out.

★1552   HUNGARIAN **€€**
(☑06 30 869 6219; www.1552.hu; Egri Vár; mains 1690-3450Ft; ☺11am-10pm) With a name like this, the stunning new 1552 has just got to be up in the castle. The upscale menu, created by Budapest-trained chef Matyás Hegyi, offers largely New Hungarian cuisine, with a polite nod to the losers way back in 1552: a handful of Turkish-inspired dishes are available as well.

Fő Tér   HUNGARIAN **€€**
(Main Square; ☑36-817 482; www.fotercafe.hu; Gerl Matyas utca 2; mains 1590-4290Ft; ☺10am-10pm) With a prominent position on Dobó István tér opposite the Minorite church, 'Main Square' adds a bit of colour to Eger's dining scene, and boasts a fine terrace with a tented roof open in summer and glassed-in during the colder months. The food is Hungarian with a contemporary taste.

ⓘ Information

Tourinform (☑36-517 715; www.eger.hu; Bajcsy-Zsilinszky utca 9; ☺9am-6pm Mon-Fri, 9am-1pm Sat & Sun, closed Sun mid-Sep–mid-Jun) Helpful office that promotes both the town and areas surrounding Eger.

ⓘ Getting There & Away

Up to seven direct trains a day connect to/from Budapest's Keleti train station (two hours).

Hungary Survival Guide

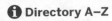

ⓘ Directory A–Z

ACCOMMODATION

➡ Hungary has a wide range of accommodation. Book a couple of months in advance if you're planning on visiting Budapest, Lake Balaton or the Danube Bend in July or August.

➡ Hotels run the gamut from luxurious five-star palaces to the run-down old socialist-era hovels that still survive in some towns.

➡ The youth hostel (*ifjúsági szállók*) scene in Budapest has exploded in the last couple of years. However, in the rest of Hungary quality hostels are rare. Useful websites for online booking include www.hostelworld.com and www.hihostels.hu.

➡ Campsites are plentiful. One of the best resources for finding a campsite in a particular part of the country is en.camping.info; another good website is www.camping.hu.

MONEY

➡ The Hungarian currency is the forint (Ft). There are coins of 5Ft, 10Ft, 20Ft, 50Ft, 100Ft and 200Ft. Notes come in denominations of 500Ft, 1000Ft, 2000Ft, 5000Ft, 10,000Ft and 20,000Ft.

➡ Credit and debit cards can be used almost everywhere and there is usually no minimum-purchase requirement.

➡ Bank ATMs are everywhere and are usually the easiest way to exchange money.

➡ Exchange cash at banks rather than at moneychangers.

➡ Tip waiters and bartenders 10% to reward good service.

OPENING HOURS

Banks 7.45am to 5pm Monday to Thursday, to 4pm Friday
Bars 11am to midnight Sunday to Thursday, to 2am Friday and Saturday
Restaurants 11am to 11pm; breakfast venues open by 8am
Shops 10am to 6pm Monday to Friday, to 1pm Saturday

PUBLIC HOLIDAYS

Hungary celebrates 10 *ünnep* (public holidays) each year.
New Year's Day 1 January
1848 Revolution/National Day 15 March
Easter Monday March/April
International Labour Day 1 May
Whit Monday May/June
St Stephen's/Constitution Day 20 August

1956 Remembrance Day/Republic Day 23 October

All Saints' Day 1 November

Christmas holidays 25 and 26 December

TELEPHONES

➜ All localities in Hungary have a two-digit telephone area code, except for Budapest, which has just a '1'.

➜ To make an intercity landline call within Hungary and whenever ringing a mobile telephone, dial the prefix 06, then dial the area code and phone number.

➜ To make an international call from Hungary, dial 00 then the country code, the area code and the number.

➜ The country code for Hungary is 36.

➜ Most North American mobile (cell) phones won't work here. Consider buying a rechargeable SIM chip at mobile-phone shops and newsagents, which cuts the cost of making local calls.

WI-FI

Almost all hostels and hotels offer internet and/or wi-fi, which is mostly free but sometimes has a small surcharge. Free wi-fi is also available at major airports, and many restaurants and cafes.

ⓘ Getting There & Away

Hungary is centrally located and has excellent air, road and rail connections to neightbouring countries. It's even possible to travel to and from Austria and Slovakia by boat along the Danube.

BORDER CROSSINGS

Hungary shares a border with seven countries. You won't have to show a passport if you're arriving from EU members Austria, Slovenia and Slovakia. The situation is different with Romania, Serbia, Croatia and Ukraine, where standard border controls are still in place.

AIR

Budapest is the main air gateway to Hungary. International flights land at Terminals 2A and 2B of **Ferenc Liszt International Airport** located on the outskirts of Budapest. **Hévíz-Balaton Airport** (SOB; ☑ 83-200 304; www.hevizairport.com; Repülőtér 1, Sármellék), in season, serves some German destinations, and is located 15km southwest of Keszthely near Lake Balaton.

LAND

Crossing the continent by bus is cheapest. Most international buses are run by Eurolines

ⓘ PRICE RANGES

The following price ranges refer to a double room with bathroom in high season. Unless otherwise stated, breakfast is included in the price.

€ less than 15,000Ft

€€ 15,000–35,000Ft

€€€ more than 35,000Ft

The following price ranges refer to a the cost of a main meal.

€ less than 3500Ft

€€ 3500–7500Ft

€€€ more than 7500Ft

and link with its Hungarian associate, **Volánbusz** (p717).

Hungarian State Railways, Magyar Államvasutak or MÁV, links up with the European rail network in all directions. Its trains run as far as London (via Munich and Paris), Stockholm (via Hamburg and Copenhagen), Moscow, Rome and İstanbul (via Belgrade). Almost all international trains bound for Hungary arrive and depart from Budapest's Keleti station; Deli handles trains to Croatia, Slovenia, Bosnia and Herzegovina and Serbia.

WATER

Hydrofoils to Bratislava and Vienna run by **Mahart PassNave** (Map p712; ☑ 1-484 4013; www.mahartpassnave.hu; V Belgrád rakpart; ☉ 9am-5pm Mon-Fri; ☒ 2) from May to late September arrive at and depart from the **International Ferry Pier** (Nemzetközi hajóállomás; Map p712; ☑ 1-484 4013; www.mahartpassnave.hu; V Belgrád rakpart; ☉ 9am-5pm Mon-Fri; ☒ 2).

ⓘ Getting Around

Hungary's domestic transport system is efficient, comprehensive and inexpensive. Towns are covered by a system of frequent buses, trams and trolleybuses. The majority of Hungary's towns and cities are easily negotiated on foot.

Hungary's **Volánbusz** (p717) bus network covers the whole country.

The national rail operator MÁV offers clean, punctual and relatively comfortable (if not ultra-modern) train services. Budapest is the hub of all the main railway lines, though many secondary train lines link provincial cities and towns.

CENTRAL & EASTERN EUROPE HUNGARY SURVIVAL GUIDE

ROMANIA

Bucharest

POP 1,900,000

Romania's capital sometimes gets a bad rap, but in fact it's dynamic, energetic and fun. You might have come to see exactly how big the Palace of Parliament is or to admire Bucharest's rise to belle époque fame, but the Romanian capital isn't just about major sights. This is a city that rewards the curious explorer, with some splendid 17th- and 18th-century Orthodox churches tucked away in quiet corners and graceful art nouveau villas. Many travellers give the city just a night or two before heading off to Transylvania, but that's not enough. Try to allow at least a few days to take in the good museums, stroll the parks and hang out at trendy cafes.

◉ Sights

Bucharest teems with museums and attractions; all are relatively cheap and many are among the nation's best. The historic thoroughfare Calea Victoriei makes a nice walk, as it connects the two main squares of the city: Piaţa Victoriei in the north, and Piaţa Revoluţiei in the centre.

★ **Palace of Parliament** HISTORIC BUILDING
(Palatul Parlamentului, Casa Poporului; ☑ tour bookings 0733-558 102; www.cic.cdep.ro; B-dul Naţiunile Unite; adult/student complete tours 55/28 lei, standard tours 35/18 lei, photography 30 lei; ⊙ 9am-5pm Mar-Oct, 10am-4pm Nov-Feb; Ⓜ Izvor) The Palace of Parliament is the world's second-largest administrative building (after the Pentagon) and former dictator Nicolae Ceauşescu's most infamous creation. Started in 1984 (and still unfinished), the building has more than 3000 rooms and covers 330,000 sq metres. Entry is by guided tour only (book in advance). Entry to

Romania

the palace is from B-dul Naţiunile Unite on the building's northern side (to find it, face the front of the palace from B-dul Unirii and walk around the building to the right). Bring your passport.

Several types of tours are available, including a 'standard' tour of the main rooms and hallways, and 'complete' tours that combine the standard tour with views of the terrace and basement. The standard tour takes around 45 minutes; add an extra 15 minutes to see the terrace and basement. Today the building houses the country's parliament and associated offices – though much of it stands unused.

★ Former Ceauşescu
Residence
MUSEUM

(Primăverii Palace; ☑ 021-318 0989; www.palatulprimaverii.ro; B-dul Primăverii 50; guided tours in English adult/child 50/40 lei; ⊙ 10am-5pm Tue-Sun; Ⓜ Aviatorilor) This restored villa is the former main residence of Nicolae and Elena Ceauşescu, who lived here for around two decades up until the end in 1989. Everything has been returned to its former lustre, including the couple's bedroom and the private apartments of the three Ceauşescu children. Highlights include a cinema in the basement, Elena's opulent private chamber and the back garden and swimming pool. Reserve a tour in advance by phone or on the website.

The overall effect is fascinating but rather depressing. The finely crafted furnishings, locally made reproductions of styles ranging from Louis XIV to art deco, feel sterile and stuffy.

Stavropoleos Church
CHURCH

(☑ 021-313 4747; www.stavropoleos.ro; Str Stavropoleos 4; ⊙ 8.30am-6pm; Ⓜ Piaţa Unirii) The tiny and lovely Stavropoleos Church, which dates from 1724, perches a bit oddly a block over from some of Bucharest's craziest Old Town carousing. It's one church, though, that will make a lasting impression, with its courtyard filled with tombstones, an ornate wooden interior and carved wooden doors.

★ Romanian
Athenaeum
HISTORIC BUILDING

(Ateneul Român; ☑ box office 021-315 6875; www.fge.org.ro; Str Benjamin Franklin 1-3; tickets 20-65 lei; ⊙ box office noon-7pm Tue-Fri, 4-7pm Sat, 10-11am Sun; Ⓜ Universitate, Piaţa Romană) The exquisite Romanian Athenaeum is the majestic heart of Romania's classical music

tradition. Scenes from Romanian history are featured on the interior fresco inside the Big Hall on the 1st floor; the dome is 41m high. A huge appeal dubbed 'Give a Penny for the Athenaeum' saved it from disaster after funds dried up in the late-19th century. Today it's home to the George Enescu Philharmonic Orchestra and normally only open during concerts, but you can often take a peak inside.

★ Grigore Antipa
Natural History Museum
MUSEUM

(Muzeul de Istorie Naturală Grigore Antipa; ☑ 021-312 8826; www.antipa.ro; Şos Kiseleff 1; adult/student 20/5 lei; ⊙ 10am-8pm Tue-Sun Apr-Oct, 10am-6pm Tue-Fri, 10am-7pm Sat & Sun Nov-Mar; 🚻; Ⓜ Piaţa Victoriei) One of the few attractions in Bucharest aimed squarely at kids, this natural history museum has been thoroughly renovated and features modern bells and whistles such as video displays, games and interactive exhibits. Much of it has English signage.

Museum of the
Romanian Peasant
MUSEUM

(Muzeul Ţăranului Român; ☑ 021-317 9661; www.muzeultaranuluiroman.ro; Şos Kiseleff 3; adult/child 8/2 lei; ⊙ 10am-6pm Tue-Sun; Ⓜ Piaţa Victoriei) The collection of peasant bric-a-brac, costumes, icons and partially restored houses makes this one of the most popular museums in the city. There's not much English signage, but insightful little cards in English posted in each room give a flavour of what's on offer. An 18th-century church stands in the back lot, as does a great gift shop and restaurant.

🛏 Sleeping

Hotels are typically aimed at businesspeople, and prices are higher here than in the rest of the country. Tips for getting discounts include booking in advance or using the hotel's website.

★ Little Bucharest
Old Town Hostel
HOSTEL €

(☑ 0786-329 136; www.littlebucharest.ro; Str Smârdan 15; dm 35-47 lei; r 105 lei; ❀ @ 🛜; Ⓜ Piaţa Unirii) Bucharest's most central hostel, in the middle of the lively Historic Centre, is super clean, white walled and well-run. Accommodation is over two floors, with dorms ranging from six to 12 beds. Private doubles are also available. The staff is travel friendly and youth oriented and can advise on sightseeing and fun. Book over the website or by email.

ROMANIA AT A GLANCE

Don't Miss

Palace of Parliament, Bucharest This is either a mind-blowing testament to the folly of dictatorship or an awe-inspiring showcase of Romanian craftsmanship. Whatever emotions are evoked by the Communist-era 'House of the People', the scale of Romania's entry into the 'World's Largest Building' competition must be seen to be believed.

Bran Castle Perched on a rocky bluff in Transylvania, Bran Castle's spectral exterior is like a composite of every horror film you've ever seen. Legend has it Vlad the Impaler (the inspiration for Count Dracula) was briefly imprisoned here, and you can follow his footsteps through an 'Escheresque' maze of courtyards and passages.

Painted monasteries of Bucovina Tucked in the eastern side of the Carpathian mountains, the Unesco-listed painted monasteries of Bucovina proudly show off Romania's unique Orthodox tradition. The churches are at one with their natural surroundings, and the dizzying kaleidoscope of colours and intricate details bring to life everything from biblical stories to the 15th-century siege of Constantinople.

Transylvania's Saxon villages & fortified churches Back in the 12th century, Saxon Germans were invited to settle parts of Transylvania to buffer the Hungarian kingdom from the threat of Tatar and Turkish attack. The architectural legacy is a row of regal fortified churches, watchtowers and impenetrable stone walls that dot the landscape between Sighişoara and Sibiu.

Braşov Gothic spires, medieval gateways, Soviet blocks and a huge Hollywood-style sign: Braşov's skyline is instantly compelling. A number of medieval watchtowers still glower over the town. Between them sparkle baroque buildings and churches, while easy-going cafes line main square Piaţa Sfatului.

Itineraries

Three Days

Three days only leaves time to explore **Bucharest** and take a short excursion to Braşov. In Bucharest, get an early start and take in the Palace of Parliament. Stroll along Calea Victoriei and take in the historic sites. Spend the second day in the leafy northern part of the capital, visiting the Former Ceauşescu Residence and the open-air National Village Museum. For the last day, take the train up to **Braşov** for a few hours.

One Week

A full week is about right to combine the capital and the highlights of Transylvania. Plan to spend at least one or two nights in **Braşov**, taking in the Black Church and admiring the city's picturesque setting. Use Braşov as a base for an excursion to nearby **Bran Castle**. From here branch out further north to see the historic town of **Sighişoara** and to admire the nearby fortified Saxon churches.

Essential Food & Drink

Mămăligă Romania's unofficial national dish is cornmeal mush (or 'polenta'), seemingly designed to warm and fill the stomach.

Sarmale Cabbage or vine leaves, stuffed with spiced meat and rice, and yeah, the *mămăligă* (see above) provides an excellent backstop for soaking up the juices.

Plum brandy Big meals traditionally begin with a shot of Romanian moonshine, *țuică*, but treat this innocent-looking liquid with respect.

Ciorbă Romanian meals often begin with a 'sour' soup called *ciorbă*. These come in several varieties: the local favourite is *ciorbă de burtă*, a garlicky tripe soup.

Getting Around

Air The Romanian national carrier Tarom (www.tarom.ro) operates a comprehensive network of domestic routes and has a network of ticket offices around the country.

Bus A mix of buses, minibuses and 'maxitaxis' – private vans holding from 10 to 20 passengers – form the backbone of the Romanian national transport system. Find an online timetable at Autogari.ro (www.autogari.ro).

Car Driving around Romania has compelling advantages, but roads are poor and driving is not ideal. If you have the chance to use alternatives like the train and bus, it can be a more relaxing option.

Train Trains are a slow but reliable way of getting around. The extensive network covers much of the country. The national rail system is run by Căile Ferate Române (CFR; www.cfrcalatori.ro); the website has an online timetable.

When to Go

Bucharest

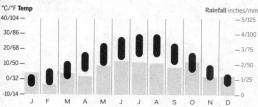

Jun–Aug Expect reliably sunny weather through the summer, but temperatures can get oppressively hot.

Mar–Jun Trees in full blossom by April; later in higher elevations. Birdwatching in the Danube Delta best in late May.

Nov–Mar Ski season runs from mid-December to early March. Cities like Braşov and Sibiu look great in the snow.

Arriving in Romania

Henri Coandă International Airport (Bucharest) Express bus 783 runs to the centre (3.50 lei, 40 minutes); taxis to the centre cost 50 to 60 lei (30 to 40 minutes); trains to Gara de Nord are 10 lei (30 minutes).

Timişoara Traian Vuia International Airport (Timişoara) Express bus E4 (2.50 lei, 30 minutes) and taxis (50 lei, 25 minutes) run to the centre.

Top Phrases

Hello. Bună ziua.

Goodbye. La revedere.

Please. Vă rog.

Thank you. Mulţumesc.

Cheers! Noroc!

Resources

Bucharest Life (www.bucharestlife.net)

Romania National Tourism Office (www.romania tourism.com)

Rural Tourism (www.ruralturism.ro)

Sapte Seri (www.sapte seri.ro)

Set Your Budget

➡ Hostel dorm room or guesthouse: 50 lei per person

➡ Street food and self-catering: 40 lei

➡ Train or bus ticket: 30 lei

➡ Museum admission: 10 lei

Central Bucharest

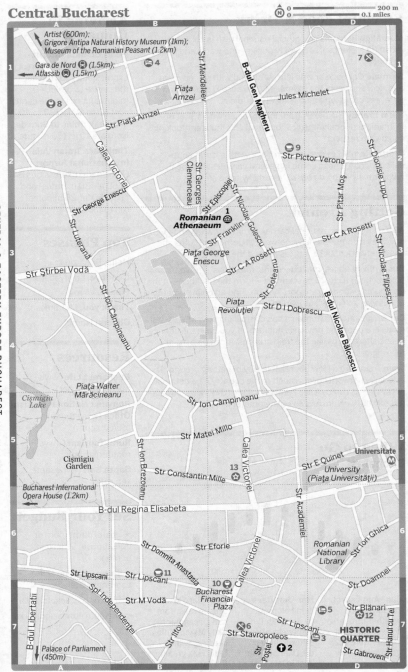

0   200 m
0   0.1 miles

Artist (600m);
Grigore Antipa Natural History Museum (1km);
Museum of the Romanian Peasant (1.2km)

Gara de Nord (1.5km);
Atlassib (1.5km)

B-dul Gen Magheru

Jules Michelet

Str Mendeleev

Piața Amzei

Str Piața Amzei

Str Georges Clemenceau

Str Pictor Verona

Str Dionisie Lupu

Calea Victoriei

Str George Enescu

Str Episcopiei

Str Nicolae Golescu

Str Pitar Moș

Romanian Athenaeum

Str Franklin

Str C A Rosetti

Str Luterană

Piața George Enescu

Str C A Rosetti

Str Nicolae Filipescu

Str Știrbei Vodă

Str Boteanu

Piața Revoluției

Str D I Dobrescu

B-dul Nicolae Bălcescu

Str Ion Câmpineanu

Piața Walter Mărăcineanu

Cișmigiu Lake

Str Ion Câmpineanu

Str Matei Millo

Cișmigiu Garden

Str Ion Brezoianu

Str Constantin Mille

Calea Victoriei

Str E Quinet

Universitate

University (Piața Universității)

Bucharest International Opera House (1.2km)

B-dul Regina Elisabeta

Str Domnița Anastasia

Str Eforie

Calea Victoriei

Str Academiei

Romanian National Library

Str Ion Ghica

Str Lipscani

Str Lipscani

Bucharest Financial Plaza

Str Doamnei

B-dul Libertății

Str M Vodă

Str Ilfov

Str Stavropoleos

Str Poștei

Str Lipscani

Str Blănari

HISTORIC QUARTER

Str Hanul cu Tei

Palace of Parliament (450m)

Spl Independenței

Str Gabroveni

Central Bucharest

Midland Youth Hostel HOSTEL **€**
(☑021-314 5323; www.themidlandhostel.com; Str Biserica Amzei 22; dm 40-60 lei; ❄✳@🛜; Ⓜ Piaţa Romană) A happening hostel, with an excellent central location not far from popular Piaţa Amzei. Accommodation is in four-, eight- or 12-bed dorms. There's a common kitchen too.

★**Rembrandt Hotel** HOTEL **€€**
(☑021-313 9315; www.rembrandt.ro; Str Smârdan 11; s/d tourist 180/230 lei, standard 260/300 lei, business 350/380 lei; ❄✳@🛜; Ⓜ Universitate) It's hard to say enough good things about this place. Stylish beyond its three-star rating, this 16-room, Dutch-run hotel faces the landmark National Bank in the Historic Centre. Rooms come in three categories – tourist, standard and business – with the chief difference being size. All rooms have polished wooden floors, timber headboards and DVD players. Book well in advance.

✖ Eating

Many restaurants are concentrated in the Old Town, with the rest spread out all around the city. Self-caterers will want to head to the daily market on Piaţa Amzei, with a good selection of fresh fruit and veg.

★**Caru' cu Bere** ROMANIAN **€€**
(☑021-313 7560; www.carucubere.ro; Str Stavropoleos 3-5; mains 20-45 lei; ⊙8am-midnight Sun-Thu, to 2am Fri & Sat; 🛜; Ⓜ Piaţa Unirii) Despite a decidedly touristy-leaning atmosphere, with peasant-girl hostesses and sporadic traditional song-and-dance numbers, Bucharest's oldest beer house continues to draw in a strong local crowd. The colourful belle-époque interior and stained-glass windows dazzle, as does the classic Romanian food. Dinner reservations are essential.

Shift Pub INTERNATIONAL **€€**
(☑021-211 2272; www.shiftpub.ro; Str General Eremia Grigorescu 17; mains 25-40 lei; ⊙noon-11pm Sun-Thu, to 1am Fri & Sat; Ⓜ Piaţa Romană) Great choice for salads and burgers as well numerous beef and pork dishes, often sporting novel Asian, Middle Eastern or Mexican taste touches. Try to arrive slightly before meal times to grab a coveted table in the tree-covered garden.

★**Artist** EUROPEAN **€€€**
(☑0728-318 871; www.theartist.ro; Calea Victoriei 147; mains 70-110 lei; ⊙noon-4pm & 5pm-midnight Tue-Sun) Located in a restored, eclectic 1880s villa on posh Calea Victoriei, this is the top fine-dining locale in Bucharest thanks to chef Paul Oppenkamp and his approach to modern cuisine, peppered with Romanian influences. The menu changes every three months, aside from the now legendary cucumber sorbet. Don't miss the spoon tasting for an artistic display of all dishes served. Reservations are a must.

🍷 Drinking & Nightlife

Origo CAFE
(☑0757-086 689; www.origocoffee.ro; Str Lipscani 9; ⊙7am-1am Sun, Tue & Wed, to 3am Thu-Sat; 🛜; Ⓜ Piaţa Unirii) Arguably the best coffee in town and *the* best place to hang out in the morning, grab a table and check your email. Lots of special coffee roasts and an unlimited number of ways to imbibe. There are a dozen pavement tables for relaxing on a sunny day.

★**Grădina Verona** CAFE
(☑0732-003 060; www.facebook.com/Gradina Verona; Str Pictor Verona 13-15; ⊙10am-midnight May-Sep; 🛜; Ⓜ Piaţa Romană) A garden oasis that is hidden behind the Cărtureşti bookshop, serving standard-issue but excellent

WORTH A TRIP

THE PAINTED MONASTERIES OF BUCOVINA

Bucovina's painted monasteries, in the northeast of the country, are among the most distinctive in all Christendom. They're cherished not only for their beauty and quality of artisanship, but also for their endurance over the centuries and overall cultural significance. The half-dozen or so monasteries, scattered over a large swath of Bucovina, date mainly from the 15th and 16th centuries, a time when Orthodox Moldavia was battling for its life with forces of the expanding Ottoman Empire.

The monasteries are hailed mainly for their colourful external frescoes, many of which have survived the region's cruel winters relatively intact. The external wall paintings served as both expressions of faith and as an effective method of conveying important biblical stories to a parish of mostly illiterate soldiers and peasants. But don't pass up the rich interiors, where every nook and cranny is filled with religious and cultural symbolism.

While several monastery complexes are spread throughout the province, the most impressive (and easiest to reach) churches are those at **Arbore** (Manastirea Arbore; ☑ 0740-154 213; Hwy DN2K 732, Arbore; adult/student 5/2 lei, photography 10 lei; ☉ 8am-7pm May-Sep, to 4pm Oct-Apr), **Humor** (Mănăstirea Humorului; Gura Humorului; adult/student 5/2 lei, photography 10 lei; ☉ 8am-7pm May-Sep, to 4pm Oct-Apr), **Voroneţ** (Mănăstirea Voroneţ; ☑ 0230-235 323; Str Voroneţ 166, Voroneţ; adult/child 5/2 lei, photography 10 lei; ☉ dawn-dusk), **Moldoviţa** (Mânăstirea Moldoviţa; Vatra Moldoviţei; adult/student 5/2 lei, photography 10 lei; ☉ 8am-7pm May-Sep, to 4pm Oct-Apr) and **Suceviţa** (☑ 0230-417 110; www.manastireasucevita.ro; Suceviţa; adult/student 5/2 lei, photography 10 lei; ☉ 8am-7pm May-Sep, to 4pm Oct-Apr). The region's biggest city, **Suceava**, is a good base for exploring the monasteries and is reachable from Bucharest by train.

espresso drinks and some of the wackiest iced-tea infusions ever concocted in Romania, such as peony flower, mango and lime (it's not bad).

Grădina Eden BAR
(www.facebook.com/gradinaeden107; Calea Victoriei 107, Palatul Ştirbey; ☉ 10pm-midnight Sun, to 5am Mon-Sat May-Sep; Ⓜ Piaţa Romană) A delightful summertime drinking garden hidden behind the derelict Ştirbey Palace. To find it, enter the gate to the palace and follow a worn footpath that runs along the palace's right side. The garden is tucked away behind some trees at the back. Line up at the bar for beer, wine or fresh lemonade, find a table and chill.

**Linea / Closer
to the Moon** ROOFTOP BAR
(☑ 0757-824 298; www.facebook.com/Linea-Closertothemoon; Calea Victoriei 17; ☉ 6pm-2am Sun-Thu, to 5am Fri & Sat) At the top of Victoria department store, Linea / Closer to the Moon is Bucharest's most popular rooftop bar displaying an ingenious cosmic theme and offering panoramic city views. Come early during summer nights as it fills up quickly; igloos are set up in winter. Food is also served.

☆ Entertainment

Control LIVE MUSIC
(☑ 0733-927 861; www.control-club.ro; Str Constantin Mille 4; ☉ 1pm-late; 🛜; Ⓜ Universitate) This is a favourite among club-goers who like alternative, turbo-folk, indie and garage sounds. Hosts both live acts and DJs, depending on the night.

Club A LIVE MUSIC
(☑ reservations 0744-517 858; www.cluba.ro; Str Blănari 14; ☉ 10.30am-5am Mon-Fri, noon-6am Sat & Sun; Ⓜ Piaţa Unirii) Run by students, this underground club is a classic and beloved by all who go there. Most weekends bring live music, with anything from rock and pop to blues and alternative.

Bucharest National Opera House OPERA
(Opera Naţională Bucureşti; ☑ box office 021-310 2661; www.operanb.ro; B-dul Mihail Kogălniceanu 70-72; tickets 12-80 lei; ☉ box office 9am-1pm & 3-7pm; Ⓜ Eroilor) The city's premier venue for classical opera and ballet. Buy tickets online or at the venue box office.

ⓘ Getting There & Away

Bucharest is Romania's main travel gateway. See p739 for international arrival and departure details.

AIR

All international and domestic flights use Henri Coandă International Airport (often referred to in conversation by its previous name 'Otopeni'). Henri Coandă is 17km north of Bucharest on the road to Braşov.

LAND

It's possible to get just about anywhere in the country by bus from Bucharest, but figuring out where your bus or maxitaxi departs from can be tricky. Bucharest has several bus stations and they don't seem to follow any discernible logic. The website **Autogari.ro** (www.autogari.ro) has an online timetable.

The central station for most national and all international trains, **Gara de Nord** (☎ reservations 021-9521; www.cfrcalatori.ro; Piaţa Gara de Nord 1; Ⓜ Gara de Nord) is accessible by metro from the centre of the city. Check the latest train schedules on either www.cfr.ro or the reliable German site www.bahn.de.

❶ Getting Around

TO/FROM THE AIRPORT

Express bus No 783 leaves every 15 minutes between 6am and 11pm (every half-hour at weekends) from Piaţas Unirii and Piaţas Victoriei and points in between. The airport is 45 to 60 minutes from the centre, depending on traffic. The express bus costs 3.50 lei each way.

There's a regular shuttle train service (35 minutes) from the main station, Gara de Nord, to Henri Coandă International Airport. The trains leave hourly at 10 minutes past the hour, starting at 8.10am and continuing until 7.10pm.

A reputable taxi should cover the distance from the centre to the airport for no more than

50 lei. Order a taxi from machines standing in the arrivals hall. You'll receive an order ticket stamped with the number of the taxi.

PUBLIC TRANSPORT

Bucharest's public transport system of metros, buses, trams and trolleybuses is operated by the transport authority **RATB** (Regia Autonomă de Transport Bucureşti; ☎ 021-9391; www.ratb.ro). The system runs from about 5am to approximately 11.30pm.

➡ The ticketing situation differs for street transport (buses, trams and trolleybuses) and for the metro.

➡ To use buses, trams or trolleybuses, you must first purchase an 'Activ' card (3.70 lei) from any RATB street kiosk, which you then load with credit that is discharged as you enter the transport vehicles. Trips cost 1.30 lei each.

➡ To use the metro, buy a magnetic-strip train ticket, which is available at ticketing machines or cashiers inside station entrances (have small bills handy). Tickets valid for two journeys cost 5 lei.

Transylvania

The northwestern Romanian province of Transylvania conjures up a vivid landscape of mountains, castles, fortified churches and a wicked, sharp-fanged nobleman of a certain ilk. A melange of architecture and chic pavement cafes punctuate the towns of Braşov and Sighişoara, while many of Transylvania's Saxon villages are dotted with fortified churches that date back half a millennium.

LOCAL KNOWLEDGE

A LITTLE BIT ABOUT DRACULA

Transylvania is best known as the stamping ground of one bloodthirsty count named 'Dracula'.

But there are two things worth point out that might come as a surprise: the first is that Dracula is real (well, sort of). The second is that he did not actually spend much time in Transylvania.

Bram Stoker's 1897 vampire novel was inspired by centuries-old superstition and the real-life exploits of Vlad Dracula. Known by his murderous moniker 'Vlad Ţepeş' (the Impaler), the 15th-century nobleman was said to have skewered up to 80,000 enemies on long spikes.

Though he was reputedly born in the Transylvanian town of Sighişoara (in a house that's still there today), the real Dracula's exploits took place largely further south, across the Carpathian Mountains, in the Romanian province of Wallachia.

Despite Dracula's wicked ways, he is considered a hero in Transylvania and throughout Romania, particularly for fending off the invading Ottoman Turks, so not everyone is exactly thrilled with the count's bloodsucking reputation.

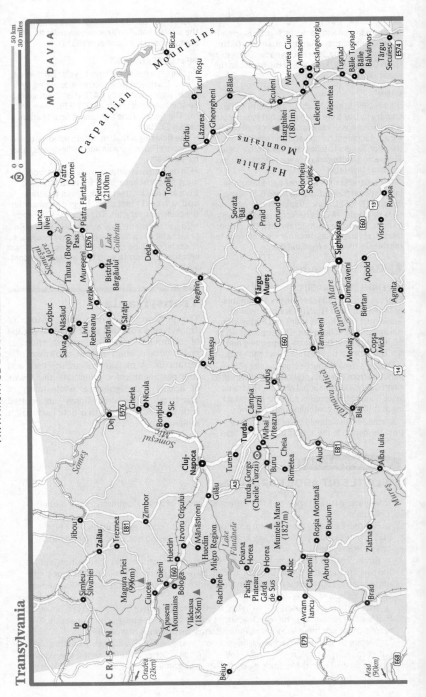

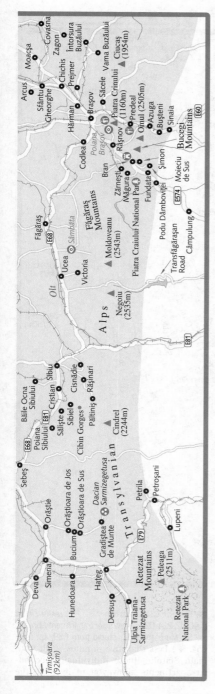

Braşov

POP 275,000

There's something whimsically enchanting about this town, with its fairy-tale turrets and cobbled streets. Dramatically overlooked by Mt Tâmpa, it's a remarkably relaxed city.

☉ Sights

Piaţa Sfatului   SQUARE

This wide square, lined with cafes, was once the heart of medieval Braşov. In the centre stands the 1420 **Council House** (Casa Sfatului), topped by the **Trumpeter's Tower**, in which town councillors would meet. These days at midday, traditionally costumed musicians appear at the top of the tower like figures in a Swiss clock.

Black Church   CHURCH

(Biserica Neagră; ☑ 0268-511 824; www.honterus-gemeinde.ro; Curtea Johannes Honterus 2; adult/student/child 10/6/3 lei; ☺10am-7pm Tue-Sat, noon-7pm Sun Apr-Sep, 10am-4pm Tue-Sat, noon-4pm Sun Oct-Mar) Romania's largest Gothic church rises triumphantly over Braşov's old town. Built between 1385 and 1477, this German Lutheran church was named for its charred appearance after the town's Great Fire in 1689. Restoration of the church took a century. Today it towers 65m high at its bell tower's tallest point. Organ recitals are held in the church three times a week during July and August, usually at 6pm Tuesday, Thursday and Saturday.

St Nicholas' Cathedral   CHURCH

(Biserica Sfântul Nicolae; Piaţa Unirii 1; ☺7am-6pm) With forested hills rising behind its prickly Gothic spires, St Nicholas' Cathedral is one of Braşov's most spectacular views. First built in wood in 1392, it was replaced by a Gothic stone church in 1495 and later embellished in Byzantine style. It was once enclosed by military walls; today the site has a small cemetery. Inside are murals of Romania's last king and queen, covered by plaster to protect them from communist leaders and uncovered in 2004.

⊨ Sleeping

Rolling Stone Hostel   HOSTEL €

(☑0268-513 965; www.rollingstone.ro; Str Piatra Mare 2A; dm/r €10/35; ℙ@☎) Powered by enthusiastic staff, Rolling Stone has clean dorm rooms that sleep between six and 10. Most rooms have high ceilings and convenient

Braşov

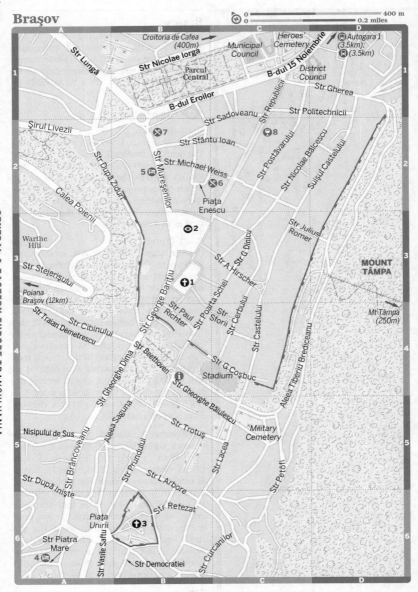

touches like lockers and reading lamps for each bed. Private doubles are comfy, or you can sleep in the wood-beamed attic for a stowaway vibe. Maps and excellent local advice are supplied the moment you step through the door.

★ **Select City Center** APARTMENT €€
(📱 0742-224 028; www.select-apartments-brasov.ro; Str Mureşenilor 17; studio from €39, apt from €54; 📶) Less than five minutes' walk from Piaţa Sfatului, these individually decorated apartments allow you to live like the

Braşov

⊙ Sights

🛏 Sleeping

🍴 Eating

🍷 Drinking & Nightlife

most glamorous of Braşov locals. Polished bathrooms, modern kitchens and spacious lounge rooms are fitted around the elegant bones of this high-ceilinged building. The apartments cultivate different atmospheres: one has a fireplace and leather love seats, another is framed by arches and flooded with natural light.

🍴 Eating

★ Bistro de l'Arte   BISTRO €€

(☑ 0720-535 566; www.bistrodelarte.ro; Piaţa Enescu 11; mains 12-35 lei; ⊙ 9am-1am Mon-Sat, noon-1am Sun; 🛜🍴) Tucked down a charming side-street, this bohemian joint can be spotted by the bike racks shaped like penny-farthings. There's an almost Parisian feel in Bistro de l'Arte's arty decor and champagne breakfasts (59 lei), though its menu picks the best from France, Italy and beyond: bruschetta, fondue, German-style cream cake, and a suitably hip cocktail list.

Sergiana   ROMANIAN €€

(☑ 0268-419 775; www.sergianagrup.ro; Str Mureşenilor 28; mains 25-40 lei; ⊙ 11am-midnight) Steaming soups in hollowed-out loaves of bread, paprika-laced meat stews, and the most generous ratio of cheese and sour cream we've ever seen in a polenta side-dish – do not wear your tight jeans for a feast at Sergiana. The subterranean dining hall, lined with brick and wood, is lively and casual – fuelled by ample German beer and loud conversation.

🍷 Drinking

Croitoria de Cafea   COFFEE

(☑ 0770-263 333; Str Iuliu Maniu 17; ⊙ 8am-7pm Mon-Fri, 9.30am-6pm Sat, to 4pm Sun) The best coffee in town can be sipped at this hole-in-the-wall cafe, which has a few wooden stools for you to perch amid bulging bags of beans.

Festival 39   BAR

(☑ 0743-339 909; www.festival39.com; Str Republicii 62; ⊙ 7am-midnight) Jazz flows from this vintage-feel watering hole and restaurant, an art-deco dream of stained-glass, high ceilings, wrought-iron finery, candelabra and leather banquettes. As good for clanking together beer glasses as for cradling a hot chocolate over your travel journal.

ⓘ Information

Tourist Information Centre (www.brasovtourism.eu; Str Prundului 1; ⊙ 10am-5pm Mon-Thu, to 2pm Fri-Sun) Cordial staff offer maps and local advice.

ⓘ Getting There & Away

Maxitaxis and minibuses are the best way to reach places near Braşov, including Bran. Braşov has two main bus stations (autogara): **Bus Station 1** (Autogara 1; ☑ 0268-427 267; www.autogari.ro; B-dul Gării 1), located next to the train station, is the main departure point for bus service to Bucharest (2½ hours); **Bus Station 2** (Autogara 2; ☑ 0268-426 332; www. autogari.ro; Str Avram Iancu 114), 1km northwest of the train station, sends half-hourly buses marked 'Moieciu-Bran' to Bran (40 minutes) from roughly 6am to 11pm.

WORTH A TRIP

FORTIFIED SAXON CHURCHES

The rolling hills stretching to the north and west of Braşov are filled with fortified churches and villages that can easily feel lost in centuries past; especially when you see a horse and cart rattle past laden with milk churns, or a shepherd ushering his flock across your path. Bus service is practically nonexistent; visitors come by hire car, taxi, bike or tour bus.

A couple of highlights get nearly all the visits, notably the fortified church at **Biertan** and the atmospheric Saxon village of **Viscri**. Much of the restoration in the area has been carried out by the Mihai Eminescu Trust, of which Britain's Prince Charles is a major driving force, along with author William Blacker (*Along The Enchanted Way*).

The train station is 2km northeast of the centre. There are convenient rail connections to both Bucharest (2½ hours) and Sighişoara (two to three hours). There are three daily trains to Budapest (13 to 16 hours) and one to Vienna (17 hours).

Bran

Just to the southwest of Braşov, the tiny town of Bran once occupied a crucial border post along the Carpathians that separated Transylvania to the north from the lands south of the peaks. It's not surprising, then, that such a gargantuan castle would arise here. More surprising is that the castle would develop such a strong association with Vlad Ţepeş (aka Dracula), who by all accounts didn't spend much time here.

⊙ Sights

Bran Castle CASTLE
(☑0268-237 700; www.bran-castle.com; Str General Traian Moşoiu 24; adult/student/child 40/25/10 lei; ⊙9am-6pm Tue-Sun, noon-6pm Mon Apr-Sep, to 4pm Oct-Mar) Rising above the town on a rocky promontory, Bran Castle holds visitors in thrall. An entire industry has sprouted around describing it as 'Dracula's Castle', though connections to either the historical Vlad Ţepeş or Bram Stoker's fictional vampire are thin. The liberties taken with Bran's reputation are quickly forgotten on a visit: you'll climb up its conical towers, admiring views over thick forest, and stroll through creaky-floored rooms furnished with bearskin rugs and 19th-century antiques.

🛏 Sleeping

The GuestHouse PENSION €€
(☑0745-179 475; www.guesthouse.ro; Str General Traian Moşoiu 7; d 140-168 lei, tr 187 lei; ᴾ☎) Six trim rooms, where modern fittings mingle with rustic touches like wooden beams, offer terrific views of Bran Castle. It's clean, friendly, and has perks for families including a kids playground and communal lounge and dining room.

ⓘ Getting There & Away

Bran is an easy DIY day trip from Braşov. Buses marked 'Bran-Moieciu' (40 minutes) depart every half-hour from Braşov's Bus Station (Autogara) 2. Return buses to Braşov leave Bran every half-hour from roughly 7am to 6pm in winter, and 7am to 10pm in summer.

Sighişoara

POP 28,100

So resplendent are Sighişoara's pastel-coloured buildings, stony lanes and medieval towers, you will rub your eyes in disbelief. Fortified walls encircle Sighişoara's lustrous merchant houses, now harbouring cafes, hotels and craft shops. Lurking behind the gingerbread roofs and turrets of the Unesco-protected old town is the history of Vlad Ţepeş, Transylvania's most notorious ruler; he was reputedly born in a house that is visitable to this day. Revered by many Romanians for protecting Transylvania from Turkish attacks, Ţepeş is better remembered as Vlad the Impaler, or Dracula, fuelling a local industry of vampire-themed souvenirs.

⊙ Sights

Citadel FORTRESS
Sighişoara's delightful medieval buildings are enclosed within its citadel, a Unesco-listed complex of protective walls and watchtowers. Walking in the citadel is today a tranquil, fairytale-like experience, but these towers were once packed with weapons and emergency supplies, guarding Sighişoara from Turkish attacks (note the upper windows, from which arrows could be fired).

From the 14th to 16th centuries each of the 14 towers and five artillery bastions was managed by a different town guild, and the walls extended 903m. Surviving today are nine towers and two bastions.

Dating from the 16th century, the **Bootmakers' Tower** (Turnul Cizmarilor; Str Zidul Cetăţii; ⊙closed to the public) was a key point of defence from the northern end. Just south, the **Tailors' Tower** (Turnul Croitorilor; Str Zidul Cetăţii; ⊙closed to the public) was built to guard over the back entrance to the citadel. As with many of the buildings here, the tower was engulfed in a massive fire in 1676 and rebuilt afterward. On the eastern edge of the citadel is the **Blacksmiths' Tower** (Turnul Fierarilor; Piaţa Muzeului; ⊙closed to the public), a pointy-roofed watchtower dating to 1631. Finally, the southerly (and top-heavy) **Tinsmiths' Tower** (Turnul Cositorarilor; Piaţa Răţuştelor; ⊙closed to the public) is one of the most easily recognisable in the citadel, both for its height (25m) and its octagonal upper level. A siege in 1704 left scars in the building that are visible to this day.

Sighişoara

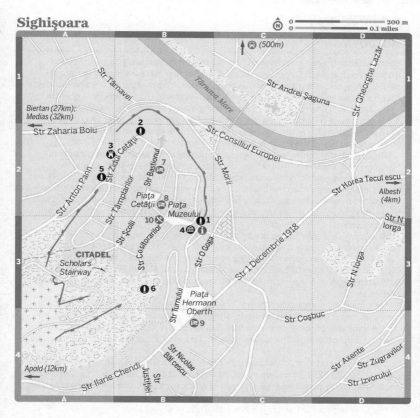

Biertan (27km); Medias (32km)

Albesti (4km)

Apold (12km)

CITADEL

Scholars Stairway

Clock Tower MUSEUM

(Turnul cu Ceas; Piaţa Muzeului 1; adult/child 14/3.50 lei; ⊙9am-6.30pm Tue-Fri, 10am-5.30pm Sat & Sun mid-May–mid-Sep, to 3.30pm mid-Sep–mid-May) The multicoloured tiled roof of Sighişoara's Clock Tower glitters like the scales of a dragon. The tower was built in the 14th century and expanded 200 years later. It remains the prettiest sight in town, offering a magnificent panorama from the top. The views are as good a reason to visit as the museum inside, a patchy collection of Roman vessels, scythes and tombstones, and a scale model of the fortified town (English-language explanation is variable).

🛏 Sleeping

Burg Hostel HOSTEL €

(☑0265-778 489; www.burghostel.ro; Str Bastionu-lui 4-6; dm 45 lei, s/d 90/110 lei, without bathroom 85/100 lei; ☜☀) A great budget choice that

MOLDOVA

Sandwiched between Romania and Ukraine, Moldova is practically as 'off the beaten track' as you can get in Europe. Attracting just a fraction of the number of visitors of neighbouring countries (just around 20,000 annually in recent years), it's a natural destination for travellers who like to plant the flag and visit lands few others have gone to.

But Moldova's charms run deeper than being merely remote. The country's wines are some of the best in Europe and a fledgling wine-tourism industry, where you can tour wineries and taste the grape, has taken root. The countryside is delightfully unspoiled and the hospitality of the villagers is authentic.

The capital, **Chişinău**, is by far Moldova's largest and liveliest city and its main transport hub. While the city's origins date back six centuries to 1420, much of Chişinău was levelled in WWII and a tragic earthquake that struck in 1940. The city was rebuilt in Soviet style from the 1950s onwards, and both the centre and outskirts are dominated by utilitarian (and frankly not very attractive) high-rise buildings. That said, the centre is surprisingly green and peaceful. The capital also has a lively restaurant and cafe scene.

Wine lovers will want to explore one of the country's two amazing wine cellars – both located within easy day-trip distance from Chişinău. The cave cellars at **Cricova** (☑ 069 077 734; www.cricova.md; Str Ungureanu 1, Cricova; ⊙10am-5pm Mon-Fri) and **Mileştii Mici** (☑ tours 022 382 333; www.milestii-mici.md; Mileştii Mici town; tours 200-500 lei; ⊙8am-5pm Mon-Fri) are both tens of kilometres long and house literally millions of bottles of wine.

For something completely different, across the Dniestr River lies the separatist, Russian-speaking region of **Transdniestr**. Although it's formally still part of Moldova, it's a time-warp kind of place, where the Soviet Union reigns supreme and busts of Lenin line the main boulevards. The region's capital, **Tiraspol**, is accessible from Chişinău by train.

The easiest way to get to Moldova is by plane. Modern **Chişinău International Airport** (KIV; ☑ 022 525 111; www.airport.md; Str Aeroportului 80/3), 16km southeast of the city centre, has flights to and from several major European cities. There are also regular train services to Chişinău from the Romanian capital Bucharest (14 hours, daily) and Moscow (28 to 32 hours, four to five daily) among a handful of other cities.

Once in Moldova, getting around can be tricky. Most locals navigate the country via a dense network of minibuses, as train travel tends to be slow and the rail network not very comprehensive.

does not compromise on charm, Burg Hostel has spacious dorms (with handy touches like plug sockets close to beds). Common areas have chandeliers made from old cartwheels, ceramic lamps, vaulted ceilings and other rustic touches. Staff are friendly and there's a relaxing courtyard cafe. Breakfast not included, but you can buy meals from the cafe.

Casa Saseasca　　　　　　　GUESTHOUSE €
(☑ 0265-772 400; www.casasaseasca.com; Piaţa Cetăţii 12; s/d from 145/177 lei; ☞) Casa Saseasca houses nine rooms with traditionally painted Saxon furniture and widescreen views of the nearby square. There's an inviting courtyard out back and a terraced restaurant at the front. Excellent value. Breakfast not included.

✖ Eating

Casa Vlad Dracul　　　　　　ROMANIAN €€
(☑ 0265-771 596; www.casavladdracul.ro; Str Cositorarilor 5; mains 24-35 lei; ⊙11am-8pm; ⊞) The link between Dracula and tomato soups, or medallions with potato and chicken roulade, we'll never quite understand. But the house where Vlad was born could have been dealt a worse blow than this atmospheric, wood-panelled restaurant. The menu of Romanian, Saxon and grilled specials is dotted with Dracula references. With a little embellishing from you, your kids will love it.

Central Park　　　　　　INTERNATIONAL €€
(☑ 0365-730 006; www.hotelcentralpark.ro; Central Park Hotel, Piaţa Hermann Oberth 25; mains 25-40 lei; ⊙11am-11pm; ℗☞) Even if you're not

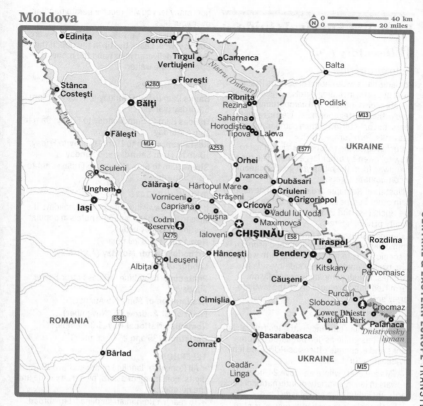

staying at the Central Park **hotel** (☑0365-730 006; www.hotelcentralpark.ro; Piaţa Hermann Oberth 25; s/d/ste €77/90/110; P❄@🛜), plan a meal here. Sighişoara is short on good restaurants and this is one of the best. The food is a mix of Romanian and international dishes, and the carefully selected wine list offers the best domestic labels. Dress up for the lavish dining room or relax on the terrace.

🔒 Shopping

★ Arts & Crafts
ARTS & CRAFTS
(www.thespoonman.ro; Str Cositorarilor 5; ⏱10am-6pm) Inside Casa Vlad Dracul, this wondrous handicraft shop is the brainchild of self-styled 'Spoonman' Mark Tudose, who employs traditional woodcarving methods to fashion Transylvanian spoons (each with a local legend behind it), as well as painted-glass icons, clay statues, painted eggs and

much more. It's a beautiful place to browse, and your best bet for finding a culturally meaningful souvenir.

ℹ Information

Tourist Information Centre (☑0788-115 511; Piaţa Muzeului 6; ⏱9am-5pm) Cordial, multilingual information service adjoining the Clock Tower, with maps and transport information.

ℹ Getting There & Away

The bus station is located next to the train station, about 15 minutes walk north of the citadel. Buses to Braşov (2½ hours) stop at the bus station three times per day.

About six trains daily connect Sighişoara with Braşov (two hours), some of which go on to Bucharest (five hours). Four daily trains go to Cluj-Napoca (four to six hours). A couple daily trains pass through town on their way to Budapest (nine hours). Buy tickets at the train station.

Romania Survival Guide

ℹ Directory A–Z

ACCOMMODATION

Romania has a wide choice of options to suit most budgets, including hotels, pensions and private rooms, hostels and campgrounds. Prices across these categories have risen in recent years, but are still lower than comparable facilities in Western Europe.

➡ Bucharest is the most expensive place to stay, followed by other large cities. The further away from the cities you go, the cheaper accommodation gets.

➡ Hostels in Romania are not as well developed as in other European countries. Large cities, like Bucharest and Braşov, do have good-quality private hostels.

➡ Campgrounds (*popas turistic*) run the gamut from a handful of nicely maintained properties in scenic areas to grungy affairs, with wooden huts packed unattractively side-by-side like sardines. Rough camping is generally not permitted, but in remote areas the laws are rarely enforced.

MONEY

➡ The Romanian currency is the leu (plural: lei), noted in this guide as 'lei' but listed in some banks and exchange offices as RON. One leu is divided into 100 bani.

➡ ATMs are everywhere and give 24-hour withdrawals in lei on a variety of international bank cards, including Visa and MasterCard.

➡ The best place to exchange money is at a bank. You'll pay a small commission, but get a decent rate. You can also change money at a private exchange booth (*casa de schimb*), but be wary of commission charges and always ask

---

> ## ℹ PRICE RANGES
>
> The following price ranges refer to a double room with a bathroom, including breakfast (Bucharest prices tend to be higher).
>
> **€** less than 150 lei
>
> **€€** 150–300 lei
>
> **€€€** more than 300 lei
>
> The following price ranges refer to an average main course.
>
> **€** less than 20 lei
>
> **€€** 20–40 lei
>
> **€€€** more than 40 lei

---

how many lei you will receive before handing over your bills.

➡ In restaurants, tip 10% of the bill to reward good service. Leave the tip in the pouch that the bill is delivered in or hand the money directly to the waiter.

OPENING HOURS

Banks 9am to 5pm Monday to Friday; to 1pm Saturday (varies)

Offices 8am to 5pm Monday to Friday; 9am to 1pm Saturday

Restaurants 9am to 11pm Monday to Friday; 10am to 11pm Saturday and Sunday

Shops 9am to 6pm Monday to Friday; 9am to 2pm Saturday

PUBLIC HOLIDAYS

If you'll be travelling during public holidays it's wise to book ahead, as some hotels in popular destinations may be full.

New Year (1 and 2 January)

Orthodox Easter Monday (April/May)

Labour Day (1 May)

Pentecost (May/June, 50 days after Easter Sunday)

Assumption of Mary (15 August)

Feast of St Andrew (30 November)

Romanian National Day (1 December)

Christmas (25 and 26 December)

TELEPHONE

➡ All Romanian landline numbers have 10 digits, consisting of a zero, plus a city code and the number.

➡ To reach a Romanian landline from abroad, dial your country's international access code, then 40 (Romanian country code), then the city code (minus the zero) and the six- (or seven-) digit local number.

➡ Mobile phone numbers can be identified by a three-digit prefix starting with 7. All mobile numbers have 10 digits: 0 + three-digit prefix (7xx) + six-digit number.

➡ Romanian mobile (cell) phones use the GSM 900/1800 network, which is the standard throughout much of Europe as well as in Australia and New Zealand, but is not compatible with most mobile phones in North America or Japan.

➡ Local SIM cards can be used in European, Australian and some American phones. Other phones must be set to roaming.

WI-FI

Romanians are justifiably proud of their country's very good internet connectivity. Nearly all hotels and hostels offer free wi-fi to guests;, as do most bars, cafes and restaurants.

ⓘ Getting There & Away

Travel to Romania does not pose any unusual problems. Bucharest has air connections with many European capitals and large cities, and train and long-haul bus services are frequent.

BORDER CROSSINGS

Romania shares a border with five countries: Bulgaria, Hungary, Moldova, Serbia and Ukraine. While Romania is a member of the European Union, it is not yet part of the EU's common customs and border area, the Schengen zone, so even if you're entering from an EU member state (Bulgaria or Hungary), you'll still have to show a passport or valid EU identity card.

AIR

➤ Romania has good air connections to Europe and the Middle East.

➤ The majority of international flights to Romania arrive at Bucharest's **Henri Coandă International Airport** (OTP, Otopeni; ✆ arrivals 021-204 1220, departures 021-204 1210; www. bucharestairports.ro; Şos Bucureşti-Ploieşti; ▣ 783). The airport is home base for Romania's national carrier **Tarom** (✆ call centre 021-204 6464, office 021-316 0220; www.tarom.ro; Spl Independenţei 17, City Centre; ⏰ 9am-5pm Mon-Fri; Ⓜ Piaţa Unirii).

➤ Several other cities have international airports that service mostly domestic flights and those to and from European cities. International airports that serve Transylvania include: Cluj's **Avram Iancu International Airport** (CLJ; ✆ 0264-307 500, 0264-416 702; www. airportcluj.ro; Str Traian Vuia 149) and **Sibiu International Airport** (SBZ; ✆ 0269-253 135; www.sibiuairport.ro; Şoseaua Alba Iulia 73).

Land

Long-haul bus services remain a popular way of travelling from Romania to Western Europe as well as to parts of southeastern Europe and Turkey. **Eurolines** (www.eurolines.ro) and **Atlassib** (✆ 021-222 8971, call centre 080-10 100 100; www.atlassib.ro; Str Gheorghe Duca 4; Ⓜ Gara de Nord) both maintain vast networks from cities throughout Europe to destinations all around Romania.

Romania is integrated into the European rail grid, and there are decent connections to Western Europe and neighbouring countries. Nearly all of these arrive at and depart from Bucharest's main station, Gara de Nord.

ⓘ Getting Around

Air Given the distances and poor state of the roads, flying between cities is a feasible option if time is a concern. Tarom operates a comprehensive network of domestic routes.

Bus A mix of buses and minibuses form the backbone of the national transport system. If you understand how the system works, you can move across the country easily and cheaply. Unfortunately, bus and minibus routes change frequently and the changes are often communicated by word of mouth. **Autogari.ro** (www. autogari.ro) is a helpful online timetable.

Train Trains are a slow but reliable way of getting around Romania. The extensive network covers much of the country, including most of the main tourist sights and key destinations. The national rail system is run by **Căile Ferate Române** (CFR; www.cfrcalatori.ro). The CFR website has a handy online timetable *(mersul trenurilor)*.

BULGARIA

Sofia

POP 1.2 MILLION

Bulgaria's pleasingly laid-back capital is often overlooked by visitors heading straight to the country's coast or ski resorts, but they're missing something special. Sofia is no grand metropolis, but it's a largely modern, youthful city, with a scattering of onion-domed churches, Ottoman mosques and stubborn Red Army monuments that lend an eclectic, exotic feel. Recent excavation work carried out during construction of the city's metro unveiled a treasure trove of Roman ruins from nearly 2000 years ago, when the city was called 'Serdica'.

⊙ Sights

★**Aleksander Nevski Cathedral** CHURCH
(pl Aleksander Nevski; ⏰ 7am-7pm; Ⓜ Sofiyski Universitet) One of *the* symbols not just of Sofia but of Bulgaria itself, this massive, awe-inspiring church was built between 1882 and 1912 in memory of the 200,000 Russian soldiers who died fighting for Bulgaria's independence during the Russo-Turkish War (1877–78). It is named in honour of a 13th-century Russian warrior-prince.

Aleksander Nevski Crypt GALLERY
(Museum of Icons; pl Aleksander Nevski; adult/child 6/3 lv; ⏰ 10am-5.30pm Tue-Sun; Ⓜ Sofiyski Universitet) Originally built as a final resting place for Bulgarian kings, this crypt now houses Bulgaria's biggest and best collection of icons, stretching back to the 5th century. Enter to the left of the eponymous church's main entrance.

BULGARIA AT A GLANCE

Don't Miss

Rila Monastery More than a thousand years of uninterrupted spiritual activity have swept through this beautiful monastery, which rises from a valley in the misty Rila Mountains. Credited with safeguarding Bulgarian culture during the dark centuries under Ottoman rule, Rila Monastery remains Bulgaria's most storied spiritual treasure.

Black Sea beaches Whether you're looking for all-day tanning, all-night clubbing or something a little more relaxing, you're sure to find some patch of sand to your liking along Bulgaria's Black Sea coast. Away from the big, brash package resorts, you'll come across charming seaside towns standing above smaller sandy coves.

Plovdiv With a pretty old town, revitalised artistic quarter and the most exhilarating nightlife outside Sofia, Bulgaria's second city has never looked finer. Ancient buildings nestle right in the centre of this seven-hilled town: a pleasant shopping street flows past its 2nd-century Roman stadium and a 15th-century mosque in an effortless blend of old and new.

Veliko Târnovo Bulgaria's long history of warring tsars and epic battles is exceptionally vivid in its former capital, Veliko Târnovo. Topped with a marvellous medieval fortress, this town of Soviet monuments, cobblestoned lanes and barely changed handicraft shops allows for a memorable trip into Bulgaria's past.

Sofia's Aleksander Nevski Cathedral Rising majestically over the rooftops of Sofia, the neo-Byzantine Orthodox church is dedicated to the memory of the 200,000 Russian soldiers who died fighting for Bulgaria's independence in the Russo-Turkish War (1877–78). An unequalled highlight of the Bulgarian capital, the church took 30 years to construct.

Itineraries

One Week

Begin in Bulgaria's lively capital, **Sofia**. Over three days, take in shimmering Aleksander Nevski Cathedral, some fascinating museums, and some of the country's best restaurants and liveliest clubs and bars. Sofia makes a good base for a day trip to resplendent **Rila Monastery**. From here, head east to **Plovdiv**, Bulgaria's second city. Spend two days immersing yourself in the charming old town, Roman ruins and bohemian nightlife. Time permitting, from here travel on to the museum village of **Koprivshtitsa**.

Two Weeks

Head north and east from here to see impressive **Veliko Târnovo**, Bulgaria's medieval capital. The centrepiece is the magnificent restored Tsarevets Fortress. If you're travelling during the summer, plan to spend the rest of your time relaxing at one of the country's seaside resorts. Connections are best to big cities like **Varna** or **Burgas**, both of which have surprisingly clean urban beaches. Don't miss the old town of **Nesebâr**, south of Varna. South of Burgas, **Sozopol** has quaint cobbled lanes and attractive beaches.

Essential Outdoors

Hiking Hiking is enormously popular in Bulgaria, and the country has some 37,000km of marked trails.

Skiing & snowboarding The ski season runs between mid-December and April. Bansko is the number one resort in the country.

Water sports During the summer, big Black Sea package resorts, as well as smaller seaside towns, offer jet-skiing, waterskiing, parasailing and windsurfing.

Rock climbing & mountaineering The Rila, Pirin and Stara Planina mountain ranges have numerous locations where you can rock climb and mountaineer. In these perilous peaks, a guide is essential.

Birdwatching The Via Pontica, which passes over Bulgaria, is one of Europe's major migratory routes for birds. Top picks for birdwatchers include spots along the Danube River and the area north of Varna on the Black Sea coast.

Getting Around

Bus The most reliable form of transport between big cities. Local buses also reach most villages, though these services are usually infrequent, or seasonal for ski or beach destinations.

Car A highly convenient way to get around, especially if your itinerary includes small Bulgarian villages. Drive on the right.

Taxi As well as short journeys within cities, engaging a local driver is a good way to reach day-trip destinations without the inconvenience of infrequent buses; make sure to agree on a fare before setting out.

Train Slower than buses and frequently delayed, trains are a scenic (if not speedy) way to cover ground in Bulgaria.

When to Go

Sofia

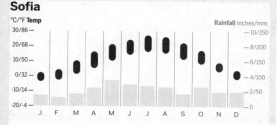

Mar–May Spring is warm and wet; Easter is a colourful time to visit.

Jun–Aug Summer is hot and dry, especially August.

Nov–Feb Winters are often icy cold, with heavy snow-falls, but January is perfect for skiing.

Arriving in Bulgaria

Serdika station (1 lv, 20 minutes); buy tickets in the station, just outside the terminal exit. Bus 84 (1 lv, 40 to 50 minutes) also travels to central Sofia; buy tickets from the driver. Taxis (10 lv to 15 lv, 30 to 40 minutes) can be booked at the OK-Supertrans counter (staff will give you a slip of paper with the three-digit code of your cab).

Varna Airport Bus 409 (1 lv, 30 minutes) runs to central Varna and towards Golden Sands. A taxi from the air-port costs 10 lv to 20 lv and takes 20 to 30 minutes.

Top Phrases

Hello. Здравейте. *(zdra·vey·te)*

Goodbye. Довиждане. *(do·veezh·da·ne)*

Please. Моля. *(mol·ya)*

Thank you. Благодаря. *(bla·go·dar·ya)*

Cheers! Наздраве! *(na·zdra·ve)*

Resources

Beach Bulgaria (www.beachbulgaria.com)

Bulgaria Travel (www.bulgariatravel.org)

Set Your Budget

➡ Dorm bed: 18–22 lv

➡ Room in a simple guesthouse: 25–50 lv

➡ Meals from cafeterias: 5–10 lv

➡ Public transport tickets: around 1 lv

Sofia

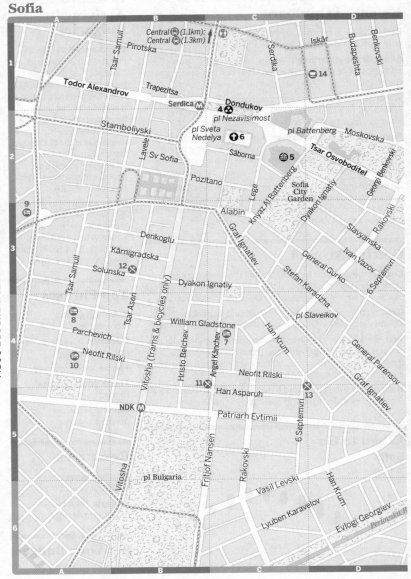

★ Sveta Sofia Church   CHURCH
(☏ 02-987 0971; ul Parizh 2; museum adult/child 6/2 lv; ☺ church 7am-7pm Mar-Sep, to 6pm Oct-Feb, museum 9am-5pm Tue-Sun; Ⓜ Sofiyski Universitet) Sveta Sofia is one of the capital's oldest churches, and gave the city its name.

A subterranean **museum** houses an ancient necropolis, that has 56 tombs and the remains of four other churches. Situated outside are the Tomb of the Unknown Soldier and an eternal flame, and the grave of Ivan Vazov, Bulgaria's most revered writer.

inside were painted between the 10th and 14th centuries. It's a busy, working church, but visitors are welcome.

Archaeological Museum　　　MUSEUM
(☑ 02-988 2406; www.naim.bg; ul Saborna 2; adult/child 10/2 lv; ☉ 10am-6pm daily May-Oct, 10am-5pm Tue-Sun Nov-Apr; M Serdika) Housed in a former mosque built in 1496, this museum displays a wealth of Thracian, Roman and medieval artefacts. Highlights include a mosaic floor from the Church of Sveta Sofia, a 4th-century BC Thracian gold burial mask, and a magnificent bronze head, thought to represent a Thracian king.

Ancient Serdica Complex　　　RUINS
(pl Nezavisimost; ☉ 6am-11pm; M Serdika) FREE This remarkable, partly covered excavation site, situated just above the Serdika metro station, displays the remains of the Roman city, Serdica, that once occupied this area. The remains were unearthed from 2010 to 2012 during construction of the metro. There are fragments of eight streets, an early Christian basilica, baths and houses dating from the 4th to 6th centuries. Plenty of signage in English.

Boyana Church　　　CHURCH
(☑ 02-959 0939; www.boyanachurch.org; ul Boyansko Ezero 3, Boyana; adult/child 10/1 lv, combined ticket with National Historical Museum 12 lv, guide 10

Sveti Georgi Rotunda　　　CHURCH
(Church of St George; ☑ 02-980 9216; www.svgeorgi-rotonda.com; bul Dondukov 2; ☉ services daily 8am, 9am & 5pm; M Serdika) Built in the 4th century AD, this tiny red-brick church is Sofia's oldest preserved building. The murals

lv; ⊙9.30am-5.30pm Apr-Oct, 9am-5pm Nov-Mar;
🚌64, 107) Tiny 13th-century Boyana Church
is included on Unesco's World Heritage list
and its 90 murals are among the very finest
examples of Bulgarian medieval artwork. A
combined ticket includes entry to both the
church and the National Museum of History,
2km away.

🛏 Sleeping

★Canapé Connection
GUESTHOUSE €

(📞02-441 6373; www.canapeconnection.com; ul
William Gladstone 12a; s/d from 50/64 lv; 🛜; 🚌1,
6, 7) Formerly a hostel, Canapé reinvented
itself as a guesthouse in 2016, retaining its
same attention to cleanliness and a refreshingly simple, rustic design. The six rooms
are divided into singles and doubles, with a
larger room upstairs to accommodate families. There's a quiet garden outside to relax
in. Note there's no breakfast, but you'll find
several coffee places nearby.

Art Hostel
HOSTEL €

(📞02-987 0545; www.art-hostel.com; ul Angel
Kânchev 21a; dm/s/d from 17/47/57 lv; @🛜; 🚌12)
This bohemian hostel stands out from the
crowd with its summertime art exhibitions,
live music, dance performances and more.
Dorms are appropriately arty and bright;
private rooms are airy and very welcoming.
There's a great basement bar and peaceful
little garden at the back.

Hostel Mostel
HOSTEL €

(📞0889223296; www.hostelmostel.com; bul
Makedoniya 2a; dm/s/d from 20/50/60 lv; 🅿🛜;
🚌1, 6, 7, 8, 10) Popular Mostel occupies a
renovated 19th-century house, and has six-
and eight-bed dorms, with either shared or
private bathrooms, as well as a single and a
couple of doubles; guests have use of a kitch-
en and a cosy lounge. Free beer, free pasta
and all-you-can-eat breakfast round out the
charms.

★Hotel Niky
HOTEL €€

(📞02-952 3058; www.hotel-niky.com; ul Neofit
Rilski 16; r/ste from 90/140 lv; 🅿❄🛜; Ⓜ NDK,
🚌1) Offering excellent value and a good
city-centre location, Niky has comfortable
rooms and gleaming bathrooms; the smart
little suites come with kitchenettes. It's a
very popular place and frequently full; be
sure to book ahead.

🍴 Eating

Sun & Moon
VEGETARIAN €

(📞0899138411; www.sunmoon.bg; ul 6 Sepemvri
39; mains 8-12 lv; ⊙8.30am-10pm Mon-Sat, to
9pm Sun; 🛜🌿; Ⓜ NDK) Very good vegetarian
cooking, a warm, student-friendly atmosphere and a sunny, streetside terrace make
this the ideal choice for a healthy, inexpensive lunch. Also has excellent homemade
bread and baked goods, and great coffee.

★Made In Home
INTERNATIONAL €

(📞0876884014; ul Angel Kânchev 30a; mains
12-22 lv; ⊙11am-9pm Mon, to 10.30pm Tue-Thur
& Sun, to 11pm Fri & Sat; 🛜🌿; Ⓜ NDK) Sofia's
very popular entrant into the worldwide,
locally sourced, slow-food trend (the name
refers to the fact that all items are made in-
house). The cooking is eclectic, with dollops
of Middle Eastern (eg hummus) and Turkish
items, as well as ample vegetarian and vegan
offerings. The playfully rustic interior feels
straight out of a Winnie-the-Pooh book. Reservations essential.

★MoMa Bulgarian Food & Wine
BULGARIAN €€

(📞0885622020; www.moma-restaurant.com; ul
Solunska 28; mains 8-22 lv; ⊙11am-10pm; 🛜🌿;
Ⓜ Serdika) An update on the traditional *me-
hana* (taverna), serving typical Bulgarian
foods such as grilled meats and meatballs,
and wines, but in a more modern and understated interior. The result is one of the
best nights out in town. Start off with a shot
of *rakia* (Bulgarian brandy) and a salad, and
move on to the ample main courses. Book
ahead – this restaurant is popular.

🍷 Drinking

One More Bar
BAR

(📞0882539592; ul Shishman 12; ⊙8.30am-2am;
🛜; Ⓜ Sofiyski Universitet) Inside a gorgeous old
house, this shabby-chic hot spot wouldn't be
out of place in Melbourne or Manhattan: an
extensive cocktail list, a delightful summer
garden and jazzy background music add to
its cosmopolitan appeal.

Fabrika Daga
CAFE

(📞02-444 0556; ul Veslets 10; ⊙8am-10pm Mon-
Fri, 10am-10pm Sat, 10am-8pm Sun; 🛜; Ⓜ Serdika, 🚌20, 22) Classic third-gen coffee roaster
with lots of exposed piping and a coffee
menu scrawled on a chalkboard. Espressos,
vacuum pots and French presses squeeze
out java drinks from a wide variety of exotic

beans. It also has a long list of salads and sandwiches, with vegan and vegetarian options. Handy spot for morning coffee and a breakfast roll or cake.

Raketa Rakia Bar BAR
(☑ 02-444 6111; ul Yanko Sakazov 15-17; ⊙11am-midnight; 🛜; 🚇11, Ⓜ Sofiyski Universitet) Unsurprisingly, this rakish communist-era retro bar has a huge selection of *rakia* (Bulgarian brandy) on hand; before you start working your way down the list, line your stomach with meat-and-cream-heavy snacks and meals. Reservations essential.

❶ Information

Sofia Tourist Information Centre (☑ 02-491 8344; www.info-sofia.bg; Sofiyski Universitet metro underpass; ⊙ 9.30am-6pm Mon-Fri; Ⓜ Sofiyski Universitet) Situated in the underpass to enter the Sofiyski Universitet metro station. Lots of free leaflets and maps, and helpful English-speaking staff.

❶ Getting There & Away

BUS

Sofia's **Central Bus Station** (Tsentralna Avtogara; ☑ info 0900 63 099; www.centralnaavtogara.bg; bul Maria Luisa 100; ⊙24hr; 🛜; Ⓜ Central Railway Station) is located beside the train station and accessed via the same metro stop. It handles services to most big towns in Bulgaria as well as international destinations.

Frequent buses depart Sofia for Plovdiv (2½ hours), Veliko Târnovo (four hours), Varna (seven hours) and more; the easy-to-navigate website www.bgrazpisanie.com has full local and international timetables and fare listings.

TRAIN

Sofia's **Central Train Station** (☑ info 0700 10 200, international services 02-931 0972, tickets 0884 193 758; www.bdz.bg; bul Maria Luisa 102a; ⊙ ticket office 7.30am-7pm; Ⓜ Central Railway Station) is the country's main rail gateway. The station is in an isolated part of town about 1km north of the centre, though it's easy to reach by metro. It's 100m (a five-minute walk) from the Central Bus Station.

Destinations are listed on timetables in Cyrillic, but departures (for the following two hours) and arrivals (for the previous two hours) are listed in English on a computer screen on the ground floor. Same-day tickets are sold at counters on the ground floor, while advance tickets are sold in the basement, accessed via an unsigned flight of stairs near some snack bars.

Sample fast train routes include Sofia to Plovdiv (2½ hours) and Varna (seven hours).

See www.bgrazpisanie.com or www.bdz.bg for domestic and international routes.

Plovdiv

POP 341,560

With an easy grace, Plovdiv mingles invigorating nightlife with millennia-old ruins. Like Rome, Plovdiv straddles seven hills; but as Europe's oldest continuously inhabited city, it's far more ancient. It is best loved for its romantic old town, packed with colourful and creaky 19th-century mansions that are now house-museums, galleries and guesthouses. But cobblestoned lanes and National Revival–era nostalgia are only part of the story. Bulgaria's cosmopolitan second city has always been hot on the heels of Sofia, and a stint as European Capital of Culture 2019 seems sure to give Plovdiv the edge.

⊙ Sights

★ **Roman Amphitheatre** HISTORIC SITE
(ul Hemus; adult/student 3/1 lv; ⊙9am-5.30pm) Plovdiv's magnificent 2nd-century AD amphitheatre, built during the reign of Emperor Trajan, was uncovered during a freak landslide in 1972. It once held about 6000 spectators. Now largely restored, it's one of Bulgaria's most magical venues, once again hosting large-scale special events and concerts. Visitors can admire the amphitheatre for free from several look-outs along ul Hemus, or pay admission for a scarper around.

Balabanov House MUSEUM
(☑ 032-627 082; ul K Stoilov 57; 5 lv; ⊙9am-6pm Apr-Oct, to 5.30pm Nov-Mar) One of Plovdiv's most beautiful Bulgarian National Revival–era mansions, Balabanov House is an enjoyable way to experience old town nostalgia as well as contemporary art. The house was faithfully reconstructed in 19th-century style during the 1970s. The lower floor has an impressive collection of paintings by local artists, while upper rooms are decorated with antiques and elaborately carved ceilings.

Ethnographical Museum MUSEUM
(☑ 032-624 261; www.ethnograph.info; ul Dr Chomakov 2; adult/student 6/2 lv; ⊙9am-6pm Tue-Sun May-Oct, to 5pm Nov-Apr) Even if you don't have time to step inside, it would be criminal to leave Plovdiv's old town without glancing into the courtyard of this stunning National Revival–era building. Well-manicured

Old Plovdiv

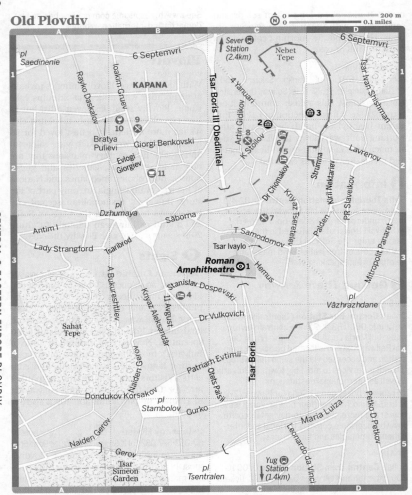

CENTRAL & EASTERN EUROPE PLOVDIV

flower gardens surround a navy-blue mansion, ornamented with golden filigree and topped with a distinctive peaked roof. There is more to admire inside, especially the upper floor's sunshine-yellow walls and carved wooden ceiling, hovering above displays of regional costumes. The ground-floor displays of agrarian instruments are a shade less interesting.

🛏 Sleeping

Hikers Hostel   HOSTEL €
(📱 0896764854; www.hikers-hostel.org; ul Sâborna 53; 14-/8-bed dm 18/20 lv; @ 🛜) In a mellow

old-town location, Hikers has wood-floored dorms and standard hostel perks such as a laundry and a shared kitchen. Bonuses such as a garden lounge, hammocks and mega-friendly staff make it a worthy option. Staff can help organise excursions to Bachkovo Monastery (southern mountains), Buzludzha Monument (central mountains) and more. Off-site private rooms (from 50 lv) are available in the Kapana area.

★ Hostel Old Plovdiv   HOSTEL €€
(📱 032-260 925; www.hosteloldplovdiv.com; ul Chetvarti Yanuari 3; dm/s/d/tr/q 22/57/76/96/116

Old Plovdiv

lv; P 🌐) This marvellous old building (1868) is more akin to a boutique historical hotel than a run-of-the-mill hostel. Remarkably restored by charismatic owner Hristo Giulev and his wife, this genial place smack bang in the middle of the old town is all about warm welcomes and old-world charm.

Dali Art Hotel BOUTIQUE HOTEL €€
(☑ 032-621 530; ul Otets Paisii 11; d/ste from 68/78 lv; P ❄ 🌐) This intimate boutique hotel, off the pedestrianised shopping street, has eight rooms furnished with the right mix of period style and modern amenities, plus reproductions of Salvador Dalí paintings. Though it's a little worn, furnishings with subtly surrealist flourishes make the hotel worthy of its name. Friendly service leaves the strongest impression. Ask ahead about the few available parking spots.

✖ Eating

Klebarnitsa Kapana BAKERY €
(☑ 0882330773; ul Ioakim Gruev 20; ☉ 9am-7pm Mon-Sat; ☑) This bakery has a sociable twist, with places to perch while you tuck into oven-warm bread, fresh pastries and other goodies.

Grazhdanski Klub BULGARIAN €€
(Citizens' Club; ☑ 032-624 139; ul Stoyan Chalukov 1; mains 8-15 lv; ☉ 8am-1am Mon-Fri, 10am-1am Sat & Sun; 🌐) A local favourite, this fabulous nook serves hefty portions of Bulgarian salads, grills and *satch* (meat and vegetables served on a hotplate), only a totter down the hill from the Roman Amphitheatre. Its cool, green courtyard is a haven in hotter months; inside is cosy.

★**Hebros Restaurant** BULGARIAN €€€
(☑ 032-625 929; ul K Stoilov 51; mains 15-27 lv; 🌐) Genteel service and a tranquil setting is exactly what you would expect from the restaurant of the boutique Hebros Hotel. Classic Bulgarian flavours are gently muddled with Western European influences, creating mouthwatering morsels such as Smilyan

WORTH A TRIP

RILA MONASTERY

Rising out of a forested valley in the Rila Mountains, Bulgaria's most famous monastery has been a spiritual centre for 1000 years. Rila Monastery's fortress-like complex engulfs 8800 sq metres, and within its stone walls you'll find remarkably colourful architecture and religious art. Visitors can't fail to be struck by its elegant colonnades, archways striped in black, red and white, and the bright yellow domes of its main church, beneath which dance apocalyptic frescoes.

The monastery compound is open from 6am to 10pm and includes the highlight **Church of Rozhdestvo Bogorodichno** (Church of the Nativity; Rila Monastery), two museums, an icon gallery, guest rooms and even a post office. The nearby 24m-high stone **Hreliova Tower** (1335), named after a significant benefactor, is the only 14th-century structure remaining here.

Most travellers visit Rila Monastery on a day trip, but you can stay at one of the monastery's **rooms** (☑ 0896872010; www.rilamonastery.pmg-blg.com; r 30-60 lv) to experience its tranquillity after the tour buses leave, or explore the hiking trails that begin here.

Handy from Sofia, the **Rila Monastery Bus** (☑ 02-489 0885; www.rilamonasterybus.com; 60 lv) ferries visitors from Sofia to the monastery, stopping at Sofia's **Boyana Church** on the way back. Departs at 9am; returns to Sofia by 5pm.

beans with parmesan, rabbit with prunes, and grilled sea bream.

Drinking

Monkey House
CAFE

(📞0889678333; ul Zlatarska 3; ⊙10am-midnight) Coffee-lovers can rest easy in the stripped-bare decor of Monkey House, purveyors of Plovdiv's best flat white. The interior is ornamented with jaunty hallmarks such as bicycles and moustachioed pillows; seats range from tree stumps and wheelbarrows to comfy chairs; and light bulbs dangle on ropes from the beamed ceiling. It's terribly good fun, and the coffee's even better. Cocktails emerge after sundown.

★ Basquiat Wine & Art
WINE BAR

(📞0895460493; https://basquiat.alle.bg; ul Bratya Pulievi 4; ⊙9am-midnight) A smooth funk soundtrack and great selection of local wines lure an arty crowd to this small Kapana bar. House wines start at 2 lv per glass; for something more memorable, the *malina* (raspberry-scented) wine packs a syrupy punch.

Getting There & Away

Most destinations of interest to travellers are served from **Yug bus station** (📞032-626 937; bul Hristo Botev 47), diagonally opposite the train station and a 15-minute walk from the centre. Popular destinations from here include Sofia (2½ hours) and Varna (seven hours).

Buses to Veliko Târnovo (4½ hours) leave from the **Sever bus station** (📞032-953 705; www. hebrosbus.com; ul Dimitar Stambolov 2), 3.5km from the old town in the northern suburbs.

From Plovdiv's **train station** (bul Hristo Botev), you can catch direct trains to Sofia (three hours) and Varna (six hours).

Koprivshtitsa

POP 2300

Behind colourful house fronts and babbling streams broods Koprivshtitsa's revolutionary spirit. This museum-village immediately pleases the eye with its numerous restored National Revival–period mansions. It's a peaceful, touristy place, but Koprivshtitsa was once the heart of Bulgaria's revolution against the Ottomans. Todor Kableshkov declared an uprising against the Turks on 20 April 1876 from Kalachev Bridge (also called 'First Shot' Bridge). Today Koprivshtitsa's streets are dotted with historic homes interspersed with rambling, overgrown lanes,

making it a romantic getaway and a safe and fun place for children.

Sights

Koprivshtitsa boasts six house-museums. To buy a combined ticket for all (adult/student 6/3 lv), visit the souvenir shop **Kupchinitsa** (near the tourist information centre) or Kableshkov House.

Oslekov House
MUSEUM

(ul Gereniloto 4; 2 lv; ⊙9.30am-5.30pm Apr-Oct, 9am-5pm Nov-Mar, closed Mon) With its triple-arched entrance and interior restored in shades from scarlet to sapphire blue, Oslekov House is arguably the most beautifully restored example of Bulgarian National Revival–period architecture in Koprivshtitsa. It was built between 1853 and 1856 by a rich merchant executed after his arrest during the 1876 April Uprising. Now a house-museum, it features informative, multilingual displays (Bulgarian, English and French) about 19th-century Bulgaria.

Kableshkov House
MUSEUM

(ul Todor Kableshkov 8; adult/student 2/1 lv; ⊙9.30am-5.30pm Tue-Sun Apr-Oct, 9am-5pm Nov-Mar) Todor Kableshkov is revered as having (probably) been the person who fired the first shot in the 1876 uprising against the Turks. After his arrest, he committed suicide rather than allow his captors to decide his fate. This, his glorious former home (built 1845), contains exhibits about the April Uprising.

Sleeping & Eating

Hotel Astra
GUESTHOUSE €

(📞07184-2033; bul Hadzhi Nencho Palaveev 11; d/apt incl breakfast 45/66 lv; 🅿) Set beautifully in a garden at the northern end of Koprivshtitsa, the hospitable Astra has large, well-kept rooms and serves an epic homemade breakfast spread of pancakes, thick yogurt and more.

Bonchova House
GUESTHOUSE €

(📞0887268069; ul Tumangelova Cheta 26; s/d/tr incl breakfast from 25/40/45 lv; 🛜) Close to the Kalachev Bridge, this homely place has bright, modern rooms and an apartment. The common room is relaxing and has a working fireplace.

Dyado Liben
BULGARIAN €€

(📞0887532096; bul Hadzhi Nencho Palaveev 47; mains 8-15 lv; ⊙11am-midnight; 🛜) Traditional fare is served at this atmospheric 1852 mansion with tables set in a warren of halls, graced with ornate painted walls and heavy, worn wood floors. Find it just across the bridge leading from the main square inside the facing courtyard.

ℹ Getting There & Away

➡ Without private transport, getting to Koprivshtitsa can be inconvenient: the train station is 9km north of the village, requiring a taxi or shuttle bus. Trains come from Sofia (2½ hours, eight daily).

➡ Alternatively, Koprivshtitsa's bus stop is central and has more frequent connections, including six daily buses to Sofia (two hours), and one daily to Plovdiv (two hours).

Veliko Târnovo

POP 68,783

Medieval history emanates from Veliko Târnovo's fortified walls and cobbled lanes. One of Bulgaria's oldest towns, Veliko Târnovo has as its centrepiece the magnificent Tsarevets Fortress, citadel of the Second Bulgarian Empire. Historic Târnovo is tucked into the dramatic bends of the Yantra River, clasped by an amphitheatre of forested hills. Bulgaria's 19th-century National Revival splendour is easy to relive along historic lanes such as ul Gurko; similarly evocative is handicraft market Samovodska Charshiya, which retains much the same atmosphere it had two centuries ago. Today's Târnovo has Bulgaria's second-largest university and is home to a multicultural expat scene. Its location between Bucharest and İstanbul has made it a backpacker favourite.

◉ Sights

★ **Tsarevets Fortress**   FORTRESS
(adult/student 6/2 lv, scenic elevator 2 lv; ⊙ 8am-7pm Apr-Oct, 9am-5pm Nov-Mar) The inescapable symbol of Veliko Târnovo, this reconstructed fortress dominates the skyline and is one of Bulgaria's most beloved monuments. The former seat of the medieval tsars, it boasts the remains of more than 400 houses, 18 churches, the royal palace, an execution rock and more. Watch your step: there are lots of potholes, broken steps and unfenced drops. The fortress morphs into a psychedelic spectacle with a magnificent night-time Sound & Light Show (p750).

Samovodska Charshiya   AREA
During its 19th-century heyday, this lane hosted dozens of vendors from local villages, carefully laying fruit and vegetables, butter and cheeses onto small carpets laid on the cobbled ground. Inns, blacksmiths and craft shops helped Samovodska Charshiya grow into Veliko Târnovo's biggest market square in the 1880s. Today it retains the nostalgic feel, with handicrafts, traditional sweets and leatherware on offer from numerous boutiques.

Veliko Târnovo
Archaeological Museum   MUSEUM
(☑ 062-682 511; www.museumvt.com; ul Ivanka Boteva 2; adult/student 6/2 lv; ⊙ 9am-6pm Tue-Sun Apr-Oct, to 5.30pm Nov-Mar) Housed in a grand old building with a courtyard full of Roman sculptures, the museum contains Roman artefacts and medieval Bulgarian exhibits, including a huge mural of the tsars, plus some ancient gold from nearby Neolithic settlements.

⌨ Sleeping

Hostel Mostel   HOSTEL €
(☑ 0897859359; www.hostelmostel.com; ul Iordan Indjeto 10; campsites/dm/s/d incl breakfast 18/20/46/60 lv; @ ⊚) The famous Sofia-based Hostel Mostel has a welcoming branch in Târnovo, with clean, modern dorm rooms and doubles with sparkling bathrooms. It's just 150m from Tsarevets Fortress – good for exploring there, but a long walk from the city centre. Service is cheerful and multilingual, and there's barbecue equipment out back.

★ **Hotel-Mehana Gurko**   HISTORIC HOTEL €€
(☑ 0887858965; www.hotel-gurko.com; ul General Gurko 33; d/apt incl breakfast from 106/149 lv; P ❄ @ ⊚) Sitting pretty on Veliko Târnovo's oldest street, with blooms spilling over its wooden balconies and agricultural curios littering the exterior, the Gurko is one of the best places to sleep (and eat) in town. Its 21 rooms are spacious and soothing, each individually decorated and offering great views.

Hotel Comfort   HOTEL €€
(☑ 0887777265; www.hotelcomfortbg.com; ul P Tipografov 5; d 40-70 lv, apt 100 lv; P ❄ ⊚) With jaw-dropping views of the fortress and surrounding hills from most rooms, plus a stellar location just around the corner from the Samovodska Charshia market square, this family-owned hotel is a winner. Room prices vary enormously, depending on their view and floor. English is spoken by the amiable staff.

Veliko Târnovo

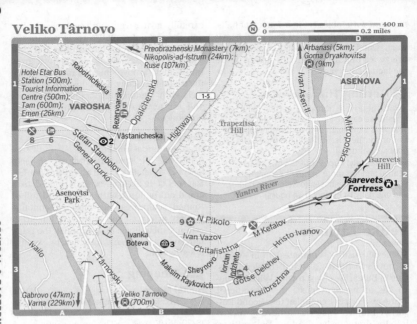

Veliko Târnovo

◉ **Top Sights**
1 Tsarevets Fortress.............................D2

◉ **Sights**
2 Samovodska Charshiya A2
3 Veliko Târnovo Archaeological
  Museum...B3

⊟ **Sleeping**
4 Hostel Mostel...................................C3
5 Hotel Comfort...................................B1
6 Hotel-Mehana Gurko A2

⊗ **Eating**
7 Ivan Asen C3
8 Shtastliveca A2

⊕ **Entertainment**
9 Sound & Light Show B2

✗ Eating

★Shtastliveca   BULGARIAN €€
(☑062-600 656; www.shtastliveca.com; ul Stefan
Stambolov 79; mains 10-20 lv; ⊙11am-midnight;
⊛) ✐ Inventive dishes and amiable service have solidified the 'Lucky Man' as a
favourite among locals and expats. Sauces
pairing chocolate and cheese are drizzled
over chicken, while strawberry and balsamic
vinegar lend piquancy to meaty dishes, and
there is a pleasing range for vegetarians.

Ivan Asen   BULGARIAN €€
(☑0882650065; www.ivan-asen.com; pl Tsar
Asen 1; mains 8-15 lv; ⊙8am-11pm) Don't be
deterred by its touristy location near Tsarevets Fortress. Stone walls and pillars infuse
it with a commanding air, while dishes are
as robust as you'd expect from a restaurant
named after the Bulgarian Empire's bolshi-
est ruler. Fill up on *satch* (a stew served on a
hotplate), roasted pork, or trout with prosciutto. Risottos and pizza also served.

⟡ Drinking & Entertainment

★Tam   BAR
(☑0889879693; ul Marno Pole 2A; ⊙4pm-3am
Mon-Sat) Open the nondescript door, and
up the stairs you'll find the city's friendliest, most-open-minded hang-out. Tam is the
place to feel the pulse of VT's arty crowd.
You might stumble on art installations, movie screenings, or language nights in English,
French or Spanish. Punters and staff extend
a genuine welcome and drinks flow late.

Sound & Light Show   LIVE PERFORMANCE
(☑0885080865; www.soundandlight.bg; ul N
Pikolo 6; 20-25 lv) Marvel as Veliko Târnovo's
medieval skyline is bathed in multicoloured

light during the Sound and Light Show. This 40-minute audiovisual display uses choral music and flashes of light in a homage to the rise and fall of the Second Bulgarian Empire.

🛈 Information

Tourist Information Centre (☑ 062-622 148; www.velikoturnovo.info; ul Hristo Botev 5; ⊙ 9am-6pm Mon-Fri, 10am-5pm Sat & Sun) Helpful English-speaking staff offering local info and advice.

🛈 Getting There & Away

BUS

The most central bus terminal is **Hotel Etar Bus Station** (www.etapgroup.com; ul Ivailo 2), with hourly buses to Sofia (three to 3½ hours) and Varna (3½ hours).

Zapad Bus Station (☑ 062-640 908; ul Nikola Gabrovski 74), about 3km southwest of the tourist information centre, runs regular buses to Plovdiv (four hours).

TRAIN

Check train schedules with the tourist information centre, or on www.bdz.bg, as Veliko Târnovo's two main train stations are located 10km apart. Irregular trains link the two stations (20 minutes, nine daily).

Gorna Oryakhovitsa train station (☑ 061-826 118), 8.5km northeast of town, is along the main line between Sofia and Varna. There are daily services to/from Sofia (four to five hours, eight daily) and Varna (3½ to four hours, five daily).

From **Veliko Târnovo Train Station** (☑ 885 39 7701), 1.5km west of town, there is one daily train to Plovdiv (4½ hours).

Varna

POP 334,700

Bulgaria's third-biggest city and maritime capital, Varna, is the most interesting and cosmopolitan town on the Black Sea coast. A combination of port city, naval base and seaside resort, it's an appealing place to while away a few days, packed with history yet thoroughly modern, with an enormous park to amble round and a lengthy beach to lounge on. In the city centre you'll find Bulgaria's largest Roman baths complex and its finest archaeological museum, as well as a lively cultural and restaurant scene.

CENTRAL & EASTERN EUROPE VARNA

WORTH A TRIP

NESEBÂR

On a small rocky outcrop about 37km northeast of Burgas (connected to the mainland by a narrow, artificial isthmus), pretty-as-a-postcard Nesebâr is famous for its surprisingly numerous, albeit mostly ruined, medieval churches. It has, inevitably, become heavily commercialised, and transforms into one huge, open-air souvenir market during the high season; outside summer, it's a ghost town.

Designated by Unesco as a World Heritage site, Nesebâr has its charms, but in summer these can be overpowered by the crowds and the relentless parade of tacky shops. With **Sunny Beach** (Slânchev Bryag) just across the bay, meanwhile, you have every conceivable water sport on hand. The 'new town' on the other side of the isthmus has the newest and biggest hotels and the main beach, but the sights are all in the old town.

Nesebâr was once home to about 80 churches, but many have been lost to time. Characteristic of the Nesebâr style are the horizontal strips of white stone and red brick, and facades decorated with green ceramic discs. The ruins, including the main church, **Sveta Sofia** (Old Metropolitan Church; ☑ 0554-46 019; www.ancient-nessebar.com; ul Mitropolitska; ⊙ dawn-dusk) **FREE**, are free to enter or to observe. Five churches – **Sveti Stefan**, **Sveti Spas**, **Christ Pantokrator**, **Sveta Paraskeva** and the **Church of St John the Baptist** – contain modest exhibitions and require a separate admission fee.

Various combined admission tickets are available that include access to the **Archaeological Museum** (☑ 0554-46 019; www.ancient-nessebar.com; ul Mesembria 2; adult/child 6/3 lv; ⊙ 9am-7pm Jun & Sep, to 8pm Jul & Aug, shorter hours Oct-May), with the **Ethnographic Museum** (☑ 0554-46 019; www.ancient-nessebar.com; ul Mesembria 32; adult/child 3/2 lv; ⊙ 10.30am-2pm & 2.30-6pm Tue-Sun Jun, to 7pm Jul-Sep, by request Oct-May) and one or more of the churches.

In summer you'll need to book accommodation in advance. Private rooms are the best option for budget travellers – locals offering rooms meet tourists off the bus.

Varna

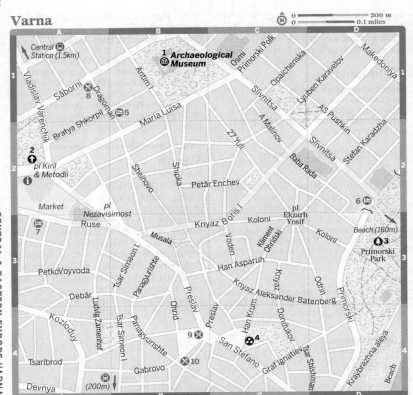

◉ Sights & Activities

Varna has a long stretch of public **beach** (☉9am-6pm), starting in the south, near the port, and stretching north some 4km. Generally, the quality of the sand and water improve and the crowds thin as you stroll north. The easiest way to access the beach is to walk south on bul Slivnitsa to **Primorski Park** and follow the stairs to the beach.

Running alongside the beach is the coastal lane, Kraybrezhna. You'll find a stretch of clubs here that have beach access and offer daybeds and umbrellas for rent (5 lv to 10 lv).

★ Archaeological
Museum   MUSEUM
(☑052-681 030; www.archaeo.museumvarna.com; ul Maria Luisa 41; adult/child 10/2 lv; ☉10am-5pm Tue-Sun Apr-Sep, Tue-Sat Oct-Mar; ☐8, 9, 109, 409) Exhibits at this vast museum, the best of

its kind in Bulgaria, include 6000-year-old bangles, necklaces and earrings said to be the oldest worked gold found in the world. You'll also find Roman surgical implements, Hellenistic tombstones and touching oddments including a marble plaque listing, in Greek, the names of the city's school graduates for AD 221. All of the exhibits are helpfully signposted in English, with excellent explanatory text. There's a large collection of icons on the second floor.

Primorski Park   PARK
(☐8, 9, 109, 409) Established in 1878, this large and attractive green space, overlooking the sea, stretches for about 8km and is said to be the largest of its kind in Europe. It's full of promenading families and old ladies knitting lace in summer, and there's always something going on. In addition to greenery and views, the park is home to the city's aquarium, zoo park and planetarium.

Varna

rafting trips. The location is an easy walk to the main sights.

Flag Hostel HOSTEL €
(☎0897408115; www.varnahostel.com; ul Bratya Shkorpil 13a, 4th fl; dm from 22 lv; [P][⊛][🛜]; 🚌8, 9, 109, 409) The Flag is a long-established, sociable spot with a party atmosphere. The three dorms are basic with comfortable single beds (no stacked bunks). Free pick-ups from the bus and train stations.

Hotel Odessos HOTEL €€
(☎052-640 300; www.odessos-bg.com; bul Slivnitsa 1; s/d from 75/90 lv; [P][⊛][🛜]) Enjoying a great location opposite the main entrance to Primorski Park, this is an older establishment with smallish and pretty average rooms, but it's convenient for the beach. Only the pricier 'sea view' rooms have balconies.

✖ Eating

★ Stariya Chinar BULGARIAN €€
(☎0876520500; www.stariachinar.com; ul Preslav 11; mains 10-20 lv; ⊗8am-midnight) This is upmarket Balkan soul food at its best. Try the baked lamb, made to an old Bulgarian recipe, or the divine barbecue pork ribs; it also boasts some rather ornate salads. Outdoor seating is lovely in summer; park yourself in the interior when the cooler weather strikes.

Orient TURKISH €€
(☎052-602 380; www.orientbg.com; ul Tzaribrod; mains 9-16 lv; ⊗8am-midnight Mon-Fri, from 9am Sat & Sun) The best place in Varna for Turkish food, including spicy kebabs, grilled meats, stews and salads. There's a nice range of appetisers, including favourites such as tabouli and hummus. Eat in or outside under the umbrellas.

Bistro Dragoman SEAFOOD €€
(☎052-621 688; www.restaurant-dragoman.net; ul Dragoman 43; mains 6-16 lv; ⊗10am-11pm; 🚌8, 9, 109, 409) This welcoming little place specialises in delicious takes on seafood and locally caught fish. This being the Balkans, grilled meats are also on the menu.

ℹ Information

Tourist Information Centre (☎052-820 690; www.visit.varna.bg; pl Kiril & Metodii; ⊗9am-7pm May-Sep, 8.30am-5.30pm Mon-Fri Oct-Apr; 🚌8, 9, 109, 409) Plenty of free brochures and maps, and helpful multilingual staff. The Tourist Information Centre also operates free three-hour walking tours of the city on select days from June to September.

Roman Thermae RUINS
(☎052-600 059; www.archaeo.museumvarna.com; cnr ul Han Krum & ul San Stefano; adult/child 5/2 lv; ⊗10am-5pm Tue-Sun May-Oct, 10am-5pm Tue-Sat Nov-Apr) The well-preserved ruins of Varna's 2nd-century-AD Roman Thermae are the largest in Bulgaria and the fourth-largest of its kind in Europe. Visitors are allowed to clamber around the various chambers of the bath complex and admire surviving pieces of the advanced floor- and water-heating systems. The baths survived in their original form for only a century or two before the complex was abandoned. It was too costly to maintain as the empire began to decline.

Cathedral of the Assumption of the Virgin CHURCH
(☎052-613 005; www.mitropolia-varna.org; pl Kiril & Metodii 2; ⊗8am-6pm; 🚌8, 9, 109, 409) Varna's cathedral (1886) is topped with golden onion domes. Note the murals (painted in 1950) and colourful stained-glass windows, though you'll have to pay 5 lv if you want to take photos inside.

🛏 Sleeping

Varna has no shortage of accommodation, although the better (more central) places get very busy during the summer months.

★ Yo Ho Hostel HOSTEL €
(☎0884729144; www.yohohostel.com; ul Ruse 23; dm/s/d from 19/39/54 lv; [@][🛜]; 🚌8, 9, 109) Shiver your timbers at this cheerful, pirate-themed place, with four- and 11-bed dorm rooms and private options. Staff offer free pick-ups and can organise camping and

WORTH A TRIP

BURGAS

For most visitors, the port city of Burgas (sometimes written 'Bourgas') is no more than an air gateway and transit point for the more obviously appealing resorts and historic towns further up and down the coast. If you do decide to stop over, you'll find a lively, well-kept city with a neat, pedestrianised centre, a gorgeous seafront park, and some interesting museums.

A clutch of reasonably priced hotels, as well as some of the best restaurants in this part of the country, makes it a practical base for exploring the southern coast, too. For a memorable meal, try **Ethno** (☑0887877966; ul Aleksandrovska 49; mains 7-20 lv; ☺11am-11.30pm; 🛜), with inviting blue-and-white surrounds that recall the city's Greek heritage, superb (English-speaking) service and a summery vibe.

Burgas' 3km-long strip of beach is surprisingly pretty for an urban beach. The water and sand tend to get nicer the further north along the coast you wander, but it's all clean and safe and patrolled by lifeguards in summer. The beach is lined with bars and fish restaurants, and umbrellas and loungers can be hired.

Nature lovers also come to Burgas for the four lakes just outside the city, which are havens for abundant bird life. You can birdwatch, kayak or take an impromptu plunge into a salt pool.

Burgas has excellent transport connections around the country. The bus and train stations are conveniently located next to each other at the southern end of the main street, ul Aleksandrovska.

❶ Getting There & Away

Varna's **central bus station** (Avtoexpress; ☑information 052-757 044, tickets 052-748 349; www.bgrazpisanie.com; bul Vladislav Varenchik 158; ☺24hr; 🚌148, 409) is about 2km northwest of the city centre. There are regular buses to Sofia (seven hours), Burgas (two hours) and all major destinations in Bulgaria; see www.bgrazpisanie.com for fares and schedules.

Facilities at Varna's **train station** (☑052-630 444; www.bdz.bg; pl Slaveikov; 🚌8, 9, 109) include a left-luggage office and cafe. Direct services are available to Sofia (seven to eight hours, seven daily) and Plovdiv (seven hours, three daily).

Sozopol

POP 5700

Ancient Sozopol, with its charming Old Town of meandering cobbled streets and pretty wooden houses huddled together on a narrow peninsula, is one of the coast's real highlights. With two superb beaches, a genial atmosphere, plentiful accommodation and good transport links, it has long been a popular seaside resort and makes an excellent base for exploring the area. Although not quite as crowded as Nesebâr, it is becoming ever more popular with international visitors. There's a lively cultural scene, too, with plenty of free concerts and other events in summer.

◉ Sights & Activities

The town's two beaches are attractive, though waves can be high for small children. The 1km-long **Harmanite Beach** (ul Ropotamo; ☺9am-6pm Jun-Sep) is wide and clean, and offers a water slide, paddleboats, volleyball nets and beach bars. The **Town Beach** (☺9am-6pm Jun-Sep) (or Northern Beach) is another pleasant curve of sand, but it's smaller, gets *very* crowded, and doesn't offer the same number of beachside cafes, restaurants and bars.

Archaeological Museum   MUSEUM
(☑0550-22 226; ul Han Krum 2; adult/child 4/1 lv; ☺8.30am-6pm Jun-Sep, 8.30am-noon & 1.30pm-5pm Mon-Fri Oct-May) Housed in a drab concrete box near the port, this museum has a small but fascinating collection of local finds from its Apollonian glory days and beyond. In addition to a wealth of Hellenic treasures, the museum occasionally exhibits the skeleton of a local 'vampire', found with a stake driven through its chest. Enter from the building's northern side.

**Southern Fortress Wall
& Tower Museum**   RUIN, MUSEUM
(☑0550-22 267; www.sozopol-foundation.com; ul Milet 50; adult/child 7 lv/free; ☺9.30am-9.30pm May-Sep) This museum occupies a former granary and part of the fortification walls of the medieval town, dating from the 5th

century AD. At this time, Sozopol was considered an important defensive post of the Byzantine Empire, with its capital at Constantinople (İstanbul). Visitors pass by some interior defensive walls and a well going back to the 3rd century BC. That said, it's a bit underwhelming. Even if you skip the museum, walk under the arch to see the sea views.

🛏 Sleeping

Sozopol has numerous private homes offering rooms. Look for signs along Republikanska in the new town, and pretty much anywhere in the Old Town.

★ Justa Hostel HOSTEL €

(☑ 0550-22 175; ul Apolonia 20; dm 20 lv; 🛜) This clean, cosy, centrally located hostel sits in the centre of the Old Town, a few minutes' walk from the beach. Dorm-bed accommodation with shared bath and shower. The price includes traditional breakfast (pancakes) and coffee.

★ Art Hotel HOTEL €€

(☑ 0878650160, 0550-24 081; www.arthotel-sbh. com; ul Kiril & Metodii 72; d/studios 85/105 lv; ❄🛜) This peaceful old house, belonging to the Union of Bulgarian Artists, is within a walled courtyard toward the tip of the peninsula, away from the crowds. It has a small selection of bright, comfortable rooms with balconies, most with sea views; breakfast is served on the terraces overlooking the sea.

🍴 Eating

The best restaurants in town are on ul Morksi Skali, on the far northeastern end of the peninsula. These are mainly traditional affairs with some spectacular views.

Panorama SEAFOOD €€

(ul Morski Skali 21; mains 8-20 lv; ⊙10am-11pm) This lively place has an open terrace with a fantastic view toward Sveti Ivan island. Fresh, locally caught fish is the mainstay of the menu. It's one of the best of many seafood spots on this street.

Ksantana SEAFOOD €€

(☑ 0550-22 454; www.ksantanabistro.com; ul Morski Skali 7; mains 10-16 lv; ⊙11am-11pm) The split-level terraces of this traditional fish restaurant afford a bird's-eye view of Sveti Ivan Island from the courtyard balcony. The restaurant can be entered at both the top and bottom of the steps and can be easy to miss.

★ Mehane Neptun BULGARIAN €€€

(☑ 0550-22 735; ul Morski Skali 45; mains 15-30 lv; ⊙10am-11pm) Occupying a promontory looking out over the sea and Sveti Ivan Island in the distance, the awesome views and the delicious fish combinations, such as mouth-watering stuffed squid, are only partly marred by the sometimes indifferent service. Try to book a sea-view table outdoors for around dusk and settle in for a memorable evening.

CENTRAL & EASTERN EUROPE SOZOPOL

❶ Getting There & Away

The small public **bus station** (☏ 0550-23 460; www.bgrazpisanie.com; ul Han Krum) is just south of the Old Town walls. Buses leave for Burgas (40 minutes) about every 30 minutes between 6am and 9pm in summer, and about once an hour in low season.

Buses also arrive and depart from spots around the new town's main square. Three or four buses go to Sofia daily and one or two depart for Plovdiv.

Fast Ferry (☏ 0889182914, booking 0885808001; www.fastferry.bg; Sozopol Harbour), operating from a kiosk at the harbour, runs ferries at least four days a week to Nesebâr (single/return from 27/54 lv, 30 minutes) between June and September.

Bulgaria Survival Guide

❶ Directory A–Z

ACCOMMODATION

Accommodation is most expensive in Sofia and other big cities, notably Plovdiv and Varna. Elsewhere, prices are relatively cheap by Western European standards.

Demand and prices are highest in coastal resorts between July and August, and in the skiing resorts between December and February. Outside the holiday seasons, these hotels often close down, or operate on a reduced basis.

Sofia has more hostels than anywhere else. You will also find hostels in Veliko Târnovo, Varna, Plovdiv and Burgas. Most are clean, modern and friendly places in central locations.

---

❶ SLEEPING PRICE RANGES

The following price ranges refer to a double room with bathroom in high season. Unless otherwise stated, breakfast is included in the price.

€ less than 60 lv

€€ 60–120 lv (to 200 lv in Sofia)

€€€ more than 120 lv (more than 200 lv in Sofia)

The following price ranges refer to a standard main course. Unless otherwise stated, service charge is included in the price.

€ less than 10 lv

€€ 10–20 lv

€€€ more than 20 lv

MONEY

➡ The local currency is the lev (plural: leva), usually abbreviated as lv. The lev is stable. For big purchases such as tours, airfares, car rentals and hotels, prices are sometimes quoted in euros, although payment is possible in leva too. Bulgaria has no immediate plans to adopt the euro.

➡ ATMs are common and can be found in all larger towns and cities.

➡ Drawing money on your own card is usually the easiest way to get local currency, though some banks may restrict how much money you can withdraw per day.

➡ In restaurants, a 10% tip for good service is common, though this may have already been added to the bill.

PUBLIC HOLIDAYS

New Year's Day 1 January

Liberation Day 3 March

Orthodox Easter March/April/May

May Day 1 May

St George's Day/Bulgarian Army Day 6 May

Cyrillic Alphabet/Culture and Literacy Day 24 May

Unification Day 6 September

Bulgarian Independence Day 22 September

Christmas 25 and 26 December

TELEPHONE

➡ To call Bulgaria from abroad, dial the international access code (which varies from country to country), add 359 (the country code for Bulgaria), the area code (minus the first zero) and then the number.

➡ To make an international call from Bulgaria, dial 00 followed by the code of the country you are calling, then the local area code, minus the first zero.

➡ Visitors from elsewhere in Europe will be able to use their mobile phones in Bulgaria. Local SIM cards are easy to buy in mobile phone stores (bring your passport) and can be used in most phones.

➡ To call a Bulgarian mobile phone from within Bulgaria, dial the full number, including the initial 0.

VISAS

Bulgaria is a member of the EU. Visas are not required for EU citizens. Citizens of Australia, Canada, New Zealand and the USA can visit visa-free for up to 90 days.

❶ Getting There & Away

BORDER CROSSINGS

Bulgaria has border crossings with Greece, Macedonia, Romania, Serbia and Turkey. Expect delays at all of these crossings, especially if you are using public transport. Delays at the Turkish border tend to be longest.

BUS

Buses travel to Bulgarian cities from destinations all over Europe, with most arriving in Sofia. You will have to get off the bus at the border and walk through customs to present your passport. When travelling out of Bulgaria by bus, the cost of entry visas for the countries concerned are not included in bus ticket prices.

TRAIN

There are a number of long-haul international trains to/from Bulgaria, including services with Serbia, Romania, Greece and Turkey. Sofia is the main hub, although trains stop at other towns. Bulgarian international train services are operated by **Bulgarian State Railway** (БДЖ; www. bdz.bg).

ⓘ Getting Around

BUS

Buses provide the most comfortable and quickest mode of public transport. They link all cities and major towns and connect villages with the nearest transport hub. There are several private companies operating frequent modern, comfortable bus services that travel between the larger towns, while older, often cramped minibuses also run on routes between smaller towns.

Biomet (www.biomet.bg) Runs between Sofia and Veliko Târnovo, Varna and Burgas.

Etap-Grup (www.etapgroup.com) Another extensive intercity network, with buses between Sofia, Burgas, Varna and Veliko Târnovo, as well as routes between Sofia and Sozopol and other resorts along the Black Sea coast.

Union-Ivkoni (www.union-ivkoni.com) Links most major towns and many smaller ones, including Sofia, Burgas, Varna and Plovdiv.

TRAIN

Bulgarian State Railways boasts an impressive network, linking most larger towns and cities. Most trains tend to be antiquated, shabby and not especially comfortable, and journey times are slower than buses. On the plus side, you will have more room to move in a train compartment, and the scenery is likely to be more rewarding.

Trains are classified as *ekspresen* (express), *bârz* (fast) or *pâtnicheski* (slow passenger). Unless you absolutely thrive on train travel or you want to visit a more remote town, use a fast or express train.

UKRAINE

Ukraine is in the headlnes a lot these days – mainly for the tragic border conflict with Russia in the country's far eastern regions. But Ukraine is a large country and much of the land is peaceful and worth a visit. Indeed, it's one of Europe's last genuine travel adventures: a poor nation, rich in colourful traditions, warm-hearted people and off-the-map experiences. You can admire the historical beauty of the capital Kyiv, sip some of Eastern Europe's best coffee in sophisticated Lviv or party on the beach in Odesa – all in just a few days.

Kyiv

POP 2.9 MILLION

In the beginning there was Kyiv (often spelled in English as 'Kiev'). Long before Ukraine and Russia came into being, its inhabitants were already striding up and down the green hills, idling away hot afternoons on the Dnipro River and promenading along Kreshchatyk – then a stream, now a main avenue. Today history continues to unfold. As revolution has come and gone, and as war in the east smoulders, Ukraine's capital has rebelled again, only this time culturally. A creative wave has swept over the city, embodied by urban art, vintage cafes and 24-hour parties. Seemingly overnight, Kyiv has become hip.

◉ Sights

Some of Kyiv's main attractions are half-day adventures and not always terribly central. So, rather than plunging right in, it's highly recommended you warm up with an initial stroll along vul Khreshchatyk and maydan Nezalezhnosti.

★ **Maydan Nezalezhnosti**　　　SQUARE
(майдан Незалежності; Independence Sq; Ⓜ Maydan Nezalezhnosti) Be it celebration or revolution, whenever Ukrainians want to get together – and they often do – 'Maydan' is the nation's meeting point. The square saw pro-independence protests in the 1990s and the Orange Revolution in 2004. But all of that was eclipsed by the Euromaidan Revolution in 2013–14, when the square was transformed into an urban guerrilla camp besieged by government forces. In peaceful times, Maydan is more about festiveness than feistiness, with weekend concerts and a popular nightly fountain show.

UKRAINE AT A GLANCE

Don't Miss

Kyiv's Kyevo-Pecherska Lavra Descend into catacombs to see mummies of much-revered saints on an excursion to the holy of holies for all eastern Slavs. Founded as a cave monastery in 1051, the lavra is packed with golden-domed churches, baroque edifices and orchards.

Lviv's historical centre Lviv is the beating cultural heart of Ukraine and the city most geared up to accept visitors. Its bustling centre is the main square, pl Rynok. Head in any direction and you will quickly stumble upon a magnificent, aromatic church: each one, it seems, belonging to a different denomination.

Kyiv's Andriyivsky Uzviz The apostle Andrew is said to have climbed this steep ascent to erect a cross and prophesy the rise of Kyiv. Today it's the haunt of artists, who install their canvases on this cobbled Montmartre-like street, which – in true decadent style – Kyivites call 'Andrew's Descent'.

Odesa's nightlife By day Odesa's museums, parks, beaches and, of course, the celebrated Potemkin Steps provide ample distraction, but it's at night that the city really comes alive. Arkadia Beach is the place to strut and pose until the wee summer hours.

Lviv's food culture Coffee, chocolate, gingerbread, strudel, cherry liqueur, beer – Lviv seems to have a festival dedicated to every naughty pleasure, but you don't have to turn up on a red-letter day to satisfy your sweet tooth. Ukraine's gastronomic capital has Eastern Europe's best coffee year-round, drunk central European style in cosy cafes.

Itineraries

One Week

Ukraine's a big country, and if you've only got a week, concentrate on **Kyiv** and Lviv. For the capital, spend the first couple of days strolling the main boulevard, vul Khreshchatyk, from Bessarabsky Rynok to Maydan Nezalezhnosti and move on to St Sophia's Cathedral. Later on, take in the Kyevo-Pecherska Lavra, and don't miss some great restaurants and bars too. Fly or take an express train to the country's western metropolis of **Lviv** for a couple days roaming the quaint cobbles and taking in those bean-perfumed coffee houses.

Two Weeks

Fourteen is a more manageable amount of time to deal with Ukraine's geography and transport. Stretch out your stay in **Lviv** and take in the city's main square, Ploshcha Rynok, as well as highlights like the Lvivarnya and the National Museum and Memorial to the Victims of Occupation. The southern Black Sea city and resort of **Odesa** is badly underrated. Here, enjoy the charms of Prymorsky Boulevar and the city's famous Potemkin Steps. By night, in summer, the beach area morphs into the country's dance-music playground.

Essential Food & Drink

Borshch A typical version of the national soup is made with beetroot, pork fat and herbs.

Bread Dark and white varieties of *khlib* (хліб) are available every day, including the white *pampushky* (soft rolls rubbed with garlic and oil and then fried), occasionally served with borshch.

Cabbage rolls *Holubtsy* (голубці) are cabbage rolls stuffed with seasoned rice and meat and stewed in a tomato and soured cream sauce.

Kasha Pretty much any grain is called *kasha* (каша), and while the word might be used to describe porridge, more commonly it turns out to be buckwheat.

Varenyky Similar to Polish pierogi, *varenyky* (вареники) are small half-moon-shaped dumplings and have more than 50 different vegetarian and meat fillings.

Getting Around

Train Cheap but slow, especially the old-school overnight services. New express trains, which travel by day, connect Kyiv with Ukraine's biggest cities. Check Ukrainian Railways (www.uz.gov.ua) for online timetables and tickets.

Bus Very cheap, with regular services, but sometimes packed to bursting and unbearably hot in summer. Handy when there is no convenient train and/or for shorter trips.

Car For daring individuals this is a good and fun way to travel around Ukraine, if you don't mind dire road quality and maniac drivers.

Air Domestic flights are convenient for travelling across the country but tend to be a bit pricey.

When to Go

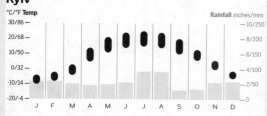

Kyiv

°C/°F **Temp**   Rainfall inches/mm

30/86 —   — 10/250
20/68 —   — 8/200
10/50 —   — 6/150
0/32 —   — 4/100
-10/14 —   — 2/50
-20/-4 —   — 0

J F M A M J J A S O N D

Jul & Aug Expect stifling heat and humidity as well as heavy thunderstorms.

Apr–Jun & Sep Spring can be chilly, but it's pleasant in Kyiv. Visit Odesa in autumn to avoid the summer crowds.

Oct–Mar Expect temperatures below zero, heavy snowfalls and hard frosts.

Arriving in Ukraine

Boryspil International Airport (Kyiv) Regular round-the-clock bus services leave from outside the terminal to the main train station. Taxis cost 650uah to the city centre (around 40 minutes).

Danylo Halytskyi International Airport (Lviv) Take trolleybus 9 to the university or bus 48 to the corner of vul Doroshenka and pr Svobody. Taxis cost around 100uah to the city centre.

Odesa International Airport Trolleybus 14 runs to the city centre between 7am and 7pm. Taking a taxi here is not recommended.

Top Phrases

Hello. Добрий день. *(do·bry den')*

Goodbye. До побачення. *(do po·ba·chen·nya)*

Please. Прошу. *(pro·shu)*

Thank you. Дякую. *(dya·ku·yu)*

Cheers! Будьмо! *(bud'·mo)*

Resources

Brama (www.brama.com)

Ukraine.com (www.ukraine.com)

Travel to Ukraine (www.traveltoukraine.org)

Set Your Budget

➡ Dorm beds: 100–250uah

➡ Cafeteria-style meal: from 80uah

➡ 100km of bus travel: 130uah

Central Kyiv

500 m
0.25 miles

Dniprovsky Park

Dnipro River

Mezhyhirya (30km)

vul Naberezhno-Khreshchatytska

PODIL

vul Voloska

vul Spaska

vul Hryhoriya Skovorody

vul Illinska

Kontraktova pl

vul Bratska

vul Sahaydachnoho

pl Poshtova

Poshtova pl

Volodymyrsky uzviz

Z hryor yysna aleya

Volodymyrska Hirka Park

vul Desyatynna

St Michael's Golden-Domed Monastery

2

vul Mykhaylivska

vul Mala Zhytomyrska

Maydan Nezalezhnosti

Maydan Nezalezhnosti

8

1

vul Borychiv Tik

4

5

Andriyivsky Uzviz

pl Mykhaylivska

pl Sofiyska

St Sophia's Cathedral

3

12

vul Velyka Zhytomyrska

vul Sofiyivska

vul Volodymyrska

vul Zhytnia

vul Prytysko-Mykilska

Kontraktova pl

vul Pokrovska

15

7

VERKHNIY GOROD

vul Vozdvyzhenska

vul Kozhumyatska

Peyzazhna aleya

pl Lvivska

vul Reytarska

vul Striletska

vul Yaroslaviv Val

vul Kostyantynivska

vul Verkhniy Val

vul Kyrylivska

vul Voznesensky uzviz

vul Petrivska

vul Kudryavska

vul Observatorna

prov Chekhovsky

vul Oleksy Honchara

vul Hlybochytsa

vul Hlybochytska

14

vul Lukyanivska

vul Sichovykh Striltsiv

vul Mykoly Rymenka

vul Bulvarno-Kudryavska

vul Yuriya Kotsyubynskoho

vul Gogolivska

vul Turgenivska

vul Dmytrivska

vul Poltavska

pl Vyacheslava Chornovola

vul Pavlivska

vul Zolotoustivska

Lukyanivska

pl Lukyanivska

Naberezhne shose

pl Poshtova

pl Evropeyska

Park Askoldova Mohyla

Park Misky Sad

Petrivska aleya

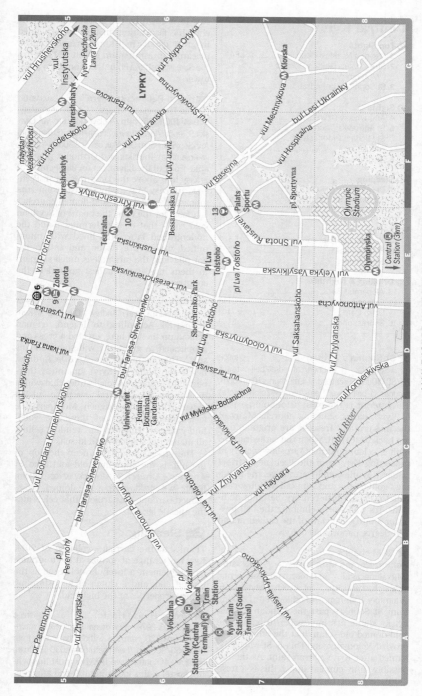

Central Kyiv

★ **St Sophia's Cathedral**   CHURCH
(pl Sofiyska; grounds/cathedral/bell tower 20/80/40uah; ⊙ cathedral & museums 10am-6pm, grounds & bell tower 9am-7pm; Ⓜ Zoloti Vorota) The interior is the most astounding aspect of Kyiv's oldest standing church. Many of the mosaics and frescoes are original, dating back to 1017–31, when the cathedral was built to celebrate Prince Yaroslav's victory in protecting Kyiv from the Pechenegs (tribal raiders). While equally attractive, the building's gold domes and 76m-tall wedding-cake bell tower are 18th-century baroque additions. It's well worth climbing the bell tower for a bird's-eye view of the cathedral and 360-degree panoramas of Kyiv.

★ **St Michael's Golden-Domed Monastery**   MONASTERY
(Михайлівський Золотоверхий монастир; www.archangel.kiev.ua; vul Tryokhsvyatytelska 6; ⊙ territory 8am-7pm; Ⓜ Poshtova Pl) Looking from St Sophia's past the Bohdan Khmelnytsky statue, it's impossible to ignore the gold-domed blue church at the other end of proyizd Volodymyrsky. This is St Michael's, named after Kyiv's patron saint. As the impossibly shiny cupolas imply, this is a fresh (2001) copy of the original (1108), which

was torn down by the Soviets in 1937. The church's fascinating history is explained in great detail (in Ukrainian and English placards) in a **museum** (14uah; ⊙ 10am-7pm Tue-Sun; Ⓜ Poshtova Pl) in the monastery's bell tower.

★ **Kyevo-Pecherska Lavra**   MONASTERY
(Києво-Печерська лавра; Caves Monastery; ☑ 044-406 6375; http://kplavra.kiev.ua; vul Lavrska 9; upper/lower Lavra 25uah/free; ⊙ 9am-7pm Apr-Sep, 9am-6pm Oct-Mar, caves 8.30am-4.30pm; Ⓜ Arsenalna) Tourists and Orthodox pilgrims alike flock to the Lavra, set on 28 hectares of grassy hills above the Dnipro River in Pechersk. It's easy to see why tourists come: the monastery's cluster of gold-domed churches is a feast for the eyes, the hoard of Scythian gold rivals that of the Hermitage, and the underground labyrinths lined with mummified monks are exotic and intriguing. For pilgrims, the rationale is much simpler: to them, this is the holiest ground in the country.

Andriyivsky Uzviz   STREET
(Андріївський узвіз; Andrew's Descent; Ⓜ Kontraktova Pl) According to legend, a man walked up the hill here, erected a cross and prophesied, 'A great city will stand on this spot.' That man was the Apostle Andrew, hence the name of Kyiv's quaintest thoroughfare, a steep cobbled street that winds its way up from Kontraktova pl to vul Volodymyrska, with a vaguely Montparnasse feel. Along the length of 'the *uzviz*' you'll find cafes, art galleries and vendors selling all manner of souvenir and kitsch.

The street's highlight, near the top of the hill, is the stunning gold and blue **St Andrew's Church** (Andriyivsky uzviz; platform 10uah; Ⓜ Kontraktova Pl), a five-domed, cross-shaped baroque masterpiece that celebrates the apostle legend.

🛌 Sleeping

Thanks to the currency collapse of 2014, Kyiv has a range of options at the midrange to complement a lovely hostel scene at the budget end, and a clutch of long-standing luxury properties at the high end.

★ **Dream House Hostel**   HOSTEL €
(☑ 095 703 2979; www.dream-family.com; Andriyivsky uzviz 2D; dm/s/d without bathroom from 240/560/900uah, d with bathroom 1030-1350uah; ✳ @ 🛜; Ⓜ Kontraktova Pl) Kyiv's most happening hostel is this gleaming 100-bed affair su-

perbly located at the bottom of Andriyivsky uzviz. An attached **cafe-bar** (Andriyivsky uzviz 2D; ⊙8am-midnight; 🛜; Ⓜ Kontraktova Pl), a basement kitchen, a laundry room, key cards, bike hire, and daily events and tours make this a comfortable and engaging base from which to explore the capital.

Veselka Hostel HOSTEL **€**
(🖉093 426 5999; www.keytogates.com.ua; vul Volodymyrska 42A; dm 160-220uah, d 650-850uah; 🖳🛜; Ⓜ Zoloti Vorota) Locations don't much better than around the corner from **Zoloti Vorota** (Golden Gate; vul Volodymyrska; adult/student 40/15uah; ⊙10am-6pm Mon-Thu, to 8am Fri-Sun; Ⓜ Zoloti Vorota) in the very centre of the city. Throw in sharp dorm rooms, bright doubles, fair prices and arguably Kyiv's most stylish common/kitchen area, and you have a real winner. It's not a particularly social hostel, but if you prefer peace over people look no further.

★**Sunflower B&B Hotel** B&B **€€**
(🖉044-279 3846; www.sunflowerhotel.kiev.ua; vul Kostyolna 9/41; s 1400-1600uah, d 1650-1850uah; 🖳@🛜; Ⓜ Maydan Nezalezhnosti) Just off maydan Nezalezhnosti but well hidden from noisy traffic and crowds, this B&B (and definitely not hotel) seems to have been designed by a super-tidy granny. The airy, light-coloured rooms have a retro feel and there are extras like umbrellas and a shoe-polishing machine that you wouldn't expect. Continental breakfast is served in your room.

 Eating

★**Puzata Khata** CAFETERIA **€**
(Пузата Хата; vul Sahaydachnoho 24; dishes 20-30uah; ⊙8am-11pm; 🖳🛜; Ⓜ Kontraktova Pl) An upscale *stolovaya*, 'Hut of the Pot Belly' is an excellent place for budget travellers to sample traditional Ukrainian cuisine. There are plenty of soups and salads, cheap veggie options, delicious pastries and even a full bar. Nothing is in English but you can just point at what you want.

★**Kyivska Perepichka** PIES **€**
(Київська перепічка; vul Bohdana Khmelnytskoho 3; perepichka 12uah; ⊙8.30am-9pm Mon-Sat, 10am-9pm Sun; Ⓜ Teatralna) A perpetually long queue moves with lightning speed towards a window where two women hand out pieces of fried dough enclosing a mouthwatering sausage. The place became a local institution long before the first 'hot dog' hit town. An essential Kyiv experience.

★**Spotykach** UKRAINIAN **€€**
(Спотикач; 🖉044-586 4095; vul Volodymyrska 16; mains 125-250uah; ⊙11am-midnight; 🖳🛜; Ⓜ Zoloti Vorota) Spotykach shed its retro-Soviet theme in 2014 and adopted a Ukrainian revolutionary theme, with pictures of Taras Shevchenko and Bohdan Khelmytsky (and Che Guevara) replacing Lenin. They do highly original takes on Ukrainian classics, including yellow-and-blue *varenyky* – the ultimate nationalist expression – and a *borshch* popsicle.

🍷 **Drinking**

Espressoholic CAFE
(vul Khoryva 25; ⊙8am-10pm; Ⓜ Kontraktova Pl) A tiny but immensely popular coffee shop in Podil with high-quality caffeinated beverages, friendly baristas and low prices. The action spills out into the street, often blending with the crowd from a neighbouring bar and pizzeria to form a mini–block party. It's a great spot to mingle with locals.

★**Closer** CLUB
(🖉067 658 8951; www.facebook.com/closerkiev; vul Nyzhnoyurkivska 31; cover 200-300uah; ⊙midnight-noon Fri & Sat; 🛜; Ⓜ Tarasa Shevchenka) More than just a nightclub, Closer is a bohemian *tour-de-force* that epitomises Kyiv's emergence as a hub of creativity and counterculture. Heavily influenced by Berlin's

CENTRAL & EASTERN EUROPE KYIV

LOCAL KNOWLEDGE

THE UKRAINIAN TABLE

Ukrainians admit theirs is a cuisine of comfort – full of hearty dishes designed for fierce winters rather than for gastronomic zing. And yet, while it's suffered from negative stereotypes of Soviet-style cabbage slop and pernicious pickles, Ukrainian cooking isn't bad. Look especially for **borshch** (борщ), the national soup made with beetroot, pork fat and herbs. **Cabbage rolls** (*holubtsy* голубці) are stuffed with seasoned rice and meat and stewed in a tomato and soured cream sauce. **Varenyky** (вареники), similar to Polish *pierogi*, are small, half-moon-shaped dumplings that have more than 50 different traditional vegetarian and meat fillings.

community of 24hr party people, Closer throws weekend raves that last well into the following afternoon. There are spaces to fit all moods, including three dance halls, a chill-out garden, and a mini-outdoor amphitheatre.

★**Alchemist Bar** COCKTAIL BAR
(vul Shota Rustaveli 12; ⊙noon-3am, to 5am Fri & Sat; 🛜; Ⓜ Palats Sportu) Kyiv's best bar is set in an intimate basement space on vibrant vul Shota Rustaveli. No pretensions, no strict *feiskontrol* (face control), just an eclectic mix of fun-loving patrons chasing good music, good drinks and good conversation. Most nights see truly excellent bands play, after which DJs take over and many people start dancing near the bar.

❶ Information

Tour Info Kiev (www.tourinfo.kiev.ua) The city runs about a dozen of these booths, including at **maydan Nezalezhnosti** (cnr vul Khreshchatyk & vul Instytutska; ⊙9am-7pm, to 5.30pm Sun) and near **Bessarabska Rynok** (cnr vul Khreshchatyk & vul Baseyna; ⊙9am-7pm, to 5.30pm Fri), and at both airports. They are of moderate usefulness, but are usually staffed by an English speaker who can answer simple questions and distribute free maps and brochures. For a small commission they also sell theatre and concert tickets as well as bus and train tickets. For more details, see www.visitkyiv.travel.

❶ Getting There & Away

AIR

Most international flights use Kyiv's main **Boryspil International Airport** (☑ 044-364 4505; www.kbp.aero), about 35km east of the city. The airport has a good website listing airlines and flight schedules. Most flights of the national carrier, **Ukraine International Airlines** (☑ 044-581 5050; www.flyuia.com; vul Lysenka 4; ⊙8am-7.30pm, to 5.30pm Sun; Ⓜ Maydan Nezalezhnosti), use this airport.

Bus

Bus Kyiv has several bus terminals, but the most useful for long-distance trips is the **Central Bus Station** (Tsentralny Avtovokzal; ☑ 044-525 5774; pl Moskovska 3; 🚌1, 12), near Demiivska metro station. Long-distance express carriers **Autolux** (☑ 044-594 9500; www.autolux.ua; Central Bus Station; ⊙6.30am-9pm) and **Gunsel** (☑ 044-525 4505; www.gunsel.com.ua; Central Bus Station) run the most comfortable buses in the business. They have frequent trips to most large regional centres; many trips go via, or continue to,

Boryspil International Airport. You can book on their websites, or buy tickets at the Central Bus Station or Boryspil International Airport.

TRAIN

You can get pretty much everywhere in the country from Kyiv's modern **train station** (Central Terminal; ☑ 044-309 7005; pl Vokzalna 2; Ⓜ Vokzalna), conveniently located near the centre at Vokzalna metro station. Heading west, the quickest way to Lviv is on the daily express day train (five hours), or there are several regular trains (eight to 13 hours). Heading south, there are night services to Odesa (eight to 12 hours).

❶ Getting Around

TO/FROM THE AIRPORT

From Boryspil International Airport catch a convenient, round-the-clock Skybus service (90uah, 45 minutes to one hour) to/from vul Polzunova outside Kyiv train station's **South Terminal** (Південний вокзал | Pivdenniy Vokzal; vul Polzunova). Departures are every 20 minutes during the day, and less frequent at night.

METRO

Although crowded, Kyiv's metro is clean, efficient and easy to use. It is also the world's deepest, requiring escalator rides of seven to eight minutes. Trains run frequently from 6am to midnight on all three lines. Blue *zhetony* (plastic tokens) costing 5uah (good for one ride) are sold by cashiers, or buy a plastic card that can be topped up at any station.

Lviv

POP 728,000

If you've spent time in any other region of Ukraine, Lviv will come as a shock. Mysterious and architecturally lovely, this Unesco World Heritage site is the country's least 'Soviet' city and exudes much of the same authentic Central European charm as Prague or Kraków. Its quaint cobbles, bean-perfumed coffee houses and rattling trams are half a continent away from the post-Soviet badlands to the east. It's also a place where the candle of Ukrainian national identity burns brightest and where Russian is definitely a minority language.

◉ Sights

★**Ploshcha Rynok** SQUARE
FREE Lviv was declared a Unesco World Heritage Site in 1998, and this old market square lies at its heart. The square was progressively rebuilt after a major fire in the early 16th century destroyed the original.

THE BLACK SEA PORT OF ODESA

Odesa is a city straight from literature – an energetic, decadent boom town. Its famous Potemkin Steps sweep down to the Black Sea and Ukraine's biggest commercial port. Behind them, a cosmopolitan cast of characters makes merry among neoclassical pastel buildings lining a geometric grid of leafy streets.

Immigrants from all over Europe were invited to make their fortune here when Odesa was founded in the late-18th century by Russia's Catherine the Great. These new inhabitants, particularly Jews, gave Russia's southern window on the world a singular, somehow 'subversive' nature.

Having weathered recent political storms, Odesa is booming again – it now substitutes for Crimea as the main domestic holiday destination. It's a golden age for local businesses, but it puts a strain on the already crowded beaches.

Odesa is a city built for strolling. Elegant **Prymorsky Boulevard** (Приморський бульвар) was designed to enchant the passengers of arriving boats with the neoclassical opulence of its architecture and old-worldish civility, which was unexpected in these parts at the time of construction in the early 19th century.

At the boulevard's eastern end, you'll spot the pink-and-white **City Hall** (bul Prymorsky), which originally served as the stock exchange. The cannon here is a war trophy captured from the British during the Crimean War. In the square in front of City Hall is Odesa's most photographed monument, the **Pushkin statue**. The plaque reads 'To Pushkin – from the Citizens of Odesa'.

Continuing along the boulevard, at the top of **Potemkin Steps** (Потьомкінські сходи) you'll reach the statue of **Duc de Richelieu** (Памятник Ришельє; bul Prymorsky), Odesa's first governor, looking like a Roman in a toga.

Underneath the eastern section of the boulevard, Istanbul park was reopened with much pomp in 2017 after a thorough Turkish-funded reconstruction that turned it into a rather manicured patch with welcoming benches, sunbeds and an impressive sandstone grotto in the middle of a fountain.

At the western end of bul Prymorsky stands the semiderelict **Vorontsov Palace** (bul Prymorsky). This was the residence of the city's third governor, and built in 1826 in a classical style with interior Arabic detailing. The Greek-style colonnade behind the palace offers brilliant views over Odesa's bustling port.

A daily Intercity+ train (seven hours) and a couple of daily overnight trains (9½ to 13 hours) connect Odesa with Kyiv. There are also services to Lviv (12 hours, four daily).

Around 40 townhouses hem the square's perimeter. Most of these three- and four-storey buildings have uniform dimensions, with three windows per storey overlooking the square. This was the maximum number of windows allowed tax free and those buildings with four or more belonged to the extremely wealthy.

★**National Museum and Memorial to the Victims of Occupation** MUSEUM (Національний музей-меморіал жертв окупаційних режимів; www.lonckoho.lviv.ua; vul Bryullova; ⊙10am-7pm Mon-Sat, 10am-5pm Sun) **FREE** This infamous building on vul Bryullova was used as a prison by the Poles, Nazis and communists in turn, but the small and very moving exhibition over two floors focuses on Stalinist atrocities in the early years of WWII. Used as a prison right up to 1996, the brutally bare cells, horrific statistics posted throughout and Nazi newsreel from summer 1941 will leave few untouched. Some English explanations.

★**Lvivarnya** MUSEUM (www.lvivbeermuseum.com; vul Kleparivska 18; 60uah, tasting session extra 35uah; ⊙10am-7pm) Revamped in 2017, the museum belonging to Lviv's brewery is an impressive, modern experience, a world away for the rickety post-Soviet repositories of the past found in many Ukrainian cities. The well-presented exhibits whet the appetite for the tasting session at the end, which takes place in an impressively renovated bar. To reach the museum, take tram 7 to St Anna Church (where vul Shevchenka peels away from vul Horodotska) then walk north along vul Kleparivska for around 600m.

★ **Lychakivsky Cemetery** CEMETERY
(Личаківський цвинтар; ☑ 032 275 5415; www.
lviv-lychakiv.ukrain.travel; vul Pekarska; adult/
student 25/15uah; ⊙9am-6pm Oct-Mar, to 8pm
Apr-Sep; 7 tram) Don't leave town until you've
seen this amazing 42ha cemetery, only a
short ride on tram 7 from the centre. This
is the Père Lachaise of Eastern Europe, with
the same sort of overgrown grounds and
Gothic aura as the famous Parisian necropolis (but containing less-well-known people).

Laid out in the late 18th century, it's packed
full of western Ukraine's great and good.
Pride of place goes to the grave of revered
nationalist poet Ivan Franko.

🛏 Sleeping

Lviv has a shortage of budget accommodation. Expect to pay twice as much here as
you would elsewhere in western Ukraine.
The hostel situation also seems to be in constant flux.

WORTH A TRIP

BELARUS

Eastern Europe's outcast, Belarus (Беларус), seems determined to avoid integration with
the rest of the continent. Taking its lead from the former Soviet Union, rather than the
European Union, this little-visited dictatorship may seem like a strange choice for travellers, but its isolation lies at the heart of its appeal.

While much of the rest of Central and Eastern Europe has charged headlong into capitalism, Belarus allows the chance to visit a Europe with minimal advertising and no litter
or graffiti.

Visitors typically begin in the capital **Minsk**, which suffered tremendous damage in
World War II and was built anew in the late 1940s and '50s as a flagship Stalinist city. The
city will almost certainly surprise you. Contrary to its dreary reputation, it's a progressive, modern and clean place. Fashionable cafes, impressive restaurants and crowded
nightclubs vie for your attention, while sushi bars and art galleries have taken up residence in a city centre once totally remodelled to the tastes of Stalin.

Minsk's main thoroughfare, **pl Nezalezhnastsi** (Independence Sq), impresses with its
sheer girth. It runs the length of the modern city, ending with a classic Lenin statue and
the imposing Belarusian government building behind it. The **Minsk Tourist Information Centre** (www.minsktourism.by) maintains a helpful website on attractions in the
city, with information in English.

Another popular destination is the southwestern city of **Brest**, a relatively prosperous
and cosmopolitan border town that looks far more to the neighbouring EU than it does
to Minsk. It has plenty of charm and has performed a massive DIY job on itself over the
past few years in preparation for its millennial celebrations in 2019.

The city's main sight is the **Brest Fortress** (Brestskaya krepost; www.brest-fortress.by;
pr Maserava) `FREE`, a moving WWII memorial where Soviet troops held out far longer
than expected against the Nazi onslaught in the summer and autumn of 1941. But there
are also several good museums here, and the impressive **Belavezhskaya Pushcha
National Park** (☑16 3156 200, 16 3156 398; www.npbp.by; cost varies per activity; ⊙ticket
office 9am-6pm) is nearby.

Outside the large cities, Belarus offers a simple yet pleasing landscape of cornflower
fields, thick forests and picturesque villages. The country also is home to Europe's largest mammal, the *zoobr* (European bison). The official **Belarus website** (www.belarus.
by) is an excellent source of general information.

Most visitors arrive in Belarus by air. The national airline **Belavia** (☑17 2202 555; www.
belavia.by; vul Nyamiha 14, Minsk) runs regular flights to and from several major European
cities, including London, Paris, Frankfurt and Vienna. Belarus is also accessible by bus
from neighbouring Poland and Lithuania.

Most visitors require a visa to visit the country, though this requirement is waived if
you arrive in Minsk by air and stay for no longer than five days. Changes in 2018 extended this to 10 days in some cases for travel in the Hrodna and Brest regions. For longer
stays, you'll need to secure a visa in advance through the Belarusian embassy of your
home country.

★ Old City Hostel
HOSTEL €

(☎032 294 9644; www.oldcityhostel.lviv.ua; vul Beryndy 3; dm/tw from 155/550uah; @🗢) Occupying two floors of an elegantly fading tenement just steps from pl Rynok, this expertly run hostel with period features and views of the Shevchenko statue from the wraparound balcony has long since established itself as the city's best. Fluff-free dorms hold four to eight beds, shower queues are unheard of, sturdy lockers keep your stuff safe and there's a well-equipped kitchen.

Dream Hostel
HOSTEL €

(☎032 247 1047; www.dream-hostels.com; vul Krakivska 5; dm from 145uah; 🗢) The Lviv branch of this national hostel chain sports spotless dorms with pine bunks equipped with reading lights and privacy-creating curtains. There's also a spacious lounge, a cafe and staff on hand to patiently answer all those questions they've answered a thousand times before. The location on busy Krakivska is perfect.

★ Saban Deluxe
GUESTHOUSE €€

(☎067 247 7777; www.sabandeluxe.com; vul Sinna 18; r 800–2100uah; P🌢🗢) This superb guesthouse 3km north of pl Rynok is an eclectic mix of old and new, 21st century and antique, jumble sale and IKEA all rolled into one. All rooms are completely different, the owner is particularly helpful and the location isn't as inconvenient as it may seem (buses run from nearby). Full board available.

🍴 Eating

Lviv is better known for its cafes than restaurants, but the food scene has seen dramatic developments in recent years, with some wonderful theme restaurants popping up across the city centre.

CENTRAL & EASTERN EUROPE LVIV

Belarus

★ **Green** VEGETARIAN €

(vul Brativ Rohatyntsiv 5; mains around 60uah; ⊙10am-9pm; ☑) Lviv's best vegetarian eatery has a relaxing, spacious dining room where you can tuck into meat-free, vegan and raw food. In the upstairs chill-out area, kick off your shoes and lounge around on cushions as you enjoy ice cream made on the premises or a late breakfast. Also runs cookery courses and Friday is concert night. Certainly a foreigner favourite.

★ **Kupol** EUROPEAN €€

(Купол; vul Chaykovskoho 37; mains 100-250uah; ⊙11am-9pm; ☎) One of the pretourism 'originals', this place is designed to feel like stepping back in time – to 1938 in particular, 'the year before civilisation ended' (ie before the Soviets rolled in). The old-world interior with its screechy parquet floors, tasselled curtains, old photos and high Austrian double doors is the perfect setting to enjoy the tasty Polish/Austrian/Ukrainian dishes. It's currently closed for renovation.

★ **Baczewski** EASTERN EUROPEAN €€

(Ресторація Бачевських; ☑ 032 224 4444; vul Shevska 8; mains 80-270; ⊙8am-midnight; ❅) Here's how you compress your Lviv cultural studies into one evening out. Start with Jewish *forschmak* (herring pate), eased down by Ukrainian *nalyvky* (digestives) and followed by Hungarian fish soup. Proceed to Polish *pierogi* (dumplings) and finish with Viennese *Sachertorte* with Turkish coffee. An essential Lviv experience. Be sure to reserve a table for dinner at this mega-popular place.

🍷 Drinking

★ **Svit Kavy** CAFE

(Світ Кави; www.svitkavy.com; pl Katedralna 6; ⊙7.45am-11pm Mon-Sat, from 8.45am Sun; ☎) Pick of the bunch on pl Katedralna, with no theme, no gimmicks, just a focus on Lviv's best coffee-making traditions (hence it's always packed with locals). Beans come from almost every continent, and if you like the drink, you can buy the unground raw ingredient in the shop next door.

★ **Pravda Beer Theatre** BREWERY

(www.pravda.beer; pl Rynok 32; ⊙10am-2am; ☎) The latest addition to Lviv's drinking scene is this dramatically industrial, multistorey beer temple right on pl Rynok. The master brewer here creates several types of beer, often given imaginative and sometimes political names such as Obama Hope and Summer Lviv. Live music is provided by the brewery's very own **orchestra**, tours run throughout the day and there's a menu of good pub food.

★ **Pyana Vyshnya** BAR

(П'яна вишня; pl Rynok 11; ⊙10am-midnight) It's easy to find this one-drink bar – just look for the crowd of people on pl Rynok holding tiny glasses of something crimson, any time of the day. The tipple in question is the namesake, 18.5% volume, bitter-sweet cherry liqueur, sold by the crystal glass (36uah) or in bottles (200uah for 0.5L).

❶ Information

Tourist Information Centre (☑ 032-254 6079; www.lviv.travel; pl Rynok 1, Ratusha; ⊙9am-8pm May-Sep, 10am-6pm Oct-Apr) Ukraine's best tourist information centre.

❶ Getting There & Away

AIR

The city's **Danylo Halytskyi International Airport** (☑ 032 229 8112; www.lwo.aero; vul Lyubinska 168) stands 7km west of the city centre. The main domestic carrier **Ukraine International Airlines** (www.flyuia.com) offers regulars flights to and from the capital, Kyiv. Internationally, Lviv is attracting an ever-increasing number of flights to European destinations, and flights service cities like Warsaw, Vienna and Munich among others.

BUS

The city's **Main Bus Station** (vul Stryska 109) is inconveniently located 7km south of the centre, though trolleybus 5 can bring you back and forth. This is the main spot for significant domestic and nearly all international coach services. Several buses daily ply the roads to Kyiv (nine hours). There are numerous external connections from here to the Czech Republic, Italy, Spain and Germany.

TRAIN

Lviv's Main Train Station is 2km west of the centre. The quickest way to Kyiv is on the daily Intercity+ express (five hours). There are also several regular trains per day, but travel times vary from eight to 13 hours. Slow daily international trains serve Bratislava, Budapest, Prague and a handful of destinations in Poland. There's a handy timetable at www.uz.gov.ua.

Ukraine Survival Guide

ℹ Directory A–Z

ACCOMMODATION

Accommodation will be your single biggest expense in Ukraine. Rooms are slightly more affordable than they once were due to more favourable exchange rates. Big cities like Kyiv and Lviv are the most expensive.

➡ Hotel rates are listed in hryvnia (uah), but you may still come across places where US dollars or euros are quoted.

➡ Hostelling is a well-established sector in Ukraine's accommodation market, especially in tourist hotspots like Kyiv and Lviv. These websites are useful for finding a hostel: **Hostelling Ukraine International** (www.hihostels.com.ua) and **Hostelworld** (www.hostelworld.com).

➡ Most so-called campsites are really former Soviet holiday camps, and slightly more formalised than most Western campers prefer. Facilities are usually poor. Wild camping is tolerated in most areas of the country, but not recommended. Lighting fires in national parks is forbidden.

MONEY

➡ The Ukrainian currency, the hryvnia (uah), is divided into 100 kopecks. Kopecks have become virtually worthless.

➡ Price inflation has been a problem in recent years and the prices in this guide may be out of date.

➡ ATMs are widespread, even in small towns. Credit cards accepted at most hotels and upmarket restaurants. The best way to manage your money is to withdraw with your card.

➡ Exchange money at banks or exchange kiosks (обмін валюти) scattered along main streets and dotting markets. Some upmarket shops have their own exchange offices, as do department stores and train stations.

➡ Tipping is not common in Ukraine.

OPENING HOURS

Banks 9am to 5pm Monday to Friday
Restaurants 11am to 11pm
Cafes 9am to 10pm
Bars 10pm to 3am
Shops 9am to 9pm daily

PUBLIC HOLIDAYS

Currently the main public holidays in Ukraine are the following.

New Year's Day 1 January
Orthodox Christmas 7 January
International Women's Day 8 March
Orthodox Easter (Paskha) April/May

ℹ PRICE RANGES

The following price ranges refer to a double room in high season. Unless otherwise stated, breakfast is included in the price.

$ less than 500uah
$$ 500–1500uah
$$$ more than 1500uah

The following price ranges refer to a main course.

$ less than 100uah
$$ 100–200uah
$$$ more than 200uah

Labour Day 1–2 May
Victory Day (1945) 9 May
Constitution Day 28 June
Independence Day (1991) 24 August
Defender of Ukraine Day 14 October

TELEPHONE

➡ Ukraine simplified the way numbers are dialled a few years ago, banishing the confusing system of Soviet-era prefixes and dialling tones. All numbers now start with 0.

➡ Ukraine's country code is +380, but the zero is always included in local codes and numbers, so you only need to add +38 when calling from outside Ukraine.

➡ To call Kyiv from abroad, dial the international access code plus 38, Ukraine's country code, plus 44, Kyiv's city code (dropping the first zero), and the number. There's no need to dial the city code if calling within that city, unless you're using a mobile.

➡ To call internationally, dial 0, wait for a second tone, then dial 0 again, followed by the country code, city code and number.

➡ European GSM phones usually work in Ukraine; double-check with your provider before leaving. However, if you're going to be making a few calls, it's more economical to get a prepaid SIM card. Top up credit using vouchers available from mobile-phone shops and news kiosks.

WI-FI

Internet service in Ukraine has improved immensely in recent years, and most hotels as well as upmarket cafes and restaurants offer free wi-fi.

ℹ Getting There & Away

The majority of visitors fly to Ukraine – generally to Kyiv. Some new direct train services to/from

770

1. Budapest, Hungary
Liberty Bridge spans the Danube River, connecting Buda Hills (p707) with Pest (p711).

2. Prague, Czech Republic
The largest monastic library in the country, Strahov Library (p675) is a baroque beauty.

3. Rila Mountains, Bulgaria
A spiritual treasure, Rila Monastery (p747) is full of colourful architecture and religious art.

4. Warsaw, Poland
Łazienki Park (p695) hosts summertime concerts in its manicured gardens.

Poland have appeared and, as it has across Europe, international bus travel has made a big comeback.

BORDER CROSSINGS

Ukraine shares borders with seven countries: Russia, Belarus, Poland, Slovakia, Hungary, Romania and Moldova. Crossing the border is a fairly straightforward (if drawn-out affair), and you should always leave ample time for delays. When heading for Belarus or Russia, always ensure you have the right visa. Despite the ongoing conflict, it is still possible to cross into Russia when travelling by train, bus or car from Kyiv.

AIR

Kyiv's Boryspil International Airport, 30km southeast of the city centre, is the country's main international air gateway. The airport is home to Ukraine's major carrier: Ukraine International Airlines (www.flyuia.com).

LAND

Both Kyiv and Lviv are connected by bus and train to destinations around Europe. The easiest points of access are via Poland, Slovakia, Hungary, Moldova and Romania.

ⓘ Getting Around

Ukraine International Airlines (www.flyuia. com), the country's largest domestic carrier, operates regular flights between Kyiv and Lviv and Odesa as well as other large cities.

For overland travel, consult the Kyiv and Lviv sections for details. All trains are operated by **Ukrainian Railways** (www.uz.gov.ua). **Bus.com. ua** (www.bus.com.ua) has bus timetables but is hard to navigate.

Russia & the Baltic Coast

Best Places to Eat

➜ Dukhan Chito-Ra (p785)

➜ Bekitzer (p794)

➜ Vegan Restoran V (p808)

➜ Miit (p823)

➜ Senamiesčio Krautuvė (p837)

Best Places to Sleep

➜ Loft Hostel 77 (p784)

➜ Soul Kitchen Hostel (p793)

➜ Tabinoya (p808)

➜ Cinnamon Sally (p821)

Why Go?

When it comes to cultural mileage, the central and north-eastern reaches of the Baltic provide as fuel-efficient a destination as you could ever hope for. First comes Russia, the big bear that lorded it over the region during the Soviet era and still casts a mighty shadow. This epic-scale nation packs a double whammy with Moscow and St Petersburg, which are among Europe's most impressive and dynamic cities, graced with imperial palaces, magnificent museums and stunning streetscapes.

In comparison, Estonia, Latvia and Lithuania are tiny. Yet in these wonderfully compact countries there are three completely distinct cultures to discover – with different languages, different traditions and markedly different temperaments. By way of example, you need only look as far as their unique and equally compelling capitals: flamboyantly baroque Vilnius, chic art-nouveau Rīga and majestically medieval Tallinn.

Fast Facts

Capitals Moscow (Russia), Tallinn (Estonia), Rīga (Latvia), Vilnius (Lithuania)

Emergency ☑112 (Estonia),

Currency Rouble (R; Russia), euro (€; Baltic States)

Languages Russian, Estonian, Latvian, Lithuanian

Visas Russia: required by all – apply at least a month in advance of your trip; Baltic states: not required for citizens of the EU, USA, Canada, Japan, New Zealand and Australia.

Time zones Russia GMT plus three hours (GMT plus four hours in summer), Baltic states GMT plus two hours (GMT plus three hours in summer)

Russia & the Baltic Coast Highlights

① Moscow Marvelling at this mega-city's historical showstoppers, such as the Kremlin and Red Square, and its cool creativity. (p776)

② St Petersburg Absorbing the amazing Hermitage and gilded palaces in this stunning old imperial capital. (p787)

③ Tallinn Exploring the Estonian capital's Old Town of polished medieval abodes. (p800)

④ Tartu Furthering your education among the

RUSSIA

Moscow

POP 12.5 MILLION

During any season, at any hour of the day, Moscow thrills visitors with its artistry and majesty. History, power and wild capitalism hang in the air alongside an explosion of creative energy, throwing up edgy art galleries and a dynamic restaurant, bar and nightlife scene.

The sturdy stone walls of the Kremlin occupy the city's founding site on the northern bank of the Moscow River. Remains of the Soviet state, such as Lenin's Tomb, are nearby in Red Square and elsewhere in the city, which radiates from the Kremlin in a series of ring roads.

⊙ Sights

⊙ The Kremlin & Red Square

★ **Moscow Kremlin**　　　　　MUSEUM
(Кремль; ☑ 495-695 4146; www.kreml.ru; R500; ⊙ 10am-5pm Fri-Wed, ticket office 9.30am-4.30pm Fri-Wed; Ⓜ Aleksandrovsky Sad) The apex of Russian political power and once the centre

---

> **DON'T MISS**
>
> ### PARK ZARYADYE
>
> Inaugurated in September 2017 was Moscow's first major new park in half a century. Covering 13 hectares, Park Zaryadye occupies a prominent site along the Moscow River just steps from Red Square and includes four different areas representing Russia's geographic zones – tundra, steppe, forest and wetlands – each flowing seamlessly into the other. Its most striking feature is the 'floating bridge', which stretches out across Moskvoretskaya nab and over the Moscow River, then loops back to Zaryadye.
>
> In addition to the parkland, Zaryadye contains a vast outdoor amphitheatre and several new museums including the **Park Zaryadye Pavilion** (Павильон парка 'Зарядье'; Moskvoretskaya ul; ⊙ 2-8pm Mon, 10am-8pm Tue-Sun) **FREE**, which provides an overview of the park and its development.

---

of the Orthodox Church, the Kremlin is not only the kernel of Moscow, but of the whole country. From here, autocratic tsars, communist dictators and modern-day presidents have done their best – and worst – for Russia.

Covering Borovitsky Hill on the north bank of the Moscow River, the Kremlin is enclosed by high walls 2.25km long, with Red Square outside the east wall. The best views of the complex are from Sofiyskaya nab across the river.

Before entering the Kremlin, deposit bags (for free) at the **left-luggage office** (Alexander Garden; ⊙ 9am-6.30pm Fri-Wed), beneath the Kutafya Tower near the main **ticket office** (Кассы музеев Кремля; Alexander Garden; ⊙ 9am-5pm Fri-Wed May-Sep, 9.30am-4.30pm Fri-Wed Oct-Apr; Ⓜ Aleksandrovsky Sad) in Alexander Garden. The entrance ticket covers admission to all five church-museums and the Patriarch's Palace. It does not include the Armoury, the Diamond Fund Exhibition or the Ivan the Great Bell Tower, which are priced separately.

Photography is not permitted inside the Armoury or any of the buildings on Sobornaya pl (Cathedral Sq).

★ **Red Square**　　　　　HISTORIC SITE
(Красная площадь; Krasnaya pl; Ⓜ Ploshchad Revolyutsii) Immediately outside the Kremlin's northeastern wall is the celebrated Red Square, the 400m-by-150m area of cobblestones that is at the very heart of Moscow. Commanding the square from the southern end is **St Basil's Cathedral** (Покровский собор, Храм Василия Блаженного; adult/student R400/150; ⊙ ticket office 11am-5pm Nov-Apr, to 6pm May-Oct; Ⓜ Ploshchad Revolyutsii). This panorama never fails to send the heart aflutter, especially at night.

Lenin's Mausoleum　　　　　MEMORIAL
(Мавзолей Ленина; www.lenin.ru; Krasnaya pl; ⊙ 10am-1pm Tue-Thu, Sat & Sun; Ⓜ Ploshchad Revolyutsii) **FREE** Although Vladimir Ilych requested that he be buried beside his mum in St Petersburg, he still lies in state at the foot of the Kremlin wall, receiving visitors who come to pay their respects. Line up at the western corner of the square (near the entrance to Alexander Garden) to see the embalmed leader, who has been here since 1924. Note that photography is not allowed and stern guards ensure that all visitors remain respectful and silent.

◎ South of the Moscow River

★ State Tretyakov
Gallery Main Branch   GALLERY
(Государственная Третьяковская Галерея; www.tretyakovgallery.ru; Lavrushinsky per 10; adult/child R500/200; ⊙10am-6pm Tue, Wed & Sun, to 9pm Thu-Sat, last tickets 1hr before closing; Ⓜ Tretyakovskaya) The exotic boyar castle on a little lane in Zamoskvorechie contains the main branch of the State Tretyakov Gallery, housing the world's best collection of Russian icons and an outstanding collection of other pre-revolutionary Russian art. Show up early to beat the queues. The neighbouring **Engineer's Building** is reserved for special exhibits.

New Tretyakov Gallery   GALLERY
(Новая Третьяковская галерея; www.tretyakovgallery.ru; ul Krymsky val 10; adult/child R500/200; ⊙10am-6pm Tue, Wed & Sun, to 9pm Thu-Sat, last tickets 1hr before closing; Ⓜ Park Kultury) Moscow's premier venue for 20th-century Russian art, this branch of the Tretyakov Gallery has much more than the typical socialist-realist images of muscle-bound men wielding scythes and busty women milking cows (although there's that, too). The exhibits showcase avant-garde artists such as Malevich, Kandinsky, Chagall, Goncharova and Popova, as well as nonconformist artists of the 1960s and 1970s who refused to accept the official style.

★ Gorky Park   PARK
(Парк Горького; ⊙24hr; 🚴; Ⓜ Oktyabrskaya) **FREE** Moscow's main city escape is not your conventional expanse of nature preserved deep inside an urban jungle. It is not a fun fair either, though it used to be one. Its official name says it all – Maxim Gorky's Central Park of Culture and Leisure. That's exactly what it provides: culture and leisure in all shapes and forms. Designed in the 1920s by avant-garde architect Konstantin Melnikov as a piece of communist utopia, these days it showcases the enlightened transformation Moscow has undergone in the recent past.

Art Muzeon & Krymskaya
Naberezhnaya   PUBLIC ART
(Ⓜ Park Kultury) **FREE** Moscow's answer to London's South Bank, Krymskaya Nab (Crimea Embankment) features wave-shaped street architecture with Scandinavian-style wooden elements, beautiful flowerbeds and a moody fountain, which ejects water randomly from many holes in the ground to the excitement of children and adults alike. It has merged with the Art Muzeon park and its motley collection of Soviet stone idols (Stalin, Sverdlov, a selection of Lenins and Brezhnevs) that were ripped from their pedestals in the post-1991 wave of anti-Soviet feeling.

★ Garage Museum of
Contemporary Art   MUSEUM
(📞495-645 0520; www.garagemca.org; ul Krymsky val 9/32; adult/student R400/200; ⊙11am-10pm; Ⓜ Oktyabrskaya) The brainchild of Moscow art fairy Darya Zhukova, Garage is one of the capital's hottest modern-art venues. In mid-2015 the museum moved to spectacular new digs in Gorky Park – a derelict Soviet-era building, renovated by the visionary Dutch architect Rem Koolhaas. It hosts exhibitions, lectures, films and interactive educational programs, featuring Russian and international artists. A good cafe and a bookstore are also on the premises.

◎ West of the Kremlin

★ Pushkin Museum of Fine Arts   MUSEUM
(Музей изобразительных искусств им Пушкина; 📞495-697 9578; www.arts-museum.ru; ul Volkhonka 12; single/combined galleries R300/550; ⊙11am-7pm Tue, Wed & Fri-Sun, to 9pm Thu; Ⓜ Kropotkinskaya) This is Moscow's premier foreign-art museum, split over three branches and showing off a broad selection of European works, including masterpieces from ancient civilisations, the Italian Renaissance and the Dutch Golden Age. To see the incredible collection of Impressionist and post-Impressionist paintings, visit the **19th & 20th Century Art Gallery** (www.arts-museum.ru; ul Volkhonka 14; adult/student R300/150; ⊙11am-7pm Tue-Sun, to 9pm Thu; Ⓜ Kropotkinskaya). The **Museum of Private Collections** (Музей личных коллекций; www.artprivatecollections.ru; ul Volkhonka 10; entry prices vary; ⊙noon-8pm Wed-Sun, to 9pm Thu; Ⓜ Kropotkinskaya) shows off complete collections donated by private individuals.

Novodevichy Convent   CONVENT
(Новодевичий монастырь; Novodevichy pr 1; adult/student R500/250, photos R300; ⊙grounds 8am-8pm, museums 9am-5pm Wed-Mon; Ⓜ Sportivnaya) The Novodevichy Convent was founded in 1524 to celebrate the taking of Smolensk from Lithuania, an important step in Moscow's conquest of the old Kyivan

RUSSIA AT A GLANCE

Don't Miss

The Kremlin The founding site of Moscow and the ultimate symbol of political power in Russia. Within its ancient walls you can admire the artistry of Russia's greatest icon painters, peer down the barrel of the gargantuan Tsar Cannon and gawk at the treasure trove that fuelled a revolution.

Red Square Stepping onto Red Square never ceases to inspire, with the Kremlin, St Basil's Cathedral, the State History Museum and the elaborate edifice of GUM all encircling a vast stretch of cobblestones. Individually they are impressive, but all together the ensemble is electrifying.

The Hermitage Perhaps the world's greatest museum, this iconic establishment's vast collection is quite simply mind-boggling. Your entry ticket also allows you to walk around the fascinating apartments and dazzling staterooms of the Romanovs.

Cruising the canals St Petersburg is a city that is best appreciated from the water. Don't miss a canal-boat tour to see some of the city's architectural gems from a different perspective. If you're in the city when the canals are frozen over, don't miss wandering along their banks for a visual treat.

Tsarskoe Selo Arguably the most beautiful of the tsarist palace areas that surround St Petersburg, Tsarskoe Selo can be an idyllic place for a day trip. Catherine Palace includes the famous Amber Room, while around it you can enjoy the gorgeous formal gardens and have a picnic in the landscaped park where Catherine the Great so loved to walk.

Itineraries

One Week

In **Moscow**, spend a day touring the Kremlin and Red Square. Viewing the spectacular collections at the Tretyakov, New Tretyakov or Pushkin art museums will take up another day. On day three size up the magnificent Novodevichy Convent and Gorky Park, home to the excellent Garage Museum of Contemporary Art. Take an overnight train to **St Petersburg**. Here spend a day taking in Nevsky pr, the polychromatic Church on the Spilled Blood and getting a view over the city from the colonnade of St Isaac's Cathedral. The Winter Palace section of the magnificent Hermitage alone deserves a day; also spend some time in the General Staff Building where the museum's Impressionist and post-Impressionist works hang.

Two Weeks

Two weeks will allow you more time in both Moscow and St Petesburg. You can also make an excursion to the old Imperial estates of **Peterhof** or **Tsarskoe Selo**. Fly to Kaliningrad where you can admire the city's reconstructed Gothic Cathedral and wander along the river to the excellent Museum of the World Ocean. Enjoy either the seaside spa town of **Svetlogorsk** or the sand dunes and forests of the **Kurshskaya Kosa National Park**.

Essential Food & Drink

Soups The are many to choose from, including the lemony, meat *solyanka* and the hearty fish *ukha*.

Bliny (pancakes) Served with *ikra* (caviar) or *tvorog* (cottage cheese).

Salads A wide variety usually slathered in mayonnaise, including the chopped potato Olivier salad.

Pelmeni Ravioli-like dumplings generally stuffed with pork or beef, eaten with sour cream and vinegar.

Central Asian dishes Try *plov* (fried rice with lamb and carrot) and *lagman* (noodles and meat in a soupy broth).

Vodka The quintessential Russian tipple.

Beer Baltika is the main brand, but there are scores of micro-breweries producing excellent craft beers.

Kvas A refreshing beerlike drink made from rye bread.

Mors A red berry juice mix.

Getting Around

Train The extensive network is the best way of getting around, with many comfortable overnight services between far-flung cities.

Air Worth considering if you need to speed up your travels (with online tickets sometimes cheaper than those for trains). Only book airlines with solid safety records.

Bus Useful for getting to places not covered by the train. Sometimes faster than local *elektrichka* (suburban) train services.

Car or taxi Sometimes the only way to get to really remote destinations.

When to Go

Moscow

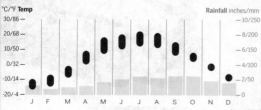

Jun–Sep Hot weather and peak season; all forms of transport should be booked in advance.

May & Oct Good time for cultural events in cities and major parades on Victory Day (9 May).

Nov–Apr Snow falls and temperatures plummet, creating the wintery Russia of the imagination.

Arriving in Russia

Sheremetyevo Airport (Moscow) Aeroexpress trains (R420, 30 minutes) run to the city every half-hour from 5am to 12.30am. Taxis cost R2000 to R2500 and take at least an hour.

Domodedovo Airport (Moscow) Aeroexpress trains (R500, 45 minutes) run to the city every half-hour from 6am to 11.30pm. Taxis cost R2000 to R2500 and take at least an hour.

Pulkovo Airport (St Petersburg) Frequent buses (R35) run to Moskovskaya metro station (R45) for a total journey time to the city centre of around 30 minutes. Taxis charge around R800 to R1000 to the centre.

Top Phrases

Hello. Здравствуйте. Zdravstvuyte.

Goodbye. До свидания. Do svidaniya.

Excuse me. Извините. Izvinite.

Sorry. Сожалею. Sozhaleyu.

Resources

Afisha (www.afisha.ru) Extensive restaurant, bar, museum and event listings for all major cities; in Russian only.

Moscow Expat Site (www.expat.ru) A mine of expat knowledge on Russia.

Set Your Budget

➡ Dorm bed: R700–800

➡ Café meal: R200–500

➡ Travel on buses and metro: R15–50

The Kremlin

A DAY AT THE KREMLIN

Only at the Kremlin can you see 800 years of Russian history and artistry in one day. Enter the ancient fortress through the Trinity Gate Tower and walk past the impressive Arsenal, ringed with cannons. Past the Patriarch's Palace, you'll find yourself surrounded by white-washed walls and golden domes. Your first stop is ❶ **Assumption Cathedral** with the solemn fresco over the doorway. As the most important church in prerevolutionary Russia, this 15th-century beauty was the burial site of the patriarchs. The ❷ **Ivan the Great Bell Tower** now contains a nifty multimedia exhibit on the architectural history of the Kremlin. The view from the top is worth the price of admission. The tower is flanked by the massive ❸ **Tsar Cannon & Bell**.

In the southeast corner, ❹ **Archangel Cathedral** has an elaborate interior, where three centuries of tsars and tsarinas are laid to rest. Your final stop on Sobornaya pl is ❺ **Annunciation Cathedral**, rich with frescoes and iconography.

Walk along the Great Kremlin Palace and enter the ❻ **Armoury** at the time designated on your ticket. After gawking at the goods, exit the Kremlin through Borovitsky Gate and stroll through the Alexander Garden to the ❼ **Tomb of the Unknown Soldier**.

Assumption Cathedral

Once your eyes adjust to the colourful frescoes, the gilded fixtures and the iconography, try to locate *Saviour with the Angry Eye*, a 14th-century icon that is one of the oldest in the Kremlin.

Arsenal

BOROVITSKY TOWER

Use the entrance at Borovitsky Tower if you intend to skip the churches and visit only the Armoury or Diamond Fund.

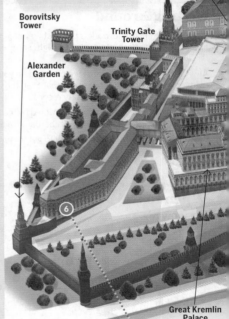

Borovitsky Tower

Trinity Gate Tower

Alexander Garden

Great Kremlin Palace

TOP TIPS

➡ **Online Purchase** Full-price tickets to the Kremlin churches and the Armoury can be purchased in advance on the Kremlin website.

➡ **Lunch** There are no eating options. Plan to eat before you arrive or stash a snack.

Armoury

Take advantage of the free audio guide to direct you to the most intriguing treasures of the Armoury, which is chock-full of precious metalworks and jewellery, armour and weapons, gowns and crowns, carriages and sledges.

Tomb of the Unknown Soldier

Visit the Tomb of the Unknown Soldier honouring the heroes of the Great Patriotic War. Come at the top of the hour to see the solemn synchronicity of the changing of the guard.

ANDREW KOTURANOV/SHUTTERSTOCK ©

Patriarch's Palace

Ivan the Great Bell Tower

Check out the artistic electronic renderings of the Kremlin's history, then climb 137 steps to the belfry's upper gallery, where you will be rewarded with super, sweeping vistas of Sobornaya pl and beyond.

Moscow River

Sobornaya pl

Tsar Cannon & Bell

Peer down the barrel of the monstrous Tsar Cannon and pose for a picture beside the oversized Tsar Bell, both of which are too big to serve their intended purpose.

Annunciation Cathedral

Admire the artistic mastery of Russia's greatest icon painters – Theophanes the Greek and Andrei Rublyov – who are responsible for many of the icons in the deesis and festival rows of the iconostasis.

Archangel Cathedral

See the final resting place of princes and emperors who ruled Russia for more than 300 years, including the visionary Ivan the Great, the tortured Ivan the Terrible and the tragic Tsarevitch Dmitry.

EKATERINA BYKOVA/SHUTTERSTOCK ©

Central Moscow

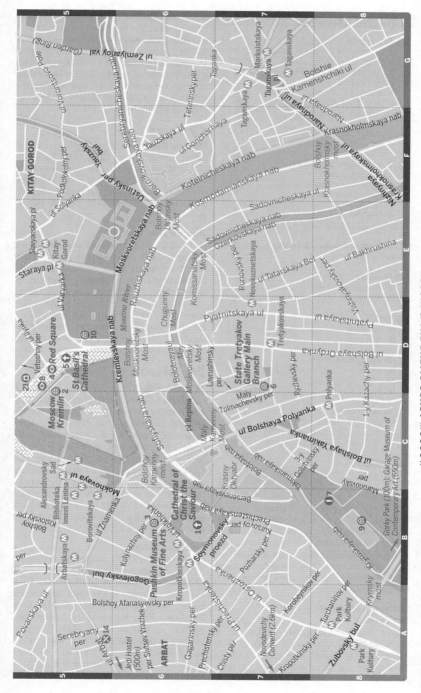

Central Moscow

Top Sights

1 Cathedral of Christ the Saviour B6
2 Moscow Kremlin C5
3 Pushkin Museum of Fine Arts B6
4 Red Square D5
5 St Basil's Cathedral D5
6 State Tretyakov Gallery Main Branch D7

Sights

19th & 20th Century Art Gallery .... (see 3)
7 Art Muzeon & Krymskaya Naberezhnaya B8
8 Lenin's Mausoleum D5
Museum of Private Collections .... (see 3)
9 New Tretyakov Gallery B8
10 Park Zaryadye Pavilion D5

Activities, Courses & Tours

11 Moscow Free Tour D4

Sleeping

12 Godzillas Hostel C2
13 Loft Hostel 77 .... B3

Eating

14 Varenichnaya No 1 .... A5
15 Zupperia D1

Drinking & Nightlife

16 32.05 .... B2
17 Enthusiast C3
18 Noor / Electro B2

Entertainment

19 Bolshoi Theatre C4
20 Moscow Tchaikovsky Conservatory B4

Shopping

21 GUM D5

Rus lands. The oldest and most dominant building on the grounds is the white Smolensk Cathedral, with a sumptuous interior covered in 16th-century frescoes. Novodevichy is a functioning monastery. Women are advised to cover their heads and shoulders when entering the churches, while men should wear long pants.

Cathedral of Christ the Saviour CHURCH
(Храм Христа Спасителя; www.xxc.ru; ul Volkhonka 15; 1-5pm Mon, from 10am Tue-Sun; M Kropotkinskaya) FREE This gargantuan cathedral was completed in 1997 – just in time to celebrate Moscow's 850th birthday. It is amazingly opulent, garishly grandiose and truly historic. The cathedral's sheer size and splendour guarantee its role as a love-it-or-hate-it landmark. Considering Stalin's plan for this site (a Palace of Soviets topped with a 100m statue of Lenin), Muscovites should at least be grateful they can admire the shiny domes of a church instead of the shiny dome of Ilyich's head.

Tours

Moscow Greeter WALKING
(www.moscowgreeter.ru) FREE Let a local volunteer show you what they love about their city! Every tour is different, as the volunteer decides (perhaps with your input) where to go. Donations are accepted, but the tour is entirely free.

Moscow Free Tour WALKING
(495-222 3466; www.moscowfreetour.com; Nikolskaya ul 4/5; guided walk free, paid tours from €31) Every day these enthusiastic ladies offer an informative, inspired 2½-hour guided walk around Red Square and Kitay Gorod – and it's completely free. It's so good that (they hope) you'll sign up for one of their excellent paid tours, covering the Kremlin, the Arbat and the Metro, or themes such as communist Moscow.

Sleeping

★ **Loft Hostel 77** HOSTEL €
(499-110 4228; www.hostel-77.com; Bldg 3a, Maly Gnezdnikovsky per 9; dm R1000-1400; M Pushkinskaya) This sweet spot offers stylish dorm rooms (if that's not an oxymoron), fully equipped with lockers, individual lights, orthopaedic mattresses and privacy curtains. Exposed brick walls and leather furniture create an attractive shabby-chic atmosphere. Multilingual staff and a super-central locale are added pluses. The only drawback is the lack of a kitchen, but the surrounding streets are packed with eateries.

Godzillas Hostel HOSTEL €
(495-699 4223; www.godzillashostel.com; Bolshoy Karetny per 6; dm R700-950, s/d R2200/2800; @; M Tsvetnoy Bulvar) Tried and true, Godzillas is Moscow's best-known hostel, with dozens of beds spread out over four floors. The rooms come in various sizes, but they are all spacious and light-filled and painted in different colours. To cater to the many guests, there are bathroom facilities on each floor, three kitchens and a big living room with satellite TV.

Jedi Hostel
HOSTEL €

(📞 929-681 0041; http://jedihostel.com; 4th fl, 2-y Smolensky per 1/4; dm/d from US$11/40; ✳ @ 📶; Ⓜ Smolenskaya) This place exudes (and requires) good vibes, with its wacky and wonderful mural-painted walls and pillow-strewn 'lounge zone'. Dorm beds are actually little 'pods' with shades that ensure complete privacy. Lockers, kitchen and laundry facilities are available. Get the door code before you show up.

✗ Eating

★ Dukhan Chito-Ra
GEORGIAN €

(📞 8-916-393 0030; www.chito-ra.ru; ul Kazakhova 10 str 2; mains R300-500; ⏱ noon-11pm; Ⓜ Kurskaya) It's a blessing when one of the most revered Georgian eateries in town is also one of the cheapest. The object of worship here is *khinkali* – large, meat-filled dumplings – but the traditional vegie starters are also great. The rather inevitable downside is that the place is constantly busy and there is often a queue to get in.

Zupperia
INTERNATIONAL €

(📞 8-915-391 8309; www.facebook.com/Zupperia; Sadovaya-Samotechnaya ul 20; soups & salads R300-400; ⏱ 8am-11pm; 📶; Ⓜ Tsvetnoy Bulvar) Designed to look like a transplant from some old-worldish European city, this unpretentious eatery is run by local celebrity chef Uilliam Lamberti. The minimalist menu includes soups, bruschettas and salads. At first glance, the place seems to consist of one long table, but there is more seating downstairs. Takeaway is available.

★ Varenichnaya No 1
RUSSIAN €

(www.varenichnaya.ru; ul Arbat 29; business lunch R290-340, mains R220-490; ⏱ 10am-midnight; ✈ 🍴; Ⓜ Arbatskaya) Retro Soviet is all the rage in Moscow, and this old-style restaurant does it right, with books lining the walls, old movies on the B&W TV, and Cold War–era prices. The menu features tasty, filling *vareniki* and *pelmeni* (Russian-style dumplings), with sweet and savoury fillings. Bonus: an excellent house-made pickled vegie plate to make you pucker.

🍷 Drinking & Nightlife

★ Noor / Electro
BAR

(📞 8-903-136 7686; www.noorbar.com; ul Tverskaya 23/12; ⏱ 8pm-3am Mon-Wed, to 6am Thu-Sun; Ⓜ Pushkinskaya) There is little to say about this misleadingly unassuming bar, apart from the fact that everything in it is close to perfection. It has it all – prime location, convivial atmosphere, eclectic DJ music, friendly bartenders and superb drinks. Though declared 'the best' by various magazines on several occasions, it doesn't feel like they care.

Enthusiast
BAR

(Энтузиаст; Stoleshnikov per 7, str 5; ⏱ noon-11pm Sun-Thu, to 2am Fri & Sat; Ⓜ Teatralnaya) Scooter enthusiast, that is. But you don't have to be one in order to enjoy this superbly laid-back bar hidden at the far end of a fancifully shaped courtyard and disguised as a spare-parts shop. On a warm day, grab a beer or cider, settle into a beach chair and let harmony descend on you.

32.05
CAFE

(📞 8-905-703 3205; www.veranda3205.ru; ul Karetny Ryad 3; ⏱ 11am-3am; Ⓜ Pushkinskaya) The biggest drinking and eating establishment in Hermitage Gardens, this verandah positioned at the back of the park's main building looks a bit like a greenhouse. In summer, tables (and patrons) spill out into the park, making it one of the city's best places for outdoor drinking. With its long bar and joyful atmosphere, the place also heaves in winter.

DON'T MISS

JEWISH MUSEUM & CENTRE OF TOLERANCE

Occupying a heritage garage, purpose-built to house a fleet of Leyland double-deckers that plied Moscow's streets in the 1920s, this vast **museum** (Еврейский музей и Центр толерантности; 📞 495-645 0550; www.jewish-museum.ru; ul Obraztsova 11 str 1a; adult/student R400/200; ⏱ noon-10pm Sun-Thu, 10am-3pm Fri; Ⓜ Novoslobodskaya), filled with cutting-edge multimedia technology, tackles the uneasy subject of relations between Jews and the Russian state over the centuries. The exhibition relates the stories of pogroms, Jewish revolutionaries, the Holocaust and Soviet anti-Semitism in a calm and balanced manner. The somewhat limited collection of material exhibits is compensated for by the abundance of interactive video displays.

DIY METRO TOUR

For just R65 you can create your own 90-minute tour around Moscow's magnificent metro stations. Many of these are marble-faced, frescoed, gilded works of art. Among our favourites are **Komsomolskaya**, a huge stuccoed hall, its ceiling covered with mosaics depicting military heroes; **Novokuznetskaya**, featuring military bas-reliefs done in sober khaki, and colourful ceiling mosaics depicting pictures of the happy life; and **Mayakovskaya**, Grand Prize winner at the 1939 World's Fair in New York.

☆ Entertainment

★ Bolshoi Theatre
BALLET, OPERA

(Большой театр; 495-455 5555; www.bolshoi. ru; Teatralnaya pl 1; tickets R100-12,000; closed late Jul–mid-Sep; Teatralnaya) An evening at the Bolshoi is still one of Moscow's most romantic and entertaining options for a night on the town. The glittering six-tier auditorium has an electric atmosphere, evoking over 240 years of premier music and dance. Both the ballet and opera companies perform a range of Russian and foreign works here.

Moscow Tchaikovsky Conservatory
CLASSICAL MUSIC

(Московская консерватория имени Чайковского; box office 495-629 9401; www. mosconsv.ru; Bolshaya Nikitskaya ul 13; Okhotny Ryad) The country's largest music school, named for Tchaikovsky of course, has two venues, both of which host concerts, recitals and competitions. The Great Hall of the Conservatory is home to the **Moscow Symphony Orchestra** (MSO; www.moscowsymphony.ru), a low-budget but highly lauded orchestra under the direction of Vladimir Ziva.

Shopping

Ul Arbat is littered with souvenir shops and stalls.

GUM
MALL

(ГУМ; www.gum.ru; Krasnaya pl 3; 10am-10pm; Ploshchad Revolyutsii) Behind its elaborate 240m-long facade on the northeastern side of Red Square, GUM is a bright, bustling shopping mall with hundreds of fancy stores and restaurants. With a skylight roof and three-level arcades, the spectacular interior was a revolutionary design when it was built in the 1890s, replacing the Upper Trading Rows that previously occupied this site.

Izmaylovsky Market
MARKET

(www.kremlin-izmailovo.com; Izmaylovskoye sh 73; 10am-8pm; Partizanskaya) Never mind the kitschy faux 'tsar's palace' it surrounds, this is the ultimate place to shop for *matryoshka* dolls, military uniforms, icons, Soviet badges, and some real antiques. Huge and diverse, it is almost a theme park, including shops, cafes and a couple of not terribly exciting museums.

ℹ Information

Discover Moscow (https://um.mos.ru/en/discover-moscow) A comprehensive site organised by the City of Moscow.

International Clinic MEDSI (495-933 7700; https://medsi.ru; Grokholsky per 1; 24hr; Prospekt Mira) Emergency service, consultations and a full range of medical specialists. On-site pharmacy with English-speaking staff.

Moscow Times (www.themoscowtimes. com) Locally published, free English-language newspaper.

Tourist Hotline (8-800-220 0001, 8-800-220 0002, 495-663 1393)

Unifest Travel (495-234 6555; www.unifest. ru; Bldg 3-4, Komsomolsky pr 16/2; 9am-9pm Mon-Fri, 10am-7pm Sat-Sun, visa support 10am-6pm Mon-Fri) On-the-ball travel company offers rail and air tickets, visa support and more.

ℹ Getting There & Away

International flights land and take off from Moscow's three airports – **Domodedovo** (Домодедово; 495-933 6666; www.domodedovo.ru), **Sheremetyevo** (Шереметьево; 495-578 6565; www.svo.aero) and **Vnukovo** (Внуково; 495-937 5555; www.vnukovo.ru).

ℹ Getting Around

TO/FROM THE AIRPORT

All three airports are accessible by the convenient **Aeroexpress Train** (8-800-700 3377; www.aeroexpress.ru; one way R420; 6am-midnight) from the city centre; a reduced rate is available for online purchase.

Alternatively, order an official airport taxi from the dispatcher's desk in the terminal (R2000 to R2500 to the city centre). If you can order a taxi by phone or with a mobile-phone app it will be about 50% cheaper. Driving times vary wildly depending on traffic.

BICYCLE

Cycling on the streets is dangerous, but it's a pleasant way to get around if you stick to the cycling routes along the river and in the city parks. Bikes are available from VeloBike (https://velobike.ru) and various rental stations around town.

PUBLIC TRANSPORT

The **Moscow Metro** (www.mosmetro.ru; per ride R55) is by far the easiest, quickest and cheapest way of getting around the city. Magnetic tickets (single ride/90-minute card R55/65) are sold at ticket booths. Save time by buying the stored value Ediny (Единый) or Troika (Тройка) cards, either of which can be topped up as you go and used on all forms of public transport.

Buses, trolleybuses and trams are useful along a few radial or cross-town routes that the metro misses, and are necessary for reaching sights away from the city centre. Tickets (R31) are sold on the vehicle by a conductor.

TAXI

Taxi cabs are affordable. Unfortunately you can't really flag down an official metered taxi in the street and most taxi drivers and dispatchers do not speak English. That said, mobile phone apps such as **Yandex.Taxi** (Яндекс.Такси; https://taxi.yandex.com) are common and easy to use.

St Petersburg

POP 4.9 MILLION

Affectionately known as 'Piter' to its locals, St Petersburg is a visual delight. The Neva River and surrounding canals reflect unbroken facades of handsome 18th- and 19th-century buildings, which house a spellbinding collection of cultural storehouses, culminating in the incomparable Hermitage. Home to many of Russia's greatest creative talents (Pushkin, Dostoevsky, Tchaikovsky), the city continues to inspire a contemporary generation of Russians, making it a liberal, hedonistic and exciting place to visit.

St Petersburg covers many islands, some real, some created through the construction of canals. The central street is Nevsky pr, which extends some 4km from the Alexander Nevsky Monastery to the Hermitage. The inner 2.5km to Moskovsky vokzal is the city's shopping centre and the focus of its entertainment and street life.

◉ Sights

◉ Historic Centre

★ State Hermitage Museum
MUSEUM

(Государственный Эрмитаж; www.hermitagemuseum.org; Dvortsovaya pl 2; combined ticket R700; ⊙10.30am-6pm Tue, Thu, Sat & Sun, to 9pm Wed & Fri; Ⓜ Admiralteyskaya) The Hermitage fully lives up to its sterling reputation. You can be absorbed by its treasures for days and still come out wanting more. The enormous collection (over three million items, only a fraction of which are on display in 360 rooms) almost amounts to a comprehensive history of Western European art. Viewing it demands a little planning, so choose the areas you'd like to concentrate on before you arrive.

★ General Staff Building
MUSEUM

(Здание Главного штаба; www.hermitagemuseum.org; Dvortsovaya pl 6-8; R300, incl main Hermitage museum & other buildings R700; ⊙10.30am-6pm Tue, Thu, Sat & Sun, to 9pm Wed & Fri; Ⓜ Admiralteyskaya) The east wing of this magnificent building, wrapping around the south of Dvortsovaya pl and designed by Carlo Rossi in the 1820s, marries restored interiors with contemporary architecture to create a series of galleries displaying the Hermitage's amazing collection of Impressionist and post-Impressionist works. Contemporary art is here, too, often in temporary exhibitions by major artists.

★ Russian Museum
MUSEUM

(Русский музей; ☎812-595 4248; www.rusmuseum.ru; Inzhenernaya ul 4; adult/student R450/200; ⊙10am-8pm Mon, 10am-6pm Wed & Fri-Sun, 1-9pm Thu; Ⓜ Nevsky Prospekt) Focusing solely on Russian art, from ancient church icons to 20th-century paintings, the Russian Museum's collection is magnificent and can easily be viewed in half a day or less. The collection includes works by Karl Bryullov, Alexander Ivanov, Nicholas Ghe, Ilya Repin, Natalya Goncharova, Kazimir Malevich and Kuzma Petrov-Vodkin, among many others, and the masterpieces keep on coming as you tour the beautiful Carlo Rossi–designed Mikhailovsky Palace and its attached wings.

★ Church of the Saviour on the Spilled Blood
CHURCH

(Храм Спаса на Крови; ☎812-315 1636; http://eng.cathedral.ru/spasa_na_krovi; Konyushennaya pl; adult/student R250/150; ⊙10.30am-6pm

The Hermitage

A HALF-DAY TOUR

Successfully navigating the State Hermitage Museum, with its four vast interconnecting buildings and around 360 rooms, is an art form in itself. Our half-day tour of the highlights can be done in four hours, or easily extended to a full day.

Once past ticket control start by ascending the grand ❶ **Jordan Staircase** to Neva Enfilade and Great Enfilade for the impressive staterooms, including the former throne room St George's Hall and the 1812 War Gallery (Room 197), and the Romanovs' private apartments. Admire the newly restored ❷ **Great Church** then make your way back to the Neva side of the building via the Western Gallery (Room 262) to find the splendid ❸ **Pavilion Hall** with its view onto the Hanging Garden and the gilded Peacock Clock, always a crowd pleaser.

Make your way along the series of smaller galleries in the Large Hermitage hung with Italian Renaissance art, including masterpieces by ❹ **Da Vinci** and ❺ **Caravaggio**. The Loggia of Raphael (Room 227) is also impressive. Linger a while in the galleries containing Spanish art before taking in the Dutch collection, the highlight of which is the hoard of ❻ **Rembrandt** canvases in Room 254.

Descend the Council Staircase (Room 206), noting the giant malachite vase, to the ground floor where the fantastic Egyptian collection awaits in Room 100 as well as the galleries of Greek and Roman Antiquities. If you have extra time, it's well worth booking tours to see the special exhibition in the ❼ **Gold Rooms** of the Treasure Gallery.

Jordan Staircase
Originally designed by Rastrelli, in the 18th century this incredible white marble construction was known as the Ambassadorial Staircase because it was the way into the palace for official receptions.

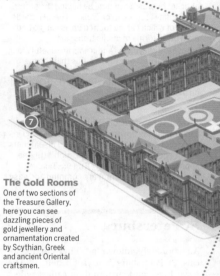

The Gold Rooms
One of two sections of the Treasure Gallery, here you can see dazzling pieces of gold jewellery and ornamentation created by Scythian, Greek and ancient Oriental craftsmen.

Great Church
This stunningly ornate church was the Romanovs' private place of worship and the venue for the marriage of the last tsar, Nicholas II, to Alexandra Feodorovna in 1895.

TOP TIPS

➡ Reserve tickets online to skip the long lines.

➡ Bring a sandwich and a bottle of water with you: the cafe isn't great.

➡ Wear comfortable shoes.

➡ Bear in mind the only cloakroom is before ticket control, so you can't go back and pick up a sweater.

Rembrandt
A moving portrait of contrition and forgiveness, *Return of the Prodigal Son* (Room 254) depicts the biblical scene of a wayward son returning to his father.

Da Vinci
Along with the *Benois Madonna*, also here, *Madonna and Child (Madonna Litta;* Room 214) is one of just a handful of paintings known to be the work of Leonardo da Vinci.

St George's Hall

Hermitage Theatre

Pavilion Hall
Apart from the Peacock Clock, the Pavilion Hall also contains beautifully detailed mosaic tables made by Italian and Russian craftsmen in the mid-19th century.

Caravaggio
The Lute Player (Room 237) is the Hermitage's only Caravaggio, and a work that the master of light and shade described as the best piece he'd ever painted.

Central St Petersburg

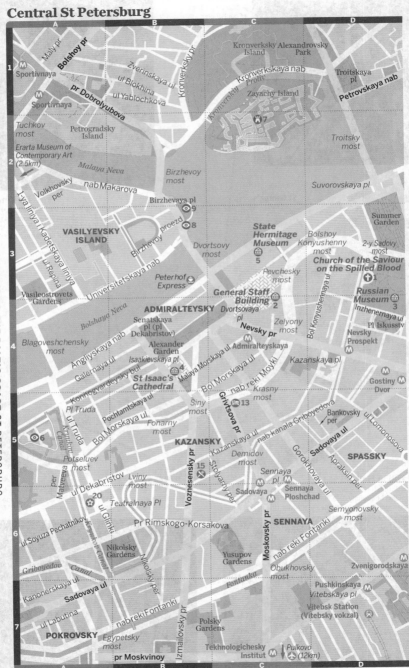

Kronverksky Alexandrovsky
Island Park

Sportivnaya
Maly pl
Bolshoy pr

Zverinskaya ul
ul Blokhina
ul Yablochkova

pr Dobrolyubova

Sportivnaya

Kronverkskaya nab

Kronverksky Proliv

Zayachy Island

Troitskaya pl
Petrovskaya nab

Tuchkov most
Petrogradsky Island

Erarta Museum of Contemporary Art (2.5km)

Malaya Neva

Birzhevoy most

Troitsky most

Suvorovskaya pl

Volkhovsky per
nab Makarova

1ya liniya Kadetskaya liniya

VASILYEVSKY ISLAND

Birzhevaya pl 9

Birzhevoy proezd 8

Summer Garden

2-y Sadovy most

State Hermitage Museum 5

Bolshoy Konyushenny most

ul Repina

Dvortsovy most

Pevchesky most

Church of the Saviour on the Spilled Blood 1

Peterhof Express

Vasileostrovets Gardens
Universitetskaya nab

Bolshaya Neva

ADMIRALTEYSKY

General Staff Building 2

Dvortsovaya pl

Zelyony most

Russian Museum 3

Inzhenernaya ul
Pl Iskusstv

Bol Konyushennaya ul

Nevsky pr

Nevsky Prospekt

Senatskaya pl (pl Dekabristov)

Admiralteyskaya

Kazanskaya pl

Gostiny Dvor

Blagoveshchensky most

Angliyskaya nab
Galernaya ul

Alexander Garden
Isaakievskaya pl 4

Malaya Morskaya ul

Bol Morskaya ul

Konnogvardeysky bul

St Isaac's Cathedral

nab reki Moyki

Krasny most

Pl Truda
6

ul Truda
Kryukov Canal

Pochtamtskaya ul
Bol Morskaya ul

Siny most

Givtsova pr 13

Bankovsky per
ul Lomonosova

Fonarny most

Potseluev most

Pochtamtskaya ul

KAZANSKY

Kazanskaya ul

nab kanala Griboyedova

Gorokhovaya ul

Sadovaya ul

SPASSKY

per Matveeva

ul Dekabristov

Lviny most

Voznesensky pr

15

Stolyarny per

Kazanskaya ul

Demidov most

Sennaya pl

Apraksin per

20

Teatralnaya Pl

Pr Rimskogo-Korsakova

Sadovaya

Sennaya Ploshchad

Semyonovsky most

SENNAYA

ul Soyuza Pechatnikov

Nikolsky Gardens

Nikolsky per

Kryukov Canal

Yusupov Gardens

Moskovsky pr

Obukhovsky most

nab reki Fontanki

Zvenigorodskaya

Griboyedov Canal

Kanonerskaya ul
Sadovaya ul

nab reki Fontanki

Fontanka

Pushkinskaya
Vitebskaya pl

Vitebsk Station (Vitebsky vokzal)

ul Labutina

POKROVSKY

Egypetsky most

pr Moskvinoy

Izmailovsky pr

Polsky Gardens

Tekhnologichesky Institut

Pulkovo (12km)

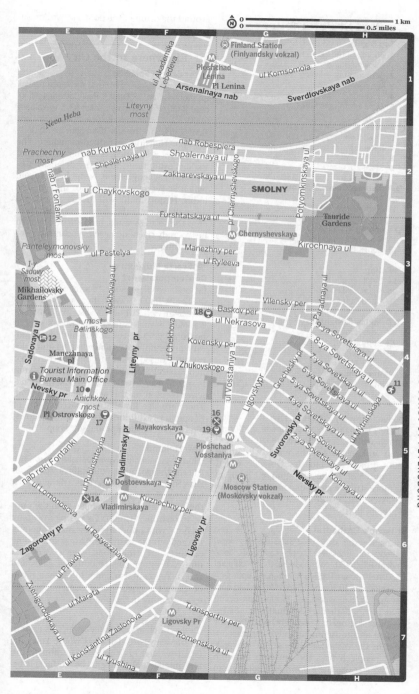

RUSSIA & THE BALTIC COAST ST PETERSBURG

Central St Petersburg

Thu-Tue; Ⓜ Nevsky Prospekt) This five-domed dazzler is St Petersburg's most elaborate church with a classic Russian Orthodox exterior and an interior decorated with some 7000 sq metres of mosaics. Officially called the Church of the Resurrection of Christ, its far more striking colloquial name references the assassination attempt on Tsar Alexander II here in 1881.

St Isaac's Cathedral   MUSEUM
(Исаакиевский собор; 📞 812-315 9732; www.cathedral.ru; Isaakievskaya pl; cathedral adult/student R250/150, colonnade R150; ⊙ cathedral 10.30am-10.30pm Thu-Tue May-Sep, to 6pm Oct-Apr, colonnade 10.30am-10.30pm May-Oct, to 6pm Nov-Apr; Ⓜ Admiralteyskaya) The golden dome of St Isaac's Cathedral dominates the St Petersburg skyline. Its obscenely lavish interior is open as a museum, although services are held in the cathedral throughout the year. Most people bypass the museum to climb the 262 steps to the *kolonnada* (colonnade)

around the drum of the dome, providing superb city views.

◎ Elsewhere in the City

Peter & Paul Fortress   FORTRESS
(Петропавловская крепость; www.spbmuseum.ru; grounds free, SS Peter & Paul Cathedral adult/child R450/250, combined ticket for 5 exhibitions R600/350; ⊙ grounds 8.30am-8pm, exhibitions 11am-6pm Mon & Thu-Sun, 10am-5pm Tue; Ⓜ Gorkovskaya) Housing a cathedral where the Romanovs are buried, a former prison and various exhibitions, this large defensive fortress on Zayachy Island is the kernel from which St Petersburg grew into the city it is today. History buffs will love it and everyone will swoon at the panoramic views from atop the fortress walls, at the foot of which lies a sandy riverside beach, a prime spot for sunbathing.

★ Erarta Museum of
Contemporary Art   MUSEUM
(Музей современного искусства Эрарта; 📞 812-324 0809; www.erarta.com; 29-ya Liniya 2; adult/under 21yr R500/350; ⊙ 10am-10pm Wed-Mon; Ⓜ Vasileostrovskaya) Erarta's superb hoard of 2300 pieces of Russian contemporary art trumps its somewhat far-flung location. Housed in an ingeniously converted neoclassical Stalinist building, the museum is spread over five floors, with the main galleries focused on the permanent collection. There are also installation spaces, plenty of temporary exhibitions, occasional shows, plus a good restaurant and gift shop.

New Holland   ISLAND
(Новая Голландия; www.newhollandsp.ru; nab Admiralteyskogo kanala; ⊙ 9am-10pm Mon-Thu, to 11pm Fri-Sun; Ⓜ Sadovaya) This triangular island was closed for the most part of the last three centuries, and has opened to the public in dazzling fashion. There's plenty going on here, with hundreds of events happening throughout the year. There are summertime concerts, art exhibitions, yoga classes and film screenings, plus restaurants, cafes and shops. You can also come to enjoy a bit of quiet on the grass – or on one of the pontoons floating in the pond.

Strelka   LANDMARK
(Birzhevaya pl; Ⓜ Vasileostrovskaya) This eastern tip of Vasilyevsky Island is where Peter the Great wanted his new city's administrative and intellectual centre to be. In fact, it be-

came the focus of the city's maritime trade, symbolised by the colonnaded Customs House (now the Institute of Russian Literature) and the Old Stock Exchange. The Strelka is flanked by the pair of **Rostral Columns** (Ростральная колонна; Birzhevaya pl; Ⓜ Vasileostrovskaya), archetypal St Petersburg landmarks.

🏃 Activities & Tours

⭐ **Peterswalk Walking Tours**　WALKING
(☑ 812-943 1229; http://peterswalk.com; from R1320) Going for over 20 years, Peter Kozyrev's innovative and passionately led tours are highly recommended as a way to see the city with knowledgeable locals. The daily Original Peterswalk (R1320) is one of the favourites and leaves daily from the **Julia Child Bistro** (☑ 812-929 0797; Grazhdanskaya ul 27; mains R310-490; ⊙ 9am-11pm Mon-Fri, from 10am Sat & Sun; 🐾🍴; Ⓜ Sadovaya) at 10.30am from April to end of September. Other tours from around R2000.

⭐ **Sputnik Tours**　WALKING
(☑ 499-110 5266; www.sputnik8.com; price varies) This online tour agency is one with a difference: it acts as a marketplace for locals wanting to give their own unique tours of their own city. Browse, select a tour, register and pay a deposit and then you are given the contact number of the guide. A superb way to meet locals you'd never meet otherwise.

⭐ **Anglo Tourismo**　BOATING
(☑ 8-921-989 4722; http://anglotourismo.com; 27 nab reki Fontanki; 1hr cruise adult/student R1900/900; Ⓜ Gostiny Dvor) There's a huge number of companies offering cruises all over the Historic Heart, all with similar prices and itineraries. Anglo Tourismo, however, is the only operator to run tours with commentary in English. Between May and September the schedule runs every 1½ hours between 11am and 6.30pm. From 1 June to 31 August there are also additional night cruises.

The company also runs walking tours including a free one starting daily from mid-May to end of September at 10.30am and lasting three hours.

Mytninskiye Bani　BATHHOUSE
(Мытнинские бани; www.mybanya.spb.ru; ul Mytninskaya 17-19; per hr R200-350; ⊙ 8am-10pm Fri-Tue; Ⓜ Ploshchad Vosstaniya) Unique in the city, Mytninskiye Bani is heated by a wood furnace, just like the log-cabin bathhouses that are still found in the Russian countryside. It's actually the oldest communal *banya* (hot bath) in the city, and in addition to a *parilka* (steam room) and plunge pool, the private 'lux' *banya* (R1000 to R2000 per hour) includes a swanky lounge area with leather furniture and a pool table.

🛏 Sleeping & Eating

⭐ **Soul Kitchen Hostel**　HOSTEL €
(☑ 8-965-816 3470; www.soulkitchenhostel.com; nab reki Moyki 62/2, apt 9, Sennaya; dm R1500-2400, d R5700-9000; 🖳🛜; Ⓜ Admiralteyskaya) Soul Kitchen blends boho hipness and boutique-hotel comfort, scoring perfect 10s in many key categories: private rooms (chic), dorm beds (double-width with privacy-protecting curtains), common areas and kitchen (all beautifully designed). The lounge is a fine place to hang out, with a record player, a big screen projector (for movie nights) and an artful design.

Baby Lemonade Hostel　HOSTEL €
(☑ 812-570 7943; http://babylemonade.epoque-hostels.com; Inzhenernaya ul 7; dm/d with shared bathroom from R600/2500, d from R3800; 🖳🛜; Ⓜ Gostiny Dvor) The owner of Baby Lemonade is crazy about the 1960s and it shows in the

> **WORTH A TRIP**
>
> ### STREET ART MUSEUM
>
> Covering 11 hectares and with 150,000 to 200,000 sq metres of walls, a large disused section of the laminated plastics factory SLOPAST is the location of the amazing **Street Art Museum** (☑ 812-448 1593; http://streetartmuseum.ru; shosse Revolutsii 84, Okhta, entrance on Umansky per; adult/student R350/250; ⊙ noon-10pm Tue-Sun May-Sep; Ⓜ Ploshchad Lenina, then bus 28, 37, 137 or 530). You'll find a wide variety of formats, from huge murals covering walls to mixed-media installations set inside a former boilerhouse. Every year the exhibition changes, with top artists from around the globe invited to contribute. Guided tours take place on weekends (at 1pm and 2pm); call ahead to ensure an English-speaking guide is on hand. The museum also hosts outdoor concerts and other big events. Check the website for the latest.

MOSCOW TO ST PETERSBURG

The fastest trains between Moscow and St Petersburg are the Sapsan services (from R1300, three to four hours, six to eight daily). There are also around 10 overnight services, which can take anywhere from seven to 11 hours (*platskart* (3rd class)/*kupe* (2nd-class sleeper) from R1570/2800). Tickets often sell out in the high months, but keep your plans flexible and you should be able to find something, even at the last minute. Many flights (from R2750) also connect the two cities and they rarely sell out.

pop-art, psychedelic design of this friendly, fun hostel with two pleasant, large dorms and a great kitchen and living room. However, it's worth splashing out for the boutique-hotel-worthy private rooms that are in a separate flat with great rooftop views.

Bekitzer
ISRAELI €

(Бекицер; ☎ 812-926 4342; www.facebook.com/bktzr; ul Rubinshteyna 40; mains R180-450; ⊗ noon-6am Mon-Fri, from noon Sat & Sun; 🛜 🗷; 🅼 Dostoyevskaya) Always crowded and spilling out into the street, this Israel-themed eatery and drinking den lures hip and joyful people with its creative cocktails, Israeli Shiraz and the best falafel wraps this side of the Baltic Sea. Other culinary temptations include sabich salad (with eggplant, egg, hummus and tahini), appetiser spreads with baba ghanoush and pitas, and rather imaginative matzah pizzas.

Obed Bufet
CAFETERIA €

(Обед Буфет; 5th fl, Nevsky Centre, Nevsky pr 114; mains R250-380; ⊗ 10am-11pm; 🛜; 🅼 Mayakovskaya) Just what St Petersburg needs: a well-organised, central and inviting cafeteria run by the city's most successful restaurant group. Here you'll find an extraordinary range of salads, soups, sandwiches, pizzas and meat dishes. There is even a 50% discount until noon and 30% after 9pm, making this a superb deal (come at 9pm for the latter, otherwise there will be no food left).

🍷 Drinking & Nightlife

★ Commode
BAR

(www.commode.club; ul Rubinshteyna 1, 2nd fl; per hr R180; ⊗ 4pm-2am Sun-Thu, to 6am Fri & Sat) Stopping in for drinks at Commode feels more like hanging out in an upper-class friend's stylish apartment. After getting buzzed up, you can hang out in various high-ceilinged rooms, catch a small concert or poetry slam, browse books in the quasi-library room, play a round of table football, or chat with the easygoing crowd that have fallen for the place.

★ Ziferblat
ANTICAFE

(Циферблат; ☎ 8-981-180 7022; www.ziferblat.net; 2nd fl, Nevsky pr 81; per min R3, per min after 1st hr R2; ⊗ 11am-midnight; 🛜; 🅼 Ploshchad Vosstaniya) A charming multiroom 'free space' that has started a worldwide trend, Ziferblat is the original anticafe in St Petersburg. Coffee, tea, soft drinks and biscuits are included as you while away your time playing chess and other board games, reading, playing instruments (help yourself to the piano and guitar) or just hanging out with the arty young locals who frequent its cosy rooms.

★ Redrum
BAR

(☎ 812-416 1126; www.facebook.com/redrumbarspb; ul Nekrasova 26; ⊗ 4pm-1am Sun-Thu, to 3am Fri & Sat; 🅼 Mayakovskaya) One of St Petersburg's best drinking dens, Redrum hits all the right notes. It has a cosy, white brick interior, a welcoming, easygoing crowd, and a stellar selection of craft brews (some two dozen on tap). There's also good pub fare on hand to go with that creative line-up of Session Indian Pale Ales, sour ales, Berliner Weisse and porters.

☆ Entertainment

★ Mariinsky Theatre
BALLET, OPERA

(Мариинский театр; ☎ 812-326 4141; www.mariinsky.ru; Teatralnaya pl 1; tickets R1200-6500; 🅼 Sadovaya) St Petersburg's most spectacular venue for ballet and opera, the Mariinsky Theatre is an attraction in its own right. Tickets can be bought online or in person; book in advance during the summer months. The magnificent interior is the epitome of imperial grandeur, and any evening here will be an impressive experience.

ℹ️ Information

American Medical Clinic (☎ 812-740 2090; www.amclinic.ru; nab reki Moyki 78; ⊗ 24hr; 🅼 Admiralteyskaya) One of the city's largest private clinics.

Tourist Information Bureau (☎ 812-303 0555, 812-242 3909; http://eng.ispb.info; Sadovaya ul 14/52; ⊗ 10am-7pm Mon-Sat; 🅼 Gostiny Dvor) There are also branches outside the

Hermitage, at St Isaac's Cathedral and at Pulkovo Airport.

ℹ Getting There & Away

International and domesitc flights touch down at **Pulkovo International Airport** (LED; ☏ 812-337 3822; www.pulkovoairport.ru; Pulkovskoye sh).

ℹ Getting Around

TO/FROM THE AIRPORT

From Pulkovo International Airport, an official taxi to the centre should cost between R800 and R1000. Alternatively, take bus 39 (35 minutes) or 39A (20 minutes) to Moskovskaya metro station for R35, then take the metro from Moskovskaya (Line 2) to anywhere in the city for R45.

PUBLIC TRANSPORT

The metro is usually the quickest way around the city. *Zhetony* (tokens) and credit-loaded cards can be bought from booths in the stations (R45).

If you are staying more than a day or two, however, it's worth buying a smart card (R60), which is good for multiple journeys to be used over the course of a fixed time period, eg 10 trips in seven days for R355.

The St Petersburg Card (https://petersburg card.com) is sold online and by the St Petersburg Tourist Centre . It gives a range of discounts on tours and sights such as the Hermitage, Peterhof and Tsarskoe Selo (the savings aren't huge), as well as acting as a stored-value card for public transport.

Buses, trolleybuses and *marshrutky* (minibuses; fares R40) often get you closer to the sights and are especially handy to cover long distances along main avenues like Nevsky pr.

TAXI

Taxi apps, such as Gett and Yandex Taxi, are all the rage in St Petersburg and they've brought down the prices of taxis in general, while improving the service a great deal.

Peterhof

The 'Russian Versailles', Peterhof (Петергоф, also known as Petrodvorets), 29km west of the city, was built for Peter the Great. A major casualty of WWII, the palace and grounds are largely a reconstruction best visited for its **Grand Cascade** (⊙11am-5pm Mon-Fri, to 6pm Sat & Sun May-Oct) and Water Avenue, a symphony of over 140 fountains and canals located in the **Lower Park** (Нижний парк; www.peterhofmuseum.ru; adult/student May-Oct R750/400, Nov-Apr free; ⊙9am-7pm). There are several additional palaces, villas and parks

here, each of which charges its own hefty admission price.

Buses and *marshrutky* to Petrodvorets (R80, 30 minutes) run frequently from outside metro stations Avtovo and Leninsky Prospekt. From May to September, the **Peterhof Express** (www.peterhof-express. com; single/return adult R800/1500, student R600/1000; ⊙10am-6pm) hydrofoil leaves from jetties behind the Hermitage and behind the Admiralty.

Pushkin (Tsarskoe Selo)

The grand imperial estate of Tsarskoe Selo (Царское Село) in the town of Pushkin, 25km south of St Petersburg, is home to the baroque **Catherine Palace** (Екатерининский дворец; www.tzar.ru; Sadovaya ul 7; adult/student R1000/350, audio guide R150; ⊙10am-4.45pm Wed-Sun), expertly restored following its near destruction in WWII. From May to September individual visits to Catherine's Palace are limited to noon to 2pm and 4pm to 4.45pm, with other times being reserved for tour groups.

From late April to October there is also an entry charge to the beautiful surrounding **Catherine Park** (Екатерининский парк; ⊙9am-6pm); otherwise this is free.

The easiest way to get to Tsarskoe Selo is by *marshrutka* (R40) from Moskovskaya metro station.

Kaliningrad Region

Sandwiched between Poland and Lithuania, the Kaliningrad Region is a Russian exclave that's both intimately attached to the Motherland and also a world apart. This 'Little Russia' – only 15,100 sq km with a population of 941,873 – offers an intriguing capital, beautiful countryside, charming old Prussian seaside resorts and splendid beaches.

Kaliningrad

POP 431,900

The capital, Kaliningrad (Калининград, formely Königsberg), was once a Middle European architectural gem equal to Prague or Kraków. Precious little of this built heritage remains, but there are attractive residential suburbs and remnants of the city's old fortifications that evoke the Prussian past.

Kaliningrad Region

⊙ Sights

The once densely populated Kant Island is now a parkland dotted with sculptures and dominated by the cathedral. A few nearby buildings – the **former Stock Exchange** (Биржа; Leninsky pr 83) from the 1870s and the neo-traditional row of shops, restaurants and hotels known as **Fish Village** (Рыбная Деревня) – hint at what this area looked like pre-WWII. Get a bird's-eye view from the 31m-high **lighthouse viewing tower** (R100; ⊙ 10am-10pm).

★ Museum of the
World Ocean   MUSEUM
(Музей Мирового Океана; ☏ 4012-538 915; www.world-ocean.ru; nab Petra Velikogo 1; adult/ student R300/150, individual vessels R150/100; ⊙ 10am-6pm Wed-Mon) Strung along the banks of the Pregolya River are several ships, a submarine, maritime machinery and exhibition halls that together make up this excellent museum. The highlight is the handsome former scientific expedition vessel *Vityaz*, moored alongside the *Viktor Patsaev*, with its exhibits relating to space research; visits to this are by guided tour (included in the admission price; every 45 minutes). The pre-atomic B-413 submarine

gives a taste of what life was like for its 300 former inhabitants.

Kaliningrad Cathedral   CHURCH
(Кафедральный собор Кёнигсберга; ☏ 4012-631 705; www.sobor-kaliningrad.ru; Kant Island; adult/student R200/100, concerts from R150; ⊙ 10am-6pm Mon-Thu, to 7pm Fri-Sun) Photos displayed inside this Unesco World Heritage Site attest to how dilapidated the cathedral was until the early 1990s – the original dates back to 1333. The lofty interior is dominated by an ornate organ used for regular **concerts**. Upstairs, the carved-wood **Wallenrodt Library** has interesting displays of old Königsberg.

🛏 Sleeping

Oh, my Kant   HOSTEL €
(☏ 4012-390 278; www.ohmykant.ru; ul Yablonevaya Alleya 34; dm/d from R500/1900; 🛜) This well-maintained hostel is one of several budget accommodation options run by the 'Oh, my Kant' group. See the website for the other properties. The setting here is a charming house in a lovely part of town, about 2km west of the centre. The dorms are airy and bright, and the kitchen and common areas are super-clean.

ℹ Information

Regional Tourism Information Centre
(☎ 4012-957 980, 4012-555 200; www.visit-
kaliningrad.ru; pr Mira 4; ⊙ 9am-8pm Mon-Fri,
11am-6pm Sat May-Sep, 9am-7pm Mon-Fri,
11am-4pm Sat Oct-Apr) Helpful, English-speaking
staff and lots of information on the region.

ℹ Getting There & Away

AIR

Khrabrovo Airport (Аэропорт Храброво/
KGD; ☎ 4012-610 620; www.kgd.aero) is 24km
north of the city. Aeroflot and other Russian
airlines offer several daily flights to Moscow's
main airports as well as to St Petersburg and
a handful of other Russian cities. Outside of
Russia, service is available to Minsk, Warsaw,
Riga and Barcelona.

BUS

Ecolines (☎ 4012-758 733; www.ecolines.
net; ul Zheleznodorozhnaya 7; ⊙ 9.30am-
10pm) and **Königs Avto** (☎ 4012-999 199;
www.kenigauto.com) operate regional
international bus services to major cities
in Poland, Lithuania, Latvia and Germany,
with onward connections to other European
destinations. Coaches for both companies
normally arrive at and depart from Kaliningrad's **South Bus Station** (Автовокзал
Южный, Yuzhny Bus Station; ul Zheleznodorozhnaya 7), though some König Avto buses
may use Kaliningrad's **International Bus
Station** (Международный Автовокзал
Калининград; ☎ 4012-999 199; www.kenig
auto.com; Moskovsky pr 184).

TRAIN

Russian Railways (p800) runs daily services
from Kaliningrad to both Moscow (20 hours,
platskart/kupe R2800/5000) and St Petersburg (24 hours, *platskart/kupe* R2700/4000).
All long-distance trains leave from the capital's
Main (South) Train Station. Note that trains to
both cities pass through EU member Lithuania
and passengers will need a re-entry visa for
onward travel to Russia. Moscow-bound trains
travel via Belarus and may require a transit visa
through that country.

ℹ Getting Around

Kaliningrad is a sprawling city and the public-transport network of buses, trams and
trolleybuses is useful for getting around. Buy
tickets (R18) from on-board conductors. Taxis
are relatively cheap; getting between destinations within the city will cost R200 to R300. **Taxi
Kaliningrad** (☎ 4012-585 858; www.taxi-kalin-
ingrad.ru) is a reliable operator.

Russia Survival Guide

ℹ Directory A–Z

ACCOMMODATION

There's a good choice of accommodation options across most major Russian cities. A dorm
bed in a hostel runs from R500 to R1000.

BUSINESS HOURS

Note that most museums close their ticket offices one hour (in some cases 30 minutes) before
the official closing time.

Banks 9am to 6pm Monday to Friday, some
open 9am to 5pm Saturday

Bars and restaurants noon to midnight

Shops 10am–8pm

GAY & LESBIAN TRAVELLERS

➡ Russia is a conservative country and being
gay is generally frowned upon. LGBT people
face stigma, harassment and violence in their
everyday lives.

➡ Homosexuality isn't illegal, but promoting
it (and other LGBT lifestyles) is. What con-
stitutes promotion is at the discretion of the
authorities.

➡ There are active and relatively open gay and
lesbian scenes in both Moscow and St Petersburg. Elsewhere, the gay scene tends to be
underground.

➡ For a good overview, visit http://english.
gay.ru.

INTERNET RESOURCES

Moscow Expat Site (www.expat.ru) A mine of
expat knowledge on Russia.

WORTH A TRIP

SVETLOGORSK & KURSHSKAYA KOSA NATIONAL PARK

It's easy to access the region's other
key sights on day trips from Kaliningrad, but if you did want to spend time
away from the city, base yourself in the
charming seaside resort of Svetlogorsk
(Светлогорск), which is only a few hours'
drive down the Baltic coast from the
pine forests and Sahara-style dunes
of the **Kurshskaya Kosa National
Park** (Национальный парк Куршская
коса; ☎ 40150-45 119; www.park-kosa.ru;
per person/car R50/300), a Unesco World
Heritage Site.

ℹ PRICE RANGES

The following price ranges are for high season double rooms with private bathroom, excluding breakfast.

€ less than R1500 (R3000 in Moscow & St Petersburg)

€€ R1500–4000 (R3000–15,000)

The following price categories are for the cost of a main course:

€ less than R300 (R500 in Moscow & St Petersburg)

€€ R300–800 (R500–1000)

Way to Russia (www.waytorussia.net) Comprehensive online travel guide.

MONEY

The Russian currency is the rouble, written as 'рубль' and abbreviated as 'руб' or 'р'. Coins come in amounts of R1 (rarely seen), R5, R10 and R50, with banknotes in values of R10, R50, R100, R200, R500, R1000, R2000 and R5000.

ATMs that accept all major credit and debit cards are everywhere, and most restaurants, shops and hotels in major cities take plastic. You can exchange dollars and euros (and some other currencies) at most banks; when they're closed, try the exchange counters at top-end hotels. You may need your passport. Note that crumpled or old banknotes are often refused.

PUBLIC HOLIDAYS

In addition to the following official days, many businesses (but not restaurants, shops and museums) close for a week of bank holidays between 1 January and at least 8 January. Bank holidays are typically declared to merge national holidays with the nearest weekend.

New Year's Day 1 January
Russian Orthodox Christmas Day 7 January
Defender of the Fatherland Day 23 February
International Women's Day 8 March
International Labour Day/Spring Festival 1 May
Victory Day 9 May
Russian Independence Day 12 June
Unity Day 4 November

SAFE TRAVEL

Petty theft and pickpockets are prevalent in both Moscow and St Petersburg, so be vigilant with your belongings.

Some police officers can be bothersome, especially to dark-skinned or foreign-looking people. Other members of the police force target tourists, though reports of tourists being hassled about their documents and registration have declined. Still, you should always carry a photocopy of your passport, visa and registration stamp. If you are stopped for any reason – legitimate or illegitimate – you will surely be hassled if you don't have these.

Sadly, racism is a problem in Russia. Be vigilant on the streets around Hitler's birthday (20 April), when bands of right-wing thugs have been known to roam around spoiling for a fight with anyone who doesn't look Russian.

TELEPHONE

The international code for Russia is 7. The international access code from landline phones in Russia is 8, followed by 10 after the second tone, followed by the country code.

Major phone networks offering pay-as-you-go deals include Beeline, Megafon, MTS and Tele2. Company offices are everywhere. It costs as little as R300 to purchase a SIM card, but bring your passport.

Local telecom rules mean mobile calls or texts from your 'home' city or region to another city or region are more expensive – essentially long-distance calls/texts. Active callers should consider purchasing a Moscow SIM while in Moscow, and a St Petersburg SIM while in St Petersburg.

Mobile phone numbers start interchangeably with either the country code (7) or the internal mobile code (8), plus three digits that change according to the service provider, followed by a seven-digit number. Nearly all Russians will give you their mobile number with an initial 8, but if you're dialling from a non-Russian number (ie your own on roaming), replace this 8 with a 7.

To call a mobile phone from a landline, the line must be enabled to make paid calls (all local numbers are free from a landline anywhere in Russia). To find out if this is the case, dial 8, and then if you hear a second tone you can dial the mobile number in full. If you hear nothing, hang up – you can't call anywhere but local landlines from here.

VISAS

Practically everyone needs a visa to visit Russia. For most travellers a tourist visa (single- or double-entry, valid for a maximum of 30 days) will be sufficient. If you plan to stay longer than a month, you can apply for a business visa or – if you are a US citizen – a three-year multi-entry visa.

To obtain a visa, everyone needs an invitation, also known as 'visa support'. Hotels and hostels will usually issue anyone staying with them an invitation voucher free or for a small fee (typically around €20 to €30). If you are not staying in a hotel or hostel, you will need to buy an invitation – this can be done through travel agents or specialist visa agencies, also for around €20.

Invitation voucher in hand, you can then apply for a visa. Start by entering details in the online form of the Consular Department of the Russian Ministry of Foreign Affairs (https://visa.kdmid.ru/PetitionChoice.aspx).

Take care in answering the questions accurately on this form, including listing all the countries you have visited in the last 10 years and the dates of the visits – stamps in your passport will be checked against this information and if there are anomalies you will likely have to restart the process. Keep a note of the unique identity number provided for your submitted form – if you have to make changes later, you will need this to access it without having to fill in the form again from scratch.

Some Russian embassies (eg those in the UK and US) have contracted separate agencies to process the submission of visa applications; these companies use online interfaces that direct the relevant information into the standard visa application form.

Consular offices apply different fees and slightly different application rules country by country. Avoid potential hassles by checking well in advance what these rules might be.

The charge for the visa will depend on the type of visa applied for and how quickly you need it. We highly recommend applying for your visa in your home country rather than on the road.

Immigration Form

Immigration forms are produced electronically by passport control at airports. If you are arriving by land, ask for the form at the border if it is not provided by the immigration officials.

Take good care of your half of the completed form as you'll need it for registration and could face problems while travelling in Russia – and certainly will on leaving – if you can't produce it.

Registration

Every visitor to Russia must have their visa registered *within seven days of arrival*, excluding weekends and public holidays. Registration is handled by your accommodating party. If staying in a homestay or rental apartment, you'll need to make arrangements with either the landlord or a friend to register you through the post office. See www.waytorussia.net/russianvisa/registration.html for how this can be done.

Once registered, you'll receive a registration slip. Keep this safe – that's the document that any police who stop you will ask to see. You do not need to register more than once unless you stay in additional cities for more than seven days, in which case you'll need additional registration slips.

Getting There & Away

AIR

There are international flights into and out of Moscow and St Petersburg.

LAND

Russia has excellent train and bus connections with the rest of Europe. However, many routes connecting St Petersburg and Moscow with points east – including Kaliningrad – go through Belarus, for which you'll need a transit visa. Buses are the best way to get from St Petersburg to Tallinn. St Petersburg to Helsinki can be done by bus or train, as well as by boat.

From Eastern Europe you are most likely to enter Russia from Estonia at Narva; from Latvia at Rēzekne; and from Ukraine at Chernihiv. You can enter Kaliningrad from Lithuania and Poland at any of seven border posts.

SEA

Between early April and late September, international passenger ferries connect Stockholm, Helsinki and Tallinn with St Petersburg.

Getting Around

AIR

Major Russian airlines have online booking and domestic flights are relatively cheap. Tickets can also be purchased at ubiquitous *avia kassa* (ticket offices). Online agencies specialising in Russian air tickets with English interfaces include **Anywayanyday** (☑ 8-800 775 7753; www.anywayanyday.com), **Pososhok.ru** (☑ 8-800 333 8118; www.pososhok.ru), One Two Trip! (www.onetwotrip.ru) and TicketsRU (www.tickets.ru).

BUS

Buses and *marshrutky* (fixed-route vans or minibuses) are often more frequent, more convenient and faster than trains, especially on short-distance routes. There's almost no need to reserve a seat – just arrive a good 30 minutes before the scheduled departure and buy a ticket. Prices are comparable to 3rd-class train fares. *Marshrutky* fares tend to be double those of buses and they usually leave when full, rather than according to a schedule. Where roads are good, *marshrutky* can be twice as fast as buses.

TAXI

The taxi situation was a pain until a few years ago, when phone apps, such as Gett and Yandex Taxi, made cabs much more affordable and easy to use. Download the various apps to your phone before using or while in Russia. Taxis can also be ordered by phone, but English-speaking operators are rare.

TRAIN

Russia's extensive train network is efficiently run by **Russian Railways** (РЖД, RZD; ☑ 8-800 775 0000; www.rzd.ru). *Prigorodny* (suburban) or short-distance trains – also known as *elektrichki* – do not require advance booking: you can buy your ticket at the *prigorodny poezd kassa* (suburban train ticket offices) at train stations.

Tickets can be bought online from RZD. Bookings open 60 days before the date of departure. You'd be wise to buy well in advance over the busy summer months and holiday periods such as New Year and early May, when securing berths at short notice on certain trains can be difficult. On long-distance trains the cheapest fares are 3rd class (*platskartny*) followed by 2nd-class sleeper (*kupe*) and 1st-class (*SV*).

At stations, you'll need your passport (or a photocopy) to buy tickets. You can buy tickets for others if you bring their passports or photocopies. Be prepared for long, slow queues. At train ticket offices ('*Zh/D kassa*', short for '*zheleznodorozhnaya kassa*'), which are all over most cities, you can pay a surcharge of around R200 and avoid the queues. Alternatively, most travel agencies will organise the reservation and delivery of train tickets for a substantial mark-up.

ESTONIA

Tallinn

POP 426,538

Estonia's capital city has charm by the bucketload, fusing the modern and medieval to come up with a vibrant vibe all of its own. It's an intoxicating mix of ancient church spires, glass skyscrapers, baroque palaces, appealing eateries, brooding battlements, shiny shopping malls, rundown wooden houses and cafes set on sunny squares – with a few Soviet throwbacks in the mix, for added spice.

◎ Sights

While most of the city's sights are conveniently located within the medieval Old Town's walls, it's worth venturing out to the further-flung attractions – and given Tallinn's relatively compact size, there's really no excuse not to. The parks, palaces and museums of Kadriorg, 2km east of Viru väljak, should be a priority.

◉ Lower Town

★ Town Hall Square   SQUARE

(Raekoja plats) In Tallinn all roads lead to Raekoja plats, the city's pulsing heart since markets began setting up here in the 11th century. One side is dominated by the Gothic town hall, while the rest is ringed by pretty pastel-coloured buildings dating from the 15th to 17th centuries. Whether bathed in sunlight or sprinkled with snow, it's always a photogenic spot.

Tallinn Town Hall   HISTORIC BUILDING

(Tallinna raekoda; ☑ 645 7900; www.raekoda.tallinn.ee; Raekoja plats; adult/student €5/2; ☉ 10am-4pm Mon-Sat Jul & Aug, shorter hours rest of year; ⓰) Completed in 1404, this is the only surviving Gothic town hall in northern Europe. Inside, you can visit the Trade Hall (whose visitor book drips with royal signatures), the Council Chamber (featuring Estonia's oldest woodcarvings, dating from 1374), the vaulted Citizens' Hall, a yellow-and-black-tiled councillor's office and a small kitchen. The steeply sloped attic has displays on the building and its restoration. Details such as brightly painted columns and intricately carved wooden friezes give some sense of the original splendour.

Town Hall Tower   VIEWPOINT

(adult/child €3/1; ☉ 11am-6pm Jun-Aug) Old Thomas (Vana Toomas), Tallinn's symbol and guardian, has been keeping watch from his perch on the town hall's weathervane since 1530 (although his previous incarnation now resides in the City Museum; p801). You can enjoy much the same views as Thomas by climbing the 115 steps to the top of the tower. According to legend, this elegant 64m minaret-like structure was modelled on a sketch made by an explorer following his visit to the Orient.

Great Guild Hall   MUSEUM

(Suurgildi hoone; ☑ 696 8693; www.ajaloomuuseum.ee; Pikk 17; adult/child €6/3; ☉ 10am-6pm, closed Wed Oct-Apr) The Estonian History Museum has filled the striking 1410 Great Guild building with a series of ruminations on the Estonian psyche, presented through interactive and unusual displays. Coin collectors shouldn't miss the old excise chamber, with its numismatic relics stretching back to Viking times, while military nuts should head downstairs. The basement also covers the history of the Great Guild itself, while Esto-

Estonia

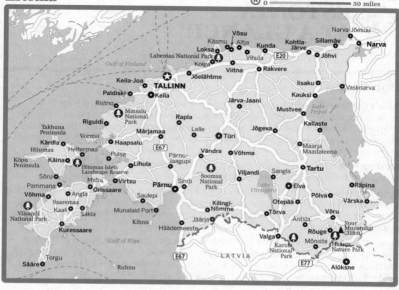

nian music, language, geography and deep history all win consideration.

Lower Town Wall
FORTRESS

(Linnamüür; ☎ 644 9867; Väike-Kloostri 1; adult/child €2/0.75; ☺ 11am-7pm Jun-Aug, shorter hours/days rest of year) The most photogenic stretch of Tallinn's remaining walls connects nine towers lining the western edge of Old Town. Visitors can explore the barren nooks and crannies of three of them (there are modest displays on weaponry and castle-craft inside) with cameras at the ready for the red-rooftop views. The gardens outside the wall are pretty and relaxing.

Holy Spirit Lutheran Church
CHURCH

(Pühavaimu kirik; ☎ 646 4430; www.eelk.ee/tallinna.puhavaimu; Pühavaimu 2; adult/child €1.50/0.50; ☺ 9am-6pm Mon-Sat when no service underway, between services Sun) The blue-and-gold clock on the facade of this striking 13th-century Gothic church is the oldest in Tallinn, dating from 1684. Inside are exquisite woodcarvings and painted panels, including an altarpiece dating to 1483 and a 17th-century baroque pulpit. Johann Koell, a former pastor here, is considered the author of the first Estonian book, a catechism published in 1535. The church hosts regular classical music concerts (try Mondays at 6pm).

City Museum
MUSEUM

(Linnamuuseum; ☎ 615 5180; www.linnamuuseum.ee; Vene 17; adult/child €4/3; ☺ 10.30am-6pm Tue-Sun Mar-Oct, to 5.30pm Nov-Feb) Tallinn's City Museum is actually split over 10 different sites. This location, its main branch, is set in a 14th-century merchant's house and traces the city's development from its earliest days. The displays are engrossing and very well laid out, with plenty of information available in English, making the hire of the audio guide quite unnecessary. Displays illuminate Estonian language, everyday life, and artefacts and cultural developments.

◎ Toompea

St Mary's Lutheran Cathedral
CHURCH

(Tallinna Püha Neitsi Maarja Piiskoplik toomkirik; ☎ 644 4140; www.toomkirik.ee; Toom-Kooli 6; church/tower €2/5; ☺ 9am-5pm May & Sep, to 6pm Jun-Aug, shorter hours/days rest of year) Tallinn's cathedral (now Lutheran, originally Catholic) had been initially built by the Danes by at least 1233, although the exterior dates mainly from the 15th century, with the

ESTONIA AT A GLANCE

Don't Miss

Tallin's Old Town A magical window into a bygone world, inducing visions of knights and ladies, merchants and peasants – not least due to the locals' proclivity for period dress. Rambling lanes lined with medieval dwellings open onto squares once covered in the filth of everyday commerce, but now lined with cafes and altogether less gory markets selling souvenirs and handicrafts.

Kadriorg Park Admire great works of art in a baroque palace built by Peter the Great before meandering through this beautiful Talllin park and gardens.

Tartu To Estonia what Oxford and Cambridge are to England, it's the presence of an esteemed ancient university and its attendant student population (with associated high japes and insobriety) that gives it its special character. There's a museum on nearly every corner of Tartu's elegant streets and, it seems, a grungy bar in every other cellar.

Pärnu When the quirky notion of sea-bathing became fashionable at the dawn of the 20th century, Pärnu became Estonia's most popular seaside resort – and it's hardly less so today. Architectural gems of that period combine with relics of the Hanseatic past to create very pleasant streets to explore, with interesting eateries and bars lurking within them.

Lahemaa National Park Providing a one-stop shop of all of Estonia's major habitats – coast, forests, plains, peatbogs, lakes and rivers – within a very convenient 80km of the capital, Lahemaa is the slice of rural Estonia that travellers on a tight schedule really shouldn't miss.

Itineraries

Three Days

Base yourself in **Tallinn** and spend your first day exploring all the nooks and crannies of the Old Town. The following day, do what most tourists don't – step out of Old Town. Explore Kadriorg Park for a first-rate greenery and art fix, then hit the wonderful Estonian Open-Air Museum. On your last day, hire a car or take a day tour to **Lahemaa National Park** where you can go hiking through forests and peatbogs and view a historic manor house.

One Week

Spend your first three days in Tallinn, then allow a full day to explore Lahemaa before bedding down within the national park. The following day, continue on to the venerable university town of **Tartu** for a night or two, making sure you see the Town Hall Square and the Estonian National Museum. Finish up in **Pärnu** where you can relax on the long, sandy beach and splash in Estonia's largest water park.

Essential Food & Drink

Kilu Pickled Baltic sprat, often served in sandwiches or as part of a breakfast buffet.

Rye bread Unlike other ryes you may have eaten, here it's moist, dense and delicious (assuming it's fresh), and usually served as a free accompaniment to every restaurant meal.

Vana Tallinn No one quite knows what the syrupy liqueur is made from, but it's sweet and strong and has a pleasant aftertaste. It's best served neat, in coffee, over ice with milk, over ice cream, or in Champagne or dry white wine.

Beer The favourite tipple in Estonia and the local product is very much in evidence. The biggest brands are Saku and A Le Coq, which come in a range of styles.

Getting Around

Bicycle Estonia is mercifully flat. Bike hire is offered in all the major cities.

Bus The national bus network is extensive, linking all the major cities to each other and the smaller towns to their regional hubs. All services are summarised on the extremely handy T pilet (www.tpilet.ee) site. Don't presume that drivers will speak English.

Car and motorcycle Estonian roads are generally very good and driving is easy. In rural areas, particularly on the islands, some roads are unsealed but they're usually kept in good condition.

Train Domestic routes are run by Elron (www.elron.ee), but it's also possible to travel between Tallinn and Narva on the Russian-bound services run by GoRail (www.gorail.ee).

When to Go

Tallinn

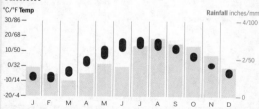

Dec–Jan Christmas markets, New Year's parties and the certainty of snow.

Jun–Jul Long, gentle, sunny days, festivals, a city open for business (and peak tourism season).

Sep The nights close in, the crowds fade, prices drop and you'll have more elbow room.

Arriving in Estonia

Tallinn Airport Bus 2 will take you to the city centre (€2) in about 20 minutes. A taxi should cost less than €10.

Ferries Most ferries and cruise ships dock at Old City Harbour (Vanasadama). There are regular buses to the city centre, while a taxi from any of the ferry terminals should cost about €5.

Tallinn Central Bus Station Bus 2 or tram 4 will get you there. Services depart from here for Latvia, Lithuania, Poland and other European destinations.

Top Phrases

Hello. Tere.

Goodbye. Nägemist.

Excuse me. Vabandage.

Sorry. Vabandust.

You're welcome. Sa oled teretulnud.

Resources

ERR (news.err.ee)

Visit Estonia (www.visit estonia.com)

Wifi Hotspots (www.wifi.ee)

Set Your Budget

➔ Budget hotel room: €20-45

➔ Two-course evening meal: €10-35

➔ Tallinn transport ticket: €1

Tallinn

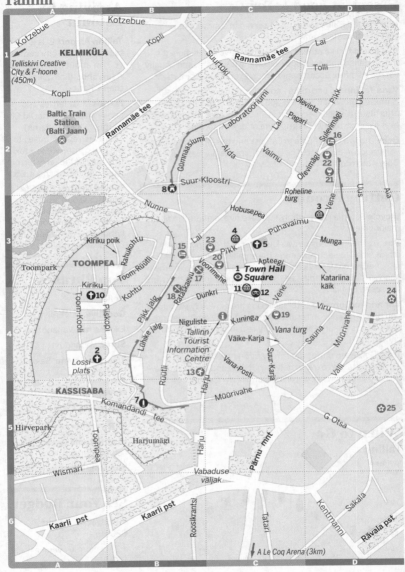

tower completed in 1779. This impressive building was a burial ground for the rich and titled, and the whitewashed walls are decorated with the elaborate coats-of-arms of Estonia's noble families. Fit view-seekers can climb the tower.

Alexander Nevsky Orthodox Cathedral
CATHEDRAL

(644 3484; http://tallinnanevskikatedraal.eu; Lossi plats 10; 8am-7pm, to 4pm winter) The positioning of this magnificent, onion-domed Russian Orthodox cathedral (completed

in droves, alongside tourists ogling the interior's striking icons and frescoes. Quiet, respectful, demurely dressed visitors are welcome but cameras aren't.

Bastion Passages　　　　　　TUNNEL
(Bastionikäigud; ☑644 6686; www.linnamuuseum.ee; Komandandi tee 2; adult/child €9/6; ☻10.30am-6pm Tue-Sun Mar-Oct) Tours exploring the 17th-century Swedish-built tunnels connecting the bastions that ring the town walls depart from the **Kiek in de Kök** (☑644 6686; www.linnamuuseum.ee; Komandandi tee 2; adult/child €6/4; ☻10.30am-6pm Tue-Sun Mar-Oct, 10am-5.30pm Nov-Feb) tower. Over the years, they've been used as fallout shelters, homeless refuges and punk rehearsal spaces. Bookings are required, and warm clothes

in 1900) at the heart of the country's main administrative hub was no accident: the church was one of many built in the last part of the 19th century as part of a general wave of Russification in the empire's Baltic provinces. Orthodox believers come here

(it's about 10°C down there) and sensible shoes are recommended. Regular tours finish in the Carved Stone Museum, showcasing tablets, statues and other historical lapidary work from Tallinn. Combined tour and tower tickets are available (€13).

City Centre

Hotel Viru KGB Museum
MUSEUM

(☑ 680 9300; www.viru.ee; Viru väljak 4; tour €12; ⊙ daily May-Oct, Tue-Sun Nov-Apr) When the Hotel Viru was built in 1972, it was not only Estonia's first skyscraper, it was the only place for tourists to stay in Tallinn – and we mean that literally. Having all the foreigners in one place made it much easier to keep tabs on them and the locals they had contact with, which is exactly what the KGB did from its 23rd-floor spy base. The hotel offers fascinating tours of the facility in various languages; bookings essential.

Linnahall
ARCHITECTURE

(City Hall; ☑ 641 2250; www.linnahall.ee; Mere pst 20) Resembling a cross between a nuclear bunker, a WWII sea-fort and some inscrutable temple to a vanished god, the Linnahall is in fact a covered concrete arena built for the 1980 Olympics. Originally named the Lenin Palace of Culture and Sport, it's an extraordinary structure – rotting, barred, weed-strewn and comprehensively graffitied. Heritage-listed and badly decayed as it is, Estonians and visitors alike are free to wander under its monumental shell. A major refurbishment is planned for spring 2019.

Rotermann Quarter
ARCHITECTURE

(Rotermanni kvartal; ☑ 626 4200; www.rotermann. eu; Rotermanni 8) With impressive contemporary architecture wedged between 19th-century brick warehouses, this development has transformed an outmoded (if historically very valuable) factory complex into the city's swankiest shopping and dining precinct. An artisan baker and butcher, together with a well-stocked cheese shop, also make it a good place to stock up on some supplies.

◉ Kadriorg Park

★ Kadriorg Art Museum
MUSEUM

(Kardrioru kunstimuuseum; ☑ 606 6400; www. kadriorumuuseum.ekm.ee; A Weizenbergi 37, Kadriorg Palace; adult/child €6.50/4.50; ⊙ 10am-6pm Tue & Thu-Sun May-Sep, to 5pm Thu-Sun Oct-Apr, to 8pm Wed year-round) Kadriorg Palace, a baroque beauty built by Peter the Great between 1718 and 1736, houses a branch of the Estonian Art Museum devoted to Dutch, German and Italian paintings from the 16th to the 18th centuries, and Russian works from the 18th to early 20th centuries (check out the decorative porcelain with Communist imagery upstairs). The pink building is exactly as frilly and fabulous as a palace ought to be and there's a handsome French-style formal garden at the rear.

★ Kumu
GALLERY

(☑ 602 6000; www.kumu.ekm.ee; A Weizenbergi 34, near Kadriorg Park; adult/student €8/6; ⊙ 10am-8pm Thu, to 6pm Wed & Fri-Sun year-round, plus 10am-6pm Tue Apr-Sep) This futuristic, Finnish-designed, seven-storey building is a spectacular structure of limestone, glass and copper, nicely integrated into the landscape. Kumu (the name is short for *kunstimuuseum*, or art museum) contains the country's largest repository of Estonian art as well as constantly changing contemporary exhibits. There's everything from venerable painted altarpieces to the work of contemporary Estonian artists such as Adamson-Eric.

Kadriorg Park
PARK

(Kadrioru park; www.kadriorupark.ee) About 2km east of Old Town, this beautiful park's ample acreage is Tallinn's favourite patch of green. Together with the baroque Kadriorg Palace, it was commissioned by the Russian tsar Peter the Great for his wife Catherine I soon after his conquest of Estonia (Kadriorg means 'Catherine's Valley' in Estonian).

◉ Other Neighbourhoods

Just past Maarjamäe the Pirita River enters Tallinn Bay and the city's favourite beach begins to unfurl. The area's other claim to fame was as the base for the sailing events of the 1980 Moscow Olympics; international regattas are still held here.

Buses 1A, 8, 34A and 38 all run between the city centre and Pirita.

Tallinn TV Tower
VIEWPOINT

(Tallinna teletorn; ☑ 686 3005; www.teletorn.ee; Kloostrimetsa tee 58a; adult/child €12/7; ⊙ 10am-7pm) Opened in time for the 1980 Olympics, this futuristic 314m tower offers brilliant views from its 22nd floor (175m). Press a button and frosted glass disks set in the floor suddenly clear, giving a view straight down. Once you're done gawping, check out the interactive displays in the space-age pods.

Daredevils can try the exterior, 175m-high 'edge walk' (€20, 10am-6pm).

★ **Estonian Open-Air Museum**   MUSEUM
(Eesti vabaõhumuuseum; ☑ 654 9101; www.evm. ee; Vabaõhumuuseumi tee 12, Rocca Al Mare; adult/ child high season €9/6, low season €7/5; ☺ 10am-8pm 23 Apr-28 Sep, to 5pm 29 Sep-22 Apr) If tourists won't go to the countryside, let's bring the countryside to them. That's the modus operandi of this excellent, sprawling complex, where historic Estonian buildings have been plucked and transplanted among the tall trees. In summer the time-warping effect is highlighted by staff in period costume performing traditional activities among the wooden farmhouses and windmills. There's a chapel dating from 1699 and an old wooden tavern, Kolu Kõrts, serving traditional Estonian cuisine.

★ **Lennusadam**   MUSEUM
(Seaplane Harbour; ☑ 620 0550; www.meremuuseum.ee; Vesilennuki 6; adult/child €14/7; ☺ 10am-7pm daily May-Sep, to 6pm Tue-Sun Oct-Apr; ℗) Surrounded on two sides by island-dotted waters, Estonia has a rich maritime history, explored in this fascinating museum filled with interactive displays. When the building, with its triple-domed hangar, was completed in 1917, its reinforced-concrete shell frame construction was unique in the world. Resembling a classic Bond-villain lair, the vast space was completely restored and opened to the public in 2012. Highlights include exploring the cramped corridors of a 1930s naval submarine, and the ice-breaker and minehunter ships moored outside.

🏃 Activities & Tours

Harju Ice Rink   ICE SKATING
(Harju tänava uisuplats; ☑ 56246739; www.uisuplats.ee; Harju; per hr adult/child €5/3; ☺ 10am-10pm Nov-Mar; ⊕) Wrap up warmly to join the locals at Old Town's outdoor ice rink – very popular in the winter months. You'll have earned a *hõõgvein* (mulled or 'glowing' wine) in the warm indoor cafe by the end of your skating session. Skate rental costs €3.

Tallinn Traveller Tours   TOURS
(☑ 58374800; www.traveller.ee) This outfit runs entertaining tours – including a two-hour Old Town walk departing from outside the tourist office (p809) (private groups of one to 15 people from €80, or there's a larger free tour, for which you should tip the engaging guides). There are also ghost tours (€15), bike tours (from €19), pub crawls (€20) and day trips as far afield as Rīga (€55).

Euroaudioguide   WALKING
(www.euroaudioguide.com; iPod rental €15) Preloaded iPods are available from the tourist office (p809) offering excellent commentary on most Old Town sights, with plenty of history thrown in. If you've got your own

RUSSIA & THE BALTIC COAST TALLINN

WORTH A TRIP

LAHEMAA NATIONAL PARK

A microcosm of Estonia's natural charms, this park takes in a stretch of deeply indented coast with several peninsulas and bays, plus 475 sq km of pine-fresh hinterland encompassing forest, lakes, rivers and peatbogs, and areas of historical and cultural interest.

Fully restored **Palmse Manor** (☑ 5559 9977; www.palmse.ee; adult/child €9/7; ☺ 10am-6pm) is the park's showpiece, housing the **visitor centre** (☑ 329 5555; www.loodusegakoos.ee; ☺ 9am-5pm daily mid-May–mid-Sep, 9am-5pm Mon-Fri mid-Sep–mid-May) in its former stables. The pretty manor house (1720, rebuilt in the 1780s) is now a museum containing period furniture and clothing. Other estate buildings have also been restored and put to new use: the distillery is a hotel, the steward's residence is a guesthouse, the lakeside bathhouse is a summertime restaurant, and the farm labourers' quarters became a tavern.

First mentioned in 1465, the fishing village of **Altja** has many restored or reconstructed traditional buildings, including a wonderfully ancient-looking tavern that was actually built in 1976. Altja's Swing Hill (Kiitemägi), complete with a traditional Estonian wooden swing, has long been the focus of Midsummer's Eve festivities in Lahemaa. The 3km circular **Altja Nature & Culture Trail** starts at Swing Hill and takes in net sheds, fishing cottages and the stone field known as the 'open-air museum of stones'.

Lahemaa is best explored by car or bicycle. The main bus routes through the park include Tallinn to Altja (€6.50, 1¾ hours, daily)

iPod, iPhone or iPad you can download the tour as an e-book (€10).

🛏 Sleeping

★ Tabinoya
HOSTEL €

(☑632 0062; www.tabinoya.com; Nunne 1; dm/d from €17/50; @🛜) The Baltic's first Japanese-run hostel occupies the two top floors of a charming old building, with dorms (the four-person one is for females only) and a communal lounge at the top, and spacious private rooms, a kitchen and a sauna below. Bathroom facilities are shared. The vibe's a bit more comfortable and quiet than most of Tallinn's hostels. Book ahead.

Tallinn Backpackers
HOSTEL €

(☑644 0298; www.tallinnbackpackers.com; Olevimägi 11; dm/r from €12/50; @🛜) In an ideal Old Town location, this place has a global feel and a roll-call of traveller-happy features: a convivial common room, free wi-fi and lockers, cheap dinners, a games room with tabletop football and a kitchen and laundry. There's also a regular roster of pub crawls and day trips to nearby attractions.

Red Emperor
HOSTEL €

(☑615 0035; www.redemperorhostel.com; Aia 10; dm/s/d from €13/22/34; @🛜) Situated above a wonderfully grungy live-music bar, Red Emperor is Tallinn's premier party hostel for those of a beardy, indie persuasion. Facilities are good, with rooms daubed with 'street art', wooden bunks named for global destinations and plenty of showers, and there are organized activities every day (karaoke, shared dinners etc). Pack heavy-duty earplugs if you're a light sleeper.

🍴 Eating

★ Vegan Restoran V
VEGAN €

(☑626 9087; www.vonkrahl.ee; Rataskaevu 12; mains €9-11; ⊘noon-11pm Sun-Thu, to midnight Fri & Sat; 🍴) Visiting vegans are spoiled for choice in this wonderful restaurant. In summer everyone wants one of the four tables on the street, but the atmospheric interior is just as appealing. The food is excellent – expect the likes of tempeh and veggies on brown rice with tomato-coconut sauce, and kale and lentil pie with creamy hemp-seed sauce.

F-hoone
PUB FOOD €

(☑53226855; www.fhoone.ee; Telliskivi 60a; mains €7-10; ⊘kitchen 9am-11pm Mon-Sat, to 9pm Sun; 🛜🍴) The trailblazing watering hole of the uberhip Telliskivi complex, the industrial-chic 'Building F' offers a quality menu of pasta, burgers, soups, salads and desserts in an always-lively atmosphere. Wash down your food with a craft beer from the extensive selection and remember to book a table on buzzing weekend evenings.

Kompressor
CRÊPES €

(☑646 4210; http://kompressorpub.ee; Rataskaevu 3; pancakes €5; ⊘11am-11pm) This Tallinn institution will plug any holes in your stomach with one of its 29 different sweet or savoury varieties of pancakes. Don't go thinking you'll have room for dessert, but do recognize this spot as a solid option for a budget drink – low on aesthetics and high on value.

🍷 Drinking & Nightlife

Tallinn's hipsters tend to leave the pricey bars of the Old Town to the tourists and head to Kalamaja instead. **Telliskivi Creative City** (Telliskivi Loomelinnak; www.telliskivi.eu; Telliskivi 60a; ⊘shops 10am-6pm Mon-Sat, 11am-5pm Sun; 🚇) is the liveliest nook but there are cosy local pubs scattered throughout the neighbourhood.

★ Levist Väljas
BAR

(☑5077372; Olevimägi 12; ⊘3pm-3am Mon-Thu, to 6am Fri & Sat, to midnight Sun) Inside this much-loved Tallinn cellar bar (usually the last pit stop of the night) you'll find broken furniture, cheap booze and a refreshingly motley crew of friendly punks, grunge kids and anyone else who strays from the well-trodden tourist path. The discreet entrance is down a flight of stairs.

★ No Ku Klubi
BAR

(☑631 3929; Pikk 5; ⊘noon-1am Mon-Thu, to 3am Fri, 2pm-3am Sat, 6pm-1am Sun) A nondescript red-and-blue door, a key-code to enter, a clubbable atmosphere of regulars lounging in mismatched armchairs – could this be Tallinn's ultimate 'secret' bar? Once the surreptitious haunt of artists in Soviet times, it's now free for all to enter – just ask one of the smokers outside for the code. Occasional evenings of low-key music and film are arranged.

DM Baar
BAR

(☑644 2350; www.depechemode.ee; Voorimehe 4; ⊘noon-4am Mon-Sat, to midnight Sun) If you just can't get enough of Depeche Mode, this is the bar for you. The walls are covered with all manner of memorabilia (including pictures of the actual band partying here) and there's a full list of DM-themed cocktails. And the soundtrack? Do you really need to ask? If you're not a fan, leave in silence.

☆ Entertainment

Tallinn's small as national capitals go, but there's still plenty to keep you stimulated. Bills, flyers and newspapers advertise events around the city, or find Tallinn's best English-language listings in the bimonthly *Tallinn In Your Pocket* (€2.50, or free at www. inyourpocket.com). There's also *Tallinn This Week* (actually also bimonthly, and free) www.culture.ee, www.concert.ee, www. draamamaa.ee and the ticketing service Piletilevi (www.piletilevi.ee).

Tallinners love live music of all genres, and summer's frequent festivals are augmented, year-round, by plenty of concert venues in and around the city. **Kultuuriklubi Kelm** (☑ 58937217; Vene 33; ☺ 6pm-1am Mon & Tue, to 3am Wed & Thu, to 5am Fri, 7pm-5am Sat, 7pm-1am Sun), **Clazz** (☑ 666 0003; Vana turg 2; ☺ 6pm-midnight Mon, to 2am Tue-Thu, to 3am Fri, 2pm-3am Sat), **Chicago 1933** (☑ 627 1266; www.chicago.ee; Aia 3; ☺ noon-midnight Mon & Tue, to 1am Wed & Thu, to 3am Fri, 2pm-3am Sat, 2pm-midnight Sun; ☎) and **Rockclub Tapper** (☑ 654 7518; www.tapper.ee; Pärnu mnt 158g; varies by event; ☺ varies by event) all host regular live shows. Touring international acts usually perform at **Tallinn Song Festival Grounds** (Tallinna lauluväljak; ☑ 611 2102; www. lauluvaljak.ee; Narva mnt 95; ☺ lighthouse 8am-4pm Mon-Fri) FREE, **A Le Coq Arena** (Asula 4c) or **Saku Suurhall** (☑ 660 0200; www.sakusuur-hall.ee; Paldiski mnt 104b).

For major classical concerts, check out what's on at the **Estonia Concert Hall** (Eesti Kontserdisaal; ☑ 614 7771; www.concert.ee; Estonia pst 4). Chamber, organ and smaller-scale concerts are held at various halls and churches around town.

ℹ Information

Tallinn Tourist Information Centre (☑ 645 7777; www.visittallinn.ee; Niguliste 2; ☺ 9am-7pm Mon-Sat, to 6pm Sun Jun-Aug, shorter hours rest of year) Has a full range of brochures, maps, event schedules and other info, for Tallinn and for Estonia generally.

ℹ Getting There & Away

AIR

Tallinn Airport (Tallinna Lennujaam; ☑ 605 8888; www.tallinn-airport.ee; Tartu mnt 101)

is 4km southeast of the Old Town. Numerous airlines fly to Tallinn from within the Baltic region and from further afield.

BOAT

Ferries head to Tallinn from Helsinki and other Baltic ports.

BUS

Regional and international buses depart from the **Central Bus Station** (Tallinna bussijaam; ☑ 12550; www.bussijaam.ee; Lastekodu 46; ☺ ticket office 7am-9pm Mon-Sat, 8am-8pm Sun), about 2km southeast of the Old Town; tram 2 or 4 will get you there. Services depart from here for Latvia and other European destinations. Main domestic routes include Tartu (€7 to €12, 2½ hours, at least every half-hour) and Pärnu (€6.50 to €11, two hours, at least hourly).

TRAIN

The **Baltic Train Station** (Balti Jaam; Toompuiestee 35) is on the northwestern edge of the Old Town. Despite the name, there are no direct services to the other Baltic states. Destinations include Tartu (€12, two to 2½ hours, eight daily) and Pärnu (€7.90, 2¼ hours, three daily).

ℹ Getting Around

TO/FROM THE AIRPORT

→ Bus 2 runs roughly every 20 minutes (6.30am to around midnight) from the A Laikmaa stop, opposite the Tallink Hotel, next to Viru Keskus. From the airport, bus 2 will take you via six bus stops to the centre and on to the passenger port. Buy tickets from the driver (€2); journey time depends on traffic, but rarely exceeds 20 minutes.

→ A taxi between the airport and the city centre should cost less than €10.

TO/FROM THE FERRY TERMINALS

Most ferries and cruise ships dock at the Old City Harbour (Vanasadama). Eckerö Line, Viking Line and St Peter Line use **Terminals A & B** (Sadama 25/2 & 3) while Tallink uses **Terminal D** (Lootsi 13), just across the marina. Linda Line ferries dock a little further west at the hulking **Linnahall** (Kalasadama).

All terminals are a short (less than 1km) walk from the Old Town, but there are also buses and tram connections. A taxi between the city centre and any of the terminals should only cost about €5.

PUBLIC TRANSPORT

Tallinn has an excellent network of buses, trams and trolleybuses running from around 6am to 11pm or midnight. The major **local bus station** is beneath the Viru Keskus shopping centre, although some buses terminate their routes on the surrounding streets. All local public transport timetables are online at www.tallinn.ee.

Public transport is free for Tallinn residents, children under seven and adults with children under three. Others need to pay, either buying a paper ticket from the driver (€2 for a single journey, exact change required) or by using the e-ticketing system. Buy a Ühiskaart (a smartcard, requiring a €2 deposit which can't be recouped within six months of validation) at an R-Kiosk, post office or the Tallinn City Government customer service desk, add credit, then validate the card at the start of each journey using the orange card-readers. E-ticket fares are €1.10/3/6 for an hour/day/five days.

The Tallinn Card includes free public transport on all services for the duration of its validity. Travelling without a valid ticket runs the risk of a €40 fine.

TAXI

Taxis are plentiful but each company sets its own fare; prices should be posted prominently. However, if you hail a taxi on the street, there's a chance you'll be overcharged; to save yourself the trouble, order a taxi by phone. Operators speak English. Well-established taxi firms include **Krooni Takso** (☑ 1212; www.kroonitakso.ee; base fare €2.50, per km €0.50-0.55) and **Reval Takso** (☑ 1207; www.reval-takso.ee; base fare €2.29, per km €0.49).

Tartu

POP 98,000

Tartu lays claim to being Estonia's spiritual capital, with locals talking about a special Tartu *vaim* (spirit) created by the time-stands-still feel of its wooden houses and stately buildings, and by the beauty of its parks and riverfront. It's also Estonia's premier university town, with students making up nearly a seventh of the population – guaranteeing a vibrant nightlife for a city of its size.

◎ Sights

◎ Old Town

★**Town Hall Square**   SQUARE
(Raekoja plats) Tartu's main square is lined with grand buildings and echoes with the chink of glasses and plates in summer. The centrepiece is the Town Hall itself, fronted by a statue of students kissing under a spouting umbrella. On the south side of the square, look out for the communist hammer-and-sickle relief that still remains on the facade of number 5.

Tartu University   UNIVERSITY
(Tartu Ülikool; www.ut.ee; Ülikooli 18) Fronted by six Doric columns, the impressive main building of Tartu University was built between 1803 and 1809. The university itself was founded in 1632 by the Swedish king Gustaf II Adolf (Gustavus Adolphus) to train Lutheran clergy and government officials. It was modelled on Uppsala University in Sweden.

Tartu University Art Museum   MUSEUM
(Tartu Ülikooli kunstimuuseum; www.kunstimuuseum.ut.ee; Ülikooli 18; adult/child €4/3; ◎ 10am-6pm Mon-Sat May-Sep, 11am-5pm Mon-Fri Oct-Apr) Within the main university building, this collection comprises mainly plaster casts of ancient Greek sculptures made in the 1860s and 1870s, along with an Egyptian mummy. The rest of the collection was evacuated to Russia in 1915 and has never returned. Admission includes entry to the graffiti-covered attic **lock-up**, where students were held in solitary confinement for various infractions.

◎ Toomemägi

Rising to the west of the town hall, Toomemägi (Cathedral Hill) is the original reason for Tartu's existence, functioning on and off as a stronghold from around the 5th or 6th century. It's now a tranquil park, with walking paths meandering through the trees and a pretty-as-a-picture **rotunda** that serves as a summertime cafe.

★**University of Tartu Museum**   MUSEUM
(Tartu Ülikool muuseum; ☑ 737 5674; www.muuseum.ut.ee; Lossi 25; adult/child €5/4; ◎ 10am-6pm Tue-Sun May-Sep, 11am-5pm Wed-Sun Oct-Apr) Atop Toomemägi are the ruins of a Gothic cathedral, originally built by German knights in the 13th century. It was substantially rebuilt in the 15th century, despoiled during the Reformation in 1525, used as a barn, and partly rebuilt between 1804 and 1809 to house the university library, which is now a museum. Inside there are a range of interesting exhibits chronicling student life.

◎ Other Neighbourhoods

★**Estonian National Museum**   MUSEUM
(Eesti rahva muuseum; ☑ 736 3051; www.erm.ee; Muuseumi tee 2; adult/child €14/10; ◎ 10am-6pm

Tartu

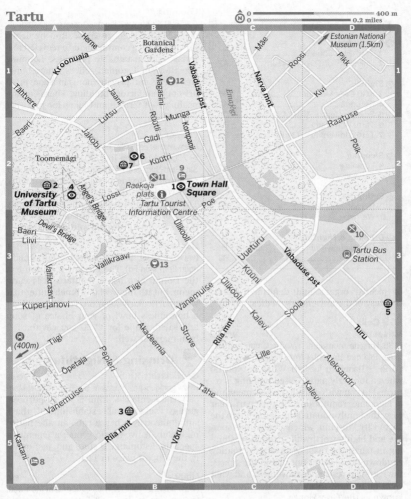

Tue & Thu-Sun, 10am-8pm Wed) This immense, low-slung, architectural showcase is a striking sight and had both Estonian patriots and architecture-lovers purring when it opened in late 2016. The permanent exhibition covers national prehistory and history in some detail. Fittingly, for a museum built over a former Soviet airstrip, the Russian occupation is given in-depth treatment, while the 'Echo of the Urals' exhibition gives an overview of the various peoples speaking tongues in the Estonian language family. There's also a restaurant and cafe.

Science Centre AHHAA   MUSEUM
(Teaduskeskus AHHAA; www.ahhaa.ee; Sadama 1; adult/child €13/10, planetarium €4, flight simulator €1; ⊙10am-7pm Sun-Thu, 10am-8pm Fri & Sat) Head under the dome for a whizz-bang series of interactive exhibits which are liable to bring out the mad scientist in kids and adults alike. Allow at least a couple of hours for button pushing, water squirting and knob twiddling. And you just haven't lived until you've set a tray of magnetised iron filings 'dancing' to Bronski Beat's *Smalltown Boy*. Upstairs there's a nightmarish collection

Tartu

of pickled organs and deformed fetuses courtesy of the university's medical faculty.

KGB Cells Museum

MUSEUM

(KGB kongide muuseum; www.linnamuuseum.tartu.ee; Riia mnt 15b, enter from Pepleri; adult/child €4/2; ⊙11am-5pm Tue-Sat) What do you do when a formerly nationalised building is returned to you with cells in the basement and a fearsome reputation? In this particular case, the family donated the basement to the Tartu City Museum, which created this sombre and highly worthwhile exhibition. Chilling in parts, the displays give a fascinating rundown on deportations, life in the gulags, the Estonian resistance movement and what went on in these former KGB headquarters, known as the 'Grey House'.

🛏 Sleeping & Eating

Terviseks

HOSTEL €

(📞565 5382; www.terviseksbbb.com; top fl, Raekoja plats 10; dm €15-17, s/d €22/44; @ 🛜) Occupying a historic building in a perfect main-square location, this excellent 'backpacker's bed and breakfast' offers dorms (maximum four beds, no bunks), private rooms, a full kitchen and lots of switched-on info about the happening places in town. It's like staying in your rich mate's cool European pad. Cheers (terviseks!) to that.

Looming

HOSTEL €

(📞5699 4398; www.loominghostel.ee; Kastani 38; dm €13-18, d €34-36; @ 🛜) 🖉 Run by urban greenies with a commitment to recycled materials and sustainable practices, Looming ('creation' in Estonian) offers smart bunk-free dorms and private rooms in a converted art-nouveau factory building. There's an appealing roof terrace and bikes for rent (per day €10).

Werner

CAFE €

(www.werner.ee; Ülikooli 11; baked items €2-5; ⊙7.30am-11pm Mon-Thu, 7.30am-1am Fri, 8am-1am Sat, 9am-9pm Sun) Upstairs there's a proper restaurant serving pasta and meaty mains, but we prefer the buzzy cafe downstairs. The counter positively groans under a hefty array of quiches and tempting cakes, plus there's a sweet little courtyard at the back.

Dorpat

BUFFET €

(www.dorpat.ee; Soola 6; buffet €5-7.50; ⊙buffet noon-2pm Mon-Fri) The elegant restaurant at the Dorpat also has a reputable a la carte menu, but it's the weekday lunch buffet that we're particularly keen on. For €5 you'll get a bottomless bowl of your choice of soup and salad, while for €7.50 you get the full bain-marie as well.

🍷 Drinking & Nightlife

Genialistide Klubi

CLUB

(www.genklubi.ee; Magasini 5; ⊙noon-3am Mon-Sat) The Genialists' Club is an all-purpose, grungy 'subcultural establishment' that's simultaneously a bar, a cafe, an alternative nightclub, a live-music venue, a cinema, a specialist Estonian CD store and, just quietly, the hippest place in Tartu.

Naiiv

BAR

(www.naiiv.ee; Vallikraavi 6; ⊙6pm-1am Mon-Wed, to 2am Thur, to 3am Fri & Sat) An imperious white cat holds court at this very cool craft beer and cocktail bar. The selection is extensive, so ask the clued up staff for suggestions on good local brews, then find a comfy sofa to sink into or head out to the small rear courtyard.

ℹ Information

Tartu Tourist Information Centre (📞744 2111; www.visittartu.com; Town Hall, Raekoja plats; ⊙9am-6pm Mon-Fri, 10am-5pm Sat & Sun mid-May–mid-Sep, 9am-6pm Mon, 9am-5pm Tue-Fri, 10am-2pm Sat mid-Sep–mid-May) Stocks local maps and brochures, books accommodation and tour guides, and has free internet access.

ℹ️ Getting There & Away

Tartu Airport (TAY; ☑ 605 8888; www.tartu-airport.ee; Lennu tn 44, Reola küla), 9km south of the city centre, offers daily Finnair services to and from Helsinki.

Regional and international (p816) buses depart from **Tartu Bus Station** (Tartu Autobussijaam; Turu 2, enter from Soola; ☺ 6am-9pm), which is attached to the Tasku shopping centre.

Major domestic routes includeTallinn (€7 to €12, 2½ hours, at least every half hour) and Pärnu (€9.60 to €12, 2¾ hours, 12 daily)

Tartu's beautifully restored wooden **train station** (☑ 673 7400; www.elron.ee; Vaksali 6), is 1.5km southwest of the Old Town at the end of Kuperjanovi street. Four express (2½-hour) and four regular (two-hour) services head to Tallinn daily (both €11).

Pärnu

POP 39,800

Local families, hormone-sozzled youths and German, Swedish and Finnish holidaymakers join together in a collective prayer for sunny weather while strolling the beaches, sprawling parks and picturesque historic centre of Pärnu (*pair*-nu), Estonia's premier seaside resort.

◉ Sights

Pärnu straddles both sides of the Pärnu River at the point where it empties into Pärnu Bay. The south bank contains the major attractions, including the Old Town and the beach. The main thoroughfare of the historic centre is Rüütli, lined with splendid buildings dating back to the 17th century.

★ Pärnu Beach   BEACH
Pärnu's long, wide, sandy beach – sprinkled with volleyball courts, cafes and changing cubicles – is easily the city's main drawcard. A curving path stretches along the sand, lined with fountains, park benches and an excellent playground. Early-20th-century buildings are strung along Ranna pst, the avenue that runs parallel to the beach. Across the road, the formal gardens of **Rannapark** are ideal for a summertime picnic.

★ Museum of New Art   GALLERY
(Uue kunstimuuseum; ☑ 443 0772; www.mona. ee; Esplanaadi 10; adult/child €4/2; ☺ 9am-9pm Jun-Aug, 9am-7pm Sep-May) Pärnu's former Communist Party headquarters now houses one of Estonia's edgiest galleries. As part of its commitment to pushing the cultural envelope, it stages an international nude art exhibition every summer. Founded by film-maker Mark Soosaar, the gallery also hosts the annual Pärnu Film Festival.

Tallinn Gate   GATE
(Tallinna Värav) The typical star shape of the 17th-century Swedish ramparts that once surrounded the Old Town can easily be spotted on a colour map as most of the pointy bits are now parks. The only intact section, complete with its moat, lies to the west of the centre. Where the rampart meets the western end of Kuninga, it's pierced by this tunnel-like gate that once defended the main road which headed to the river-ferry crossing and on to Tallinn.

🏃 Activities

Tervise Paradiis Veekeskus   WATER PARK
(www.terviseparadiis.ee; Side 14; adult/child 3hr €16/11, 1 day €21/17; ☺ 10am-10pm Jun-Aug, from 11am Sep-May) At the far end of the beach, Estonia's largest water park beckons with pools, slides, tubes and other slippery fun. It's a big family-focused draw, especially when bad weather ruins beach plans. The large resort also offers spa treatments, fitness classes and ten-pin bowling.

Hedon Spa   SPA
(☑ 449 9011; www.hedonspa.com; Ranna pst 1; treatments from €30; ☺ 9am-7pm Mon-Sat, to 5pm Sun) Built in 1927 to house Pärnu's famous mud baths, this handsome neoclassical building has recently been fully restored and opened as a day spa. All manner of pampering treatments are offered, only some of which involve mud.

🛏️ Sleeping & Eating

Konse Motel & Camping   CAMPGROUND €
(☑ 5343 5092; www.konse.ee; Suur-Jõe 44a; sites €18, r with/without bathroom from €52/40; 🅿️@🛜) Crammed beside the river about 1km from the centre, Konse offers camping and a variety of rooms, all with kitchen access. It's not an especially charming spot but there is a sauna (per hour €15), and bike (per day €10) and rowboat (per hour €10) rental.

★ Piccadilly   CAFE €
(☑ 442 0085; www.kohvila.com; Pühavaimu 15; dishes €4-8; ☺ 9am-8pm Mon-Thu, 11am-11pm Fri-Sat, 11am-8pm Sun; ☑) Piccadilly offers

Pärnu

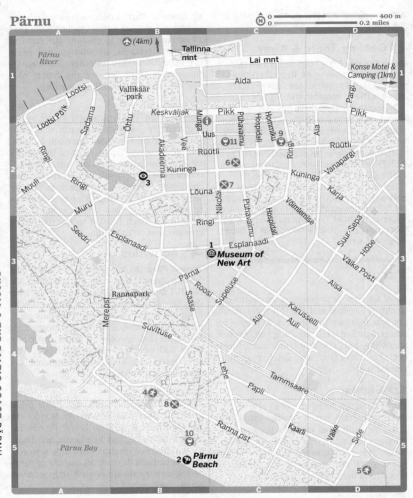

RUSSIA & THE BALTIC COAST PÄRNU

a down-tempo haven for wine-lovers and vegetarians and an extensive range of hot beverages. Savoury options include delicious salads, sandwiches and omelettes, but really it's all about the sweeties, including moreish cheesecake and handmade chocolates.

Steffani　　　　　　　　　　　　PIZZA €
(www.steffani.ee; Nikolai 24; mains €6-8; ⊙11am-midnight Sun-Thu, to 2am Fri & Sat; ⊛) The queue out front should alert you – this is a top choice for thin-crust and pan pizzas, particularly in summer when you can dine

alfresco on the big, flower-filled terrace. The menu also stretches to pasta and, oddly, burritos. During summer it also operates out of a **beach branch** (Ranna pst 1; mains €6-8).

🍷 Drinking & Nightlife

Veerev Õlu　　　　　　　　　　　PUB
(Uus 3a; ⊙11am-midnight Mon-Sat, from 1pm Sun) Named after the Rolling Stones, the 'Rolling Beer' wins the award for the friendliest and cosiest pub by a long shot. It's a tiny rustic space with good vibes, cheap beer and the occasional live folk-rock band (with compulsory dancing on tables, it would seem).

Pärnu

Puhvet APTEK   BAR

(www.aptek.ee; Rüütli 40; ⊙8pm-2am Wed & Thu, to 5am Fri & Sat) Drop by the old 1930s pharmacy to admire the clever restoration that has turned it into a smooth late-night haunt. Fabulous decor (including original cabinets, vials and bottles) competes for your attention with cocktails and DJs.

Sunset   CLUB

(www.sunset.ee; Ranna pst 3; ⊙11pm-6am Fri & Sat Jun-Aug) Pärnu's biggest and most famous summertime nightclub has an outdoor beach terrace and a sleek multifloor interior with plenty of nooks for when the dance floor gets crowded. Imported DJs and bands keep things cranked until the early hours.

ⓘ Information

Pärnu Tourist Information Centre (☑447 3000; www.visitparnu.com; Uus 4; ⊙9am-6pm mid-May–mid-Sep, 9am-5pm Mon-Fri, 10am-2pm Sat & Sun mid-Sep–mid-May) A very helpful centre stocking maps and brochures, booking accommodation and rental cars (for a small fee), and providing a left-luggage service (per day €2). There's a small gallery attached as well as a toilet and showers.

ⓘ Getting There & Away

Buses stop at the corner of Pikk and Ringi, but the main **bus station ticket office** (Ringi 3; ⊙8am-7.30pm Mon-Fri, to 5pm Sat, 9am-5pm Sun) is about 100m away (look for the red 'bussijaam' sign). International coaches head from here to as far afield as St Petersburg and Vilnius. Domestic destinations include Tallinn (€6.50 to

€11, two hours, at least hourly) and Tartu (€9.60 to €12, 2¾ hours,12 daily).

Three daily trains run between Tallinn and Pärnu (€7.60, 2¼ hours), but this isn't a great option given that **Pärnu station** (Liivi tee) is an inconvenient 5km east of the town centre in a difficult to find and to access spot on a major road.

Estonia Survival Guide

ⓘ Directory A–Z

ACCOMMODATION

If you like flying by the seat of your pants when you're travelling, you'll find July and August in Estonia very problematic. The best accommodation books up quickly and in Tallinn, especially on weekends, you might find yourself scraping for anywhere at all to lay your head. In fact, Tallinn gets busy most weekends, so try to book about a month ahead anytime from May to September (midweek isn't anywhere near as bad).

Budget catagory accommodation (€) has double rooms and/or dorm beds for less than €35.

PUBLIC HOLIDAYS

New Year's Day (Uusaasta) 1 January

Independence Day (Iseseisvuspäev) Anniversary of 1918 declaration on 24 February

Good Friday (Suur reede) March/April

Easter Sunday (Lihavõtted) March/April

Spring Day (Kevadpüha) 1 May

Pentecost (Nelipühade) Seventh Sunday after Easter (May/June)

Victory Day (Võidupüha) Commemorating the anniversary of the Battle of Võnnu (1919) on 23 June.

St John's Day (Jaanipäev, Midsummer's Day). Taken together, Victory Day and St John's Day on 24 June are the excuse for a week-long midsummer break for many people.

Day of Restoration of Independence (Taasiseseisvumispäev) On 20 August, marking the country's return to Independence in 1991.

Christmas Eve (Jõululaupäev) 24 December

Christmas Day (Jõulupüha) 25 December

Boxing Day (Teine jõulupüha) 26 December

TELEPHONE

There are no area codes in Estonia; if you're calling anywhere within the country, just dial the number as it's listed. All landline phone numbers have seven digits; mobile (cell) numbers have seven or eight digits and begin with 5. Estonia's country code is 372.

TOURIST INFORMATION

In addition to the info-laden, multilingual website of the Estonian Tourist Board (www.visitestonia.

> **ⓘ PRICE RANGES**
>
> ....
>
> The following price ranges refer to a double room in high (but not necessary peak) seaon.
>
> € less than €35
>
> €€ €35–100
>
> The following eating price ranges refer to a standard main course.
>
> € less than €10
>
> €€ €10 to €15

com), there are tourist offices in most cities and many towns and national parks throughout the country. At nearly every one you'll find English-speaking staff and lots of free material.

ⓘ Getting There & Away

AIR

Eleven European airlines have scheduled services to Tallinn year-round, with additional routes and airlines added in summer. There are also daily flights between Helsinki and Tartu.

LAND
Bus

Ecolines (www.ecolines.net), Lux Express & Simple Express (www.luxexpress.eu) and Toks (http://toks.lt) offer services between Estonia and the other Baltic states.

Train

Valga is the terminus for both the Estonian and Latvian rail systems, but the train services don't connect up. From Valga, Estonian trains operated by Elron (http://elron.ee) head to Tartu, while Latvian trains operated by Pasažieru vilciens (www.pv.lv) head to Valmiera, Cēsis, Sigulda and Rīga. There are also direct trains to Tallinn from St Petersburg and Moscow.

SEA

Tallinn has ferry connections to Helsinki and other Baltic ports.

ⓘ Getting Around

BUS

➡ The national bus network is extensive, linking all the major cities to each other and the smaller towns to their regional hubs.

➡ All services are summarised on the extremely handy T pilet (www.tpilet.ee) site.

➡ Don't presume that drivers will speak English.

➡ Concessions are available for children and seniors.

TRAIN

Train services have been steadily improving in recent years. Domestic routes are run by Elron (www.elron.ee), but it's also possible to travel between Tallinn and Narva on the Russian-bound services run by GoRail (www.gorail.ee)

LATVIA

Rīga

POP 703,500

The Gothic spires that dominate Rīga's cityscape might suggest austerity, but it is the flamboyant art nouveau that forms the flesh and the spirit of this vibrant cosmopolitan city, the largest of all three Baltic capitals. Like all northerners, it is quiet and reserved on the outside, but there is some powerful chemistry going on inside its hip bars and modern art centres, and in the kitchens of its cool experimental restaurants. Standing next to a gulf named after itself, Rīga is a short drive from the jet-setting sea resort of Jūrmala, which comes with a stunning white-sand beach. But if you are craving solitude and a pristine environment, gorgeous sand dunes and blueberry-filled forests, begin right outside the city boundaries.

◉ Sights

◉ Old Rīga (Vecrīga)

★ **Rīga Cathedral**   CHURCH
(Rīgas Doms; ☑ 6722 7573; www.doms.lv; Doma laukums 1; €3; ⊙ 10am-5pm Oct-Jun, 9am-6pm Sat-Tue, 9am-5pm Wed & Fri, 9am-5.30pm Thu Jul-Sep) Founded in 1211 as the seat of the Rīga diocese, this enormous (once Catholic, now Evangelical Lutheran) cathedral is the largest medieval church in the Baltic. The architecture is an amalgam of styles from the 13th to the 18th centuries: the eastern end, the oldest portion, has Romanesque features; the tower is 18th-century baroque; and much of the rest dates from a 15th-century Gothic rebuilding.

★ **Art Museum Rīga Bourse**   MUSEUM
(Mākslas muzejs Rīgas Birža; ☑ 6732 4461; www.lnmm.lv; Doma laukums 6; adult/child €6/3; ⊙ 10am-6pm Tue-Thu, Sat & Sun, to 8pm Fri) Rīga's lavishly restored stock exchange building is a worthy showcase for the city's art treasures. The elaborate facade features a coterie

of deities that dance between the windows, while inside, gilt chandeliers sparkle from ornately moulded ceilings. The Oriental section features beautiful Chinese and Japanese ceramics and an Egyptian mummy, but the main halls are devoted to Western art, including a Monet painting and a scaled-down cast of Rodin's *The Kiss*.

★ **Arsenāls Exhibition Hall**   GALLERY
(Izstāžu zāle Arsenāls; ☑ 6732 4461; www.lnmm.lv; Torņa iela 1; adult/child €3.50/2; ☺ 11am-6pm Tue, Wed & Fri, to 8pm Thu, noon-5pm Sat & Sun) Behind a row of spooky granite heads depicting Latvia's most prominent artists, the imperial arsenal, constructed in 1832 to store weapons for the Russian tzar's army, is now a prime spot for international and local art exhibitions, which makes it worth a visit whenever you are in Rīga. Also check out the massive wooden stairs at the back of the building – their simple yet funky geometry predates modern architecture.

★ **Blackheads House**   HISTORIC BUILDING
(Melngalvju nams; ☑ 6704 3678; www.melngalvjunams.lv; Rātslaukums 7) Built in 1344 as a veritable fraternity house for the Blackheads guild of unmarried German merchants, the original house was decimated in 1941 and flattened by the Soviets seven years later. Somehow the original blueprints survived and an exact replica of this fantastically ornate structure was completed in 2001 for Rīga's 800th birthday.

Rīga History & Navigation Museum   MUSEUM
(Rīgas vēstures un kuģniecības muzejs; ☑ 6735 6676; www.rigamuz.lv; Palasta iela 4; adult/child €4.27/0.71; ☺ 10am-5pm May-Sep, 11am-5pm Wed-Sun Oct-Apr) Founded in 1773, this is the oldest museum in the Baltic, situated in the old cathedral monastery. The permanent collection features artefacts from the Bronze Age all the way to WWII, ranging from lovely pre-Christian jewellery to preserved hands removed from Medieval forgers. A highlight is the beautiful neoclassical Column Hall, built when Latvia was part of the Russian empire and filled with relics from that time.

Cat House   HISTORIC BUILDING
(Kaķu māja; Miestaru iela 10/12) The spooked black cats mounted on the turrets of this 1909 art nouveau–influenced building have become a symbol of Rīga. According to local legend, the building's owner was rejected from the Great Guild across the street from

exacted revenge by pointing the cats' butts towards the hall. The members of the guild were outraged, and after a lengthy court battle the merchant was admitted into the club on the condition that the cats be turned in the opposite direction.

Museum of Decorative Arts & Design   MUSEUM
(Dekoratīvi lietišķās mākslas muzejs; ☑ 6732 4461; www.lnmm.lv; Skārņu iela 10/20; adult/child €5/2.50; ☺ 11am-5pm Tue & Thu-Sun, to 7pm Wed) The former St George's Church houses a museum devoted to applied art from the art nouveau period to the present, including an impressive collection of furniture, woodcuts, tapestries and ceramics. The building's foundations date back to 1207 when the Livonian Brothers of the Sword erected their castle here. Since the rest of the original knights' castle was levelled by rioting citizens at the end of the same century, it is the only building that remains intact since the birth of Rīga.

◎ **Central Rīga (Centrs)**

Pilsētas Kanāls (City Canal)   PARK
Pilsētas kanāls, the city's old moat, once protected the medieval interior from invaders.

> **DON'T MISS**
>
> ### ART NOUVEAU RĪGA
>
> Just when you thought that Old Rīga was the most beautiful neighbourhood in town, the city's audacious art nouveau district (focused around Alberta iela, Strēlnieku iela and Elizabetes iela) swoops in to vie for the prize. Rīga boasts over 750 Jugendstil (art nouveau) buildings, making it the city with the most art nouveau architecture in the world.
>
> **Alberta iela** is like a huge painting that you can spend hours staring at, as your eye detects more and more intriguing details. But this must-see Rīga sight is a rather functional street with residential houses, restaurants and shops. The master responsible for most of these is Mikhail Eisenstein (father of filmmaker Sergei Eisenstein). Named after the founder of Rīga, Bishop Albert von Buxthoeven, the street was the architect's gift to Rīga on its 700th anniversary.

 LATVIA AT A GLANCE

Don't Miss

Rīga Over 750 buildings in Latvia's capital – more than any other city in Europe – boast the flamboyant and haunting art nouveau style of decor. Spend a breezy afternoon snapping your camera at the imaginative facades in the city's Quiet Centre district to find an ethereal (and almost eerie) melange of screaming demons, enraptured deities, overgrown flora and bizarre geometrical patterns.

Jūrmala While the sanatorium craze has come and gone, Jūrmala remains an uber-popular place to pamper oneself silly, with unending menus of bizarre services (chocolate massages?). Even if you're not particularly keen to swim at the shallow beach, it's well worth the day trip from the Latvian capital to check out the wonderful old wooden mansions and witness the ostentatious presentations of the nouveau riche.

Cēsis With its stunning medieval castle, cobbled streets, green hills and landscaped garden, Cēsis is simply the cutest little town in the whole of Latvia. There's also the whole of Gauja National Park around it to explore.

Sigulda Known locally as the 'Switzerland of Latvia', Sigulda offers scenic trails, extreme sports and 13th-century castles steeped in legends. Don't miss riding the cable car across the valley for an awesome aerial perspective.

Kuldīga Joining swarms of fish trying to jump over the Ventas Rumba waterfall, the widest (and possibly the shortest) in Europe. The Old Town's picturesque streets make it a favourite spot to shoot Latvian period-piece films.

Itineraries

Three Days

Spend a morning wandering among the twisting cobbled lanes that snake through medieval **Old Rīga**. After a leisurely lunch, wander beyond the ancient walls, passing the Freedom Monument as you make your way to the grand boulevards that radiate from the city's castle core. Head to the Quiet Centre, where you'll find some of Rīga's finest examples of art nouveau architecture. Don't miss the Rīga Art Nouveau Centre.

On your second day, fine-tune your bargaining skills during a visit to the Central Market, where you can haggle for anything from wildberries to knock-off T-shirts. Have a walk through the small Spīķeri district then take a relaxing boat ride along the Daugava and the city's inner canals. For a late lunch, wander through the Quiet Centre all the way up to Miera iela to enjoy the city's emerging hipster cafe culture near the sweet-smelling Laima chocolate factory.

On day three pack your swimsuit and head out of town to the silky sands in **Jūrmala**.

One Week

Spend a couple of extra days exploring some of Rīga's lesser-known nooks. Head out to **Gauja National Park** for an action-packed day of castle-ogling mixed with adventure sports. In **Sigulda** get the blood rushing on the Olympic bobsled track. Also make an excursion to the fortress ruins in **Cēsis**.

Essential Food & Drink

Black Balzām The jet-black, 45%-proof concoction is a secret recipe of more than a dozen fairy-tale ingredients. A shot a day keeps the doctor away, so say most of Latvia's pensioners.

Mushrooms A national obsession; mushroom-picking takes the country by storm during the first showers of autumn.

Smoked fish Dozens of fish shacks dot the Kurzeme coast – look for the veritable smoke signals rising above the tree line. Grab 'em to go; they make the perfect afternoon snack.

Alus Each major town has its own beer. You can't go wrong with Užavas (Ventspils' contribution).

Kvass A beloved beverage made from fermented rye bread.

Getting Around

Buses Much more convenient than trains if you're travelling beyond the capital's clutch of suburban rail lines. Updated timetables are available at www.autoosta.lv and www.1188.lv.

Car and motorcycle Driving is on the right-hand side. Headlights must be on at all times. Be sure to ask for 'benzene' when looking for a petrol station – gāze means 'air'.

Train Convenient for a limited number of destinations, most notably Jūrmala, Gauja National Park and Daugavpils. All train schedule queries can be answered at www.pv.lv as well as at www.1188.lv.

When to Go

Rīga

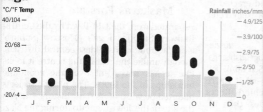

°C/°F Temp
Rainfall inches/mm

40/104 — — 4.9/125
— 3.9/100
20/68 — — 2.9/75
— 2/50
0/32 — — 1/25
-20/-4 — — 0

J F M A M J J A S O N D

Dec–Jan Spend the holidays in the birthplace of the Christmas tree, and try some bobsledding.

Jun & Jul The all-night solstice sees locals flocking to their coastal cottages for beach-lazing and midnight sun.

Sep Sip lattes at the season's last alfresco cafes.

Arriving in Latvia

Rīga International Airport is in the suburb of Skulte, 13km southwest of the city centre. To the city bus 22 (€2, 25 minutes) runs at least every 30 minutes and stops at several points around town. A taxi ride between the airport and the centre typically costs €12.

Rīga central train station Convenient to Old and Central Rīga. International destinations include Moscow (€142, 16 hours, daily), St Petersburg (€107, 15 hours, daily) and Minsk (€66, 12 hours, daily).

Top Phrases

Hello. Sveiks.

Goodbye. Atā.

Excuse me. Atvainojiet.

Sorry. Piedodiet.

You're welcome. Nav par ko.

Resources

Lattelecom (Lattelekom; www.lattelecom.lv) Latvia's main communications service provider has set up wi-fi beacons at every payphone around the city.

Latvia (www.latvia.travel) Latvia's official tourism website.

Set Your Budget

➡ Budget hotel room: 25Ls

➡ Two-course evening meal: 10Ls

➡ Museum entrance: 1.50Ls

➡ City transport ticket: 0.70Ls

Latvia

Today, the snaking ravine has been incorporated into a thin belt of stunning parkland splitting Old and Central Rīga. Stately Raiņa bulvāris follows the rivulet on the north side, and used to be known as 'Embassy Row' during Latvia's independence between the world wars.

Freedom Monument   MONUMENT
(Brīvības bulvāris) Affectionately known as 'Milda', Rīga's Freedom Monument towers above the city between Old and Central Rīga. Paid for by public donations, the monument was designed by Kārlis Zāle and erected in 1935 where a statue of Russian ruler Peter the Great once stood.

Rīga Art Nouveau Museum   MUSEUM
(Rīgas jūgendstila muzejs; www.jugendstils.riga. lv; Alberta iela 12; adult/child May-Sep €6/4, Oct-Apr €3.50/2.50; ⊙10am-6pm Tue-Sun) If you're curious about what lurks behind Rīga's imaginative art nouveau facades, then it's definitely worth stopping by here. Once the home of Konstantīns Pēkšēns (a local architect responsible for over 250 of the city's buildings), the interiors have been completely restored to resemble a middle-class apartment from the 1920s. Enter from Strēlnieku iela; push No 12 on the doorbell.

Nativity of Christ Cathedral   CHURCH
(Kristus Piedzimšanas katedrāle; ☑6721 1207; www.pravoslavie.lv; Brīvības bulvāris 23; ⊙7am-7pm) With gilded cupolas peeking through the trees, this Byzantine-styled Orthodox cathedral (1883) adds a dazzling dash of Russian bling to the skyline. During the Soviet period the church was converted into a planetarium but it's since been restored to its former use. Mind the dress code – definitely no shorts; women are asked to cover their heads.

◉ Maskavas Forštate

Separated from the Old Town by the Central Railway Station, Rīga's 'Moscow Suburb' is in fact one of its oldest central districts, though unlike the rest of the centre it looks like it has never got over the economic hardships of the 1990s. The place also feels haunted because of its dark history – it was the site of the Jewish ghetto during the Nazi occupation of Latvia.

★ Rīga Central Market   MARKET
(Rīgas Centrāltirgus; ☑6722 9985; www.rct.lv; Nēģu iela 7; ⊙7am-6pm) Haggle for your huckleberries at this vast market, housed in a series of WWI Zeppelin hangars and spilling outdoors as well. It's an essential Rīga ex-

perience, providing bountiful opportunities both for people-watching and to stock up for a picnic lunch. Although the number of traders is dwindling, the dairy and fish departments, each occupying a separate hangar, present a colourful picture of abundance that activates ancient foraging instincts in the visitors.

Spīķeri
AREA

(www.spikeri.lv) The shipping yard behind the Central Market is the latest district to benefit from a generous dose of gentrification. These crumbling brick warehouses were once filled with swinging slabs of hanger meat; these days you'll find hip cafes and start-up companies. Stop by during the day to check out **Kim?** (2116 7138; www.kim. lv; Maskavas iela 12/1; €3; noon-6pm Wed-Sun, to 8pm Tue) – an experimental art zone that dabbles with contemporary media – or come in the evening to peruse the surplus of farm produce at the **night market**.

Latvian Academy of Science
HISTORIC BUILDING

(Latvijas Zinātņu Akadēmija; www.panoramariga.lv; Akadēmijas laukums 1; adult/child €5/1; 9am-10pm Apr-Nov) Rising above the Moscow suburb, this Stalinesque tower is in fact a not-so-welcome present from the Russian capital, which has seven towers like it, only bigger. Construction of what is often dubbed 'Stalin's birthday cake' commenced in 1951 but wasn't completed until 1961, by which time Stalin had run out of birthdays. Those with an eagle eye will spot hammers and sickles hidden in the convoluted facade. The wonderful viewing terrace at floor 17 is Rīga's best vantage point.

Tours

E.A.T. Rīga
WALKING, CYCLING

(22469888; www.eatriga.lv; tours from €20) Foodies may be initially disappointed to discover that the name stands for 'Experience Alternative Tours' and the focus is on off-the-beaten-track themed walking tours (Old Rīga, Art Nouveau, Alternative Rīga, Retro Rīga). But don't fret – Rīga Food Tasting is an option. It also offers a cycling tour of Jūrmala.

Rīga Bike Tours
CYCLING

(28225773; www.rigabiketours.com; Riharda Vagnera iela 14; 10am-6pm) These folks run daily bicycle tours of Rīga that last for three hours and cost €15 (€10 with your own bike). Longer cycling tours of Latvia are also on offer. Their useful office operates under Rīga Explorers Club brand.

Riga Culture Free Tour
CULTURAL TOUR

(2883 4052; www.rigaculturefreetour.lv;) **FREE** A daily English-language walk conducted by local cultural experts. It lasts for two hours and begins at noon from Rainis monument on Esplanāde.

Retro Tram
CULTURAL

(6710 4817; www.rigassatiksme.lv/en/services/retro-tram; €2) Two routes, aboard a restored tram, meander through the art nouveau district and on to Mežaparks. Free guided walking tours of the art nouveau district are available on weekends and public holidays, departing five time a day from the Ausekļa tram stop.

Sleeping

★ Cinnamon Sally
HOSTEL €

(2204 2280; www.cinnamonsally.com; Merķeļa iela 1; dm €11-17; @) Convenient for the train/bus stations, Cinnamon Sally comes with perfectly clean rooms, very helpful staff and a common area cluttered with sociable characters. It might feel odd to be asked to take off your shoes at the reception, but it's

Rīga

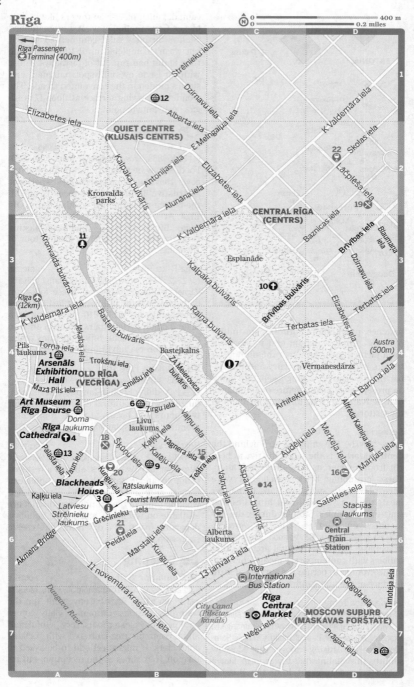

RUSSIA & THE BALTIC COAST RĪGA

N 0 ————— 400 m
0 ————— 0.2 miles

Riga Passenger Terminal (400m)

Strēlnieku iela

Dzirnavu iela

Alberta iela

Elizabetes iela

QUIET CENTRE (KLUSAIS CENTRS)

E Melngaiļa iela

Antonijas iela

Elizabetes iela

Kronvalda parks

Alunāna iela

K Valdemāra iela

CENTRAL RĪGA (CENTRS)

Kalpaka bulvāris

Esplanāde

Baznīcas iela

K Valdemāra iela

Skolas iela

Lāčpleša iela

22

Brīvības iela

Blaumaņa iela

Dzirnavu iela

Kalpaka bulvāris

Elizabetes iela

Tērbatas iela

Raiņa bulvāris

10

Brīvības bulvāris

Tērbatas iela

Austra (500m)

Rīga (12km)

K Valdemāra iela

Bastejā bulvāris

Bastejkalns

ZA Meierovica bulvāris

7

Vērmanesdārzs

Arhitektu

K Barona iela

Alfrēda Kalniņa iela

Marijas iela

Torņa iela

Pils laukums

1

Arsenāls Exhibition Hall

Maza Pils iela

Trokšņu iela

OLD RĪGA (VECRĪGA)

Smilšu iela

Art Museum 2
Rīga Bourse

6 Zirgu iela

Doma laukums

Rīga Cathedral 4

Jēkaba iela

Palasta iela

13

Jauna iela

18

Līvu laukums

Vāgnera iela

Valņu iela

Kaļķu iela

Kaļēju iela

Teātra iela

Valņu iela

Aspazijas bulvāris

15

9

5

Kungu iela

20

Blackheads House

3

Ratslaukums

Tourist Information Centre iela

Grēcinieku

Kaļķu iela

Latviešu Strēlnieku laukums

21

Peldu iela

Marstaļu iela

Kungu iela

Alberta laukums

17

14

Audēju iela

Merķeļa iela

Satekles iela

Stacijas laukums

16

Central Train Station

Akmens Bridge

11 novembra krastmala iela

13 janvāra iela

Rīga International Bus Station

Gogoļa iela

Daugava River

City Canal (Pilsētas kanāls)

5

Rīga Central Market

Nēģu iela

MOSCOW SUBURB (MASKAVAS FORŠTATE)

Prāgas iela

Timoteja iela

8

Rīga

all part of its relentless effort to create a homey atmosphere.

★ **Naughty Squirrel** HOSTEL €

(☑ 6722 0073; www.thenaughtysquirrel.com; Kalēju iela 50; dm €12-16, r €45-51; ✳ @ 🛜) Slashes of bright paint and cartoon graffiti brighten up the city's capital of backpackerdom, which buzzes with travellers rattling the foosball table and chilling out in the TV room. Sign up for regular pub crawls, adrenaline-charged day trips to the countryside and summer BBQs.

Riga City Camping CAMPGROUND €

(☑ 6706 7519; www.rigacamping.lv; Ķīpsalas iela 8; sites per adult/child/tent €4/2/6; ⊙ mid-May–mid-Sep; @ 🛜) Located on Ķīpsala across the river from Old Rīga, this large camp site is surprisingly close to the city centre and offers plenty of room for campers and campervanners. Discounts are available for those staying more than three nights.

✖ Eating

★ **Miit** CAFE €

(www.miit.lv; Lāčplēša iela 10; mains €5; ⊙ 7am-9pm Mon, to 11pm Tue-Thu, to 1am Fri, 9am-11pm Sat, 10am-6pm Sun) Rīga's hipster students head here to sip espresso and blog about Nietzsche amid comfy couches and discarded bicycle parts. The two-course lunch is a fantastic deal for penny-pinchers – expect a soup and a main course for under €5.

Austra INTERNATIONAL €

(www.facebook.com/eatdineaustra; Krišjāna Barona iela 41/43; mains €5-9; ⊙ noon-4pm Mon & Tue, to 11pm Wed-Fri, 11am-11pm Sat, to 5pm Sun) The inventive fusion food served in this small unpretentious place achieves the quality of a fashionable upmarket restaurant, but goes for the price of a cafeteria. The €5 two-course lunches are one of the best deals in town.

LIDO Alus Sēta LATVIAN €

(☑ 6722 2431; www.lido.lv; Tirgoņu iela 6; mains around €5; ⊙ 11am-10pm; 🛜) The pick of the LIDO litter (Rīga's ubiquitous smorgasbord chain), Alus Sēta feels like an old Latvian brew house. It's popular with locals as well as tourists – everyone flocks here for cheap but tasty traditional fare and homemade beer. Seating spills onto the cobbled street during the warmer months.

🍷 Drinking & Nightlife

★ **Folksklub Ala Pagrabs** BEER HALL

(☑ 2779 6914; www.folkklubs.lv; Peldu iela 19; ⊙ noon-1am Mon & Tue, to 3am Wed, to 4am Thu, to 6am Fri, 2pm-5am Sat, 2pm-1am Sun) A huge cavern filled with the bubbling magma of relentless beer-infused joy, folk-punk music, dancing and Latvian nationalism, this is an essential Rīga drinking venue, no matter what highbrowed locals say about it. The bar strives to reflect the full geography and diversity of Latvian beer production, but there is also plenty of local cider, fruit wine and *šmakouka* moonshine.

★ **Kaņepes Kultūras Centrs** BAR

(☑ 6734 7050; www.kanepes.lv; Skolas iela 15; ⊙ 3pm-2am or later) The crumbling building of a former musical school, which half of Rīgans over 40 seem to have attended, is now a bar with a large outdoor area filled with an artsy studenty crowd. Wild dancing regularly erupts in the large room, where the parents of the patrons once suffered through their violin drills.

Egle
BEER GARDEN

(www.spogulegle.lv; Kaļķu iela 1a; ⊙ 11am-1am Mon-Sat, to midnight Sun) Split between a noisier half with live music most nights (everything from folk to rockabilly), and a quieter half (which generally closes early), this is the best of Old Rīga's open-air beer gardens. It shuts up shop when the weather gets really horrible.

☆ Entertainment

Rīga in Your Pocket and *Rīga This Week* have the most up-to-date listings for opera, ballet, guest DJs, live music and other events around town. The tourist office in the Black-heads House (p817) can help travellers book tickets at any concert venue around town. Several operators offer bar and club tours if you'd rather have someone else arrange your big night out. Backpackers staying at sociable digs might find hostel-organised pub crawls and parties.

ℹ Information

Tourist Information Centre (☑ 6703 7900; www.liveriga.com; Rātslaukums 6; ⊙ 10am-6pm Oct-Apr, 9am-7pm May-Sep) Dispenses tourist maps and walking-tour brochures, helps with accommodation, books and day trips, and sells concert tickets. It also stocks the Rīga Card, which offers discounts on sights and restaurants, and free rides on public transport. Satellite offices can be found in Līvu laukums (May to September only) and at the bus station.

ℹ Getting There & Away

AIR
Rīga airport (Starptautiskā Lidosta Rīga; ☑ 1817; www.riga-airport.com; Mārupe District; ☑ 22) is 13km southwest of the city centre.

BOAT
Rīga's **passenger ferry terminal** (☑ 6732 6200; www.portofriga.lv; Eksporta iela 3a), located about 1km downstream (north) of Akmens Bridge, offers service to Stockholm aboard Tallink (www.tallink.lv; three to four weekly).

BUS
Buses depart from Rīga's **international bus station** (Rīgas starptautiskā autoosta; ☑ 9000 0009; www.autoosta.lv; Prāgas iela 1), located behind the railway embankment just beyond the southeastern edge of Old Rīga. Latvian destinations include Cēsis (€4.15, two hours, every 30 minutes), Kuldīga (€6.40, 2½ to 3¼ hours, hourly), Sigulda (€2.15, one hour, every 45 minutes) and Ventspils (€7.55, three to four hours, hourly).

TRAIN
Rīga's **central train station** (Centrālā stacija; ☑ 6723 2135; www.pv.lv; Stacijas laukums 2) is convenient to Old and Central Rīga. Visit www.ldz.lv to view the timetables and prices for long-haul international and domestic trains. Local destinations include Cēsis (€3.50, two hours, four daily) and Jūrmala (Majori; €1.40, 30 minutes, two to three per hour).

ℹ Getting Around

TO/FROM THE AIRPORT
The cheapest way to get from Rīga airport to the centre is bus 22 (€2, 25 minutes), which runs at least every 30 minutes and stops at several points around town, including the Stockmanns complex and on the river side of the Old Town. A taxi ride between the airport and the centre typically costs €12.

BICYCLE
Zip around town with **Sixt Bicycle Rental** (Sixt velo noma; ☑ 6767 6780; www.sixtbicycle.lv; per 30min/day €1/10). A handful of stands are conveniently positioned around Rīga and Jūrmala; simply choose your bike, call the rental service and receive the code to unlock your wheels.

PUBLIC TRANSPORT
The centre of Rīga is too compact for most visitors even to consider public transport, but trams, buses or trolleybuses may come in handy if you are venturing further out. For routes and schedules, consult www.rigassatiksme.lv. Tickets cost €1.15 (€0.30 for ISIC-holding students). Unlimited tickets are available for 24 hours (€5), three days (€10) and five days (€15). Tickets are available from Narvessen newspaper kiosks as well as vending machines on board new trams and in the underground pass by the train station.

TAXI
Taxis charge €0.60 to €0.80 per kilometre. Insist on having the meter on before you set off. Meters usually start running at around €1.50. It shouldn't cost more than €5 for a short journey (like crossing the Daugava for dinner in Ķīpsala). There are taxi ranks outside the bus and train stations, at the airport and in front of a few major hotels in Central Rīga, such as Radisson Blu Hotel Latvija.

Jūrmala

POP 56,000

The Baltic's version of the French Riviera, Jūrmala (pronounced *yoor*-muh-lah) is a 32km strip of 14 townships with Prussian-style villas, each unique in shape and decor. Even during the height of communism,

KULDĪGA

Famed locally for its cute shrunken Niagara, lovely old Kuldīga is a place where your immersion into the epoch of chivalry won't be spoiled by day-tripping camera-clickers – the place is simply too far from Rīga.

In its heyday, Kuldīga served as the capital of the Duchy of Courland (1596–1616), but it was badly damaged during the Great Northern War and never quite able to regain its former lustre. Today this blast from the past is a favourite spot to shoot Latvian period-piece films.

There's not a lot to do here except to stroll the streets and the park in the grounds of the old castle (of which nothing much remains), admiring the sculpture garden and gazing down on pretty **Ventas Rumba**. Said to be Europe's widest waterfall, it stretches for 249m, but is only a couple of metres high. During spawning season salmon would have little difficulty launching themselves up and over it, giving Kuldīga the curious epithet 'city where salmon fly'.

Buses run to/from Rīga (€6.40, 2½ to 3½ hours, every two hours) and Ventspils (€3, 1¼ hours, seven daily).

Jūrmala was always a place to 'sea' and be seen. On summer weekends, vehicles clog the roads when jetsetters and day-tripping Rīgans flock to the resort town for some serious fun in the sun.

If you don't have a car or bicycle, you'll want to head straight to the heart of the action – the townships of Majori and Dzintari.

◉ Sights & Activities

Besides its 'Blue Flag' beach, Jūrmala's main attraction is its colourful art nouveau **wooden houses**, distinguishable by frilly awnings, detailed facades and elaborate towers. There are over 4000 wooden structures found throughout Jūrmala (most are lavish summer cottages), but you can get your fill by taking a leisurely stroll along **Jūras iela**, a 1km-long pedestrian street connecting Majori and Dzintari.

Ķemeri National Park   NATIONAL PARK
(Ķemeru nacionālais parks; ☑6673 0078; www.kemerunacionalaisparks.lv) Beyond Jūrmala's stretch of celebrity summer homes lies a verdant hinterland of drowsy fishing villages, quaking bogs and thick forests. At the end of the 19th century Ķemeri was known for its curative mud and spring water, attracting visitors from as far away as Moscow.

Baltic Beach Spa   SPA
(☑6777 1446; www.balticbeach.lv; Jūras iela 23/25; treatments from €15; ☉7am-10pm) Attached to a beachfront resort, this is the largest treatment centre in the Baltic, with three rambling storeys full of massage rooms, saunas, yoga studios, swimming pools and spa pools.

❶ Information

Tourist Office (☑6714 7900; Lienes iela 5; ☉9am-5pm Mon-Fri, 10am-5pm Sat, 10am-3pm Sun) Located across from Majori train station, this helpful office has scores of brochures outlining walks, bike routes and attractions. Staff can assist with accommodation bookings and bike rental. A giant map outside helps orient visitors when the centre is closed.

❶ Getting There & Around

BICYCLE

Six Rent a Bicycle (sixbicycle.lv) has several locations in Jūrmala. The most useful one is across the square from Majori station. You can also drop its bikes here if you rode them from Rīga.

MINIBUSES

From Rīga take minibuses (30 minutes) in the direction of Sloka, Jaunķemeri or Dubulti and ask the driver to let you off at Majori. These vans depart every five to 15 minutes between 6am and midnight and leave opposite Rīga's central train station. Catch the bus at Majori train station for a lift back. From 9am to midnight, minibuses also connect Jūrmala to Rīga International Airport.

BOAT

The river boat **New Way** (☑2923 7123; www.pie-kapteina.lv; adult/child €15/10) departs from Rīga Riflemen Sq and docks in Majori near the train station. The journey takes one hour, and only runs on weekends.

TRAIN

Two to three trains per hour link Jūrmala to Central Rīga. Take a suburban train bound for Sloka,

Tukums or Dubulti and disembark at Majori station (€1.50, 30 to 35 minutes).

Sigulda

POP 17,800

With a name that sounds like a mythical ogress, it comes as no surprise that the gateway to the **Gauja National Park** (www.entergauja.com) is an enchanting spot with delightful surprises tucked behind every dappled tree. Locals proudly call their town the 'Switzerland of Latvia', but if you're expecting the majesty of a mountainous snow-capped realm, you'll be rather disappointed.

Instead, Sigulda mixes its own brew of scenic trails, extreme sports and 800-year-old castles steeped in legends.

◉ Sights

Sigulda sprawls between its three castles, with most of the action occurring on the east side of the Gauja River near New Sigulda Castle. Take your own walking tour for an abridged version of Sigulda's greatest hits, and don't forget to take a ride on the **cable car** (☎2921 2731; Poruka iela 14; one way adult/child €8/5; ☺10am-6.30pm May-Oct, to 5pm Nov-Apr) across the valley for an awesome aerial perspective.

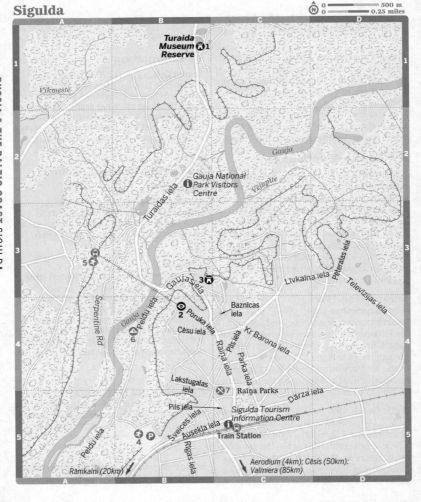

Sigulda

0 — 500 m
0 — 0.25 miles

Turaida Museum Reserve 1

Vikmeste

Gauja

Gauja National Park Visitors Centre

Turaidas iela

Veļupīte

Livkalna iela

Peterlas iela

Televīzijas iela

Gaujas iela 3

Baznīcas iela

2 Poruka iela

Serpentine Rd

Peldu iela

Gauja

6

Cēsu iela

Kr Barona iela

Raiņa iela

Pils iela

Parka iela

Lakstugalas iela

7 Raiņa Parks

Darza iela

Pils iela

Sveices iela

Ausekļa iela

Sigulda Tourism Information Centre

Train Station

Peldu iela

4

Rīgas iela

Aerodium (4km); Cēsis (50km); Valmiera (85km)

Rāmkalni (20km)

★**Turaida Museum Reserve**   CASTLE
(Turaidas muzejrezervāts; ☑ 67971402; www.turaida-muzejs.lv; Turaidas iela 10; adult/child summer €5/1.15, winter €3/0.70; ⊙ 9am-8pm May-Sep, 9am-7pm Oct, 10am-5pm Nov-Mar, 10am-7pm Apr) Turaida means 'God's Garden' in ancient Livonian, and this green knoll capped with a fairy-tale castle is certainly a heavenly place. The red-brick castle with its tall cylindrical tower was built in 1214 on the site of a Liv stronghold. A museum inside the castle's 15th-century granary offers an interesting account of the Livonian state from 1319 to 1561, and additional exhibitions can be viewed in the 42m-high Donjon Tower, and the castle's western and southern towers.

Sigulda Medieval Castle   CASTLE
(Pils iela 18; adult/child €2/1; ⊙ 9am-8pm May-Sep, 9am-5pm Mon-Fri, to 7pm Sat & Sun Oct, 9am-5pm Nov-Apr) Constructed between 1207 and 1209 by the Livonian Brothers of the Sword, this castle lies mainly in picturesque ruins after being severely damaged during the Great Northern War. Some sections have been restored and you can now walk along the front ramparts and ascend a tower at the rear where there are wonderful views over the forested Gauja Valley. See if you can spy Krimulda Manor and Turaida Castle poking through the trees.

🏃 **Activities**

Sigulda is prime hiking territory, so bring your walking shoes. Many outfitters around Sigulda offer bicycle and mountain-bike rentals costing around €15 per day. Brochures detailing hiking, cycling and hiking routes are available at the tourist office.

Sigulda

◎ **Top Sights**

Bobsled Track   ADVENTURE SPORTS
(Bob trase; ☑ 6797 3813; www.bobtrase.lv; Šveices iela 13; ⊙ noon-5pm Sat & Sun) Sigulda's 1200m bobsled track was built for the Soviet team. In winter you can fly down the 16-bend track at 80km/h in a five-person Vučko **soft bob** (per adult/child €10/7, from November to March). Summer speed fiends can ride a wheeled **summer bob** (per adult/child €10/7, from May to September).

Aerodium   ADVENTURE SPORTS
(☑ 2838 4400; www.aerodium.lv; 2min/4min €45/65) The one-of-a-kind aerodium is a giant wind tunnel that propels participants up into the sky as though they were flying. Instructors can get about 15m high, while first-timers usually rock out at about 3m. To find the site, look for the sign along the A2 highway, 4km west of Sigulda.

Cable Car Bungee Jump   ADVENTURE SPORTS
(☑ 2838 3333; www.bungee.lv; Poruka iela 14; bungee jump from €60; ⊙ from 6.45pm Thu-Sun May-Oct) Take your daredevil shenanigans to the next level with a 43m bungee jump from the bright-orange cable car that glides over the Gauja River. For an added thrill, jump naked.

🛏 **Sleeping & Eating**

Kempings Siguldas Pludmale   CAMPGROUND €
(☑ 2924 4948; www.makars.lv; Peldu iela 2; per person/tent/car/caravan €6/3/3/6; ⊙ mid-May–mid-Sep) Pitch your tent in the grassy camping area beside the sandy beach along the Gauja. The location is perfect; however, there's only one men's and one women's bathroom for the scores of campers. Two-person tents can be hired for €4.50 per day. There's a second camping area up the river in Līgatne that's owned and operated by Makars as well. Ask at this location for directions.

Kaķu Māja   LATVIAN €
(www.cathouse.lv; Pils iela 8; mains around €3; ⊙ 8am-9pm) A top spot for a cheap bite, the 'Cat's House' has pick-and-point bain-marie meals and an attached bakery with pastries, pies and cakes. On Friday and Saturday nights, the restaurant in the back busts out the disco ball and morphs into a nightclub until 2am.

ℹ **Information**

Gauja National Park Visitors Centre (☑ 6130 3030; www.gnp.lv; Turaida iela 2a; ⊙ 9am-7pm

RUSSIA & THE BALTIC COAST SIGULDA

May-Sep, to 6pm Oct-Apr) Sells maps to the park, town and cycle routes nearby.

Sigulda Tourism Information Centre (☑ 6797 1335; www.tourism.sigulda.lv; Ausekļa iela 6; ⊙ 9am-6pm; ☎) Located within the train station, this extremely helpful centre has stacks of information about activities and accommodation.

ⓘ Getting There & Around

Buses trundle the 50-odd kilometres between Sigulda's bus station and Rīga (€2.15, one hour, every 30 minutes between 8am and 10.30pm).

One train per hour (between 6am and 9pm) travels the Rīga–Sigulda–Cēsis–Valmiera Line. Destinations from Sigulda include Rīga (€2.35, one to 1¼ hours) and Cēsis (€2, 40 minutes).

Sigulda's attractions are quite spread out, and after a long day of walking, bus 12 will become your new best friend. It plies the route to/from New Sigulda Castle, Turaida Castle and Krimulda Manor hourly during business hours (more on weekends).

Cēsis
POP 19,500

Not only is sweet little Cēsis (tsay-sis) one of Latvia's prettiest towns, but it's also one of its oldest. Nestled within the forested confines of Gauja National Park, its cobbled lanes wend around a sturdy castle, a soaring church spire and a lazy lakeside park.

◉ Sights

★ **Cēsis Castle** CASTLE
(Cēsu pils; ☑ 6412 1815; www.cesupils.lv; adult/ student €6/3.50, tours from €35; ⊙ 10am-6pm

daily May-Sep, 10am-5pm Tue-Sat, 10am-4pm Sun Oct-Apr) It is actually two castles in one. The first is the sorrowful dark-stone towers of the old Wenden castle. Founded by Livonian knights in 1214, it was sacked by Russian tsar Ivan the Terrible in 1577, but only after its 300 defenders blew themselves up with gunpowder. The other is the more cheerful castle-like 18th-century manor house once inhabited by the dynasty of German counts von Sievers. It houses a museum that features original fin de siècle interiors.

After visiting the old and the new castles, take a walk through the landscaped **castle park** with a pond inhabited by the cutest of paddle steamers that takes people around for €2.20. Just as cute is the hilltop **Russian Orthodox Church of Transfiguration**, which the von Sievers built at their family cemetery (like many Germans on Russian service they converted to Orthodoxy).

St John's Church CHURCH
(Svētā Jāņa baznīca; www.cesujana.lelb.lv; ⊙ 11am-5pm) Switch on your imagination in this 13th-century church where armour-clad Livonian knights prayed and buried their dead in what then was a lonely island of Christianity surrounded by the lands of pagans. Currently the home of the town's Lutheran community, the church contains tombs of the order's grand masters and top bishops.

🛏 Sleeping & Eating

Glūdas Grava MOTEL €
(☑ 27036862; www.gludasgrava.lv; Glūdas iela 6a; r €50) An unusual one. A garage has

OFF THE BEATEN TRACK

DAUGAVPILS

Latvia's second-largest city has an undeserved reputation as a grim Soviet Gotham City – mostly among Latvians who have never been to it. In reality it has a fairly well-preserved historical centre and a mighty fortress, reminding of the times when it was a provincial Russian imperial town with a thriving Jewish community. Native son Mark Rothko became one of America's most notable 20th-century artists: his name is attached to the **contemporary art centre,** (www.rothkocenter.com; Mihaila iela 3; adult/ student €8/4, half-price for people born on 24 Apr & 25 Sep; ⊙ 11am-7pm Wed-Sat, to 5pm Tue & Sun) one of the country's best.

Four trains a day depart Daugavpils' **train station** (☑ 1188; Stacijas iela) for Rīga (€7, three to four hours). Other services include St Petersburg in Russia (€49, 10 hours, daily) and Minsk in Belarus (€43, nine hours, three weekly).

From the **bus station** (☑ 6542 3000; www.buspark.lv; Viestura iela 10) buses run to/ from Rīga (€9, 3¾ hours, hourly) as well as Vilnius in Lithuania (€12, 3½ hours, two daily).

Cēsis

Cēsis

⊙ Top Sights

⊙ Sights

⊟ Sleeping

⊗ Eating

been transformed into five studios with glassy front walls and individual entrances. Each studio is equipped with a kitchen and sleeps up to four people. There is no reception – so book your stay on its website or on www.booking.com and it will come back with instructions about how to access the keys.

Mākslas Telpa Mala CAFE €
(www.facebook.com/telpamala; Lielā Skolas iela 4; mains €3-4; ☉noon-7pm Wed & Thu, to 1am Fri, to 2am Sat, to 5pm Sun) A truly heart-warming place inside an old wooden house featuring an antiquated tiled wood stove. Cheapish lunch food is on offer, along with craft beer, Latvian cider and fruit wine. We also liked the Latvian rock classics (not something you would hear in your average cafe) for the soundtrack. A small souvenir and cloth shop is attached.

ⓘ Information

Cēsis Tourism Information Centre (☎6412 1815; www.tourism.cesis.lv; Pils laukums 9; ☉10am-5pm daily May-Sep, 10am-5pm Tue-Sat, to 4pm Sun Oct-Apr) Within the Cēsis Castle.

ⓘ Getting There & Away

Cēsis' bus and train stations can be found in the same location: at the roundabout connecting Raunas iela to Raiņa iela. There are up to five trains per day between 6.35am and 9pm linking Cēsis and Rīga (€3.50, two hours). Bikes are allowed on board. Two or three buses per hour between 6.15am and 10.20pm ply the route from Cēsis to Rīga, stopping in Līgatne and Sigulda.

Ventspils

POP 42,500

Fabulous amounts of oil and shipping money have turned Ventspils into one of Latvia's most beautiful and dynamic cities. Although locals nurse their Užavas beer and claim that there's not much to do, tourists will find a weekend's worth of fun in the form of brilliant beaches, interactive museums and winding Old Town streets dotted with the odd boutique and cafe.

⊙ Sights

Ventspils Beach BEACH
For Liepāja, the wide stretch of dazzlingly white sand south of the Venta River is what the Louvre is for Paris – its main treasure. During the warmer months, beach bums of every ilk – from nudist to kiteboarder – line the sands to absorb the sun's rays. Backed by

a belt of dunes and a lush manicured park, the Blue Flag beach feels as pristine and well cared for as an urban beach can get.

Livonian Order Castle CASTLE
(Livonijas ordeņa pils; ☑ 6362 2031; www.ventspilsmuzejs.lv; Jāņa iela 17; adult/child €2.10/1.10; ⊙10am-6pm Tue-Sun) This blocky building doesn't look obviously castle-like from the outside, but the 13th-century interior is home to a cutting-edge interactive local history and art museum. During Soviet rule the castle was used as a prison and an exhibit in the stables recounts its horrors (in Latvian only). An adjacent Zen rock garden will soothe your soul afterwards.

🛏 Sleeping & Eating

Piejūras Kempings CAMPGROUND €
(☑ 6362 7925; Vasarnīcu iela 56; tent sites per person €5, 4-person cottage from €40; @) This charming campus of grassy tent grounds and pine cottages is a full-service operation with an on-site laundrette, bicycle rental, and tennis, volleyball and basketball courts.

Skroderkrogs LATVIAN €€
(☑ 6362 7634; Skroderu iela 6; mains €6-13; ⊙11am-10pm) If you're after big serves of Latvian comfort food in a pleasant local setting (candles and flowers on tables fashioned from old sewing machines), this is the place to come.

❶ Information

Tourist Information Centre (☑ 6362 2263; www.visitventspils.com; Dārzu iela 6; ⊙8am-6pm Mon-Fri, 10am-4pm Sat & Sun) In the ferry terminal.

❶ Getting There & Away

Ventspils' **bus terminal** (☑ 6362 9904; Kuldīgas iela 5) is served by buses to/from Rīga (€7.50,

---

❶ PRICE RANGES

The following price ranges refer to the cost of a double room with private bathroom.

€ less than €40

€€ €40–80

Eating price ranges are based on the average price of a main dish.

€ less than €7

€€ €7–14

2¾ to four hours, hourly) and Kuldīga (€3, 1¼ hours, five daily).

Stena Line (www.stenalinetravel.com) runs ferries to Nynashamn, Sweden (from €17, 12 hours, 12 weekly).

Latvia Survival Guide

❶ Directory A–Z

ACCOMMODATION
We highly advise booking ahead during the high season (summer). Rates drop significantly in the colder months. Budget range accommodation (**€**) cost less than €40.

Check out www.camping.lv for details on pitching a tent.

INTERNET RESOURCES
11188 (www.1188.lv) Latvia's top search engine
Latvian Tourism Development Agency (www.latvia.travel)
Latvia Institute (www.li.lv)

PUBLIC HOLIDAYS
New Year's Day 1 January
Easter March/April
Labour Day 1 May
Restoration of Independence of the Republic of Latvia 4 May
Mothers' Day Second Sunday in May
Whitsunday A Sunday in May or June
Līgo Eve (Midsummer festival) 23 June
Jāņi (St John's Day and Summer Solstice) 24 June
National Day Anniversary of proclamation of Latvian Republic, 1918, on 18 November
Christmas (Ziemsvētki) 25 December
Second Holiday 26 December
New Year's Eve 31 December

TELEPHONE
Latvian telephone numbers have eight digits; landlines start with '6' and mobile numbers start with '2'. To make any call within Latvia, simply dial the eight-digit number. To call a Latvian telephone number from abroad, dial the international access code, then the country code for Latvia (371) followed by the subscriber's eight-digit number.

❶ Getting There & Away

AIR
There are direct flights to over 50 destinations within Europe from **Rīga International Airport** (Starptautiskā Lidosta Rīga; ☑ 1817; www.riga-airport.com; Mārupe District; ▣ 22).

LAND

There are no border controls between Latvia and both Estonia and Lithuania. However, we advise carrying your travel documents with you at all times, as random border checks do occur.

International trains head from Rīga to Moscow (€142, 16 hours, daily), St Petersburg (€107, 15 hours, daily) and Minsk (€66, 12 hours, daily). There are no direct trains to Estonia; you'll need to change at Valka.

SEA

Ferry services from Rīga and Ventspils connect Latvia to Sweden.

ⓘ Getting Around

BUS

Buses are much more convenient than trains if you're travelling beyond the capital's clutch of suburban rail lines. Updated timetables are available at www.autoosta.lv and www.1188.lv.

CAR & MOTORCYCLE

➧ Driving is on the right-hand side.

➧ Headlights must be on at all times.

➧ Local car-hire companies usually allow you to drive in all three Baltic countries, but not beyond.

TRAIN

Rīga's network of commuter rails makes it easy for tourists to reach day-tripping destinations. Latvia's further attractions are best explored by bus. Train schedule queries can be answered at www.pv.lv as well as at www.1188.lv.

LITHUANIA

Vilnius

☑ / POP 546,700

Europe's largest baroque old town is at Vilnius' heart. Viewed from a hot air balloon, the skyline – pierced by countless Orthodox and Catholic church steeples – looks like a giant bed of nails. Adding to this heady mix is a combination of cobbled alleys, crumbling corners, majestic hilltop views, breakaway states and traditional artists' workshops – all in a city so small you'd sometimes think it was a village.

It has not always been so happy here, though. There are reminders of loss and pain too, from the horror of the KGB's torture cells to the ghettos where the Jewish community was concentrated before being murdered by the Nazis. Yet the spirit of freedom and resistance has prevailed, and the city is forging a new identity, combining the past with a present and future that involves world cuisine, a burgeoning nightlife and shiny new skyscrapers.

⊙ Sights

⊙ Cathedral Square & Gediminis Hill

At the base of Gediminas Hill sprawls Cathedral Square (Katedros aikštė), dominated by Vilnius Cathedral and its 57m-tall **belfry** (☑8-6001 2080; www.bpmuziejus.lt; Katedros aikštė; adult/student €4.50/2.50; ☉10am-7pm Mon-Sat May-Sep, to 6pm Oct-Apr). The square buzzes with local life, especially during Sunday morning Mass.

★ Palace of the Grand Dukes of Lithuania   MUSEUM

(Valdovų Rumai; ☑5-262 0007; www.valdovurumai.lt; Katedros aikštė 4; adult/student €3/1.50, guided tour €22; ☉museum 10am-6pm Tue, Wed, Fri & Sat, to 8pm Thu, to 4pm Sun) On a site that has been settled since at least the 4th century AD stands the latest in a procession of fortified palaces, repeatedly remodelled, extended, destroyed, and rebuilt over the centuries. What visitors now see is a painstaking restoration of its final grand manifestation, the baroque palace built for the Grand Dukes in the 17th century. While the gleamingly white complex is evidently new, it contains fascinating historical remains, and is a potent symbol of revitalised, independent Lithuania.

Europa Tower   LANDMARK

(Konstitucijos Prospektas 7) There's an observation deck at 114m; this is the highest skyscraper in the Baltics.

Vingis Park   PARK

(www.vilniausparkai.lt; MK Čiurlionio gatvė 100) At the western end of Čiurlionio gatvė is the wooded Vingis Park, surrounded on three sides by the Neris. The park has a large open-air amphitheatre used for the Lithuanian Song and Dance Festival (in July). Take trolleybus 7 from the train station or 3 from the Gedimino stop on Vilniaus gatvė to the Kęstučio stop (the second after the bridge over the river), then walk over the footbridge from the end of Treniotos gatvė.

LITHUANIA AT A GLANCE

Don't Miss

Vilnius The Lithuanian capital's Old Town is one of the best places to get lost in throughout the Baltics. Old and new seem to coexist seamlessly here: whether you're looking for that thrift-shop boutique, an organic bakery, a cosy little bookshop or just a quiet spot to have a coffee, they're all likely to be standing side-by-side down some cobblestone alleyway.

Curonian Split Lithuania's loveliest seaside retreat is a long, thin strip of rare and majestic sand dunes that lines the southeastern corner of the Baltic Sea. Come here to recharge your batteries and renew your faith in the redemptive powers of wind, water, earth and sky.

Hill of Crosses More a mound than a mountain, this bump on the flat Lithuanian countryside is covered in crosses by the tens of thousands. The location takes on even more significance when you realise that the crosses planted here represent not just religious faith but an affirmation of the country's very identity.

Kaunas With a compact Old Town, an abundance of artistic and educational museums, and a fascinating history, Kaunas is worthy of your time. A sizeable student population provides plenty of energy, and some rough edges give it that extra bit of spice.

Trakai With its red-brick, fairy-tale castle, Karaites culture, quaint wooden houses and pretty lakeside location, Trakai is a must-see just 28km from the capital.

Itineraries

Three Days

Spend the first day exploring **Vilnius**' Old Town, not missing the Cathedral, the Gates of Dawn and the university's 13 courtyards, followed by lunch on an Old Town terrace. At dusk, hike (or ride the funicular) up Gediminas Hill for a city-spire sunset. On the second day, discover Jewish Vilnius with visits to the Tolerance Centre, Holocaust Museum and Choral Synagogue. On day three journey out of town to **Trakai** for its island castle and the homesteads of the Karaite people.

One Week

Follow the three day itinerary as above perhaps adding an extra day to relax in Vilnius. Travel cross-country to the awe-inspiring **Hill of Crosses**, then head to the seaside and the sand dunes of the **Curonian Spit National Park** for two or three days. Heading back east spend a night each in the old Prussian capital of **Klaipėda**, which offers the remains of a castle and a cobbled Old Town, and **Kaunas**, another historic town with a lively student vibe.

Essential Food & Drink

Cepelinai (tsep-e-lin-ay) Sometimes jokingly called zeppelins, these are parcels of thick potato dough stuffed with cheese, meat or mushrooms and topped with a rich sauce of onions, butter, sour cream and bacon bits.

Kugelis Borrowed from German cuisine, this 'cannon ball' dish bakes grated potatoes and carrots in the oven.

Koldūnai (kol-doon-ay) Hearty ravioli stuffed with meat or mushrooms.

Virtiniai Stodgy dumplings.

Alus Beer is the most widespread drink, local brands being Švyturys, Utenos and Kalnapilis.

Midus (mead) Honey boiled with water, berries and spices, then fermented with hops to produce an alcoholic drink of 10% to 15% proof, is Lithuania's oldest and most noble drink.

Getting Around

Bicycle Touring cyclists will find Lithuania mercifully flat. In rural areas, some roads are unsealed but they're usually kept in good condition. Bike hire is offered in all the major cities.

Bus The national bus network is extensive, linking all the major cities to each other and the smaller towns to their regional hubs. Most services are summarised on the extremely handy website Bus Tickets (www.autobusubilietai.lt).

Car and Motorcycle Lithuanian roads are generally very good and driving is easy. Four-lane highways link the main cities of Vilnius, Kaunas and Klaipėda.

Train Lithuanian Rail website (www.litrail.lt) is a model of user-friendliness and has routes, times and prices in English.

When to Go
Vilnius

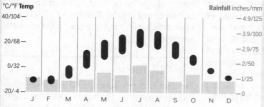

Jun–Aug The days are long, the nights are short and the Baltic Sea's waters are warm – or at least swimmable.

Apr & May Weather is cool until late in spring.

Sep–Nov Ideal weather with sunny days and chilly nights. There's also the Mama Jazz festival in Vilnius.

Arriving in Lithuania

Vilnius Airport Bus 1 runs between the airport and the train station; trains run to the central station every 30 minutes between 6am and 11.30pm. On-board tickets cost €0.72 and the trip is only 10 minutes. A taxi to the centre, 5km away, will cost €10 to €15.

Vilnius train station Opposite the bus station. There is no direct or convenient rail link between Vilnius and Rīga or Tallinn.

Top Phrases

Hello. Sveki.

Goodbye. Viso gero.

Excuse me. Prašau.

Sorry. Atsiprašau.

You're welcome. Prašom.

Resources

Lithuanian Travel (www.lithuania.travel) Lithuania's leading tourism portal.

Wifi Hot Spots (www.wifi.lt)

Set Your Budget

➡ Budget hotel room: €40

➡ Two-course meal: €10

➡ City transport ticket: €0.64

Map of Lithuania showing cities including Rīga, Jelgava, Liepāja, Klaipėda, Šiauliai, Panevėžys, Kaunas, Vilnius, and surrounding countries Latvia, Russia, Poland, Belarus.

Vilnius Cathedral
CATHEDRAL

(Vilniaus Arkikatedra; ☑ 5-261 0731; www.katedra.
lt; Katedros aikštė 1; crypts adult/child €4.50/2.50;
⏰ 7am-7pm, crypts 10am-4pm Mon-Sat) Known
in full as the Cathedral of St Stanislav and
St Vladislav, this national symbol occupies
a spot originally used for the worship of
Perkūnas, the Lithuanian thunder god. Sev-
enteenth-century St Casimir's Chapel, with
its a baroque cupola, coloured marble and
frescoes of the saint's life, is the showpiece,
while the crypts are the final resting place
of many prominent Lithuanians, including
Vytautas the Great (1350–1430). The website
has details of Mass.

National Museum
of Lithuania
MUSEUM

(Lietuvos Nacionalinis Muziejus; ☑ 5-262 7774;
www.lnm.lt; Arsenalo gatvė 1; adult/child €2/1;
⏰ 10am-6pm Tue-Sun) Building on the collections complied by the Museum of Antiquities since 1855, this splendid museum shows
artefacts from Lithuanian life from Neolithic times to the 20th century. It has special
collections devoted to the country's different
folk traditions, to numismatics (including
some of the very first Lithuanian coins)
and to burial goods. A statue of Mindaugas,
Lithuania's sole king, stands guard over the
entrance.

◉ Old Town

Eastern Europe's largest Old Town deserves
its Unesco status. The area, stretching 1.5km
south from Katedros aikštė, was built up in
the 15th and 16th centuries, and its narrow
winding streets, hidden courtyards and lavish old churches retain the feel of bygone
centuries. One of the purest pleasures the
city has to offer is aimlessly wandering Old
Town backstreets.

★ Vilnius University
HISTORIC BUILDING

(Vilniaus Universitetas; ☑5-219 3029; www.
muziejus.vu.lt; Universiteto gatvė 3; architectural
ensemble adult/child €1.50/0.50; ☉9am-6pm
Mon-Sat Mar-Oct, 9.30am-5.30pm Mon-Sat Nov-
Feb) Founded in 1579 during the Counter-
Reformation, Vilnius University was run by
Jesuits for two centuries and became one
of the greatest centres of Polish learning.
It produced many notable scholars but was
closed by the Russians in 1832 and didn't
reopen until 1919. Today it has 23,000 students and Lithuania's oldest library, shelv-
ing five million books (including one of two
originals of *The Catechism* by Martynas
Mažvydas, the first book ever published in
Lithuanian).

St Anne's Church
CHURCH

(Šv Onos Bažnyčia; ☑8-676 74463; www.onosba-
znycia.lt; Maironio gatvė 8-1; ☉10.30am-6.30pm
Tue-Sat, 8am-7pm Sun May-Sep, 4.30-6.30pm
Tue-Fri, 10.30am-6.30pm Sat, 8am-5pm Sun Oct-
Apr) This gorgeous, late-15th-century Gothic church is a tiny confection of red brick,
glass and arches, dwarfed by the Bernadine
Church outside which it stands. Marrying
33 different kinds of brick into a whole
that many regard as the most beautiful in
Vilnius, it's reputed that Napoleon was so
charmed by St Anne's that he wanted to relocate it to Paris.

St Casimir's Church
CHURCH

(Šv Kazimiero Bažnyčia; ☑5-212 1715; www.
kazimiero.lt; Didžioji gatvė 34; ☉10am-6.30pm
Mon-Sat, 8am-6.30pm Sun Apr-Sep, 4pm-6.30pm
Mon-Sat, 8am-2pm Sun Oct-Mar) This striking
church is the city's oldest baroque place
of worship. St Casimir's dome and cross-
shaped ground plan defined a new style
for 17th-century churches when the Jesuits
built it between 1604 and 1615. It was destroyed and rebuilt several times over the
centuries and has recently emerged from
another bout of renovation.

Gates of Dawn
HISTORIC BUILDING

(Aušros Vartai; ☑5-212 3513; www.ausrosvartai.
lt; Aušros Vartų gatvė 12; ☉6am-7pm) **FREE** The
southern border of Old Town is marked by
the last-standing of five portals that were
once built into the city walls. A suitably
grand way to enter one of the best-preserved
sections of the Old Town, it's also the site of
the Gate of Dawn Chapel of Mary the Mother of Mercy and the 'Vilnius Madonna', a
17th-century painting of Our Lady said to
work miracles.

☞ Tours

Two-hour walking tours of the Old Town in
English (€10), starting at 11am on Monday,
Wednesday, Friday and Sunday from mid-
May to mid-September, are organised by any
Tourist Information Centre. They also sup-
ply audio guides (€10) for self-guided tours
and hand out free copies of thematic walk-
ing tours, including Jewish Vilnius, Musical
Vilnius, and Castles & Palaces of Vilnius.

☷ Sleeping

Litinterp
B&B €

(☑5-212 3850; www.litinterp.lt; Bernardinų gatvė 7-2; s/d/tr €20/36/54; ☉office 8.30am-9pm

---

JEWISH VILNIUS

Over the centuries Vilnius developed into one of Europe's leading centres of Jewish life
and scholarship, until the community was wiped out by the occupying Nazis and their
Lithuanian sympathisers during WWII. The former Jewish quarter lay in the streets west
of Didžiojigatvė, including present-day Žydų gatvė (Jews St) and Gaono gatvė, named
after Vilnius' most famous Jewish resident, Gaon Elijahu ben Shlomo Zalman (1720–97).

The **Tolerance Centre** (☑5-262 9666; www.jmuseum.lt; Naugarduko gatvė 10/2; adult/
concession €4/2; ☉10am-6pm Mon-Thu, to 4pm Fri & Sun), in a beautifully restored former
Jewish theatre, houses thought-provoking displays on the history and culture of Jews
in Lithuania before the Shoah (Holocaust), plus occasional exhibitions. The **Holocaust
Museum** (Holokausto Muziejus; ☑5-262 0730; www.jmuseum.lt; Pamėnkalnio gatvė 12; adult/
child €3/1.50; ☉9am-5pm Mon-Thu, 9am-4pm Fri, 10am-4pm Sun), in the so-called Green
House, is an unvarnished account detailing the suffering of Lithuanian Jews in an un-
edited display of horrific images and letters by local survivors. Vilnius' only remaining
synagogue, the **Choral Synagogue** (Choralinė Sinagoga; ☑5-261 2523; Pylimo gatvė 39;
donations welcome; ☉10am-2pm Mon-Fri), was built in a Moorish style in 1903 and survived
because it was used as a medical store.

Vilnius

New Town / **Old Town** map

Map labels:
Neris River · Europa Tower (500m) · Žvejų gatvė · Žygimantų gatvė · Lukiškių gatvė · Gynėjų gatvė · Rinktinės gatvė · Lukiškių aikštė · NEW TOWN · Vienuolio gatvė · 22 · Vilniaus gatvė · Jasinskio gatvė · 17 · Goštauto gatvė · Gedimino prospektas · Neris River · Vingis Park (400m) · Pakalnės gatvė · Kudirkos gatvė · 6 · Tourist Information Office Old Town · 21 · Totorių gatvė · Vrublevskio gatvė · 3 · 11 · 1 · 7 · Palace of the Grand Dukes of Lithuania · Pylimo gatvė · Vilniaus gatvė · Liejyklos gatvė · Vilnius University · 2 · Pilies gatvė · Čiurlionio gatvė · Kalinausko gatvė · Rasų gatvė · Konarskio gatvė · Savanorių prospektas · Basanavičiaus gatvė · Traku gatvė · Vokiečių gatvė · OLD TOWN · 18 · Vivulskio gatvė · Vingrių gatvė · 14 · Rotušės aikštė · Ševčenkos gatvė · Švitrigailos gatvė · Vytenio gatvė · 10 · 19 · Tourist Information Office Town Hall · 9 · Smolensko gatvė · Naugarduko gatvė · Mindaugo gatvė · Aguonų gatvė · 4 · Ligoninės gatvė · 20 · Arklių gatvė · Aušros Vartų gatvė · 23 · Žemaitės gatvė · Algirdo gatvė · Raugyklos gatvė · Pylimo gatvė · 5 · 12 · Šopeno gatvė · Kauno gatvė · Vilkpėdės gatvė · Panerių gatvė · (3km) · Vilnius Bus Station · Train Station · Pelesos gatvė

Mon-Fri, 9am-3pm Sat; 🛜) This bright, clean and friendly establishment has a wide range of options in the heart of the Old Town. Rooms with shared bathroom can be a little cramped, but those with en suite are generously large. Guests can check in after office hours providing they give advance notice, and mini kitchens and a left-luggage service are available. Breakfast is €3.

Filaretai Hostel

HOSTEL €

(📞 6865 5589; www.filaretaihostel.com; Filaretų gatvė 17; dm/s/d/tr per person without bathroom €10/20/15/12; 🅿 @ 🛜) Affiliated with the Lithuanian Hostels Association, Filaretai occupies a quaint old villa 15 minutes' walk (uphill) from Old Town. Dorms are five- to eight-bedded; bed linen is provided, towels are extra, and there's a communal kitchen and washing machine. To get here take bus 34 from the bus and train stations to the seventh stop.

Come to Vilnius

HOSTEL €

(📞 8-6202 9390; www.cometovilnius.eu; Šv Stepano gatvė 15; dm/d/tr €16/35/43; @ 🛜) Bright colours, timber furnishings, proximity to transport and free pancakes, hot drinks,

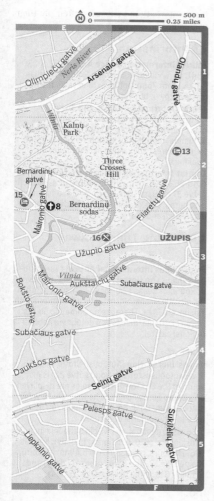

towels and wi-fi are the draws at this decent indie hostel. Prices fall slightly in the low season.

✗ Eating

★ Senamiesčio Krautuvė LITHUANIAN €
(☑ 5-231 2836; www.senamiesciokrautuve.lt; Literatų gatvė 5; ☉ 10am-8pm Mon-Sat, 11am-5pm Sun) Look no further than this wonderful, quiet hobbit-hole for the very best Lithuanian comestibles, many unique to the country. Cured meats, fresh sausages, cheeses, fresh fruit and vegetables, honey and preserves, breads and pastries: all are arranged in ir-

resistible profusion around the walls of this snug trove on Literatų gatvė.

Kmyninė BAKERY €
(☑ 6404 9042; Užupio gatvė 38; bread or cookies per kilo €3.50-7; ☉ 7.30am-9pm Mon-Fri, from 8am Sat & Sun; ☏) This sweet little bakery, named for the caraway seeds so beloved in Central and Eastern Europe, is a great place to pick up moist, sweet rye breads, Lithuanian cookies and *sakotis,* the traditional cake that looks a little like a Christmas tree.

Pietausim LITHUANIAN €
(☑ 6260 5652; www.pietausim.lt; J Jasinskio gatvė 16; mains €4; ☉ 11am-2.30pm Mon-Fri) Like a Soviet-era canteen, but with sleek decor and a bustling, youthful clientele, Pietausim bangs out great-value Lithuanian food to the lunchtime *cognoscenti.* Baked fish, *šaltibarščiai* (cold beetroot soup), salads

and more: all gets hoovered up by the early afternoon, so get in quickly.

Drinking & Nightlife

Bukowski
BAR

(8-640 58855; www.facebook.com/bukowski-pub; Visų Šventų gatvė 7; ⊗4pm-2am Mon-Thu, to 4am Fri & Sat, to midnight Sun) The eponymous Barfly is the spiritual patron of this charismatic boho bar in a less-trodden pocket of the Old Town. It has a back terrace for finer weather, great beers on tap, a full program of poetry, music and other events, and a welcoming, unpretentious atmosphere. One of Vilnius' best.

Būsi Trečias
MICROBREWERY

(⊡618 11266; www.busitrecias.lt; Totorių gatvė 18; ⊗11am-11pm Sun-Wed, to midnight Thu, to 2am Fri & Sat) Locals know this microbrewery-pub is a great place to get a cheap, sustaining Lithuanian lunch. It also offers charismatic wooden decor, 12 varieties of beer (including lime, raspberry and caramel) and courtyard tables for the warmer months.

Brodvėjus
CLUB

(www.brodvejus.lt; Vokiečių gatvė 4/Mėsinių gatvė 4; ⊗8pm-3am Sun, Tue & Wed, to 4am Thu, to 5am Fri & Sat) Live bands, karaoke, DJs and raucous late nights make this an institution in the heart of the Old Town.

☆ Entertainment

The tourist office publishes events listings, as does the *Baltic Times* (www.baltictimes.com).

Lithuanian National Opera & Ballet Theatre
OPERA

(Lietuvos Nacionalinis Operos ir Baleto Teatras; ⊡5-262 0727; www.opera.lt; Vienuolio gatvė 1; ⊗box office 10am-7pm Mon-Fri, to 6.30pm Sat, to 3pm Sun) This stunning (or gaudy, depending on your taste) Soviet-era building, with its huge, cascading chandeliers and grandiose dimensions, is home to Lithuania's national ballet and opera companies. You can see world-class performers for as little as €4 (or as much as €200...)

Lithuanian National Philharmonic
CLASSICAL MUSIC

(Lietuvos Nacionalinė Filharmonija; ⊡5-266 5233; www.filharmonija.lt; Aušros Vartų gatvė 5; ⊗box office 10am-7pm Tue-Sat, to noon Sun) Lithuania's premier venue for orchestral, chamber and sacral music. But it's not all classical: prominent international jazz acts often ply their trade here.

Information

Tourist Information Office Airport
(⊡5-230 6841; www.vilnius-tourism.lt; Rodūnios kelias 2-1; ⊗10am-7pm) Not as extensive as the head office in town, but very useful.

Tourist Information Office Old Town
(⊡5-262 9660; www.vilnius-tourism.lt; Vilniaus gatvė 22; ⊗9am-6pm) The head office of Vilnius' tourist information service is great for brochures, advice and accommodation bookings.

Tourist Information Office Town Hall
(⊡5-262 6470; www.vilnius-tourism.lt; Didžioji gatvė 31; ⊗9am-1pm & 2-6pm) Good for maps, brochures, bike rentals, accommodation booking, advice and more.

ⓘ Getting There & Away

AIR

From **Vilnius International Airport** (Tarptautinis Vilniaus Oro Uostas; ⊡6124 4442; www.vno.lt; Rodūnios kelias 10a; ☎; ⌨1, 2), 5km south of the city, there are international connections with Tallinn and Rīga. There are no domestic flights within Lithuania, unless you detour via another regional capital.

BUS

Vilnius' **bus station** (Autobusų Stotis; ⊡1661; www.autobusustotis.lt; Sodų gatvė 22) is just south of the Old Town. Timetables are displayed on a board here and on the handy website www.autobusubilietai.lt. Several bus lines run from here to international destinations.

Buses to destinations within Lithuania include Druskininkai (€10, two hours, 15 daily), Kaunas (€6, 1¾ hours, regularly from 5.45am to 11pm), Klaipėda (€18, four to 5½ hours, 17 daily) and Šiauliai (€13, three to 4½ hours, 15 daily).

TRAIN

The **train station** (Geležinkelio Stotis; ⊡5-269 2121; www.litrail.lt; Geležinkelio gatvė 16) is opposite the bus station. There is no direct or convenient rail link between Vilnius and Rīga or Tallinn. Direct daily services within Lithuania to/from Vilnius include Kaunas (€6, 1½ hours, 14 daily), Klaipėda (€16, four hours, three daily) and Trakai (€1.70, 40 minutes, up to 10 daily).

ⓘ Getting Around

TO/FROM THE AIRPORT

Bus 1 runs between the airport and the train station; bus 2 runs between the airport and the northwestern suburb of Šeškinė via the Žaliasis bridge across the Neris and on to Lukiškių aikštė. Have small change handy for a ticket (€1 from the driver).

Trains run to the central station every 30 minutes between 6am and 11.30pm. On-board tickets cost €0.72 and the trip is only 10 minutes.

Taxi rates vary depending on whether you hail one from out the front of the arrivals hall (about €15), or call a reputable firm in advance (around €10).

BICYCLE

Bikes can be easily hired and returned at the 37 orange **Cyclocity** (☑ 8-800 22008; www. cyclocity.lt; ☺ Apr-Oct) stations across Vilnius. Either credit cards or Cyclocity Cards (available by advance subscription) can be used to hire a bike. A three-day ticket is €2.90.

Velo-City (☑ 8-674 12123; www.velovilnius. lt; Palangos gatvė 1; per hr/24hr €5/12; ☺ 10am-8pm Apr-Sep, by appointment Oct to Mar) is a well-established bike-hire operation on the edge of the Old Town with decent, well-maintained bikes.

PUBLIC TRANSPORT

The city is efficiently served by buses and trolleybuses from 5.30am or 6am to midnight; Sunday services are less frequent. Single-trip tickets cost €1 from the driver, €0.64 if you have a Vilniečio Kortelė (an electronic ticket sold at kiosks; see www.vilniusticket.lt for details) or nothing if you have a Vilnius City Card with public transport included (sold in tourist information centres). Fare evaders risk a small fine.

Quicker minibuses shadow most routes. They pick up/drop off passengers anywhere en route (not just at official bus stops) and can be flagged down on the street. Tickets costs €1 from the driver.

For destinations within the Old Town, you'll normally have to hoof it.

For route details see www.vilniustransport.lt or pick up a transport map from tourist offices.

TAXI

Taxi rates in Vilnius can vary; they are generally cheaper if ordered in advance by telephone than if hailed directly off the street or picked up at a taxi stand. Ask the hotel reception desk or restaurant to call one for you. Reliable companies include **Ekipažas** (☑ 1446; www.ekipazastaksi. lt) and **Mersera** (☑ 278 8888).

Trakai

POP 5400

With its red-brick, fairy-tale castle, Karaites culture, quaint wooden houses and pretty lakeside location, Trakai is a must-see just 28km from the capital.

Most of the town stands on a 2km-long, north-pointing tongue of land between Lake Luka (east) and Lake Totoriškių (west). Lake Galvė opens out from the northern end of the peninsula and boasts 21 islands.

Gediminas probably made Trakai his capital in the 1320s and Kęstutis certainly based his 14th-century court here. Protected by the 82-sq-km **Trakai Historical National Park** (☑ 528-55 776; www.seniejitrakai.lt), Trakai today is a quiet town, outside summer weekends.

◉ Sights

★ Trakai Castle CASTLE

(Trakų Pilis; www.trakaimuziejus.lt; adult/senior/ student & child €7/3.50/3.50; ☺ 10am-7pm May-Sep, 10am-6pm Tue-Sun Mar, Apr & Oct, 9am-5pm Tue-Sun Nov-Feb; ♿) The centrepiece of Trakai is its picture-postcard Island Castle atop an island on Lake Galvė. The painstakingly restored red-brick Gothic castle probably dates from around 1400, when Gran Duke Vytautas needed stronger defences than the peninsula castle afforded. A footbridge links it to the shore and a moat separates the triangular outer courtyard from the main tower with its cavernous central court and a range of galleries, halls and rooms. Some house the Trakai History Museum, which charts the history of the castle.

Church of the Visitation of the Blessed Mary CHURCH

(Birutės gatvė 5) Founded around the same time as Trakai Castle, and also by Grand Duke Vytautas, this grand, 15th-century parish church has a large collection of ecclesiastical art, including the Trakai Mother of God, a revered image thought to have been donated by Vytautas himself.

Karaite Ethnographic Museum MUSEUM

(Karaimų etnografinė paroda; ☑ 528-55 286; www. trakaimuziejus.lt; Karaimų gatvė 22; adult/child €2/1; ☺ 10am-6pm Wed-Sun Apr-Oct, to 5pm Nov-Mar) The Karaite Ethnographic Museum traces the ancestry of the Karaites, a Judaic sect and Turkic minority originating in Baghdad, which adheres to the Law of Moses. Their descendants – some 380 families – were brought to Trakai from the Crimea around 1400 to serve as bodyguards. Only 12 families (60 individuals) still live in Trakai and their numbers – 280 throughout Lithuania – are dwindling rapidly.

ℹ Information

Tourist Information Centre (☎ 528-51 934; www.trakai-visit.lt; Karaimų gatvė 41; ⊙ 9am-6pm May-Sep, 8am-5pm Mon-Fri, from 10am Sat & Sun Oct-Apr) Lavishly stocked with brochures, staffed by English speakers who can organise everything from boat trips to accommodation, and with an adjoining handicrafts shop, this little office by the lake has everything you need.

ℹ Getting There & Away

Up to 10 daily trains (€1.48, 30 minutes) travel between Trakai's **train station** (☎ 7005 5111; Vilniaus gatvė 5) and Vilnius.

Kaunas

POP 353,000

Kaunas (kow-nas), a sprawling city 100km west of Vilnius at the confluence of the Nemunas and Neris Rivers, has a compact Old Town, an abundance of artistic and educational museums, and a fascinating history. A sizeable student population provides plenty of energy, and some rough edges give it that extra bit of spice.

◉ Sights

◉ Old Town

Rotušės aikštė, a large, open square at the heart of the Old Town, is lined with pretty 15th- and 16th-century German merchants' houses and is centred on the 17th-century former **town hall** (Kauno rotušė; ☎ 37-424 263; www.kaunas.lt; Rotušės aikštė 15). The first two floors also serve as a wedding hall (Saturdays usually see a procession of brides and grooms in their finery) and there's a small ceramics museum in the cellar.

St Francis Xavier Church & Monastery CHURCH
(☎ 37-432 098; www.jesuit.lt; Rotušės aikštė 7-9; tower €1.50; ⊙ 4-6pm Mon-Fri, 7am-1pm & 4-6pm Sun) The southern side of Rotušės aikštė is dominated by the twin-towered St Francis Xavier Church, college and Jesuit monastery complex, built between 1666 and 1720. Take a peek inside and then climb the tower for the best aerial views of Kaunas.

Sts Peter & Paul Cathedral CHURCH
(Šventų Apaštalų Petro ir Povilo Arkekatedra Bazilika; ☎ 37-324 093; www.kaunoarkikatedra.lt; Vilniaus gatvė 1; ⊙ 7am-9pm) With its single tower, this church owes much to baroque reconstruction, especially inside, but the original 15th-century Gothic shape of its windows remains. The largest Gothic building in Lithuania, it was probably founded by Vytautas around 1410 and now has nine altars. The **tomb of Maironis** stands outside the south wall.

◉ New Town

Kaunas expanded east from the Old Town in the 19th century, giving birth to the modern centre and its striking 1.7km pedestrian street, **Laisvės alėja** (Freedom Ave).

★**MK Čiurlionis National Museum of Art** GALLERY
(MK Čiurlionio Valstybinis Dailės Muziejus; ☎ 37-229 475; www.ciurlionis.lt; Putvinskio gatvė 55; adult/child €4/2; ⊙ 11am-5pm Tue, Wed & Fri-Sun, to 7pm Thu) In this, Kaunas' leading gallery, you'll find extensive collections of the romantic paintings of Mikalojus Konstantinas Čiurlionis (1875–1911), one of Lithuania's greatest artists and composers, as well as Lithuanian folk art and 16th- to 20th-century European applied art.

Museum of Devils MUSEUM
(Velnių Muziejus; ☎ 37-221 587; www.ciurlionis.lt; Putvinskio gatvė 64; adult/child €3/1.50; ⊙ 11am-5pm Tue, Wed & Fri-Sun, to 7pm Thu; 🖐) Diabolical is the best word to describe the collection of 3000-odd devil statuettes in this museum, collected over the years by landscape artist Antanas Žmuidzinavičius (1876–1966). While the commentary aims for a pseudo-intellectual veneer, linking the devils to Lithuanian folklore, the fun of this museum is all about the spooky masks and stories. Great for kids.

◉ Outside the Centre

Museum of the Ninth Fort MUSEUM
(IX Forto Muziejus; ☎ 37-377 750; www.9fortomuziejus.lt; Žemaičių plentas 73; adult/child €3/1.50; ⊙ 10am-6pm Wed-Mon Apr-Oct, 10am-4pm Wed-Sun Nov-Mar) A poignant memorial to the tens of thousands of people, mainly Jews, who were murdered by the Nazis, the excellent Museum of the Ninth Fort, 7km north of Kaunas, comprises an old WWI-era fort and the bunker-like church of the damned. Displays cover deportations of Lithuanians by the Soviets and graphic photo exhibitions track the demise of Kaunas' Jewish

Kaunas

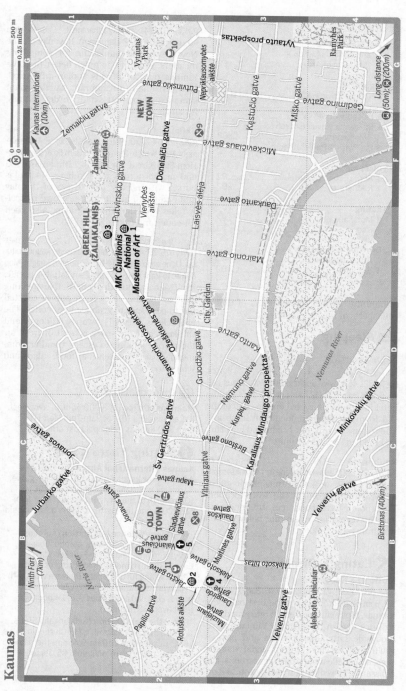

Map labels:

Kaunas International (10km)

Žemaičių gatvė

Vytautas Park

Vytauto prospektas

Žaliakalnis Funicular

Putvinskio gatvė

Nepriklausomybės aikštė

Kęstučio gatvė

Miško gatvė

Gedimino gatvė

Long-distance (50m); (200m)

Ramybės Park

NEW TOWN

Donelaičio gatvė

Mickevičiaus gatvė

GREEN HILL (ŽALIAKALNIS)

Putvinskio gatvė

Vienybės aikštė

MK Čiurlionis National Museum of Art

Daukanto gatvė

Laisvės alėja

Savanorių prospektas

Ožeškienės gatvė

Maironio gatvė

City Garden

Kanto gatvė

Nemunas River

Gruodžio gatvė

Nemuno gatvė

Kurpių gatvė

Karaliaus Mindaugo prospektas

Birštono gatvė

Minkovskių gatvė

Šv Gertrūdos gatvė

Jonavos gatvė

Jurbarko gatvė

Veiverių gatvė

Birštonas (40km)

Mapu gatvė

Vilniaus gatvė

Daukšos gatvė

OLD TOWN

Sladkevičiaus gatvė

Muitinės gatvė

Aleksoto gatvė

Aleksoto tiltas

Veiverių gatvė

Aleksoto Funicular

Ninth Fort (7km)

Neris River

Papilio gatvė

Rotušės aikštė

Jakšto gatvė

Valančiaus gatvė

Muziejaus gatvė

Daugirdo gatvė

Jonavos gatvė

N

500 m
0.25 miles

0
0

Kaunas

◎ Top Sights
1 MK Čiurlionis National
  Museum of Art E2

◎ Sights
2 Kaunas Town Hall.................................B2
  Maironis's Tomb ....(see 5)
3 Museum of Devils E1
4 St Francis Xavier Church &
  Monastery..B3
5 Sts Peter & Paul Cathedral.................B2

🛏 Sleeping
6 Apple Economy Hotel..........................B2
7 Radharanė B2

🍴 Eating
8 Motiejaus Kepyklėlė B2
9 Radharanė F2

🍷 Drinking & Nightlife
10 Kultūra Kavinė.....................................G2
11 Skliautas B2

community. Various guided tours of different aspects of the fort are offered.

🛏 Sleeping

**Apple Economy
Hotel** HOTEL €
(📞37-321 404; www.applehotel.lt; Valančiaus gatvė 19; s/d from €34/42; P ✿ @ 🛜) This simple hotel in a quiet courtyard on the edge of the Old Town is a recommended no-frills option. The rooms are tiny, but bright and cheerful, and the beds are very comfy.

Radharanė GUESTHOUSE €€
(📞37-320 800; www.radharane.lt; M Daukšos gatvė 28; d €49-56; P @ 🛜) Atmospheric guesthouse with an excellent Old Town location. The rooms have been recently renovated and the vegetarian restaurant below is well worth investigating.

🍴 Eating & Drinking

Motiejaus Kepyklėlė BAKERY €
(📞8-616 15599; Vilniaus gatvė 7; ⊙8am-7pm Mon-Sat, 9am-6pm Sun) Perhaps the best bakery in Kaunas, Motiejaus has settled into grand new redbrick digs in the heart of Vilniaus gatvė. Alongside Lithuanian cookies and pastries you'll find excellent international dainties such as canneles, cupcakes, macaroons and croissants. The coffee can also be counted on.

Radharanė VEGETARIAN €
(📞37-362 941; www.radharane.lt; Laisvės alėja 40; mains €4-6; ⊙11am-9pm) If you're in the New Town and hankering for something meatless, you can't do much better than the Kaunas outpost of this Indian-influenced, Hare Krishna-run restaurant. Curries, giant samosas, soups and salads: order blithely, it's all good.

Skliautas BAR
(📞37-6864 2700; Rotušės aikštė 26; ⊙4pm-midnight Mon-Wed, to 2am Thu, to 3am Fri & Sat, 11am-11pm Sun) Great for cheap Lithuanian food and a boisterous atmosphere, Skliautas bursts with energy most times of the day and night, and in summer its crowd basically takes over the adjoining alley. Also good for coffee and cake.

Kultūra Kavinė CAFE
(📞8-676 25546; www.facebook.com/kauno.kultura; Donelaičio gatvė 14-16; ⊙noon-midnight Mon & Tue, to 2am Wed-Fri, 3pm-2am Sat; 🛜) It calls itself a cafe, but this alternative meeting spot covers the bases from pub to cocktail bar to cosy spot to grab a cup of coffee. The clientele is skewed towards students and thinkers, and the space is a bit of fresh air for anyone looking to escape trendier, commercial bars. Excellent bar food, salads and wings, too.

ℹ Information

Main Post Office (📞8-700 55400; www.post.lt; Laisvės alėja 102; ⊙9am-7pm Mon-Fri, to 2pm Sat) Kaunas' principal post office.

ℹ Getting There & Away

Kaunas International Airport (📞8-612 44442; www.kaunas-airport.lt; Vilniaus gatvė, Karmėlava; ⊙6am-midnight; 🚌 29, 29E) is 10km north of the city centre. Bus 29 or minibus 120 run to the centre of town; a taxi should cost around €18.

The **long-distance bus station** (Autobusų Stotis; 📞37-409 060; www.autobusubilietai.lt; Vytauto prospektas 24; ⊙ticket office 6am-9.30pm) handles intercity buses within Lithuania and further afield. Daily services within Lithuania include Klaipėda (€14, 2¾ to four hours, 20 daily) and Vilnius (€6, 1¾ hours, at least every 30 minutes).

From the **train station** (Geležinkelio Stotis; 📞7005 5111; www.litrail.lt; MK Čiurlionio gatvė 16; ⊙ticket office 4.10am-9.45pm) there are 14 trains daily to/from Vilnius (€5, 1¼ to 1¾ hours).

THE HILL OF CROSSES

One of Lithuania's most awe-inspiring sights is the legendary **Hill of Crosses** (Kryžių kalnas; ☎ 41-370 860; Jurgaičiai). The sound of the thousands of crosses – which appear to grow on the hillock – tinkling in the breeze is wonderfully eerie.

Planted here since at least the 19th century and probably much older, the crosses were bulldozed by the Soviets, but each night people crept past soldiers and barbed wire to plant more, risking their lives or freedom to express their national and spiritual fervour. Some of the crosses are devotional, others are memorials (many for people deported to Siberia), and some are finely carved folk-art masterpieces.

The hill is 10km north of Šiauliai, 2km east off the road to Joniškis and Rīga, in the village of Jurgaičiai. To get here, take one of up to eight daily buses from Šiauliai bus station to Joniškis and get off at the Domantai stop, from where the hill is a 2km walk. The return taxi fare from Šiauliai is €18 to €22; ask Šiauliai tourist office to order one for you by telephone to avoid paying more than you should.

Šiauliai is reachable by bus from Vilnius (€15, 3¾ hours, six daily), Kaunas (€10, 2¾ hours, 20 daily) and Klaipėda (€11, three hours, eight daily). For accommodation, consult the **Tourist Information Centre** (☎ 41-523 110; http://tic.siauliai.lt; Vilniaus gatvė 213; ⊙ 9am-6pm Mon-Fri, 10am-4pm Sat Sep-May, plus 10am-2pm Sun Jun-Aug).

ℹ Getting Around

Buses and trolleybuses run from 5am to 11pm, and tickets cost €0.70 from the driver. Alternatively, you can buy a *Kauno Miesto Kortelė* (Kaunas City Card) from a Kauno Spauda or Naversen kiosk for €1.74, top it up, and pay only €0.58 per trip. While the City Card is cheaper, it's only really worth it if you'll be in Kaunas for an extended stay.

Minibuses shadow routes and run later than regular buses; drivers sell tickets for €0.87, and will stop wherever you wish. For information on public transport, including routes and timetables, see the website Kaunas Public Transport (www.kvt.lt).

Klaipėda

POP 161,300

Lithuania's third-largest city is a mix of old and new. This former Prussian capital (when it was named Memel) has retained a distinct German flavour in the architecture of its heavily cobbled Old Town and one remaining tower of its red-brick castle. It's also Lithuania's only port of call for *Titanic*-sized cruise ships, and a vital sea link for cargo and passenger ferries between Lithuania, Scandinavia and beyond.

Most people will only catch a glimpse of Klaipėda (klai-pey-da) as they rush headlong for the ferry to Curonian Spit, but spend a few hours – or even better, a day – and you'll be justly rewarded.

◉ Sights

Klaipėda Castle Museum MUSEUM
(Klaipėda Pilies Muziejus; ☎ 46-410 527; www.mlimuziejus.lt; Pilies gatvė 4; adult/child €1.74/0.87; ⊙ 10am-6pm Tue-Sat) This small museum is based inside the remains of Klaipėda's old moat-protected castle, which dates back to the 13th century. It tells the castle's story through the ages until the 19th century, when most of the structure was pulled down. You'll find fascinating photos from WWII and the immediate postwar years, when the city was rebuilt by Soviet planners.

History Museum of Lithuania Minor MUSEUM
(Mažosios Lietuvos Istorijos Muziejus; ☎ 46-410 524; www.mlimuziejus.lt; Didžioji Vandens gatvė 6; adult/child €1.45/0.72; ⊙ 10am-6pm Tue-Sat) This small museum traces the origins of 'Lithuania Minor' (Kleinlitauen) – as this coastal region was known during several centuries as part of East Prussia. It exhibits Prussian maps, coins, artefacts of the Teutonic order, traditional weaving machines and traditional folk art.

Švyturys BREWERY
(☎ 46-484 000; www.svyturys.lt; Kūlių Vartų gatvė 7) Klaipėda is home to the country's oldest operating brewery, where its biggest beer, Švyturys, has been brewed since 1784. Organised by the tourist office, tours of the brewery are 1½ to two hours, cost €10 per

Klaipėda

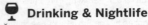

Klaipėda

◎ Sights
1 History Museum of Lithuania
Minor B2
2 Klaipėda Castle Museum A3

✴ Eating
3 Katpėdėlė A1

◎ Drinking & Nightlife
4 Žvejų Baras B1

person (including tastings), and leave any time between 10am and 4pm Monday to Friday.

🛏 Sleeping & Eating

Klaipėda Hostel
HOSTEL €

(☑655 94407; www.klaipedahostel.com; Butkų Juzės gatvė 7/4; dm/d €12/30; 🅿@🛜) This friendly hostel close to the bus station looks terrible from the outside but is very homey and pleasant inside. Two small dorms sleep 12 people and there's one double, as well as a kitchen and free tea and coffee. Book in advance; no credit cards accepted.

Katpėdėlė
LITHUANIAN €

(☑8-618 28343; www.katpedele.lt; Žvejų gatvė 12; mains €4-9; ⊙11am-10pm Sun-Wed, to 11pm Thu,

to 1am Fri & Sat; 🛜) It may be a franchise, but Katpėdėlė does the Lithuanian standards really well, and makes the most of a brick merchant's building in a prime spot by the Danė. Try the grilled pork neck with thyme and whiskey sauce, or the salmon with peanuts.

🍷 Drinking & Nightlife

Žvejų Baras
BAR

(☑699 98762; www.zvejubaras.lt; Kurpių gatvė 8; ⊙5pm-midnight Sun-Wed, to 2am Thu, to 4am Fri & Sat) The beautiful, lead-lit, timbered interior of this portside pub (the name means 'Fisherman's Bar') is one of Klaipėda's nicest places to catch live music, or chat over a few interesting beers.

ℹ Information

Tourist Office (☑46-412 186; www.klaipedainfo.lt; Turgaus gatvė 7; ⊙9am-6pm Mon-Fri) Exceptionally efficient tourist office selling maps and locally published guidebooks, and arranging accommodation, tours and more. Operates reduced hours outside high season, closing on Sundays.

ℹ Getting There & Away

The train and bus stations are situated near each other in the modern part of town, about 2km north of Old Town. Three daily trains run to Vilnius (€18, 4 hours). There are regular bus services to Vilnius (€18, four to 5½ hours, 17 daily) and Kaunas (€14, 2¾ to four hours, 20 daily).

Curonian Spit National Park

This magical sliver of land, covered by pine forest, hosts some of Europe's most precious sand dunes and a menagerie of elk, deer and avian wildlife. Recognised by Unesco as a World Heritage site, the fragile spit is divided evenly between Lithuania and Russia's Kaliningrad region, with Lithuania's half protected as **Curonian Spit National Park** (☑46-402 256; www.nerija.lt; Smiltynės gatvė 11, Smiltynė; ⊙9am-noon & 1-6pm Tue-Sat).

Smiltynė, where the ferries from Klaipėda dock, draws weekend crowds with the fascinating **Lithuania Sea Museum** (Lietuvos Jūrų Muziejus; ☑46-490 740; www.juru.muziejus.lt; Smiltynės gatvė 3; adult/student Jun-Aug €10/5, Sep-May €7/3.50; ⊙10.30am-6.30pm Tue-Sun Jun-Aug, shorter hours rest of year; 👪) inside a 19th-century fort. Further south, the village of **Juodkrantė** is scented with the tempting smells of smoked fish (*žuvis*) and home to a 6500-strong colony of grey herons and cormorants, while picture-perfect **Nida** is close by the unmissable 52m-high **Parnidis Dune**, with its panoramic views of the 'Lithuanian Sahara' – coastline, forest and sand extending towards Kaliningrad.

The tourist office in Klaipėda can help arrange transport and accommodation.

Curonian Spit is accessible only via boat or ferry (there are no bridges linking the spit to the mainland). From Klaipėda, two ferries run regularly: a passenger ferry, known as the 'Old Ferry', goes to Smiltynė; and a vehicle ferry, the 'New Ferry', connects to a point on the spit around 2km south of Smiltynė, and departs from a port 2km south of Klaipėda's Old Town.

Regular buses run to villages on the spit, including Nida (€3.40) and Juodkrantė (€1.40), but these depart from **Smiltynė** (Smiltynės gatvė), meaning you'll first have to use the passenger ferry to get to the bus.

Ift the weather is fine, cycling is a great way to explore the spit. There is a well-marked trail that runs the entire length of the spit from Smiltynė to Nida via Juodkrantė (about 50km). Hire bikes in Klaipėda and take them across the lagoon via the passenger ferry for free.

Lithuania Survival Guide

❶ Directory A–Z

ACCOMMODATION

Book ahead in the high season for Vilnius and the Curonian Spit. High-season prices are around 30% higher than low-season prices. Prices are higher in Vilnius.

Budget accommodation in Lithuania (**€**) is less than €50.

INTERNET RESOUCES
State Tourism Department (www.tourism.lt)

LGBT TRAVELLERS

The scene is low-key and underground. For general information, chat rooms and guides, contact Vilnius-based **Lithuanian Gay League** (☑ 5-261 0314; www.gay.lt), which publishes a solid online entertainment guide in English.

PUBLIC HOLIDAYS
New Year's Day 1 January
Independence Day (Nepriklausomybės diena) 16 February; anniversary of 1918 independence declaration
Lithuanian Independence Restoration Day 11 March
Easter March/April
International Labour Day 1 May
Mothers' Day First Sunday in May
Fathers' Day First Sunday in June

RUSSIA & THE BALTIC COAST LITHUANIA SURVIVAL GUIDE

DON'T MISS

ŽEMAITIJA NATIONAL PARK

The 200-sq-km Žemaitija National Park, a magical landscape of lake and forest, is as mysterious as it is beautiful. It's easy to see why it spawns fables of devils, ghosts and buried treasure.

The draw here is twofold. You can swim, boat and bike around at your leisure, as well as pay a visit to one of the country's newest and most bizarre attractions: the **Cold War Museum** (Šaltojo Karo Muziejus; ☑ 8-677 86574; www.zemaitijosnp.lt; Plokštinė; adult/child €5/2.50; ⊙ 8am-noon & 12.45-5pm Mon-Thu, 8am-noon & 12.45-3.45pm Fri), housed in what was once a Soviet nuclear missile base.

The best access point is the small town of **Plateliai**, on the western shore of the lake of the same name, and home to the helpful **Žemaitija National Park Visitor Centre** (☑ 448-49 231; www.zemaitijosnp.lt; Didžioji gatvė 8; ⊙ 8am-5pm Mon-Fri).

About 20km northeast of the park is **Samogitian Calvary** (Žemaičių Kalvarija), built on the site of 9th- to 13th-century burial grounds. Pilgrims come here during the first two weeks of July to climb the seven hills, where 20 chapels form a 7km 'Stations of the Cross' route in commemoration of Christ's life, death and resurrection.

Plungė, the nearest city, is best reached by train from Klaipėda (€4, one hour, four daily) and from Vilnius (€13, four hours, two daily). There are several buses that run daily from Kaunas (€13, four hours). From Plungė, there are limited bus services onward to Plateliai.

> ## ⓘ PRICE RANGES
>
> The following price ranges refer to the cost of a double room with private bathroom.
>
> **€** less than €50
>
> **€€** €50–100
>
> The following meal price ranges are based on a typical main meal.
>
> **€** less than €7
>
> **€€** €7–14

Feast of St John (Midsummer) 24 June
Statehood Day 6 July; commemoration of coronation of Grand Duke Mindaugas in the 13th century
Assumption of Blessed Virgin 15 August
All Saints' Day 1 November
Christmas (Kalėdos) 25 and 26 December

TELEPHONE

➡ To call a landline within Lithuania, dial 8 followed by the city code and phone number.

➡ To call a mobile phone within Lithuania, dial 8 followed by the eight-digit number.

➡ To make an international call dial 00 before the country code.

➡ Mobile companies Bitė (www.bite.lt), Telia (www.telia.lt) and Tele2 (www.tele2.lt) sell pre-paid SIM cards. Tele2 offers free roaming with its prepaid cards, making it the best choice for those travelling in Estonia, Latvia and Poland too. It also offers the cheapest rates.

ⓘ Getting There & Away

AIR

Between them, airBaltic and Estonian Air connect Vilnius with Tallinn up to five times daily, and Rīga up to seven times daily.

Ryanair handles the bulk of Kaunas airport's traffic, operating flights to/from 11 European destinations.

BOAT

From Klaipėda's **International Ferry Port** (46-323 232; www.dfdsseaways.lt; Perkėlos gatvė 10), **DFDS Seaways** (46-323 232; www.dfdsseaways.lt; Šaulių gatvė 19) runs big passenger and car ferries regularly to Kiel and Sassnitz (in Germany), and to Karlshamn (in Sweden).

BUS

Simple Express (www.simpleexpress.eu) Budget bus carrier offering arguably the lowest prices to Lithuania from destinations in the Baltic, including daily buses to Vilnius from Rīga and Tallinn and to Kaunas from Rīga.

TRAIN

Many international train routes, including to Warsaw and Moscow, pass through Belarus and require a transit visa.

See Lithuanian Rail (www.litrail.lt) for further information.

ⓘ Getting Around

BICYCLE

Touring cyclists will find Lithuania mercifully flat. Some roads are unsealed, but they're usually kept in good condition. Bike hire is offered in all the major cities.

BUS

Most services are summarised on the handy website Bus Tickets (www.autobusubilietai.lt).

CAR & MOTORCYCLE

Lithuanian roads are generally very good and driving is easy, though winter poses particular problems for those not used to driving in ice and snow. Four-lane highways link the main cities of Vilnius, Kaunas and Klaipėda, and the drive from Vilnius all the way to the Baltic coast (330km) generally takes three to four hours. Car hire is offered in all the major cities.

PUBLIC TRANSPORT

Lithuanian cities generally have good public transport, with buses, trolleybuses and minibuses. A ride usually costs around €1.

TRAIN

Services link Vilnius to Kaunas, Klaipėda and Trakai. Whether you take the bus or the train depends very much on the route. For common train journeys like Vilnius to Kaunas or to Klaipėda, the train is often more comfortable and better value than the bus. For other routes, the opposite might be true.

Survival Guide

Directory A–Z

Accommodation

Europe offers the fullest possible range of accommodation for all budgets. Book up to two months in advance for a July visit or for ski resorts over Christmas and New Year.

Hotels Range from the local pub to restored castles.

B&Bs Small, family-run houses generally provide good value.

Hostels Enormous variety from backpacker palaces to real dumps.

Homestays and farmstays A great way to really find out how locals live.

Price Ranges

Rates in our reviews are for high season and often drop outside high season by as much as 50%. High season in ski resorts is usually between Christmas and New Year and around the February to March winter holidays. Price categories are broken down differently for individual countries – see each country for full details.

Reservations

During peak holiday periods, particularly Easter, summer and Christmas – and any time of year in popular destinations such as London, Paris and Rome – it's wise to book ahead. Most places can be reserved online. Always try to book directly with the establishment; this means you're paying just for your room, with no surcharge going to a hostel- or hotel-booking website.

B&Bs & Guesthouses

Guesthouses (pension, Gasthaus, chambre d'hôte etc) and B&Bs (bed and breakfasts) offer greater comfort than hostels for a marginally higher price. Most are simple affairs, normally with shared bathrooms.

In some destinations, particularly in Eastern Europe, locals wait in train stations touting rented rooms. Just be sure such accommodation isn't in a far-flung suburb that requires an expensive taxi ride to and from town. Confirm the price before agreeing to rent a room and remember that it's unwise to leave valuables in your room when you go out.

B&Bs in the UK and Ireland often aren't really budget accommodation – even the lowliest tend to have midrange prices and there is a new generation of 'designer' B&Bs, which are positively top end.

Camping

Most camping grounds are some distance from city centres; we list easily accessible camping grounds only, and have included sites where it's common for travellers to bed down en masse under the stars (for example, on some Greek islands).

National tourist offices provide lists of camping grounds and camping organisations. Also see www.coolcamping.co.uk for details on prime campsites across Europe.

There will usually be a charge per tent or site, per person and per vehicle. In busy areas and in busy seasons, it's sometimes necessary to book in advance.

Camping other than at designated grounds is difficult in Western Europe, because it's hard to find a suitably private spot.

Camping is also illegal without the permission of the local authorities (the police or local council office) or the landowner. Don't be shy about asking; you might be pleasantly surprised.

BOOK YOUR STAY ONLINE

For more accommodation reviews by Lonely Planet authors, check out http://lonelyplanet.com/hotels/. You'll find independent reviews, as well as recommendations on the best places to stay. Best of all, you can book online.

PRACTICALITIES

Bargaining Isn't common in much of Europe, but is known in and around the Mediterranean. In Turkey it's virtually a way of life.

Dining Europeans take their time over dining (especially in the Mediterranean) enjoying food, family, talk and wine. Fast food, though present, is less popular.

Dress Dress modestly when visiting churches or other religious buildings. Europeans are more inclined to dress up than North Americans, be it for a business meeting or a night out at the theatre.

Tipping Less prevalent in Europe than other parts of the world. No need to leave lavish tips in restaurants or to tip the bus driver.

Greetings Vary greatly from country to country, though, in general, greetings are fairly formal and bound by long-standing etiquette.

Smoking Forbidden in enclosed public places in most European countries although enforcement differs from country to country. Smoking is often allowed in designated areas outside bars and restaurants.

In some countries, such as Austria, the UK, France and Germany, free camping is illegal on all but private land, and in Greece it's illegal altogether but not enforced. This doesn't prevent hikers from occasionally pitching their tent, and you'll usually get away with it if you have a small tent, are discreet, stay just one or two nights, decamp during the day and don't light a fire or leave rubbish. At worst, you'll be woken by the police and asked to move on.

In Eastern Europe free camping is more widespread.

Homestays & Farmstays

You needn't volunteer on a farm to sleep on it. In Switzerland and Germany there's the opportunity to sleep in barns or 'hay hotels'. Farmers provide cotton undersheets (to avoid straw pricks) and woolly blankets for extra warmth, but guests need their own sleeping bag and torch. For further details visit Abenteuer im Stroh (www.schlaf-im-stroh.ch).

Italy has a similar and increasingly popular network of farmstays called *agriturismi*. Participating farms must grow at least one of their own crops. Otherwise accommodation runs the gamut from small rustic hideaways to grand country estates. See www.agriturismo.it for more details.

Hostels

Hostels are great places to meet other travellers and pick up all kinds of information on the region you are visiting. They often usurp tourist offices in this respect.

There's a vast variation in hostel standards across Europe. HI Hostels (those affiliated to Hostelling International; www.hihostels.com) often offer the cheapest (secure) roof over your head in Europe and you don't have to be particularly young to use them. That said, if you're over 26 you'll frequently pay a small surcharge (usually about €3) to stay in an official hostel. Nonmembers likewise pay a few extra euros to stay, which will be set against future membership. After sufficient nights (usually six), you automatically become a member. To join, ask at any hostel or contact your national hostelling office, which you'll find on the HI website – where you can also make online bookings.

Hostel rules vary per facility and country, but some ask that guests vacate the rooms for cleaning purposes or impose a curfew. In many countries, sheets and quilts are automatically provided – sleeping bags are forbidden due to the spread of bed bugs. Many offer breakfast (not always included in nightly rates). Dorms are generally single sex and mixed; be sure to stipulate your preference when booking.

Europe has dozens of private hostels, often design-driven with plenty of private rooms (often with private bathroom), 'dorms' maxing out at four beds and trendy cafes or coffee shops attached.

Hotels

Hotels are usually the most expensive accommodation option, though at the lower end there is little to differentiate them from guesthouses or even hostels.

Cheap hotels around bus and train stations can be convenient for late-night or early-morning arrivals and departures, but some are also unofficial brothels or just downright sleazy. Check the room beforehand and make sure you're clear on the price and what it covers.

Discounts for longer stays are usually possible and hotel owners in southern Europe *might* be open to a little bargaining if times are slack. In many countries it's common for business hotels (usually more than two stars) to slash their rates by up to 40% on Friday and Saturday nights.

University Accommodation

Some university towns rent out their student accommodation during the holiday periods. This is a popular practice in France, the UK and many Eastern European countries. University accommodation will sometimes be in single rooms (although it's more commonly in doubles or triples) and might have cooking facilities. For details ask at individual colleges or universities, at student information offices or local tourist offices.

Customs Regulations

The European Union (EU) has a two-tier customs system: one for goods bought duty-free to import to or export from the EU, and one for goods bought in another EU country where taxes and duties have already been paid.

➡ Entering or leaving the EU, you are allowed to carry duty-free 200 cigarettes, 50 cigars or 250g of tobacco; 2L of still wine plus 1L of spirits over 22% alcohol or another 4L of wine (sparkling or otherwise); 50g of perfume, 250cc of eau de toilette.

➡ Travelling from one EU country to another, the duty-paid limits are 800 cigarettes, 200 cigars, 1kg of tobacco, 10L of spirits, 20L of fortified wine, 90L of wine (of which not more than 60L is sparkling) and 110L of beer.

➡ Non-EU countries often have different regulations and many countries forbid the export of antiquities and cultural treasures.

Discount Cards

See p39 for information about discount cards for students, transport and camping.

Electricity

Europe generally runs on 220V, 50Hz AC, but there are exceptions. The UK runs on 230/240V AC, and some old buildings in Italy and Spain have 125V (or even 110V in Spain). The continent is moving towards a 230V standard. If your home country has a vastly different voltage you will need a transformer for delicate and important appliances.

The UK and Ireland use three-pin square plugs. Most of Europe uses the 'europlug' with two round pins. Greece, Italy and Switzerland use a third round pin in a way that the two-pin plug usually – but not always in Italy and Switzerland – fits. Buy an adapter before leaving home; those on sale in Europe generally go the other way, but ones for visitors to Europe are also available – airports are always a good place to buy them.

Embassies & Consulates

Generally speaking, your embassy won't be much help in emergencies if the trouble you're in is remotely your own fault. Remember, you're bound by the laws of the country you're in.

In genuine emergencies you might get some assistance, but only if other channels have been exhausted. For example, if you need to get home urgently, a free ticket is exceedingly unlikely – the embassy would expect you to have insurance. If you have all your money and documents stolen, it might assist with getting a new passport, but a loan for onward travel is out of the question.

Food

European cuisine is extremely varied, reflecting the multitude of different countries and regions spread across the continent. The Mediterranean diet is listed as an 'Intangible Cultural Heritage' by Unesco and has a number of variants, including Italian, Spanish and Greek. French food is practically a religion. Nordic food is the trendy new upstart of the culinary world. The UK excels in cosmopolitan Asian flavours and has invented its own brand of spicy Anglo-Indian cuisine. Wherever you go in Europe, eating is not just a pleasure, but a valuable insight into the local history and culture.

Eating price ranges in our reviews are based on the price of a main meal. Price categories are broken down differently for individual countries – see each country for full details.

Health

Good health care is readily available in Western Europe and, for minor illnesses, pharmacists can provide valuable advice and sell over-the-counter medication. They can also advise if you need specialised help and point you in the right direction. The standard of dental care is usually good in Europe.

While the situation in Eastern Europe is improving since the EU accession of many countries, quality medical care is not always readily available outside major cities. Embassies, consulates and five-star hotels can usually recommend doctors or clinics.

Condoms are widely available in Europe, however emergency contraception may not be, so take the necessary precautions.

Recommended Vaccinations

No jabs are necessary to visit Europe. However, the World Health Organization (WHO) recommends that all travellers be covered for diphtheria, tetanus, measles, mumps, rubella and polio, regardless of their destination. Since most vaccines don't produce immunity until at least two weeks after they're given, visit a physician at least six weeks before departure.

Tap Water

Tap water is generally safe to drink in Western Europe. However, bottled water is recommended in most of Eastern Europe and is a must in some countries, including Russia and Ukraine, where the giardia parasite can be a problem. Do not drink water from rivers or lakes as it may contain bacteria or viruses.

Insurance

It's foolhardy to travel without insurance to cover theft, loss and medical problems. There are a wide variety of policies, so check the small print.

Some policies specifically exclude 'dangerous activities', which can include scuba diving, motorcycling, winter sports, adventure sports or even hiking.

Check that the policy covers ambulances or an emergency flight home.

Worldwide travel insurance is available online at www.lonelyplanet.com/travel-insurance. You can buy, extend and claim online anytime – even if you're already on the road.

Internet Access

Internet access varies enormously across Europe. In most places you'll be able to find wireless (wi-fi, also called WLAN in some coun-

tries), although whether it's free varies greatly.

Where the wi-fi icon appears, it means that the establishment offers free wi-fi that you can access immediately or by asking for the access code from staff.

Access is generally straightforward, although a few tips are in order. If you can't find the @ symbol on a keyboard, try AltGr + 2, or AltGr + Q. Watch out for German and some Balkans keyboards, which reverse the Z and the Y positions. Using a French keyboard is an art unto itself.

Where necessary in relevant countries, click on the language prompt in the bottom right-hand corner of the screen or hit Ctrl + Shift to switch between the Cyrillic and Latin alphabets.

Legal Matters

Drugs are often quite openly available in Europe, but that doesn't mean they're legal. The Netherlands is most famed for its liberal attitudes, with coffeeshops openly selling cannabis even though the drug is *not*

technically legal. However, a blind eye is generally turned to the trade as the possession and purchase of small amounts (5g) of 'soft drugs' (ie marijuana and hashish) is allowed and users won't be prosecuted for smoking or carrying this amount. Don't take this relaxed attitude as an invitation to buy harder drugs; if you get caught, you'll be punished. Since 2008 magic mushrooms have been banned in the Netherlands.

Spain also has pretty liberal laws regarding marijuana, although its use is usually reserved for private 'cannabis clubs'.

In Belgium the possession of up to 3g of cannabis is legal, but selling the drug isn't, so if you get caught at the point of sale, you could be in trouble. Switzerland, Portugal, Ukraine, Malta, Luxembourg, Estonia, Austria and the Czech Republic have also decriminalised possession of marijuana, however, selling remains illegal.

Getting caught with drugs in some parts of Europe can lead to imprisonment. If in any doubt, err on the side of caution, and don't even think about taking drugs across international borders.

LGBT Travellers

Across Western Europe you'll find very liberal attitudes towards homosexuality. London, Paris, Berlin, Munich, Amsterdam, Madrid and Lisbon have thriving gay communities and pride events. The Greek islands of Mykonos and Lesvos are popular gay beach destinations. Gran Canaria and Ibiza in Spain are big centres for both gay clubbing and beach holidays.

Eastern Europe, and in particular Russia, tends to be far less progressive. Outside the big cities, attitudes become more conservative and discretion is advised, particularly in Turkey.

Money

The euro, used in 19 EU states as well as four other non-EU states (Andorra, Monaco, San Marino and Vatican City), is made up of 100 cents. Notes come in denominations of €5, €10, €20, €50, €100, €200 and €500, though any notes above €50 are rarely used on a daily basis. Coins come in 1c, 2c, 5c, 10c, 20c, 50c, €1 and €2.

Denmark, the UK and Sweden have held out against adopting the euro for political reasons, while non-EU nations, such as Albania, Belarus, Norway, Russia, Switzerland, Turkey and Ukraine also have their own currencies.

ATMs

Across major European towns and cities international ATMs are common, but you should always have a backup option, as there can be glitches. In some remote areas ATMs might be scarce.

Much of Western Europe now uses a chip-and-pin

system for added security. You will have problems if you don't have a four-digit PIN and might have difficulties if your card doesn't have a metallic chip. Check with your bank.

Always cover the keypad when entering your PIN and make sure there are no unusual devices attached to the machine, which can copy your card's details or cause it to stick in the machine. If your card disappears and the screen goes blank before you've even entered your PIN, don't enter it – especially if a 'helpful' bystander tells you to do so. If you can't retrieve your card, call your bank's emergency number, if you can, before leaving the ATM.

Cash

It's a good idea to bring some local currency in cash, if only to cover yourself until you get to an exchange facility or find an ATM. The equivalent of €150 should usually be enough. Some extra cash in an easily exchanged currency is also a good idea, especially in Eastern Europe.

Credit Cards

Visa and MasterCard/Eurocard are more widely accepted in Europe than Amex and Diners Club; Visa (sometimes called Carte Bleue) is particularly strong in France and Spain.

There are, however, regional differences in the general acceptability of credit cards; in Germany for example, it's rare for restaurants to take credit cards. Cards are not widely accepted off the beaten track.

To reduce the risk of fraud, always keep your card in view when making transactions; for example, in restaurants that do accept cards, pay as you leave, following your card to the till. Keep transaction records and either check your statements when you return home or check your account online while on the road.

Letting your credit-card company know roughly where you're going lessens the chance of fraud – or of your bank cutting off the card when it sees (your) unusual spending.

Debit Cards

It's always worthwhile having a Maestro-compatible debit card, which differs from a credit card in deducting money straight from your bank account. Check with your bank or MasterCard (Maestro's parent) for compatibility.

Exchanging Money

Euros, US dollars and UK pounds are the easiest currencies to exchange. You may have trouble exchanging some lesser-known ones at small banks.

Importing or exporting some currencies is restricted or banned, so try to get rid of any local currency before you leave. Get rid of Scottish pounds before leaving the UK; nobody outside Britain will touch them.

Most airports, central train stations, big hotels and many border posts have banking facilities outside regular business hours, at times on a 24-hour basis. Post offices in Europe often perform banking tasks, tend to open longer hours and outnumber banks in remote places. While they always exchange cash, they might baulk at handling travellers cheques not in the local currency.

The best exchange rates are usually at banks. *Bureaux de change* usually – but not always – offer worse rates or charge higher commissions. Hotels and airports are almost always the worst places to change money.

International Transfers

International bank transfers are good for secure one-off movements of large amounts of money, but they might take three to five days and there will be a fee (about £25 in the UK, for example). Be sure to specify the name of the bank, plus the sort code and address of the branch where you'd like to pick up your money.

In an emergency it's quicker but more costly to have money wired via an Amex office (www.americanexpress.com), Western Union (www.westernunion.com) or MoneyGram (www.moneygram.com).

Taxes & Refunds

When non-EU residents spend more than a certain amount (around €75, but amounts can vary from country to country) they can usually reclaim any sales tax when they are leaving the country.

Making a tax-back claim is a very straightforward procedure. First make sure the shop offers duty-free sales (often a sign will be displayed reading 'Tax-Free Shopping'). When making your purchase, ask the shop attendant for a tax-refund voucher, filled in with the correct amount and the date. This can be used to claim a refund directly at international airports, or stamped at ferry ports or border crossings and mailed back to you for a refund.

Travellers Cheques

It's become more difficult to find places that cash travellers cheques. In parts of Eastern Europe only a few banks handle them, and the process can be quite bureaucratic and costly.

That said, having a few cheques is a good back-up. If they're stolen you can claim a refund, provided you have a separate record of cheque numbers.

Amex and Thomas Cook are reliable brands of travellers cheques, while cheques in US dollars, euros or British pounds are the easiest

to cash. When changing them ask about fees and commissions, as well as the exchange rate.

Opening Hours

Opening times vary significantly between countries. The following is a general overview.

Shops & businesses 9am–6pm Monday to Friday, to 1pm or 5pm Saturday. In smaller towns there may be a one- to two-hour closure for lunch. Some shops close on Sunday. Businesses also close on national holidays and local feast days.

Banks 9am to between 3pm and 5pm Monday to Friday. Occasionally shut for lunch.

Restaurants noon to midnight.

Bars 6pm to midnight or sometimes later.

Museums close Monday or (less commonly) Tuesday.

Post

From major European centres, airmail typically takes about five days to reach North America and about a week to reach Australasian destinations, although mail from such countries as Albania or Russia can be much slower.

Courier services such as DHL are best for essential deliveries.

Public Holidays

There are large variations in statutory holidays in Europe. The following holidays are the most common across the board.

New Year's Day 1 January

Good Friday March/April

Easter Sunday March/April

May Day 1 May

Pentecost/Whitsun May/June

Christmas Day 25 December

Safe Travel

Travelling in Europe is usually very safe.

Discrimination

In some parts of Europe travellers of African, Arab or Asian descent might encounter unpleasant attitudes that are unrelated to them personally. In rural areas travellers whose skin colour marks them out as foreigners might experience unwanted attention.

Attitudes vary from country to country. People tend to be more accepting in cities than in the country. Race is also less of an issue in Western Europe than in parts of the former Eastern Bloc. For example, there has been a spate of racially motivated attacks in St Petersburg and other parts of Russia in recent years.

Drugging

Although rare, some drugging of travellers does occur in Europe. Travellers are especially vulnerable on trains and buses where a new 'friend' may offer you food or a drink that will knock you out, giving them time to steal your belongings.

Gassings have also been reported on a handful of overnight international trains. The best protection is to lock the door of your compartment (use your own lock if there isn't one) and to lock your bags to luggage racks, preferably with a sturdy combination cable.

If you can help it, never sleep alone in a train compartment.

Pickpockets & Thieves

Theft is definitely a problem in parts of Europe and you have to be aware of unscrupulous fellow travellers. The key is to be sensible with your possessions.

➡ Don't store valuables in train-station lockers or luggage-storage counters

CALLING EMERGENCY

The phone number ☎112 can be dialled free for emergencies in all EU states. See individual countries for country-specific emergency numbers.

and be careful about people who offer to help you operate a locker. Also be vigilant if someone offers to carry your luggage: they might carry it away altogether.

➡ Don't leave valuables in your car, on train seats or in your room. When going out, don't flaunt cameras, laptops or other expensive electronic goods.

➡ Carry a small day pack, as shoulder bags are an open invitation for snatch-thieves. Consider using small zipper locks on your packs.

➡ Pickpockets are most active in dense crowds, especially in busy train stations and on public transport during peak hours. Be careful in these situations.

➡ Spread valuables, cash and cards around your body or in different bags.

➡ A money belt with your essentials (passport, cash, credit cards, airline tickets) is usually a good idea. However, so you needn't delve into it in public, carry a wallet with a day's worth of cash.

➡ Having your passport stolen is less of a disaster if you've recorded the number and issue date or, even better, photocopied the relevant data pages. You can also scan them and email them to yourself. If you lose your passport, notify the police immediately to get a statement and contact your nearest consulate.

➡ Carry photocopies of your credit cards, airline tickets and other travel documents.

Scams

Most scams involve distracting you – either by kids running up to you, someone asking for directions or spilling something on you – while another person steals your wallet. Be alert in such situations.

In some countries, especially in Eastern Europe, you may encounter people claiming to be from the tourist police, the special police, the supersecret police, whatever. Unless they're wearing a uniform and have good reason for accosting you, treat their claims with suspicion.

Needless to say, never show your passport or cash to anyone on the street. Simply walk away. If someone flashes a badge, offer to accompany them to the nearest police station.

Unrest & Terrorism

Civil unrest and terrorist bombings are relatively rare in Europe, all things considered, but they do occur. Attacks by extremists in the UK, France, Germany, Belgium and Russia have occurred in recent years. Keep an eye on the news and avoid areas where any flare-up seems likely.

Telephone

If your mobile phone is European, it's often perfectly feasible to use it on roaming throughout the continent.

If you're coming from outside Europe, it's usually worth buying a prepaid local SIM in one European country. Even if you're not staying there long, calls across Europe will still be cheaper if they're not routed via your home country and the prepaid card will enable you to keep a limit on your spending. In several countries you need your passport to buy a SIM card.

In order to use other SIM cards in your phone, you'll need to have your handset unlocked by your home provider. Even if your phone is locked, you can use apps such as Whatsapp to send free text messages internationally wherever you have wi-fi access or Skype to make free international calls whenever you're online.

Europe uses the GSM 900 network, which also covers Australia and New Zealand, but is not compatible with the North American GSM 1900 or the totally different system in Japan and South Korea. If you have a GSM phone, check with your service provider about using it in Europe. You'll need international roaming, but this is usually free to enable.

You can call abroad from almost any phone box in Europe. Public telephones accepting phonecards (available from post offices, telephone centres, news stands or retail outlets) are virtually the norm now; coin-operated phones are rare, if not impossible, to find.

Without a phonecard, you can ring from a telephone booth inside a post office or telephone centre and settle your bill at the counter. Reverse-charge (collect) calls are often possible. From many countries the Country Direct system lets you phone home by billing the long-distance carrier you use at home. These numbers can often be dialled from public phones without even inserting a phonecard.

Time

Europe is divided into four time zones. From west to east:

UTC (Britain, Ireland, Portugal) GMT (GMT+1 in summer)

CET (the majority of European countries) GMT+1 (GMT+2 in summer)

EET (Greece, Turkey, Bulgaria, Romania, Moldova, Ukraine, Belarus, Lithuania, Latvia, Estonia, Kaliningrad, Finland) GMT+2 (GMT+3 in summer)

MSK (Russia) GMT+3 (GMT+4 in summer)

At 9am in Britain it's 1am (GMT/UTC minus eight hours) on the US west coast, 4am (GMT/UTC minus five hours) on the US east coast, 10am in Paris and Prague, 11am in Athens, midday in Moscow and 7pm (GMT/UTC plus 10 hours) in Sydney.

Toilets

Many public toilets require a small fee either deposited in a box or given to the attendant. Sit-down toilets are the rule in the vast majority of places. Squat toilets can still be found in rural areas, although they are definitely a dying breed.

Public-toilet provision is changeable from city to city. If you can't find a toilet, simply drop into a hotel or restaurant and ask to use theirs.

Tourist Information

Unless otherwise indicated, tourist offices are common and widespread, although their usefulness varies enormously.

Travellers with Disabilities

Cobbled medieval streets, 'classic' hotels, congested inner cities and underground subway systems make Europe a tricky destination for people with mobility impairments. However, the train facilities are good and some destinations boast new tram services or lifts to platforms. Download Lonely Planet's free Accessible Travel guide from http://lptravel.to/AccessibleTravel. The following websites can help with specific details.

Accessible Europe (www.accessibleurope.com) Specialist European tours with van transport.

DisabledGo.com (www.disabledgo.com) Detailed access information for thousands of venues across the UK and Ireland.

Mobility International Schweiz (www.mis-ch.ch) Good site (only partly in English) listing 'barrier-free' destinations in Switzerland and abroad, plus

SCHENGEN

Twenty-six European countries are signatories to the Schengen Agreement, which has effectively dismantled internal border controls between them. They are Austria, Belgium, the Czech Republic, Denmark, Estonia, Finland, France, Germany, Greece, Iceland, Italy, Hungary, Latvia, Liechtenstein, Lithuania, Luxembourg, Malta, the Netherlands, Norway, Poland, Portugal, Slovakia, Slovenia, Spain, Sweden and Switzerland.

The UK and Ireland, as well as Russia and much of Eastern Europe, are not part of the Schengen Agreement. Visitors from non-EU countries will have to apply for visas to these countries separately.

Citizens of the US, Australia, New Zealand, Canada and the UK only need a valid passport to enter Schengen countries (as well as the UK and Ireland). However, other nationals, including South Africans, can apply for a single visa – a Schengen visa – when travelling throughout this region.

Non-EU visitors (with or without a Schengen visa) should expect to be questioned, however perfunctorily, when first entering the region. However, later travel within the zone is much like a domestic trip, with no border controls.

If you need a Schengen visa, you must apply at the consulate or embassy of the country that's your main destination, or your point of entry. You may then stay up to a maximum of 90 days in the entire Schengen area within a six-month period. Once your visa has expired, you must leave the zone and may only reenter after three months abroad. Shop around when choosing your point of entry, as visa prices may differ from country to country.

If you're a citizen of the US, Australia, New Zealand or Canada, you may stay visa-free a total of 90 days, during six months, within the entire Schengen region.

If you're planning a longer trip, you need to enquire personally as to whether you need a visa or visas. Your country might have bilateral agreements with individual Schengen countries allowing you to stay there longer than 90 days without a visa. However, you will need to talk directly to the relevant embassies or consulates.

While the UK and Ireland are not part of the Schengen area, their citizens can stay indefinitely in other EU countries, only needing paperwork if they want to work long-term or take up residency.

wheelchair-accessible hotels in Switzerland.

Mobility International USA (www.miusa.org) Publishes guides and advises travellers with disabilities on mobility issues.

Society for Accessible Travel & Hospitality (SATH; www.sath. org) Reams of information for travellers with disabilities.

Visas

➡ Citizens of the USA, Canada, Australia, New Zealand and the UK need only a valid passport to enter nearly all countries in Europe, including the entire EU.

➡ Belarus and Russia require a prearranged visa before arrival and even an 'invitation' from (or booking with) a tour operator or hotel. It's simpler and safer to obtain these visas before leaving home.

➡ Australians and New Zealanders can obtain a visa on arrival in Ukraine from Boryspil International Airport (Kyiv).

➡ Transit visas are usually cheaper than tourist or business visas but they allow only a very short stay (one to five days) and can be difficult to extend.

➡ All visas have a 'use-by' date and you'll be refused entry afterwards. In some cases it's easier to get visas as you go along, rather than arranging them all beforehand. Carry spare passport photos (you may need from one to four every time you apply for a visa).

➡ Visas to neighbouring countries are usually issued immediately by consulates in Eastern Europe, although some may levy a hefty surcharge for 'express service'.

➡ Consulates are generally open weekday mornings (if there's both an embassy and a consulate, you want the consulate).

➡ Because regulations can change, double-check with the relevant embassy or consulate before travelling.

Volunteering

If you want to spend more time living and working in Europe, a short-term volunteer project might seem a good idea, say, teaching English in Poland or building a school in Turkey. However, most voluntary organisations levy high charges for airfares, food, lodging and recruitment (from about €250 to €800 per week), making such work impractical for most shoestringers. One exception is WWOOF International (www.wwoof. org), which helps link volunteers with organic farms in Germany, Slovenia, the Czech Republic, Denmark, the UK, Austria and Switzerland. A small membership fee is required to join the national chapter but in exchange for your labour you'll receive free lodging and food.

For more information, Lonely Planet publishes *Volunteer: A Traveller's Guide to Making a Difference Around the World*.

Women Travellers

➡ Women might attract unwanted attention in Turkey, rural Spain and southern Italy, especially Sicily, where many men view whistling and catcalling as flattery. Conservative dress can help to deter lascivious gazes and wolf whistles; dark sunglasses help avoid unwanted eye contact.

➡ Marriage is highly respected in southern Europe, and a wedding ring can help avoid unwanted attention, along with talk about 'my husband'.

Hitchhiking alone is not recommended anywhere.

➡ Female readers have reported assaults at Turkish hotels with shared bathrooms, so women travelling to Turkey might want to consider a more expensive room with private bathroom.

➡ Journeywoman (www. journeywoman.com) maintains an online newsletter about solo female travels all over the world.

Work

EU citizens are allowed to work in any other EU country, but there can still be tiresome paperwork to complete. Other nationalities require special work permits that can be almost impossible to arrange, especially for temporary work. However, that doesn't prevent enterprising travellers from topping up their funds by working in the hotel or restaurant trades at beach or ski resorts, or teaching a little English – and they don't always have to do this illegally.

The UK, for example, issues special Tier 5 (Youth Mobility Scheme) visas to citizens from Australia, Canada, New Zealand, Japan, Hong Kong, South Korea and Taiwan aged between 18 and 30, valid for two years of work (see www.gov.uk/tier-5-youth-mobility/overview). Your national student-exchange organisation might be able to arrange temporary work permits to several countries.

If you have a grandparent or parent who was born in an EU country, you may have certain rights of residency or citizenship. Ask that country's embassy about dual citizenship and work permits. With citizenship, also ask about any obligations, such as military service and residency. Beware that your home country may not recognise dual citizenship.

Seasonal Work

➡ *Work Your Way Around the World* by Susan Griffith gives practical advice.

➡ Typical tourist jobs (picking grapes in France, working at a bar in Greece) often come with board and lodging, and the pay is essentially pocket money, but you'll have a good time partying with other travellers.

➡ Busking is fairly common in major European cities, but it's illegal in some parts of Switzerland and Austria. Crackdowns even occur in Belgium and Germany, where it has been tolerated in the past. Some other cities, including London, require permits and security checks. Talk to other buskers first.

Useful websites:

EuroJobs (www.eurojobs.com) Links to hundreds of organisations looking to employ both non-Europeans (with the correct work permits) and Europeans.

Natives (www.natives.co.uk) Summer and winter resort jobs, and various tips.

Picking Jobs (www.pickingjobs. com) Includes some tourism jobs.

Season Workers (www.season workers.com) Best for ski-resort work and summer jobs, although it also has some childcare jobs.

Ski-jobs.co.uk (www.ski-jobs. co.uk) Mainly service jobs such as chalet hosts, bar staff and porters. Some linguistic skills required.

TEACHING ENGLISH

Most schools prefer a bachelor's degree and a TEFL (Teaching English as a Foreign Language) certificate.

It is easier to find TEFL jobs in Eastern Europe than in Western Europe. The British Council (www.british council.org) can provide advice about training and job searches. Alternatively, try the big schools such as Berlitz (www.berlitz.com) and Wall Street English (www. wallstreetenglish.com).

Transport

GETTING THERE & AWAY

Europe is one of the world's major destinations, sporting many of its busiest airports with routes fanning out to the far corners of the globe. More adventurous travellers can enter from Asia on some epic long-distance train routes. Numerous ferries jockey across the Mediterranean between Europe and Africa.

Flights, cars and tours can be booked online at www.lonelyplanet.com/bookings.

Air

To save money, it's best to travel off-season. This means, if possible, avoid mid-June to early September, Easter, Christmas and school holidays.

Regardless of your ultimate destination, it's sometimes better to pick a recognised transport 'hub' as your initial port of entry, where high traffic volumes help keep prices down. The busiest, and therefore most obvious, airports are London, Frankfurt, Paris and Rome. Sometimes tickets to Amsterdam, Athens, Barcelona, Berlin, İstanbul, Madrid and Vienna are worth checking out.

Long-haul airfares to Eastern Europe are rarely a bargain; you're usually better flying to a Western European hub and taking an onward budget-airline flight or train. The main hubs in Eastern Europe are Budapest, Moscow, Prague and Warsaw.

Most of the aforementioned gateway cities are also well serviced by low-cost carriers that fly to other parts of Europe.

Main European airports:

Schiphol Airport, Amsterdam (www.schiphol.nl)

Frankfurt Airport, Frankfurt (www.frankfurt-airport.com)

Heathrow Airport, London (www.heathrow.com)

Barajas Airport, Madrid (www.aeropuertomadrid-barajas.com)

Aéroport de Charles de Gaulle, Paris (www.easycdg.com)

Leonardo da Vinci Airport, Rome (www.adr.it)

Land

It's possible to reach Europe by various train routes from Asia. Most common is the Trans-Siberian Railway, connecting Moscow to Siberia, the Russian Far East, Mongolia and China.

It is also possible to reach Moscow from several Central Asian states and İstanbul from Iran and Jordan. See www.seat61.com for more information about these adventurous routes.

Border Crossings

Border formalities have been relaxed in most of the EU but still exist in all their original

---

CLIMATE CHANGE & TRAVEL

Every form of transport that relies on carbon-based fuel generates CO_2, the main cause of human-induced climate change. Modern travel is dependent on aeroplanes, which might use less fuel per kilometre per person than most cars but travel much greater distances. The altitude at which aircraft emit gases (including CO_2) and particles also contributes to their climate change impact. Many websites offer 'carbon calculators' that allow people to estimate the carbon emissions generated by their journey and, for those who wish to do so, to offset the impact of the greenhouse gases emitted with contributions to portfolios of climate-friendly initiatives throughout the world. Lonely Planet offsets the carbon footprint of all staff and author travel.

bureaucratic glory in the more far-flung parts of Eastern Europe.

In line with the Schengen Agreement, there are officially no passport controls at the borders between 26 European states, namely: Austria, Belgium, the Czech Republic, Denmark, Estonia, Finland, France, Germany, Greece, Iceland, Italy, Hungary, Latvia, Liechtenstein, Lithuania, Luxembourg, Malta, the Netherlands, Norway, Poland, Portugal, Slovakia, Slovenia, Spain, Sweden and Switzerland.

Sometimes, however, there are spot checks on trains crossing borders, so always have your passport. The UK was a nonsignatory to Schengen and thus maintains border controls over traffic from other EU countries (except Ireland, with which it shares an open border), although there is no customs control. The same goes for Ireland. For more details see www.schengenvisainfo.com.

Most borders in Eastern Europe will be crossed via train, where border guards board the train and go through compartments checking passengers' papers. It is rare to be asked for bribes, but occasionally in Belarus or Moldova you may face a difficulty that can only be overcome with a 'fine'.

Sea

There are numerous ferry routes between Europe and Africa, including links from Spain to Morocco; Italy and Malta to Tunisia; and France to Morocco and Tunisia. Check out www.traghetti-web.it for comprehensive information on all Mediterranean ferries. Ferries are often filled to capacity in summer, especially to and from Tunisia, so book well in advance if you're taking a vehicle across.

Passenger freighters (typically carrying up to 12 passengers) aren't nearly as competitively priced as airlines. Journeys also take a long time. However, if you have your heart set on a transatlantic journey, TravLtips Cruise and Freighter (www.travltips.com) has information on freighter cruises.

GETTING AROUND

In most European countries the train is the best option for internal transport. On the down side, Europe's fast and efficient rail network is rarely a bargain – book well in advance and/or use a rail pass wisely.

Air

Low-cost carriers have revolutionised European transport. Each has a similar pricing system – namely that ticket prices rise with the number of seats sold on each flight, so book as early as possible to get a decent fare.

Some budget airlines fly to smaller, less convenient airports on the outskirts of their destination city, or even to the airports of nearby cities. Check the exact location of the departure and arrival airports before you book.

Many flights leave at the crack of dawn or arrive inconveniently late at night.

Departure and other taxes (including booking fees, checked-baggage fees and other surcharges) soon add up and are included in the final price by the end of the online booking process – usually a lot more than you were hoping to pay. With careful choosing and advance booking you can get excellent deals. For a comprehensive overview of which low-cost carriers fly to or from which European cities,

check out the excellent www.flycheapo.com.

Bicycle

Cycling is one of the most pleasurable means of getting around Europe. For more information, including on transporting your bicycle to Europe and cycling routes in situ, see p45.

Rental & Purchase

It is easy to hire bikes throughout most of Europe. Many Western European train stations have bike-rental counters. It is sometimes possible to return the bike at a different outlet so you don't have to retrace your route. Hostels are another good place to find cheap bike hire.

There are plenty of places to buy bikes in Europe, but you'll need a specialist bicycle shop for a bike capable of withstanding a European trip. Cycling is very popular in the Netherlands and Germany, and those countries are good places to pick up a well-equipped touring bicycle.

European prices are quite high (certainly higher than in North America), however non-European residents should be able to claim back value-added tax (VAT) on the purchase. A growing number of European cities have bike-sharing schemes where you can casually borrow a bike from a docking station for short hops around the city for a small cost. Most schemes have daily rates, although you usually need a credit card as deposit. Large bike-sharing schemes include Paris' Vélib (Europe's biggest) and London's Santander Cycles.

Transporting a Bicycle

For major cycling trips, it's best to have a bike you're familiar with, so consider bringing your own rather than buying on arrival.

If coming from outside Europe, ask about the airline's policy on transporting bikes before buying your ticket. From the UK to the Continent, Eurostar (the train service through the Channel Tunnel) charges £30 to send a semi-dismantled bike as registered luggage with you. Book ahead.

You can also transport your bicycle with you on Eurotunnel through the Channel Tunnel for around £20. With a bit of tinkering and dismantling (eg removing wheels), you might be able to get your bike into a bag or sack and take it on a train as hand luggage.

Alternatively, European Bike Express (www.bike-express.co.uk) is a UK-based coach service where cyclists can travel with their bicycles to various drop-off and pick-up points in France and northern Spain.

Once on the Continent, local and regional trains usually allow bikes to be transported as luggage, subject to space and a small supplementary fee (€5 to €15). Off-peak hours are best. Some cyclists have reported that Italian and French train attendants have refused bikes on slow trains, so be prepared for regulations to be interpreted differently in different countries.

Not all fast trains and international trains can accommodate bikes; they might need to be sent as registered luggage and may end up on a different train from the one you take. When booking your train ticket, always check if the train you are taking accepts bikes (denoted on timetables in France with a bike symbol).

Boat

Several different ferry companies compete on the main ferry routes, resulting in a comprehensive but complicated service. The same ferry company can have a host of different prices for the same route, depending on the time of day or year, validity of the ticket and length of your vehicle. Vehicle tickets usually include the driver and often up to five passengers free of charge.

It's worth booking ahead where possible as there may be special reductions on off-peak crossings and advance-purchase tickets. On English Channel routes, apart from one-day or short-term excursion returns, there is little price advantage in buying a return ticket versus two singles.

Rail-pass holders are entitled to discounts or free travel on some lines. Food on ferries is often expensive (and lousy), so it is worth bringing your own. Also be aware that if you take your vehicle on board, you are usually denied access to it during the voyage.

Lake and river ferry services operate in many countries, Austria and Switzerland being just two. Some of these are very scenic.

Bus
International Buses

Often cheaper than trains, sometimes substantially so, long-distance buses also tend to be slower and less comfortable. However in Portugal, Greece and Turkey buses are often a better option than trains. Eurolines (www.eurolines.com) is Europe's biggest organisation of international buses, bringing together national companies all over Europe.

National Buses

Domestic buses provide a viable alternative to trains in most countries. Again, they are usually slightly cheaper and somewhat slower. Buses are generally best for short hops, such as getting around cities and reaching remote villages, and they are often the only option in mountainous regions.

Reservations are rarely necessary. On many city buses you usually buy your ticket in advance from a kiosk or machine and validate it on entering the bus.

Car & Motorcycle

Travelling with your own vehicle gives flexibility and is the best way to reach remote places. However, the independence does sometimes isolate you from local life. Also, cars can be a target for theft and are often impractical in city centres, where traffic jams, parking problems and getting thoroughly lost can make it well worth ditching your vehicle and using public transport. Various car-carrying trains can help you avoid long, tiring drives.

Campervan

One popular way to tour Europe is for a group of three or four people to band together and buy or rent a campervan. London is the usual embarkation point. Look at the ads in London's free magazine TNT (www.tntmagazine.com) if you wish to form or join a group. TNT is also a good source for purchasing a van, as is Loot (www.loot.com).

Some secondhand dealers offer a 'buy-back' scheme for when you return from the Continent, but check the small print before signing anything and remember that if an offer is too good to be true, it probably is. Buying and reselling privately should be more advantageous if you have time. In the UK, DUInsure (www.duinsure.com) offers a campervan policy.

Fuel

➡ Fuel prices can vary enormously (though fuel is always more expensive than in North America or Australia).

➡ Unleaded petrol only is available throughout Europe. Diesel is usually cheaper, though the difference is marginal in Britain, Ireland and Switzerland.

➡ Ireland's Automobile Association maintains a webpage of European fuel prices at www.theaa.ie/aa/motoring-advice/petrol-prices.aspx.

Insurance

➡ Third-party motor insurance is compulsory. Most UK policies automatically provide this for EU countries. Get your insurer to issue a Green Card (which may cost extra), an internationally recognised proof of insurance, and check that it lists every country you intend to visit. You'll need this in the event of an accident outside the country where the vehicle is insured.

➡ Ask your insurer for a European Accident Statement form, which can simplify things if worst comes to worst. Never sign statements that you can't read or understand – insist on a translation and sign that only if it's acceptable.

➡ For non-EU countries, check the requirements with your insurer. Travellers from the UK can obtain additional advice and information from the Association of British Insurers (www.abi.org.uk).

➡ Take out a European motoring assistance policy. Non-Europeans might find it cheaper to arrange international coverage with their national motoring organisation before leaving home. Ask your motoring organisation for details about the free services offered by affiliated organisations around Europe.

➡ Residents of the UK should contact the RAC (www.rac.co.uk) or the AA (www.theaa.co.uk) for more information.

Residents of the US, contact AAA (www.aaa.com).

Leasing

Leasing a vehicle involves fewer hassles than purchasing and can work out much cheaper than hiring for longer than 17 days. This program is limited to certain types of new cars, including Renault and Peugeot, but you save money because leasing is exempt from VAT and inclusive insurance plans are cheaper than daily insurance rates.

To lease a vehicle your permanent address must be outside the EU. In the USA, contact Renault Eurodrive (www.renault-eurodrive.com) for more information.

Purchase

Buying a car and then selling it at the end of your European travels may work out to be a better deal than renting one, although this isn't guaranteed and you'll need to do your sums carefully.

The purchase of vehicles in some European countries is illegal for non-nationals or non-EU residents. Britain is probably the best place to buy as secondhand prices are good there. Bear in mind that British cars have steering wheels on the right-hand side. If you wish to have left-hand drive and can afford to buy a new car, prices are generally reasonable in Greece, France, Germany, Belgium, Luxembourg and the Netherlands.

Paperwork can be tricky wherever you buy, and many countries have compulsory roadworthiness checks on older vehicles.

Rental

➡ Renting a car is ideal for people who will need cars for 16 days or less. Anything longer, it's better to lease.

➡ Big international rental firms will give you reliable service and good vehicles. National or local firms can often undercut the big companies by up to 40%.

➡ Usually you will have the option of returning the car to a different outlet at the end of the rental period, but there's normally a charge for this and it can be very steep if it's a long way from your point of origin.

➡ Book early for the lowest rates and make sure you compare rates in different cities. Taxes range from 15% to 20% and surcharges apply if rented from an airport.

MOTORCYCLE TOURING

Europe is made for motorcycle touring, with quality winding roads, stunning scenery and an active motorcycling scene. Just make sure your wet-weather motorcycling gear is up to scratch.

➡ Rider and passenger crash helmets are compulsory everywhere in Europe.

➡ Austria, Belgium, France, Germany, Luxembourg, Portugal and Spain require that motorcyclists use headlights during the day; in other countries it is recommended.

➡ On ferries, motorcyclists rarely have to book ahead as they can generally be squeezed on board.

➡ Take note of the local custom about parking motorcycles on pavements (sidewalks). Though this is illegal in some countries, the police often turn a blind eye provided the vehicle doesn't obstruct pedestrians.

HITCHING FOR CASH

In parts of Eastern Europe including Russia, Ukraine and Turkey, traditional hitchhiking is rarely practised. Instead, anyone with a car can be a taxi and it's quite usual to see locals stick their hands out (palm down) on the street, looking to hitch a lift. The difference with hitching here, however, is that you pay for the privilege. You will need to speak the local language (or at least know the numbers) to discuss your destination and negotiate a price.

➡ If you rent a car in the EU you might not be able to take it outside the EU, and if you rent the car outside the EU, you will only be able to drive within the EU for eight days. Ask at the rental agencies for other such regulations.

➡ Make sure you understand what is included in the price (unlimited or paid kilometres, tax, injury insurance, collision damage waiver etc) and what your liabilities are. We recommend taking the collision damage waiver, though you can probably skip the injury insurance if you and your passengers have decent travel insurance.

➡ The minimum rental age is usually 21 years and sometimes 25. You'll need a credit card and to have held your licence for at least a year.

➡ Motorcycle and moped rental is common in some countries, such as Italy, Spain, Greece and southern France.

Road Conditions & Road Rules

➡ Conditions and types of roads vary across Europe. The fastest routes are generally four- or six-lane highways known locally as motorways, autoroutes, autostrade, autobahnen etc. These tend to skirt cities and plough through the countryside in straight lines, often avoiding the most scenic bits.

➡ Some highways incur tolls, which are often quite hefty (especially in Italy, France and Spain), but there will always be an alternative route. Motorways and other primary routes are generally in good condition.

➡ Road surfaces on minor routes are unreliable in some countries (eg Greece, Albania, Romania, Ireland, Russia and Ukraine), although normally they will be more than adequate.

➡ Except in Britain and Ireland, you should drive on the right. Vehicles brought to the Continent from any of these locales should have their headlights adjusted to avoid blinding oncoming traffic (a simple solution on older headlight lenses is to cover up a triangular section of the lens with tape). Priority is often given to traffic approaching from the right in countries that drive on the right-hand side.

➡ Speed limits vary from country to country. You may be surprised at the apparent disregard for traffic regulations in some places (particularly in Italy and Greece), but as a visitor it is always best to be cautious. Many driving infringements are subject to an on-the-spot fine. Always ask for a receipt.

➡ European drink-driving laws are particularly strict. The blood-alcohol concentration (BAC) limit when driving is usually between 0.05% and 0.08%,

but in certain areas (such as Gibraltar, Bulgaria and Belarus) it can be zero.

➡ Always carry proof of ownership of your vehicle (Vehicle Registration Document for British-registered cars). An EU driving licence is acceptable for those driving through Europe. If you have any other type of licence, you should obtain an International Driving Permit (IDP) from your motoring organisation. Check what type of licence is required in your destination prior to departure.

➡ Every vehicle that travels across an international border should display a sticker indicating its country of registration. A warning triangle, to be used in the event of breakdown, is compulsory almost everywhere.

➡ Some recommended accessories include a first-aid kit (compulsory in Austria, Slovenia, Croatia, Serbia, Montenegro and Greece), a spare bulb kit (compulsory in Spain and France), a reflective jacket for every person in the car (compulsory in France, Italy and Spain) and a fire extinguisher (compulsory in Greece and Turkey).

Hitching

Hitching is never entirely safe and we don't recommend it. Travellers who decide to hitch should understand that they are taking a small but potentially serious risk. It will be safer if they travel in pairs and let someone know where they plan to go.

➡ A man and woman travelling together is probably the best combination. A woman hitching on her own is taking a larger than normal risk.

➡ Don't try to hitch from city centres; take public

transport to the suburban exit routes.

→ Hitching is usually illegal on highways – stand on the slip roads or approach drivers at petrol stations and truck stops.

→ Look presentable and cheerful, and make a cardboard sign indicating your intended destination in the local language.

→ Never hitch where drivers can't stop in good time or without causing an obstruction.

→ It is often possible to arrange a lift in advance: scan student noticeboards in colleges or check out services such as www. carpooling.co.uk or www. drive2day.de.

Local Transport

European towns and cities have excellent local-transport systems, often encompassing trams as well as buses and metro/subway/underground-rail networks.

Most travellers will find areas of interest in European cities can be easily traversed by foot or bicycle. In Greece and Italy, travellers sometimes rent mopeds and motorcycles for scooting around a city or island.

Taxis

Taxis in Europe are metered and rates are usually high. There might also be supplements for things such as luggage, time of day, location of pick-up and extra passengers.

INTERNATIONAL RAIL PASSES

A rail pass is a good idea if you are travelling extensively throughout Europe. Normal point-to-point tickets are valid for two months, and you can make as many stops as you like en route; make your intentions known when purchasing and inform train conductors how far you're going before they punch your ticket.

Supplementary charges (eg for some express and overnight trains) and seat reservation fees (mandatory on some trains, a good idea on others) are not covered by rail passes.

European rail passes also give reductions on Eurostar, the Channel Tunnel and on certain ferries.

Eurail

Eurail (www.eurail.com) passes can be bought only by residents of non-European countries and should be purchased before arriving in Europe. The most comprehensive of the various Eurail passes is the 'Global Pass' covering 28 countries.

The pass is valid for a set number of consecutive days or a set number of days within a period of time. Those under 26 years of age can buy a Eurail Youth pass, which only covers travel in 2nd-class compartments. Those aged 26 and over must buy the full-fare Eurail pass, which entitles you to travel 1st class.

Alternatively, there is the Select pass, which allows you to nominate two, three or four bordering countries in which you wish to travel, and then buy a pass allowing five, six, eight or 10 travel days in a two-month period. The five- and six-day passes offer an attractive price break, but for more expensive options, the continuous pass becomes better value.

Two to five people travelling together can get a Saver version of all Eurail passes for a 15% discount.

InterRail

InterRail (www.interrail.eu) offers passes to European residents for unlimited rail travel through 30 European and North African countries (excluding the pass-holder's country of residence). To qualify as a resident, you must have lived in a European country for six months.

While an InterRail pass will get you further than a Eurail pass along the private rail networks of Switzerland's Jungfrau region (near Interlaken), its benefits are limited. A Swiss Pass or Half-Fare Card might be a necessary addition if you plan to travel extensively in that region.

For a small fee, European residents can buy a Railplus Card, entitling the holder to a 25% discount on many (but not all) international train journeys. It is available from counters in main train stations.

Good bus, rail and under-ground-railway networks often render taxis unnecessary, but if you need one in a hurry, they can be found idling near train stations or outside big hotels. Lower fares make taxis more viable in some countries such as Spain, Greece, Portugal and Turkey.

Train

Express Trains

Eurostar (www.eurostar.com) links London's St Pancras International station, via the Channel Tunnel, with Paris' Gare du Nord (2¼ hours, up to 25 a day) and Brussels' international terminal (one hour 50 minutes, up to 12 a day). Some trains also stop at Lille and Calais in France. There are also several trains a week from London to Disneyland Paris; London to Bordeaux (with a change of train in Paris); London to Marseilles via Lyon and Avignon; and seasonal trains between London and several French ski resorts (December to April). Eurostar trains also link London St Pancras with Rotterdam and Amsterdam Centraal Station, both with a change of train in Brussels.

The train stations at St Pancras International, Paris and Brussels are much more central than the cities' airports. So, overall, the journey takes as little time as the equivalent flight, with less hassle.

Eurostar in London also sells tickets onward to some Continental destinations. Holders of Eurail and InterRail passes are offered discounts on some Eurostar services; check when booking.

Within Europe, express trains are identified by the symbols 'EC' (EuroCity) or 'IC' (InterCity). The French TGV, Spanish AVE and German ICE trains are even faster, reaching up to 300km/h. Supplementary fares can apply on fast trains (which you often have to pay when travelling on a rail pass), and it is a good idea (sometimes obligatory) to reserve seats at peak times and on certain lines. The same applies for branded express trains, such as the Thalys (between Paris and Brussels, Bruges, Amsterdam and Cologne), and the Freccia trains in Italy.

If you don't have a seat reservation, you can still obtain a seat that doesn't have a reservation ticket attached to it. Check which destination a seat is reserved for – you might be able to sit in it until the person boards the train.

Overnight Trains

There are usually two types of sleeping accommodation: dozing off upright in your seat or stretching out in a sleeper. Again, reservations are advisable, as sleeping options are allocated on a first-come, first-served basis. Couchette bunks are comfortable enough, if lacking in privacy. There are four per compartment in 1st class, six in 2nd class.

Sleepers are the most comfortable option, offering beds for one or two passengers in 1st class, or two or three passengers in 2nd class. Charges vary depending upon the journey, but they are significantly more costly than couchettes.

In the former Soviet Union, the most common options are either 2nd-class *kupeyny* compartments – which have four bunks – or the cheaper *platskartny*, which are open-plan compartments with reserved bunks. This 3rd-class equivalent is not great for those who value privacy.

Other options include the very basic bench seats in *obshchiy* (*zahalney* in Ukrainian) class and 1st-class, two-person sleeping carriages (*myagki* in Russian). In Ukrainian, this last option is known as *spalney*, but is usually abbreviated to CB in Cyrillic (pronounced *es-ve*). First class is not available on every Russian or Ukrainian train.

Security

Sensible security measures include always keeping your bags in sight (especially at stations), chaining them to the luggage rack, locking compartment doors overnight and sleeping in compartments with other people. However, horror stories are very rare.

Language

ALBANIAN

Note that uh is pronounced as the 'a' in 'ago'. Also, ll and rr in Albanian are pronounced stronger than when they are written as single letters. Albanian is also understood in Kosovo.

Hello.	*Tungjatjeta.*	toon·dya·*tye*·ta
Goodbye.	*Mirupafshim.*	mee·roo·*paf*·sheem
Please.	*Ju lutem.*	yoo *loo*·tem
Thank you.	*Faleminderit.*	fa·le·meen·de·reet
Excuse me.	*Më falni.*	muh *fal*·nee
Sorry.	*Më vjen keq.*	muh vyen kech
Yes./No.	*Po./Jo.*	po/yo
Help!	*Ndihmë!*	ndeeh·muh
Cheers!	*Gëzuar!*	guh·*zoo*·ar

I don't understand.
Unë nuk kuptoj. oo·nuh nook koop·*toy*

Do you speak English?
A flisni anglisht? a flees·nee ang·*leesht*

How much is it?
Sa kushton? sa koosh·*ton*

Where's ...?
Ku është ...? koo *uhsh*·tuh ...

Where are the toilets?
Ku janë banjat? koo ya·nuh ba·nyat

BULGARIAN

Note that uh is pronounced as the 'a' in 'ago' and zh as the 's' in 'pleasure'.

Hello.	Здравейте.	zdra·*vey*·te
Goodbye.	Довиждане.	do·*veezh*·da·ne
Please.	Моля.	*mol*·ya
Thank you.	Благодаря.	bla·go·dar·*ya*
Excuse me.	Извинете.	iz·vee·*ne*·te
Sorry.	Съжалявам.	suh·zhal·*ya*·vam
Yes./No.	Да./Не.	da/ne
Help!	Помощ!	*po*·mosht
Cheers!	Наздраве!	na·*zdra*·ve

I don't understand.
Не разбирам. ne raz·*bee*·ram

Do you speak English?
Говорите ли английски? go·vo·ree·te lee ang·*lees*·kee

How much is it?
Колко струва? *kol*·ko *stroo*·va

Where's ...?
Къде се намира ...? kuh·*de* se na·*mee*·ra ...

Where are the toilets?
Къде има тоалетни? kuh·*de* ee·ma to·a·*let*·nee

CROATIAN & SERBIAN

Croatian and Serbian are very similar and mutually intelligible (and using them you'll also be understood in Bosnia and Hercegovina, Montenegro and parts of Kosovo). In this section the significant differences between Croatian and Serbian are indicated with (C) and (S) respectively. Note that r is rolled and zh is pronounced as the 's' in 'pleasure'.

Hello.	*Dobar dan.*	daw·ber dan
Goodbye.	*Zbogom.*	*zbo*·gom
Please.	*Molim.*	*mo*·lim
Thank you.	*Hvala.*	*hva*·la

WANT MORE?

For in-depth language information and handy phrases, check out Lonely Planet's *Europe Phrasebook*. You'll find it at **shop.lonelyplanet.com**, or you can buy Lonely Planet's iPhone phrasebooks at the Apple App Store.

Excuse me.	Oprostite.	o·*pro*·sti·te
Sorry.	Žao mi je.	zha·o mi ye
Yes./No.	Da./Ne.	da/ne
Help!	Upomoć!	u·po·moch
Cheers!	Živjeli!	zhi·vye·li

I don't understand.
Ja ne razumijem.   ya ne ra·*zu*·mi·yem

Do you speak English?
Govorite/Govoriš li   go·vo·ri·te/go·vo·rish
engleski? (pol/inf)   li en·gle·ski

How much is it?
Koliko stoji/   ko·*li*·ko sto·yi/
košta? (C/S)   kosh·ta

Where's ...?
Gdje je ...?   gdye ye ...

Where are the toilets?
Gdje se nalaze   gdye se na·la·ze
zahodi/toaleti? (C/S)   za·ho·di/to·a·le·ti

CZECH

An accent mark over a vowel in written Czech indicates it's pronounced as a long sound. Note that oh is pronounced as the 'o' in 'note', uh as the 'a' in 'ago', and kh as the 'ch' in the Scottish *loch*. Also, r is rolled in Czech and the apostrophe (') indicates a slight y sound.

Hello.	Ahoj.	uh·hoy
Goodbye.	Na shledanou.	nuh·skhle·duh·noh
Please.	Prosím.	pro·seem
Thank you.	Děkuji.	dye·ku·yi
Excuse me.	Promiňte.	pro·min'·te
Sorry.	Promiňte.	pro·min'·te
Yes./No.	Ano./Ne.	uh·no/ne
Help!	Pomoc!	po·mots
Cheers!	Na zdraví!	nuh zdruh·vee

I don't understand.
Nerozumím.   ne·ro·zu·meem

Do you speak English?
Mluvíte anglicky?   mlu·vee·te uhn·glits·ki

How much is it?
Kolik to stojí?   ko·lik to sto·yee

Where's ...?
Kde je ...?   gde ye ...

Where are the toilets?
Kde jsou toalety?   gde ysoh to·uh·le·ti

DANISH

All vowels in Danish can be long or short. Note that aw is pronounced as in 'saw', and ew as the 'ee' in 'see' with rounded lips.

Hello.	Goddag.	go·da
Goodbye.	Farvel.	faar·vel
Please.	Vær så venlig.	ver saw ven·lee
Thank you.	Tak.	taak
Excuse me.	Undskyld mig.	awn·skewl mai
Sorry.	Undskyld.	awn·skewl
Yes./No.	Ja./Nej.	ya/nai
Help!	Hjælp!	yelp
Cheers!	Skål!	skawl

I don't understand.
Jeg forstår ikke.   yai for·*stawr* i·ke

Do you speak English?
Taler De/du   ta·la dee/doo
engelsk? (pol/inf)   eng·elsk

How much is it?
Hvor meget koster det?   vor *maa*·yet *kos*·ta dey

Where's ...?
Hvor er ...?   vor ir ...

Where's the toilet?
Hvor er toilettet?   vor ir toy·le·tet

DUTCH

It's important to distinguish between the long and short versions of each vowel sound. Note that ew is pronounced as the 'ee' in 'see' with rounded lips, oh as the 'o' in 'note', uh as the 'a' in 'ago', and kh as the 'ch' in the Scottish *loch* (harsh and throaty).

Hello.	Dag.	dakh
Goodbye.	Dag.	dakh
Please.	Alstublieft.	al·stew·*bleeft*
Thank you.	Dank u.	dangk ew
Excuse me.	Pardon.	par·*don*
Sorry.	Sorry.	so·ree
Yes./No.	Ja./Nee.	yaa/ney
Help!	Help!	help
Cheers!	Proost!	prohst

I don't understand.
Ik begrijp het niet.   ik buh·*khreyp* huht neet

Do you speak English?
Spreekt u Engels?   spreykt ew *eng*·uhls

How much is it?
Hoeveel kost het?   hoo·*veyl* kost huht

Where's ...?
Waar is ...?   waar is ...

Where are the toilets?
Waar zijn de toiletten?   waar zeyn duh twa·*le*·tuhn

ESTONIAN

Double vowels in written Estonian indicate they are pronounced as long sounds. Note that air is pronounced as in 'hair'.

Hello.	*Tere.*	te·re
Goodbye.	*Nägemist.*	nair·ge·mist
Please.	*Palun.*	pa·lun
Thank you.	*Tänan.*	tair·nan
Excuse me.	*Vabandage.* (pol)	va·ban·da·ge
	Vabanda. (inf)	va·ban·da
Sorry.	*Vabandust.*	va·ban·dust
Yes./No.	*Jaa./Ei.*	yaa/ay
Help!	*Appi!*	ap·pi
Cheers!	*Terviseks!*	tair·vi·seks

I don't understand.
Ma ei saa aru.   ma ay saa a·ru

Do you speak English?
Kas te räägite   kas te rair·git·te
inglise keelt?   ing·kli·se keylt

How much is it?
Kui palju see maksab?   ku·i pal·yu sey mak·sab

Where's ...?
Kus on ...?   kus on ...

Where are the toilets?
Kus on WC?   kus on ve·se

FINNISH

In Finnish, double consonants are held longer than their single equivalents. Note that ew is pronounced as the 'ee' in 'see' with rounded lips, and uh as the 'u' in 'run'.

Hello.	*Hei.*	hay
Goodbye.	*Näkemiin.*	na·ke·meen
Please.	*Ole hyvä.*	o·le hew·va
Thank you.	*Kiitos.*	kee·tos
Excuse me.	*Anteeksi.*	uhn·tayk·si
Sorry.	*Anteeksi.*	uhn·tayk·si
Yes./No.	*Kyllä./Ei.*	kewl·la/ay
Help!	*Apua!*	uh·pu·uh
Cheers!	*Kippis!*	kip·pis

I don't understand.
En ymmärrä.   en ewm·mar·ra

Do you speak English?
Puhutko englantia?   pu·hut·ko en·gluhn·ti·uh

How much is it?
Mitä se maksaa?   mi·ta se muhk·saa

Where's ...?
Missä on ...?   mis·sa on ...

Where are the toilets?
Missä on vessa?   mis·sa on ves·suh

FRENCH

The French r sound is throaty. French also has nasal vowels (pronounced as if you're trying to force the sound through the nose), indicated here with o or u followed by an almost inaudible nasal consonant sound m, n or ng. Syllables in French words are, for the most part, equally stressed.

Hello.	*Bonjour.*	bon·zhoor
Goodbye.	*Au revoir.*	o·rer·vwa
Please.	*S'il vous plaît.*	seel voo play
Thank you.	*Merci.*	mair·see
Excuse me.	*Excusez-moi.*	ek·skew·zay·mwa
Sorry.	*Pardon.*	par·don
Yes./No.	*Oui./Non.*	wee/non
Help!	*Au secours!*	o skoor
Cheers!	*Santé!*	son·tay

I don't understand.
Je ne comprends pas.   zher ner kom·pron pa

Do you speak English?
Parlez-vous anglais?   par·lay·voo ong·glay

How much is it?
C'est combien?   say kom·byun

Where's ...?
Où est ...?   oo ay ...

Where are the toilets?
Où sont les toilettes?   oo son ley twa·let

GERMAN

Note that aw is pronounced as in 'saw', ew as the 'ee' in 'see' with rounded lips, while kh and r are both throaty sounds in German.

Hello.		
(in general)	*Guten Tag.*	goo·ten taak
(Austria)	*Servus.*	zer·vus
(Switzerland)	*Grüezi.*	grew·e·tsi
Goodbye.	*Auf Wiedersehen.*	owf vee·der·zey·en
Please.	*Bitte.*	bi·te
Thank you.	*Danke.*	dang·ke
Excuse me.	*Entschuldigung.*	ent·shul·di·gung
Sorry.	*Entschuldigung.*	ent·shul·di·gung
Yes./No.	*Ja./Nein.*	yaa/nain
Help!	*Hilfe!*	hil·fe
Cheers!	*Prost!*	prawst

I don't understand.
Ich verstehe nicht.   ikh fer·shtey·e nikht

Do you speak English?
Sprechen Sie Englisch?   shpre·khen zee eng·lish

How much is it?
Wie viel kostet das?   vee feel kos·tet das

Where's ...?
Wo ist ...?   vaw ist ...

Where are the toilets?
Wo ist die Toilette?   vo ist dee to·a·le·te

GREEK

Note that dh is pronounced as the 'th' in 'that', and that gh and kh are both throaty sounds, similar to the 'ch' in the Scottish loch.

Hello.	Γεια σου.	yia su
Goodbye.	Αντίο.	a·di·o
Please.	Παρακαλώ.	pa·ra·ka·lo
Thank you.	Ευχαριστώ.	ef·kha·ri·sto
Excuse me.	Με συγχωρείτε.	me sing·kho·ri·te
Sorry.	Συγνώμη.	si·ghno·mi
Yes./No.	Ναι./Όχι.	ne/o·hi
Help!	Βοήθεια!	vo·i·thia
Cheers!	Στην υγειά μας!	stin i·yia mas

I don't understand.
Δεν καταλαβαίνω.   dhen ka·ta·la·ve·no

Do you speak English?
Μιλάς Αγγλικά;   mi·las ang·gli·ka

How much is it?
Πόσο κάνει;   po·so ka·ni

Where's ...?
Που είναι ...;   pu i·ne ...

Where are the toilets?
Που είναι η τουαλέτα;   pu i·ne i tu·a·le·ta

HUNGARIAN

A symbol over a vowel in written Hungarian indicates it's pronounced as a long sound. Double consonants should be drawn out a little longer than in English. Note that aw is pronounced as in 'law', eu as the 'u' in 'nurse', and ew as 'ee' with rounded lips. Also, r is rolled in Hungarian and the apostrophe (') indicates a slight y sound.

Hello. (to one person)
Szervusz.   ser·vus

Hello. (to more than one person)
Szervusztok.   ser·vus·tawk

Goodbye.	Viszlát.	vis·lat
Please.	Kérem. (pol)	key·rem
	Kérlek. (inf)	keyr·lek
Thank you.	Köszönöm.	keu·seu·neum

Excuse me.   Elnézést   el·ney·zeysht
   kérek.   key·rek

Sorry.   Sajnálom.   shoy·na·lawm

Yes.   Igen.   i·gen

No.   Nem.   nem

Help!   Segítség!   she·geet·sheyg

Cheers! (to one person)
Egészségedre!   e·geys·shey·ged·re

Cheers! (to more than one person)
Egészségetekre!   e·geys·shey·ge·tek·re

I don't understand.
Nem értem.   nem eyr·tem

Do you speak English?
Beszél/Beszélsz   be·seyl/be·seyls
angolul? (pol/inf)   on·gaw·lul

How much is it?
Mennyibe kerül?   men'·nyi·be ke·rewl

Where's ...?
Hol van a ...?   hawl von o ...

Where are the toilets?
Hol a vécé?   hawl o vey·tsey

ITALIAN

The r sound in Italian is rolled and stronger than in English. Most other consonants can have a more emphatic pronunciation too (in which case they're written as double letters).

Hello.	Buongiorno.	bwon·jor·no
Goodbye.	Arrivederci.	a·ree·ve·der·chee
Please.	Per favore.	per fa·vo·re
Thank you.	Grazie.	gra·tsye
Excuse me.	Mi scusi. (pol)	mee skoo·zee
	Scusami. (inf)	skoo·za·mee
Sorry.	Mi dispiace.	mee dees·pya·che
Yes.	Sì.	see
No.	No.	no
Help!	Aiuto!	ai·yoo·to
Cheers!	Salute!	sa·loo·te

I don't understand.
Non capisco.   non ka·pee·sko

Do you speak English?
Parla inglese?   par·la een·gle·ze

How much is it?
Quant'è?   kwan·te

Where's ... ?
Dov'è ... ?   do·ve ...

Where are the toilets?
Dove sono i   do·ve so·no ee
gabinetti?   ga·bee·ne·tee

LATVIAN

A line over a vowel in written Latvian indicates it's pronounced as a long sound. Note that air is pronounced as in 'hair', ea as in 'ear', wa as in 'water', and dz as the 'ds' in 'adds'.

Hello.	Sveiks.	svayks
Goodbye.	Atā.	a·taa
Please.	Lūdzu.	loo·dzu
Thank you.	Paldies.	pal·deas
Excuse me.	Atvainojiet.	at·vai·nwa·yeat
Sorry.	Piedodiet.	pea·dwa·deat
Yes./No.	Jā./Nē.	yaa/nair
Help!	Palīgā!	pa·lee·gaa
Cheers!	Priekā!	prea·kaa

I don't understand.
Es nesaprotu. — es ne·sa·prwa·tu

Do you speak English?
Vai Jūs runājat angliski? — vai yoos ru·naa·yat ang·li·ski

How much is it?
Cik maksā? — tsik mak·saa

Where's ...?
Kur ir ...? — kur ir ...

Where are the toilets?
Kur ir tualetes? — kur ir tu·a·le·tes

LITHUANIAN

Symbols on vowels in written Lithuanian indicate that they're pronounced as long sounds. Note that ow is pronounced as in 'how'.

Hello.	Sveiki.	svay·ki
Goodbye.	Viso gero.	vi·so ge·ro
Please.	Prašau.	pra·show
Thank you.	Ačiū.	aa·choo
Excuse me.	Atleiskite.	at·lays·ki·te
Sorry.	Atsiprašau.	at·si·pra·show
Yes./No.	Taip./Ne.	taip/ne
Help!	Padėkit!	pa·dey·kit
Cheers!	Į sveikatą!	ee svay·kaa·taa

I don't understand.
Aš nesuprantu. — ash ne·su·pran·tu

Do you speak English?
Ar kalbate angliškai? — ar kal·ba·te aang·lish·kai

How much is it?
Kiek kainuoja? — keak kain·wo·ya

Where's ...?
Kur yra ...? — kur ee·ra ...

Where are the toilets?
Kur yra tualetai? — kur ee·ra tu·a·le·tai

MACEDONIAN

Note that r is pronounced as a rolled sound in Macedonian.

Hello.	Здраво.	zdra·vo
Goodbye.	До гледање.	do gle·da·nye
Please.	Молам.	mo·lam
Thank you.	Благодарам.	bla·go·da·ram
Excuse me.	Извинете.	iz·vi·ne·te
Sorry.	Простете.	pros·te·te
Yes./No.	Да./Не.	da/ne
Help!	Помош!	po·mosh
Cheers!	На здравје!	na zdrav·ye

I don't understand.
Jас не разбирам. — yas ne raz·bi·ram

Do you speak English?
Зборувате ли англиски? — zbo·ru·va·te li an·glis·ki

How much is it?
Колку чини тоа? — kol·ku chi·ni to·a

Where's ...?
Каде е ...? — ka·de e ...

Where are the toilets?
Каде се тоалетите? — ka·de se to·a·le·ti·te

NORWEGIAN

In Norwegian, each vowel can be either long or short. Generally, they're long when followed by one consonant and short when followed by two or more consonants. Note that aw is pronounced as in 'law', ew as 'ee' with pursed lips, and ow as in 'how'.

Hello.	God dag.	go·daag
Goodbye.	Ha det.	haa·de
Please.	Vær så snill.	veyr saw snil
Thank you.	Takk.	tak
Excuse me.	Unnskyld.	ewn·shewl
Sorry.	Beklager.	bey·klaa·geyr
Yes./No.	Ja./Nei.	yaa/ney
Help!	Hjelp!	yelp
Cheers!	Skål!	skawl

I don't understand.
Jeg forstår ikke. — yai fawr·stawr i·key

Do you speak English?
Snakker du engelsk? — sna·ker doo eyng·elsk

How much is it?
Hvor mye koster det? — vor mew·e kaws·ter de

Where's ...?
Hvor er ...? — vor ayr ...

Where are the toilets?
Hvor er toalettene? — vor eyr to·aa·le·te·ne

POLISH

Polish vowels are generally pronounced short. Nasal vowels are pronounced as though you're trying to force the air through your nose, and are indicated with n or m following the vowel. Note also that r is rolled in Polish.

Hello.	Cześć.	cheshch
Goodbye.	Do widzenia.	do vee·dze·nya
Please.	Proszę.	pro·she
Thank you.	Dziękuję.	jyen·koo·ye
Excuse me.	Przepraszam.	pshe·pra·sham
Sorry.	Przepraszam.	pshe·pra·sham
Yes./No.	Tak./Nie.	tak/nye
Help!	Na pomoc!	na po·mots
Cheers!	Na zdrowie!	na zdro·vye

I don't understand.
Nie rozumiem.　　　nye ro·zoo·myem

Do you speak English?
Czy pan/pani mówi　chi pan/pa·nee moo·vee
po angielsku? (m/f)　po an·gyel·skoo

How much is it?
Ile to kosztuje?　　ee·le to kosh·too·ye

Where's ...?
Gdzie jest ...?　　　gjye yest ...

Where are the toilets?
Gdzie są toalety?　　gjye som to·a·le·ti

PORTUGUESE

Most vowel sounds in Portuguese have a nasal version (ie pronounced as if you're trying to force the sound through your nose), which is indicated in our pronunciation guides with ng after the vowel.

Hello.	Olá.	o·laa
Goodbye.	Adeus.	a·de·oosh
Please.	Por favor.	poor fa·vor
Thank you.	Obrigado. (m)	o·bree·gaa·doo
	Obrigada. (f)	o·bree·gaa·da
Excuse me.	Faz favor.	faash fa·vor
Sorry.	Desculpe.	desh·kool·pe
Yes./No.	Sim./Não.	seeng/nowng
Help!	Socorro!	soo·ko·rroo
Cheers!	Saúde!	sa·oo·de

I don't understand.
Não entendo.　　　nowng eng·teng·doo

Do you speak English?
Fala inglês?　　　faa·la eeng·glesh

How much is it?
Quanto custa?　　　kwang·too koosh·ta

Where's ...?
Onde é ...?　　　　ong·de e ...

Where are the toilets?
Onde é a casa de　ong·de e a kaa·za de
banho?　　　　　　ba·nyoo

ROMANIAN

Note that ew is pronounced as the 'ee' in 'see' with rounded lips, uh as the 'a' in 'ago', and zh as the 's' in 'pleasure'. The apostrophe (') indicates a very short, unstressed (almost silent) i. Moldovan is the official name of the variety of Romanian spoken in Moldova.

Hello.	Bună ziua.	boo·nuh zee·wa
Goodbye.	La revedere.	la re·ve·de·re
Please.	Vă rog.	vuh rog
Thank you.	Mulţumesc.	mool·tsoo·mesk
Excuse me.	Scuzaţi-mă.	skoo·za·tsee·muh
Sorry.	Îmi pare rău.	ewm' pa·re ruh·oo
Yes./No.	Da./Nu.	da/noo
Help!	Ajutor!	a·zhoo·tor
Cheers!	Noroc!	no·rok

I don't understand.
Eu nu înţeleg.　　　ye·oo noo ewn·tse·leg

Do you speak English?
Vorbiţi engleza?　　vor·beets' en·gle·za

How much is it?
Cât costă?　　　　kewt kos·tuh

Where's ...?
Unde este ...?　　　oon·de yes·te ...

Where are the toilets?
Unde este o toaletă?　oon·de yes·te o to·a·le·tuh

RUSSIAN

Note that zh is pronounced as the 's' in 'pleasure'. Also, r is rolled in Russian and the apostrophe (') indicates a slight y sound.

Hello.	Здравствуйте.	zdrast·vuyt·ye
Goodbye.	До свидания.	da svee·dan·ya
Please.	Пожалуйста.	pa·zhal·sta
Thank you.	Спасибо	spa·see·ba
Excuse me./ Sorry.	Извините, пожалуйста.	eez·vee·neet·ye pa·zhal·sta
Yes./No.	Да./Нет.	da/nyet
Help!	Помогите!	pa·ma·gee·tye
Cheers!	Пей до дна!	pyey da dna

I don't understand.
Я не понимаю.　　　ya nye pa·nee·ma·yu

Do you speak English?
Вы говорите
по-английски? | vi ga·va·*reet*·ye
pa·an·*glee*·skee

How much is it?
Сколько стоит? | *skol'*·ka *sto*·eet

Where's ...?
Где (здесь) ...? | gdye (zdyes') ...

Where are the toilets?
Где здесь туалет? | gdye zdyes' tu·al·*yet*

I don't understand.
Ne razumem. | ne ra·*zoo*·mem

Do you speak English?
*Ali govorite
angleško?* | a·lee go·vo·*ree*·te
ang·*lesh*·ko

How much is it?
Koliko stane? | ko·lee·ko sta·ne

Where's ...?
Kje je ...? | kye ye ...

Where are the toilets?
Kje je stranišče? | kye ye stra·*neesh*·che

SLOVAK

An accent mark over a vowel in written Slovak indicates it's pronounced as a long sound. Note also that uh is pronounced as the 'a' in 'ago', and kh as the 'ch' in the Scottish *loch*. The apostrophe (') indicates a slight y sound.

Hello.	*Dobrý deň.*	do·bree dyen'
Goodbye.	*Do videnia.*	do *vi*·dye·ni·yuh
Please.	*Prosím.*	pro·seem
Thank you.	*Ďakujem*	dyuh·ku·yem
Excuse me.	*Prepáčte.*	pre·pach·tye
Sorry.	*Prepáčte.*	pre·pach·tye
Yes./No.	*Áno./Nie.*	a·no/ni·ye
Help!	*Pomoc!*	po·mots
Cheers!	*Nazdravie!*	nuhz·druh·vi·ye

I don't understand.
Nerozumiem. | nye·ro·zu·myem

Do you speak English?
*Hovoríte po
anglicky?* | ho·vo·ree·tye po
uhng·lits·ki

How much is it?
Koľko to stojí? | kol'·ko to sto·yee

Where's ...?
Kde je ...? | kdye ye ...

Where are the toilets?
Kde sú tu záchody? | kdye soo tu za·kho·di

SLOVENE

Note that r is pronounced as a rolled sound in Slovene.

Hello.	*Zdravo.*	zdra·vo
Goodbye.	*Na svidenje.*	na svee·den·ye
Please.	*Prosim.*	pro·seem
Thank you.	*Hvala.*	hva·la
Excuse me.	*Dovolite.*	do·vo·lee·te
Sorry.	*Oprostite.*	op·ros·tee·te
Yes./No.	*Da./Ne.*	da/ne
Help!	*Na pomoč!*	na po·moch
Cheers!	*Na zdravje!*	na zdrav·ye

SPANISH

Note that the Spanish r is strong and rolled, th is pronounced 'with a lisp', and v is soft, pronounced almost like a 'b'.

Hello.	*Hola.*	o·la
Goodbye.	*Adiós.*	a·dyos
Please.	*Por favor.*	por fa·vor
Thank you.	*Gracias.*	gra·thyas
Excuse me.	*Perdón.*	per·don
Sorry.	*Lo siento.*	lo syen·to
Yes./No.	*Sí./No.*	see/no
Help!	*¡Socorro!*	so·ko·ro
Cheers!	*¡Salud!*	sa·loo

I don't understand.
Yo no entiendo. | yo no en·tyen·do

Do you speak English?
*¿Habla/Hablas
inglés?* (pol/inf) | a·bla/a·blas
een·gles

How much is it?
¿Cuánto cuesta? | kwan·to kwes·ta

Where's ...?
¿Dónde está ...? | don·de es·ta ...

Where are the toilets?
*¿Dónde están los
servicios?* | don·de es·tan los
ser·vee·thyos

SWEDISH

Swedish vowels can be short or long – generally the stressed vowels are long, except when followed by double consonants. Note that aw is pronounced as in 'saw', air as in 'hair', eu as the 'u' in 'nurse', ew as the 'ee' in 'see' with rounded lips, and oh as the 'o' in 'note'.

Hello.	*Hej.*	hey
Goodbye.	*Hej då.*	hey daw
Please.	*Tack.*	tak
Thank you.	*Tack.*	tak

Excuse me.	Ursäkta mig.	oor·shek·ta mey
Sorry.	Förlåt.	feur·lawt
Yes./No.	Ja./Nej.	yaa/ney
Help!	Hjälp!	yelp
Cheers!	Skål!	skawl
I don't understand.		
Jag förstår inte.		yaa feur·shtawr in·te
Do you speak English?		
Talar du engelska?		taa·lar doo eng·el·ska
How much is it?		
Hur mycket kostar det?		hoor mew·ke kos·tar de
Where's ...?		
Var finns det ...?		var finns de ...
Where are the toilets?		
Var är toaletten?		var air toh·aa·le·ten

TURKISH

Double vowels are pronounced twice in Turkish. Note also that eu is pronounced as the 'u' in 'nurse', ew as the 'ee' in 'see' with rounded lips, uh as the 'a' in 'ago', r is rolled and v is a little softer than in English.

Hello.	Merhaba.	mer·ha·ba
Goodbye.	Hoşçakal.	hosh·cha·kal
	(when leaving)	
	Güle güle.	gew·le gew·le
	(when staying)	
Please.	Lütfen.	lewt·fen
Thank you.	Teşekkür ederim.	te·shek·kewr e·de·reem
Excuse me.	Bakar mısınız.	ba·kar muh·suh·nuhz
Sorry.	Özür dilerim.	eu·zewr dee·le·reem
Yes./No.	Evet./Hayır.	e·vet/ha·yuhr
Help!	İmdat!	eem·dat
Cheers!	Şerefe!	she·re·fe
I don't understand.		
Anlamıyorum.		an·la·muh·yo·room

Do you speak English?		
İngilizce konuşuyor musunuz?		een·gee·leez·je ko·noo·shoo·yor moo·soo·nooz
How much is it?		
Ne kadar?		ne ka·dar
Where's ...?		
... nerede?		... ne·re·de
Where are the toilets?		
Tuvaletler nerede?		too·va·let·ler ne·re·de

UKRAINIAN

Ukrainian vowels in unstressed syllables are generally pronounced shorter and weaker than they are in stressed syllables. Note that ow is pronounced as in 'how' and zh as the 's' in 'pleasure'. The apostrophe (') indicates a slight y sound.

Hello.	Добрий день.	do·bry den'
Goodbye.	До побачення.	do po·ba·chen·nya
Please.	Прошу.	pro·shu
Thank you.	Дякую.	dya·ku·yu
Excuse me.	Вибачте.	vy·bach·te
Sorry.	Перепрошую.	pe·re·pro·shu·yu
Yes./No.	Так./Ні.	tak/ni
Help!	Допоможіть!	do·po·mo·zhit'
Cheers!	Будьмо!	bud'·mo

I don't understand.		
Я не розумію.		ya ne ro·zu·mi·yu
Do you speak English?		
Ви розмовляєте англійською мовою?		vy roz·mow·lya·ye·te an·hliys'·ko·yu mo·vo·yu
How much is it?		
Скільки це він/вона коштує? (m/f)		skil'·ki tse vin/vo·na ko·shtu·ye
Where's ...?		
Де ...?		de ...
Where are the toilets?		
Де туалети?		de tu·a·le·ti

Behind the Scenes

SEND US YOUR FEEDBACK

We love to hear from travellers – your comments keep us on our toes and help make our books better. Our well-travelled team reads every word on what you loved or loathed about this book. Although we cannot reply individually to your submissions, we always guarantee that your feedback goes straight to the appropriate authors, in time for the next edition. Each person who sends us information is thanked in the next edition – the most useful submissions are rewarded with a selection of digital PDF chapters.

Visit **lonelyplanet.com/contact** to submit your updates and suggestions or to ask for help. Our award-winning website also features inspirational travel stories, news and discussions.

Note: We may edit, reproduce and incorporate your comments in Lonely Planet products such as guidebooks, websites and digital products, so let us know if you don't want your comments reproduced or your name acknowledged. For a copy of our privacy policy visit lonelyplanet.com/privacy.

ACKNOWLEDGEMENTS

Climate map data adapted from Peel MC, Finlayson BL & McMahon TA (2007) 'Updated World Map of the Köppen-Geiger Climate Classification', *Hydrology and Earth System Sciences*, 11, pp1633–44.

Illustrations pp86–7, pp322–3, pp330–1, pp388–9, pp404–5, pp414–15, pp484–5, pp496–7, pp508–9, pp510–11, pp780–1, pp788–9 by Javier Zarracina; pp60–1 by Javier Zarracina and Michael Weldon.

Cover photograph: Vespa scooter, Douglas Carr/Alamy ©

THIS BOOK

This 10th edition of Lonely Planet's *Europe on a Shoestring* guidebook was curated by Mark Baker, Korina Miller, Simon Richmond, Andrea Schulte-Peevers, Andy Symington, Brana Vladisavljevic and Nicola Williams. This guidebook was produced by the following:

Managing Destination Editor Jennifer Carey

Destination Editors Daniel Fahey, Gemma Graham, Niamh O'Brien, Tom Stainer, Anna Tyler, Brana Vladisavljevic, Clifton Wilkinson

Senior Product Editors Anne Mason, Elizabeth Jones

Product Editor Alison Ridgway

Senior Cartographer Mark Griffiths

Book Designer Michael Weldon

Assisting Editors Kate Chapman, Pete Cruttenden, Bruce Evans, Samantha Forge, Shona Gray, Sandie Kestell, Cath Lanigan, Amy Lysen, Susan Paterson

Assisting Cartographers Laura Bailey, Anita Banh

Assisting Book Designer Katherine Marsh

Cover Researcher Naomi Parker

Thanks to Carolyn Boicos, Adriaan Boogert, Victoria Dickson, James Hardy, Clara Monitto, Claire Murphy, Kirsten Rawlings, John Taufa

Index

NOTES

Map Legend

Sights

- Beach
- Bird Sanctuary
- Buddhist
- Castle/Palace
- Christian
- Confucian
- Hindu
- Islamic
- Jain
- Jewish
- Monument
- Museum/Gallery/Historic Building
- Ruin
- Shinto
- Sikh
- Taoist
- Winery/Vineyard
- Zoo/Wildlife Sanctuary
- Other Sight

Activities, Courses & Tours

- Bodysurfing
- Diving
- Canoeing/Kayaking
- Course/Tour
- Sento Hot Baths/Onsen
- Skiing
- Snorkelling
- Surfing
- Swimming/Pool
- Walking
- Windsurfing
- Other Activity

Sleeping

- Sleeping
- Camping
- Hut/Shelter

Eating

- Eating

Drinking & Nightlife

- Drinking & Nightlife
- Cafe

Entertainment

- Entertainment

Shopping

- Shopping

Information

- Bank
- Embassy/Consulate
- Hospital/Medical
- Internet
- Police
- Post Office
- Telephone
- Toilet
- Tourist Information
- Other Information

Geographic

- Beach
- Gate
- Hut/Shelter
- Lighthouse
- Lookout
- Mountain/Volcano
- Oasis
- Park
- Pass
- Picnic Area
- Waterfall

Population

- Capital (National)
- Capital (State/Province)
- City/Large Town
- Town/Village

Transport

- Airport
- Border crossing
- Bus
- Cable car/Funicular
- Cycling
- Ferry
- Metro station
- Monorail
- Parking
- Petrol station
- S-Bahn/Subway station
- Taxi
- T-bane/Tunnelbana station
- Train station/Railway
- Tram
- Tube station
- U-Bahn/Underground station
- Other Transport

Routes

- Tollway
- Freeway
- Primary
- Secondary
- Tertiary
- Lane
- Unsealed road
- Road under construction
- Plaza/Mall
- Steps
- Tunnel
- Pedestrian overpass
- Walking Tour
- Walking Tour detour
- Path/Walking Trail

Boundaries

- International
- State/Province
- Disputed
- Regional/Suburb
- Marine Park
- Cliff
- Wall

Hydrography

- River, Creek
- Intermittent River
- Canal
- Water
- Dry/Salt/Intermittent Lake
- Reef

Areas

- Airport/Runway
- Beach/Desert
- Cemetery (Christian)
- Cemetery (Other)
- Glacier
- Mudflat
- Park/Forest
- Sight (Building)
- Sportsground
- Swamp/Mangrove

Note: Not all symbols displayed above appear on the maps in this book

Andrea Schulte-Peevers

Germany, Austria & Benelux Born and raised in Germany and educated in London and at UCLA, Andrea has travelled the distance to the moon and back in her visits to some 75 countries. She has earned her living as a professional travel writer for over two decades and authored or contributed to nearly 100 Lonely Planet titles as well as to newspapers, magazines and websites around the world. She also works as a travel consultant, translator and editor. Andrea's destination expertise is especially strong when it comes to Germany, Dubai and the UAE, Crete and the Caribbean Islands. She makes her home in Berlin.

Andy Symington

Scandinavia, Spain & Portugal Andy has written or worked on over a hundred books and other updates for Lonely Planet (especially in Europe and Latin America) and other publishing companies, and has published articles on numerous subjects for a variety of newspapers, magazines and websites. He part-owns and operates a rock bar, has written a novel and is currently working on several fiction and non-fiction writing projects. Andy, from Australia, moved to northern Spain many years ago. When he's not off with a backpack in some far-flung corner of the world, he can probably be found watching the tragically poor local football side or tasting local wines after a long walk in the nearby mountains.

Nicola Williams

France & Switzerland, Plan, Survival Guide Border-hopping is a way of life for British writer, runner, foodie, art aficionado and mum-of-three Nicola Williams, who has lived in a French village on the southern side of Lake Geneva for more than a decade. Nicola has authored more than 50 guidebooks on Paris, Provence, Rome, Tuscany, France, Italy and Switzerland for Lonely Planet and covers France as a destination expert for the *Telegraph*. She also writes for the *Independent, Guardian,* lonelyplanet.com, *Lonely Planet Magazine, French Magazine, Cool Camping France* and others. Catch her on the road on Twitter and Instagram at @tripalong.

Contributing Writers & Researchers

Isabel Albiston, Kate Armstrong, Alexis Averbuck, Carolyn Bain, Oliver Berry, Abigail Blasi, Greg Bloom, Cristian Bonetto, Kerry Christiani, Gregor Clark, Michael Stamatios Clark, Fionn Davenport, Sally Davies, Marc Di Duca, Belinda Dixon, Peter Dragicevich, Mark Elliott, Steve Fallon, Emilie Filou, Duncan Garwood, Anthony Ham, Paula Hardy, Damian Harper, Anita Isalska, Anna Kaminski, Catherine Le Nevez, Jessica Lee, Ali Lemer, Tom Masters, Virginia Maxwell, Craig McLachlan, Hugh McNaughtan, Isabella Noble, John Noble, Becky Ohlsen, Zora O'Neill, Lorna Parkes, Christopher Pitts, Josephine Quintero, Leonid Ragozin, Kevin Raub, Tim Richards, Daniel Robinson, Brendan Sainsbury, Tamara Sheward, Helena Smith, Regis St Louis, Mara Vorhees, Benedict Walker, Greg Ward, Richard Waters, Donna Wheeler, Neil Wilson

Brana Vladisavljevic curated the Balkans chapter.

OUR STORY

A beat-up old car, a few dollars in the pocket and a sense of adventure. In 1972 that's all Tony and Maureen Wheeler needed for the trip of a lifetime – across Europe and Asia overland to Australia. It took several months, and at the end – broke but inspired – they sat at their kitchen table writing and stapling together their first travel guide, *Across Asia on the Cheap*. Within a week they'd sold 1500 copies. Lonely Planet was born.

Today, Lonely Planet has offices in Franklin, London, Melbourne, Oakland, Dublin, Beijing and Delhi, with more than 600 staff and writers. We share Tony's belief that 'a great guidebook should do three things: inform, educate and amuse'.

OUR WRITERS

Mark Baker

Central & Eastern Europe Mark Baker is a freelance travel writer with a penchant for offbeat stories and forgotten places. He's originally from the United States, but now makes his home in the Czech capital, Prague. He writes mainly on Eastern and Central Europe for Lonely Planet as well as other leading travel publishers, but finds real satisfaction in digging up stories in places that are too remote or quirky for the guides. Prior to becoming an author, he worked as a journalist for the *Economist*, *Bloomberg News* and *Radio Free Europe*, among other organisations. Instagram: @markbakerprague Twitter: @markbakerprague Blog: www. markbakerprague.com

Korina Miller

Italy, Greece & Turkey Korina grew up on Vancouver Island and has been exploring the globe independently since she was 16, visiting or living in 36 countries and picking up a degree in Communications and Canadian Studies, an MA in Migration Studies and a diploma in Visual Arts en route. As a writer and editor, Korina has worked on nearly 60 titles for Lonely Planet and has also worked with LP.com, BBC, the *Independent*, the *Guardian*, BBC5 and CBC, as well as many independent magazines, covering travel, art and culture. She has currently set up camp back in Victoria, soaking up the mountain views and the pounding surf.

Simon Richmond

Great Britain & Ireland, Russia & the Baltic Coast Journalist and photographer Simon Richmond has specialised as a travel writer since the early 1990s and first worked for Lonely Planet in 1999 on its *Central Asia* guide. He's long since stopped counting the number of guidebooks he's researched and written for the company, but countries covered include Australia, China, India, Iran, Japan, Korea, Malaysia, Mongolia, Myanmar (Burma), Russia, Singapore, South Africa and Turkey. For Lonely Planet's website he's penned features on topics from the world's best swimming pools to the joys of Urban Sketching – follow him on Instagram to see some of his photos and sketches.

OVER PAGE MORE WRITERS

Published by Lonely Planet Global Limited
CRN 554153
10th edition – October 2018
ISBN 978 1 78657 640 8
© Lonely Planet 2018   Photographs © as indicated 2018
10 9 8 7 6 5 4 3 2 1
Printed in China

Although the authors and Lonely Planet have taken all reasonable care in preparing this book, we make no warranty about the accuracy or completeness of its content and, to the maximum extent permitted, disclaim all liability arising from its use.